ASSER International Sports Law Series

For further volumes:
http://www.springer.com/series/8858

Andre M. Louw

Ambush Marketing and the Mega-Event Monopoly

How Laws are Abused to Protect Commercial Rights to Major Sporting Events

T·M·C·ASSER PRESS

Springer

Andre M. Louw
School of Law, Howard College Campus
University of KwaZulu-Natal
King George V Avenue
Durban 4041
South Africa

ISSN 1874-6926
ISBN 978-90-6704-863-7 ISBN 978-90-6704-864-4 (eBook)
DOI 10.1007/978-90-6704-864-4

Library of Congress Control Number: 2012936963

Published by T.M.C. Asser Press, The Hague, The Netherlands www.asserpress.nl
Produced and distributed for T.M.C. Asser Press by Springer-Verlag Berlin Heidelberg

Printed on acid-free paper

Springer is part of Springer Science+Business Media (www.springer.com)

Series Information

Books in the *ASSER International Sports Law Series* chart and comment upon the legal and policy developments in European and international sports law. The books contain materials on interstate organisations and the international sports governing bodies, and will serve as comprehensive and relevant reference tools for all those involved in the area on a professional basis.

The Series is developed, edited and published by the ASSER International Sports Law Centre in The Hague. The Centre's mission is to provide a centre of excellence in particular by providing high-quality research, services and products to the sporting world at large (sports ministries, international—intergovernmental—organisations, sports associations and federations, the professional sports industry, etc.) on both a national and an international basis. The Centre is the co-founder and coordinator of the Hague International Sports Law Academy (HISLA), the purpose of which is the organisation of academic conferences and workshops of international excellence which are held in various parts of the world. Apart from the Series, the Centre edits and publishes *The International Sports Law Journal.*

Series Editors
Dr. Robert C. R. Siekmann, Director Asser International Sports Centre
e-mail: r.siekmann@asser.nl

Dr. Janwillem Soek
e-mail: J.soek@asser.nl

M. A. van der Harst LL.M.
e-mail: m.van.der.harst@asser.nl

Editorial Office
ASSER International Sports Law Centre
T.M.C. Asser Institute
P.O. Box 30461
2500 GL, The Hague
The Netherlands
www.sportslaw.nl

Series Information

Books in the ASSER International Sports Law Series chart and comment upon the legal and policy developments in European and international sports law. The books contain materials on inter-state organisations and the international sports governing bodies, and will serve as comprehensive and relevant reference tools for all those involved in the area on a professional basis.

The Series is developed, edited and published by the ASSER International Sports Law Centre in The Hague. The Centre's mission is to provide a centre of excellence in particular by providing high quality research, services and products to the sporting world at large (sports ministries, international intergovernmental organisations, sports associations and federations, the professional sports industry, etc.) on both a national and an international basis. The Centre is the co-founder and coordinator of the Hague International Sports Law Academy (HISLA), the purpose of which is the organisation of academic conferences and workshops of international excellence which are held in various parts of the world.

For my father, the biggest sports fan ever,
with all my love
Thanks for everything

Preface

My homeland was invaded by a foreign power 2 years ago, amidst much fanfare, publicity and excitement. The world sat watching with avid interest to see events unfold, although few spectators were even mildly concerned about these developments and, ultimately, boredom over the resultant spectacle appeared to be the order of the day. The invader was expected (had been invited, in fact), it brought no tanks or guns (although quite a few private jets were to be seen), and its uniform was more bespoke three-piece suits than combat camouflage. While the operation had taken longer to plan than the D-Day landings (more than 6 years in the making), the invasion and subsequent regime change lasted only a month. FIFA had come to South Africa, and my country would never be the same again.

This book started as the germ of an idea that festered amid some interesting debates with postgraduate students in seminars on intellectual property law, where we explored the fascinating world of 'ambush marketing' (well, I found it fascinating, it's mostly impossible to divine the thoughts of a student). From subsequent reading on ambush marketing and IP rights in sport I developed an interest in the commercialisation of sport in its various guises; in the sometimes extremely interesting ways in which businesses have managed to 'unofficially' market their products and services in relation to major sports events and the likewise intriguing ways in which rights holders have proceeded to protect their often considerable investment in these events by means of recourse to the law. Fascination, however, gradually blossomed into disbelief, caused mainly by one specific aspect of ambush marketing: The ways in which the law—specifically in the form of domestic legislation in the countries that have hosted recent major events—has been used, or abused, in order to protect the privately 'owned' commercial rights of event organisers and sponsors at the expense of the rights of just about everyone else.

Upon further reading I found more, and ever more blatant, examples of this, and started to see a pattern of significant economic and political power at work in the world of sport. I have come to the conclusion (and I am not alone in this respect) that those governing world sport and those who plough millions of dollars into major events as sponsors and 'commercial partners' in order to put on the biggest shows on earth have for some time now been hard at work behind the scenes creating very powerful and influential cliques, and have often rabidly protected their power and financial interests by various means involving the law. I am no conspiracy theorist, and I am not suggesting that some dark forces or *illuminati* are at work here. I just believe that the modern political economy of international sport has assumed dimensions which may require urgent intervention in the public interest, and in the interests of sport. As a lawyer and a teacher of law I have found them extremely worrying.

Following FIFA's brief but tempestuous invasion of my country I felt the need to take up arms. The pen is mightier than the sword, and the laptop is mightier still. So I did what academics are wont to do. I wrote a paper, which was published as a series of articles in a local South African law journal, on the legal implications of commercial monopolies in events such as the FIFA World Cup, and on the (what I view to be) deplorable legislation that my country's democratically elected lawmakers have passed and which has been employed in order to protect and maintain one such monopoly. These articles have formed the basis for this book, and I wish to thank the publishers of the *Obiter* journal, at the Law Faculty of the Nelson Mandela Metropolitan University in Port Elizabeth, for their kind permission to use some of that material in this attempt to expand the discussion and to include other jurisdictions and other events in the purview.

Further reading on the subject in researching this book has surprised me into finding that very little work has been done to date by the legal fraternity, *from a critical perspective*, in respect of assessing the legitimacy of the current state of affairs regarding commercial rights to sports mega-events and how the law is employed to protect such rights. In trawling the Internet I have found literally hundreds of articles, opinion pieces and blog postings on ambush marketing, from across the world. The reader is encouraged to search for these, there's some very interesting stuff out there. From this bounty of source material I have tried to piece together what I hope is an interesting if possibly rather long-winded exploration of the nature and implications of the commercial juggernaut that is the modern sports mega-event, and of the activities of those involved in staging and financing these spectacles. While I also found a number of examples of scholarly writing on the subject emanating from both the legal and marketing fraternities, a definitive and all-encompassing critical treatise on the legal and other issues involved has eluded me. This book is not such a work, although I fervently hope that, while not providing a comprehensive and all-encompassing source on the subject, it might serve at the very least to provoke further thinking, reading, writing and debate in the interests of development of the law for purposes of its application to such events in future.

I wish to sincerely thank my colleague, mentor and friend, Tanya Woker, who first suggested that I should write this book (although I am constantly looking for ways to get back at her for the months of hard work that her suggestion inspired).

A number of persons either expressed very flattering interest in the work, assisted me in writing it, or provided helpful information which I managed to use in the process. I wish to express, in no particular order, my sincere gratitude to

Nandan Kamath, Phillip Johnson, Dalton Odendaal, Tim Burrell, Ari Sliffmann, Brian Pelanda, Susan Corbett, Joe Cobbs, Simon Boyes and Kim Skildum-Reid, most of whom offered to assist me although my own busy academic schedule unfortunately prevented me from doing their offers justice. My thanks go also to Kadephi Majola and to Christopher Rodel (for helping me find some of the research material, which turned out to be very helpful); to the good folks at Google; and to Jo-Anne Du Plessis for her extremely thoughtful comments early in the process. Thanks also to Dawn Southgate and the UK's Chartered Institute of Marketing for providing me with material. A special and heartfelt word of thanks goes to Willene Holness, for her tireless and invaluable assistance in compiling the index for the book.

I wish to specifically single out a few individuals who assisted me greatly in preparing the manuscript, mostly by reading draft sections or chapters before its submission to the publisher. First, my heartfelt thanks to Jon Heshka, professor of law at Thompson Rivers University in Kamloops, British Columbia. Jon not only provided me with copies of some of his own writings on ambush marketing and expressed an avid interest in this project from the time of our first correspondence in late 2010, he also went way beyond the call of duty and agreed to read through advanced drafts of some of the chapters of this book to help save me embarrassment upon releasing it on unsuspecting readers. Jon will always be welcome for a beer or two at my place if he's ever in the neighbourhood, if only so I can apologise for mentioning his name here. My thanks go also to Wim Alberts, and to Roshana Kelbrick (for sacrificing her well-deserved beach holiday) for their thoughtful comments on the contents of Chap. 5.

I wish to also sincerely thank David Becker, at the time of writing the head of legal services for the International Cricket Council and someone with an intimate knowledge of both the law and practice of ambush marketing, from both 'sides of the fence'. David took time out of a busy schedule to provide me with extremely valuable information (unfortunately at the eleventh hour in my preparation of the manuscript; we had planned to meet earlier but my own commitments unfortunately did not allow for this). David was instrumental in assisting me to inject some much-needed objectivity into the analysis and also, specifically, in informing me of some of the most prominent characteristics of the 'modern ambush' from his experience particularly in respect of the 2011 ICC Cricket World Cup event (which I've tried to discuss briefly in the concluding chapter).

In particular I also wish to thank Felipe Dannemann Lundgren, whose avid interest in the project and extremely generous and selfless assistance in updating me on recent developments in Brazil will always be greatly appreciated. He did so much more than just guide me through impenetrable Portuguese-language texts. In light of the scope of the project and the way in which some chapters simply snowballed into near unmanageable Tolstoy-like ramblings, my inability to do real justice to the relevant Brazilian law in the short section as contained in Chap. 4 is in no way attributable to Felipe. I hope that he will not be too disappointed in the result.

Finally, I also wish to thank Philip van Tongeren and Marjolijn Bastiaans at Asser Press, and, of course, Rob Siekmann, for their interest in and support for the project (and, especially, for the much-appreciated hands-off approach and the significant trust placed in me to finish the manuscript, substantially on time if a little 'warts and all').

As always, a heartfelt word of thanks and of immense love to my family, especially my long-suffering parents (I love you dearly), brothers, sisters-in-law, nephew, and the little ones. Thanks also to my friends (especially Dave and Willene, Hugo and Eloise and Martin and Claudia).

I hope, for once, that more people will read this book than have assisted me in writing it or have supported me along the way. Despite all their assistance, the mistakes, omissions and no doubt glaring errors are, of course, my own.

Durban, South Africa, Summer 2012 Andre M. Louw

About the Author

Andre M. Louw is an academic at the School of Law of the University of KwaZulu-Natal in Durban, South Africa. He holds the degrees BA, LL.B, LL.M and LL.D (in sports law, from the University of Stellenbosch).

Andre teaches contract law and sports law, and has taught some intellectual property law. His research interests are, exclusively, in the area of sports law, and he has contributed articles to various law journals on a diverse range of issues within the field. He is an attorney of the High Court, South Africa; a member of the British Association for Sport and Law; and a member of the editorial board of the *International Sports Law Journal.*

Andre is also the author of *Sports Law in South Africa* (Kluwer Law International, 2010).

Contents

Abbreviations

AIPPI	International Association for the Protection of Intellectual Property
BCCI	Board of Control for Cricket in India
BCCLA	British Columbia Civil Liberties Association
BOA	British Olympic Authority
BOCOG	Beijing Organising Committee for the 2008 Beijing Olympic Games
CBF	Brazilian Football Federation (Confederaçao Brasileira de Futebol)
CIM	Chartered Institute of Marketing (United Kingdom)
COC	Canadian Olympic Committee
CONAR	Brazilian Advertising Standards Authority
FIFA	Federation Internationale de Football Associations
ICC	International Cricket Council
ICCDIL	ICC Development International Ltd
INTA	International Trademark Association
IOC	International Olympic Committee
IP	Intellectual Property
IPC	International Paralympic Committee
IPL	Indian Premier League (cricket competition)
IRB	International Rugby Board
ISL	International Sports and Leisure (sports marketing rights agency)
LOAR	London Olympics Association Right
LOC	Local Organising Committee (2010 FIFA World Cup South Africa)
LOCOG	Organising Committee for the 2012 London Olympic Games
MEMA	Major Events Management Act, 2007 (New Zealand)
MMA	Merchandise Marks Act, 1941 (as amended) (South Africa)
NFL	National Football League (United States)
NOC	National Olympic Committee
NZRFU	New Zealand Rugby Football Union
OCOG	Organising Committee for the Olympic Games
ODA	Olympic Delivery Authority (for the 2012 London Olympic Games)
OHIM	Office for Harmonisation in the internal market
OSPA	Olympic Symbol etc (Protection) Act, 1995 (United Kingdom)

SROC	Sports Rights Owners Coalition
TOP	The Olympic (Partner) Programme
UEFA	Union of European Football Associations
USOC	United States Olympic Committee
VANOC	Organising Committee for the 2010 Vancouver Winter Olympic Games

Chapter 1
Introduction

Two Million Reasons Not to Wear Reebok

> August 1992—Barcelona:
>
> Officials of the United States Olympic Committee announced that if … Nike endorsers composing half of the American [basketball] "Dream Team" did not relent and wear the official, American flag-bedecked awards ceremony jackets also bearing the emblem of Reebok, the athletic-shoe company against which Nike had conducted a holy war for much of a decade, the players would not be allowed atop the medals stand when some 600 million television viewers in 193 countries heard the "Star-Spangled Banner" begin. But Michael Jordan and the other Nike guys on the Dream Team refused to budge. "We won't wear Reebok," Jordan said …
>
> Here was a sports moment meant to reside above the marketplace, an event indicative of sport's traditional purity of purpose: the flag unfurled and the national anthem on the public-address system, the tears of young athletes glistening in the arc lights. And yet certain ostentatiously remunerated basketball players seemed willing to deny the nation this experience because of loyalty not to the flag, to the "glory of sport" or "honour of our teams," as the Olympic oath has it, but to a company in Oregon that markets their shoes. Charles Barkley … managed to underscore the perception that mammon was about to triumph over patria in Barcelona by proclaiming that he had no less than "two million reasons not to wear Reebok."[1]

The Olympic Truce (or *Ekecheiria*—the 'laying down of arms') was first established in ancient times by the signing of a treaty between kings to ensure the safety of athletes, pilgrims and the masses when travelling to and from the Olympic Games, and for the duration of their participation in and attendance of the event. This ancient custom, with all its considerable feel-good PR value, was revived in modern times, and since 1993 the Truce is declared for each instalment of the Games by a special resolution (proposed by the government of the host

[1] Katz 1994, p. 16.

A. M. Louw, *Ambush Marketing and the Mega-Event Monopoly*, ASSER International Sports Law Series, DOI: 10.1007/978-90-6704-864-4_1,

nation) of the United Nations General Assembly, and signed by all UN member states.[2]

We all know what weight UN resolutions carry when it comes to international armed conflict. It should therefore come as no surprise that the revival of the Truce has been rather less than a spectacular success. It appears to have much the same deterrent effect as those pesky speed cameras on many of our modern roads, and to be generally subjected to about as much respect as most grown-ups reserve for Santa Claus. In the 115 years to date of the modern era of the Olympics, the Games have been cancelled on three occasions due to war, have been blighted on five occasions by mass boycotts and twice by terrorist attacks, and virtually every instalment of the Summer, Winter and Paralympic Games has occurred in the midst of violations of the Truce.[3] Apart from this rather shabby treatment of such an intrinsically laudable symbolic institution by the governments and militia of the world, the Olympic Games and other comparable international sports mega-events have also come to be characterised by a rather ironic breach of the peace by the very custodians of such events. Every 4 years or so, and mostly behind the scenes (although increasingly publicly) the organisers of these events declare a no-holds-barred, albeit bloodless, war.

The war is a commercial one. Hit squads of those modern and most scary of warriors—lawyers—and sundry other 'suits' are deployed to all corners of the globe to take the fight to 'ambush marketers' or those who engage in 'guerrilla marketing' tactics. Cease-and-desist letters are dispatched by the thousands (old news reel footage of the Stalin organ in action comes to mind), threatening the unfortunate recipients with all species of dire consequences for having had the audacity to attempt to associate a product or service with such grand publicity-generating events or to have used a depiction of the sacred Five Rings or words such as 'world' or 'cup' or even 'summer' or 'gold' in an advertising campaign. Sometimes threats turn to legal action and courts the world over have sporadically been faced with pitched battles in the war between the sporting and corporate world's big boys, and the various unfortunate souls who may have inadvertently stumbled into the crosshairs. While some of the 'ambushers' are seasoned and very shrewd campaigners unworthy of our sympathy (anything but some shrinking little Bambi caught in the headlights), some allegations of 'transgressions' or

[2] 'In 1993, the United Nations officially revived the ancient tradition of Ekecheiria by adopting an unbinding resolution to restore the Olympic Truce, whereby countries agree to cease all hostilities during the course of the Games. Since then, the United Nations adopts a similar resolution specific to the Olympiad at hand in which the Olympic Truce is used as an international appeal for peace … The Olympic Truce resolution was established on November 7, 1995, when the United Nations amended a previous resolution to include in the agenda of its 52nd session an item entitled "Building a peaceful and better world through sport and the Olympic ideal." This resolution specified that a new resolution calling on a renewed commitment to Olympic Truce be passed every two years in advance of each Summer and Winter Olympic Games.'—Burleson 2009, p. 33.

[3] From an article entitled 'A legacy far greater than medals and prizes,' 15 December 2010, available on the web site http://www.epolitix.com.

'infringements' are often reminiscent of the much-publicised search for the mythical WMD from our recent past. Sometimes ordinary people or the odd entrepreneur may wonder why this particular rather large pitfall of modern marketing was never on the syllabus at elementary school while they were being taught never to talk to strangers, and that fingers and wall plugs go together like dinosaurs and meteor showers. Bright (sometimes award-winning) marketers and advertising executives may feel the pinch and may even get the impression that fascism is alive and well and has found a new home in the corridors of power of world sport.

This war is a very real (and sometimes very dirty) one, although for the most part it goes unnoticed by members of the public. As the incident regarding the Nike-sponsored 'Dream Team' recounted in the by-line to this chapter illustrates, big money and the commercial interests of athletes have assumed such a prominent role in sports, and in the mega-event context, that traditional notions of the primacy of national pride and of sporting achievement are becoming peripheral and sometimes subordinate to brand allegiance and the event as marketing platform. When Joe Soap tunes in to watch the Games he often has no clue of the skirmishes behind the scenes. These intrigues have, however, become part and parcel of the modern sports mega-event, and it might not be long before the fascinating slash and parry of the battle to protect the vastly lucrative commercial rights to these spectacles itself attains the status of an official Olympic event.

It is now cliché to say that 'it is cliché to say that sport is big business.' It would not be an exaggeration to characterise the biggest sport of all, football, as the world's single most popular and ubiquitous form of recreational entertainment across all strata of nationality, class, race, creed, religious persuasion and—even that most divisive of distinctions—club affiliation. The other major entertainment sectors also regularly capitalise on the popularity of sport: Hollywood has in recent years gone gaga for American football (with films like *Any Given Sunday*, *Varsity Blues* and *Friday Night Lights*), motor racing (*Days of Thunder*), rugby union (*Invictus*), football (want to learn to *Bend it like Beckham*, anyone?), golf (*The Legend of Bagger Vance*, *Tin Cup* and *The Greatest Game ever Played*) and a host of other sports (including those intrepid Jamaican bobsled boys). Even popular music and video games (compare the hugely successful *FIFA* and *Pro Evolution Soccer* franchises, or the *Madden NFL* monopoly currently enjoyed by Electronic Arts in the USA) have managed to join the gravy train in exploiting the phenomenal popularity of sport. In fact, sport has in recent decades managed to very successfully cross into the realm of popular culture, and celebrity athletes are, well, celebrities, some of the world's best-paid entertainers.

Apart from the blockbuster commercial success of leagues and competitions that are hosted on an ongoing annual or seasonal basis (prime examples being the English Premier League football competition, American football's Super Bowl and baseball's (always ambitiously named) 'World Series,' the FIA Formula 1 world championship and, more recently, the Indian Premier League cricket tournament), the pinnacle of elite sport, globally, is found in the quadrennial world championship events such as the Olympic Games and the FIFA football World Cup.

These and a selected few other events have reached such an iconic status and scope that they have garnered the handle 'mega-event.' While their success may be attributable to the national pride factor (they serve, after all, to crown world champions), it is probably more realistic a view to observe that the events have simply attained the status and expectation of *über*-spectacles, a 'grand show' on a global stage. They serve to focus the attention of the world media, sports fans and, importantly, consumers (which we all ultimately are), like no other modern-day public spectacles. One writer observed in the mid-1990s that the Olympic Games and FIFA's World Cup 'have become the most known, watched, romanticised, revered, commercialised, mediatised, nationalistic, passionately followed, and critiqued mega sporting events'[4]—that is quite a mouthful. Nations and cities feverishly bid for the privilege (if sometimes only perceived) to host these events. They generate billions of dollars in revenues for their organisers and for the corporations that 'jump on the brand wagon' by paying astronomical amounts to associate themselves and their products and services with these 'feel-good' occasions that provide such unprecedented marketing opportunities to captive television and other media audiences on a global scale. Sometimes, these events even make money for their hosts. But it seems that there is a dark side to these extravaganzas, and it is not fanciful to say that public and scientific opinion on the benefits is rather ambivalent:

> Sports mega-events have been largely developed by undemocratic organisations, often with anarchic decision-making and a lack of transparency, and more often in the interests of global flows rather than local communities. In this respect they represent a shift from public funds to private interests. Such organisations represent part of the ideological assault on citizenship that has occurred since the 1980s, which prefers global consumers to local publics.[5]

For some, the mega-events provide what is possibly an unrivalled opportunity to generate profits and to wield substantial economic and even political power. These events are the biggest of the big in sports business. They represent the pinnacle of the sport-media-business alliance that was formed in the late twentieth-century. Through the idea of packaging, via the tripartite model of sponsorship rights, exclusive broadcasting rights and merchandising, sponsors of the Olympic Games and football World Cup have been attracted by the association with the sports and the vast global exposure that these mega-events achieve.[6] Those who control the staging and those who provide much of the financing for these events are the all-powerful international governing bodies and their commercial partners. This book will examine the relationship between these role-players and the legitimacy (in terms of laws in various jurisdictions) of such commercial relationships and their protection by the law.

---

4 Real 1996.

5 Horne and Manzenreiter 2006, p. 18.

6 Horne and Manzenreiter *supra* 5.

One of the most powerful organisations in world sport, FIFA, has in recent years generated much interest from various quarters in its activities in presenting its World Cup, which is the world's biggest single-sport event. FIFA itself, like its counterparts in other popular sporting codes, is a rather anomalous entity, which represents a non-governmental organisation that, in essence, has no status in the global polity as either a nation state or one of the recognised non-governmental organisations (or NGOs) that perform official functions and enjoy recognition in terms of international law. FIFA, as a sports governing body, is a transnational entity based on principles of voluntary association of private individuals and groups of individuals, which is registered in a canton in Switzerland as a non-profit organisation, although it generates revenues (and profits, although they don't like to call it that) which exceed those reported by some multinational corporations, and often exerts economic and political power that dwarfs the influence of smaller nations in the developing world.

This book is not about FIFA, just as it is not about the International Olympic Committee or any of the other sports mega-event organisers (or, as they've charmingly been called, the 'quadrennial anagrams'[7]) whose activities will be discussed in the chapters that follow. It is also not about Coca-Cola, Kia, McDonalds, VISA or any of the other large multinational corporations who so love to associate their brands with sports mega-events. I am not a marketing expert, and this book will not provide guidance on how best to engage in sports sponsorship or (ambush) marketing.

What this book is about is the way in which sports mega-events have in the past few decades become major global brands, which, like other such brands, are dependent on the protection of the law in respect of the creation of a monopoly of control over elements of popular culture. Others have in recent years written, critically, about the ways in which corporate entities have eroded the public commons of literature, music and various other areas of human endeavour, through the sometimes rabid enforcement of intellectual property rights and other means. This book will examine similar developments in what I view to be an especially germane context. Sport—especially top level international competition—represents one of the best examples of an activity fundamentally situated within the public domain. It also provides a prime example of an area where corporate commercial interests have 'hijacked' the public interest to a significant degree—sports clothing manufacturer Nike, for example, which has been so dominant in sports branding and (ambush) marketing since the 1990s, has been described as a 'company that swallows cultural space in giant gulps.'[8]

Sport is one of the most popular and prominent means by which we pursue recreation and entertainment, as participants, or (for those of us who are less active-minded) as couch potato fans, those who wager a few dollars on matches or as water cooler pundits around the office. Aside from the weather (and politics),

---

[7] Skildum-Reid 2009.

[8] Klein 2001, p. 51.

few topics hold more general interest and potential to spice up small talk. Is it any surprise that any news bulletin worth its salt will include the general news of the day, a segment on financial news, and a segment on sport? It is hard to imagine a field of human activity that can be more aptly characterised as being, fundamentally, grounded and positioned so squarely within the public domain. In fact, law-makers and courts in various jurisdictions have described the basis for the power that those governing sport (the organisations like FIFA) wield as being a 'sacred trust' to administer the relevant sporting code in the public interest. Even the very definition of a 'mega-event' acknowledges this public dimension to such grand shows:

> "Mega-events" are large-scale cultural (including commercial and sporting) events which have a dramatic character, mass popular appeal and international significance. They are typically organised by variable combinations of national governmental and international non-governmental organisations and thus can be said to be important elements in "official" versions of public culture.[9]

In this light, it is interesting to consider the fact that mega-events and the vast amount of publicity that they generate are now often claimed to be commercial (read: private, and lucrative) property, and I will argue that controversial laws have started to actually protect them as such in various jurisdictions (even though, traditionally, there exists no such thing as a 'property right to a spectacle').

One observer has expressed the opinion that the allocation of hosting rights to the football World Cup resembles a franchise system, with FIFA constituting the monopolistic supplier and exclusive holder of property rights to the event.[10] This type of system has apparently also been accepted by the Olympic insiders, and is justified as necessary in order to guarantee the success of the Games.[11] Such a claim to a 'property right' to the World Cup event is echoed in FIFA's own founding documents (which variously claim ownership of *inter alia* 'every kind of

---

9 Roche 2000, p. 1.

10 Kurscheidt 2006, p. 7.

11 Former IOC Executive Board member (and vice-president) Dick Pound, expressed it as follows:

> In recent years, we have begun to think of the Olympics as a special form of franchise, in which the IOC is the franchisor and the host cities are the franchisees. It is up to us [the IOC] to define the basic parameters and standards we expect, and to see that these standards are met and even exceeded by our franchisees. Above all, we must be sure that no franchisee devaluates the Olympic franchise.

Pound 2006, p. 163.

financial right,'' marketing rights' and 'promotional rights' related to the event[12]) and in court papers in litigation where FIFA has attempted to protect such property through claims of the 'considerable goodwill in terms of common law' of their event. The IOC also views the Games as its property,[13] and rights to associate brands with the Olympics are sold to commercial partners at the rate of hundreds of millions of dollars (e.g. an approximate total of US$866 million in sponsorship investment in the Beijing Games of 2008, an event that lasted, in 'real time,' a little more than 2 weeks[14]). Most of these sponsorship deals, nowadays, are framed in the form of category exclusivity arrangements based on a groundbreaking Olympic sponsorship model created in the 1980s, which provides sponsors (in return for the hefty price tag) with the means of very effectively excluding their competitors from such events.[15] The attraction for sponsors is clear, and in no small measure connected with the nature of the rights grantors (the governing bodies) and their stance on claiming the existence of and protection for their 'property rights' to the events:

> Because sport with its self-governance has an exceptional and internationally acknowledged status, enjoying monopolistic elements in its governance and management, advertisers can indirectly enjoy similar benefits. For instance, being the sole provider of certain category of products that is allowed to enjoy the benefits of associating with a certain sport or event. Also, when the rights are acquired from a sole existing seller and in packages, it is arguably easier to conduct advertising campaigns, the strategy usually by default unanimously covering all the channels for the message to reach the audience. In most cases it is probably also easier to negotiate, enter into agreements and implement them, when a sole rights holder needs to be contracted, provided that the acquirer is able to provide substantial financial injections.[16]

---

[12] Article 74 (entitled 'Rights') of FIFA's Statutes (August 2009 version in force at the time of writing) provides as follows:

> Article 74(1) FIFA, its Members and the Confederations are the original owners of all of the rights emanating from competitions and other events coming under their respective jurisdiction, without any restrictions as to content, time, place and law. These rights include, among others, every kind of financial rights, audiovisual and radio recording, reproduction and broadcasting rights, multimedia rights, marketing and promotional rights and incorporeal rights such as emblems and rights arising under copyright law.
>
> (2) The Executive Committee shall decide how and to what extent these rights are utilised and draw up special regulations to this end. The Executive Committee shall alone decide whether these rights shall be utilised exclusively, or jointly with a third party or entirely through a third party.

[13] Compare Article 40(a) of the Host City Contract for the 2012 London Olympic Games, which provides that '[t]he City, the NOC and the OCOG acknowledge, without limiting any provision of the Olympic Charter, that the Games are the exclusive property of the IOC.'

[14] Harris et al 2009, p. 74.

[15] Sponsorship exclusivity will be more closely examined in Chaps. 2 and 6.

[16] Gradauskaite 2010, para 34.

It is difficult to imagine a more perfect textbook example for students of marketing and advertising of a surefire campaign which enjoys universal media coverage and is pitched at (and, generally, positively received by) a captive target audience seemingly perpetually insatiable for images and sound-bites associated with sports entertainment and popular culture. As I said, I know very little about marketing, maybe they do teach this in the classrooms; if they do not then maybe they should.

At the heart of these commercial arrangements is to be found a monopoly, and an extremely lucrative one at that. The Hollywood film industry and other entertainment sectors tend to concentrate the power to make and distribute films and other entertainment products in the hands of a few powerful studios, record companies or design houses, and protect the property that they create by means of the enforcement of the (limited) monopoly rights that the law provides for what has come to be known as intellectual property. However, an inherently monopolistic international sports governing body, which is by definition the self-proclaimed sole entity entitled to officially control the relevant sporting code (and especially its world championship competition—the mega-event), enjoys unprecedented power to exploit the commercial spin-offs of such competitions to the exclusion of all others. And this sometimes happens by way of a self-fulfilling prophecy, whereby an organisation that claims in its statutes that it is 'the original owner of all of the rights emanating from competitions and other events … without any restrictions as to content, time, place *and law*'[17] often appears to manage to usurp or coerce the law-making powers of event host nations in order to protect its fiefdom and the interests of its 'elite club' of commercial partners. I love telling my students about how these organisations frequently go so far as claiming (with varying success) immunity from laws in certain jurisdictions, in respect of their general day-to-day activities ranging from doping control to selling broadcasting rights or regulating the employment of professional athletes. But nowhere has this 'immunity' been achieved more completely than in the context of the staging of mega-events, where we have increasingly seen event organisers demand the passing of their very own, tailor-made laws by sovereign legislatures. *That* is the real subject of this book.

It is debatable whether there exists, anywhere, a more perfect example of an iron-clad commercial monopoly (which is protected by means of special laws) than the sports mega-event. Ironically, however, in light of the fact that legislatures have frequently engaged with these events in the process of passing such protecting laws, these monopolies appear to have managed to avoid significant legal scrutiny in most jurisdictions. This book will ask the pertinent question 'Why?,' and I will argue that the time has come for the legal fraternity and host governments to seriously question the continued legitimacy of the status quo when it comes to mega-event commercial rights protection and the role of the law.

17 Article 74(1) of the FIFA Statutes (2009).

One reason for the lack of critical engagement with these issues that arise in the context of the sponsorship of sport may be due to the fact that the very study of sports sponsorship has possibly been 'staunchly positivistic' and 'lacking in self-reflectivity':

> For most researchers sport sponsorship is seen as a neutral harmless task in which sponsors provide money to sport and in turn get to link their product to an athlete, team or event. Sport is seen to benefit because it receives a needed infusion of money. Commercial sponsors benefit because of their association with the popularity of sport, the visibility of the event or the high profile nature of the athlete(s) involved … The conceptual underpinning of such an understanding of the process of sport sponsorship is based in the notion that these types of transactions … involve an exchange relationship … By basing ideas about sponsorship on the concept of exchange, scholars who have studied this practice have provided an image of neutrality and of choices that are limited only by the skill of the people involved in the sponsorship transactions. Such a view ignores the underlying inequalities of power that are part of the sponsorship process, presents an overly simplistic account of the complexities of such interactions and neglects to address how structures of domination and exploitation shape and mediate these relationships.[18]
>
> Sponsorship is different from philanthropy: It is a strategic action from which the sponsor expects commercial benefits to accrue. Looking critically at this process will … show that the cheques are not free but can come at a cost to the sport and often involve broader social costs. A [critical rather than positivistic approach to sponsorship research] will need to move away from the bland surveys that characterise much of what passes for sponsorship research, to engage with more interpretative approaches.[19]

As mentioned, I am not a marketing or sponsorship researcher, and as such this book does not constitute sponsorship research in the strict sense of the word. My interest lies with the critical evaluation of what is, apparently, often viewed in mainstream discourse as sacred truths or *fait accompli*. Much of this book is about 'ambush marketing.' While I do not want to come across as a big fan of such much-maligned practices, I do often feel a measure of disappointment and sometimes even pure disgust at some allegedly expert writers' treatment of the subject—one more often than not encounters bald and unsubstantiated views condemning such marketing and vilifying the 'ambushers.' As observed above regarding the experience of sponsorship research to date, the same can possibly be said for research on ambush marketing:

> As the amount of money invested in sponsorship, and therefore the importance of brand protection has increased, so too has research in this area. However, despite the increasing interest, literature on ambush marketing has remained highly descriptive with little to no integration of theory. To date, the ambush literature has mainly focused on five themes: (1) definitions and explanations of the phenomenon …; (2) consumer reaction and sponsors recall …; (3) ethical issues …; (4) strategies and remedies for ambush marketing …; and (5) legal issues.[20]

---

[18] Slack and Amis 2004, p. 270.

[19] Ibid. 284.

[20] From Seguin et al 2009, p. 241.

While this book will largely focus on this last-mentioned area, namely legal issues regarding ambushing, I hope that it will do so by adding to the 'integration of theory' rather than merely being another 'highly descriptive' text on the subject. Most troubling about the vilifying and pejorative approach to ambush marketing in the literature is the frequently repeated but seldom interrogated truism that 'ambush marketing' is bad for sports and bad for mega-events, and that absent 'proper' (read: all-comprehensive, often draconian) legal protection against such marketing the sponsors will fly south for a long and dark winter in which sports mega-events will consequently and inevitably go the way of the dodo (sorry, I strangled some metaphors there I'm sure). I hope that my approach to the issues will go some way towards providing a measure of the type of critique called for in the above quoted passage in the context of sports sponsorship research, and that it might provide some much-needed balance in the debate about the ethics and legality of ambush marketing.

Central to the commercial value of mega-events for sponsors is the right to associate their brands, products and services with the relevant event. 'Association rights' have in recent years developed from a practical consequence of the working of the law (in the form of the threat of litigation for contravention of statutory trade mark rights and common law protections found in actions such as 'passing off' and other prohibited forms of unlawful competition) to what appears to be a new form of pseudo-property, in some cases created specially in mega-event specific legislation. What was previously not recognised as a substantive legal right—i.e., an event organiser's liberty to decide to contract with a commercial entity for purposes of sponsorship or endorsement, or not—has apparently been transformed into a legally protected right to associate with an event; a right that can be infringed by anyone—and I do mean anyone—who has not in fact entered into such a contract. The sometimes rabid protectionism as displayed by the event organisers (and there are many examples referred to in this book) reminds me of James Boyle's reference (made in the context of copyright as intellectual property) to the fact that 'the legal system's default setting is that "all rights are reserved" to the author' (or creator of the event, in this case).[21]

It appears to be accepted that the mega-event provides a sought-after platform (in the meaning of a 'mechanism that allows for the presentation of information and its transmission from a sender to a receiver'), and Price has explained that these platforms have enormous value if they are successful in attracting large, indeed massive, audiences and serving the need of their sponsors, whether they are selling goods or ideas or have the potential to do so.[22] He further explains, with reference to the Olympic Games, how this platform may be appropriated by persons who have not contributed to its creation:

> [T]he emphasis is on the effort (and this is a rough distinction) not to create a platform, but rather to appropriate one that was already established or constructed for another purpose,

---

[21] Boyle 2008, p. 181.

[22] Price 2008, p. 87.

> turning the message from that of its sponsors to those of others, commercial entities or global civil society groups. It is that specific irony—the notion of hijacking or piggy-backing—that becomes of interest with respect to the Olympics. The central idea is to find a platform that has proven highly successful in establishing a major constituency for one purpose and then convert that constituency to a different, unintended objective. The cost of creating the platform (very likely considerable) is borne by one player, but the benefits are then obtained by another. The Olympic Games, which offer advocacy groups opportunities for alliances among disparate groups that make up global civil society, provides an important example of this phenomenon. Embedded in this idea are a variety of sub-notions: (a) that the Olympic Games are such a platform; (b) that one can identify a dominant narrative that is the intended and approved narrative for which the platform was designed; and (c) in contrast, one can categorize other uses of the platform as counter-narrative in ways that are worthy of distinction. In other words, there is some (possibly illusionary) accepted use for the Olympics that is crowded out or violated and that it is possible to tell, sometimes in advance of the event, who the contenders are for the secondary use.[23]

This book will evaluate (and question) the notion of 'ambush marketing' as such a 'counter-narrative' in respect of the sport mega-event as platform for commercial exploitation, and the event organisers' frequent condemnation of ambushing as 'piggy-backing,' 'filching' and 'misappropriation of goodwill' of events. In essence, I will consider, on the one hand, the justification for the stigmatised view of ambushing as expressed by event organisers and the ethical and legal aspects; on the other I will examine the legitimacy of the apparently claimed 'property right' to a sports event, of the commercial monopoly in such events and, more pointedly, of the ways in which laws have been and continue to be used in order to protect such monopolies in a number of jurisdictions against ambushing. I will do so by examining the public interest in such events (and the public interest grounding of such events) as well as the frequent conflicts between private commercial interests and universally accepted human rights.

My Aims with the Book

A major focus of the book (to which I will specifically devote a chapter, Chap. 8) is the proper demarcation of the legally protectable thematic space around sports mega-events. I will examine both what sponsors pay for (and should rightly receive in return for their sponsorship fee), as well as the legitimacy of the special protection granted to organisers and sponsors in order to optimise exploitation of the potential commercial value of such thematic space. A key thread in this evaluation will be to determine what it is about these events that is actually deserving of legal protection. The public domain element of this thematic space is an ever-shrinking one in light of the legislative intervention by host governments and law-makers, and the 'special interest legislation' against ambushing

---

[23] Ibid. 89.

significantly skews the commercial playing field as well as the wider social and cultural dimension of the sports mega-event in favour of a generally small group of primarily large multinational corporations and monopolistic sports governing bodies (with narrow commercial interests which may easily ignore and impinge on wider societal goals and imperatives). I generally object to the 'propertization' of all kinds of elements of events (such as organisers' persistent claims of 'rights,' some of which, frankly, do not exist in terms of general legal principles in most jurisdictions), which includes, *inter alia*, the worrying trend towards monopolisation of language re events and claims to control the 'conversation' around the event (which claims face stiff challenges from the modern social media). Somewhere during the past few decades the eminently public-centred sports mega-event became a private money-spinner *par excellence*. While developing nations continue to bid for the right (or is it a privilege?) to host these events, the mega-event has become a creature that does not necessarily bring with it the benefits that voters and tax-payers in these nations should be entitled to expect, while auguring significant implications for the civil liberties and fundamental rights of such host nation citizens.

At the risk of displaying a lack of objectivity, I strongly believe that the current model of commercial exploitation of events and the continuing trend of legal legitimisation and protection thereof has been insufficiently justified to date and, in fact, has not been subjected to proper and in-depth scrutiny by the legal fraternity. I believe that the time is ripe for radical law reform in this regard, and I hope that this book will go some way towards providing the necessary impetus for such a process.

I tend to subscribe to the apparently growing consensus view of some marketing experts, such as (specifically) the outspoken Kim Skildum-Reid, namely that the most successful way to avoid or combat ambushing is by proper leveraging of sponsorship rights, rather than the prohibitive and potentially restrictive efforts at erecting legally reinforced walls around events. The answer may not lie (or not primarily, at least) in use of the sometimes blunt instrument of the law. I have strong objections against the conduct and track record of some of the major event organisers (such as FIFA) in respect of aggressive rights protection programmes which often display a marked lack of forethought or even common sense. Recent research suggests that some of the problems relating to the pejoratively characterised 'ambushing' of events are probably more properly ascribable to marketing clutter caused by these very organisations, as a result of their efforts to ostensibly milk every last possible dollar from rights exploitation rather than providing fewer official sponsors with more 'bang for their buck.' The law-makers have, for the most part, not displayed a sufficient sense of sovereignty, of accountability to their domestic constituencies and of respect for the rule of law, and have compounded the problem through largely indiscriminate acceptance of the now standard, non-negotiable demands for special legal protection of events in the form of bid guarantees. The result is an environment where conduct by members of the public (tax-paying contributors to the hefty bills to host mega-events), which would otherwise not fall foul of normal and universally-accepted legal principles, has been outlawed in order to protect narrow commercial interests of sometimes dubious legitimacy in terms of legal principles. Ironically, while support for better leveraging of sponsorship rights as a primary means to deter and combat ambushing is gaining ground (although not yet sufficiently within the legal fraternity), the special laws passed for events may in fact deter sponsors from pursuing this route. The *sui generis* event legislation tends to provide a safety net whereby event organisers and sponsors may be growing lazy in respect of their rights exploitation and enforcement/protection efforts. Not only does this foster a tendency to automatically resort to the ubiquitous cease-and-desist letters, it also promotes a rigid attitude of 'all rights reserved' (and the claiming of legal remedies for things that are/should not be protected by law). Such legislation may be fostering a culture of entitlement with very little basis in law.

The continuing trend for mega-events (of which the FIFA World Cup and Olympic Games are prime examples) to spawn sometimes ludicrous and widely-condemned incidents of very public *faux pas* in the form of overly-aggressive rights enforcement by event organisers is troubling, and cannot be good for the reputation of these events (or of the legal system) in the long run. As a South African I am embarrassed to have to point to the 'Bavaria babes' debacle experienced in this country in June 2010, during the opening round of FIFA's 2010 showcase. While this was a clear case of an orchestrated campaign to gain publicity for a brand (although I am loath to call it an 'ambush' in the traditional sense of the word, if one considers that strong anti-ambushing legislation such as that found in South Africa departs radically from the traditional notion of an 'ambush' as involving deception of the public as to official sponsorship or affiliation to the event) the response by both FIFA and the South African authorities was heavy-handed and lacked any sense of appreciation of the 'bigger picture.' While the widely reported public perception that such response back-fired will hopefully serve as food for thought for event organisers in future, I would like to see legislatures actively resisting calls for the type and level of protection that would facilitate such responses by event organisers.

My message to event organisers and sponsors who are concerned about ambushes is simple: *Less can be more*.

Limit, to the extent necessary, the number of sponsors in order to reduce clutter, but ensure that those sponsors get exactly what they pay for and that you will 'have their backs' when their rights are threatened. While no event organiser has to date managed to prove or even make a really convincing argument that ambush marketing actually threatens the continued existence of their events (because, as they tend to claim, it threatens to alienate sponsors), I would suggest that such proper support for sponsors' contractual rights would negate this risk in most cases. After all, not even the risk of competitors having a way in to grab a small slice of the pie (which, after all, is business as usual outside the context of the mega-event in free market economies) takes away from the fact that these events provide a probably unmatched and ideal marketing platform for the official sponsors.

Allow, in the domestic context of the host nation, for more freedom for smaller firms to participate in the commercial opportunities that arise from the event, with an objective, unprejudiced (and not a knee-jerk, over-protective) approach to inclusiveness. Rather work with the large sponsors to find ways of leveraging the publicity value of the event, to which such activities of smaller firms in fact contributes. Maybe one can even find ways for small firms and multinational sponsors to partner up in the process of marketing their mutually beneficial links to the event.

But also know that the historical fact of your status of event organiser and monopoly regulator of 'the game' may not entitle you to claim all aspects of the event as your exclusive property. You will not be able to avoid all potential 'ambushes,' but you as organiser and your sponsors will be much happier if you realise and openly acknowledge this fact. When you enter the market of commercial exploitation of events you must accept that others also inhabit this market, and may have stronger pre-existing rights to pursue their trade. FIFA, for example, was recently forcibly reminded of this fact by the German federal Supreme Court in the final throes of its protracted litigation against confectionary maker Ferrero (which I'll discuss briefly in Chap. 5). You cannot, simultaneously, claim very substantial government and public support (financial and otherwise) in order to encamp in a particular country and then attempt to aggressively ring-fence nearly all possible ways of riding the wave of event publicity. The citizen and entrepreneur in the host nation do not want to have to pay a premium to be an extra in what is increasingly becoming, simply, someone else's corporate marketing video. Show respect for the host nation and its people, and let your commercial footprint (just like your carbon footprint) be a small one and not be redolent, primarily, of what may be perceived (rightly or wrongly) as selfish and crass commercialism.

With that in mind, however, by all means enforce your generally-accepted and applicable existing legal rights, but do not demand special treatment under the laws of a host nation unless you can provide sufficient and reasoned motivation for this, bearing in mind that such protection often comes at great social, financial and other costs to others who inhabit that domain (which you are, after all, visiting temporarily). And let that process of motivating for strong and special legal protection be a democratic and participatory one, which involves all stakeholders, including the consumer public and small businesses in the host nation or city.

More fundamentally, make sure that your very system of sponsorship exclusivity is above board and does not invite potential legal challenge. Ensure that fair opportunities for participation in cutting the commercial cake are provided and that more guests (both invited and uninvited—but only if well-behaved) are allowed at the table. Allow opportunities to a wide spectrum of potential commercial partners, and do not create the perception of perpetuating a closed shop where only the 'big boys' are perceived to benefit from the event. With less aggressive enforcement against small 'ambushers' as a largely PR-focused exercise, and principled action against the large commercial actors (who may be serial ambushers of events but are rarely if ever actually sued, to which Nike can attest), may come a legitimisation of the concept and importance of commercial rights and the need for their protection in the public zeitgeist.

As for the risks to event organisers, recent events have again shown the dynamic nature of ambushing and of the legal implications. For example, I understand that the 2011 ICC Cricket World Cup has raised specific issues regarding the unauthorised commercial use of news footage of matches by the media, which has implicated practices of media accreditation.[24] While this is not something new, the level of the problem appears to have been unprecedented, and may well lead to litigation in the near future. This just shows that only time will tell how future events will be affected. The viral internet marketing campaign and prevalence of social media, for example, will undoubtedly pose not only opportunities but also new risks to event organisers and sponsors. The large and prominent ambushing campaign, in the traditional sense of illegitimately associating a brand with an event by means of deceiving consumers and infringing use of organisers' IP, is largely a thing of the past. The 'ambushers' have grown more sophisticated, and the event organisers and sponsors should follow suit. This does not, however, mean that these parties should lobby for more and more stringent 'catch-all' laws to enclose 'their' event in an artificially constructed bubble. Legal advisors should be more creative in finding ways in which existing laws can protect events without resorting to the political power of event organisers (and their hosting bid evaluators) and the economic power of multinational sponsors being used to demand dubious new event-specific laws.

The Style and Approach of the Book

I have tried very hard to avoid this book turning into a textbook on ambush marketing or legal aspects of sport sponsorship. I believe there is a need for such works (and they do exist—English barrister and intellectual property law expert Philip Johnson has written a very good one, which was updated recently), but this is not one of them. What I have tried to produce is an informative and (hopefully) interesting account of the subject, including some description of the development of commercial exploitation of major events and the real experience of ambushing of such events in recent years, which also includes critical analysis and evaluation of the state of laws in this respect with a view to assessing the legitimacy of legal responses to ambush marketing. I have attempted to avoid the sometimes judgmental (and, in my view, rather simplistic) point of departure of many commentators who appear to accept, without more, that all 'ambush marketing' of events is evil and must be combated ruthlessly and, apparently, at all costs. As the title of the book suggests, I have attempted to subject the very targets of such 'ambushing' campaigns—the events and their commercialisation—to critical scrutiny. At the very real risk of displaying a lack of objectivity on the

[24] On which I will say more in Chap. 10.

issue, I will argue that the apparently sacrosanct nature of these mega-events and of the commercial rights that are exploited in relation to them should be re-evaluated.

My contention throughout is that one should remember that these are largely private commercial interests that are at stake, and that attempts to protect these interests, primarily through the use of legal instruments (specifically legislation), should clearly and sufficiently balance these private interests and the greater public interest in mega-events and sport, more generally. While I am no supporter of ambush marketing and have a healthy respect for rights and commercial property legitimately created, nurtured or obtained (often at great cost), I do hope that the reader will consider that not all conduct that may be described by those with vested interests (namely sports organisations and their commercial partners) as 'ambush marketing' is necessarily an evil that needs to be eradicated. Morals, ethics and also the rule of law need to be reappraised in this context, and the abuse of the legal and/or legislative process at the cost of the public good or of accepted principles of the law, where this happens, should be addressed as a matter of urgency.

I have also tried to keep the style rather informal, light-hearted and sometimes irreverent in places. The subject matter, in my opinion, lends itself very well to this. I hope that the reader will enjoy some of the accounts of 'ambushes' of events that we have seen in recent years and of the responses thereto. I believe this is a serious book that deals with a serious subject matter, but I feel that it need not put the reader to sleep in the process.

As regards the focus areas of the book, it needs first to be said that the project turned out to be quite a daunting one. Developing what started as a series of articles in a domestic law journal (about one specific mega-event and the relevant legal framework in one particular jurisdiction) into a work that attempts to cover multiple different mega-events and various jurisdictions was quite a substantial task. I had somewhat less than 9 months to do the research and writing, something that (in hindsight) I probably needed about 4 years (a mega-event quadrennial) to do properly and comfortably. I sincerely hope that the end product does not display any major gaps or errors and, if so, that others may take up the challenge to further develop anything of use they may find in this work.

I need to include two short disclaimers regarding the focus of the book. The first relates to the events covered. My intention was to include discussion on the commercialisation of most of the international mega-events in sport, namely the Olympic Games, the FIFA football World Cup, the IRB Rugby World Cup, the ICC Cricket World Cup, the Commonwealth Games and the Asian Games. Other relevant events, although different in nature from those mentioned, include the FIA formula 1 world motor racing championship and American football's Super Bowl. Unfortunately, time and the suggested scope of a work of this nature would not allow for in-depth and separate discussion of all these events, individually. I have thus attempted to extrapolate common practices and models of commercialisation in respect of all of these events, with the Olympic Games featuring as a template for other events (as it has done in practice). Where relevant and required I have attempted to then include some discussion of particular aspects of other specific events that may be meaningful in respect of the subject and the process of evaluating the relevant laws and legal responses to 'ambushes' or other such (perceived) threats to commercial interests of the stakeholders in these events.

The second disclaimer relates to the jurisdictions covered in the book. Given more time and scope I would have loved to include a separate chapter on each of the jurisdictions relevant to the discussion, where I could examine the common law, legislative and other bases for protection of commercial rights to mega-events specific to the relevant systems. Ultimately I had to select the relevant jurisdictions (based, primarily, on their hosting of mega-events in recent years or future hosting where bids have been awarded at the time of writing and resultant development of law specific to such events) and include discussion of them in a piecemeal fashion. I decided that, for example, it would be more prudent to discuss anti-ambush marketing legislation in the different jurisdictions by lumping relevant statutes and other legislative instruments together under a relevant and related topic. For example, instead therefore of comprehensively describing the content of such legislation as passed in e.g. the UK, South Africa and India, respectively (although Chap. 4 contains discussion of such laws in these and other jurisdictions), relevant aspects of the different pieces of legislation have been lumped together in e.g. the discussion of potential intellectual property rights implications of such instruments or how they may affect freedom of expression guarantees in the relevant jurisdictions. The reader who is interested in a more descriptive and comprehensive source of information on the contents of the relevant legislation in a particular jurisdiction is therefore advised to consult other available sources. This book will, hopefully, provide a meaningful evaluation of the relevant legislation in the various jurisdictions in a more focused manner, which should provide not only analysis of the legitimacy and efficacy of specific instruments but should also be of interest to comparative law scholars.

Finally, this book was not written with a specific target market in mind. It is not aimed specifically or exclusively at students, or academics, or legal practitioners, or sports organisations, or potential event host governments or sponsors. In a perfect world someone will read this book; and that someone will, preferably, be involved in future bidding for the rights to host a sports mega-event or in preparation for the hosting of such an event where these rights have already been awarded. I guess that my ideal target market would be the law-makers who are faced with the issue of juggling the pressure from event organisers and rights holders to obtain special legal protection for their commercial interests, and the interests, rights and liberties of the public and of small business enterprises, the media and others. For this reason I have tried to include some suggestions aimed specifically at such lawmakers, in the final chapter. It is hoped that the subject and its treatment will be of wider interest and relevance, however, and that all of these persons will find something of value here. Actually, I'm just hoping that someone (anyone!) will buy it.

What You Will Find in the Chapters

Chapter 2 will proceed to examine the commercial arrangements relating to sports mega-events between sports organisations and their commercial partners, primarily the sponsors who spend hundreds of millions of dollars to associate their products and services with these international spectacles. It will start with a brief discussion of how the commercial exploitation through sponsorship of these events works, after which I will provide some brief description of the (short) history of the development of the modern mega-vent sponsorship model in the Olympic Games context. The final section of the chapter will examine (again, very briefly) how sponsorship works, and will then focus on a central concept in the evaluation of the legality of ambush marketing and of the law's responses to it, namely sponsorship exclusivity to events. The legal implications of such exclusivity will be further examined in Chap. 6.

Chapter 3 will provide, as background for the later chapters, a largely descriptive overview of the definitions and practices of ambush marketing and of the legal bases for protection available to sports organisations and their commercial partners. The final section will set the scene for critical analysis of the legitimacy of anti-ambushing laws as undertaken in the later chapters, by briefly but seriously interrogating the question of whether all forms of 'ambushing,' as marketing efforts by non-sponsors around events is often characterised, are in fact legally and ethically 'wrong.' I believe that this is a crucially important exercise, as the chapters that follow will examine criticisms that have been expressed in recent years regarding the sometimes draconian and excessive protections that international sports organisations have been able to impose on the governments of host nations for major events, in furthering or maintaining the commercial interests of such organisations and of their commercial partners (especially that powerful new animal, the 'official supporter' or 'global partner'; such 'linguistic contortions' aimed at creating an aura of altruistic patronage rather than commercial interest in the face of prolonged criticism of the commercialisation of events such as the Olympic Games[25]).

Chapter 4 examines the ways in which domestic laws in various countries treat ambush marketing of events. It starts off by examining the way in which special legal protection has been obtained in those systems, in recent years, where *sui generis* event legislation has been passed under significant pressure from the event organisers who now demand the creation of such special laws as an absolute *sine qua non* in order to obtain the rights to host these events. The latter half of the chapter will undertake description of the legal treatment of ambush marketing in ten different jurisdictions. These range from countries that have passed such special anti-ambushing laws to countries where event organisers have been forced to resort to only the existing laws available on the statute book or in terms of the

[25] Magdalinski and Nauright 2004, p. 195.

common law or otherwise. Some of the special laws discussed in this chapter will be the subject of more in-depth critical scrutiny in the later chapters.

Chapter 5 is the first of three chapters which will each focus on a specific aspect of the impact of special legal protection of commercial rights to events. This chapter will critically examine the ways in which such special laws not only supplement but often significantly alter the fundamental precepts, characteristics and working of intellectual property laws. IP rights are, of course, important in the context of event sponsorships and also of ambush marketing. I will examine, however, the recent trend of phenomenal expansion of IP laws and of IP rights and the protection which they provide to event organisers and their commercial partners by means of *sui generis* event legislation, from a critical perspective. My conclusion is that this expansion is illegitimate and unjustifiable in this context, and provides a major cause for concern regarding the legitimacy of special event protection laws.

Chapter 6 continues this more specific evaluation of the nature and effects of special anti-ambushing laws, by focusing on the potential competition law (or anti-trust) implications of such laws. In Chap. 2, I examine how the mega-event sponsorship model functions, and I hint at the fact that the modern sports mega-event is a commercial monopoly through which event organisers (and sponsors) pursue excessive market control in interests of the pursuit of profit. This chapter will continue this examination and will include consideration of the (potential) role of competition law in this context.

Chapter 7 will conclude the more specific consideration of the impact of special event commercial rights protection on traditional legal principles, by briefly examining the potential human rights implications of such laws. I will examine issues such as the impact of anti-ambushing laws on free speech, and on constitutionally protected property rights and the freedom of trade. I hope that this discussion will, if only obliquely, focus attention on the urgent need for the legal fraternity to seriously consider the implications and legitimacy of mega-event commercial monopolies in the context of the global political economy and, specifically, developmental states such as South Africa, India and Brazil, who are more and more frequently bidding for and successfully acquiring the rights to host mega-events, and then called upon to pass laws which undermine fundamental principles of their hard-fought constitutional democracies.

Chapter 8 will conclude the examination of the legal implications of special anti-ambushing laws by focusing on what is currently the pinnacle of international legal developments in respect of special event commercial rights protection, namely the relatively new legal creature that has come to be known as the 'association right' to an event. I will critically examine a number of aspects of these very substantial and controversial new pseudo-intellectual property rights, which I believe require closer scrutiny and serious consideration. These include the issue of the legitimacy of using the mechanism of public power (in the form of legislation) to protect narrow, private commercial interests to events; the questions of what such laws are aimed at protecting and what they in fact seek to outlaw; and the considerable costs of such special laws in the greater scheme of the public interest in the staging of sports mega-events.

Chapter 9 will seek to inject some sense of objectivity into my evaluation of the legitimacy of these special event laws, which may be refreshing if the reader feels that such objectivity is lacking in the sometimes scathing criticism of anti-ambushing laws and practices as contained in the earlier chapters. I will briefly examine the stock argument of event organisers that is so often invoked in support of aggressive campaigns to protect commercial rights to events against ambushes (namely that ambush marketing threatens the very existence of the mega-event through the potential for ambushing to alienate the official sponsors—what I will refer to as the 'survival of the Games' argument). I will further examine the legitimacy of claims to rights and claims for their protection by law in the face of the commercial monopoly enjoyed by such event organisers. I will not beat around the bush in expressing my opinion that these justifications for strong anti-ambushing laws are mostly illusory, if not disingenuous.

Chapter 10, the final chapter, will contain some conclusions regarding the legitimacy of anti-ambushing laws and of the mega-event monopoly. I will briefly summarise the objections raised in the preceding chapters and will even try, although rather superficially, to include some suggestions for addressing the problems that exist. As I will state repeatedly throughout the book, I am not a supporter of ambush marketing in the sense of efforts by unscrupulous opportunists to 'free-ride' off the publicity value of events if such 'ambushes' take the form of deception and the creation of consumer confusion about the support provided by these marketers to the event or to the efforts of those who put on the show. I do believe, however, that many other forms of conduct by legitimate marketers and individuals are nowadays called 'ambushing,' but are in fact undeserving of this largely pejorative label and even less so of the often brutal reaction by law-makers and law enforcers. In this chapter I will also briefly examine expectations for the future regarding ambush marketing and sports mega-events. I will examine a seemingly unrelated (although, I will argue, very relevant) development in one specific jurisdiction, which, it will be submitted, may hold significant implications for this ongoing process of ever-increasing monopolisation of events. This involves a new law in France, which envisages the creation of a 'sports event organiser's right' in the context of the regulation of sports betting. I will speculate to what extent such development might serve to create precedent or a model for international sports organisations to claim a 'proprietary right to a spectacle' in the future, and how this might contribute to the further monopolisation of events and of ring-fencing of the commercial and other value of such events. On the other side of the event organiser/ambush marketer divide I will also briefly consider future prospects for mega-event ambushing primarily with reference to the use of the internet and, more specifically, social media.

In this concluding chapter I will attempt to suggest ways in which we can avoid the untenable and, frankly, despicable trend of the law increasingly being used virtually as a blunt instrument in the back pocket of sports event organisers and multinational corporations. While my suggestions will, for the most part, be rather sketchy and undeveloped, I hope that they may spark some debate and may serve at least as a basis for development of further and more meaningful ideas on how to address the problems that currently exist in the sports mega-event milieu.

So relax, put on some background music (you could use your Visa® card to buy a copy of Shakira's 'Waka Waka'© and pour yourself a Budweiser® while you snack on a Big Mac®), and let's take a look at the ways in which laws protect the commercial monopoly that is the sports mega-event. I will only ask that you keep an open mind, and suspend disbelief as we delve, along the way, into some examples of the sometimes rabid protection of these commercial 'rights' and how the interests of the public and of sports fans have been relegated to a very distant and apparently unimportant concern. Ancient Rome had its gladiatorial games where the populace were politically (and very professionally) seduced and drugged by the entertainment spectacle while all sorts of horrors and misdemeanours were perpetrated at their expense. I will argue that little has changed in the past couple of millennia, and that the modern sports mega-event remains an unfortunate smokescreen for greed and corruption, which, worryingly, constitutes neither a natural culmination of the ethos and spirit of sport and of major sports events such as the Olympic Games, nor a high point in the global pursuit of the supremacy of the rule of law.

References

All internet-based sources referred to, were last visited in or before December 2011

Boyle J (2008) The public domain: enclosing the commons of the mind. Yale University Press, New Haven

Burleson C (2009) Ekecheiria revival: re-establishing the ancient Olympic truce in modern-day peacekeeping. Proceedings of the 17th international seminar on Olympic studies for postgraduate students, vol 26, International Olympic Academy, 1–30 July 2009

Gradauskaite J (2010) The advertising appeal of sports and the legal limits of the incorporation of sports in advertising. Entertain Sports Law J 8(1). ISSN 1748-944X. http://www2.warwick.ac.uk/fac/soc/law/elj/eslj/issues/volume8/number1/gradauskaite/gradauskaite.pdf

Harris P, Schmitz S, O'Hare R (2009) Ambush marketing and London 2012: a golden opportunity for advertising, or not? Entertain Law Rev 20(3):74

Horne J, Manzenreiter W (eds) (2006) Sports mega-events: social scientific analyses of a global phenomenon. Blackwell Publishing Ltd/The Sociological Review, Oxford

Katz D (1994) Just do it: the Nike spirit in the corporate world. Adams Media Corporation, Holbrook

Klein N (2001) No logo. Flamingo Books, London

Kurscheidt M (2006) The world cup. Paper presented at the Copenhagen conference on the social and economic impact of hosting mega sports events, 1 Sept 2006

Magdalinski T, Nauright J (2004) Commercialisation of the modern Olympics. In: Slack T (ed) The commercialisation of sport. Routledge, London

Pound RW (2006) Inside the Olympics. Wiley, Toronto

Price ME (2008) On seizing the Olympic platform. In: Price ME, Dayan D (eds) Owning the Olympics: narratives of the New China. Digitalculturebooks, Ann Arbor, pp 86–114

Real M (1996) The postmodern Olympics: technology and the commodification of the olympic movement. Quest 48(1):9–24, as quoted by Symons C, Warren I (2006) "David v. Goliath": the gay games, the Olympics and the ownership of language. Entertain Sports Law J

Roche M (2000) Mega-events and modernity: Olympics and expos in the growth of global culture. Routledge, London

Seguin B, Gauthier M, Ellis D, Parent MM (2009) Power play: an examination of power and ambush marketing. Conference proceedings, 17th EASM conference 2009

Skildum-Reid K (2009) Why ambush marketing legislation will never work (and what will). Posted 5 August 2009. Available online at the time of writing at http://blog.powersponsorship.com/index.php/2009/08/why-ambush-marketing-legislation-will-never-work/

Slack T, Amis J (2004) Money for nothing and your cheques for free? A critical perspective on sports sponsorship. In: Slack T (ed) The commercialisation of sport. Routledge, London

Chapter 2
The Commercial Monopoly in Sports Mega-Events

> [The world football governing body was] not driven by any selfless goal of global equity within FIFA, more by the entrepreneurial motivation and machiavellian global networking of FIFA's bosses and their business allies ... In such contexts and circumstances, global markets for sports business and for major sponsors have expanded with little or no reference to the wider constituencies of sport, or to the ruling forum of individual sports organisations. Benefits may have accrued to under-resourced areas of the football world, but such expansion has been driven by the commercial interests of an incestuous network of sports leaders, administrators and commercial entrepreneurs.[1]

2.1 Introduction

These are challenging times for those who roam the corridors of power in the highest echelons of international sport, with some international sports federations (notably the two biggest players, the International Olympic Committee and FIFA) having experienced crises of governance and well-publicised allegations of corruption and mismanagement in the past decade or so. The Salt Lake City Olympic Games, of course, comes to mind. More recently we saw a widespread furore over bribes in the bidding for 'Fair Play'-loving FIFA's 2022 World Cup, which, after some FIFA officials were suspended clearly did not bother President Sepp Blatter too much. He subsequently responded to criticism of the organisation by saying that all FIFA's 'successes' have created 'a lot of envy and jealousy in our world because you cannot satisfy everybody'; 'the success story of FIFA can continue because we are in a comfortable situation' and 'we have the power and the

[1] Tomlinson 2005, p. 59, 60.

A. M. Louw, *Ambush Marketing and the Mega-Event Monopoly*,
ASSER International Sports Law Series, DOI: 10.1007/978-90-6704-864-4_2,

instruments to go against any attacks that are made'.[2] 'Herr Sepp', who was named in March 2011 by *The Times* in the top spot of its 'Sport Power 100' list of the one hundred most influential people in sport, is presently still firmly ensconced in FIFA House, described as 'a $100 m bunker remote from the eyes of the world'.[3] Undoubtedly, he is correct in his convictions of the untouchable nature of his fiefdom. The major international sports governing bodies often appear to weather the storms of criticism and to be able to function, to a significant degree, outside the realm of domestic regulation, as the many calls for a 'sporting exception' to the application of the EU Treaty in recent years attests. Two significant reasons for this is the lack of transparency in respect of the governance of an organisation such as FIFA as well as the very nature of the beast, as was observed by Transparency International in a rather scathing August 2011 report:

> FIFA is both a non-governmental, non-profit organisation and a global company with huge revenues, unprecedented reach, political clout and enormous worldwide social influence. But unlike a multinational company, answerable to shareholders, FIFA's mandate comes from the member federations represented by officials (i.e. presidents and delegates, mostly working on a voluntary basis) from all over the world, elected bottom up. This means that FIFA is answerable to the 208 national football associations who themselves are partly dependent on the funds that FIFA allocates to them. This lack of mandatory accountability to the outside world makes it unlikely that change will come either from within the organisation or from the grassroots of the football organisations. Moreover, the scale and specific structure of FIFA makes it difficult to adapt what is considered best business practice to the governance challenges it is facing.[4]

Despite the scandals and the controversies, the silver lining to all of these woes attendant to a modern Internet-based society of social networking, blogging, WikiLeaks and widespread access to dirty little secrets, may be the prospect of an even larger paycheque for sports administrators in future. It appears that there are important recent developments regarding the commercialisation of major events, which deserve critical consideration. This phenomenon is systemic and widespread, which might lead cynical observers to question the extent to which sport as a social activity has apparently largely lost touch with the fact that it was, until relatively recently still, at least notionally, rooted in 'Corinthian ideals' and the much-vaunted 'spirit of Olympism'. We are concerned here primarily with what is

[2] See the report dated 6 January 2011, available online at http://uk.reuters.com/article/2011/01/06/uk-soccer-asian-congress-blatter-idUKTRE70525X20110106.

[3] From Scott, M 'FIFA crisis: Storm clouds gather as big hitters fight to clear names', 29 May 2011 in *The Guardian*—available online at the time of writing at http://www.guardian.co.uk/football/2011/may/29/fifa-crisis-storm-clouds-gather?INTCMP=ILCNETTXT3487.

[4] Schenk, S *Safe Hands: Building Integrity and Transparency at FIFA* Report by Transparency International (August 2011) at 2—copy available at the time of writing for download on their web site at http://www.transparency.org/news_room/latest_news/press_releases/2011/2011_08_16_independent_group_fifa_reform.

often referred to as the development of the 'Olympic brand'[5] or its equivalent in sports such as football, with its FIFA World Cup.

Examples of the excesses that have been experienced with the influx of money in sport abound. Cynical observers may feel that commercialisation appears to be making a mockery of the 'sacred trust' which has traditionally formed the basis for sports governing bodies' trusteeship over sporting codes,[6] and big money has also contributed significantly to the increased scrutiny of the activities of such organisations by the media and others. Amidst the allegations of greed and corruption that have so frequently been levelled at those at the very top in the largest and most elite of these bodies,[7] I hesitate to express a view on the morality or otherwise of the ever-increasing role of money in sport. I am, personally, not averse to this; if one considers the vast entertainment value of sport across the globe it would be fatuous to condemn money in sport and to ignore consumer choice and the rights

---

[5] See, for example, the arguably rather arrogant view of Michael Payne, former marketing director of the International Olympic Committee, writing in Payne 2006, p. 187:

'[B]y the time the athletes and media arrived at Salt Lake [for the 2002 winter Olympic Games], the world found what it wanted: a city and an organising committee that fully understood its responsibilities in staging the Games; that they were mere custodians of the Olympic brand, and were tasked with nurturing it, polishing it and eventually returning it back to the [International Olympic Committee]—stronger, and in better shape, than when they had received it'.

[6] It is interesting to note what (it is submitted) may amount to a rather blatant recent example of the way in which the pursuit of profit has assumed a dominant role over the promotion of sport for the greater good: The South African organisers of the 2010 FIFA World Cup apparently experienced difficulty in negotiations with FIFA regarding ticket prices for the event. While the local organisers (and other forums across Africa) had insisted that tickets should be affordable to the masses, FIFA apparently pegged the prices, insisting on the maximisation of profits in order to finance their own activities for the four years until the next World Cup in 2014. Apparently, FIFA emphasised the fact that the event is a FIFA event and that South Africa has little bargaining power in this respect—even to the point of stating that the organisation could take away the World Cup if they chose (from a briefing to the parliamentary Portfolio Committee on Sport and Recreation, Cape Town, 14 June 2005). It appears that there is widespread dissatisfaction amongst host countries of the FIFA World Cup in respect of the organisation's history of imposing rigid demands on hosts in the interest of maximising FIFA profits from the event. On a study tour to France by members of the Parliamentary Portfolio Committee on Sport and Recreation (visit undertaken in June 2005, to investigate issues surrounding France's hosting of the FIFA World Cup in 1998 with a view to preparations for World Cup 2010 in South Africa), members of the delegation were specifically warned by the Director-General of the French Football Federation that FIFA was imposing increasingly rigid regulations in this regard (e.g. that the organisation would receive all the revenues from television rights for the event). The delegation was reportedly advised that South Africa should not agree to a blanket acceptance of all FIFA's rules and conditions, in order to ensure that the country would derive sufficient economic benefit from the event. See the minutes of the discussion of the Committee, 11 August 2005 (available online at http://www.pmg.org.za/viewminute.php?id=6094).

[7] Compare the latest in a number of critical exposes, British investigative journalist Andrew Jennings's *Foul! The Secret World of FIFA: Bribes, Vote Rigging and Ticket Scandals*, Harper Sport, London, 2006; see also (in respect of the International Olympic Committee) Jennings's *The New Lords of the Rings* Pocket Books 1996.

of those savvy enough to try and turn a profit in the face of such abundance. This does not, however, mean that all degrees of the apparently largely unchecked expansion of the commercial elements of sport should not be open to scrutiny and even treated with a healthy dose of suspicion on occasion.

A watershed moment in the commercialisation of international sport and its mega-events was the 1984 Olympic Games in Los Angeles, which, despite the then still notionally 'amateur' status of the competition, was the first instalment of the Games where no public money was required to host the event and where the International Olympic Committee managed to show a more than USD 200 million profit. This was due mainly to the efforts of the president of the Organising Committee, Peter Ueberroth, who managed to an unprecedented degree to leverage the commercial potential of the Games by means of expensive corporate sponsorship fees, different categories of sponsorship and the promise of exclusivity within each level.[8] Interestingly, the 1984 Games also saw the first really mainstream media attention for what would be dubbed 'ambush marketing'—which we will examine in Chap. 3—when Kodak upstaged official Olympic sponsor Fuji. More will be said about developments surrounding the Los Angeles Games and the commercialisation model that it spawned in the discussion below.

More generally, the professional sports industry in recent decades has simply exploded to the point of the astronomical amounts that make up today's sports broadcasting market (internationally, the major source of income for those governing sport). In English football, the entry of BSkyB into the market of broadcasting Premier League matches (in 1992) facilitated a phenomenal increase in the TV rights fees. In the 15-year period between 1986 and 2001, the rights fee increased from GBP 6.3 million for a 2-year period to GBP 1.1 billion over 3 years (or from GBP 3.1 million to GBP 367 million per year).[9] The Premier League rights became even dearer in recent years, with the League's sale of broadcasting rights for the 2010–2013 period raising GBP 1.78 billion in respect of domestic television rights and a further GBP 1.4 billion representing the sale of overseas broadcasting rights.[10] In the United States, television money represents the NFL's most lucrative revenue source, and in agreements with CBS, Fox, NBC, ESPN, and Direct-TV the NFL earns more than USD 3.75 billion per season.[11] Even a traditionally less mainstream commercial sport such as cricket has in the past

[8] See Crow and Hoek 2003, p. 2; Johnson 2007, p. 4; see also the discussion in Pound 2006, Chap. 6.

[9] See Walters 2004, p. 17.

According to recent reports (see *The Observer*, 12 February 2007), at the time of writing BSkyB and Setanta Sports are reportedly paying £1.7 billion to hold the exclusive rights to screen live matches of the English Premiership in Britain for the next 3 years. Broadcasters in 208 other countries have reportedly recently doubled their payments to secure English Premiership rights, to a combined £625 million.

[10] See the report available online at the time of writing at http://www.independent.co.uk/sport/football/premier-league/premier-league-nets-16314bn-tv-rights-bonanza-1925462.html.

[11] Fortunato and Martin 2011.

decade felt the effects of the boom in TV rights revenues. It was announced on 1 March 2006 that Indian sports and media agency Nimbus Communications Limited had concluded a deal with the Board of Control for Cricket in India to acquire the global media rights to all international and domestic cricket played in India until 2010. Nimbus prevailed over media giants such as ESPN Star Sports and Sony Entertainment Television, and paid USD 612 million for the media rights.[12] This agreement was the single biggest commercial deal in the history of cricket, but took only 2 years to be eclipsed by the more than USD 1 billion 10-year broadcasting deal in respect of the phenomenally successful Indian Premier League (or IPL). In 2008, amidst the beginning of a global recession, *Sport Business* reported that the IOC president had announced that television income for the 2010 and 2012 Games was USD 3.8 billion, an increase of 40% on the USD 2.6 billion the IOC had received for the 2006 and 2008 Games.[13]

And the top international professional athletes also appear to draw those with deep pockets like moths to a flame. It is not only the players in successful leagues who benefit from the lucrative broadcasting rights deals (e.g. where players in the English Premier League see significant salary hikes from the influx of TV money—one response to news of the record EPL 2010–2013 broadcasting rights deal was that the 'sighs of relief were audible in Porsche dealerships from Wilmslow to Berkeley Square'[14]). The individual stars also earn huge amounts from personal endorsement contracts. David Beckham reportedly earned, over and above his playing salary, in the region of GBP 33,300 *per week* back in 2003 while under contract with Manchester United, *solely for the use of his image on club merchandise*.[15] Tiger Woods has for a number of years earned by far more income from sponsorship and endorsement deals than from actual tournament winnings (in fact, when Mr. Woods won the Australian Masters tournament in November 2009, which preceded a 2-year win drought for the great player, it was reported that his appearance fee to play in the event significantly exceeded the amount of the winner's cheque). And then there's the story (which reflects less on Tiger than on shady corporate social responsibility and rampant commercialism in sport) of Nike workers in Thailand who wrote to Woods, expressing their 'utmost respect for your skill and perseverance as an athlete' but pointing out that they would need to work 72,000 years 'to receive what you will

[12] See the report available online on the web site of the Asser Sports Law Centre at http://www.sportslaw.nl (last visited 8 March 2006).

[13] See http://www.sportbusiness.com/news/167610/olympic-tv-revenue-to-increase.

[14] Nick Harris '£1.78bn: Record Premier League TV deal defies economic slump' The Independent, 7 February 2009—available online at the time of writing at http://www.independent.co.uk/sport/football/premier-league/163178bn-record-premier-league-tv-deal-defies-economic-slump-1569576.html.

[15] See the short article by Andrew Braithwaite and Sonya Pennington 'Image Rights: Do they exist and who should own them?', available online at http://www.sportandtechnology.com/page/0035.html [last accessed 27 February 2007].

earn from [your Nike] contract'.[16] Of course, recent events appear to have overtaken the world's most well-known golfer, as sponsors dropped him like a hot potato following his marital infidelity scandal, and it appears that 'Tigergate' may forever change the way sports sponsors approach the athlete endorsement brand. When the athlete signed an endorsement deal with Rolex in late 2011 it was reported that he had slumped to a ranking of 2,775th most effective product spokesperson according to online consumer polls.[17]

Apart from the sports broadcasting and athlete endorsement markets, the growth in sports sponsorship spending, generally, has been so phenomenal as to remind one of the dot.com boom. Burton and Chadwick[18] provide some figures on sponsorship growth in the past 20-odd years. They state that global sponsorship spending in 1984 (an auspicious year, as we will see) amounted to approximately USD 2 billion. The 2008 international sponsorship industry was calculated to be worth USD 43.5 billion, a growth of USD 19.1 billion over the previous six years. And, as the authors observe, marketing expenditures in leveraging and promoting sponsorship are generally agreed to at least equal, if not exceed, the amount spent securing rights, making sponsorship's overall estimated market value nearly USD 100 billion per annum.[19] PriceWaterhouseCoopers has reportedly declared that 'sports marketing has exploded into a multi-billion dollar business, with the global sports market expected to see revenues of $141 billion by 2012'.[20] Rather ironically, recent years have seen the media branching out into the role of participants as broadcasting corporations and networks have purchased clubs and teams.[21] Not to be outdone, sports teams have entered the broadcasting industry to corner an even bigger slice of the economic pie.[22] It is now truly cliché to remark that sport

[16] Taken from Pilger, J 'Why sharks should not own sport' on the *truth-out* web site at http://www.truth-out.org/why-sharks-should-not-own-sport58820.

[17] See the report by Vranicka, S 'Tiger scores a comeback', 6 October 2011, *The Wall Street Journal*—available online at http://online.wsj.com/article/SB10001424052970203388804576613220984785418.html.

[18] Burton and Chadwick 2009, p. 3.

[19] Ibid.

[20] Gannon 2010, p. 67.

[21] Rupert Murdoch (Fox, Sky and Star TV networks) has at times had holdings in British and German football clubs, major league baseball teams in the United States and rugby league clubs in Australia. Silvio Berlusconi was at one time the principal owner of AC Milan football club, and has also had a major stake in Sportal, the Internet sport company. Canal Plus, the French television station, owned the Paris St. Germain football club. See Mark Marqusee 'Sport as Apocalypse', available online at http://www.frontlineonnet.com/fl1716/17161100.htm.

See also Downward and Dawson 2000, p. 37.

[22] E.g. Manchester United football club and the New York Yankees baseball franchise, both of which have entered the Internet and broadcasting business. See, in general, Sect. 2.5 of the final report of the Sports Directorate of the Netherlands Ministry of Health, Welfare and Sport, entitled *The Balance Between the Game and the Money* (2000).

has become big business.[23] In fact, it is so cliché that, were I a journalist, one observer would have my pay docked and press pass revoked for stating the 'mind-numbingly obvious'[24]—which just proves the point, I guess.

Along with the influx of money has come an attitude of (sometimes rabid) protectionism in respect of the interests of the governing bodies and their commercial partners who bankroll major events. In recent years this has been encountered in the form of the responses by those governing sporting codes to initiatives by private promoters in the establishment of unofficial, 'breakaway' leagues and competitions (compare the Board of Control for Cricket in India's responses to the Indian Cricket League or ICL). These responses have raised competition law and restraint of trade concerns regarding the banning of players as well as efforts to deny access to facilities for the hosting of such unofficial competitions.[25] A related development is the efforts by governing bodies and their commercial partners to protect the commercial exploitation of the publicity value of major events. Commentators elsewhere have criticised the apparently limitless expansion of protection (legislative and otherwise) of the commercial interests of international sports organisations and these partners—especially in the context of anti-ambush marketing measures, which will be the specific focus of Chap. 3—and it appears that current developments in one jurisdiction may point towards the potential for even increased future claims of 'monopolies' in major events.[26] I view such developments with concern, and it is submitted that what may currently be just a blip on the radar screen should be watched very closely indeed by the legal fraternity and sports-loving public.

The modern era has seen an apparent worldwide backlash against some of the more invidious aspects of capitalism and free markets, especially anti-competitive behaviour. Many countries have adopted competition laws and governmental competition authorities are playing an ever more visible and significant role in clamping down on cartels and monopolies and in addressing abuse of dominance by firms and undertakings, ranging from bread manufacturers to mobile phone

---

[23] Philip Knight, founder of the Nike Corporation, characterised sport in the mid-1990s as 'the dominant entertainment in the world'. Gratton and Taylor 2000, p. 3 remarked the following in 2000:

'Sport is now recognised as an important sector of economic activity, part of the increasingly important leisure industry which accounts for over a quarter of all consumer spending and over 10% of total employment in the UK, and brings in over £20 billion per annum in foreign exchange. Sport is not the largest sector of the leisure industry, but it is among the fastest growing'.

In respect of commercialisation of sporting competition, Downward and Dawson 2000, pp. 36, 37 identify sports leagues' main sources of revenue (historically) as gate receipts, merchandising, sponsorship, the sale of TV rights, transfer fees and the sale of match schedules to the gaming industry.

[24] Andrews 2004, p. 3.

[25] For more on these developments and their legal implications, see Louw 2009, par. 353–364, 406–412, 485–490.

[26] See discussion of the apparent development of a 'sports event organiser's right' in Chap. 10.

service providers, in the interests of consumers. Sport has not failed to escape the scrutiny of competition authorities, and those who abhor the abuse of power by those with significant commercial clout should seriously consider the legitimacy of the conduct of organisations or commercial entities that so often claim promotion of the common good as a veiled attempt to justify the much baser generation of profits. Events like the Olympic Games and the football World Cup have become powerful global brands. We must consider to what extent these brands that are so fundamentally based (and dependent) on the public's support of the sport should be protected and advanced, apparently, with scant regard for the rights and interests of members of the public or for wider societal and developmental goals in the domestic jurisdictions where these nomadic events may encamp at any given time.

The main focus areas of this book, namely anti-ambush marketing measures and the often rabid protection of exclusive commercial interests in sporting events by means of special laws, are at the crossroads of the interaction between such developments in competition law and other fields of law. A significant aspect of the fight against ambush marketing involves the use of intellectual property (or IP) rights[27]; and these rights are, traditionally, fundamentally about the creation of (limited) monopolies.[28] A further aspect that requires special consideration is the fact that such issue of monopolisation of sporting events by means of (e.g.) anti-ambush marketing measures is, in the sporting context, situated squarely within an inherently monopoly-based global industry. I (and others) have elsewhere discussed the fundamental monopolistic governance role and functions of (international) sports governing bodies in terms of the 'European Model of Sport', and I have characterised these organisations as monopoly regulators with inherent market dominance.[29] While 'monopolisation' of major sporting events might, therefore, appear to be a natural consequence or function of the very milieu within which these organisations operate, it must be remembered that recent years have seen the development of an increasingly strained dichotomy between the commercial function of sports organisations and their traditional role as 'custodians of the game' in the respective sports, in the (at least professed) interests of the public.

It is contended that the ever-increasing efforts at commercialisation of major events by sports governing bodies and their commercial partners is fostering a culture of greed and opportunism surrounding such events, which is inimical to the very *raison d'etre* for the events and their traditional role of providing a showcase

---

[27] See the discussion in section Chap. 5.

[28] As it has been put, succinctly, in the American context:

'Both patent and copyright law limit competition and therefore increase or at least stabilize prices for a product or service. Patents and copyrights are the only constitutionally mandated monopolies, created with the recognition that unfettered competition would drain creators of their financial incentive to create'. Vaidhyanathan 2003, p. 87

[29] The International Olympic Committee of the 1970 s, for example, has been described as an organisation 'with an extremely limited product increasingly in global demand'—see Magdalinski and Nauright 2004, p. 193.

to the public of the best in sporting talent and athletic endeavours. For example, much has been made promotionally in recent years of football as the 'beautiful game', and the status of football as the game of the people has often been touted, especially with reference to African football (which has been blighted in recent times by the proverbial 'slave trade' of players to especially European clubs). One would be hard-pressed to find, in the era following the fall of the Berlin Wall, a more symbolically loaded development in respect of the global appeal of sport as a uniting, universal force, than the decision to host the football World Cup on the last remaining bastion, the African continent. FIFA's much-celebrated first foray onto African soil with the 2010 FIFA World Cup South Africa had, however, already prior to the event been characterised by apparently deep-seated apathy for the interests of the masses and, frankly, apparent attempts (not only by FIFA and its commercial partners but also by other service providers) to simply milk the commercial potential of the popularity of the event for all it is worth. Examples range from controversy surrounding ticket pricing by FIFA[30] to an investigation by South African competition authorities into allegations of collusion by the country's major airlines in hiking airfares with a view to the event,[31] as well as reports of exorbitant rates set by private accommodation service providers threatening the potential uptake by foreign tourists for the event. While such apparently short-sighted scrambling for what will surely promise to be no more than short-term gains may be understandable in respect of small businesses, the more systemic and institutionalised pursuit of profit associated with the commercial arrangements of major sports governing bodies and their multi-million dollar sponsors and partners is much more worrying.

The attempts to protect the commercial rights and interests associated with mega- events, as discussed in this book, relate mainly to two legal bases: The first is intellectual property protection in respect of licensing schemes involving the intellectual properties created for and associated with such events (primarily registered trademarks and copyrighted works, and ranging from official marks, emblems and event posters to mascots and event anthems). The second relates to

[30] FIFA is no stranger to controversy surrounding the sale of tickets to its World Cup events. The European Competition Commission ruled against the French local organising committee (the CFO) established by FIFA and the French football federation for purposes of the hosting of the 1998 FIFA World Cup in France, in respect of its mandate in respect of ticket sales. The Commission ruled that the CFO had infringed Article 82 of the EC Treaty (see discussion in the text below) by applying discriminatory arrangements in the sale of tickets to the general public, which involved the imposition of unfair trading conditions on consumers outside France which resulted in the limitation of the market to the prejudice of such consumers—Commission Decision of 20 July 1999, Case IV/36.888—*1998 Football World Cup*); see the discussion in Gardiner et al. 2006, pp. 360–362.

[31] It was reported on 7 April 2010 that competition authorities had raided the offices of South African Airways and its low-cost local subsidiary Mango Airlines in order to obtain evidence in respect of such collusion investigation (and it was speculated that these two companies were at risk of losing indemnity for their participation in such investigation on the basis of alleged withholding of evidence).

purely contractual rights created between sports governing bodies and their commercial partners, rights that are enforceable only between such contracting parties in light of the privity of contract. These rights are the genesis of sponsorship exclusivity in relation to events,[32] which, as we will see, is central to any review of the legitimacy of legal protection of commercial rights to events.

The discussion in the following chapters will evaluate the legitimacy of the measures used to protect these contractual rights, especially, in respect of such measures' consequences for outside parties and the public at large. But first we need to consider how the system functions in practice.

2.2 Commercial Rights to Mega-Events: The 'Nuts and Bolts' of How It Works

In examining the immense scale of commercialisation of modern sport, we need to focus our attention on the 'crown jewels' of international sport, the mega-events. It is hard to find a comprehensive and truly definitive definition of the (sports) mega-event (referred to by some as a 'hallmark event' or 'marquee event') for the present context of this discussion. Roche has offered the following definition, which seems to have found general favour:

> "Mega-events" are large-scale cultural (including commercial and sporting) events which have a dramatic character, mass popular appeal and international significance. They are typically organised by variable combinations of national governmental and international non-governmental organisations and thus can be said to be important elements in "official" versions of public culture.[33]

More succinctly, O'Reilly et al. define it (in the sponsorship context) as 'a property that garners significant international media exposure, offers sponsors millions of dollars in promotional value and has a global impact'.[34] A working committee of the International Association for the Protection of Intellectual Property (AIPPI) recently defined 'major sports events' as 'sports events to which a high level of both spectator interests and interests by all forms of media to cover the event are attached and the realisation of which is dependent on substantial contributions of official sponsors'.[35] The following does well to sum up the main

---

[32] As has been observed: 'Simply put, [sponsorship] exclusivity is difficult to control, but it would be impossible without contractual stipulations'. Graham et al. 1995, p. 103.

[33] Roche 2000, p. 1.

[34] O'Reilly, N; McCarthy, L; Seguin, B; Lyberger, M 'Sponsorship and the Super Bowl: A longitudinal analysis' (2005) at 55—available online at the time of writing at http://luxor.acadiau.ca/library/ASAC/v26/03/26_03_p052.pdf

[35] In guidelines published by the AIPPI's Working Committee, Project Q210 ('The protection of major sports events and associated commercial activities through trademarks and other IPR'; in a call for country reports compiled for purposes of a draft resolution to be submitted to the AIPPI

characteristics (and a little bit of history) of such events, including the motivation of those who bid to host these spectacles:

> Nations around the world try to use large events in order to regenerate and promote particular places. Mega-events, otherwise referred to as hallmark tourist events… or special events… are major fairs, festivals, expositions, cultural and sporting events that are most often held on a one-off basis… The event is the celebration or presentation of a theme and usually organised only once at a particular location and for a pre-determined period. Consequently, they have no permanent and uniform organisational structures; usually they are established some years preceding the event and cease following it. Notwithstanding its temporal nature (being a one-off event at a certain location), in the hope of a significant economic return, cities are willing to make enormous investments not only in the event itself, but also in the physical infrastructure in relation to the mega-event. This phenomenon, however, does not have a very long tradition; one can see a certain evolution in the impact of mega-events. For example, at the beginning of the history of the best known mega-event, the modern Olympic Games, it was small-scale, relatively poorly organised and its urban impact was minimal. It has become gradually larger-scale, better organised, and only in the mid 1900s started to include flag-ship building projects (sports facilities) and consequently attract more attention. Since 1960, the Games have often been used as a trigger for large-scale urban improvements and, as a consequence, had a much more substantial impact on the landscape and urban environment of the host cities… Ever since the 19th century (starting with the Olympics and Expos, joined by the football World Cup), mega-events served nation building, identity and citizenship construction functions, which have remained important through to modern times. Already the participation of a nation (represented by athletes, artists, sport teams, exhibitors) at such events are regarded as very important national symbols, but it is even more the case in terms of the ability of a nation to act as a host for a mega-event. The mega-event obsession of today is the most spectacular in the tense intercity and international competition during the bidding processes to win the right to stage them.[36]

In respect of attractiveness to sponsors (the focus of this chapter) the following has been observed in respect of the Olympic Games as sponsorship product, which identifies some of the distinguishing features of such a mega-event:

> [T]he Olympic Games may be the most unique, prestigious sporting event with which a sponsor may wish to identify. Its worldwide audience, relative infrequency, human drama and patriotic overtones making it highly desirable to marketers.[37]

In essence, the sports mega-event—which has also been referred to as 'the leisure industry's "super-nova"'[38]—is a large sporting event that is international in nature (in having international teams or individual athletes compete and/or with the intention of crowning a world champion). It is not organised on an annual (or more frequent) basis, and is hosted by countries or cities that bid for the right to host the event. It is also organised under the auspices of an international

(Footnote 35 continued)
Exco meeting in Buenos Aires, October 2009)—available online at the time of writing at https://www.aippi.org/download/commitees/210/WG210English.pdf.

[36] Nemeth 2010.

[37] McDaniel and Kinney 1998.

[38] Horne and Manzenreiter 2006, p. 3.

organisation (either one that governs the relevant sporting code in the case of single-sport events, or which governs the competition in the particular event in the case of multi-sport events). Two central features of these events are that they are deemed to have significant consequences for the host city, region or nation where they occur, and that they attract considerable media coverage.[39] In fact, if one considers that the president of the International Olympic Committee in 2005 predicted that the total value of television rights to the Olympics would rise to USD 3.5 billion in 2012, it is not surprising that media representatives easily outnumber athletes at the Games (e.g. more than 16,000 press and broadcasting reporters were involved with the 2000 Sydney Games).[40] Host broadcasters have dedicated increasing numbers of broadcasting feed hours to the two-week long Games, with the 2008 Beijing instalment totalling 5,000 h. It is the ability of these events to reach billions of viewers across the globe (e.g. cumulative totals of 40 billion and nearly 29 billion, respectively, for the 2004 Athens Olympics and the 2002 FIFA World Cup, and 35,000 and 41,000 h, respectively, of programming dedicated to these two events[41]), which makes them so important and valuable as promotional tools. Corporate sponsors pay huge amounts of money to obtain the right to advertise their products and services by means of the marketing vehicle that these events provide.

When I use the term 'sports mega-event' in this book I am referring to the following (and similar) events, based on their size and the popularity of the relevant sporting code or the competition[42]

- The Olympic Games;
- The FIFA football World Cup;
- The ICC Cricket World Cup;
- The IRB Rugby World Cup;
- UEFA's Euro (European) football championship;
- The Commonwealth Games;
- The Asian Games;
- The American football Super Bowl; and
- The NCAA men's basketball tournament ('March Madness').[43]

---

[39] Ibid. 2.

[40] Ibid. 5.

[41] Ibid. 3.

[42] Compare the following classification:

'Mega-sporting events include specialist world-level international sports competitions (e.g. the World Cup competitions in soccer, athletics, rugby and Grand Prix events for horseracing and motor racing) and also the 'world regional-level' versions of these events. These are mainly connected to the multi-sport Olympics, such as the Asian Games, the Pan-American Games and the Commonwealth Games, and to a lesser degree to the world-level specialist events such as the European zone competition for the soccer World Cup'. Malfas et al. 2004, p. 211.

[43] In 2011 the NCAA agreed to a 14-year, USD 10.8 billion deal with CBS and Turner Sports for the US broadcast rights.

More to the point, in respect of the subject matter of this book, these events are the ones that attract 'the big sponsors and so the big money' and they are 'sufficiently important to the body politic and the public for legislative time to be dedicated to protecting the brand'.[44] Of course, much of what will be said here about the commercialisation of sports events and the use of law to protect commercial rights is also relevant in respect of other sporting 'events', i.e. competitions or leagues which are presented on a more regular (e.g. annual) basis. Examples are the FIA Formula 1 World Championship, the English football Premier League competition, the Indian Premier League cricket competition, the Tri-Nations rugby competition, etc.

With such (very loose) definition and terminology in mind, the focus should shift to an examination of the commercialisation of these events. The gist of the commercial exploitation of mega-events can be succinctly distilled to two distinct rights, namely the right to associate with and the right to broadcast.[45] By way of illustration, by far the two largest sources of revenue for FIFA in respect of its 2010 World Cup South Africa[46] were the sale of broadcasting rights (a total of more than USD 2.4 billion) and the sale of 'marketing rights' relating to sponsor investment (a total of more than USD 1 billion).[47]

In essence, the commercial arrangements surrounding a mega-event such as the football World Cup or Olympic Games involve a monopoly regulator of the commercial rights connected to such an event (e.g. FIFA, the sole rights holder and regulator in respect of the football competition, in terms of rights claimed in the organisation's founding documents[48]) inviting bids from would be sponsors and broadcasters to obtain rights to broadcast or to associate with (for the purposes of commercial exploitation of such association) the event to the exclusion of all

[44] Johnson 2008, p. 29.

[45] Broadcasting rights to sports mega-events will not be considered in this book.

[46] With event-related revenue the single largest source of income for the organisation (at 93% of the total for the relevant period).

[47] Source: *FIFA Annual Financial Report 2010*—available online at the time of writing at www.fifa.com.

[48] Compare Article 74 of the FIFA Statutes (August 2009 version, currently in force at the time of writing), and discussion in Chap. 3. See also the description of FIFA in the preamble to the 2010 FIFA World Cup South Africa By-laws as published by the eThekwini Municipality for the host city of Durban, which describes FIFA as 'both the world governing body of association football and the lawful owner of the world-wide Marketing Rights, Media Rights and all other commercial rights in respect of the [World Cup] Competition'. Such description does, of course, not qualify such 'rights' in respect of their nature and status (i.e. the personal nature—read: unenforceability against third parties—of contractual rights flowing from commercial agreements with sponsors). FIFA's web site (at www.fifa.com) proclaims that 'The FIFA World Cup and all other FIFA competitions are privately funded—without state subsidies for either FIFA or the Local Organising Committee. FIFA carries the costs of staging the Event and in exchange retains all commercial rights'.

others.[49] I shall leave aside, for now, the potential competition law or anti-trust issues regarding such arrangement (which will be considered elsewhere in this book[50]) or other potential problems regarding the 'free and fair' nature of the auctioning off of these rights by the governing bodies concerned.[51]

Underlying and demarcating both the boundaries and the 'rules of the game' in the rights bidding process are rules set by the sports organisation which are aimed at 'legislating' to all and sundry—i.e. interested sponsors or commercial partners and everyone else—what 'rights' may or may not be up for grabs, and from whom such 'rights' must be obtained. For example, Rule 7 of the Olympic Charter[52] provides as follows regarding 'Rights over the Olympic Games and Olympic Properties':

> 7.1 The Olympic Games are the exclusive property of the IOC which owns all rights and data relating thereto, in particular, and without limitation, all rights relating to their organisation, exploitation, broadcasting, recording, representation, reproduction, access and dissemination in any form and by any means or mechanism whatsoever, whether now

---

[49] Gardiner et al. 2006, p. 458 explain the value of sports sponsorship for sponsors as follows: '[T]he sponsor's association is with the sponsored party's sports event and also with the emblems, logos and mascots (the event marks) that identify and distinguish the particular sports body and its event … Sports sponsorship results in a transfer of the essential values and properties of the sponsored party and its events to the sponsor's business organisation and, ultimately, to its products and/or services, thereby raising the sponsor's profile and standing in the community (offering public relations opportunities and advantages) and amongst its existing and potential customers … [The value of sports sponsorship] also lies in the fact that the sponsor is given exclusivity in the particular product or service category in respect of which the sponsorship rights are granted by the owner of the rights'.

[50] In Sect. 2.4 in this chapter and in Chap. 6.

[51] It should be noted in passing that the bid processes in respect of commercial rights to major events are not always transparent and have, allegedly, at least once in the past been manipulated in an apparently anti-competitive manner by FIFA executives in respect of the football World Cup (See discussion of the bid process for the sale of television broadcasting rights to the 2002 and 2006 FIFA World Cups in Jennings 2006, Chap. 7). It has also been reported that Match Event Services, which was FIFA's exclusive official accommodation provider for the 2010 World Cup and no stranger to controversy, was apparently appointed without any tender process. Rob Rose writes (in Schulz-Herzenberg 2010, pp. 99, 100) as follows:

'While [Match Event Services] officially warns accommodation providers to keep room rates low because tourists are 'sensitive to pricing', an investigation by the author has confirmed that tourists will have to pay Match 1000% more than they would normally pay for accommodation in certain cases, such as for units at South Africa's Kruger National Park. Match Event Services is owned entirely by a family-owned UK-registered company called Byrom PLC. The circumstances of its appointment remain cloudy: there was never any public tender for the multi-million rand contract, for example. Riding on those coat-tails is the closely linked Match Hospitality, which has FIFA's official stamp of approval to provide exclusive hospitality packages to large companies seeking to impress clients at the South African event. Not only does Match Hospitality refuse to disclose its exact shareholding structure, but it has emerged that one of the four shareholders in the company is Infront Sports and Media, a company headed by Philippe Blatter—nephew and godson of the FIFA supremo'.

[52] The Olympic Charter in force from 11 February 2010 (currently in force at the time of writing).

existing or developed in the future. The IOC shall determine the conditions of access to and the conditions of any use of data relating to the Olympic Games and to the competitions and sports performances of the Olympic Games.

7.2 The Olympic symbol, flag, motto, anthem, identifications (including but not limited to "Olympic Games" and "Games of the Olympiad"), designations, emblems, flame and torches… shall be collectively or individually referred to as "Olympic properties". All rights to any and all Olympic properties, as well as all rights to the use thereof, belong exclusively to the IOC, including but not limited to the use for any profit-making, commercial or advertising purposes. The IOC may license all or part of its rights on terms and conditions set forth by the IOC Executive Board.

In addition, By-law 3 to Rule 41 of the Olympic Charter provides as follows:

Except as permitted by the IOC Executive Board, no competitor, coach, trainer or official who participates in the Olympic Games may allow his person, name, picture or sports performances to be used for advertising purposes during the Olympic Games.

The IOC clearly and unequivocally claims a 'property right' in the Games. Compare Article 40(a) of the Host City Contract for the 2012 London Olympic Games, which provides that '[t]he City, the NOC and the OCOG acknowledge, without limiting any provision of the Olympic Charter, that the Games are the exclusive property of the IOC'. It is clear that the cumulative effect of the above provisions is that the IOC appropriates all rights to the Games (which 'rights' are themselves created in the Charter—we will see later that in most jurisdictions there exists no independent basis for legal recognition of such property outside of such founding documents) to itself and assumes the role of the exclusive provider of licenses or consent to the use of such rights in relation to the event, while also prohibiting the very persons whose performances at the event form the core of its entertainment product from entering into any commercial arrangements with anyone who has not taken the official route of negotiating for and obtaining access to such 'rights' from the IOC. One Olympic insider[53] has characterised the last-quoted by-law above as the very backbone for the feasibility of the practice of providing category exclusivity[54] to event sponsors (specifically in the context of the category of apparel sponsorships), which is central to the commercial monopoly in mega-events and will be discussed in more detail below.[55] The IOC's own *Technical Manual on Brand Protection* in respect of the Games is at pains to

[53] See the response by John Coates (president of the Australian Olympic Committee and Executive Board Member of the International Olympic Committee) to an article by Malcolm Maiden ('The Olympic monopoly and why it harms sport', *Sydney Morning Herald*, 20 November 2009—available online at the time of writing at http://www.smh.com.au/business/the-olympic-monopoly-and-why-it-harms-sport-20091119-iowz.html), available online at the time of writing on the web site of the Australian Olympic Committee at http://corporate.olympics.com.au/news.cfm?ArticleID=10495.

[54] See the discussion in Sect. 2.4.

[55] Former Olympic marketing manager Michael Payne has also been emphatic in stressing the importance of sponsorship exclusivity for the success of the Olympic commercialisation model—see Payne 2006, pp. 142, 143.

emphasise the importance of category exclusivity for the Olympic marketing programme:

> Official Olympic marketing partners are granted exclusive Olympic marketing rights within a given product category, for a specifically defined territory on a national, multinational, or worldwide scale. This is an essential characteristic of Olympic marketing, and the value of the rights granted to the Olympic marketing partners is directly related to the Olympic Family's ability to protect that exclusivity. Ambush marketing occurs when this exclusivity is violated by any entity.[56]

Lawyers should tread lightly when assessing such claims of rights in the founding documents of sports governing bodies to consider that not all the 'rights' claimed necessarily have wider legal substance (in the meaning of being enforceable against all the world as opposed to only the parties to these commercial agreements). This is especially important in those jurisdictions where no proprietary right to an event is recognised by-law. It has been pointed out that sponsors need to be satisfied that the sponsored party can show a good title to rights being granted, and that the sponsorship agreement should contain a warranty by the event rights grantor to the effect that it is free and able to grant the particular sponsorship rights,[57] because '[p]roving title to commercial rights in a sporting event may be easier in theory than in practice'.[58] Gardiner et al. refer to the fact that a potential sponsor of broadcast coverage of the FIFA World Cup will be faced with a 'bald statement' contained in FIFA's Statutes (namely, that 'FIFA, its member associations, confederations and clubs own the exclusive rights to broadcast and transmissions of events'), and that '[i]nquiries beyond this statement will produce a blank'.[59] Of course, organisations like the IOC and FIFA clearly do commonly enjoy legal protection for their intellectual property (e.g. symbols such as the Olympic Rings, or event logos for the football World Cup) as well as common law protection in the form of e.g. unlawful competition or passing off. But these wide claims of rights in the Olympic Charter or the FIFA Statutes often imply wider protection than is traditionally to be found in most jurisdictions. For example, FIFA consistently claimed 'marketing rights' in respect of their 2010 World Cup event in South Africa, which 'rights' do not exist in terms of the

---

56 The version available at the time of writing on the web site of http://www.gamesmonitor.org.uk in respect of the 2012 London Olympics, in Section IV: Ambush Marketing Prevention, at p. 13 (this document refers to an updated version of the Manual which was scheduled for publication in July 2005, although such updated version (if it exists) is not available online at the time of writing).

57 The sponsor or other purchaser of rights should generally obtain a warranty from the event organiser that it is entitled to hold the event at the venue, that it controls access to the event, and that it own trademarks and other relevant intellectual property rights relating to the event (and, in addition, an undertaking from the event organiser that it will take specific steps to combat unauthorised commercial exploitation of the event, for example by means of ticket terms regulating access and participation agreements regarding teams and athletes)—see Becker 2006, p. 23.

58 Gardiner et al. 2006, p. 449.

59 Ibid.

domestic law of the host nation.[60] It is these types of rights that, in fact, exist only by virtue of sponsorship and other licensing arrangements with sponsors and other commercial partners; they are really no more than contractual rights (most often in the form of *pacta de non petendo*, or agreements not to take legal action against 'rights holders' for exploitation of such 'rights' in marketing relating to the event). In this way this last category of 'rights' are important to consider, as it could be argued that the governing bodies' apparent belief in the creation of these legally ambiguous concepts may have formed the basis for what we have come to know in recent times as 'association rights' to events. Such association rights will be discussed elsewhere.[61]

Through the event rights bidding processes, large multinational corporations that are able to afford the very substantial rights fees enter into agreements with the sports organisation which effectively close the market (and often for a long period of time[62]) to all non-sponsors, e.g. also small business entities in the particular country or geographical area where the event is to be hosted, which entities are rarely able to compete on a level playing field (or at all) with the official sponsors and commercial partners in terms of the financial outlay required by the sports organisation. Vassallo et al. are quite direct in describing the big bucks scenario surrounding modern mega-event sponsorships: 'Clearly the stakes are high and event organisers are reaping the rewards. Just as clearly, small companies cannot afford to be sponsors'.[63] And as it has also been succinctly described: 'Since such sponsorships are extremely expensive and often are long-term commitments, this advertising strategy is available only to a handful of large corporations... The little guy need not apply'.[64] So, basically, if you can't pay, you can't play.

This clear bias towards the larger, predominantly multi-national corporations able to afford to pay for such rights has invoked the ire of a variety of stakeholders when it comes to the passing of special legislation to protect such corporate interests from ambush marketing by 'unofficial sponsors'. For example, the following criticism was expressed regarding the protection for the 2012 London Olympic Games: '[T]his sort of legislation is insulting. It is specific and unprecedented protection for a small group of internationally based, predominately non-UK companies to the detriment of all other businesses'.[65] When evaluating such arrangements one is confronted with

---

60 See Burrell, T 'FIFA's money grab a blatant foul', *Daily News*, 12 April 2010.

61 See, specifically, the discussion in Chap. 8.

62 Organisations such as the International Olympic Committee and FIFA enter into long-term contracts which span multiple major events with their most attractive high profile sponsors (e.g. VISA is currently involved in a long-term agreement with FIFA as a 'FIFA Partner' in the financial services segment until the year 2014; Coca-Cola earlier entered into a 16-year deal with FIFA at a cost of USD 500 million).

63 Vassallo et al. 2005, p. 1354.

64 Fortunato and Richards 2007, p. 34.

65 Marina Palomba, legal director of the UK's Institute for Advertising Practitioners, quoted in a report entitled 'UK businesses upset over London Olympics Law', 25 August 2005, available online at the time of writing on the web site of www.GamesBids.com at http://www.gamesbids.com/eng/other_news/1125074698.html.

the potential for serious abuse of economic power in an apparently significantly skewed competitive environment founded upon the notion of providing exclusivity[66]:

> [A]dvertising appears to offer advantages as a predatory strategy for economically dominant corporations that wish to maintain or advance their position in a particular marketplace. A sponsorship agreement that grants exclusivity for a brand within a product category to a contained audience exacerbates an already problematic issue.[67]

By way of example of the size of corporate entities involved and the scale of their investment in mega-events-related commercial rights, it has been observed that sponsors who participate in the TOP ('The Olympic Partner') programme,[68] which is the highest level of Olympic sponsorship that provides international exposure to brands and gives sponsors the right to sponsor one quadrennial cycle of the Winter and Summer Games, invest between USD 200–300 million for the privilege (with the sponsorship fee amounting to more than USD 70 million and a further investment of between three and four times that amount in activation expenditures ('leveraging the brand') such as marketing programmes to give effect to the sponsorship). Some observers suggest that successful activation and leveraging may require sponsors to spend anywhere up to a 10:1 ratio of leveraging to sponsorship fee when discussing major sport properties.[69] This for *an event that, in real time, lasts just over two weeks*. One source claims that, between 1980 and 2000, the IOC generated nearly USD 15 billion from its marketing and licensing programmes.[70] Accordingly, and in common parlance, what may be compared to a very exclusive and elite 'old boys' club' is created to profit from the event.

Having created such a phenomenally mutually beneficial commercial partnership by means of contract, the next link in the chain of establishing a system for the generation and maintenance of such monopolistic arrangements is that the interests of the members of such club are vigorously protected by (ever-increasingly rigid and far-reaching[71]) legislation and other anti-ambush marketing measures in the host country. Such legislation is obtained through very real pressure by the sports organisation on the host government by means of rigid requirements

---

66 See discussion of sponsorship exclusivity in relation to mega-events in Sect. 2.4.

67 Fortunato and Richards, p. 36.

68 See the discussion in Sect. 2.3.

69 Seguin et al. 2005.

70 Magdalinski and Nauright 2004, p. 194.

71 Compare the voluminous Major Sporting Events Bill 2009 of the Parliament of Victoria in Australia (the status of which in the legislative process is at the time of writing unknown to the author). This document runs to over 200 sections, dealing with safety at sporting events, ambush marketing, ticketing etc. By way of illustration of the types of ambush marketing conduct prohibited by this Bill, compare the wording of section 38, which provides that it is an offence for a person to use protected event logos or images or protected event references without authorisation, if such use would (*inter alia*) 'suggest a sponsorship-like arrangement to a reasonable person' (section 38(1)(e) of the Bill).

(demanded as a matter of course) related to the provision of guarantees in the bidding process.[72] Andriychuck explains it as follows[73]:

> [T]he very format of auctions for the selection of organisers of major sports events enables rights holders to leverage their commercial power in order to reach better protection of their media products… Inasmuch as competition for the right to hosting the major sports

---

[72] The New Zealand Rugby Football Union failed to secure co-hosting rights to the 2003 IRB Rugby World Cup due to its inability to guarantee "clean stadia" for the event to the IRB. As part of New Zealand's successful bids to host the 2011 Rugby World Cup and the 2015 ICC Cricket World Cup a commitment was given to ensure adequate provisions were in place to protect sponsors. New Zealand subsequently passed much-criticised and very extensive anti-ambush marketing legislation in the form of the Major Events Management Act, 35 of 2007. Since the promulgation of the Act three events have to date been identified as protected events, namely the 2011 Rugby World Cup, the FIFA U-17 Women's World Cup and the FIBA U-19 World Championship—see the report by Ironside "Ambush Marketing Law Passes First Test"—available online at the time of writing at http://www.baldwins.com/ambush-marketing-law-passes-first-test (posted 2009-09-04). The Hon Trevor Mallard, New Zealand's Minister for the Rugby World Cup, was quoted as explaining the need for this legislation as follows:

'[T]he legislation will make New Zealand more attractive to major event organisers. Without it, New Zealand's success when bidding for similar events in the future, may be at risk. It is impossible to host major events these days without enormous financial contributions from large sponsors. These companies will not provide sponsorship dollars if others are allowed to manipulate public perceptions by falsely suggesting a link with these events'.

From the undated (last updated 2009-09-16) report entitled "Proposed Ambush Marketing Bill Explained" http://www.med.govt.nz/templates/MultipageDocumentTOC41944.aspx. Kelbrick 2008, pp. 38, 39 refers to the criticism voiced by the New Zealand Law Society in response to the promulgation of this very extensive Act. The Law Society recognised that the justification for the Act was that some major international events could not be hosted unless such legislation existed, and suggested (which suggestion was not accepted) that an event should only be declared a protected event in terms of the Act if the relevant Minister is satisfied that this is necessary in order to secure hosting rights in respect of the specific event—from the New Zealand Law Society Submission on the Major Events Management Bill (see Kelbrick 2008, p. 39, note 74).

In respect of the position in Australia, Curthoys and Kendall 2001 observe the following (at par. 43) in showing that the relevant legislative amendments prior to the Sydney 2000 Olympics were, primarily, in order to serve the commercial interests of event organisers and their sponsors:

'The [Sydney 2000 Games (Indicia and Images) Protection Act] itself is a comment on the power of the advertising dollar associated with the Olympic symbol and the Sydney 2000 Games—this intersection being made explicit in sub-section 3 of the Act which provides:

(1) The objects of this Act are:
    (a) to protect, and to further, the position of Australia as a participant in, and a supporter of, the World Olympic and Para-Olympic movements; and
    (b) to the extent that it is within the power of the Parliament to assist in protecting the relations and ensuring the performance of the obligations of the Sydney 2000 Games bodies with and to the World Olympic and Para-Olympic movements, in relation to the holding of the Sydney 2000 Games.
(2) These objects are to be achieved by facilitating the raising of licensing revenue in relation to the Sydney 2000 Games through the regulation of the use for commercial purposes of the indicia and images associated with the Games'.

[73] Andriychuck 2009, p. 133.

> events is highly fierce, because the very commercially attractive market is at stake, the conditions regarding legislative restriction of unauthorised broadcasting and unselected merchandising can be imposed by the event organisers during the tender procedure. The country/city, which wins the auction, would become bound by the obligation to provide the strongest protection for media rights. Such restrictions from event organisers, to a large extent, is a forced measure. Rights holders seek to protect their investment and maximise revenue. The lack of legal protection forces them to lobby ad hoc legislation of a highly political nature.

It is commonly accepted nowadays that this 'political and economic coercion' takes place and that the chances of obtaining hosting rights without committing to passing special event protection laws are slim to nil. Is it any coincidence that the Brazilian Congress passed its special *Olympic Act*, 2009 just one day before the IOC officially selected Rio de Janeiro to host the 2016 Games?[74] Stuart and Scassa confirm the sense of coercion in observing the following:

> [T]he IOC has successfully used its coercive power to achieve the extraordinary outcome whereby sovereign states enact national legislation solely for the protection of the Olympic brand, its revenues and those of commercial organisations associated with the Games. In the light of comprehensive pre-existing legislation, many consider these additional legal instruments wholly unnecessary. Such is the allure and perceived, though often illusory, material benefit of hosting the Olympic Games, that national authorities are willing to expend significant scarce resources, such as time and tax revenues, to protect the [intellectual property rights] of an external agency: the IOC.[75]

Canadian law academic Jon Heshka has reminded me that such coercion may be overstated when viewed in respect of the host governments' complicity in passing these laws: 'Bidding countries go into the process with their eyes wide open cognizant of the conditions to which they would be expected to comply. They may not be happy about it and indeed they may pinch their noses while passing it but pass it they do'.[76] I have to agree, but would submit that this does not detract from the coercive nature of the demands made by event organisers and, at best, it serves only to show poor judgment and/or a lack of concern for the potential impact of such laws for their citizens on the part of such governments.

Accordingly, while we have seen that commercial rights to mega-events are, essentially, self-proclaimed and -created contractual rights that arise from sports governing bodies' founding documents and are subsequently incorporated in contracts with sponsors and commercial partners, such rights are further clothed with a public visage through ostensible legal legitimacy by means of another high profile contract. This is the hosting contract entered into between the governing body and the host nation or city government. While such rights, therefore, in essence remain contractual in nature, the relevant government is contractually obligated to enact relevant domestic laws to give effect to these rights, which is where the lawmakers then become actively involved. For example, in the 2010

74 See Bacalao-Fleury 2011, p. 200.

75 Stuart and Scassa 2011, par. 18.

76 From personal correspondence, December 2011.

football World Cup bid, South African national government departments provided a total of 17 guarantees to FIFA, which were subsequently (as per FIFA's requirements) consolidated in the 2010 FIFA World Cup South Africa Special Measures Act.[77] These guarantees included, for present purposes, FIFA's ownership of media and marketing rights (Ministry of Communications; Ministry of Trade and Industry) and exploitation of marketing rights (Ministry of Trade and Industry).[78] As was subsequently observed by a South African court, in examining the public nature of the functions performed by the Local Organising Committee (or LOC) for the event, which was incorporated as a company:

> [T]he legislation passed by various legislative authorities such as the bye-laws passed by the local authorities of Johannesburg and Tshwane, give legislative underpinning to the LOC's obligations to FIFA. Unlike an ordinary private contract only enforceable by the parties to that contract, in this case many of the LOC's contractual obligations, having been captured in substance in legislation, have become enforceable against the public at large.[79]

The special event legislation and legislative efforts to provide *sui generis* protection for the relevant event encompasses a wide a range of measures. These generally include everything from tax breaks for event organisers and their partners (see below), special immigration measures aimed at facilitating entry into and egress from the host nation for event organisers and their officials, and special laws facilitating not only the protection of existing rights but also the establishment of new rights for event organisers. For example, a questionnaire as part of the bid requirements sent to applicants to host UEFA's Euro 2012 championship included special treatment for the organisation and its sponsors in respect of the registration of intellectual property such as trademarks relating to the event. This included demands for written guarantees from relevant government departments regarding the appointment of a dedicated set of examiners to administer all registrations relating to the Euro 2012 tournament and to consider any opposition by UEFA to registrations; guarantees to expedite all registrations and opposition proceedings brought by UEFA (which are to take no longer than 6 months); and government guarantees to 'monitor all applications for intellectual property registrations… in order to quickly identify applications which conflict with any UEFA application or registration and that it shall reject any such conflicting application without UEFA having to take any action'.[80] In South Africa, the governmental guarantees not only included the express undertaking to ensure the passing of laws to protect FIFA against ambush marketing and the provision of personnel to assist in the protection of 'marketing rights, broadcast rights, marks and other intellectual

[77] Act 12 of 2006.

[78] For more on the FIFA 2010 bid guarantees, see Davies 2009, pp. 38–40.

[79] *M and G Media Ltd v 2010 FIFA World Cup South Africa Organising Committee Ltd* South Gauteng High Court Case No. 09/51422 (unreported at the time of writing) at par. 123.

[80] Guarantee 12 as contained in the Phase II Questionnaire as part of the UEFA European Football Championship 2012 Final Tournament bid requirements.

property rights'. It also included guarantees relating to tax breaks and special customs clearances, and even an undertaking by the Minister of Tourism to 'ensure that the hotel prices for the FIFA delegation are 20% less than the frozen rate at 1 January 2010'.[81] Such special treatment of event organisers brought about under the threat of the withholding of events in a bidding process must surely provide some food for thought to fair-minded persons who subscribe to the rule of law and to the principle of equal treatment for all before the law. More will be said in this regard in Chap. 4.

Once host government guarantees and the passing of special legislation have been obtained, the final link in the chain of ensuring universal application of such purely contractual rights to individuals and business entities situated outside the relevant contractual matrices then swiftly falls in place. Following the establishment of the required legislative framework, the sports federations or their local event organisers employ a veritable army of top flight local lawyers in the host jurisdiction to protect these 'rights' (often by focusing their efforts on the 'small fry' rather than the powerful non-sponsor corporations that may be skirting the bounds of legitimate marketing relating to events but who also have the deep pockets to enter into protracted and expensive litigation). FIFA in 2003 reported a budget of USD 13 million in 'Rights protection—rights delivery', with averages of between USD 5 and USD 6 million budgeted annually for protection of the 2006 World Cup, in addition to around USD 9 million per year in general legal expenses.[82] That's quite a chunk of change which I'm sure will cover substantial postage fees for all those threatening letters that are invariably sent out to would be infringers. Although that might be a tad optimistic—the (impressively named) Atlanta Centennial Olympic Properties Sponsor Protection Department reportedly sent out approximately 4,000 such letters during the 1996 Atlanta Games.[83]

The lawyers are generally an advance guard, which proceeds to establish the required 'legal climate' for commercial rights protection of the events well before the actual event. One of FIFA's local lawyers for the 2010 World Cup in South Africa has been quoted as observing that 'Many of the legal elements we saw in South Africa are now prerequisites for a country wishing to host major sporting events. As a law firm you cannot hope for a better instruction'.[84] Environmentalists may baulk at the mountain of paperwork created, which ranges from countless applications to register trademarks and designs and to the dispatch of threatening letters to perceived infringers of the event organisers' rights. As Johnson explains, it is an advisable tactic for organisations like FIFA to make sweeping trademark applications (i.e. in a large number of categories for goods

---

81 *M and G Media Ltd v 2010 FIFA World Cup South Africa Organising Committee Ltd* supra at par. 107.

82 Schwab 2006, p. 8.

83 Tripodi and Sutherland 2000, pp. 412–422.

84 Mike du Toit, partner of South African firm ENS, as quoted in a report entitled 'Sporting Chance', available on the web site of the International Bar Association at http://www.ibanet.org/Article/Detail.aspx?ArticleUid=1a43e1e6-e207-4aa7-a21f-6d0435bba7e7.

and services) in the relevant jurisdiction(s) roughly 4–5 years before the end of the event (as 'non-use' provisions in trademark laws generally require non-use over a period of 5 years), as this can serve to cover the 'whole field of sponsorship' (the application can cover all conceivable goods or services which might attract sponsorship, while also closing the field to potential 'ambushers' of the event in respect of less likely goods or services).[85] Jon Heshka points out that 'The monopolistic and draconian nature of [the special event laws] serves to legally protect and enhance the interests of international companies. What the laws do is to widen the gap between 'big business' (official top flight sponsors and high-end ambushers) and small and medium-sized enterprises, appreciating it is the [small and medium enterprises] who are promised the benefits of hosting the mega-event but who make an easy target if they stray outside the lines of these laws'.[86]

Some of the efforts to create 'special' rights in respect of the events may seem strange. The London Organising Committee for the 2012 Olympic Games (or LOCOG), for example, has even commissioned its own font (called '2012 Headline'), which is used on the cover of all its guidance material and also on the words 'London' and 'Paralympic games' inside the 2012 logo, which enjoys copyright protection. Accordingly, permission should be sought from LOCOG to use any of these.[87] It was reported that by November 2009, more than 6 months before the start of the 2010 FIFA World Cup in South Africa (and only shortly after the end of the 2009 Confederations Cup), FIFA had already registered more than thirty event-related marks for its 2014 World Cup in Brazil with the Brazilian Institute for Intellectual Property, and that the cease-and-desist letters were already flying out of the lawyer's offices in Brazil.[88] Kelbrick[89] observes that, for example, FIFA's tactics are to threaten litigation in respect of every reference to its events, and that the organisation 'singles out smaller concerns with few financial or legal resources to defend themselves', and the author quotes a statement by FIFA's legal counsel prior to the 2006 FIFA World Cup:

> Big companies know where the grey zones are because they are well-advised … We don't touch the grey areas … [M]any companies, especially the smaller firms, won't take risks with this.[90]

---

[85] Johnson 2007, p. 26.

[86] Heshka is a law professor at the Thompson Rivers University in British Columbia, and has published on ambush marketing and the 2010 Vancouver Winter Olympic Games—from personal correspondence with the author, December 2011.

[87] Montagnon, R and Smith, J 'Marketing, advertising and the Olympics: How to avoid falling at the first hurdle', April 2010, available online at the time of writing at http://www.herbertsmith.com/NR/rdonlyres/24175EF6-DA81-4B1B-8C75-F39DEACC4DD2/14743/FeatureOlympicswithcopy.pdf.

[88] See the report dated 2 June 2010 available online at the time of writing at http://www.v-brazil.com/world-cup/2014/cbf-files-lawsuits-for-ambush-marketing/.

[89] Kelbrick 2008.

[90] Martin Stopper as quoted by Doreen Carvajal in the *International Herald Tribune*, 31 May 2006.

In light of the fact that when FIFA encountered an alleged ambush by the South African subsidiary of electronics giant LG Electronics in respect of the 2006 World Cup in Germany, FIFA only followed the complaint procedure of the Advertising Standards Authority rather than to instigate litigation,[91] it is interesting to note the controversial litigation instituted by FIFA in South Africa in respect of alleged ambush marketing of the 2010 World Cup event against what can only be termed 'small players'.[92] This might be ascribable to a belief that FIFA's local legal representatives had formulated a foolproof litigation strategy in the light of the extensive and extremely stringent South African anti-ambush marketing legislation (which will be discussed elsewhere). In recognition of the potential for a public relations nightmare and backlash following from such heavy-handed tactics, some sports governing bodies and event organisers appear to display more common sense in this regard. The 2012 London Olympics organisers refrained from taking legal action against a Dorset sausage maker who in 2007 used a sign featuring a 'five rings' logo made up of sausage links; in the words of a senior London 2012 sponsorship lawyer '[w]e don't want to be seen to be heavy-handed—we will choose a case carefully', and '[i]f we had taken legal action against the sausage maker it would not have looked very professional'.[93] The IOC's response to FIFA's handling of the Bavaria ambush in Johannesburg (see below), however, was to reiterate its zero tolerance approach to ambushing on the basis that ambushing threatens grassroots sport through its potential to decrease event revenues from sponsorship.[94] The ICC's head legal counsel was recently quoted as stating that the organisation had decided to take a more common sense approach in respect of attempts to ambush the 2011 Cricket World Cup than that followed by FIFA in South Africa.[95] One wonders why, in the light of the frequently negative press that follows reports of event organisers flexing their muscle against small fry 'infringers' or 'ambushers', common sense appears to be in such short supply. When faced with such 'pedantic sabre-rattlers',[96] the words of a well-known intellectual property law expert bear considering: 'Possessing a right does

---

[91] See discussion in Chap. 3.

[92] As discussed in Sect. 4.4.5 in Chap. 4.

[93] Dalton Odendaal, as quoted in an April 2008 BBC report (available online at the time of writing at http://news.bbc.co.uk/2/hi/business/7364391.stm).

[94] 'IOC vows to continue ambush marketing crackdown', 22 June 2010, available online at the time of writing at http://www.sports-city.org/news_details.php?news_id=12128&idCategory=1.

[95] David Becker was quoted as follows in an interview available online at http://www.sportzpower.com/?q=content/interview-david-becker-head-legal-icc-0&page=0%2C1:

'We did review the procedures and guidelines during the 2010 FIFA World Cup and have taken valuable lessons from them. We are determined to strike the right balance between protecting our sponsors and recognising the public's rights to interact with and enjoy the event. Our team will be carefully accessing every situation and dealing with each case according to our established protocols. A common-sense approach will be taken based on the individual circumstances of each case'.

[96] From a posting ('How the World Cup ambushed itself', 18 June 2010) on marketing guru Kim Skildum-Reid's blog at http://blog.powersponsorship.com.

not mean that it is a good idea to enforce it always, and to the hilt. Discretion may be nine parts of possession'.[97] The danger of over-zealous enforcement by event organisers has been observed by an American commentator in the Olympic context:

> Every time the [United States Olympic Committee] and IOC attack ambush marketers, they dilute the value of their brand to sponsors, because research reveals fan support for sponsors is greatest when they believe that without the sponsors the property would go away. The more heavy-handed, commercially driven and powerful the Olympic movement appears, the less consumers believe in the need to support its sponsors.[98]

The more blatant the enforcement message from event organisers as communicated to the fans, the crasser the commercialisation of events will appear. In the context of the FIFA World Cup it was once observed that 'football supporters, already enraged by the number of tickets doled out to sponsors rather than real fans, may object if they find themselves as extras in somebody else's corporate video'.[99] A case in point on the issue of ill-conceived enforcement, which matter was eventually quickly and quietly disposed of through a reported settlement, is FIFA's response to the 'Bavaria girls' stunt during the 2010 FIFA World Cup South Africa in the opening round of the tournament.[100] FIFA was subsequently lambasted for its conduct towards the young women involved (along with the alleged conduct of the South African police) and the consensus seems to be that FIFA's not unexpected response was Bavaria's biggest asset in ensuring the success of its publicity stunt. In a similar vein, compare the provocative advertisement promoting a gay dating web site ('ManCrunch'), 'where many, many men come out to play', which was rejected by CBS before the 2010 Super Bowl but garnered huge public attention due to the controversy surrounding the decision not to air the ad.[101] The ad was subsequently 'all over the internet'—more than one observer has called this an advertisement that was probably never made with the intention of being screened. Such stories raise the question why event organisers engage in heavy-handed responses to ambushing and, specifically, in the litigation that (infrequently) results from organisers' claims of attempted ambushes by often insignificant little entities that would, left to their own devices, most probably just

[97] From an address presented by Professor David Vaver, Reuters professor of Intellectual Property and Information Technology Law, Oxford University, at the Victoria University of Wellington, 30 August 2000—available online at the time of writing at http://kirra.austlii.edu.au/nz/journals/VUWLawRw/2001/2.html.

[98] Lesa Ukman, writing (16 February 2010) on the IEG sponsorship blog available online at http://www.sponsorship.com/About-IEG/Sponsorship-Blogs/Lesa-Ukman/February-2010/The-Other-Side-Of-The-Current-Ambush-Marketing-Deb.aspx.

[99] 'Ambush marketing: War minus the shooting', *The Economist*, 16 February 2006, available online at the time of writing at http://www.economist.com/node/5536128.

[100] See discussion in Chap. 7.

[101] The CBS rejection letter noted that 'CBS Standards and Practices has reviewed your proposed Super Bowl ad and concluded that the creative is not within the Network's Broadcast Standards for Super Bowl Sunday'.

fade into the background of event lore. Some event organisers may be savvy enough to avoid potential negative publicity fall-out; might that be the reason for the IOC's complete lack of action over what appeared to be a clear ambush in the form of Comedy Central comedian Stephen Colbert's 'Vancouverage 2010' shows during the 2010 Vancouver Winter Olympics?[102]

Such efforts at pursuing legal action against small fry 'ambushers' of events may be viewed as having a deterrent effect. A 2010 brand protection survey[103] conducted amongst leading sports marketers, sports leagues and corporate sponsors found that, when asked 'What measures are being used to ensure brand protection in your organisation?', 16% of respondents indicated the answer 'Selectively targeting perpetrators to make an example'.[104] Of course, a cynical view might be that such litigious posturing may be one (or both) of two things. The constant barrage of threats of legal action may be a shrewd tactic not unknown to trademark owners, namely the use of 'strike suits' to stifle competition.[105] It may also be little more than a clear message meant for the official sponsors. When one examines the nature of the rights granted to official sponsors in return for the sponsorship investment, one might conceivably ask what benefit does Coca-Cola (for example) receive for its USD 100 million investment in an Olympics sponsorship? As I've remarked above, in essence what the sponsor receives is a *pactum de non petendo*, or a contractual undertaking from the event organiser to not sue it for associating itself or its product or service with the event in its marketing. The sponsorship rights are a license to do what would otherwise be unlawful. The actual tangible benefits received in exchange for the sizeable investment are less easy to identify; it appears to be limited to the provision of access to support in the sponsor's marketing campaigns (e.g. access to logos and event *indicia*) and the provision of hospitality packages. This, of course, is the garnishing that adorns the agreement not to get sued; it is the sponsorship property for which the big bucks are paid. In this light, would it be fanciful to speculate that high profile litigation (or threats of such litigation) against nobodies who effectively pose a very limited

---

[102] See the short piece available online at the time of writing at http://www.deep-alliance.com/?p=624. Canadian law professor Jon Heshka explains that Colbert was also the official sponsor of the US Speed-skating team and had raised more than USD 300,000 for the team, and he suggests that VANOC would have been outgunned by Colbert and they wisely chose not to go after him (from personal correspondence with the author, December 2011).

[103] A survey was conducted by the Chief Marketing Officer (CMO) Council (a six-month qualitative and quantitative research campaign, 'Doing Away With Foul Play in Sports Marketing', aimed at sensitising sports sponsors and franchises to trademark trespassing, property rights violations and online scams, frauds and infringements) with the assistance of MarkMonitor. The CMO Council surveyed more than 180 senior-level sports marketers across relevant industries for an assessment of how brands are safeguarding themselves and whether those measures are effective. The study also drew from interviews with executives at top leagues and corporate sponsors. See Gannon, N 'Foul play in sports branding—the marketer's perspective' October/November 2010 *World Trademark Review* 67.

[104] Gannon 2010, p. 68.

[105] See the discussion in Sect. 5.2.2 of Chap. 5.

threat to the event organiser and the sponsors may be little more than attempts by the organisers to justify the sponsorship investment? I.e. that such litigation may actually often be a marketing exercise on the part of the event organiser in order to show its sponsors that it is serious about protecting the sponsorship investment (and maybe even an element of 'See what would happen if you had not paid the millions you have?')? Bikoff et al., in referring to the Bavaria ambush at the 2010 FIFA event, observe that 'aggressive enforcement is necessary to appease official sponsors injured by such activities and to protect the value of future endorsements'.[106] As mentioned, this is speculation, although it may be generous to attempt to explain conduct by event organisers that sometimes seems to beggar belief in terms of the apparent lack of common sense. In rare cases, threatened or actual litigation might even be used in order to turn an 'ambusher' into an official sponsor.[107]

Also, it should be noted that some observers actually encourage use of the litigation route by event organisers. McKelvey and Grady, for example, state that 'the deterrent effects of bringing a highly publicised lawsuit against an ambush marketer may seem self-evident', but they question why event organisers have brought so few law suits against 'ambush marketers'. One possible reason that they advance is the risk of adverse court rulings (such as that encountered by FIFA in its wrangling with chocolate-maker Ferrero before the German federal supreme court in respect of its claims to trademark protection for its 'Fussball WM 2006' mark).[108]

Apart from the potential for litigation to enforce anti-ambushing laws being rather skewed in respect of its target defendants, warnings about the potential for a discrepancy in respect of the impact of such laws have been expressed for years. For example, compare the following opinion expressed at the time of the tabling of the London Olympics and Paralympic Games Bill[109]:

---

106 Bikoff et al. 2010, p. 91.

107 Chase and Kernit 2010, p. 386 recount a case in the USA involving the United States Olympic Committee:

'[I]n *United States Olympic Committee v. Asics America Corporation* [No. CV-08-00522 Complaint (C.D. Cal. 9th May, 2008)], the USOC sued Asics for running multiple print and Internet advertisements supporting its endorsed athletes'accomplishments in connection with the 2008 Olympics… [T]hese advertisements included a print advertisement featuring a photograph of Asics-endorsed marathoner Ryan Hall that stated: "Good luck in the 2008 Summer Olympic Games. From all your fans at Asics", as well as congratulatory messages on Asics' website for its endorsers making the US Olympic team. Although the USOC voluntarily dismissed its complaint, the parties apparently settled their differences, as Asics subsequently entered into a multi-year agreement with USA Field Hockey, the national governing body for field hockey affiliated with the USOC, to become the "Official Partner and Exclusive Sponsor of footwear, apparel, and accessories"'.

108 McKelvey and Grady 2008, p. 581. See further Chap. 5.

109 For discussion of the London Olympic and Paralympic Games Act, 2006, see Sect. 4.4.3 in Chap. 4.

> Sponsors need protection but it is a question of balance. Is this bill going too far? We are concerned about an overreaction to the problem and, of course, the bill favours the multinational companies with deep pockets.[110]

This criticism may have been prophetic, especially if one considers this same observer's prediction at the time that '[i]t is possible that any unauthorised association with [the London 2012 Games] could contravene the law—even a pub advertising that it is screening an event'.[111] Five years later FIFA managed to obtain just such special protection in respect of the screening of matches in its 2010 World Cup in South Africa. In early 2010 the draft Liquor Control Policy for the 2010 FIFA World Cup was gazetted by the South African Department of Trade and Industry,[112] to be greeted by public outcry especially from the hospitality industry. Initial reactions to what was perceived as a requirement for existing liquor license holders to obtain a costly special license during the event were highly critical (in reaction to the draft policy's wording, which required venues hosting 'any public viewing event' where matches are broadcast 'to the general public or otherwise' to obtain a special license). The DTI attempted to set the record straight by explaining that the liquor control policy would only require a special license in respect of venues such as pubs, clubs, bars and restaurants that intend to charge an admission fee or similar surcharge for the screening of 2010 World Cup games (which establishments would require the permission of FIFA for this purpose). According to reports, such license would have to be obtained at a cost of ZAR50000 each and 2% of traders' revenues.

When one considers the potential need for new laws it is traditional to not only focus on the relevant mischief it is proposed to address, but also to consider and weigh the potential costs and benefits for the public at large. One often wonders whether this process occurs with the hosting of mega-events. We will see later that a specific requirement for the designation of the 2010 FIFA World Cup as a 'protected event' for purposes of the relevant legislation[113] was that it was deemed to be in the public interest to do so. The reality, however, is that very little benefit for the public was to be seen from this event, and FIFA's conduct during and surrounding the event was widely criticised for the organisation's apparent monopolisation of all related commercial opportunities and blatant disregard for the interests of ordinary South Africans, apparently with the full blessing of the South African government. Mark James has observed the following in respect of the legislative protection for the commercial rights to the 2012 London Olympic Games[114]:

---

[110] Marina Palomba, legal director of the UK's Institute for Practitioners in Advertising, as quoted in 'Olympics Bill to blitz 'ambush advertising'', *Daily Telegraph*, 9 July 2005.

[111] Ibid.

[112] *Government Gazette* No. 32878 Vol. 535 (18 January 2010).

[113] The Merchandise Marks Act, 1941 (as amended in 2002), discussed in Chap. 4 and elsewhere in this book.

[114] Which will be discussed in more detail in Chap. 4 and elsewhere in this book.

> [S]ome sections of the London Olympic and Paralympic Games Act 2006 appear to have been inserted at the behest of a purely private body, the International Olympic Committee, rather than on the basis of a rational legal justification. Why the Olympic and Paralympic Games are so special that the use of their symbols and sales of tickets to their events need legislative protection—protections not previously extended to other national or international sporting or cultural events held in the UK—has never been fully debated either in Parliament or before the courts.[115]

I will further examine the process of legislating for special, extended, rights protection for mega-events in Chap. 4, but for present purposes it is hoped that the reader will consider such wider public interest in events that are, after all, sporting in nature and at least ostensibly targeted at the fans (and, one hopes, not only at fans as potential consumers of soft drinks or purchasers of sports utility vehicles):

> There is a perception that no event can now be successfully held without draconian protections against so called ambush marketing. This has led to international federations being able to demand rights even after countries have been awarded the right to host the event in question. There is an argument, which host countries appear to be ignoring, that these often private and highly profitable businesses are changing the intellectual property laws of host nations to protect the event holders' investment and profits... Like most laws there is a fine balance between protecting rights holders and allowing free and fair competition.[116]

In evaluating the impact of the legal framework for commercial rights protection in the host country (and particularly such special legislation as demanded by the rights grantors through their hosting requirements), it should be noted that such requirements also generally include demands for income for the sports organisations from commercial rights exploitation to be completely tax-free. Compare, for example, Article 49(a) of the Host City Contract for the 2012 London Olympic Games:

> The City and/or the OCOG shall bear all taxes, including direct and indirect taxes, whether they be withholding taxes, customs duties, value added taxes or any other indirect taxes, whether present or future, due in any jurisdiction on a payment to be made to the IOC or any third party owned and/or controlled by the IOC, including Olympic Broadcasting Services and Meridian Management SA, with respect to the revenues generated in relation to the Games. In particular, if a withholding tax, a value added tax or any other indirect tax is due to the Host Country, to Switzerland or to any other jurisdiction on a payment to be received by the IOC or any of the above-noted third parties pursuant to this Contract and/or pursuant to an agreement with an Olympic sponsor, broadcaster or other commercial partner, the payment shall be increased and paid by the OCOG so that the IOC or such third party, after the applicable tax, receives an amount that equals the amount it would have received had there been no such tax. The City and/or the OCOG shall indemnify the IOC or such third party for any direct taxes and/or indirect taxes that could be borne by the IOC or such third party in the Host Country, so that if the IOC or such third party is liable

115 James 2010, p. 10.

116 Palomba, M 'Is ambush marketing dead?' Reed Smith Advertising Compliance Team Client Alert No. 10-097 (May 2010)—available online at the time of writing at http://www.advertisingcompliancelaw.com/uploads/file/10-097%20ReACTS%20-%20Is%20ambush%20marketing%20dead.PDF.

for the payment of direct taxes and/or indirect taxes in the Host Country, it shall be put in the same situation as if such direct and/or indirect taxes had not been due.[117]

Compare also paragraph 4.4 (contained in Chap. 4: Government Guarantees) of South Africa's Bid Book for the 2010 FIFA World Cup South Africa:

The Government guarantees that South Africa and its tax authorities (including any governmental authority with jurisdiction over the assessment, determination, collection or imposition of any taxes, duties or other levies) shall not impose any kind of taxes, duties or other levies on FIFA, FIFA's subsidiaries, the FIFA Delegation and the Host Broadcaster. They are to be treated as tax exempt persons/entities. In particular South Africa and its tax authorities recognise… that the exploitation of FIFA's Marketing and Broadcasting Rights shall not subject FIFA, FIFA's subsidiaries and the Host Broadcaster to any kind of taxation in the country… The government guarantees that it will, if required by FIFA, issue in advance written, unconditional and binding tax rulings on the above or any other tax issues relating to FIFA. In addition, the government, as well as 'the South African Football Association], guarantee that they will provide FIFA, the Commercial Affiliates and the Broadcast Rights Holders, including the Host Broadcaster, with the highest level of administrative assistance and support with regard to the handling of any tax issues related to the organisation of the 2010 FIFA World Cup™.[118]

---

[117] Article 49(b) of the London 2012 Host City Contract further provides as follows:

'Payments to be made by the IOC or certain third parties: The City and/or the OCOG shall bear all taxes, whether they be withholding taxes, customs duties, value added taxes or any other indirect taxes, whether present or future, due in any jurisdiction on a payment to be made by the IOC or any third party owned and/or controlled by the IOC, including without limitation Olympic Broadcasting Services and Meridian Management SA, with respect to the revenues generated in relation to the Games, including without limitation pursuant to any agreement with an Olympic sponsor, supplier, licensee, broadcaster or other commercial partner. The amount of a payment to be made by the IOC or any of the above-noted third parties pursuant to this Contract shall not be increased by any taxes due on such payment. If the IOC or such third party is liable for the payment of such tax, the net payment received by the City, the NOC or the OCOG shall be reduced by an amount corresponding to such tax or, if the payment to the City, the NOC or the OCOG has already been made, the tax subsequently paid by the IOC or such third party shall be reimbursed in full to the IOC or such third party by the City, the NOC or the OCOG, as the case may be'.

[118] Another example of such a provision for tax exemption can be found in section 16(1) of Jamaica's.

ICC Cricket World Cup West Indies 2007 Act, 2006:

'Income arising from [Cricket World Cup 2007] earned by:

(a) CWC 2007 Inc., ICC and its members, [ICC Development (International) Ltd], [Global Cricket Corporation Ltd] and [the West Indies Cricket Board] and its members and their respective advisers not ordinarily resident in Jamaica;
(b) a member of a squad;
(c) a CWC 2007 official; or
(d) the staff of ICC, IDI or GCC, shall be exempt from taxes of every description'. See also article 21 of the Russian Federation's 'Olympic and Paralympic Law' (Federation Law 310-FZ) for the hosting of the 2014 Sochi winter Olympic Games, which adds the following to Part Two of the Tax Code of the Russian Federation:

'The organisations who are foreign organisers of the Olympic Games and the Paralympic Games according to Article 3 of the Federal Law "On the Organisation and Holding of the XXII Olympic Winter Games and the XI Paralympic Winter Games 2014 in Sochi, the

In fact, in England's (ultimately unsuccessful) bid to host the 2018 FIFA World Cup, FIFA controversially demanded as a government guarantee exemption from a key piece of UK money-laundering legislation, the Proceeds of Crime Act, 2002. The FIFA demand required that the government must provide for 'the unrestricted import and export of all foreign currencies to and from the UK, as well as the unrestricted exchange and conversion of these currencies into US dollars, euros or Swiss francs', which allowance would apply to hundreds of individuals ranging from the delegates and staff of FIFA, its confederations and member associations, match officials, as well as an unspecified number of unnamed 'FIFA Listed Individuals'. This guarantee has been described as 'an incredible carve-out from existing laws',[119] the reason for which was unexplained. But this is not an isolated case. It was reported in September 2009 that FIFA was embroiled in a stalemate with the Brazilian tax service, Receita Federal, regarding the claimed tax exemptions for the 2014 FIFA World Cup. The Brazilian government had agreed to the tax exemptions for FIFA, but FIFA subsequently demanded that all its contractors (i.e. including its commercial partners) should be completely exempted, which Receita Federal refused to allow. In another illustration of the substantial power wielded by the event organiser, it was subsequently reported that the sports minister had announced in April 2010 that a draft law was to be sent to Congress for approval in order to meet FIFA's demand for a full exemption of its contractors, and in May 2010 it was reported that the law had been passed.[120]

The Dutch government, which was also unsuccessful in its bid to host the 2018 FIFA World Cup, must have upset Mr. Blatter when they published the details of FIFA's required government guarantees in bidding for the event. In a draft form letter in the name of the Netherlands government and addressed to FIFA (entitled 'Government Guarantee No. 3: Tax Exemption', available on the Internet at the time of writing[121]) the following is found:

> FIFA and/or FIFA Subsidiaries, irrespective of whether resident in the Netherlands or not, will be fully exempt from any Taxes in the Netherlands. FIFA and/or FIFA Subsidiaries will be treated as fully Tax exempt entities. The full Tax exemption is not limited to the Events and is not limited time-wise.
>
> The exemption stated in this section shall encompass all revenues, profits, income, expenses, costs, investments and any and all kind of payments, in cash or otherwise,

(Footnote 118 continued)
Development of Sochi as a Mountain Climate Resort and the Amendment of Certain Legislative Acts of the Russian Federation" shall not be deemed to be taxpayers in relation to the transactions made as part of the organisation and holding of the XXII Olympic Winter Games and the XI Paralympic Winter Games 2014 in Sochi'.

119 See the report by Scott, M 'FIFA's demand to be exempt of UK money-laundering legislation' *The Guardian*, 1 December 2010, available online at the time of writing at http://www.guardian.co.uk/football/2010/dec/01/fifa-government-government-exemptions?INTCMP=ILCNETTXT3487.

120 From a report available online at the time of writing at http://www.v-brazil.com/world-cup/2014/fifa-claims-full-tax-exemption/.

121 At https://zoek.officielebekendmakingen.nl/blg-63037.html.

including through (i) the delivery of goods or services, (ii) accounting credits, (iii) other deliveries, (iv) applications, or (v) remittances, made by or to FIFA and/or FIFA Subsidiaries.

Paragraph 3 of the document makes it clear that the above exemption shall 'in particular and without limitation' mean that '[n]o Taxes will be levied on any profits made by FIFA and/or FIFA Subsidiaries'.

Of course, FIFA can probably not be faulted for the energy expended on obtaining such tax exemptions—it has been estimated that FIFA left South Africa with a GBP 2 billion tax-free profit[122] from what some observers called FIFA's 'African tax bubble'.[123] Also, one should remember that the big boys in international sports governance tend to base themselves in friendly tax havens—FIFA is registered (as a 'non-profit organisation') in a tax-friendly Swiss canton; the Dublin-based International Rugby Board is incorporated under the laws of the Isle of Man; and the International Cricket Council recently moved from its historic base at Lords Cricket Ground in London to that paragon of a cricketing mecca, Dubai.

The end result of such tax exemption and related arrangements, as demanded by the relevant sports governing body, is that members of the public and entrepreneurs in the host nation are effectively deprived of most opportunities to benefit financially from the hype and excitement around such events—ironically, while these same persons are often by means of their tax dollars forced to assist to foot the bill for the often vastly expensive infrastructure, stadium construction, transport etc. expenses that are necessitated by bid guarantees. And, of course, the rationale for footing the bill is the direct and indirect benefits to be accrued from hosting the mega-event which are disingenuously promised in order to build support for hosting it.[124]

This is highly ironic (some might say obscene) when one considers that budgeting for mega-events in government bids appear to often (if not always) constitute masterpieces of pseudo-science, painting an extremely rosy picture which subsequently, invariably, turns out to be anything but realistic. Some respected sports economists have suggested that after the-event audits of economic impact serve an important role, because they 'can serve as filters through which the hyperbole that may be present in some prospective economic impact estimates can be captured and eliminated'.[125] That may be fine for the next potential mega-event

---

[122] See, for example, the report available online at the time of writing at http://www.guardian.co.uk/football/2010/jul/18/fifa-world-cup-sepp-blatter.

[123] See, for example, the discussion on the Tax Justice Network website (e.g. at http://taxjustice.blogspot.com/2010/10/fifa-versus-south-africa-total-victory.html).

[124] My thanks to Jon Heshka for reminding me of this point (from personal correspondence with the author, December 2011).

[125] Baade, R A and Matheson, V 'Bidding for the Olympics: Fool's Gold?' (at 7)—Undated paper available online at the time of writing at http://harbaugh.uoregon.edu/Readings/Sports/olympics.pdf.

host (assuming they'll learn from the past), but does little for the taxpayer who may have just been subjected to a huge and long-term debt by politicians. In the later chapters I will express criticism of the fact that, contrary to the traditional notion of what constitutes illegitimate 'ambush marketing' of events, the modern day special legislation passed to outlaw such conduct generally does not require proof by event organisers that consumers (the public) have actually been deceived by means of misrepresentation by the ambusher. In this light it is ironic to consider whether event organisers, rather than ambushers, should not be exposed to legal sanctions for deception of the consumer public when it comes to possible misrepresentation of the scale of potential benefits their events may bring (although the host nations or city governments are, of course, largely complicit in this regard). Leaving that issue aside, the result of such rosy forecasts of boom times is that taxpayers are presented after the fact with highly inflated costs which are to be borne by the domestic tax base. Compare the South African government's extremely optimistic stadium infrastructure budget for the 2010 event, as one example. Even though '[the South African Football Association] has developed a sophisticated financial model to facilitate a clear, credible and accurate understanding of the business imperatives involved in staging the 2010 FIFA World Cup' and such model 'created in accordance with the highest international standards, is inherently flexible and can be easily configured to reflect the impact of changing economic conditions in various scenarios through to 2010',[126] the initial amount budgeted for all stadium upgrades and refurbishments, namely ZAR 1.1 billion, eventually ballooned to an impressive ZAR 16.5 billion (half the South African government's 2010 national budget for defence and, more troubling in a developing nation with such pervasive socio-economic problems, approximately 20% of the national housing and community amenities budget for the same year). South Africa's deputy president was quoted in media reports as attributing the escalation to increasing material costs,[127] which seems to make a nonsense of the 'sophisticated financial model' developed for the bid budgeting exercise. A South African economist recently made the following rather worrying assessment:

> [T]he difference between the original budget and current estimated expenditure indicates that the original budget was hopelessly incorrect. The total tangible costs for the South African government was supposed to be "minimal", estimated at ZAR 2.3 billion in 2003. Currently the 2010 estimated cost for the South Africa government is ZAR 39.3 billion—a whopping 1,709% increase from the original estimate.[128]

---

[126] Chap. 7 of the South African government's Bid Book for the 2010 FIFA World Cup South Africa.

[127] Tolsi, N 'The World Cup Bid Book fiasco' 13 June 2010, *The Mail and Guardian* (available online at the time of writing at http://www.mg.co.za/article/2010-06-13-the-completely-miscalculated-world-cup-bid-book-that-cost-us-a-bundle).

[128] Cottle, E 'A preliminary evaluation of the impact of the 2010 FIFA World Cup South Africa', 2 September 2010—available online at the time of writing at http://www.sah.ch/data/D23807E0/ImpactassessmentFinalSeptember2010EddieCottle.pdf.

Of course, this is not even to mention the fact that economists, more fundamentally, question the very use of sports mega-events to boost local economies in circumstances where often the required investments should be made by governments without the need for such drivers. These events are extremely expensive to stage, and one may justifiably ask whether the money can be better spent. It was observed, for example, that when Rio de Janeiro won the right to host the 2016 Olympic Games with a USD 15 billion bid, this represented a sum equal to over USD 2,000 for each citizen of Rio, even before the expected cost overruns.[129]

Such developments are, however, of little concern to the sports governing bodies, who may often have 'flown the coop' by the time that the true implications of hosting mega-events enters the public consciousness.[130] In terms of the government guarantees required to obtain hosting rights, governments are (possibly in many cases, justifiably) left to face the public outcry when the true facts come out, and when, in any event, it is too late to do anything about prior commitments and legal obligations entered into in the heady fiesta atmosphere of mega-event bidding. The taxpayers, generally, keep paying for a long time after the events, and the mega-event hangover is a persistent one. South Africa's public broadcaster employed the slogan 'Feel it, it is here' in the run-up to and during the 2010 World Cup. It might not be inappropriate for the national revenue service to print, on their future tax return forms (and for some time to come), the slogan 'Feel it, it is *still* here'.

Of course, members of the public only tend to get hot under the collar when they are actually allowed access to information about their governments' dealings in the bidding process. There is an apparent widespread trend to lock away such information from the prying eyes of democratically elected host governments' constituencies, which one might suggest adds insult to injury. The South African government's Bid Book for the 2010 FIFA World Cup was subsequently posted on the web site of the *Mail and Guardian* newspaper, after reportedly unsuccessful efforts by the democratic governance and rights unit of the University of Cape Town to obtain access to the document in terms of the Promotion of Access to Information Act, 2 of 2000 (or 'PAIA'). The *Mail and Guardian* also obtained a court order from the South Gauteng High Court in Johannesburg a week before the opening matches of the 2010 World Cup to obtain access to the Local Organising Committee's tender awards for the event (where the court ruled that '[r]efusing access to these records would enable the organiser of this event to keep from the public eye documents which may disclose evidence of corruption, graft and incompetence in the organisation of the World Cup, or which may disclose that

---

[129] Rose and Spiegel 2010, p. 12.

[130] It was reported in October 2010 that the nine South African host cities for the tournament were considering taking legal action to recover an amount of approximately ZAR 500 million from FIFA, which FIFA had allegedly contractually undertaken to pay the host cities for certain construction work, for 'rehabilitation' of parts of the host cities after the event, and in respect of the host cities' alleged entitlement to 10% of revenues from ticket sales during the event.

there has been no such malfeasance'[131]). The Local Organising Committee not only argued that it was 'too busy' to provide such information, but also attempted to defend a claim for access to such documents in terms of PAIA on the basis that the Local Organising Committee was not part of government and was not performing a public function in its organising of the World Cup. Its legal counsel argued unsuccessfully (not surprisingly) that FIFA was essentially a 'Swiss club' and that the hosting agreement was between FIFA and the South African Football Association, and not the South African government.[132] The Games Monitor web site in respect of the 2012 London Olympic Games[133] reports that the 2012 London Host City Contract requirements were successfully kept from the public and elected representatives by the Mayor of London from July 2005 to December 2009, on the grounds of allegedly being exempted from public disclosure in terms of section 41 of the Freedom of Information Act of 2000 as 'information provided in confidence'. This position was successfully challenged and, at the time of writing, the Host City Contract is available from the Greater London Authority.[134] Of course, 'secret' commercial contracts in international sport are nothing new; compare the elusive Concorde agreement in Formula 1 motor sport, which has, in its various incarnations, managed to baffle pundits outside the hallowed halls since 1981.

The restrictions imposed in the form of bid guarantee requirements for mega-events are also not only financial; issues such as 'spring-cleaning' by event organisers through the forced removal of the homeless from the precincts of event venues,[135]

---

[131] See the *Mail and Guardian* report available online at the time of writing at http://mg.co.za/article/2010-06-08-mg-wins-bid-to-access-world-cup-tender-documents; *M and G Media Ltd v 2010 FIFA World Cup South Africa Organising Committee Ltd* South Gauteng High Court Case No. 09/51422 (unreported at the time of writing).

[132] From a report available online at the time of writing at http://mg.co.za/article/2010-05-24-loc-too-busy-for-mg-court-battle.

[133] See http://www.gamesmonitor.org.uk/node/935.

[134] At http://www.london.gov.uk/freedom-information.

[135] See the report by Raquel Rolnik, United Nations Special Rapporteur on adequate housing, of March 2010, which calls on FIFA and the IOC (and host governments) to ensure that mega-events such as the football World Cup and the Olympic Games do not lead to the displacement of the poor, through forced evictions, criminalisation of homeless persons and informal activities, and the dismantling of informal settlements—see the report entitled 'Olympics and World Cup soccer must take up cause of right to housing—UN expert', 9 March 2010, available on the web site of the UN News Centre at www.un.org [accessed 20 March 2010]. It was reported on 7 April 2010 that the City of Cape Town's efforts to move the residents of informal settlements had caused controversy and were claimed to be aimed at removing an 'eyesore' for tourists in the run-up to the 2010 FIFA World Cup. City officials denied that such efforts were aimed at city beautification for the event, and claimed that they were part of a longer term strategy to provide permanent housing for such residents.

At the time of writing (in early 2011) a major Indian housing advocacy group was in the process of taking a claim for compensation and rehabilitation to the high court of Delhi, arguing that a programme of forced evictions ahead of the 2010 Commonwealth Games violated rights. The Housing and Land Rights Network produced a report in February 2011, alleging that the severe restrictions on the informal economic activities sector[136] and often extensive restrictions on freedom of expression and of the media (e.g. through extremely restrictive accreditation requirements) are, sadly, nothing new (also not in respect of the 2010 football World Cup event).[137]

The preceding discussion of how the commercial monopolies to sports mega-events are established may appear to be very negatively slanted against those involved. It is by no means the intention here to deny the existence and value of the very real commercial interests and expense that are at stake in staging some of the greatest entertainment spectacles on earth. However, what I find troubling is the apparent and all-pervasive trend to seek to, at least ostensibly, protect such interests at all costs and by trumping all other considerations and interests—including, especially, the public interest in the hosting of major events—which I submit needs to be considered much more critically. Specifically, it will be contended here that the apparently sacrosanct nature of such events and of the commercial interests of those hosting and sponsoring them should be more closely scrutinised, from a legal perspective, as I will attempt to do in the later chapters. The fact that FIFA and other international sports governing bodies conduct 'business as usual' in all the jurisdictions where they operate, does not take away from the fact that Mr. Blatter et al.—if they want to conduct such business in South Africa, Brazil, Qatar or anywhere else—must respect and comply with the relevant host nation's laws as well as accepted principles of international law.

The following section will briefly examine how and why the modern mega-event sports sponsorship model developed in recent years, with a view to evaluating, in the chapters that follow, the legal implications of such model and how it operates for the rights and interests of parties other than the event organisers (sports organisations) and their commercial partners.

2.3 The Development of the Modern Mega-Event Sponsorship Model

Sponsorship involvement with sport and sports mega-events has been around for many years, and this book will not undertake a historic overview of developments in this field. Coca-Cola, for example, is very proud of its continuous involvement

(Footnote 135 continued)
forced evictions by the local government had violated people's rights and even led to a number of deaths before the games in October 2010. Four months before the games, authorities in the city of Delhi announced that street vendors and other stall holders were a 'major security risk' and would be evicted—see the report available online at the time of writing at http://www.radioaustralia.net.au/asiapac/stories/201102/s3144899.htm.

[136] Compare the very extensive restrictions on informal street traders as contained in the various 2010 host city municipal by-laws, as referred to in Chap. 7.

[137] See the discussion on human rights implications of mega-events commercial rights protection in Chap. 7.

with the Olympic Games since as far back as 1928, while Kodak was already there in 1896, and sports equipment manufacturer A.G. Spalding managed to wangle the job of director of sport for the US Olympic team at the Games of 1900 and to orchestrate the selection of his products as 'official' equipment for the 1904 Games in St Louis. The 1924 Games in Paris saw outrage on the part of the International Olympic Committee at the level of in-stadium advertising, which prompted it to proclaim a 'clean venue' policy which is still in force today. When former IOC president Samaranch (ever-vigilant in chasing the 'hidden pot of gold' for the Olympic movement) went so far as to direct an enquiry to Coke's head of marketing as to how much more it would pay if the IOC were to allow venue advertising, Coke threatened to cancel its Olympic sponsorships if the IOC ever scrapped the clean venue policy as it would change 'what makes the Games so special'.[138]

The modern phenomenon of commercial sponsorship arrangements between sports governing bodies and corporate sponsors, however, had its genesis in a landmark agreement signed in Lausanne on 28 May 1985 between the International Olympic Committee and Horst Dassler's[139] sports marketing company, ISL Licensing AG of Switzerland. ISL, which specialised in sports sponsorship marketing, was founded shortly after the 1982 FIFA football World Cup, and established its reputation through exclusive marketing contracts with FIFA and the European and South-American football confederations. In a bid to extend its global reach ISL targeted the Olympic movement and the Olympic symbol of the five rings as the most recognised and powerful symbol in world sport, and envisioned a global sponsorship programme of the Olympics which would provide a second main revenue source for the IOC, apart from television rights revenues.[140]

The May 1985 agreement[141] facilitated the implementation of a new sponsorship programme for the Olympic Games, which came to be known as The Olympic Programme (or 'TOP', later known as 'The Olympic Partner Programme') and was to become the model for modern mega-event commercial rights exploitation also beyond the Olympic Games. These developments were instrumental in the International Olympic Committee's 'transformation from the instrument of peace and goodwill envisioned by its founder... to a transnational nongovernmental commercial giant of imposing power and influence in global sporting matters'.[142] It has, however, been hinted that the modern Olympic movement may, in fact, have been created on a platform at least partly influenced by commercialism, which holds a measure of irony in light of later developments: When de Coubertin devised the Olympic five-ring symbol he wrote (in 1913) of how the rings

---

[138] Payne 2006, pp. 143, 144.

[139] Son of Adi Dassler (founder of Adidas) and brother to Rudi (founder of Puma). See the discussion in Chap. 9.

[140] See Schaus and Wenn 2007, p. 316.

[141] Which was to become known as 'TOP I' and which operated from 1985–1988—see the discussion in the text below.

[142] From the preface to Barney et al. 2004.

represent 'the five parts of the world, now won over by Olympism, ready to accept its fruitful rivalries'. An alternative suggestion is that the Baron got the inspiration for the Olympic symbol from an advertisement for Dunlop tyres which depicted angels holding interlaced bicycle tyres representing continents.[143] Be that as it may, '[t]he IOC's decision to embrace commercialisation and create an innovative marketing programme has changed the essence of the organisation… on the verge of bankruptcy in the 1970s, the IOC went from an "amateur" run sport organisation to a multi-billion dollar international corporation'.[144] As has been mentioned above, the global sponsorship industry was estimated to amount to more than USD 43 billion in 2008, from a rather more humble figure of USD 2 billion in 1984.[145] The Olympic Games has been a pioneering sponsorship product in contributing to the globalised appeal of sport, and of the sports mega-event, as marketing tool, and its explosion in magnitude in the past few decades.

TOP was officially inaugurated at the 1988 Seoul Olympics, and was devised at a time when the International Olympic Committee was experiencing serious financial problems and when hosting the expensive Games was not an attractive option for potential host cities (e.g. only Los Angeles bid for the 1984 Games, but it managed to report a USD 225 million surplus).[146] This came in the wake of the most recent instalments of the Games at the time, which had been financial disasters, compare Moscow in 1980 and Montreal in 1976. Montreal mayor Jean Drapeau famously assured taxpayers that 'The Olympics can no more have a deficit than a man can have a baby'. Ah, those lovable politicians—the City of Montreal was ultimately faced with an unenviable CDN 990 million deficit, and it reportedly took more than 30 years to repay the debt incurred to host the Games (earning the Olympic Stadium known as the Big 'O' the nickname of the Big 'Owe'[147]). Not all post-1984 Games have managed to avoid the potential pitfall for their host taxpayers, however (it was reported, for example, that Nagano, host city of the 1998 Winter Games, faced severe financial consequences for hosting such a big event and taxpayers suffered debts of up to GBP 20,000 per household to balance the city's books!).[148] Along with the financial implications, the IOC was also faced with other serious issues—after the terrorist attack at the 1972 Munich Summer Games, voters of Colorado rejected the right to host the 1976 Winter Games even after it was awarded to the state, and the IOC had to scramble to find any willing host.[149]

---

[143] Payne 2006, p. 112.

[144] Seguin and O'Reilly 2008, p. 62.

[145] Burton and Chadwick 2009, p. 3.

[146] See Johnson 2008, p. 3. At the time fewer cities were interested in bidding for the Games: Munich, Madrid, Montreal and Detroit bid for the 1972 Games, Montreal, Los Angeles and Moscow bid for 1976, Moscow and Los Angeles for 1980, and only Los Angeles bid for 1984.

[147] Taken from http://www.atkearney.com/index.php/Publications/building-a-legacy.html.

[148] Malfas et al. 2004, p. 213.

[149] See Matheson, V A and Baade, R A 'Mega-sporting events in developing nations: Playing the way to prosperity?' (draft document, March 2003)—available online at the time of writing at http://web.williams.edu/Economics/wp/mathesonprosperity.pdf.

On the commercialisation side of things, the Montreal Games, which saw the first time that the Olympic symbol and trademarks were granted protection by the legislature in a host country,[150] was characterised by an aggressive campaign by the local organising committee to source sponsorship from the private sector in order to facilitate its goal of 'self-financing the Games'. As a result, the organisers had obtained signed agreements with 628 companies each for a fee of CDN 50,000 (the total corporate sponsorship initiative netted revenues of barely CDN 5 million dollars after the deduction of administrative and management costs).[151] Los Angeles was an anomaly in respect of the commercial facet of the Games. Because of the growing reputation of the Olympics as a proverbial black hole sucking in money as if it was going out of fashion, interest in hosting the event was conspicuously absent. The city of Los Angeles, the state of California and the US government had made it clear that no public money would be provided to finance the event. The IOC had no replacement host city to fall back on, and consequently the Los Angeles Olympic Organising Committee (or LAOOC) enjoyed unprecedented bargaining power in negotiating its contract with the IOC. It could insist that its own lawyers draw up the contract, which included cast-iron guarantees against losses that would otherwise have fallen on the shoulders of tax-payers. The Games were handed to the LAOOC as an independent organising committee which accepted financial responsibility jointly with the US Organising Committee (USOC), which sought financial guarantees from private industry to cover losses, as opposed to such burden falling on the city of Los Angeles (which was contrary to the Olympic Charter[152]).[153] The organisers directly approached private sponsors to pay for the rights to use Olympic symbols in their marketing, but chairman of the local organising committee, Peter Ueberroth (who would go on to be named *Time* magazine's Man of the Year for 1984, and to be appointed as Major League Baseball's 6th Commissioner in late 1984), had learnt from the mistakes of Montreal, where the organisers, by sourcing a large number of corporate sponsors for relatively small individual sponsorship fees, had failed to generate significant revenues.[154] Ueberroth's marketing campaign led to contracts with 35 commercial 'partners', 64 'suppliers' and 65 companies holding licenses (with each product category enjoying designated rights and exclusivity), and the Los Angeles marketing programme alone generated USD 157 million in the form of cash, equipment, goods, 'value-in-kind' products and services provided.[155]

From the phenomenal commercial success of the LA Games came the realisation that the Olympics could be a real money-spinner. In fact, this was rather serendipitous at a time when another major concern for the IOC (apart from the

[150] The Olympic Act passed by the Parliament of Canada on 27 July 1973.

[151] Barney et al. 2004, p. 155.

[152] The host city contract was subsequently amended by the IOC.

[153] De Lange 1998, p. 105.

[154] Barney et al. 2004, p. 155.

[155] Ibid. 160.

high cost of hosting its spectacle) was the fear that the Olympic Movement had heretofore placed all its eggs in a rather shaky basket—in the 1970s the sale of television broadcasting rights to the Games was the source of nearly 98% of Olympic revenues, and there were fears that broadcasters might in future at some point decide to refuse to pay what was then (and still is) spiralling rights fees.[156] One should consider the context; apart from the Los Angeles experience the IOC was also at the time particularly obsessed with the protection of the symbols of its Games as its 'property'. It had only recently managed (after involved machinations) to obtain trademark protection for the Olympic symbols in Switzerland, as a prelude to its lobbying of governments which would culminate in the WIPO[157]-administered Nairobi Treaty on the Protection of the Olympic Symbol in 1981[158] (the movement to protect the Olympic symbols at the time was aimed primarily at developing Olympic merchandising rights rather than to protect the event against unauthorised commercial conduct by outsiders such as ambush marketing,[159] discussed later). The IOC was at the time facing the prospect of the expiry of copyright protection in respect of the Five Rings symbol in 1987, fifty years after the death of its creator (the founder of the modern Olympic Movement, Baron Pierre de Coubertin).[160] So the race was on to obtain proper protection for its intellectual property, and then to ensure that such property would yield revenues through their commercial exploitation.

As mentioned above, the inception of the TOP programme must be understood in light of developments in financing the expensive to-host Games since the mid-twentieth century, and more specifically in the post-World War II era. The first television broadcast (by means of a closed circuit system) of the summer Games had occurred at the last instalment of the Games before the interruption of the war years (the infamous 'Nazi Olympics' in Berlin in 1936).[161] At the time, the Third Reich was only capable of delivering live feed from one of three cameras, and that only while the sun was shining. It appears to be commonly accepted that what would come to constitute the foremost source of revenue for Olympics organisers and the IOC, namely television broadcasting rights, first attained a measure of official recognition at the first post-war Games, the 1948 Olympics in London,

---

[156] Barney et al. 2004, p. 163.

[157] The World Intellectual Property Organisation, a specialised agency of the United Nations established by the WIP Treaty adopted in Stockholm on 14 July 1967.

[158] Adopted on 26 September 1981, which in its Article 1 places an obligation on states party to the Treaty 'to refuse or to invalidate the registration as a mark and to prohibit by appropriate measures the use, as a mark or other sign, for commercial purposes, of any sign consisting of or containing the Olympic symbol, as defined in the Charter of the International Olympic Committee, except with the authorisation of the International Olympic Committee'.

[159] Johnson 2008, p. 25.

[160] See Barney et al. 2004, pp. 156–163.

[161] This television broadcast was famously fictionalised as the first major television broadcast to emanate from Earth and to be received by an alien civilisation, in the 1997 Warner Bros Pictures film *Contact*, directed by Robert Zemeckis.

when the BBC was charged the then huge sum of one thousand pounds for the rights to broadcast the event by the organising committee. When the BBC subsequently pleaded poverty but wrote a cheque in payment, the local organisers reportedly (in classic British gentleman fashion) never cashed the cheque.[162] The IOC appeared to recognise the potential value of television and the money it could bring to the event and its organisers. Although the IOC president of the time who was elected to the position shortly after the 1948 Games, the controversial Avery Brundage,[163] was apparently sceptical of the appropriateness of the IOC's involvement in the marketing of TV rights, Rule 49 of the Olympic Charter was amended in 1958 to make provision for the negotiation of television rights by each organising committee.[164]

Toohey and Veal recount an amusing incident at the first live broadcast of the winter Games (in Cortina in 1956), which might be a metaphor for the love-hate relationship between the purists (reverence of the amateur ethos of the Games) and commercialism in the form of the television and media industries: the final torch bearer reportedly tripped on a television cable placed on the ice surface of the Olympic stadium and dropped the torch, temporarily extinguishing the Olympic flame…[165]

While the inevitable influx of large amounts of money into the organisation of the Olympics by means of television revenues would play a significant role in the development of the Games as the world's pre-eminent social/cultural spectacle, developments regarding commercialisation that followed would serve to also pose one of the biggest challenges to the Olympic Movement in modern times. The exposure that television (and, more recently, other digital media) has brought to the event is the prime driver behind the involvement of corporate sponsors, especially the large multi-national corporations who are best placed to capitalise on the international exposure provided by broadcasts that truly circle the globe and reach billions of potential consumers. This is easy to grasp if one considers that the revenues from the sale of broadcasting rights to the Games escalated from USD 1.2 million for the 1960 Rome Games to more than USD 1.7 billion for Beijing in 2008.[166]

The IOC's interest in the development of a marketing programme such as TOP is commonly attributed to Juan Antonio Samaranch's increased anxiety over the IOC's nearly sole reliance on television revenues at the time (when approximately 95–98% of its revenues derived from this, rather mercurial and unpredictable,

---

162 Toohey and Veal 2007, pp. 153, 154.

163 Brundage, who had been IOC vice-president since 1942 and who was elected president in 1952, was famously instrumental in the removal of the only two Jewish competitors in the US team for the 400 meter race at the Berlin Olympics of 1936. He has been labelled a Nazi sympathiser, who was also opposed to the inclusion of women in the Games.

164 Ibid. Rule 49 of the Olympic Charter (7 July 2007, in force at the time of writing) deals with 'Media Coverage of the Olympic Games'. Rule 49.2 provides that '[a]ll decisions concerning the coverage of the Olympic Games by the media rest within the competence of the IOC'.

165 Ibid.

166 From the 2010 edition of the IOC's *Olympic Marketing Fact File*, available online at the time of writing at http://www.olympic.org/Documents/fact_file_2010.pdf.

source). Recent instalments of the Games at the time had been tainted or affected by geopolitical baggage and the previous two administrations of the organisation (under Brundage and Lord Killanin) had fought a running battle with organising committees regarding the apportionment of such revenues (not to mention the vagaries of the periodic contract negotiations with broadcasters).[167] A newly-formed IOC Commission on New Sources of Financing made recommendations in favour of the concept of a worldwide sponsorship programme based on a proposal developed by ISL, and the IOC's Executive Board approved this in principle at the IOC's Session in New Delhi in March 1983.[168] The IOC was clearly swayed in its decision to finally accept the ISL proposal for a global programme with multinational corporate sponsors by the success of the LAOOC to source private sponsorships to cover the costs of the Los Angeles Games. Negotiations, quite involved and protracted, followed with the NOCs to sign up to the new programme, although the US Olympic Committee (USOC) was a constant thorn in the IOC's side due to its reluctance to give up its already lucrative marketing programme in the United States (and fears that, while TOP would benefit the NOCs in countries without proper marketing campaigns, the USOC would gain few benefits from its association with the programme that it did not already enjoy at the time). The USOC was also sceptical about the IOCs insistence for it to participate in this new international programme which would see mostly American-based multinational corporations as its headline sponsors, and USOC felt that it was entitled to a greater share of revenues than would be paid to other NOCs participating in TOP.[169] The USOC's position would appear to have been justified. Houlihan observes that, at the time of the Salt Lake City bribery scandal in the late 1990s the IOC was concerned about the response from America when the US government launched its own investigation through a series of congressional hearings and the involvement of the FBI. The IOC was 'acutely aware' of the fact that 60% of all its commercial revenue came from the States, which provided 9 of the 11 largest corporate sponsors at the time and accounted for the bulk of broadcasting income.[170] Dick Pound explains that most of the IOC's difficulties with the introduction of TOP arose out of the negotiations with the NOCs as to what their shares would be, but once 'everyone was equally unhappy, we knew we had it pretty well right'.[171] The continued importance of the American market for the Olympics bosses is illustrated by NBC's USD 2 billion Olympics broadcasting rights fee for the 2010–2012 period, which dwarfs the broadcasting rights fees paid in all other territories or countries.[172]

---

[167] Schaus and Wenn 2007, p. 316.

[168] Ibid.; Barney et al. 2004, pp. 170, 171.

[169] See Barney et al. 2004, pp. 171–179.

[170] Houlihan 2004, p. 66.

[171] Pound 2006, p. 150.

[172] From the 2010 edition of the IOC's *Olympic Marketing Fact File*, available online at the time of writing at http://www.olympic.org/Documents/fact_file_2010.pdf.

Along with the introduction of TOP the IOC also adopted a new system in order to ensure maximum benefit from the new sponsorship revenue source. 1992 was the last year in which the summer and winter Olympics took place in the same year; since then it has been staggered so that there is currently a 2-year cycle between mega-events (the summer Olympics take place in the same year as UEFA's Euro football championship, while the winter Olympics shares its year with the FIFA World Cup finals and the Commonwealth Games).

TOP was not only a response to the growing realisation of the potential for massive sponsorship revenues to be generated in respect of the Games, but also an attempt to address a practical hurdle to the sourcing and management of sponsorships that had been identified by Organising Committees (the 'OCOGs').[173] The Olympic sponsorship activities were dependent on the use of the Olympic symbols (notably the five rings), and sponsors in essence bought the right to associate with the Games by using these symbols in their promotional campaigns. The practical problem, however, lay in the fact that the rights to use and license the use of the Olympic symbols were vested in the National Olympic Committees (or 'NOCs'). The Olympic Charter required that any marketing activities by an OCOG in the territory of a NOC required the consent of the local NOC. Accordingly, the relevant OCOG for the Games, along with its potential sponsors, had to individually negotiate the use of symbols with each relevant NOC within whose territory such use was to take place. This clearly created huge problems for sponsors, especially large multinational corporations such as Kodak, Coca-Cola and McDonalds, who had enjoyed long association with the Games and desired truly international exposure from such association in future. Accordingly, the TOP programme was created by the IOC in response to requests by the major sponsors to simplify the international marketing programme.[174] These sponsors reportedly also indicated that they would be willing to contribute much more to the Olympic Movement if the IOC could offer exclusivity on a world-wide basis.[175] As a result, the TOP programme introduced the concept of category exclusivity[176] of Olympic sponsorships, whereby sponsors would receive exclusive international rights within certain product or service categories (i.e. banking services, soft drinks or apparel). The TOP Programme was initially centred around 44 international product or service categories, which categories are susceptible of sponsorship on an international basis, by reason of the nature of the product or service or of the size and international scope of the corporations dealing therein.[177] Prior to the establishment of the TOP programme, fewer than ten NOCs in the world had a

---

173 Organising Committee for the Olympic Games.

174 This issue of 'centralising' negotiations for sponsorship rights was specifically cited as one of the reasons for the IOC Executive Board's approval of the recommendation to pursue the ISL proposal for a new global sponsorship programme—see Barney et al. 2004, p. 171.

175 Pound 1986, p. 84.

176 See discussion in Sect. 2.4.

177 Pound 1986, p. 85.

source of marketing revenue, and the programme also saw OCOGs launch independent marketing programmes for the first time while the IOC now required the relevant OCOG to form a joint marketing programme with the host country NOC.[178] The 2010 edition of the IOC's *Olympic Marketing Fact File* describes the working of the TOP programme as follows:

> The TOP programme provides each Worldwide Olympic Partner with exclusive global marketing rights and opportunities within a designated product or service category. The global marketing rights include partnerships with the IOC, all active NOCs and their Olympic teams, and the two OCOGs and the Games of each quadrennium. The TOP Partners may exercise these rights worldwide and may activate marketing initiatives with all the members of the Olympic Movement that participate in the TOP programme.

The TOP programme leaves space—although limited—for local or domestic sponsorships outside of the programme, whereby sponsors can obtain rights outside the categories on the international list. This does, however, not preclude the earning of revenues by OCOGS in respect of the 'worldwide exclusive' categories under TOP. Separately, the OCOGs receive 50% of the revenue from the IOC's worldwide sale of marketing rights across about ten business categories under TOP. In return for surrendering marketing rights for these business categories in their territories, the 203 NOCs which participate in the Games each receive a share of the 20% of TOP revenue that is allocated to the NOCs.[179] By way of example, the Australian Olympic Committee's share of TOP for the 2005–2008 quadrennial amounted to approximately one-third of its total revenue from sponsorship sales and licensing (in the amount of AUD 34 million).[180] In addition, the OCOGs also receive 50% of the broadcast revenue, after the costs for the Host Broadcaster have been deducted. Since the Sydney Olympics the IOC has become the Host Broadcaster (or producer of content) of the Games through its joint venture (it holds 80%) in Olympic Broadcasting Services (OBS). After the costs of OBS are deducted, the 50% payments to the OCOGs are made and the 12.75% of United States broadcast fees is paid to the USOC, the IOC pays a further share of broadcasting revenues to the international federations with sports on the Olympic programme (a total of around USD 296 million to 26 international federations for the 2012 London Games and USD 121 m to seven international federations for the 2010 Vancouver winter Games).[181]

Since the inception of the new TOP sponsorship model—which one observer has referred to as 'a corporatization and McDonaldization of the world sporting

[178] See the 2010 edition of the IOC's *Olympic Marketing Fact File* (available online at the time of writing at http://www.olympic.org/Documents/fact_file_2010.pdf).

[179] See the letter by John Coates, president of the Australian Olympic Committee and Executive Board Member of the International Olympic Committee, available online the time of writing on the web site of the Australian Olympic Committee at http://corporate.olympics.com.au/news.cfm?ArticleID=10495.

[180] Ibid.

[181] Ibid.

event'[182]—all subsequent instalments of the Olympic Games (except Athens in 2004) have either broken even or made a profit for its organisers.[183] In the 2005–2008 Olympic quadrennial, the 12 TOP sponsors paid a total of USD 866 million in sponsorship fees, of which revenues approximately 40% was allocated by the IOC to national Olympic committees and 50% to local organising committees.[184]

The 'TOP I programme', the first TOP programme, operated from 1985–1988, was supported by nine multinational corporate partners and generated USD 97 million for the Olympic movement. TOP II (1989–1992) comprised twelve corporate partners (including eight of the original sponsors from TOP I) and generated USD 175 million. TOP III (1993–1996) comprised ten corporate partners and generated more than USD 350 million, while TOP IV (1997–2000), with its eleven corporate partners, generated more than USD 550 million to the movement. TOP V, which concluded in 2004, had ten worldwide corporate partners and reportedly generated more than USD 600 million.[185] As mentioned above, in the 2005–2008 Olympic quadrennial, the twelve TOP sponsors paid a total of USD 866 million in sponsorship fees. At the time of writing, the TOP VII programme, which is in place during the 2009–2012 Olympic quadrennium (where TOP VII Partners sponsor the 2010 Olympic Winter Games in Vancouver and the 2012 Olympic Games in London), is nearing conclusion.

The IOC severed its relationship with ISL in 1996, and established (and holds stock in) Meridian Management (now IOC Television and Marketing Services, SA), which drives the commercial marketing programme of the IOC. The current Olympic sponsorship model encompasses six revenue-generating programmes as sources of funding. These are the following:

- IOC-managed broadcast partnerships;
- The TOP programme of international partners of the Olympic Movement;
- The IOC's official supplier and licensing programme;
- Domestic sponsorship programmes run by the individual OCOGs;
- Ticketing programmes in the host country; and
- Licensing programmes in the host country.[186]

A significant benefit for the IOC in selling the TOP programme to the members of the Olympic Movement (although, as mentioned, this was a tough sell for the USOC) has been the distribution of revenues by the IOC to OCOGs and NOCs. At

---

182 Gruneau 1984, p. 36.

183 Ibid. 24–25. The Winter Games in Albertville in 1992 reportedly made a USD 57 million loss. By way of example, the Sydney 2000 Summer Games cost an estimated USD 3.24 billion to present (including a bid cost of USD 12.6 million) and broke even; The Salt Lake City Winter Games of 2002 cost an estimated USD 1.3 billion to present (including a USD 7 million bid cost) and showed an estimated USD 100 million profit—see Davis 2008, p. 68.

184 See Davis 2008, pp. 163, 164.

185 Schaus and Wenn 2007, pp. 317, 318.

186 Davis 2008, p. 156.

the time when negotiations were still ongoing in order to get the NOCs on board with the programme, the IOC was promising that more than 70% of its revenue share from the programme would be distributed to NOCs. In the period between the 1993–1996 and 2001–2004 quadrennials the IOC has retained 8% of the total revenues generated by all the above programmes and 92% of such total revenues have been allocated to NOCs, OCOGs and international federations.[187] The revenue distribution model and the TOP programme have facilitated a significant revenue injection for NOCs, many of whom at the time of the introduction of TOP had no sponsorship income, by means of e.g. a fixed fee and flat fee per athlete participating in the Games being paid to the NOCs by the IOC from sponsorship income in terms of TOP.[188]

The revenues generated by domestic sponsorships is larger than that from the TOP programme (e.g. in the 2001–2004 quadrennial, USD 796 million compared to USD 663 million). As an indication of the extent of the success of all six the above revenue streams, the total revenues in the 2001–2004 quadrennial were approximately USD 4,189 million (of which more than half was generated through the broadcast programme).[189]

Along with TOP, which operates on the corporate sponsorship side of things (the focus of this book), a significant development occurred in the late 1990s in respect of the IOC's other main revenue stream, the sale of broadcasting rights to the Games. In 1995, America's National Broadcasting Company (NBC), which had been involved in constant bidding wars with its rivals ABC and CBS in the 1980s and early 1990s, made a very lucrative offer to Samaranch, which was attractive for the measure of financial security it promised to provide the IOC in respect of future Games. NBC offered, in a package deal, USD 1.25 billion for the US rights to the 2000 Sydney summer Games and the 2004 Salt Lake City winter Games, an offer that was time-sensitive and also included a prohibition on discussion with NBC's competitors (which now included the Fox television networks). The IOC felt that it could not pass up the advantages of this deal, and within months the parties also discussed a package deal in respect of the US broadcasting rights to 2004, 2006 and 2008, which culminated in a USD 2.3 billion agreement (which the parties called 'the Sunset Project').[190] It subsequently proved that the IOC's acceptance of the NBC package deal (which was to form the template for negotiations with other broadcasters in 1996 and 1997 and which culminated in similar deals in respect of the other international markets) had been shrewd. Schaus and Wenn observe that the Sunset Project brought with it three distinct advantages for the IOC. First, it allowed for a more realistic cost planning process in future bid competitions, as the money from television rights available to future host cities was known (up to and including 2008). Secondly, the security provided by this

[187] Ibid. 157.

[188] Pound 1986, p. 85.

[189] Davis 2008, p. 157.

[190] Schaus and Wenn 2007, pp. 312, 313.

arrangement assisted the IOC's budgeting committee, who now knew how much television revenue was available in the medium term, Thirdly, this arrangement proved very valuable when the Salt Lake City scandal broke in 1998, as the television contracts for future events were already in place and the IOC was not forced to deal with a compromised negotiating environment in respect of television rights for the upcoming Games.[191] David Andrews explains how profitable the deal was for NBC, which managed to purchase the right to 'creatively suture the network's trademark peacock logo to the accumulated and emotive symbolism of the Olympic rings'.[192] He recounts how NBC managed, with this huge capital investment, to become a puppet-master that could manipulate the 1996 Atlanta Games into a product aimed primarily at female viewers because the female market provided its best chance of lifting Olympic ratings. The IOC, understandably, acquiesced; as its marketing supremo Dick Pound put it: 'If you owe the bank $10,000 you're a customer, if you owe them $10 billion you're a partner'.[193]

The IOC sells television rights to the Games on an exclusive territorial basis to television organisations who bid for the rights, thereby becoming rights holders in respect of such broadcasts who acquire the right to broadcast the Games on free-to-air television, cable television and closed circuit television (and, to a limited extent, satellite and high definition television). Such rights generally include pre-Olympics events and cultural events associated with the Games.[194] Following the Sydney Olympics the IOC has become the Host Broadcaster (or producer of content) of the Games through its joint venture (it holds 80%) in Olympic Broadcasting Services (OBS). After the costs of OBS are deducted, the 50% payments to the OCOGs are made and the 12.75% of United States broadcast fees is paid to the USOC, the IOC pays a further share of broadcasting revenues to the international federations with sports on the Olympic programme.[195] Other sports organisations involved in mega-event organising are less generous in sharing the proceeds of broadcasting rights deals and of marketing arrangements such as the IOC's TOP programme. For example, in respect of the football and rugby union world cup events, all broadcasting rights fees and worldwide marketing revenue is retained by the 'owners' of the events, namely FIFA and the International Rugby Board respectively, and is used for the development of their games worldwide. All venue (and infrastructure) costs are borne by the host country, a frequent bone of contention in recent years.[196]

---

191 Ibid.

192 Andrews 2004, p. 18.

193 Ibid.

194 See the discussion of the 2000 Sydney Olympics in Still et al. (2009), pp. 182, 183.

195 See the letter by John Coates, president of the Australian Olympic Committee and Executive Board Member of the International Olympic Committee, available online the time of writing on the web site of the Australian Olympic Committee at http://corporate.olympics.com.au/news.cfm?ArticleID=10495.

196 Ibid.

Of course, in light of the above, one needs to consider where the corporate culture of the Olympic Games (and, indeed, the other mega-events such as the FIFA World Cup) is heading. I've referred to a number of changes brought about to the Olympic Movement in the interests of commercialising the Games during the past few decades. Examples are the decision to allow professional athletes at the Games (in 1981, when NOCs were given the right to pick the athletes to participate), the decision to allow category exclusivity of sponsorship in 1983 (which, as we've seen was so phenomenally successful in Los Angeles in 1984), and the decision to stagger the winter[197] and summer Games (i.e. to shorten the cycle between these events and provide more frequent opportunity for corporate sponsors to obtain marketing opportunities to two separate major events rather than two events in the same year). One must ask: Where is it all heading? Apart from the increase in sponsorship fees (compare, for example, that it was reported that to purchase a space for a company logo on a sponsor medal stand for the 2002 and 2004 winter and summer Olympics cost USD 55 million or 10 times the amount charged in 1984), it can be expected that sponsors will start to claim increasingly expansive leverage in order to ensure a return on the vast amounts of money invested. When M&M Mars sought permission for its M&M characters to jump out behind marathon runners and appear on television as the athletes passed through city streets at the 1992 Barcelona Games, the IOC refused, concerned that such crass advertising could devalue the Games' marketing image. The company dropped its sponsorship and directed its investment into marketing youth soccer, as it felt that it would not obtain the required returns from an Olympic sponsorship.[198] In light of the increasingly cluttered marketing environment surrounding these mega-events (which I will refer to again in the later chapters) and the ever-escalating rights fees paid by sponsors, it is to be expected that such 'creativity' in respect of efforts to heighten brand awareness and exposure—if that is what it is—will be seen more and more at these events in years to come. I believe that event organisers will be under severe pressure to maintain (or aspire to) the moral high ground in respect of commercialism, especially when their own efforts at generating profits from the events continue apace and serve as the invitation to corporate sponsors to join the party. When your 'guests' are charged exorbitant fees for the privilege of your company or to visit 'the place to be seen', it is hard to ask them not to smoke in your house or play their music too loud.

---

[197] A separate Winter Olympics dates from 1924—figure skating and ice hockey were Olympic events before 1924, but the larger programme hosted by France in 1924 was so successful that the IOC in 1925 retroactively labelled it the Winter Olympics and subsequently solicited separate bids to host the Winter Olympics. As has been observed (with a bit of tongue-in-cheek, I'm sure): 'The 1928 Olympics were hosted by Amsterdam, which was not a good location for downhill skiing, and the Winter Olympics were held in St. Moritz, Switzerland'—Pomfret et al. 2009, p. 11.

[198] From an article by Phillips, R 'Big business demands a corporate Olympics', 16 March 1999, available online at http://www.wsws.org/articles/1999/mar1999/olym-m16.shtml; see also Payne 2006, p. 144.

2.4 Category Exclusivity of Sponsorships of Mega-Events

As mentioned above, a major component of the Olympic commercialisation model that developed with the TOP programme is the system of category exclusivity of sponsorships to the Olympic Games and to related properties[199] of the Olympic Movement. This measure of exclusivity is the very object of the legal protection against ambush marketing of events (which we'll consider in the chapters that follow). I will accordingly briefly examine this phenomenon, which has come to characterise the modern commercialisation model in respect of all sports mega-events, by way of background to the discussion in the chapters that follow. But before I attempt to do so, let's first ask 'What is sponsorship?'

Sponsorship is often defined as an investment in cash (the 'sponsorship fee') or kind ('value-in-kind' denoting the provision of products, services or other facilities) in an activity in return for access to the 'exploitable commercial and marketing potential' associated with that activity.[200] Those capable of being sponsored (e.g. a sports team, athlete or, in the context of this book, a sports mega-event) are referred to, in marketing speak, as 'properties', and the ability for the sponsor to associate itself with such a property is known as a 'right'.[201] The sponsor obtains a right to associate with the event organiser's event marks (such as logos, emblems and mascots), combined with 'designations' (i.e. the right of the sponsor to describe itself 'official sponsor' in advertising and promotional literature and on product packaging, labelling and merchandising material).[202] The 2010 edition of the IOC's *Olympic Marketing Fact File* contains the following definition of Olympic sponsorship:

> Olympic sponsorship is an agreement between an Olympic organisation and a corporation, whereby the corporation is granted the rights to specific Olympic intellectual property and Olympic marketing opportunities in exchange for financial support and goods and services contributions. Olympic sponsorship programmes operate on the principle of product category exclusivity. Under the direction of the IOC, the Olympic Family works to preserve the value of Olympic properties and to protect the exclusive rights of Olympic sponsors.[203]

The sponsored event provides its sponsors with 'unsurpassed visibility, invaluable exclusivity and impressive associative and branding potential'.[204] Some commentators in the late 1990s predicted that sports sponsorship would become

[199] I use the word 'properties' here in the sense that it is understood in the sponsorship industry. As will be clear from discussion elsewhere in this book I am not convinced that what the sports mega-event rights grantors (the international sports governing bodies) and rights holders (the sponsors or commercial partners) refer to as their 'property' necessarily always enjoys such status in the legal sense.

[200] Lewis and Taylor 2007, p. 706 (par. D5.4).

[201] Ibid.

[202] Gardiner et al. 2006, pp. 446, 447.

[203] Available online, at the time of writing, at http://www.olympic.org/Documents/fact_file_2010.pdf.

[204] Schwab 2006, p. 7.

the optimal positioning tool for international marketers seeking to communicate global messages, which seems accurate at the time that I write this.[205] The sports mega-event provides a 'platform' upon and around which a marketing campaign is based in order to leverage the rights sold:

> The sponsorship is a payment that buys the company a platform that offers a central theme around which a focused, integrated promotional message can be communicated through an array of different communication vehicles. Leveraging the platform involves developing a promotion plan which specifies the role of each vehicle and the extent to which it will be used.[206]

This leveraging of the sponsorship is sometimes also referred to as 'activation' or 'maximisation' in order to complete the integration of the event sponsorship into the sponsor's overall communications programme.[207] Leveraging around a mega-event can be done very successfully, or sometimes less so—compare the case of Sony (sometimes perceived as 'owning football' or the 'go-to brand for football fans'), who made much of 3D coverage of the 2010 FIFA World Cup but failed to release its 3D televisions in time for the event, with the result that Australians who watched the tournament in 3D did so on a Samsung TV.[208]

The mega-event, therefore, offers a 'thematic space'[209] (something I will examine more closely in Chap. 8) for the commercial exploitation of the marketing value of the event for sponsors (such marketing value being determined by and consisting of a number of factors, including the advertising reach in respect of the size of the broadcast market, the nature and characteristics of the event, etc.). In recent years the reach of the event in terms of garnering and capturing public (consumer) attention has increased significantly. The '360 degree commissioning of sports content' (producing content that can be delivered across platforms such as television, the Internet and mobile devices)[210] and the interactive nature of the Internet and the role played by web sites (such as YouTube, fan-sites, fantasy league sites, etc.) and, especially, social media such as Facebook and Twitter,[211] means that the mega-event thematic space has become extremely pervasive and lucrative as a marketing tool. And it is aimed increasingly at a 'younger demographic of digital natives'.[212]

---

[205] Farrelly and Quester 1997, pp. 5–7.

[206] Crompton 2004a, p. 9.

[207] See Masterman 2009, p. 305 et seq.

[208] See Avenell, P 'Sharp slips under Sony's radar to steal Euro 2012 sponsorship', available online at the time of writing at http://www.current.com.au/2011/05/25/article/Sharp-slips-under-Sonys-radar-to-steal-Euro2012-sponsorship/OBRIXLDFAM.

[209] Which, in marketing terms, one could define as 'the definitional categories within which products and services are positioned, categorized, and described, and within which they are, therefore, considered for purchase by consumers'—see http://welshmktg.com/WMA_thematic_spaces.pdf.

[210] Boyle and Haynes 2009, p. 63.

[211] More will be said about the (potential) role of social media in this regard in Chap. 10.

[212] Boyle and Haynes 2009, p. 63.

The sponsorship of the event is viewed as a mutually-beneficial exercise, whereby the event organiser directly earns revenues by means of the sponsorship fees paid, and the sponsor is provided with access to the thematic space in order to further leverage its investment with dedicated marketing or otherwise. Crompton has explained the underlying theory of sponsorship as follows:

> The central concept underlying sponsorship is exchange theory, which is one of the most prominent theoretical perspectives in the social sciences. It has two main precepts: (i) two or more parties exchange resources, and (ii) the resources offered by each party must be equally valued by the reciprocating parties. In response to the first precept of exchange theory, sport organisations and businesses have multiple resources that they may use as "currency" to facilitate an exchange. The sport facility or event may offer businesses increased awareness, image enhancement, product trial or sales opportunities. Companies in return may offer support through investments of money, media exposure, or in-kind services. The second precept of exchange theory suggests that a corporate partner will ask two questions, "What's in it for me?" and "How much will it cost me?" The trade-off is weighed between what will be gained and what will have to be given up. A key feature of this second precept is that the exchange is perceived to be fair by both sides.[213]

This role of the exchange theory, however, may be open to criticism as ignoring some of the realities of the sponsorship market (a few of which we will encounter elsewhere in this book when considering the relationships between event organisers, 'official sponsors' and 'ambush marketers', and when evaluating the interests of these stakeholders in the sports sponsorship market):

> By basing ideas about sponsorship on the concept of exchange, scholars who have studied this practice have provided an image of neutrality and of choices that are limited only by the skill of the people involved in the sponsorship transactions. Such a view ignores the underlying inequalities of power that are part of the sponsorship process, presents an overly simplistic account of the complexities of such interactions and neglects to address how structures of domination and exploitation shape and mediate these relationships.[214]

While the above characterisation of inequalities in the relationship and exploitation may very well hold true, others argue that the sports sponsorship relationship should be approached as a strategic alliance, where the corporate sponsor and sports property should be encouraged to take 'a deliberate, collaborative approach to instigating a partnership that emphasises a mutual understanding of both parties' objectives and commitment to a long-term vision'.[215]

Such issues of theory aside, the benefits for potential sponsors of sports or sports-related sponsorships, as a form of 'life-styled marketing' (i.e. which targets consumers through their lifestyles), are well-recognised, and probably account for the phenomenal world-wide growth of the industry which has seen sponsorship reach an estimated expenditure of USD 44.8 billion in 2009 (and capturing nearly a 20% share of overall marketing budgets.[216] The previous section has briefly

---

[213] Crompton 2004b, p. 268.

[214] Slack and Amis 2004, p. 270.

[215] Cobbs 2011 (my thanks to the author for providing me with an advance copy of the article).

[216] Cobbs 2011, relying on an IEG *Sponsorship Report* 2009.

considered the evolution of the modern mega-event sponsorship model. The value of sport, for sponsorship and otherwise, was realised during the last two decades of the 20th century and those governing 'the game' lost little time in capitalising on this unique product:

> Sports were once cheap production numbers that drew viewers to their screens in millions. Those days have long since gone. While negotiating various deals with television, major sports governing organisations must have been taking notes. They quickly learnt that the same principles that applied to marketing beer or shaving foam, also applied to sports… From the 1980s, sports began marketing themselves, turning themselves into commodities; not commodities with use-values, but ones with symbolic values. Consumers were sold images they could blend with their personal histories or their identities: sports became a means of self-expression, a statement of lifestyle… Sports used the same techniques as car makers, soft drink manufacturers and computer companies, attempting to manipulate consumer "needs", using art and design to create agreeable images and packaging their products to make them appealing. Today, it is virtually impossible to find a major sport that does not have a logo.[217]

Sport as entertainment shows significantly unique characteristics that are different from other entertainment products. One of its central virtues is the role of competition and the entertainment value of unscripted competitions. This key requirement for the entertainment value of the sports product forms the rationale behind some of the measures and practices which provide fertile soil for the application of law to sport, such as doping control, gender testing and anti-corruption measures aimed at curbing match fixing. However, it has been observed that the core of the sports entertainment product has moved beyond this 'uncertainty of outcomes' regarding the sporting competition, to include 'a product/service associated with the excitement of the event'.[218] This is well-illustrated in the context of sporting mega-events such as the FIFA football World Cup, where significant marketing and revenue-generating activities relate solely to the hype and excitement of the event as opposed to the actual on-field competition. The very entertainment product provided by sports teams (and individual star athletes) can also be differentiated from the entertainment product provided by other industries, in terms of the impact on the psyche of the relevant consumers of the product.[219] As one observer remarked:

---

217 Cashmore 2010, p. 372.

218 Schaaf 1995, p. 22.

219 Sutton et al. 1997, p. 15 describe the phenomenon of 'fan identification' in professional team sports as follows:

'Fan identification is defined as the personal commitment and emotional involvement fans have with a sport organisation. When a customer identifies closely with an organisation, a sense of connectedness ensues and he or she begins to define him- or herself in terms of the organisation… Sport differs from other sources of entertainment through evoking high levels of emotional attachment and identification… Sport promotes communication, involves people jointly, provides common symbols, a collective identity and a reason for solidarity'.

> Sports marketing is unique because of the way sports fans follow their teams. They identify with and gain allegiance to sports teams and individuals. People don't have the same enthusiasm for Holiday Inn.[220]

And this phenomenon has even more verity in the context of the modern technology and Internet-based society. In such an environment, merchandising images become key dialogic resources: 'Widely disseminated, textured through the process of audience adaptation, these signifiers enable like-minded individuals to identify one another and coalesce into what public choice theorists would recognise as interest groups'.[221] For the potential sponsor of a sports event this may, for example, be a more subtle ('less commercial') alternative to normal advertising which, due to the phenomenal popularity of sport, still achieves a significant measure of brand exposure. Sponsorship, generally, is a form of 'below-the-line' advertising which is not carried by the traditional media—rather than paying for actual brand advertising in the media, the sponsor can raise awareness indirectly (e.g. by having its name mentioned in an event title where the sponsorship involves event naming rights, or in the venue title where it involves stadium naming rights, or having its name applied—on the periphery of the viewer's vision—to a top golfer's bag). Or, sometimes, rather more directly—compare the 7–11 sponsorship of the Chicago White Sox baseball team, where the team owners agreed to start all their home games at 7.11 pm. Such generally more 'subtle' means of bringing the brand to the attention of sports fans may be preferable as being perceived as being less intrusive than actual mainstream advertising, and the repetitive encountering of the brand by the spectator whose attention remains on the sporting action free from the distraction of annoying advertisements may have a subliminal effect in creating brand awareness as well as a more positive consumer perception of the brand than might be the case with 'in your face' advertising.[222]

It was also realised that, with the proliferation of media (e.g. television networks in the 1990s and, more recently, the Internet and mobile media), has come a significant amount of advertising 'clutter', and that sponsorship provides an alternative to advertising which can go some way towards avoiding this problem.[223] In fact, clutter, which leads to fragmentation of the market and difficulty for the consumer in diffusing messages, has been identified by some of the TOP Olympic sponsors as a major concern regarding Olympic-related marketing. Even though ambush marketing (which will be discussed in Chap. 3) is one source of clutter, it was identified that the large number of sponsorships granted by the IOC

---

[220] Hofacre, writing in Burnett J, Menon A, Smart DT 1993, p. 22.

[221] Cooper Dreyfuss 1996, p. 139; Coombe 1991, p. 1877.

[222] For some interesting discussion of an example of why advertising during broadcasts may have an ever-increasing bad rap amongst consumers (at least in the United States), see Bollier 2005, pp. 197–201 ('The quest for perfect control').

[223] See Mullin et al. 2000.

also contributes to the problem.[224] In fact, some sponsors indicated that they were less concerned about ambush marketing than with what they viewed as the 'increasingly cluttered environment' of Olympic sponsorship.[225] Some marketing experts have characterised the usefulness of sponsorship as a strategic tool to achieve a competitive advantage as being based largely on its heterogeneous distribution, inimitability, imperfect mobility, and pre-emptive limits to competition, which qualities, taken together, characterise sponsorship as a 'scarce resource that provides the capacity to differentiate affiliating sponsors' brands from their competitors in the minds of consumers'.[226] In this light, the dangers of advertising clutter in the realm of mega-event sponsorship should be clear.

Another benefit of a sports product for the sponsor is what is referred to as 'brand association transfer':

> In addition to brand exposure, many authors suggest that developing and communicating an association between the sponsoring brand and a sponsored property, such as a league or a team, is an objective that can be achieved through a sponsorship... [S]ponsorship goals assume that the target audience—the "consumers" or fans—will transfer their loyalty from the sponsored property or event to the sponsor itself. To help achieve this transfer, the sponsorship often permits the advertiser to communicate its association to a league or team by being able to place that logo on product packaging and in its advertisements. The popularity and the positive image and reputation of these sports teams and events can precipitate and indeed foster a similar favourable feeling by fans and consumers alike towards their brand.[227]

And this can translate into increased sales by changing the very way in which consumers think about a product (which is particularly pertinent in the sports merchandising market but also relevant in respect of sponsorship):

> Research indicates that achieving a brand association transfer through sponsorship strategies potentially could influence consumers' behaviour, including increasing purchases of the sponsoring brand product... Loyalty towards a preferred team may have beneficial consequences for corporate sponsors. Consistent with the idea of in-group favouritism, higher levels of team identification among attendees of a sporting event appear to be positively related to intentions to purchase a sponsor's products.[228]

FIFA's web site (at www.fifa.com) explains that licensing of event marks in the event merchandising market makes a lot of sense:

---

224 See Seguin and O'Reilly 2008.

225 Ibid. 72.

226 Cobbs 2011, with reference to Amis, J; Pant, N and Slack, T 'Achieving sustainable competitive advantage: A resource-based view of sport sponsorship' 11(1) *Journal of Sport Management* (1997), pp. 80–96; and Fahy, J; Farrelly, F and Quester, P 'Competitive advantage through sponsorship: A conceptual model and research propositions' 38(8) *European Journal of Marketing* (2004), pp. 1013–1030.

227 Fortunato and Richards 2007, pp. 40, 41. See also O'Reilly, N; McCarthy, L; Seguin, B; Lyberger, M 'Sponsorship and the Super Bowl: A longitudinal analysis' (2005) at 55—available online at the time of writing at http://luxor.acadiau.ca/library/ASAC/v26/03/26_03_p052.pdf.

228 Ibid. 41. See also Grohs et al. 2004, pp. 119–138.

> Research has shown that applications of sports event symbols to packaging and products—or as a component of an advertising campaign—provide a significant marketing advantage: consumers are more than 50% more likely to buy the products. This is now widely recognised, with the result that the licensing of sport marks has become a significant aspect of the sports marketing business.

The lifestyle element of sports sponsorship is also further accentuated by the social and cultural significance of mega-events, which draws in consumers who want to be involved in such historic events by 'owning a piece' of the event. In the Olympic context, it has been observed that most spectators only ever witness a mediated version of the Games, and the Olympic movement has through its licensing of symbols broadened opportunities for viewers to 'participate' personally—spectators can 'relish their Olympic experience by drinking official Olympic beer, nibbling on official Olympic mascot cheese shapes, wearing official Olympic clothing, sitting on official Olympic rugs, clutching official Olympic toys while talking to friends on official Olympic telecommunications devices'.[229] This might explain why (or how) revenues from licensing for the OCOGS has increased from USD 18 million for Seoul in 1988 to USD 163 million for Beijing in 2008 (where over 8,000 different items of merchandise were available from 1,000 retail units across China and beyond, and reportedly netted more than USD 100 million in royalties).[230] This side of the commercial exploitation of events, namely the sports merchandising industry, thrives on the licensing of intellectual property and is a significant money-spinner for event organisers or sports rights holders. It can, however, also generate legal challenges (for example, in respect of competition or antitrust law issues, which I will examine in more detail later). The following description found in the judgment of the U.S. Court of Appeals for the 7th Circuit in *American Needle, Inc v NFL*[231] of the rise of merchandising in one of the major American professional sports leagues does well to explain the trend, and the potential for disputes:

> Realising that the success of the NFL as a whole was in their best interests, in the early 1960s the individual teams sought to collectively promote the NFL Brand—that is, the intellectual property of the NFL and its member teams—to compete against other forms of entertainment. With this promotional effort in mind, in 1963 the NFL teams formed NFL Properties: a separate corporate entity charged with (1) developing, licensing, and marketing the intellectual property the teams owned, such as their logos, trademarks, and other indicia; and (2) "conduct[ing] and engag[ing] in advertising campaigns and promotional ventures on behalf of the NFL and [its] member [teams]." Among other things, the NFL teams authorised NFL Properties to grant licenses to vendors so the vendors could use the teams' intellectual property to manufacture and sell various kinds of consumer products that bear the teams' logos and trademarks—products such as team jerseys, shirts, flags, and, as pertinent here, headwear, like baseball caps and stocking hats. For a while after its

[229] Magdalinski and Nauright 2004, p. 185.

[230] From the 2010 edition of the IOC's *Olympic Marketing Fact File*, available online at the time of writing at http://www.olympic.org/Documents/fact_file_2010.pdf; see also Bacalao-Fleury 2011, p. 198.

[231] 538 F.3d 736 (2008) at 737–738—for more on this case, see the discussion in Chap. 6.

establishment, NFL Properties granted headwear licenses to a number of different vendors simultaneously; one of those vendors was American Needle, which held an NFL headwear license for over 20 years. But then in 2000, the NFL teams authorised NFL Properties to solicit bids from the vendors for an exclusive headwear license. Reebok won the bidding war, and in 2001 the NFL teams allowed NFL Properties to grant an exclusive license to Reebok for ten years. NFL Properties thus did not renew American Needle's headwear license, or the licenses of the other headwear vendors. American Needle responded to the loss of its headwear license by filing an antitrust action against the NFL, NFL Properties, the individual NFL teams, and Reebok. As relevant here, American Needle claimed that the exclusive headwear licensing agreement between NFL Properties and Reebok violated § 1 of the Sherman Antitrust Act, which outlaws any "contract, combination… or conspiracy, in restraint of trade."

I have touched on sports merchandising here because the above-mentioned range of disparate products and services marketed through use of reference to or association with the mega-event as marketing vehicle or platform highlights the fact that mega-events nowadays are characterised by a veritable publicity 'carpet-bombing' by the event organiser (such as FIFA or the IOC), sponsors, and the local organisers. This brings to mind the words of Justice Frankfurter on the use of trademarks, expressed nearly 70 years ago:

> [W]e live by symbols, [and] it is no less true that we purchase goods by them. A trademark is a merchandising short-cut which induces a purchaser to select what he wants, or what he has been led to believe he wants. The owner of a mark exploits this human propensity by making every effort to impregnate the atmosphere of the market with the drawing power of a congenial symbol.[232]

I will revisit the relevance of such marketing strategies in the context of ambush marketing and of allegations of infringement of modern 'association rights' to mega-events in Chap. 8, where I will try and throw some light on the thematic space of the mega-event as marketing tool and object of legal protection.

For the sponsor or supplier the 'official' designation of its involvement with the event lends a measure of prestige for being selected by e.g. Olympic authorities as being good enough to be associated with the Games, while the consumer is left with a perception that such official status denotes superior quality of the product or service. Of course, this 'official' status and exclusivity of the merchandise sometimes goes to extremes—compare the use of a 'genetic stamp' by incorporation of DNA material of Olympic swimmer Dawn Fraser into the labels of Olympic merchandise sold prior to the 2000 Sydney Olympics.

When sponsorship consists of exclusive rights to such an already attractive marketing vehicle, the sponsor will enjoy a high level of exposure accompanied by the significant benefits of a lack of competition and the avoidance of the clutter associated with normal advertising.[233] For the rights grantors (the sports organisations) the benefits of providing exclusive exploitation rights are obvious,

---

[232] *Mishawaka Rubber and Woollen Manufacturing Co. v S S Kresge Co.* (1942) 13 US 203, at 205.

[233] See Mullin et al. 2007, p. 322.

namely, primarily, the higher rights fees that can be charged in terms of the greater value provided. While their legal advisors need to be alert to potential conflicts (e.g. the provision of conflicting rights to competing sponsors), which might in itself cause clutter and expose the organisations to litigation, the substantial cost of exclusive rights provide a significant source of revenues in respect of mega-events. Michael Payne, former marketing director of the IOC, has stressed the importance of exclusivity for sponsors of the Games:

> Exclusivity has been one of the cornerstones of the Olympic Movement's marketing programmes. The knowledge that a company can invest in the Olympic movement and be certain that they are not going to be undermined by a last-minute surprise promotional campaign by their competitor, was a key factor in driving the value of Olympic sponsorships. The TOP programme was designed to be as ambush-proof as possible, providing partners with one of the highest levels of protection of any major sports property.[234]

Category exclusivity of sponsorships can be defined as 'the right of a sponsor to be the only company within its product or service category associated with the sponsored property'.[235] These rights as granted to sponsors may also sometimes be referred to as 'sector rights':

> [S]ponsors with sector or category rights enjoy uncompetitive status with the event in that they are the sole representation from the sector/market in which they operate. These rights offer sector, market or category exclusivity for the sponsor. Title or presenting sponsors may also have these rights... These rights, once seen as a negotiable right, are now generally viewed as being a prerequisite. Sector exclusive sponsors can sit more comfortably into an event sponsorship programme and work together productively and so most events now understand that they will not be able to attract any level of sponsor without ensuring that they have exclusive sector rights.[236]

The development of event sponsorship since the introduction of exclusivity at the highest level of global sports sponsorship (with the 1988 Seoul Olympic Games, as mentioned earlier) has brought this form of sponsorship to the fore, to the extent of having created an expectation of such rights on the part of event sponsors. Masterman notes that it is arguable that 'while sector exclusivity is not entirely 100% used at all events it is, nevertheless, now a virtual necessity... The implications for event managers are that, whereas previously this might have been the cutting edge in recruiting a sponsor, the fact now is that sponsors expect such status as standard'.[237] I would suggest that this expectation plays an important role in respect of the pejorative and highly critical view of 'ambushing' of events that one encounters amongst event sponsors as well as the often overly-aggressive

---

[234] Payne 2006, pp. 142, 143.

[235] Govoni 2004, p. 32; see also Carrie Urban Kapraun 'Fun with category exclusivity', 7 October 2009, writing on the IEG sponsorship blog available online at the time of writing at http://www.sponsorship.com.

[236] Masterman 2009, p. 286.

[237] Masterman 2009, p. 300.

responses to alleged 'ambushes' on the part of event organisers (both of which we will examine more closely in Chap. 3). If sponsors expect exclusivity and that it is their privilege to exclude all competitors from the sponsored event, the organisers will naturally feel bound (and contractually so) to deliver such a state of affairs (not only because this expectation allows the organisers to demand a higher sponsorship fee). I would also suggest that this expectation on the part of sponsors has played a central role in what I will argue (in Chap. 8) to be the bloated and unrealistic conception amongst sponsors and event organisers of the scope of the thematic space of the modern sports mega-event. And, in Chap. 10, I will refer to the observation by some commentators that this sponsor expectation may, in fact, be a significant danger to the funding of sports mega-events in future.

Joe Cobbs explains what category exclusivity is and how it works, and why it is so important for the parties involved:

> In the context of commercial sponsorship, a designation of product category exclusivity acts to exclude competitors within a sponsor's product or service category from a controlled sports environment. In such cases, the sponsored team or event agrees to refrain from affiliating with any of the sponsor's rivals within a product or service category. Such category exclusivity has been recognised as among the most valued rights afforded corporate sponsors of sport, and therefore, sponsors often pay a premium price to achieve such a restricted promotional position… To ensure three of the four strategic elements [of sponsorship, namely] (heterogeneous distribution, imperfect mobility, and limits to competition), sponsored enterprises often offer multi-year product category exclusivity to potential corporate partners in exchange for a price premium. Category exclusive sponsorships contain an agreement by the sponsored enterprise to forgo any potential promotional affiliation with a corporate partner's competitors in a defined product/service category for the duration of the sponsorship arrangement. In doing so, the sponsored enterprise has confined both the distribution and mobility of their sponsorship resource. A common additional clause that grants the sponsor the right of first acceptance/refusal to continue the relationship at the conclusion of the initially specified term also sets a strict limit to competition for the sponsorship resource going forward. Many corporate sponsors are not only willing to marginally increase their right payment for this type of rival exclusion, but research has shown product/service category exclusivity to be the most important criteria in sponsorship selection.[238]

Such exclusivity can extend throughout the property (e.g. the mega-event) and cover all sponsor benefits, or different levels of exclusivity may exist (e.g. whereby a sponsor may enjoy exclusivity within a certain category of product or service—for example, telecommunications services or sporting apparel—but where other sponsors (competitors) may, for example, have advertising rights in respect of broadcasts of the event). The benefits of exclusivity for the sponsor may also differ according to the nature of the product or service and its potential relationship to the sponsored property:

> Exclusivity avoids competitive interference that would be incurred in other media contexts. For some industries, such as beer, soda, and credit cards, the characteristic of exclusivity provides not only brand exposure but the additional advantage of selling their

[238] Cobbs 2011.

> product through point of-purchase at the stadium without competition. Other exclusivity agreements could include an athlete only using his or her sponsors' equipment, i.e., Tiger Woods only using Nike golf balls, or a league only using its sponsors' product or service, i.e., the NFL only having Reebok manufacture its licensed headwear.[239]

I will later (in Chap. 6) examine the potential competition (antitrust) implications of sponsorship exclusivity arrangements, and it should be borne in mind that this nature of the product or service and the resultant benefits of exclusivity for the sponsor in any given case may be relevant in this regard (e.g. in respect of determination of the relevant market for purposes of anti-trust review, and of the impact of such arrangements on that market—compare pouring rights and equipment sponsorship exclusivity, which may both have a more limited impact and/or may relate to a smaller market than other forms of product/service exclusivity deals with a wider reach beyond the event venue or playing field). As Fortunato and Martin observe:

> [P]erhaps in antitrust cases that concern sports leagues the courts will begin to recognise a distinction based on the product category. A beer sponsorship with a team is limited by geography, for example, while a sponsorship with a clothing manufacturer has fewer limitation of that sort any more.[240]

The exclusivity of the arrangement derives, of course, from negative contractual obligations undertaken by the rights grantor to refrain from granting similar rights to other potential sponsors (and such purported grants of rights would, therefore, constitute breach of the sponsorship contract[241] and, I would suggest, might even be argued to constitute a form of ambush marketing *vis a vis* the existing exclusive sponsor).

Once it is established that category exclusivity is on offer, sponsor and rights grantor should negotiate and agree upon which categories will be covered as well as the extent of the exclusivity within such categories. It is usually in a sponsor's best interest to have total category exclusivity, but that may be prohibitively expensive from the perspective of the would be sponsor, or it may not be in the best interest of the property, it may not be possible because of existing agreements with third parties, or the rights grantor might not control certain aspects of the property for the purposes of granting exclusive rights. Total category exclusivity is the most costly form of sponsorship, and not having any category exclusivity could significantly lower both the cost and the value of a sponsorship.[242] Of course, it is not only the above-mentioned potential constraints to the availability of category exclusivity which might determine whether (or the extent to which) exclusivity is

---

239 Fortunato and Martin 2011.

240 Ibid.

241 Compare the facts of *Force India Formula 1 Team Ltd v Etihad Airways and Aldar Properties* [2010] EWCA Civ 1051.

242 Kapraun supra.

obtained. Potential sponsors will make a determination of their need for exclusivity based on their objective with the relevant sponsorship. If the potential sponsor is convinced that an association with the property (e.g. mega-event) will affect its target audience's perception of the sponsor or their purchase intent, it should pursue category exclusivity as a means of locking out competitors from associating with the property. If its objective is more focused it may not make sense to pay the premium for exclusivity (e.g. where the sponsor is simply trying to leverage a particular soft drink brand it may not make sense to demand and pay for exclusivity within a category that might include energy drinks, fruit juices, etc.). Other than that, it has been observed that exclusivity is not a rigid status; depending on the negotiating power of the event it may be possible to 'segment very finely certain market sectors and still achieve exclusivity'—the example cited is the Wimbledon tennis event, which in 2005 had seven distinct official drink sponsors (in 2008 there were five, in categories including official wine, official water, official champagne, official coffee and official still soft drink).[243]

Finally, in respect of the cost of exclusivity there is another aspect that has received little attention to date, namely that the protection of exclusivity (by the rights grantors, local organisers etc. in terms of the commercial agreements providing such exclusivity) may in fact be counter-productive from the sponsor's perspective, i.e. by being a factor in raising the cost of such exclusive sponsorships. The rights grantors, though, are unlikely to ever raise such an argument (in the interest of maintaining maximum revenues from sponsorship) and the potential sponsors are faced with a monopolistic supply of opportunities for sponsorship from the rights grantor governing bodies.

In respect of sports mega-events it is important to note that, while the category exclusivity sponsorship model has become the norm, the extent of exclusivity provided may differ from event to event and between the different sports governing bodies who act as rights grantors in respect of mega-events. As discussed above, the IOC's TOP programme in respect of the Olympic Games, which pioneered this form of exclusivity for mega-events, provides far-reaching benefits to sponsors regarding the exclusivity of their rights and the exclusion of competitors. A TOP sponsor pays a premium, but receives exclusivity that is international and extends across the structure of the Olympic Movement and includes different entities. A TOP sponsor obtains global category exclusivity that extends to the IOC, to all National Olympic Committees (NOCs) and their national Olympic teams, to the relevant Organising Committee (or OCOG) in respect of the Games, and to the Olympic Games event itself, while also providing preferential access to Olympic Games broadcasts (i.e. a 'right of first refusal' in respect of broadcast sponsorship or advertising in order to prevent 'ambushing' of event broadcasts by competitors). What the TOP sponsor does not receive is category exclusivity in respect of the

[243] Masterman 2009, pp. 300, 301.

sponsoring of individual athletes or of national governing bodies for participating sporting codes.[244]

FIFA pioneered its own (what one observer calls) 'exclusive competitive sponsorships' at the 1972 FIFA World Cup in Mexico,[245] but in recent years has followed the lead of the Olympic Movement's TOP model. In contrast to TOP, sponsors of FIFA's football World Cup receive considerably less 'bang for their buck' in respect of exclusivity of their rights. A 'FIFA Partner' for the World Cup (the highest level of corporate sponsor for the event) has category exclusivity that extends to FIFA, the FIFA World Cup and all other FIFA tournaments (for example, the Confederations Cup which precedes each instalment of the football World Cup as a 'dress rehearsal'). It does not extend to regional football confederations (such as UEFA), country federations, individual national teams, club teams, players or qualifying matches leading into the World Cup.[246] Of course, there are other differences between event organisers' treatment of sponsors. One example where FIFA sponsors receive more for their outlay than the IOC's sponsors relates to the IOC's 'clean venue' policy which is not in place for FIFA's events. The IOC, ostensibly in the interests of promoting the focus on sport rather than commercialisation (and, one might assume, largely as a result of the earlier criticism of the swiftly creeping commercialism surrounding the Games during the last decades of the 20th century), does not allow any advertising within its venues,[247] which clearly impacts on the marketing value received by sponsors (also from event broadcasts). A positive spin-off from the clean venue requirements is that broadcasters can charge a premium to fewer (official) sponsors, who are given a right of first refusal to sponsor event broadcasts, because of the removal of clutter and the potential for such sponsors to fully leverage their involvement in the event.[248] The Union of European Football Associations (UEFA) has taken broadcast sponsorship protection a step further, by buying and controlling all advertising time during matches, and allotting time to sponsors (protecting

244 See Kapraun supra, writing on the IEG sponsorship blog available online at the time of writing at http://www.sponsorship.com. The 2010 edition of the *Olympic Marketing Fact File* contains the following description of the TOP programme and the benefits that it brings to TOP sponsors:

'The TOP programme provides each Worldwide Olympic Partner with exclusive global marketing rights and opportunities within a designated product or service category. The global marketing rights include partnerships with the IOC, all active NOCs and their Olympic teams, and the two OCOGs and the Games of each quadrennium. The TOP Partners may exercise these rights worldwide and may activate marketing initiatives with all the members of the Olympic Movement that participate in the TOP programme'.

245 Schwab 2006, p. 6.

246 Ibid.

247 See Rule 51.2 of the Olympic Charter (2010):

'No form of advertising or other publicity shall be allowed in and above the stadia, venues and other competition areas which are considered as part of the Olympic sites. Commercial installations and advertising signs shall not be allowed in the stadia, venues or other sports grounds'.

248 Magdalinski and Nauright 2004, p. 196.

sponsors from potential ambush campaigns and also forcing them to better leverage their investment).[249]

The benefits arising from sponsorship of sport, especially when coupled with category exclusivity, for sponsors and sports federations alike should be clear:

> Because sport with its self-governance has an exceptional and internationally acknowledged status, enjoying monopolistic elements in its governance and management, advertisers can indirectly enjoy similar benefits. For instance, being the sole provider of certain category of products that is allowed to enjoy the benefits of associating with a certain sport or event. Also, when the rights are acquired from a sole existing seller and in packages, it is arguably easier to conduct advertising campaigns, the strategy usually by default unanimously covering all the channels for the message to reach the audience. In most cases it is probably also easier to negotiate, enter into agreements and implement them, when a sole rights holder needs to be contracted, provided that the acquirer is able to provide substantial financial injections.[250]

By way of summary, therefore, the main advantages of category exclusivity sponsorship for potential sponsors in the marketing marketplace are the following:

- The sponsor receives a high measure of brand exposure through its official status and the often significant rights afforded official sponsors (e.g. the rights to use event logos and intellectual property in its advertising and other marketing campaigns);
- Apart from the brand exposure, research has shown that sports represent a conducive environment for sponsors to achieve brand association transfer, where (in essence) the fans transfer their loyalty to the sports product (e.g. a team like Manchester United or an event like the Olympic Games) to the sponsor's brand;
- It has also been shown that, through such brand association transfer, the sponsorship can influence consumers' behaviour in a positive manner;
- The sponsor also receives, by dint of the exclusivity of the sponsorship, the ability to exclude its competitors, in essence creating an environment for the marketing of its brand without fear of competition (compare, for example, arrangements which prohibit competitors of official sponsors to buy advertising time in respect of event broadcasts). In addition, these exclusivity arrangements contain legal obligations for event organisers (rights grantors) to actively take steps to protect such exclusivity in the interests of protecting the sponsor's investment (this is why event hosting bids include demands for organisers or host governments to establish a legal framework conducive to commercial rights protection for the event, and hosting contracts create legally enforceable obligations in this regard); and
- Sports sponsorship, and specifically sponsorship exclusivity as discussed here, provides an ideal opportunity for would be sponsors to obtain rights to the commercial exploitation of a desirable property, which rights can often be tailored to best suit the sponsor's needs (more so than in other sponsorship or marketing environments):

In addition to the brand exposure, the image association possibilities, and the possibility of influencing purchasing behaviour that have been demonstrated by scholars, another aspect that makes sponsorship a particularly attractive strategy for many corporations is that all of the parameters of the sponsorship agreement are negotiable. This flexibility in negotiations makes the promotion much more malleable than other forms of marketing communication. Indeed, it is the sponsoring corporation's

---

249 Burton and Chadwick 2009, p. 9.

250 Gradauskaite 2010, par. 34.

responsibility to negotiate and attempt to control for factors that could otherwise hinder the success of a sponsorship agreement. In other words, it is a custom-fit strategy where sponsors can be surgically selective in choosing their sponsorships and bargaining for the best conditions. Like most other aspects of these agreements, exclusivity is a frequently negotiable element for the sponsoring corporation.[251]

The importance of sponsorship exclusivity for the hosting of sports mega-events was acknowledged in a 2009 resolution issued by the International Association for the Protection of Intellectual Property (AIPPI) in response to a working committee's examination of the efficacy of trademark and unlawful competition protection for major sports events in different jurisdictions:

> The value of the sponsorship of major sports events will partially depend on the nature of the exclusive rights which can be licensed or awarded to official sponsors. One of the important issues with major sports events is therefore the value which sponsors place on the exclusive rights available to them. The value of the exclusive right available to official sponsors will depend, *inter alia*, on its scope and enforceability.[252]

While sponsorship exclusivity is thus a key component of the commercial exploitation of mega-events, I do not believe it to be immune from legal scrutiny. When we consider the law's protection of commercial rights to sports mega-events in the chapters that follow, it will emerge that this notion of sponsorship exclusivity is central to the exercise of determining the legitimacy of such protection. More specifically, in Chap. 6, I will re-examine the concept of sponsorship exclusivity in the context of a competition (antitrust) law review of mega-event rights protection. Sponsors and organisers may often jealously guard the exclusivity provided in these agreements, which may include, *inter alia*, provisions making athlete eligibility for top-level competition dependent on toeing the line in using only official sponsors' equipment[253] or even disparagement of exclusive sponsors' competitors.[254] The potential competition law implications of such conduct (and of the agreements they aim to enforce) should be clear.

---

[251] Fortunato and Richards 2007, p. 42.

[252] AIPPI Resolution on Question Q210: 'The protection of major sports events and associated commercial activities through Trade Marks and other IPR', adopted at the AIPPI Executive Committee meeting in Buenos Aires, 14 October 2009—English version available online at the time of writing at https://www.aippi.org/download/commitees/210/RS210English.pdf.

[253] Compare the recent litigation involving the Dutch badminton federation and its exclusive equipment sponsor Yonex, which is discussed in Chap. 6.

[254] Compare the antitrust litigation between *TYR Sports, Inc v Warnaco Swimwear, Inc* et al. 679 F. Supp. 2d. 1120 (2009), which included federal antitrust claims in terms of the Sherman Act, of conspiracy and disparagement against Warnaco (manufacturer of the Speedo brand of clothing), U.S. Swimming and the U.S. national swimming coach. The plaintiff's claims included allegations (which it failed to prove in evidence) that U.S. Swimming had refused it to advertise in its official magazine, *Splash*, the largest-selling swimming magazine in the USA, and that photographs in the magazine had been airbrushed to remove the logos of competitors of Speedo from view. It was also alleged that Schubert, the U.S. national swimming coach had prior to the 2008 Beijing Games told athletes that 'I would strongly advise them to wear the [Speedo] at trials, or they may end up at home watching [the Olympics] on NBC'.

2.5 Conclusion

Developments in respect of the marketing of the Olympic Games during the last two decades of the twentieth century were pivotal in establishing the trends and practices in commercialisation of sports mega-events today. More specifically, it should also be clear that the developments described above have contributed significantly to the establishment of the current model of commercial monopolies regarding such events. First, the TOP programme emanated from fears regarding the uncertainty of the television rights market and was, specifically, developed in an attempt to address potential problems for the IOC (in respect of expectations as to the revenues to be derived from future Games) caused by the open market and free competition between broadcasters and media companies. TOP itself is based in the very exclusivity of rights granted to a limited number of corporate sponsors to associate with the Games. Furthermore, as described above, the long-term sale of television rights in the form of package deals (such as that first seen with the Sunset Project) has become the norm, and such ring-fencing of rights happens not only in respect of broadcasting rights but also in the context of sponsorship programmes modelled on TOP (for example, VISA is currently a TOP Olympic Partner until 2020).

In the next chapter we will examine ambush marketing of sports events and developments in this regard in recent years (in respect of both 'ambushing' practices and the measures used to combat them). It will be shown that, in fact, 'ambush marketing' appears to have come to exist in large part as a result of the above development of the modern mega-event sponsorship model. When the IOC first moved to category exclusivity of sponsorships and the commercial value of the related rights skyrocketed, many businesses (also those who may in the past have been actively involved in sports sponsorship) found themselves on the outside looking in, and unable to afford the now hefty price tag of involvement in sports-related marketing. Octagon's head of Olympic marketing, Bob Heussner, observed that when the TOP programme was first implemented in Seoul in 1988, entry level was about GBP 8 million, which had escalated to GBP 53 million (and a multiple of that amount to activate) in 2008.[255] Apart from the prohibitive cost of mega-event sponsorship, the TOP model as it has developed is of course also restrictive in terms of the number of sponsors who may attain involvement with the event. We have seen that the 'all comers welcome' approach followed at the Montreal Games (which saw a total of 628 sponsors and suppliers involved, providing a paltry USD 7 million) and in Sarajevo in 1984 (where the organising committee signed 447 foreign and domestic sponsorship agreements)[256] was seen

[255] From the short article entitled 'Bush-Whackers', 21 August 2008 in *Marketing Week* (available online at the time of writing at http://www.mad.co.uk/Main/Home/Articlex/17d67f5e4e9e42fc9cd8d88de18c2749/'Bush-whackers.html).

[256] See the 2010 edition of the IOC's *Olympic Marketing Fact File* (available online at the time of writing at http://www.olympic.org/Documents/fact_file_2010.pdf).

to be unsuccessful, and that the number of sponsors for subsequent Games has been limited in order to charge a premium for the granting of exclusive rights. Club membership, simply, is not open to everyone, and only the wealthiest applicants need apply.

While the Olympic Movement's (and other sports organisations') move to the TOP programme type of event commercialisation model accordingly brought with it very significantly increased income, such development also saw those who so frequently and vocally complain about and who so actively seek to combat ambush marketing, to a significant extent, having been the masters of their own fate.[257] Exclusivity of opportunities and rights to the sports product has served to create a lack of opportunities for many, and has apparently seen necessity as the mother of invention in respect of often creative new forms and ways of sports-related marketing and advertising.[258] It should also be noted that, apart from the fact that category exclusivity in a sense created ambush marketing, such sponsorship arrangements may also serve to facilitate ambushing and the efficacy of an ambush campaign. Johnson has observed, for example, that the complexity and fluidity of sponsorship category arrangements (in the context of the Football Association's rather involved system) make it difficult for consumers to understand who is, and who is not, an official sponsor.[259] The proliferation of official sponsors in a multitude of sponsorship categories may serve to create advertising clutter, thereby in fact adding value to an ambusher's campaign by causing the ability to create confusion amongst consumers regarding its own status or involvement with the event.

The sports organisations' and official sponsors' response to the 'ambush' may be attributable, on the one hand, to greed (i.e. wanting an even bigger slice of the

---

[257] Johnson observes that '[t]he rise of ambush marketing was a result of the increasing sophistication of sports sponsorship', and '[t]he rise of ambush marketing is directly related to the media attention given to sporting events'—Johnson 2007, p. 6. Elsewhere (Johnson 2008, p. 24) Johnson also observes:

'In real terms ambush marketing is the result of exclusive sponsorship deals. Sport has involved some form of sponsorship from the very beginning. The early days of sports marketing, during the 1950s and 1960s, witnessed a substantial growth in sponsorship deals and those wanting to be sponsors, but during this period anyone who wanted to become a sponsor could arrange some sort of deal. Accordingly, everyone was welcome and the varying levels of competition that existed meant that there was no need to ever ambush an event. The problem with this open access model was that it did not provide sufficient funds to host major sporting events and, in particular, the Olympic Games. By the late 1970s the International Olympic Committee had serious financial problems and hosting the Olympic Games was seen as an albatross around the neck of the host city'.

[258] See, for example, Barney et al. 2004, p. 236:

'The question of whether ambush marketing is an unethical or imaginative practice is widely debated within the sponsorship industry. Arguments for or against ambush marketing vary widely depending on whether one adopts a narrow or broad view of the practice itself. One thing remains certain, however: the growth of Olympic sponsorship expenditure world-wide has been accompanied by a parallel growth in the practice of ambush marketing'.

[259] Johnson 2007, p. 6.

pie or trying to close the door on the competition) or, on the other hand, to a justified fear of sabotage and misappropriation of expensive to obtain rights and a resultant threat to revenue streams that are integral to the ability to host such spectacles. We will consider these possibilities in more detail below, after a brief examination, in the following chapter, of what ambush marketing is—and what it is not.

References

All internet-based sources referred to, were last visited in or before December 2011.

Andrews D (2004) Sport in the late capitalist movement. In: Slack T (ed) The commercialisation of sport. Routledge, London

Andriychuck O (2009) The legal nature of premium sports events: "IP or not IP—that is the question". In: Blackshaw I, Cornelius S, Siekmann R (eds) TV rights and sport: legal aspects. T.M.C Asser Press, The Hague

Bacalao-Fleury, CE (2011) Brazil's Olympic Trials: An Overview of the Intellectual Property Challenges posed by the 2016 Rio de Janeiro Games. Univ Ill J Law Technol Policy 1:191

Barney RK, Wenn SR, Martyn SG (2004) Selling the five rings. University of Utah Press, Salt Lake City

Becker D (2006) The essential legal guide to events. Dynamic Publishing Ltd, Atlanta

Bikoff JL, Heasley DK, Delaney MT, Marano PV, Konoshima T (2010) From the gridiron to gold medals: enforcing sports trademarks. World Trademark Rev (26):87–91

Bollier D (2005) Brand name bullies: the quest to own and control culture. Wiley, Hoboken

Boyle R, Haynes R (2009) Power play: sport, the media and popular culture. Edinburgh University Press, Edinburgh

Burton N, Chadwick, S (2009) A typology of ambush marketing: the methods and strategies of ambushing in sport. Centre for the International Business of Sport Working Paper Series No. 10

Cashmore E (2010) Making sense of sports, 5th edn. Taylor and Francis, Hoboken

Chase CR, Kernit R (2010) Fighting for what is left of exclusivity: strategies to protect the exclusivity of sponsors in the sports industry. J Spons 3(4):379–393

Cobbs J (2011) Legal battles for sponsorship exclusivity: the cases of the World Cup and NASCAR. Sport Manag Rev 14(3):287–296. Elsevier Ltd—in-press at the time of writing

Coombe RJ (1991) Objects of property and subjects of politics: intellectual property laws and democratic dialogue. Tex Law Rev 69:1853

Dreyfuss RC (1996) We are symbols and inhabit symbols, so should we be paying rent? Deconstructing the Lanham Act and rights of publicity. Columbia-VLA J Law Arts 20:23

Crompton JL (2004a) Sponsorship ambushing in sport. Manag Leis 9:1–12

Crompton JL (2004b) Conceptualizations and alternate operationalizations of the measurement of sponsorship effectiveness in sport. Leis Stud 23(3):267–281

Crow D, Hoek J (2003) Ambush marketing: a critical review and some practical advice. Mark Bull 14:1–14

Curthoys J, Kendall CN (2001) Ambush marketing and the Sydney 2000 games (indicia and images) protection act: a retrospective. Murdoch Univ Elec J Law 8(2). http://www.murdoch.edu.au/elaw/issues/v8n2/kendall82.html

Davies G (2009) Managing the alchemy of the 2010 Football World Cup. In: Pillay U, Tomlinson R, Bass O (eds) Development and dreams: the urban legacy of the 2010 Football World Cup. HSRC Press, Cape Town

Davis JA (2008) The Olympic games effect: how sports marketing builds strong brands. Wiley, Singapore

De Lange P (1998) The games cities play. C P de Lange Inc, South Africa

Downward P, Dawson A (2000) The economics of professional team sports. Routledge, London

Farrelly FJ, Quester P (1997) In the name of the game. Asia Aust Mark J 5(1):5–7

Fortunato JA, Martin SE (2011) American needle v NFL: legal and sponsorship implications. Univ Denver Sports Entertain Law J 9:73

Fortunato JA, Richards J (2007) Reconciling sports sponsorship exclusivity with antitrust law. Tex Rev Entertain Sports Law 8:33

Gannon N (2010) Foul play in sports branding—the marketer's perspective' World Trademark Rev 27:67

Gardiner S et al (2006) Sports law, 3rd edn. Cavendish Publishing, London

Govoni NAP (2004) Dictionary of marketing communications. Sage Publishing, Thousand Oaks

Gradauskaite J (2010) The advertising appeal of sports and the legal limits of the incorporation of sports in advertising. Entertain Sports Law J. ISSN 1748-944X

Graham S, Goldblatt JJ, Delpy L (1995) The ultimate guide to sport event management and marketing. Irwin Professional Publishing, Chicago

Gratton C, Taylor P (2000) Economics of sport and recreation. E and FN Spon, London

Grohs R, Wagner U, Vsetecka S (2004) Assessing the effectiveness of sports sponsorships: an empirical examination. Schmalenbach Bus Rev 56:119–138

Gruneau R (1984) The McDonaldization of the Olympics. In: Tomlinson A, Whannel G (eds) Five-ring circus—money, power and politics at the Olympic games. Pluto Press, London, as referred to in Tomlinson A (2005) The making of the global sports economy: ISL, adidas and the rise of the corporate player in world sport. In: Silk ML, Andrews DL, Cole CL (eds) Sport and corporate nationalisms. Berg Publishing, Oxford

Hofacre, writing in Burnett J, Menon A, Smart DT (1993) Sports marketing: a new ball game with new rules. J Advert Res 33(5):21–35

Horne J, Manzenreiter W (eds) (2006) Sports mega-events: social scientific analyses of a global phenomenon. Blackwell Publishing Ltd, Oxford

Houlihan B (2004) Sports globalisation, the state and the problem of governance. In: Slack T (ed) The commercialisation of sport. Routledge, London

James M (2010) Sports law. Palgrave Macmillan, Basingstoke

Jennings A (1996) The new lords of the rings. Pocket Books, Great Britain

Jennings A (2006) Foul! the secret world of FIFA: bribes, vote rigging and ticket scandals. Harper Sport, London

Johnson P (2007) Ambush marketing: a practical guide to protecting the brand of a sporting event. Sweet and Maxwell, London

Johnson P (2008) Look out! it's an ambush. Int Sports Law Rev 2/3:24–29 (Sweet & Maxwell Ltd)

Kelbrick R (2008) Ambush marketing and the protection of the trade marks of international sports organizations—a comparative view. CILSA 41(1):24–48

Lewis A, Taylor J (2007) Sport: law and practice. Tottel Publishing, Edinburgh

Louw AM (2009) South Africa. In: International encyclopaedia of sports law. Kluwer Law International, Deventer

Magdalinski T, Nauright J (2004) Commercialisation of the modern Olympics. In: Slack T (ed) The commercialisation of sport. Routledge, London

Malfas M, Theodoraki E, Houlihan B (2004) Impacts of the Olympic games as mega-events. Munic Eng 157(ME3):209–220

Masterman G (2009) Strategic sports event management: Olympic edition. Elsevier, London

McDaniel L, Kinney L (1998) The implications of recency and gender effects in consumer response to ambush marketing. Psychol Mark 15(4):385–403

McKelvey S, Grady J (2008) Sponsorship program protection strategies for special sport events: are event organizers outmaneuvering ambush marketers? J Sport Manag 22:550–586

Mullin B, Hardy S, Sutton W (2000) Sports marketing, 2nd edn. Human Kinetics, Champaign

Nemeth A (2010) Mega-events, their sustainability and potential impact on spatial development: the European capital of culture. Int J Interdiscip Soc Sci 5(4):265–278

Payne M (2006) Olympic turnaround. Praeger Press, Westport

Pomfret R, Wilson JK, Lobmayr B (2009) Bidding for sports mega-events. University of Adelaide school of economics research paper 2009–30, paper presented at the first European conference in sports economics at university Paris 1 (Panthéon Sorbonne), 14–15 Sept 2009

Pound RW (1986) The international Olympic marketing programme. Olymp Rev 220:84–86

Pound RW (2006) Inside the Olympics. Wiley, Toronta

Roche M (2000) Mega-events and modernity: Olympics and expos in the growth of global culture. Routledge, London

Rose AK, Spiegel MM (2010) The Olympic trade effect. Finance Dev 47(1):12–13

Schaaf D (1995) Sports marketing: it's not just a game anymore. Prometheus Books, Amherst (as quoted in Mason DS (1999) What is the sports product, and who buys it? Eur J Mark 33(3/4): 402–415)

Schaus GP, Wenn SR (eds) (2007) Onward to the Olympics: historical perspectives on the Olympic games. Wilfrid Laurier University Press, Waterloo

Schulz-Herzenberg, C (ed) (2010) Player and referee: conflicting interests and the 2010 FIFA world cup™ monograph, vol 169. South African Institute for Security Studies

Schwab F (2006) FIFA's trademark tactics. World Trademark Rev 3:6

Seguin B, O'Reilly NJ (2008) The Olympic brand, ambush marketing and clutter. Int J Sport Manag Mark 4(1):62

Seguin B, Teed K, O'Reilly N (2005) National sport organizations and sponsorship: an identification of best practices. Int J Sport Manag Mark 1(2):69–92

Slack T, Amis J (2004) Money for nothing and your cheques for free? A critical perspective on sports sponsorship. In: Slack T (ed) The commercialisation of sport. Routledge, London

Sports Directorate of the Netherlands Ministry of Health, Welfare and Sport (2000) The balance between the game and the money

Still M, Jordan K, Ryston-Pratt T (2009) TV rights related to major sports events: the example of the Olympic games. In: Blackshaw I, Cornelius S, Siekmann R (eds) TV rights and sport: legal aspects. TMC Asser Press, The Hague

Stuart SA, Scassa T (2011) Legal guarantees for Olympic legacy. Entertain Sports Law J 9(1). http://www2.warwick.ac.uk/fac/soc/law/elj/eslj/issues/volume9/number1/stuart/

Sutton WA, McDonald MA, Milne GR, Cimperman J (1997) Creating and fostering fan identification in professional sports. Sports Mark Q 6:1

Tomlinson A (2005) The making of the global sports economy: ISL, Adidas and the rise of the corporate player in world sport. In: Silk ML, Andrews DL, Cole CL (eds) Sport and corporate nationalisms. Berg Publishing, Oxford

Toohey K, Veal AJ (2007) The Olympic games: a social science perspective, 2nd edn. CAB International, Wallingford

Tripodi JA, Sutherland M (2000) Ambush marketing—an Olympic event. J Brand Manag 7(6):412–422

Vaidhyanathan S (2003) Copyrights and copywrongs: the rise of intellectual property and how it threatens creativity. New York University Press, New York

Vassallo E, Blemaster K, Werner P (2005) An international look at ambush marketing. Trademark Report 95:1338

Walters G (2004) The professional footballers' association: a case study of trade union growth. Football Governance Research Centre, University of London, Birkbeck

Chapter 3
Ambush Marketing of Sports Mega-Events

Serious sport has nothing to do with fair play. It is bound up with hatred, jealousy, boastfulness, disregard of all rules and sadistic pleasure in witnessing violence. In other words, it is war minus the shooting.

George Orwell.

3.1 Introduction

In the previous chapter we encountered the commercial arrangements that event organisers enter into with corporate sponsors (and broadcasters) in order to commercially exploit an association with their showcase events. We have seen that these events are some of the most powerful promotional and marketing vehicles available to brands in the modern world, and that billions of dollars are spent in the sports sponsorship market in order to obtain rights and to leverage such rights with a view to pursuing profit maximisation. The central characteristic of these arrangements, as we have seen, is the exclusivity of the rights granted, and the sponsors' (and rights grantors') ability to exclude non-sponsors from associating with the event and thereby riding on the coattails of a 'product' for which they do not pay. In recent years a number of books have been written on the subject and the rather colourful term 'ambush marketing' has entered the lexicon of the sports industry, the legal fraternity and public discourse around mega-events.

We now need to consider the position of these 'non-sponsors', who pose the single largest threat to the commercialisation of events in the eyes of the governing bodies and their commercial partners. As a couple of commentators rather quaintly illustrated by posing the following scenario, in a thinly veiled reference to the FIFA World Cup (which is reminiscent of a 2002 piece by Abram Sauer posted on *Brandchannel*):

> Imagine you're having a party. You invite heaps of brilliant, interesting people having relevance to your business which you are promoting. Imagine on the night of your party

A. M. Louw, *Ambush Marketing and the Mega-Event Monopoly*,
ASSER International Sports Law Series, DOI: 10.1007/978-90-6704-864-4_3,

your archrival arrives, with all his friends. Imagine watching in awe as the freeloader takes credit for your expense and effort. Now imagine that party just cost you $65 million.[1]

What follows is a very brief overview; this chapter does not provide a 'how to' guide for ambushers, nor a 'how to' guide on how to protect against ambushing. I do not intend going over the same ground as covered in other excellent works regarding the available legal avenues and other ways that are open to event organisers and sponsors to combat ambush marketing.[2]

My aim here is rather to sketch the necessary background for purposes of the evaluation in the rest of this book of the legality of the current system of commercial rights exploitation in respect of mega-events, and their protection by the law. A key element of such protection is found in special anti-ambush marketing legislation in the various jurisdictions, which will be considered in detail in the later chapters. Here, I will briefly examine what is understood by the term ambush marketing, and then what the common (traditional) legal bases are for protecting against ambush marketing. In light of a growing realisation of the loaded nature of the term (e.g. '[t]he earliest definitions of ambush marketing were pejorative, implying unethical business conduct laden with the evil intent (thus supporting the perspective of event organizers and official sponsors)'[3]), I would suggest a little more circumspection in our consideration of the nomenclature and of the examples encountered in practice. While some commentators have approached the subject with an apparent strongly-held conviction that ambush marketing is simply 'wrong' (with one observer, for example, declaring unequivocally that '[t]here is no doubt that the practice of ambush marketing is an unethical business practice'[4]), the latter part of the chapter will ask whether all examples of what is often rather flippantly referred to as 'ambushing' are, in fact, ethically and (more importantly) legally 'wrong'.[5] This is a crucial issue to consider in the process of determining the legitimacy of the use of special laws to combat such conduct. Before we get to

---

[1] Dean-Wales, C and Dean, O, in an undated piece entitled 'Ambush marketing: Virtue or vice?', posted on the web site of South African brand advisors Scarab Origination, available online at the time of writing at http://www.scarabsa.com/news_ambush_marketing.htm.

[2] Compare, for example, the comprehensive, detailed and extremely useful treatment of the subject by Johnson (2007).

[3] McKelvey and Grady 2008, p. 553.

[4] Seth 2010, p. 456.

[5] Compare the following observation:

'Ambush marketing is not a legal category nor a well circumscribed marketing practice. It is an expression invented by its victims/detractors. "Guerilla *(sic)* marketing", "parasite marketing", "piggy-back marketing", "gorilla marketing" and in relation to TV broadcasts and digital means of communication, "viral marketing" are other expressions to describe the same practice. "Ambush" or "guerilla" *(sic)* have dramatic connotations to warfare and imply morally questionable behaviour. These expressions are not neutral and contribute to the stigmatisation of practices fought by the organisers of large sport events, such as the International Olympic Committee, FIFA and UEFA… There have been many definitions of ambush marketing. These definitions usually lack objectivity and fail to take in consideration the endless variety of the phenomenon'. From Kobel at 4.

that point, however, let's consider what exactly we are talking about when we discuss the ambushing of a sports event.

3.2 What Is 'Ambush Marketing'?

Ambush or 'parasitic'[6] marketing, or 'event piracy'[7] (or, a personal favourite, 'corporate shoplifting'[8]) is not unique to sport or to sports mega-events, and can occur in respect of any size and type (e.g. cultural, social, charity or, probably even, political) event. The term seems to crop up more and more frequently nowadays, and sometimes in the strangest of contexts. Shortly before the April 2011 British royal wedding of HRH Prince William of Wales and Miss Catherine Middleton, retail analysts suggested that the event could generate GBP 620 million for the UK economy (taking into account sales of engagement and wedding-related merchandise, food, drink, travel and tourism). One pair of observers, writing on intellectual property implications of the event, felt the need to specifically remark that ambush marketing was not expected to be a problem seeing that the event had no sponsors—so '[i]t does not seem that there will be any anti-ambush marketing legislation to protect royal rights in the run-up to the wedding'.[9]

Not only events can be ambushed, however. In fact, at the time of writing, the Court of Justice of the European Union has just ruled in the case between Interflora and Britain's Marks and Spencer retail group over claims that M and S had purchased certain search terms which, in terms of Google's 'AdWords' technology, would return ads for M and S's flower business when users search for Interflora. The ECJ held that M and S's conduct could constitute a trademark infringement and could also constitute free-riding on the reputation of a well-known mark.[10] While this terminology was nowhere used in the case, I would suggest that the facts, in effect, would support claims that internet users' Google

---

[6] So called because 'detractors argue that ambushers are obtaining nourishment from the host event without giving anything in return'—Crompton 2004, p. 1. The IOC began using the term 'parasite' rather than 'ambush' marketing, but its Marketing Department decided that the word 'ambush' 'actually got the message across more effectively'—from the minutes of the meeting of the IOC's New Sources of Finance Commission held in Lausanne, 25 June 1993 (at p. 36), as referred to by Barney et al. 2004, p. 376, note 32.

[7] From an article entitled 'The rights stuff' on the FIFA web site, available online at the time of writing at http://www.fifa.com/aboutfifa/federation/news/newsid=1105906.html.

[8] From a blog posting by Andy Sutherden, available online at http://blogs.hillandknowlton.com/hank/2011/11/15/ambush-marketing-keeping-us-all-on-our-toes/.

[9] Montagnon, R and du Boulay, E 'IP and the royal wedding: A marriage of inconvenience?' From the March 2011 *News Brief*, available online at the time of writing at http://www.herbertsmith.com/NR/rdonlyres/6754B8FC-5380-4718-96C0-DC4E872A9D92/18238/NewsbriefMARCH1.PDF.

[10] *Interflora, Inc., Interflora British Unit v Marks and Spencer plc, Flowers Direct Online Ltd* C-323/09 (22 September 2011).

searches were subjected to ambush marketing.[11] A similar case by luxury brands forming part of the Richemont Group (including Cartier and Alfred Dunhill) against retailer Aspinal of London had gone to the UK High Court in April 2011.[12]

It is, however, in the context of large sports events that ambush marketing has achieved most prominence in the past few decades. Ambushing of the biggest mega-events such as the Olympic Games and FIFA's World Cup are now so common that certain media sources even keep a running tally of ambushing. Compare the following assessment of the performance of (in this case) official sponsors at the 2008 Beijing Games by the Global Language Monitor's Trend-topper Mediabuzz, which reads like a sports match score update:

> In medal round of our competition, Lenovo performed a Phelpsian move pulling away from the crowd. In fact its media awareness grew over 2100% since our baseline "snapshot" on the last day of 2007. The strength of the Johnson and Johnson brand was also remarkable at No. 2. McDonald's brand equity was leveraged in clever and interesting ways, especially with their spectacular kick-off event. And, once again, Coca-Cola proved itself in the distance events, placing at or near the top for another Olympiad.[13]

---

[11] See the report 'Interflora sues Marks and Spencer over keywords, 15 October 2010, available online at the time of writing at http://www.theepochtimes.com/n2/content/view/44278/. It was reported in March 2011 that Advocate General Niilo Jääskinen of the European Court of Justice had recommended that some restrictions be placed on the rights of advertisers to use the names of rivals as keywords to generate sponsored links on Internet search engines (Pfanner, E 'Advertisers in Europe may face limits in use of keywords', *New York Times*, 24 March 2011). For interest's sake, it can be noted that Widmaier and Schechter (in their country report on the United States prepared for the Working Committee of the International Association for the Protection of Intellectual property (AIPPI), Project Q210 ('The protection of major sports events and associated commercial activities through trademarks and other IPR'; reports compiled for purposes of a draft resolution to be submitted to the AIPPI Exco meeting in Buenos Aires, October 2009)—available online at the time of writing at https://www.aippi.org/download/commitees/210/GR210usa.pdf) note that there is currently a disagreement among the U.S. Courts of Appeals as to whether a defendant's use of a trademark as a search engine keyword to trigger the display of sponsored advertisements on the search results page does or does not constitute use in commerce sufficient to expose that defendant to Lanham Act (federal trademark) liability. This issue pertains to all trademarks protected under the Lanham Act and therefore applies also to any marks and designations relating to Major Sporting Events. Briefly stated, the Second Circuit, in *1-800 Contacts, Inc. v. WhenU.com, Inc.*, 414 F.3d 400 (2d Cir. 2005), has held that keyword use is not use in commerce, and thus not actionable under the Lanham Act, while most courts outside the Second Circuit have found that using a trademark as a keyword to trigger sponsored advertisements does constitute use in commerce. *See, e.g., Google, Inc. v. Am.*

Blind and Wallpaper Factory, Inc., 2007 WL 1159950, *6 (N.D. Cal. Apr. 18, 2007) (finding that Google's sale of trademarked terms in the AdWords program is a use in commerce for purposes of the Lanham Act); *J.G. Wentworth S.S.C. LP v. Settlement Funding LLC*, 2007 WL 30115, 85 U.S.P.Q.2d 1780, 1785 (E.D. Pa. 2007) (finding that participating in Google's AdWords program constitutes trademark use).

[12] Although LMVH, the French owner of the Luis Vitton brand, had failed in a similar action against Google.

[13] Available online at the time of writing at http://www.languagemonitor.com/trendtopper/olympic/.

Much has been written in recent years about ambush marketing in a number of jurisdictions, and I will only include a very brief summary here for those readers who are less familiar with this phenomenon, and in order to provide some background to the discussion later in this book on legal responses to ambush marketing.

It has been observed that ambush marketing is 'an amorphous concept', and that 'the meaning of the term is so uncertain that most articles on the subject start by defining what the term means often by using examples of such practices'.[14] It has even been said that '[a]lthough widely used, the term "ambush marketing" is virtually meaningless in a practical sense and it has no legal referent'.[15] Jon Heshka reminds me that the situation seems to be analogous to US Supreme Court Justice Potter Stewart's 'I know it when I see it' definition of obscenity in *Jacobellis v. Ohio*.[16] I will try to be original, and will refrain from listing a number of the (sometimes amusing and entertaining) examples encountered in recent years, which are commonly to be found in the literature, but I do need to include mention of some of the definitions used to date. Max Duthie[17] has defined this practice as follows:

> "Ambush marketing" is the unauthorised trading off the goodwill or exposure of another's event. It is a form of "free-riding" where an advertiser seeks to associate itself with an event, or just share some of the event's publicity, without paying for the right to do so.

Philip Johnson[18] defines it as 'a planned campaign by an organisation to associate itself indirectly with an event in order to gain at least some of the recognition and benefits that are associated with being an official sponsor'. A more comprehensive description of the type of conduct involved is provided by Townley et al.[19]:

> Ambush marketing, or parasitic marketing, consists, in the sports context, of the unauthorized association by businesses of their names, brands, products, or services with a sports event or competition through any one or more of a wide range of marketing activities. The association is unauthorized in the sense that the controller of the commercial rights of such an event, usually the relevant governing body, has neither sanctioned nor licensed it, either itself or through its commercial agents. The term *ambush* has been applied because of the tendency for such activities to be devised by competitors of official sponsors or suppliers of sports events and to take place during the build up to or during the event itself; thus maximum commercial impact is achieved. The activity is often carefully planned to take advantage of inadequacies in an event's commercial

---

[14] Johnson 2008, p. 24.

[15] See Wood, Z; Hoek, J and Mossaidis, C 'Ambush marketing: A re-definition and research agenda', undated paper available online at the time of writing at http://smib.vuw.ac.nz:8081/WWW/ANZMAC2004/CDsite/papers/Wood1.PDF.

[16] 378 US 184 (1964). Heshka is a law professor at Thompson Rivers University in British Columbia—from personal correspondence with the author, December 2011.

[17] Duthie 2003, p. 171.

[18] Johnson 2007, p. 7.

[19] Townley et al. 1998, p. 333. See also Vassallo et al. 2005, p. 1339 et seq.

program and real or apparent loopholes in the legal protection available to event owners and sponsors.[20]

In the context of the Olympic Games, the following definition is found in the IOC's *Technical Manual on Brand Protection*[21]:

> The term *ambush marketing*… includes all intentional and unintentional attempts to create a false or unauthorised commercial association with the Olympic Movement or the Olympic Games. Ambush marketing includes: *(a)* a non-partner company's use of creative means to generate a false association with the Olympic Games, *(b)* a non-partner company's infringement of the various laws that protect the use of Olympic imagery and indicia, and *(c)* a non-partner company's activities that intentionally or unintentionally interfere with the legitimate marketing activities of Olympic partners.

Ambushing was defined in the agreement between the South African Football Association and FIFA for the organisation of the 2010 FIFA World Cup as meaning 'marketing, promotional, advertising and public relations activities in words, sound or any other form relating to the Championship, which are intended to capitalize on any form of association with the Championship, but which are undertaken by a person or an entity which has not been granted the right to

---

[20] For further description of what constitutes ambush marketing, see also Chap. 2 ('Definition, extent and effects of ambush marketing') in Scaria 2008, p. 28 et seq. In South Africa, the long awaited Safety at Sports and Recreational Events Act was passed in 2010. While this Act does not contain provisions regarding ambush marketing, the earlier Safety at Sports and Recreational Events Bill, 2005 contained provisions regarding ambush marketing of sports events. Sections 19 and 22 of the Bill provided for safety and security planning for events and security measures, amongst which were contained certain provisions relating to ambush marketing (e.g. regarding a prohibited and restricted item policy in respect of access points, a spectator and vehicle search policy, and the enforcement of an ambush marketing policy within a stadium or venue and its precinct, which is designed to protect, amongst others, the proprietary and commercial interests of an event organizer and an accredited event sponsor). The Bill defined ambush marketing as follows:

'[A]n intentional act or an attempt on the part of a person which utilizes or attempts to utilize the commercialization, publicity or public interest in an event arranged, organized or sponsored by others to obtain an unauthorized and unpaid for commercial benefit from, or association with, an event, without any official involvement or connection with such event'.

Paragraph 1.1.6 of the City of Johannesburg 2010 FIFA World Cup South Africa By-Laws contained the following definition:

'"Ambush Marketing" means marketing, promotional, advertising or public relations activity in words, sound or any other form, directly or indirectly relating to the Competition, and which claims or implies an association with the Competition and/or capitalises or is intended to capitalise on an association with, or gains or is intended to gain a promotional benefit from it to the prejudice of any sponsor of, the Competition, but which is undertaken by a person which has not been granted the right to promote an association with the Competition by FIFA and whose aforesaid activity has not been authorised by FIFA'.

[21] The version available at the time of writing on the web site of http://www.gamesmonitor.org.uk in respect of the 2012 London Olympics, at p 9 (this document refers to an updated version of the Manual which was scheduled for publication in July 2005, although such updated version (if it exists) is not available online at the time of writing).

promote an affiliation with the Championship by FIFA'.[22] In guidelines published recently by a working committee of the International Association for the Protection of Intellectual Property (AIPPI), on the use of trade mark protection for major sports events, ambush marketing is defined as 'all activities not authorised by the right holders in the fields of marketing, promotion and advertising in any form in connection with Major Sports Events which somehow seeks to benefit from the goodwill or general interest in the Major Sports Event'.[23]

While we're engaged with such colourful terms, in the realm of 'ambushers' and 'parasites', it is apparently important not to confuse an 'ambush' with 'guerrilla marketing'[24]:

> Guerrilla marketing and tactical marketing are legitimate forms of advertising and sales promotions that may be unconventional and which are intended to get maximum results from minimal resources. Some would argue they are a means for smaller businesses to compete against the large multi-national companies who are able to afford official sponsorship status of major events. The difficulty is deciding where such activity crosses the line and becomes ambush marketing likely to infringe the various laws and regulations now protecting nearly all major event holders and their sponsors.[25]

Modern marketing techniques have developed to the point where guerrilla marketers have to compete with viral marketers, ambient marketers, stealth marketers and, of course, ambush marketers. It may be no simple task to tell these guys apart, although the 'ambushers' appear to have generally been singled out as miscreants deserving of very public drawing and quartering.

Chadwick and Burton[26] recently suggested an 'updated breakdown of ambushing', in which they classify three distinct categories of ambushes (direct, indirect, and incidental) each including different specific types of ambushes or ambushing activity:

- *Direct ambushing*
  This is when a brand intentionally tries to make itself seem associated with an event or property for which it has purchased no rights and is not an official

---

[22] As quoted in *M and G Media Ltd v 2010 FIFA World Cup South Africa Organising Committee Ltd* South Gauteng High Court Case No. 09/51422 (unreported at the time of writing) at par. 108 note 42.

[23] Working Committee, Project Q210 ('The protection of major sports events and associated commercial activities through trademarks and other IPR'; in a call for reports compiled for purposes of a draft resolution to be submitted to the AIPPI Exco meeting in Buenos Aires, October 2009)—available online at the time of writing at https://www.aippi.org/download/commitees/210/WG210English.pdf.

[24] See Drake and Wells 2008.

[25] Palomba, M 'Is ambush marketing dead?' Reed Smith Advertising Compliance Team Client Alert No. 10-097 (May 2010)—available online at the time of writing at http://www.advertisingcompliancelaw.com/uploads/file/10-097%20ReACTS%20-%20Is%20ambush%20marketing%20dead.PDF.

[26] Simon Chadwick and Nicholas Burton 'Ambushed' in *The Wall Street Journal*, 25 January 2010—available online at the time of writing at http://online.wsj.com/article/SB10001424052970204731804574391102699362862.html#articleTabs%3Dcomments. See also Burton and Chadwick 2009.

sponsor, either in order to attack its rivals (who are official sponsors) or in order to capitalise on the public interest generated by the event. In this category the authors include the following four types of ambushes:

- *Predatory ambushing*—i.e. an intentional attack on a rival's official sponsorship in an effort to gain market share and to confuse consumers as to who the official sponsor is;
- *Coattail ambushing*—i.e. an attempt by a brand to directly associate itself with a property or event by using a legitimate link (for example, an existing individual athlete or team sponsorship) other than becoming an official sponsor of the property or event;
- *Property infringement*—i.e. the intentional unauthorized use of protected intellectual property (such as logos or unauthorised use of symbols or words relating to an event); and
- *Self-Ambushing*—i.e. marketing activities by an official sponsor above and beyond what has been agreed on in the sponsorship contract.

• *Indirect ambushing*
The authors describe this category of ambushing as the intentional association of a brand with an event or property through suggestion or indirect reference, including the following types of ambushes:

- *Associative ambushing*—i.e. the use of imagery or terminology to create an allusion that an organization has links to a sporting event or property;
- *Distractive ambushing*—i.e. the setting up of a promotional presence at or near an event without making specific reference to the event itself, its imagery or themes, in order to intrude upon public consciousness and gain awareness from the event's audience;
- *Values ambushing*—i.e. the use of an event or property's central value or theme to imply an association with the property in the mind of the consumer;
- *Insurgent ambushing*—i.e. the use of surprise street-style promotions at or near an event; and
- *Parallel property ambushing*—i.e. the creation or sponsorship of an event or property that is somehow related to the ambush target event and competes with it for the public's attention.

• *Incidental ambushing*
The authors describe this category of ambushing activity as instances when consumers think that a brand is a sponsor or is associated with an event or property without any attempt on the brand's part to establish such a connection (which can be harmful to event sponsors as it may cause cluttering of the marketing environment). They include the following types of 'ambushes' in this category:

- *Unintentional ambushing*—e.g. where media coverage will for example mention equipment or clothing used by an athlete, or a company that is providing a service in support of an event, causing consumers to think (wrongly) that the company is an official sponsor of the event; and

– *Saturation ambushing*—i.e. where 'ambushers' increase their advertising and marketing at the time of an event; they make no reference to the event itself and avoid any associative imagery or suggestion, but the goal seems to be to capitalize on the increased broadcast media attention and television audiences surrounding the event.

According to more conventional thinking ambush marketing practices are generally distinguished as taking one of two forms, namely association and intrusion cases.[27] In both cases the commonly-perceived harm caused to official sponsors is that (as sponsors contend) the ambush marketing 'can prevent delivery of category exclusivity and harm the brand awareness and image building objectives they have by introducing increased promotional clutter surrounding an event'.[28] We have seen how much of an investment is made in order to ensure exclusivity for sponsors of mega-events, so the negative perception of ambushing by official sponsors is understandable. There is more than just an element of outrage at free riding without paying similar amounts for the right to do so; the proliferation of commercial branding surrounding an event and the confusion it may cause may in fact directly detract from the value of what the official sponsor receives for their outlay.

There appears to be a growing realisation amongst sponsorship researchers that the traditional definitions of ambush marketing are unsatisfactory, because there does not seem to be a truly common understanding of the term and because such definitions are outdated in light of the practical experience of ambushes (which may range 'from the clever to the contrived'[29]). This is understandable if one considers the creative element of 'ambushing'; the fact that, especially in light of legal and other responses by event organisers and official sponsors in recent years, the 'ambusher' much like the guerrilla fighter seems to be constantly on the move, ducking and diving and re-strategising in order to ensure the success of its campaigns. How do you cope with a guy like Kym Illman and his company Messages on Hold? Kym is proud of his unofficial title of Australia's 'king of ambush marketing', and admits that 'I've had people stand behind cricketers in Kenya with t-shirts on, and we've even put fake sick on the floor at the cricket to clear a couple of rows so we could get enough space to ensure TV coverage'.[30] You've just got to love the Aussies. Or how about the Tongan national rugby union team's antics at the 2007 IRB Rugby World Cup? Members of the team, which was sponsored by Irish bookmaker Paddy Power, dyed their hair green to reflect their sponsor's

[27] See Schwab 2006, p. 7; Dean, O 'Legal aspects of ambush marketing', published on the web site *Legal City*, 11 February 2000 [available online at http://www.legalcity.net—last accessed 15 February 2007]; Kelbrick 2008, p. 26.

[28] Grady et al. 2010, p. 146.

[29] Schwab 2006, p. 7.

[30] See http://www.mediaman.com.au/profiles/ambush_marketing.html.

colours, and one player, Epeli Taione, felt the fashion statement wasn't enough and legally changed his name to Paddy Power![31] The bookmaker had agreed to sponsor the cash-strapped Tongan team for a five-figure sum, provided Taione was re-named, and it subsequently offered odds of 7-1 against its new namesake's team winning the Cup (not a classic example of brand loyalty by the sponsor).[32]

With the closing of avenues for ambushing (e.g. through developments such as the introduction of exclusion zones around venues, or the closing down of opportunities for sponsorship of broadcasts of events by rivals of official event sponsors), ever more creative thinking is required in order to place the ambusher's message in the public eye. In light of the apparent uncertainty amongst researchers regarding the process of defining ambushing, Chadwick and Burton suggest that "'ambush" marketing as a title may be somewhat misleading; rather, the French "*pseudo-parrainage*", or pseudo-sponsorship, is perhaps more applicable'. They propose the following definition:

> Ambush marketing is a form of associative marketing which is designed to capitalize on the awareness, attention, goodwill, and other benefits, generated by having an association with an event or property, without an official or direct connection to that event or property.[33]

I will continue to discuss ambushing with reference to the accepted terminology of association and intrusion ambushes, although it is worth noting that differences of opinion exist regarding the nomenclature used. One might suggest that ambush marketing is something that might be less susceptible to exact, scientific, quantification. It might, simply, be something—much like a duck—that one knows when one sees it, although, of course, for the lawyer such an understanding of the concept is problematic, especially as it has become more and more common for ambush marketing to be criminalised in special event legislation.[34] If one considers the *nulla poena sine culpa* principle it is unacceptable for conduct which is not sufficiently clearly defined by the law to be criminalised. I will return to consideration of the issue elsewhere.

Ambush marketing by *association* occurs where a marketer misleads the public into thinking it is an authorised sponsor associated with an event (the ambush marketer's conduct is aimed at or has the effect of creating the impression in the minds of the public that the ambush marketer or his product or brand is in some way associated with the sporting event, most commonly an impression that it is an

---

31 See Storey 2010, p. 46.

32 See the report 'Paddy to power Tonga to victory?', 4 September 2007, available online at the time of writing at http://news.bbc.co.uk/2/hi/uk_news/northern_ireland/6977125.stm.

33 Burton and Chadwick 2009, p. 10.

34 See the discussion in Chap. 4 and elsewhere in this book.

official sponsor of the event).[35] Clearly, this type of ambush marketing would usually constitute (at least in theory) 'passing off' in the traditional sense.[36] In the South African context, for example, the 2006 FIFA World Cup in Germany saw an association ambush complaint by FIFA to the Advertising Standards Authority (or 'ASASA')[37] against electronics giant LG Electronics (Pty) Ltd, which had run a competition in terms of which the winners could win a trip to the final of the FIFA World Cup in Germany. The competition was advertised with extensive use of allusions to the event, even though LG was not an official event sponsor. LG withdrew the allegedly offending promotional material and the matter was viewed by the ASASA as resolved (without a finding on whether such conduct in fact constituted ambush marketing in terms of its Sponsorship Code).[38] Ambush marketing first came to prominence (following an attempt to ambush at the 1996 Comrades marathon) in South Africa during the 2003 ICC Cricket World Cup, which was officially sponsored by inter alia Pepsi. The event saw much-publicized instances of anti-ambush marketing measures aimed at protecting official event sponsors, which included the controversial instance of a spectator being escorted

---

[35] Grady et al. 2010, p. 145 distinguish between the 'broad conception' of ambushing (in essence, creating a perception of association with the event) and a more pejorative form:

'An alternative conceptualisation of what constitutes ambush marketing reflects a more pejorative view of the practice, in that it is seen not simply as any unpaid association with an event, but specifically as actions whereby companies intentionally seek to create actual perceptions of official sponsorship ties that do not exist. Such actions might be, for example, using notable athletes affiliated with an event in one's advertising, engaging in congratulatory advertising (ie running advertisements congratulating Olympic medalists), or offering premiums thematically tied to an event. Note that this view of ambush marketing goes further than the broader conceptualisation in that, for an act to be considered an ambush, the ambusher should be intending to create perceptions of official sponsorship ties, or engaging in activities that actually create such perceptions'.

[36] Scaria describes ambush marketing, from a theoretical perspective, as referring to 'a company's attempt to capitalize on the goodwill, reputation and popularity of a particular event by creating an association with it ...' (Scaria 2008, p. 29)—classic passing off language. See, more generally, the discussion in Sect. 3.3.5 in the text below.

[37] Section 3.7 of the ASA's Sponsorship Code (available on the internet) defines ambush marketing as follows:

'The attempt of an organization, product or brand to create the impression of being an official sponsor of an event or activity by affiliating itself with that event or activity without having paid the sponsorship rights-fee or being a party to the sponsorship contract'.

[38] Article 11.1 of Clause 10 of the ASA Sponsorship Code provides that 'no organization, other than an official sponsor, may directly or by implication create an impression that its communications relate to a specific event or create an impression that they are an official sponsor of such event', and Article 11.1.4 of Clause 10 provides that '[n]o organization, other than an official sponsor ... may launch event-related sales promotions to give the impression of sponsoring such event'. See the article by Schimmel, G and Green, C 'Ambushed by a ticket?' *Without Prejudice* June 2008, p. 17–18.

from a match at the Centurion stadium for opening a can of Coca-Cola.[39] Ironically, the situation in 2003 was diametrically opposite to what had happened at the 1996 cricket World Cup, where Coca-Cola was an official event sponsor and Pepsi launched a massive advertising campaign (with extensive use of the slogan 'Nothing official about it'), which included concluding sponsorship agreements with individual players who took part in the event (e.g. iconic Indian batsman Sachin Tendulkar). Events at the 1996 ICC World Cup came to be known as the 'Cola wars'.[40] While Coca-Cola was a sponsor of the event, hot air balloons were launched at cricket grounds bearing the branding of their rivals, Pepsi. Between that event and the 2003 World Cup, Pepsi had become one of cricket's 'Global Partners', the top bracket of sponsors, by signing a seven-year deal with Rupert Murdoch's Global Cricket Corporation.[41] As Pepsi's conduct has been described—'the poacher had turned gamekeeper'—and the organisers of the 2003 event were obliged to stamp out ambush marketing in favour of event sponsors such as Pepsi.[42] The saga continued in 2010 at FIFA's Coca-Cola-sponsored World Cup in South Africa, where it was reported that Pepsi cans were handed out to World Cup volunteers at the beachfront Fan Fest in Durban, which a city spokesperson described as a 'delivery error' from suppliers and nothing sinister or deliberate. Many of the city's World Cup volunteers reportedly had their bags searched and the Pepsi cans in their free lunch packs were confiscated and thrown into rubbish bins at the venue. The ambiguous conduct of sponsors and ex-sponsors of mega-events is no new phenomenon, with 'official sponsors' and 'ambush marketers' often fulfilling one or the other role in different events (compare the sponsorship histories of Fuji and Kodak, and Nike and Adidas, in the context of the Olympic Games).

Ambush marketing by *intrusion* occurs when a marketer makes use of the publicity surrounding an event to give exposure to its own brand, trademarks etc. The ambush marketer attempts to ride on the coat-tails, as it were, of the event and of the interest and publicity it generates. This can be done in a myriad ways; e.g. through in-store promotions, advertising in the different media, competitions offered to consumers, etc. (i.e. such conduct is not limited to activities at the relevant stadium or venue). One example of intrusion ambushing that is often cited is that of the unauthorized use of airspace at an event by for example using a branded blimp to 'intrude' in such airspace and advertise a product or brand which

[39] A Johannesburg businessman felt the sting of measures enforced in terms of the new legislation during the tournament at the match between Australia and India on 15 February 2003, when he was evicted from Centurion stadium for drinking Coca-Cola and refusing a request by security personnel to surrender cans of the soft drink (he was, however, subsequently readmitted to the stadium).

[40] For more on the long-standing marketing feud between the two cola brands, specifically in respect of the American Super Bowl event, see McKelvey 2006, pp. 114–123.

[41] The GCC had bought the sponsorship and television rights to ICC events as part of a seven-year deal at a cost of USD 550 million.

[42] See Hartman 2004, p. 417.

has no official connection with the event or its official sponsors. Not surprisingly, sports federations and event organisers have in recent years responded by requiring host governments to enact and enforce special civil aviation regulations in respect of mega-events. Australia passed the Olympic Arrangements Act[43] in the run-up to the 2000 Sydney Olympics, which banned flying banners and skywriting above official locations by placing a temporary restriction on the airspace over competition venues.[44] Compare also the rather intimidating provisions contained in section 20 of Jamaica's ICC Cricket World Cup West Indies 2007 Act, 2006:

> No person shall, during a match period or such other period as the said Minister may determine, operate an aircraft within or cause an aircraft to enter, restricted airspace without an air traffic clearance... The said Minister shall not issue an air traffic clearance for restricted airspace ... unless he is of the opinion that the operation of the aircraft within the restricted airspace will not adversely affect the efficient organization and staging of [Cricket World Cup 2007], any [Cricket World Cup 2007] activity *or any commercial arrangement relating to such activity*... A person who contravenes [these provisions] commits an offence and is liable on summary conviction in a Resident Magistrate's Court to a fine not exceeding one million dollars. [Emphasis added].

Intrusion ambushes represent a very broad category of possible marketing practices, with no *numerus clausus* of conduct that may be deemed to constitute an 'ambush' and thus draw potential sanctions in terms of legal action or even criminal proceedings, depending on the relevant laws in the domestic jurisdiction where an event is hosted. As a result, these 'intrusion' cases are in my view most problematic when considering the legitimacy of commercial rights protection against ambush marketing. However, because intrusion ambushes do not require deception of the public, the burden of proof in intrusion cases may be considerably more difficult to discharge. This will be illustrated later, when we will see that anti-ambush marketing legislation in South Africa includes a provision that specifically and directly prohibits ambushing by intrusion,[45] and we will see that this provision is highly problematic and, it is submitted, highlights the difficulties of outlawing this specific form of ambush marketing.

One commentator has suggested that the practice of ambushing can be classified, broadly, as taking one of three forms:

- Advertising promotion in relation to an event;
- Appropriation of the prestige and status of an event without the authorisation of its organisers and sponsors; and
- The creation of a false impression of legitimate association or participation in the event.[46]

---

[43] Act 1 of 2000.

[44] See Vassallo et al. 2005, p. 1352.

[45] Section 15A(2) of the Merchandise Marks Act, 1941 (as amended in 2002)—see the discussion in Chap. 4 and elsewhere in this book.

[46] Mendes 2010, p. 19.

Crompton[47] has identified seven distinct areas or opportunities for ambushing an event, which I will briefly list here, as these different opportunities are not only relevant to the potential 'ambusher's' strategy but also to the available legal responses by event organisers and rights holders. They are the following:

- Sponsorship of the broadcast of the event;
- Purchasing advertising in and around event broadcasts;
- Sponsoring entities other than the event organiser;
- Purchasing advertising space in locations that are in close proximity to event venues;
- Thematic advertising and implied allusion to the event;
- Creation of a counter attraction; and
- Accidental ambushing.

It seems that ambush marketing, in its myriad forms, is so ubiquitous that it has attracted the attention of regulators at all levels in recent years. For example, the International Chamber of Commerce's *Consolidated Code of Advertising and Marketing Communication Practice*[48] expressly recognises ambushing and discourages it. For example, its Article 15 provides as follows:

> Marketing communication should not make unjustifiable use of the name, initials, logo and/or trademarks of another firm, company or institution. Marketing communication should not in any way take undue advantage of another firm's, individual's or institution's goodwill in its name, brands or other intellectual property, or take advantage of the goodwill earned by other marketing campaigns without prior consent.

Article B3 of the Code (in the section that deals with sponsorship) is entitled 'Imitation and confusion', and provides that '[s]ponsors and sponsored parties, as well as other parties involved in a sponsorship, should avoid imitation of the representation of other sponsorships where such imitation might mislead or generate confusion, even if applied to non-competitive products, companies or events, and Article B4 ('"Ambushing" of sponsored properties') reads:

> No party should seek to give the impression that it is a sponsor of any event or of media coverage of an event, whether sponsored or not, if it is not in fact an official sponsor of the property or of media coverage.

This wide range of areas where ambushing can occur highlight the need for a well-planned, comprehensive and forward-thinking strategy to counter ambushing by both event organisers and the official sponsors. The event organiser grants rights to sponsors and the huge cost of such rights warrants proactive rights protection by the organiser. From the sponsor's perspective the investment in the event (not only in the form of these huge rights fees but also further leveraging of such rights—which is nowadays estimated to amount on average to between three

---

[47] Crompton 2004.

[48] ICC Document 240-46/330, published August 2006, available online at the time of writing on the website of the ICC at http://www.iccwbo.org/policy/marketing/id8532/index.html.

and five times the amount of the rights fees) warrants active steps to protect these rights. Responses (although the term should not be read to imply only action after the fact; both rights grantors and sponsors need to be proactive and pre-emptive in their treatment of potential ambushes) range from contractual regulation of rights to public education campaigns regarding ambushing, and to recourse to the law. If one considers the huge hullabaloo over 'ambushing' during the past decade and more it is strange to note that a survey conducted amongst leading sports marketers, sports organisations and corporate sponsors as recently as 2010 found that an 'astounding' 30% of marketers do not participate in any programmes to protect their brands against event ambushing.[49] Others, and FIFA is a prominent example which I refer to throughout this book, are much more aggressive in their attempts to curb the activities of anyone without 'official' status in respect of their events. Even if they are not always used (or used effectively) there is a range of measures and safeguards available to those involved. The following section will briefly examine the most common grounds or mechanisms available in law to event organisers and sponsors.

3.3 The Available (Traditional) Legal Bases for Protection Against Ambush Marketing

Protection against ambush marketing can be based on a number of common law grounds, on applicable legislation or on straightforward shrewd event planning. These include the following (which will only be examined briefly below):

- Regulation of rights to events in the founding documents of the relevant sports organisation;
- The use of contractual regulation (by means of the matrix of sponsorship and event management contracts surrounding an event, and the practice of 'saturation sponsorship' by official event sponsors);
- Protection of relevant intellectual property (IP) rights related to the event;
- Ticketing terms and conditions;
- Venue security and (media) accreditation;
- Common law passing off and unfair competition actions;
- Advertising and sponsorship codes of practice;

[49] A survey conducted by the Chief Marketing Officer (CMO) Council (a six-month qualitative and quantitative research campaign, 'Doing Away With Foul Play in Sports Marketing', aimed at sensitising sports sponsors and franchises to trademark trespassing, property rights violations and online scams, frauds and infringements) with the assistance of MarkMonitor. The CMO Council surveyed more than 180 senior-level sports marketers across relevant industries for an assessment of how brands are safeguarding themselves and whether those measures are effective. The study also drew from interviews with executives at top leagues and corporate sponsors. See Gannon 2010, p. 69.

- Specific legislation (including umbrella event legislation and *sui generis* event protection—which will be discussed in Chap. 4); and
- Planning laws (and e.g. municipal by-laws).[50]

In addition to these weapons in the organisers' legal arsenal, recent years have also seen an emphasis on public education campaigns aimed at educating the public about official sponsors' rights and the alleged evils of ambush marketing (often coupled with 'naming and shaming' campaigns against alleged ambushers, which have been more or less successful on a number of occasions).

The following section contains a few brief words on each of the above possible legal bases for protection, by way of background to the critical evaluation of legal responses to ambush marketing in the form of special legislation (to be undertaken in Chap. 4).

3.3.1 Claims of Rights in the Founding Documents of International Sports Organisations

An international sports governing body is empowered, through the monopoly system of governance which is such a fundamental characteristic of the 'European Model' of sports organisation, to claim rights in events which are organised under its auspices by its domestic member federations. As an example,[51] Article 74 (entitled 'Rights') of FIFA's Statutes[52] provides as follows:

> Article 74:
>
> (1) FIFA, its Members and the Confederations are the original owners of all of the rights emanating from competitions and other events coming under their respective jurisdiction, without any restrictions as to content, time, place and law. These rights include, among others, every kind of financial rights, audiovisual and radio recording,

[50] This last mechanism will not be examined here, but Chap. 7 will include brief discussion of the ambush marketing provisions contained in the host city municipal By-Laws that were in place for the 2010 FIFA World Cup South Africa™.

[51] Rule 7.1 of the Olympic Charter (7 July 2007, in force at the time of writing) provides as follows in respect of 'Rights over the Olympic Games and Olympic Properties':

'The Olympic Games are the exclusive property of the IOC which owns all rights and data relating thereto, in particular, and without limitation, all rights relating to their organisation, exploitation, broadcasting, recording, representation, reproduction, access and dissemination in any form and by any means or mechanism whatsoever, whether now existing or developed in the future. The IOC shall determine the conditions of access to and the conditions of any use of data relating to the Olympic Games and to the competitions and sports performances of the Olympic Games'.

The By-Laws to Rule 7 regulate the licensing of use of the Olympic Properties to National Olympic Committees in their respective territories.

[52] The August 2009 version of the FIFA Statutes, currently in force at the time of writing.

reproduction and broadcasting rights, multimedia rights, marketing and promotional rights and incorporeal rights such as emblems and rights arising under copyright law.

(2) The Executive Committee shall decide how and to what extent these rights are utilised and draw up special regulations to this end. The Executive Committee shall alone decide whether these rights shall be utilised exclusively, or jointly with a third party or entirely through a third party.

The wide ambit of the rights claimed in terms of this provision should be obvious: Reference is made to 'all of the rights emanating from competitions and other events', to 'every kind of financial rights' and 'marketing and promotional rights', and FIFA's Executive Committee 'shall alone decide' how these rights shall be utilised. Compare also the wide wording of the similar provisions of Rule 7 of the Olympic Charter, which has been referred to elsewhere.[53] However, it should be noted that such provisions are only binding on the member federations of the relevant sports organisation. Such extensive rights as claimed in the statutes of a sports governing body cannot create legal obligations for third parties (e.g. corporations and other business undertakings that have no contractual relationship with the relevant organisation or its members), unless, of course, the contents of such documents are incorporated into domestic laws (compare the 'Olympic law' enacted by Turkey to boost its numerous unsuccessful bids for the Games,[54] which incorporates the provisions of the Olympic Charter into the country's domestic laws).

Accordingly, while seemingly significant and while the relevant sports organisations will always emphasise the existence of such provisions in the context of their efforts to combat ambush marketing, such provisions probably hold little sway over the potential conduct of ambush marketers who, by their very definition, have no association with the relevant event and thus have no existing contractual obligations in that regard.

3.3.2 Contractual Regulation of Commercial Rights to an Event

Major sporting events generate a matrix of contracts between the relevant parties, including host nation (and city) agreements, sponsorship agreements, venue management agreements, participation agreements (between event organisers and participating teams or domestic federations), broadcasting rights agreements, etc. One means for sponsors and commercial partners to attempt to exhaustively ring-fence their commercial interests in an iron-clad web of contracts is the practice of 'saturation sponsorship' (i.e. the process of event sponsors securing exclusive rights at all levels of the 'stakeholder food chain'). In this way, sponsors acquire a

---

[53] In Chap. 2.

[54] Turkey's Parliament enacted the first Olympic law in the world (on 5 May 1992) guaranteeing the full cost of staging the Games and the government has set aside fixed sources of revenues for facilities.

broad portfolio of rights in respect of athletes, teams, event organisers and broadcasters. Of course, such 'saturation' tactics can also be employed by an ambusher to set up a future ambush. One example may be Pepsi's recent sponsorship of the Asian Games, allowing it to use 'Team China' in its marketing up to the end of 2007. With that connection established, it subsequently launched (from September 2007) its cans in a colour it termed 'China Red', as part of its 'Passion of 1.3 Billion, Red for China' campaign, extending the association in the minds of the public in the run-up to the 2008 Beijing Olympic Games.[55]

One component of the practice of saturation sponsorship is ensuring that event regulations and participation agreements (e.g. between the organisers of the event and participating teams) restrict the rights that participants may grant to their own sponsors,[56] including for example restricting the participants' use and licensing of their image rights during or leading up to the event. Such arrangements are not always easy to implement and may lead to legal challenge from pre-event rights holders in terms of e.g. existing athlete or team sponsorship agreements.[57] In the run-up to the 2011 ICC Cricket World Cup[58] (in October 2010) the ICC's head legal counsel sent a memo to all players participating in the event, warning them about ambush marketing and calling on them to avoid conduct which might adversely affect official sponsors' commercial interests. The memo made it clear that the following was prohibited:

> At all times Squad Members may **not** allow their name, likeness or image to be used by any third party in any advertising or endorsement (or for any other commercial purpose) **in such a way that gives rise to a direct or implied association with the Event**;
>
> **During the period of 7 days prior the first match of the Event and the departure date of the Team**, Squad Members may **not** allow their name, likeness or image to be used by any third party in any advertising or endorsement (or for any other commercial purpose) **wearing Team Kit, Team Uniform or Practice Kit (or any other clothing confusingly similar thereto**);
>
> Squad Members may **not** display the **branding, marks or insignia of any third party (apart from an approved kit manufacturer, Team Sponsor or Team logo) while on the field of play**. [Emphasis in the original].

---

[55] See 'Marks, set, ambush—associating your brand with the Olympics', 9 July 2010, available online at the time of writing at http://www.wragge.com/analysis_6124.asp.

[56] In order to avoid the negative effects of what is referred to as conflict marketing (i.e. where publicity gained by e.g. an official team sponsor detracts from the publicity derived by official event sponsors); while this practice involves official sponsors and is distinguishable from ambush marketing, its impact can be as damaging to event sponsors.

[57] Compare the ICC's problems in the run-up to the 2003 ICC Cricket World Cup, in respect of individual players' personal sponsorships (especially sub-continent players). Compare also the problems experienced in the dispute between the ICC and Cricket Australia in the run-up to the 2007 ICC Cricket World Cup in the Caribbean, regarding the position of Cricket Australia's own exclusive team sponsor, Travelex (see the report of the ruling of the International Cricket Council's Dispute Resolution Committee in *Cricket Australia v ICC Development (International) Ltd*, 2007 (*World Sports Law Review*, 2 (May), SLR 61–75, Sweet and Maxwell).

[58] Co-hosted by India, Sri Lanka and Bangladesh.

Players would be allowed to 'appear in any advertising or endorsement (or other commercial activity) in their generic 'cricket whites' or in any other casual, formal or leisure wear, provided that… [t]hey are not appearing in the national colours of a Team; and [t]here is no direct association with the Event or any use of the ICC or Event marks/logos'.[59] The memo was intended to draw players' attention to the provisions regarding ambush marketing of the Members Participation Agreement (or MPA) between the member boards and the ICC for the 2011 event (specifically, clause 1.5 and Item 2 of Schedule 4 to the MPA). The MPA had had a chequered past since its introduction in 2006 (the Board of Control for Cricket in India (BCCI) had initially refused to sign the MPA in the run-up to the 2003 ICC World Cup, when it objected to a clause which prevented its players from advertising products from rivals of the ICC's official sponsors for three months on either side of the World Cup—after protracted negotiations the BCCI sent a team to the event after it was agreed that the clause would only apply for the duration of the event, but the official commercial rights holder (Rupert Murdoch's Global Cricket Corp.) withheld money from the ICC and the BCC had to accept liability for all damages that might have arisen from claims made by sponsors of the World Cup on account of the amended conditions[60]). Similar disputes had arisen in respect of the ICC Champions Trophy event held in September 2002, regarding the Indian team's sponsorship by Sahara (which was in conflict with an event sponsorship by South African Airways) and the prohibition on endorsement activity by players for periods before and after the event. Such conflict of pre-existing sponsorships can affect team selection—in 2005 a similar dispute led to the dropping of a number of leading players from the West Indies cricket team because they were sponsored by a competitor of the official event sponsor for a series the team was scheduled to play in.[61] In 2006, India faced losing the right to co-host the 2011 tournament due to another refusal by the BCCI to sign the MPA due to commercial rights issues relating to their players. Indian team captain, Mahendra Singh Dhoni, invoked the ire of the ICC a few days before the start of the 2011 ICC World Cup tournament in February 2011, for promoting Sony and Aircel (rivals to the ICC's official sponsors), and was given a warning by the ICC.[62]

---

59 Memo from David Becker, ICC head legal counsel, 26 October 2010 (available online at the time of writing at http://static.icc-cricket.yahoo.net/ugc/documents/DOC_4F4A49058EED67A652B676DB54524966_1293679965894_945.pdf.

60 See Kaur, B 'Apprehending an ambush: How to defend against ambush marketing' *Brands in the Boardroom 2010* pp. 56–59 at 58 (www.iam-magazine.com)—available online at the time of writing at http://www.iam-magazine.com/issues/Article.ashx?g=a96dceed-1e54-456c-bd75-6a38f819d228.

61 See Becker 2006, pp. 158–159.

62 See the report available online at the time of writing at http://iccworldcupliveupdates.blogspot.com/2011/02/icc-cricket-world-cup-2011-dhoni-warned.html.

An interesting variation is a resolution passed at the 2010 Olympic Assembly in Colorado Springs in September 2010, where the US National Governing Body (NGB) Council unanimously passed an anti-ambush resolution in cooperation with the US Olympic Committee (USOC). The resolution states that the USOC and the US NGBs won't consent to their sponsors airing comparative or disparaging advertising, and to disallow use of their marks, emblems and designations in such advertising by their respective sponsors and to work to ensure that all advertising around the Olympic Games conforms to the spirit of the Games.[63] One assumes that such a resolution would be backed by a specific clause in sponsorship agreements prohibiting such advertising, which may be an effective way of addressing the issue although it would not affect the conduct of outside parties or 'ambushers'.

Athlete or team participation agreements may also place restrictions on equipment sponsors. During the 2011 IRB Rugby World Cup in New Zealand, England and Samoan national team players (and brothers) Manu and Alesana Tuilagi were both fined $10,000 for wearing unapproved OPRO branded mouth-guards during the tournament, breaching the event's terms of participation. The mouth-guard manufacturer was accused of ambush marketing but denied the allegations and vowed to pay the players' fines.

Another, important, example of combating ambush marketing by means of contractual regulation of rights is the use of broadcasting contracts to control broadcast sponsorship in order to exclude the possibility of broadcast sponsors upstaging event sponsors and being perceived as sponsoring the event while paying much less for the privilege or not contributing to the coffers of the event organiser[64] (for example, by providing official event sponsors with a right of first refusal in respect of sponsorship of the broadcasts of the event, or, as the IOC does, prohibiting in the broadcasting agreement the use of the phrase 'broadcast sponsor', and variations thereof[65]).

From the event organiser's perspective and in respect of broadcasting rights agreements (and, this issue will be revisited elsewhere in this book), it is important to note that most legal systems[66] do not recognize a 'proprietary right to a spectacle' in respect of sports events. While such a right to a sports event which is worthy and capable of protection against misappropriation appears to enjoy some

---

[63] See the report on the Team USA website, dated 24 September 2010, available online at the time of writing at http://www.teamusa.org/news/2010/09/24/national-governing-body-council-passes-anti-ambush-resolution-with-u-s-olympic-committee/38693.

[64] As happened during the 1984 Olympics when Kodak sponsored the ABC television coverage of the event while Fuji was the official event sponsor. Sony managed to be perceived as the official sponsor of the 1991 IRB rugby World Cup through its sponsorship of broadcasts, even though it was not an official sponsor of the event.

[65] Burton and Chadwick 2009, p. 11.

[66] Notably the UK and Australia—compare *Victoria Park Racing v Taylor* (1937) C.L.R. 479; *Australian Broadcasting Corp v Lenah* (2001) 208 C.L.R. 199.

form of recognition in the United States of America[67] and some civil law jurisdictions provide a measure of assistance to event organizers by providing that copyright in sports broadcasts vest in the event organizer,[68] in jurisdictions such as the United Kingdom, Canada, South Africa, Australia, New Zealand, Germany, Switzerland, Sweden, Japan and others the rights to broadcast a sporting event or to disseminate news regarding the results and action on the field of play must be protected by means of other mechanisms and/or through a combination of other, recognized, legal rights.[69] This appears to have received express recognition in the recent landmark judgment of the Court of Justice for the European Union in the *Football Association Premier League (FAPL) v Karen Murphy* broadcasting rights case.[70] The ECJ held that sports events (in this case, English Premier League football matches) do not qualify for copyright protection as protectable works:

> [S]porting events cannot be regarded as intellectual creations classifiable as works within the meaning of the Copyright Directive. That applies in particular to football matches, which are subject to rules of the game, leaving no room for creative freedom for the purposes of copyright. Accordingly, those events cannot be protected under copyright. It is, moreover, undisputed that European Union law does not protect them on any other basis in the field of intellectual property.[71]

The court acknowledged that sporting events 'have a unique and, to that extent, original character which can transform them into subject-matter that is worthy of protection comparable to the protection of works, and that protection can be granted, where appropriate, by the various domestic legal orders'.[72] It seems that this is, at least to a significant extent, what *sui generis* anti-ambush marketing laws

---

[67] On the basis of *International News Service v Associated Press* 248 US 215, 63 L Ed 211, 39 S Ct 68 (1918); *Pittsburgh Athletic Co v KQV Broadcasting Co* 24 F Supp 490 (WD Pa 1937). See also *Twentieth Century Sporting Club v. Transradio Press Service,* 300 N.Y.S. 159 (N.Y. Sup. Ct. 1937); *Johnson-Kennedy Radio Corp. v. Chicago Bears Football Club.* 97 F.2d 233 (7th Cir. 1938); *Mutual Broadcasting System v. Muzak*, 30 N.Y.S.2d 419 (Sup. Cot. N.Y. County 1941); *Southeastern Broadcasting Co. v. Oil Center Broadcasting Co.*, 210 S.W.2d 230 (Tex. Civ. App. 1947); *Liberty Broadcasting System v. National League Clubs,* 1952 Trade Cases (CCH) 67,278 (N.D. Ill. 1952); and *Nat'l Exhibition Co. v. Fass,* 143 N.Y.S.2d 767 (N.Y. Sup. Ct. 1955). Lewis and Taylor *Sport: Law and Practice* Cavendish Publishing 2003 at 405, 583 and 679; Johnson, P *Ambush Marketing: A Practical Guide to Protecting the Brand of a Sporting Event* Sweet and Maxwell, London (2008) at 2–3.

[68] Notably Spain, the Netherlands and France—see the discussion in Hewitt 2005, pp. 32, 33.

[69] Hewitt supra discusses the failed lobby in England by the Association for the Protection of Copyright in Sports for the recognition of copyright in sports events similar to other types of 'works' under the applicable copyright legislation (e.g. literary, artistic and musical works), which was rejected in the 1952 Gregory Report (a report of the Committee on Copyright Protection which led to the Copyright Act of 1965). See also, generally, Becker 2006, pp. 5–7.

[70] Judgment of the Grand Chamber (4 October 2011) available online at the time of writing at http://eur-lex.europa.eu/LexUriServ/LexUriServ.do?uri=CELEX:62008CJ0403:EN:HTML.

[71] At par. 98, 99 of the judgment.

[72] At par. 100 of the judgment.

in various jurisdictions appear to do, although such laws have yet to create a special 'property right' to a sports event.

In light of this, and as has been explained in the context of English law, the development of a valuable and viable commercial programme around a sports event necessitates a foundational matrix of different rights, as follows[73]:

(i) Access rights to the venue: The event organizer must have the right to exclusive possession of the venue and must be able to control access to the venue—see discussion in the following section in the text below;
(ii) Contractual restrictions on participants and official event sponsors: Restrictions on participants are aimed mainly at ensuring that the commercial value of the event is not diluted by athletes' personal sponsorship or endorsement deals,[74] while restrictions on official partners are aimed at ensuring that they do not overstep their own contractual rights nor inadvertently assist others in hijacking the goodwill in the event (e.g. through ambush marketing). It is interesting to note that as early as 1932, in respect of the Los Angeles Olympic Games of that year, the official supplier agreement entered into between suppliers and the Los Angeles Organising Committee contained injunction clauses against publicly advertising contracted products with the Olympic emblems included[75]; and
(iii) The creation (by means of contract), protection and enforcement of copyright, trade mark and other intellectual property rights that may subsist in the elements that go to make up a sports event.

As Cloete et al. have observed,[76] the justification for legal measures to combat ambush marketing—i.e. to protect the exclusivity of official sponsors' rights and the often very substantial commercial outlay in associating with sporting events—is well illustrated in the South African context with reference to the facts of the case of *Motor Racing Enterprises (Pty) Ltd (in liquidation) v NPS (Electronics) Ltd.*[77] This case also illustrates the effects of poor protection by the rights grantor of the rights granted to a sponsor. The appellant was the organizer of the South African leg of the FIA's Formula 1 Grand Prix, and the respondent had agreed to

[73] See Lewis and Taylor 2003, p. 584.

[74] Which is why, for example, the official guidelines to brand and content protection (available at the time of writing at http://static.icc-cricket.yahoo.net/ugc/documents/DOC_78EA5B38294E6DA3B05BD9BBEED292E4_1289140599475_38.pdf) distributed by the International Cricket Council in respect of its ICC Cricket World Cup 2011 (co-hosted by India, Bangladesh and Sri Lanka) contains the following:

'It is important to note that a formal or pre-existing association with any of the fourteen participating national teams or the tournament venues does not permit a team partner or team sponsor any right to use the ICC Cricket World Cup IPR (other than the specific rights such team is authorised by the ICC to license) without the prior authorisation of the ICC'.

[75] Barney et al. 2004, p. 33. Although such injunction clause failed to assist the Olympic organisers in the most prominent (and ultimately important) case of such use of the Olympic symbols at that event, the Helms Bakery case (see the discussion in Sect. 6.2.1 in Chap. 6).

[76] Cloete et al. 2005, p. 179.

[77] 1996 (4) SA 950 (A).

sponsor the event at a cost of ZAR 22 million (or around USD 3 million) payable in instalments, which extended well beyond the date upon which the event was to take place. The respondent obtained naming rights, the exclusive right to be official sponsor of the race, and that all public references to the race were to indicate the respondent's sponsorship. The appellant, however, took no steps to ensure that public reference to the race referred to the respondent's sponsorship, and also allowed another sponsor to erect advertisements around the track that gave the impression that such sponsor was the official sponsor of the event. The appellant claimed an order for specific performance against the respondent for payment of the outstanding instalments, and the respondent raised the defence of the *exceptio non adimpleti contractus*. The court upheld this defence on a finding that the parties' obligations in terms of the sponsorship contract were reciprocal. As Cloete et al. observe, the end result was that the appellant was liquidated and South African motor sport suffered irreparable harm[78] (the country has to date never again hosted a Formula 1 race, although it appears at the time of writing that negotiations have been initiated by a motor sport development company, which was recently established under the auspices of the Gauteng provincial government, to re-introduce the South African Formula 1 Grand Prix at the Kyalami race-track in Johannesburg in the near future). Other examples abound of the impact that ambush marketing can have in respect of the promotional value derived by official sponsors in respect of major events.[79]

The major problem for sponsors in respect of 'saturation sponsorship' (as described above) is, of course, the prohibitive cost involved.[80] These rights can be (and usually are) very expensive; exclusivity carries a hefty price tag. It does however hold a number of advantages. For example, event (and title) sponsors can avoid the dangers of being upstaged by broadcast sponsors.[81] In respect of applicable legislative protection in the relevant jurisdiction, other sponsors' conduct in respect of individual participants or teams might not constitute ambush marketing in terms of the applicable legislation (i.e. see section 15A of the Merchandise Marks Act in South Africa,[82] which prohibits showing a connection

---

78 Cloete et al. 2005, p. 179.

79 E.g. Vassallo et al. 2005, p. 1340 refer to a survey that showed that three out of five companies most associated with the 1994 Lillehammer Winter Olympics in Norway were not official sponsors, at a time that official sponsors were paying USD 40 million to be so associated with that event.

80 Note also Scaria's observation on the practicalities involved (Scaria 2008, p. 30):

'It is virtually impossible for a sponsor to buy rights to all avenues leading to the public's awareness of a given sponsorship property. In such situations, all except that which is specifically purchased is for grabs and this is what ambush marketers capitalize on'.

81 Compare the events surrounding the 1991 IRB Rugby World Cup, where Sony was not the event sponsor but was perceived by the public to be the main event sponsor while it was only the sponsor of TV coverage of the event (and had paid much less for these rights than the event sponsors).

82 See the discussion in Sect. 4.4.5 in Chap. 4.

with or deriving publicity from an 'event'). In such cases the protection afforded by means of contract might be of value.

Of course, it should be borne in mind that a major impediment to the use of contract to obtain all-encompassing protection against ambush marketing is the role of a principle which is firmly entrenched in most legal systems, namely privity of contract. Any commercial rights granted or licensed to a party to the relevant contract can only be enforced against the other parties to that contract; while such contracts may create or vest rights for purposes of determining *locus standi* in a civil action against ambush marketers, the contract per se does not provide grounds for a contractual claim in this regard.[83] Apart from the privity of the rights created in such contracts, a further hurdle might be the fact that alleged infringers of such rights may also be viewed as not having any knowledge thereof. In the Indian case of *ICC Development (International) Ltd v Arvee Enterprises and Philips*[84] the International Cricket Council (ICC) claimed that Philips' ticket distribution scheme was reserved for sponsors and that in depriving sponsors of this exclusive right, Philips was preventing the ICC from fulfilling its contractual obligations. The court ruled in favour of Philips on the ground that the ICC had failed to provide material evidence to show that Philips had notice of the terms and conditions set out in the contracts between the ICC and its sponsors. Nowadays, such exclusive contractual arrangements between event organisers and sponsors are so

[83] Apart from the enforcement of guarantees that an event organizer and rights holder may have provided in respect of the exclusivity of rights licensed to e.g. sponsors. It is debatable (and purely speculative here) whether ambush marketing activities might provide a sponsor party to a commercial agreement regarding an event with an alternative claim against the ambush marketer, relating to such contract. It is, for example, accepted in South African law that '[a] delictual [tort] remedy is available to a party to a contract who complains that a third party has intentionally and without lawful justification induced another party to the contract to commit a breach thereof' (*Atlas Organic Fertilizers (Pty) Ltd v Pikkewyn Ghwano (Pty) Ltd* 1981 (2) SA 173 (T) at 202. See also *Dun and Bradstreet (Pty) Ltd v SA Merchants Combined Credit Bureau (Cape) (Pty) Ltd* 1968 (1) SA 209 (C)). South African courts generally require the defendant's actions or conduct in interfering with the contractual rights of the plaintiff to be *intentional* (therefore with the clear intention to interfere with the parties' contractual rights and cause the plaintiff damage) in order to found liability under this delictual action (*Union Government v Ocean Accident and Guarantee Corporation Ltd* 1956 (1) SA 577 (A)). Just some examples of specific forms of conduct that may found liability under this delict are the intentional inducement, enticement or instigation of a contracting party to breach the agreement, bribing an employee of a competitor to sell trade secrets, or enticing employees of a competitor to leave its service. The inducement element may, of course, provide some problems to prove in such a scenario. Vassallo et al. 2005, pp. 1344, 1345 note that ambush marketing may lead to liability in terms of the tort of tortuous interference with contractual relations (in the United States). Although this tort has apparently not yet been utilised in this context, the authors refer to the Canadian case of *National Hockey League et al. v Pepsi-Cola Canada Ltd* 70 B.C.L.R. (2d) 27 (1992), affirmed 59 C.P.R. (3d) 216 (1995), where the possible application of a remedy of this nature was mentioned (although the court held that Pepsi's conduct did not satisfy the requirements for the tort in light of the official sponsor (Coca-Cola)'s limited contractual rights on the facts).

[84] (2003) VII AD (Del) 405.

common and well-known, of course, that the outcome of a future case on similar facts may be different.

3.3.3 Control of (Access to) Event Venues

Access control to events constitutes an effective way to combat some of the practices favoured by ambush marketers. Three aspects of such control can be distinguished, namely contractual control of access to broadcasters by means of broadcasting rights contracts, spectator access control through the means of ticket terms, and media accreditation.

The event organizer must have the right to exclusive possession of the venue (either through rights of ownership or through an agreement of lease or other basis), and must be able to control access to the venue, and to stop unauthorized persons entering the venue and exploiting the commercial value of the event. In some cases legislation may come to the aid of organisers or sponsors who own the physical spaces inside or around an event venue.[85] Where the event organizer is not owner of the venue (e.g. as is the case with FIFA and the local stadia for the 2010 World Cup), its agreement with the local organizer or venue owner will include requirements to provide a 'clean venue' for the duration of the event.[86] Access control includes the imposition of terms and conditions of entry (usually imposed by means of contractual provisions incorporated on tickets or by means of prominent notices at the venue) which may be utilized to prevent those who enter the venue from commercially exploiting e.g. footage of action on the field of play obtained through the use of private recording or broadcasting equipment (and also, increasingly, to prohibit ambush marketing, as was the case in respect of ticket

---

[85] Compare, for example, the old Transfer of Property Act of 1882 in India, which might assist the owners of stadium walls and perimeter boards—see Shwetashree Majumder and Harsimran Kalra 'The ambush marketing debate', on the web site *Managing Intellectual Property*, 1 September 2010 (available online at the time of writing at http://www.managingip.com/Article/2665113/The-ambush-marketing-debate.html?ArticleId=2665113&p=2).

[86] Compare the position in respect of the Ellis Park stadium in Johannesburg. It was reported in June 2008 that the most lucrative stadium naming rights deal to date in South Africa had been concluded (apparently following two years of negotiation) in respect of the historic Ellis Park rugby stadium, which is now known as the Coca-Cola Park stadium. Coca-Cola International had apparently paid GBP 30 million for the naming rights in a four year deal. The deal does not include the 2010 FIFA World Cup South Africa™, as FIFA has prohibited the use of corporate names for stadia during the event (corporate use will be interrupted during the Exclusive Use Period when FIFA regulations require a 'clean' stadium free of non-FIFA sponsor advertising and marketing rights in terms of the agreement between FIFA and the South African bid committee, and corporate sponsors will not be compensated by FIFA in this regard)—see the report by Moholoa, R 'Blow to corporate stadium names', *The Sowetan*, 7 March 2007.

terms for events ranging from the ICC Cricket World Cup 2007 to the A1 Grand Prix World Cup of Motorsport event in Malaysia[87]). Such control of access rights to the venue may include accreditation of members of the media or of e.g. sports photographers,[88] and in the absence of proper contractual control event organizers may come unstuck and find little sympathy from the law in the event of trespassers.[89]

While it should be remembered that the law generally requires that such imposed terms as contained in tickets or notices should be clearly brought to the attention of spectators at the time of the purchase of the tickets (i.e. reasonable steps should be taken by the event organizer),[90] such ticket terms can provide event organizers with a powerful tool to combat ambush marketing (or for other related purposes[91]). A more worrying aspect, as raised by McKelvey and Grady, is that ticket terms which prohibit 'ambush marketing' by spectators often don't define the term, which arguably leaves it up to the event organizer to determine what is and is not to be deemed ambush marketing activity regardless of the legality of such activity.[92] While individual spectators will rarely engage in

---

[87] Clause 14 of the standard Ticket Terms and Conditions for this event, which was held at the Sepang International Circuit, stated that 'the Ticket Holder shall not engage in any form of Ambush Marketing (Ambush Marketing is an activity by a party which utilizes the publicity value of an event without having any official involvement or connection with the event) and shall not breach or infringe the rights of any sponsors, Suppliers, broadcasters or other parties commercially associated with the event or the venue, nor conduct any unauthorized promotions or other commercial activity'.

[88] The International Rugby Board's 'draconian' media accreditation rules for the 2007 IRB Rugby World Cup in France attracted wide-spread criticism from international press freedom groups. It was reported prior to the 2010 FIFA World Cup that FIFA and local South African media were locked in a stand-off over restrictive terms and conditions imposed by FIFA in respect of media accreditation for the event. At issue appeared to be provisions in the accreditation agreement that would bind publications to the same rules that would bind journalists attending matches and official FIFA events as well as a clause providing that behaviour harmful to FIFA or the Local Organising Committee could be punished by summary withdrawal of accreditation (from a report on www.legalbrief.co.za—25 November 2009). For more on media accreditation to major sporting events, see the discussion on the role of the fundamental right to freedom of expression in Chap. 7.

[89] As in the old English case of *Sports and General Press Agency v Our Dogs Publishing Co.* [1917] 2 KB 125—see Hewitt 2005, p. 34.

[90] For some South African case law on this, see *King's Car Hire v Wakeling* 1970 (4) SA 640 (N); *Bok Clothing Manufacturers (Pty) Ltd v Lady Land Ltd* 1982 (2) SA 565 (C); *Durban's Water Wonderland (Pty) Ltd v Botha* 1999 (1) SA 982 (A).

[91] A popular ambush technique in the United States is to promote a sweepstakes in which event tickets are a prize. To prevent this, the National Collegiate Athletic Association (NCAA) issues tickets to its annual basketball tournament games as revocable licenses. Under the terms printed on the back, the ticket may be revoked if it is used as a sweepstakes prize without the NCAA's permission. The NCAA brought state law breach of contract and unfair competition claims against a company that nonetheless gave away the tickets as part of a promotion, but the parties settled before the merits of this approach could be determined.

[92] McKelvey and Grady 2008, p. 572.

attempts to ambush an event, shrewd marketers can use (and have done so in the past) groups of spectators in an ambush marketing campaign. Examples are beer maker Bavaria's 'orange lederhosen' campaign amongst Dutch football fans at the 2006 FIFA World Cup in Germany (and the similar stunt by Bavaria at the 2010 FIFA World Cup in South Africa, discussed elsewhere), and the practice of 'message on hold' advertising (where fans are paid to hold up banners or other forms of messages containing advertising for competitor brands etc.).[93] Ticket terms and conditions can also be used to found a basis for cancellation of tickets used in unauthorised competitions (e.g. where a non-event sponsor offers tickets to an event as a prize and impliedly creates an impression of association with the event) or to found breach of contract claims against such competition organisers.[94]

Related to the imposition of contract terms by means of ticket terms or notices, it should be noted that potential ambush marketers may of course also elect to make use of disclaimers in a promotional campaign regarding their lack of official sponsor-status, as a possible means to avoid liability for ambush marketing. The potential efficacy of such disclaimers, however, is open to some doubt[95] (although it would clearly be a question to be decided on a case-by-case basis[96]).

Finally, in respect of combating ambush marketing at event venues, it should also be noted that organisers often deploy 'hit squads' to police the venue and remove or conceal offending advertising or products for sale:

> [Olympic] Games organizers are required to provide a clean venue. This is not just a venue devoid of the advertising messages and media, but control of all forms of commercial activity, including concessions, franchises, and type of food sold in restaurants. Such agreements will even specify the credit card to be accepted and the brand of soft drink to be served. Once a clean venue has been achieved and sponsor brands installed, the next

---

93 See Johnson 2007, p. 11. As Johnson points out, this practice was in fact named after an Australian company (Messages on Hold) which pioneered this form of advertising.

94 Vassallo et al. 2005, p. 1341 discuss the argument pursued by the relevant sports event organiser in the matter of *NCAA v Coors Brewing Co.* 2002 US Dist. LEXIS 21059 (S.D. Ind. October 25, 2002), where Coors had used NCAA Men's Basketball tournament tickets as a prize in a promotional campaign. The NCAA claimed that this constituted breach of a revocable license in light of the wording on the tickets (the matter was eventually settled). In respect of the 210 FIFA World Cup, see Schimmel, G and Green, C 'Ambushed by a ticket?' *Without Prejudice* June 2008 supra at 17:

'FIFA has strict processes around the purchase of tickets, so tickets that are resold, or given away in unauthorised competitions, may well be cancelled. This is because their use is against the General Terms and Conditions relating to the ticket sale, which will have been signed by the person purchasing the ticket. The innocent consumer who believes that he or she has won a ticket to a match may well be turned away at the stadium. Hence, the initial advertising for the competition could be regarded as misleading'.

Regulations prohibiting the unauthorised promotion and resale of tickets for the 2010 FIFA World Cup were proclaimed in April 2009.

95 See Vassallo et al. 2005, p. 1355.

96 Compare the successful use of a disclaimer as found by the court in the Canadian case of *National Hockey League v Pepsi-Cola Canada* (1995) 122 DLR (4th) 412.

task is to police infringements of agreements. To this end special ambush hit squads are used to monitor all venues at which Olympic events are taking place.[97]

The IOC's clean venue requirements, of course, relate to the prohibition of advertising (the IOC does not allow visible advertising within its venues, first banning such advertising in outrage at in-stadium advertising at the 1924 Olympics in Paris).[98] Michael Payne, former marketing manager of the IOC, has expressed pride in the IOC's ability to maintain its clean venue policy in the face of the global television audience for the Games and the 'growing commercial pressures' (and he relates an amusing instance where he had to authorise an IOC manager to break into a McDonalds restaurant in the Atlanta Games Olympic village to switch off a neon sign so that it wouldn't show up on television in the athletes parade during the opening ceremony).[99] In contrast to the IOC, other governing bodies such as FIFA also require venues to be 'clean', but in the sense of not containing advertising by competitors of its official sponsors in order to facilitate re-branding the venue for its rights holders. FIFA also prohibits the use of corporate names for stadia in terms of existing stadium naming rights agreements during its events (e.g. corporate use is interrupted during the Exclusive Use Period of the World Cup event when FIFA regulations requires a clean stadium free of non-FIFA sponsor advertising and marketing rights in terms of the agreement between FIFA and the local organising committee, and corporate sponsors are generally not compensated by FIFA in this regard).[100] This practice was started at the 2006 FIFA World Cup in Germany, where more than half the stadia were re-named to 'FIFA WM Stadion', seeing the removal of billboards and other signage of existing stadium naming rights holders to the venues in what was described by one FIFA representative as a 'culture shock' for the host cities.[101]

McKelvey and Grady observe that 'perhaps no tactic of sponsorship program protection has seen a more proactive and arguably aggressive approach' than on-site policing at event venues by means of 'ambush patrols'.[102] Efforts to preserve a

---

[97] Michael Payne, marketing director of the International Olympic Committee, describing one of the legs of the IOC's strategy to protect the Olympic Games from ambush marketing, in Payne 1998. Canadian law professor John Heshka points out that it is noteworthy that the IOC invokes the language of war in defending its intellectual property rights through the use of special ambush 'hit squads'. Such repetitive use of hyperbolic terms and appropriation of rights which it may not necessarily possess has normalized its heavy-handed approach—from personal correspondence with the author, December 2011.

[98] See Rule 51.2 of the Olympic Charter (2010):

'No form of advertising or other publicity shall be allowed in and above the stadia, venues and other competition areas which are considered as part of the Olympic sites. Commercial installations and advertising signs shall not be allowed in the stadia, venues or other sports grounds'.

[99] Payne 2006, pp. 141–143.

[100] For more on in-stadium advertising at (mega-)events, see the case study of the 2000 Sydney Olympic Games and of the 1999 FIFA Under-17 World Football Championships in new Zealand in Scherer et al. 2005.

[101] As recounted in McKelvey and Grady 2008, p. 567.

[102] McKelvey and Grady 2008, p. 565.

clean venue include policing not only what clothing spectators may wear or what signs they may carry, but also the beverages they plan to consume at the event—a potentially risky tactic.[103] The 2003 ICC Cricket World Cup in South Africa saw a much-publicised (and criticised) episode of a spectator being ejected from a match for refusing to relinquish his Coca-Cola cans to security staff attempting to protect Pepsi's sponsorship of the event, and similar plans are apparently in place for the 2012 London Olympics.[104] International Rugby Board officials reportedly patrolled match venues at the 2007 IRB Rugby World Cup with masking tape, covering 'offending' clothing labels on players' tracksuits (something that the IOC has also been reported to engage in). One wonders how far the use of masking tape may potentially go, when considering that athletes are sometimes contractually prohibited from engaging in much more than just wearing illicit logos on their clothing. The Olympic Charter, in the bye-laws to Rule 51, includes a prohibition on athletes' use of advertising on clothing, and this provision has even been cemented into domestic laws (for example, in the Olympic Act passed by the Russian Federation for purposes of the hosting of the 2014 Sochi Winter Games[105]). Olympic athletes are required to enter into Team Member Agreements prior to the Games, as a condition of selection and participation at the event. Such agreement, which incorporates elements of the Olympic Charter, sets down rules about the athlete's behaviour and includes respect for official sponsors, for example:

> Athletes may not wear, have tattooed, branded, painted, shaved, cut, pierced, applied or affixed to, into or onto their body (including… spectacles or contact lenses) any name, logo or design of any commercial or political entity.[106]

While seemingly rather bizarre, the event organisers have had to play catch-up with developments in practice through the use of these types of provisions. Linford

---

[103] McKelvey and Grady 2008, p. 565.

[104] According to Dalton Odendaal, senior sponsorship lawyer for London 2012, as quoted in an April 2008 BBC report (available online at the time of writing at http://news.bbc.co.uk/2/hi/business/7364391.stm).

[105] Article 6(2) of the 'Olympic and Paralympic Act', Federal Law No. 310-FZ (approved by the Federation Council on 23 November 2007) provides as follows:

'During the period of the holding of the Olympic Games and the Paralympic Games, any advertising on sportswear, accessories or sports equipment to be used by athletes or other participants in the Olympic Games and the Paralympic Games shall be permitted only in instances and upon the terms stipulated by the Olympic Charter'.

[106] From the document entitled 'Protecting Sponsors at the London 2012 Olympics', by solicitor Liz Ellen, as available online at the time of writing on the web site of international law firm Mishcon de Reya at http://www.mishcon.com/assets/managed/docs/downloads/doc_2413/Protecting_Sponsors_at_the_London_2012_Olympics_doc_(2).pdf). See Bye-law 1 to Rule 51 of the Olympic Charter (2010), which provides as follows:

'No form of publicity or propaganda, commercial or otherwise, may appear on persons, on sportswear, accessories or, more generally, on any article of clothing or equipment whatsoever worn or used by the athletes or other participants in the Olympic Games, except for the identification… of the manufacturer of the article or equipment concerned, provided that such identification shall not be marked conspicuously for advertising purposes'.

Christie, the then defending 100 metres champion, famously appeared at a press conference during the 1996 Atlanta Olympic Games wearing blue contact lenses with the Puma logo clearly visible in the centre of each eye. Normally such athlete conduct is subject to truly scary sanctions in the wide world of sports—compare Chicago Bears linebacker Brian Urlacher, who was fined USD 100,000 by the NFL for wearing a cap that promoted a sponsor not authorized by the league during the 2007 Super Bowl media day![107]

There must, however, surely be some rational, common sense limit as to how far it all goes. At the 2008 Beijing Olympics enforcement efforts included the IOC reportedly ensuring 'that fixtures and fittings that aren't made by official sponsors, including toilet bowls and paper dispensers, are being covered by grey tape at the sports venues, and patrols are dispatched daily to ensure they stay that way'[108]—this was not the first time that manufacturers' logos on toilets had come under scrutiny.[109] This must, surely, be one of the least glamorous and rewarding jobs in the world, and presumably one not frequently boasted about at dinner parties by those involved. Although they'll probably enjoy swopping stories of their adventures with the car guards at the Kaiserslautern stadium in Germany where, during the 2006 FIFA World Cup, as the Australian team and their entourage entered the stadium in their official Hyundai team bus, the Mercedes-Benz behind them carrying their equipment and training supplies was barred from entering.[110]

Another, related form of protection against ambushing for event organisers and official sponsors is to be found in the 'marketing exclusion zones' or 'exclusive use zones' that are increasingly being instituted around event venues (i.e. an area within which commercial activities by non-sponsors and any other parties who have no commercial arrangements in place with the event organiser are prohibited on match days or otherwise—this includes advertising, street vending and other activities). Host cities' justification for imposing on their citizens often harsh and seemingly draconian rules to regulate the conduct and the freedom of movement of those on the ground in host cities range from sometimes involved and high-browed explanations of the obligations undertaken in host city contracts and the imminent dangers of ambush marketing, to the flowery sales talk of Bid Books ('London will become a Host City with an unmistakable air of celebration and excitement… We want to create a backdrop fit for celebration on a truly global scale'[111]), and to the

---

[107] As referred to by McKelvey and Grady 2008, p. 571.

[108] The IOC's marketing chairman for the event, Gerhard Heiberg, as quoted on the www.GamesBids.com web site (available online at the time of writing at http://www.gamesbids.com/eng/other_news/1216133637.html).

[109] McKelvey and Grady 2008, p. 565 recount how brand names of toilets were covered with tape at the curling site for the 2006 winter Olympics in Turin.

[110] Schwab 2006, p. 8.

[111] From the UK Department of Culture, Media and Sport's consultation document on Regulations on Advertising Activity and Trading Around London 2012 March 2011 at 5—available online at the time of writing at http://www.culture.gov.uk/images/publications/ConDoc_Regulations_on_Advertising_and_Trading_London_2012-section1-7.pdf.

more prosaic and downright blunt (e.g., in justifying the need for street trading regulations in London for the 2012 Olympics: 'To ensure the free flow of spectators to venues we need to limit the number of additional people taking up space on the pavements'[112]). While involving a form of control over access to venues, these exclusion zones are usually created in terms of legislation or municipal host city by-laws, and as such will be discussed in more detail in Chap. 4 and elsewhere[113] below.

3.3.4 Advertising and Sponsorship Codes of Practice

Advertising watchdog agencies can play an important role in cases of alleged ambushing, as a non-judicial (and less expensive) means of having complaints by official sponsors or governing bodies adjudicated. In the UK, for example, the 2009 Six Nations rugby tournament saw a complaint to the UK's Advertising Standards Authority (or ASA) by the Rugby Football Union against the makers of Fuller's London Pride Ale, which concerned a regional magazine ad depicting a pair of rugby posts and containing text stating (inter alia) 'Support English Rugby'. The complainants claimed that this was an attempt at ambushing the event and the England rugby team, in light of the fact that Fuller's was not an official sponsor, and was allegedly attempting to imply such an association and that it was endorsed by the England team. Fuller's response was that it had not used trade marks or included any claims of being an 'official sponsor' or 'official partner' of the event, and that it had actively supported English rugby for a decade and was the official beer for several English rugby clubs and competitions. The ASA found that readers of the ad were unlikely to be misled into thinking that Fuller's were an official sponsor or partner of the England rugby team and that it was also not misleading because Fuller's did in fact support English rugby. The ASA rejected the complaint.[114]

Similar advertising industry watchdog organisations are found in many jurisdictions. Section 3.1 of the Advertising Standards Authority of South Africa (ASASA)'s *Sponsorship Code* (a code of conduct for those engaged in sponsorship in inter alia sport)[115] defines 'sponsorship' as follows:

> Sponsorship is a form of marketing communication whereby a sponsor contractually provides financial and/or other support to an organization, individual, team, activity, event and/or broadcast in return for rights to use the sponsor's name and logo in connection with a sponsored event, activity, team, individual, organization or broadcast. The objective of investing in sponsorship is to create a positive association between a sponsor's image, product or brand and a sponsored event or activity, team, individual, organization or broadcast, within the sponsor's target market in order to attain marketing and corporate objectives.

---

[112] Ibid.

[113] In Chap. 7.

[114] See http://asab.org.uk/ASA-action/Adjudications/2009/7/Fuller-Smith-and-Turner-plc/TF_ADJ_46480.aspx.

[115] The Code is available on the ASA's web site at http://www.asasa.org.za.

The ASASA is an independent body established and funded by the advertising industry 'to ensure that its system of self-regulation works in the interests of the public'. The ASASA runs a Sponsorship Dispute Resolution Committee and a Sponsorship Appeals Committee, which consists of member of the signatories to the Code within the advertising industry, and rulings are made by peers. While the Code is not legally enforceable, the ASASA may advise persons of their rights and obligations. Rulings by the ASASA or a Committee may include orders for the withdrawal of advertising as well as other sanctions on members of the industry (e.g. withholding advertising space or referral to a disciplinary hearing).[116] While this code of conduct is therefore hardly a primary weapon in the arsenal of sponsors, who will need to enforce their rights through the applicable branch of intellectual property law (e.g. copyright or trade mark protection), common law actions (e.g. in cases of passing off) or actions for breach of contract, it does provide a possible avenue for action against persons or organizations within the advertising industry in cases of questionable practices relating to sports sponsorship. This may include cases of ambush marketing. The ASASA hears an average of 4,000 complaints per year, of which approximately 96% are brought by members of the public, and 4% from competitors of business undertakings. Roughly 47% of such complaints relate to instances of alleged misleading claims in advertising.

The ASASA in 2008 heard a complaint related to (sports) sponsorship (in terms of its Sponsorship Code) in football. The dispute arose out of an advertisement by mobile phone network MTN, which ran a newspaper advertisement during 2007 with the bold heading 'Turning Young Men into Bafana Bafana'.[117] Rival mobile telephone network Vodacom, the official national team sponsor, brought a complaint against MTN, claiming that the advertisement infringed Vodacom's sponsorship rights which it had obtained from the SA Football Association (SAFA). It was also alleged that SAFA had registered the word 'Bafana Bafana' as a trade mark for mobile phone services and that Vodacom had been given the right to use the mark in advertising, and that MTN's advertisement constituted infringement of such trade mark. The ASASA ruled against MTN (which was not an official football sponsor associated with the national team), and the ruling was taken on appeal to the ASASA's Sponsorship Appeals Committee. The Appeals Committee upheld the ruling in May 2008, finding that MTN's conduct implied a joint sponsorship of the national football team by MTN and Vodacom, and as such constituted ambush marketing.[118] The Committee held that MTN was in breach of

---

[116] See, generally, the provisions of the Code.

[117] Referring to the popular nickname of the national football team (and translated, roughly, as 'our boys').

[118] From a briefing by Ms Lillian Mlambo, ASA Communications Manager, Cape Town, 23 June 2008.

the Sponsorship Code's provision regarding 'Imitation and Confusion', which provides that 'imitation of the representation of other sponsorships should be avoided if this misleads or generates confusion, even when applied to non-competitive products, companies or events'.

The Committee's ruling has been criticized as being confusing; e.g. the Committee's finding that Vodacom could not claim an exclusive right to the use of the words 'Bafana Bafana', but that a competitor in the same industry was not entitled to use those words to promote its own event.[119] It also appears that the Committee ruled that sponsorship is under no statutory control, but solely under the control of the ASASA Sponsorship Code, which ignores the role of the relevant ambush marketing legislation.[120] ASASA also heard a similar complaint against Hyundai, who had made an ad depicting a Bafana player in the national team jersey. The ad was viewed as clear case of ambush marketing, and Hyundai withdrew it and vowed not to engage in similar ads in future without the SA Football Association's consent.[121]

It is debatable to what extent the ASASA Sponsorship Code may serve to address instances of illegitimate sports sponsorship activities in future and, specifically, to what extent its available processes for lodging complaints will serve as a satisfactory avenue for redress for those whose commercial or other interests are affected by such sponsorship conduct or activities.[122] Industry watchdogs such as the ASASA and its counterparts in other countries (for example, the Advertising Standards Council of India; or CONAR, the Brazilian Advertising Self-Regulation Council, which is a private entity created in 1980 by local advertisers, advertising agencies and media companies, and which has specific ambush marketing rules in terms of its Code of Ethics) are sometimes viewed as mostly toothless bodies, due mainly to the lack of the level of meaningful sanctions that the law provides. Their role in respect of combating ambush marketing (especially in the light of the other possible measures that are available to sponsors, sports governing bodies and commercial partners) might be a marginal one.

---

[119] From a report available on *Marketingweb*, 5 June 2008.

[120] Such as the Merchandise Marks Act, 1941 (as amended), which is discussed below.

[121] See the report 'Ambush marketing crackdown in South Africa...', 28 July 2009, available online at the time of writing at http://burtonsportsmgmt.blogspot.com/2009/07/ambush-marketing-crackdown-in-south.html.

[122] In November 2009 the ASA rejected a claim in terms of its Advertising Code by SA Rugby against beer maker Windhoek Lager, relating to the use of the (national) colours green and gold in its advertising (and reference to Windhoek Lager as 'the green and gold beer'). SA Rugby had claimed that Windhoek had attempted to create the impression of an association with the national team, the Springboks, while Castle Lager has been the official sponsor since 1992. The ASA rejected the claim but advised SA Rugby to submit a claim in terms of the ASA Sponsorship Code. It is expected that, in line with the earlier finding in the Bafana Bafana matter, Windhoek's conduct will probably be found to contravene the Sponsorship Code's 'Imitation and Confusion' provisions.

3.3.5 *Intellectual Property Rights and Common Law Unlawful Competition Protection*

Very little will be said here regarding these two very important potential sources of remedies against ambush marketing, as both intellectual property (IP) rights protection and the common law action for unlawful competition (specifically passing off) will be examined in more detail in Chap. 5 and elsewhere below, in the context of evaluating the legitimacy of legislative anti-ambush marketing protection in different jurisdictions.

Crow and Hoek[123] have identified the fact that intellectual property protection against ambush marketing has a limited role in many cases, especially when event organisers or sponsors are confronted with the more imaginative of 'ambush' marketing strategies:

> Before the introduction of specific legislation to address the potential for ambush marketing, event owners and sponsors had to rely on trademark and fair trading statutes. However, very few ambushers use the exact logos or insignia of the event owner; instead, ambushers typically create alternative devices that connote the event or team without breaching registered trademarks. The New Zealand "Ring Ring" case[124] illustrates the imaginative use of a visual device that, on close reading clearly refers to the Olympic Ring symbol… Similarly, Pepsi's use of [National Hockey League] teams' home towns,[125] instead of the team names themselves, avoided breaching trademarked names.

This limitation of IP law to provide comprehensive protection against ambush marketing is also well explained by Majumder and Kalra:

> The inadequacy of a traditional IP law framework to provide protection to an event and the rights licensed to the sponsor lie at the sub-stratum of what IP represents. IP protection

[123] Crow and Hoek 2003, p. 11.

[124] In the parody case of *New Zealand Olympic and Commonwealth Games Association, Inc v Telecom New Zealand* (1996) F.S.R. 757 the New Zealand Olympic Association (NZOA) sought an action against Telecom New Zealand regarding one of its highly publicized advertisements. The advertisement, which was published in several magazines and newspapers, featured the word 'Ring' in positions strikingly similar to those of the five rings of the Olympic symbol, in the following manner:

Ring Ring Ring
Ring Ring

[The word 'ring' was used as a play on the ringing of a telephone, in light of the advertiser's product.] Beneath the word arrangement was the slogan, 'With Telecom mobile, you can take your own phone to the Olympics'. The NZOA alleged that the advertisement amounted to passing off because it quite clearly suggested a falsified association between Telecom and the Olympics. The court, in adjudicating upon the issue of passing off, found that the typical newspaper reader tended to browse advertisements and would not read them in a closely focused way. Accordingly, the advert would simply be mildly amusing and seem like a cartoon or clever device to the reader. Further it was held that it is 'a long way from brief amusement to an assumption that this play on the Olympic five circles must have been with the authority of the Olympic organization, or through sponsorship of the Olympics'.

[125] See the *National Hockey League* case referred to in note 83 above.

> typically envisages two constants and one variable—the proprietor's trade/service mark and the goods or services to which it is applied are the constant, while the variable is the identical/similar trade or service mark that a third party adopts to give off an impression of affiliation to the proprietor. The introduction of a third dimension, for example an event, which circumscribes a trade mark owner's right, nullifies the traditional enquiry as to the identity of an infringer. Typically, in an ambush marketing scenario, the ambush marketer uses his own trade mark as his purpose is not to give off an impression of affiliation with the sponsor's trade mark but to create a nexus between the event and his own mark. Thus there can be no confusion or deception between the two trade marks *per se*—consumer confusion is at best in the context of the relationship between the sponsor and the ambush marketer to the event for which they are both using their marks. Thus there can be no infringement.[126]

In other cases, of course, where ambush marketers clearly misappropriate intellectual property or infringe on IP rights of event organisers or sponsors, relief may be available in terms of such IP rights, for example in South Africa in terms of mainly the Trade Marks Act[127] and the Copyright Act.[128] Organisations such as FIFA have thus prioritised its programme to register trademarks and otherwise protect the IP rights in its logos, emblems etc.[129] Generally, event organisers are

---

[126] Shwetashree Majumder and Harsimran Kalra 'The ambush marketing debate', on the web site *Managing Intellectual Property*, 1 September 2010 (available online at the time of writing at http://www.managingip.com/Article/2665113/The-ambush-marketing-debate.html?ArticleId=2665113&p=2).

[127] Act 194 of 1993.

[128] Act 98 of 1978.

[129] Compare the following description of initiatives in this regard as available on FIFA's web site (at http://www.fifa.com/aboutfifa/marketing/marketing/rightsprotection/index.html):

'After its sporadic beginnings in 1994 with 258 cases across 39 countries, the problem [of ambush marketing and abuse of IP] first became a major concern when the 1998 FIFA World Cup ™ was held in France and 773 infringements of registered marks were discovered in 47 countries. Eight years on, 3,300 rights infringements were uncovered in 84 countries in relation to the 2006 FIFA World Cup ™. By contrast, when the 2002 event took place in Japan and Korea, there had been 1,884 cases in 94 countries, and with three and a half years to go until the 2010 FIFA World Cup™, there have already been 127 cases of rights' abuses, 70% of them in the host nation, South Africa. 19 of these incidents related to counterfeit products that have been confiscated by South African customs, thus illustrating the efficiency of FIFA's rights protection programme… FIFA has been implementing its rights protection programme in close collaboration with various authorities—within the host nation and elsewhere—including police forces, customs authorities, patent offices and public prosecutors. More than 150 international specialists help the FIFA rights protection team to register marks and protect them at local level… FIFA's rights protection programme is founded on national and international mark protection laws and anti-trust laws. The trademarks registered by FIFA bear the ™ insignia to make it easier for users around the globe to recognise that these marks are protected. FIFA has registered a raft of picture and word marks for its many competitions—no easy or cheap undertaking. For the Official Emblem of the 2010 FIFA World Cup ™, a total of 1,808 commercial samples were checked in a range of markets so as to avoid any nasty and costly surprises after the mark's registration… Following months of exchanges between top international legal specialists on intellectual property, it was finally possible to register the definitive design with the relevant patent offices in May 2006—just before the 2006 FIFA World Cup ™ kicked off in Germany. The Official Emblem that was publicly unveiled on 7 July 2006 has since been protected in an unprecedented

encouraged to obtain IP protection for relevant material such as emblems, logos, anthems, official event mascots, etc., through e.g. trade mark or design registration. Upon acquisition of such rights, organisers can then license the IP for use by official sponsors in terms of the relevant sponsorship agreements.

I will not examine the requirements for registration of trademarks or the relevant trademark infringement provisions as found in different legal systems here, nor the copyright protection of e.g. symbols (or the *sui generis* protection that is available elsewhere for certain well-known symbols such as the Olympic Rings).[130] The reader is referred to detailed discussion elsewhere[131] (and I will deal in more detail with the role of trademark law in Chap. 5).

Mention has been made above of the fact that ambush marketing (especially association ambushes) will often constitute passing off under the common law. Where an ambush marketer attempts to deceive the public into believing that it is associated with an event, the event organiser or official sponsor will often have a remedy if it is able to show 'the classical trinity of reputation (or goodwill), misrepresentation and damage'.[132] As the traditional formulation of the wrong of passing off by the then Appellate Division in the South African case of *Capital Estate and General Agencies (Pty) Ltd v Holiday Inns Inc*[133] provides:

> The wrong known as passing off consists in a representation by one person that his business (or merchandise, as the case may be) is that of another, or that it is associated with that of another, and, in order to determine whether a representation amounts to a passing off, one enquires whether there is a reasonable likelihood that members of the public may be confused into believing that the business of the one is, or is connected with, that of another … Whether there is a reasonable likelihood of such confusion arising is, of course, a question of fact which will have to be determined in the light of the circumstances of each case.

The relevance of the passing off action in the context of ambush marketing is well illustrated in another South African case, the 1994 judgment of the (then) Transvaal Provincial Division of the High Court in *Federation Internationale de*

(Footnote 129 continued)
153 countries and in several hundred product categories. By comparison, the "laughing faces" emblem of the 2006 FIFA World Cup ™ was protected in 124 nations. Meanwhile, the FIFA World Cup Trophy, the most recognisable sporting trophy in the world, has over 700 mark protection entries in 134 countries'.

[130] Compare the protection of the Olympic symbol in terms of the Nairobi Treaty on the Protection of the Olympic Symbol, 1980, which is administered by the World Intellectual Property Organisation (WIPO)—for more on this treaty, see Johnson 2007, p. 99 et seq.

[131] See Johnson 2007, Chaps. 2 and 3; Kelbrick 2008; Scaria 2008, Chap. 3.

[132] As per Harms JA in *Caterham Car Sales and Coach Works Ltd v Birkin Cars (Pty) Ltd* 1998 (3) SA 938 (SCA). For further discussion of the passing off action in the context of ambush marketing, see Johnson 2007, par 3-03 to 3-22; Scaria 2008, pp. 67–76.

[133] 1977 (2) SA 916 (A) at 929. See also *Premier Trading Co (Pty) Ltd v Sporttopia (Pty) Ltd* 2000 (3) SA 259 (SCA).

Football Association (FIFA) and Others v Bartlett and Others.[134] In this matter FIFA, along with a number of foreign companies involved in the licensing of trade marks, emblems and other intellectual property associated with the football World Cup, sought relief against the respondent, Bartlett, who had designed a trade mark in 1965 which consisted of the words 'world cup' superimposed on a map of the world device. In 1969, Bartlett had registered the trade mark in the South African trade marks registry, in class 25 (for use in respect of 'men's clothing and footwear') and in class 28 (in respect of 'soccer equipment'). In 1989 Bartlett assigned the trade marks with goodwill to a company of which he was a director, and also afforded the right to exploit the trade marks between June 1993 and December 1994 to a sportswear marketing and manufacturing company.

The applicants alleged that Bartlett and the other respondents had embarked on a campaign of unlawful conduct in South Africa which was calculated to cause serious irreparable damage to them. It was alleged that the respondents were, by their conduct and in certain correspondence, making misrepresentations to the effect that they held the licensing rights in South Africa in respect of World Cup USA 1994, and that Bartlett was attempting to extract commission and royalty payments from the applicants' sponsors and sub-licensees. The applicants sought (inter alia) the following relief:

(i) An interdict based on passing off and unlawful competition;
(ii) An order in terms of section 18 of the (then applicable) Trade Marks Act[135] to the effect that the words 'world cup' contain 'matter common to the trade or otherwise of a non-distinctive character'. The applicants sought an order to the effect that an amendment be made of the registered trade marks by adding a disclaimer stating that '[r]egistration of the trade mark shall give no right to the exclusive use of the words "world cup" separately and apart from the mark'; and
(iii) (in the alternative), an order for the expungement of the Bartlett trade marks from the trade marks register on the grounds of non-use in terms of the (then applicable) section 36(1)(b) of the Trade Marks Act.

The court, in evaluating the evidence in respect of the claim based on unlawful competition, evaluated the state of South African law at the time with regard to the practice of character merchandising. The same court had in 1981, in the case of *Lorimar Productions Inc and Others v Sterling Clothing Manufacturers (Pty) Ltd*,[136] held that character merchandising was not so well-known in South Africa that the court could 'without proper evidence in this regard assume that the man in the street will have any knowledge thereof'. In *Bartlett*, the court by way of Joffe J held that markets may have changed in the years since Lorimar, and that a mass of evidence was available to conclude that character merchandising had taken hold in

[134] 1994 (4) SA 722 (TPD). See also the brief discussion of this case in Kelbrick 2008. See also discussion in Sect. 4.4.5 of Chap. 4 regarding the matter of *FIFA v Metcash Trading Africa (Pty) Ltd*, South Gauteng High Court, Case No. 53304/07.

[135] Act 62 of 1963. This Act was replaced by the Trade Marks Act 194 of 1993.

[136] 1981 (3) SA 1129 (T).

South Africa and that the man in the street would have knowledge thereof and would make the link between the merchandising property and the events or circumstances which made it famous (and that such link is established by licensing or a license).[137] The court described the practice of character merchandising as follows:

> Character merchandising is defined as being the business of merchandising popular names, characters and insignia in order to enhance the sales of consumer products in relation to which such names and characters are used... The association of a famous person or character with a consumer product can boost that product's sales considerably. The fame and popularity of the name or character in question enhances the desirability of the product from the consumer's point of view. The association between the name or character, which can be referred to as the 'merchandising property', and the consumer product is usually created by depicting the merchandising product prominently on the product. A typical merchandising product is the well-known cartoon character Mickey Mouse. As the proprietor of the merchandising property has already invested substantial time and money in developing and popularizing such character, and it is the fame and desirability of the merchandising property which will promote the sale of the goods to which it is applied, the proprietor of the merchandising property charges a royalty of license fee for the use of his merchandising property. The royalty is payable in terms of a license agreement under which the owner of the merchandising property authorizes the licensee to utilize the merchandising property in relation to his goods ... It appears that the consumer makes a connection and an association between the character and its creator or owner and the products featuring the character.[138]

The court continued to hold as follows:

> Although not constituting character merchandising in the strict sense, licensing the use of properties such as the Barcelona Olympic Games logo, the Olympic rings device, the Davis Cup tennis logo and logos associated with other major international sporting events, such as the World Cup soccer tournament, can be regarded as character merchandising in the broad sense. [W]hen an event like the World Cup soccer tournament is in the public eye, use of the insignia symbolizing such an event in relation to clothing and similar goods will cause the public to believe that such goods have a trade connection with the events symbolized by the insignia. A link is established between the goods featuring the merchandising property and the person who or entity which is the original source of the material which launched the merchandising property on its path to fame and fortune.[139]

On this basis, the court found that the respondents' character merchandising conduct *in casu* constituted the tort of passing off, with reference to the definition of passing off as formulated in the earlier *Capital Estate* case.[140] The court reiterated that the unlawfulness of passing off, as a form of wrongful competition, is to be found in the fact that 'it results, or is calculated to result, in the improper filching of another's trade and an improper infringement of his goodwill and/or

[137] At 738B of the *Bartlett* judgment.

[138] At 736E-J of the *Bartlett* judgment.

[139] At 737B-D of the judgment.

[140] 1977 (2) SA 916 (A).

because it may cause injury to the other's trade reputation'.[141] On the basis of this the court held that the respondents were guilty of passing off and unlawful competition, sufficient to grant the order claimed by the applicants[142]:

> The evidence clearly established that the applicants and their licensees have a reputation and goodwill in South Africa. This is established by the fact that various prominent retailers ... are anxious to obtain and pay for licenses from the applicants for the purpose of manufacturing and marketing clothing bearing the World Cup insignia. Furthermore, by reason of the fact that applicants are engaged in character merchandising, it is sufficient to create in the public's mind a link between the merchandising product and the applicants. As a result of the conduct of [respondents] the applicants are likely to suffer injury or damage. Firstly, the applicants and their licensees are likely to lose revenue and, secondly, because of the uncertainty created by their conduct, potential licensees are refraining from entering into licensing agreements with the applicants, thereby depriving the applicants of income.

Accordingly, the court made an order prohibiting the respondents from using the words 'world cup' together with the words '1994' and/or '94' and/or 'America' and/or 'USA'. The court's further findings regarding the respondents' use of the registered trade marks and of copyright infringement will not be discussed here.

I will not say more here about passing off and its possible role in providing a cause of action against ambush marketers of sports mega-events. It does bear noting, however, that claims based in passing off have been unsuccessful in this context in the past (compare the *National Hockey League v Pepsi-Cola Canada* case as well as the *New Zealand Telecom* case, which I refer to elsewhere), and that proving passing off may be problematic for event organisers or official sponsors. Ellis et al. explain that 'a company seeking to draft on the goodwill associated with a particular event is not attempting to suggest that their products or services are those of their competitor, the official sponsor. On the contrary, they want to promote themselves as the source of their own products and services—they simply want to benefit from the larger audiences attracted to the event in question. This makes the tort of passing off, particularly the element of misrepresentation, difficult to establish'.[143] In addition, damage or a likelihood of damage to the goodwill of the event organiser or official sponsor may be very difficult to establish, especially by means of survey evidence in the relatively short time frame of a mega-event (and a mega-event ambush campaign).[144]

---

[141] With reference to *Brian Boswell Circus (Pty) Ltd and Another v Boswell Wilkie Circus (Pty) Ltd* 1985 (4) SA 466 (A).

[142] At 739I–740B of the judgment.

[143] Ellis et al. 2011, p. 300.

[144] See Corbett and van Roy 2010, p. 352.

3.3.6 The Use of a Combination of Grounds

At this point the reader should note that ambush marketing protection for mega-events is usually focused on employing a combination of the above-mentioned protection measures (i.e. through contractual arrangements, reliance on intellectual property rights, unfair competition law as well as available legislative provisions—which will be discussed in the next chapter). The IOC developed a three-pronged protection strategy to protect it against ambush marketing (inspired, in significant measure, by Nike's high profile and highly successful ambushing campaigns in respect of the Games):

> Our basic philosophy was that the best defence is a good offence. If a company deliberately overstepped the line we would take no hostages, to set a clear example to the rest of the industry. The second element was to build a fortress around the rights package and block all loopholes. We needed to get the house in order long before a host city was even appointed. We needed to invest in prevention, rather than being caught in a highly expensive and high profile cure. Third, we designed an advertising communications campaign to educate the public on who the sponsors are and let the marketing industry understand the risks and consequences of taking on the Olympic Movement with any unauthorised campaign. There is no doubt that the IOC adopted a very aggressive attitude in protecting its rights and those of the Olympic partners.[145]

McKelvey and Grady have observed that 'the conclusion of each successive major sporting event—arguably beginning with the 1996 Olympic Games in Atlanta—has provided an evolving roadmap to new and arguably more effective sponsorship program protection strategies'.[146] The authors identify as the main components of such strategies a number of the avenues discussed above (namely pre-event education and public relations initiatives; on-site policing ranging from confiscation of non-sponsor products and signage to the creation of 'clean zones'; the use of contractual language in athlete participation agreements and on spectators' tickets; and the enactment and enforcement of special trademark protection legislation).[147] An example of the legal strategy accompanying (and forming an integral part of) such a rights protection programme is well illustrated in the following, 'insider's' description by Dean,[148] of FIFA's aggressive domestic campaign in this regard in respect of the 2010 football World Cup in South Africa, which does well to show how specific (*sui generis*) legal protection can be used by event organisers to facilitate the task of hamstringing potential ambushers:

> The first step was to ensure that [FIFA] could make the most of the favourable [legal landscape to protect against ambush marketing in South Africa]. This meant taking

[145] Payne 2006, p. 145.

[146] McKelvey and Grady 2008, p. 560.

[147] Ibid.

[148] Owen Dean, partner of Spoor and Fisher (one of the large intellectual property law firms representing FIFA in South Africa), writing in Dean, O 'FIFA scores opening goal' *Without Prejudice* May 2009 p. 4–5.

> comprehensive steps to put measures in place to enable it to assert its rights in connection of the 2010 tournament. This entailed embarking on an extensive trade mark registration programme covering trademarks such as SOUTH AFRICA 2010, WORLD CUP 2010. Once the official emblem had been devised, steps were taken to register it widely as a trade mark as well as a design under the Designs Act. To supplement these measures, application was made to the Minister of Trade and Industry to declare the principal trade marks associated with the event as prohibited marks under s15 of the Merchandise Marks Act. All these measures were, however, somewhat secondary to the main thrust of its plan of attack which was to utilise the provisions of s15A of the [Merchandise Marks Act[149]] which empowers the Minister of Trade and Industry to designate major sporting events as so called "protected events"… This object was achieved in May 2006, when the Minister of Trade and Industry published a notice declaring the event to be protected. Having done all the ground work for the implementation of its game plan, the next step was to harmonise and synchronise its players with the game plan. This entailed preparing a template for a civil court case to be brought against an ambush marketer. In so doing groundbreaking causes of action and arguments were formulated. In particular, a method had to be devised to enable FIFA to pursue a civil claim against an ambush marketer based on the anti-ambush marketing provisions of s15A of the Merchandise Marks Act, that create a criminal offence.[150] An unlawful competition argument was formulated utilising the principle that, in breaching the criminal provisions and thus entering into direct competition with FIFA's sponsor's for the 2010 World Cup, ambush marketers were perpetrating conduct which was objectively unlawful, being a criminal offence, and were causing damage to FIFA by prejudicing its relations with its sponsors.

Accordingly, through the use of a whole arsenal of legal measures, sports organizations can establish a well-oiled and imposing juggernaut—a whole, special legal strategy—in order to pre-empt, discourage or challenge ambush marketing practices. Apart from (but allied with) resort to the legal measures, educational campaigns are increasingly important (compare the distribution of FIFA's 'Public Information Sheet', containing a guide to FIFA's protected marks for the 2010 event,[151] and a similar, expensive, public education campaign that was embarked upon by the organisers of the 2004 UEFO Euro football tournament hosted in Portugal). The marketing department of the organisers of the 2008 Beijing Olympic Games, BOCOG, and the China Advertising Association jointly issued an official 'Anti-Ambush Advertising Initiative' in July 2008, which urged advertising companies and practitioners to support business ethics and not to engage in any commercial activity that could mislead the public, provide, or create ambush concepts or advertisements or play 'edge ball' with marketing activities of official Olympic sponsors. VANOC, the organisers of the 2010 Vancouver winter Olympics, was praised for its education campaign and its reportedly more

---

149 See the discussion in Sect. 4.4.5 in Chap. 4.

150 It is very interesting to note that, as Johnson observes (Johnson 2007, p. 141, note 97), the Explanatory Memorandum to the amendment Bill which inserted section 9(d) of the Trade Practices Act (see above) expressly stated that passing off would not be available under the common law in the event of a breach of trade practices law. It is unclear why or to what extent a similar consideration should not apply in respect of the Merchandise Marks Act.

151 Federation Internationale de Football Association (FIFA) 2010 *FIFA World Cup South Africa FIFA Public Information Sheet* (a guide to FIFA's Official Marks).

circumspect approach to potential ambushers. It seems that there has been a growing realisation that, important as the law is in combating ambushing, there may be other, less drastic, methods that are more likely to bring results. Gannon observes this in the context of IP education campaigns in new markets, with specific reference to the efforts of the American NBA in its expansion of the game of basketball into Asian markets:

> [W]hile the threat of legal penalty is necessary to preserve brand integrity in the short term, the mere punishment of offenders is not a long-term solution. No matter how sympathetic lawmakers and courts may be towards official rights holders, IP law cannot keep up with the growing challenges of digital media. Furthermore, it is impossible for the biggest global brands to keep an eye on violators all over the world. Sports properties that rely solely on defensive enforcement will always be playing catch-up. Instead, executives from the most admired sports properties and brands have shifted their focus to prevention and education. As many leagues expand internationally and corporate sponsors launch global advertising campaigns, they are entering markets where legal infrastructure does not necessarily exist, at least at the same maturity as in western countries. Consumers, lawmakers, media and businesses simply do not have a developed understanding of rights protection. While this makes enforcement difficult, smart brands are treating these challenges as opportunities to create new, loyal fans. The NBA has had incredible success expanding its brand and growing the game of basketball internationally, including in Asia, where many counterfeiting operations and online scams originate. They have done so by emphasising IP education and the development of legal infrastructure in their new markets… [T]he NBA spent years devoting significant efforts to stanch the major leak of counterfeit goods from China to the international community. More recently, however, it has focused on developing a good framework on the ground that can support an authorised licensed NBA business in China. This is a better long-term solution… and has helped the NBA to tap into millions of new fans.[152]

The IOC first adopted auditing programmes at the Salt Lake City winter Games in 2002, which included photo audits of commercial activity within the Olympic venues and mystery shopper programmes to detect unauthorised merchandise.[153] It is often prudent for event organisers to follow a 'soft-handed approach' in this regard when dealing with e.g. businesses in the area where an event will be staged.[154] But a more gung ho approach is sometimes employed, as event organisers also more and more frequently use 'name and shame' campaigns against ambushers. Crompton refers to the US Olympic Committee's tendency to threaten ambushers 'with campaigns which would consist of half or full page advertisements in many of the country's major newspapers featuring a photograph of an ambushing company's CEO under the headline, "Thief!"',[155] and compare the IOC's campaign against Nike in 1996 when the retailer dropped their 'didn't win silver, lost gold' campaign in the face of the public exposure. Such name and shame campaigns, may, however, be less than successful and decidedly

152 Gannon 2010, p. 70.

153 Crow and Hoek 2003, p. 11.

154 For an example from the United States, see McKelvey and Grady 2008, pp. 561, 562.

155 Crompton 2004, p. 10.

ill-advised. Jon Heshka observes the following regarding the name and shame campaign by the organisers of the 2010 Vancouver winter Olympics, VANOC, against yoga wear manufacturer Lululemon's perceived ambushing of the event:

> The "name and shame" tactic might make VANOC's lawyers feel like they are doing something in response to being ambushed but it really just plays into the hands of the illicit marketer. Rather than being buried in an avalanche of advertising related to the Olympics, the effect of this approach is to amplify the ambusher's message and make it a major news story. This ill-conceived strategy gives the story "legs" enabling the ambusher even more and longer media exposure and puts the conflict on the front pages of the newspaper instead of being dissolved in the miasma of marketing clutter. The rationale and effectiveness of the "name and shame" tactic is suspect. The legal goal is obviously to protect the intellectual property rights vested in the Olympics so that official sponsors get the maximum return on their investment, and VANOC benefits insofar as being the beneficiary of the sponsorship fees. Underlying the strategy is a dogma that prevents them from seeing the trap set by the ambush marketer.[156]

Another prime example of this type of negative fall-out is that of FIFA's response to the orange-clad 'Bavaria girls' at the 2010 FIFA World Cup, which I refer to elsewhere. And the IRB 'bullies' were roundly criticised for the heavy fines meted out to two participants, brothers Alesana and Manu Tuilagi, during the 2011 IRB Rugby World Cup, for wearing unofficial mouth-guards as part of an alleged 'ambush' (which was vehemently denied by both the players and the company concerned, and which saw fans fundraising to pay the players' fines and people on the internet wanting to know the brand of the mouth-guard so they could support it in defiance of the penalties imposed).[157] Due to an apparent lack of common sense and/or overzealousness born from the extremely wide scope of legal protection provided by lawmakers, event organisers who frequently employ the 'big bad wolf' approach[158] to 'ambushers' are often victims of a self-inflicted PR nightmare—the so called 'Streisand effect'.[159] As a South African Constitutional Court judge expressed it in a case involving a parody defence to a trademark dilution claim (in respect of the sale of t-shirts that parodied a well-known beer brand):

> [O]ne must recognise that litigation could be a risky enterprise for a meritorious trademark owner as well as the prankster. Applicants seeking to interdict the abusive use of their trademarks stand to be involved in lengthy litigation in which every manner of accusation could be made against them by persons from whom no costs could ultimately be recovered. Furthermore, any businesses seen as trying to block free speech could hardly be surprised if the media tended to champion their opponent's cause. Indeed, the very act of

---

156 Heshka 2010, p. 37.

157 See the report 'Harsh fines could backfire on IRB 'bullies'', 4 October 2011, available online at the time of writing at http://tvnz.co.nz/rugby-world-cup/harsh-fines-could-backfire-irb-bullies-4441266.

158 McKelvey, S 'As Games approach, time to reconsider ambush marketing', 28 January 2010, available online at http://www.sportsbusinessdaily.com/Journal/Issues/2010/01/20100118/Opinion/As-Games-Approach-Time-To-Reconsider-Ambush-Marketing.aspx.

159 With apologies to Jon Heshka's wife (whom I understand is a fan). For the reader unfamiliar with this term, see some examples at http://www.thestreisandeffect.com/.

> invoking the heavy machinery of the law might be regarded as being in conflict with the image of freedom, liveliness and good cheer associated with their product brand. Thus, in the present matter simply bringing the proceedings… risked being more tarnishing of [the beer brand's] association with bonhomie and cheerfulness than the sale of 200 hundred T-shirts could ever have done. The principle of litigator beware, however, faces any person contemplating legal action.[160]

I would suggest that the event organisers, such as FIFA, who are in the business of selling a celebration of their sport (which, one would assume, is replete with 'bonhomie and cheerfulness'), should take particular heed of this warning. In fact, as Chap. 7 will show, the UK government has even expressly justified its far-reaching street trading and advertising restrictions as being in the interests of protecting the 'celebratory look and feel of the Games', even to the point of claiming (in my view, quite dubiously) that this justifies potential infringement of fundamental free speech and other rights. Aggressive rights protection measures which sometimes baffle the senses and often severely curtail civil liberties do not have any place in such celebrations.

Of course, it might bear mentioning that an arch cynic (I'm not yet sure whether I answer to this tag) might find something sinister in cases where event organisers make such a public and apparently self-defeating song and dance of cases of ambushing. One method employed in marketing circles to test the efficacy of both sponsorship and ambushes is that of 'recall and recognition',[161] whereby consumer surveys are used to determine the extent of recall by consumers of marketing efforts and their recognition of the role of the relevant marketer *vis a vis* an event. The cynic might argue that such apparently short-sighted conduct by event organisers, which frequently actually serves to raise consumer awareness of the relevant 'ambush', could very well be perpetrated in the hope that surveys would show up the ambush (in cases where a lack of response by the event organiser would otherwise leave the 'ambush' very much under the radar), and thus provide ammunition for future anti-ambushing campaigns or even calls for special legislative protection. I am speculating, rather cynically, and will leave this issue for now.

Apart from the frequent threats of shock and awe, event organisers are also increasingly focusing their efforts on deploying specialist teams of high profile legal advisors in order to take the offensive to the ambush marketers. A 2006 report in UK publication *The Lawyer* colourfully explained the make up and remit of FIFA's rights protection team, under its then head of legal affairs at Marketing

---

160 As per Sachs J in *Laugh It Off Promotions CC v South African Breweries International (Finance) BV t/a Sabmark International and Another* (CCT42/04) [2005] ZACC 7; 2006 (1) SA 144 (CC); 2005 (8) BCLR 743 (CC) (27 May 2005) at par. 104.

161 See Lingling Wei 'Legal regulation of ambush marketing: Where is the base?' Paper presented at the 6th Annual European Policy for Intellectual Property Conference, 8–9 September 2011, Brussels—copy available online at http://www.epip.eu/conferences/epip06/papers/Parallel%20Session%20Papers/WEI%20Lingling.pdf.

and Television, Tom Houseman, and its use of prominent sports industry lawyers in the fight against ambush marketing:

> Houseman's legal dream team lines up in a conventional formation. The defence receives, logs and monitors potential IP infringements. This work is handled in-house in the main. The midfield is made up of permanent trademark advisers—lone playmakers that, according to Houseman, "bridge the gap between the in-house and private practice lawyers". UK trademark adviser David Gill is an ex-Fifa employee and as a result can offer a real insight into how IP works within Fifa's business, according to Houseman. These lawyers hold many of the keys to Fifa's outsourced work and so are important figures for law firms on the outside looking in. Fifa has outsourced some of its work to firms in the major European jurisdictions of Germany, the UK, France, Italy and Spain. Fifa typically turns to Hammonds for its strikers. The national firm handles Fifa's pressing priorities, including the illegal trade in match tickets, ambush marketing and match ticket competitions not sanctioned by Fifa… In the run-up to the World Cup, Hammonds has beefed up its Fifa client team, which now comprises eight lawyers at any one time. And there is plenty of work, with the World Cup just a week away. "At the moment we're getting two or three instructions a day," says Hammonds sports solicitor Stephen Sampson. Hammonds' association with the football body stems from partner Alasdair Bell, who was Uefa's main outside counsel for several years. When he joined Hammonds in 2004 from Olswang, he took the work with him. But Fifa is changing the way it handles its IP and Olswang has been the firm to capitalise in the UK. Olswang partner David Zeffman has been quick off the mark and has scored the mandate to advise Fifa on the auction of its broadcast rights for the 2010 and 2014 World Cups. Houseman, whose first major tournament as an in-house lawyer was Euro 2000, is hopeful that he will have less to do in the future.[162]

FIFA was successful in following the litigation route in South Africa in the run-up to the 2010 World Cup event.[163] While FIFA appears to have had few qualms in doing so in the context of South African business entities attempting to associate themselves or derive benefit from the 2010 event, it should be noted that litigation may not always be advisable for event organizers. A significant practical risk of the litigation route for an organization like FIFA (aside from the costs involved as well as the lengthy duration of such cases) may be the possibility of alienating large corporations who, while not current official sponsors of the relevant event, might want to sponsor the organiser's future events.[164]

In recent years use has also been made of specialist external agencies to assist sports organisations in monitoring and combating potential IP infringement and ambush marketing attempts or activities in respect of events. For example, the International Cricket Council has on a number of occasions contracted the services of Bangalore-based Copyright Integrity International[165] (whose web site describes the organisation as 'a world leader in protecting valuable digital assets and

---

[162] Moshinsky, B 'Forget Argentina and Brazil—this is the real World Cup-winning team', 29 May 2006, *The Lawyer*—available online at the time of writing at http://www.thelawyer.com/forget-argentina-and-brazil-this-is-the-real-world-cup-winning-team/120125.article.

[163] See the discussion in Sect. 4.4.5 in Chap. 4.

[164] Vassallo et al. 2005, p. 1354 mention this possible risk for event organisers in respect of large corporations.

[165] On the web at http://www.copyrightintegrity.com.

intellectual property rights from the threat of online piracy and unlicensed use'), also most recently in respect of the ICC Cricket World Cup 2011 hosted on the Asian sub-continent.

From the perspective of legal theory, one can distinguish three types of legal protection for mega-event commercial interests, which is an important distinction to bear in mind in the evaluation in the later chapters of the legitimacy of the relevant legal protection for event organisers and sponsors. The first is the use of proprietary legal rights of such parties, primarily in the form of intellectual property rights such as trademarks, designs and copyright. The second is the use of non-proprietary measures in the form of pure liability rules, such as the law of passing off in common law systems, fair trade practices laws and breach of contract.[166] The third—which will be considered in more detail in Chap. 8—is the use of *sui generis* event legislation to provide a novel form of legal protection, one that may be akin to the first form of protection (by creating new, statutory 'quasi-IP rights') while also showing certain elements reminiscent of the second. It is especially the proprietary characteristic of the protections afforded by such legislation (i.e. the creation of a new form of ownership of something that, traditionally, cannot be owned by anyone) that is problematic and deserves more in-depth critical theoretical consideration in the later chapters.

It is such legislation that has in recent years been passed in different jurisdictions (including, specifically, the above-mentioned South African legislation—the most stringent currently to be found anywhere) that is most problematic in terms of evaluating the legitimacy of what amounts to state-driven and sanctioned measures to protect narrow commercial interests to mega-events. Anti-ambush marketing legislative protection is not immune to criticism regarding the reach and scope of the measures imposed and their possible effects on the rights of persons and parties other than event sponsors.[167] In particular, it should be noted that the current South African legislative protection which was employed in respect of the 2010 FIFA World Cup South Africa, for example, might be open to constitutional challenge in respect of the effect of restrictions imposed on the rights of others (e.g. in respect of the right of freedom of expression, freedom of trade and occupation, and the right of property, as guaranteed in the South African Bill of Rights[168]). This is especially poignant in the context of South Africa's developmental state with its high levels of poverty, and the urgent need to encourage alternatives to formal employment (e.g. encouraging opportunities for street vendors surrounding major tournaments, although the prevalence of illegal importation of counterfeit goods such as sporting apparel remains problematic). Such considerations are of prime

[166] Louise Longdin specifically refers to this distinction in discussing New Zealand's Major Events Management Act, 2007 (discussed in Chap. 4)—see Longdin 2009, p. 731.

[167] E.g. see the discussion of what Phillip Johnson calls horizontal and vertical 'creep' in respect of the adoption of new legislation on ambush marketing based on developments in other jurisdictions, in Johnson 2008; see also the discussion in Chap. 4.

[168] In sections 16, 22 and 25, respectively, of the Constitution of the Republic of South Africa, 1996.

importance in a number of the other jurisdictions which have elected to employ such special event legislation, including, especially, Brazil, which at the time of writing is wrestling with its own demands from FIFA regarding rights protection and the passing of special legislation for this purpose. It should be noted in this context that the sports industry is in various jurisdictions already subjected to limitations or restraints on freedom of contract, specifically in order to promote the public interest. Examples are sports broadcasting regulations which limit the sale of exclusive broadcasting rights in respect of 'listed events' that are viewed as being of national interest,[169] the prohibition of certain prohibited sponsors in respect of events (e.g. tobacco sponsorship) and competition law restraints on the collective selling of broadcasting rights.[170] The special event legislation which protects narrow commercial rights would appear to be something of an anomaly in this context.

In light of the specific importance of special anti-ambushing event legislation, and its particular place in consideration of the legitimacy of legal responses to 'ambush marketing' of events, the next chapter will specifically consider such legislation as found in a number of jurisdictions. But we must first, in the following section, examine a fundamental issue regarding ambush marketing, which is central to the evaluation of the legitimacy of the applicable laws which I will undertake in the chapters that follow.

3.4 Is All 'Ambushing' Necessarily Ethically, and Legally, Wrong?

Having briefly considered some of the commonly encountered definitions in the literature and the concept of ambush marketing, it remains to consider whether all 'ambushing' is in fact objectionable and, more specifically for purposes of the review in the later chapters, whether it should be outlawed and attract the often substantial civil penalties or even criminal sanctions as found in some jurisdictions. I referred above to intrusion ambushes and, particularly, the fact that they may be problematic in respect of discharging the burden of proof when challenged because of the absence of the element of deception of the public as to a commercial association with an event. However, at a more fundamental level, which is relevant to the question of whether or the extent to which legal regulation

[169] In the South African context, consider the Independent Communications Authority of SA (or ICASA)'s position paper and regulations on 'Sports Broadcasting Rights' of 2003 (Notice 2029, *Government Gazette* No. 25249, 25 July 2003), specifically par.3 and 4. At the time of writing, ICASA has conducted hearings with a view to the publication of updated sports broadcasting rights regulations [compare the discussion paper in this regard which was published as General Notice 1238 of 2008, Government Gazette No. 31483, 2 October 2008 ('Review of Sports Broadcasting Rights Regulations—Discussion Document, September 2008')].

[170] See Hewitt 2005, pp. 35, 36.

(especially by means of legislation) is appropriate and legitimate, it should also be noted that cases of intrusion 'ambushing' may in fact involve conduct that is not even morally or ethically questionable.[171] It has been observed that the very term 'ambush marketing' is an ambiguous one, which raises a number of questions when one considers the practical reality of many of the practices labelled in this way: If a non-sponsor's activity is legal, should it still be deemed to be ambush marketing? If there is no purposeful intent to confuse consumers as to a non-sponsor's association with an event, is it still ambush marketing? If the non-sponsor is legitimately sponsoring a team within a league, well within the league's sponsorship guidelines, is it still ambush marketing? Is it ambush marketing only because the event organizer says it is?[172]

It has been noted that many writers regard the distinction between the narrow (association ambushes) and broader definitions (the latter including intrusion cases) of ambush marketing as important:

> Ambush marketing in the narrow sense commonly contravenes intellectual property and/or trade practices laws, giving a cause of action to the event organiser. In contrast, ambush marketing in the broad sense includes many activities that do not infringe any intellectual property rights or make any misrepresentation as to sponsorship. Furthermore, these activities may involve the use of rights that have been purchased legitimately and at considerable expense. Examples of this broader form of ambush marketing include sponsoring a participating team or athlete, sponsoring the stadium or broadcast, engaging in a campaign that coincides with the event, purchasing advertising time during or around the event broadcast, or giving away tickets in promotions or contests… Given broader definitions of the phrase, the naming of conduct as 'ambush marketing' should not be seen as automatically suggesting that such activity is unethical or 'wrong'. This is a crucial point, as the word 'ambush' may seem pejorative … To the extent that government elects to intervene in these commercial activities and relationships, decisions need to be made about the appropriate level of legislative intervention.[173]

In fact, the person commonly credited with coining the term 'ambush marketing', Jerry Welsh,[174] was apparently at pains to acknowledge this aspect:

> Though today's world considers ambush marketing as something akin to commercial theft, [Welsh] disagrees with this view and explains that in the world of modern marketing,

---

[171] Compare, for example, the finding of the Delhi High Court in India in the matter of *ICC Development (International) Ltd v Arvee Enterprises and Philips* 2003 (26) P.T.C. 245 (Del.), where Philips had offered ICC Cricket World Cup 2003 tickets in a promotional campaign. The court held that there was no likelihood of confusion that Philips was a sponsor of the event, and dismissed passing off and unfair trading claims. In respect of the practice of ambush marketing, the court held that this practice was distinguishable from passing off, as there is no element of deceit in ambush marketing but merely opportunistic commercial exploitation of an event. The court held that this is not contrary to the public interest, and that as long as an official sponsor's trade marks are not used, ambush marketing is not illegal and in line with commercial advertising as free speech in terms of the Indian Constitution—see Vassallo et al. 2005, p. 1347.

[172] McKelvey and Grady 2008, p. 553.

[173] See Frontier Economics 2007, pp. 13, 14.

[174] The marketing strategist who was manager of global marketing for American Express in the 1980s.

sponsor and ambusher are not moral labels to be assigned by the self-appointed arbiters of ethics, but merely the names to be given to two different and complementary, though competing roles played by competitors vying for consumer loyalty and recognition in the same thematic space. According to him, the roots of ambush marketing can be found in the escalating prices and the "distressed imagery of category-exclusive sponsorships".[175]

It has been observed that Welsh subsequently tended to get rather upset with the generally negative perception of ambush marketing and chose to unequivocally pin his colours to the mast of the 'ambushers'. He has been quoted as stating that competitors of official sponsors have 'not only a right, but an obligation to shareholders to take advantage of [major] events', and that 'all this talk about unethical ambushing is … intellectual rubbish and posturing by people who are sloppy marketers'.[176] Similar sentiments have been expressed by Canadian observer Maurice Cardinal, who, in the context of the Olympic Games, prefers to refer to what the IOC calls 'ambush marketing' as alternative ways of 'leveraging Olympic momentum':

> A growing group of mostly large companies do it regularly and with great success. Some business executives maintain, and rightly so, independently leveraging Olympic momentum improves the IOC business model by keeping Olympic organizations on their toes.[177]

American marketing expert and author of an entertaining book on ambush marketing, Kim Skildum-Reid, would appear to agree with this last-expressed opinion, observing that successful ambushes would appear to highlight gaps in the official sponsors' campaigns and a failure to properly leverage such official rights.[178] Jolan Storch, writing about the 2010 Vancouver Winter Games, succinctly explains:

> When Coca-Cola pays the IOC $60 million for worldwide Olympic marketing rights, that's $60 million Pepsi didn't spend that allows them to hire some awesome creative folks to design a campaign that will take advantage of the public attention drawn by the Games, without using even one Olympic ring. The official sponsor has now paid millions for the Olympic rights, but also needs to adequately budget to activate those rights. If they cut back on their activation budget or produce less than stellar creative, it leaves a big hole for their competitors to grab the public's attention. In my view, those who cut back on their activation budgets for Vancouver lost the value of their original investment in the Games and were ripe to be ambushed.[179]

---

175 As per Scaria 2008, p. 30.

176 Crow and Hoek 2003, p. 5 (quoting from Meenaghan 1996).

177 Cardinal, M 'Olympic Brand Ambush Marketing is… (A) a Mortal Sin (B) Good Business Sense (C) None of the Above', *Vancouver Observer*, 29 November 2009 (available online at the time of writing at http://www.vancouverobserver.com/politics/commentary/2009/11/29/olympic-brand-ambush-marketing-isa-mortal-sin-b-good-business-sense-c).

178 From comments posted on Skildum-Reid's sponsorship blog at http://blog.powersponsorship.com.

179 Storch, J 'It's an ambush! Or is it?' *Marketing*, 17 May 2010—available online at http://www.macleoddixon.com/documents/Storch.pdf.

The point about the importance of proper leveraging is, in fact, borne out by recent qualitative research amongst TOP sponsors in respect of the Olympic Games.[180] Seguin and O'Reilly remark (in the Olympics context):

> [A] number of studies… have found a high level of confusion regarding sponsorship… [R]ecent studies… have observed that consumers do not care about ambush marketing and that Olympic organisers are responsible for the lack of consumer awareness and support for sponsors. Perhaps the IOC's emphasis on maximising revenue streams from both sponsorship and broadcasting rights, as opposed to properly protecting the exclusivity of its sponsors, contributed to this confusion.[181]

In this way, the threat of ambushing would appear to provide an opportunity for rights grantors and official sponsors alike to fine-tune exploitation of rights in the marketplace. As Schmitz observes:

> Arguably, ambush marketing provides a positive free market force. By exposing to official sponsors and event organizers the true scope of exclusivity that any sponsor can reasonably expect to enjoy, ambushers in effect help quantify the true market value of Olympic sponsorship while participating in the marketing blitz in a manner they deem most cost effective for their company. As it becomes clear to potential sponsors of future Olympic Games that event organizers will not be able to stop all ambush marketing efforts, this should be a factor that is accounted for in determining the fees to be paid for official sponsorship.[182]

In similar vein, Crompton is of the view that '[t]here is no doubt that ambushing has resulted in more extensive and creative use of the platform that sponsorship provides for integrated promotion, and to much cleaner, tighter contracts between properties and sponsors'.[183] However, some commentators have observed that the passing of event legislation by domestic lawmakers to protect against ambush marketing (which will be discussed in detail in the next chapter) may in fact hamper the official sponsors' protection and leveraging of their investment:

> Event-specific legislation not only provides official sponsors with a significant practical advantage by minimising the risk of ambush, but may in fact provide a disincentive against the need strategically and creatively to compete against their competition by providing a psychic 'safety net'. Ironically, by insisting on unprecedented trademark protection to eliminate marketing competition, the Olympic movement may be unwittingly demotivating its official sponsors to fully maximise and leverage their association with the Games.[184]

As Ellis et al. observe, there has 'recently been a move towards the use of anti-ambush marketing legislation as the ultimate form of brand protection'.[185] I would

[180] See Seguin and O'Reilly 2008.

[181] Ibid. 67.

[182] Schmitz 2005, p. 208.

[183] Crompton 2004, p. 10.

[184] Grady et al. 2010, p. 153.

[185] Ellis et al. 2011, p. 300.

suggest that this 'psychic safety net'[186] of anti-ambush marketing protection in *sui generis* event legislation (which we will consider in detail in the later chapters) contributes to a laziness or sense of entitlement that is commonly present amongst trademark holders. A distinction must be drawn between a trademark holder's need to engage in commercial communication with customers (i.e. to send messages about the quality, source and value of goods) and 'his desire to extract all the consumer surplus that inheres in his mark'.[187] And as Amis et al. note: '[I]t is important not to regard sponsorship as being a uni-dimensional purveyor of an association between the sponsor and the sponsored. The ways of exploiting the relationship are limited only by a manager's imagination'.[188] Not only should sponsors ensure that they properly leverage the sponsorship in order to limit the possible benefits for an ambusher, it is advisable for sponsors to not restrict their thinking in such a limited (and limiting) way to just the association with the event. This is an interesting issue when one considers the new statutory 'association rights' to events created in some recent mega-event host countries, which appear for the most part to take an extremely one-dimensional view of the sponsors' relationship to the event and seems to, pedantically, target only this association as the be-all-and-end-all of protecting the event against ambushing. I will examine these rights in more detail in Chap. 8.

In the context of considering the merits of event organisers' stigmatised view of the ethics and morality of ambush marketing, it is interesting to note that Maurice Cardinal, writing in the context of the 2010 Vancouver Winter Olympic Games, attempts to expose the IOC's alleged hypocrisy on the subject of ambushing by asking why, if ambush marketing is such a 'mortal sin' of unethical behaviour, the IOC elected to make Nike (one of the world's most infamous exponents of sports ambushing campaigns to date, which has been rumoured to have its own ambush marketing director[189]) an official Olympic sponsor.[190] In fact, the IOC reportedly

---

[186] See also Ellis et al. 2011, p. 306.

[187] Cooper Dreyfuss 1990, p. 424.

[188] Amis et al. 1999, p. 257.

[189] See Shank 1999, Chap. 12.

[190] Dick Pound is quite proud of the IOC's move to involve Nike as official sponsor, even after Nike's controversial 'You don't win silver. You lose gold' ambush campaign at the 1996 Atlanta Games:

'We… did our best to convince Nike that it would be better for them to become mainstream and support the efforts of aspiring Olympic athletes, since they did have superb product lines. This paid an unexpected dividend… when, in the middle of the Salt Lake City crisis, the 2000 Games sponsor, Reebok, suddenly withdrew its sponsorship, for reasons unrelated to the crisis. We immediately got through to our Nike contacts and said there was an opportunity for them, if they could act quickly. We put together a full sponsorship deal for Sydney in forty-eight hours, working round the clock, and were able to make it public in the midst of the crisis, thus showing the ongoing value of the Olympics despite the furor. Even the Australians were impressed with this ability to replace one of their sponsors so quickly and effectively. It also saved expensive and time-consuming litigation with Reebok, whose officials were equally stunned by the speed with which they became irrelevant'. (Pound 2006, pp. 162, 163)

also recruited Peter Bratschi, former Nike sports marketing head for Asia Pacific, to assist in co-ordination of its education campaign to Chinese businesses about ambush marketing for the 2008 Beijing Games, because 'he knows what this is about'.[191] This may all be indicative of a rather strange love-hate relationship between Nike and the Olympic powers-that-be: The IOC also granted a waiver of one of the fundamental principles of its Charter (that no one other than official sponsors can use Olympic athletes in advertising during the Games) to Nike to use Olympic athletes in its advertising during the Adidas-sponsored Beijing Olympics, which has been characterised as an 'extraordinary' step.[192] Cardinal encourages small businesses to investigate ways to 'unofficially' leverage Olympic fever, and proudly espouses the philosophy that 'if you have to pay for the Olympics' (a reference to the increased taxes imposed to finance the Games) 'you should benefit too'.[193]

It seems that, much like beauty, the 'ambush' is in the eye of the beholder (or, should that be 'beer-holder', if one considers the frequency of alcohol sponsors' ambushing antics, such as the Bavaria ambush of Budweiser's sponsorship at the 2010 FIFA World Cup?).[194] In light of the developing scholarly opinions and debate amongst marketing practitioners on ambushing one currently finds, at one end of the spectrum, the use of pejorative terms such as 'parasitic marketing', while at the other end one finds much less emotionally charged language such as 'parallel marketing'.[195] It has been observed that '[f]rom the industrial perspective, how people think about ambush marketing mainly depends on who they are'.[196]

(Footnote 190 continued)

Most interesting, for me, from this anecdote is that it appears to show that an open and transparent bidding process for the right to be a top level Olympic sponsor does not always take place….

191 From a report entitled 'IOC to crack down on Beijing 2008 "ambush marketing"', 17 January 2008, available at the time of writing on the www.GameBids.com web site at http://www.gamesbids.com/eng/other_news/1200686224.html.

192 From the short article entitled 'Bush-Whackers', 21 August 2008 in *Marketing Week* (available online at the time of writing at http://www.mad.co.uk/Main/Home/Articlex/17d67f5e4e9e42fc9cd8d88de18c2749/'Bush-whackers.html).

193 Ibid.

194 See the discussion in Chap. 7.

195 See, for example, the following depiction of such development:

'What has emerged through scholarly research, as well as debate among practitioners, is an evolution in our understanding of the concept of ambush marketing, as well as a fleshing out of the ambiguities that surround the practice. From the earliest definitions of ambush marketing as a pejorative term involving "unauthorized" practices has emerged not only an acknowledgment of the considerable vagueness that surrounds the concept but also a conceptual framework of ambush marketing that more accurately reflects the balancing of sponsors' contractual rights against the rights of non-sponsors to maintain a market presence during an event through legal and competitive business activities'. McKelvey and Grady 2008, p. 554.

196 Ning, C 'Conceptual and Semantic Analysis in Ambush Marketing Utilizing LEXIMANCER Software Tool', available online at the time of writing at http://anzmac2010.org/proceedings/pdf/anzmac10Final00022.pdf.

Event organisers and sponsors invariably label conduct as ambushing—their *bête noire* when it comes to commercial exploitation of their events—while non-sponsors appear to have fewer qualms about the legitimacy (and ethics) of what is seen as a powerful marketing tool in the struggle to keep ahead of the competition. In a qualitative study by Seguin and O'Reilly prior to the 2002 winter Olympics, which included a survey and interviews with Olympic marketing executives and the top marketing execs from five of the TOP sponsors at the time, it emerged that the sponsors apparently view ambush marketing not as unethical behaviour but rather as a competitive business practice.[197] One such TOP executive reportedly observed that the 'positioning of ambush marketing as unethical is an interesting public relations ploy created to level the playing fields'.[198] It has been observed that the event organisers' and official sponsors' pejorative rhetoric is robust and emotionally charged, with characterisation of ambushing ranging from 'like leaches they suck the lifeblood and goodwill out of the institution' to 'it is a form of theft practiced by corporate pariahs'.[199] FIFA characterised a Pepsi TV and press ad campaign in Argentina (which put the words 'Tokyo 2002' alongside famous footballers and other football imagery and associated them with the Pepsi logo) as 'below the belt', and in June 2002 a court banned the ads because it suggested a 'presumed sponsorship relationship' between Pepsi and the FIFA World Cup that could cause confusion among consumers.[200]

Another issue that must be raised here (and which will be revisited in Chap. 9) is the question of what the actual impact of ambush marketing is for sponsors and governing bodies. I will examine the justification for anti-ambush marketing protection by means of special legislation, with reference specifically to the rather hackneyed, 'knee-jerk reaction argument' that is so often encountered in the literature, namely that ambush marketing threatens to alienate sponsors and to lead to the imminent downfall of mega-events (the 'survival of the Games' argument). I will do so in the interest of what I view to be the urgent necessity to bring a measure of objectivity and balance to the debate about ambush marketing and of the law's response, which in my view is severely lacking in current discourse and the literature. In this regard there appears to be a twinkling of hope that the issue will enjoy more critical attention in future. For example, the following has been observed in criticism of the existing research on ambush marketing:

> [A]lthough the discussion of ambush marketing is necessarily rooted in the discussion of sport sponsorship, there is a dearth of research into the actual impact of ambush marketing, from a practical, managerial, or strategic perspective... [M]ost disconcerting [is the fact that] no definitive understanding of ambush marketing exists, and recent developments in

[197] Seguin and O'Reilly 2008, p. 62.

[198] Ibid. 70.

[199] Crompton 2004, p. 10.

[200] Day, J 'FIFA foils Pepsi ambush', 11 June 2002, *The Guardian* (available online at the time of writing at http://www.guardian.co.uk/media/2002/jun/11/advertising.marketingandpr).

sport marketing have raised renewed concerns over the actual impact of ambushing on sponsors, and what specifically constitutes ambush marketing.[201]

From the discussion in later chapters the reader will note that I am an enthusiastic member of the school of thought that subscribes to the belief that what is traditionally labelled 'intrusion' ambush marketing (as discussed above) is something that probably needs to be removed from the purview of anti-ambush marketing efforts and, specifically, should not attract the aggressive legal responses we have seen to date. This will be particularly clear in my later evaluation of the applicable anti-ambush marketing legislation in South Africa in the form of the Merchandise Marks Act,[202] which is probably (currently) the most stringent and far-reaching anti-ambushing legislation to be found anywhere in the world. I have serious concerns about the wide-spread attitude amongst those who purport to be opponents of 'ambushing', namely the inclusion of otherwise perfectly legal (and possibly harmless) conduct in their definitions of what allegedly should be combated and outlawed. Compare the following description of what one source refers to as 'indirect ambush marketing' (which source describes 'direct ambush marketing' as 'an intentional use of symbols and trademarks associated with the mass event so as to give the consumers the wrong impression as to the actual sponsors of the event'):

> [Indirect ambush marketing] consists in adjusting the message to the nature of the event in the manner which does not directly breach the rights of the organizers or sponsors of the event but uses the event as a pretext for the ambusher's own marketing purposes.[203]

I simply must ask: *What is wrong with that?* If there is no breach of the rights of organisers or official sponsors (and no infringement of a legal prescript) why should such conduct be specially outlawed and subjected to the stigmatised and often overkill treatment by event organisers and even members of the legal fraternity? More troubling, why should there be calls for special laws (as discussed in Chap. 4) to make such otherwise perfectly legal conduct illegal, or even to criminalise it? I support the distinction that Jolan Storch draws: 'There are two types of ambush marketing: the blatant and the suggestive. The blatant ambush marketing campaign uses an official trademark without the right to do so. It is the suggestive ambush marketing that is much more difficult to evaluate'.[204] In Chap. 8 I will discuss the thematic space of the sports mega-event and the folly of event organisers who try to ban any reference to the event. The 'suggestive ambush' is something that I believe (and I'll try to explain this in the later chapters) should not even be a blip on the radar of the legal fraternity.

---

[201] Burton and Chadwick 2009, p. 5.

[202] Merchandise Marks Act, 1941, as amended in 2002 prior to South Africa's hosting of the 2003 ICC Cricket World Cup—see the discussion in Chap. 4 and elsewhere in the book.

[203] From the *Harvard Business Review Polska*, Listopad 2009 (at 122)—available online at the time of writing at http://www.gala-marketlaw.com/pdfs/GALA_Warsaw%2018_09_09.pdf.

[204] Storch, J 'It's an ambush! Or is it?' *Marketing*, 17 May 2010—available online at http://www.macleoddixon.com/documents/Storch.pdf.

However, it should be noted that there appears to currently be a realisation, more generally, of a shift in perception of ambush marketing from previously-held convictions regarding the (un)ethical nature of such conduct and, potentially more relevant for this book, its legality. This appears to be due, in part, to the nature of ambushing cases in recent years and the motivation of the 'ambushers'. Burton and Chadwick observe:

> [W]hereas previously ambush marketing's primary aim has been seen as a means of confusing consumers as to whom officially sponsors an event, or to detract from an official sponsorship's media awareness and derive the same brand association benefits as official sponsors, contemporary ambush marketing appears to have evolved into a marketing communication vehicle unto its own... [A]mbush marketing can be viewed as an alternative to sponsorship for companies, depending on their budget, interests, and brand image; for some organizations, taking a more bold, daring approach to marketing their products or services, utilizing unauthorized and defiant means such as ambushing, represents an alternative means of gaining some of the same benefits of association with an event as sponsorship, while maintaining a connection with their own brand ethos... In examining past ambush campaigns ... a distinct shift in paradigms is evident; whilst early in ambush marketing's history, predatory and coat-tail ambush strategies were most prominent, more recently ambush marketing has taken a decided emphasis on associative marketing and the overall capitalization on the value of sporting events. Cases from the 1980s through to the mid-1990s appear to represent a clearer and better-defined competitive relationship between ambusher and ambushee, with a number of attacks explicitly attacking a rival's sponsorship... However, more contemporary examples, perhaps in line with the dramatic increase in sponsorship value over time, a more indirect, opportunistic approach now more accurately describes ambush marketing... Brands, this shift would seem to indicate, have taken a much stronger focus on gaining and encouraging some benefit from a presumed association with an event, in place of early suggestions that ambushers sought primarily to detract from sponsorship and negatively impact a sponsor's returns. While in some cases this is surely still a main focus, in capturing attention and drawing consumer awareness away from sponsors, ambushers are ultimately affecting the activities of sponsors, our findings point away from intentional confusion and distraction, towards a broader, more opportunistic and benefit-driven perspective of ambushing.[205]

Pelanda questions the legitimacy of the event organisers' traditional, pejorative view of 'ambushing':

> Event sponsors, corporate stakeholders, and commentators have discussed the issue of so called "ambush marketing," which is alleged to occur during high profile international athletic events such as the Olympics, primarily under the premise that the practice transgresses or at least skirts some, albeit unidentified, ethical boundaries, regardless of whether governments legally permit or prohibit certain forms of it. The International Olympic Committee and many commentators have applied the term to a myriad of different corporate marketing strategies used during such events, all of which to varying degrees purportedly interfere with or dilute "official" corporate sponsorships. The pervasive liberal use of the term "ambush marketing" is problematic because it cloaks an overly broad range of marketing practices with a presumed shroud of negativity and illegality. Generalizing any commercial activity that seeks to capitalize on the occurrence of high profile sporting events without authorization from event organizers as "ambush marketing" suggests a definitive conclusion about the legality and/or the ethicality of the

[205] Burton and Chadwick 2009, pp. 17, 18.

> practice… The power to define ambush marketing and the categories of activities it encompasses is important because it carries with it the ability to influence the formation of law… Both inside and outside the legal world, words matter, and the term "ambush marketing" is used too loosely both by commentators and event organizers and sponsors… Despite the glaring contradiction between the accepted definition of ambush marketing and its frequent application, the parties that stand to benefit from the overly broad use of the term nevertheless control the discourse. These parties are event organizers such as national Olympic committees in need of securing sponsorship contracts, and companies willing to invest in expensive sponsorship agreements. Although these parties claim that they are concerned with the consumer confusion supposedly caused by the marketing practices they label as "ambushes," what they seem to actually be concerned with is attaining the power to quell all unauthorized speech relating to the high profile athletic events that they promote, regardless of the likelihood of any such confusion. The controversy over ambush marketing has simply been manifested by the unrealistic expectation of being able to restrict the speech of third parties that event organizers and corporate sponsors have for the sponsorship contracts that they have negotiated.[206]

In fact, one marketing pundit a few years ago speculated that the rise of a more 'professional' and organised approach by specialised agencies to leveraging Olympic sponsorship may have created a new dimension of business, namely 'Olympic assault marketing'.[207] Crow and Hoek,[208] back in 2003, observed that commercial pragmatism may, over time, overcome some of the emotion associated with the issue of ambush marketing. They referred to Meenaghan,[209] who in 1996 had pointed out that many of the activities previously labelled 'ambush marketing' (for example, competitive advertising during and around sponsored events), are now seen as legitimate activities. The authors suggested that 'event owners have accepted that the level of brand competition that exists in other media is also likely to occur in sponsorship and associated activities'.[210] While the current shift in perception regarding the legitimacy of ambushing may be, at least in part, attributable to commercial pragmatism, it should be noted that event organisers have nearly ten years on from the publication of Crow and Hoek's article most definitely not yet 'accepted' the brand competition highlighted by ambushing. In light of this apparent shift in perceptions, which has apparently not yet permeated the thinking of the event organisers, it is submitted that the traditional approach of event organisers (and legislatures) in responding to ambushing needs to be re-examined. As Jon Heshka points out, event rights owners' lawyers probably don't care overly much about such nuanced practicalities. They only concern themselves with (mis)calculated cost/benefit decisions, and leave it to 'Marketing' to figure

---

[206] Pelanda, B L 'Ambush marketing: Dissecting the discourse', undated 2011 paper available online at the time of writing at http://works.bepress.com/brian_pelanda/.

[207] Lefton, T 'McCann-Erickson digs into Olympics niche with its new Q^5 group' *Sportsbusiness Journal*, 6 May 2002 (see also Barney et al. 2004, p. 394, note 37).

[208] Crow and Hoek 2003.

[209] Meenaghan 1996.

[210] Crow and Hoek 2003, p. 9.

out ways to optimally exploit the IP rights given to them.[211] Grady et al. also appear to recognise the 'paradigm shift' referred to above, but go further to suggest—in my view, correctly—that this should inform the (legal) responses to ambush marketing:

> Through over a decade of academic research and practitioner debate, the concept of ambush marketing has evolved to become significantly less emotionally charged and pejorative as the sport marketplace has come to accept the nuances and realities of the practice within a competitive marketplace (the notion of 'commercial pragmatism'). One of the few notable exceptions remains the Olympic movement, which can maintain its unwavering stance on ambush marketing because of the absolute leverage it holds over potential host cities throughout the bid process. As a result, by conceding to the requirement to enact event-specific legislation, governments not only embrace the Olympic movement's stigmatised definition of ambush marketing as unethical and immoral, but also threaten to make illegal competitive business behaviour that would otherwise be deemed normal, fair, acceptable and legal... The IOC holds substantial leverage through the bid process whereby it requires host countries to enact event specific legislation. This one-sided process, it can be argued, does not achieve a fair balance between all of the stakeholder interests. It significantly tips the balance in favour of the Olympic movement... The requirement to enact event-specific legislation is foisted upon the host country's legislature, and the host country essentially must buy into the perspective of ambush marketing as defined by the Olympic movement. This view is increasingly at odds with the current conceptualisation of ambush marketing in the practitioner and academic literatures as an effective alternative to purchasing sponsorship rights. Whereas in the past ambush marketing was largely viewed as an unethical business practice to be condemned, there has been a considerable shift in industry perspective, reflected in the academic literature, to an increasingly less negative and pejorative view of the practice.[212]

Jerry Welsh has suggested an alternative definition for ambush marketing, which, I would suggest, bears serious consideration as more closely reflecting an objective understanding of the role of this practice in the marketing arena, devoid of the stigma and reflexive pejorative treatment by sports governing bodies:

> Ambush Marketing ought to be understood simply as a marketing strategy with its programmatic outcomes, occupying the thematic space of a sponsoring competitor, and formulated to vie with that sponsoring competitor for marketing pre-eminence. Successful ambush strategies feed on ill-conceived sponsorships and inept sponsors; in that regard, Ambush Marketing is the natural result of healthy competition and has the long-range effect of making sponsored properties more valuable, not less, in that successful ambushes, over time, help to weed out inferior sponsorship propositions.[213]

---

[211] Canadian law professor Jon Heshka, from personal correspondence with the author, December 2011.

[212] Grady et al. 2010, pp. 150, 151, 153, 154.

[213] From Welsh, J 'Ambush Marketing: What it Is; What it Isn't', available online at the time of writing on the web site of Welsh Marketing Associates at http://welshmktg.com/WMA_ambushmktg.pdf (see also Welsh, J. (2002) 'In defense of ambush marketing' *Sponsorship Report*, 21(11), 1, 4–5).

This view accords with the contemporary views of other marketing experts, in recognising the element of self-inflicted harm from 'ambushing' by official sponsors and event organisers where the sponsored properties are either insufficiently protected or insufficiently leveraged, or both.[214] Welsh highlights, in his forthright way, the limitations inherent in the rights that sponsors routinely buy, and the rights that event organisers are able to provide:

> The point to understand is that, in buying a sponsorship, a company buys only that specific, packaged product, offered as it is, with its constituent parts and attendant rights (and its liabilities). In sponsoring, the company does not thereby purchase the rights to all avenues leading to the public's awareness of that property; and, more importantly, the company does not buy the rights to the entire thematic space in which the purchased property is usually only one resident. In other words, all else other than that which is specifically purchased is up for commercial grabs. That's as it should be in sponsorship and as it is in the larger world of both commerce and life: when you own and license Kermit you have only given the rights you own to one specific frog—not to all frogs, and maybe not even to all green ones.[215]

Of course, this view is most definitely not shared by the sports governing bodies—compare the reference above by Grady et al. to 'the Olympic movement's stigmatised view of ambush marketing', and also FIFA's alleged attempts to monopolise its World Cup event as criticised in litigation surrounding the 2010 event in South Africa. The respondent in the case of *FIFA v Executive African Trading*[216] (the case involving an application for an interdict against the respondent by FIFA, claiming that the respondent's registered design of a keychain bearing the numerals '2010', the ornamentation of a vuvuzela trumpet and soccer balls, infringed FIFA's common law rights and intellectual property in the event) pointedly raised this:

> [A] repeated refrain throughout [FIFA's] founding affidavits is that [FIFA] is the "owner" of the FIFA world cup 2010 which, in turn, is one of the footholds of [FIFA's] alleged intellectual property rights in and to the numerals 2010 coupled with anything representing the game of soccer... [FIFA] is wrong in believing that it is the sole owner of the tournament. The FIFA world cup 2010 is not a private event falling into [FIFA's] private fiefdom and sole domain. The South African public also has a substantial stake in the tournament. After all, it is surely common cause that vast stadiums, roads and the like have been built across the country utilizing public funds running into billions of Rand... As to the numerals 2010, in association with features denoting the game of soccer, in my submission the relevant numerals and symbols are part of the *res communes* and should be seen as *res extra commercium*. They are consequently not capable of ownership by a private person.[217]

---

214 Compare comments posted on Skildum-Reid's sponsorship blog at http://blog.powersponsorship.com and referred to elsewhere.

215 Welsh, writing on http://welshmktg.com/WMA_ambushmktg.pdf supra.

216 *Federation Internationale de Football Association (FIFA) v Executive African Trading CC and Another* Case No. 52308/07 North Gauteng High Court, Pretoria—see the discussion in the section on special anti-ambushing laws in South Africa in Sect. 4.4.5 in Chap. 4.

217 From the Respondent's Heads of Argument in the application (11.3 par. 33–35). I thank Dr. Tim Burrell, counsel for the Respondent, for providing me with the relevant documentation.

A view similar to that held by Welsh would appear to have found favour in the Indian case of *ICC Development (International) Ltd v Arvee Enterprises and Philips*,[218] which involved claims of unlawful ambush marketing and passing off against the defendant's use of cricket World Cup tickets as prizes in a promotional campaign:

> So far as the plea of ambush marketing is concerned, the phrase ambush marketing is used by marketing executives only. It is different from passing off. In the passing off action, there is an element of overt or covert deceit whereas ambush marketing is opportunistic commercial exploitation of an event. The ambush marketer does not seek to suggest any connection with the event but gives his own brand or other insignia, a larger exposure to the people, attached to the event, without any authorization of the event organizer. However, in such cases, there is no deception, therefore, the defendants' conduct cannot be categorized as wrongful or against public interest. It is now well settled that commercial advertisement is a form of commercial speech. It is a part of the freedom of speech and expression guaranteed under Article 19(1)(a) [of the Indian Constitution]. The 'World Cup' or the event is not protected by any international treaty or domestic law, unlike the word Olympics and its logo, which is protected under the Emblems and Names [Prevention of Improper Use] Act, 1950. It is for the Legislature to determine how far to curtail legitimate fair competition and freedom of speech. From the material on record, the advertising campaign offering tickets of the event as prizes without using the logo or the mark of the plaintiff cannot be held to be unlawful.[219]

In fact, against the backdrop of the discussion in the previous chapter of the potential anti-competitive nature and effects of the system of sponsorship exclusivity in respect of mega-events, it is ironic to note that what the event organisers like to call unethical, immoral and unlawful 'ambush marketing' may in fact have the opposite competition effect:

> The irony of ambushing is that it has resulted in much tighter contract agreements and more emphasis on leveraging the platform in which sponsors have invested. In short, the adage that 'competition makes us better' appears to fit the ambushing phenomenon. There has been a realization that purchase of sponsorship rights is the beginning of a promotion process, not the end. If a company does not invest resources to exploit the platform that a sponsorship provides, it is likely to have wasted its investment, because ambushing competitors are given the opportunity to usurp its position in the eyes of the public.[220]

---

[218] 2003 (26) PTC 245 (Del).

[219] The plaintiffs also claimed that they had been using the words 'World Cup' since 1975 in the game of cricket and had used it exclusively, therefore the term 'Cricket World Cup' is associated with the plaintiffs and that the defendants by making use of the impugned words were guilty of passing off the indicia, marks and identity of the plaintiffs and the World Cup, thereby causing irreparable harm and injury to them. The court held that the word 'World Cup' is a generic term; the generic nature of these words can be judged from the fact that they have been used to refer to several other international sporting events (including, for example, the FIFA World Cup). The plaintiffs therefore had no trademark in the said words. The words belong to one genus and such words can neither be brand names nor have any protection by means of a registered trade mark. This last accords with the view of the South African court in *FIFA v Bartlett and others* 1994 (4) SA 722 (TPD) (discussed in the text above) at 742C that the words 'world cup' are simply of such a descriptive character in South Africa that they cannot fulfil the function as a trade mark.

[220] Crompton 2004, p. 11.

And supporters of a competitive marketplace might be tempted to ask 'whether it is reasonable, in our current competitive climate, to expect companies like American Express, Visa, and MasterCard or AT and T and Sprint to compete full throttle 365 days of the year but stay home doing nothing when a major event occurs'.[221] As Teresa Scassa observes:

> Recent anti-ambush marketing legislation goes well beyond prohibiting head-to-head competition between rivals in the marketplace and captures a very broad range of activity. What is captured by the law may go well beyond what is generally considered unethical. It may also stifle legitimate (and beneficial) competition.[222]

At this point it bears mentioning that one must, of course, be careful in assessing the veracity of the arguments regarding the ethics or morality of ambush marketing with due consideration of the perspectives of the different parties (and, specifically, their respective self-interests). As mentioned, the event organisers' 'stigmatised' view is clearly motivated by the interest of these organisations in exploiting the commercial value of the events. From the 'ambushers'' perspective the motivation in favour of the ethics of ambushing also, clearly, derives from attempts to justify their marketing efforts from a commercial motivation. An example of the slanting of views based on commercial considerations may be found in the context of the media, and one should consider that the media's treatment of ambush marketing may also illustrate a special perspective based on underlying commercial considerations:

> The media often are reluctant to accept and acknowledge the role of sponsors of a sport. They believe that to credit sponsors in editorial coverage could potentially harm their advertising revenue, since companies are spending their communications money on the sponsorship rather than on advertising. The prevailing philosophy is, "When you are in the business of selling media time or space, you don't want to give away time or space". As a general rule, broadcast media will not credit title sponsors unless the event or sponsor purchases advertising time during the broadcast.[223]

And, of course, the media can also engage in ambushing of events (as occurred recently in respect of the alleged commercial misuse of broadcast footage by news media during the 2011 ICC Cricket World Cup, which may form the subject of litigation in the near future). While such partisan motives may seem to complicate the question in attempting to make an objective assessment of the ethics and morality of ambush marketing, I would suggest that it should not be overstated. At least the protagonists are clearly identified and we know where they stand and where they are coming from. While such commercially-motivated views are important, I believe that the legal debate is less complex than the ethical one.

---

221 Bischoff et al. 2005, p. 19.

222 Scassa 2011, p. 364.

223 Crompton 2004, p. 3. In fact, as Crompton points out (at 4), the media may also actively encourage ambushing (if not expressly prohibited by its contract with the event organiser) by, for example, aggressively soliciting advertising of event broadcasts by competitor non-official sponsors, because this provides an opportunity for generating greater advertising revenues.

For the lawyer, the determination of whether ambush marketing should be unlawful and, more importantly, whether it should be outlawed and even criminalised by means of e.g. special legislation, should simply be made on the basis of legal principles and without undue emphasis on the commercial interests involved. I believe that this determination regarding the legality of ambush marketing should take due notice of the motivations of the stakeholders, but legal scrutiny should infuse the exercise with first principles of law. Which is why I find it unacceptable that legal commentators can in this day and age still, brazenly, define ambush marketing in a pejorative sense without mention of the possibility that an 'ambush' may very well be nothing of the kind. Compare the apparent unqualified (I would suggest thoughtless) acceptance of a blameworthy intent on the part of the 'ambusher' and of consumer confusion, in the definition provided by Bacalao-Fleury in a late 2011 law journal article, which states that 'Ambush marketing is a deceitful advertising strategy that involves confusing consumers regarding a company's status as an official sponsor of an event… [C]onsumers are deliberately confused and deceived by the "free riders" as to their status as an official sponsor'.[224] I will examine the problematic issues surrounding these aspects of (and assumptions about) ambushing in the later chapters.

Before stepping off the point about the stigmatised view of ambushing and the pejorative use of the term by event organisers, I wish to highlight one final issue, namely the ironic fact that those pointing the accusatory finger at 'ambushers' are probably rarely squeaky clean themselves. Former IOC head of marketing, Michael Payne, proudly recalls a couple of incidents involving Olympic officials' conduct which raise some serious questions about 'ambushes' and what meaning, exactly, the IOC ascribes to the term. Payne recalls that in the run-up to the 1984 Games, which I've discussed in more detail earlier, local organising committee supremo Peter Ueberroth encountered resistance from the Greek Olympic Committee to his plans to sell advertising opportunities in respect of each of the different stages of the Olympic torch relay (which was eventually sponsored by telecommunications company AT and T at USD 3,000 per slot and raised an amount of nearly USD 11 million for charities). The Greek authorities were of the view that this was shameless commercialism and a 'sacrilege against the Olympic ideal', and they refused to allow the Los Angeles organisers to come and light the flame at Olympia. Payne recounts that, after weeks of negotiations with the Greek Committee had failed, Samaranch 'concocted a simple plan':

> Two Swiss students were sent to Olympia to light the flame, photographing and filming the whole exercise to verify the authenticity of the process. The students brought the flame back to Lausanne in a miner's lamp. Samaranch then presented the Greek Committee with a simple choice. The Greeks were told to either allow Ueberroth to come to Olympia and light the flame in the traditional manner, or the IOC would dispatch the flame from the IOC headquarters in Lausanne. The Greek Committee accepted Samaranch's proposal. Samaranch advised Ueberroth that his "little problem" had been solved.[225]

224 Bacalao-Fleury 2011, p. 197.

225 Payne 2006, pp. 126, 127.

Is anyone reminded of the often-maligned, devious tactics of 'ambushers' of events? In similar vein, Payne also recalls that in the days before the IOC's demands for host cities and governments to enact aviation regulations to protect the airspace over Olympic venues, it was not always easy to enforce the grounding of airships:

> Fuji and Reebok airships turned up in Barcelona [at the 1992 Games]. They fully expected to be allowed to fly over the city for the duration of the Games, ambushing Kodak and the local sports brands. *No legislation was passed forbidding air ships from passing over the city*. But it was rumoured that the local air traffic controllers obtained the Games tickets they needed, while the requisite permissions for the offending air ships languished in an in-tray for 17 days. No doubt the Fuji and Reebok executives were left wondering what on earth had happened. They probably didn't enjoy explaining to their senior management why they had spent millions of pesetas on a grounded air ship.[226] [Emphasis added].

Again there is the implication of an apparent moral outrage on the part of an event organiser, directed at conduct which is not, in fact, illegal. While some might find the 'ingenuity' displayed by the IOC in these cases amusing, I would suggest that Payne's thinly veiled glee in recounting these events rather serves to highlight the fact that the Olympic movement might be a far from blameless proponent of the labelling of 'ambush marketing' as immoral or unethical behaviour. While for the Olympics' head honchos the end, very clearly, justifies the means, I would suggest that the assumed moral high ground may, in fact, be a quicksand of ambiguity and self-interest.

To return to the issue of the legitimacy (or not) of ambush marketing, and in less anecdotal terms, it also bears mentioning that research seems to indicate that the earlier view of the significant threat posed by ambush marketing to mega-events may need to be reconsidered in light of other factors which may pose a greater threat. Mention was made earlier of Seguin and O'Reilly's qualitative study of the Olympic marketing programme, which included a survey of the views of some of the TOP sponsors in respect of ambush marketing.[227] A significant finding of this research is the major role of advertising clutter, which is viewed as a pervasive threat to sponsorship investment and to the Olympic brand. While these sponsors recognised the fact that ambush marketing contributes to clutter (and vice versa), the Olympic movement's management of the Olympic brand was highlighted:

> Ambush marketing, originally considered as a major threat to the Olympic marketing programme, was found to be less of a concern than the hundreds of associations (TOP, NOC, OCOGS, athletes, etc.) who could legitimately use Olympic symbols and imagery in their marketing communications programme. The brand equity model… suggests that the commercial equity of the Olympic brand is significantly reduced by clutter. Our analysis leads us to believe the most effective way to manage ambush marketing and clutter is for the IOC to engage in strategic brand management.[228]

---

[226] Ibid. 149.

[227] Seguin and O'Reilly 2008.

[228] Ibid. 78–79.

A similar view was expressed nearly a decade earlier:

> With so many sponsors promoting their Olympic involvement simultaneously, there is high probability of confusion from clutter as well as an erosion of any perceived uniqueness from Olympic association in the minds of consumers. With so many companies in the mental equation, a kind of camouflage is created for the ambush marketers. The large number of deals may be inevitable given the funds that Olympic organisers need to raise but there are times when event organisers contribute to this confusion by allowing competitive companies to sponsor the same event.[229]

In short, a prime reason for the problems experienced by marketers in obtaining brand equity may be the fact that there simply are too many sponsors. We have considered the practice of granting category exclusivity of sponsorships to mega-events like the Olympic Games and the FIFA World Cup (in Chap. 2). While I will attempt (in Chap. 6) to highlight the potential problems with sponsorship exclusivity from a legal (primarily competition law) perspective, a practical impediment may be that the event organisers, in attempting to exploit to the hilt the commercial value of the mega-events as brands, are simply slicing the wedges of the pie too thin. While the official sponsors may therefore enjoy significant potential to exclude their competitors from associating with the event by means of such exclusivity, the actual value of the rights that they pay for, in terms of its marketing and promotional value, may be obscured by the clutter caused by an over-leveraging of the offering of sponsorship rights by the event organiser. I would suggest that this goes hand in hand with an apparent attitude on the part of event organisers that their events (which, as the reader will recall, these organisations love to describe as their property) create a virtually unlimited opportunity for commercial exploitation, as long as such exploitation does not take place by those who don't pay for the privilege. I believe this was illustrated in recent litigation in South Africa regarding an alleged ambush of the 2010 FIFA World Cup. In the previously mentioned *FIFA v Executive African Trading*[230] case (involving an application for an interdict against the respondent by FIFA, claiming that the respondent's registered design of a key holder bearing the numerals '2010', the ornamentation of a vuvuzela trumpet and soccer balls, infringed FIFA's common law rights and intellectual property in the event as well as constituting ambush marketing in contravention of the relevant legislation), it appears that FIFA attempted to establish a claim of passing off in the market of commemorative key holders even though FIFA itself does not produce such merchandise and also had not licensed any manufacturers to produce souvenir key holders in respect of its event. The following claim was made in the affidavit by the main deponent in

---

229 Tripodi and Sutherland 2000, p. 417.

230 *Federation Internationale de Football Association (FIFA) v Executive African Trading CC and Another* Case No. 52308/07 North Gauteng High Court, Pretoria—see discussion in Sect. 4.4.5 of Chap. 4.

support of FIFA's application,[231] which common law legal practitioners familiar with the passing off action should find surprising:

> [W]hen in due course [FIFA] grants a license for the manufacture of key holders, such key holders will be of a similar nature and effect to the articles depicted in [the Respondent's allegedly] offending designs. When such key holders are produced and sold with the permission of [FIFA], the public will correctly connect them in the course of trade with [FIFA].[232]

Similarly, in another supporting affidavit filed by Miguel Portela, FIFA's rights protection programme manager, it was stated that 'it is probable that [FIFA] will grant licenses in respect of key holders for the 2010 FIFA World Cup'.[233]

It is clear that FIFA was not attempting to base its passing off or unlawful competition claim on an existing reputation, but was attempting to close the market for commemorative key holders to all and sundry by means of an ill-suited legal avenue. Leaving aside the issue of the quality of the legal advice received by FIFA (upon which I will not express an opinion), it is submitted that this approach illustrates the attitude commonly found amongst event organisers about the nature and extent of their 'property' right to the event, and that such blatantly exclusionary approach to the issue of entrepreneurs' access to opportunities for commercial exploitation of an event appears thoroughly ingrained. Which brings to mind the following observation by Rochelle Cooper Dreyfuss on the sports industry's apparent obsession with the exploitation of image (in her discussion of the use of publicity rights and the expansion of trademark rights in this regard):

> [O]verzealous protection can distort the incentive structure in which purveyors [of commercially valuable images] operate, stimulating them to devote their resources to exploiting their images instead of continuing in the work for which the images became known. Recent developments in professional sports furnish one example, for both teams and players now earn so much money through control over their logos, names and likenesses, which make it appear that there may be little need to actually engage in athletics very often. Thus, until 1994, a World Series had been played in baseball every year since 1903. Until recently, the only interruption in the hockey season was the 1992 season's ten day strike. Yet, 1995 saw both sports suffering from debilitating work stoppages. The cities where the teams played were hurt, the merchants who depend on operating the franchises within the stadiums were hurt, and fans were devastated. But revenue from images apparently gave both the players and the teams the financial ability to hold out.[234]

This was expressed in the mid-1990s, and I would suggest that the phenomenon is even more prevalent today.

In the mega-event context I believe that over-leveraging of sponsorship allocation opportunities by event organisers, coupled with under-leveraging of such sponsorship investments by the sponsors, may be significant factors in the dilution of

---

[231] Affidavit by David Murray, who had left FIFA's employ by the time of the hearing of the case in March 2011.

[232] At par. 27.1 of Murray's affidavit.

[233] In par. 54 of Portela's replying affidavit.

[234] Cooper Dreyfuss 1996, p. 145.

sponsorship value, which event organisers love to ascribe to ambush marketing in the process of demanding special legal protection for their events. When one adds another factor to the mix, namely the stigmatised view of 'ambushing' (i.e. all 'non-official' marketing surrounding the event) and event organisers' aggressive campaigns to paint the 'ambushers' with the brush of opprobrium, one is confronted with a climate of suspicion and knee-jerk reaction to any such unofficial marketing or commercial activity within the thematic space of the event. This leads to the otherwise innocent and even ethical conduct of small business, entrepreneurs and individuals being outlawed by overly-wide special event laws, and efforts at enforcement of such often draconian laws further feed the anti-ambushing machine in a self-fulfilling prophecy which tends to demonise 'ambushing' without sufficient consideration of the consequences to the rights and interests of the public.

3.5 Conclusion

I have in this chapter provided a brief overview of ambush marketing as it is understood in the literature, with a special emphasis on distinguishing the main forms of such conduct (even though, as mentioned, 'ambushing' is not always easy to define or to pin down in practice, due in part to the increasingly clever campaigns devised by the ambushers). An important issue in this regard is the fact that the traditional concept of the 'intrusion ambush' is a slippery one. Having now also considered the apparent development of a more rounded or objective discourse regarding the ethics and legality of ambushing, the point I wish to make is that the clever modern 'ambush' of an event, as well as a myriad other unintentional commercial activities which take place within the thematic space occupied by the sports mega-event, exists within a definite 'grey zone' in terms of legal regulation. While the event organisers love to point to this grey zone as a reason for special legal protection (with the implication that it constitutes a lawless frontier where their valuable commercial interests and rights are subjected to indiscriminate rape and pillage), I would like the reader to consider whether there is in fact anything ominous in the existence of such zone. Does it not simply constitute a vacuum of legal regulation which exists for the very reason that the law has no place there? When anti-ambushing laws are passed to address conduct which, traditionally, has never been outlawed, this does not automatically imply that the law is, quite legitimately, simply developing to keep pace with commercial realities and to ensure substantive justice for rights holders. Maybe it just means that the law-makers have been coerced into outlawing that which should not be outlawed at all.

In the following chapter I will consider the passing of such special laws to protect mega-events, and I will briefly examine the current state of such laws in a number of jurisdictions. In the later chapters I will return to an evaluation of the legitimacy of such laws, in light of what was said above regarding the ethical and legal legitimacy of ambush marketing.

References

All internet-based sources referred to, were last visited in or before December 2011

Amis J, Slack T, Berrett T (1999) Sport sponsorship as distinctive competence. Eur J Mark 33(3/4): 250–272

Bacalao-Fleury CE (2011) Brazil's Olympic trials: an overview of the intellectual property challenges posed by the 2016 Rio de Janeiro games. Univ Ill J Law Technol Policy 1:191

Barney RK, Wenn SR, Martyn SG (2004) Selling the five rings. University of Utah Press, Salt Lake City

Becker D (2006) The essential legal guide to events. Dynamic Publishing Ltd, Atlanta

Bischoff JB, Curry JP, Berzins, I (2005) Dispatch from the trademark wars: ambush marketing and the arena of sports. Metrop Corp Couns Newslett 19. (February 2005)

Burton, N, Chadwick, S (2009) A typology of ambush marketing: the methods and strategies of ambushing in sport. Centre for the International Business of Sport Working Paper Series No. 10

Cloete R et al (2005) Introduction to sports law in South Africa. LexisNexis Butterworths, Durban

Cooper Dreyfuss R (1990) Expressive genericity: trademarks as language in the Pepsi generation. Notre Dame Law Rev 65:397

Cooper Dreyfuss R (1996) We are symbols and inhabit symbols, so should we be paying rent? Deconstructing the Lanham Act and rights of publicity. Columbia-VLA J Law Arts 20:123

Corbett S, Van Roy Y (2010) Events management in New Zealand: one law to rule them all? J Bus Law 4:338–362

Crompton JL (2004) Sponsorship ambushing in sport. Manag Leis 9:1–12

Crow D, Hoek J (2003) Ambush marketing: a critical review and some practical advice. Mark Bull 14:1–14

Drake S, Wells C (2008) The complete idiot's guide to guerrilla marketing. Alpha Books, Indianapolis

Duthie M (2003) It's just not cricket: ambushing the ambushers in South Africa. Freehills Patent & Trade Mark Attorneys. (June 2004)

Ellis D, Scassa T, Seguin B (2011) Framing ambush marketing as a legal issue: an Olympic perspective. Sport Manag Rev 14(3):297–308

Federation Internationale de Football Association (FIFA) (2010) 2010 FIFA world cup South Africa FIFA Public information sheet. (a guide to FIFA's Official Marks)

Frontier Economics Pty Ltd, Melbourne (2007) Ambush marketing legislation review, a report prepared for IP Australia and the Australian Government's Department of Communications, Information Technology and the Arts

Gannon N (2010) Foul play in sports branding—the marketer's perspective. World Trademark Rev 27:67

Grady J, McKelvey S, Bernthal MJ (2010) From Beijing 2008 to London 2012: examining event-specific Olympic legislation *vis à vis* the rights and interests of stakeholders. J Spons 3(2):144–156

Heshka J (2010) Rules and rogues. Marketing 37

Hewitt I (2005) Commercialisation of major sports events: does the law help or hinder the event organiser? Sport Law J 13(1):32–39

Johnson P (2007) Ambush marketing: a practical guide to protecting the brand of a sporting event. Sweet and Maxwell, London

Johnson P (2008) Look out! It's an ambush. Int Sports Law Rev 2/3:24–29

Kelbrick R (2008) Ambush marketing and the protection of the trade marks of international sports organizations—a comparative view. CILSA 41(1):24–28

Kobel P (2007) International report on question B: ambush marketing too smart to be good? Should certain ambush marketing practices be declared illegal and if yes, which ones and

under what conditions? International Report to the International League of Competition Law, Catania Congress 2007
Lewis A, Taylor J (2003) Sport: law and practice. Cavendish Publishing, London
Longdin L (2009) Public law solutions to private law problems: major event regulation subverts IP's internal balance. J Intell Prop Law Pract 4(10):726–742
McKelvey SM (2006) Coca-Cola vs. PepsiCo: a "Super" battleground for the cola wars? Sports Mark Q 15(2):114–123
McKelvey S, Grady J (2008) Sponsorship program protection strategies for special sport events: are event organizers outmaneuvering ambush marketers? J Sport Manag 22:550–586
Meenaghan T (1996) Ambush marketing—a threat to corporate sponsorship. Sloan Manag Rev 38:103–113
Mendes PPM (2010) Brazil moves fast to fight ambush marketing. World Intell Prop Rev 18–21
Payne M (1998) Ambush marketing: the undeserved advantage. Psychol Mark 15(4):323–331
Payne M (2006) Olympic turnaround. Praeger Publishers, Westport
Pound RW (2006) Inside the Olympics. Wiley, Montreal
Scaria AG (2008) Ambush marketing: game within a game. Oxford University Press, Oxford
Scassa T (2011) Ambush marketing and the right of association: clamping down on references to that big event with the all the athletes in a couple of years. J Sport Manag 25:354–370
Scherer J, Sam M, Batty R (2005) Sporting sign wars: advertising and the contested terrain of sporting events and venues. Int J Sport Manag Mark 1(1–2):17–36
Schmitz JJ (2005) Ambush marketing: the off-field competition at the Olympic games. Northwest J Technol Intell Prop 3:203
Schwab F (2006) FIFA's trademark tactics. World Trademark Rev 3:6. (Sept/Oct 2006)
Seguin B, O'Reilly NJ (2008) The Olympic brand, ambush marketing and clutter. Int J Sport Manag Mark 4(1):62–84
Seth R (2010) Ambush marketing—need for legislation in India. J Intell Prop Rights 15:455–463
Shank M (1999) Sports marketing: a strategic perspective. Prentice Hall, London
Storey S (2010) Pilfering, piracy and prevention: developments in combating ambush marketing. Sport Law J 18(1):40–54
Townley S, Harrington D, Couchman N (1998) The legal and practical prevention of ambush marketing in sports. Psychol Mark 15(4):333–348
Tripodi JA, Sutherland S (2000) Ambush marketing—"An Olympic event". J Brand Manag 7(6):412–422
Vassallo E, Blemaster K, Werner P (2005) An international look at ambush marketing. Trademark Rep 95:1338

Chapter 4
Harnessing Special Laws to Protect Commercial Rights to Sports Mega-Events

> [B]y conceding to the requirement to enact event-specific legislation, governments not only embrace the Olympic movement's stigmatised definition of ambush marketing as unethical and immoral, but also threaten to make illegal competitive business behaviour that would otherwise be deemed normal, fair, acceptable and legal.[1]
>
> By requiring countries to introduce legal measures to protect sponsors from ambush marketing, the IOC is able to protect their rights over those of all others despite the broader public policy obligations inherent in the creation of legislation.[2]
>
> The extensive legal protections that are now sought by those opposed to ambush marketing have, for reasons of fundamental principle, not been considered appropriate in traditional laws. Arguably, ambush marketing legislation raises other ethical and political questions including the question of when it is ethically acceptable for the state to provide favourable legislative regimes for selected businesses. Existing consumer laws and intellectual property laws, which have traditionally been used to address marketing issues, have always maintained a balance between individual freedoms, the public interest and state coercion. Legislation that will specifically address ambush marketing may affect that balance and, therefore, needs to be introduced with caution.[3]

4.1 Introduction

In the previous chapter, we briefly examined a few of the generally-applicable legal bases for protection against ambush marketing of sports mega-events. The latter section of this chapter will consider the current state of the law in a number of selected jurisdictions, as background to the critical evaluation of the legitimacy of relevant laws in the chapters that follow. Such overview will undertake a brief, descriptive discussion of special laws that have been passed in order to protect commercial rights to sports mega-events (specifically in the form of anti-ambush

[1] Grady et al. 2010, pp. 150–151.
[2] Ellis et al. 2011, p. 302.
[3] Corbett and Van Roy 2010, p. 339.

A. M. Louw, *Ambush Marketing and the Mega-Event Monopoly*,
ASSER International Sports Law Series, DOI: 10.1007/978-90-6704-864-4_4,

marketing legislation), and of anti-ambushing litigation as pursued by the relevant event organisers in those jurisdictions. Please note that this rather limited focus is necessitated by the limitations of this book; broader analysis of applicable laws in these (and other jurisdictions) is simply beyond the scope of this work and the interested reader is advised to consult other available texts in this regard. The focus of this book is on commercial monopolies in mega-events and, more specifically, the special dispensation through which laws are employed to protect and maintain such monopolies. Accordingly, the focus of the jurisdiction review in this chapter is limited: When discussing anti-ambush marketing legislation, I will concentrate on special legislation passed specifically for this purpose and which applies, exclusively, in the context of (mega-) events (i.e. I will not focus, for example, on more generally-applicable laws such as domestic intellectual property laws, consumer protection legislation, trade practises legislation, etc.—except where this is especially relevant in a particular jurisdiction). Similarly, discussion of anti-ambushing litigation will not focus on litigation involving related issues (such as, for example, case law regarding event organisers' trademarks,[4] etc.), but rather on those occasions where the event organisers have sought to enforce special laws passed for their events.

But first we need to consider the processes through which event organisers obtain such special commercial rights protection for their sporting spectacles, and the legitimacy of domestic law-makers' acquiescence in and active support for aggressive commercial rights protection programmes which may not be in the best interests of those situated beyond the event organiser/commercial partner relationship, specifically their constituencies in the form of host nation citizens and business enterprises.

4.2 'We Want Special Laws, or Else...'

The potential pressure to guarantee effective anti-ambush marketing measures that may be exacted by international sports governing bodies over aspirant host cities or even national governments is very real, and may constitute a metaphorical elephant in the room at many a venue where bids are negotiated or adjudicated. The events hosting bid process is anything but a painless one; it drags on for what may seem an inordinately long period of time (although everything's relative, of course, and successful applicant hosts who are faced with the mammoth task of preparation may disagree) and its effects are significant for economies and market

[4] Which means that I will not discuss, for example, important litigation in the European context such as FIFA's attempts to obtain trademark protection for its marks in respect of the 2006 FIFA World Cup Germany against Italian confectionary manufacturer Ferrero. I will briefly discuss this matter in Chap. 5.

conditions. For example, compare the bidding for Olympic Games hosting rights[5]:

> A bid proposal from a prospective host city and national Olympic Committee typically occurs about nine years prior to the games. The IOC usually receives several bids and takes 2 years to evaluate these… The final decision is itself a global televised media event. As soon as the announcement is made and the winning bid chosen, a 7-year-long sprint begins. The announcement is a trigger… that signals the beginning of the race. It is an exogenous shock upon the market and the industries that deliver the physical amenities, goods and services, and structures and systems which are required to put on the event. The event has a broad and deep effect on the entire economy… The announcement is invariably received as good news for the winning city, region, and country—but it produces a market dominated by scarcity, time compression, and limited access.[6]

While the economic effects of a successful bid are significant, the cost of unsuccessful bids can also be staggering—New York City's failed bid to host the 2012 Games reportedly cost in the region of USD 50 million, while Chicago's similarly ill-fated bid for the 2016 Games reportedly cost double that amount.[7] In the context of the discussion in the previous chapter, it should be noted that this phenomenal cost of bidding and bid preparations may include early preemptive steps against potential ambushing of the event:

> New York tried to future proof its possible 2012 Olympics. In its failed bid for the Games, it provided a considerable degree of ambush protection by securing the majority of outdoor media that would be available in the city in 2012. It did this in 2005, 7 years ahead, on index linked prices and managed temporarily to book 95% of the 600,000 advertising signage available.[8]

As if the self-inflicted crisis of labour, financial investment and inevitable bouts of stress-induced insomnia for local organisers and city fathers is not bad enough for the successful applicants, in recent years it has become par for the course for event organisers (and their commercial partners) to enforce strict demands of a 'safe haven' for their events. This does not relate solely to issues of security (an increasingly important issue in international sport), infrastructure readiness (the trains and planes should run on time) and guaranteed public interest (i.e. full stadia where TV cameras won't have to pan over unsightly empty seats), but also to commercial rights protection.[9] Bacalao-Fleury declares that 'Hosting the Olympic Games requires more than a great sports tradition, for the IOC will only choose the candidate that best satisfies the legal and infrastructure requirements of the Olympic Charter. Those requirements include the candidate's ability to protect and enforce any intellectual property rights related to the

---

[5] For some fascinating information on individual Olympic bids (both successful and unsuccessful), see www.gamesbids.com.

[6] Dollinger, MJ; Li, X; Mooney, C H 'Mega-events and entrepreneurial rents: Lessons from the Beijing Olympics' (draft document, April 2009—available online at the time of writing at http://www.indiana.edu/~rccpb/uschinacooperation/papers/P8%20Dollinger.pdf.

[7] See http://money.cnn.com/2009/10/02/news/economy/chicago_olympics_rejection/index.htm.

[8] Masterman 2009, p. 311.

[9] See Johnson 2008, p. 27.

Olympic Games.'[10] When Crow and Hoek wrote in 2003 that '[event-related marketing activities] not prohibited by law or the terms of the contract [between event organiser and official sponsor], would be legitimate marketing tactics,'[11] they possibly did not foresee the extent to which event organisers would proceed to obtain, through legislative licence in the jurisdictions where their events are held, a means of stopping those gaps in what had previously been an area where domestic laws did not require intervention. The scope for 'legitimate marketing practices' around mega-events is an ever-shrinking space, due largely to such efforts by the event organisers to extend legal protection for their commercial interests. Stuart and Scassa describe the total of 17 bid guarantees that the IOC requires from a successful Games bid government, and they observe that the category dealing with commercial rights protection (including marketing and sponsorship and the protection of intellectual property against ambushing) 'incorporate the IOC's most comprehensively stated legal prerequisites… It is via the consistent delivery of these particular guarantees that, since 1993, the IOC's coercive power is most evident.'[12]

One specific and key area where such coercive power is prevalent relates to the 'clean zone' (or 'marketing exclusion zone') requirements for event venues and their precincts. McKelvey and Grady explain the standard operating procedure followed by organisations, such as the IOC and FIFA, in the bidding process for their events (although, as the authors point out, such requirements have also been set, for example, in respect of the American Super Bowl as well as the NCAA championships[13]):

> Event organizers are increasingly using the host site bid process to ensure that host countries and cities enact special legislation establishing "clean zones." Although ordinances establishing clean zones are publicly positioned by event organizers as a means of controlling excessive commercialism (and sometimes providing for public safety), the underlying purpose is to protect event organizers and their official sponsors from unauthorized businesses' ability to engage in ambush marketing. For instance, as part of the Olympic bid process, the bidding city must provide detailed answers to questions relating to measures that will be taken to prevent ambush marketing. Among other application requirements, the "Candidate City" must demonstrate that it has "obtained unconditional commitments from all public or private entities (e.g., government authorities, advertising space owners, etc.) within the territory, to protect the Olympic image and prevent ambush marketing"[14]

Schwab explains the use of such zones at the 2006 FIFA World Cup in Germany, where this concept made its debut at FIFA's world championship event:

---

[10] Bacalao-Fleury 2011, p. 192.

[11] Crow and Hoek 2003, p. 11.

[12] Stuart and Scassa 2011, para 13.

[13] Compare Section X: para A ('Ambush marketing') of the National Collegiate Athletics Association (NCAA)'s Championship Host City Bid Specifications for its Division 1 football championship (2010-11/2012-13)—available online at the time of writing at http://www.ncaa.org/wps/wcm/connect/b9e19d004f406167a72aff51e8cf77e3/Bid+Specifications.pdf?MOD=AJPERES&CACHEID=b9e19d004f406167a72aff51e8cf77e3.

[14] McKelvey and Grady 2008, p. 568.

> One of the more visible and controversial measures taken by FIFA and implemented by German host cities was the establishment of controlled territories around the FIFA stadia. No competing unofficial goods or services could be promoted, marketed or sold within the confines of these zones as, according to FIFA's marketing regulations, "uncontrolled distribution and/or sales in the immediate vicinity of the stadium … may constitute so-called ambush marketing activities." Surrounded by a two-metre high outer security perimeter, the stadium grounds themselves were handed over to FIFA several weeks before the start of the first matches. However, the stadia constituted only a portion of the total controlled territories surrounding each event. While FIFA's marketing regulations deny that it imposed an exclusion zone of two kilometres around the stadia, FIFA clearly controlled large areas in their vicinity, within which it could make use of its domiciliary rights.[15]

Sliffman explains that the bid request package that is sent to all cities interested in hosting the NFL's Super Bowl requires that the host committee work together with the local government to create anti-ambushing 'clean zones,' which encompass a one-mile radius around the event's facility as well as 'on the property of area airports, within a [six]-block radiu[s] of the NFL Headquarters Hotel and around the location of NFL Experience.'[16] Super Bowl host cities are required to provide, within these clean zones, prohibitions on temporary structures, prohibitions on temporary signage and prohibitions on inflatables and on the use of advertising banners or signage as building wraps. It is also provided that host cities must establish a 'preventive fund', i.e. if such prohibitions cannot be obtained, the Host Committee must provide a fund of USD 1 million for the NFL to use to prevent ambush marketing.[17] More will be said in Chap. 7 regarding the implications of such 'clean zones' for the citizens of host cities, particularly from the perspective of their human rights implications.

Another manifestation of the creation of special legal protection for commercial rights to events relates, more generally, to the extension of protection for intellectual property (which will be examined more closely in Chap. 5). Since the Sydney Olympics in 2000 the IOC also demands specific legislation to protect its event against unauthorised commercial exploitation, and its lead has been followed by other event organisers (such as FIFA and UEFA). As it has been aptly put, we are confronted here with 'the manipulation of governments by sport organisations that make enactment of event-specific legislation "a cost of doing business" in exchange for hosting the event.'[18] In fact, the bargaining power of event organisers is such that applicant host nations or cities are not only forced to accede to demands for special legislation in order to qualify to be awarded hosting rights. Johnson observes that 'international federations are in such a strong position that they can demand ambush marketing protection even after the event has been

[15] Schwab 2006, p. 8.

[16] Sliffman 2012.

[17] Ibid.

[18] Grady et al. 2010, p. 149.

awarded to a particular country.'[19] No wonder then that it was reported in the South African parliament in August 2005 that during a governmental World Cup fact-finding mission to 1998 hosts, France, the director-general of the French Football Federation, Jacques Lambert, advised South Africa and the federations to remain 'firm' with FIFA because the 'requirements from FIFA were increasing.' It was reported that German authorities, hosts of the 2006 football showcase, had also warned the South African government to be wary of FIFA and the extent of its demands.

Bid requirements now more often than not contain specific requirements regarding a suitable or satisfactory legal framework and an environment within which attempts to ambush the event or to infringe on e.g. broadcasting rights and intellectual property can be properly (and harshly) dealt with. By way of illustration, compare the provisions of Article 41(a) of the Host City Contract for the 2012 London Olympic Games, which preceded the passing of the London Olympic Games and Paralympic Games Act, 2006:

> The City, the NOC and/or the OCOG have ensured, or shall ensure, not later than 31st December 2005, that the Olympic Symbol, the terms "Olympic" and "Olympiad" and the Olympic motto are protected in the name of the IOC and/or that they have obtained, from the Government and/or the competent national authorities of the Host Country, adequate and continuing legal protection to the satisfaction of the IOC and in the name of the IOC. The NOC confirms that, in accordance with the Olympic Charter, should such domestic legal protection exist or be expressed in the name of or for the benefit of the NOC, the NOC shall only exercise such rights in accordance with the instructions received from the IOC. The City, the NOC and/or the OCOG shall ensure that the above-noted legal protection provides for a procedure which allows intellectual property disputes, concerning the above-noted properties, to be solved in a timely manner, in particular before and during the actual period of the Games.

According to the IOC's Technical Manual on Brand Protection[20] in respect of the Games, the local organising committees (or OCOGs) are required to work towards obtaining legislative protection for Olympic marks and other commercial rights. For example, the Manual provides that '[t]he OCOG must draft legislation for the protection of Olympic intellectual property, including restrictions on company, business and Internet site names—and, if possible, Games-specific legislation in addition to existing copyright and trademark laws,' and '[t]he OCOG must consult with the geographical names board (or similar appropriate agency) to restrict the registration of place names containing Olympic-related words.'[21] OCOGs are required to 'plan and petition new legislation':

---

[19] Johnson 2008, p. 28.

[20] The version available at the time of writing on the web site of http://www.gamesmonitor.org.uk in respect of the 2012 London Olympics (this document refers to an updated version of the Manual which was scheduled for publication in July 2005, although such updated version (if it exists) is not available online at the time of writing).

[21] The 2005 version of the Manual at 16.

> The OCOG must work for legislation that:
>
> – allows the OCOG to obtain an injunction to prevent an unauthorised user from manufacturing or distributing goods that improperly bear Olympic identification, without the necessity of proving damage;
> – enables OCOGs to work with NOCs and national customs offices to prevent the import of goods that improperly bear Olympic identification;
> – requires the unauthorised user to provide the OCOG with damages, or an account of profits, or both.[22]

And OCOGs must 'prepare cease-and-desist orders that cite the appropriate legislative support of OCOG marketing programmes.'[23] The Manual also requires candidate cities to 'work for legislative protection of Olympic-related emblems, trademarks, slogans, etc., including the emblem of the bid committee and the word "Olympic."'[24] The importance of the Host City Contract should not be underestimated, as it forms the basis for legislative protection of intellectual property which can be significantly at variance with the existing laws of the host nation (city); it is the instrument upon which wide-ranging changes in domestic laws are based due to the IOC's stringent demands. For example, while the United States does not currently have special anti-ambush marketing legislation in place at either federal or state level, the following provision is to be found in the proposed Illinois legislation which was drafted in pursuance of the IOC's bid city requirements for the (ultimately unsuccessful) Chicago 2016 Olympics bid:

> The State, in accordance with law and to the extent of the State's authority, and subject to the limitations of this Article agrees that, if requested by the candidate city, the bid committee, or the OCOG, it shall permit any member of the General Assembly to introduce legislation necessary to: (i) effectively reduce and sanction ambush marketing, (ii) eliminate illegal street vending during the period beginning 2 weeks before the games through the end of the games; and (iii) control advertising space (including, but not limited to, billboards and advertising on public transport) as well as air space and that any such legislation will be introduced as soon as possible...[25]

Wang[26] noted that 'as an international organisation, the IOC's intellectual property standards are its own, separate and apart from the nation that happens to host the games in any given year.' The IOC is able to dictate the level of intellectual property protection in the respective host countries, thus allowing the IOC to achieve 'a standard of international protection for its own trademark through the Host City Contract.'[27]

---

[22] Ibid. 58.

[23] Ibid.

[24] Ibid. 21.

[25] Illinois Compiled Statutes (65 ILCS 120) 2016 Olympic and Paralympic Games Act; section 5-10(12).

[26] Wang 2005, pp. 300–301.

[27] See McKelvey and Grady 2008, p. 575.

At this point I should include a brief reference to the fact that, of course, while the mega-event organisers have been very successful in their efforts to demand legal protection for what they view as their property, they have not (yet) attained a complete immunity from the normal domestic laws in all host nations, which might affect sponsors' interests. For example, Budweiser, which has come to be associated with the football World Cup for some years, had to sell its rights to the 1998 FIFA World Cup in France to electronics giant Casio, because French legislation placed restrictions on alcohol advertising. Even in the face of the substantial power posed by the event organisers and the strict bidding requirements that they set, it will be interesting to see how similar restrictions are dealt with in future (when one considers, for example, that Muslim and Arab middle-East countries are expected to bid for future mega-events—Qatar will be hosting the 2022 FIFA World Cup[28]).

Similar requirements (demands) for the passing of legislation to protect the commercial rights of event organisers and their sponsors are set by the other relevant international sports organisations in respect of their mega-events. Schwab, for example, doesn't mince words in observing that 'a lack of rights protection legislation would have rendered Africa a nonstarter as a candidate' to host the 2010 FIFA World Cup,[29] and a South African court specifically examined the contractual obligation placed by FIFA on the Local Organising Committee for the 2010 FIFA World Cup to 'secure and maintain good relations, the collaboration and clear lines of communication with the competent national and local government authorities, including, but not limited to, competition authorities, police departments, trading standards and customs authorities and other such parties.'[30] One of the clearest examples of the pressure on potential host law-makers to pass such legislation in conformity with the organisers' requirements can be found in

[28] It has been reported that, while alcohol is not illegal in Qatar, the government has tightened regulations on alcohol consumption in an attempt to stop Qatari citizens, especially young people, from drinking. It is an offence to drink or be drunk in public. Qataris are not allowed in bars while foreigners are asked to present their passports or a membership card to gain entry. A spokesperson for Qatar's World Cup bid was quoted as stating that alcohol would be available in 'a flexible approach' to all fans that come to Qatar, at fan zones.

[29] Schwab 2006, p. 9.

[30] Par. 31.1.4 of the Association Agreement for the hosting of the 2010 FIFA World Cup South Africa, entered into in 2003 between FIFA and the South African Football Association (whose rights and obligations were later assigned to the Local Organising Committee, a company), as quoted in *M&G Media Ltd v 2010 FIFA World Cup South Africa Organising Committee Ltd* South Gauteng High Court Case No. 09/51422 (unreported at the time of writing) at par. 118.

respect of the 2014 Glasgow Commonwealth Games.[31] The New Zealand Rugby Football Union failed to secure cohosting rights to the 2003 IRB Rugby World Cup due to its inability to guarantee 'clean stadia' for the event to the IRB,[32] and it is interesting to note that New Zealand subsequently passed much-criticised and very extensive anti-ambush marketing legislation in the form of the Major Events Management Act, 2007[33] and was ultimately successful in obtaining the rights to host the IRB Rugby World Cup in 2011 and to cohost the 2015 ICC Cricket World Cup.

---

[31] The Glasgow Commonwealth Games Act, 2008, when in Bill form (tabled in parliament on 9 November 2007), contained the following (for example) in respect of the Commonwealth Games Federation's requirements for regulating street trading around Games event venues—note the references to the organisers' demands:

> Current legislation only relates to street trading/peddling, as controlled in Scotland under the Civic Government (Scotland) Act 1982 and the Pedlars Acts. The Commonwealth Games Federation require the prevention of street vending which would necessitate control by the Scottish Ministers over street trading, and the prevention of markets, fairs, pedlars or trading on public or private land from taking place in the vicinity of Games venues during the Games period. The Scottish Ministers do not have power to direct how councils exercise their discretionary powers under the 1982 Act. The penalties associated with these offences are also unlikely to discourage attempts to target the Games. Relying on current legislation would, therefore, not deliver the Government's obligations under the Host City Contract and risk legal action by the Commonwealth Games Federation. Failure to control street vending around Games events during the Games period could also threaten the image of the Games and undermine Scotland's ability to attract major events in the future… As the introduction of legislation necessary to eliminate street vending is a requirement of hosting the 2014 Commonwealth Games, there is no alternative to the introduction of a prohibition on street trading that would deliver the policy objectives.

[32] See Crow and Hoek 2003, p. 4.

[33] As part of New Zealand's successful bids to host the 2011 Rugby World Cup and the 2015 ICC Cricket World Cup a commitment was given to ensure adequate provisions were in place to protect sponsors. Since the promulgation of the Act three events have to date been identified as protected events, namely the 2011 Rugby World Cup, the FIFA U-17 Women's World Cup and the FIBA U-19 World Championship—see the report by Ironside, S I 'Ambush Marketing Law Passes First Test,' available at http://www.baldwins.com/ambush-marketing-law-passes-first-test (posted 4 September 2009). The Hon Trevor Mallard, New Zealand's Minister for the Rugby World Cup, was quoted as explaining the need for this legislation as follows:

> [T]he legislation will make New Zealand more attractive to major event organisers. Without it, New Zealand's success when bidding for similar events in the future, may be at risk. It is impossible to host major events these days without enormous financial contributions from large sponsors. These companies will not provide sponsorship dollars if others are allowed to manipulate public perceptions by falsely suggesting a link with these events.

From the undated (last updated 16 September 2009) report entitled 'Proposed Ambush Marketing Bill Explained,' available online at http://www.med.govt.nz/templates/MultipageDocumentTOC41944.aspx.

Such widespread demands for special laws are not unproblematic from a legal perspective. As has been observed, the legal footing for the expectation of 'clean venues' for their events by event organisers is 'at best, shaky, and is destined to be challenged sooner than later.'[34] At the time of the announcement of the results of the 2018 and 2022 FIFA football World Cup bids, in late 2010, there was reportedly speculation that one reason for the failure of the Low Countries bid (a joint bid by the Netherlands and Belgium) was an alleged lack of government support for the bid; one could interpret this as including a lack of confidence on the part of FIFA and/or its commercial partners that these potential hosts would be willing to pass the type of anti-ambushing legislation as seen in countries like South Africa (especially after the near diplomatic row involving the Dutch government following the Bavaria ambushing stunt during the 2010 FIFA World Cup South Africa, discussed elsewhere in Chap. 8). Was the following (contained in an undated letter by the Dutch government addressed to FIFA's president suggesting changes to FIFA's wording of its demanded government guarantee in respect of 'Legal issues and Indemnification')[35] fatal to the Low Countries bid?

> Chapter B of Government Guarantee No. 6 is replaced as follows:
>
> 'We confirm that all FIFA's intellectual property rights are protected according to the Host Country's intellectual property laws. For acquiring copyright protection no formalities need to be fulfilled. With regard to patent, trademark rights and design rights, it is up to FIFA to take care of the formalities (timely registering those rights with the responsible authorities to acquire the protection) and to make sure that the material requirements for obtaining the protection are fulfilled.
>
> Since all FIFA's Intellectual Property rights are or can be protected according to Dutch law, there is no need for any "special protection"... There is no specific "ambush marketing law" in Dutch and Belgian legislation. We consider "ambush marketing" to be covered by a) intellectual property laws, more specifically the copyright and trademark law, b) unfair competition law, more specifically misleading and comparative advertising law and the unfair commercial practices Law, and c) general tort law.

FIFA's response (by way of its head of commercial legal services, Jörg Vollmüller, in a letter to the Holland-Belgium Bid Foundation dated 16 September 2010[36]) was that the watered-down version of FIFA's required governmental guarantee in respect of commercial rights protection constituted non-compliance with the organisation's bid requirements. FIFA declared that its template for government guarantees contain 'the indispensable minimum requirements in respect of the governmental support necessary to host and stage a FIFA World Cup™,' and that 'any modifications or deviations from such FIFA templates wording or required content and the consequential lack of Government support

[34] Marcus 2010, p. 31.

[35] A copy of this (draft) letter is available at the time of writing on the web site of investigative journalist (and perennial thorn in FIFA's side) Andrew Jennings, at http://www.transparencyinsport.org/The_documents_that_FIFA_does_not_want_fans_to_read/PDF-documents/(8)Legal-Issues-and-Indemnification.pdf.

[36] Available online at the time of writing at http://www.transparencyinsport.org/The_documents_that_FIFA_does_not_want_fans_to_read/PDF-documents/(10)FIFA-aan-NL.pdf.

have an effect on the manner in which the requirements on these matters are met and may therefore represent a significant shortfall from the FIFA requirements which the Legal Working Group will have to address in its evaluation report.'[37] Even though the Dutch Minister of Health, Welfare and Sport responded (in a letter dated 19 October 2010[38]) the Holland-Belgium bid was, of course, ultimately unsuccessful—although I wouldn't want to imply that this was due (only) to the refusal to commit to FIFA's demands for special laws to protect its commercial rights. FIFA's response is not surprising; as one commentator observed with reference to the Bavaria babes scenario and the Dutch government's stance: 'Wearing clothes of your own bearing the trademark of a party that is not an official sponsor will not constitute trademark infringement. Therefore, if the Netherlands will indeed host the World Cup tournament in 2018/2022, the Bavaria babes can delve up their Dutch dresses once again.'[39]

Marcus[40] poses the question, more generally, whether it is fair for a country with world-class sporting facilities, a strong sporting history, financial support, an efficient transportation system, five-star hotels and a visionary post-event legacy plan to be rejected from hosting a sports mega-event because it does not intend to enact brand protection legislation. He observes that, even though the objectives of event organisers may be legitimate (which I would submit is not a given), they are bordering on 'micro-managing' the hosting of their events, which is a reflection of the changed priorities of modern sporting culture:

> Previously, the salient factor in bidding was the quality of facilities. While that remains a central feature, the paramount consideration is now the protection of commercial interests so that brand protection and strong intellectual property security are pertinent, perhaps indispensable elements of a bid package.[41]

Before we consider the legitimacy of these requirements for the passing of special anti-ambushing legislation, and for the sake of completeness, it bears mentioning that such legislation can take a number of different forms or types. The first distinction relates to the focus of the legislation (such legislative instruments share the object of protecting the commercial interests of the event organisers and sponsors, but they may relate to different foci). Some such legislation, for example, is aimed specifically at protecting intellectual property of the event organisers or

---

[37] Ibid.

[38] A copy of which is available online on the website of the Dutch government at https://zoek.officielebekendmakingen.nl/blg-84443.html?zoekcriteria=%3fzkt%3dEenvoudig%26pst%3d%26vrt%3dcommercial%2brights%2bFIFA%26zkd%3dInDeGeheleText%26dpr%3dAfgelopenDag%26sdt%3dDatumBrief%26ap%3d%26pnr%3d1%26rpp%3d10&resultIndex=0&sorttype=1&sortorder=4.

[39] Van der Zaal, R 'How Will The Government Deal With Ambush Marketing if the World Cup Comes to the Netherlands?' Kennedy van der Laan newsletter September 2010—available online at http://www.kvdl.nl/PdfCreator.aspx?guid=%7B05DDAA4E-7354-4B1E-BACB-1FEB9263BC6C%7D.

[40] Ibid. 26.

[41] Ibid. 27.

sponsors. It does so in order to provide additional protection, beyond general intellectual property laws (i.e. existing copyright and trademark statutes). Examples, in the context of the Olympic Games, are the Olympic Symbol etc. (Protection) Act, 1995 in England, the Ted Stevens Olympic and Amateur Sports Act, 1998, in the United States,[42] the Regulations on the Protection of Olympic Symbols, 2002[43] in China, and the Emblems and Names [Prevention of Improper Use] Act, 1950[44] in India.

The second type of legislative instrument is the one which I will focus on in the later chapters when evaluating the legitimacy of special event legislation to protect commercial rights, namely legislation that is aimed at providing specific protection against ambush marketing. This type of instrument can be in the form of either an event-specific statute (compare the London Olympic and Paralympic Games Act, 2006, Vancouver's Olympic and Paralympic Marks Act, 2007 or Brazil's Olympic Act, 2009[45]) or an 'umbrella' statute which covers more than one event (events must usually be designated as 'protected' in order to be covered by the provisions of such statute), such as New Zealand's Major Events Management Act, 2007. In this category one also finds legislation aimed at protecting directly against ambush marketing by means of specific provisions, although the statute itself is not specific to (sports) (mega-)events, for example unfair trade practises legislation (such as South Africa's amended Merchandise Marks Act, 2002, which arguably provides the most stringent and far-reaching protection against ambush marketing currently to be found anywhere in the world).

Finally, one finds other legislative instruments aimed at or directly relevant to ambush marketing protection, such as municipal host city by-laws (which, for example, may contain wide and far-reaching restrictions on commercial and other activities in exclusive use zones around event venues).[46] At the time of writing there has been much controversy over the UK Government's draft Regulations on Advertising and Trading Activity around London 2012, which was published for

---

[42] 36 U.S.C. 380 (the Amateur Sports Act, 1978, was amended in 1998 to become the Ted Stevens Olympic and Amateur Sport Act, in order, *inter alia*, to provide protection for the Salt Lake City winter Olympic Games, by providing the US Olympic Committee with the right to sue companies for even appearing to associate with the Games). The United States Supreme Court famously (and controversially) upheld an injunction in terms of the Act preventing San Francisco Arts and Athletics (SFAA) from using the word 'Olympic' to promote the 'Gay Olympic Games,' in *San Francisco Arts and Athletics v. United States Olympic Committee*, 483 U.S. 522 (1987). The Court concluded that the United States Olympic Committee does not have to prove that unauthorsed use of the word Olympic was confusing.

[43] Decree No. 245, State Council of the Peoples' Republic of China, 2002, released by the State Council on 4 February 2002 (implemented 1 April 2002).

[44] The symbol of the International Olympic Committee, including the interlaced five rings, are protected in terms of Item 21 of the Schedule to the Act.

[45] Act 12,035 of 2009 (effective as of 2 October 2009, and in force until 31 December 2016).

[46] See the discussion in Sect. 4.4.5 in respect of the 2010 FIFA World Cup South Africa.

public comment in early 2011.[47] Burton and Chadwick[48] point out that UEFA spearheaded the use and enforcement of marketing exclusion zones surrounding stadia and event host sites, as a result of serial ambusher Nike's Euro 1996 and 1998 FIFA World Cup promotions around match venues (Nike famously—allegedly, I should add—went as far as having a building constructed especially for the purpose of an ambushing stunt[49]). These exclusion zones have also been implemented for the Olympic Games,[50] and are now seen as a required element of any Olympic host bid, as part of anti-ambush marketing legislation. These exclusion zones have forced ambushers to become more creative and have encouraged greater planning for larger, more ambitious ambush campaigns.[51]

These different types of legislative instruments will be considered in more detail in the sections that follow and the later chapters.

4.3 Evaluating the Legitimacy of Demands for Special Legal Protection of Commercial Rights to Mega-Events

The reasons for the increased calls for specific event legislation by sports governing bodies are twofold. First, of course, 'event-specific legislation is designed to protect the sport organisation and event brand equity for the ultimate purpose of maximising revenue.'[52] Second, the experience in recent years has been one of often creative ambushes of events by shrewd 'ambushers' who have managed to skirt the boundaries of existing laws such as, for example, intellectual property laws and the common law of unlawful competition. There has been a realisation that such more traditional forms of legal protection often simply do not provide sufficient safeguards in such cases. More sophisticated forms of ambush marketing have developed so that they do not contravene any existing law; or enforcement is

[47] See more discussion on these regulations in the section on ambush marketing legislation in the United Kingdom later in this chapter, and in Chap. 7.

[48] Burton and Chadwick 2009, p. 9.

[49] Nike is often cited as an example of a major multinational corporation that apparently has few scruples when it comes to 'ambushing' their competitors in respect of sporting events: The company has been credited with having its own 'director of ambush marketing,' and during the 1996 Atlanta Olympic Games it not only produced a commercial web site (Nike@Lanta) but also erected its name and logo on a building overlooking Atlanta's Olympic Park—the building was apparently constructed specifically for the purpose of ambush marketing!—see Shank 1999, pp. 373–374.

[50] Rather drastic steps are sometimes taken to ensure a 'clean slate' for advertising by official sponsors and the elimination of potential ambushers' messages. For example, in preparation for the 2004 Athens Olympic Games more than USD 750,000 was spent removing and cleaning billboards throughout the city, in an effort to prevent non-sponsors from grabbing the limelight during the event.

[51] Burton and Chadwick 2009, p. 9.

[52] Grady et al. 2010, p. 147.

unlikely, given uncertainty regarding the application of the law, the timing of the event, and/or the costs of litigation.[53] This involves practical problems related to the grinding of the wheels of justice, which may make the availability of a legal remedy, where appropriate, a largely academic matter after the fact. For example, it was observed that a lack of event-specific street trading regulations in a host city may defeat the very purpose of existing by-laws in the process of combating ambush marketing by intrusion into the precincts of event venues—'under current legislation some types of illegal advertising can be removed only after 28 days' notice—this is a longer time frame than the Olympic or Paralympic Games.'[54] Similarly, the time constraints inherent in traditional forms of litigation to protect event organisers' rights (such as, for example, a claim for an injunction in respect of alleged trademark infringement) may make a nonsense of the practical value of such remedies in a high pressure mega-event staging environment where time may be of the essence.

Marcus highlights the importance of commercial rights protection in the context of the selection of host nations or cities for mega-events. He observes that, while the reasons for choosing one bidding territory over another are not usually given after the event is awarded, certain fundamental issues surface, namely

- Whether the particular country's culture is a 'protective' one when it comes to sports brands and marketing;
- Whether the bidding nation has a track record of strong intellectual property protection; and
- Whether the bidding nation has an effective law enforcement policy and practise.[55]

He concludes that the practise of enacting protective legislation for sports events is well entrenched, and that 'the only distinction from one bid to another is whether the legislation already exists or new legislation must be introduced.'[56] *Sui generis* event commercial rights protection has become the norm for the hosting of sports mega-events, even though the rationale for such special laws is not always sufficiently (and transparently) explained, and one is faced with a situation where the apparently automatic introduction of new legislation has become *de rigueur*.[57]

---

[53] See the recent ambush marketing legislation review prepared for the Australian government—Frontier Economics 2007, Chap. 2.

[54] From the UK Department of Culture, Media And Sport's consultation document on Regulations on Advertising Activity and Trading Around London 2012 March 2011 at 5—available online at the time of writing at http://www.culture.gov.uk/images/publications/ConDoc_Regulations_on_Advertising_and_Trading_London_2012-section1-7.pdf.

[55] Marcus 2010, p. 27.

[56] Ibid.

[57] See the discussion of Phillip Johnson's views on 'vertical and horizontal creep' in respect of the introduction of special event legislation, in the text below.

Another important reason for the potential ineffectiveness of, specifically, more general intellectual property laws, is what has been described as the 'third dimension' that events bring to the equation in the context of ambush marketing.[58] Traditionally, IP rights infringements involve e.g. an infringement by X of Y's copyright in a work (for example, by means of unlawful copying or publication of the relevant work) or through X using, for example, a trademark that is confusingly similar to Y's registered trademark. In the case of ambush marketing of an event, however, the 'ambusher' would usually not be infringing the intellectual property of its competitor (e.g. an official sponsor). The deception or confusion relates to association with *the event* and not with the official sponsor.[59] And as Ellis et al. observe, 'association with the event is created by more oblique references or juxtapositions'[60] rather than direct use of protected IP. The 'ambusher' is alleged to have created confusion over their (official) involvement or association with an event, which it is then claimed prejudices both the event organisers (rights grantors) and the official sponsors or commercial partners (rights holders) due to the dilution of the value of their investment and a potential loss of revenues that would otherwise have been payable in terms of an official rights grant contract (as well as negatively affecting the efficacy of the official sponsor's advertising through the creation of a cluttered marketing environment surrounding the event). This third dimension is also relevant in respect of the efficacy of other forms of legal protection, as it may affect the availability of remedies. In the context of consumer protection legislation (e.g. aimed at prohibiting unfair trading) such remedies are usually afforded to consumers and not to competitors (i.e. an official sponsor may not have a leg to stand on in respect of an ambush which may harm its interests but strictly speaking falls outside the ambit of the relevant law). Ambush marketing also appears to be problematic in respect of pigeon-holing such conduct under other legal doctrines:

> Ambush marketing is often qualified as parasitism. But parasitism usually takes place between competitors, whilst ambush marketing does not necessarily involve competitors. Ambush marketing first means association with an event, not with specific parties. Another difference with traditional parasitism is that authorised sponsors did not contribute through their own work or efforts, to the reputation of the event or to the values associated with the event. The sponsor only financed the event (and this in a relatively small proportion as compared to broadcasting rights). The party who created the reputation and who can claim rights over the values associated with the Olympic Games or the World Cup, are the [IOC] and [FIFA]. Therefore the phenomenon is more akin to some sort of free rider issue.[61]

---

[58] Shwetashree Majumder and Harsimran Kalra 'The ambush marketing debate,' on the web site *Managing Intellectual Property*, 1 September 2010 (available online at the time of writing at http://www.managingip.com/Article/2665113/The-ambush-marketing-debate.html?ArticleId=2665113&p=2).

[59] See also Corbett and Van Roy 2010, p. 351.

[60] Ellis et al. 2011, p. 300.

[61] Kobel 2007, p. 8.

I would submit, however, that this potential for existing laws to be insufficient in the face of creative ambushes does not provide enough reason *per se* for legislatures to pass new and often very far-reaching and even draconian laws aimed at stopping the (perceived) gaps. There is always the argument that where existing laws do not cover specific conduct such conduct should, in fact, simply not be outlawed. It is a rather scary prospect to imagine a world where increasingly restrictive legislation is constantly passed to address perceived inadequacies of existing laws that fail to cover conduct that the lawmaker (or those lobbying for such new laws) views to be unlawful but which, in fact, is not unlawful in terms of the existing law and also constitutes an apparent 'grey area' in the public perception of the moral or ethical dimensions of the conduct sought to be outlawed. Longdin observes the following (in the context of New Zealand's extensive anti-ambush marketing legislation and the conflicting views of detractors and proponents of special legislation and the need for special legislative regulation in this regard):

> Implicit (and sometimes explicit) on both sides of the fence are two assumptions. The first is that lack of special protection for particular kinds of economic activity and for particular forms of investment over that given to any player in a market economy constitutes a gap in the law that courts or legislatures must fill whenever asked. This is to ask judges and legislators to take a considerable leap of faith. The 'gap' may exist for perfectly valid social or economic reasons. The case for legal protection must be made. It cannot simply be asserted. The second assumption, obviously fallacious once stated but all the more tenacious for that, is that all harms deserve compensation. Neither form of a priori reasoning is an appropriate starting point for an analysis of [New Zealand's Major Events Management Act, 2007] (or indeed for the analysis of the social utility or economic efficiency of IP in general).[62]

Clearly this is a balancing act and a slippery slope to negotiate, and especially problematic when it raises concerns relating to legislative fairness in the context of the protection of narrow commercial interests at the potential expense of significant public interests. As one commentator observed in respect of the legislative anti-ambushing protection enacted for the 2010 Vancouver winter Olympic Games[63]:

> Special interest legislation, particularly legislation blatantly designed to protect a select group of corporate interests at the expense of free speech, should have no place in a government focused on trust and accountability. Protecting the investment of Olympic corporate sponsors may be a worthwhile goal, yet there is a price to be paid for eliminating

[62] Longdin 2009, p. 728. For more on the New Zealand legislation, see the discussion in Sect. 4.4.4.

[63] For more detailed discussion of the Vancouver legislation, see Sect. 4.4.7.

court-ordered safeguards and granting control over generic words to a private entity. Canadian Olympic organizers have pledged to "own the podium" in 2010, yet Canadians might ask whether they must own words such as "winter" in order to do so.[64]

In what will surely seem a weird stance for a lawyer to take, I simply cannot support the following approach as advocated by respected commentators on ambush marketing. McKelvey and Grady question why event organisers have brought so few law suits against 'ambush marketers.' One possible reason that they advance is the risk of adverse court rulings (such as that encountered by FIFA in its wrangling with chocolate-maker Ferrero before the German federal supreme court in respect of its claims to trademark protection for its 'Fussball WM 2006' mark, which will be examined in Chap. 5). The authors refer to the danger of the 'vagaries of the courts' and declare:

> [C]ourts, when faced with the decision of protecting the intellectual property rights of event organizers and their official sponsors to the detriment of the free enterprise rights of local businesses, are just as likely to side with the latter. It is therefore incumbent upon event organizers to exert as much leverage as possible during the bid process to ensure that special trademark legislation and other forms of advertising restrictions anticipate and address, as specifically as possible, the legal gray areas of ambush marketing that could result in unfavorable judicial interpretation.[65]

The 'legal grey areas' that they refer to exist because the legal systems of many jurisdictions simply do not outlaw conduct that event organisers and their commercial partners view as threats to their commercial interests, with the objective of maximising the returns from such events. A view that advocates lobbying (read: strict demands) for special legislation which seeks to effectively limit the power of courts to say so is destructive of the rule of law, and highly dubious. To illustrate the point, another observer has also recently commented on the dearth of case law where event organisers, in the various jurisdictions, have actually proceeded to the point of litigation against 'ambushers,' in a discussion of the reasons why ambush marketing has managed to 'survive' in the face of legal responses. Seth[66] refers to the well-known Canadian case of *NHL v Pepsi-Cola, Canada*[67]—note the loaded use of language:

> Corporations have been extremely adept at protecting themselves from legal challenges against ambush marketing. For example, in the [*NHL v Pepsi* case] the popular strategy of using disclaimers such as 'the company is not an official sponsor and has not paid to

[64] Michael Geist, Canada Research Chair in Internet and E-commerce Law at the University of Ottawa, Faculty of Law, writing on his free speech blog ('Special interest law undermines the Olympic spirit,' 19 March 2007—available online at the time of writing at http://www.michaelgeist.ca/index.php?option=com_topics&task=view&id=10041&Itemid=75&startmonth=&startyear=&endmonth=&endyear=&intersect=0&topic%5B%5D=10041&limit=10&limitstart=50).

[65] McKelvey and Grady 2008, p. 581.

[66] Seth 2010, pp. 457, 458.

[67] 92 DLR 4th 349—see discussion elsewhere in this book.

> affiliate with the event' was successful in helping Pepsi get away scot free. Besides, since the two products were not similar, Pepsi wriggled out of the allegation of trade mark infringement and passing off. The problem is that always at least one condition of any of the above mentioned claims or any other potentially applicable claims remains unfulfilled thereby leading to a failed action by the claimant… The above case laws *(sic)*[68] show that in the absence of specific legislation for ambush marketing, defendants get away thereby leaving the plaintiffs with no guaranteed remedy.

My response, with all due respect, is simply to observe that this lack of objectivity is troubling. Such a clearly biased view implies that ambush marketing is bad; if the law doesn't say so then the law must be wrong. If you sue someone for an alleged breach of contract and it turns out that you had never even entered into a contract with them, would you blame the court for throwing out your case? This approach flatly ignores the fact that Pepsi's conduct simply *did not constitute ambush marketing in the eyes of the law*. The disclaimer served to refute claims of an attempt to confuse as to an association, and the legal requirements for passing off and trademark infringement were not met. Such subjective views on the proper role for the law based on apparently deep-seated antagonism to the practise of 'ambushing' (which view is quite common in the literature), in my view, ultimately shows contempt of the rule of law. If you want to lobby for changes to the law, do so with recourse to substantive reasons why the law needs to change, rather than a pre-conceived conception that the conduct you despise shouldn't be tolerated. As has been observed, whatever route of legal protection for event commercial rights is taken 'the onus remains on event organisers to strike the balance between satisfying the needs of event partners while adhering to the broad spectrum of legal principles.'[69]

Leaving aside, for now, the legitimacy of such special anti-ambushing legislation (which will be considered in more detail elsewhere in this book), it remains to consider the sports governing bodies' frequent calls for special treatment of their commercial stock-in-trade. While it is, in my view, no argument to suggest that such legislative lobbying is justifiable in light of the fact that it happens only in isolated cases involving specific high profile showcases, it should be noted that, in any event, efforts at obtaining special legal protection for the commercial interests of sports sponsors is much more ubiquitous.

Apart from the pressure exerted on potential event host nations or cities in the event bidding process to ensure a suitable domestic legal environment for the purposes of commercial rights protection, which takes place on an *ad hoc* basis in respect of individual mega-event bid procedures, the sports organisations are also continually active in respect of the lobbying of lawmakers for the purposes of strengthening rights protection more generally. An early example of a permanent

---

68 The author refers to the above-mentioned *NHL v Pepsi* case and a few other cases where claims based on 'ambush marketing' were not accepted by courts (e.g. in India).

69 Marcus 2010, p. 28.

sports rights holders association hails from the American professional sports leagues. In 1992 the NFL, National Basketball Association (NBA), National Hockey League, Major League Baseball and Collegiate Licensing Association formed the Coalition to Advance the Protection of Sports Logos, specifically to deal with trademark defence of its constituents. Since its inception, the organisation has seized more than 9 million pieces of illegal merchandise with logos from its members, valued at more than USD 334 million, and it is described as a best practise example for sports brand protection by means of proactive (and litigious) responses to threats of IP infringement.[70] Less focused on the courts and more on the law-makers is the (initially low-profile but increasingly active) Sports Rights Owners Coalition (or SROC),[71] which was formed in 2006 and has as its members all the largest international sports governing bodies (except for the Olympic Movement)[72] and a number of the most prominent domestic sports federations and professional leagues[73] found worldwide. SROC describes itself as providing a forum through which sports bodies can share information and experiences, with the purpose to enable discussion and sharing of best practise on key legal, political and regulatory issues; raising awareness of new developments and innovation in sports rights; and in order to enable sports to take joint action to protect and promote their rights. The following is contained on the organisation's web site:

> SROC members are looking to National Governments and international Treaty Organisations such as the European Union, WTO and WIPO to:
>
> - Fully recognise, protect and promote the special nature of sport and sports rights;
> - Provide comprehensive protection for sports rights, including their names, logos and marks;
> - Prevent the theft of sports events broadcasts by pirates;
> - Outlaw ambush marketing and ticket touting/scalping; and
> - Create a regime for sports betting that enables sport to protect its integrity, and establishes a fair return to sports for the use of their events by betting operators.

SROC, for example, lobbied the European Parliament's Select Committee on Culture, Media and Sport in January 2008 by means of (unsuccessful) calls for the granting of *sui generis* copyright protection to sports events as a whole, and has criticised the EU's White Paper on Sport for its failure to adequately address

---

70 Gannon 2010, p. 70.

71 On the web at http://sroc.info/index.html.

72 Members include FIFA, the International Rugby Board, the International Cricket Council, the International Association of Athletics Federations and the International Tennis Federation.

73 Including UEFA, the Bundesliga, the England and Wales Cricket Board, Cricket Australia, the English Rugby Football Union, the Football Association (or FA), the Premier League, Formula 1 motor racing, the NBA, NFL and Major League Baseball, the Indian Premier League (cricket), the European Tour (golf), the British Horse Racing Authority and the Wimbledon and Roland Garros tennis championships.

broadcasting and media issues relating to sport.[74] SROC enjoys observer status with the World Intellectual Property Organisation (WIPO) to monitor copyright issues regarding sport, and has been accepted into the European Observatory on Counterfeiting and Piracy (the EU group which combats illegal internet file-sharing). More recently SROC has, controversially, been involved in calls for the creation of a 'sports betting right' with consequent revenues to be paid to sports event organisers by bookmakers, and its justification on the basis of the maintenance of sporting integrity has not been well received by the sports betting industry, who apparently feel that such calls are disingenuous and used to mask an agenda of the sports industry to increase revenues. SROC members, such as FIFA, the Premier League and the England and Wales Cricket Board have been pressing governments about a 'fair return' for betting, arguing that their tournaments are intellectual properties and that bookmakers should pay for the right to take bets on the events. The stakes are quite high, if one considers that it is estimated that if such a levy had been in place for the 2010 FIFA World Cup South Africa, FIFA would have earned between GBP 10 and 20 million from such source in respect of betting in the UK alone.[75] These SROC members are calling for a 'sports betting right' similar to the one that has been introduced in France, with sporting bodies able to negotiate a return of about 1.5% of turnover. It has been reported that insiders in respect of England's (failed) 2018 FIFA World Cup bid were of the opinion that the French legislation had been a factor in France being awarded the 2016 European Championships by UEFA.[76]

The sense of frustration in respect of certain issues regarding sports rights protection is understandable—compare SROC's concerns regarding digital piracy,[77] and the problem of counterfeit goods is so prevalent that at the 2010 Commonwealth Games in Delhi the fake 'branded' clothing hit the streets even before the official stuff could make it out there.[78] But these continual efforts at greater protection for sports (event) rights are indicative of a more general attitude among the large sporting organisations regarding the apparent imperative for domestic lawmakers to respect what are often self-created commercial rights, the substantial value of which is based on monopolistic practises (relating, from the sport organisation's perspective, to its sole control of the sporting code's pinnacle international competition or event, and from the sponsor's perspective, to

[74] See Andriychuck 2009, pp. 122–123.

[75] See Blitz, R 'World Cup bid team eyes betting levy' *Financial Times Online*, 14 October 2010, available online at the time of writing at http://www.ft.com/cms/s/0/3910bf12-d7c2-11df-b478-00144feabdc0.html#axzz1B2QRCxWz.

[76] Ibid.

[77] See the report (compiled by Envisional Ltd and NetResult Ltd) entitled *Background Report on Digital Piracy of Sporting Events* (2008), available on the SROC web site at the time of writing at http://sroc.info/resources/OECD%20Sports%20Piracy%20CaseStudy%20-%20FINAL%20VERSION%20-%20NOVEM-BER%202008.pdf.

[78] Police raids pursuant to a Delhi High Court order of 2 July 2010 found a proliferation of fake branded goods.

sponsorship exclusivity arrangements) and the protection of which is not often clearly for the benefit of the relevant governments or their citizens (as opposed to the relevant sports organisations and their commercial partners). SROC frequently justifies its calls for greater rights protection with reference to investment in sport. Compare the following (in the context of online content protection):

> Investment in sport at every level—investing in talent development and in people and facilities at the grassroots, as well as at the elite levels—is dependent on achieving the proper returns due to the creators of sporting content.[79]

Reference to 'proper returns due to the creators of sporting content' can, however, be construed by the cynic as indicative of an attitude of entitlement on the part of monopolists who create the very value of what they peddle by means of the creation of a closed shop of potential beneficiaries, while calling for the law to protect such arrangements with little tangible evidence of the serving of a greater good beyond the relevant sport. SROC clashed (during the 2007 IRB Rugby World Cup) with its nemesis in respect of media exploitation of sport, the News Media Coalition (or NMC), members of which threatened a boycott of the 2007 event in protest against the stringent restrictions imposed in respect of media reporting. SROC members were accused of attempting to impose censorship on the news media (e.g. with reference to calls by Cricket Australia around the same time for rights to sell cricket match images directly to book publishers—the News Media Coalition expressed concerns that such restrictions would give the right to sports officials to approve photographs used in books on the sport along with the accompanying text) while (as was claimed) the sports organisations had a mercenary motive (i.e. they were developing their own web sites and online video programmes and were allegedly interested in protecting their ability to reap revenue from new media content).[80] The News Media Coalition responded to claims by SROC that the news media were starting to inappropriately (read: commercially) exploit sports images; one of NMC's organisers, Andrew Moger, observed that in Europe 'many of the stadiums for games are publicly funded and therefore the public is a significant stakeholder… I think there are temptations to sidestep that recognition because it's not necessarily convenient for [the sports organisations] to recognize.'[81]

Finally, with all due regard for the huge problems of piracy and counterfeiting of sports brands, maybe some of the event organisers and rights holders should just

---

[79] From the Sports Rights Owners Coalition's Submission to the European Commission's Content Online Consultation (2007)—available online at the time of writing at http://ec.europa.eu/avpolicy/docs/other_actions/col_2008/ngo/sroc_en.pdf.

[80] See Carvajal, D 'Sports groups clash with media over pictures,' *The New York Times*, 16 December 2007 (available online at the time of writing at http://www.nytimes.com/2007/12/16/technology/16iht-COALITION17.1.8762446.html?_r=1).

[81] Ibid.

'chill' and take the extremely rosy (or is it ironic?) view expressed by one industry player:

> According to [Marc Reeves, international commercial director at the National Football League (NFL)], who says that protecting sponsorship rights is the league's brand protection priority, being forced to address knock-off goods is actually indicative that the NFL is doing something right: "We're still actively trying to grow our sport and our brand internationally," he explains. "It's a good sign if [counterfeit merchandise] is something we have to deal with. It means we're growing."[82]

Mention was made above of the significant pressure often exerted on potential mega-event hosts (i.e. those bidding for the rights to host) to ensure a comprehensive legal environment to protect commercial rights, specifically in the form of specific anti-ambushing legislation. There appears to be both a carrot and stick approach; a potential host faces losing in its bid to host an event if it does not provide sufficient guarantees of legal protection of commercial rights, but a successful applicant may also be further 'encouraged' to step up enforcement efforts. McKelvey and Grady remarked on the fact that the success (or failure) of Beijing's efforts to protect Olympic intellectual property could have a lasting financial legacy as the failure to fulfil provisions of the Beijing Host City Contract related to intellectual property protection meant that the city could lose certain subsidies that are contingent on enforcement results (with promised subsidies including USD 118 million for sustainable development and USD 400 million for healthcare improvements in Beijing, among other subsidies).[83] In the face of such considerations host legislatures pass new and special legislation to protect commercial rights to mega-events. It is, however, not a cut-and-dried issue that specific legislation to protect events *should* be passed in addition to existing common law and other legal mechanisms. Politicians and legislatures need to consider that the mere fact that more and more countries have in the past couple of decades in fact proceeded to pass such legislation (Australia and South Africa are frequently cited as two of the first to do so, for the 2000 Sydney Olympics and the 2003 ICC cricket World Cup, respectively) does not on its own provide a convincing argument for new events legislation. While calls for such legislation were made, for example, in India prior to both the 2010 Commonwealth Games in Delhi[84] and the ICC Cricket World Cup 2011, the ICC's own outside legal counsel for the latter event was (even though supportive of such legislation) at pains to point out the intricacy of the considerations involved:

---

82 Gannon 2010, p. 68.

83 McKelvey and Grady 2008, pp. 575–576.

84 See Kaur, B 'Apprehending an ambush: How to defend against ambush marketing' *Brands in the Boardroom 2010* 56–59 at 59 (www.iam-magazine.com)—available online at the time of writing at http://www.iam-magazine.com/issues/Article.ashx?g=a96dceed-1e54-456c-bd75-6a38f819d228.

> [A]rguing in favour of an anti-ambush marketing law, it isn't enough to say that India must legislate just because other countries have. There really isn't a black-and-white moral or ethical argument against ambush marketing. So, the case for legislation must be made on rational economic grounds in the public interest and in the specific Indian context... The most significant risks of special interest legislation are unintended consequences and over-reaching effects. For the wholesome enjoyment of the event, an equilibrium must be found that both protects sponsors and provides other participants necessary freedoms to interact with the event. By its essence, the law would need to be limited by time (around the event in question), would need to "grandfather" legitimate uses that preceded the legislation, must distinguish, as you rightly said, between impermissible suggestions of business associations on the one hand and legitimate non-commercial, journalistic and other public interest uses on the other. The eventual success of the law will be in the success of the events protected and the fostering of an environment that promotes many more similar events finding a home in India. Importantly, if one is to reconcile the public interest with limits on freedom and curbs on creativity and innovation engendered by an anti-ambush marketing law, the protected event should not lose the spirit of the staging in trying to enforce laws with hyper-technical precision.[85]

It is refreshing to see reference to the public interest in events and recognition of the fact that a proper weighing up of this public interest and the private, commercial interests of event host organisations and their commercial partners should take place. Also, organisations such as FIFA have a rather poor track record when it comes to avoiding the perils of the warning posed in the last line of the above quote; it should always be noted that while having the relevant legislation in place may provide event organisers with a measure of peace of mind as to how safe their safe haven may be, calls for the enforcement of such legislation through legal and even criminal action may turn into a public relations nightmare where it is done pedantically and without employing common sense. That being said, and more fundamentally, it is debatable to what extent the weighing up of the relevant public and private interests was properly done in some of the cases where countries have passed event-specific legislation.

We need to remember that there is a very significant public interest element to the hosting of sports mega-events (which will be examined in more detail elsewhere in the later chapters), and also that those usually hardest hit by special event legislation, such as anti-ambush marketing statutes, are entrepreneurs and members of the public in the host nations which pass such laws. Hewitt[86] has examined the protection of commercial rights to sporting events in the context of English law, and expresses the following view of the current state of the law:

> On balance, and in a pragmatic manner, the law does "help" rather than "hinder" the organiser of a major sports event. However, the law's support is not positive; it is largely passive. It is the responsibility of the event organiser to develop a sophisticated and careful contractual matrix in order to acquire its "rights." The event organiser must rely on

---

[85] The ICC's outside legal counsel for the 2011 cricket World Cup event, Nandan Kamath, as quoted in an e-mail interview (in his capacity, at the time, of director of sports consultancy GoSports) with *The Hindu Business Line*, 8 May 2008 (available online at the time of writing at http://www.thehindubusinessline.com/catalyst/2008/05/08/stories/2008050850110300.htm).

[86] Hewitt 2005, pp. 32–33.

diligence and bargaining strength. The law does not help the weak or careless. There is little evident policy—apart from support of freedom of contract and limited remedies against more extreme forms of misrepresentation. Should English law do more? The large sums paid in practice for sports broadcasting and sponsorship "rights" suggest that there is no case for reform generally. However, the dependence of major events on commercial revenue (and the public importance of such events) means that greater protection of rights granted to "official" counterparties is highly desirable. Constructive legal developments would be:

- continuing expansion of the boundaries of passing off to counter "ambush marketing" of kinds which misrepresent an association with a sporting event; and
- the introduction of special legislation to assist "protected events" along the lines of the model for the South African Cricket World Cup (at least where public funding or guarantees for that event are substantial).[87]

I cannot agree with the author's contention that the public importance of the events and the substantial degree of public funding or guarantees in fact justify special legislation to protect the private commercial interests of sponsors of such events. To me it simply does not make sense to argue that the more public funding an event receives, the more those very members of the public who are paying for it should be so severely restricted in respect of their dealing with the thematic space of the event (as we find in the often draconian special event legislation in some jurisdictions, as discussed later), especially when one considers that what is being protected is primarily the private commercial interests of sponsors and event organisers. The argument seems illogical. The event organisers, however, will (and do) argue that it is actually the event itself that is ultimately being protected by such means, as ambush marketing threatens both the value of sponsorship as well as future interest from sponsors). Are they arguing that protection of the survival of the mega-event is in the public interest? If so, how can they ignore the impact of special legislation on members of the public in respect of free speech and other implications? The argument would seem to be that it is in the greater public interest to limit the rights of some members of the public (a 'greater good' argument), although I would dispute the veracity of such reasoning in the current context, not least because the organisers' claims that ambush marketing actually threatens the survival of events is a rather tenuous one which does not seem to be borne out by real and convincing evidence in practise[88] (an issue I will examine in more detail in Chap. 9). Remember also that this argument has in recent years been advanced in a climate where event organisers consistently make huge profits (although they'll seldom call it that) from the commercialisation of the events, a relevant factor indeed.

Apart from the fundamental issue of whether we need such special event legislation and whether it is legally tenable, which will be re-examined in later chapters, it is also important to consider the apparent trend of lawmakers in recent years to provide ever-increasingly wide and stringent commercial rights protection

[87] Ibid. 39.

[88] Grady et al. 2010.

to mega-events. In this regard I am in agreement with Johnson's warning against the dangers of what he refers to as 'vertical and horizontal creep.'[89] Johnson states that the expansion and development of the sort of special legislative protection of events as discussed here clearly comes from the strong bargaining position of the international federations, who have made the protection granted to the brand of a major event pivotal to any bid being successful, by requiring guarantees to be made to the federations that legislation will be put in place. Johnson is of the view that the ability of international federations to make these demands has directly led to horizontal and vertical creep.[90]

'Horizontal creep' (as defined by Johnson) refers, simply, to the fact that 'the protection afforded to an event in one country is used to justify protection in another country.'[91] As an example, Johnson refers to the London Olympic and Paralympic Games Act, 2006. When the UK law-makers considered this in Bill form, it was apparent that the special legislative protection granted in Australia for the 2000 Sydney Olympics was viewed as having struck a proper balance in respect of legal protection against ambush marketing. As Johnson notes, many amendments were proposed simply on the basis that they represented what was in the Australian legislation, and on occasion, the Australian legislation was seen as a norm and so deviations from that norm had to be justified.[92] Illustrative of the author's point in respect of the 'creep' that is taking place, the London Act also subsequently fulfilled a similar role when it came to consideration of special event legislation for later events, notably the Olympic and Paralympic Marks Act passed for the 2010 Vancouver winter Olympics, and New Zealand's Major Events Management Act, 2007. Johnson rightly acknowledges that such legislative creep also happens in other areas, for example in the Commonwealth, where intellectual property legislation in the former British dominions and colonies had, at one point, been based on the equivalent UK legislation. But, importantly, he points out that this process is somehow different in relation to special anti-ambush marketing legislation:

> It appears that instead of using foreign law as a basis of domestic law and making some tweaks, legislators are using foreign law as a benchmark (or starting point) and then granting further protection, each new benchmark being another rung in the ladder of increased protection.[93]

Johnson further argues that a process of 'vertical creep' can also be divined in respect of such special legislative protection for events. This arises where a country hosts two or more events in succession, and where strong legal protection is granted in respect of one event and is then subsequently demanded in relation to a later (potentially, less prestigious) event. An example of this, again, is the

[89] Johnson 2008.

[90] Ibid. 26.

[91] Johnson 2008, p. 27.

[92] Ibid.

[93] Ibid.

London Act. Johnson predicted that the broad protection granted to the London Olympics is likely to be mirrored by the protection granted for the Glasgow Commonwealth Games in 2014—this prediction proved accurate, in the form of the Glasgow Commonwealth Games Act, 2008,[94] which (for example) contains provisions regarding 'authorised advertising' around the event and creates an offence in the form of 'unauthorised advertising'[95] and, more importantly, creates an 'association right' to the event which is identical to that created in the London legislation of 2006.[96] In fact, this was expressly done—the Glasgow Act, in Bill form, specifically stated that this was the objective.[97] Scotland Office minister Ann McKechin was quoted in a January 2009 press release regarding the anti-ambushing objectives of the Act:

> In order to meet the requirements laid down by the Commonwealth Games Federation and protect the intellectual property rights of the 2014 Games it is necessary to create an 'association right'—a form of intellectual property protection similar to that already conferred on the London 2012 Olympics that proactively safeguards economic interests where copyright and trademarks cannot.[98]

This is simply a convenient overstatement of the reality of the situation which faced the Scottish legislature—it is simply not accurate to say that 'it is necessary to create' an association right similar to that which was created for the 2012 London Olympics; there are surely many different and viable options as to how best to provide commercial rights protection for such an event which does not involve placing on the statute books a novel and far-reaching statutory creature such as that found in the London legislation. In fact, the UK's Advertising Association, which prepared a submission to the Scottish legislature during the preparation of the Glasgow legislation, specifically observed that '[o]f

[94] Which received Royal Assent on 10 June 2008.

[95] Compare the provisions of section 10 of the Act:

10 Ban on advertising in the vicinity of Games locations:

(1) It is an offence to advertise in the vicinity of a Games location at a prohibited time ("the advertising offence").
(2) Ministers may by regulations ("the advertising regulations")
   (a) exempt types of advertising from the advertising offence,
   (b) make such further provision as they think fit in relation to advertising in the vicinity of Games locations.
(3) The advertising offence does not apply to advertising by the Organising Committee or the Commonwealth Games Federation (so long as that advertising is done in accordance with any conditions imposed by the advertising regulations).

[96] The association right was created by means of the Glasgow Commonwealth Games Act 2008 (Games Association Right) Order, 2009 (Order 1969 of 2009).

[97] See para 13 of the 'Policy objectives of the Bill,' as contained in the Glasgow Commonwealth Games Bill tabled in Parliament on 9 November 2007.

[98] See 'Scotland Office to legislate to protect Glasgow 2014 image,' 26 January 2009, available online at the time of writing at http://www.scotlandoffice.gov.uk/scotlandoffice/11390.html.

the material to which the [Advertising Association] has had access thus far, which includes the [Commonwealth Games Federation Brand Protection Games Manual]… but not the Host City Contract itself, the Association can find nothing that would contractually require the Scottish Government to introduce an association right for the Commonwealth Games.'[99] The Advertising Association specifically called for a requirement that the Scottish ministers should provide a comprehensive justification as to why the existing body of law covering intellectual property rights was deemed to be insufficient to protect the Commonwealth Games and its sponsors,[100] as opposed to such a special association right, but it appears that this went unheeded (to the best of my knowledge).

This last is a very clear example of what Johnson refers to. Such creep is ironic, and problematic from the perspective of legal principles. The special protection provided by legislation only a decade ago for the Olympic Games was granted because the Olympics was seen as a unique event which had unique dignity and unique value in popular culture. As Johnson points out, however, the reality is that 'if Scotland wants to host the Games, the UK Government cannot say that it considers the Commonwealth Games to be less significant than the Olympics.'[101] It is effectively compelled to give it at least the same protection. In this way, legislation that was unique and aimed at addressing special problems relating to a special event on a once-off basis, is used as the benchmark for future legislation which is developed to cover a wide range of events which, quite possibly, do not have the same characteristics or pose the same problems as such a huge event as the Olympic Games. In fact, Johnson points out that this process has seen similar protection as that provided for major events (such as the 2004 EURO football championship in Portugal) provided to smaller events such as an under-21 football tournament, and that when the World Swimming Championships were awarded to Melbourne, legislation was passed which ensured that it had equivalent provision to the Commonwealth Games. The eventual outcome, he predicted, is the following:

> This vertical creep has only recently begun, but will ultimately result in generic ambush marketing legislation being enacted by restating the same provisions and passing similar legislation, probably more generous to event organisers, every time a new event is hosted. Indeed, such a step has been taken in New Zealand with the passage of the Major Events Management Act 2007… The problem is how the protection has been granted and the way countries are incrementally extending protection and the events that are protected. If one country broadens its protection it becomes increasingly difficult for the next host nation not to do likewise.[102]

---

[99] In para A.3.1 of this submission document, which is available online at the time of writing at http://www.adassoc.org.uk/aa/index.cfm?LinkServID=5737B08E-19B9-F84A-0C664664F83A91B0&showMeta=0.

[100] Ibid. at par. A.5.2.

[101] Johnson 2008, p. 27.

[102] Johnson 2008, p. 28.

More fundamentally, this 'creep' is displayed in the very model of commercial rights exploitation to mega-events. We considered, in Chap. 2, the system of exclusivity of sponsorships of such events, and the fact that 'ambush marketing' developed as a result of such exclusivity (which, in any event, poses some interesting competition law questions to be revisited in later chapters). Phillips has highlighted the apparent absurdity of increased calls for legislative protection of the commercial monopolies in mega-events:

> Because the acquisition of [exclusive sponsorship rights] requires the party acquiring it to pay an extremely large sum, the payment of that sum itself provides a justification for the imposition upon competitors of the acquiring party of wider restraints upon competition than those which intellectual property laws require. The imposition of these wider restraints upon competition makes the exclusive right of Olympic sponsorship even more valuable to prospective sponsors, who in turn will be prepared to pay more for the acquisition of those rights.[103]

Philips highlights the 'notion of circularity' inherent in how this system functions: 'The more you pay, the more protection you need; the more protection you get, the more you pay.'[104] It is a self-fulfilling prophecy that event organisers and their sponsors increasingly demand more comprehensive protection of what they respectively view as their property or their financial investment in mega-events, and that legislatures are similarly increasingly providing such protection. In fact, there is currently no prospect of this process letting up any time soon, and with the mega-events consistently increasing in size and in respect of the costs to stage such spectacles it is doubtful that this trend will dissipate anytime soon—unless governments and the legal fraternity take active steps to retard the process and to restore a measure of normalcy to the mega-events commercialisation context.

Recent research suggests that the event legislation (and, I would suggest, also the measure of creep that Johnson refers to) is the direct result of a significantly skewed power relationship in respect of the hosting of events, between the event organisers or rights holders and host governments and national sports organisations. The following was observed in the context of the 2010 Vancouver Winter Olympic Games:

> The ability of the IOC to influence governments to pass anti-ambush legislation with little consultation through implicit promises in the bid phase, as well as the creation of strict controls by VANOC [the Vancouver Olympics Organising Committee] over Olympic marketing materials suggests a measure of asymmetrical power between the IOC/VANOC and other stakeholders. However, a reluctance to engage in conflict over such measures of control suggests acceptance by the [national sports organisations] that this asymmetry is unavoidable… It appears that [national sports organisations] accept this asymmetry as unavoidable which then leads to the perception of a constructive working relationship with VANOC around the issue of fighting and preventing ambush marketing. However, to complete the cycle, this acceptance and constructive working relationship then continues to reinforce and feed the original asymmetrical power relationship by offering little

---

103 Phillips 2006.

104 Ibid.

> resistance. Further questions must be asked in this area to help determine the positive and/or negative impacts of asymmetry and the potential for the relationships to change if negative outcomes, for instance questions around the overextension of power in creating anti-ambush legislation, are identified.[105]

I would support the need for research to examine this apparently (and mystifyingly) skewed dynamic between sports event organisers and sovereign states, as called for by Ellis et al., who observe rather dryly that '[t]he ability of the IOC to make such a request [for special anti-ambushing laws] and for governments to simply obey with little fanfare points to an interesting and dynamic power relationship between the two parties.'[106] In light of this power relationship and the coercive nature of the power wielded by mega-event organisers, I find it troubling that Stuart and Scassa, seemingly without interrogating the legitimacy of the *status quo*, advocate the use of such coercive power by the IOC in demanding Olympic legacy legislation to be passed by host governments.[107] The end seems laudable, but the means would be problematic.

Before I revisit the issues of the legal legitimacy of the commercial monopolisation of mega-events and of the law's protection and maintenance of such monopolies in the later chapters, we should briefly consider the current state of the law regarding special protection for commercial rights to mega-events against ambush marketing in a number of jurisdictions.

4.4 The Special Legislation to Protect Commercial Rights to Mega-Events: An Overview of Selected Jurisdictions

This section will undertake a brief examination of the relevant special event legislation that has been passed in various selected jurisdictions in recent years primarily to protect the commercial rights to such events against ambush marketing.[108] Such legislation is often referred to as providing *sui generis* protection to event organisers and their commercial partners, i.e. a special form of protection, specific to the particular event or to events more generally, which provides discrete grounds for protection distinct from other, more general, legal

---

[105] From Seguin et al. 2009, p. 242.

[106] Ellis et al. 2011, p. 307.

[107] See Stuart and Scassa 2011.

[108] For the interested reader, relatively recent information on ambush marketing protection in a wider selection of jurisdictions (a total of 37 countries) is available in the form of country reports to the International Association of Intellectual Property Protection (AIPPI)'s Working Committee, Project Q210 ('The protection of major sports events and associated commercial activities through trademarks and other IPR'; reports compiled for purposes of a draft resolution to be submitted to the AIPPI Exco meeting in Buenos Aires, October 2009)—available online at the time of writing at https://www.aippi.org/?sel=questions&sub=listingcommittees&viewQ=210#210.

bases (e.g. copyright or trademark protection, unlawful competition protection or protection against unfair trade practises). Such *sui generis* protection often goes beyond the level of protection offered by the more traditional legal bases—sometimes (often) controversially so.

A recent country survey of trademark protection for major sports events, undertaken by the International Association for the Protection of Intellectual Property,[109] provides a useful quick reference source to determine the level of event protection available for trademarks and related commercial rights to events in different jurisdictions. The respondent countries can be classified into three groups, depending on the level of such special legal protection that is currently available or expected to be incorporated in future:

- A number of countries (namely Belgium, Denmark, Estonia, Finland, France, Indonesia, Korea, Latvia, Mexico, Panama, Singapore, Sweden, Switzerland and Thailand) have no special provisions that exist in their national statutory law or case law in respect of such protection for sports events;
- A number of other countries (including Argentina, Australia, Canada, Czech Republic, Germany, Hungary, Italy, Paraguay, Poland, Portugal, Romania, Russia, Turkey, the United Kingdom and the United States) reported that their national law, at the outset, does not provide specific protection for trademarks or other designations relating to sports events, but that special legislation in some cases had been adopted in relation to a particular event (i.e. *sui generis* legislation), which either had already been hosted or was planned to be hosted, and where it has been a requirement for being appointed host of the event that special legislation had been or would be adopted;
- Of the respondent countries, only Italy,[110] New Zealand and South Africa reported a special legal regime for such trademark protection of sports events.

In this section I will briefly discuss the available legal protection in a number of countries from the last two of these above groups. The jurisdictions selected for purposes of this review are the following:

- Brazil
- China
- India
- Canada
- Australia
- New Zealand
- The Russian Federation
- South Africa

---

[109] Ibid.

[110] The Italy country report mentioned special protection of signs which have acquired notoriety in extra-commercial contexts, i.e. well-known signs used in the artistic, literary, scientific, political or sports field (which also comprises trademarks or other designations relating to major sports events).

- The United Kingdom
- The United States

I will provide a brief description of the relevant legislative instruments with a view to the analysis, in the following chapters, of the legal impact of such instruments on the rights of parties other than the event organisers and their commercial partners (and the public, generally). I have selected the legislation that I view to be most relevant and important for purposes of such analysis, based on the nature, extent and reach of the legislative provisions and on the relevance of the specific jurisdictions in respect of their future hosting of mega-events (notably Brazil and the UK in respect of the upcoming instalments of the Olympic Games and FIFA World Cup). For this last reason (and the limitations inherent in the scope of this chapter) I have not included an important jurisdictional block in the global context, namely the European Union. The interested reader is advised to consult specialist texts for more information on relevant legislation and developments in specific EU jurisdictions.[111]

In addition to the legislation review, I will include very brief discussion (where relevant or applicable) of the most prominent event-related litigation to date in each of these jurisdictions in terms of such anti-ambush marketing legislation.

4.4.1 The Applicable Anti-Ambush Marketing Legislation in Brazil[112]

Brazil has been selected to host the 2014 FIFA World Cup tournament, and the city of Rio de Janeiro will host the 2016 Olympic and Paralympic Games. This last is especially historic, as it will be the first time since the inception of the Olympic

[111] Such as, for example, generally, the potential application of the EU's Unfair Commercial Practices Directive (Directive No. 2005/29/EC) or the Trademarks Directive (Directive 2008/95/EC); or, more specifically, Portugal's anti-ambushing legislation for UEFA's EURO 2004 competition (Law Decree 86/2004); Italy's anti-ambushing law for the 2006 Turin winter Games (Law Decree 167/2005—no longer in force); and Hungary's (aborted when it was not awarded the hosting rights) draft legislation for UEFA's EURO 2012 competition (under the proposed legislation, any reference to the UEFA or the championship which would have suggested a contractual, commercial, organisational or financial relationship with the UEFA was prohibited, and standing to sue was granted to UEFA and the official sponsors, with remedies similar to those under trademark law (no criminal sanctions and no enforcement agency were foreseen)). I will include brief discussion of the well-known dispute(s) between FIFA and Ferrero in terms of German trademark registrations in Sect. 5.2.

[112] Information regarding special legal protection for the upcoming 2014 FIFA World Cup Brazil and the 2016 Rio de Janeiro Olympic Games is rather sketchy at the time of writing. I would, however, like to sincerely thank Felipe Dannemann Lundgren (of Dannemann Siemsen attorneys, Rio de Janeiro—http://www.dannemann.com.br) for his extremely helpful assistance in providing me with information regarding the relevant laws in Brazil at the time of writing (and for assisting me in respect of the translation of Portuguese language texts in this regard).

Games that it will be hosted on the South American continent. With the world's two largest sports mega-events scheduled to take place in this jurisdiction within a short 2 year-period, it can be expected that Brazilian lawmakers will be faced head-on with the issue of commercial rights protection for these events and, more specifically, how to best combat potential ambush marketing campaigns. At the time of writing reports on Brazil's expected investment in infrastructure for the FIFA World Cup are sketchy, reported variously as expected to be in the region of USD 9.5 billion (more than double that of the South African government's investment for the 2010 FIFA event) or nearly USD 19 billion (according to Brazil's sports minister, quoted in July 2010),[113] while expected investment in infrastructure for the 2016 Olympics has reportedly been estimated to amount to USD 15 billion.[114]

At the time of writing in 2011 it appears that the Brazilian Olympics organisers' domestic sponsorship programme is progressing well. It was announced in March 2011 that the Embratel-Claro consortium was appointed as official Tier One telecommunications service provider for the 2016 Games. The financial details of the deal were not disclosed but the two companies 'are set to have paid at least more than double the GBP 80 million that BT did to be the Tier One sponsor in the same category for London 2012.'[115] Bradesco, Brazil's second largest bank, signed a GBP 205 million deal to become the first sponsor in December 2010. It was successful in its bid to become a Tier One sponsor, paying the minimum amount set by the Rio 2016 Organising Committee to become the official finance and insurance services partner (which is more than twice what Lloyds TSB paid for the same category at London 2012).

Similarly, by April 2011 four major Brazilian companies (Marfrig, Oi, Banco Itaú and Nescau) had signed up to the National Supporter programme as domestic sponsors of the 2014 FIFA World Cup.

The importance of these two upcoming mega-events is clear, and the Brazilian government can be expected to take the inevitable demands for commercial rights protection by the event organisers seriously—especially as the IOC and FIFA have to date been the most vocal proponents of special protection for the commercial rights to their events and are no strangers to aggressive rights enforcement campaigns. It should, however, be noted that it has been observed that there are certain 'cultural differences' between FIFA and the Brazilian football authority, Confederaçao Brasileira de Futebol, in respect of the attitude to persons associating themselves with events—the one (guess which) being very fond of cease-and-desist letters, and the other having a more tolerant attitude in a country with many competing tournaments whilst most other football federations follow a single

113 See http://fifa2014bra.blogspot.com/2010/07/brazil-to-invest-us-187-billion-in.html.

114 From a report available online at the time of writing at http://www.mondaq.com/article.asp?articleid=117458.

115 From a report dated 5 March 2011 available online at the time of writing at http://www.insidethegames.biz/summer-olympics/2016/12153-rio-2016-signs-deal-with-consortium-to-become-telecommunications-sponsor.

unified structure.[116] One commentator has observed that 'the Brazilian doctrine avoids a literal translation of ambush marketing, because the term "ambush" has a pejorative meaning in Portuguese. Consequently, it makes the distinction between marketing of lawful and unlawful association.'[117] It is also interesting to note that Bacalao-Fleury quotes a former US ambassador to the UN who characterised the country as 'a prominent member of the axis of IP evil' because of its 'flagrant disregard' for intellectual property rights.[118] While the author observes that this arose out of tensions between the Brazilian government and pharmaceutical companies that produce anti-retroviral medicines, it remains to be seen how conducive the Brazilian political and judicial environment will be to the approach of FIFA and the Olympic Movement to IP and commercial rights protection for their events.

In this section I will not elaborate upon the Civil Code or other statutory protections that exist and are available for the protection of the interests of the event hosts and official sponsors (such as, e.g. trademark and copyright protection[119]). The Code provides protection against undue enrichment, unfair competition and the doctrine defined as parasitic exploitation, although these protections are generic and do not provide special sanctions, and are not aimed at the specific instances of ambushing which may present in practise in respect of a sports mega-event.[120] The Brazilian Federal Constitution[121] also expressly guarantees everyone's right to property, which includes intellectual property (unlike, for example, the South African Constitution, which does not expressly protect IP rights although it is generally accepted that such rights are included in the protection provided by the fundamental right to property in section 25 of the Bill of Rights).

An important provision is to be found in the general sport law (the *Pelé Act*, see below), which in its Article 87 provides that names and symbols of sports or sports practise administration entities, also professional athletics names or nicknames, have legal protection, valid across the Brazilian territory and for an undetermined

---

[116] Kobel 2007, p. 54.

[117] Mendes 2010, p. 19.

[118] Bacalao-Fleury 2011, pp. 202–203. See also Smith 2011, p. 46.

[119] The protection of the name of an event is secured regardless of its registration as a trademark by the organizer, and there is legal protection of the name, prize or symbol, which is intrinsic to any sports event (see Article 87 of the Pele Act, referred to in the text below). Brazil's Copyright Law (Law 9610/98), in turn, provides for the protection of a wide range of intellectual works (including copyright protection for the Olympic symbols and mascots). The ownership of works of authorship by legal entities (as it is the case of the entities organizers of sports events) is obtained through the formalsation of the assignment of rights by the author, whereas the assignee is secured patrimonial rights in the work, which include the 'exclusive right to use, enjoy and dispose of the literary, artistic or scientific work.' Inasmuch as the sports event organizer is the legal owner of copyrights in symbols, mascots and songs, it will have the prerogative of preventing the protected work from being used without its authorsation—see http://www.mondaq.com/article.asp?articleid=117458.

[120] Mendes 2010, p. 20.

[121] In Article 5.

period, with no need for registration. Brazilian lawmakers have already at the time of writing proceeded to enact special event legislation with a view to these two upcoming events, and I will, in keeping with the approach in the rest of this chapter, focus the discussion on these new or pending laws.

Following the approval by the Brazilian Congress (by means of a legislative decree in June 1984[122]) of the Nairobi Treaty on the Protection of the Olympic Symbol, the principles of the Nairobi Treaty have been incorporated in the Intellectual Property Law[123] and the general sports Act, known as the *Pelé Act*.[124] These provisions secures the Brazilian Olympic Committee (BOC) and the Brazilian Paralympic Committee (BPC) the exclusive use of registered trademarks and the right to use flags, slogans, anthems and Olympic and Paralympic symbols, as well as the expressions 'Olympic Games,' 'Olympics,' 'Paralympic Games' and 'Paralympics.'

Brazil's Industrial Property Law (Law 9279/96),[125] in section 124, XIII, does not consider names, prizes or symbols of sporting, artistic, cultural, social, political, economic or technical official or officially recognised events, as well as imitations likely to cause confusion, to be registrable as marks, except when authorised by the competent authority or entity promoting the event. In terms of this provision, trademark registration of terms directly related to major sports events can be cancelled when the event organiser's consent is not obtained. Use of a trademark by non-official sponsors (e.g. ambushers) can be prohibited, as the Brazilian legislation not only secures exclusivity over trademarks and symbols related to sports events, but also provides several tools to assure the compliance with this right, since the infringement of intellectual property is punished within the civil and criminal code. Title V of the Industrial Property Law describes crimes against industrial property and, specifically chapters III and VI address crimes against marks and unfair competition. Non-authorised use of registered trademarks is unlawful, as stated in article 189 of the Industrial Property Law.[126] There is no need to prove that the reproduction of registered marks was made to gain economic advantage, since it does not require this purpose for the crime to be established. The available protection for Olympic marks and for sports events and event organisers is not limited to trademark goods and services classification, and there are no fair use provisions.[127]

---

[122] Legislative Decree No. 21, 4 June 1984.

[123] Law 9279/96.

[124] Law 9615/98.

[125] See further Bacalao-Fleury 2011, p. 200 et seq.

[126] See the country report on Brazil prepared for the Working Committee of the International Association for the Protection of Intellectual Property (AIPPI), Project Q210 ('The protection of major sports events and associated commercial activities through trademarks and other IPR'; reports compiled for purposes of a draft resolution to be submitted to the AIPPI Exco meeting in Buenos Aires, October 2009)—available online at the time of writing at https://www.aippi.org/download/commitees/210/GR210brazil.pdf.

[127] Ibid.

Finally, in respect of the applicable regulatory regime relevant to ambush marketing, CONAR (the Brazilian advertising standards body)'s Code of Self-Regulation specifically refers to and condemns ambush marketing:

> This Code condemns the unlawful and illegitimate advertising benefits obtained by means of "piggy-backing" and/or "ambushing," through the invasion of the editorial or commercial space of the communication vehicle.

Like its counterparts elsewhere, however, this Code has no legal force, the majority of the decisions of the regulatory authority are administratively enforced and its sanctions are limited.[128]

Just one day before Rio was awarded the right to host the 2016 Games, the national Congress passed Law 12.035 (of 1 October 2009), also known as the *Olympic Act*.[129] This Act, which was enacted to deal primarily with logistical and operational issues relating to the hosting of the Games, contains a number of specific provisions designed to protect the official symbols of the Olympic movement and to curb ambush marketing during the Games.[130] In terms of Article 6 of the Act, federal authorities are responsible to control, oversee and suppress any unlawful acts which violate the rights of the symbols in connection with the Rio 2016 Games. The Act broadly defines these symbols as follows:

(i) all graphically distinctive signs, flags, mottos, emblems and anthems used by the International Olympic Committee;
(ii) the names 'Olympic Games,' 'Paralympic Games,' 'Rio 2016 Olympic Games,' 'Rio 2016 Paralympic Games,' 'XXXI Olympic Games,' 'Rio 2016,' 'Rio Olympics,' 'Rio 2016 Olympics,' 'Rio Paralympics,' 'Rio 2016 Paralympics' and other abbreviations and variations and also those equally relevant which may be created for the same purposes, in any language, including those in connection with the internet and website domains;
(iii) the name, emblem, flag, anthem, motto and trademarks and other symbols of the Rio 2016 Organising Committee; and
(iv) the mascots, trademarks, torches and other symbols in connection with the XXXI Olympic Games, Rio 2016 Olympic Games and Rio 2016 Paralympic Games.

Article 7 provides that, unless prior and express authority is obtained from the Rio 2016 Games Organising Committee or the IOC, the use of any symbols in connection with the Rio 2016 Games, whether or not for commercial use, is expressly forbidden. Article 8 provides further, and extensive, anti-ambush marketing protection:

---

[128] Mendes 2010, p. 20.

[129] Lei No. 12.035, de I de Outubro de 2009, DIARIO OFICIAL DA UNIAO [D.O.U.] de 1.10.2009. (Braz.).

[130] For information regarding this Act, see the report available online at the time of writing at http://bakerxchange.com/ve/ZZ65K69t60CSjbuY616/VT=0/page=5.

The prohibition provided for in Article 7 extends to the use of terms and expressions that, even though not included in the list of symbols mentioned herein, have sufficient similarity as to cause undue association of any products and services, or even of any company, transaction or event, with the Rio 2016 Games or with the Olympic Movement.

This provision accordingly appears to make use of an 'association right' to the Games, by vesting the right to authorise the use of terms and expressions with 'sufficient similarity' to the listed symbols and expressions in the event organisers. More will be said later in this chapter and in Chap. 8 about the 'association rights' to sports mega-events as created by *sui generis* event legislation in other jurisdictions. For present purposes it is interesting to note that Article 8 of the *Olympic Act* speaks of an 'undue association,' and also that it extends to the use of terms and expressions which have sufficient similarity to the listed symbols to cause such an undue association, even if such terms or expressions are not employed for commercial use. This is interesting, and could have broader potential free speech implications than might be the case with other such special event legislation. I also remark (in Chap. 8) on the fact that, in my view worryingly, the association rights to events appear for the most part to ignore not only the requirement for event organisers to show deception of consumers by potential infringing ambushers, but also to ignore the element of harm to the event organisers. I would suggest that Article 8 perpetuates this trend by outlawing 'undue' association (and not the deception of consumers as to an association or the creation of consumer confusion in this regard), and also by expressly including non-commercial use (which, I would suggest, by definition means that use of such terms and expressions which may be outlawed include use which may, in fact, cause no economic harm to the Olympics organisers).

Apart from the above provisions, the Olympic Act does not expressly provide for special protection for sports or Olympic related patents, nor does it prescribe sanctions against Olympic trademark and copyright infringement, and the Industrial Property Law will deal with any such issues.[131] The Brazilian Olympic Committee has also requested the Brazilian Senate to expand the protection under the Olympic Act to include new terms or expressions whose use or combination with other elements may lead to a false association with the Rio Games 2016 (such terms or expressions including 'Games,' 'Summer Games,' 'Rio,' '2016,' 'two thousand and sixteen,' 'twenty sixteen,' 'medals,' 'gold medal,' 'silver medal,' 'bronze medal' and 'sponsor'). At the time of writing (in 2011) the Senate had not yet issued a response to this request. It has been observed that the above protection for sports-related and event-related symbols (in respect of the Olympic Games and otherwise) is potentially insufficient to effectively deal with ambush marketing, as not all ambushes make use of the misappropriation or reproduction of symbols (i.e. such legal protection does not cover cases of intrusion ambushing).[132]

---

131 Bacalao-Fleury 2011, p. 202.

132 Mendes 2010, p. 20.

Bacalao-Fleury is not convinced that the anti-ambushing protection as contained in the Olympic Act is sufficient:

> [T]he Olympic Act's scope on ambush marketing is limited to mere prohibitions of certain practices, but does not prescribe sanctions for these violations. Consequently, the unfair competition provisions of the Industrial Property Law may be used to determine sanctions. However, the scope of the useful IPL's unfair competition sanctions is limited to those cases where (i) a person or entity "uses [or imitates] another person's advertising phrase or sign... in order to create confusion among the products or establishments;"' or (ii) "attributes to himself, for advertising purposes, a reward or distinction that he has not received." As a consequence, Brazil's current legal framework is insufficient to deal with some of the more sophisticated ambush marketing practices. For instance, "sponsoring individual players at sporting events so that they are wearing the ambush marketer's logo [or] sponsoring a news conference where team players are invited to speak" are ambush-marketing practices that create confusion in consumers, but would go unpunished under Brazilian laws.[133]

It appears that FIFA, for one, is (not surprisingly) attempting to remedy this situation of possible gaps in the anti-ambushing legal framework through proposed legislation (at the time of writing) for its 2013 Confederations Cup and 2104 World Cup events. A Bill was reported as being pending before the Brazilian Senate, aimed at defining rules for advertisements and marketing campaigns during the 2014 FIFA World Cup and the 2013 Confederations Cup. Bill 394/2009 was filed on 3 September 2009, and on 7 January 2011 was awaiting the appointment of a Rapporteur. It provides for the use of advertising space, names, flags, mottos, anthems, trademarks, logos and symbols relating to FIFA and the 2014 FIFA World Cup and the 2013 FIFA Confederations Cup, and the organisers, rights holders, teams and athletes participating in the events.

Article 3 of the Bill defines FIFA as the sole and exclusive proprietor of all the rights related to the 2014 FIFA World Cup Brazil. Article 3(1) grants FIFA and its partners the exclusive right to use a number of terms, including 'World Cup Soccer,' 'World Cup,' 'World Cup 2014,' 'Cup 2014,' 'Brasil 2014.' Similar rights are granted in favour of the Brazilian Soccer Confederation (CBF) in respect of terms such as 'Seleção Brasileira,' 'Equipe Brasileira' and 'Seleção.' Any association of products or services with the protected terms is prohibited, regardless of whether such use is unintentional or whether disclaimers such as 'non-authorized' or 'non-official' are added. The Bill does, however, provide for exceptions for non-profit uses by natural persons and uses exclusively for information, critique or opinion purposes by the media. A 'grandfather clause,' protecting the owners of prior rights over such names is also foreseen. Similar to the Olympic Act, Senate Bill No. 394 also grants the event organizers (in this case FIFA and CBF) with special rights over terms, which are considered by some to be

[133] Bacalao-Fleury 2011, p. 210.

descriptive and lacking distinctive character, which raises the possibility of future freedom of expression challenges to the legislation in terms of the relevant provisions of the Brazilian Constitution (Article 5 (IV) and (IX) of the Federal Constitution).[134]

On 14 September 2011 a special Bill dealing with the 2014 FIFA World Cup and the 2013 FIFA Confederations Cup was sent to the Brazilian Congress. At the time it was reported that there were severe disagreements between FIFA and the Brazilian Government on this legislation, and it was not expected that it would be passed into law before sometime in 2012.[135] This Bill, the *Lei Geral da Copa*,[136] deals extensively with commercial rights protection, with 25 of the 46 Articles in the Bill dedicated to intellectual property. The Bill provides, *inter alia*, for the following:

- Article 3 provides that the Brazilian Trademark Office (BTO) will declare 'the FIFA emblem'; 'the Confederations Cup 2013' and 'World Cup 2014' emblems; and the official mascots of the 'Confederations Cup 2013' and 'World Cup 2014' as highly reputed trademarks with special protection in all fields of activity. This declaration will be in effect until 31 December 2014;
- According to Article 5, §1, II, FIFA will not have to prove that its trademarks are highly reputed (as ordinarily foreseen in Article 125 of the Brazilian Industrial Property Law);
- Article 7 provides that FIFA's trademark applications will be examined on an expedited basis by the BTO (within 30 days after publication in the IP Journal);
- In terms of Article 10, FIFA will be exempted from paying official fees to the BTO for the examination of its trademark applications;
- Interestingly, although under section III of the Bill FIFA is granted exclusive rights over the images and sounds of the events, it will be obliged to allow other broadcasters (in addition to the official broadcaster) to exhibit small passages of the matches and of the opening ceremony, as long as such broadcast is for information purposes and restricted to 30 s. It was reported that this was a major point of disagreement between FIFA and the Brazilian Government (with FIFA clearly chafing at such carve-out from its exclusive control of who would be able to exhibit images of the events);
- Section IV of the Bill provides for criminal offences relating to the reproduction or imitation of any of FIFA's official symbols; ambush marketing 'by association'; and ambush marketing 'by intrusion.'

Article 18 defines 'ambush marketing by association' quite broadly, namely to 'disclose trademarks, products or services, with economic or advertising purposes, by means of direct or indirect association with the "Events" or "Official Symbols," without the authorisation of FIFA or of a person indicated by FIFA,

---

[134] From a summary of the contents of the Bill by Lundgren, F D 'Event Marks: A Necessary Form of Protection against Ambush Marketing?' A thesis submitted to the Munich Intellectual Property Law Centre, 13 September 2010 (available online at the time of writing at http://oami.europa.eu/ows/rw/resource/documents/QPLUS/network/universities/felipe_danneman_lundgren_miplc.pdf).

[135] I wish to thank Felipe Dannemann Lundgren for his extremely helpful assistance in sourcing information regarding the contents of the Bill, as contained in the text that follows.

[136] Full text (in Portuguese) available online at the time of writing at http://www.copa2014.gov.br/sites/default/files/publicas/sobre-a-copa/biblioteca/pl_lei-geral-da-copa.pdf.

inducing third parties to believe that such trademarks, products or services are approved, authorized or endorsed by FIFA.'

Article 19 of the Bill provides for special protection against intrusion ambushing. It provides for the criminalisation of certain conduct, including to 'expose trademarks, businesses, establishments, products, services or to practice any promotional activities not authorized by FIFA or by a person indicated by FIFA, attracting, by any means, public attention in the Official Places of the Events, with the objective of obtaining economic or advertising advantage' [Unofficial translation from the Portuguese text[137]]. The Bill provides for criminal penalties of 3 months to a year imprisonment, or a fine. This new crime will be valid only until 31 December 2014. Even though the penalties for infringement are in line with those provided in respect of criminal offences in terms of the Industrial Property Law,[138] an informed observer has expressed the opinion that it is doubtful whether the establishment of this criminal liability by means of an ordinary law will be considered constitutional in view of the Brazilian Federal Constitution (although the issue will probably not confront the Superior Courts before the end of the FIFA World Cup in 2014, if at all).[139]

The further progress of this proposed legislation for the 2013 Confederations Cup and 2014 World Cup events will be watched with interest, although I can unfortunately not include more detailed or definite information thereon at the time of going to press.

The Brazilian courts have to date heard a number of cases relating to commercial rights protection of events, with other such litigation currently pending. On 2 September 2009 the Rio de Janeiro Court of Appeals confirmed the decision of the court of first instance which had ordered injunctive relief for the organising committee of the 2007 Pan-American Games (which were hosted in Rio) against the Rio de Janeiro International Airport Taxi Service, to stop unauthorised use of the trademark 'RIO 2007.' The Court of Appeals confirmed that such unauthorised use constituted both a trademark infringement as well as ambush marketing, by creating an undue association with the Pan-American Games as if the defendant were an official sponsor of the event. Damages were awarded on the basis of the amount that the defendant would have had to pay for a licence to use the mark.[140]

The same court also heard a case brought by the Brazilian Olympic Committee (COB) prior to the 2008 Beijing Olympic Games against a supermarket chain, Guanabara, for its use of the word 'Olimpíadas' and of an 'Olympic' torch in a TV

---

[137] Courtesy of Felipe Dannemann Lundgren.

[138] Articles 183, 187 and 189—see Bacalao-Fleury 2011, p. 201.

[139] Courtesy of Felipe Dannemann Lundgren.

[140] See Antonella Carminnati and Jose Eduardo de V. Pieri 'Brazil in the Spotlight of Ambush Marketing'—available online at the time of writing at http://www.bmapi.com.br/bmapi/arquivos/Artigos/ANI-Brazil_in_the_Spotlight.pdf.

advertisement. As this matter was instituted before the coming into force of the new Olympic Act, COB claimed in terms of its exclusive power to use Olympic symbols under the Nairobi Treaty, the Brazilian Sports Act and on the basis of ambush marketing. The court rejected these claims (*inter alia*, on the basis that the Nairobi Treaty protected the Five Rings symbol and not the Olympic torch—which does enjoy protection under the new Olympic Act—and that COB had previously failed in its application for a trademark of the word 'Olimpíadas' on the basis of its being descriptive; and the court also held that COB had failed to show that the Olympic symbols merited special protection (as it claimed), and failed to prove consumer confusion as to an implied association by Guanabara as an official sponsor of the Beijing Games).[141]

In May 2010 it was reported that the Brazilian Football Confederation (or CBF) was planning to file a number of lawsuits against large corporations on the basis of alleged ambush marketing regarding the 2010 FIFA World Cup South Africa. The companies had used the words 'World Cup' and/or unauthorised depictions of players in the Brazilian national uniform in their advertising (some of the companies were direct competitors of CBF's official sponsors of the national team), and FIFA and the CBF were planning to take action. It was reported at the time that FIFA had by November 2009 registered nearly thirty expressions, marks and logos with the Brazilian Institute for Intellectual Property, and had started sending out its famous cease-and-desist letters to alleged infringers using the World Cup trademark, and it was speculated that the outcome of these matters would serve to provide jurisprudence for purposes of the 2014 FIFA World Cup.[142]

FIFA has been very busy in its 2014 World Cup preparations. Apart from the reports of a large number of trademark registrations (and cease-and-desist letters), and FIFA's dispute with the Brazilian Tax Service regarding demands for a full tax exemption for all its contractors (which exemption was subsequently granted with the approval of Congress), FIFA appears to have been busy trying to avoid potential problems regarding its commitments to its official event sponsors. It was also reported in late 2009 that FIFA was involved in trying to obtain exemptions for its sponsors from a municipal law (which had been in force since January 2008) in Sao Paolo, the so-called 'Clean City Law,' in terms of which there is a ban on outdoor advertising on billboards in certain parts of the city. FIFA demanded that its sponsors be exempted in order to allow them to advertise in respect of the World Cup. A commission was appointed to consider FIFA's demand, but one report suggests that it was indicated that a law providing for exceptions could be

---

[141] *Comitê Olímpico Brasileiro (COB) v. Casas Guanabara Comestíveis Ltda*. Décima Quinta Câmara Cível do TJ/RJ. Appeal No. 2009.001.52062, Rel. Des. Celso Ferreira Filho (6 October 2009).

[142] From a report dated 2 June 2010, available online at the time of writing at http://www.v-brazil.com/world-cup/2014/cbf-files-lawsuits-for-ambush-marketing/.

passed for purposes of the World Cup.[143] This is not the only such effort, however, as FIFA was reportedly also lobbying the Brazilian government for an exemption to another law which would affect one of its sponsors. Law 12.299[144] was approved by Brazil's president in July 2010, with a view to promoting safety and security at sports events (replacing an earlier 2003 Act which has reportedly gone largely unheeded). While such an Act would appear to be good news for FIFA in the run-up to its 2014 event, Article 13 of the law posed a problem. This section prohibits alcohol at sports events (and confirms an earlier compromise effected by the Brazilian Football Confederation with prosecuting authorities in 2008 to ban alcohol at football matches). FIFA could have none of that, of course. Budweiser is one of its main sponsors (and also owns a number of the major Brazilian beer brands). Reminiscent of FIFA's heavy-handed attempts to protect, essentially, the interests of Budweiser at the time of beer-maker Bavaria's ambush marketing stunt at the 2010 World Cup in South Africa (discussed elsewhere),[145] FIFA has demanded suspension of the law in respect of the 2014 event (FIFA's contract with Budweiser requires that its beer must be sold in stadiums during the event).[146]

With two more years to go before the 2014 FIFA World Cup, all the relevant legal instruments for commercial rights protection in respect of the event are not yet in place at the time that this book goes to press. Developments in this regard, and especially also in respect of possible ambush marketing litigation in the run-up to this event and the 2016 Olympic Games, will be watched with interest. The potential for ambush marketing or other threats to these events' commercial rights is currently purely speculative (although counterfeiting and piracy may prove to be especially problematic[147]). Bacalao-Fleury, who is of the opinion that the 2016 Rio Games is not sufficiently protected against potential rights infringements, has warned that Brazil's approach to intellectual property rights is 'selective and capricious,' and that the relevant policy-makers should note that 'the attitude of Brazilian people will have a significant impact upon Olympic-related intellectual

[143] See the report available online at the time of writing at http://www.v-brazil.com/world-cup/2014/fifa-wants-more-publicity-freedom/. The Olympic Act referred to in the text above provides that during the period between 5 July and 26 September 2016, the contracts executed for the use of advertising space in airports or federal areas of interest to the Rio 2016 Games are suspended under the condition of a duly grounded request submitted by the Rio 2016 Organising Committee for the exclusive use of the space.

[144] The Portuguese text of which is available online at the time of writing at http://www.planalto.gov.br/ccivil/_Ato2007-2010/2010/Lei/L12299.htm.

[145] Budweiser must be getting quite used to attempts to ambush its affiliation with the FIFA World Cup; it also saw a campaign by Kirin Ichiban beer claiming to be the 'un-official' sponsor of the 2002 FIFA World Cup in Korea and Japan.

[146] From the rather naively titled article ('Can FIFA change laws in Brazil?'—the easy answer is YES) available online at the time of writing at http://www.v-brazil.com/world-cup/2014/can-fifa-change-laws-in-brazil/.

[147] See Bacalao-Fleury 2011, p. 208 et seq.

property on the road to the 2016 Games.'[148] The author feels strongly that much needs to be done:

> The 2016 Rio de Janeiro Olympic Games will provide Brazil with one of its greatest challenges in its recent history. Providing effective measures to protect Olympic-related intellectual property will challenge the Brazilian government to a profound revision of its policies and legal framework in the area... in order to combat Olympic trademark infringements and ambush marketing, Brazil must adopt an integral approach that coordinates law enforcement, customs, education and an efficient judiciary. Finally, before Brazil can claim that it is "ready to host the Games of celebration," it must initiate the above transformations itself.[149]

Depending on the level of prevalence of rights disputes, I would suggest that Brazil might very well become an extremely important jurisdiction in the context of future developments in mega-event rights protection due to a number of factors (including, as mentioned, the fact that the world's two largest sporting events will be hosted within this jurisdiction within a short two-year period, as well as the fact that Brazil is a developing nation and part of the BRICS group of nations,[150] and that socio-economic factors and developmental needs may very well serve to place the event organisers' demands for special commercial rights laws (especially if coupled with aggressive enforcement campaigns in the lead-up and during these events) in the spotlight of international scrutiny). In fact, if the policy- and law-makers fail to achieve Bacalao-Fleury's above-quoted ambitions for the formulation of a 'fully compliant' jurisdiction, I would suggest that the resultant, expected, cases of potential infringement of the rights of FIFA, the Olympic Movement and their commercial partners may provide fruitful opportunity for ambush marketing litigation (and even constitutional challenges to the relevant anti-ambushing laws). This might go some way towards providing clarity on the question of the legality of anti-ambushing laws, both in Brazil and elsewhere. Only time will tell.

4.4.2 Anti-Ambush Marketing Protection in India

India currently (at the time of writing) does not have special anti-ambush marketing event legislation. The astute reader may wonder why I include this jurisdiction in the discussion of jurisdictions that employ such legislation, and I will try to explain.

While India has not legislated specifically to deal with ambush marketing, this country hosted two of the recent international sports mega-events (the 2010 Delhi

[148] Ibid. 211.

[149] Ibid. 213.

[150] The political grouping of leading emerging economies, consisting of Brazil, Russia, India, China and South Africa.

Commonwealth Games, and the 2011 ICC Cricket World Cup, co-hosted with Sri Lanka and Bangladesh). Its courts have also, on occasion, considered claims based on ambush marketing. What differentiates this jurisdiction, however, is the fact that despite increasing calls from legal quarters for special anti-ambushing legislation the Indian legislature has to date not taken this step, and protection for event organisers and their sponsors is grounded in common law and other, more general, statutory provisions. India thus constitutes an exception to the rule in the class of recent mega-event host countries in respect of the nature of event protection afforded by the law-makers. Developments in this jurisdiction warrant close scrutiny, as it is expected that special legislation will probably be passed at some point in the near future if India expects to host future mega-events. I will not discuss the available grounds for protection in any detail, and will simply list them here (and the interested reader is advised to consult specialist sources on Indian law for more information).

The first type of protection available to event organisers or sponsors is found in the relevant Indian intellectual property statutes, primarily the Copyright Act, 1957[151] and the Trademarks Act, 1999 (and, while India does not currently possess specific counterfeit goods legislation, such cases can be brought in terms of the infringement provisions contained in section 29 of the Trademarks Act). There may also be recourse to the common law action for passing off or in terms of the more generally-applicable trade practises provisions of the Monopolies and Restrictive Trade Practises Act, 1969.[152] Section 36A(1)[153] of this last Act defines an ‘unfair trade practice’ as a trade practise which, for the purpose of promoting the sale, use or supply of any good or for the provision of any services, adopts any unfair method or unfair or deceptive practise. Such unfair or deceptive practises include representing ‘that the goods or services have sponsorship, approval, performance, characteristics, accessories, uses or benefits which such goods or services do not have,’[154] or representing ‘that the seller or supplier has a sponsorship or approval or affiliation which such seller or supplier does not have.’[155] Proof of loss or damage to a consumer is not an essential ingredient of an unfair trade practise in terms of section 36A(1) of the Act.[156] The Monopolies and Restrictive Trade Practices Commission[157] is empowered to investigate claims of unfair trade practises[158] and may make certain orders in this regard.[159]

[151] Act 14 of 1957 (as amended).

[152] Act 54 of 1969.

[153] Inserted in the Act by Act 30 of 1984.

[154] Section 36A(1)(iv).

[155] Section 36A(1)(v).

[156] *Director-General of Investigation and Registration v Cement Corp. of Gujarat Ltd.* (1994) 80 Comp Cas 15 (MRTPC).

[157] Established in terms of section 5 of the Act.

[158] Section 36B of the Act.

[159] Section 36D.

In addition, India has the Emblems and Names (Prevention of Improper Use) Act, 1950,[160] which serves to prevent the improper use of certain emblems and names for professional and commercial purposes, and provides protection to the 'name and emblem of the International Olympic Committee consisting of five interlaced rings.'[161] Section 3 of this Act prohibits the use, for the purpose of any trade, business, certain callings or professions, or in the title of any patent, or in any trademark or design, of any names or emblems specified in the Schedule to the Act or any colourable imitation thereof without the previous permission of the Central Government. Section 4 of the Act prohibits any competent authority from registering any company, firm or other body of persons which bears a prohibited name; or from registering a trademark or design which bears any prohibited emblem or name; or from granting a patent in respect of any invention which bears a title containing any prohibited emblem or name, if the use of such name or emblem is in contravention of section 3. Section 5 of the Act provides that a contravention of section 3 is punishable by a fine.

Indian courts have a on a few occasions been faced with ambush marketing claims. Following the earlier high profile ambushing of the 1996 ICC Cricket World Cup (with Pepsi's 'Nothing official about it' campaign which did not impress official sponsor Coca-Cola much), some notable claims were brought in respect of the 2003 ICC Cricket World Cup, and in the context of the ICC's protracted sponsorship dispute with Indian national cricketers at the time in the run-up to the 2003 World Cup hosted in South Africa (which was referred to in Chap. 3). The Delhi high court dismissed an interim application by the ICC seeking to restrain Britannia Industries (an Indian biscuit manufacturer) and its authorised departmental stores from using the logo, mark and mascot of the 2003 event in their promotional schemes. The ICC's commercial rights subsidiary, ICC Development International Ltd (ICCDIL), had alleged that Britannia and its authorised departmental stores were misrepresenting their association with them by using the World Cup logo and other marks etc. on their promotional material without permission, and that this constituted ambush marketing. The ICCDIL alleged that the 'Britannia Khao World Cup Jao' marketing campaign amounted to an act of unfair trade practise in addition to depriving the authorised sponsors of the enjoyment of the exclusivity granted to them as official sponsors. The High Court refused to recognise ambush marketing as a cause of action for the plaintiff, and also held that it had not made out a case for the interim injunction prayed for (on the basis of a lack of evidence to refute the defendant's claims that it was in fact licenced to use the relevant event logos by an exclusive licensing agent of the ICC). The court found that, based on the contracts placed in evidence, it was evident that Britannia had acquired the right to use black and white stripes (as per

[160] Act 12 of 1950.

[161] Paragraph 21 of the Schedule to the Act.

the ICC's zebra-inspired event logo) and even the event mascot on the packaging of biscuits manufactured by it.[162]

In the only successful claim for relief in a case relating to ambush marketing in India to date, the Delhi High Court granted a copyright infringement claim by the ICC against a service station for use of the ICC's logo in promotional material. In *ICC Development (International) Ltd. v Ever Green Service Station*[163] the court granted an injunction preventing the defendants from using the logo of the 'ICC World Cup 2003' consisting of black and white strips and the event mascot 'Dazzler,' holding these to be 'artistic works' protected under Section 2(c) of the Copyright Act, 1957. Event slogans may, similarly, be capable of protection as 'literary works' under the Copyright Act. [This judgment may be especially interesting when one considers that the mascot for the 2010 Delhi Commonwealth Games, a cute Bengal tiger by the name of Shera, bears a striking resemblance to Hobbes from Bill Watterson's *Calvin and Hobbes* comic strip. Maybe it's just me…]

The most important ambush marketing case in India to date is the 2003 Delhi High Court matter of *ICC Development (International) Ltd. v Arvee Enterprises Ltd. & Philips,*[164] in which the ICCDIL brought suit against electronics company Philips for its 'Philips: Diwali Manao World Cup Jao' campaign, and its 'Buy a Philips audio system, win a ticket to the World Cup' advertisements (which also used a pictorial depiction of a 'Cricket World Cup 2003' ticket with fictional seat and gate numbers), which the plaintiff claimed constituted unfair competition, passing off and ambush marketing. The court held that the use of the slogans simply pointed to the fact that a purchaser of the defendant's products may win a prize, and that there was no likelihood of confusion that Philips was a sponsor of the event (which they weren't). The court agreed with Philips's argument that the words 'world cup' are generic and are used in the context of several international sporting events, such as the FIFA World Cup, and their use is descriptive and not proprietary to the ICC. The court held that ICC's mark had not been misappropriated and confusion among the public was not established. The court accordingly dismissed the passing off and unfair trading claims. The ICC also pleaded that the Philips ticket distribution scheme was reserved for sponsors and that in depriving sponsors of this exclusive right, Philips was preventing the ICC from fulfilling its contractual obligations. The court's preliminary ruling on this point was also in favour of Philips, on the ground that the ICC had failed to provide material evidence to show that Philips had notice of the terms and conditions set out in the contracts between the ICC and its sponsors. The court dismissed a further claim by the ICC, which contended that it owned publicity rights in all its events which had commercial value and that Philips was wrongfully exploiting the ICC's persona.

[162] See the report 'ICC plea for stay on use of World Cup logo rejected,' 4 December 2002, available online at the time of writing at http://www.rediff.com/cricket/2002/dec/04reject.htm.

[163] 2003 (26) PTC 228 (Del).

[164] (2003) VII AD (Del) 405.

The court rejected this plea on the basis of its opinion that non-living entities are not entitled to publicity right protection for an event.[165] In respect of the claim of intrusion ambush marketing, the court held that this practise was distinguishable from passing off, as there is no element of deceit in intrusion ambush marketing but merely opportunistic commercial exploitation of an event. The court held that this is not contrary to the public interest and that as long as an official sponsor's trademarks are not used (which Philips had not done), ambush marketing is not illegal and it is in line with commercial advertising as free speech in terms of the Indian Constitution[166]:

> So far as plea of "ambush marketing" is concerned, the phrase "ambush marketing" is used by marketing executives only. It is different from passing off. In the passing off action, there is an element of overt or covert deceit whereas the ambush marketing is opportunistic commercial exploitation of an event. The ambush marketer does not seek to suggest any connection with the event but gives his own brand or other insignia, a larger exposure to the people, attracted to the event, without any authorization of the event organizer. The organizers call it ambush marketing by the defendant, for promoting his brand or product without incurring financial obligation like the official sponsors. The ambush marketing may be inside the stadium like clash between official and personal endorsements or outside the stadium. However, in such cases, there is no deception, therefore, the defendants' conduct cannot be categorised as wrongful or against public interest. It is now well settled that commercial advertisement is form of "commercial speech." It is a part of the freedom of speech and expression guaranteed under Article 19(1)(a). However, unlike the First Amendment under the United States Constitution, our Constitution lays down in Article 19(2) the restrictions which can be imposed by law to restrict such rights... The 'World Cup' or the Event is not protected by any International treaty or domestic law, unlike the word "Olympics" and its logo, which is protected under the Emblems and Names {Prevention of Improper Use} Act, 1950. It is for Legislature to determine how far to curtail legitimate fair competition and freedom of speech. From the material on record, the advertising campaign offering tickets of the Event as prizes without using the logo or the mark of the plaintiff cannot be held to be unlawful.[167]

It is unclear whether an Indian court would currently or in future take a similar view of conduct such as that at issue in the *Philips* case, and it is possible that the approach in respect of recognition of ambush marketing as constituting an independent cause of action might change in future. Of course, it is also possible that a claim against ambushing can be brought under different grounds in law (such as, for example, a trademark infringement claim based on dilution of an event organiser or sponsor mark).

---

[165] A more recent dispute between adidas and Nike over an endorsement deal with Indian cricket star batsman Sachin Tendulkar has led to calls for a review of Indian law's treatment of publicity rights—see Safiyuddin and Bhandare 2008, p. 8.

[166] See Vassallo et al. 2005, p. 1347; see also Kaur, B 'Apprehending an ambush: How to defend against ambush marketing' *Brands in the Boardroom 2010* 56-59 at 57 (www.iam-magazine.com)—available online at the time of writing at http://www.iam-magazine.com/issues/Article.ashx?g=a96dceed-1e54-456c-bd75-6a38f819d228.

[167] From par. 10 of the court's order (by Agarwal J, dated 1 January 2003).

More recently, on 16 April 2010, in an ambush-related matter in respect of the 2010 Commonwealth Games the Delhi High Court granted an injunction against use of the domain name www.commonwealthgames2010.org in *The Organising Committee Commonwealth Games 2010 Delhi v Gets Holidays & Another.*[168] A WIPO domain name dispute panel also ruled in favour of the Delhi Commonwealth Games organisers in respect of another disputed domain name in September 2010.[169]

The phenomenally successful Indian Premier League (IPL) cricket competition has, predictably, also been at the forefront of ambushing. Brand owners have inevitably tried to cash in on the success of the IPL marks or events, a notable example being the launch of a range of biscuits under the name '20–20'[170] by confectionery company Parle Products (reminiscent of the Britannia biscuits case referred to earlier). The BCCI also filed suit against an online gaming company (and Rediff.com for a domain registration) in May 2008, which released a Twenty20 cricket game under the name Indian Fantasy League—Indian Fantasy Cricket. The Madras High Court restrained the company from using the name Indian Fantasy League as a trademark or domain name, and from using a logo depicting a batsman playing a shot, concluding that the name and logo were deceptively similar to the BCCI's IPL mark and logo.[171]

It is interesting to note that India has to date not passed special anti-ambushing legislation, especially in light of the above position taken by the Delhi High Court in 2003 regarding ambush marketing (which one might expect would make event organisers distinctly nervous). Some have criticised the current legal position (e.g. 'the current intellectual property regime is only partially successful to combat ambush marketing and hence a *sui generis* approach has to be taken and new laws

---

168 See Nigam 2011, p. 61.

169 WIPO Arbitration and Mediation Centre, *Organising Committee Commonwealth Games 2010 Delhi v. PrivacyProtect.org/netlinkblue digital energy (p) limited*, Case No. D2010-1194 (14 September 2010). The panel found, *inter alia*, the following:

'Like the Olympic games, the Commonwealth Games are traditionally known by the name of the host city followed by the year of the games… Given the age-old tradition of identifying games with the name of the hosting city, the use of name of the city of "Delhi" in the disputed domain name followed by the words "Commonwealth Games," in the Panel's view, makes the disputed domain name confusingly similar to the Complainant's mark. The domain name in the present dispute is an obvious transposition of the terms used in the Complainant's mark 2010 COMMONWEALTH GAMES DELHI. The disputed domain name <delhi-commonwealth-games.com> undeniably refers to the event being hosted by the Complainant, and the transposition of words does not alter this underlying character. Neither does the substitution of hyphens for the space between the words in the disputed domain name make any material alteration to its basic characteristic that it is similar to the Complainant's mark. The Panel accordingly finds that the disputed domain name <delhi-commonwealth-games.com> is confusingly similar to the Complainant's mark 2010 COMMONWEALTH GAMES DELHI.'

170 The IPL is a Twenty20 (or twenty-over-a-side) competition.

171 See Safiyuddin and Bhandare 2008, pp. 7–8; 'BCCI moves HC against Rediff's online game,' 28 May 2008, *The Times of India*—available online at the time of writing at http://timesofindia.indiatimes.com/sports/cricket/ipl-2011/news/BCCI-moves-HC-against-Rediffs-online-game/articleshow/3079631.cms.

to be framed in the lines of South Africa, Australia, etc'[172]). The reader might find it strange in light of event organisers' inevitable demands in the bidding for mega-events for comprehensive legal protection against ambushing, that Delhi was awarded the rights to host the 2010 Commonwealth Games and India was awarded the right to co-host the 2011 ICC Cricket World Cup. The ICC, in fact, reportedly made a conscious decision not to push for special legislation for the 2011 World Cup. Legal counsel for the ICC reported that no major ambush marketing was experienced at the 2011 ICC Cricket World Cup (co-hosted by India),[173] and that the most noteworthy commercial rights issue that confronted the organisers was the use and commercialisation of match footage by Indian news channels and violations of news access guidelines/regulations. Such conduct was reportedly by news broadcasters and not the official broadcaster, and media accreditation was withdrawn at one point given the nature of commercialisation of footage in the name of fair use/ fair dealing.[174] At the time of writing it appears likely that legal action might follow or, at the very least, that the ICC will likely take active and special steps to address this particular type of 'ambush' in respect of future events. However, it is interesting to consider that India might provide an example of a high risk ambushing jurisdiction which has avoided the passing of *sui generis* event legislation, but yet has also apparently been able to cope with the problems of ambushing through more traditional legal means. This might serve as a good subject for future research regarding the need for special commercial rights protection for mega-events.

4.4.3 The Applicable Anti-Ambush Marketing Legislation in the United Kingdom

Special ambush marketing protection in the form of *sui generis* legislation has been passed for both the upcoming (at the time of writing) mega-events to be hosted in the United Kingdom, namely the 2012 London Olympic Games and the 2014 Glasgow Commonwealth Games. The UK is currently experiencing what some like to refer to as a 'golden sporting decade,' with other major events to be hosted between 2011 and 2020 including the 2014 Ryder Cup at Gleneagles in Scotland, the IRB Rugby World Cup 2015 and the ICC Cricket World Cup in 2019. At the time of writing it is unclear whether special legislation will be passed to provide special protection for commercial rights to these other events. In respect

---

[172] Bhattacharjee 2003, p. 382. See also Seth 2010; 'Should we legislate on ambush marketing?' *The Hindu Business Line*, available online at the time of writing at http://www.thehindubusinessline.in/catalyst/2008/05/08/stories/2008050850110300.htm; 'Ambush marketing—Growth in India,' available online at http://www.gala-marketlaw.com/joomla4/index.php?option=com_content&view=article&id=306&Itemid=306.

[173] Following the reports of ambush advertising by Indian national team players in the weeks before the start of the event, which prompted the intervention of the ICC—see discussion elsewhere in Chap. 3.

[174] My thanks to Nandan Kamath for providing this information.

of the London Olympics, especially, I will only include a brief overview here, as further discussion is found in Chap. 8 and elsewhere in the book where relevant.

4.4.3.1 The 2012 London Olympic Games

The 2012 Olympic Games legislative protection is twofold. The first is found in the Olympic Symbol etc. (Protection) Act 1995[175] (or 'OSPA'), which created a general 'Olympic association right,' which provides protection to the Olympic symbol, the Olympic motto and certain key words such as 'Olympiad' and 'Olympian' and prevents representations of anything similar that is likely to create an association with the Olympic Games or the Olympic Movement in the public mind.[176] It provides similar protection for the Paralympic Games (i.e. for the Paralympic marks and symbols).[177] This is a form of 'quasi-trademark protection' for such symbols and marks.

The second, and most important for present purposes, is the London Olympic Games and Paralympic Games Act, 2006[178] (which I will refer to throughout as the 'London Act'), which created the 'London Olympics association right' (commonly known by the acronym 'LOAR'), which prohibits representations from being made in relation to goods or services which are likely to suggest to the public that there is an association between those goods or services and the London Olympic Games or Paralympic Games. This right vests in the London Organising Committee of the Olympic Games (LOCOG). The protection under the 1995 Act was introduced to fulfil an obligation made as part of the unsuccessful bid for the 'Manchester 2000 Games,' and the protection under this Act was extended to the Paralympic insignia under the 2006 Act. The protection by means of 'association rights' is thus in two forms:

(i) The Olympic Association Right (the 'OAR,' under the 1995 Act) and the Paralympic Association Right (the 'PAR,' under the amended 1995 Act); and
(ii) The London Olympic Association Right (the 'LOAR,' under the 2006 Act).

LOCOG is proprietor of the LOAR. Together with the British Olympic Association and British Paralympic Association, LOCOG is the joint proprietor of the OAR/PAR until 31 December 2012.[179] LOCOG's *Brand Protection* guidelines,[180] issued in April 2010, describe its role as follows:

---

175 19 July 1995.

176 The general Olympic association right is the right constituted under section 1(1) of the Olympic Symbol etc. (Protection) Act 1995.

177 See schedule 3 section 6 of the London Olympic and Paralympic Games Act, 2006 (which inserted a section 5A in the Olympic Symbol etc. (Protection) Act, 1995 to make provision for Paralympic Games words and marks).

178 Which received Royal Assent on 30 March 2006.

179 Section 40(8) of the London Act.

180 Available online at the time of writing at http://www.london2012.com/documents/brand-guidelines/statutory-marketing-rights.pdf.

> LOCOG is a private, limited liability company with only 3% (approx.) of its revenue coming from the public sector (which represents funding for the Paralympic Games specifically). The remaining 97% is raised privately, through sponsorship, merchandise sales, ticket sales and broadcasting revenues etc. The… statutory provisions [as contained in OSPA and the London Act] are intended to secure LOCOG's ability to raise this revenue. LOCOG must raise money by selling rights of association to the 2012 Games to sponsors, by selling official merchandise and by selling tickets. In order to maximise sponsorship revenue it is essential that the association which can be granted to sponsors is exclusive. LOCOG must therefore be able to prevent others from creating an unauthorised association with the Games and thereby profiting from the Games for free to the detriment of those who have lawfully acquired such rights.

The UK authorities' seriousness about complying with IOC requirements for the Games is well illustrated by the London Act, which in its 2005 Bill form received its first reading in Parliament a mere 8 days after London was announced as the 2012 host city. The protection of sponsors' and event organisers' commercial rights to the Games in terms of the legislation is wide-ranging, and serves to supplement the traditional bases for protection against ambush marketing. Whereas most brands must seek to protect their intellectual property rights through the limited auspices of registered trademarks, design rights, or copyright and passing off claims, the London Act gives unprecedented powers to LOCOG to prevent ambush marketing at the 2012 Games.[181] Such protection includes the following:

- The various association rights (the OAR and PAR in terms of the 1995 Act, and the LOAR in terms of the London Act of 2006);
- The advertising regulations issued in terms of the London Act 2006;
- The street trading regulations issued in terms of the London Act 2006; and
- The ticket touting offences created in the London Act 2006.

I will not focus here on the street trading, advertising and ticket regulation aspects of the legislation, although these will be touched on where relevant in the later chapters.

Both the 1995 Act and the 2006 Act contain the same definition of the meaning of 'association' for the purposes of the association rights referred to. The definition of 'association' is broad, as it captures any concept of a contractual or commercial relationship, or corporate or structural connection, or the provision of financial or other support, in relation to the Olympic (or Paralympic) Games.[182] The Act specifically excludes the making of a statement 'which accords with honest practises in industrial or commercial matters, and does not make promotional or

[181] Ellen, L 'Protecting Sponsors at the London 2012 Olympics,' January 2010 (at 10), available online at the time of writing at http://www.mishcon.com/assets/managed/docs/downloads/doc_2413/Protecting_Sponsors_at_the_London_2012_Olympics_doc_(2).pdf.

[182] Section 1(2)(a) of Schedule 4 of the London Act 2006.

other commercial use of a representation relating to the London Olympics by incorporating it in a context to which the London Olympics are substantively irrelevant.'[183]

For purposes of infringement of these various rights relating to association with the Games the following should be noted:

- The OAR and PAR are infringed by use of a 'controlled representation'[184] in the course of trade. A 'controlled representation' is defined in the 1995 Act (in respect of infringement of the association right) as referring to 'a representation of the Olympic symbol, the Olympic motto or a protected word, or… a representation of something so similar to the Olympic symbol or the Olympic motto as to be likely to create in the public mind an association with it'[185] (infringement occurs where such a controlled representation is made in the course of trade and without the required consent). The controlled representations include the five rings emblem, the words 'Olympics' and 'Paralympics' and variations thereof, and the official mottos, or anything so similar that would also create an association with the Olympics. According to LOCOG, 'use in the course of trade' bears its ordinary meaning, and includes use of a controlled representation in advertising and on goods, and in relation to the supply of services.[186] It seems likely that interpretation of 'use in the course of trade' will be interpreted in the same way as in trademark law, i.e. where use takes place in the context of a commercial activity with a view to an economic advantage, and not as a private matter.[187] The effect of the legislation is that use of a 'controlled representation' in the course of trade is deemed to infringe, and the burden of proof is on the user to show that, in the particular circumstances, no such association is made out, or that one of the defences under the 1995 Act applies.[188] However, it is difficult to imagine circumstances where use of the five Olympic rings, for example, would not create such an association.[189]

---

[183] Section 1(2)(b) of Schedule 4.

[184] The expression 'controlled representation' is defined in section 3 of the 1995 Act, as amended by para 3 of Schedule 3 to the 2006 Act and applied and modified in relation to the London Olympics association right by para 10 of Schedule 4 to that Act.

[185] Section 3(1) of the 1995 Act.

[186] The 1995 Act, in section 3(2), defines 'use' of a 'controlled representation' as including when a person
(a) affixes it to goods or the packaging thereof,
(b) incorporates it in a flag or banner,
(c) offers or exposes for sale, puts on the market or stocks for those purposes goods which bear it or whose packaging bears it,
(d) imports or exports goods which bear it or whose packaging bears it,
(e) offers or supplies services under a sign which consists of or contains it, or
(f) uses it on business papers or in advertising.'

[187] See the article by Hussey, G and Snaith, T 'Marketing With the London 2012 Olympic Games (or Not Associating With a Sporting Event to be Held in the UK Next Year),' January 2011, available online at the time of writing at http://www.bnai.com/MarketingLondon2012 Olympics/default.aspx.

[188] See section 4 of the 1995 Act.

[189] Hussey and Snaith *supra.*

- The test for infringement of the LOAR under the 2006 London Act is different to that of the OAR/PAR. It is less prescriptive and, as a result, more uncertain.[190] The LOAR is infringed by use in the course of trade of *any* representation in a manner likely to suggest an association with the London Olympics.[191] Section 2(1) of Schedule 4 of the London Act provides that '[a] person infringes the London Olympics association right if in the course of trade he uses in relation to goods or services any representation (of any kind) in a manner likely to suggest to the public that there is an association between the London Olympics and… goods or services, or.. a person who provides… goods or services.' So, unlike the 1995 Act, the 2006 Act does not set out certain ring-fenced representations the use of which would automatically raise a presumption of infringement. The test is broader and applies to use of any representation, visual or verbal, that suggests an association with the London Olympics. Hussey and Snaith point out that this was not always the intended outcome. The original London Olympics Bill did contain particular words and phrases the use of which would give rise to a presumption of infringement. These provisions were watered down[192] during the Bill's passage through parliament, and what remains is a set of words which when used in combination are deemed to be 'listed expressions.'[193] Examples include 'London 2012,' 'Summer Games' and 'London Games.' Use of a listed expression is not fatal in deciding whether there has been infringement of the LOAR, but will be taken into account by the court when deciding whether there has been an infringement of the association right (the Act provides that for the purpose of considering whether a person has infringed the London Olympics association right 'a court may, in particular, take account of his use of a combination of expressions of a kind specified'[194]). LOCOG must thus still prove that the prohibited association has taken place. From a practical point of view, use of a listed expression may be a red flag to LOCOG when deciding whether or not to bring an action for infringement of the LOAR.[195] The LOAR could therefore be infringed even if marketers do not use a listed expression, which gives LOCOG flexibility to bring a claim for infringement of the LOAR even where there is no use of such an expression. LOCOG has indicated that the decision as to whether a prohibited association has been made will be dictated by the context and circumstances of any given case, but has provided some guidance on factors which it thinks could give

---

[190] Ibid.

[191] Paragraph 10(2)(a) of Schedule 4 of the London Act 2006 provides that 'a reference to a controlled representation is a reference to a visual or verbal representation (of any kind) likely to create in the public mind an association between the London Olympics and… goods or services, or… a provider of goods or services.'

[192] I.e. earlier proposals for the use of such words to trigger a presumption of infringement of the LOAR were not accepted, and the effect of such words was also limited to providing courts with the power to take such words into account in determining whether infringement is present.

[193] The Act contains two groups of words, and use of words from the first group (para 3(3) of Schedule 4) in conjunction with words from the second group (para 3(4) of Schedule 4) is at issue. The listed words in Table A are 'Games,' Two Thousand and Twelve,' '2012' and 'Twenty Twelve'; the listed words in Table B are 'Gold,' 'Silver,' Bronze,' 'London,' 'Medals,' 'Sponsor' and 'Summer.' The combined use of words refers to use of a word from the first group combined with either another word from the first group or a word from the second group (i.e. it does not refer to the use of more than one word from the second group in combination).

[194] Paragraph 3(1) of Schedule 4 of the London Act 2006.

[195] Hussey and Snaith *supra.*

rise to such an association. These include use of the colours of the Olympic rings, use of Olympic related imagery (for example, the Olympic torch), and images of venues or places associated with the London Games.[196] It is interesting to speculate as to which types of potentially infringing 'representations' might conceivably be prosecuted. It has, for example, been observed that even the use of '30th' or 'XXX' (the 2012 Games are the 30th Games of the Olympiad) has been identified by LOCOG as a potential indicator of the creation of an infringing association.[197] Other contributory factors which LOCOG will take into account are the timing of the marketing activity and past conduct of the would-be infringer. It must be remembered that this guidance comes from LOCOG (the enforcer of the LOAR), and not from the legislation or the courts, a point specifically acknowledged by LOCOG in its brand protection guidelines issued to the public. Accordingly, other factors which LOCOG has mentioned as relevant (such as past conduct, the nature of the product advertised and the timing of the advertisement—particularly publication or broadcast 'before or during' the Olympics) and which are not contained in either the 1995 or 2006 Acts, will have await judicial consideration.[198]

Finally, as mentioned (but an important point to note) in respect of infringement, is the difference in respect of the incidence of the burden of proof with respect to the different association rights. With the OAR and PAR there is a presumption of infringement unless the user can show that a defence applies or that its use was not likely to create an association with the Olympics/Paralympics. The LOAR is infringed when an unauthorised non-sponsor, in the course of trade, creates an association between their business, goods or services and London 2012. It is for LOCOG to show that an infringement has occurred by proving that such an association has been made.

It is important to note the available defences in respect of potential claims of infringement of the different association rights as provided for by these two statutes. The general defences in respect of the different association rights created by the 1995 and 2006 Acts, respectively, can be classified in three categories[199]:

(i) Defences to infringement common to both the LOAR and the OAR/PAR:

- **Honestly made statement**: It will not be an association if a business only makes a statement that accords with honest commercial practises in industrial or commercial matters, and does not make promotional or other commercial use of a representation in relation to the Olympics/Olympic movement/London Olympics by incorporating it in a context to which these are substantively Irrelevant.[200]
- **Journalism/information**: Neither the OAR/PAR nor LOAR are infringed by use of a controlled representation (OAR/PAR) or a representation likely to create an

[196] See LOCOG's *Brand Protection Guidelines*, April 2010—available online at the time of writing at http://www.london2012.com/documents/brand-guidelines/statutory-marketing-rights.pdf.

[197] Montagnon, R and Smith, J 'Marketing, advertising and the Olympics: How to avoid falling at the first hurdle,' April 2010, available online at the time of writing at http://www.herbertsmith.com/NR/rdonlyres/24175EF6-DA81-4B1B-8C75-F39DEACC4DD2/14743/FeatureOlympicswithcopy.pdf.

[198] Ibid.

[199] I will follow the useful formulation provided by Montagnon, R and Smith, J 'Marketing, advertising and the Olympics: How to avoid falling at the first hurdle,' April 2010, *supra*, at 4–6.

[200] See para 1(2)(b) of Schedule 4 of the 2006 London Act; section 4(3)(b) of the 1995 Act.

association (LOAR), if contained in publishing or broadcasting a report of a sporting or other event forming part of the Olympic Games; or in publishing or broadcasting information about the Olympic Games.[201]

- **Incidental use**: The LOAR will not be infringed by a representation made as an incidental inclusion in a literary work, dramatic work, artistic work, sound recording, film or broadcast, within the meaning of Part I of the UK Copyright, Designs and Patents Act, 1988[202] (the defence of 'incidental use' will be judged in the same way as it is under this Act in relation to copyright. A court will ask whether the inclusion was genuinely incidental, what was the motivation for including a particular image or word, was use fleeting or insubstantial and was any commercial advantage gained. It is likely that this defence will be limited in scope.[203]
- **Continuous use**: This defence applies where a business had been using a controlled representation, or a phrase or other representation that might otherwise create an association with the Olympics, Paralympics or London Olympics, since before the introduction of the relevant right (for example, a café has always been called 'Olympic Café'). Such a business should be able to continue to use such representations without fear of action by LOCOG.[204]
- **Registered or prior rights**: Use of registered rights or other prior rights will also be a defence to allegations of infringement.[205]

(ii) Defence to infringement available only in respect of the OAR/PAR:
Where controlled representations in the meaning of the Act are used infringement is presumed, but it is a defence to infringement of the OAR and PAR that use was in a context not likely to suggest an association.

(iii) Defences to infringement available only in respect of the LOAR:
The following are all defences available specifically in respect of the LOAR, provided that in each case that the use must be in accordance with honest commercial practises:

- Use of a person's or business's own name or address;
- Use as an indication of characteristics of the goods or services (for example, kind, quality, intended purpose, value, geographical origin, time of production of goods or of rendering of services); or
- Use necessary to indicate the intended purpose of a product or service.[206]

For more information on LOCOG's expected interpretation of these defences and its stance on conduct that it believes would potentially infringe its rights in terms of the legislation, the reader is referred to the Brand Protection guidelines

---

[201] Paragraph 8(1) of Schedule 4 of the 2006 London Act (note that, in terms of par. 8(2), this defence does not apply to advertising material which is published or broadcast at the same time as, or in connection with, a report or information); section 4 of the 1995 Act.

[202] Paragraph 8(1)(c) of Schedule 4 of the London Act 2006; section 4(1) and (2) of the 1995 Act.

[203] Montagnon and Smith *supra* at 5.

[204] Paragraph 10(1)(c) of Schedule 4 of the London Act 2006; section 4(11) and (12) of the 1995 Act.

[205] Paragraph 10(1(c) of Schedule 4 of the London Act 2006; section 4(13) and (14) of the 1995 Act.

[206] Paragraph 7 of Schedule 4 of the London Act 2006.

published by LOCOG (the April 2010 version of which runs to more than 60 pages, and which has pretty and colourful pictures for the slow reader).[207] In 2009 a Waltham removal firm, Olympic Removals, which has been using the Five Rings in its logo for more than 22 years, was admonished by the LOCOG to paint over the logo on its vans or face legal action, and in 2010 a London greasy spoon, the 'Cafe Olympic,' was facing threats of action by the LOCOG although it claimed that it had been granted permission by the local Council to change its name to include the Olympic reference after London was awarded the right to host the 2012 Games. Travel agents had already been told to drop references to the Games in their advertising.[208]

In addition to the London Olympics Association Right the London Act, 2006 also makes provision for the passing of advertising regulations. Section 19 provides that the Secretary of State shall make regulations about advertising in the vicinity of London Olympic events, in making such regulations, the Secretary of State shall, *inter alia*, 'aim to secure compliance with obligations imposed on any person by the Host City Contract' and 'have regard to any requests or guidance from the International Olympic Committee.'[209] While the Act provides that such regulations shall specify or provide criteria for determining the nature of the advertising in respect of which the regulations apply,[210] the Act provides that the regulations may apply 'in respect of advertising of any kind including, in particular, advertising of a non-commercial nature, and… announcements or notices of any kind.'[211] This displays the wide reach of the expected regulation of advertising for the event. At the time of writing such advertising regulations have yet to be issued. The Department for Culture, Media and Sport published, in March 2011, a consultation document on 'Regulations on Advertising Activity and Trading around London 2012' for public comment by the end of May 2011.[212] The three stated objectives with the proposed regulations were 'ensuring Games events have a consistent celebratory look and feel,' preventing people from engaging in ambush marketing, and ensuring people can easily access Games venues. I will refer again to these grounds for justification of the regulation in the later chapters.

Infringement of the anti-ambush marketing provisions (in the form of the association rights and the regulation of advertising) is a serious matter. Section 21 of the Act makes it an offence to contravene any regulations on advertising passed in terms of section 19, and a person guilty of such an offence (i.e. to whom one of the

---

[207] Available online at the time of writing at http://www.london2012.com/documents/brand-guidelines/statutory-marketing-rights.pdf.

[208] See the report in *travelweekly*, dated 18 March 2010, available online at the time of writing at http://www.travelweekly.co.uk/Articles/2010/03/18/33285/olympic-trademark-rules-shackle-travel-agents.html.

[209] Section 19(2) of the London Act 2006.

[210] Section 19(3)(b).

[211] Section 19(4).

[212] Available online at the time of writing at http://www.culture.gov.uk/images/publications/ConDoc_Regulations_on_Advertising_and_Trading_London_2012-section1-7.pdf.

defences does not apply[213]) shall be liable on summary conviction to a fine not exceeding GBP 20,000 (and convicted on indictment, to an unlimited fine).[214] A similar fine is prescribed for contravention of street trading regulations passed in terms of section 25 of the Act.[215] No criminal penalties are available in respect of infringement of the LOAR,[216] although infringement of the OAR and PAR may lead to criminal sanctions[217] (in respect of goods, not services[218]). Civil penalties are available and may be incurred on infringement of the OAR, the PAR and/or the LOAR (including damages or account of profits, as well as injunctions and orders for delivery up of offending assets, erasure of an offending sign and disposal of goods).

The enforcement provisions contained in section 22 (dealing with enforcement of advertising regulations) and section 28 (dealing with enforcement of regulations on street trading) are similarly extensive and far-reaching, compare section 22(1):

(1) A constable or enforcement officer may

(a) enter land or premises on which they reasonably believe a contravention of regulations under section 19 is occurring (whether by reason of advertising on that land or premises or by the use of that land or premises to cause an advertisement to appear elsewhere);
(b) remove, destroy, conceal or erase any infringing article;
(c) …;
(d) use, or authorise the use of, reasonable force for the purpose of taking action under this subsection.

An 'enforcement officer' is defined in the Act as a person designated for such purposes by the Olympic Delivery Authority (established in terms of Schedule 1 of the London Act 2006), and may therefore clearly be someone other than a police

---

213 Section 21(2) provides that it shall be a defence for a person charged with an offence under section 21(1) to prove that the contravention of the regulations occurred without his knowledge, or despite his taking all reasonable steps to prevent it from occurring or (where he became aware of it after its commencement) from continuing.

214 Section 21(3) of the Act.

215 Section 27 of the London Act 2006.

216 Storch observes that 'Although the language used in the UK legislation reads like criminal law, the legislation does not contain criminal sanctions.'—Storch, J 'It's an ambush! Or is it?' *Marketing*, 17 May 2010—available online at http://www.macleoddixon.com/documents/Storch.pdf.

217 It will be a criminal offence if, with a view to gain for itself or another, or with intent to cause loss to another and without the consent of the proprietor, a person applies a controlled representation to goods or packaging, labels, business paper in relation to goods, or material to be used to advertise goods. There are other related offences regarding the selling, hiring, distributing, offering or exposing for sale of such goods or packaging, as well as applying controlled representations to material intended for labelling or packaging goods, or business paper (in relation to goods) or for advertising goods. Use of such in the course of business or possessing such material is also an offence. It is a defence to the criminal offences in terms of the 1995 Act to show belief, on reasonable grounds, that the use of the representation in the manner in which it was used, or was to be used, was not an infringement of the OAR or PAR.

218 Section 8 of the 1995 Act.

officer. The powers of entry of a constable or enforcement officer are further circumscribed in section 22 (i.e. such person must take reasonable steps to establish the identity of an owner, occupier or person responsible for the management of the relevant land or premises or of any infringing article on the land or premises, and must give any owner, occupier or responsible person identified such opportunity as seems reasonable to the constable or enforcement officer in the circumstances of the case to end the contravention of the regulations (whether by removing, destroying or concealing any infringing article or otherwise)).[219] The power to enter premises may be exercised in relation to a dwelling only in accordance with a warrant issued by a justice of the peace, and a justice of the peace may issue a warrant only if satisfied on the application of a constable or enforcement officer that there are reasonable grounds to believe a contravention of regulations under section 19 is occurring in the dwelling or on land that can reasonably be entered only through the dwelling; that the constable or enforcement officer has complied with the requirements of attempting to establish the identity of the relevant owner or occupier and of providing them with a reasonable opportunity to end the contravention of the advertising regulations; that the constable or enforcement officer has taken reasonable steps to give notice to persons likely to be interested of his intention to apply for a warrant; and that it is reasonable in the circumstances of the case to issue a warrant.[220]

Special regulations relating to enforcement were published in late 2010 under the OSPA 1995 and the 2006 London Acts. These are known as the Olympics, Paralympics and London Olympics Association Rights (Infringement Proceedings) Regulations 2010,[221] which came into force on 8 November 2010. They give the courts new powers in relation to goods and materials that are found to infringe the London Olympics association right. The High Court is empowered to order the erasure, removal, obliteration or destruction of any offending representations, and LOCOG may apply to the court for the delivery up of infringing goods or articles, which may then be destroyed. In particular, the Regulations provide for the following powers for the High Court in England and Wales, the High Court in Northern Ireland and the Court of Session in Scotland:

- Where a person has infringed the London Olympic association right, the court may order erasure (or 'obliteration') of a representation that infringes the association right (i.e. the relevant logo or mark) from infringing goods, material or articles. In the event of non-compliance with the order, or if the court believes that compliance is unlikely, the court may order the goods to be delivered up for destruction; and
- LOCOG may, up to 31 December 2012, apply to the court for an order that infringing goods, material or articles in a person's possession in the course of a business be delivered up to it, or to such person as the court directs. In addition, the organising committee may apply to the court for an order that infringing goods or material which

[219] Section 22(3).

[220] Section 22(4).

[221] Text available online at the time of writing at http://www.legislation.gov.uk/uksi/2010/2477/made.

have been delivered up may be destroyed or forfeited. If the court decides that no such order should be made the person who had possession of the articles before they were delivered up is entitled to their return. In considering what order (if any) should be made after delivery up of goods, the court shall consider whether other remedies available in an action for infringement of the London Olympics association right would be adequate to compensate the London Organising Committee and any licencee and protect their interests.[222] Licencees are those persons who have been granted consent by LOCOG to associate with the Games in terms of the legislation. LOCOG has an unfettered discretion regarding which persons it authorises to use the representation of association,[223] although members of the IOC's TOP programme must be included.[224]

It is clear that these regulations provide quite substantial powers to the courts and to the LOCOG in respect of enforcement of the relevant statutory association rights to the Games, and it remains to be seen to what extent such enforcement will be required and/or take place during and around the time of the event. It has been observed that 'without these Regulations, the Court may not be able to make orders that provide a sufficient deterrent and remedy to infringements of the LOAR.'[225] This refers to the problem commonly experienced by event organisers in respect of ambush marketing campaigns, where time factors and practical considerations may make traditional legal action (e.g. claims for injunctions) problematic, in respect of obtaining real and effective relief where time is of the essence. An important point to note, however, relates to a remedy that is available in terms of the 1995 and 2006 Acts which is not available in respect of some other such *sui generis* anti-ambushing legislation (for example, the far-reaching South African legislation discussed in Sect. 4.4.5), although section 48 of the Sydney 2000 Games (Indicia and Images Protection) Act of 1996 contained a similar provision. This relates to the availability of a remedy against groundless threats. Section 16 of the 1995 Act (which also applies to the LOAR in terms of the 2006 Act[226]) provides as follows:

Section 16 Remedy for groundless threats of infringement proceedings.

(1) Where the proprietor [of the association right] threatens another with proceedings for infringement of the Olympics association right other than

  (a) the application to goods or their packaging of a controlled representation,
  (b) the importation of goods to which, or to the packaging of which, such a representation has been applied, or
  (c) the supply of services under a sign which consists of or contains such a representation, any person aggrieved may bring proceedings for relief under this section.

(2) The relief which may be applied for is any of the following

---

[222] Regulation 4(2).

[223] See para 4(2)(b) of Schedule 4 of the London Act 2006.

[224] See Johnson 2007, p. 133.

[225] See Laurie, A 'LOCOG gets set to ambush unauthorised marketing in the lead-up to London Olympics,' January 2011, available online at the time of writing at http://www.ashursts.com/publication-item.aspx?id_Content=5657.

[226] Paragraph 10(1)(h) of Schedule 4 of the London Act 2006.

(a) a declaration that the threats are unjustifiable,
(b) an injunction against the continuance of the threats, and
(c) damages in respect of any loss he has sustained by the threats;

(3) A plaintiff under this section shall be entitled to the relief applied for unless the defendant shows that the acts in respect of which proceedings were threatened constitute (or if done would constitute) an infringement of the Olympics association right.
(4) The mere notification of the rights conferred by this Act shall not constitute a threat of proceedings for the purposes of this section.

Mention is made elsewhere in this book[227] of the potential chilling effect of *sui generis* anti-ambushing legislation on the freedom of expression and freedom of trade rights of individuals and businesses, and of the wide-spread practise of event organisers (FIFA being a prime example) to tend to send large numbers of cease-and-desist letters to potential 'ambushers.' A provision such as this goes some way towards discouraging such trend where there is a lack of good grounds for potential legal action (i.e. in less serious or blatant attempts at 'ambush'), although its true value is of course dependent on the public's knowledge of the availability of such remedy. Also, it bears mentioning that I agree with Teresa Scassa who, also noting the potential chilling effects of the London Act and its 'association right,' observes that this arguably laudable inclusion of a provision to deal with groundless threats 'would seem to be recognition of the potential overbreadth of the right.'[228]

It is clear from the above that the protection of the 2012 London Games against ambush marketing in terms of special legislation (i.e. over and above the more traditional bases such as intellectual property laws and unlawful competition and passing off) is very extensive. The legislation has come in for strident and sustained criticism from various quarters since its inception. The UK's Chartered Institute of Marketing (or 'CIM'), for example, published an agenda paper in September 2008 entitled *The Event that dare not speak its Name: Marketing and the Olympics*,[229] which criticised the extent of the anti-ambushing protection provided by the Act. The CIM noted that a Spring 2008 Marketing Trends Survey of marketing companies in the UK at the time showed that only 14% of companies polled had a fairly good understanding of the provisions of the London Act (with 40% expressing total ignorance of its provisions). It also observed that, while the Act's objective of combating ambush marketing was laudable, the Act 'has been executed in a heavy-handed, blanket way that fails to give allowance to the (by Olympic standards) miniscule efforts of small and medium-sized companies to gain some benefit from the presence of the Games' (and observing that 'even official suppliers to the event are not entitled to associate their companies with the Games in advertising, promotions or even in formal discussions with other companies when seeking other business').[230] The CIM especially criticised the Act's

227 See Chap. 7.

228 Scassa 2011, p. 360.

229 Chartered Institute of Marketing *Shape the Agenda* Issue 14, 2008.

230 The agenda paper at 6.

listed expressions provisions, observing that the IOC is throwing the baby out with the bath water: 'Major corporate sponsors do not need such draconian legislation from a body that seems keener to protect large international companies than support its own grass roots businesses and entrepreneurs.'[231] The CIM commented, specifically, on the potential chilling effect of the Act. Even though the LOCOG had indicated that it would follow a common sense approach in deciding which cases of reference or attempted association with the Games to prosecute, it was observed that 'the only guaranteed safe way for marketers to respond will be to steer clear of anything associative at all.' This would put small and medium-sized enterprises in a no-win situation: 'They won't be able to afford to become a sponsor; being a supplier does not confer any exemptions to the rules; and by the nature of being an SME, few will be able to afford the risk, however small, of litigation.'[232] It concluded that the London Act is 'a piece of legislation that seems unnecessarily restrictive, and goes far beyond its valid remit of preventing ambush marketing and preserving the investment value of official sponsors.'[233] More recently, in April 2011, the CIM published a further report entitled *Ambush Marketing and the Law*, authored by its director for research, Mark Blayney Stuart, which makes for interesting reading regarding the commercial rights protection for the 2012 Games.

Without wishing to detract from the wide range and reach of all these provisions referred to, the gist of the London 2012 anti-ambushing protection is found in the concept of the 'association rights' that have been created, specifically the more general London Olympics Association Right (LOAR) in terms of the 2006 London Act. One observer has described the LOAR as 'an unusual beast—a time limited, *sui generis* right designed solely for economic reasons.'[234] As mentioned, this right is infringed by the use without consent, in the course of trade, and in relation to goods and services, of any representation of any kind that is likely to suggest to the public that there is an association between the London Games and particular goods or services or a person providing them.[235] As wide as the potential reach of these provisions appear to go, the London Act's protection is in places eclipsed by other such legislation (compare, for example, section 15A(2) of the South African Merchandise Marks Act, discussed in Sect. 4.4.5: While the London Act contains an exception to infringement of the LOAR in respect of existing registered trademarks,[236] the Merchandise Marks Act extends its protection to also

[231] Ibid.

[232] The agenda paper at 7.

[233] At 14.

[234] Cookson 2011, pp. 149–150.

[235] Paragraph 2(1) of Schedule 4 of the 2006 Act.

[236] Paragraph 6 of Schedule 4 of the London Act 2006, which provides as follows:

> The London Olympics association right is not infringed by the use of a trademark registered under the Trademarks Act 1994 (c. 26) in relation to goods or services for which it is registered.

cover the 'abuse' of a registered mark by its owner). It should be clear that legislative prohibitions and/or restrictions of such ambit hold the potential to significantly affect the rights and interests of members of the public and of business enterprises, and need to be treated very seriously by the legal fraternity. For lawyers, of course, it will remain to be seen how exactly the LOAR will function in practise once courts are confronted with cases of potential infringement, and there is currently (at the time of writing) still a significant measure of uncertainty in this regard:

> [The *sui generis* London association right] is more far reaching than traditional trademark law as it is not limited to a registered mark (or something confusingly similar). The LOAR may be infringed by use of terms that, on their own, would not receive trademark protection as they may be considered generic or descriptive, such as "Summer Games"... Although the LOAR has a wider scope than trademark legislation, it is also open to wider interpretation and so demonstrating an association may be more difficult than showing trademark infringement, where use of identical marks on identical goods or services does not require the trademark owner to demonstrate association or confusion. There is also a total absence of any case law in the area to determine the scope of the rights.[237]

But apart from the role of the courts, more worryingly, is the fact that significant power is in the hands of LOCOG to determine which conduct it will view as infringing its association rights and which cases it will decide to prosecute, which has been criticised *inter alia* on the basis of the apparently wide disparity between LOCOG's understanding of what is prohibited and what the common law (of passing off, specifically) would outlaw.[238] It was reported in October 2011 that about 50 cases of alleged ambush marketing are investigated by the LOCOG every month (with between 50 and 100 cases of alleged ambushes or contraventions of the legislation, many in video, print and online, being examined at any one time) in respect of the 2012 Games. Of these, 5% have been deemed serious infringements—based on factors such as the company's marketing power, whether they are a direct competitor of an Olympic sponsor and if the violation is judged intentional.[239] One of LOCOG's two senior brand protection lawyers, Farisha Constable, was quoted in late 2011 as stating that LOCOG's response to suspected infringements is not aggressive but fair: 'We are really pragmatic and really

---

237 See the country report on the United Kingdom prepared for the Working Committee of the International Association for the Protection of Intellectual property (AIPPI), Project Q210 ('The protection of major sports events and associated commercial activities through trademarks and other IPR'; reports compiled for purposes of a draft resolution to be submitted to the AIPPI Exco meeting in Buenos Aires, October 2009)—available online at the time of writing at https://www.aippi.org/download/commitees/210/GR210united_kingdom.pdf.

238 See, for example, Hussey, G and Snaith, T 'Marketing With the London 2012 Olympic Games (or Not Associating With a Sporting Event to be Held in the UK Next Year),' January 2011, available online at the time of writing at http://www.bnai.com/MarketingLondon2012Olympics/default.aspx.

239 Kortekaas, V 'Digital "ambush marketing" threatens Games,' 9 October 2011, *Financial Times*—available online at the time of writing at http://www.ft.com/intl/cms/s/0/f1879b92-ee78-11e0-a2ed-00144feab49a.html#axzz1dg1w0GLD.

proportionate in our response.'[240] This was against the backdrop of earlier reports that the brains behind the Great Exhibition 2012 (a festival to celebrate the UK's people, culture and history which is to run concurrent with the 2012 Olympics), Julie Benson, had invoked the ire of LOCOG when she applied to register GREAT EXHIBITION 2012 as a trademark. LOCOG informed her that she could not use '2012,' on the basis of the IOC's Community Trademark (registered in 2005, shortly before the announcement of the success of the London bid) for '2012' which is registered across all classes of goods and services. It was also claimed that Benson's trademark would infringe the London Act's association right, and Benson was quoted as stating that LOCOG had informed her that under the Act it 'could use "association" in the broadest of terms.'[241]

It is impossible to judge the merits of these cases without further information, and I would assume that many more cease-and-desist letters have been sent, which of course have implications in respect of their chilling effect and may therefore significantly enlarge the LOCOG's regulatory footprint. These and other considerations are crucial to determining the legitimacy of an approach to event commercial rights protection as encapsulated in the UK legislation, and I will revisit problematic aspects of association rights to events, more generally, in Chap. 8 and elsewhere in the chapters that follow.

4.4.3.2 The 2014 Glasgow Commonwealth Games

The city of Glasgow in Scotland is to host the twentieth edition of the Commonwealth Games,[242] from 23 July to 3 August 2014. As part of the bidding process, the Scottish government gave a commitment in terms of the Host City Contract with the Commonwealth Games Federation that, should Glasgow succeed, legislation necessary to prohibit ambush marketing, eliminate street vending and control advertising space during the period of the Games would be in place no later than 30 June 2010. In line with special event legislation passed for the 2012 London Olympics (as discussed in the previous section above), the Glasgow Commonwealth Games Act, 2008[243] was passed to regulate a number of aspects relating to the hosting of the event, including such commercial rights protection (over and above the existing Scottish legislative and common law protections that are available[244]). The organising committee for the event, Glasgow 2014 Ltd

[240] Smith 2011, p. 43.

[241] Ibid.

[242] The Commonwealth Games is the only international multi-sport event for which the Scottish government bids separately from the UK government.

[243] Bill passed by Parliament on 30 April 2008; received Royal Assent on 10 June 2008.

[244] Example, the Town and Country Planning (Scotland) Act 1997, the Trademarks Act 1994, the Trade Descriptions Act 1968, the Control of Misleading Advertising Regulations 1988 and the common law of passing off.

(or 'G2014'), a company incorporated in June 2007, has been granted association rights to the event.

The Glasgow Commonwealth Games Act 2008 (Games Association Right) Order 2009 (or 'the Order')[245] came into force on 20th January 2010.[246] The Order gives G2014 a right known as the 'Glasgow Commonwealth Games Association Right' which provides that unless a defence applies, G2014 can prevent people or organisations from creating associations with the Games without its authorisation. This 'special and exclusive legal right' known as the Glasgow Commonwealth Games Association Right (or 'GCGAR') applies to the use of certain representations made in the course of business, intended to suggest to the public that an association exists between the Games and any goods or services. Examples would be uses of certain images or words in advertising or on the goods or packaging themselves. The right is to remain in force from 20 January 2010 until 6 months after the closing ceremony of the Games in 2014.[247]

The Order follows an approach nearly identical to the provisions of the London Olympic and Paralympic Games Act, 2006 in terms of giving substance and meaning to the Glasgow association right. The Act, when in Bill form, expressly stated that the intention was to provide protection similar to that found in section 33 of the London Act.[248] For example, it also contains two lists of expressions which, if used in combination, 'may be likely to be considered to be an association with the Games.'[249] The right itself is described (in section 4 of the Order) in identical terms to the London Olympics Association Right (or 'LOAR') as per the wording of the relevant provisions of the 2006 London Act. The defences are also similarly worded; compare section 9 of the Order, which provides that the Glasgow association right is not infringed by

245 No. 1969 of 2009; text available online at the time of writing at http://www.legislation.gov.uk/uksi/2009/1969/contents/made.

246 In order to meet the requirements laid down by the Commonwealth Games Federation and protect the intellectual property rights of the 2014 Commonwealth Games it was felt to be necessary to create an association right, similar to that provided for the London 2012 Olympic and Paralympic Games. As intellectual property is a reserved matter under the Scotland Act, 1998 and so that this protection could apply across the UK, an Order had to be taken forward by the Scotland Office under Section 104 of the Scotland Act in consequence of the 2008 Act—source: http://www.ipo.gov.uk/pro-policy/policy-information/policy-notices/policy-notices-old/policy-notices-glasgow/policy-notices-section104.htm.

247 See the public guidance document published by Glasgow 2014 Ltd, available online at the time of writing at http://www.glasgow2014.com/assets/3da51308-65ca-47d1-9f2d-98e113d47023.pdf.

248 See para 13 of the 'Policy objectives of the Bill,' as contained in the Glasgow Commonwealth Games Bill tabled in Parliament on 9 November 2007.

249 List A containing the words 'Games,' 'Two Thousand and Fourteen,' '2014' and 'XXth'; List B containing the words 'Glasgow,' 'medals,' 'Sponsors,' 'Gold,''Silver,' and 'Bronze'—compare para 3(3) and (4) of Schedule 4 of the London Act 2006 (as discussed in the previous section in the text above).

(a) the use by a person of the person's own name or address;
(b) the use of indications concerning the kind, quality, quantity, intended purpose, value, geographical origin, time of production of goods or of provision of services, or other characteristics of the goods or services;
(c) the use of a representation which is necessary to indicate the intended purpose of a product or service; provided, in each case, that the use is in accordance with honest practises in industrial or commercial matters. It, similarly, also provided for exceptions to infringement in the case of prior use,[250] prior existing rights[251] and in respect of journalism (and informational use) and incidental use.[252]

The Order makes provision for civil claims that may be brought by G2014 in the event of infringement of the association rights, and remedies include an interdict; count, reckoning and payment; damages; and delivery up and destruction of infringing goods, material or articles. Interestingly, the Order provides that all such relief is available 'as is available in respect of the infringement of any other property right.'[253] The Order furthermore provides for similar orders for erasure, delivery up and disposal of infringing goods[254] as provided for in the regulations passed in terms of the London Act, 2006.[255]

Also similar to the position in respect of the London Act, 2006, the Order protects the public against groundless threats of infringement by the organising committee, by giving a right to apply to the court if they consider they are being unreasonably threatened with proceedings.

Finally, the anti-ambushing protection for the Glasgow Commonwealth Games in terms of the Act also includes provisions regulating street trading, advertising and ticket touting, similar to the London Act, 2006, as well as including similarly wide provisions regarding the enforcement powers (e.g. in respect of search and seizure) granted to enforcement officers (although, interestingly, the Act defines an 'enforcement officer' as 'individuals designated as such by the Organising Committee,'[256] and does not expressly include police officers as per the London Act).

The Glasgow Commonwealth Games legislation, and the association right that it creates, were clearly modelled on the protection provided for the 2012 London Olympic Games, and due to the similarity between these instruments no more will be said here regarding the 'Glasgow association right.'

---

[250] Section 10 of the Order.

[251] Section 11 of the Order.

[252] Section 12 of the Order.

[253] Section 14(2) of the Order.

[254] Sections 15–17 of the Order.

[255] The Olympics, Paralympics and London Olympics Association Rights (Infringement Proceedings) Regulations 2010—text available online at the time of writing at http://www.legislation.gov.uk/uksi/2010/2477/made.

[256] Section 21 of the Glasgow Commonwealth Games Act, 2008.

4.4.4 *The Applicable Anti-Ambush Marketing Legislation in New Zealand*

Reference was made earlier in this chapter to the fact that the New Zealand Rugby Football Union failed to secure cohosting rights to the 2003 IRB Rugby World Cup due partly to its inability to guarantee 'clean stadia' for the event to the IRB.[257] Australia, the other potential co-host at the time, agreed to provide clean venues for the matches it was hosting but, after months of negotiation, the invitation to the NZRFU had to be withdrawn after it refused to agree to the clean venue policy due to prior contractual obligations with corporate box-holders. Realisation dawned that effective anti-ambushing measures needed to be established in a legal framework which would make the country more attractive for event organisers as a future host, in light of these organisers' habitual requirement of such protection in the bidding process. The New Zealand Parliament subsequently passed much-criticised and very extensive anti-ambush marketing legislation in the form of the Major Events Management Act, 2007—which one observer colourfully calls a 'statutory sledgehammer'[258]—due largely to the impetus of the country's (successful) bids to host the 2011 IRB Rugby World Cup (to be held in September–October 2011) and the 2015 ICC Cricket World Cup (which will be co-hosted by New Zealand).[259] The passing of such legislation was a requirement in terms of these bids. It appears that, with this legislation, the New Zealand legislature has succeeded in its mission of making the country (which has, in any event, always had a proud and impressive sporting tradition—as this Springbok rugby supporter will grudgingly admit) a more attractive potential host nation. Johnson has described the nature and value of the relevant legislation in this jurisdiction:

> The ambush marketing restrictions in new Zealand are incredibly broad and could be used to prevent most types of ambush. From an event organiser's perspective they represent the gold standard in prevention of ambush marketing. Indeed, from a sponsorship perspective it makes New Zealand the ideal place to host an event, but more importantly it is likely to push up the bar for countries hosting other major sports events.[260]

I will briefly provide an overview of the main points of interest in respect of this very extensive legislative protection (as with the other jurisdictions considered in this section I will not focus on other, more traditional bases for anti-ambush protection in terms of New Zealand law, but rather on the *sui generis* commercial rights protection as contained in the legislation referred to).

---

[257] See Crow and Hoek 2003, p. 4.

[258] Longdin 2009, p. 728.

[259] See the report quoting new Zealand's Minister for the Rugby World Cup, Trevor Mallard, available online at the time of writing at http://www.med.govt.nz/templates/MultipageDocumentTOC____41944.aspx.

[260] Johnson 2007, p. 143.

The Major Events Management Act, 2007[261] (or 'MEMA') is an example of 'umbrella legislation,' which is not event-specific (i.e. special legislation aimed at a single event, such as, for example, the legislation passed in countries like Australia and the UK in respect of specific instalments of the Olympic Games). The Act makes provision for designation of events by the relevant government official as 'major events,' thereby triggering the protection afforded by the Act.[262] MEMA also differs from other non-event specific anti-ambushing legislation (e.g. that found in South Africa) which employs more generally-applicable legislation by means of provisions relating specifically to events. Other than, for example, general unfair trade practises legislation, MEMA deals exclusively with major events.

I will briefly discuss the most important provisions of MEMA in respect of special anti-ambushing provisions. Section 7 of MEMA deals with the declaration of major events, and provides as follows:

> 7 (1) The Governor-General may, by Order in Council made on the recommendation of the Economic Development Minister after consultation with the Commerce Minister and the Sports Minister, declare that an event is a major event.
>
> (2) An Order in Council under subsection (1) must identify the major event and the major event organiser.
>
> (3) The Economic Development Minister may only make a recommendation if
>
> (a) an event organiser has applied for an event to be declared to be a major event under this Act; and
>
> (b) the event activities will take place, at least in part, in New Zealand; and
>
> (c) the Minister is satisfied that the event organiser has the capacity and the intention to
>
> (i) successfully and professionally stage and manage the event; and
>
> (ii) use all practicable measures available under the existing law to prevent unauthorised commercial exploitation of the major event and to protect its intellectual property and other legal rights (including, for example, registering relevant trade marks).
>
> (4) Before making a recommendation, the Economic Development Minister must take into account whether the event will
>
> (a) attract a large number of international participants or spectators and therefore generate significant tourism opportunities for New Zealand;
>
> (b) significantly raise New Zealand's international profile;
>
> (c) require a high level of professional management and co-ordination;
>
> (d) attract significant sponsorship and international media coverage;
>
> (e) attract large numbers of New Zealanders as participants or spectators;
>
> (f) offer substantial sporting, cultural, social, economic, or other benefits for New Zealand or New Zealanders.

---

[261] Act 35 of 2007, which received Royal Assent on 28 August 2007 and came in force on 29 August 2007 (section 2 of the Act).

[262] Section 7 of the Act.

Once an event has been declared a major event, it enjoys protection against ambush marketing by association (in subpart 2 of Part 2 of the Act) and against ambush marketing by intrusion (in subpart 3 of Part 2 of the Act) for the protection period[263] of the event. The latter relates mainly to clean zones, clean transport routes, advertising and street trading in the vicinity of event venues (which is prohibited if not done with the written authorisation of the major event organiser), and will not be discussed here. The Act also contains provisions regarding ticket scalping, pitch invasions and the throwing of missiles. As part of the association ambush protection measures the Act contains provisions regarding the declaration of major event emblems and words (in section 8)[264] and regarding association with the event (section 10). Section 10, the most important provision for present purposes, provides as follows:

> 10 (1) No person may, during a major event's protection period, make any representation in a way likely to suggest to a reasonable person that there is an association between the major event and
>
> (a) goods or services; or
> (b) a brand of goods or services; or
> (c) a person who provides goods or services.
>
> (2) In subsection (1), a person who makes a representation includes a person who
>
> (a) pays for, commissions, or authorises the representation; or
> (b) receives consideration for the placement or the location of the representation.

An 'association' is defined in the Act[265] as 'a relationship of connection, whether direct or implied, such as an approval, authorisation, sponsorship, or commercial arrangement and includes offering, giving away, or selling a ticket to a major event activity in connection with the promotion of goods or services.'

According to section 11 of the Act, a court may presume that a representation is in breach of section 10 (i.e. is an unauthorised and prohibited representation of an association with the event) if it includes a major event emblem; or a major event word or major event words; or a representation that so closely resembles a major event emblem, a major event word, or major event words as to be likely to deceive or confuse a reasonable person.[266] Importantly, in respect of the potential use of disclaimers regarding a lack of official sponsorship or affiliation with a protected event, section 11(2) expressly provides that this presumption applies 'even if the representation is qualified by words like "unauthorised" or "unofficial," or other words that are intended to defeat the purpose of section 10.'

---

263 See MEMA section 9.

264 Part 3 of MEMA (read with the schedules to the Act) deals with permanently protected emblems and words relating to the Olympic Games, Commonwealth Games and other such events.

265 Section 4.

266 MEMA section 11(1).

Contravention of the provisions of sections 10 and 11 (by someone who knowingly breaches section 10) constitute a criminal offence, which is punishable upon summary conviction to a fine not exceeding NZD 150,000. A civil action may also be brought for contravention of section 10 (and the other anti-ambushing provisions of the Act relating to advertising and street trading[267] and ticket scalping[268]), in which case the remedies a court may order include an injunction on any terms that the court thinks fit, and either damages or an account of profits.[269] An order for erasure may also be applied for,[270] as well as an order for delivery up.[271] Section 55 of the Act also provides for a direction for corrective advertising in the case of a breach of section 10 by the making of a prohibited representation of association:

> 55 (2) If the court is satisfied that a person has breached section 10, the court may order that person or any other person involved in the breach to do either or both of the following:
>
> (a) disclose information specified in the order about a civil proceeding for a breach of section 10;
>
> (b) publish corrective statements.
>
> (3) The information or corrective statements ordered by the court under subsection (2) are to be published or disclosed to the public, or to a particular member of or class of the public
>
> (a) at the person's own expense; and
>
> (b) in the manner specified in the court order; and
>
> (c) at the times specified in the order; and
>
> (d) in the terms specified in the order or determined in accordance with the order.

A major event organiser may apply to the court for relief in respect of the Act (including in terms of a breach of section 10). A major event sponsor[272] may request the major event organiser's permission for the sponsor to take proceedings for relief, in which case the defendant has all the defences that would be available against proceedings by the major event organiser, available against such sponsor.[273] In civil proceedings alleging a breach of the Act, a court may, on the application of any person against whom the proceedings are brought, make a declaration that the bringing of proceedings is unjustified and make an order for

---

267 Sections 17–20 of the Act.

268 Section 25 of the Act.

269 MEMA section 52.

270 MEMA section 53.

271 MEMA section 56.

272 Defined in section 4 of the Act as 'a person who has the written authorisation of the major event organiser to make a representation suggesting an association between the major event and that person, or goods or services provided by that person.'

273 MEMA section 49.

the payment of damages for any loss suffered by the person against whom the proceedings are brought.[274]

The Act also contains provisions regarding enforcement and enforcement officers[275] (whose powers are more limited than in the case of the London Olympic and Paralympic Games Act, 2006, as discussed earlier in this chapter) and search warrants.[276]

The Act makes provision for a number of exceptions to infringement in terms of sections 10 and 11. These sections do not apply if

- the association between the major event and the goods, services, brand of goods or services, or person who provides goods or services has the written authorisation of the major event organiser; or
- the representation has the written authorisation of the major event organiser; or
- the representation is of the nature of a personal opinion made by a natural person for no commercial gain; or
- in accordance with honest practises in industrial or commercial matters, the representation

  (i) is necessary to indicate the intended purpose of goods or services; or
  (ii) is made by an existing organisation continuing to carry out its ordinary activities; or
  (iii) is for the purposes of reporting news, information, criticism, or a review (including promoting that news, information, criticism, or review) in a newspaper or magazine, or by means of television, radio, film, the Internet, or other means of reporting; or
  (iv) in the case of a word or emblem (provided that the word or emblem is not being used in combination with other words or emblems with the intention of suggesting an association that breaches section 10), comprises the whole or part of the proper name of any town or road or other place in New Zealand; or the legal or trade name (not being used for the purpose of defeating the intention of the Act) of the person making the representation; or an existing registered trademark.[277]

It has been observed that New Zealand courts will likely follow orthodox statutory interpretation principles in respect of MEMA, which would include an approach of purposive interpretation focusing on the purposes of the Act (as contained in section 3) and the criteria for declaration of an event as a protected major event (in section 7), in respect of demarcating the scope and limits of the exceptions and defences in the Act.[278]

---

[274] MEMA section 51(1).

[275] In subpart 3 of Part 4 of the Act.

[276] Subpart 6 of Part 4 of the Act.

[277] MEMA section 12. Section 14 furthermore provides that it is a defence to an action or a prosecution for a breach of section 10, in relation to a representation that is an advertisement, if the defendant proves that the defendant's business includes publishing or arranging for the publication of advertisements; and that the defendant received the representation in the ordinary course of that business and did not know, and had no reason to believe, that publishing it would constitute a breach of section 10. Section 14 overrides the presumption in section 11 of the Act.

[278] Hughes 2010, p. 16.

Section 15, finally, provides that a registering authority must not register an incorporated or unincorporated body under a name if the use by that body of that name, or of any word in that name, would breach section 10; or an emblem on the application of any person if the use of that emblem by that person would breach section 10. This prohibition applies only during the major event's protection period, but also applies to any application for registration that was filed or lodged before the start of the protection period; but is not registered at the start of the protection period.

The protection provided by MEMA is clearly extensive, and its value for potential mega-event organisers is clear. It provides compliance with mega-event hosting requirements, *in anticipando*, and may serve to strengthen future New Zealand event bids for that reason. To date (in early 2011), four events have been hosted as protected major events in terms of the Act.[279] MEMA will encounter its first real test in late 2011 when the 2011 IRB Rugby World Cup will be hosted in New Zealand. The first charge to be laid under MEMA saw a person who imported counterfeit Rugby World Cup merchandise being fined NZD 20,000 by the Auckland District Court (and his company was also fined NZD 20,000) in September 2010[280] (although it appears that this conviction was on a formal proof hearing after the importer apparently disappeared[281]). The IRB and local events organisers' publicity material in respect of this event is replete with references to MEMA,[282] and an intensive public education campaign regarding ambush marketing and MEMA's potential role has been put in place for the event (including by the NZ Commerce Commission, aimed at businesses).

This very far-reaching statute has, however, been the subject of rather scathing criticism from a number of legal commentators.[283] Louise Longdin has pulled no punches in condemning the particularity of this Act as a mechanism aimed at providing protection for the narrow commercial interests of the few at the potential cost of the rights and freedoms of members of the public, which she views as an illegitimate use of legislative powers:

> MEMA is a misguided attempt to provide a public law solution to a private law problem and the mismatch shows. This temporary renting out of the coercive powers of the state ironically takes us back to the world before the enactment of the Statute of Monopolies in 1623 in which a chronically cash-strapped Crown disbursed one-off privileges to those prepared to pay for them.[284]

---

[279] The 2008 FIFA under-17 women's World Cup, the 2009 FIBA under-19 World Championship, the 2010 ICC under-19 Cricket World Cup, and the 2010 World Rowing Championships.

[280] See http://www.bellgully.com/resources/resource.02678.asp.

[281] See Hughes 2010, p. 16.

[282] The Rugby World Cup MEMA Guide is available (at the time of writing) online at http://www.rugbyworldcup.com/mm/Document/Tournament/0/MEMAGuide_10232.pdf.

[283] See, for example, Corbett and Van Roy 2010.

[284] Longdin 2009, p. 742.

The author has also observed the following in her examination of MEMA's radical departure from the existing law and highlights the fact that such legislation constitutes a dangerous precedent in the international landscape of mega-event rights protection when one considers Johnson's warning about legislative creep as referred to earlier in this chapter:

> Given that New Zealand is a relative late-comer to the world of major events management legislation, one might suppose that the drafters of its statute would choose to draw on the experience of other jurisdictions in which major event management laws have attracted strong criticism for providing an excessive level of protection for sponsors, eroding freedom of commercial speech, and not properly balancing the interests of all stakeholders not just those with a direct interest in the event such as the international sponsoring organization, the national organizing committee and financial underwriters. This has not been the case.[285]

Despite this MEMA promises to compound the problem in terms of such creep, as this Act has been cited with apparent approval by many proponents of strong and aggressive event rights protection and it may well provide the model for further expansion of legal protection of events in other jurisdictions in future.

4.4.5 The Applicable Anti-Ambush Marketing Legislation in South Africa

In the run-up to the 2003 ICC Cricket World Cup South Africa (and under reported pressure from the ICC), South Africa enacted legislation (by means of rather far-reaching amendments to existing legislation) specifically to deal with ambush marketing.[286] This legislation was reportedly already mooted at the time of the country's hosting of the 1995 IRB Rugby World Cup but it appears that there was a lack of political will to pass it at the time by the then newly-established first democratic South African parliament. The South African legislation can be characterised as 'umbrella legislation' (i.e. non-event-specific[287]), as opposed to *sui generis*, event-specific legislation that has been passed in other jurisdictions in recent years.[288]

---

[285] Ibid. 727.

[286] According to one of the drafters of the relevant legislation (the Merchandise Marks Amendment Act, see below), the relevant legislation had originally been prepared with a view to the 1995 IRB Rugby World Cup, but had not found favour with the powers that be and was eventually only passed prior to the 2003 cricket World Cup—from a note posted by Dr. Owen Dean on the afro-ip.blogspot (at the time of writing available on the internet at http://afro-ip.blogspot.com/2009/10/fifa-v-metcash-owen-deans-response.html).

[287] Compare also the Major Events Management Act (35 of 2007) (New Zealand).

[288] Example, compare the Sydney 2000 Games (Indicia and Images) Protection Act, 1996 (Australia), Law Decree 86/2004 of April 17, 2004 (on the protection of the insignia of 'EURO 2004') (Portugal); Law of August 17, 2005 No.167 (Measures for the protection of the Olympic symbol in relation to the Turin 2006 Olympics) (Italy); the London 2012 Olympic Games and Paralympics Games Act, 2006 (UK); and the ICC Cricket World Cup West Indies 2007 Act, 28 of 2006 (Parliament of the Republic of Trinidad and Tobago, 1 November 2006).

In respect of, specifically, association ambush marketing,[289] the Trade Practises Amendment Act 26 of 2001 inserted a new section 9(d) into the Trade Practises Act,[290] which provision prohibits a person from making, publishing or displaying false or misleading statements, communications or advertisements which suggest or imply a contractual or other connection with a sponsored event or the person sponsoring such event.[291] The application of this provision is wide, as is illustrated by section 1 of the Act, which defines an 'advertisement' to mean the following:

> Any written, illustrated, visual or other descriptive material or oral statement, communication or representation or reference distributed to members of the public or brought to their notice in any manner whatsoever and which is intended to
>
> (a) promote the sale or leasing of goods or encourage the use thereof or draw attention to the nature, properties, advantages or uses of goods or to the manner in, condition on or prices at which goods may be purchased, leased or otherwise acquired; or
> (b) promote or encourage the use of any service or draw attention to the nature, properties, advantages or uses of any service or the manner in, conditions on or prices at which any services is rendered or provided.

The new section 9(d) of the Trade Practises Act represents one of the first (if not the first) examples of the creation of a statutory association right in respect of events (which differs from, for example, the association rights created by the UK legislation in respect of the 2012 London Olympic Games and the legislation passed in Australia for the 2000 Sydney Olympic Games, as it is not specific to an event but covers events, generally). As Johnson[292] points out, this provision represents a 'bold step,' and a 'turning point in the prevention of ambush marketing' in light of later developments regarding the creation of statutory event association rights. Schwab described South Africa's legal system (and its anti-ambushing laws) as 'one of the most potent infringement regimes ever.'[293]

More generally (and in order to specifically also address intrusion ambush marketing), the Merchandise Marks Amendment Act 61 of 2002 (amending the Merchandise Marks Act, 1941[294]) was promulgated in order to increase the powers of the Minister to regulate the use of trademarks in respect of *inter alia* sporting events. This amendment followed from (and incorporated) draft legislation which was formulated by the Association of Marketers and submitted to the Department of Sport and Recreation and the Department of Trade and Industry. The main

289 See the discussion in Chap. 3.

290 Act 76 of 1976.

291 Contravention of section 9(d) constitutes a criminal offence and is subject to hefty fines or imprisonment.

292 Johnson 2008, p. 26.

293 Schwab 2006, p. 9.

294 Act 17 of 1941 (as amended).

thrust of the Amendment Act was to amend the definition of an 'event,' which is defined to include the following[295]:

> [A]ny exhibition, show or competition of a sporting, recreational or entertainment nature which is
>
> (a) held or to be held in public;
> (b) likely to attract the attention of the public or to be newsworthy; and
> (c) financed or subsidized by commercial sponsorship, and includes any broadcast[296] of such exhibition, show or competition.

The Amendment Act inserted section 15A in the Merchandise Marks Act, 1941, and provides as follows:

> Abuse of trade mark in relation to event:
>
> 15A (1)
>
> (a) The Minister may, after investigation and proper consultation and subject to such conditions as may be appropriate in the circumstances, by notice in the Gazette designate an event as a protected event and in that notice stipulate the date
>
> (i) with effect from which the protection commences; and
> (ii) on which the protection ends, which date may not be later than 1 month after the completion or termination of the event.
>
> (b) The Minister may not designate an event as a protected event unless the staging of the event is in the public interest and the Minister is satisfied that the organisers have created sufficient opportunities for small businesses and in particular for those of the previously disadvantaged communities.
>
> (2) For the period during which an event is protected, no person may use a trade mark in relation to such event in a manner which is calculated to achieve publicity for that trade mark and thereby to derive special promotional benefit from the event, without the prior authority of the organiser of such event.
> (3) For the purposes of subsection (2), the use of a trade mark includes
>
> (a) any visual representation upon or in relation to goods or in relation to the rendering of services;
> (b) any audible reproduction of the trade mark in relation to goods or to the rendering of services; or
> (c) the use of the trade mark in promotional activities, which in any way, directly or indirectly, is intended to be brought into association with or to allude to an event.

---

[295] Section 1(a) of the Amendment Act. Section 1(b) of the Amendment Act provides for the insertion of the definition of a 'protected event' (namely an event designated as such by the Minister in terms of section 15A).

[296] It seems that specific inclusion of 'broadcast' in this provision would imply that a competing (or any other) marketer can be prohibited from sponsoring the broadcast of an event; and also from buying advertising slots during such a broadcast (see above definition as read with section 15A(2) and 15A(3) below). Compare the events surrounding the 1991 IRB Rugby World Cup as referred to in the text above.

Section 15A(2), as quoted above, is probably the most far-reaching (and controversial) anti-ambushing provision of the Act, and will be referred to extensively thorughout the later chapters of this book. Section 15A(4) provides that any contravention of subsection (2) is a criminal offence, which offence is punishable by a fine of ZAR 60,000 or up to 3 years imprisonment for a first offence or a fine of ZAR 100,000 or up to 5 years imprisonment for a subsequent offence.[297]

The 2010 FIFA World Cup South Africa™ was declared such a protected event[298] in terms of section 15A(1)(a).[299] The Minister's powers in respect of section 15A were furthermore extended specifically for purposes of the FIFA World Cup 2010, by means of the 2010 FIFA World Cup South Africa Second Special Measures Act 12 of 2006,[300] in terms of which the duration of protection for the event was extended from the 1 month period provided for in section 15A(1)(a)(ii) to a period of 6 months following the end of the event.[301] The Minister has also declared the use of certain words and emblems to be prohibited in terms of the Merchandise Marks Act.[302] The phrases that have been prohibited include '2010 FIFA World Cup South Africa,' 'Football World Cup,' 'FIFA World Cup,' '2010 FIFA World Cup' and 'Soccer World Cup,' and such prohibition relates to use of such phrases in connection with the 2010 event and only applies to 'activities connected to 2010 FIFA World Cup South Africa in the area of Football or Soccer 2010 FIFA World Cup.'[303] Furthermore, the prohibition does not apply to the media, provided the reportage is fair and not imbued with unscrupulous business enterprising.[304]

Apart from the relevant provisions of the above two statutes (which are the primary anti-ambushing measures), further protection is also found in section 29 of the recently-enacted (and very far-reaching) Consumer Protection Act, 2008,[305] which contains provisions regarding the marketing of goods or services and also

---

[297] A court finding a person guilty of this offence may also order confiscation of goods in respect of which the offence was committed (e.g. promotional material).

[298] It should be noted that the protection provided in terms of section 9(d) of the Trade Practses Act (see discussion in the text above) does not require designation of an event as 'protected.'

[299] Notice 683 of 2006 (Government Gazette No. 28877, 25 May 2006).

[300] In terms of section 2 of this Act, which provides as follows:

> If the Minister of Trade and Industry declares the 2010 FIFA World Cup South Africa a protected event in terms of section 15A(1) of the Merchandise Marks Act, 1941 … he or she may, notwithstanding section 15A(1)(a)(ii) of that Act, stipulate by notice in the *Gazette* a date later than one month but not later than six months after the completion or termination of the final competition as the date on which the protection afforded by such a declaration ends.

[301] The 2010 FIFA World Cup was played from 11 June to 11 July 2010.

[302] Notice 1791 of 2007—Government Gazette No. 30595, 14 December 2007.

[303] Ibid.

[304] Ibid.

[305] Act 68 of 2008 (the Act referred to has in the meantime come into force).

prohibits ambush marketing by association with an event. Section 29 of this Act, which is found in Part E (which deals with consumers' 'right to fair and responsible marketing'), provides as follows:

> S29. A producer, importer, distributor, retailer or service provider must not market any goods or services
>
> (a) in a manner that is reasonably likely to imply a false or misleading representation concerning those goods or services ...; or
> (b) in a manner that is misleading, fraudulent or deceptive in any way, including in respect of ... the sponsoring of any event.

Finally, it should also be noted here that the Counterfeit Goods Act 37 of 1997 provides additional protection, which may also be relevant in combating ambush marketing, even though it should be noted that this statute is not uncontroversial (with one commentator observing that it is 'fascist and open to rampant abuse'[306]—a powerful weapon to place in the hands of an apparently trigger-happy organisation such as FIFA?). The designation as a 'protected event' in terms of the Merchandise Marks Act might also mean that no person may register any domain name or have content on their web site which is likely to be associated with such an event without obtaining authorisation from the event organisers.[307] This raises the issue of protection against ambush marketing by means of the internet (or, as it has been called, the practise of 'new age' ambush marketing[308]), which will not be discussed here.

By way of summary, it is clear that legislative protection against ambush marketing in South Africa is very extensive when compared to certain other jurisdictions.[309] Especially section 15A of the Merchandise Marks Act is quite far-reaching, making provision as it does *inter alia* for prohibition of the use ('abuse') of a marketer's own trademark. Note that the London Olympics association right

---

306 Johannesburg attorney Ron Wheeldon, writing in a roundtable discussion on South African IP law ('Staying ahead in the rainbow nation' May/June 2007 *World Trademark Review* 38 at 39):

> [The Counterfeit Goods Act] is a powerful weapon in the hands of trademark owners—perhaps too powerful. In fact, I regard it as fascist and open to rampant abuse. The complaint procedure is *ex parte*. A complainant makes a complaint to an 'inspector,' who may apply to a magistrate or judge for a seizure warrant. This is then executed by the police, accompanied by the inspector and a 'knowledgeable person' who can tell the real from the fake. Properly applied, it is an effective remedy against people against whom it is typically impossible to use normal civil procedure against, such as itinerant street vendors, flea markets and inner city buildings of obscure ownership and tenancy where much of the counterfeit clothing is produced or finished. In some ways, though, the act is a double-edged sword as a trademark owner can find itself suddenly deprived of its genuine goods.

307 See the article by Glazier, D 'FIFA threatens World Cup domain owner,' 5 October 2006 (available on the web site of http://www.itweb.co.za—accessed 8 April 2009); Reimers, M 'FIFA scores its first goal' *Without Prejudice* February 2008 pp. 31–32.

308 See Gardiner et al. *Sports Law* 3rd ed Cavendish Publishing Ltd (2006) at pp. 470–472.

309 See e.g. Johnson 2007, p. 234; Vassallo et al. 2005, p. 1348.

(discussed in Sect. 4.4.3) does not go this far, as the London legislation specifically recognises, as an exception to infringement of the right, that '[t]he London Olympics association right is not infringed by the use of a trademark registered under the Trademarks Act 1994 (c. 26) in relation to goods or services for which it is registered.'[310] Section 15A also clearly provides quite substantial protection against ambush marketing, and its real value for event organisers lies in the fact that it covers both the so-called 'association' cases as well as 'intrusion' cases (compare the wording of section 15A(2) as quoted above)—although I am sceptical of the legitimacy of this extension, as I'll explain in the later chapters. This has assuaged earlier criticism of the shortcomings of the previously available grounds to combat ambush marketing (such as action under the Trademarks Act, the Copyright Act, unlawful competition and passing off, etc.) as well as of other suggested legislative amendments at the time.[311] There are five main differences between the protection provided by the MMA and normal trademark law, as summarised by a report by the South African country reporters to the International Association for the Protection of Intellectual Property (AIPPI),[312] namely:

- Protection is available notwithstanding the absence of consumer confusion, which is a general requirement for trademark infringement;
- There would be protection of the event mark or sponsor trademark even in the absence of registration;
- Protection would be extended, in principle, to all classes, whilst in normal practise a trader only has protection for a limited number of types of goods or services;
- It is not necessary to prove that a mark has been used as a trademark; and
- It is not necessary to prove that the use of the mark causes detriment or takes unfair advantage of the relevant protected mark.

The template of this far-reaching legislative mechanism has been followed elsewhere,[313] and due to the extremely stringent nature of the Merchandise Marks Act's treatment of ambush marketing its provisions will be revisited elsewhere in the chapters that follow.

The 2010 FIFA World Cup South Africa, not unexpectedly, provided fertile soil for ambush marketing campaigns, and saw two prominent such ambushes which

---

[310] Schedule 4, par. 6 of the London Act.

[311] See the article by Owen Dean, 'Legal aspects of ambush marketing,' published on the web site *Legal City*, 11 February 2000 [available online at http://www.legalcity.net—last accessed 15 February 2007].

[312] Report by Alberts, W and Parker, L to the Working Committee, Project Q210 ('The protection of major sports events and associated commercial activities through trademarks and other IPR'; reports compiled for purposes of a draft resolution to be submitted to the AIPPI Exco meeting in Buenos Aires, October 2009)—available online at the time of writing at https://www.aippi.org/download/commitees/210/GR210south-africa.pdf.

[313] Compare the nearly identical wording of section 25(2) and (3) of the ICC Cricket World Cup West Indies 2007 Act, 28 of 2006, which was passed by the Parliament of the Republic of Trinidad and Tobago, 1 November 2006.

both proved extremely successful. I'm sure very few industry insiders and ambush observers were surprised to see Nike's *Write the Future* viral marketing campaign, which saw a video (featuring a stellar cast of international footballers, some of whom were already sponsored by competitors of Nike[314]) released on YouTube a month before the tournament kicked off and accompanying print ads with high production value, and enjoyed millions of views on the internet within a two-week period. The campaign extended to social networks Facebook and Twitter and was interactive (fans could 'write the future' of their favourite players and selected submissions were displayed in lights on the electric facade of the Life Centre building in Johannesburg). The campaign was generally lauded as extremely successful, and consumer surveys showed that Nike enjoyed higher recognition than official sponsors such as its competitor Adidas (which was reported to have paid an estimated USD 351 million for the rights to the 2010 and 2014 FIFA World Cup tournaments) and Sony. In fact, Nielsen research indicated that at the start of the tournament Nike had generated more buzz than *any* of the tournament's official partners and sponsors—all of whom paid expensive sponsorship fees.[315] Adidas managed to overtake Nike 2 weeks into the tournament (although much of the buzz around the brand was about the problems with its official match ball—not the best marketing exposure imaginable for a sporting goods manufacturer).[316] (In late 2011 Nike was again, true to form, and as a non-sponsor, showing 13 times more brand equity associated with the London 2012 Olympics than the official partner, Adidas.)[317]

The second prominent ambush campaign at FIFA's 2010 event, which has since featured widely in the ambush marketing literature, was Dutch brewer Bavaria's stunt involving attractive young ladies with their little orange dresses at the Netherlands-Denmark opening-round match in Johannesburg. This matter will not be discussed here, but will be revisited where relevant in the later chapters.

FIFA engaged in litigation in South Africa on three occasions in respect of the 2010 football World Cup, in which cases actions based on contravention of

---

[314] Joseph Fesenmair, co-head of the sports law practse at Bird and Bird in Munich, has been quoted as observing the following about the *Write the Future* campaign:

> 'What was significant in that campaign... was the use of players already contracted to other companies—for example, for their boots—but whose feet were never shown. The dominant sports companies may be keen to maximise their exposure during major events but they are also careful not to tread on each others' toes.' From the report entitled 'Sporting Chance,' available on the web site of the International Bar Association at http://www.ibanet.org/Article/Detail.aspx?ArticleUid=1a43e1e6-e207-4aa7-a21f-6d0435bba7e7.

[315] See the NielsenWire report available online at the time of writing at http://blog.nielsen.com/nielsenwire/media_entertainment/nike-ambushes-official-world-cup-sponsors/.

[316] See http://blog.nielsen.com/nielsenwire/online_mobile/world-cup-sponsors-recover-from-competitor-ambushes/.

[317] According to the 'First ambush marketing rankings for London 2012,' 10 October 2011—available at http://www.languagemonitor.com/global-english/3436/.

section 15A of the MMA were brought in conjunction with other (mainly common law unlawful competition) claims.

In April 2009 it was reported that FIFA had obtained a court order against a tavern in Pretoria, the Eastwoods Tavern which is situated close to the Loftus Versfeld rugby stadium (a 2010 FIFA World Cup match venue), to remove World Cup-related signage. The tavern had placed the words 'World Cup 2010' beneath the main sign on its roof, and had erected banners featuring the flags of prominent football-playing nations with the numeral '2010' and the words 'Twenty Ten South Africa' on them. An application was launched in the Gauteng North High Court claiming interdicts against the tavern owners on the grounds of infringing FIFA's registered trademarks ('WORLD CUP 2010,' 'SOUTH AFRICA 2010' and 'TWENTY TEN SOUTH AFRICA'), for passing off under the common law, and unlawful competition through the violation of section 15A of the Merchandise Marks Act and Section 9(d) of the Trade Practises Act. The matter was settled and a consent order granted.[318] One observer has remarked that it appears strange that the words detailed in the consent order are not protected by the General Notice by which the Minister of Trade and Industry prohibited the use of certain words in terms of section 15A of the Merchandise Marks Act.[319]

A potentially important test case regarding the ambit and interpretation of the 2010 FIFA World Cup anti-ambush marketing protection measures was brought in the Gauteng North (formerly Pretoria) High Court.[320] This matter involved an application by FIFA against South African retail group Metcash Trading Africa for an order prohibiting the use of a mark, 'Astor 2010 Pops,' on lollipops.[321] The mark is a registered trademark and depicts the South African national flag in the zero numerals contained in '2010,' and the get-up of the lollipops further contains soccer balls depicted on the background to the device. Metcash claimed to have used the 'Astor' trademark since 1985 in respect of the marketing of its goods, which mark was claimed to enjoy a substantial reputation in the market place.[322]

FIFA applied for the following orders:

- To restrain the Respondent from infringing its registered trademark (to the 'South Africa 2010 Bid & Device')[323] by making unauthorised use, in the course of trade, of

[318] See the report available online at http://www.themarketingsite.com/live/content.php?Item_ID=8980 (accessed 23 April 2009).

[319] From a blog posting by Johannesburg law professor Roshana Kelbrick on 8 May 2009 on the afro-ip blogspot (available at http://afro-ip.blogspot.com—accessed on 9 April 2010).

[320] The matter was argued on 12 December 2008, with judgment only being handed down on 1 October 2009.

[321] *Federation Internationale de Football Association (FIFA) v Metcash Trading Africa (Pty) Ltd* [2009] ZAGPPHC 123 (Gauteng North High Court). My thanks to Deon Bouwer of Bouwers Inc, attorneys for the Respondent, for kindly providing me with copies of the parties' heads of argument and supporting documentation in this matter.

[322] Par. 1 of the Respondent's heads of argument.

[323] Registered trademark number 2003/04015.

the mark '2010 Pops' and/or '2010' in conjunction with depictions of the South African flag and/or depictions of soccer balls in relation to the product;
- To restrain the Respondent from passing its product off as being those of FIFA or as being products made under licence, or as being connected or associated with FIFA or with the 2010 World Cup; and
- To restrain the Respondent from competing unlawfully with FIFA by contravening section 15A of the Merchandise Marks Act, 1941, and/or section 9(d) of the Trade Practises Act, 1976.

FIFA's claims therefore related to whether the Respondent's conduct constituted a statutory trademark infringement in terms of section 34(1) of the Trademarks Act, 1993,[324] whether such conduct constituted passing off, or whether it constituted unlawful competition in contravention of the Merchandise Marks and Trade Practises Acts (i.e. the standard causes of action as per the template for civil actions against potential ambush marketers as developed by FIFA and its local legal representatives as an integral part of its anti-ambush marketing strategy).

FIFA claimed that its World Cup tournaments have received significant publicity and public interest in South Africa and that, as a result of an enormous repute and goodwill in the 2010 event, there are 'strong common law rights in that event,' which vest in FIFA.[325] As a result, FIFA claimed that the Respondent's use of its trademark and packaging would cause the general public to believe that there is some association between the Respondent's product and FIFA as the organizer of the 2010 event (i.e. 'passing off').[326] In respect of determination of the likelihood of deception or confusion with the public, FIFA argued that such confusion or deception can exist in members of the public believing that the Respondent's goods are endorsed by FIFA (i.e. such as in cases of character merchandising).[327]

Metcash denied that its conduct constituted passing off, mainly on the basis, firstly, that FIFA does not market lollipops and, secondly, that the law relating to passing off provides that one may use offending marks if you clearly distinguish your goods from that of another. In this last respect, Metcash claimed that the 'Astor' trademark clearly distinguishes its product from those of FIFA. FIFA, for its part, argued that the use of the 'Astor' mark had no bearing on its contention that an impression of endorsement has been created (as it is only logical to assume that all licencees or sponsors of a sports tournament would use their own trademarks on the licenced products, as payment of the licence fee is done for the expected promotional gain to one's own marks), and that Metcash's first contention was irrelevant in light of the fact that a common field of activity is not required to prove passing off.[328]

---

[324] Act 194 of 1993. Section 34 of the Act is referred to elsewhere in Sect. 7.2.3.

[325] At par. 11.1 of the Applicant's heads of argument.

[326] Par. 15.2 of the Applicant's heads of argument.

[327] Par. 17 of the Applicant's heads of argument.

[328] *Capital Estates and General Agencies (Pty) Ltd & Others v Holiday Inns Inc* 1977 (2) SA 916 (A).

In respect of the section 15A prohibition as contained in the Merchandise Marks Act, Metcash argued that proper recognition should be given to the difference in scope between the protection afforded by section 15(1) and section 15A of the Act. It contended that section 15A merely restricts use of a trademark in respect of a protected event where such use is made in relation to the event, and to derive special promotional benefit from the event. According to its argument, this protection is less than that provided for in section 15(1), which allows the Minister of Trade and Industry to prohibit, either absolutely or conditionally, the use of the South African national flag or of any mark, word, letter or figure or any arrangement or combination thereof in connection with an event.[329] Metcash referred to the fact that FIFA had earlier applied to the Minister for a blanket prohibition in terms of section 15(1)(b) of the Act of any use of 'South Africa 2010' or of the depiction of a football 'for any purpose and in any context other than use by [FIFA] or its mandataries,' but that the Minister had refused to grant such a prohibition and instead restricted the terms of the prohibition so as to exclude the 'South Africa 2010' emblem, the picture of a football and the word marks 'South Africa 2010' and 'SA 2010.'[330] This appears to be par for the course, as sports governing bodies apparently prefer to take a 'shotgun approach' in respect of requested protection, then settling for what they can manage to obtain.[331]

The prohibition which was published by the Minister was also qualified, in that it restricted the use of such marks only to 'activities connected to the 2010 FIFA WORLD CUP SOUTH AFRICA in the area of FOOTBALL or SOCCER 2010 FIFA WORLD CUP.'[332] Accordingly, the Respondent's argument went that FIFA was seeking to rely on section 15A of the Act, which provides a lesser form of protection, to afford it protection which extends beyond the scope of the protection which it sought but failed to obtain in terms of section 15(1) of the Act.

Metcash denied claims that the mark connotes a formal connection with the 2010 FIFA World Cup event and constitutes ambush marketing. It argued that the football connotation of the 'Astor' mark relates to a football development programme for under-privileged youths, which it had launched in 2005 at the same time as its '2010 Pops' confectionery (and that the '2010' reference was included to refer to the year when such initiative is planned to terminate).[333] FIFA denied such alleged significance of the reference to the year 2010, as it claimed that this was not publicised in Metcash's promotional material.

---

[329] Par. 26 *et seq.* of the Respondent's heads of argument.

[330] Ibid. par. 34.

[331] Compare the London 2012 Olympics association right—Johnson explains how the Olympic contract between the IOC and host countries now requires the passing of legislation to 'effectively reduce and sanction' ambush marketing, and that the broad protection requested in respect of the London 2012 Olympic Games proved to be controversial and that the protection afforded in terms of the London Olympic Games and Paralympic Games Act, 2006 was considerably watered down from the original proposal (see Johnson 2007, pp. 128–129).

[332] Ibid. par. 35.

[333] At par. 2 et seq. of the Respondent's heads of argument.

In a similar vein, Metcash argued that its conduct does not fall foul of section 9(d) of the Trade Practises Act, as its lollipops are marketed with reliance on its well-known 'Astor' mark in a market place within which its association with football is well known, and accordingly its usage of the mark cannot be said to imply or suggest a contractual or other connection or association with the 2010 event. Metcash further argued that FIFA's assertion that any reference to 'South Africa' and the year 2010 creates a connotation of the sort proscribed in section 9(d) was not backed up with any evidence.

Metcash further argued that section 15A of the Merchandise Marks Act must be read in light of the Constitution, and that the restriction on the use of their trademark (which was registered in 2004, prior to the date that the 2010 event was declared a protected event) violated Metcash's right of property[334] in respect of its trademark as well as its freedom of expression.[335] With reference to the courts' method of statutory interpretation in light of the Constitution[336] (which requires that, in the event of competing interpretations, a court must read down a statute so as to ensure an interpretation consistent with the Constitution), Metcash argued that a proper interpretation of section 15A as only prohibiting use of a trademark which is unfair and likely to result in material harm to FIFA's marks would constitute a justifiable limitation of its rights under section 36 of the Bill of Rights.[337] However, Metcash contended that FIFA's 'broad and limitless' interpretation of the section's prohibition limits its rights 'in an extremely invasive manner which could not ... be justified on any limitations exercise.'[338] In terms of the provisions of the Bill of Rights, FIFA bears the onus to prove justification of any limitation of Metcash's fundamental rights, which Metcash contended it had failed to do.

The hearing of the matter was argued on the basis of the third prong of FIFA's claim (namely that Metcash's conduct constituted unlawful competition in light of alleged contravention of section 15A of the Merchandise Marks Act), and the issue

---

334 In terms of section 25 of the Bill of Rights.

335 In terms of section 16 of the Bill of Rights.

336 With reference to *Govender v Minister of Safety and Security* 2001 (4) SA 273 (SCA) and *S v Coetzee* 1997 (3) SA 527 (CC).

337 The limitation clause, which provides as follows:

'S 36(1) The rights in the Bill of Rights may be limited only in terms of law of general application to the extent that the limitation is reasonable and justifiable in an open and democratic society based on human dignity, equality and freedom, taking into account all relevant factors, including:
(a) the nature of the right;
(b) the importance of the purpose of the limitation;
(c) the nature and extent of the limitation;
(d) the relation between the limitation and its purpose; and
(e) less restrictive means to achieve the purpose.
(2) Except as provided in subsection (1) or in any other provision of the Constitution, no law may limit any right entrenched in the Bill of Rights.'

338 At par. 45 of Respondent's heads of argument.

to be determined was held to be whether Metcash had contravened the section of the Act.[339] After a 10 month wait, Msimeki J ruled on the application on 1 October 2009, in what can in this observer's view only be characterised (respectfully) as a rather disappointingly superficial judgment. The court held that Metcash had contravened section 15A(2) and ordered that Metcash be 'restrained from competing unlawfully' with FIFA. One aspect of the learnt judge's order which I find particularly disappointing concerns the circular reasoning contained in FIFA's anti-ambushing strategy. FIFA's contention that a contravention of section 15A should lead to an automatic finding of unlawful competition against Metcash was accepted without more (with the words that FIFA's contention in this regard 'has merit').[340] FIFA's following contention also found favour with the Court:

> [R]egard must be had to the fact that licensees and sponsors of a world cup tournament use their own trademarks on the licensed products to promote their own trade marks and businesses. The examples are: MTN, FNB and TELKOM. The use of its trade mark by the Respondent, according to the Applicant, shows that it intended its pops to be associated with soccer and 2010 soccer world cup. If the Respondent had only intended its pops to be associated with soccer only, *then the need would not have been there to mention 2010 world cup.*[341] [My emphasis]

The Court's acceptance of this contention,[342] without more, is quite interesting in light of the fact that (in respect of the section in italics above) Metcash's get-up of the lollipops did not in fact include a reference to the '2010 World Cup,' aside from the use of the numerals '2010' and a stylised depiction of the South African flag. FIFA had argued that Metcash's 'selling of confectionery products under the trademark 2010 pops coupled with the partial depiction of the South African flag and depictions of soccer balls ("the offending marks") ... constitutes unlawful competition in that [Metcash] is thereby contravening section 15A of the MMA.' The court accepted FIFA's contention that, in the event of such conduct being contrary to this provision, it would amount to unlawful competition. Nowhere is mention made of the fact that neither the (partial depiction of) the South African flag nor depictions of soccer balls are protected marks in respect of the World Cup; nor is it explained why soccer balls and the South African flag appear to have been held to allude to the 2010 World Cup.

It is, in my view, a pity that the court did not feel the need to consider, more fundamentally, the potential problems with the reach of the provision as contained in section 15A(2), even though Metcash's arguments did raise the interpretation of

---

[339] At par. 3 of the court's order (by Msimeki J, dated 1 October 2009). Roshana Kelbrick [in a blog posting on 8 May 2009 on the afro-ip blogspot (available at http://afro-ip.blogspot.com—accessed on 9 April 2010)] has suggested that the other two grounds of FIFA's claim, which were 'not necessarily abandoned,' would appear 'more tenuous than generally admitted in FIFA press reports.

[340] At par. 7 of the court's order.

[341] At par. 8 of the court's order (emphasis added).

[342] Ibid.

the section and what its restrictions amount to. The following was said by the judge regarding the gist of the matter before the court:

> The nub of the matter, is whether [Metcash's] conduct is calculated to achieve publicity for the trademark which results in the deriving of special promotional benefit from the event without the prior authority of the organizer of the event. If the answer is yes, then the conduct is unlawful, as [FIFA] submitted, irrespective of any damage to the "trade mark" of [FIFA]. I agree.[343]

While it is of course correct that a contravention of section 15A(2) amounts to unlawful conduct, this unqualified acceptance of FIFA's submission is rather disappointing. While, as has been shown, section 15A(2) does not require FIFA to show 'damage' or that Metcash's conduct infringed a FIFA trademark, it is doubtful whether the absence of these elements should justify a finding that contravention of the section constitutes unlawful competition with FIFA and its sponsors and licencees.

In short, and in my view, the main objections to the judgment in *Metcash* is its lack of reasons and its failure to engage with the possible challenges to the legitimacy of the statutory provision beyond simply enquiring whether Metcash's conduct contravened the provision. With all due respect, the judgment reads like a mere rubber-stamping of FIFA's arguments by the learnt judge, apparently without proper consideration (and explanation for the rejection) of Metcash's arguments relating to the manner in which FIFA was attempting to enforce the provision and that it was attempting to achieve protection that it was not legally entitled to in light of the Minister's earlier decision regarding protected marks for the 2010 event. Kelbrick has also expressed disappointment in the court's failure to engage with the constitutional arguments raised by Metcash, with reference to the elements of the section 36 limitations test as set out in the Bill of Rights.[344] Other commentators have taken issue with the court's rather sparse treatment of the constitutional freedom of

---

[343] At par. 11 of the court's order.

[344] Roshana Kelbrick observed the following on 8 May 2009 on the afro-ip blogspot (available at http://afro-ip.blogspot.com—accessed on 9 April 2010):

> [Msimeki J] unfortunately gave no further consideration to the question of whether section 15A is unconstitutional. This is a pity. The limitations contained in section 36 of the Constitution include the nature of the right (all holders of SA trade marks: here [on the *FIFA v Metcash* facts], a trade mark used from 2004, 2 years before the section 15A prohibition commenced); the importance of the purpose of the limitation (for FIFA, through sponsors and licensees, to make money); the nature and extent of the limitation (4.5 years absolute prohibition); the relation between the limitation and the purpose (there was a mere allegation that the staging of the event is in the public interest and no evidence was submitted that the organisers have created sufficient opportunities for small businesses and in particular those of the previously disadvantaged communities, in fact media coverage suggests the contrary); and less restrictive means to achieve the purpose (no equivalent relief is available in terms of any other legislation or common law—the provision is extraordinarily wide and no equivalent relief is available in terms of any other legislation or common law—for example trade mark rights are much narrower in scope and the applicant's registered trade mark does not give any such protection because of the disclaimers.

speech issues which were implicated in the case but probably not properly aired, and lament the fact that the case did not go on higher review:

> [Metcash] argued that the Constitution required a narrower interpretation of the section than the broad casting of the ambush marketing net which FIFA was fishing with—arguing that where legislation restricts the rights to freedom of expression or property, it must be interpreted narrowly so as to give the widest possible protection to the right to freedom of expression. The ambush marketing clauses in the relevant legislation are framed in fairly broad language, so the manufacturer argued that they could conceivably prohibit a significant amount of commercial expression. This argument was summarily dismissed in the judgment on the basis that a broader interpretation was justified in the interests of the greater public, which benefited from the hosting of the event, and by the fact that the protection was limited in duration to the period around the tournament. Unfortunately, this decision was not appealed and the challenges to this interpretation were not tested before the Constitutional Court, so the true scope of the clause remains open to debate.[345]

At the time of writing, another matter relating to alleged ambush marketing in respect of the 2010 World Cup has recently died a quiet (although disquieting) death in the Gauteng North High Court,[346] where it had been set down for a hearing on the merits[347] on 23 April 2010[348] but was withdrawn from the roll by FIFA and re-enroled for a hearing in March 2011. This matter, which promised to provide the first meaningful consideration of the legitimacy of FIFA's claims for protection in terms of its litigation template, involved an application by FIFA against a Cape Town entrepreneur, Grant Abrahamse, whose business, Executive African Trading CC, is the registered rights holder in respect of the shape and configuration (of the outline of) a keychain in the shape of a vuvuzela[349] with the numerals '2010' superimposed on it (which design was registered roughly 6 months after South Africa was awarded the 2010 bid in 2004).

Enquiry during the finalisation of this book revealed that the case was finally set down for a hearing before Bertelsmann J in the Gauteng court on 8 June 2011. The respondent's attorney recounts that FIFA's two senior counsel arrived to say that

345 Haman and Marriott 2010, p. 74.

346 *Federation Internationale de Football Associations (FIFA) v Executive African Trading (EAT) CC* Case No. 52308/07.

347 The High Court made a ruling in favour of FIFA on procedural issues relating to FIFA's application in October 2008, and the respondent's appeal against such ruling was overturned in June 2009.

348 The court papers filed by the parties in this matter run to more than 550 pages, and Respondent's contention that oral argument in the matter will likely take up more than a single court day has necessitated a court date later than the originally scheduled hearing date of 24 March 2010.

349 The iconic, mass-produced local plastic trumpet which South African football supporters love to blow at football matches and which promises to be an enduring element of the legacy of (good or bad) World Cup memories for foreign visitors to the 2010 event (interestingly, FIFA reportedly received numerous complaints about the noise levels created by vuvuzelas at the 2009 FIFA Confederations Cup event, but the organisation has ruled that the vuvuzela will not be banned from the 2010 World Cup, despite the findings of recent research that the noise levels created by the vuvuzela are potentially harmful and may cause permanent hearing loss).

they had decided to withdraw the case and contended that each party should pay its own costs, which the learnt judge, despite the respondent's lengthy protestations, ordered. In respondent's attorney's words: 'And that, I am afraid, was that.'

It had been hoped that this case would bring much-needed clarity to South African law on ambush marketing and the application of the Merchandise Marks Act, specifically (especially after the, what I view to be, rather superficial judgment in the earlier *Metcash* case). It provided a rare opportunity for a South African court to deal fully with the many issues which had to be debated and such judgment may eventually have proved to hold something of value to future hosts of the football World Cup or to provide some guidance in respect of the reach of the anti-ambush marketing legislation for purposes of possible future events to be hosted in South Africa. I would suggest the outcome of this matter raises the urgent need for the South African anti-ambushing legislation to incorporate a provision such as that found in the UK legislation for the 2012 London Games (as discussed in Sect. 4.4.3), relating to a remedy for groundless threats in cases of alleged ambushing.[350] Without wishing to display a lack of objectivity and to imply that FIFA had no grounds for its legal action, I believe that the respondent in this matter (who had reportedly incurred hundreds of thousands of Rands worth of legal costs in defending FIFA's aggressive legal action) was hard done by. I believe other future mega-event host jurisdictions can also take something from this.

---

[350] Section 16 of the 1995 Act provides for a 'Remedy for groundless threats of infringement proceedings,' as follows:

> 16(1) Where the proprietor [of the association right] threatens another with proceedings for infringement of the Olympics association right other than
>
> (a) the application to goods or their packaging of a controlled representation,
> (b) the importation of goods to which, or to the packaging of which, such a representation has been applied, or
> (c) the supply of services under a sign which consists of or contains such a representation, any person aggrieved may bring proceedings for relief under this section.
>
> (2) The relief which may be applied for is any of the following
>
> (a) a declaration that the threats are unjustifiable,
> (b) an injunction against the continuance of the threats, and
> (c) damages in respect of any loss he has sustained by the threats;
>
> (3) A plaintiff under this section shall be entitled to the relief applied for unless the defendant shows that the acts in respect of which proceedings were threatened constitute (or if done would constitute) an infringement of the Olympics association right.
> (4) The mere notification of the rights conferred by this Act shall not constitute a threat of proceedings for the purposes of this section.

4.4.6 The Applicable Anti-Ambush Marketing Legislation in Australia

In addition to federal protection of the Olympic symbols (the Olympic Insignia Protection Act, 1987[351]), Australia was the first jurisdiction to pass legislation especially for the purposes of a specific instalment of the Olympic Games dealing with protection of intellectual property and commercial rights against ambush marketing, in the form of the Sydney 2000 Games (Indicia and Images) Protection Act, 1996[352] (since repealed). Other such legislation was also passed, federally or by state legislatures, in respect of specific sporting events, including the Melbourne 2006 Commonwealth Games (Indicia and Images) Protection Act, 2005 and the Australian Grands Prix Act, 1994. The Melbourne Commonwealth Games Act was the first to provide for protection against persons engaging in conduct which would suggest that they have sponsorship, association or affiliation with the Games[353] (unlike the Sydney 2000 Act). For purposes of this chapter I will not include discussion of the earlier Australian legislation in respect of these mega-events, which have since 'expired' (have been repealed having served its function for such events), although it should be noted that (as Johnson observes[354]) this provides guidance on what Australian governments will do in relation to future events. I will also not consider legislation dealing with specific events other than sports events (such as South Australia's Adelaide Festival Corporation Act, 1998,[355] which contains special protection for logos and insignia[356]). For present purposes I will just focus briefly on two recent legislative enactments by the state legislatures in Victoria and New South Wales, respectively.

The state legislature of Victoria passed the Major Sporting Events Act, 2009,[357] which is a voluminous statute aimed at consolidating other existing event-related legislation in order to provide a comprehensive event management Act for purposes

[351] Act 27 of 1987 (which came into force on 23 June 1987), as amended by the Olympic Insignia Protection Amendment Act, 1994.

[352] Act 22 of 1996 (repealed in terms of para 17 of Schedule 3 to the Statute Law Revision Act 8 of 2007).

[353] In section 56L of the Melbourne 2006 Act.

[354] Johnson 2007, p. 137.

[355] Act 73 of 1998 (which commenced on 1 April 1999).

[356] Section 24 of the Act provides that a person must not, without the consent of the Adelaide Festival organising corporation, in the course of a trade or business, use a name in which the corporation has a proprietary interest under the Act for the purpose of promoting the sale of services or the provision of any benefits; or sell goods marked with official insignia; or use official insignia for the purpose of promoting the sale of goods or services. A maximum penalty of AUSD 20,000 is set. The section also provides that a person must not, without the consent of the corporation, assume a name or description that consists of, or includes, official insignia (with the same penalty provided for).

[357] Act 30 of 2009, which was assented to on 23 June 2009 and which came into force on 24 June 2009.

of the hosting of future events in the state (which has for years proudly proclaimed itself to be Australia's sports events capital). The Victorian government characterised this as 'the most comprehensive major sporting event-related legislation in the world.'[358]

The protections found in the Act will apply to an event for which a 'major sporting event order' has been made[359] (although not all of the myriad protections found in the Act will automatically apply to each such declared event; the protection offered is to be tailored in relation to the importance of the event). Orders may be made by the Governor in Council, on the recommendation of the Minister of Sport, Recreation and Youth Affairs. To make such a recommendation, the Minister must be of the opinion that the order is in the public interest and that the event is a major event at an international, national or state level. The Minister must also have regard to certain features of the event before recommending that an order must be made, including its size, the likely number of spectators, the likely media coverage, the projected economic impact, the contribution to Victoria's international profile as a host of major events, the experience and expertise of the event organiser and factors affecting the operational organisation of the event (such as traffic and security management plans).

Among the commercial rights protection measures included in the Act are the following:

- Provisions relating to unauthorised advertising:
  The Act supplements existing provisions relating to aerial advertising,[360] and it also prohibits unauthorised advertising on buildings and structures within a

---

[358] See Hore, P and Wood, P 'Victoria takes aim at ambush marketers' 7 May 2009 *Sports, Entertainment and Marketing Insights* (available online at the time of writing at http://www.claytonutz.com/publications/newsletters/sports_entertainment_and_marketing_insights/20090507/victoria_takes_aim_at_ambush_marketers.page).

[359] Compare the order published in the Victoria Government Gazette No. section 503, 20 December 2010 (A major sporting event order by the Governor in terms of section 7(1) of the Act to declare a number of key cricket matches (Boxing Day tests and international T20 matches) at Melbourne Cricket Ground between 2010 and 2015 as major sporting events, and in terms of section 8(2)(c) as aerial advertising events).

[360] Section 125 provides as follows:

> (1) During the aerial advertising limitation time for an aerial advertising event, a person must not display commercial aerial advertising, or cause commercial aerial advertising to be displayed, without an aerial advertising authorisation if
>
> (a) that advertising is within sight of the aerial advertising venue or an event area where the aerial advertising event is being conducted; and
> (b) that advertising is displayed in such a manner that the content can be seen by the human eye without the aid of optical apparatus other than contact lenses or spectacles.

protected event, venue or area.[361] Unauthorised advertising on certain vessels in the vicinity of an event is also prohibited. Event organisers are given authority to remove or obliterate any unauthorised advertising within an event area. It is also a criminal offence under the Act to possess 'prohibited items' in an event area or venue without authorisation. This includes a flag or banner larger than 1 metre by 1 metre (or with a handle longer than one metre) and any items that are in such a quantity that a reasonable person could infer that they are to be used for commercial purposes.

– Unauthorised use of event logos:
The minister may declare that specified logos, images or references connected to an event are protected,[362] if the minister is satisfied that such logos, images or references relate to and are sufficiently connected to the identity and conduct of the major sporting event; and the event has commercial arrangements that are likely to be adversely affected by unauthorised use of logos, images or references.[363] Section 38(1) provides for the creation of an offence in respect of the unauthorised use of such logo, image or references:

A person must not use

(a) protected event logos or images or protected event references in relation to an event to which this Division of this Part applies; or
(b) any thing that is substantially identical to or deceptively similar to protected event logos or images or protected event references in relation to an event to which this Division of this Part applies
if the use
(c) is for commercial purposes; or
(d) is for promotional, advertising or marketing purposes, whether or not for commercial gain; or
(e) would suggest a sponsorship-like arrangement to a reasonable person.

---

361 See section 116 of the Act:

(1) … [D]uring an advertising limitation period for an event to which this Part applies, a person who is the owner or occupier or the holder of a lease or licence relating to a building or structure in an area which is an event venue to which this Part applies or an event area to which this Part applies must not cause or permit any advertising material to be affixed to or placed on, or to remain on, the building or structure except as authorised or permitted by the event organiser of that event.
(2) The event organiser of an event to which this Part applies may obliterate or remove any advertising material on a building or structure in contravention of subsection (1) in

(a) an event venue to which this Part applies; or
(b) an event area to which this Part applies.

(3) In exercising its powers under subsection (2), an event organiser must cause as little damage as possible.

362 Section 31(1).

363 Section 31(3).

Apart from the cases where the required authorisation for use of logos, image or references in respect of an event has been obtained, the Act provides in section 36(2) that the any person may use such without authorisation

(a) if the use is incidental to

  (i) the provision of information, including the reporting of news and the presentation of current affairs; or
  (ii) the purposes of criticism and review, including criticism or review in a newspaper, magazine or similar periodical, a broadcast or a film;

(c) if the use is for

  (i) the purposes of professional advice; or
  (ii) research or study purposes; or
  (iii) educational purposes.[364]

- Authorised broadcasting:
  Section 43 of the Act provides that a person must not broadcast, telecast or transmit by any means whatever any sound or image of an event to which this Division of this Part applies or any part of that event at or from a place within or outside an event venue or an event area for that event unless the person has a broadcasting authorisation, and is acting in accordance with that broadcasting authorisation. This prohibition does not apply if the broadcast, telecast or transmission is not for profit or gain, or for a purpose that includes profit or gain and

  (a) is not a substantial part of the event; or
  (b) is for the purpose of

    (i) criticism or review; or
    (ii) parody or satire; or
    (iii) the reporting of news; or
    (iv) a judicial proceeding or the giving or receiving of legal advice; or
    (v) providing official library services for a member of Parliament; or
    (vi) private and domestic use.[365]

The Act expressly provides that its above provisions relating to event logos, image and references do not affect other avenues of legal recourse for event

[364] Use by any such person covered by section 36(2) will not be authorised use if it is for promotional, marketing or commercial purposes; or suggests a sponsorship-like arrangement.
[365] Section 43(2) of the Act.

organisers, including intellectual property laws[366] and passing off.[367] In respect of ambush marketing protection, more generally, section 37 of the Act provides that it is an offence to engage in conduct that suggests sponsorship, approval or affiliation with an event, and that a person must not engage in conduct which would suggest to a reasonable person that goods or services (or any person) have a sponsorship, approval or affiliation that they do not have with an event, or the event organiser of an event to which the Act applies, or any event or activity associated with an event to which the Act applies.[368] The penalty for this offence is a fine, calculated in terms of a formula of penalty units (which differs in respect of whether the perpetrator is a natural person or a body corporate). An authorised applicant may apply to the Supreme Court, County Court or Magistrates' Court for the grant of an injunction restraining a person from engaging in conduct that constitutes a contravention of section 37.[369] The court is also empowered to make an order for corrective advertising,[370] and to award damages in an action for damages[371] or make an order for an account of profits.[372]

The state legislature of New South Wales also recently promulgated event legislation, in the form of the Major Events Act, 2009.[373] On major difference between this Act and the Victoria legislation above is that the Major Events Act is not specific to sporting events, and covers major events of a sporting, cultural or other nature.

---

[366] Section 28.

[367] Section 30 of the Act provides as follows:

30(1) Nothing in this Part affects the use of any logos or images or references by a person on or after the commencement of a major sporting event order in relation to an event to which this Part… applies if, immediately before that commencement, the person would have been entitled to prevent another person from passing off by means of the use of the logos or images or the references, or of similar logos or images or references, goods, services or a business as the goods, services or business of the first-mentioned person.

(2) In an action or proceedings in respect of passing off brought against the event organiser of an event to which this Part… applies or a person authorised to use protected event logos or images or protected event references arising out of the use of logos or images or references referred to in subsection (1), it is a defence if the event organiser or the person authorised to use protected event logos or images or protected event references satisfies the court that at the time of the use, the event organiser or the person authorised to use protected event logos or images or protected event references was not aware that the person bringing the action or proceedings was entitled to prevent the passing off.

[368] Section 37(1) and (2).

[369] Section 45 of the Act.

[370] Section 47.

[371] Section 48.

[372] Section 49.

[373] Act 73 of 2009, assented to on 28 October 2009.

Section 5 of the Act provides for the declaration of a major event[374] by means of regulation, and the relevant minister is empowered to make such regulation after consideration of a number of factors relating to the event.[375] The objects of the Act are set out in section 3, and include 'to prevent unauthorised commercial exploitation of major events at the expense of event organisers and sponsors.'[376] This Act also contains a range of provisions relating to different aspects of the staging of major events, and I will focus briefly on those relating to commercial rights protection.

The Act, in its Division 4 (sections 37–42) provides for commercial and airspace controls in respect of major events. This includes provisions regulating advertising on buildings and structures at or in the vicinity of event venues, control over the sale and distribution of articles in certain public spaces ('controlled areas'), control of airspace and prohibition on aerial advertising, and regulated 'commercial and other activities.'[377] Section 42 deals with the use of the official title and insignia of a major event, and provides as follows:

> (1) A person must not use any official title, or official insignia, of a major event for a commercial purpose without the written consent of the responsible authority.
> (2) A consent under this section:
>
> (a) may be given with or without conditions (including conditions requiring payment to the responsible authority or another person), and

---

[374] Rally Australia, part of the FIA's World Rally Championship, which was held in September 2009 in the Northern Rivers region of New South Wales, was declared a major event in terms of the Act.

[375] In terms of section 5(3) of the Act the Minister may have regard to the following matters before determining whether to recommend the making of a regulation under section 5(1):

(a) the potential size of the event;
(b) the likely number of spectators for the event;
(c) the possible media coverage of the event;
(d) the possible economic impact of the event;
(e) the potential contribution to New South Wales's international profile as a host of major events;
(f) the commercial arrangements for the event, if known;
(g) the views of the event organiser, including the organiser's event management experience and expertise;
(h) possible factors affecting the operational organisation of the event, such as the following:

(i) preparation of road and transport plans;
(ii) the need for emergency management plans;
(iii) the need for security plans and consultation with police and emergency services;

(i) if known, the views of local councils directly affected by the event in relation to the arrangements made or to be made for the event; and
(j) the possible need for consultation and agreements to be made between the event organiser and affected local councils in relation to the event, including any agreements about the restoration of event venues and facilities.

[376] Section 3(d) of the Act.

[377] Section 41 of the Act.

(b) may be revoked by the responsible authority for breach of a condition by notice in writing given personally or by post to a person who has the benefit of the consent.

The 'official insignia' of an event is defined as 'a logo, symbol or other design approved by the responsible authority for the purposes of this section by notice published in the Gazette,' and the 'official title' as 'the title of the major event approved by the responsible authority for the purposes of this section by notice published in the Gazette.'

This is the extent of the Act's regulation of conduct that might constitute ambush marketing of a major event, and it may be notable that it does not include such extensive provisions regarding commercial matters such as advertising and commercial reference to an event (implying sponsorship or affiliation) as contained in Victoria's Major Sporting Events Act as discussed above.

4.4.7 The Applicable Anti-Ambush Marketing Legislation in Canada

The Canadian jurisdiction is an important one for purposes of the subject of this book. The 1976 Montreal Olympic Games was more than just a footnote in any account of the development of the modern mega-event commercialisation model (albeit probably a good case study on 'how not to do it' for event organisers). The British Columbia Supreme Court also saw an early ambush marketing case (*National Hockey League v Pepsi-Cola Canada*[378]), which has been extensively cited in the literature and referred to in litigation in other jurisdictions, and which judgment's refusal of a claim for ambushing has possibly played some role in the relative dearth of ambush marketing litigation in the United States in recent years. I will not discuss this case here (I will do so, where relevant, elsewhere in the chapters that follow), but will focus on the most recent mega-event to be hosted in this jurisdiction and the legal measures introduced in relation to it.

Canadian law provides the normal forms of protection of intellectual property (trademarks and copyright), unfair competition[379] etc. which may be relevant in cases of ambushing of mega-events, but will not be discussed here. In addition to these laws, the Canadian legislature passed the Olympic and Paralympic Marks Act, 2007[380] (the 'Vancouver Act,' also sometimes referred to in the literature as

[378] *National Hockey League* et al. *v Pepsi-Cola Canada Ltd* 70 B.C.L.R. (2d) 27 (1992), affirmed 59 C.P.R. (3d) 216 (1995).

[379] Compare, for example, section 52 of the Competition Act (R.S., 1985, c. C-34), which provides that 'no person shall, for the purpose of promoting, directly or indirectly, the supply or use of a product or for the purpose of promoting, directly or indirectly, any business interest, by any means whatever, knowingly or recklessly make a representation to the public that is false or misleading in a material respect.'

[380] Olympic and Paralympic Marks Act, 2007 c.25, which received Assent on 22 June 2007 (text available online at the time of writing at http://laws.justice.gc.ca/PDF/Statute/O/O-9.2.pdf).

'Bill C-47') for purposes of the 2010 Vancouver winter Olympic Games, which was hosted in Vancouver, British Columbia from 12 to 28 February 2010. The Act is described as an Act 'respecting the protection of marks related to the Olympic Games and the Paralympic Games and protection against certain misleading business associations,' and it contains a number of Olympic-related words and marks in schedules to the Act which enjoy(ed) varying degrees of protection in terms of the Act. One commentator, less generously, characterised the 'broad sweep of the Act' as making it 'a trap for the unwary.'[381]

Schedule 1 of the Act contains a number of words and figurative marks related to the Olympic and Paralympic Games (including Olympic-related words and the Olympic motto and the marks of the Olympic and Paralympic movements and of the Canadian Olympic and Paralympic committees). The marks in this schedule and the provisions of the Act relating to this schedule remain in force to date (and may thus be employed for the protection of possible future Olympic Games to be hosted in Canada). Schedules 2 and 3 of the Act contained trademarks specific to the 2010 Vancouver Games[382] and generic Olympic terms, respectively. The provisions of the Act dealing with these last two schedules expired on 31 December 2010 (i.e. the Act contained 'sunset' provisions[383] in respect of the protection granted to the 2010 Vancouver winter Games).

The two main anti-ambush marketing provisions of the Act are contained in sections 3 and 4. Section 3 of the Act (which deals with 'prohibited marks') provides as follows (which prohibition does not apply to the Olympic and Paralympic Games organising committees or the Canadian Olympic Committee and Canadian Paralympic Games committee[384]):

> 3 (1) No person shall adopt or use in connection with a business, as a trade-mark or otherwise, an Olympic or Paralympic mark or a mark that so nearly resembles an Olympic or Paralympic mark as to be likely to be mistaken for it.
> (2) No person shall use in connection with a business, as a trade-mark or otherwise, a mark that is a translation in any language of an Olympic or Paralympic mark.

The Act[385] makes provision for a number of exceptions to infringement of the prohibition contained in section 3, *inter alia* the following:

- Approved use (i.e. use, adoption or registration of a mark with the requisite consent of the Games organising committee or the Canadian Olympic Committee or Canadian Paralympic Committee)[386];

---

[381] MacDonald, R A 'Olympic and Paralympic Marks Act comes into force,' 5 February 2008, on the *World Trademark Review*'s 'Daily' blog.

[382] Registered and owned by either the Vancouver Gamers Organising Committee ('VANOC') or the Vancouver Whistler 2010 Bid Corporation.

[383] In section 13 of the Act.

[384] Section 3(3) of the Act.

[385] In sections 3(4), (5) and (6).

[386] Section 3(4)(a).

- Prior use (e.g. use of a trademark by an owner or licensee of the trademark if an owner or licensee of the trademark used it before 2 March 2007 and the use subsequent to that date is in association with the same wares or services as those for which the trademark was used before that date; the wares or services in respect of which it is registered under the Trademarks Act,[387] or any other wares or services of the same general class as that for which it is registered or was, before that date, used)[388];
- the use by a person of their address, the geographical name of their place of business, an accurate indication of the origin of their wares or services, or an accurate description of their wares or services to the extent that the description is necessary to explain those wares or services to the public[389];
- the use by an individual of their name[390];
- the use of an Olympic or Paralympic mark or a translation of it in any language in the publication or broadcasting of a news report relating to Olympic Games or Paralympic Games, including by means of electronic media, or for the purposes of criticism or parody relating to Olympic Games or Paralympic Games, is not a use in connection with a business[391]; and
- the inclusion of an Olympic or Paralympic mark or a translation of it in any language in an artistic work, within the meaning of the Copyright Act,[392] by the author of that work, is not in itself a use in connection with a business if the work is not reproduced on a commercial scale.[393]

Section 4 of the Act contains the main anti-ambush marketing ('association') provision and provides as follows:

4 (1) No person shall, during any period prescribed by regulation, in association with a trade-mark or other mark, promote or otherwise direct public attention to their business, wares or services in a manner that misleads or is likely to mislead the public into believing that

(a) the person's business, wares or services are approved, authorized or endorsed by an organizing committee, the [Canadian Olympic Committee, or 'COC'] or the [Canadian Paralympic Committee, or 'CPC']; or
(b) a business association exists between the person's business and the Olympic Games, the Paralympic Games, an organizing committee, the COC or the CPC.

Mouritz[394] has observed that section 4 creates, without expressly saying so, an association right to the Olympic Games similar to that created by the London Olympic and Paralympic Games Act, 2006 (discussed in Sect. 4.4.3).

Section 4(2) provides that in determining whether a person has contravened the provisions of section 4(1) as set out above, the court shall take into account any

---

387 R.S. 1985 c. T-13 (as amended).

388 See sections 3(4)(b) and (c).

389 Section 3(4)(g).

390 Section 3(4)(h).

391 Section 3(5).

392 R.S. 1985 c. C-42 (as amended).

393 Section 3(6).

394 Mouritz 2008, p. 12.

evidence that the person has used, in any language, a combination of expressions set out in Part 1 of Schedule 3; or the combination of an expression set out in Part 1 of Schedule 3 with an expression set out in Part 2 of that Schedule. Part 1 of Schedule 3 to the Act contained (prior to its expiry on 31 December 2010 in terms of section 13 of the Act) a list of terms, which include 'Games,' '2010,' 'Twenty-ten,' '21st,' 'Twenty-first,' 'XXIst,' '10th,' 'Tenth,' 'Xth,' and 'Medals.' Part 2 of Schedule 3 contained a list of terms (which are generic words[395]) which included 'Winter,' 'Gold,' 'Silver,' 'Bronze,' 'Sponsor,' 'Vancouver' and 'Whistler.'[396,397] The Vancouver Act therefore, similar to the London Act in respect of the 2012 London Olympic Games (discussed in Sect. 4.4.3), provides courts with the power to take into account the use of certain terms or combination of terms in determining whether an unauthorised and prohibited association with the Games has been made[398] (and also does not provide for any presumption of infringement in this regard, *contra* the earlier draft provisions of the London Act in Bill form).

Section 5 of the Vancouver Act provides that if a court finds, on application, that an act has been done in contravention of sections 3 or 4, it may make any order that it considers appropriate in the circumstances, including an order providing for relief by way of injunction and the recovery of damages or profits, for punitive damages, for the publication of a corrective advertisement and for the destruction, exportation or other disposition of goods or materials in respect of which such act was done. If an interim or interlocutory injunction is sought in respect of an act that is claimed to be contrary to section 3 or 4, an applicant is not required to prove that they will suffer irreparable harm[399] (this last provision applied until 31 December 2010).

There are a number of important distinctions between the specific protection of Olympic and Paralympic marks compared to normal trademark protection in Canada in terms of its Trademarks Act, 1985[400]:

- A trademark registration provides protection against 'use' of the registered trademark or a confusing trademark. The Trademarks Act requires use of the mark as a 'trademark' by the infringing party (use for the purpose of distinguishing the wares or services from the wares and services of others). The Vancouver Act is broader in that it protects against the use of the mark 'as a trademark or otherwise';

---

395 For discussion of the protection of such generic terms, specifically in the context of trademark law, see Chap. 5.

396 Some of the 2010 Vancouver winter Olympics events were staged in the resort town of Whistler.

397 The Canadian Trademarks Office recently advised that effective 1 January 2011, it will no longer object to marks that consists of or so nearly resembles an Olympic or Paralympic mark listed in Schedule 2 or 3 of the Act. However, that does not mean that such applications will automatically be approved by the Office, as a number of the Schedule 2 and 3 marks are still the subject of advertised official marks.

398 See para 3(1) of Schedule 4 of the London Act 2006.

399 Section 6 of the Act.

400 Trademarks Act, 1985 (R.S., 1985, c. T-13).

- Protection under the Trademarks Act not only involves assessing the degree of resemblance between the marks in issue, but also consideration of all surrounding circumstances including the wares, services and channels of trade in association with which the marks are used. Since the protection provided to Olympic or Paralympic Marks is not in respect of certain specified wares or services, it appears that the primary issue will be the degree of resemblance between the marks;
- A registration under the Trademarks Act must be renewed every 15 years (and is always subject to challenge by third parties on a variety of grounds including failure to use and/or lack of distinctiveness). Official marks are protected indefinitely under the Trademarks Act. Except for the marks in Schedule 2 of the Vancouver Act, which expired on 31 December 2010, there is no specified term for the protection provided to Olympic or Paralympic Marks pursuant to the Act (and there is no specified procedure to challenge the protection provided to them).[401]

The Vancouver Act was roundly criticised by civic associations such as the British Columbia Civil Liberties Association (or BCCLA), who pushed for rights to peaceful protest against the 2010 Vancouver Games. The city of Vancouver passed the Vancouver 2010 Olympic and Paralympic Winter Games Bylaw[402] in June 2009 to restrict the distribution and exhibition of unapproved advertising material and signs in any Olympic area during the Games (aimed at combating ambush marketing). The BCCLA filed a lawsuit in October 2009 against the City of Vancouver over free speech concerns regarding anti-Olympic protest groups. The action was subsequently withdrawn in January 2010 after the by-laws were amended (e.g. through the deletion of provisions that banned signs that didn't celebrate the Olympics over huge swaths of the downtown core of the city). A Vancouver pizzeria, Olympia Pizza, invoked the ire of the Canadian Olympic Committee more than a year before the passing of the Vancouver Act over its use of the Olympic rings and torch in its logo and advertising, and was used by the 2010 winter Games organisers, VANOC, as an example in justifying the call for federal anti-ambushing legislation.[403] VANOC's commercial rights manager was quoted after the 2010 Vancouver Games as stating that his department (Commercial Rights Management, or the Brand Protection unit of VANOC) handled an estimated 3,200 cases of potential ambushing of the event, most of which were resolved without publicity. He estimated that there were 50–60 merchandise seizures involving 20,000–30,000 units that were knockoffs or contained illegally used trademarks. There were also high-profile cases of alleged ambush marketing

---

[401] See the country report on Canada prepared for the Working Committee of the International Association for the Protection of Intellectual property (AIPPI), Project Q210 ('The protection of major sports events and associated commercial activities through trademarks and other IPR'; reports compiled for purposes of a draft resolution to be submitted to the AIPPI Exco meeting in Buenos Aires, October 2009)—available online at the time of writing at https://www.aippi.org/download/commitees/210/GR210canada.pdf.

[402] Text available online at the time of writing at http://vancouver.ca/COMMSVCS/bylaws/2010/2010.htm.

[403] See, e.g. 'VANOC seeks law to combat trademark misuse,' 26 October 2006, available online at the time of writing at http://www.canada.com/theprovince/news/story.html?id=1b3b83c2-b428-4ef2-89f1-69e5df35cb9b.

by non-sponsors, from yoga wear company Lululemon Athletica[404] to Scotiabank (while Royal Bank of Canada was an official sponsor, having paid CND 110 million in 2005 for the rights, Scotiabank ran a photo and story-submitting contest called 'Show Your Colours' that used images of fans in red and white cheering a sporting event and included a former Olympic ice hockey champion[405]).[406] VANOC publicly scolded a number of companies for what it viewed as ambushing (and Red Bull even pulled some Olympic-related tweets on Twitter as a result). The run-up to the Games even saw an objection by the Canadian Olympic Committee to the logo of a Vancouver-based gay men's chat line, which the COC claimed looked like an Olympic wrestling pictogram used during the 1976 Summer Games in Montreal. While VANOC have been criticised for its overly zealous clampdown on alleged ambushers,[407] it has also been praised for an educative and consultative approach, including the use of a novel scoring system to evaluate potential ambushes.[408] Despite such efforts, however, and the event-specific legislation in the form of the Vancouver Act, the Games were rife with ambush marketing activity. It was noted that '(s)ix of the top 10 brands at… [the] Vancouver Games were ambushers, or brands with no official affiliation with the Olympics, according to the TrendTopper MediaBuzz Ambush Index, a list put out by the Austin-Texas-based Global Language Monitor, which ranks perceived Olympic sponsors according to their presence in the global media.'[409] The top ambushers at the Games were Red Bull and the Martin Scorsese film 'Shutter Island' (which forged its Olympic linkage by running innumerable prime-time ads during NBC's exclusive coverage of the event).

4.4.8 The Applicable Anti-Ambush Marketing Legislation in the Russian Federation

Russia's largest resort city, Sochi, in Krasnodar Krai on the Black Sea coast, was announced in July 2007 as the host city for the 2014 Winter Olympics. The city is

[404] See the discussion in Chap. 7.

[405] See the report dated 15 January 2010 available online at the time of writing at http://www.ngnews.ca/Business/Personal-finance/2010-01-15/article-799431/Olympics-organizers-accuse-Scotiabank-of-ambush-marketing-with-new-campaign/1.

[406] See the undated report by Mackin, B 'Vancouver Olympic law expires with 2010'—available online at the time of writing at http://slam.canoe.ca/Slam/Olympics/News/2010/12/31/16720396.html?cid=rsssportsolympics.

[407] See Heshka, J 'Rules and Rogues,' *Marketing Magazine*, 1 February 2010 at 37.

[408] See, for an example, the short report posted online at http://www.brandstoke.com/2010/02/23/olympic-scorecard-how-to-judge-ambush-marketing/.

[409] Fitzgerald, T 'Who won in Vancouver: Ambushers,' 23 March 2010, available online at the time of writing at http://www.medialifemagazine.com/artman2/publish/Alternative_media_43/Who_really_won_in_Vancouver_Ambushers_printer.asp.

also to host the Russian Formula 1 Grand Prix and will be a host city for FIFA's 2018 World Cup. From early on the Sochi Olympic bid has been criticised for a variety of reasons, ranging from the expected environmental impact of the Games to the fact that the city had been the site in 1864 of a reported massacre of ethnic Circassians by ethnic Russians, which the Circassians (with the support of Georgians) are attempting to have declared a genocide. Despite the behind-the-scenes drama, the Games organisers had by late 2011 already raised more than USD 1 billion in domestic sponsorships, and the city has been described as the 'biggest construction site in the world' with a 50,000-strong force working around the clock, 7 days a week. In the proud tradition of Olympic host one-upmanship, it was reported that Sochi's domestic torch relay, the longest in Olympic history, would be a 120-day, 17,000 mile journey across Russia involving 14,000 torch bearers. The flame will go to the top of Russia's highest mountain, Mount Elbrus, and the bottom of the world's deepest lake, Lake Baikal, and the head of the organising committee was also quoted as saying that plans that the flame would be taken into space were in the process of negotiations.[410]

Apart from the earlier wide-spread opposition to the Games, the Russian Federation is actively supporting the hosting of the event and, in line with the IOC's demands, has passed special legislation for purposes of its organisation. The 'Olympic Law' (Federal Law No. 310-FZ)[411] covers various aspects regarding the staging of the Games, including, of course, ambush marketing protection for the event. In keeping with the brief overview of relevant legislation in the rest of this chapter I will only focus here on the main provisions dealing with commercial rights protection and ambush marketing.

Article 5(2) of the Act (which I will call the 'Sochi Act') provides that one of the main functions of the Sochi 2014 organising committee is to 'ensure, in conjunction with the Olympic Committee of Russia and the Paralympic Committee of Russia, the protection of the exclusive intellectual property rights belonging to the International Olympic Committee and the International Paralympic Committee during the organisation and holding of the Olympic Games and the Paralympic Games.' Article 6 provides for a 'clean zone' around event venues during the Games,[412] and also contains an interesting (and rather unusual) provision which confirms the restrictions on athlete advertising as contained in Rule

[410] From a report on the gamesbids.com website, 14 October 2011, available online at http://www.gamesbids.com/eng/other_news/1216135928.html.

[411] Approved by the Federation Council on 23 November 2007.

[412] Article 6(1), which provides as follows:

> During the period of the holding of the Olympic Games and the Paralympic Games, the placement (distribution) of advertising outside, inside, above or within one thousand meters from the Olympic facilities and the sites of sports events and ceremonies of the Olympic Games and the Paralympic Games shall be permitted only provided that an agreement to this effect has been concluded with the International Olympic Committee or an organisation authorised thereby.

51 (and its bye-laws) of the Olympic Charter.[413] I am speculating, but this provision may have been inspired by the dispute in the run-up to the 2010 Vancouver winter Games between VANOC and Hockey Canada regarding the IOC's rules against the use of national federations' logos on uniforms during the Games. Article 6(3) deals with advertising and contains the following:

> Any advertising which contains false information concerning the association of an advertiser with the Olympic Games and the Paralympic Games, including in the capacity of a sponsor, or concerning the approval of consumer properties of advertised goods (works, services) by the International Olympic Committee, the International Paralympic Committee, the Olympic Committee of Russia, the Paralympic Committee of Russia, the Organising Committee "Sochi 2014," shall be deemed to be misleading.

The Act does not contain any further provisions which explain the effect of such a determination that advertising is misleading, and it is unclear what the consequences shall be for the advertiser. In the absence of such further information one is left with a rather tautological statement (that 'advertising which contains false information ... shall be deemed to be misleading'), which appears to float, untethered, in the text of the Act. Article 7(2) contains the following, which refers to association with the Games:

> The use of Olympic and/or Paralympic symbols, including for identification of legal entities and individual entrepreneurs or goods, works or services produced, performed or rendered by them (in trade names, commercial signage, trademarks, service marks, appellations of places of origin) or otherwise, as long as such use creates an impression that such persons are associated with the Olympic Games and the Paralympic Games, shall be permitted only provided that an agreement to this effect has been concluded with the International Olympic Committee and/or the International Paralympic Committee or organisations authorised thereby.

And article 7(3) provides that '[a]ny use of Olympic and/or Paralympic symbols in violation of requirements of [Article 7(2) above] shall be deemed to be unlawful.'

The wording of Article 7(2) is interesting, if only for the fact that it, firstly, appears to provide less protection than it might seem at first glance and, secondly, for the fact that it approaches the requirement of consent to associate with the Games differently from other such legislation in the other jurisdictions discussed in this chapter. It should be noted that the section does not prohibit or declare unlawful any attempt to associate with the Games (e.g. by a non-sponsor who tries to deceive the public regarding sponsorship or affiliation of the event), but only where such conduct involves the 'use of Olympic and/or Paralympic symbols.' At the time of writing, the event's official website also only contains a request to

---

[413] Article 6(2) provides as follows:

> During the period of the holding of the Olympic Games and the Paralympic Games, any advertising on sportswear, accessories or sports equipment to be used by athletes or other participants in the Olympic Games and the Paralympic Games shall be permitted only in instances and upon the terms stipulated by the Olympic Charter.

members of the public to report 'unauthorised use of Olympic symbols.'[414] Clearly the ambit of protection provided by this section is much narrower than, for example, what we have seen in the case of the London Act and other such legislation. All that Article 7(2) apparently prohibits is conduct that would normally be actionable in terms of intellectual property laws (i.e. unauthorised use of copyrighted or trademarked symbols). The Olympic and Paralympic symbols are protected under Russian law just like any other item of intellectual property in terms of Part IV of the Civil Code of the Russian Federation. For this reason the potential value of Article 7(2) in order to combat ambush marketing is, frankly, negligible; as we see elsewhere in this book, the truly challenging cases of ambushing are the less blatant ones, where the 'ambusher' does not use intellectual property of the event organiser but more subtly implies sponsorship or affiliation with the event. Also, if one considers the wording of this section, it is clear that it only mentions a prohibition on such unauthorised use of the Olympic or Paralympic symbols 'as long as such use creates an impression that such persons are associated with the Olympic Games and the Paralympic Games.' I find this proviso strange. Upon my reading of the clear language of the provision it, in effect, implies that anyone may use the relevant symbols, and that permission is only required where such use creates an impression of association and [when read with Article 7(3) of the Act] that any such use of the symbols without the requisite permission but when it does not create an impression of association is not unlawful in terms of the Act. One is left with very little protection for such symbols, apart from existing grounds such as intellectual property laws. And as Jolan Storch observes, the Act appears not to cover the use of disclaimers: 'Maybe something has been lost in the translation, but it seems they have enacted legislation that will only catch misleading advertising if the consumer is left with the impression that the advertiser was an official sponsor, which would be difficult to prove and provide an out for advertisers who specify that they are not official sponsors.'[415] Accordingly, I fail to see the purpose of this provision. In a recent survey of countries to determine the level of special trademark protection for major sports events, undertaken by the international Association for the Protection of Intellectual Property (or AIPPI), the country reporter for the Russian Federation also observed that protection provided by the above provision of the Sochi Act is narrower than is the case with other trademarks, since only actual use of Olympic or Paralympic symbols is prohibited without an agreement with the international committees (using confusingly similar symbols is not prohibited by law), and such a use is prohibited

---

[414] At http://sochi2014.com/en/games/legal/protection/feedback/.

[415] Storch, J 'It's an ambush! Or is it?' *Marketing*, 17 May 2010—available online at http://www.macleoddixon.com/documents/Storch.pdf.

only in cases where it creates an impression that the legal entity or individual entrepreneur is associated with the Olympics or Paralympics events.[416]

Secondly, it also appears rather strange that Article 7(2) only refers to permission for the use of the relevant symbols to be obtained from the International Olympic Committee or the International Paralympic Committee. We have seen that other such legislation in the other jurisdictions require authorisation for associating with the Games to be obtained from the relevant local organising committee (e.g. LOCOG in the case of the 2012 London Olympics and VANOC in the case of the 2010 Vancouver winter Games). The major problematic issue for event organisers such as the IOC in respect of ambushing of the Games is found in the domestic context, i.e. the city and country where the Games take place. Apart from the IOC's TOP programme of global sponsors, a significant source of revenue for the organisers is the domestic sponsorship market, and it is in order to protect such sponsors that *sui generis* event legislation such as this is required. Legislation like the London Act, the Vancouver Act and the Sochi Act do not have extra-territorial application; the host legislature cannot pass legislation that applies beyond its borders. I therefore find it strange that the Sochi Act does not provide for a requirement for the local organising committee to authorise use of event symbols, etc. The provision does mention organisations authorised by the IOC or the IPC, but it does not emphasise the power of the local organising committee to consent to use of the symbols.

The final anti-ambushing provision of the Sochi Act is found in Article 8, which takes a rather interesting approach which is not found in the legislation from the other jurisdictions. Article 8 is entitled 'The Ensuring of Fair Competition in Connection with the Olympic Games and the Paralympic Games,' and provides as follows:

> The following shall be treated as unfair competition and shall entail the consequences envisaged by the antimonopoly legislation of the Russian Federation:
>
> (1) the sale, exchange or other introduction of goods involving unlawful use of Olympic and/or Paralympic symbols;
> (2) misrepresentation, including by creating a false impression that a manufacturer or an advertiser of goods is associated with the Olympic Games and/or the Paralympic Games, including in the capacity of a sponsor.

In light of what has been said above about the content of Article 7(2) and its apparently limited ambit [and considering that Article 6(3) as quoted above only deals with advertising that is deemed to be misleading], Article 8(2) contains the most significant anti-ambush marketing provision of the Sochi Act. Article 8(2)

---

[416] See the country report for the Russian Federation submitted to the AIPPI Working Committee, Project Q210 ('The protection of major sports events and associated commercial activities through trademarks and other IPR'; in response to a call for reports compiled for purposes of a draft resolution to be submitted to the AIPPI Exco meeting in Buenos Aires, October 2009)—available online at the time of writing at https://www.aippi.org/download/commitees/210/GR210russia.pdf.

declares that a misrepresentation and/or creation of a false impression of association with the Games is to be treated as unfair competition in terms of competition laws. This approach is not found in any of the other *sui generis* event statutes from the other jurisdictions. Most of those jurisdictions as discussed here grant common law unlawful competition (or passing off) protection which would normally cover such misrepresentations or consumer deception regarding sponsorship or affiliation. It is unclear what the effect is of this provision, and whether it in fact provides anything more than the existing competition laws in the Russian Federation. If not, such a provision would be largely *pro non scripto*. Not being an expert on Russian competition law, I assume that the reference to 'antimonopoly legislation' in this provision is to the Federal Law on Protection of Competition, 2006 (or the 'Protection of Competition Act').[417] This Act[418] defines 'unfair competition' as 'any actions of economic entities (groups of persons) aimed at getting benefits while exercising business activity, contradicting with the legislation of the Russian Federation, business traditions, requirements of respectability, rationality and equity and which inflicted or can inflict losses to the other economic entities-competitors or harmed or can harm their business reputation *(sic)*.' Article 14 of the Protection of Competition Act prohibits unfair competition, providing as follows:

> 14 (1) Unfair competition is not permitted, including:
>
> (i) dissemination of false, inaccurate, or distorted information, which can inflict losses on economic entity or cause damage to its business reputation;
> (ii) misrepresentation concerning the nature, method, and place of manufacture, consumer characteristics, quality and quantity of a commodity or concerning its producers;
> (iii) incorrect comparison of the products by an economic entity, manufactured or sold by it, with the products manufactured or sold by other economic entities;...

A case based on unfair competition is based on a petition submitted by an economic agent regarding the actions of its competitor that are covered by the definition of unfair competition, to the Russian Federation's federal antimonopoly service, FAS (also referred to as 'the Commission'). The petitioner presents available evidence regarding the breach of the legislation on unfair competition. The case is then heard by the FAS, under the Chairmanship of a Deputy Head of FAS Russia, and members of the Commission. Having considered the case, the Commission makes a collegial decision. If necessary, the Commission may issue a determination, which is mandatory.

At the time of writing I am not aware of any litigation or other significant developments in respect of the enforcement of the anti-ambushing provisions of

[417] Law 135-FZ, approved by the Federation Council on 14 July 2006 (and amended in July 2009), which replaced the Law of the RSFSR No. 948-1 On Competition and Limitation of Monopolistic Activity in Commodities Markets (1991).

[418] In Article 4(9).

the Sochi Act. The Sochi organisers have apparently decided to take a leaf out of VANOC's book in respect of the strategy for its brand protection programme, with an emphasis on public and business education regarding ambushing and sponsorship (and e.g. the establishment of a toll-free hotline). Sochi's overall brand protection programme ('Excellence in Sports and the Preparation and Execution of the 2014 XXIInd Olympic Winter Games and XIth Paralympic Winter Games in Sochi') was approved by the Presidium of the Presidential Council for the Development of Physical Culture and Sport on 4 February 2008, and the programme was officially launched publicly on 21 April 2008. While it is unclear how successful such programme will be, it does appear safe to say at this point in time that Sochi promises to raise many of the same problems and issues regarding ambushing as have been experienced in other host cities to date. The Sochi 2014 organisers announced in February 2009 that it had sourced its first domestic sponsorship for the event, a record-breaking USD 460 million deal in the telecommunications category with state-controlled long-distance telephone company Rostelecom and Russia's number three mobile carrier, Megafon (the two companies had pledged USD 260 million in sponsorship, plus a further USD 200 million to develop infrastructure in the region). The 2012 London Olympics, no slouch in the fast acquisition of domestic sponsors, had announced its first domestic sponsorship (with Lloyds TSB) 591 days after winning the 2012 bid, and Sochi's announcement shaved 14 days off that mark.[419] As mentioned above, the USD 1 billion mark in domestic sponsorships was reached by late 2011 and the head of the organising committee was quoted as predicting a USD 300 million profit from the event.

Upon a simple reading of the Sochi Act, however, and as mentioned, it appears to contain a rather strange approach to ambush marketing. At the very least it can be said that it does not appear—unlike the case with some of the other legislation in the other jurisdictions discussed in this chapter—that the drafters of the Sochi Act were guided by anti-ambushing legislation found elsewhere. The approach of the Act is very different and, I would submit, rather confusing in that it appears to provide not only significantly less protection than found elsewhere (not necessarily a bad thing, of course) but also to provide only marginally more protection than is to be found in the common law or other domestic legislation. I have discussed the mega-event organisers' requirements of legal protection against ambush marketing in event bidding (specifically also by the IOC), and it is debatable whether the Sochi Act in fact satisfies such requirements (although I am not aware of any objections by the Olympic organisers to the legislation). I will not speculate on the potential impact of this Act in respect of combating possible attempts at ambushing of the 2014 Games, beyond the above general remarks regarding the potential ambit of these provisions as they stand.

---

[419] See the report available online at the time of writing at http://www.synergy-sponsorship.com/blog/category/sochi-2014/.

Finally, the evaluation report of the IOC's Evaluation Commission on the 2014 Games bids declared, in respect of the Sochi bid, that comprehensive legislation exists to protect Olympic intellectual property rights in Russia. Federal law stipulates that the Russian Olympic Committee controls the use of all Olympic intellectual property in Russia and provides specific measures to combat ambush marketing. It also declared that '[a] guarantee has been provided that the Parliament (State Duma) would enact additional legislation to further strengthen sanctions against ambush marketing in the Russian Federation and, in particular, in Sochi and the Krasnodar Region, no later than 1 January 2012.'[420] It is unclear at the time of writing whether any additional commercial rights protection measures will be enacted in this regard.

4.4.9 The Applicable Anti-Ambush Marketing Legislation in China

Having for decades been for many in the Western world a faceless leviathan largely hidden behind the Bamboo Curtain and the legacy of Chairman Mao, the People's Republic of China only gained global prominence as an international mega-event host[421] with the 2008 Beijing summer Olympic Games, which was hosted in the Chinese capital from 8 to 24 August 2008. The Beijing Olympics was something of an anomaly in the sphere of (sports) mega-events, as it is commonly acknowledged that it is not only the costliest Olympics ever hosted (with estimates in the region of USD 40 billion dwarfing the next-costliest 2004 Athens Games' USD 15 billion[422]), but it will probably also represent the most money ever to be invested in the hosting of the Games. The Beijing Games had the largest Olympics television audience ever, although there was no global or supranational coverage and domestic broadcasters across the world were subject to extensive territorial copyright restrictions in respect of access (which was also the case with online coverage).

In a move that would seem highly ironic to anyone who has ever encountered the flood of counterfeit goods (such as slightly off-colour Man United t-shirts and suspiciously cheap copies of *Pirates of the Caribbean* and other family favourites) originating from China, the Chinese National Copyright Administration introduced rigorous copyright restrictions and enforcement in respect of Olympic broadcasts

---

420 IOC 2014 Evaluation Commission Report (2007) at 17—available online at the time of writing at http://www.olympic.org/Documents/Reports/EN/en_report_1187.pdf.

421 Apart from the hosting of the Asian Games (the second largest multi-sports event in the world after the Olympic Games), which were held in Beijing in 1990 (and in Guangzhou in 2010).

422 See Rabinovich, S 'Beijing Games to be costliest, but no debt legacy,' 5 August 2008, available online at the time of writing at http://www.reuters.com/article/2008/08/05/us-olympics-cost-idUSPEK25823820080805.

(with some internet reports at the time alleging that notices had been sent out warning individuals of a 100,000 yuan[423] fine for uploading Olympic Games video to the Internet). This approach is understandable if one considers that one of the major concerns of the relevant stakeholders prior to the event was the often-perceived as rather lax intellectual property law regime in China,[424] which one observer in the run-up to the event called 'the undisputed global centre for IP rights infringement.'[425] Predictably, the host nation—(in)famous for its widespread 'Shanzhai culture'—also had to step up the protection offered by its laws for the commercial interests of the Olympic Movement and its commercial partners, a natural development if one considers that, having been awarded the rights to host the 2008 Beijing Games in 2001, China had joined the World Trade Organisation in 2001 and was making a concerted effort to fulfil its obligations to protect and enforce intellectual property rights.[426] Accession required significant amendments to China's IP rights protection regime to make it more compliant with the WTO's TRIPs agreement, with the most notable of these changes being updates to the Trademark Law and its Implementing Regulations, which included the following:

- expansion of the scope of registrable subject matter to include three-dimensional marks, combinations of colours, and certification and collective marks;
- allowing appeals to the courts of the Trademark Review and Adjudication Board's decisions;
- increased recognition and protection of well-known marks;
- allowing foreign mark owners to apply to local administrative agencies directly for enforcement; and
- implementation of temporary restraining measures in the form of pre-suit preliminary injunctions.[427]

Apart from such changes to its IP laws, China did not pass special, comprehensive *sui generis* anti-ambush marketing legislation for the 2008 Games, and currently no such legislation is in place. The organisers staked their efforts at combating ambushing around the Games on a combination of the use of special Olympic symbols protection and 'non-law enforcement methods.'

The Beijing municipality issued regulations on protection of Olympic intellectual property, which came into force on 1 November 2001. A month before China joined the WTO, the Chinese government issued a local rule concerning the protection of Olympic-related IP rights (the so-called 'Beijing Rule'), which was implemented on

[423] Roughly USD 15,000 at the time of writing.

[424] See, for example, Mey 2009.

[425] Sun 2008, p. 46.

[426] Which came at a time of other intellectual property law developments in China, including the second revision of the Chinese Trademark Law, promulgated on October 27, 2001, which contained (in its Article 13) the first express legal protection for well-known trademarks that was fully consistent with the TRIPS agreement (even though one commentator has observed that 'international commentators were not satisfied with that progress'—see Zhang 2010, p. 959).

[427] Sun 2008, p. 46.

November 1 2001. After accession, China brought in at least 10 regulations and rules nationwide protecting Olympic-related IP rights. This new framework made use of the existing enforcement system provided by bodies such as the State Intellectual Property Office (SIPO), the General Administration of Customs and the State Administration for Industry and Commerce (SAIC).[428] According to the Beijing regulations the use of a name identical or similar to the Olympic Symbols by corporations, social groups, websites, business entities, or as building, geographical area and venue names were prohibited. The regulations also prohibited the use of the Olympic intellectual property in any advertising or promotional activities including charity and non-profit-making events. The law also encouraged the reporting of suspected or actual infringing activities relating to the Olympic Symbols (an aspect not covered by the earlier trademark, patent or copyright laws. The Preparatory Office of the Beijing Organising Committee for the Olympic Games (or BOCOG) released a statement on 20 August 2001 to the effect that any use of the Olympic rings, the name of the Olympic Games, the Olympic flags, the Olympic Motto or the Olympic songs, even if such use was exclusively for non-commercial purposes, was only permitted with prior consent of the IOC. The regulations thus restricted both commercial and non-commercial use of the Olympic symbols.[429] In addition to the Beijing regulations, a *Customs Clearance Notice for Beijing Olympic Materials* was also passed.[430]

At national legislative level, the Regulations on the Protection of Olympic Symbols of 2002[431] (hereinafter 'the Regulations') were adopted by the State Council for purposes of the 2008 Games in order to provide special protection to Olympic symbols against commercial exploitation, in furtherance of the requirements of the Olympic Charter and the Beijing Host City Contract. In addition to these regulations, Olympic symbols are also protected according to provisions of other laws and administrative regulations such as the copyright law of the People's Republic of China,[432] trademark law of the People's Republic of China,[433] the patent law of the People's Republic of China[434] and the Regulations on Administration of Special Symbols[435,436] (in terms of this last, the period for protection for special symbols is 4 years). Protection against ambush marketing, generally,

[428] Ibid.

[429] Source: The *China IP Bulletin 2008* on the web site of Deacons Legal Services, available online at the time of writing at http://www.deacons.com.hk/eng/knowledge/knowledge_302.htm.

[430] *Customs Clearance Notice for Beijing Olympic Materials* (July 29, 2008), http://english.customs.gov.cn/publish/portal191/tab28300/module60424/info121218.htm.

[431] Adopted at the 54th Executive Meeting of the State Council on 30 January 2002, promulgated by Decree No. 345 of the State Council of the People's Republic of China on 4 February 2002, and effective as of 1 April 2002.

[432] Copyright Act (Republic of China), 2006.

[433] Trademark Law of the Republic of China, last revised 2001.

[434] Patent Law of the Republic of China, last revised 2008.

[435] Regulations on the Administration of Special Symbols (Promulgated by Decree No. 202 of the State Council of the People's Republic of China on July 13, 1996).

[436] Article 14 of the Regulations.

may also be available in terms of the Law against Unfair Competition of the People's Republic of China, 1993.[437] Other than these instruments Chinese law does not currently provide for any special anti-ambush marketing protection.

The protection provided by the Regulations extends to the Five Rings, the Olympic flag, the motto, emblem and even the Olympic anthem. Certain words are also protected (such as 'Olympic,' 'Olympiad,' and 'Olympic Games'). Emblems of the Chinese Olympic Committee (or COC) and of the 2008 Games are also protected through the means of rights vesting jointly in the IOC, the COC and the BOCOG (the 2008 Beijing Organising Committee). The Regulations provide for an exclusive right in respect of the relevant symbols for the respective rights holders, and provide that 'no one may use Olympic symbols for commercial purposes ... without the authorization of the right holders.'[438] Any licencee with the right to use any of the Olympic Symbols must be recorded with the Chinese Trademark Office under the Procedures for Recordal and Administration of Olympic Symbols (issued on 22 April 2002). Article 5 of the Regulations defines 'use for commercial purposes' of the symbols to mean use for profit-making purposes in the following ways:

> 5 (1) The use of Olympic symbols in goods, packages or containers of goods or trade documents of goods;
> (2) The use of Olympic symbols in services;
> (3) The use of Olympic symbols in advertising, commercial exhibition, profit-making performance and other commercial activities;
> (4) Selling, importing or exporting goods bearing Olympic symbols;
> (5) Manufacturing or selling Olympic symbols.

Article 5(6) contains the closest approximation of China's Olympic symbol regulations to an 'association right' in respect of the Games, by specifically including in such 'use for commercial purposes' the following:

> Other acts that might mislead people to think there are sponsorship or other supporting relations between the doers and the right holders of Olympic symbols.

---

[437] Article 5 of which provides as follows:

> Article 5: An operator may not adopt the following unfair means to carry on transactions in the market and cause damage to competitors:
>
> (1) Passing off the registered trademark of another person;
> (2) Using, without authorisation, the name, packaging or decoration peculiar to well-known goods or using a name, packaging or decoration similar to that of well-known goods, so that his goods are confused with the well-known goods of another person, causing buyers to mistake them for the well-known goods of the other person;
> (3) Using, without authorisation, the business name or personal name of the other person on his own goods, leading people to mistake them for the goods of the other person;
> (4) Forging or falsely using, on his goods, symbols of quality such as symbols of certification and symbols of famous and high-quality goods, falsifying the origin of his goods, and making false representations which are misleading as to the quality of the goods.

[438] Article 4 of the Regulations.

The Regulations created an institution, the Administration for Industry and Commerce (AIC) which is responsible for the protection of the Olympic Symbols. The enforcement rights of the AIC are similar to those conferred under the existing laws protecting IPRs in China, which include the rights to investigate, order cessation of infringing activities, confiscation and destruction of the infringing goods and related tools, with the special right to impose a fine up to five times of the illegal income, or if there is no illegal income, a fine of not more than RMB 50,000.[439] Any use of Olympic Symbols to commit fraud or other illegal activities could attract criminal liability.[440]

Section 13 of the Regulations provides as follows in respect of loss caused through infringement:

> The amount of compensation for the loss caused by infringement of the exclusive rights of Olympic symbols shall be determined on the basis of the loss that the right holder has suffered from the infringement or the profit that the infringer has obtained through the infringement, including the reasonable expenses paid for checking the infringement; where the loss suffered by the infringe or the profit obtained by the infringer are difficult to determine, the compensation shall be reasonably determined with reference to the licensing fees for using Olympic symbol (*sic*).

Interestingly, the Regulations do not expressly provide for exceptions to infringement, apart from use for commercial purposes under a licence (i.e. consent to use by the right holder(s)[441]). This leaves a wide swath of potential conduct that may fall foul of the provisions. While all use for a purpose other than 'commercial purposes' as defined in the Regulations would appear to be exempted, this raises questions as to the position in respect of types of conduct (use of symbols) which are generally exempted from infringement of association rights and other anti-ambushing provisions in other jurisdictions (for example, use of symbols in reporting by the media, and prior or existing use). In light of the lack of ambush marketing litigation and consideration of these Regulations by courts of law it is unclear to what extent such conduct may constitute infringement under the Regulations.

The 2008 Beijing Games were significantly commercialised in the sense of the up-take of global and domestic sponsorships, which was described as follows:

> It seems like the marketing opportunity of the century: Thousands of athletes compete in the capital of a country whose 1.3 billion citizens are sports-mad, increasingly affluent, and eager to spend on new clothing, gadgets, and other consumer goods. That's why a dozen multinationals such as Coca-Cola, Lenovo, McDonald's, and Samsung have laid out as much as $100 million each to be global sponsors of the Beijing Olympics this summer. An additional 11—including Volkswagen, Adidas, and Air China—have paid as much as

[439] Wikipedia explains the distinction between the yuan and Renminbi (RMB) as analogous to that between the pound and sterling; the pound (yuan) is the unit of account while sterling (Renminbi) is the actual currency.

[440] *China IP Bulletin 2008*—available online at http://www.deacons.com.hk/eng/knowledge/knowledge_302.htm.

[441] See Article 8 of the Regulations.

> $50 million each for the right to link ads within China to the Games. Dozens of other companies have less extensive tie-ups, ranging from the "official wine supplier" (Great Wall) to Guangzhou Liby Enterprise Group, which is an official provider of detergent for sheets, shorts, and other laundry.[442]

A special concern for sponsors at the Beijing Games was the effect of marketing clutter. While one major reason for this was the wide-spread sponsorship of individual participating athletes by non-event sponsors (firms like Nike and Chinese sneaker manufacturer Li Ning), one observer commented wryly that 'It doesn't help that the Beijing organising committee offers five levels of sponsorship, and a total of 49 companies have signed up.'[443]

The Beijing Games saw quite vigorous enforcement of IP rights in respect of the Games and active policing of attempts to ambush the event. It was reported that the BOCOG registered in the region of 200 'Olympic Symbols' and six special marks that included the five event mascots (and BOCOG issued a proclamation detailing how the mascots could be used and by whom). These symbols were registered across a total of 44 classes, and, in addition, the Trademark Office recorded 483 Olympic licensing agreements.[444] In addition to the creation of the AIC, the BOCOG also created a Legal Affairs Department, to manage contracts, combat IP infringement and to protect the IOC's interests, along with a Brand Protection Department specifically to deal with ambush marketing. On 3 July 2008 BOCOG's marketing department and the China Advertising Association jointly issued an official 'Anti-Ambush Advertising Initiative,' which urged advertising companies and practitioners to support business ethics. They were not to engage in any commercial activity that could 'mislead the public, provide, or create ambush concepts or advertisements or play "edge ball" with marketing activities of official Olympic sponsors.'[445] BOCOG''s director of legal affairs was quoted as explaining the authority's powers in terms of BOCOG and the city of Beijing's regulations to control advertising in event venue precincts (BOCOG's *Proposal for Regulating Ambush Marketing*, announced on 15 March 2008, which prohibited several types of marketing):

> BOCOG will work in conjunction with the Beijing municipal government to prevent ambush marketing by controlling outdoor advertisings on road signs, neon lights, billboards, bus stops, mobile outdoor advertising, and buses. During the Olympics, advertising near the Olympic venues ..., regardless of long-term agreements, BOCOG and the municipal government have the power to prohibit position and content of advertisements. They can be torn down or replaced with contents approved by BOCOG. Furthermore, advertising banners hanging outside buildings are also within the scope of control. Within

---

[442] Balfour, F 'Ambush in Beijing' *Bloomberg Businessweek*, 13 March 2008—available online at the time of writing at http://www.businessweek.com/magazine/content/08_12/b4076054803579.htm.

[443] Ibid.

[444] Sun 2008, 48.

[445] Yang, H 'Non-law enforcement methods to tackle Olympic ambush marketing,' *China Intellectual Property Magazine* (June 2008)—available online at the time of writing at http://www.chinaipmagazine.com/en/journal-show.asp?id=381.

controlled Olympic areas, unauthorized advertising material containing names or logos of business establishments is not allowed to be distributed, including advertising by a group of people wearing the same logo on their clothes. BOCOG has the right to requisition or block this marketing as deemed necessary. The rights of BOCOG trace back to a promise made to the IOC by the Beijing municipal government. The standard adopted by the IOC as to whether an advertisement is inappropriate is not based on legal grounds. If ambush marketing is suspected, action can be taken against it.[446]

Between 2004 and 2007 the AIC in China handled and investigated a reported 1,357 cases relating to violations of the Olympic symbols involving counterfeit merchandise with a value of RMB 10.72 million.[447] People could report infringements via the Beijing 2008 website—in what is to my knowledge a unique approach, people reporting infringements to the government were entitled to receive a reward of up to RMB 100,000 on the condition that certain requirements were satisfied[448]—and it was reported that the city of Beijing, in 2007, issued 1 million yuan (approximately USD 151,000) in fines to those flouting Olympic copyright rules.[449] It was reported prior to the Games that small-scale 'ambushing' (in the form of references to the event in a commercial context ranging from advertising campaigns to restaurant menus—including dishes such as 'Short Track Speed Skating Sprint' and 'Discus Mushroom') was rife.[450] Many 'ambushers' avoided the ire of BOCOG in terms of the Olympic symbol regulations by simply using images of athletes in their advertising. Despite these cases, ambush marketing at the Beijing Games is most often discussed in the literature with reference to what turned out to be the most prominent perpetrator, a regular poster boy for ambushing at the event. Li Ning, former Chinese Olympic gymnast, was (ironically) chosen to light the Olympic flame. Li Ning's eponymous sportswear company, while not an official Games sponsor, supplied the clothing and footwear for sportscasters on China's CCTV 5 channel (the broadcaster who enjoyed exclusive broadcasting rights on the mainland), and even programme guests had to wear the company logo. An Ipsos Chinese consumer survey prior to the Games found that the local sportswear manufacturer's slogan 'Anything is possible' was more successful than that of official sponsor Adidas ('Impossible is nothing'), and Li Ning was viewed by 82% of consumers as an official Olympics sponsor as opposed to

[446] Ibid.

[447] *China IP Bulletin 2008*—available online at http://www.deacons.com.hk/eng/knowledge/knowledge_302.htm.

[448] Huang, J and Marr, T 'Trade mark developments in China' Allens Arthur Robertson *Intellectual Property Bulletin* (July 2008), available online at the time of writing at http://www.aar.com.au/pubs/ip/ipbulljul08.htm#Trade_.

[449] See the report entitled 'Olympic sponsors steeled for ambush,' 4 June 2008, available online at the time of writing at http://www.abc.net.au/news/stories/2008/06/04/2264673.htm?site=olympics/2008.

[450] Yang *supra* (http://www.chinaipmagazine.com/en/journal-show.asp?id=381).

69% recognition of Adidas.[451] As one blogger described Li Ning's grand entrance at the Games the day after the opening ceremony:

> To understand the enormity of last night's torch lighting ceremony, with potentially billions of eyes watching as former Chinese gymnast Li Ning flew through the Beijing night, consider this: Imagine the year is 1996. Reebok is the official sponsor of the Games. They've spent quite a bit of money trying to convince the world to buy Reebok shoes and clothing. The Atlanta organizing committee is keeping things hush about who will light the torch. And then, imagine this: Nike CEO Phil Knight parachutes into the Opening Ceremonies, torch in hand, and lights the Olympic flame. The next day, everyone's talking about Nike, and nobody's talking about Reebok.[452]

Of course, life being stranger than fiction, Li Ning was wearing Adidas clothing at the time... [Li Ning appears to be a bit of a 'serial ambusher': Gymnasts at the 2010 Asian Games in Guangzhou who were sponsored by Li Ning were investigated after they used hand signals (by putting a hand on their chest with thumb up and fingers pointed like a gun during competition and medals ceremonies) apparently aimed at mimicking Li Ning's L-shaped logo—one gymnast was quoted as explaining that 'This is a gesture that's required as part of the deal with our sponsor.'[453]]

The aggressive enforcement against ambushing encountered at the Beijing Games makes sense when one considers that it was observed that, while most instalments of the Olympic Games leave a legacy of infrastructure for the host nation, it was hoped that the enforcement of the Olympic intellectual property rights in China and the new regulations protecting the Olympic symbols would leave a legal legacy, leading to stronger enforcement of IP in China.

4.4.10 Applicable Anti-Ambush Marketing Protection in the United States of America

There is currently no special, generally-applicable anti-ambush marketing legislation in force in the United States, either at federal or state level,[454] and this

---

[451] Ibid.

[452] Dan Oshinsky 'The greatest free ad ever,' posted 9 August 2008, available online at the time of writing at http://blogs.rockymountainnews.com/2008_summer_olympics_blog/archives/2008/08/the-greatest-free-ad-ever.html#. See also Masterman 2009, pp. 311–312.

[453] Chang, A 'Chinese gymnasts spark ambush marketing inquiry,' *Deseret News*, 17 November 2010—available online at the time of writing at http://www.deseretnews.com/article/700082791/Chinese-gymnasts-spark-ambush-marketing-inquiry.html.

[454] I referred earlier in this chapter to the unsuccessful bid by Chicago to win the rights to host the 2016 Olympic Games (which were awarded to Rio de Janeiro). During the bid process Illinois legislation was prepared to deal with ambush marketing. Compare the following, as contained in Illinois Compiled Statutes (65 ILCS 120) 2016 Olympic and Paralympic Games Act; section 5–10(12):

jurisdiction may even be characterised as a 'tolerant legal regime'[455] in respect of ambushing. Apart from state-based unfair competition law (similar to what is known in other systems as 'passing off'), such protection is available specifically for Olympic symbols, words and other indicia in terms of the Ted Stevens Olympic and Amateur Sports Act, 1998 (the 'Ted Stevens Act'),[456] apart from which, more general protection is to be found in the federal trademark statute.[457] There is no event-specific anti-ambushing protection to be found currently in US law.

The Ted Stevens Act in its current form originated in the 1978 Amateur Sports Act, which was the culmination of more than a decade of legislative lobbying by the former IOC president, Avery Brundage, for special protection of the Olympics in the United States.[458] A primary rationale for the Act was to provide additional revenue to fund US Olympic Committee (or 'USOC') athlete development programmes and produce world-class competitors at summer and winter Olympic Games. In theory, the USOC would become less reliant on government subsidies through the enhanced commercial protection of Olympic insignia, phrases and related intellectual property. It was reported in 2008 that USOC owns approximately 120 active federally registered trademarks (with another 15–20 pending applications at the time).[459] The 1978 Act replaced previous criminal penalties for unauthorised uses of the terms 'Olympic,' 'Olympiad,' 'Citus Altius Fortius,' the Olympic rings, or any associated USOC insignia, with civil remedies under existing trademark provisions of the Lanham Act, 1946.[460] The Ted Stevens Act provides, *inter alia*, for the powers of the US Olympic Committee (referred to in

(Footnote 454 continued)

> The State, in accordance with law and to the extent of the State's authority, and subject to the limitations of this Article agrees that, if requested by the candidate city, the bid committee, or the OCOG, it shall permit any member of the General Assembly to introduce legislation necessary to: (i) effectively reduce and sanction ambush marketing, (ii) eliminate illegal street vending during the period beginning 2 weeks before the games through the end of the games; and (iii) control advertising space (including, but not limited to, billboards and advertising on public transport) as well as air space and that any such legislation will be introduced as soon as possible….

[455] Bischoff et al. 2005, p. 19.

[456] 36 U.S.C. § 220501 et seq. (the Amateur Sports Act, 1978, was amended in 1998 to become the Ted Stevens Olympic and Amateur Sport Act, in order, *inter alia*, to provide protection for the Salt Lake City winter Olympic Games).

[457] The Lanham Act (Title 15 US Code)—see the discussion in the text below.

[458] For the history behind the Act, see Gandert, D.J. 'The Court's Yellow Card for the United States Soccer Federation: A Case for Implied Antitrust Immunity' (2011) *ExpressO* (available at: http://works.bepress.com/daniel_gandert/1)—forthcoming at the time of writing.

[459] McKelvey and Grady 2008, p. 558.

[460] See Symons, C and Warren, I '"David v. Goliath": The Gay Games, the Olympics and the Ownership of Language' *Entertainment and Sports Law Journal* (April 2006), text available online at the time of writing at http://www.bl.uk/sportandsociety/exploresocsci/sportsoc/mega/articles/clicklogo.pdf.

the Act as 'the corporation') to exclusive use of and to authorise the use of Olympic symbols. Section 106(a) provides as follows:

(a) Exclusive Right of Corporation—Except as provided in subsection (d) of this section, the corporation has the exclusive right to use

(1) the name "United States Olympic Committee";
(2) the symbol of the International Olympic Committee, consisting of five interlocking rings, the symbol of the International Paralympic Committee, consisting of three TaiGeuks, or the symbol of the Pan-American Sports Organization, consisting of a torch surrounded by concentric rings;
(3) the emblem of the corporation, consisting of an escutcheon having a blue chief and vertically extending red and white bars on the base with 5 interlocking rings displayed on the chief; and
(4) the words "Olympic," "Olympiad," "Citius Altius Fortius," "Paralympic," "Paralympiad," "Pan-American," "America Espirito Sport Fraternite," or any combination of those words.

Section 106(b) provides that USOC 'may authorise contributors and suppliers of goods or services to use the trade name of the corporation or any trademark, symbol, insignia, or emblem of the International Olympic Committee, International Paralympic Committee, the Pan-American Sports Organization, or of the corporation to advertise that the contributions, goods, or services were donated or supplied to, or approved, selected, or used by, the corporation, the United States Olympic team, the Paralympic team, the Pan-American team, or team members.' USOC is entitled to file civil action for remedies in trademark law against anyone who, without the consent of USOC, 'uses for the purpose of trade, to induce the sale of any goods or services, or to promote any theatrical exhibition, athletic performance, or competition, the Olympic symbols or words described in section 106(a), including any 'combination or simulation of those words tending to cause confusion or mistake, to deceive, or to falsely suggest a connection with the corporation or any Olympic, Paralympic, or Pan-American Games activity'[461]; or 'any trademark, trade name, sign, symbol, or insignia falsely representing association with, or authorisation by, the International Olympic Committee, the International Paralympic Committee, the Pan-American Sports Organization, or the corporation.'[462] Section 106(c)(d) provides for exemptions relating to pre-existing and geographic reference rights.[463]

---

[461] Section 106(c)(3) of the Act.

[462] Section 106(c)(4).

[463] Section 106(d) Pre-Existing and Geographic Reference Rights:

(1) A person who actually used the emblem described in subsection (a)(3) of this section, or the words or any combination of the words described in subsection (a)(4) of this section, for any lawful purpose before September 21, 1950, is not prohibited by this section from continuing the lawful use for the same purpose and for the same goods or services.

USOC's enforcement of its rights in terms of the Act has been quite rigorous. It is also important to note that the Act contains no 'fair use' provisions, and unlike trademark law, the courts have held that consumer confusion need not be shown by USOC in order to prosecute a civil claim for unauthorised use of the protected symbols or words:

> Congress has given the USOC heightened exclusivity in regard to its trademarks as an incentive for the USOC to produce a high quality product that will in turn benefit the people of the United States and the world: as the Olympic charter states, "to educate young people through sport in a spirit of better understanding between each other and of friendship, thereby helping to build a better and more peaceful world." In practical terms, this heightened exclusivity means that if the USOC objects to the use of one of its trademarks by another party, the USOC does not need to show that confusion among consumers is likely to occur (the standard test for trademark infringement) to have the legal grounds on which to demand that the use be stopped.[464]

The special nature of the protection afforded to the USOC's exclusive rights to the use of Olympic symbols and words has been acknowledged by the courts. The US Supreme Court, in *San Francisco Arts & Athletics, Inc. v USOC*[465] (the 'Gay Olympics case') held that the protection provided by the Act is more than that provided to 'normal' trademarks, holding that the 'legislative history demonstrates that Congress intended to provide the USOC with exclusive control of the use of the word 'Olympic' without regard to whether an unauthorised use of the word tends to cause confusion.' In this case the plaintiff, San Francisco Arts & Athletics

---

(Footnote 463 continued)

(2) A person who actually used, or whose assignor actually used, the words or any combination of the words described in subsection (a)(4) of this section, or a trademark, trade name, sign, symbol, or insignia described in subsection (c)(4) of this section, for any lawful purpose before September 21, 1950, is not prohibited by this section from continuing the lawful use for the same purpose and for the same goods or services.

(3) Use of the word "Olympic" to identify a business or goods or services is permitted by this section where

  (A) such use is not combined with any of the intellectual properties referenced in subsection (a) or (c) of this section;
  (B) it is evident from the circumstances that such use of the word "Olympic" refers to the naturally occurring mountains or geographical region of the same name that were named prior to February 6, 1998, and not to the corporation or any Olympic activity; and
  (C) such business, goods, or services are operated, sold, and marketed in the State of Washington west of the Cascade Mountain range and operations, sales, and marketing outside of this area are not substantial.

[464] Thomas, P E 'Marketers beware: Avoid the Olympic temptation,' August 2008, available online at the time of writing at http://www.fredlaw.com/areas/trademark/Articles/trade_0808_pet.html.

[465] 483 U.S. 522 (1987).

(SFAA), a non-profit California corporation, promoted the 'Gay Olympic Games,' to be held in 1982, by using those words on its letterheads and mailings, in local newspapers, and on various merchandise sold to cover the costs of the planned Games. The USOC informed the SFAA of the existence of the Act and requested that it terminate use of the word 'Olympic' in its description of the planned Games. When the SFAA failed to do so, the USOC brought suit in Federal District Court for injunctive relief. The court granted the USOC summary judgment and a permanent injunction. The Court of Appeals affirmed, holding (based on the language of the Act) that the Act granted the USOC exclusive use of the word 'Olympic' without requiring the USOC to prove that the unauthorised use was confusing and without regard to the defenses available to an entity sued for a trademark violation under the Lanham Act.[466] The court also found that the USOC's 'property right' in the word and its associated symbols and slogans can be protected without violating the First Amendment.[467] SFAA argued that the word 'Olympic' is a generic word that constitutionally cannot gain trademark protection under the Lanham Act, and that the First Amendment prohibits Congress from granting a trademark in the word. The court held that when a word acquires value as the result of organisation and the expenditure of labour, skill and money by an entity, that entity constitutionally may obtain a limited property right in the word. Congress reasonably could conclude that the commercial and promotional value of the word 'Olympic' was the product of the USOC's talents and energy, the end result of much time, effort and expense. In view of the history of the origins and associations of the word 'Olympic,' Congress' decision to grant the USOC a limited property right in the word falls within the scope of trademark law protections.[468] The court held that Congress reasonably could find that since 1896, the word 'Olympic' has acquired what in trademark law is known as a secondary meaning—it 'has become distinctive of [the USOC's] goods in commerce ... Congress' decision to grant the USOC a limited property right in the word 'Olympic' falls within the scope of trademark law protections, and thus certainly within constitutional bounds.[469] Mark Lemley, writing on trademarks and the American courts' tendency to treat trademarks as property in their own right rather than as advertisements or referents for the goods to which they are attached, refers to the *San Francisco Arts & Athletics* case as 'an isolated and perhaps unique Supreme Court reference,' attributable to the fact that the Ted Stevens Act provides much broader protection

---

466 483 U.S. 530.

467 See, for more detailed discussion of this case, Symons, C and Warren, I '"David v. Goliath": The Gay Games, the Olympics and the Ownership of Language' *Entertainment and Sports Law Journal* (April 2006), text available online at the time of writing at http://www.bl.uk/sportandsociety/exploresocsci/sportsoc/mega/articles/clicklogo.pdf. For further discussion of this case in the context of the potential free speech implications of anti-ambush marketing legislation, see Chap. 7.

468 483 U.S. 532–533.

469 483 U.S. 534–535; see also Symons and Warren *supra* par. 42.

than the Lanham (Trademark) Act (see discussion in the text below);[470] which might not be surprising if one considers the American courts' apparent tendency to provide 'special' treatment to the Olympic Games and its organisers.[471] More will be said in Chap. 5 about the implications of the *San Francisco Arts & Athletics* case in respect of the court's view on USOC's control over words.

Justice Brennan, in a strong dissent, was less convinced that there was no violation of the free speech guarantee, and had no hesitation in declaring the USOC's language monopoly 'substantially overbroad.'[472] The court did not adjudicate the SFAA's claim that the USOC's enforcement of its rights was discriminatory in violation of the equal protection component of the Due Process Clause of the Fifth Amendment to the US Constitution, because it held that the USOC is not a governmental actor to which the Constitution applies. This last is rather controversial—the USOC has for years relied on the fact that it does not receive direct federal funding (in a law suit in 2001[473] USOC agreed to admit that they received federal financial assistance, although such admission was limited to a small, L-shaped parking lot located at One Olympic Plaza in Colorado Springs, that had been gifted to them by the federal government[474]), although reports suggest that considerable lobbying takes place in Washington, DC by USOC, which maintains a Washington-based office.[475]

In short, it has been observed that the Ted Stevens Act enjoys special status when compared to normal trademark protection. In contrast to 'ordinary' trademarks protected only under the Lanham Act (see the discussion in the text below), protection of the Olympic indicia under the Ted Stevens Act does not end if the marks are abandoned or become generic. These marks remain protected for as long as the Ted Stevens Act remains in force, and the only way in which their protection would cease would be for Congress to repeal the Act or for a court to declare the Act to be invalid (although, as mentioned, the U.S. Supreme Court specifically held in the *San Francisco Arts & Athletics* case that the Act is valid and constitutional).[476]

By way of illustration of the stringent reach of the protection afforded by the Ted Stevens Act (or, at least, USOC's interpretation thereof): One of the exemptions [section 106(d)(3)] relates to Washington state, and is aimed at providing room for exemption for businesses on the Olympic Peninsula (Olympia,

---

470 Lemley 1999, p. 1705 (text, and at fn 95).

471 Compare *Martin v IOC* 740 F.2d 670 (9th Cir. 1984).

472 483 U.S. 562.

473 See the report available online at the time of writing at http://findarticles.com/p/articles/mi_m0EIN/is_1999_Nov_4/ai_57234622/.

474 See Jefferies, P 'It's only money,' Summer 2002, available online at http://findarticles.com/p/articles/mi_hb6643/is_3_18/ai_n28944593/.

475 See the report by Bogardus, K and Snyder, J 'Olympic lobbying a year-round sport' *The Hill*, 16 February 2010, available online at the time of writing at http://thehill.com/business-a-lobbying/81369-lobbying-for-olympics-is-a-year-round-sport.

476 Widmaier and Schechter 2009.

Washington, was founded and named in 1850), although this did not stop the USOC from opposing a trademark application to register the name of a local newspaper, *The Olympian*, on the basis that it was alleged that consumers would be confused as to USOC sponsorship. In 2007 USOC also sent a cease-and-desist letter to Olympic Cellars Winery, an Olympic Peninsula winery which had been using the name for 15 years (and USOC gave the winery permission to register its olympiccellars.com domain name in 1999). Ultimately, the USOC and Olympic Cellars were able to reach an agreement, in terms of which the winery can continue to operate as Olympic Cellars, sell wine via the Internet, keep its website domain name and sell to its wine club as long as its sales and marketing of 'Olympic Cellars' branded wines beyond its local area are not deemed 'substantial.'[477] As the winery owner was quoted: 'I can't significantly grow my wine brand that uses the winery name, Olympic Cellars. It will be forced to remain small even though the term OLYMPIC is our birthright and heritage, where we live, and part of our local culture.'[478]

It is clear that the Ted Stevens Act provides for a *sui generis* form of protection of Olympic symbols and words in favour of USOC, which, according to the courts,[479] extends well beyond the protection afforded to trademarks (the plaintiff need not prove likelihood of confusion, use of its mark in commerce or distinctiveness, and the defendant does not have access to the normal Lanham Act trademark infringement defences such as abandonment, lack of secondary meaning or genericness[480])[481] and, controversially, establishes a property right in the form of a monopoly in such indicia which vests in a non-governmental organisation.

Apart from such special protection provided by the Ted Stevens Act, U.S. courts have also held that the Act provides an implied immunity from antitrust laws to national sports governing bodies.[482]

Despite the lack of generally-applicable special protection against ambush marketing and, apart from the above-mentioned special protection for the Olympic symbols, the US jurisdiction does provide protection against the most insidious forms of ambushing (association ambushing), as most countries do. The federal

---

[477] See the short piece by Karau, D R, dated August 2008, available online at the time of writing at http://www.fredlaw.com/areas/trademark/Articles/trade_0808_drk2.html.

[478] Ibid.

[479] See also *USOC v Toy Truck Lines, Inc.* 237 F.3d 1331 (Fed. Cir. 2001); *USOC v American Media, Inc.* No. 01-K-281, 2001 US Dist. LEXIS 11523 (D. Colo. August 3, 2001).

[480] *San Francisco Arts & Athletics, Inc., v. U.S. Olympic Committee*, 483 U.S. 522, 531 (1987).

[481] See Widmaier and Schechter 2009.

[482] See *Behagen v. Amateur Basketball Ass'n of the United States*, 884 F.2d 524 (10th Cir. 1989) (this case was decided before the 1998 amendments to the Amateur Sports Act, but the relevant portions of the act were not changed with the amendments); *Jes Properties, Inc. v. USA Equestrian, Inc.* 458 F.3d 1224, 1227 (11th Cir. 2006); see also Gandert, D.J. 'The Court's Yellow Card for the United States Soccer Federation: A Case for Implied Antitrust Immunity' (2011) *ExpressO* (available at: http://works.bepress.com/daniel_gandert/1)—forthcoming at the time of writing. See, however, *ChampionsWorld LLC, v. United States Soccer Federation, INC.,* et al.; N.D.Ill.; Case No. 06 C 5724, 2010 U.S. Dist. LEXIS 73253; 7/21/10.

trademark statute, the Lanham Act,[483] provides twofold protection against ambushing. Where a trademark is infringed (although such cases are nowadays likely to be rare in the context of savvy 'ambushers') action can be brought under section 32[484] for trademark infringement (although a major practical hurdle for event organisers is the requirement of showing consumer confusion by means of costly and time-consuming consumer surveys[485]). For all trademarks or other designations relating to sports events that are protected only under the Lanham Act (and not under the Ted Stevens Act), the owner of the mark must prove both distinctiveness and use in commerce of its mark in order for the mark to be valid and enforceable in court. These requirements, which are precisely the same as for any other trademarks whether or not they are related to sporting events, are as follows[486]:

- A mark is inherently distinctive, and thus protectable without a showing of secondary meaning, if it is fanciful, arbitrary, or suggestive[487];
- A descriptive term can be protected only if it has acquired distinctiveness[488];
- A mark is used in commerce in connection with goods if it is placed in any manner on the goods, their containers, associated displays, or on the tags or labels affixed thereto, or on documents associated with the goods or their sale; and
- the mark is used in commerce in connection with services if it is used or displayed in the sale or advertising of services and the services are rendered in commerce.[489]

American professional sports teams began to licence their names and images in the 1950s, and their original licensing activities were based on a theory of 'false endorsement' or 'false advertising' derived from the law of unfair competition.[490] Professional sports teams and leagues authorised their licencees to sell merchandise 'endorsed' by the team or the league, and much of the 'logoed' merchandise of the 1950s and 1960s was commissioned by the professional teams and leagues themselves to sell directly to their fans, and the leagues and teams produced no consumer goods on their own.[491] Widmaier and Schechter[492] refer to the development of a 'rich body of case law' concerning the application of the Lanham Act

[483] Title 15 of the US Code (15 U.S.C.), enacted in 1946 and amended in 1988.

[484] 15 U.S.C. § 1114.

[485] See McKelvey and Grady 2008, p. 559.

[486] See Widmeier and Schechter 2009.

[487] *Abercrombie & Fitch Co. v. Hunting World, Inc.*, 537 F.2d 4 (2d Cir. 1976).

[488] Ibid.; s*ee also* Sec. 2(e) of the Lanham Act, 15 U.S.C. Sec. 1052(e).

[489] 15 U.S.C. § 1127.

[490] MacCambridge 2004, pp. 183–185.

[491] See the undated paper by Hylton, J G 'The over-protection of intellectual property rights in sport' (Marquette University Law School/National Sports Law Insititute)—available online at the time of writing at http://shiac.com/files/arablexsportiva-presentations/004003.pdf.

[492] The authors of the country report on the United States prepared for the Working Committee of the International Association for the Protection of Intellectual property (AIPPI), Project Q210 ('The protection of major sports events and associated commercial activities through trademarks and other IPR'; reports compiled for purposes of a draft resolution to be submitted to the AIPPI

to sports event-related marks, encompassing a wide range of issues from standard trademark infringement to the sale of sports emblems unattached to any goods, ambush marketing, appropriation of player names and performance, and the unlicenced broadcasting of major sports events. The first of these cases, which was instrumental in establishing an interesting variation of the test for likelihood of confusion in a trademark case, was heard in 1975. In *Boston Professional Hockey Association, Inc., v. Dallas Cap & Emblem Manufacturing, Inc.*,[493] the Court of Appeals for the Fifth Circuit established a standard for the likelihood of confusion element that was specifically adapted to marks and designations relating to major sporting events. The defendant sold embroidered cloth emblems bearing hockey team marks owned by the plaintiff. The court stated that '[t]he difficulty with this case stems from the fact that a reproduction of the trademark itself is being sold, unattached to any other goods or services,' noting that the Lanham Act and case law was not geared towards such an unattached use of a mark by itself.[494] The court overturned the earlier judgment of the lower court in this matter that held that such protection in terms of trademark law would be 'tantamount to a copyright monopoly'.[495] The court developed a test for likelihood of confusion to accommodate this particular situation:

> 'The confusion question here is conceptually difficult. It can be said that the public buyer knew that the emblems portrayed the teams' symbols. Thus, it can be argued, the buyer is not confused or deceived. This argument misplaces the purpose of the confusion requirement. The confusion or deceit requirement is met by the fact that the defendant duplicated the protected trademarks and sold them to the public knowing that the public would identify them as being the teams' trademarks. The certain knowledge of the buyer that the source and origin of the trademark symbols were in plaintiffs satisfies the requirement of the act. The argument that confusion must be as to the source of the manufacture of the emblem itself is unpersuasive, where the trademark, originated by the team, is the triggering mechanism for the sale of the emblem.'[496]

This approach, which constituted a 'radical break with traditional trademark law,' was sharply criticised on that ground in subsequent court decisions.[497] Hylton notes the apparent absurdity of the approach:

(Footnote 492 continued)
Exco meeting in Buenos Aires, October 2009)—available online at the time of writing at https://www.aippi.org/download/commitees/210/GR210usa.pdf.

493 510 F.2d 1004 (5th Cir. 1975).

494 Ibid. at 1010.

495 *Boston Professional Hockey Assn. v. Dallas Cap & Emblem Mfg.*, 360 F.Supp. 459 (N. D. Tex. 1973), which held as follows (at 464):

'In this area of the economy the protection of the trademark law must give way to the public policy favoring free competition. To hold that plaintiffs can prohibit the imitation of the team symbols because of the trademark registration would be to grant to the mark owners protection which is tantamount to a copyright monopoly. Plaintiffs therefore have no right to relief under the Lanham Act against the defendant's copying and selling emblems denoting their team symbols.'

496 The *Boston Hockey* case supra at 1012.

497 Widmaier and Schechter 2009.

> In the early 1970s, professional teams and leagues began to file lawsuits against manufacturers who were making use of teams names and logos without license. What is most interesting about these cases is that they allege, not false adverting or unfair competition, but violations of the Lanham Act, the federal trademark statute. Beginning in 1975, American courts started to agree that the unlicensed attachment of names or logos to clothing constituted an actionable trademark claim. In so ruling, courts discovered that the existing trademark statute provided the holder a right against "dilution" as well as against fraud or "passing off." Why this change in attitude occurred when it did is a fascinating question, especially as no change had occurred in the text of the Lanham Act itself. As the market for such apparel exploded, the new "property" interest in the mark itself made it possible for sports teams to reap large profits which otherwise would have gone uncaptured or else required uncertain tort actions. Moreover, in 1995, the United States Congress confirmed this expansion of property rights of trademark holders with the Federal Trademark Dilution Act, which essentially codified recent case law.[498]

The *Boston Hockey* rule, which made proving likelihood of confusion substantially easier for plaintiffs, was applied in a number of subsequent cases.[499] After this development, the traditional test in terms of the Lanham Act requiring proof of likely consumer confusion as to source, and doing away with presuming such proof, has gradually been reinstated.[500] Plaintiffs in cases involving marks and designations relating to sports events are likely to prevail only if they put forth solid evidence supporting a finding of likelihood of consumer confusion.[501]

In addition to a straightforward trademark infringement claim, it is important to note in an evaluation of US protection against ambush marketing that a Lanham Act action can also be brought in cases of false association (i.e. protection against association ambushes) in terms of section 43[502] of the Act, which is based on the theory of unfair competition and covers cases of false association, false authorisation or false advertising. This section (which does not apply only to registered trademarks, as opposed to the provisions of section 32 of the Act, and may provide grounds for protecting also, for example, trade dress or the design and shape of a product without a requirement of registration[503]) deals with false designations of origin and false descriptions and in its modern guise includes remedies for trademark holders in respect of e.g. dilution and cyber-piracy. It provides as follows in section 43(a)(1):

> (1) Any person who, on or in connection with any goods or services, or any container for goods, uses in commerce any word, term, name, symbol, or device, or any

---

498 Hylton, J G 'The over-protection of intellectual property rights in sport' (Marquette University Law School/National Sports Law Insititute)—undated paper available online at the time of writing at http://shiac.com/files/arablexsportiva-presentations/004003.pdf.

499 Such as *University of Georgia Athletic Association v. Laite* 756 F.2d 1535 (11th Cir. 1985).

500 See, e.g. *National Football League v. Governor of the State of Delaware* 435 F. Supp. 1372, 1381 (D. Del. 1977); and *Boston Athletic Ass'n v. Sullivan* 867 F.2d 22, 33 (1st Cir. 1989).

501 See Widmaier and Schechter 2009.

502 15 U.S.C. § 1125.

503 Merges et al. 2003, p. 546.

combination thereof, or any false designation of origin, false or misleading description of fact, or false or misleading representation of fact, which

(a) is likely to cause confusion, or to cause mistake, or to deceive as to the affiliation, connection, or association of such person with another person, or as to the origin, sponsorship, or approval of his or her goods, services, or commercial activities by another person, or
(b) in commercial advertising or promotion, misrepresents the nature, characteristics, qualities, or geographic origin of his or her or another person's goods, services, or commercial activities, shall be liable in a civil action by any person who believes that he or she is or is likely to be damaged by such act.

These provisions of the Lanham Act provide potential remedies for ambush marketing that results in consumer confusion, or the likelihood of consumer confusion, regarding the relationship between the company being advertised and the targeted sporting event. Here it bears mentioning that it has been observed that this provision has come to cover a great deal of ground, and that in respect of the issue of consumer confusion (with reference to the *Ferrari v Roberts* judgment[504]—not a sports case, although a 'sports car' case) the courts in deciding § 43(a) cases 'have shown a willingness to believe in an astonishingly stupid consumer.'[505] US courts also recognise a company's First Amendment right to engage in commercial speech if consumer confusion is not threatened. The courts have formulated the following elements for a claim under § 43(a):

- The defendant must have made a false or misleading statement of fact in advertising;
- That statement must have actually deceived or had the capacity to deceive a substantial segment of the audience;
- The deception must have been material, in that it was likely to influence the purchasing decision;
- The defendant must have caused its goods to enter interstate commerce; and
- The plaintiff must have been or is likely to be injured as a result.[506]

Apart from obtaining relief by way of injunction, a plaintiff can claim monetary damages if it can show actual consumer reliance on the false advertisement and a resulting economic impact on its business.

There are exceptions to infringement of a trademark relating to 'fair use.' Specifically, section 33[507] of the Act provides for a statutory fair use defence, where a defendant can show that 'the use of the name, term, or device charged to be an infringement is a use, otherwise than as a mark, of the party's individual name in his own business, or of the individual name of anyone in privity with such party, or of a term or device which is descriptive of and used fairly and in good faith only to describe the goods or services of such party, or their geographic origin.' This fair use defence is specified as one of the limited number of defences

---

504 *Ferrari S.p.A. Esercizio Fabriche Automobili E Corse v. Roberts* 944 F.2d 1235 (6th Cir. 1991), *cert. denied,* 505 U.S. 1219 (1992).

505 Cooper Dreyfuss 1996, p. 133.

506 *United Industries Corp. v. Clorox Co.*, 140 F.3d 1175, 1180 (8th Cir. 1998).

507 15 U.S.C. § 1115(b)(4).

available to a defendant against a claim of infringement of an incontestable registration, but it is also regularly used as a defence against any trademark infringement claim, including a non-incontestable registrations and a § 43(a) infringement claim. This defence prevents a trademark owner from monopolising or appropriating a descriptive word or phrase, and the defence is available only in actions involving descriptive terms and only when the term is used in its descriptive sense rather than its trademark sense.[508] Apart from the statutory fair use defence, and as a result of its narrow scope, the courts have formulated additional fair use defences to trademark infringement claims, namely 'nominative fair use'; comparative advertising as fair use; and parody as fair use. Statutory fair use or nominative fair use can only be used when the use of the trademark does not imply affiliation or sponsorship with the owner's product or services, and will not confuse the reader into thinking the owner of the mark has something to do with the use (accordingly, such defences may not be available in trademark infringement claims in cases of ambush marketing).

Generally, of course, legal protection against ambush marketing may implicate freedom of expression issues, and the protection of freedom of speech under the First Amendment to the U.S. Constitution is important to consider. If a defendant makes use of a plaintiff's mark—including a mark relating to a sports event, or one of the marks enumerated in the Ted Stevens Act—for the purposes of criticism, news reporting, parody, art or another purpose recognised under the First Amendment, then such use does not form the basis of liability for infringement or dilution under the Lanham Act. The U.S. Trademark Dilution Revision Act[509] also contains a number of specific exemptions from dilution liability for uses such as comparative advertising, parody and non-commercial speech. These exemptions apply fully to any famous marks and designations relating to sports events that may be sought to be protected under such dilution provisions.[510] It has also been observed that even in situations where the defendant's commercial use of the plaintiff's mark or designation is established, the free speech clause of the First Amendment can still bar the plaintiff's assertion of trademark and related intellectual property rights related to a sports event.[511]

---

[508] *Zatarains, Inc. v. Oak Grove Smokehouse, Inc.*, 698 F.2d 786 (5th Cir. 1983) at 791 [relying on *Soweco, Inc. v. Shell Oil Co.*, 617 F.2d 1178, 1185 (5th Cir. 1980)].

[509] 15 U.S.C. Sec. 1125(c).

[510] See Widmaier and Schechter 2009.

[511] Widmaier and Schechter 2009 refer to *C.B.C. Distribution and Marketing, Inc. v. Major League Baseball Advanced Media, L.P.*, 505 F.3d 818 (8th Cir. 2007), where the Court of Appeals for the Eighth Circuit held in 2007 that the defendant's First Amendment rights superseded the rights of Major League Baseball and the players represented in the Major League Baseball Players Association. The defendant sold fantasy sports products, including fantasy baseball, 'incorporat[ing] the names along with performance and biographical data of actual major league players' (at 820 of the judgment). The court held that the plaintiffs had stated a cause of action for violation of the players' right of publicity by (1) using their names as symbols of their identities, (2) without consent, and (3) with the intent to obtain a commercial advantage (at 822-23). Nevertheless, the court found that 'CBC's first amendment rights in offering its

Clearly, and unlike the Ted Stevens Act in respect of its protection of Olympic symbols, § 43(a) does require a plaintiff to show consumer confusion or likelihood of such confusion, so the interplay between § 43(a) and First Amendment free speech defence would appear to be limited, and would turn on such element of confusion. Schmitz (who refers to the Olympics context) has highlighted the fact that the potential of § 43(a) to provide remedies in ambush marketing cases may be limited:

> One of the problems with challenging ambush marketers under the Lanham Act is that the consumer protection-oriented approach may fail to provide courts with an appropriate rationale to find for trademark holders. Specifically, the "likelihood of confusion" analysis often does not apply to the facts of ambush cases. Ambushers often do not use or display the Olympic marks but instead create a false association with the marks and the Olympics. Additionally, survey evidence of actual consumer confusion may not be probative of whether consumers care about the identity of the actual sponsors or the impact it may have on their respective consumer behavior.[512]

Schmitz observes that the court's opinion in the 1994 case of *MasterCard International, Inc. v. Sprint Communications Co.*[513] demonstrates the willingness of courts to protect sponsorship and licensing contracts under § 43(a) even though there may be no actual consumer confusion—although Schmitz observes that this case is 'by no means a clear precedent for ambush marketing cases.'[514] MasterCard, a 1994 FIFA World Cup sponsor, successfully enjoined Sprint, a 1994 World Cup partner, from issuing 'card-based payment and account access devices' with 'World Cup '94' trademarks based upon MasterCard's agreement with FIFA's official licensing agency at the time, ISL, that MasterCard had the exclusive rights to use the 'World Cup '94' trademarks on 'card-based payment and account access devices,' which was interpreted to include any telephone credit card. Although the court mentioned consumer confusion caused by the public's belief that the World Cup organisers approved of Sprint's use of its trademarks, Schmitz observes that, in reality, consumers were probably not confused. Consumers could be confused about the sponsorship only to the extent that they thought about it, and likely, most consumers did not care whether Sprint officially sponsored the 1994 World Cup. Instead, the court used § 43(a) to protect MasterCard's investment.[515]

(Footnote 511 continued)
fantasy baseball products supersede the players' rights of publicity.' Widmaier and Schechter declare that this case shows that the First Amendment can act as a bar to the assertion of legitimate interests in protecting marks and designations relating to sports events (here, Major League Baseball games) against commercial exploitation by unauthorsed third parties.

512 Schmitz 2005, p. 207.

513 *MasterCard Int'l, Inc. v. Sprint Communications Co.*, 1994 WL 97097 (S.D.N.Y. 1994), affirmed, 23 F.3d 397 (2d Cir. 1994).

514 Schmitz 2005, p. 208.

515 Schmitz 2005, pp. 207–208.

Apart from the above-mentioned *MasterCard* case, American courts have heard few cases specifically involving ambush marketing to date. Not unlike the position in other jurisdictions which lack far-reaching, direct legislative protection against ambushing, there are important practical reasons for the apparent reluctance of event organisers and rights holders to take the litigation route:

> [T]here is a reluctance to take legal action against ambush marketers, for a number of reasons. Ambush marketers have increasingly launched more sophisticated campaigns that blur the lines between legal marketing activity and marketing that constitutes trademark infringement or false association. Because ambushers rarely use the actual trade marks of the property, a pure trademark infringement claim is often unavailable, thus leaving the ambush campaign in a legal grey area. Additionally, many ambush campaigns last only for a short period of time, which makes the time and cost of litigation to prevent such a campaign prohibitive. Further, ambush marketers can take the simple step of including a disclaimer in their marketing campaigns and, while not a foolproof defence, there is some judicial support around the use of disclaimers as a valid defence. Because litigation can bring uncertain results, is very costly and the ambush marketer may welcome the extra publicity that it receives, properties are hesitant to sue over ambush marketing.[516]

McKelvey and Grady also mention the fear of adverse judicial rulings as a possible reason for the reluctance to sue on the basis of ambush marketing, with reference to the outcome of the Canadian *NHL v Pepsi-Cola Canada Ltd* case,[517] discussed elsewhere.

Ambush marketing in the major American professional sports leagues and at collegiate athletics level is, of course, nothing new. In probably one of the most prominent cases of alleged 'ambushing' in American professional sports, 'maverick' owner of the Dallas Cowboys franchise, Jerry Jones, was sued for USD 300 million in 1995 by NFL Properties[518] for signing sponsorship contracts with non-official NFL sponsors such as Pepsi, Dr Pepper and Nike (which deals were viewed to ambush NFL sponsors Coca-Cola and Reebok). Jones, who was labelled 'a rogue and a thief' by the NFL rights holders, dubbed the league 'an illegal cartel that puts its monopolistic kibosh on competition.'[519] Jones was adamant that his attempts to maximise his investment in the franchise, which related to stadium-specific deals in respect of the Cowboys, did not violate the NFL's league-wide deals with e.g. Coca-Cola. These efforts were part of developments at the time in terms of which a small coalition of owners led by Jones began to challenge the NFL to release the local marketing rights back to the individual teams. In an attempt to force this issue on NFL Properties, Jones embarked on a series of highly-publicised sponsorship signings that made companies like Pepsi, Nike, American Express, AT&T and Dr. Pepper official sponsors of the Dallas Cowboys stadium (a clever

---

516 Chase and Kernit 2010, p. 385.

517 42 C.P.R. (3d) 390, 1992 C.P.R. Lexis 1773 (British Columbia Supreme Court).

518 The entity established in 1963 by means of the NFL Trust Agreement, with the purpose of managing a system through which all revenues generated through broadcasting, licensing, and sponsorship related to the NFL would be shared equally among all the NFL teams.

519 Sandomir, R 'Jones's war with NFL may be over' *The Journal Record* 11 December 1996.

manoeuvre designed to associate these companies with the Dallas Cowboys while not violating the legal provisions of the team's agreement with NFL Properties).[520] NFL Properties sued Jones and the Cowboys for violating the Trust Agreement the club signed in 1982 authorising the NFL to negotiate commercial uses of the team's name, helmet, uniform and slogans, and for what it claimed amounted to ambush marketing (in light of the fact that Jones's stadium sponsorship deals were with competitors of the league's official sponsors). The case was eventually settled out of court, with the NFL recognising Jones' right to sell sponsorships to the Dallas Cowboys stadium, but the matter had wider implications. In 2002, spurred by the continued lobbying of Jones and newer franchise owners, the NFL agreed to cede local marketing rights back to the individual teams, creating the opportunity for individual teams to sell its trademark rights to whomever they choose, including competitors of NFL official league-wide sponsors.[521]

Professional sports leagues attempt to combat ambushing by means of player endorsements and advertising of non-official sponsors through agreements with their players. The NFL, for example, has policies in place which prohibit players from engaging in promotional conduct or ambushing (i.e. 'wearing, displaying, promoting or otherwise conveying their support of a commercially identified product during a game while they're on the field'), which was enforced in 2009 when Captain Morgan rum attempted to run a promotional campaign using players to strike the famous 'Captain's pose' after scoring a touchdown, in return for making a 'charitable donation' to the Gridiron Greats fund (in the amount of USD 10,000, with totals escalating to USD 25,000 in the playoffs and USD 100,000 in the Super Bowl—a bargain compared to the cost of Super Bowl broadcast advertising).[522] Such restrictions on endorsement and advertising activities by players are also to be found in collective bargaining agreements in other leagues.[523]

The National Collegiate Athletics Association (NCAA) sued a major brewer in *NCAA v Coors Brewing Co.*,[524] a contract-based claim. The NCAA sued Coors after Coors allegedly gave away tickets to the NCAA men's basketball championships as a promotional prize in the Coors Light 'Tourney Time Sweepstakes.' NCAA tickets expressly prohibit this practise, which is stated on the ticket-back. While McKelvey and Grady characterised this as a matter that promised to provide 'a novel opportunity to establish the legal parameters of ambush marketing,'[525] the

---

520 McKelvey 2006, p. 116.

521 McKelvey 2006, p. 117.

522 See the report available online at the time of writing at http://content.usatoday.com/communities/thehuddle/post/2009/11/nfl-to-captain-morgan-players-ambush-marketing-wont-be-tolerated/1.

523 See, for example, the provisions in force between the US Soccer Federation and its national team players, referred to below in discussion of the June 2010 litigation between US Soccer and The Sporting Authority in respect of the 2010 FIFA World Cup.

524 02-CV-01325, Complaint (S.D. Ind. 26th August, 2002).

525 McKelvey and Grady 2008, p. 559.

parties settled the case without an admission of wrongdoing by Coors (although it was reported that Coors had paid USD 75,000 to the NCAA in 2003 in settlement of the claims).[526] More recently, in December 2009, former NBA star Michael Jordan sued two Chicago-area grocery stores for placing advertisements in a *Sports Illustrated* commemorative issue celebrating Jordan's induction into the Basketball Hall of Fame where such advertisements offered congratulations to Jordan and featured his name, his number 23 jersey from his playing career and images of basketball shoes meant to resemble his branded 'Air Jordans' (with both advertisements tying the congratulatory message into marketing slogans for the stores concerned). Jordan brought claims for, *inter alia*, violations of his right of publicity under Illinois state law, trademark infringement, false endorsement and deceptive business practises.[527]

Chase and Kernit[528] recount that, although lawsuits targeting ambush marketing campaigns are risky (and rare), there have been a few circumstances where an event organiser or rights holder has successfully sued an ambush marketer in the USA over the wrongful taking of the property's goodwill. In *University of Georgia Athletic Association v Laite*[529] the Eleventh Circuit Court of Appeals upheld an injunction against a wholesaler of novelty beers, preventing the wholesaler from selling cans of 'Battlin' Bulldog Beer' featuring a logo of a cartoon snarling bulldog with a sweater emblazoned with the letter 'G' that the University claimed was too similar to its bulldog mascot and logo. Although the logos were not exactly the same, the total context of the use, which included the University's official colours, was found to be too similar. The court further found that the wholesaler intended to capitalise on the goodwill of the university's football team. The authors also mention *National Football League v. Coors Brewing Company*,[530] where the Second Circuit Court of Appeals upheld the NFL's injunction against Coors for its use of the phrase 'Official Beer of NFL Players' in marketing materials because the court found that Coors' intent was to capitalise on the goodwill of the NFL trademark. Coors had entered into an agreement with the

---

[526] A similar more recent case was also settled—see *Philadelphia Eagles, LLC v. Equity Communications LP*, 09-CV-04968, Complaint (D. N. J. 25th September, 2009) (judgment on consent granted 1 December 2009).

[527] *Jordan v. Jewel Food Stores, Inc.*, 2009-L-015549, Complaint (Ill. Cir. Court 21st December, 2009), removed to the US District Court for the Northern District of Illinois, No. 10-CV-00340 (N.D. Ill. 19th January, 2010); and *Jordan and Jump 23, Inc. v. Dominick's Finer Foods, LLC*, No. 2009-L-015548, Complaint (Ill. Cir. Court 21st December, 2009), removed to the US District Court for the Northern District of Illinois, No. 10-CV-00407 (N.D. Ill. 20th January, 2010)—see Chase and Kernit *supra* 385.

[528] Chase and Kernit 2010, pp. 385–386.

[529] 756 F.2d 1535 (11th Cir. 1985).

[530] 205 F.3d 1324 (2d Cir. 1999).

NFL professional players' union to use the phrase. The court determined that Coors' use of the NFL trademark went beyond merely descriptive use. Other cases (such as the one filed by Powerbar, Inc, an Olympic sponsor, against Nabisco in respect of Nabisco's adverts for its 'Fig Newton' cookies in respect of the 2000 Sydney Olympics[531]) were settled and did not bring judgments in order to shape case law relating to ambushing.

More recently, the 2010 FIFA World Cup South Africa saw a case of alleged ambush marketing in which the U.S. Soccer Federation ('U.S. Soccer') instituted legal action against U.S. sports goods retailer, The Sports Authority, Inc. (or 'TSA') for an alleged ambush involving its registered trademarks and which threatened the interests of U.S. Soccer's exclusive sponsor (Dick's Sporting Goods) as well as tortiously infringing its collective bargaining agreement with national team players competing in the FIFA World Cup. TSA had run advertisements (including on Facebook and Youtube) of national player Taylor Twellman wearing the U.S. national soccer uniform and sporting registered trademarks. In June 2010 U.S. Soccer filed suit in the U.S. District Court for the Northern District of Illinois, in *U.S. Soccer Federation Inc. v. TSA Stores Inc.*,[532] accusing TSA of seeking an unfair competitive edge and interfering with endorsement contracts through infringing ads, and claiming unfair competition and trademark infringement under the Lanham Act, as well as claiming unjust enrichment and relief in terms of Illinois common law claims. U.S. Soccer alleged that 'consumers will mistakenly believe that TSA's use of the U.S. Soccer mark and U.S. Soccer national team uniform featuring that mark to [be] affiliated, connected with or sponsored by U.S. Soccer, which it most definitely is not,' and claimed that in addition to causing consumer confusion, TSA had interfered not only with U.S. Soccer's collective bargaining agreement with its players (collective agreement between U.S. Soccer and the US National Soccer Team Players Association)[533] but also with its exclusive licensing deal with official sponsor

[531] *USOC v. Nabisco, Inc.*, Case No. C 00 3086 (N.D. Cal., Aug. 25, 2000).

[532] Case number 10-cv-03755, U.S. District Court for the Northern District of Illinois (filed 17 June 2010).

[533] Which agreement (in force until 31 December 2010) contained the following provision:

> (a) Because of [U.S. Soccer's] concern that the public might be misled to believe that a particular product or event is endorsed or sponsored by [U.S. Soccer] and the need of [U.S. Soccer] to preserve its reputation and integrity as the National Governing Body for the sport of soccer in the United States, Player agrees that Player shall not:
>
> (i) use the name or logos of the Team or [U.S. Soccer] for any purpose…
> (ii) use any uniform of the Team or [U.S. Soccer] for any purpose other than appearing in a match as requested by [U.S. Soccer] unless Player shall have received prior written consent and approval of [U.S. Soccer.]…

Dick's Sporting Goods, the only apparel outlet with permission to display U.S. Soccer marks. TSA had, allegedly, received a cease-and-desist letter on 11 June 2010, and continued to authorise the broadcast of an infringing advertisement on 12 June, during the United States and England match, and the action was filed in order to restrain the defendant from continuing its alleged infringement in respect of the U.S.-Slovenia match on 18 June. U.S. Soccer's first claim under the Lanham Act was for infringement in terms of 15 U.S.C. § 1114(1) (section 32),[534] as follows:

> TSA has displayed, and continues to display, the U.S. Crest Logo Mark in its advertisements without a valid license or the consent of U.S. Soccer. TSA's actions are likely to have caused and will continue to cause confusion, mistake and deception both among consumers intending to purchase official U.S. Soccer sporting goods and as to the affiliation, connection, sponsorship, partnership and/or association of TSA with U.S. Soccer.

(Footnote 533 continued)

(iii) make any endorsements or commercial appearances, sponsor any products, or use or consent to use by any third party of any name, picture or likeness of Player in which Player appears, either alone or with others, in the official Team uniform, or any attire which closely resembles or is confusingly similar to the official Team uniform, or in any attire whatsoever bearing or displaying the marks and/or logos of either [U.S. Soccer] or the Team unless Player(s) shall have received the prior written consent and approval of [U.S. Soccer.]...

(v) engage in marketing efforts, alone or with others, as the Team or in his capacity as a Team player that will lead someone to believe that [U.S. Soccer] has endorsed a business, product or service. Nothing in this Agreement shall be deemed to give any Player or the Players Association the right, without [U.S. Soccer's] prior written consent, to state or imply that [U.S. Soccer] has endorsed a product, service, or business.

[534] § 1114(1), which deals with remedies and infringement in respect of registered marks, provides as follows:

> Any person who shall, without the consent of the registrant
>
> (a) use in commerce any reproduction, counterfeit, copy, or colorable imitation of a registered mark in connection with the sale, offering for sale, distribution, or advertising of any goods or services on or in connection with which such use is likely to cause confusion, or to cause mistake, or to deceive; or
>
> (b) reproduce, counterfeit, copy, or colorably imitate a registered mark and apply such reproduction, counterfeit, copy, or colorable imitation to labels, signs, prints, packages, wrappers, receptacles or advertisements intended to be used in commerce upon or in connection with the sale, offering for sale, distribution, or advertising of goods or services on or in connection with which such use is likely to cause confusion, or to cause mistake, or to deceive, shall be liable in a civil action by the registrant for the remedies hereinafter provided.

Its second claim was for infringement of section 43(a) of the Lanham Act, in the following terms:

> TSA's use of the U.S. Soccer Marks and the National Team uniform, which consumers currently exclusively associate with U.S. Soccer, in its advertisement has likely caused and will continue to cause confusion, mistake and deception among consumers intending to purchase official U.S. Soccer sporting goods as to the affiliation, connection, sponsorship, partnership and/or association of TSA with U.S. Soccer.

The court granted a temporary restraining order and a preliminary injunction in favour of the plaintiff.

Overall, it is clear that legal protection against ambush marketing is available in the United States although, apparently, such protection has not often been utilised to date (which might seem strange in such a litigious society). It remains to be seen whether the US law-makers will enact special event commercial rights protection by means of legislation or other measures in future, which might depend on whether any mega-event bids will be awarded to a US city (compare the recent, unsuccessful, Chicago and New York Olympic Games bids)—this is likely in light of the event bidding requirements of organisers such as the IOC and FIFA (as discussed earlier in this chapter), although the United States is a jurisdiction that might necessitate and allow for differences in approach (compare, for example, the unique position of the US Olympic Committee as compared to other NOCs, and the special relevance of this jurisdiction as source or home base of a number of multinational TOP sponsors of the Olympic Games as well as in respect of the broadcasting market). If this happens it is reasonable to expect that any such legislation would likely be subjected to judicial scrutiny in respect of e.g. free speech guarantees in terms of the US Constitution, and I would speculate that special event legislation along the lines of, for example, the 2012 London Olympics legislation and its 'association right' would be less likely to be accepted as providing a monopoly in words or language as is the case under the Ted Stevens Act.

Finally, it bears mentioning that one commentator, Brian Pelanda, recently observed that the dearth of case law on ambush marketing in the United States might be attributable to the problematic nature of the very conception of ambushing as found in the literature:

> On its face, [the classic definition of ambush marketing] describes the practise of false association which is explicitly prohibited by United States law under the Lanham Act, and for which a substantial body of case law exists. Yet despite the innumerable cited instances of alleged ambush marketing over the last thirty years, "there is almost no ambush marketing case law in the United States." Clearly, there must be a disconnect between the all-too-frequent allegations of "ambush marketing" as defined above, and the reality of the marketing strategies often alleged to be "ambushes."[535]

[535] Pelanda, B L 'Ambush marketing: Dissecting the discourse,' undated 2011 paper available online at the time of writing at http://works.bepress.com/brian_pelanda/.

Pelanda argues that a prime reason for the absence of ambushing case law may be attributable to a 'fundamental flaw that pervades most analyses of the alleged threat posed by ambush marketing': While critics argue that what is often termed ambush marketing tactics are particularly threatening because they cause consumer confusion as to a non-sponsoring company's association with an event, few ambush cases have ever been litigated primarily because complainants have not even been able to meet even the Lanham Act's low threshold of proving any such likelihood of consumer confusion. I will, in Chap. 8, return to this issue of consumer confusion (or the lack thereof) in ambushing cases and in the special anti-ambushing legislation, which issue I view to be relevant more widely than just in the context of America's Lanham Act.

Pelanda argues that the United States requires no special anti-ambushing laws, and that all cases of alleged ambushing should be tested against the confusion as to sponsorship or affiliation-provisions of the Lanham Act, as discussed above. He feels that the Lanham Act's likelihood of confusion test 'is a more than reasonable standard that both protects event organizers and sponsors and free speech in the competitive free market,' and that its approach should guide lawmakers elsewhere as well:

> Because U.S. law adequately balances free speech interests with consumer confusion, and because it protects markholders and businesses from actions by competitors designed to deceive consumers, U.S. law should serve as a model for the international community to follow in regard to dealing with ambush marketing. Commentators and athletic event organizers such as the IOC should wield their allegations of ambush marketing more precisely and more sincerely if they wish to be taken more seriously by the legal community.[536]

4.5 Conclusion

The previous section provides a very brief overview of special (or the not so special) ambush marketing protection for sports events in a number of prominent jurisdictions. I will revisit such special event legislation, and especially the new statutory association rights to events, in Chap. 8.

In the next chapter I will briefly examine the issue of intellectual property rights protection in respect of ambush marketing and, specifically, I will evaluate the legitimacy of the special event legislation in the light of traditional principles underlying IP law. Chapter 6 will undertake a similar exercise in respect of competition (anti-trust) laws, and Chap. 7 will do so with reference to the human

[536] Ibid.

rights implications of such legislation and the aggressive protection of commercial rights to mega-events against ambush marketing.

References

All internet-based sources referred to, were last visited in or before December 2011

Andriychuck O (2009) The legal nature of premium sports events: "IP or not IP—that is the question." In: Blackshaw I, Cornelius S, Siekmann R (eds) TV rights and sport: legal aspects. T.M.C. Asser Press, The Hague

Bacalao-Fleury CE (2011) Brazil's Olympic trials: an overview of the intellectual property challenges posed by the 2016 Rio de Janeiro Games. Univ Ill J Law Technol Policy 1:191

Bhattacharjee S (2003) Ambush marketing: the problem and the projected solutions vis a vis intellectual property law—a global perspective. J Intellect Prop Rights 8:375–388

Bischoff JB, Curry JP, Berzins I (2005) Dispatch from the trademark wars: ambush marketing and the arena of sports. Metrop Corp Couns Newslett 19. (February 2005)

Burton N, Chadwick S (2009) A typology of ambush marketing: the methods and strategies of ambushing in sport. Centre for the International Business of Sport Working Paper Series No. 10

Chase CR, Kernit R (2010) Fighting for what is left of exclusivity: strategies to protect the exclusivity of sponsors in the sports industry. J Spons 3(4):379–393

Cookson B (2011) Erasing ambush marketing. J Intellect Prop Law Pract 6(3):149–150

Cooper Dreyfuss R (1996) We are symbols and inhabit symbols, so should we be paying rent? Deconstructing the Lanham Act and rights of publicity. Columbia-VLA J Law Arts 20:123

Corbett S, Van Roy Y (2010) Events management in New Zealand: one law to rule them all? J Bus Law 4:338–362

Crow D, Hoek J (2003) Ambush marketing: a critical review and some practical advice. Marketing Bulletin 1–14

Ellis D, Scassa T, Seguin B (2011) Framing ambush marketing as a legal issue: an Olympic perspective. Sport Manag Rev 14(3):297–308

Frontier Economics (2007) Ambush marketing legislation review (Prepared for IP Australia and the Department of Communications, Information Technology and the Arts)

Gannon N (2010) Foul play in sports branding—the marketer's perspective. World Trademark Rev 67–71

Gardiner S et al (2006) Sports Law, 3rd ed. Cavendish Publishing Ltd, London

Grady J, McKelvey S, Bernthal MJ (2010) From Beijing 2008 to London 2012 examining event-specific Olympic legislation vis à vis the rights and interests of stakeholders. J Spons 3(2):144–156

Haman M, Marriott D (2010) The 2010 World Cup—practical lessons in brand protection. World Trademark Rev 72–77

Hewitt I (2005) Commercialisation of major sports events: does the law help or hinder the event organiser? Sport Law J 13(1):32–33

Hughes G (2010) Brands at war. N Z Lawyer (150):14–16

Johnson P (2007) Ambush marketing: a practical guide to protecting the brand of a sporting event. Sweet & Maxwell, London

Johnson P (2008) Look out! It's an ambush. Int Sports Law Rev 2/3:24–29

Kobel P (2007) International report on question B: ambush marketing too smart to be good? Should certain ambush marketing practices be declared illegal and if yes, which ones and under what conditions? International report to the international league of competition law, Catania Congress

Lemley MA (1999) The modern Lanham Act and the death of common sense. Yale Law J 108:1687

Longdin L (2009) Public law solutions to private law problems: major event regulation subverts IP's internal balance. J Intellec Prop Law Pract 4(10):726–742

MacCambridge M (2004) America's game: the epic story of how pro football captured a nation. Random House, New York

Marcus JT (2010) Ambush marketing: an analysis of its threat to sports rights holders and the efficacy of past, present and proposed anti-infringement programmes. Sport Law J 18(1):25

Masterman G (2009) Strategic sports event management: Olympic edition. Elsevier (Butterworth-Heinemann), London

McKelvey SM (2006) Coca-Cola vs. PepsiCo: a "Super" battleground for the Cola wars? Sports Mark Q 15(2):114–123

McKelvey S, Grady J (2008) Sponsorship program protection strategies for special sport events: are event organizers outmaneuvring ambush marketers? J Sport Manag 22:550–586

Mendes PPM (2010) Brazil moves fast to fight ambush marketing. World Intellec Prop Rev

Merges RP, Menell PS, Lemley MA (2003) Intellectual property in the new technological age, 3rd edn. Aspen Publishers, New York

Mey BP (2009) China, the "intellectual property black hole" hosts the XXIX Olympiad: measures the People's Republic of China undertook to secure the protection of Olympic-related intellectual property rights. J World Intellect Prop 12(2):153–173

Mouritz A (2008) Challenging the legal enforceability of the Vancouver 2010 Olympic Games anti-ambush marketing provisions. Sport Law J 1(16):10–19

Nigam KV (2011) Official sponsors clean bowled by ambush marketing. World Intellect Prop Rev Annual 60–61

Phillips J (2006) Play the game, kill the competition. J Intellect Prop Law Pract 1(2):79

Safiyuddin M, Bhandare S (2008) Branding in India spiced up by Indian Premier League. World Trademark Rev 5. (July/Aug 2008)

Scassa T (2011) Ambush marketing and the right of association: clamping down on references to that big event with the all the athletes in a couple of years. Journal of Sport Management 25:354–370

Schmitz JJ (2005) Ambush marketing: the off-field competition at the Olympic games. Northwestern Journal of Technology & Intellectual Property 3:203

Schwab F (2006) FIFA's trademark tactics. World Trademark Rev 3:6

Seguin B, Gauthier M, Ellis D, Parent MM (2009) Power play: an examination of power and ambush marketing. Conference proceedings, 17th EASM conference 2009

Seth R (2010) Ambush marketing—need for legislation in India. Journal of Intellectual Property Rights 15:455–463

Shank MD (1999) Sports marketing: a strategic perspective. Prentice Hall Inc, Upper Saddle River

Sliffman AJ (2012) Unconstitutional hosting of the super bowl: anti-ambush marketing clean zone's violation of the first amendment. Marq Sports Law Rev 22(1):257–285

Smith A (2011) Ramping up trademark protection at the Olympics. World Trademark Rev 33:42–46

Stuart SA, Scassa T (2011) Legal guarantees for Olympic legacy. Entertain Sports Law J 9(1). http://www2.warwick.ac.uk/fac/soc/law/elj/eslj/issues/volume9/number1/stuart/

Sun C (2008) Get set to defend your rights: protection and enforcement before, during and after the Beijing games. World Trademark Rev 45

Vassallo E, Blemaster K, Werner P (2005) An international look at ambush marketing. Trademark Rep 95:1338

Wang SH (2005) Great Olympics, new China: intellectual property enforcement steps up to the mark. Loyola Los Angel Int Comp Law Rev 27:291–322

Widmaier U, Schechter PC (2009) 'United States'—country report on the United States prepared for the Working Committee of the International Association for the Protection of Intellectual property (AIPPI), Project Q210 ('The protection of major sports events and associated commercial activities through trademarks and other IPR'; reports compiled for purposes of a draft resolution to be submitted to the AIPPI Exco meeting in Buenos Aires, October 2009)—available online at the time of writing at https://www.aippi.org/download/commitees/210/GR210usa.pdf

Zhang AG (2010) The judicial determination and protection of well-known marks in China in the 21st century. Univ Louisville Law Rev 48:959

Chapter 5
Mega-Event Rights Protection and Intellectual Property Laws

> In common law legal systems, IP rights exist not to protect the interests of any particular market player or players but to strike a balance between the need to encourage innovation and creativity and discourage consumer deception through the granting of temporary and limited legal monopolies and the potentially adverse effect on the wider economy that such monopolies can entail… In the nature of things, no IP regime gets this balance right all the time… [E]ven where the balance in the view of some commentators is wrongly struck, there is at least the saving grace that, because these are laws of general application, any favouring of owners over consumers or competitors will apply equally to all forms of economic activity. The problem [special event legislation such as New Zealand's Major Events Management Act, 2007] poses for the internal coherence of IP law as a whole is that, by outflanking this debate, it encourages losers in the lobbying contest that usually accompanies legislative changes to IP regimes to believe that the solution to their problems is a freestanding custom-built statute of their own. That is a problem for the future.[1]

> In an acquisitive society, the drive for monopoly advantage is a very powerful pressure. Unchecked, it would no doubt patent the wheel, copyright the alphabet, and register the sun and the moon as exclusive trademarks.[2]

5.1 Introduction

This chapter does not contain detailed discussion of the use of intellectual property rights to exploit the commercial value of a major sporting event, or the various forms of intellectual property protection (e.g. the ones most relevant in this context, namely trademarks, copyright or registered designs) that are available to event organisers and/or sponsors in order to protect against ambush marketing. It will also not examine the ins and outs of such litigation, or related aspects regarding IP law as a means to combat ambushing of events (such as, e.g. the extent to which event organisers may enjoy 'special' trademark protection for their

[1] Longdin 2009, p. 728.
[2] Brown 1948, p. 1206.

A. M. Louw, *Ambush Marketing and the Mega-Event Monopoly*,
ASSER International Sports Law Series, DOI: 10.1007/978-90-6704-864-4_5,

marks as well-known or famous marks). The interested reader is referred to more specialised texts in this regard.[3] The main reason for avoiding a focus on such more practical examination of the role of intellectual property rights in combating ambush marketing is the fact that, generally and in all but the most blatant cases of ambushing, IP rights actually play a rather limited role in the modern mega-event context.[4] Examples of blatant association ambushes of events (such as the sale of unauthorised or counterfeit merchandise that incorporates a registered event or sponsor trademark or design, and false endorsement advertising that misrepresents that an athlete supports a company's products or services) are activities that are 'traditionally considered piracies' and—leaving aside detection and enforcement issues—are areas in which IP (or trade practises) law already provides a remedy.[5] So, while IP rights are central to the protection against ambushing in terms of the available legal responses, in practise they play a limited role in the cases of creative ambushes which do not make use of event IP or in those cases which are now, because of the legislation, treated as 'ambushing' but may very well, in fact, be nothing of the sort.

I have also referred (in the previous chapter) to the theoretical disconnect between 'ambush marketing' of an event and the theory of IP infringement (i.e. the fact that ambushing relates mainly to creating an impression of association with an event rather than infringement in the normal sense of the word of a sponsor's or event organiser's IP), but there is also a practical reason why IP rights may become less relevant to the combating of ambushing in those jurisdictions that have proceeded to pass strong event legislation. Louise Longdin explains this in the context of New Zealand's Major Events Management Act (or MEMA, discussed in the previous chapter), which Act requires the relevant Minister, in deciding whether to declare an event as protected in terms of the Act, to consider the capacity and intention of the event organiser 'to use all practicable measures available under the existing law to prevent unauthorised commercial exploitation of the major event and to protect its IP and other legal rights'. She points to the fact that such legislation may effectively sideline the relevant IP laws or the chances of event organisers electing to use them:

---

[3] See, e.g., Johnson 2007, Chaps. 2 and 3 (a second and updated edition of which has just been published as Johnson, P *Ambush Marketing and Brand Protection: Law and Practice* Oxford University Press (November 2011)); Scaria 2008, Chap. 3; see also Lewis and Taylor 2007, chapter D1 (especially D1.36–D1.132; Gardiner et al. 2006, Chaps. 10 and 11.

[4] Kobel does well to sum this up in the context of the use of trademarks:

'A commonly held view is that trademark law is simply irrelevant because ambush marketers carefully avoid referring to trademarks. Court practice however shows that users of ambush marketing technique are not always subtle and often refer to protected trademarks. The situation may be relatively clear and does not require long developments when ambush marketers are referring to competitors' trademarks. In such cases, the likelihood of confusion is obvious and protection is straightforward…In reality, ambush marketers refer to the event itself, possibly to the name of the event organiser. In these cases claiming protection under trademark law is less obvious.' Kobel 2007, p. 20

[5] See the report by Frontier Economics 2007, p. 14 (referring to Townley et al. 1998, p. 335).

> Practical realities require one to ask, why would the event organiser wish to pursue rights whose inadequacy from its point of view was the reason for enacting the legislation in the first place? Few corporates are likely to want to exchange the uncertainties and inbuilt limitations of IP law and allied liability rules for the satisfyingly draconian and instant remedies provided by MEMA.[6]

This chapter will rather focus on evaluating the legitimacy of commercial monopolisation of events (a combination of the anti-competitive characteristics of event commercialisation as discussed in Chap. 2, and the legal measures employed to protect such monopolies as discussed in Chap. 4) on a more fundamental level, against the background of the traditional notions and considerations that underlie intellectual property laws. It will be my objective to evaluate to what extent the exclusive sponsorship and other commercial arrangements around mega-events, as well as the use of intellectual property rights in order to maintain and protect such arrangements, are consonant with the traditional notions that underpin IP law and what it serves to protect. This is especially poignant in light of developments in the past decade whereby specific legislation has been passed in a number of jurisdictions in order to provide special protection to major sports events and their associated intellectual property, as discussed in the previous chapter. We have seen that such anti-ambush marketing protection has derived mostly from special laws that were passed to strengthen intellectual property rights protection (for example, of Olympic symbols—compare the erstwhile Australian legislation for the 2000 Sydney Games and the current UK legislation for the 2012 London Games), and that such IP element of the legislation remains a fundamental part of such protection.

In the broader context, other authors have in recent years bemoaned the frequently apparent excesses in the enforcement of intellectual property laws primarily by large multinational corporations, and the ways in which such laws (apparently contrary to notions and philosophies that have traditionally been accepted as justifying (but also limiting) the protection of IP) have increasingly been used to monopolise aspects of popular culture and to promote narrow commercial interests over the public good.[7] One American observer ascribes this trend (in the United States) to the changing face of the economy (from an agriculture-based economy, through a transformation to an industrial-based economy in the nineteenth century to an economy based on information processing 'as the principal source of American jobs') and to the transformation of the US from a net consumer of intellectual property to a net producer ('more Americans had an interest in "pirating" copyrighted or patented materials produced by foreigners than had an interest in protecting copyrights or patents against "piracy" by foreigners').[8] Legislators are increasingly testing the bounds between aggressive IP

---

[6] Longdin 2009, p. 731.

[7] See, for example, Bollier 2005; Lessig 2004; Vaidhyanathan 2003; see also Spinello and Bottis 2009, Chaps. 1 and 4.

[8] William W Fischer III 'The growth of intellectual property: A history of the ownership of ideas in the United States' (at 10–11), Harvard University, paper available online at the time of writing at http://cyber.law.harvard.edu/people/tfisher/iphistory.pdf.

rights enforcement and human rights, with much-criticised legislation (such as the UK's Digital Economy Act of 2010[9]) gradually serving to restrict personal freedoms in the digital domain in the interests of protecting forms of intellectual property (and means of infringing the associated rights) which would have been inconceivable mere decades ago. Leaving aside the frequently contentious modern IP issues (such as those relating to copyright in respect of music and literature and the scourge of internet file-sharing, for example, or of IP rights in respect of medicines and the ongoing battles involving the patented vs. the generic) it is no great stretch of the imagination to characterise the world as having become a brand-mad environment. One need only watch a random selection of hip-hop music videos to encounter the Generation Y preoccupation with conspicuous consumption (the 'bling factor') and its reverence for the almighty brand. It is not surprising then that WIPO reported in May 2009 that it had reached the one-million mark for international trademark registrations.

Along with such growth (or as a result) there have been calls for a constant reexamination of the parameters for IP protection in the light of recent extensions in various jurisdictions.[10] Add to this the trend of an apparent 'free-for-all' in litigious societies (e.g. where an American toy manufacturer might feel justified in suing a Danish pop group for naming their song after a well-known children's doll[11]), and the stage is set for IP rights becoming—if not in fact then at least in terms of perceptions—unmanageable. To make matters worse, and apart from IP expansion, one is also confronted with the frequent overlapping of different IP rights to protect the same 'property'.[12] American commentators have also criticised the 'propertization' of IP rights in respect of their scope and duration. Michael Carrier mentions a number of examples, including what he refers to as the extension to cyberspace of common law doctrines, such as trespass to chattels, proposed legislation that would create *sui generis* protection for uncopyrightable

---

[9] Digital Economy Act 2010 c. 24 (Royal Assent 8 April 2010).

[10] Compare the following observation by David Vaver, Reuters professor of Intellectual Property and Information Technology Law, Oxford University, in a public address at the Victoria University of Wellington, 30 August 2000—available online at the time of writing at http://kirra.austlii.edu.au/nz/journals/VUWLawRw/2001/2.html:

'The recent expansion of intellectual property has come to be more an end in itself than a means to the end of stimulating desirable innovation. The question whether existing protections should be scaled back or re-contoured, because the activities that they supposedly foster would occur anyway and would be more widely distributed throughout society, is hardly asked any more. If intellectual property were seen as a form of subsidy—a willingness by society at large to provide economic benefits to one sector in return for the prospect of larger benefits to all—then few would question the need to keep intellectual property under constant review to ensure the scheme was working well. It would not be enough to say that intellectual property as a whole was returning social benefits that outweighed its costs as a whole. As with any other subsidy, each element within the scheme would need to be examined to see if it passes its own A level—and with distinction. A strong case for such systematic reviews must surely exist.'

[11] *Mattel Inc v. MCA Records Inc.* 296 F.3d 894 (9th Cir. 2002).

[12] See, for example, the discussion Tawfik 2008, p. 267 *et seq.*

databases, and judicial and legislative protection of software licences that limit access and use.[13] I would suggest that one can add to this list the protection of event organisers' 'intellectual property' in *sui generis* mega-event legislation, upon which I will elaborate below.

In this light of an apparently burgeoning international resistance to IP's unbounded growth, it is interesting to note how IP laws have in the past few years increasingly been *expanded upon* to protect and maintain commercial monopolies in sports mega-events. This is probably not surprising if one notes that the realm of sport has increasingly become a playground for IP lawyers—one American observer opines that 'It seems as though it has become impossible to maintain one's sports savvy without a grounding in intellectual property law'; and that 'one could teach a course on intellectual property law utilizing [only] sports cases'.[14] In the United States, for example, Congress only explicitly extended copyright to broadcasts of live sporting events as recently as 1976 (by means of the revamped Copyright Act),[15] and courts have also ruled that the special techniques of sports broadcasting—instant replays, split screen shots and commentary by announcers—constitute 'creativity' for authorship purposes.[16] Other areas of IP law—notably trademark law—have shown even more rapid expansion in the sports context.

Some sports-related IP claims would, however, appear to be rather preposterous. Compare the recent settlement arrived at after the City of Dunedin in Florida and course management of the local 'St. Andrews' golf course received a demand of USD 75,000 and threats of impending legal action from the St. Andrews Links Trust in Scotland (one would assume that any 'consumer confusion' as to which course one was playing would be averted by the differences in prevailing weather, at the very least). It was reported in March 2011 that the New Zealand Rugby Union had concluded an agreement with a Maori tribe, which holds intellectual property rights to the 'haka' war dance, to allow the national All Blacks team to continue its long-standing tradition (practised since 1905) of performing the dance prior to its matches to intimidate its opponents (there had been concerns that the tribe would take steps to protest such use during the 2011 IRB Rugby World Cup, to be hosted in New Zealand). And then there is the legal action by India's Sports Ministry in April 2009 against the Indian Premier League cricket tournament's organisers—the Ministry objected to the 'Building India' tagline in the logo of the event title sponsor, real estate developer DLF,[17] specifically objecting to having it

[13] Carrier 2004, p. 9.

[14] Das 2000, pp. 1074–1075.

[15] 17 U.S.C. § 102(a)(6).

[16] See Hylton, J G 'The over-protection of intellectual property rights in sport' (Marquette University Law School/National Sports Law Institute)—undated paper available online at the time of writing at http://shiac.com/files/arablexsportiva-presentations/004003.pdf

[17] Real estate developer DLF Group won the title sponsorship of the IPL for a 5-year period after its successful bid of over USD 50 million for the rights.

on the bowlers' run-up area where players would frequently tread on the word 'India', to the chagrin of the government.[18]

Many of the 'rights' associated with the commercialisation of sport (such as, primarily, the copyright in sports broadcasts which are a significant component of what has come to be known as 'sports broadcasting rights'—although this latter term has little actual substance in legal theory in most jurisdictions)[19] are based in IP law. In fact, one could argue that IP, and not 'the game', is actually the end product of the modern major professional sports league or event organiser. One of the heavy hitters in American professional sports, NBA Commissioner David Stern, explained the role of IP in professional sport in the following unequivocal terms in a 2000 interview, when asked about the effect of the mergers of major production companies in the entertainment industry at the time:

> The fierce protection of our intellectual property is the largest issue that now confronts us; and I hope that some of the outdated views of looking at sports leagues in a certain way as competitors, as they seek to compete in this broader [entertainment] marketplace, will not be applied. We all generate a fair amount of intellectual property. It is our end product, and we are actually out there competing with enterprises that are many times our size in doing that. Each of [the professional hockey, basketball, baseball and football] leagues is in the magazine business. Each of our leagues is in the network production business. Each of our leagues is in the cable business. We are in the trading card business. We are in a variety of businesses that all of these entertainment companies are in, although we are considerably smaller than even the smallest of them… On the one hand, these mergers may be healthy for them, and I think they are, and probably good for us because there are now strong competitors for our rights, we need the ability to develop and compete on a global basis as we create the intellectual property that is the product of the presentation of our games.[20]

Such a prominent role for intellectual property in the modern sports industry may account for some of the claims of a rather bizarre scope of such rights in this context in recent years. World-renowned IP law expert David Vaver has observed that around the time of the 1996 Atlanta Olympic Games there was speculation in the legal journals that intellectual property rights could be extended to cover sports

[18] See the report in the *Hindustan Times* of 12 April 2010, available online at the time of writing at http://www.hindustantimes.com/News-Feed/cricketnews/Stop-treading-on-India-Sports-Ministry-tells-IPL/Article1-529045.aspx

[19] Another example is found in sports 'image rights' of athletes in the various jurisdictions. Although 'publicity rights' enjoy varying degrees of recognition in the United States at state and federal levels, UK law (for example) recognises no such right, but 'image rights' are accepted in practise (apparently as a form of quasi-IP right) even though there is little theoretical basis for its existence.

[20] From a round-table interview with the four major professional league commissioners in the American Bar Association's publication, Vol. 14 No. 2 *Antitrust* (Spring 2000) at 10 (available online at the time of writing at http://www.americanbar.org/content/dam/aba/publishing/antitrust_magazine/antitrust_14-2_full.authcheckdam.pdf).

moves.[21] Not only could one enjoy a patent for a new golf club or ball, but for the actual way of swinging a golf club:

> Many a golf game might no doubt be livened up as intellectual property lawyers take to the greens to scrutinize each swing and to serve legal process on whichever player comes close to the bunker of patent law; but the cure for dullness in sporting events is surely better found outside the intellectual property sphere.[22]

Gardiner et al. pose the question of the patentability of Bernard Langer's inverted putting grip, of Johnny Wilkinson's 'cradle kick', of Shane Warne's 'flipper' and of Dick Fosbury's 'Fosbury flop' high-jump technique.[23] A group of American IP lawyers argued that the method 'for sailing an America's Cup yacht wherein the yacht sails 10 degrees closer to the wind, for high-jumping higher or for skiing downhill 10 per cent faster' could easily be classified as a 'useful process' within the meaning of the federal patent statute.[24] James Foster, American 'inventor' of the 'Arena football' indoor football game, managed to obtain a patent for the game,[25] and one American commentator has mooted the possibility of providing IP protection for a team's playbook of 'scripted sports moves'.[26]

---

[21] With reference to Kunstadt et al. 1996, c1; Phelps 'Can Copyright Move in Mysterious Ways?' (1996) 63 Copyright World 17. See also Kukkonen, C A 'Be a Good Sport and Refrain from Using my Patented Putt: Intellectual Property Protection for Sports Related Movements' 80 *J. Pat. & Trademark Off. Soc'y* 808 (1998); Das 2000; Weber, L J 'Something in the Way She Moves: The Case for Applying Copyright Protection to Sports Moves' 23 *Colum.-VLA J.L. & Arts* 317 (1999–2000).

[22] From an address presented by Professor Vaver at the Victoria University of Wellington, 30 August 2000—available online at the time of writing at http://kirra.austlii.edu.au/nz/journals/VUWLawRw/2001/2.html.

[23] Gardiner et al. 2006, p. 415

[24] Kunstadt et al. 1996.

[25] US Patent no. US4911443 (A) (published 27 March 1990). The patent expired on 30 September 2007. The abstract of the patent contained the following:

'A new game is disclosed, involving substantially the same rules as American football (e.g., NFL or NCAA) except that kicks or passes into the end zone may be deflected back onto the playing field as a playable ball by a rebounding assembly that surrounds the goalposts. Upon an attempted field goal, an errant kick will result in the ball hitting the rebounding assembly instead of passing between the vertical uprights of the goalpost. The reflected ball can be caught before it hits the ground by only players of the team defending the goal. Once caught, the defending team may advance the ball toward the opposite goal in accordance with the normal rules of American football. If the ball reflected off of the rebounding assembly hits the ground before it is caught by a player of the team defending the goal, the ball is free for players of either team to advance. In order to ensure that an errant kick results in the rebounding of the ball back into the playing field, the rebounding assembly is comprised of resilient material that returns much of the kinetic energy to the ball after it impacts the rebounding assembly. The rebound assembly for playing the game is comprised of a goal post substantially similar to that used in American football, with the exception that the instant goal is provided with a ball rebound net extending outwards from each side of the goal post, along the extremity of the end zone to substantially the entire width of the playing field.' See http://v3.espacenet.com/publicationDetails/biblio?CC=US&NR=4911443&KC=&FT=E.

[26] Das 2000.

Leaving aside such patent (excuse the pun) absurdity, I believe that the current scope of ambush marketing legislation in various jurisdictions is an example of the dangers inherent in unchecked expansion of narrow commercial interests at the expense of the public interest in what I view to be one of the most prominent (remaining) examples of a phenomenon that belongs squarely within the social and cultural commons, namely the international sports mega-event. In light of the fact that trademarks are a form of IP that is especially relevant in this context of event protection it is interesting to note, as one commentator has observed, that '[a]lthough no other intellectual property regime pose so many legal tests that depend upon public consciousness [as trademark law], no other form of intellectual property provides so little corresponding recognition of a public domain.'[27] The ever-increasing expansion of commercial rights protection for mega- (and other) sports events by means of special, *sui generis* legislative protection (as discussed in the previous chapter) needs to be considered against the backdrop of the following judgement expressed by Johnson, which emphasises the significant public interest in *not* providing overly wide protection as a matter of course:

> [In recent years] minor and minority events are being offered protection for their brands in much the same way as the major events. This is all well and good for the event organisers moreover simply because the sponsorship involved less money this does not mean, in itself, that the event's brand is less worthy of protection. But this approach does not take sufficient account of the public interest in allowing certain people, possibly even traders, to make associations with such a brand. Intellectual property law has always had at its heart the balance of interests between the right holder and the public. Yet the justification for granting these pervasive rights is the expense and cultural importance of the major sporting events. It does not seem that sufficient consideration has been given to the appropriate threshold for protection. At some point it has to be possible to say: No, this event does not deserve protection.[28]

We need to, similarly, consider just exactly what it is that has always been at the heart of intellectual property laws, as we see how recent legislation in respect of mega-events has attempted to expand protection to 'intellectual property' not traditionally recognised as such and protected by the law. Before I embark on an examination of the traditional theoretical and/or philosophical underpinnings of IP laws, I will briefly examine the ways and extent to which modern mega-event commercial rights protection goes beyond IP law. The following two sections will examine, first, the possibility of mega-events constituting a 'special case' deserving of recognition of a special form of IP right (with relaxed requirements for its establishment, discrete from the requirements of eligibility for other IP rights), and, second, the extension of traditional IP law by means of specific provisions of the *sui generis* event legislation which we encountered in the previous chapter's discussion of the various recent and future mega-event host jurisdictions.

---

[27] Wilf 1999.

[28] Johnson 2008, p. 29.

5.2 Do Event Organisers Enjoy a Special IP Right in the Name of Their Event?

Elsewhere in the earlier chapters, I have referred to the IP rights that vest in event organisers and their official sponsors. These include, primarily, registered trademarks and copyright in intellectual property ranging from event logos, symbols and slogans, to mascots and event anthems. When it comes to combating ambush marketing by means of such IP rights, event organisers and sponsors may have a variety of legal remedies available. For example, when it comes to registered trademarks, an ambusher's activity may conceivably open it up to potential liability through straightforward trademark infringement claims, or to claims of dilution of a mark or of false advertising (compare section 43 of the Lanham Act in the United States, as discussed in Sect. 4.4.10 in Chap. 4).

Apart from these and other IP rights, which are uncontroversial and relatively unproblematic for the relevant rights holders to enforce provided they have done their homework (e.g. have attended to applications for registration of marks, for example, well in advance of the event) and are willing to incur the costs of litigation (in financial terms as well as in potential negative publicity). In recent years, however, event organisers have increasingly been demanding something more, and more event-specific, in line with the trend to claim property rights and 'ownership' of their events. The organisers have started to claim the existence of, and protection for, what has been referred to as 'event marks'. While FIFA, for example, enjoys IP rights to its name, it has for the past decade started to claim such IP rights to the name of its event or of terms or combinations of words which conjure up its event (for example, 'FIFA World Cup', or 'World Cup 2010', or 'South Africa 2010'). At the time of writing FIFA's website actually lists (or refers to) its event marks as 'assets' of the organisation.[29]

Such calls have thus far had mixed success amongst law-makers and before the courts, but we need to consider such developments in the process of examining the IP law implications of mega-events rights protection as established by the law in

---

[29] 'The world of FIFA's Marketing Assets and Programmes is manifold. For the most part it includes the creation and marketing of all FIFA Marks, of which the Event Marks for the various FIFA tournaments are developed in cooperation with the respective Local Organising Committee. In particular, these are the Official Trophies, Official Mascots, Official Emblems, Official Posters and related programmes (e.g. Fan Fest, Trophy Tours).'—at http://www.fifa.com/aboutfifa/marketing/marketing/fifaassets/index.html

The England and Wales Cricket Board (EWCB), who devised the modern 'Twenty20' format of cricket and the name, registered the name as a trademark, although deciding (apparently for reasons of financial constraint), to limit their rights to the European Union. They therefore only filed a U.K. trademark application and a CTM application for the trademark Twenty20. As one observer commented tongue-in-cheek (in light of cricket's level of popularity in Europe): 'No doubt, when the French version of the game takes off in France and the Bulgarian version is the talk of Sofia, the royalties will begin to roll in'—see http://www.jenkins.eu/mym-autumn-2008/snippets.asp.

the various jurisdictions and, more specifically, by means of the *sui generis* event legislation.

5.2.1 What is an 'Event Mark'?

German jurist Karl-Heinz Fezer[30] argues that recognition should be given to an 'event mark', as a special mark in respect of an event that is registrable independently of other trademarks. In effect, Fezer argues that event marks should be recognised as a new category of trademark (and one with different registration requirements—see below), which would negate the need for special protection of commercial rights to events related to e.g. event logos, symbols and names by means of the *sui generis* legislation such as we have encountered in the previous chapter. An example would be registration of an event mark in the form of 'Brazil 2014' or 'World Cup 2010', distinct from other FIFA marks or the FIFA name or logo itself. Or compare the attempts by the organising committee for the 2012 London Olympic Games to register the number '2012' as a trademark (which was apparently abandoned after the UK Trademark Office indicated that that they were likely to refuse the application on the ground that the mark lacked distinctiveness (i.e. is 'generic').[31]

An 'event mark' may be understood as any 'signal used to identify an event, a presentation and/or a performance, in which the event organizer has the interest to use (and protect) the trademark in connection with a large number of products and services'.[32] Fezer suggests that such an event mark should be recognised in two possible forms, namely a product event mark (or *Veranstaltungswarenmarken*) and a service event mark (or *Veranstaltungsdienstleistungsmarken*). The first is also referred to as a 'merchandising mark', and the second as a 'sponsoring mark'.[33] Service event marks identify services related to the 'organization, performance, execution, development and partial financing' of the event (i.e. are 'sponsoring marks', while product event marks are used to identify merchandising products related to the event (i.e. 'merchandising marks'). According to Fezer, these are two completely different forms of marks. Sponsoring (and the use of the sponsoring mark) serves as an instrument for the financing of a product of the event organizer through sponsors (by means of sponsoring agreements), while merchandising marks serve to identify products of the event organizer itself. Merchandising marks identify the origin of the products as originating from the event organizer

---

30 Fezer 2003, 2007. My discussion of Fezer's writing in the text relies on discussion of it by Lundgren 2010.

31 See Blackshaw 2010.

32 Trautmann, K 'Die eventmarke—Markenschutz von sponsoring und merchandising' *Hartung-Gorre Verlag*, Konstanz (2008) 85—as quoted by Lundgren 2010, p. 42.

33 See Lundgren 2010, pp. 41–42.

itself, while sponsoring marks are used to signify to the public the sponsorship role and affiliation of official partners of the event.[34] According to Fezer, sponsoring marks would serve to individualise the services of organisation and financing of an event. Such events' organisation service marks (or *allgemeine Veranstaltungsdienstleistungsmarke*) identify an organisational commercial activity. The organisation and financing of an event are protectable services as such (in terms of class 41 of the Nice international trademark classification) and, therefore, would be entitled to protection through registration.[35] Fezer draws a parallel between service (sponsoring) event marks and the general commercialisation of products mark (*Handelsdienstleistungsmarke*),[36] in light of the recognition by the European Court of Justice that the concept of 'services' in respect of registration of a trademark covers services provided in connection with retail trade in goods.[37] Fezer argues that, similar to the general commercialisation of products mark, sponsoring marks should be deemed as registrable to identify services of 'organization and financing of events'.[38]

Fezer's suggested new category of trademark has, however, been received with less than enthusiasm. Lundgren[39] succinctly explains both Fezer's understanding of the basis for registrability of his suggested new form of mark as well as the criticism of other commentators which Fezer's 'event mark' has evoked.

Fezer's suggested mark should be evaluated with due regard for the traditional nature, and functions, of a trademark. Trademarks are a form of intellectual property that is distinct from the other IP rights, such as patents, trade secrets and copyright. These latter rights are designed to protect and/or reward something new, inventive or creative (whether in the form of an idea, a physical creation or an expression). By contrast, a trademark does not 'depend upon novelty, invention, discovery or any work of the brain… [and] requires no fancy or imagination, no genius, no laborious thought'.[40] Trademark protection is awarded merely to those who were the first to use a distinctive mark in commerce.[41] The traditional functions of a trademark (as accepted in the American context and in other systems) are the following:

(1) to identify one seller's goods and distinguish them from goods sold by others;
(2) to signify that all goods bearing the trademark come from a single, albeit anonymous, source;

---

[34] Fezer as discussed by Lundgren 2010, pp. 42–43.

[35] Lundgren 2010, p. 43.

[36] Ibid.

[37] *Praktiker Bau-und Heimwerkermarkte AG v Deutsches Patent und Markenamt* C418/02 (7 July 2005).

[38] Lundgren 2010, p. 44.

[39] Lundgren 2010, p. 50 *et seq*.

[40] As observed in the *Trade-Mark Cases* 100 U.S. 82, 93–94 (1879), quoted in Merges et al. 2003, p. 530.

[41] Ibid.

(3) to signify that all goods bearing the trademark are of an equal level of quality; and
(4) as a prime instrument in advertising and selling of goods.[42]

The source origin function is viewed as central to the function of a trademark (compare the definition of a trademark in the federal trademark statute, the Lanham Act[43]), while the signifying of the quality of a product or service by reference to a trademark has in recent years assumed a more important role.[44] Lundgren observes that German law recognises much the same functions as in US trademark law, although it places more emphasis on the trademark owner's rights in relation to the traditional source-identifying function. He quotes a German Federal Constitutional Court decision of 1979 which noted that 'marks do not merely denominate the source of a product, but are an "expression of an entrepreneur's achievement motivation"',[45] and, similarly, the 11th recital of the EU Trademarks Directive[46] provides that the function of trademarks is 'in particular, to guarantee the trademark as an indication of origin' (without excluding other possible functions).

Lundgren explains Fezer's understanding of trademark functions as going beyond the traditional origin function, which serves to differentiate products from different companies in the market, and to include the guarantee of quality and advertising functions as legally protected functions of a mark. As a symbol of communication of a commercial activity, the trademark not only identifies the products of a given trademark owner, but also confirms the authenticity of that product as belonging to a certain supplier. In this way, the reasoning goes that event marks identify the commercial activity of the event's organizer, and the main function of an event mark is to convey information to consumers about the organisation and financing of the event. Through sponsorship agreements the event organizer authorises and legitimates its sponsors to communicate to the public their contribution to the financing of the event, as 'official sponsors' or commercial

---

42 McCarthy, J Thomas *McCarthy on Trademarks and Unfair Competition* § 2:10 (2d ed.) 1984 at 104 (as referred to by Lundgren 2010, p. 44).

43 Section 45 of the Lanham Act provides as follows:
'The term "trademark" includes any word, name, symbol, or device, or any combination thereof
(1) used by a person, or
(2) which a person has a bona fide intention to use in commerce and applies to register on the principal register established by this Act;
to identify and distinguish his or her goods, including a unique product, from those manufactured or sold by others and to indicate the source of the goods, even if that source is unknown.'

44 Although recent developments in American trademark law such as the enactment of the Trademark Law Revision Act, 1988 and the Federal Trademark Dilution Act, 1995 illustrate the trademark law's struggle with making necessary adjustments, and accepting a deviation from the consumer confusion model—see Rayle 2000.

45 Lundgren 2010, p. 45.

46 First Council Directive 89/104/EEC, of 21 December 1988.

partners.[47] This approach, accordingly, seems to focus less on the source of origin function of an event mark (the use of an event mark by a sponsor, either to identify goods produced by him, or services offered by him, would not necessarily be intended to identify the origin of the goods or services as having been produced or offered by him) and more on the guarantee of quality function (i.e. as a means to guarantee that the goods or services identified by the event mark are recognised as products of merchandising and sponsoring). As Lundgren explains, in a natural competition system such as that of the European Union, companies must be in a position to attract consumers by means of the quality of its products and services, which is only possible through trademarks which communicate a message to consumers about the quality and authenticity of such products and services.[48] Fezer's justification for the special event mark is summarised as follows with reference to European trademark case law[49]:

> The recognition of event marks as a new form of protection of the efforts dispensed in the organization, financing and realization of an event would, therefore, find harbour in the wider understanding of the origin function in the jurisprudence of the European Court of Justice and the German Federal Supreme Court… [A]ccording to Fezer, both the European Court of Justice and the German Federal Supreme Court, recognize the advertising function as one of the core functions of trademarks, which would be another argument in favour of the registrability of event marks. The European case law recognizes the right of trademark owners to protect the *luxury image* and high reputation of their products. In the *Dior* decision, for example, the European Court of Justice recognized a "general advertising right of distributors of branded goods". In the *BMW* decision, it was expressly recognized that the owner of a trademark cannot restrict a third party from making use of the brand to communicate to the public services of repair or maintenance of the product, but "as long as the mark is not used in a way to imply that there is a commercial relation between the trademark owner and the third party", in other words, that the third party is an authorized representative of the trademark owner. In the realm of event marks, this advertising function would serve as means for the sponsors to identify and communicate their sponsoring efforts. Thus, if the event mark is used by non-official sponsors, the public might be led to think that there is some sort of relation between the event organizer, as owner of the event mark, and that company (non-sponsor), what is certainly not desirable, since it might create a risk of false association to consumers and, therefore, negatively affect the enormous investments made by the official sponsors.[50]

I believe that it would not be inapt to compare Fezer's conception of an 'event mark' as explained above to the development in (*inter alia*) American law to recognise a new meaning for trademarks. This is especially relevant in respect of so-called 'merchandising rights' (which, not surprisingly, have featured prominently in the sports context):

---

[47] Lundgren 2010, pp. 46–47.

[48] Ibid.

[49] In the *Dior* case (ECJ, Rs. C-337/95, Slg. 1997, I-6013, GRUR Int. 1998, 140—*Dior/Evora*) and the *BMW* case (ECJ. Rs. C-63/97, Slg. 1999, I-0905, GRUR Int. 1999, 438—*BMW*).

[50] Lundgren 2010, pp. 47–48.

> [T]here are a limited series of cases in which trademarks themselves have clearly become the valuable commodities. Sports team logos are obvious examples, as is the Nike "swoosh." People buy products like hats and tee-shirts because they have the logo emblazoned on them. This is a rather striking reversal of the normal role of trademark law. Rather than identifying the good with a particular manufacturer, and thereby guaranteeing its quality, the identifier is itself the product. There is no reason to think that the Dallas Cowboys (or their licensee, who may not be identified at all) manufacture particularly high-quality hats, or even hats of constant quality. Rather, the logo stands alone as a thing that customers value in and of itself. Traditional trademark theory has a tough time dealing with this use of trademarks. If the goals of trademark law are to prevent consumer confusion, or to maintain product quality standards, there is no particular reason to give trademark owners the right to control such merchandising of their marks unless consumers in fact view the mark as an identifier of source… But at least some of the cases that have been decided do appear to give trademark owners of sports logos an exclusive "merchandising right". [T]here is no question that an enormous amount of licensing activity proceeds on the *assumption* that they have such a right. The effect of such a merchandising right is to give trademark "owners" something they have never traditionally had: the right to control the use of the mark in totally unrelated circumstances.[51]

I would suggest that Fezer's event mark raises similar concerns regarding the proper role and function of trademarks. If special protection is granted to FIFA in respect of e.g. the term 'FIFA 2014', as a special trademark with discrete registration requirements, such protection would appear to be based on a conception of the term as identifier of the event as the product itself (and worthy of protection in its own right).While this is, in my view, sufficiently problematic, one must also remember that such protection for generic terms (such as 'South Africa 2010' or 'World Cup') also hold wider free speech and competition implications. Furthermore, I would suggest that Fezer's event mark raises similar issues as to the development of a 'doctrine' of merchandising rights distinct from a requirement of consumer confusion as to sponsorship or affiliation (which I will discuss in Chap. 8 when examining 'association rights' to mega-events), which may be problematic in respect of traditional notions of the role and functions of trademarks:

> [A]t least some courts have taken the merchandising right so far as to conclude that "consumer confusion" may occur where consumers are not in fact confused about the relationship between the two products, but nonetheless believe that the defendant might have needed a license to use the mark. This right stems not from the traditional rationales for trademark protection, but from a sense of trademarks (or sports logos, at least) as valuable things that can be owned in and of themselves. In these cases, trademark law is used to assert exclusive ownership rights over any commercial use of the mark in question, whether or not the use is "trademark use" or is likely to cause confusion as to the source. Merchandising rights divorce trademarks from the goods they supposedly advertise and therefore from trademark theory as well.[52]

Criticism of Fezer's suggested event mark by other commentators centres on its differentiation of such a special mark from other trademarks, generally, in respect

---

[51] Lemley 1999, pp. 1706–1707.

[52] Ibid. 1707–1708.

of the requirements for registration of the mark, as well as the potential anti-competitive effects of recognition of such a concept.

The first point of criticism relates to the lack of distinctiveness of such event marks, e.g. 'World Cup 2014'. It is settled law that a trademark must be distinctive, so that consumers can identify the mark in relation to products or services and must be able to recognise the origin of the product or service and link it to a certain source. Section 8(2) of the German Trademark Act, for example, lists as an absolute ground for refusal of registration of a mark any mark which is 'devoid of any distinctive character as to the goods or services', and this requirement is mirrored in the EU regulations on the Community Trademark.[53] Similarly, the definition of both a trademark and a service mark in terms of section 45 of the Lanham Act (in the United States) requires the ability for the mark to identify and distinguish the relevant goods or services from the goods manufactured or sold or the services provides by others [i.e. a mark will be distinctive if it is either inherently distinctive, or has acquired distinctiveness through secondary meaning (it has become associated with a single source by the public)]. As Lundgren points out, critics of Fezer's event mark argue that such marks lack distinctiveness (even if the understanding of indication of origin is interpreted in a broader sense, taking into account the dynamic nature of transactions in the modern economy and the extent to which trademarks are assigned nowadays, the owner of the trademark must still at least be considered responsible for the quality of the goods or services which are identified by the mark.[54] It could be argued that, specifically in respect of event marks, such as FIFA's contentious 'Fussball WM 2006' and 'WM 2006' (see the discussion in Sect. 5.2.2 below), the capability of the mark to indicate commercial origin may be minimal compared to its primary capacity of evoking the event as such.[55]

Apart from a lack of distinctiveness, critics of Fezer's event mark also view it to be too descriptive in nature to be capable of registration. It is also settled law that marks that are merely descriptive of the goods or services in conjunction with which it is used are not capable of registration, primarily because such registration would unduly trammel the rights and freedoms of persons other than the mark's proprietor. Such a requirement is likewise found in the German Trademark Act,[56]

---

[53] See Article 7 of the Council Regulation (EC) No. 207/2009 (26 February 2009).

[54] Lundgren 2010, pp. 50–51

[55] Kur 2008, p. 204—as referred to by Lundgren 2010, p. 51.

[56] See Article 8(2) Item 2, which prohibits the registration of 'trademarks which consist exclusively of signs or indications which may serve, in trade, to designate the kind, quality, quantity, intended purpose, value, geographical origin, the time of production of the goods or of the rendering of the services, or to designate other characteristics of the goods or services.'

EU trademark law[57] and the Lanham Act.[58] Lundgren explains that criticism of Fezer's event mark on the basis of its descriptiveness relates to the absolute prohibition of registration of descriptive marks which is based on the public interest to keep those marks free for use by anyone. The grant of an exclusive right over a descriptive mark to a certain party could lead to negative restrictions on competition, and it may be argued that if exclusive protection is granted to marks, such as 'WM 2006' or 'World Cup 2014', etc., other organizers of world cups in the relevant year would not be able to make use of those signs, a patently unfair scenario.[59]

A final basis for criticism of the concept of an event mark relates to the potential anti-competitive effect of such a creature. Lundgren refers to the fact that this is an important consideration, not only in respect of the availability of terms such as 'World Cup' in the sporting context (i.e. the fact, as referred to above, that other event organisers in sports such as rugby union, cricket, golf and field hockey, to name a few, have consistently used this term for their world championships), but in terms of more general principles of IP law. An important consideration for both courts and registering authorities in the European context is found in a trademark doctrine from German law which has found its way into the jurisprudence of the ECJ (even though the ECJ has indicated that its application should be more limited than its traditional application in German law[60]). This is the 'public interest' doctrine (sometimes described as 'the need to keep free', or 'doctrine of availability', or *Freihaltebedürfnis* in German law). This doctrine relates to an objection against providing a right of exclusive use over something that it would be against the public interest to monopolise. In practise, it could be applied in cases of terms which do not satisfy the distinctiveness requirement for a trademark but have been consistently used to such an extent and for such a long period by a certain firm that it acquires distinctiveness in respect of such firm's product or service

[57] See Article 7(1)(c) of the provisions on the Community Trademark. In the 'Baby-Dry' case of *Procter & Gamble Co. v OHIM* Case 393/99 the ECJ examined the importance of individual words or aspects of a trademark in determining whether it is descriptive, and found that what was important was the overall effect of the mark and not the components of its make-up. The court held that the words Baby and Dry in that case were a 'lexical invention bestowing distinctive power on the mark so formed'.

[58] Section 2(e) of the Lanham Act (15 U.S.C. §1052) allows for the refusal of registration of a mark which (1) when used on or in connection with the goods of the applicant is merely descriptive or deceptively misdescriptive of them, (2) when used on or in connection with the goods of the applicant is primarily geographically descriptive of them, except as indications of regional origin may be registrable under section 4, (3) when used on or in connection with the goods of the applicant is primarily geographically deceptively misdescriptive of them, (4) is primarily merely a surname, or (5) comprises any matter that, as a whole, is functional.

[59] Lundgren 2010, p. 52.

[60] See the views of Advocate General Ruiz-Jarabo Colomer as expressed in his opinion in C-102/07 *Adidas AG, Adidas Benelux BV v. Marca Mode CV, C&A Nederland CV, H&M Hennes & Mauritz Netherlands BV and Vendex KBB Nederland BV* (delivered on 16 January 2008) at 33–45.

(i.e. it would normally become capable of registration), but where registration would serve to monopolise the use of such term against the public interest (the interest of other traders in commerce). In such cases, a court may refuse to allow the firm to obtain exclusive rights to use the term, or a registering authority could refuse to register the mark and thus to grant a monopoly in the use of the term which would be against the public interest. The ECJ has held that this doctrine or criterion is only to be used in the process of determining whether a mark is descriptive and not in the process of determining distinctiveness (i.e. distinctiveness depends solely on consumer perception).[61] Lundgren quotes Kur[62] as observing that 'granting an exclusive right in a term referring to an immensely popular event implies a huge competitive advantage to the person or entity owning that right, and thus it raises misgivings under the aspect of the public interest in keeping such signs free for general use'. The author concludes:

> The question is whether such potential restriction of competition would be justified in order to protect the legitimate interests of organizers of major events. At a first glance, from a pure trademark perspective, it seems that the negative effects of granting such exclusive rights would overcome the positive effects, especially when one thinks that event organizers and sponsors would still be able to guarantee reasonable exclusivity and protection over the reputation of their events, through the use of official logos and expressions like "official sponsors". If non-sponsors would make use of official logos or misleading expressions, there is little doubt that they would be compelled to stop such practice under both trademark and unfair competition legal provisions.[63]

Finally, Lundgren also mentions that trademark registrations are renewable for an indefinite period and that lenient registration requirements, such as those proposed by Fezer could lead to undesirable situations, with limited remedies to correct them, and ultimately the establishment of 'an eternal monopoly right over a term' which should be kept free for use by all interested parties.[64]

It appears that there are significant objections to the recognition, in legal theory, of a special 'event mark'. The German Federal Supreme Court (*Bundesgerichtshof*) rejected the creation of a new registration category to accommodate 'event marks' in its April 2006 judgment in the *FIFA v Ferrero* case concerning FIFA's 'Fussball WM 2006' trademark[65] (see the discussion in the section that follows in the text below). The court expressly stated that no lower registration requirements should be applied to this type of mark, which would need to meet the same requirements as any ordinary marks in terms of § 3 and § 8 of the German Trademark Act in order to be eligible for registration.

---

[61] Case C-329/02 P: *SAT.1 SatellitenFernsehen GmbH v Office for Harmonisation in the Internal Market (Trade Marks and Designs) (OHIM)* Judgment of the Court (Second Chamber), 16 September 2004.

[62] Kur 2008, p. 201.

[63] Lundgren 2010, p. 54.

[64] Ibid.

[65] BGH, Beschluss v. 27.04.2006—I ZB 96/05—FUSSBALL WM 2006. MarkenR 2006, 395.

I would add that Lemley's following criticism of an aspect of the process of 'propertizing' trademarks in American law (and which should ring a bell with anyone who has been following developments in recent years regarding domain name registrations and cyber-squatting) is germane here to the potential effect of recognising an 'event mark' for FIFA in, say, the term 'Brazil 2014':

> Treating trademarks as property… creates abundant incentives for opportunistic behavior. If trademarks are property, it becomes harder to explain why they do not always belong to whoever grabs them first. The property theory has already led some people to register marks not to be used to identify the source of goods, but solely to lock up the use of the trademarked phrase itself. Thus, one legal entrepreneur has registered "Class of 2000" as a trademark and claims the right to prevent anyone else from selling merchandise bearing the phrase. Another has registered the ubiquitous yellow smiley-face and is collecting money from those who use it. Still another (not the movie producer) claims the exclusive right to sell merchandise with the word "Titanic" on it. Under traditional trademark law, these claims are frivolous. Trademark law protects source identification; it does not allow people to own designs or phrases outright and to prevent their use regardless of context. Get a copyright, if you can; if not, too bad. But as trademarks continue to be treated as property, it becomes harder and harder to come up with a convincing reason why one should not be allowed to register "Class of 2000" or the smiley-face and prevent anyone else from using them without a license.[66]

The relevant considerations in evaluating a call for special IP protection for organisers in the form of an 'event mark' are similar to those referred to in the ambush marketing literature in criticism of aspects of the strong *sui generis* event legislation, specifically also in respect of the new statutory creation of 'association rights' to some events, and these aspects (such as the competition implications of event rights protection) will be considered in more detail in the later chapters. For present purposes, I will conclude discussion of Fezer's event mark with reference to the following words of Mark Lemley (and I will suggest that what is said about the Dallas Cowboys football franchise is equally apt in the context of FIFA or other mega-event organisers' claims to special protection for their 'event marks'):

> The "Dallas Cowboys" trademark identifies a football team. The team can of course use trademark law to prevent competition by another team using the same name or even to prevent consumer confusion as to affiliation or sponsorship. But when trademark law reaches beyond that—when it precludes a haberdasher from selling a hat with the "Cowboys" logo, even when the circumstances preclude a finding of consumer confusion—it has left its theoretical foundations. The haberdasher is not using the "Cowboys" logo as a trademark; she is simply reproducing it. Consumers are not confused, at least assuming she uses an appropriate disclaimer and makes no false reference to an "official licenced NFL product." Nor can the trademark owner make a plausible case that this competing sale will weaken the connection between the mark and the team. True, the Cowboys might make less money than they would if trademarks were absolute property

[66] Lemley 1999, pp. 1696–1697.

> rights, and they might argue that this "discourages investment." But so what? The point of trademark law has never been to maximize profits for trademark owners at the expense of competitors and consumers. And the investment at issue in these cases is *not* investment in the quality of the underlying product (the team), but in merchandising the brand itself.[67]

While the 'event mark' currently appears to be a nonentity in terms of legal recognition as a 'special' form of IP right (or, at least, a trademark with special registration requirements), one might need to watch future developments closely. I am not in favour of the creation of 'new' IP rights in cases where the would-be proprietors lobby for adaptation or wholesale revamping of the law in order to address perceived threats to new and apparently ever-expanding opportunities for commercial exploitation. The following was observed about a similar trend in the context of 'privately legislated intellectual property rights' to information (with reference to e.g. database rights) in the American context, which sentiments I view to be apt in the current context of calls by event organisers for a 'new' type of mark worthy of legal protection:

> [T]oday's most commercially valuable information goods often fit imperfectly within the classical patent and copyright paradigms, a development that prods both courts and legislators to devise ad hoc means of avoiding a perceived threat of market failure. One response is to tinker with the existing doctrinal structures of these paradigms to accommodate information goods that have little, or nothing, in common with "inventions" or "works of authorship" in the traditional and ordinary sense. A second, and now perhaps dominant, response is to enact new, hybrid intellectual property rights, based on modified patent and copyright principles, to protect deviant subject matter that cannot meet either the "nonobviousness" test of eligibility in patent law or the "originality" eligibility test in copyright law. These two responses introduce a powerful, high-protectionist tilt into the world-wide intellectual property system, which threatens to undermine the balance between incentives to create and free competition that has traditionally governed investment and technical innovation in the US economy. Whether the new balance will adequately stimulate the development of the information economy… or merely substitute a chronic and socially costly state of overprotection for a perceived risk of chronic underprotection… remains to be seen.[68]

In Chap. 10 I shall mention recent developments in certain jurisdictions (notably France) in the recognition of a 'sports event organiser's right', which has been particularly relevant in the field of sports betting and the apparent realisation by sports governing bodies and event organisers that this practise (which has experienced phenomenal growth in recent years) constitutes an extremely lucrative potential new revenue stream. Such developments may turn out to be relevant to any future consideration of potential recognition of a special 'event mark' for the organisers.

---

67 Ibid. 1708.

68 Reichmann and Franklin 1999, pp. 890–891.

5.2.2 Sepp Blatter and the Chocolate Factory

I referred, in Chap. 2, to the tendency of event organisers, when faced with potential ambush marketing, to focus their enforcement efforts through the means of litigation filed against 'small players' (i.e. to avoid taking legal action against large corporations whom the organisers might claim are ambushing their events, but who also have the deep pockets to defend such legal action). Recent years have seen 'name and shame' campaigns instituted against large corporate 'ambushers' as opposed to undoubtedly expensive litigation against the smaller offenders. It might be worth noting that, in the rare cases where event organisers have sued large corporations for alleged ambushing (compare Pepsi-Cola in Canada, the Phillips electronics corporation in India and Telecom New Zealand in New Zealand), the outcomes of such law suits have gone against the organisers. There may be a range of reasons for the apparent preference to target small fry, of which fear of adverse judgments may only be one.[69] But the cynic might argue that the most plausible is that such potential defendants are more likely to cave under the threats of financial ruin (and that reports of settlements or court orders against these persons can have a snow-ball PR effect to deter other 'ambushers'). And there is some irony in this:

> A law that is potentially unconstitutional either because it is outside the jurisdiction of the enacting government or because it violates rights to freedom of expression may be challenged on these grounds. Even without grounds for a constitutional challenge, it is also possible to argue that the allegedly offending conduct is not captured by the terms of the law. Yet in order to make these arguments in court, it is necessary to be able to afford the high cost of legal counsel and litigation. These costs are not easily affordable by small or even mid-sized businesses, although they may well be a worthwhile cost of doing business for a large company hoping to benefit substantially from a high profile advertising campaign during the peak of public interest in the major event. The consequence may be that small and mid-sized businesses who receive cease and desist letters with respect to conduct which may or may not be ambush marketing, will be more likely to cease and desist from the activity because they are not in a position to defend themselves. Ironically, these companies may be the ones that the public would be least likely to expect to be Olympic sponsors as they are unlikely to be in direct competition with Olympic sponsors… It is the conduct of large companies that compete with existing sponsors that is likely to have the greatest impact on event sponsors; yet these companies are in the best position to seek legal advice to circumvent or to challenge laws aimed at restricting ambush marketing.[70]

Such threatened (and real) legal action by event organisers or sponsors may, however, be little more than a manifestation of a blanket attempt to stifle competition, something that is known in trademark circles in the United States as the use of 'strike suits'. While not wishing to make a bald allegation and ascribe such a devious intention to football's governing body, the following description must

[69] See, e.g., McKelvey 2006, p. 119.

[70] Ellis et al. 2011, p. 305.

surely sound familiar to lawyers and those who have followed developments in respect of FIFA's rights protection programmes for its recent World Cup events (a December 2010 report by two Brazilian commentators observed that it was reported that FIFA has brought 2,500 lawsuits in the past 3 years to protect the 'World Cup' mark[71]):

> In the normal course of conduct, the trademark holder sends a cease-and-desist letter to an offending user of a mark and objects to that usage. If the other party ignores the letter or responds that it will not cease use, an infringement or dilution lawsuit may result. This is the normal, rational course of conduct in trademark litigation. Today, trademark holders are using this course of conduct to expand their trademark rights, not just to object to truly objectionable uses. That is, some trademark holders send thousands of cease-and-desist letters to the point that there are now "sample" cease-and-desist letters available on the internet. These cease-and-desist letters are followed by hundreds of trademark infringement filings. These cases are almost never prosecuted to a conclusion on their merits. In fact, if prosecuted to a trial on their merits, the trademark holder/plaintiff would likely lose because they are not very meritorious claims. This conduct is referred to as a "strike suit." These lawsuits and, in the trademark context, cease-and-desist letters have a different objective than to merely stop the use or conduct of the would-be defendant. Their objective is to raise the cost of market entrance or continuation for the competitor.[72]

A case in point may be the rather Dickensian matter of Cape Town businessman Grant Abrahamse. Abrahamse, when reportedly attempting to settle claims by FIFA of ambush marketing in respect of his 'vuvuzela' registered keychain design in the face of threats of legal action which allegedly had his 5-year-old daughter in tears over the conduct of FIFA's lawyers, was reportedly presented with an account for a licensing fee (payable in advance) of ZAR 250,000 per annum—roughly USD 30,000—and for 50% of the proceeds from each of the trinkets sold, as well as an account for FIFA's legal fees (allegedly totalling ZAR 175,000 at the time). To be fair, though, FIFA has defended itself against allegations relating to its David versus Goliath jousting in this case by pointing out that 'unlike other countries, the laws of South Africa do not allow for [invalidation actions for cancellation of design registrations] to be heard at the local patent office—the High Court is the only forum to hear such cases'.[73] To add insult to injury, FIFA withdrew its case[74] against Abrahamse's business in June 2011 and obtained a court order that each party should pay their own costs. This gentleman's involuntary dealings with FIFA have by all accounts left him considerably out of pocket, and without an opportunity to vindicate his new-found reputation as an 'ambush marketer'.

---

[71] Lopes, T C & Lima, E L 'Ambush marketing in times of World Cup and Olympic Games' *IP Frontline* 21 December 2010—available online at the time of writing at http://www.ipfrontline.com/depts/article.aspx?id=24693&deptid=3#.

[72] Port 2008, p. 4.

[73] An unnamed FIFA source as quoted in a report in *World Intellectual Property Review* January/February 2010 at 10.

[74] *Federation Internationale de Football Associations (FIFA) v Executive African Trading (EAT) CC* Case No. 52308/07, Gauteng North High Court.

However, as mentioned, the apparent strong-arm tendency in focusing on 'soft' targets for legal action might be attributable to realisation of the tenuous nature of some of the organisers' claims of rights to events and of a fear of adverse findings by domestic courts (compare, for example, unsuccessful ambush marketing litigation as referred to above in jurisdictions such as Canada,[75] India[76] and New Zealand[77]). An organisation such as FIFA might, after all, simply sit back and concentrate on its bottom line, secure in the strength of perceptions regarding its moral (or legal) high ground, if nothing more:

> By and large, it is understood that FIFA is relatively happy with the way in which it could control marketing activity that took place in South Africa prior to and during the [2010 FIFA] World Cup. Although the [South African ambush marketing] legislation was not fully or properly tested by the courts, this played into FIFA's hands: the uncertainty as to how the courts would interpret other marketing activities allowed FIFA to scare potential ambush marketers into submission through the dispatch of strongly worded yet cost-effective letters of demand... South Africa's ambush marketing laws are much stricter than those of any other host nation, but unfortunately were not fully tested before the courts to see whether they would stand up to rigorous challenge. In this sense, FIFA may have done well to stay away from the courts, as it can now hold up the South African laws as an example of the types of measures and legislation it can expect of proposed future host nations. By all accounts, the proposed Brazilian laws on ambush marketing [for the 2014 FIFA World Cup and the 2016 Rio Olympic Games] are equally strict, if not more so, than those in force in South Africa.[78]

It is been observed that lawyers found it significant that FIFA at the 2010 World Cup in South Africa came down so heavily on the 'Bavaria girls' (*a la* the orange dress stunt) but left Nike (*a la* the huge and undoubtedly expensive *Write the Future* campaign) alone, as Nike's campaign arguably presented a much more obvious challenge and FIFA, in any event, controlled match coverage so could have avoided any images of the women, who were wearing branding so subtle as to be invisible except up close,[79] to be broadcast.

The dangers for event organisers are well illustrated by FIFA's well-known and protracted spat with the German subsidiary of Italian confectionery company Ferrero (proprietor of brands such as Ferrero Rocher, Kinder and Tic Tac), Ferrero GmbH, where FIFA appeared to bite off more than it could chew.[80]

FIFA had prior to its World Cup event in Germany in 2006 registered a number of marks, primarily 'WM 2006' and 'Fussball WM 2006', both nationally in Germany as trademarks and as community trademarks at European level ('WM' is a common abbreviation of *Weltmeisterschaft* (the German word for 'world

---

[75] The *National Hockey League v Pepsi-Cola Canada* case, discussed elsewhere.

[76] See the *ICC Development v Phillips & Arvee* case, discussed elsewhere.

[77] See the *New Zealand Telecom* case, discussed elsewhere.

[78] Haman and Marriott 2010, p. 77.

[79] See the report entitled 'Sporting Chance', available on the web site of the International Bar Association at http://www.ibanet.org/Article/Detail.aspx?ArticleUid=1a43e1e6-e207-4aa7-a21f-6d0435bba7e7

[80] See, generally, Schatte 2009.

championships') and 'Fussball' means 'football'). The registrations covered a wide range of goods and services (in the region of 850) in 36 different classes, including many typical merchandising products. This is tame compared to pharmaceutical giant Pfizer, which reportedly has approximately 40 000 live trademarks, but it is still an impressive number for a sports governing body. Event organisers, of course, do not register trademarks because they wish to produce and market event-related goods themselves (although this may be the case). They do so in order to enable them to licence the use of the mark by others, which is why Johnson advises that one of the first things an event organiser should do when a new event has been scheduled is to ensure that trademark applications have been made in respect of those marks which might have commercial value to official sponsors or ambush marketers.[81] FIFA has been extremely active in this regard, and in seeking to protect such registered marks:

> In the years leading up to the 2006 World Cup, FIFA fought for exclusivity for its own trademarks, logos and official mascot, and has sought to protect its intellectual property as well as the rights of its official sponsors. Indeed, FIFA allotted over $1.5 million for registering and enforcing these marks and other IP rights, and has established close relationships with government customs authorities around the world to protect and enforce its trademarks. FIFA's legal team was very active in the registration and protection of its own official World Cup trademarks. However, despite the registration of several word marks, six official emblems, three official event titles, three official mascot poses, one logo and one image of a trophy, recent case law has since limited FIFA's monopoly on World Cup-related marks.[82]

Some of FIFA's registrations were rather surprising (as observed by one blogger on the IPKat website), and are indicative of the 'catch-all' approach of event organisers, generally, in respect of attempts to protect all conceivable (and some, inconceivable) potential avenues for commercial exploitation of their brands[83]:

Class 5—feminine hygienic products; fungicides, herbicides; deodorants for non-personal use.
Class 8—electric or non-electric razors, including razor blades; depilatory devices; tweezers; curling tongs; kitchen scissors.
Class 10—nursing bottles; condoms.
Class 31—Foodstuff for animals; fresh berries; fresh vegetables; flowers; litter for animals.
Class 34—Matches; lighters; cigarette cases, ashtrays, smoker's articles made of non-precious metal; cigarettes; tobacco.[84]

---

[81] Johnson 2007, p. 15.

[82] Schwab 2006, p. 8.

[83] Kobel 2007, pp. 21–22 refers to the fact that the community trademark 'Olympic Games' has been registered in the 42 existing classes and 'London 2012' was registered in the UK and as a Community trademark in every single class.

[84] The German *Bundesgerichtshof* held (in its decisions of April 27, 2006, I ZB 96/05 and I ZB 97/05) that registration of 'WM 2006' and 'Fussball WM 2006' for 850 products or services was not in bad faith and valid, as it was not made to damage a third party but with a view to protect the trademark in relation to all listed products and services.

FIFA-branded condoms might have been a witty accompaniment to the 'Fick FUFA' t-shirts which were printed as a non-profit venture by an anonymous Cape Town artist during the 2010 FIFA World Cup, in protest of FIFA's alleged monopolisation of all aspects of the tournament in South Africa.

The registration of marks such as the 'WM 2006' mark was part of a revised strategy by FIFA, implemented in 2001, to register broader words marks which do not include the name identifier 'FIFA' in respect of its events.[85] Ferrero GmbH (hereinafter simply 'Ferrero') had also registered similar marks (it had for some years, since 1982, in fact, distributed free collectible stickers with its Hanuta and Duplo chocolate wafers showing players in the German national football team, with a logo that combined a depiction of a football with a reference to the World Cup tournament, including the year it was held). Not surprisingly, FIFA was less than enamoured with the chocolate giant and the matter went to court. The organisation may have been emboldened by early success in another matter regarding the unlicenced sale of souvenir coins bearing the phrase 'WM 2006 Germany' following a 2004 decision from the Hamburg Appeal Court,[86] but FIFA was to find the dispute with Ferrero tough going in later years.

5.2.2.1 The Initial Litigation in Germany

FIFA sued Ferrero in infringement proceedings in respect of its registered marks, and Ferrero launched a counter-attack calling for the cancellation of FIFA's marks, which claims had to be heard by the German Trademark Office. The German Trademark Office revoked both trademarks completely. FIFA appealed the decision to the Federal Patent Court (*Bundespatentgericht*), which reversed the decisions in part. It agreed with the view of the German Trademark Office that the trademarks were not distinctive with regard to goods and services that were closely related to the football championships and the tournament event (not only 'sporting events' in class 41, but for example also media products and goods such as sports shoes). However, with regard to goods and services that had less of a connection the court reversed the decision of the Trademark Office.

FIFA promptly appealed the Federal Patent Court's judgment to the German Federal Supreme Court (the *Bundesgerichtshof*). Lundgren explains the details of

85 Lundgren 2010, p. 19.

86 Case GRUR-RR 2004, 362, where the court found that there was a likelihood of confusion with FIFA's registered mark 'WORLD CUP 2006 GERMANY'. Although the court did not comment on the validity of FIFA's mark, it cautioned that such a phrase might, in some cases, be considered descriptive and therefore not eligible for trademark protection—see Schwab, F 'FIFA's trademark tactics' September/October 2006 *World Trademark Review* 6 at 8.

the *Bundesgerichtshof* judgment[87] in respect of the 'Fussball WM 2006' mark, which I will quote here extensively[88]:

> On April 27, 2006, shortly before the start of the FIFA World Cup in Germany, the German Federal Supreme Court rendered decisions on the validity of trademarks "FUSSBALL WM 2006" and "WM 2006". Regarding trademark "FUSSBALL WM 2006", the Court decided to cancel the entire registration, in relation to all goods and services covered. In the Court's opinion, trademark "FUSSBALL WM 2006" consisted of a common term to identify the happening of the World Cup Soccer in Germany in 2006. Arguably, the public in general was used to the use of such type of sign to identify major sports events like the FIFA World Cup. The term "Fussball WM 2006" was simply referencing a major sporting event and did not imply a message about commercial origin. Moreover, the sign "FUSSBALL WM 2006" was a mere description of the event happening that year in Germany and could not serve as an indication of source (*Herkunftshinweis*). In view of this, the term could not be registered as a trademark, in the terms of § 8 (2) (1) and (2) of the German Trademark Act (very similar to article 7 (b) and (c) of the Community Trademark Regulation—CTMR)... [H]owever, even terms which are considered to be devoid of any distinctive character or considered to be of descriptive nature can become eligible for registration through acquired distinctiveness. This is foreseen in section 8 (3) of the German Trademark Act and article 7 (3) of the Community Trademark Regulation. However, in the matter before the German Federal Supreme Court, this was of no help to the petitioner. FIFA was not able to prove acquired distinctiveness of the term "FUSSBALL WM 2006". According to the Court, only evidence of the fame acquired by trademarks containing the term FIFA or the official logo of the soccer world cup to be held that year in Germany was submitted. In view of this, the argument of "acquired distinctiveness" was promptly rejected by the Court. Following on the grounds to reject FIFA's appeal, the Court stated that even if a broader interpretation of the concept of "indication of source" would be adopted (in accordance with the latest European jurisprudence), the sign "FUSSBALL WM 2006" would still lack distinctive character, since the event organizer (FIFA) did not have responsibility over the quality of the products and services offered under the disputed mark. Considering that products and services bearing the signs "FUSSBALL WM 2006" and "WM 2006" were ultimately manufactured and offered by the official sponsors of the event (which were the only ones entitled to make use of the marks), and not by FIFA, responsibility over them remained vested in the sponsors and not in the event organizer. In fact, this seems to be one of the main reasons why the Court rejected FIFA's claims. A careful reading of the decision suggests that if FIFA would have contractually reserved its right to control and inspect the quality of the products and services offered under the licensed marks, and effectively made use of this right, then the Court might have been more inclined to recognize the fulfilment of the indication of origin requirement. However, this was not the case and FIFA had absolutely no control over the products commercialized under its marks by the official sponsors. Finally, the court rejected the creation of a new registration category to accommodate "event marks" and expressly stated that no lower registration requirements should be applied to this type of marks. Like any other ordinary mark, "event marks" would need to meet the requirements of § 3 and § 8 of the German Trademark Act, in order to be eligible for registration.[89]

---

[87] BGH, Beschluss v. 27.04.2006—I ZB 96/05—FUSSBALL WM 2006. MarkenR 2006, 395.

[88] At the time of writing I was unable to obtain an English language copy of the relevant judgments discussed here. My sincere thanks to Felipe Dannemann Lundgren for permission to reproduce relevant sections from the text of his LL.M thesis as referred to previously.

[89] Lundgren 2010, pp. 20–23.

It may be especially important to note that the court did not consider it decisive that FIFA was the only association that would be organising football world championships in the year 2006 (FIFA had in fact relied on its monopoly, referred to in Chap. 2 and in Chap. 6, in this regard in order to prove that its marks were distinctive). Secondary meaning regarding the marks was not discussed. The Federal Supreme Court examined a survey presented by FIFA, but it did not accept the questionnaire it was based on.

The *Bundesgerichtshof* subsequently (on the same day) delivered judgment[90] in the case regarding the trademark 'WM 2006'. Lundgren explains that its judgment on this mark was practically identical to the 'Fussball WM 2006' decision, both on the grounds and on the wording. The main difference was the Court's finding that in relation to 'WM 2006' the general public's association with the event taking place that year in Germany was not so strong and direct as in the case of the 'Fussball' mark, and it ordered the cancellation of the mark only in relation to certain products and services, which were closely connected with the event itself, and referred the issue back to the German Patent Court to decide in relation to which products protection could be granted. The Court held that the 'WM 2006' mark was eligible for registration to identify products which were not directly and closely connected to the event itself.[91]

Johnson[92] has criticised the German Supreme Court judgment for having apparently considered both a lack of distinctiveness and descriptiveness at the same time, which the author states is not the correct approach.[93] He also believes that the court set a high standard for distinctiveness which does not accord with the views of the European Court of Justice.[94] Johnson also points out that similar event marks have been registered in other jurisdictions, such as the UK (he refers to the 'London 2012' and 'Glasgow 2014'[95] marks—interestingly, the LOCOG had initially attempted to register '2012' as a trademark but abandoned the application after the UK Intellectual Property Office indicated that the application would likely be refused). Although such marks have not been challenged to date in court proceedings, they have not been found to be inherently objectionable. Schwab observes that FIFA did not show specific concern at this unfavourable decision by the *Bundesgerichtshof* (in light of the fact that it had secured Community trade-mark registrations and that German courts had recognised the wording 'WM 2006' as a 'special commercial designation' in Germany), but that the press reported that after the Supreme Court decision some of FIFA's licencees requested a significant reduction of their licence fees as they perceived that there had been damage to

[90] BGH, Beschluss v. 27.04.2006—I ZB 97/05—WM 2006.

[91] Lundgren 2010, pp. 23–24

[92] Johnson 2007, p. 23.

[93] Relying on the authority of Case C329/02 *SAT.1 SatellitenFernsehen GmbH*; and *Linde AG v Deutsches Patent-und Markenamt* (C53/01).

[94] Particularly in the case of *Erpo Mobelwerk* (C63/02).

[95] UK Application No. 2433070, registered 7 November 2007.

their exclusive right to use the marks.[96] I would imagine that was not a good day to be at FIFA House.

5.2.2.2 The Proceedings Before the EU Trademark Authorities

As mentioned, the unfavourable decisions in the German jurisdiction did not have too great an effect on FIFA, as it could still rely on its Community Trademarks. The Office for Harmonization of the Internal Market (OHIM) rejected Ferrero's applications for a revocation of the following marks: 'Germany 2006', World Cup Germany', 'World Cup 2006' and 'WM 2006'. The grounds upon which the registrations were challenged were that the signs in question were descriptive and lacked distinctive character. The Cancellation Division (decisions of the OHIM Cancellation Division in October 2005[97]) found that, even though marks consisting of a year, *simpliciter*, or of a geographical location may not be distinctive or may be descriptive of the goods or services, this did not apply to the relevant marks under consideration. The words 'Germany' and '2006' did not form a grammatically correct expression and as such could not be descriptive of the World Cup event. It was also held that the words do not describe a football championship as no reference to football appears with these words. While the words suggested that something was happening in Germany in 2006 or that a world championship of some nature was to take place in that country in that year, this did not deprive the words of a distinctive character. The media interest in the 2006 World Cup caused the public to connect the relevant event-related marks with FIFA as the tournament organiser.[98]

These decisions were subsequently taken on appeal to the OHIM Board of Appeals, which were all upheld in June 2008.[99] FIFA subsequently (in September 2008) applied for the annulment of the decisions of the First Board of Appeal.[100]

Article 63 of Council Regulation (EC) No 40/94[101] on the Community Trademark provides that the Court of Justice of the EU may act as an appeal body regarding the decisions of the OHIM's Boards of Appeal. FIFA subsequently appealed to the ECJ, but its appeals against the OHIM in the Ferrero cases[102] were ordered (by the president of the Third Chamber, in an order of the general court on 16 December 2010) to be removed from the register, which was duly done in

---

[96] Schwab 2006, p. 9.

[97] Decisions of the Cancellation Division of 28 October 2005—No. 972C 002152817 and No. 969C 002155521.

[98] See the decisions of the OHIM Cancellation Division referred to; Johnson 2007, p. 22.

[99] OHIM Board of Appeals—Cases R 1466/2005-1, R 1467/2005-1, R 1468/2005-1, R 1469/2005-1 and R 1470/2005-1 (20 June 2008).

[100] Cases T-445/08; T-446/08 and T-447/08 (action brought on 29 September 2008).

[101] Of 20 December 1993.

[102] Joined cases T-444/08 to T-448/08.

February 2011. I have (at the time of writing) not been able to ascertain whether these matters have finally been settled between FIFA and Ferrero, but it is assumed that this is indeed the case.[103]

5.2.2.3 FIFA Before the German Courts, Again

The above rulings were, however, not the end of the saga involving these two parties. In an action that mirrored the earlier litigation, FIFA subsequently applied for the cancellation of Ferrero's marks relating to the football World Cup event. Ferrero had, in 2004 and 2005, registered a total of eight words and device marks relating to both the 2006 (Germany) and 2010 (South Africa) instalments of FIFA's franchise. Ferrero also applied to register three additional marks, including the mark 'Südafrika 2010' in reference to the 2010 World Cup.

FIFA sought to cancel Ferrero's World Cup trademark registrations and to secure its agreement to a withdrawal of its pending applications arguing that the confectionery company had no rights to register the marks. FIFA claimed that Ferrero's trademark registrations and applications infringed its earlier rights and constituted an infringement of German unfair competition law. Birgit Clark[104] explains the unfolding of this matter and its eventual culmination in a November 2009 German Federal Supreme Court judgment, which went against FIFA:

> The Court of First Instance, the Regional Court of Hamburg… decided in FIFA's favour and ruled that the defendant's actions had unfairly obstructed the claimant's freedom to operate on the market under section 4 No. 10 [of the German Act of Unfair Competition (UWG)]. The court of appeal, the Higher Regional Court of Hamburg… dismissed the claim and held that FIFA could base its claim neither on its earlier trademark registrations nor on the protection of 'work titles'. The Higher Regional Court disagreed with the Court of First Instance and emphasized that it could not be established that the defendant's trademark registration aimed to obstruct the claimant in the market. The defendant's trademark registrations predominantly served to safeguard its established business practices. Even though the specifications of the defendant's trademarks were wider than its actual business activities, a certain level of expansion was permissible.

---

[103] According to Articles 77–78 of the Rules of Procedure of the Court of Justice the President of the Court shall order the case to be removed from the register in the event of a settlement. Article 77 provides that if, before the Court has given its decision, the parties reach a settlement of their dispute and intimate to the Court the abandonment of their claims, the President shall order the case to be removed from the register and shall give a decision as to costs in accordance with Article 69(5), having regard to any proposals made by the parties on the matter. Article 78 provides that if the applicant informs the Court in writing that he wishes to discontinue the proceedings, the President shall order the case to be removed from the register and shall give a decision as to costs in accordance with Article 69(5).

[104] Writing on the weblog of the *Journal of Intellectual Property Law and Practice*, 8 January 2010—available online at the time of writing at http://jiplp.blogspot.com/2010/01/world-cup-trade-mark-dispute-1-0-says.html.

> In its decision of 12 November 2009, the German Federal Supreme Court agreed with the Higher Regional Court's reasoning. The Federal judges found that there was no likelihood of confusion between the parties' trademarks under section 14, German Trademark Act; nor could FIFA successfully base its claim on the 'work title rights' it owned for 'WM 2010', 'GERMANY 2006', and 'SOUTH AFRICA'. FIFA was also barred from making claims under unfair competition law, including the so-called 'general clause' of section 3 UWG... Ferrero's trademarks did not influence the relevant trade circles to assume that it was an official sponsor of the World Cup tournaments, nor did the defendant unfairly block FIFA's efforts to market the World Cup events via licensing through third party sponsors. The court emphasised that FIFA's basic constitutional right to exploit its World Cup tournaments commercially did not extend to the point that it could prevent all types of third party exploitation of the sport event.'[105]

Reinholz explains that the decision is particularly significant with regard to competition rights: 'This case relates, in effect, to the extent of an organiser's marketing rights to "his" event. As German law does not recognise specific "sports organisers' rights", sports associations such as FIFA, are using Competition Law in order to obtain wider-reaching rights than are currently afforded them by Trademark and Copyright Law.'[106] Ferrero proceeded to run a (by all accounts very successful) football-themed marketing campaign at international and South African airports during the 2010 FIFA World Cup South Africa.[107]

Finally, it should be noted that the FIFA/Ferrero litigation is not the only example of such challenges to event mark registrations, and not even the only such litigation in which Ferrero has been involved. Ferrero has also reportedly challenged UEFA's Euro championship Community Trademark registration for *Europameisterschaft* (although I have no further knowledge of the outcome of this matter at the time of writing). It has, however, been observed that 'The particularly interesting aspect of Ferrero's challenge to the EM 2008 mark is that they (Ferrero) were an official sponsor of the recently held championships. How the cancellation action was greeted in UEFA's corridors of power can only be imagined. However, if I were Cadbury I would be preparing my bid to sponsor EURO 2012 now'.[108]

It will be interesting to follow future progress of both trademark registrations by event organisers in respect of event-related marks, such as those at issue in the FIFA/Ferrero spat, along with developments in Europe regarding the potential

---

[105] In respect of the reference to the protection of 'work titles' under German law and their potential relevance to sports events, see also the AIPPI Q210 *Germany* country report (at 12)—available online at https://www.aippi.org/download/commitees/210/GR210germany_en.pdf.

[106] Reinholz, F 'No legal grounds for FIFA's objection to football stickers in chocolate bars', 2 December 2009—available online at the time of writing at http://www.haerting.de/de/suche/index.php?we_objectID=1494.

[107] See the online report available at http://www.travelretaildubai.com/confectionery/ferrero-s-fifa-promotions-prove-a-big-hit-with-soccer-fans-1.685553.

[108] See the snippet from the Autumn 2008 edition of the *Make Your Mark* trademark newsletter available online at http://www.jenkins.eu/mym-autumn-2008/snippets.asp.

recognition of a 'sports event organiser's right' (which I'll revisit in Chap. 10). I would suggest that these developments may be very important in the greater scheme of future event commercial rights protection and of ambush marketing of events.

5.3 'IP+ Protection' in *Sui Generis* Mega-Event Legislation

In the previous chapter we briefly considered some of the *sui generis* event legislation that have been enacted in different jurisdictions in order to provide special protection for commercial rights and interests in sports mega-events. Phillip Johnson has examined the apparent trend in such legislative measures against ambush marketing to more and more frequently provide what the author calls 'IP +' protection for events[109]—i.e. protection that provides something more than what IP rights offer. These 'IP+' rights (which the author also refers to as 'quasi-intellectual property rights') refer primarily to 'association rights'[110] to events, and have been developed by certain legislatures since 2000. Johnson grants South Africa the (dubious?) distinction of being the first country to take the 'bold step' of creating a protectable association right to a major event (i.e. by prohibiting any association to be made with such event if unauthorised), by means of the amendment to section 9 of its Trade Practices Act, 1976,[111] which Johnson calls 'clearly … a turning point in the prevention of ambush marketing'.[112]

Following on this legislation, other jurisdictions have also proceeded to pass legislation to protect association rights to a number of events, by means of event-specific legislation (e.g. in respect of the 2006 Melbourne Commonwealth Games, the EURO 2004 football tournament in Portugal, the 2006 Turin Winter Olympics in Italy, the 2010 Vancouver Winter Olympics and the 2012 London Olympic Games), or by means of 'umbrella' legislation (e.g. New Zealand's oft-maligned Major Events Management Act of 2007, or the more recent legislation in Australian states Victoria and New South Wales).

---

[109] Johnson 2008.

[110] Compare the 'London 2012 Olympics Association Right' (discussed in Sect. 4.4.3 of Chap. 4) created in terms of the London Olympic Games and Paralympic Games Act, 2006, which the legal advisor to a number of 2012 Olympics sponsors has characterised as a new 'IP right'—see David Stone 'The Olympic Games cannot survive without sponsors and those sponsors need legal protection' *The Lawyer*, 16 January 2006. I will examine such association rights in more detail in Chap. 8.

[111] The Trade Practices Amendment Act 26 of 2001 inserted section 9(d) in the Trade Practices Act, 76 of 1976, which provision prohibits a person from making, publishing or displaying false or misleading statements, communications or advertisements which suggest or imply a contractual or other connection with a sponsored event or the person sponsoring such event. See the discussion in Sect. 4.4.5 of Chap. 4.

[112] Johnson 2008, p. 26.

A provision such as section 9 of the South African Trade Practices Act[113] to an extent blurs the line between the protection of intellectual property related to an event (e.g. a FIFA trademark) and the common law 'passing off' action, by constituting a legislative prohibition against deceiving or misleading the public regarding association with an event. It is 'IP+' (i.e. 'something more than IP') protection because liability in terms of such provision does not require any IP infringement (i.e. there need not be any trademark, copyrighted work or registered design at issue; what is prohibited is creating confusion regarding an association, howsoever caused), and also because this type of provision that deals with an association with an event is often aimed at protecting something more than the traditionally recognised intellectual property of events organisers (e.g. by claiming protection against the use of generic terms which would/do not qualify for IP protection in terms of originality and distinctiveness requirements).[114] Such provisions have been enacted in different jurisdictions, ostensibly, as a result of a realisation that existing legal protection in terms of the common law (e.g. unlawful competition) or more general legislation (e.g. deceptive trade practises legislation and IP statutes) does not provide satisfactory protection against the often novel and creative efforts of 'ambushers'.[115] A prime example, which I have briefly

---

[113] For other legislative provisions that outlaw 'association ambushes' in South Africa, see Section 29 of the Consumer Protection Act, 68 of 2008, which is found in Part E of the Act (which deals with consumers' "right to fair and responsible marketing") and contains provisions regarding the marketing of goods or services. This section also prohibits ambush marketing by association with an event, and provides as follows:

'S29. A producer, importer, distributor, retailer or service provider must not market any goods or services

(a) in a manner that is reasonably likely to imply a false or misleading representation concerning those goods or services ...; or

(b) in a manner that is misleading, fraudulent or deceptive in any way, including in respect of ... the sponsoring of any event.'

Section 41 of the Act (dealing with 'False, misleading or deceptive representations') contains the following:

'S 41(3). ... [I]t is a false, misleading or deceptive representation to falsely state or imply, or fail to correct an apparent misapprehension on the part of a consumer to the effect, that

(a) the supplier of any goods or services has any particular status, affiliation, connection, sponsorship or approval that they do not have.'

[114] Mouritz 2008 (see discussion in the text below).

[115] Compare the discussion on the event-specific legislation that was prepared for the Sydney 2000 Olympic Games in Curthoys and Kendall 2001; see also Frontier Economics 2007, p. 17:

'[M]any legally-savvy companies are unlikely to be ... explicit in their ambush marketing tactics. Much concern about ambush marketing instead relates to far more subtle practices for which: (1) the application of existing law is uncertain or highly fact-dependent; or (2) there is no contravention of any law at all. The breadth of conduct that falls within this category demonstrates the creativity of marketers in finding ways to leverage off an event, either without infringing any law, or where legal uncertainty (combined with the time and cost of litigation) dissuades any enforcement action by the event organiser.'

considered earlier, is the very 'special' protection of the Olympic Games provided for by the United States Congress.[116]

Apart from the motivation for extension of legal protection based on such practical experience, there is another reason for the apparent (or claimed) inefficacy of existing IP law to protect against ambushing of events. In Chap. 4 I explained that traditional IP rights infringements involve e.g. an infringement by X of Y's copyright in a work (for example, by means of unlawful copying or publication of the relevant work) or through X using, for example, a trademark that is confusingly similar to Y's registered trademark. In the case of ambush marketing of an event, however, the 'ambusher' would usually not be infringing the intellectual property of its competitor (e.g. an official sponsor). The deception or confusion relates to association with *the event* and not with the official sponsor. The 'ambusher' is alleged to have created confusion over their (official) involvement or association with an event, which it is then claimed prejudices both the event organisers (rights grantors) and the official sponsors or commercial partners (rights holders) due to the dilution of the value of their investment and a potential loss of revenues that would otherwise have been payable in terms of an official rights grant contract (as well as negatively affecting the efficacy of the official sponsor's advertising through the creation of a cluttered marketing environment surrounding the event). Accordingly, one reason advanced for calls for special protection for events, also in the form of 'IP+' legislation, is to address the differences between traditional IP infringement cases and what is experienced in the case of ambushing of events.

Finally, a convincing rationale for extended protection is found in the practical consideration of the nature of IP-related litigation in the context of the time factor when events are ambushed. Injunctions or interdicts, while a speedy legal process, may be as unsatisfactory as proceeding by way of protracted legal action in e.g. a case of unlawful competition or passing off. An ambush campaign that occurs in the midst of a two-week long Olympic Games event confronts the event organisers and sponsors with a situation where time is of the essence and where the damage may be done long before a court can pronounce on a matter; the horse may have bolted long before the barn door is closed by way of a court order, which may become academic in nature, especially where an order for damages may be problematic in the context of proving and quantifying harm. Sarah Storey explains (with reference to Canada's Olympic and Paralympic Marks Act enacted for the 2010 Vancouver Winter Games[117] and that country's trademark legislation) the

[116] In the form of the Ted Stevens Act (see the discussion in Sect. 4.4.10 in Chap. 4). Compare the view expressed in *San Francisco Arts and Athletics, Inc. v. United States Olympic Comm.*, 483 U.S. 522, 531 (1987), in terms of which, unlike traditional claims under the Lanham Act, under the Ted Stevens Act 'the USOC need not prove that a contested use [of its registered marks] is likely to cause confusion, and an unauthorised user of the [marks] does not have available the normal statutory defences.'

[117] The 'Vancouver Act', discussed in Sect. 4.4.7 of Chap. 4.

need for differences in approach in special event legislation, specifically in respect of the availability of effective injunctive relief for event organisers:

> Trademark law is designed to deal with marks belonging to companies that trade on an ongoing basis, not those associated with major sporting events that last only weeks or even days. A well-timed ambush can have a big public impact, thereby significantly harming the sports rights owner and its commercial partners, and every day that an ambush is allowed to continue during a major event, the harm compounds. In the case of ongoing businesses, it is more likely that damages could be sufficient to remedy the harm.[118]

In essence, the problems with a 'modern' ambush marketing campaign can be summarised as follows:

> [M]any legally-savvy companies are unlikely to be... explicit in their ambush marketing tactics. Much concern about ambush marketing instead relates to far more subtle practices for which: (1) the application of existing law is uncertain or highly fact-dependent; or (2) there is no contravention of any law at all. The breadth of conduct that falls within this category demonstrates the creativity of marketers in finding ways to leverage off an event, either without infringing any law, or where legal uncertainty (combined with the time and cost of litigation) dissuades any enforcement action by the event organiser.[119]

I understand these problems (although, of course, I have lingering concerns over the need for and legitimacy of providing a novel legal remedy in those cases where 'there is no contravention of any law at all') and have a measure of empathy with the event organisers and their sponsors. I even understand the resultant need for special legislation to add something to the existing law where such problems pose the potential for the existing law to be found lacking in the face of practical considerations; I have never supported the possibility of encountering a 'right without a remedy', which simply makes little sense and at the very least would not bode well for the public's perception of the law, of its sense of justice and of the legitimacy of the legal system. I am, however, extremely concerned at the ways in which such new *sui generis* event legislation has been shaped in order to address these problems. The need for law reform should not be construed as a *carte blanche* licence for law-makers to import wholesale changes to existing legal principles on a casuistic basis (especially not when due to lobbying—in fact, demands—by commercial actors, born of self-interest), especially where such law reforms come at a potentially significant social cost. Where such new laws provide 'IP+' protections we must critically evaluate the legitimacy of what, exactly, has been added to the existing laws, and the potential consequences. In evaluating this trend in light of the fundamental principles of IP law I will briefly revisit the relevant legislation in the different jurisdictions to illustrate the extension of IP law by this means.

In a recent review undertaken by a working committee of the International Association for the Protection of Intellectual Property (AIPPI) on the suitability of

---

118 Storey 2010, p. 50.

119 See Frontier Economics 2007, p. 17.

existing trademark and unfair competition protection for major sports events in a number of jurisdictions,[120] the following was highlighted as deserving of attention:

> When determining whether there is a need for adoption of rules which address specific problems arising from the characteristics of trademarks which relate to Major Sports Events, the following may be considered:
>
> - whether the fact that the current classification system does not recognise the concept of merchandising products or services justifies that the scope of services of "organisation of Sports Events" in class 41 is extended to cover the products and services related to such an event,[121]
> - whether it is desirable to narrow the requirement of distinctiveness for trademarks which relate to Major Sports Events, regard being had to the substantial value attached to those trademarks and to the linking of a business with the name of the Major Sports Events,[122]
> - whether it is desirable to extend the period relating to the use requirement which is usually 5 years due to the fact that the registration of a trademark which relates to a Major Sports Event is usually accomplished up to 8 years before the taking place of the event and accordingly up to 8 years before the actual commencement of use of those trademarks, or whether this reason for non use should be seen as a valid reason for such nonuse.
> - whether the fact that the use of the trademarks relating to Major Sports Events takes place for a limited period of time, i.e. while the event in question takes place, combined with the risk of other traders' attempt to benefit financially from the event, justifies the adoption of specific remedies in case of infringement of a trademark which relates to a Major Sports Event,
> - whether the legal consequences of infringements of trademarks which relate to Major Sports Events should be different from the legal consequences of infringements of other trademarks due to the sums of money involved with the sponsoring of Major Sports Events.

These questions emphasise the special considerations which may be relevant not only in respect of determining the suitability of existing IP law (such as trademark law) to deal with ambushing of sports mega-events, but also hint at areas where proponents of special protection for events propose an extension of the normal, accepted principles relating to such IP rights. I will not examine all of these aspects, which are beyond the scope of this chapter, but will consider instances where special events legislation in the various jurisdictions has proceeded to extend IP protection for events. These relate to different aspects, including the requirements for the establishment of protection, matters relating to infringement of the relevant rights, the protection of the generic or commonplace (mainly in respect of words and descriptions of events), and some practical aspects

---

[120] See the guidelines of the Working Committee, Project Q210 ('The protection of major sports events and associated commercial activities through trademarks and other IPR'; in a call for reports compiled for purposes of a draft resolution to be submitted to the AIPPI Exco meeting in Buenos Aires, October 2009)—available online at the time of writing at https://www.aippi.org/download/commitees/210/WG210English.pdf.

[121] See discussion in the text in Sect. 5.3.1.2 heading (iv) below.

[122] See discussion in the text in Sect. 5.3.1.2 heading (iii) below.

in respect of enforcing the relevant rights. In what follows I will briefly consider these different aspects of IP rights with reference to the following:

- Requirements relating to the establishment of IP protection and the scope of protection:

Here I will briefly discuss the following:

  - The requirements of copyright relating to originality and expression of ideas in a tangible form (and of 'substantiality' in respect of copying);
  - The registration requirement for trademark protection;
  - The use requirement for trademark protection;
  - The requirement relating to distinctiveness and descriptiveness in respect of trademarks;
  - The system of class registrations for trademarks; and
  - The role of disclaimers or endorsements in respect of trademark registrations.

- More practical considerations relating to IP infringement proceedings before the courts:

Here I will briefly consider the following:

  - The exceptions to infringement (particularly, the issue of 'fair use');
  - The requirement of consumer confusion in trademark cases; and
  - The requirement to prove harm in infringement cases.

These issues will be briefly discussed in turn below.

5.3.1 Requirements for Establishment and the Scope of Protection

The main forms of intellectual property rights that are relevant and come to the fore in the protection of commercial aspects of mega-events are trademarks, copyright and registered designs. These may relate to a variety of material related to an event, including marks, such as organisers' logos and symbols, slogans, event-specific designations which identify the name, year and location of the event, sponsors' trademarks, event anthems, mascots, etc. Johnson, for example, suggests that an event organiser should consider registering 'at least the following word marks' in respect of its event:

- Event + Year (e.g. 'FIFA World Cup 2006');
- Event + Location (e.g. 'World Cup Germany');
- Event + Number (e.g. '12th FINA World Championship');
- Event (e.g. 'Rugby World Cup' or 'Wimbledon'); and
- Location + Year (e.g. 'London 2012').[123]

[123] Johnson 2007, pp. 15–16.

These marks are listed in the order of the likelihood of being registered, which conjures up the requirements for their registration, which will be discussed below. As illustrated in the above discussion of the *FIFA v Ferrero* saga, marks such as 'World Cup Germany' or 'London 2012' may have very dubious claims to protection by means of trademark registration.

This type of material is central to the mega-event as a brand, as well as, more functionally, in respect of the ways in which the event is commercially exploited by the relevant rights holders. As mentioned in Chap. 2, the gist of the organiser/sponsor or organiser/merchandiser contract is twofold, namely the provision of a licence (consent) to use the relevant event marks, logos, symbols etc. in marketing or merchandising (including the granting of designation rights to call itself a sponsor), and an agreement not to sue (or *pactum de non petendo*) provided by the organiser in respect of such use. The subject matter of the licence so provided is the event-related material referred to, and the main basis for protection of such material is found in IP law. The event organiser is able to licence use (on an exclusive basis) of its IP rights to sponsors and merchandisers. A further, extremely important source of commercial value is, of course, found in the rights provided to broadcasters to broadcast the event (which brings with it the further marketing and sponsorship opportunities related to broadcasts). The core of such broadcasting rights is also found in the realm of IP, namely copyright to broadcasts (coupled with contractual arrangements regarding the provision of access to the event to broadcasters in order to facilitate such broadcasts). As mentioned earlier, this book does not focus on the legal issues pertaining to the broadcasting of mega-events.

The mentioned forms of IP rights are all subject to different requirements for their establishment. Primarily, this relates to registration (of trademarks and designs) or other requirements in respect of copyright (which, generally, does not require registration). These requirements can be technical and won't make for riveting reading, and I will not elaborate too much on them here. The interested reader is referred to other, more specialised texts in this regard.[124] As specific requirements may differ depending on the relevant legal regime and jurisdiction (e.g. the USA, UK, EU, New Zealand or South Africa), I will extrapolate only the most general, standard requirements here as opposed to more specific variables depending on special legal provisions in the different jurisdictions. By painting broad strokes, the discussion will simply provide a brief overview of the general requirements for the establishment of IP rights in respect of trademarks, copyright and design, with a view to considering the extent to which the extension of IP protection in *sui generis* event legislation differs and provides an alternative framework for the establishment of rights to events for organisers and sponsors. The 'rights' (including restrictions in respect of protected words and symbols and even the newfangled 'association rights') as created in the *sui generis* event

[124] For example, Johnson 2007, which discusses the specific requirements relating to trademarks (in Chap. 2) and copyright and designs (in Chap. 3).

legislation in fact serves to allow organisers to side-step some of the rigorous requirements for the establishment of IP rights in respect of their events. Reminiscent of Fezer's suggested 'event mark' (discussed earlier in this chapter) with its relaxed registration requirements, the protection offered in terms of this legislation provides a significant expansion on the traditional IP regime, specifically in respect of the establishment of rights. And, as Longdin observes (in a passage quoted at the beginning of this chapter), such legislation poses the problem of outflanking the debate between the monopolies inherent in IP rights and the wider societal interests and those of other players in the economy, which 'encourages losers in the lobbying contest that usually accompanies legislative changes to IP regimes to believe that the solution to their problems is a freestanding custom-built statute of their own'.

Along with the requirements for the establishment of IP rights we should also consider how and to what extent the protection afforded by means of special event legislation expands on the scope of protection that would normally be provided by IP rights.

5.3.1.1 Copyright: Originality, Expression in Tangible Form and 'Substantial Copying'

Copyright can provide a type of 'catch-all' protection for event-related material, such as words, emblems, logos, symbols, depictions of mascots, anthems, recorded event films and live broadcasts, which would enjoy copyright protection without the requirement for registration as long as the relevant material is eligible for protection (i.e. as a specific type of copyrighted work, such as a literary, artistic or musical work, or a film or broadcast) and satisfies the requirements for protection. The gist of such requirements relates to originality and the expression of an idea in the form of a physical or tangible embodiment. It is trite that the originality requirement does not equate to novelty or to artistic, literary, musical or aesthetic merit. Originality may be expressed (and sought) in different ways in the different jurisdictions, but generally the law requires something ranging from a modicum of creativity to the expenditure of 'sweat of the brow' (i.e. effort, labour and skill, or 'industriousness') in creating the work. Basically, a work will be sufficiently 'original' to carry copyright if it was not copied from another, prior work. Although it is not necessarily so straightforward, as recognised by a Canadian court:

> The plain meaning of the word "original" suggests at least some intellectual effort, as is necessarily involved in the exercise of skill and judgment... "Original"'s plain meaning implies not just that something is not a copy. It includes, if not creativity per se, at least some sort of intellectual effort... when used to mean simply that the work must originate from the author, originality is eviscerated of its core meaning. It becomes a synonym of "originated", and fails to reflect the ordinary sense of the word.[125]

[125] *CCH Canadian Ltd* v *Law Society of Upper Canada* [2002] FCA 187 (14 May 2002) par. 18.

As regards the requirement for physical embodiment of the work in a tangible medium,[126] one is faced with copyright's famous 'idea/expression dichotomy', and the maxim that there is no such thing as copyright in ideas. The idea itself cannot be copyright and copyright can only be established when the idea is embodied in a 'work' in tangible form.

When one considers the nature of the protection provided to event organisers in the special event legislation, however, it appears that the protection provided, which is analogous or akin to IP protection, is not based on the traditional notions of IP relating to the aspects, such as the requirements for establishment of subject matter capable of IP protection, and in respect of the accepted notions of what constitutes infringement of such IP. This is especially clear if one compares such legislative protection to copyright. South Africa's Merchandise Marks Act provides that, during the period for which an event is a protected event, 'no person may use a trademark in relation to such event in a manner which is calculated to achieve publicity for that trademark and thereby to derive special promotional benefit from the event, without the prior authority of the organiser of such event'. 'Use' of a mark is defined in the Act as including 'any audible reproduction of the trademark in relation to goods or to the rendering of services', or 'the use of the trademark in promotional activities, which in any way, directly or indirectly, is intended to be brought into association with or to allude to an event'. It is clear from these definitions that, unlike the requirement in copyright law that for an infringement to occur the protected work must be copied and that infringement refers to taking the expression of an idea in tangible form (copying of a 'substantial part' of a 'work', as is generally required) rather than the idea *simpliciter*, an infringement in terms of s 15A(2) can take place where there is no tangible expression of an idea at issue. The would-be infringer need not substantially reproduce a mark (i.e. an artistic work) or logo (i.e. a literary work) of the event organiser (and need not substantially reproduce such mark or logo in a tangible form); mere reference to the event (as opposed to an aspect of the event which qualifies as intellectual property of the event organiser) can constitute infringement. This negates not only copyright's requirement for the establishment of protection (expression of an idea in tangible form by the author) but also the requirement of copying of the copyright-protected work for purposes of liability for infringement.

A similar situation pertains in respect of the other 'association rights' to events created by special event legislation. When one considers the 'rights' to mega-events as created in the special event legislation it is clear that there is little or no connection to the requirements for copyright to subsist—in essence these rights are not connected with any material which may form the subject of copyright. Let us

[126] Which requirement, of course, might not apply depending on the nature of the relevant work (e.g. South African copyright law does not require this in respect of two distinct classes of 'works' recognised in the Copyright Act 98 of 1978, namely broadcasts and programme-carrying signals).

take, for example, the London Olympics association right as created in the London Olympic and Paralympic Games Act, 2006 (as discussed in Chap. 4). This right prohibits representations from being made in relation to goods or services which are likely to suggest to the public that there is an association between those goods or services and the London Olympic Games or Paralympic Games. Similar to the rights created and conferred under IP laws (for example, copyright), this right provides its proprietor, LOCOG, with the right to take legal action to prohibit others from performing acts which may infringe on the interests of the rights holder deriving from the exclusivity of its entitlements in dealing with such 'property'. Whereas a central right which is vested in the copyright holder is the right to prevent copying of the work, the association right in respect of the London Games similarly provides LOCOG with the right to prevent what would amount to a *reproduction of the association with the event* (which, the assumption would go, by its nature vests in the organiser or creator of the event and those licenced to associate themselves with the event) through making an unauthorised representation. The statute, however, creates this protection without requiring any underlying copyright-protected work or a work capable of copyright protection. What is protected is association with the event, and the event itself cannot be copyrighted. There is no required 'outlay' by an author, in the form of a work that is reduced to tangible form. There is no requirement of originality in respect of a protected work (the event, or the association with the event, performs the function of a protected work, although not qualifying for such protection in terms of the principles of copyright law) or that the 'work' must be reduced to some tangible form. The same is true of the association right to a 'protected event' in terms of section 10(1) of New Zealand's Major Event Management Act, 2007 (or 'MEMA'), which provides as follows:

> 'No person may, during a major event's protection period, make any representation in a way likely to suggest to a reasonable person that there is an association between the major event and
>
> (a) goods or services; or
> (b) a brand of goods or services; or
> (c) a person who provides goods or services.'

All that is required in terms of MEMA to vest the association right in the organiser of the event is the declaration of the event as protected (in terms of section 7 of the Act), upon which declaration the association right automatically vests in the event organiser.

The apparent disconnect with the precepts of copyright law as displayed by special legislative event protection is clearer when one examines the provisions of the special event legislation which deal with protected words or symbols. Section 3(1) of the Vancouver Act (discussed in Chap. 4) provides that '[n]o person shall adopt or use in connection with a business, as a trademark or otherwise, an Olympic or Paralympic mark or a mark that so nearly resembles an Olympic or Paralympic mark as to be likely to be mistaken for it'. The protection provided is similar to the copyright holder's right to prohibit copying of the copyrighted work.

The Act, however, does not require originality for the protected marks or their expression in tangible form. As such, this Act also provides a basis for protection without requiring compliance with requirements for the establishment of a 'work' or subject matter that is capable of protection in terms of traditional principles of IP law. Similar considerations apply to other event legislation (compare the prohibition on '[o]ther acts that might mislead people to think there are sponsorship or other supporting relations between the doers and the right holders of Olympic symbols' in Article 5(6) of China's Olympic Regulations for the 2008 Beijing Games, which clearly could include various forms of conduct which would not amount to infringement of copyright by means of copying of a protected copyright work—while the wording of the provision would appear to imply that it applies to acts which constitute use of such Olympic symbols its ambit is clearly wider and might include conduct not including use of symbols which may qualify for copyright protection).

I will not elaborate on the role of copyright here, beyond pointing out that it appears that the special protection afforded to events by the *sui generis* event legislation (I refer here to the use of provisions dealing with protected words or symbols, and the special 'association rights'[127]) are clearly not grounded in the theoretical construct of copyright law. In as far as this special protection is 'IP+' (i.e. it provides more robust protection than copyright, and also does so without requiring adherence to the normal requirements for the establishment of copyright) it bears little resemblance to the precepts of copyright.

5.3.1.2 Trademark Law

(i) Registration

The different jurisdictions all require that trademarks must be registered in order to enjoy protection under trademark laws in addition to other, existing grounds for protection (which include, primarily, unfair competition law in terms of e.g. the common law, and legislative trade practises protection). It is generally not possible to acquire extra-territorial protection for a registered trademark, and apart from limited exceptions[128] there is no such thing as an international trademark registration. This has necessitated the wide-spread, simultaneous 'blanket filing' of trademark applications in various jurisdictions by mega-event organisers in respect

---

[127] Which are further examined in Chap. 8.

[128] Namely a trademark filing in terms of the Madrid Protocol of 1989 (*Protocol relating to the Madrid Agreement concerning the International Registration of Marks*—a filing treaty and not a substantive harmonsation treaty)—for more information, see http://www.uspto.gov/trademarks/law/madrid/index.jsp)—or the filing of a Community trademark in the EU. It should be noted also that a number of 'event marks' may qualify for protection as famous marks although unregistered in various jurisdictions in terms of Article 6bis of the Paris Convention or in terms of Article 16 of the TRIPS agreement, although discussion of this issue is beyond the scope of this chapter.

of each specific event, a crucial part of the domestic commercial rights protection programmes of event organisers. The registration requirement serves a number of important functions which facilitate scrutiny of applications to exclude registration based on absolute (e.g. where a prospective trademark includes protected matter, such as protected Olympic or Red Cross symbols or a national flag)[129] or relative (e.g. where a prospective mark would infringe on an already registered, existing mark) grounds. Such scrutiny generally involves the registering authorities as well as other trademark holders or applicants for trademark protection, who have the right to object to a pending application.

I will not discuss the registration requirement for trademarks here, but will simply note that the protection provided to event organisers in *sui generis* event legislation does not require registration of protected marks or symbols. The protection is automatic by means of promulgation of the relevant legislation or, in the case of legislation such as that found in South Africa[130] and New Zealand,[131] upon declaration of the event as 'protected' by the relevant government official. Importantly, this means that the normal 'safety mechanisms' inherent in trademark registration procedures are absent. There is, for example, no provision for interested parties to object to the registration of a mark as in the case with normal trademark registrations, and the question of whether an event is to be protected relate to the nature and characteristics of the relevant event and of its anticipated economic, cultural and other characteristics or benefits rather than an investigation into the merits of invoking the statutory protection for event organisers and sponsors in respect of the relevant symbols or words. MEMA, for example, in its section 7(4) provides that New Zealand's Economic Development Minister must, before making a recommendation for the declaration of an event as a major event in terms of the Act, consider whether the event will

- attract a large number of international participants or spectators and therefore generate significant tourism opportunities for New Zealand;
- significantly raise New Zealand's international profile;
- require a high level of professional management and co-ordination;
- attract significant sponsorship and international media coverage;
- attract large numbers of New Zealanders as participants or spectators;
- offer substantial sporting, cultural, social, economic, or other benefits for New Zealand or New Zealanders.'

MEMA does not require an investigation into the merits of protection of the relevant protected symbols, logos etc. (the use of which is prohibited by the Act when declared to be 'major event emblems or words') in line with normal trademark registration considerations. Section 8 of the Act provides that the

---

[129] Compare the provisions of section 3 of the UK Trademarks Act, 1994.

[130] The Merchandise Marks Act, 1941 (as amended)—see the discussion in Sect. 4.4.5 in Chap. 4.

[131] The Major Events Management Act, 2007—see the discussion in Sect. 4.4.4 in Chap. 4.

Minister, in making a recommendation regarding the declaration of major event emblems and words by means of an Order in Council in terms of section 8(1) of the Act, must take into account the extent to which, in relation to the major event, emblems and words require protection in order to

(a) obtain maximum benefits for New Zealanders:
(b) prevent unauthorised commercial exploitation at the expense of either a major event organiser or a major event sponsor.

It is interesting to note that MEMA suggests that wider consultation should take place in considering whether to declare words or emblems as protected than in deciding whether a specific event should be declared a major event under the Act. Section 8(2)(c) requires that the Minister may only make such a recommendation after consultation with the Commerce Minister, the relevant major event organiser and 'persons the Minister considers are likely to be substantially affected by the recommendation'. Paradoxically, however, section 8(4) provides that a failure to comply with subsection (2)(c) does not affect the validity of an Order in Council made under subsection (1)! In fact, it may be that the only issue relevant to the protection afforded to words and symbols which is expressly to be considered in the process of declaring an event as protected in terms of the Act is whether the Minister is satisfied that the event organiser has the capacity and the intention to 'use all practicable measures available under the existing law to prevent unauthorised commercial exploitation of the major event and to protect its intellectual property and other legal rights (including, for example, registering relevant trademarks)'.[132] As has been pointed out, however, this provision appears to be rather nonsensical, as event organisers will surely be less likely to pursue the measures provided in terms of existing law in the face of the special protection afforded by the Act (they would be less likely to 'exchange the uncertainties and inbuilt limitations of IP law and allied liability rules for the satisfyingly draconian and instant remedies provided by MEMA').[133] MEMA's wide and accommodating approach towards allowing for restrictions on the use of major event emblems and words appears to have been specifically intended. Longdin notes that when MEMA was first introduced into the House in Bill form it was conceded that the net cast by the legislation was intended to be wide, 'going far beyond trade-marking legislation in order to protect commercial interests'.[134]

South Africa's Merchandise Marks Act, similarly, contains provisions which necessitate consideration of the nature of the event in the process of declaring it as being protected in terms of the Act. Section 15A(1)(b) provides that the Minister of Trade and Industry may not designate an event as a protected event 'unless the staging of the event is in the public interest and the Minister is satisfied that the organisers have created sufficient opportunities for small businesses and in

[132] MEMA section 7(3)(c)(ii).

[133] Longdin 2009, p. 731.

[134] Ibid. 732, referencing HD Parker, Vol. 637 *Hansard* 7494 (20 February 2007).

particular for those of the previously disadvantaged communities'. This requirement does not relate to the nature and characteristics of prohibited words, symbols etc. in respect of a protected event. The relevant provision which regulates the Minister's power to declare such material as prohibited, section 15(1)(b) (which gives the Minister the power to prohibit either absolutely or conditionally the use of 'any mark, word, letter or figure or any arrangement or combination thereof, in connection with any trade, business, profession, occupation or event, or in connection with a trademark, mark or trade description applied to goods), expressly provides that the Minister may do so 'after such investigation as he or she may think fit'. No guidance is provided as to which considerations may, or may not, be taken into account by the Minister in respect of the prohibition of use of such material. When the Minister made the relevant determination in respect of the 2010 FIFA World Cup it was declared by the Minister that 'in deciding on this matter, I will also consider principles contained in the Trademarks Act, 1993... dealing with issues considered before trademarks are granted or not granted'.[135] Note the use of 'also'—neither the Act nor the relevant Government Notice contain any further information regarding the issues the Minister would need to consider in deciding on whether to prohibit a word, symbol etc. The Minister's statement of intent to consider trademark principles is a non-compulsory one, and it is unclear which (or to what extent) principles were considered in the process. Kelbrick points out that the preamble to the 2010 FIFA World Cup South Africa Special Measures Act 11 of 2006 emphasised the South African government's duty to pursue major developmental goals as reflected in initiatives to eradicate poverty and that 'the Government must strike a balance between the broad national interests of the Republic and the specific interests of FIFA when implementing its guarantees' to host the World Cup, but it is unclear how the very restrictive effect of the prohibited marks in terms of the MMA on (small) enterprise feature in this regard.[136]

(ii) The Requirement of Use

It is generally required for purposes of registration of a trademark that the relevant mark has been used in commerce, or that the applicant should be able to show a *bona fide* intention to so use the mark in commerce. Trademark rights must be maintained through actual lawful use of the trademark, and such rights will cease if a mark is not actively used for a period of time (normally 5 years in most jurisdictions), on a 'use-it-or-lose-it' basis. Compare, for example, the definition of a 'trademark' in section 45 of the Lanham Act in the United States, and the provisions of section 6A of the UK Trademarks Act, 1994 (as amended).[137] In the case of an application for registration, failure to actively use the mark in the lawful

[135] Government Notice 787 of 2007, *Government Gazette* 30001 (21 June 2007).

[136] Kelbrick 2008, p. 332.

[137] See also section 32(3) of the UK Act, which requires a declaration during the application for registration of a trademark to the effect that 'the trademark is being used, by the applicant or with his consent, in relation to those goods or services, or that he has a *bona fide* intention that it should be so used.'

course of trade, or to enforce the registration in the event of infringement, may also expose the registration itself to become liable for an application for the removal from the register after a certain period of time on the grounds of 'nonuse'.[138]

A pertinent issue that arises in respect of trademark registrations by event organisers for marks related to events is the issue of use, or more properly, of use by parties other than the event organiser as trademark proprietor. As mentioned earlier, event organisers tend (and are advised) to register their event-related marks in a large number of goods and service trademark categories, in order to facilitate the licensing of such marks to others (primarily their official sponsors and merchandisers in respect of the event) and to close the field to potential ambushers. Trademark law generally allows for the licensing of the use of marks, although there may be pitfalls for mark owners. Careless licensing may impact on the reputation of the mark and of its proprietor's business undertaking or brand. 'Naked licensing' occurs when third parties are allowed to use a trademark without restriction; when the quality of goods or services provided under a mark by third parties is not controlled, or when rights in a mark are assigned, in whole or part, without the goodwill of the business symbolised by the mark. Naked licensing severs a mark from its source-identifying function, and thus may result in the loss of trademark rights through abandonment. Trademark laws usually allow for use by a licencee to substitute for use by the trademark proprietor (whose own nonuse would thus not lead to viable claims for cancellation of the mark).[139]

When one considers the special legislative event protection, specifically of 'marks', symbols and words that obtain special protection through prohibitions on use, it is important to note that such protection does not require use or even a *bona fide* intention to use on the part of event organisers. As mentioned earlier, these protections kick in when the relevant legislation is published or when the relevant event is subsequently declared to be protected, and opportunities for consideration of the scope of protection (and, importantly, with due consideration of the interests of parties other than the event organiser and its sponsors) are usually much more limited than in the case of a trademark application. The use requirement in trademark law is aimed at preventing a situation of unfair stifling of competition (i.e. a trademark proprietor is not permitted to register a mark when there is no intention to use such mark and purely for the purpose of preventing others from registering the mark or from using it, by means of infringement proceedings). It also goes to the heart of the functions of a trademark; if trademarks signify, primarily, the source or origin of goods or services upon which a mark is affixed or in connection with which it is used, then it makes sense that the failure to actually use a mark would justify the expunging of such mark. The absence of this check in the case of protected symbols through the means of the *sui generis* legislation serves to facilitate just such a tactic of perceived overkill by event organisers. One

[138] Compare the provisions of section 46 of the UK Trademarks Act, 1994.

[139] See, for example, the provisions of section 46(1)(a) of the UK Trademarks Act in respect of its reference to the consent of the proprietor.

is inevitably reminded of FIFA's passing off claim in the recent South African case concerning a football-themed keychain design.[140] FIFA attempted to establish a claim of passing off in the market of commemorative key holders even though FIFA itself does not produce such merchandise and also had not licenced any manufacturers to produce souvenir key holders in respect of its event. The following claim was made in the affidavit by the main deponent in support of FIFA's application[141]:

> [W]hen in due course [FIFA] grants a licence for the manufacture of key holders, such key holders will be of a similar nature and effect to the articles depicted in [the Respondent's allegedly] offending designs. When such key holders are produced and sold with the permission of [FIFA], the public will correctly connect them in the course of trade with [FIFA].[142]

Similarly, in another supporting affidavit filed by Miguel Portela, FIFA's rights protection programme manager, it was stated that 'it is probable that [FIFA] will grant licences in respect of key holders for the 2010 FIFA World Cup'.[143] To the best of my knowledge FIFA has to date never provided such licences for the 2010 event.

Johnson explains that it is an advisable tactic for event organisers like FIFA to make sweeping trademark applications (i.e. in a large number of categories for goods and services) in the relevant jurisdiction(s) roughly 4–5 years before the end of the future event (as 'nonuse' provisions in trademark laws generally require nonuse over a period of 5 years), as this can serve to cover the 'whole field of sponsorship' (the application can cover all conceivable goods or services which might attract sponsorship, while also closing the field to potential 'ambushers' of the event in respect or less likely goods or services).[144] It was reported that by November 2009, more than 6 months before the start of the 2010 FIFA World Cup in South Africa (and only shortly after the end of the 2009 Confederations Cup), FIFA had already registered more than thirty event-related marks for its 2014 World Cup in Brazil with the Brazilian Institute for Intellectual Property, and that cease-and-desist letters were already being dispatched to would-be infringers of FIFA's rights in Brazil.[145] The mega-event 'carpet-bombing' of trademark applications and registrations is a common strategy as part of the modern-day commercial rights programme, and it contributes to the process of contracting the

---

140 *Federation Internationale de Football Association (FIFA) v Executive African Trading CC & Another* Case No. 52308/07 North Gauteng High Court, Pretoria (which case was subsequently withdrawn in June 2011—see the discussion in Sect. 4.4.5 in Chap. 4).

141 Affidavit by David Murray, who had left FIFA's employ by the time of the scheduled hearing of the case in March 2011.

142 At par. 27.1 of Murray's affidavit.

143 In par. 54 of Portela's relying affidavit.

144 Johnson 2007, p. 26.

145 See the report dated 2 June 2010 available online at the time of writing at http://www.v-brazil.com/world-cup/2014/cbf-files-lawsuits-for-ambush-marketing/.

space for commercial activity surrounding events by non-licenced persons and businesses,[146] while also holding potential freedom of (commercial) expression implications.[147] Such practise, however, is at least subject to normal IP law principles such as those of the rigours of the registration process and the opportunity for the filing of objections to registration of certain marks.

Finally, another point worth noting in respect of the use of trademarks is the fact that there has been considerable debate in recent years, in various jurisdictions, about whether only use of a trademark as a trademark (i.e. 'trademark use') should be able to constitute infringement, or whether courts should recognise infringement through other ('non-trademark') uses of a mark.[148] This issue has featured, for example, in the protracted litigation in the UK and before the ECJ in the well-known *Arsenal FC v Reed* case, and the South African Supreme Court of Appeal has characterised the dilution provisions in the South African Trademarks Act[149] as protecting not only the source-identifying function of a registered mark but also 'the economic value of a trademark, more particularly its reputation and its advertising value or selling power'[150] (while the Constitutional Court in the same case held that this provision also protects the 'unique identity and reputation' of a registered mark, as related, *inter alia*, to its selling power[151]). The point I wish to make here is that the protection afforded by the *sui generis* event legislation, which does not require use of a trademark by event organisers to trigger the extensive protections of commercial rights afforded, also serves to circumvent this debate as to the forms of usage of the mark for purposes of infringement proceedings.

In summary, the material protected by means of provisions of special event legislation relating to prohibited words or symbols, or the 'association rights' to events which are aimed at protecting commercial aspects of events, do not require the use of marks by event organisers, and as such may be open to abuse which may hold significant anti-competitive implications.

(iii) Distinctiveness Versus Descriptiveness

This facet of trademark law will not be discussed in any detail here, and I will elaborate on some relevant issues in Sect. 5.3.2 later in this chapter (in examining the ways in which special event legislation tends to provide legal protection for the generic and the commonplace). I wish to simply highlight the fact that these two

---

[146] See, more generally, the discussion in Chap. 8.

[147] See the discussion in Chap. 7.

[148] See, for example, on this debate in South African law and with reference to case law from other jurisdictions, Alberts, W 'Origin of the species: Trademark infringement after the *Bergkelder* case', undated paper available online at the time of writing at http://www.bowman.co.za/LawArticles/Publications/Trademark%20Article.pdf.

[149] Act 194 of 1993; section 34(1)(c).

[150] *Laugh It Off Promotions CC v South African Breweries International (Finance) t/a Sabmark International* 2005 (2) SA 46 (SCA) par. 13.

[151] *Laugh It Off Promotions CC v South African Breweries International (Finance) t/a Sabmark International* 2005 (8) BCLR 743 (CC) par. 40; see Alberts (note 148 above).

requirements in respect of trademarks also bear special consideration in the context of evaluating the extension of IP protection by means of the *sui generis* event legislation.

Trademark laws generally require that a mark cannot be registered as a trademark if it is not sufficiently distinctive.[152] This requirement is related to and may have its genesis in the source-identifying function of a trademark,[153] i.e. a mark that distinguishes the goods or services of the mark proprietor from the goods or services of other traders. This function of a trademark focuses on its ability to signify the origin of goods or services; trademarks have been succinctly described as 'a flag planted to identify the fact that you are in a particular trader's territory.'[154] Some claim that trademarks are 'property purely of consumers' minds', as they 'exist only to the extent that consumers perceive them as designations of source'[155]; or that 'A trademark has no inherent meaning. Its meaning is derived from the association that the mark has with the goods and services it identifies'.[156] The importance of the source-identifying function is bolstered by/based upon a prime economic rationale of trademarks, namely their function of reducing search costs for consumers by distinguishing the goods or services available in the market and allowing for informed choice on the part of the consumer. Of course, one should take care to consider that the traditional meaning of the 'source' or 'origin' of products or services, and the connotations of such meaning for consumers, is dynamic, and has changed over the past 50 years or so:

> The source at issue today is no longer an identifiable individual or entity—in other words, the mark on the bottom of a piece of pottery is not a shorthand for "John the cooking pot seller"—but rather serves to indicate the identity or essence of the product itself. A consumer who encounters the "Pepsi" or "Cadillac" mark probably does not think of the particular place of manufacture of the product or the owner of the mark—assuming those are the same entity in an age of outsourcing—but references instead some set of qualities of the product itself. One might say, "I drink Pepsi because I think it tastes better than other soft drinks" or "I buy Cadillacs because I think they're well-built cars that also impress my friends," but this is a different sense of "source" from the one that describes the place to which a buyer returns to buy more of the same goods. To be sure, the product itself must come from a manufacturer, and so there is a connection of sorts between the set of qualities attached to the product and some sort of producer, but it is not at all clear that the consumer always cares which set of hands is responsible for creating a product, so long as its qualities are consistent.[157]

[152] Compare section 1(1) of the UK Trademarks Act, 1994, which requires that a mark should be 'capable of distinguishing goods or services of one undertaking from those of other undertakings'.

[153] A trademark must distinguish the proprietor's goods or services from those of other traders. By signifying the origin of goods or services a trademark also fulfils this function, by distinguishing the goods and services of the originator from goods and services of others.

[154] *Mars GB Ltd v Cadbury Ltd* [1987] RPC 377 402, as quoted by Alberts (note 148 above).

[155] Beebe 2005, 2021.

[156] Baird 1993, p. 772.

[157] Heymann 2011, p. 388.

And, sticking with cars…:

> A trademark's primary function is denotative. As the typical explanation goes, when a consumer sees the "Mercedes" trademark, she identifies the car as one manufactured by the entity that makes Mercedes automobiles. (This is, of course, the Mercedes-Benz company, a division of the German corporation Daimler AG, but a consumer need not know this in order for the trademark to serve its denotative function).[158]

References to the source-identifying function of a trademark may need to incorporate some such conception of other qualities of the mark and of their role in making the mark distinctive, which qualities combine to make the mark something attractive to consumers. This includes not only the denotative function of a mark referred to above, but also the connotative (which calls to mind the collection of qualities that give the mark its power of differentiation).[159] Even expanded notions of the functions of trademarks—e.g. recognition of its role in identifying sponsorship or affiliation (compare section 43 of the Lanham Act in the United States[160]) or in signifying the quality of goods or services (compare luxury trademarks such as Louis Vuitton, Dunhill and Rolls Royce)[161]—require distinctiveness of the mark in order to fulfil its functions. An indistinctive mark would not be able to communicate any useful information to the consumer which would assist such consumer to make a choice between goods or services in the market.

Coupled with the requirement of distinctiveness is the general requirement in trademark law that a mark is not eligible for registration if it is merely descriptive of the goods or services for which it is sought to be registered. The reason is clear; where a mark would simply describe the relevant goods or services in connection with which it is used, it cannot distinguish such goods or services from others within the *genus* of goods or services, and it would thus not be sufficiently distinctive. A descriptive mark is not inherently distinctive and a secondary meaning (as source identifier, i.e. consumers would identify the product or service as deriving from a single source) would generally be required.[162]

In the mega-event context (and that of registered trademarks in respect of events), we have seen that FIFA has in recent years encountered problems regarding its registration of marks in respect of its World Cup 2006 and World Cup 2010 events. In Sect. 5.2.2 above we considered the protracted litigation involving FIFA and Ferrero in the German courts and before the Office for the Harmonisation of the Internal Market (in respect of FIFA's Community trademarks), and

---

158 Ibid. 393.

159 Ibid.

160 See the discussion in Chap. 8.

161 Alberts (note 148 above) refers to other functions of trademarks, including the use of a mark to fulfil an advertising, psychological or guarantee function, or as a communication tool (with reference to *Elleni Holding BV v Sigla SA* [2005] ETMR 51 par. 40), or to make a lifestyle statement (with reference to Phillips *Trade Marks: A Practical Anatomy* (2003) 27).

162 See, generally on American law in this regard, Merges et al. 2003, p. 546 *et seq.*; see also Article 15(1) of the TRIPS agreement.

we saw that the German Federal Supreme Court found that the mark 'Fussball WM 2006' was a mere description of the event happening that year in Germany and could not serve as an indication of source. The mark could consequently not be registered as a trademark in terms of sections 8(2)(1) and (2) of the German Trademark Act (very similar to Article 7(b) and (c) of the Community Trademark Regulation). It was also held that FIFA had failed to prove that the mark had become eligible for registration through acquired distinctiveness, in terms of section 8(3) of the German Trademark Act (and article 7(3) of the Community Trademark Regulation). FIFA's registered mark was accordingly cancelled.

Similar concerns exist in respect of the protected marks, words and symbols in respect of *sui generis* event legislation, in light of the distinctiveness and descriptiveness trademark requirements. In Sect. 5.3.2 below I will briefly examine the provisions of the relevant legislation (compare MEMA's major event word and symbol provisions[163] or those found in the Vancouver Act[164] and the London Act[165]) in respect of the tendency to provide protection to generic terms which, generally, lack distinctiveness for trademark purposes and simply describe the relevant events. While FIFA may have (and has, in the past had) problems in arguing that the words 'World Cup' are distinctive, terms such as 'Olympic', 'Olympic Games' and 'Olympiad' may justifiably be claimed to have inherent distinctiveness for the Olympic Movement. The same, however, is not true for many of the other words prohibited by event legislation and protected on a similar basis (for example, words like 'sponsor', 'medal', gold' or 'silver'), and these provisions raise serious concerns over the basis for protection (which so substantially lacks grounding in the normal principles of IP laws) and the effects of such protection (especially in respect of the free speech and freedom of trade implications—see Chap. 7). These provisions are an important example of how the *sui generis* event legislation provides significantly 'IP+' protection for event organisers, by prohibiting the use of material that would otherwise not be deemed worthy or capable of protection in terms of IP laws.

(iv) Registration in Specified Classes of Goods or Services

The *International Classification of Goods and Services for the Purposes of the Registration of Marks* was established by an Agreement concluded at the Nice Diplomatic Conference, on June 15, 1957 (subsequently revised at Stockholm (in 1967) and at Geneva (in 1977), and amended in 1979). The countries that are party to the Nice Agreement constitute a Special Union within the framework of the *Paris Union for the Protection of Industrial Property*. They have adopted and apply the Nice Classification for the purposes of the registration of marks. Each of the countries party to the Nice Agreement is obliged to apply the Nice Classification in

[163] Major Events Management Act, 2007 section 8 and the Schedule to the Act.

[164] Olympic and Paralympic Marks Act (Bill C-47); Schedule 3 ('Generic Olympic Terms') and section 3.

[165] London Olympic Games and Paralympic Games Act, 2006; Schedule 4 par. 3 (the 'listed expressions').

connection with the registration of marks, either as the principal classification or as a subsidiary classification, and has to include in the official documents and publications relating to its registrations of marks the numbers of the classes of the Classification to which the goods or services for which the marks are registered belong. Use of the Nice Classification is mandatory not only for the national registration of marks in countries party to the Nice Agreement, but also for the international registration of marks effected by the International Bureau of WIPO, the African Intellectual Property Organisation (OAPI), the African Regional Intellectual Property Organisation (ARIPO), the Benelux Organisation for Intellectual Property (BOIP) and the European Union Office for Harmonisation in the Internal Market (Trademarks and Designs) (OHIM). The Nice Classification is also applied in a number of countries not party to the Nice Agreement. Currently, the 9th edition of the Nice Classification is in force (since 1 January 2007).[166]

An applicant for registration of a trade or service mark must specify the registration of their mark in one or more of the product (class 1–34) or service (class 35–45) classes, depending on the intended use of the mark in respect of a variety of goods or services. Protection of the trademark is generally limited to the relevant class(es) within which the mark is registered. Registration, of course, brings significant benefits for the trademark holder. In the absence of registration of a mark, legal action based on e.g. unfair competition law requires that the mark holder (trader)'s reputation has to be established in every court action that is brought against imitators. A registered mark may, depending on the relevant trademark laws of a particular jurisdiction, provide benefits to the registered mark proprietor in the form of presumptions in litigation (relating to e.g. ownership of the mark and an exclusive right to use the mark). A trademark registration also puts competitors on notice that the trader claims exclusive rights in its name or the brand, and often notice of that right is all that is needed to bring infringing conduct to an end. The registration will also, in most cases, block others seeking to register the same or confusingly similar name or mark. Both these last two benefits are especially relevant in combating ambush marketing of an event. Finally, and of special relevance in the context of the commercial exploitation of sports events, a registered trademark will also be a valuable asset for event organisers, as it is much easier to value, sell, and licence than a mere common law mark, i.e. an unregistered trademark.

In respect of the staging of major sports events, event organisers can register their marks in Class 41, which includes the services of organisation of sports competitions. In recent years there have, however, been calls to expand the classification of such organisation of events to include merchandising in relation to such events. A FIFA lawyer,[167] for example, called for such extension at a

[166] Source: The website of the World Intellectual property Organisation (WIPO), at http://www.wipo.int/classifications/nice/en/about_the_ncl/preface.html.

[167] Richard Buchel, former intellectual property counsel to Adidas and counsel for FIFA and other international sports federations in respect of their global rights protection programmes.

workshop of the International Association for the Protection of Intellectual property (AIPPI) held in Berlin in September 2005[168]:

> On the registration side, it would be worth considering… a simplification in the classification system in relation to sporting events; as the Marks are indeed referring to a single and very specific Event, the products and services to be designated will always be connected to such event. The current classification system does not recognise the concept of merchandising products or services. We therefore would suggest to consider extending the scope of the services of "organisation of sporting events" in class 41 to also cover the products and services related to such Event. This interpretation would be in line with recent requirement of OHIM on "Event Marks" which requested a Disclaimer to be added to the specification of goods and services stating "all the aforementioned goods/services to be related to or connected with the Sporting Event organised by the Applicant". This modification would substantially reduce the costs of the application programmes, and would be more in accordance with the specific nature of the Marks referring to Major Sporting Events.[169]

Essentially the argument goes that allowing a trademark registration for an event mark in class 41 in relation to the organising of a sports event to include merchandising in respect of such event would negate the necessity for event organisers to make a large number of applications for marks in other classes (both in order to obtain the trademarks for purposes of licensing use of such marks to their event sponsors, but also in the form of defensive mark registrations to provide a basis for trademark infringement claims against potential ambush marketers).

The issue was subsequently canvassed by the working committee of the AIPPI on its Question 210: *Protection of Major Sports Events and associated commercial activities through Trademarks and other IPR* in a call for country reports (which received 37 such reports). Only the Swedish and Singapore country reporters unequivocally supported an amendment to the trademark classification system for major sports events. The Swedish group observed that many trademarks held by the International Olympic Committee are registered in all classes. The trademarks are used for many products and services—taking all sponsors into consideration—but not in all classes and for all goods and services. It was of the opinion that an adjustment of the classification system 'to cover not only organising sports events but also all other activities and marketing material which are of interest to major sports events would be an appropriate measure to facilitate for major sports events and other events without having a negative effect on society or third parties'.[170] The Singapore group were of the opinion that it would be reasonable to adapt the trademark registration system both to facilitate a shorter registration period for event-related marks and by changing the classification system. It is observed that, as the trademarks and signs which relate to Major Sports Events are heavily used

---

168 AIPPI Forum, 23–25 September 2005, Berlin.

169 From a summary of the presentations at the AIPPI Forum event, available at https://www.aippi.org/download/berlin2005/f1_cover.pdf.

170 From the Sweden country report, available online at the time of writing at https://www.aippi.org/download/commitees/210/GR210sweden.pdf.

only during the run-up period of the event and a short period thereafter, it may be reasonable to adopt these two suggested changes, with the effect that 'the existing trademark system is customised to accommodate the registration and use of specific trademarks in respect of a specific event for a specific period only'.[171] A large number of country reports were not in favour of changing the classification system (suggesting that it would be impractical and unnecessary). The German and Spanish groups were of the view that the present Nice classification system already sufficiently considers the goods and services that are relevant in relation to major sports events, while the Swiss group had the following to say on the subject:

> By extending e.g. the scope of services of "organisation of sports events" in class 41 to cover (merchandising) products and services related to such an event the subject matter of trademark protection becomes indefinite. The specific goods and services, in their interplay with the similarity of the signs in question, define whether or not there is a likelihood of confusion and, thus, determine the scope of trademark protection. Any vagueness regarding the goods/services renders it impossible to evaluate whether a potential new trademark will be infringing or not. Further, it seems perfectly acceptable to require a right owner to specify the goods and services for which his trademark shall enjoy protection and to have its trademark registered in all the relevant classes.[172]

It remains to be seen whether there will be further developments regarding calls for the classification in class 41 to be amended in future in the face of lobbying by event organisers for the explicit recognition of event merchandising (in respect of which the issue of the 'specificity' of sport in the European Union and the 'soft competence' stance of the EC *White Paper on Sport* of 2007 and its apparent view that the specific nature, characteristics and needs of sport will continue to be recognised, although not warranting a general exemption from the application of EU law) might be relevant). The Sports Rights Owners Coalition (SROC) expressed disappointment that the White Paper had 'failed to address the key issues' on sports rights more widely and that the White Paper's Action Plan did not include a set of actions related to intellectual property (even though the White Paper specifically recognises the value of sports rights), which calls have found support from other quarters within the sports industry and elsewhere.[173] For present purposes, I wish to turn to brief consideration of the relevance of protection

---

[171] From the Singapore country report, available online at the time of writing at https://www.aippi.org/download/commitees/210/GR210singapore.pdf.

[172] From the Switzerland country report, available online at the time of writing at https://www.aippi.org/download/commitees/210/GR210switzerland.pdf.

[173] Including, in the UK, the Culture, Media and Sport committee of the House of Commons, which included the following in its conclusions/recommendations on the White Paper on Sport:

'Intellectual property rights represent a large and increasing proportion of the income generated by sport. We share the view that it is disappointing that the White Paper does not give greater recognition to this, and we believe that it is therefore essential that sport has a seat at the table in all consultations and policy-making relating to intellectual property.' [See the report of the Culture, Media and Sport committee, 7th Report of Session 2007–2008 (2008), available online at the time of writing at http://www.parliament.the-stationery-office.co.uk/pa/cm200708/cmselect/cmcumeds/347/347.pdf].

provided by the *sui generis* event legislation in respect of the trademark classification system.

Protection provided to event organisers in special event legislation in the form of restrictions or prohibitions on the use of words or symbols (compare MEMA's major event word and symbol provisions[174] or those found in the Vancouver Act[175] and the London Act[176]) and the association rights to events, are not dependent on registration of such words or symbols as marks in specific classes of goods or services. The application of such protection also is not dependent on the types of goods or services involved in the case of a claim of infringement. Use of a prohibited term (e.g. 'Olympian') is prohibited in respect of any and all goods or services. And 'goods and services' in respect of the prohibition of making a representation that is likely to create an association with the event, is not further defined or refined in MEMA,[177] the London Act or the Vancouver Act.[178] South Africa's Merchandise Marks Act,[179] of course, also does not limit the prohibition on 'abuse' of a mark as contained in section 15A(2) to specific classes of goods or services only, which extends protection, in principle, to all classes.[180] And section 15(1)(b)'s prohibition on the use of words or numerals 'in connection with any trade, business, profession, occupation or event, or in connection with a trademark, mark or trade description applied to goods' is far-reaching, and clearly includes a prohibition on use as a trademark for goods and services. However, unlike trademarks, no class is specified. So if viewed as a type of trademark, these words and numerals are protected in respect of all goods and all services.[181]

The result is that event organisers are provided with special and more far-reaching protection than they would otherwise obtain through IP laws (specifically, through registration of the relevant marks as trademarks), or, at least, a level of protection that they would only be able to obtain at great cost and effort through the means of extensive (and expensive) 'blanket' trademark applications. In this light I would suggest that the above-mentioned calls for amendment of the Nice classification system in Class 41 to include merchandising of products and services in respect of sports events are ill-founded and insufficiently motivated, in light of

174 Major Events Management Act, 2007 section 8 and the Schedule to the Act.

175 Olympic and Paralympic Marks Act (Bill C-47); Schedule 3 ('Generic Olympic Terms') and section 3.

176 London Olympic Games and Paralympic Games Act, 2006; Schedule 4 par. 3 (the 'listed expressions').

177 See section 10.

178 See section 3.

179 Merchandise Marks Act, 2002—see discussion in Sect. 4.4.5 of Chap. 4.

180 See the report by Alberts, W and Parker, L to the Working Committee, Project Q210 ('The protection of major sports events and associated commercial activities through trademarks and other IPR'; reports compiled for purposes of a draft resolution to be submitted to the AIPPI Exco meeting in Buenos Aires, October 2009)—available online at the time of writing at https://www.aippi.org/download/commitees/210/GR210south-africa.pdf

181 See Kelbrick 2008, pp. 331–332.

the fact that the *sui generis* event legislation already provides extended protection to the organisers. Coupled with the existing and well-entrenched practise of event organisers to undertake such a blanket applications strategy for purposes of exploiting sponsorship and merchandising opportunities to events and in respect of defensive registrations to combat ambushing, over and above the special legislative protection which is demanded as a matter of course as a requirement in the bidding process for events, I would suggest that event organisers would be hard-pressed to show a real and pressing need for further special protection as a special, and especially deserving, class of mark owners.

(V) The Role of Disclaimers/Endorsements

Most trademark registration systems make use of a trademark disclaimer (or endorsement) system, whereby the ambit of protection provided in respect of the registered mark can be expressly limited. This may happen, for example, where a trademark consisting of more than one word may contain objectionable content relating to one of the words, but is capable of being registered in its entirety as being distinctive and satisfying the other requirements for registration. In such a case the following would be a typical disclaimer: 'No claim is made to the exclusive right to use '______' apart from the mark as shown'. In essence, trademark disclaimers are a way to include matter that may be otherwise incapable of registration (e.g. components that are unregisterable because they are descriptive, merely descriptive, deceptively descriptive, geographically descriptive, generic, a surname or meeting other grounds for refusal). A disclaimer may be limited to pertain to only certain classes, or to only certain goods or services. A disclaimer has legal consequences in respect of registration of a mark but does not affect the substance of a mark (i.e. it does not divide or separate portions of a mark from other portions[182]), although it has been observed that the presence of a disclaimer may have the psychological effect of weakening the breadth of a mark or may be deemed as an admission that the part(s) disclaimed is or are descriptive.[183] In the United States, for example, statutory provision is made for the use of trademark disclaimers,[184] and the function of the practise has been described as follows:

> As used in trade mark registrations, a disclaimer of a component of a composite mark amounts merely to a statement that, in so far as that particular registration is concerned, no

---

[182] *United States Steel Corp. v Vasco Metals Corp.* 394 F.2d 1009 (1968).

[183] Brookman 2003, pp. 5–49

[184] See Title 15: Commerce and Trade of the US Code, 15 U.S.C. §1056, which provides as follows:

(a) The Director may require the applicant to disclaim an unregistrable component of a mark otherwise registrable. An applicant may voluntarily disclaim a component of a mark sought to be registered.
(b) No disclaimer, including those made under subsection (e) of section 7 of this Act, shall prejudice or affect the applicant's or registrant's rights then existing or thereafter arising in the disclaimed matter, or his right of registration on another application if the disclaimed matter be or shall have become distinctive of his goods or services.

> rights are being asserted in the disclaimed component standing alone, but rights are asserted in the composite; and the particular registration represents only such rights as flow from the use of the composite mark.[185]

Similarly, provision is made in the EU's Community Trademark Regulations for disclaimers[186]: The circumstances when a disclaimer is not required are, firstly, that the disclaimer should not relate to the entire trademark, but only to a part thereof, and, secondly, that this part should not be distinctive *per se*. A trademark for which the applicant relinquishes a right altogether should not be registered. The disclaimer has a uniform effect for the entire European Union, even in countries where the element would be distinctive. In any procedure regarding likelihood of confusion, however, the similarity of trademarks cannot be established on the basis of this element.[187]

When considering the nature of *sui generis* legislative event protection (in respect of both provisions governing prohibited words or symbols as well as the association rights to events) it is clear that such protection is frequently provided for material that would normally not be capable of registration as trademarks. I will consider the protection provided to generic words and terms in more detail later in this chapter. The point to be noted here, however, is that such protection appears to leapfrog the *via media* of trademark disclaimers: At the one end of the spectrum one finds material capable of being registered as trademarks; at the other one finds such generic material that may be descriptive or otherwise lack distinctiveness for purposes of trademark registration. Disclaimers would provide a middle ground in terms of which the event organiser would otherwise have been able to obtain protection, albeit limited, for its mark, but not to the extent of acquiring exclusive rights to the use of material that is incapable of registration and consequently would trample on the rights of others (e.g. by unduly limiting competition). The *sui generis* event legislation, however, generally follows the approach of providing blanket protection for a vast range of event-related material

---

185 *Sprague Electric Co. v. Erie Resistor Corp.* 101 USPQ 486, 486–487 (Comm'r Pats. 1954).

186 Council Regulation (EC) No 207/2009 (26 February 2009); Article 37(2), which provides as follows:

'Where the trade mark contains an element which is not distinctive, and where the inclusion of that element in the trade mark could give rise to doubts as to the scope of protection of the trademark, the Office may request, as a condition for registration of said trade mark, that the applicant state that he disclaims any exclusive right to such element. Any disclaimer shall be published together with the application or the registration of the Community trade mark, as the case may be.'

187 Even in the absence of a disclaimer a trademark may not monopolise elements which should not be capable of exclusive use. The European Court of Justice found (in the *Chiemsee* case—joined cases C-108/97 and C-109/97, judgment of 4 May 1999) in principle that there were public interests why a particular sign should not be reserved to one undertaking alone as a trademark. This applied both to the sign on its own as well as in combination with other elements. Signs which may not be reserved to one undertaking alone include descriptive indications or non-distinctive elements, but also to sign elements in which there are other public interests, for example, national emblems or of indications of geographical origin.

in the form of words and symbols which may contain generic words, but without including any disclaimer regarding the scope of the exclusivity granted to event organisers or their sponsors in respect of such material. As such, the legislation displays an ill-motivated preference for the commercial interests of these parties at the expense of the public and other traders.

Kelbrick highlights the anomalous nature of the protection afforded to (and claimed by) FIFA under the Merchandise Marks Act in respect of its 2010 World Cup in South Africa, and which clearly illustrates a significant departure from the normal requirements for registration of a trademark and of the ambit of the protection afforded by a registered mark. This includes the impact of such protection in the context of trademark disclaimers (or endorsements):

> [R]ecent [trademark] applications by FIFA are substantially broader in their ambit [than marks including the name FIFA and/or the name of the host country of the World Cup event along with the words 'world cup']. They include the phrase 'world cup' *simpliciter* and the numerals '2010'. Arguably the phrase 'South Africa 2010 World Cup' is entitled to this kind of blanket protection—but on what basis is 'world cup' or '2010' so entitled? To exclude others from using these words or numerals 'in connection with any trade, business, profession, occupation or event, or in connection with a trademark, mark or trade description applied to goods' [in the words of section 15(1)(b) of the Merchandise Marks Act] is far-reaching. It clearly includes a prohibition on use as a trademark for goods and services. *However, unlike trade marks, no class is specified. So if viewed as a type of trade mark, these words and numerals are protected in respect of all goods and all services. Again, if viewed as trade marks, these words or emblems are not subject to the tests for registrability imposed by the Trade Marks Act. Neither are they subject to the endorsements recorded against the same words or emblems registered in terms of that Act. Thus, words and numerals such as world cup, South Africa, and 2010 are not subject to disclaimers. Prohibition of use of the phrase 'world cup' will also effectively prohibit use of the Bartlett trade mark registrations by their registered proprietor.*[188] *But the prohibition is not merely on use 'as a trademark'. Section 15(1)(b), couched in substantially wider language, apparently prohibits any commercial use of these words or symbols. If these FIFA applications are granted, South Africa 2010 cannot be used to describe a vintage or a flight schedule; neither can the words 'twenty ten' be used as a trade description for goods.*[189] [My emphasis]

Kelbrick posed a reminder (writing in late 2007) that the Minister of Trade & Industry had declared that, in deciding on protection to be provided to FIFA in respect of protected words and phrases in terms of the MMA, he would consider principles contained in the Trademarks Act, 1993 dealing with issues considered before trademarks are granted or not granted.[190] She pointed to the extremely wide range and the nature of the words FIFA sought to be protected, and observes:

> It is debatable whether any words for which protection is sought qualify for registration as trade marks, either at all or without disclaimers. If the Minister does deal with the FIFA application using this approach, it seems unlikely that protection will be granted to any of the proposed words or numerals other than the acronym FIFA.

---

188 See discussion of the *FIFA v Bartlett* case in Sect. 3.3.5 in Chap. 3.

189 Kelbrick 2008, pp. 331–332.

190 As per Notice 787 of 2007—*Government Gazette* 30001, 21 June 2007.

This prediction proved accurate, although FIFA did manage to obtain protection for more than just its own name. The Minister eventually declared the use of a limited number of words and emblems to be prohibited in terms of the MMA, from the much broader list of words and emblems for which FIFA had claimed protection.[191] The phrases that were prohibited include '2010 FIFA World Cup South Africa', 'Football World Cup', 'FIFA World Cup', '2010 FIFA World Cup' and 'Soccer World Cup' (from a much broader list applied for by FIFA[192]). Such prohibition related to use of such phrases in connection with the 2010 event and only applied to 'activities connected to 2010 FIFA World Cup South Africa in the area of Football or Soccer 2010 FIFA World Cup'.[193] Furthermore, the prohibition did not apply to the media, provided 'the reportage is fair and not imbued with unscrupulous business enterprising'.[194]

This more limited protection than what FIFA had claimed did, however, not assist a number of South African entrepreneurs who were subsequently confronted by rather ambitious claims by FIFA's lawyers. Kelbrick mentions media reports that 'lawyers acting for FIFA have barred about 20 entrepreneurs from using 2010 as part of the name of their business, many of whom adopted these numerals before they had alleged other significance', and of how FIFA objected to a company name 'South African Dream 2010' registered 3 years before South Africa won the rights to stage the 2010 event.[195] Mention was made earlier of the litigation against a Cape Town businessman in respect of his registered design for a vuvuzela-shaped keychain with the numerals '2010' and of the large number of cease-and-desist letter that were reportedly sent out by FIFA in South Africa. Such litigious posturing can have a chilling effect on the commercial conduct of individuals and businesses, and may in fact facilitate a wider *de facto* protection than the event organiser may, in law, be entitled to. From anecdotal evidence it would seem that the layman at the time of the 2010 FIFA World Cup and in the preceding months may generally have been under the impression that FIFA did in fact enjoy legal protection for words and phrases such as '2010', 'World Cup' and South Africa 2010'. For FIFA this would have been a case of mission accomplished even though it was provided with much more limited protection for its 'event marks' by

---

[191] Notice 1791 of 2007—Government Gazette No. 30595, 14 December 2007.

[192] Which included '2010 FIFA WORLD CUP SOUTH AFRICA', 'WORLD CUP 2010', 'RSA 2010', 'FOOTBALL WORLD CUP', 'FIFA WORLD CUP', 'SOUTH AFRICA 2010', 'SA 2010', 2010 FIFA WORLD CUP', 'AFRICA 2010', 'SOCCER WORLD CUP', WORLD CUP', 'SOUTH AFRICA WORLD CUP', 'WORLD CUP SOUTH AFRICA', '2010', 'TWENTY TEN', 'CAPE TOWN 2010', 'BLOEMFONTEIN 2010', 'MANGAUNG 2010', 'DURBAN 2010', 'JOHANNESBURG 2010', 'NELSPRUIT 2010', 'MBOMBELA 2010', 'POLOKWANE 2010', 'PIETERSBURG 2010', 'PORT ELIZABETH 2010', 'NELSON MANDELA BAY 2010', 'PRETORIA 2010', 'TSHWANE 2010', 'RUSTENBURG 2010', 'CONFEDERATIONS CUP', 'WIN IN AFRICA FOR AFRICA', and 'FOOTBALL FOR A BETTER WORLD'.

[193] Kelbrick 2008, pp. 331–332.

[194] Ibid.

[195] Kelbrick 2008, p. 332.

the Minister in terms of the MMA than had been requested, and would have probably obtained even less protection if application had been made for registration of these same 'marks' as trademarks. Things heated up and public sentiment appeared to turn against FIFA, and the *Business Report* ran the following report (on April 1st, of course…):

> Three South African calendar manufacturers say they will fight Fifa in court over the soccer body's claim that it has trademark rights to the date "2010". The dispute, which has been simmering since the beginning of the year, came to a head last week when Fifa's marketing arm issued the businesses with lawyers' letters demanding a total of R2.7 million in royalties. Fifa maintains that use of the date for commercial purposes, such as in calendars, is a breach of the special legislation approved last year to protect its branding ahead of the world cup. However managing director of Cape Town publishing firm Paragon, Goolam Allie, said on Thursday that the claim was "spurious". "They are definitely chancing their arm," he said. "We have spoken to our lawyers, and we will fight them all the way." He said Paragon was one of three firms he knew of that had received the lawyers' letters, and the other two, both in Johannesburg, had also vowed to contest the claim. Paragon had in the run-up to 2010 printed close to 85 000 desk and wall calendars, all bearing the 2010 date. "What does Fifa want us to put there instead?" he asked. "Or are they saying we must give the calendars away for free?"
>
> Patent attorney Richard Track said a date was regarded as "common goods" when it came to intellectual property, and as such could never enjoy copyright protection. Only when it was linked to an event in a phrase such as "2010 soccer world cup" did it become a trademark.
>
> Fifa's South African spokeswoman Delia Hunter said in response that the body was committed to freedom of expression, but that it had to protect its commercial rights. "We are obliged to act in the interests of our licencees, who have paid substantial amounts of money to share in the branding around the cup," she said.
>
> The move against the calendar manufacturers follows a similar Fifa letter two weeks ago to Kulula.com over an ad in which the low-cost airline called itself the "unofficial national carrier of the you-know-what", with stylised pictures of a soccer stadium and vuvuzelas. Kulula has discontinued the campaign.
>
> So the question is—is this an April fool's joke or for real?—[South African Press Association]

On a more serious note, trademark disclaimers would provide the space within which many such forms of commercial conduct by smaller enterprises and entrepreneurs could take place, reflecting a balancing act between the extremes of blanket protection for all event-related material for event organisers (or, to the extent as currently provided by the *sui generis* legislation), on the one hand, and of a significant lack of protection for event organisers on the grounds of the refusal of registration of such (e.g. generic or descriptive) material as trademarks. The legislation, however, generally opts for the first without providing significant exceptions which would stimulate economic activity by other parties in the mega-event milieu. One is reminded of the following words of Dreyfuss (in the context of a 'fair use' defence in trademark cases), which I would submit are germane in considering the poverty of *sui generis* event protection in respect of recognising other, more reasonable and fair options besides 'all-out' protection of commercial rights to events, as would be provided by trademark disclaimers:

> It is elementary trademark law that the right to a mark depends on its use *in commerce,* that is, in a communication between merchant and customer.' Also a part of basic trademark law is the idea that marks are infringed only when the unauthorised use is also in commerce, and then only when the use is not one that "fairly and in good faith... describe[s] the goods" (the fair use defence). Similarly, statutory rights of publicity often contain specific exemptions that depend on context. There are, however, many of what *The Pepsi Generation* called "hybrid" uses—uses that are neither purely commercial nor purely expressive—that are currently thought likely to give rise to confusion. With a better understanding of expressive needs and interpretive strategies, it should be possible to construct a taxonomy of such uses, with the idea that some can be safely returned to the public domain.[196]

Of course, legal advisors will often be less than enamoured with disclaimers suggested (required) by registering authorities and may prudently advise their clients not to blindly accept the registration of a disclaimer to a mark. Compare the following suggestion:

> Although disclaimed subject matter may still be protected under various theories, a disclaimer should be approached as, in essence, a donation of the subject words or elements to the public domain. Accordingly, anyone tempted to disclaim should ask herself, "Would I be upset if my direct competitor started using those terms in its own marketing?" If the answer is yes, then she should strongly consider taking a stand against the requirement.[197]

It should, however, be noted that my objection to the failure of *sui generis* event legislation to leave room for trademark disclaimers relates to the fact that this legislation, generally, in the relevant provisions are in fact *taking something out of the public domain*, and ringfencing it by granting event organisers and their sponsors rights to exclusive use. I would suggest that the decision of what should, and should not, be in the public domain should not be left up to event organisers and their legal advisors, in deciding whom to sue for infringing their specially crafted 'rights'. Ian Cockburn, in an undated piece on the WIPO website, refers to FIFA's unsuccessful pursuit of exclusive trademark rights to its 'Fussball WM 2006' and 'WM 2006' marks in respect of the 2006 FIFA World Cup Germany,[198] in stating that 'It is important to learn from these decisions that no matter the size of your company or its influence you cannot capture language, which is descriptive, nor can you monopolise an entire market simply by registering a trademark'.[199] I would agree, but would add 'except when you are able to demand that lawmakers make an exception if they want to host your showcase events'. Then who would need a registered trademark?

---

196 Cooper Dreyfuss 1996, pp. 150–151.

197 Karol, P 'Resisting the trademark disclaimer temptation', 28 February 2011, available online at the time of writing at http://sunsteinlaw.blogspot.com/2011/02/resisting-trademark-disclaimer.html.

198 See the discussion in Sect. 5.2.2 earlier in this chapter.

199 Cockburn, I 'Two apples, a football tournament and a bunch of trademarks', undated, available online at the time of writing at http://www.wipo.int/sme/en/documents/trademarks.htm.

5.3.1.3 Off to Court: Practical Considerations in Enforcing the Relevant Rights Against Would-be Infringers

Having briefly considered some substantive differences between IP rights and the special protection provided to event organisers in the *sui generis* event legislation, I need to turn to slightly more practical issues regarding the enforcement of the relevant rights. Mega-event organisers, to varying degrees, are no strangers to aggressive enforcement of commercial rights to their events, including litigation to protect IP such as trademarks. Such enforcement efforts are, in principle, unproblematic; where the law provides a right, it should provide a remedy. But the manner in which event organisers proceed to enforce their rights may warrant scrutiny.

I referred earlier in this chapter to the cynical (and sinister) strategy of using 'strike suits' as employed by some American trademark holders. Kenneth Port, in his provocative 2008 article, refers to this an example of what he calls 'trademark extortion', which includes other strategies and methods to stifle competition (all of which may be reminiscent of the conduct of commercial rights protection programmes by mega-event organisers in recent years). Is it fanciful to say that the following description, if not representing the reality of event organisers' protection strategies (which it might), reflects the apparent objective of such efforts?:

> Although much is said about litigious Americans, the ratio of trademark cases that reach a trial on the merits continues to go down, all while the total number of cases filed continues to go up. Of course, there may be several causes for the shrinking per centage of cases that make it to a trial on the merits (e.g. money, time, etc.). Another possible cause of this decrease is the prevalence of strike suit conduct. This strike suit conduct is also prevalent in the registration stage of the trademark before the Patent and Trademark Office (PTO). In this case, a trademark holder objects to the registration of a mark. The objection is based on the idea that the trademark holder has to plough a wide path through commerce in the United States. The wider this path is, the better it is for the existing trademark holder—better in the sense that the more third parties acquiesce to its use, the stronger the mark becomes. As the trademark holder ploughs this wide swath through American commerce by means of strike suit conduct in litigation…, cease-and-desist letters, or objecting to the registration of marks before the PTO, the trademark holder's mark becomes that much more distinctive and strong. *As this conduct occurs, gradually, but assuredly, the actual scope of protection of the trademark broadens. As the trademark scope broadens, the mark becomes more distinctive. As it becomes more distinctive, it becomes more likely that a skilled litigant will be able to argue that it has become famous. Once famous, it becomes subject to protection from dilution. Once a mark is protected from dilution, it has reached the zenith of its power to exclude others, regardless of whether the goods in connection with which the marks are used are in competition. That is, once the mark becomes famous and eligible for dilution protection, competition no longer is relevant. This is the holder's intended life cycle of trademarks.* [My emphasis][200]

The strong, special protection provided by *sui generis* event legislation adds a worrying dimension by providing expanded protection to event organisers in a climate of aggressive rights enforcement. As mentioned, this does not relate solely to the substance of the 'rights' provided but also to the more practical aspects of

[200] Port 2008, pp. 5–7.

litigation to enforce them. I will proceed to focus on three aspects relating to the enforcement of these rights, namely what event organisers are required to prove when claiming infringement of their rights (or, more accurately, what they do not need to prove) and what conduct is exempted from liability for infringement.

(i) No Such Thing as 'Fair Use'?

Copyright law knows the concept of 'fair use' as a limitation on the exclusive rights of the copyright holder, which provides exceptions to infringement of copyright in order to further important societal goals (such as freedom of speech) and to prevent the stifling of culture and of the pursuit of knowledge and innovation.[201] In the United States, Title 17 of the US Code (in 17 U.S.C. § 107) provides for fair use (as an affirmative defence to a copyright infringement claim[202]) in terms of a four-factor test that has its roots in a classic US copyright case[203]:

> Notwithstanding the provisions [of the Code dealing with the rights of copyright owners and their rights of attribution and integrity], the fair use of a copyrighted work, including such use by reproduction in copies or phonorecords or by any other means specified by that section, for purposes such as criticism, comment, news reporting, teaching (including multiple copies for classroom use), scholarship, or research, is not an infringement of copyright. In determining whether the use made of a work in any particular case is a fair use the factors to be considered shall include
>
> (1) the purpose and character of the use, including whether such use is of a commercial nature or is for nonprofit educational purposes;
> (2) the nature of the copyrighted work;
> (3) the amount and substantiality of the portion used in relation to the copyrighted work as a whole; and
> (4) the effect of the use upon the potential market for or value of the copyrighted work.
>
> The fact that a work is unpublished shall not itself bar a finding of fair use if such finding is made upon consideration of all the above factors.

Fair use provides for limited use of copyright material for a number of purposes, including commentary, criticism, news reporting, research, teaching and scholarship. In recent years, the doctrine has become a stalwart for opponents of the expansion of IP laws in attempting to further the limitation of monopolies imposed by means of the use of copyright. The American 'fair use' doctrine is of wider application that the equivalent 'fair dealing' found in common law jurisdictions, which tend to provide specific categories of use of a copyright work as exempted from infringement provisions.[204]

American trademark law also knows a trademark fair use defence, which is narrower in scope than the copyright fair use doctrine.[205] Fair use occurs when a

[201] For a more detailed discussion, see Fisher 1988.

[202] *Campbell v Acuff-Rose Music, Inc.* 510 U.S. 578 (1994).

[203] *Folsom v. Marsh* 9 F.Cas. 342 (1841).

[204] Compare section 12(1) of South Africa's Copyright Act 98 of 1978; section 29 of the UK's Copyright, Designs and Patents Act, 1988.

[205] See, generally, Ewelukwa 2006, p. 109 *et seq.*

descriptive mark is used in good faith for its primary, rather than secondary, meaning, and where no consumer confusion is likely to result.[206] In terms of the Lanham Act the defence may be asserted where the infringing term is 'used fairly and in good faith only to describe to users the goods or services of [a] party, or their geographical origin.'[207] The defence is available only in respect of descriptive terms and where they are used in a descriptive sense rather than in the trademark sense. It prevents trademark owners from appropriating descriptive terms for their exclusive use to the detriment of others who may need to use the terms to describe their own goods or services (i.e. the primary descriptive sense of such terms must remain open to use by others).[208] Fair use of a trademark may also include nominative use of the mark (i.e. where use of a term is necessary for purposes of identifying another producer's product, not the user's own product,[209] in order to discuss such other person's product or in comparative advertising) or parody.[210] The US Supreme Court has held that a finding of a likelihood of consumer confusion as to the origin of goods does not foreclose the fair use defence and the defendant need not prove absence of a likelihood of confusion in order to rely on the defence.[211]

A similar fair use defence is available in other systems (such as in the United Kingdom,[212] and in respect of the European 'Community Trademark'[213]).[214] More detailed discussion of the trademark fair use defence (and of the differences in its scope and application in various jurisdictions) is beyond the scope of this chapter, and the interested reader is advised to consult specialist texts in this regards.

It is clear from a reading of the relevant provisions of the *sui generis* event legislation which deal with exceptions to liability for infringement of provisions relating to prohibited words or symbols, and to association rights to events, that such exceptions are generally modelled on the trademark fair use defence. For example, compare the wording of section 11(2)(b) of the UK Trademarks Act, 1994 (which exempts the 'the use of indications concerning the kind, quality, quantity, intended purpose, value, geographical origin, the time of production of goods or of rendering of services, or other characteristics of goods or services') with that of Paragraph 7 of Schedule 4 of the London Act, 2006[215] ('[u]se as an indication of characteristics of the goods or services (for example, kind, quality,

206 Compare *Zatarain's, Inc v Oak Grove Smokehouse, Inc* 698 F.2d 786 (5th Cir. 1983).

207 15 U.S.C. § 1115(b)(4) (section 33(b)(4) of the Lanham Act).

208 See Merges et al. 2003, p. 550

209 See *New Kids on the Block v News America Publishing, Inc* 971 F.2d 302 (9th Cir. 1992).

210 See *L.L. Bean, Inc V Drake Publishers, Inc* 811 F.2d 26 (1st Cir. 1987).

211 *KP Permanent Make-Up, Inc. v. Lasting Impression I, Inc.* 543 U.S. 111 (2004).

212 See section 11 of the Trademarks Act, 1994.

213 See section 12 of the European Council Regulation (EC) No. 40/94.

214 See Ewelukwa 2006, p. 134 *et seq.*

215 London Olympic Games and Paralympic Games Act, 2006 (see the discussion in Sect. 4.4.3 of Chap. 4).

intended purpose, value, geographical origin, time of production of goods or of rendering of services)'). Compare also the proviso found in Article 12[216] of the EC Regulation on the Community Trademark,[217] which exempts certain uses of a Community trademark by an alleged infringer ('provided he uses them in accordance with honest practises in industrial or commercial matters') with the wording of section 12(d) of New Zealand's Major Events Management Act, 2007 (which exempts certain conduct of an alleged infringer from the association right provisions in section 10 and the presumption of liability in the case of the use of major event emblems and words in section 11, where such conduct is 'in accordance with honest practises in industrial or commercial matters'). These similarities strengthen the view that the event association rights are a statutory invention 'akin to trademark rights' (as was claimed by the London Organising Committee for the 2012 Games in a recent domain name dispute).

It should, however, be noted that such 'fair use' type exemptions are not unproblematic. First, and generally, one should consider that while such exemptions may appear to provide 'entitlements' in respect of conduct related to events, it is not unduly cynical to observe that the prohibited conduct (i.e. where such exemptions do not apply) are significant carve-outs from what would otherwise in any event fall within the public domain. When one compares, for example, the prohibition on use of generic words or terms (such as that contained in Schedule 3 of the Vancouver Act,[218] in Schedule 4 of the London Act, and in Parts 2 and 3 of the schedule to MEMA), it is clear that the relevant legislation has removed matter from the public domain and placed it within the exclusive control of event organisers and those acting upon their authorisation. The exemptions to liability for the use of such matter should not be characterised as entitlements but should rather be viewed as a generally extremely narrow remainder of the public domain. In this light these exceptions appear less benign and less clearly equivalent to doctrines of fair use in IP law. As was observed earlier, the American trademark fair use defence (apart from its extension to nominative use) is available in respect of descriptive terms and where they are used in a descriptive sense rather than in

---

[216] Which deals with limitation of the effects of a Community trademark, and provides as follows:

'A Community trademark shall not entitle the proprietor to prohibit a third party from using in the course of trade:

(a) his own name or address;

(b) indications concerning the kind, quality, quantity, intended purpose, value, geographical origin, the time of production of the goods or of rendering of the service, or other characteristics of the goods or service;

(c) the trademark where it is necessary to indicate the intended purpose of a product or service, in particular as accessories or spare parts, provided he uses them in accordance with honest practises in industrial or commercial matters.'

[217] European Council Regulation (EC) No. 40/94 (20 December 1993), as codified by Council Regulation (EC) No 207/2009 (26 February 2009).

[218] Olympic and Paralympic Marks Act (Bill C-47), 2007—see the discussion in Sect. 4.4.7 of Chap. 4.

the trademark sense, and it prevents trademark owners from appropriating descriptive terms for their exclusive use to the detriment of others who may need to use the terms to describe their own goods or services. Clearly, efforts by event organisers, such as FIFA and the IOC to prevent the use of reference to their events, in a descriptive sense, by e.g. travel agents and accommodation service providers, is not consonant with such a perception of what constitutes fair use in terms of IP law. Also, while an exception to infringement of association rights relating to the reporting of news[219] is common in the legislation and would appear to protect freedom of speech, such provisions lose some of their shine when one reads about the extent of their recognition in practise by event organisers—compare FIFA's requirement for media accreditation that journalists reporting on its World Cup should not bring the organisation into disrepute,[220] and the IRB's stringent press accreditation rules for the 2007 IRB Rugby World Cup which included restrictions on the number of photographs journalists were allowed to take during a match.

Second, and more specifically, one needs to consider that not all the association right and other restrictive provisions of the *sui generis* legislation in fact make provision for exceptions to liability, and that for some of these legislative restrictions there appears to be no such thing as 'fair use'. Corbett and van Roy refer to the extensive protections afforded to major event emblems and words in terms of MEMA, and 'inadequate quasi-"fair dealing" exceptions' to those protections.[221] But other such statutes may in fact offer even less in the nature of fair use exemptions.

Even though the London Act contains exceptions to infringements of its association right to the 2012 Olympic Games,[222] certain aspects of the right appear to negate or severely limit the scope for 'fair use'. This evident in the wide meaning accorded to a 'representation'[223] and to 'association', and the fact that not only does the Act not require an intention to infringe or deception of consumers[224]

---

[219] Compare section 12(d)(iii) of MEMA, which exempts a representation in accordance with honest practises in industrial or commercial matters, which is 'for the purposes of reporting news, information, criticism, or a review (including promoting that news, information, criticism, or review) in a newspaper or magazine, or by means of television, radio, film, the Internet, or other means of reporting'.

[220] See the piece by Guy Berger 'FIFA should embrace coverage, not curb it', *Mail & Guardian*, 20 May 2010, available online at the time of writing at http://mg.co.za/article/2010-05-20-fifa-should-embrace-coverage-not-curb-it; Menary, S 'South African media concerned over FIFA press accreditation rules', 29 January 2010, available online at http://www.playthegame.org/news/detailed/south-african-media-concerned-over-fifa-press-accreditation-rules-4645.html?type=98&cHash=c9506774c256cf7a569efc3a4e1fc363; da Silva, I S 'FIFA accused of "bullying", dictatorial tactics', 1 February 2010, available online at http://www.bizcommunity.com/Article/196/147/44260.html.

[221] Corbett and Van Roy 2010, p. 352.

[222] See, generally, Schedule 4 to the Act (and, specifically, para 7 of Schedule 4).

[223] For example a representation can be of any kind (including a verbal representation), as long as it is made 'in a manner likely to suggest to the public that there is an association'.

[224] The representation must objectively create the association.

for purposes of establishing an infringement, it is also clear that disclaimers would not exclude liability. Paragraph 1(2)(a) of Schedule 4 to the Act provides as follows:

> The concept of an association between a person, goods or a service and the London Olympics includes, in particular
>
> (i) any kind of contractual relationship,
> (ii) any kind of commercial relationship,
> (iii) any kind of corporate or structural connection, and
> (iv) the provision by a person of financial or other support for or in connection with the London Olympics.

Seeing that a disclaimer would not exclude liability for infringement,[225] would mere reference to the Games by an 'ambush marketer' who is a competitor of an official sponsor or service provider (for example, a London hotel advertising 'special rates and a shuttle service to and from anywhere in London for the duration of the Olympic Games') create an indirect association in respect of 'any kind of commercial relationship' with the Games? Paragraph 1(2)(b) of Schedule 4 provides that a person does not suggest an association between a person, goods or a service and the London Olympics only by making a statement which accords with honest practises in industrial or commercial matters, and does not make promotional or other commercial use of a representation relating to the London Olympics by incorporating it in a context to which the London Olympics are substantively irrelevant. Would such a reference to the Games fall within the very narrow exception described here? The advertisement is made in a context where the Olympics is not 'substantively irrelevant'; the hotel is offering a service for the duration of the Games because of the expected influx of tourists and the expected heightened competition between accommodation providers for the duration of the event. While no right-minded person would read the above hypothetical ad as representing an association with the Games (e.g. that the hotel is a sponsor or an official service provider), the definition of an association as quoted above is wide enough to lead to liability. As Johnson points out, the list is exemplary rather than exhaustive, and so an association can occur in other cases.[226] And there would be little prospect of a 'fair use' type defence, as the representation is made in the course of trade and for a commercial purpose. It is submitted that the hotel management would have a hard time convincing a court that the advertisement merely makes use of 'indications concerning the… quality…, intended purpose [or] value' of its services[227] which accords with honest practises in commercial matters, especially if such court may 'take into account' that the advertisement made use of a combination of the listed expressions in the Act.[228] At best, the scope for a defence of 'fair use' by our hotelier would be very narrow.

[225] Johnson 2007, p. 131.
[226] Ibid. 130.
[227] In the meaning of para 7(b) of Schedule 4 to the Act.
[228] Paragraph 3(1) of Schedule 4.

The issue of the limits of a fair use defence is even more acute in the context of the protection provided for a protected event in terms of section 15A(2) of South Africa's Merchandise Marks Act, 2002. As discussed elsewhere, this section prohibits the use of a trademark in relation to such event in a manner which is calculated to achieve publicity for that trademark and thereby to derive special promotional benefit from the event, without the prior authority of the organiser of such event. As I have argued elsewhere, this provision does not provide exemption from liability for non-commercial use of such mark. Section 15A(3) provides that 'use' as defined in s 15A(2) includes certain forms of use in relation to goods or services, and includes 'the use of the trademark in promotional activities, which in any way, directly or indirectly, is intended to be brought into association with or to allude to an event'. It does not exclude non-commercial use of a mark. Accordingly, it is also immaterial whether the use of the mark 'accords with honest practises in commercial matters'. As also argued elsewhere, the extremely wide ambit of the prohibition in s 15A(2) does not require the showing of consumer deception (what is prohibited is the use of a mark in relation to an event in a manner calculated to achieve publicity for that mark, and deriving 'special promotional benefit' from the event); there is no mention of consumers or the public perception of such use of the mark). Also, there is clearly no requirement for the event organiser to show an intention to associate with the event (i.e. to 'ambush'); the only intention referred to in s 15A(2) is that the use of the mark must be in a manner 'calculated to achieve publicity' for that mark—i.e. one of the normal functions or purposes of the use of a trademark. Section 15A(3) provides that use of a mark includes any use which 'in any way, directly or indirectly, is intended to be brought into association with or to allude to any event'. This last intention is defined extremely widely—there is no indication that it refers to the normal intention to deceive consumers inherent in the traditional notions of what constitutes ambush marketing (i.e. an intention to deceive consumers or the public into believing that the ambusher is an official sponsor or otherwise officially affiliated with the event)—and reference to indirectly alluding to an event simply casts the net too wide. I would suggest that the scope for a 'fair use' defence by an alleged infringer of the s 15A(2) prohibition is extremely narrow, if not non-existent.

Finally, one needs to consider the 'clean zone', advertising and airspace restrictions and regulation as found in the *sui generis* event legislation. These restrictions, discussed elsewhere in this book, are of course extensive and peremptory in their application, and they forbid wide swaths of commercial activity within specified geographical areas near event venues and for specified time periods around the mega-event, with limited scope for exceptions from liability. Compare section 22 of MEMA, which exempts certain advertising in clean zones around a major event (as prohibited in sections 18–20 of the Act):

Sections 18–20 do not apply to advertising

(a) if, in accordance with honest practises in industrial or commercial matters, the advertising is done by an existing organisation continuing to carry out its ordinary activities; or
(b) on articles of clothing (including shoes) or other personal items being worn, carried, or used by

 (i) a member of the public, unless that item is being worn, carried, or used in co-ordination with other persons with the intention that the advertising intrude on a major event activity or the attention of the associated audience; or
 (ii) a person who is a participant in, or who is officiating at, a major event activity; or
 (iii) a volunteer engaged in the management or conduct of a major event activity; or

(c) in a newspaper or magazine, or on a television, radio, or electronic device, being used for personal use, unless it is being used with the intention that the advertising intrude on a major event activity or the attention of the associated audience; or
(d) on a train, boat, or vehicle, provided that that train, boat, or vehicle is being used to carry out its ordinary activities in its usual manner; or
(e) on an aircraft that is used for an emergency that involves a danger to life or property necessitating the urgent transportation of persons or medical or other supplies for the protection of life or property.

These exceptions are all narrowly framed and pertain to very specific situations, and are anything but a general fair use defence. MEMA's restriction on street trading in a clean zone during a clean period (in section 17 of the Act) contains only one express exception, namely 'operating an existing business out of existing permanent premises of that business'. These types of restrictions as found also in the other *sui generis* legislation,[229] generally, leave no room for any fair use-type defence for would-be infringers. The absence of such a defence is especially poignant in respect of the clean zone and clean stadia rules of event organisers who demand either complete absence of stadium advertising (compare the IOC) or re-branding of event venues. FIFA has, since its 2006 World Cup in Germany, demanded clean venues (not devoid of all advertising, but only of advertising by non-sponsors of its event) which have necessitated re-branding or the removal of advertising from existing stadia. Existing stadium naming rights holders, therefore, have seen their rights being severely restricted for the period of FIFA's 'exclusive use period' in respect of such stadia; by the obliteration of their names from stadia they suffer a severe diminution of the sponsorship value for which they have invariably paid large sums of money. Such restrictions on the existing rights of rights holders who are not official sponsors of the relevant mega-event equate to a denial of the status of prior rights (which, generally, constitute grounds for a 'fair

[229] Compare the provisions dealing with advertising regulations in section 19 *et seq.*, and the provisions dealing with street trading as found in sections 25–31 of the London Olympic Games and Paralympic Games Act, 2006.

use' defence in other contexts), and are of dubious legitimacy.[230] This also reminds one, again, of the wide ambit of the anti-ambushing provision contained in s 15A(2) of South Africa's Merchandise Marks Act. By prohibiting the use of a trademark by such a mark's proprietor in certain circumstances, this provision completely ignores any 'prior use' exception to infringement. The very object of the section is to prohibit the use by a (intellectual) property owner of its property, notwithstanding the fact that such proprietor's rights may be prior in time (and should thus, in principle, enjoy preference—*qui prior in tempore est potior in iure*) to those of the mega-event organiser.

(ii) The Requirement of Consumer Confusion[231]

A central concept to the functioning of trademark laws in the different jurisdictions is that of consumer confusion. I have referred to the fact that one of the key functions of a trademark is its source-distinguishing function. We briefly considered the importance of distinctiveness as a requirement in the establishment of trademark rights earlier; this requirement flows from the central function of a trademark to denote the origin of products or services in respect of which the mark is used, in order for consumers to be able to make purchasing decisions based on factors such as the reputation of the producer or service provider, the consumer (and other consumers') experience of the brand, etc. As a result of this core function of trademarks the issue of consumer confusion is central to the law relating to trademark infringement (as well as being an important factor for registering authorities in determining whether a mark qualifies for registration).

In the United States a 'likelihood of confusion' test is used, both as the standard required to prove infringement of a trademark and as one of several examinations conducted by the U.S. Patent and Trademark Office in determining whether to approve an applicant's trademark application. Early American cases and statutes had taken a restrictive view of trademark rights and trademark infringement was originally limited to the use of a name or mark identical to the trademark in the same of identical goods, where the infringer's use was intended to deceive consumers. Since 1905 (when the requirements of identicality and intention to deceive were dropped) American law has, in what has been referred to as part of the

---

[230] Compare the following from the resolution adopted by the committee calling on the Board of Directors of the International Trademark Association (INTA) to issue guidelines regarding ambush marketing legislation, dated 10 November 2010, available on the INTA web site at the time of writing at http://www.inta.org/Advocacy/Pages/AmbushMarketingLegislation.aspx—see **Appendix A** at the end of this book:

'[P]roperty owners and others are often forced to breach existing agreements and incur associated expenses for which there is no compensation. Such signs and advertisements that predate the special event are clearly not attempts by the owner or advertiser to interfere with the rights of the sponsors to a particular event and should not be considered "ambush marketing." Ambush marketing legislation should make reasonable accommodation for these pre-existing rights.'

[231] More will be said in Chap. 8 about the role (or lack thereof) of consumer confusion in respect of association rights to mega-events as created in the *sui generis* event legislation.

process of 'propertization' of trademark law, extended the protection afforded to trademark holders, *inter alia* by introducing the likelihood of confusion standard for infringement.[232] The test, in essence, is aimed at determining whether the relevant consuming public would likely be confused or mistaken about the source of a product or service sold using the mark in question, in which case likelihood of confusion exists, and the mark would be deemed to have been infringed.[233] In order to determine the likelihood of consumer confusion the courts consider a variety of factors (including the strength of the mark; proximity of the goods; similarity of the marks; evidence of actual confusion; marketing channels used; the type of goods and the degree of care likely to be exercised by the purchaser; the defendant's intent in selecting the mark; and likelihood of the expansion of the relevant product lines).[234] Trademark law seeks to proactively prevent consumer confusion, and thus does not require proof of actual consumer confusion in order for infringement of another's trademark to occur. All that is necessary is for the trademark owner to be able to prove that a hypothetical, 'reasonably prudent' consumer would likely be confused by the use of the same or a similar trademark on potentially competing products. Infringement is not limited to confusion of consumers as to source, but includes confusion of any kind with respect to consumers or potential consumers. Courts have even found a likelihood of confusion to exist where the public at large could be confused, even though the actual purchasers themselves are not confused. It also bears noting that likelihood of confusion may also relate to confusion as to sponsorship or affiliation,[235] as expressly provided in section 43(a) of the US federal trademark statute, the Lanham Act (which is especially relevant in the context of the subject of commercial rights protection for sports mega-events, and which will be discussed in more detail below and in Chap. 8).

The UK Trademarks Act, 1994 provides for infringement of a trademark by the use of an identical mark in relation to identical goods or services, or of a similar mark in relation to similar goods or services, where 'there exists a likelihood of confusion on the part of the public, which includes the likelihood of association with the trademark'.[236] The EU's Community Trademark Regulations (CTMR)

---

[232] Merges et al. 2003, pp. 531–532.

[233] Even if there is no likelihood of confusion (i.e. no trademark infringement), one may still be liable for using another's trademark if you are blurring or tarnishing their mark under the state and/or federal dilution laws.

[234] See Merges et al. 2003, p. 615 *et seq.*; *AMF Inc. V Sleekcraft Boats* 599 F.2d 341 (9th Cir. 1979).

[235] Compare also the 11th recital of the EU's Community Trademark Regulations (CTMR), Council Regulation (EC) No 207/2009 (26 February 2009), which provides as follows:

'A Community trade mark is to be regarded as an object of property which exists separately from the undertakings whose goods or services are designated by it. Accordingly, it should be capable of being transferred, subject to the overriding need to prevent the public being misled as a result of the transfer.'

[236] UK Trademarks Act, 1994 c. 26; section 10(2).

also prohibits the registration of a mark that is 'of such a nature as to deceive the public',[237] and confers on the proprietor of a registered trademark the right to prevent the use by another in the course of trade of 'any sign where, because of its identity with, or similarity to, the Community trademark and the identity or similarity of the goods or services covered by the Community trademark and the sign, there exists a likelihood of confusion on the part of the public; the likelihood of confusion includes the likelihood of association between the sign and the trademark'.[238] The wording of trademark legislation in other systems may differ (e.g. South Africa's Trademarks Act,[239] which refers also to likelihood to 'deceive'[240]) but generally sets a similar standard in respect of confusion.[241] The concept of confusion in UK trademark law was recently extended significantly by the Chancery Division's recognition, in the *OCH-Ziff v OCH Capital* case,[242] of the possibility of a claim for what has come to be known in the US jurisprudence since the 1970 s as 'initial interest confusion' being available in terms of Article 9(1)(b) of the CTMR. The court defined initial interest confusion as 'confusion on the part of the public as to the trade origin of the goods or services in relation to which the impugned sign has been used arising from use of the sign prior to purchase of those goods or services, and in particular confusion arising from use of the sign in advertising or promotional materials'.[243] The court in *OCH-Ziff* rejected the argument that initial interest confusion should not constitute infringement as there is a lack of harm to the trademark proprietor where such confusion is cleared

[237] Council Regulation (EC) No 207/2009; Article 7(1)(g) ('Absolute grounds for refusal').

[238] Ibid. Article 9(1)(b).

[239] Trademarks Act 194 of 1993.

[240] Section 34(1)(a), which provides that infringement would include 'the unauthorised use in the course of trade in relation to goods or services in respect of which the trademark is registered, of an identical mark or of a mark so nearly resembling it as to be likely to deceive or cause confusion'.

[241] See also Article 16(1) of the TRIPS agreement.

[242] *OCH-ZIFF Management Europe Ltd v OCH Capital LLP* [2010] EWHC 2599 (Ch) (20 October 2010).

[243] At par. 87 of the *OCH-ZIFF* judgment. The court (by way of Arnold J, in par. 81) provided a well-known hypothetical example of initial interest confusion which was discussed in the judgment of Circuit Judge O'Scannlain in *Brookfield Communications, Inc v West Coast Entertainment Corp* 174 F. 3rd 1036 (9th Cir., 1999) at 1064, involving two video rental stores:

'Suppose West Coast's competitor (let's call it 'Blockbuster') puts up a billboard on a highway reading 'West Coast Video: 2 miles ahead at Exit 7' where West Coast is really located at Exit 8 but Blockbuster is located at Exit 7. Customers looking for West Coast's store will pull off at Exit 7 and drive around looking for it. Unable to locate West Coast, but seeing the Blockbuster store right by the highway entrance, they may simply rent there. Even consumers who prefer West Coast may find it not worth the trouble to continue searching for West Coast since there is a Blockbuster right there. Customers are not confused in the narrow sense: they are fully aware that they are purchasing from Blockbuster and they have no reason to believe that Blockbuster is related to, or in any way sponsored by, West Coast. Nevertheless, the fact that there is only initial consumer confusion does not alter the fact that Blockbuster would be misappropriating West Coast's acquired goodwill.'

up before the point of purchase. It held that confusion arising from an advertisement is capable of causing damage to the trademark proprietor even if such confusion would be dispelled prior to any purchase:

> Although there will be no diversion of sales in such circumstances, there are at least two other ways in which the trademark proprietor may be damaged. The first is that a confusing advertisement may affect the reputation of the trademarked goods or services. It is irrelevant for this purpose whether the defendant's goods or services are objectively inferior to those of the trademark proprietor. The second is that such confusion may erode the distinctiveness of the trademark.[244]

A notable exception to trademark law's requirement of consumer confusion is to be found in dilution provisions, which are aimed at preventing the erosion of the communication and advertising functions of trademarks. Compare section 34(1)(c) of South Africa's Trademarks Act, which provides for infringement by dilution where use of a mark takes unfair advantage of or is detrimental to the distinctive character or repute of a famous registered mark, notwithstanding the absence of confusion.

The issue of consumer confusion is one that has largely been neglected in the literature regarding ambush marketing of sports mega-events. This is specifically true of analysis of *sui generis* event legislation to date. I will consider this issue in more detail in Chap. 8 (in respect of the 'association rights' to mega-events), but will include a few brief words here in my discussion of how the legislation tends to expand upon IP laws and the scope of protection provided by normal IP rights such as trademarks. A specific aspect relates to the element of proof of consumer confusion in cases of alleged infringement of association rights.

I have on a few occasions in the earlier chapters referred to what has been described as the 'third dimension' that events bring to the equation in the context of ambush marketing.[245] Traditionally, IP rights infringements involve e.g. an infringement by X of Y's copyright in a work (for example, by means of unlawful copying or publication of the relevant work) or through X using, for example, a trademark that is confusingly similar to Y's registered trademark. In the case of ambush marketing of an event, however, the 'ambusher' would usually not be infringing the intellectual property of its competitor (e.g. an official sponsor). The deception or confusion relates to association with *the event* and not with the official sponsor. The 'ambusher' is alleged to have created confusion over their (official) involvement or association with an event, which it is then claimed prejudices both the event organisers (rights grantors) and the official sponsors or commercial partners (rights holders) due to the dilution of the value of their investment and a potential loss of revenues that would otherwise have been payable in terms of an official rights grant contract (as well as negatively affecting

---

244 *OCH-Ziff* supra at par. 101.

245 Shwetashree Majumder & Harsimran Kalra 'The ambush marketing debate', on the web site *Managing Intellectual Property*, 1 September 2010 (available online at the time of writing at http://www.managingip.com/Article/2665113/The-ambush-marketing-debate.html?ArticleId=2665113&p=2).

the efficacy of the official sponsor's advertising through the creation of a cluttered marketing environment surrounding the event). I would suggest that the form of consumer confusion that may be present in cases of ambushing would primarily be initial interest confusion (as referred to above). While proof of actual harm through diversion of sales of event-related goods or services to event organisers caused by ambush advertising may be elusive, the argument would go that (as observed in the *OCH-Ziff* case) such advertising may affect the reputation of event-related trademarked goods or services (or of the event itself) and may erode the distinctiveness of event-related marks (an argument relating to the adverse effects of advertising clutter).

A study of legal responses to ambush marketing of sports mega-events concerns, primarily, issues which resonate with a specific branch of trademark protection that has developed in recent years, namely the law relating to use of a trademark to denote sponsorship or affiliation. This is one of the 'new categories of confusion'[246] that have developed in trademark law in recent times. The Lanham Act in the United States makes specific provision for protection of marks in the function of denoting sponsorship, and also for consumer confusion in this regard,[247] rather than merely the source of a product or service in the more limited, traditional, sense. This development of the law has been criticised as leading to a vague conception of consumer confusion and as being contrary to core principles of trademark law.[248] Lemley and McKenna believe that a loose application by courts of confusion as to sponsorship and affiliation (which they refer to as 'irrelevant confusion') threatens to make the very scope of the application of trademark law overly wide:

> Confusion about some relationships simply shouldn't matter because it doesn't affect consumers decisions to purchase the defendant's goods or services. Yet the "sponsorship or affiliation" formulation allows for no such distinctions, threatening ultimately to swallow up all uses of another's mark.[249]

The *sui generis* protection of mega-events through special legislation is—at least ostensibly—similarly aimed at protecting against consumer confusion over sponsorship and affiliation. The special legislation that we encountered in Chap. 4 generally protect against unauthorised 'association' (in commercial dealings) with a protected event. The London Act, for example, grants the London Olympic Games Organising Committee a right 'to use any representation (of any kind) in a manner likely to suggest to the public that there is an association between the

---

246 See Luepke 2008, p. 794.

247 Lanham Act, Title 15, chapter 22 of the US Code. See the meaning of source in respect of 'related companies in section 5 of the Lanham Act; see section 43(a) of the Act; see Lemley and McKenna 2010, p. 413.

248 Lemley and McKenna 2010, pp. 427–428.

249 Ibid. 428.

London Olympic or Paralympic Games and goods and services, or a person who provides goods or services'.[250] The prohibited 'association' includes any kind of contractual relationship, commercial relationship, corporate or structural connection or the provision of financial or other support for or in connection with the Games.'[251] New Zealand's Major Events Management Act,[252] in section 10, similarly provides that no person may, during a major event's protection period, make any representation in a way likely to suggest to a reasonable person that there is an association between the major event and goods or services (or a brand of goods or services or a person who provides goods or services). Similarly, China's Protection of Olympic Symbols Regulations, 2002 (which were passed to meet its obligation to protect the Olympic intellectual property under the Host City Contract for the 2008 Olympic Games in Beijing) prohibits the use of Olympic names and logos for 'implied commercial purposes',[253] and prohibits 'activities that might be deemed by others as an existing sponsorship or other supportive relationship'.[254] It is clearly the relationship of sponsorship or affiliation (e.g. by means of licensing in the context of event-related merchandising) that is involved here.

Such legislation prohibits deception of the public as to association in the form of sponsorship or affiliation. What is particularly interesting, however, is that deception (and actual confusion of the public) is often not required for purposes of infringement—compare the London Act, which does not require that the association caused by a representation should be misleading (i.e. it does not matter whether consumers are confused or not), the representation must objectively create the association, and even a disclaimer to the effect that the would-be infringer of the association right is in no way officially involved with the Games would not suffice to exclude liability. There are two notable exceptions. The first is the legislation passed to protect the 2010 Vancouver winter Olympics. Section 4(1) of the Olympic and Paralympic Marks Act (or 'Bill C-47') states that no person shall, during the time period of the legislation, in association with the protected trademarks or other mark, promote or otherwise direct public attention to their business, wares or services in a manner that *misleads or is likely to mislead the public into believing* that (a) the person's business, wares or services are approved, authorised or endorsed by any of the Olympic organising committees, or (b) a business association exists between the person's business and the Games or any of the organising committees. The second example of an anti-ambushing provision which appears to emphasise the issue of deception of the public is contained in

[250] Schedule 4, par. 1(1) of the Act.

[251] Schedule 4, par. 1(2).

[252] Public Act 35 of 2007, discussed in Chap. 4.

[253] In Article 2.

[254] In Article 9.

section 6(3) of the Russian Federation's 'Olympic and Paralympic Law'[255] passed for the 2014 Sochi Winter Games.[256]

This issue of consumer confusion[257] (or rather the lack of a *de facto* requirement of such confusion in most special event legislation aimed at combating ambush marketing) raises an interesting question against the backdrop of Lemley and McKenna's criticism of the expansion of American trademark law to include confusion over sponsorship or affiliation. They argue that this expansion ignores a crucial requirement in terms of traditional notions of trademark protection, namely the *effect* of such consumer confusion on the consumer's actions, and that 'sponsorship and affiliation confusion has taken on a life of its own, leading courts to declare as infringing a variety of practises that might be confusing in some sense, but that do not affect consumers' decision-making process.'[258] As mentioned earlier, in traditional terms registered trademarks are intended to protect against consumer confusion because the use of an infringing mark (by a competitor or otherwise, depending on the circumstances) poses *a threat of actual harm to consumers*. Their confusion might lead them to decide to purchase the infringing party's goods or services, which may be of inferior quality or otherwise objectionable when not originating from the stable of the mark holder.

The association rights created by *sui generis* legislative events protection, arguably, create statutory protection that is akin to registered trademark rights (this was submitted recently by the London organising committee in a cyber-squatting

---

[255] Federal Law No. 310-FZ (approved by the Federation Council on 23 November 2007).

[256] Which provides as follows:

'Any advertising which contains false information concerning the association of an advertiser with the Olympic Games and the Paralympic Games, including in the capacity of a sponsor, or concerning the approval of consumer properties of advertised goods (works, services) by the International Olympic Committee, the International Paralympic Committee, the Olympic Committee of Russia, the Paralympic Committee of Russia, the Organising Committee "Sochi 2014", shall be deemed to be misleading.'

[257] In fairness, it should be noted here that some are of the view that trademark law has moved away from its traditional consumer protection rationale. Catherine Ng argues, rather convincingly, that developments in both the use of trademarks and in trademark laws have served to sideline the traditional requirement of consumer confusion as to the source of goods or services. These developments include the role of company law (i.e. modern corporate structures are often opaque and corporate management unknown to the public, which serves to 'alienate' the source of trademarked goods or services), the law's acceptance of trademark licensing (which, by definition, permits co-existence of multiple sources for one trademark) and franchising. She observes the following in arguing for a reassessment of the rationales for trademark law and a re-rationalisation of the boundaries for protection:

'Without a secure consumer protection rationale which presumes that consumer demand is trained more on the desirability of the goods than the desirability of their marks, the rationale [of trademark law] for advancing efficient distribution of economic resources… needs to be reconsidered. Where a mark is desired by and its goods incidental to the consumer, the consumer's economic votes may favour promoting the marks more than producing the goods which fulfil material needs.'

See Ng 2008, pp. 223–237.

[258] Lemley and McKenna 2010, p. 414.

dispute before the WIPO arbitration and mediation centre[259]). I would submit that the same criticism can be expressed in regard to such legislative protection and, more specifically, the fact that its focus is not on protecting the public (consumers) against harm deriving from confusion as to the origin of goods or services but rather the connection between the sponsor or merchandising licencee and the event organiser. What the legislation aims to protect is nothing more than the right (or ability) of the event organiser to licence association with the event to sponsors or licencees. And claims that this type of consumer confusion may warrant such protection for event organisers are tenuous, at best, as Lemley and McKenna try to illustrate in the context of alleged infringement of the trademark of a producer where the use of a mark suggests to consumers a relationship of sponsorship or affiliation with such producer.[260]

I would submit that, similar to what Lemley and McKenna refer to, what association rights to events seek to protect is little more than the event organiser's loss of potential revenues from non-sponsors, where the point of departure is an assumption that the event organiser owns the whole of the thematic space around an event and is therefore entitled to control all reference to the event.[261] Allied to this is the substantial interest of event organisers to keep the existing sponsors happy by presenting a no-nonsense, 'zero tolerance' front against 'ambushers'. The argument that ambushing causes harm to event organisers in the form of a loss

---

[259] *The London Organising Committee of the Olympic Games and Paralympic Games Limited v. H&S Media Ltd* Case No. D2010-0415 (the Administrative Panel decision dated 29 April 2010)—report available online at the time of writing at http://www.wipo.int/amc/en/domains/decisions/text/2010/d2010-0415.html. See also the discussion earlier in this chapter, which makes the point that the wording of the exceptions to infringement of association rights and provisions regarding restrictions on the use of event symbols and words, as found in the *sui generis* event legislation, often closely mirrors the wording of statutory trademark fair use provisions.

[260] Lemley and McKenna 2010, pp. 438–439 state:

'[S]tudies suggest that any harm to producers [or event organisers in this context] from confusion about sponsorship or affiliation is quite attenuated: producers suffer no lost sales, and they are unlikely to suffer any reputational consequences absent additional information suggesting control over the partner. If a mall cookie vendor advertises that its cookies contain M&Ms, for example, consumers might or might not assume that Mars had entered into a deal with the cookie company, but whether they do or not they are unlikely to blame Mars if they don't like the cookies. *The only sense, then, in which a mark owner is harmed by third-party uses that suggest sponsorship or affiliation is that third-party uses might interfere with the mark owner's own ability to develop and derive value from such relationships. In other words, the only likely loss to trademark owners from affiliation confusion is the loss of revenue the trademark owner could have made by licensing the mark to the putative affiliate. This is a claim to market control, not a claim of harm resulting from confusion or even an injury to consumers at all.* We think this circular claim to licensing revenue is insufficient to justify trademark protection, particularly in light of the significant costs such protection entails… Our point is not that consumers can never be harmed by confusion regarding non-quality-related relationships. Rather, the point is that the sort of attenuated confusion at issue in sponsorship and affiliation cases does not *necessarily* or even often harm consumers or the market for quality products. The benefits of expanding confusion law to this class of cases are correspondingly smaller.' [Emphasis added].

[261] See Kobel 2007, pp. 7–8.

of potential revenues that would otherwise have been payable in terms of an official rights grant contract is, in my view, contentious at best. This justification for such legislative protection as found in the *sui generis* legislation does not explain the legislation's failure to exempt cases where clear disclaimers are used by alleged 'ambushers'. The argument of event organisers goes that 'the ambusher is taking something for which they should have paid us', but in cases of the use of disclaimers the 'ambusher' is making it clear not only that they did not pay, but also that they did not take. A clear disclaimer such as that employed by Pepsi and examined by the Canadian court in the *NHL v Pepsi-Cola Canada* case would surely serve to remove any suggestion of consumer confusion for reasonable consumers. This was, after all, the basis for the court's finding in that case that Pepsi's 'ambush marketing' was not actionable as passing off, because there was no likelihood of consumer confusion. Absent such consumer confusion and the possibility that confusion might cause harm to event organisers (which, remember, has hardly been satisfactorily proven to date as a general proposition), one is left with a situation where the event organisers can at best claim that they have been prejudiced by the ambusher's association with the event on the basis that the ambusher is free-riding. But this assumes a meaning of 'association' with the event along the lines of the broad and robust understanding of the term in e.g. the London Act (with its extremely limited concept of exceptions to infringement), which I would suggest, is especially suspect in cases where there is a clear disclaimer of the unofficial status of an 'ambusher's marketing campaign. Absent consumer confusion one is left with the inevitable question: If the 'ambusher' has clearly not acted in a way that would suggest to consumers that it is an official sponsor (i.e. it has not acted contrary to accepted principles of law relating to fair competition and to infringement of IP rights), what exactly has it taken from the event organiser, and how is the organiser impoverished as a result? I will examine this question in more detail in Chap. 8.

I would suggest that Lemley and McKenna are spot-on in their assessment of the problems inherent in an approach to trademark infringement which so significantly ignores actual consumer confusion and its effects on the consumer. This is especially evident in the *sui generis* event legislation. Compare again the London Act's test for infringement of the association right, which requires only that a representation should be 'likely to suggest' an association with the Olympics; compare also the even more blatantly dismissive treatment of consumer confusion in South Africa's Merchandise Marks Act, whose s 15A(2) contains not a single iota of a requirement to show such element in infringement proceedings—it is the mere use of a mark in the prohibited manner, *per se*, that is outlawed. Corbett and van Roy also criticise the lower evidential threshold in terms of MEMA as compared to New Zealand's Trademarks Act.[262] They point out that it is, in terms of section 10 of MEMA, an offence to any representation in a way 'likely to suggest to a reasonable person' that there is a prohibited association (and

[262] Trademarks Act, 2002.

that courts are directed to presume such association where there is use of a protected major event emblem or word), and that this appears to be a lower evidential threshold to that contained in the Trademarks Act, namely to establish 'likely to deceive'.[263]

With no further attention given to potential consumer confusion and why it needs to be outlawed, the legislation significantly and, in my view, illegitimately, expands the event organisers' protection beyond what IP laws allow. This brings the rationale for *sui generis* event protection (e.g. in the form of association rights to events) in conflict with the purpose of the confusion standard in trademark law. Trademark law frequently refers to the confusion of consumers or the probable confusion of consumers. The reason for this is that trademark law is not as much about protecting business interests as it is to protect consumers. By providing a business with the incentive of increased profits by the grant of exclusive rights in a mark, and imposing a duty upon that owner to stop others from using that same mark on competing products, trademark law gives consumers some amount of control over the quality of products they buy. A prime economic justification for trademark rights is the role of trademarks in lowering consumer search costs—knowing a mark and being able to distinguish the products or services in respect of which such mark is used (and their source of origin) saves the consumer time, and allows her to make informed purchase decisions. For this reason, the standard for determining whether or when a trademark right is being infringed has entirely to do with whether or not a consumer is going to be confused, and thus deprived of making informed purchasing decisions. Pelanda expresses doubts about the legitimacy of wide anti-ambushing protection which includes the outlawing of mere reference to events in marketing (what many commentators would characterise as falling under the umbrella of an 'intrusion ambush') when considered in the light of trademark law:

> The ability to prevent a company from even referencing the existence of the Olympics in a way that does not cause confusion would be a dramatic departure from trademark law's primary rationale of preventing consumer confusion as to source of origin or sponsorship... [T]rademark law is only intended to prohibit commercial competition that is unfair, i.e. practises that are likely to confuse consumers, not to provide a competition-free commercial environment.[264]

In conclusion I wish to consider one other aspect relating to the lack of a requirement to prove consumer confusion in ambushing cases, in terms of the

---

[263] Corbett and Van Roy 2010, p. 351.

[264] Pelanda, B L 'Ambush marketing: Dissecting the discourse', undated 2011 paper available online at the time of writing at http://works.bepress.com/brian_pelanda/. The author refers to the opinion of American courts regarding the function of trademark law: *Two Pesos v. Taco Cabana*, 505 U.S. 763, 767–768 (1992) (The Lanham Act was intended to make "actionable the deceptive and misleading use of marks" and "to protect persons engaged in... commerce against unfair competition" (citing § 45, 15 U.S.C. § 1127)); *Mattel Inc. v. MCA Records Inc.*, 296 F.3d 894, 904 (9th Cir. 2002) ("trademark law grants relief only against uses that are likely to confuse").

legislation under discussion. As I will further examine in the later chapters,[265] there is a growing realisation in marketing circles that although ambush marketing is viewed as a significant threat to sponsors' investment in mega-events, another important threat is that of the marketing and advertising clutter produced (to a significant extent) by event organisers' tendency to over-exploit commercial value to events by saturating sponsorship opportunities in the form of a plethora of categories for sponsorship. This was, in fact, highlighted in an empirical study conducted amongst executives of some of the Olympic TOP sponsors.[266] This consideration is not only important in respect of the element of determining harm (and causation in respect of such harm) in cases of ambushing; it may also be very relevant in determining consumer confusion and the causes of such confusion.

(iii) The Requirement of Harm[267]

The requirement of proof of harm in trademark infringement cases is not based on the consumer protection function of trademarks, but rather on the sub-function of a trademark, namely to protect the goodwill of the trademark proprietor. This last relates to the reputation of the trademark holder (although, in respect of such reputation, the trademark also protects consumers in the sense of providing a measure of quality assurance).

In American law a trademark proprietor is in principle entitled to injunctive relief in cases of infringement. This is based around a property rule, which means that infringers cannot claim a right to use a trademark upon payment of damages; because trademarks serve to protect the plaintiff's business goodwill, infringers who 'trade on or dilute (and thus appropriate and destroy) a plaintiff's goodwill cannot simply "buy back" that goodwill with money… Once it is dissipated, it is gone forever'.[268] It has been held that 'to satisfy the irreparable harm requirement, [plaintiffs] must demonstrate that absent a preliminary injunction they will suffer an injury that is neither remote nor speculative, but actual and imminent, and one that cannot be remedied if a court waits until the end of trial to resolve the harm'.[269] Irreparable harm presupposes harm that cannot be adequately redressed by means of monetary damages. Not surprisingly, in light of the 'property rule' nature of trademark law as displayed in the jurisprudence, courts have in practise developed a presumption of irreparable harm which would entitle the plaintiff to injunctive relief once confusion has been proven in trademark infringement cases.[270] This has placed the owners of intellectual property in a stronger position than other litigants (as courts generally view pre-trial relief such as injunctions as

---

265 In Chaps. 8 and 9.

266 Seguin and O'Reilly 2008, p. 62.

267 I will not be discussing the issue of proof of harm in cases of trademark dilution (and in respect of famous or well-known marks) here.

268 Merges et al. 2003, p. 726.

269 *Faiveley Transp. Malmo AB v. Wabtec Corp.* 559 F.3d 110 (2d Cir. 2009) 118.

270 Stoll-DeBell et al. 2009, pp. 119–120.

an extraordinary remedy, which should be granted sparingly).[271] In recent years, however, the American courts have shown a difference of opinion following the judgment in a patent case,[272] which has spilled over into trademark law, regarding proof of harm. The Supreme Court has departed from the traditional approach, whereby proof of infringement would entitle a plaintiff to a permanent injunction without proof of irreparable harm, to find on equitable principles that no such injunction should be awarded without proof of harm.[273] The 11th Circuit of the Court of Appeals subsequently observed that a strong case can be made that this patent law judgment's holding 'necessarily extends to the grant of preliminary injunctions under the Lanham Act',[274] and, more recently, the 2nd Circuit also followed this route,[275] although the position currently appears to be unsettled.[276]

In the previous section I expressed the opinion that the issue of consumer confusion is one that has largely been neglected in the literature regarding ambush marketing of sports events. This is also (and probably even more so) true of the issue of proof of harm by event organisers and/or their sponsors in cases of ambushing. Much of the literature, in fact (and as observed in Chap. 3), proceeds from the apparent *assumption* that ambushing causes harm to event organisers and to the events themselves. Actual proof of such harm, however, has been largely lacking to date. I would suggest that this context of event commercial rights protection is directly analogous to one of the key problems with trademark dilution law, namely 'that it provides a remedy without a supportable theorisation of the harm'.[277]

South Africa's Merchandise Marks Act again provides a good example of the over-reach of special event legislation in protecting event organisers against ambushing. I have mentioned that fact that section 15A(2)'s prohibition on the use of a mark in relation to a protected event, which is calculated to achieve publicity for such mark and thereby derives special promotional benefit for such mark, is prohibited, and that this section does not require consumer confusion (e.g. in respect of an association with the event) and does not allow for a 'fair use' exemption (seeing that the section is also not limited to commercial use). Section 15A(2) is also rather anomalous in terms of the issue of harm to event organisers by the conduct of whoever infringes the prohibition. There is no

---

[271] Ross 2000, par. 11.01.

[272] *eBay, Inc. v. MercExchange, L.L.C.* 126 S. Ct. 1837 (U.S. 2006). This is reminiscent of the 9th Circuit's similar refusal to uphold a presumption of irreparable harm for purposes of an injunction in a copyright case, in *Sun Microsystems, Inc v Microsoft, Inc* 188 F.3d 1115 (9th Cir. 1999).

[273] Compare, also, *Amoco Prod. Co. v Village of Gambell* 480 U.S. 531 (1987) at 545 (not a trademark case).

[274] *North American Medical Corp. v. Axiom Worldwide* 2008 U.S. App. LEXIS 7370.

[275] *Salinger v Colting* 2010 WL 1729126 (2d Cir. April 30, 2010) (a copyright case involving J D Salinger's *Catcher in the Rye*).

[276] See Stoll-DeBell et al. 2009, pp. 121–125; see also Williams 2009, p. 571.

[277] Farley 2006, p. 1184.

requirement of harm to the event organiser, and the protection afforded to such organiser has no relation to the normal principles of infringement of rights. There is no requirement for the user of a mark in contravention of the prohibition to use their mark in a way that e.g. infringes the intellectual property of an event organiser. In theory, the organiser would be protected against such use of a mark even where it owns no intellectual property in respect of the event. The 'special promotional benefit' that a mark user might gain from the use of the mark is not tethered to the rights or interests of the event organiser, unless one reads into the provision an implicit assumption that the special promotional benefit derived by the mark user in some way takes something away from the event organiser (a classic 'free-riding' argument). It is difficult to pinpoint just what this something might be (although it appears to be 'publicity value' of the event, which I would suggest, is problematic[278]).

I won't consider this issue any further here, although I will again return to the question of proof of harm (or, rather, a lack of such requirement in *sui generis* event legislation) in Chap. 8. The issue of harm to event organisers deriving from ambushing of events will also feature in Chap. 9, where I will briefly consider the arguments in defence of the event organisers' mega-event monopoly and of aggressive rights protection in respect of such events.

5.3.1.4 Summary

By way of summary, it is clear that special event protection by means of the *sui generis* legislation found in various jurisdictions as discussed in Chap. 4 generally encompasses 'IP+' protection for event organisers. This often significantly extends the rights of event organisers and sponsors beyond what IP law provides or would provide, relating to both the requirements for the establishment of protection and the scope of such protection, as well as practical elements of enforcement of the relevant rights:

- The restrictions on the use of protected words or symbols generally require only the declaration of an event as protected (in the case of the more generic event legislation) or automatically pertain once the relevant event-specific statute comes into force. There is no requirement for such protected words or symbols to pass the test for copyright protection (e.g. in respect of requirements for originality) or to undergo a process of application for registration (such is the case for trademarks and for registered designs). Significantly, this removes the content and scope of such protection from public purview in terms of the normal trademark registration process and the mechanisms for scrutiny of applications;
- Normal restrictions on the extent of IP protection, for example disclaimers or endorsements as to the scope of registered trademarks and the limitation inherent in the registering of trademarks in respect of specific classes of goods or services, do not apply to such protected words or symbols;

[278] Which I will examine in more detail in Chap. 8.

- The scope of 'fair use' defences as normally found in the case of e.g. a copyrighted work or a trademark are much narrower, and in some cases apparently completely absent (with some special event legislation not allowing for e.g. a prior use exception);
- The association rights to events do not require infringement in the normal IP sense. Use of a trader's own mark, for example, which contravenes a prohibited association right does not require that such trader infringe the copyright of an event organiser's or sponsor's mark through unauthorised copying of such mark (i.e. all that is required is a representation that is likely to suggest an association with the event). In the context of the normal trademark laws, infringement of such association rights also does not require consumer confusion in the normal sense. In Chap. 8 I will discuss this issue of consumer confusion in more detail, but for present purposes it bears mentioning that the likelihood of consumers being under the impression that a trader or 'ambusher' is associated with an event does not, in terms of the event legislation, require that such impression should include confusion regarding the source of the trader's goods or services, which confusion in fact affects the consumer's purchasing decisions. The most stringent example of such a provision, section 15A(2) of South Africa's Merchandise Marks Act, in fact prohibits mere allusion to a protected event even if accompanied by an explicit disclaimer disavowing an association with the event. Such provision has no parallel in IP law;
- Infringement also, generally, does not require proof of harm. There is an absence of a requirement to prove that the defendant's conduct was to the detriment of the event organiser or sponsor, and there often appears to be an implicit assumption that infringing use takes unfair advantage of the relevant protected mark (or the event, generally, which raises questions as to the actual subject of such protection—which will be examined in more detail in Chap. 8);
- Apart from protected words and symbols and the association rights, the special event legislation generally also include 'clean zone' provisions around event venues, and far-reaching advertising and other (e.g. airspace) restrictions and regulation. These provisions prohibit trading in ways that are extremely restrictive and go far beyond the protection that an event organiser would be able to obtain through normal IP rights such as registered trademarks, by preventing other (even non-competing) traders from conducting virtually any form of commercial trading (including non-IP infringing conduct) within a certain geographical area and for a certain period of time. Such provisions are applied without requiring infringement of event organisers' rights; they constitute a blanket ban comprising a form of strict liability which does not require any unlawful conduct by traders (the unlawfulness of such trading derives solely from the relevant clean zone regulations in such event legislation).

5.3.2 *Turning Words into Property; or the Development of a 'Monopoly on Language'*

It is a well-known principle of intellectual property laws relating to trademarks and copyright that the mere commonplace is not deserving of legal protection. There is no such thing as a trademark in a generic term (i.e. a mark that denotes the class or *genus* of the goods or services to which the mark is affixed). No one can trademark the name 'Computer' in respect of a computer product, or 'Briefcase' in respect of a briefcase—these terms are generic ab initio.[279] Marks that are capable of registration as trademarks can also lose their ability to denote the relevant goods or services as a trademark when they become generic over time (through the process of 'genericide'). Just ask the inventors of the yo-yo, plexiglass, escalator, cellophane, linoleum or zipper marks (or, maybe you should first 'google' them?).[280] In fact, apropos the title of this book, the US Ninth Circuit in 1982 invalidated the Parker Brothers trademark 'Monopoly' on the ground that it had become the generic name of a certain type of board game.[281] In the law of copyright it is trite that the mere commonplace in the form of facts cannot enjoy copyright protection.[282]

The rationale behind this disdain that IP law holds for the generic and the commonplace can be attributed to a number of reasons. First, in the case of trademarks, it is clear that a generic word or term, by definition, is not capable of performing the key function of a trademark, namely to distinguish the goods or services marketed under the mark from the goods or services of another. If a mark depicts a *genus* of goods or services it can clearly not, simultaneously, manage to denote a specific good or service within that class as originating from a specific source. In this way the relevant mark can also not contribute to the economic rationale for recognising and protecting trademarks, if it does not lower the consumer's search costs and does not prevent consumer confusion. Finally, there is the issue of the potential anti-competitive effects of being able to trademark a generic term. The rights granted to the trademark holder would create an undue advantage while at the same time unduly restricting everyone else from using a term that is required in order to depict a class of goods or services. This would limit the use of language by consumers without any saving grace. Copyright also requires a measure of 'originality' in the creation of a work capable of protection. While copyright laws generally do not require novelty and only set the bar for the requirement of 'originality' at a modicum of creativity, a measure of 'sweat of the brow' is required for the copyright holder to claim the protection of the law. Similar notions of avoiding undue restrictions on the use of language apply—being able to claim copyright in the words 'Main Street' would simply place an undue burden on others, who might be required to include complex GPS co-ordinates on their letterheads in order to avoid infringing the copyright of another.

---

[279] Of course, the more arbitrary and unusual the use of the relevant word the more likely it might be capable of registration as a trademark (e.g. 'Diesel' for clothing goods, or 'Apple' for computers). The more a mark describes the good or service that it labels, the less strong the trademark protection it will receive, and the more freedom others have to use the same word for other purposes.

[280] Firms such as Google and Xerox have taken active steps in recent years to educate consumers (and e.g. the compilers of online dictionaries) as to the fact that their trademarks and brands are not for generic use, in order to prevent future claims of genericide—see Stim 2010, p. 428

[281] *Anti-Monopoly, Inc v General Mills Fun Group, Inc* 684 (F.2d) 1316 (9th Cir. 1982).

[282] Although the issue has come to the fore in recent years in various jurisdictions, specifically in the context of database rights.

It was predicted a decade ago that the internet—that great scourge of modern times—is facilitating a change in trademark law in respect of the 'propertization'[283] of language (as IP):

> The Internet is facilitating a new attitude into word ownership that will spill over into American trademark law and eventually erode its core conceptual boundaries. [The] Internet domain name system is fostering a much more pro-property view of word ownership than currently exists under trademark law, and… this new attitude will not be easily quelled. The Internet readily embraces the idea of language as a commodity. Words on-line is not much different than pork bellies. Both commodities can be bought, sold, stored and swapped with ease. The domain name business.com was recently sold for $7.5 million, wine.com fetched $3 million and wallstreet.com $1.03 million. GreatDomains.com, a popular online auction house, lists thousands of words for sale on its web site and reports scores of daily transactions. None of this is permitted by trademark law.[284]

When one considers the extent to which mega-event organisers have claimed rights to their events one encounters a worrying trend towards comparable claims of exclusive rights to the commonplace (even though the phenomenon of attempting to monopolise language is nothing new[285]). Elsewhere in this book I discuss the notion of the thematic space of events, in the context of attempting to quantify what sponsors are actually paying for when they fork out the big bucks to associate their brands with events, and to demarcate which aspects of events should be open to claims of 'ownership' or exclusive use by both the sponsors and the event organisers (and which should not). It appears, from both the claims of these organisers and from the protection provided in recent years by law-makers in various jurisdictions, that much of the commonplace and the generic are now apparently deemed to be included within such thematic space of events. It is not fanciful to say that the event organiser's lexicon appears to be constructed around an attitude that 'the legal system's default setting is that "all rights are reserved"'[286]—this, apparently, also applies to language.

In 2007 a British author, Robert Ronsson, wrote a children's science-fiction book entitled *The Donovan Twins: Olympic Mind Games*, about a 13-year-old boy who knows that the world is in danger from an alien invasion in 2012 and has to hide out in the safest place in the UK—London's Olympic Village—if he is to emerge from the shadow of his super-achieving twin sister and defeat the forces

[283] Claims of the propertization of IP law relate to developments in recent years which have expanded the duration and scope of initial IP rights to approach unlimited dimensions (for example, in the American context)—see Carrier 2004. I use the term here to denote the (purported) creation of a veritable right of ownership to language and words.

[284] Franklyn 2001, p. 1251.

[285] Compare the words of Sir Herbert Cozens-Hardy MR:

'Wealthy traders are habitually eager to enclose part of the great common of the English language and to exclude the general public of the present day and of the future from access to the enclosure.' *In re Joseph Crosfield & Sons, Ltd. ("Perfection")*, [1910] 1 Ch. 130, 141 (A.C. 1909), cited in *British Sugar P.L.C. v. James Robertson & Sons, Ltd.*, [1996] R.P.C. 281, 284 (Ch.).

[286] The phrasing of Boyle 2008, p. 181 (expressed in the context of copyright law).

committed to the world's destruction. Sound good? Apparently not to the London Olympics organising committee. LOCOG's brand manager sent Ronsson an e-mail threatening legal action for copyright infringement over the use of the Olympic reference, although it was subsequently decided that it would be 'disproportionate' to prosecute the author. There is a saying about the road to hell being paved with good intentions, and Mr. Ronsson must now be a great believer in this. The furore arose after the author and his publisher decided, in light of the Olympic connotations of the work, to donate £ 1 from every book sold to a local sports charity; when the charity queried the use of the word Olympic, the LOCOG got involved. One blogger put things in perspective, observing that 'a simple search on Amazon proves that 4 305 books have been published with Olympic in the title, 103 DVDs, 34 video games and 179 music items. It appears that the Olympic team had been a little lax in enforcing its brand'.[287] Rather less stoic about this affair was David Edgar, playwright and president of the Writer's Guild, who expressed strong condemnation of LOCOG's attitude to what it narrowly views as its sacrosanct intellectual property:

> The email to Robert Ronson was written by the Olympic organising committee's manager of brand protection, concerned to "ensure that there was no confusion" as to whether the novel was "an official licenced product", presumably in case the committee seeks to declare Ian McEwan or Martin Amis official novelist to the 2012 Olympics at some point... By declaring images, titles and now words to be ownable brands,... various organisations and individuals are contributing to an increased commodification and thus privatisation of materials previously agreed to be in the public domain. For scientists, this constrains the use of public and published knowledge, up to and including the human genome. For artists, it implies that the only thing you can do with subject matter is to sell it. As a consequence, people's view of what representation does becomes narrowly literal... Consulted by its British branch about the Olympic Mind Games case, the International Olympic Committee expressed two major concerns: that the word Olympic was used in the title of a work of fiction and that "there is no such thing as Olympic mind games". Clearly, the IOC hasn't grasped what the word "fiction" means. Most expression involves reference to something real in the world. Most of our "experience" and indeed our "imagination" are formed from the image-making of others. Writers and other artists are rightly concerned about protecting their own copyright, but they should be equally concerned with the shrinking of the public domain. Ronson's refusal to be cowed into changing the title of his novel is a victory for the idea that there is more to free expression than the right to advertise.[288]

I would assume that, had the LOCOG proceeded to institute litigation against Mr. Ronsson and if a court were to grant it protection of the exclusive use of the Olympic reference (which is quite conceivable in light of the wide ambit of the London Act), this would be a case that would qualify for inclusion in Rochelle Cooper Dreyfuss's description of developments in publicity rights and product get-up protection through trademark law (in the USA) having the effect of '[divesting]

---

[287] See http://wondering-mind.blogspot.com/2007/12/masterclass-self-publishing-olympic.html.

[288] Edgar, D 'You can't use the "O-word"', *The Guardian*, 8 October 2007 (available online at the time of writing at http://www.guardian.co.uk/commentisfree/2007/oct/08/comment.olympics2012).

the public domain… of symbols that, by virtue of shared cultural understandings, serve valuable linguistic and symbolic functions'.[289] Cases like this beg the question: Should we allow language to become property of the rich and litigious? Should we countenance—ridiculous as it may sound—a 'monopoly on language'?

It appears to be generally acknowledged that the law's protection of intellectual property, by its very nature, holds freedom of speech implications:

> [M]ost intellectual property rules—copyright law, trademark law, right of publicity law, and trade secret law—are speech restrictions: They keep people from publishing, producing, and performing the speech that they want to publish, produce, and perform. The laws may be well motivated and often beneficial, but they are speech restrictions nonetheless, as many courts have acknowledged.[290]

If one accepts this, as I think one must, it seems reasonable to suggest that any laws or legal protection of subject matter that goes *beyond* IP rights—such as the 'IP+' protection in *sui generis* event legislation for words, emblems and other things relating to mega-events—have the potential to be even more restrictive of free speech. I will not elaborate on freedom of speech as a constitutional or fundamental human rights issue here (I will do so elsewhere[291]). My point here is simply that the use of IP in the mega-event anti-ambush marketing context or of statutory 'IP+' 'rights' in event legislation to limit freedom over the use of language is a worrying trend, which holds wider implications that go well beyond a narrow objective-based view of protecting commercial interests of sponsors or event organisers. And it is not only those cases where event organisers threaten action against persons like Mr. Ronsson based on a conception of 'owning' words or phrases which require our attention. I will discuss the new-fangled statutory 'association rights' to mega-events in more detail elsewhere.[292] An important consideration when it comes to determining the legitimacy of association rights to events is the chilling effect that such rights may have, generally in respect of the freedom of expression, and more specifically also in respect of advertising. This is especially relevant in the context of restrictions placed on the use of language (e.g. where use of generic terms is prohibited, as we have seen in the context of various *sui generis* event statutes in various jurisdictions). Mention was made in Chap. 4 of the special event legislation passed for purposes of the 2014 Glasgow Commonwealth Games, and of the special Order issued subsequently which creates an association right to this event similar to that created in the legislation for the 2012 London Olympic Games. The UK's Advertising Association prepared a submission to the Scottish legislature during the preparation of the Glasgow legislation, and specifically raised this issue[293]:

---

[289] Cooper Dreyfuss 1996, p. 136.

[290] Volokh 2003, p. 698.

[291] In Chap. 7.

[292] See Chap. 8.

[293] In para A.1.3 of this submission document, which is available online at the time of writing at http://www.adassoc.org.uk/aa/index.cfm?LinkServID=5737B08E−19B9-F84A-0C664664F83A91B0&showMeta=0.

> In addition to being unnecessary, the [Advertising Association] is deeply concerned that the creation of an association right for the Glasgow Commonwealth Games, as Scottish Ministers currently propose, is disproportionate and risks damaging the wider advertising sector by introducing intellectual property rights over words and numerals in common usage. In so doing, *association rights intentionally create an atmosphere of legal doubt for companies engaged in legitimate advertising having no desire to create any misleading or false associations with sponsored events, thereby impacting detrimentally upon the advertising economy.* The AA anticipates that the association right contained within Section 33 ("London Olympics association right") of the 2006 Act is (and will continue to have) precisely this UK-wide effect. The same UK-wide effect would be created were equivalent rights granted to the Glasgow Commonwealth Games thereby perpetuating the problems identified above. [My emphasis]

And one is faced with the question of whether the Olympic Movement (and the rest of us) really needs a provision such as section 28 of New Zealand's Major Events Management Act. This section makes it an offence for anyone, without the authorisation of the NZ Olympic Committee, to 'display, exhibit, or otherwise use' any word in trade that 'so closely resembles any emblem or word' in the schedule to the Act 'as to be likely to deceive or confuse any person'. The protected words in the Schedule include words like 'Olympic Gold', 'Commonwealth', 'Games', 'Melbourne', 'Beijing', '2006', '2008', 'Twentieth' and 'Twenty-sixth'. Anyone convicted of the offence is liable on summary conviction to a fine not exceeding NZD 150,000.[294] Yes, section 30 of the Act contains exceptions to infringement,[295] but one should not forget that the words prohibited by section 28

[294] MEMA section 31.

[295] Section 30 provides as follows:

'Section 28 does not apply to the display, exhibition, or use of any emblem or word if

(a) the display, exhibition, or use is expressly authorised by or under any Act or by the Governor-General by Order in Council; or
(b) immediately before 18 December 1998, either
    (i) that display, exhibition, or use was expressly authorised by any consent, permission, approval, or authority given by a person lawfully entitled to give it; or
    (ii) the emblem or word was registered under any statutory authority; or
(c) the emblem or word is part of the description of any sporting or recreational facilities operated by a local authority or community organisation; or
(d) the display, exhibition, or use is for the purposes of, or associated with, the reporting of news or criticism or a review in a newspaper or magazine, or by means of television, radio, film, the Internet, or by other means of reporting by a person who ordinarily engages in the business of such reporting; or
(e) the display, exhibition, or use is for the purposes of, or associated with, a radio or television programme, an Internet website, or a film, book, or article for publication in a newspaper or magazine, relating to a person who was a member or official of the New Zealand team that competed at an Olympic Games or Commonwealth Games; or
(f) in the case of a word, the word comprises the whole or part of the proper name of any town or road or other place in New Zealand; or
(g) in the case of a word, the word is the surname or initials (not being used for the purpose of defeating the intention of this section) of a foundation member of the body or of the person engaging in the business, trade, or occupation.'

constitute a radical carve-out of matter that, prior to the passing of MEMA, was in the public domain. In that light the exceptions in section 30 start to appear flimsy and technical, and one wonders whether such extensive protection of the commercial interests of sports bosses through restrictions on the use of language can ever be legitimate in a twenty first century democracy. How legitimate is it that academic commentators would have to speculate over such issues in this day and age and in a modern constitutional democracy?

> Thankfully, the MEMA permits the use of a major event emblem or word if "the representation is of personal opinion made by a natural person for no commercial gain". Ordinary citizens are thus reasonably secure from legal action if they should happen to mention a major event word in conversation with their friends. It is possible that this exception might apply to academic and student research and criticism.[296]

When one considers the central role of trademarks as IP in the mega-event rights protection milieu, it is important to acknowledge the multi-dimensional nature of this construct and the fact that it should be treated differently from other forms of (tangible) property. This is especially germane when we are confronted with the free speech implications of IP rights (and of trademarks) and its relevance to language:

> Since the trademark holder both invents and sustains the worth of the mark, it is his or her claims to private ownership that must be protected. Similar arguments about the investment of labor are often used to legitimize tangible property. But here it is employed to bolster private entitlements to language and iconography. Intellectual property... is different. As a form of expression, there is a clear and ever-present public role in shaping language. Trademarks are even one step further from tangible property than other species of intellectual property. Peculiar to trademarks, the communicative sign is a placeholder for a robust but intangible cultural relationship between producer and consumer.[297]

In light of these considerations regarding the role of both traditional IP rights and the new statutory form of protection of the mega-event, we need to examine to what extent words are 'propertized' in this context. It also bears consideration whether 'it can be argued that Major Sports Events do not constitute a foundation for a redistribution of rights between official sponsors and other traders whereby third party traders are excluded from using certain words which form part of common language usage, and it may be argued that third parties should be able to use a sport event in advertising or other commercial activities as long as they respect the rights and legitimate interests of the organisers and sponsors'.[298]

---

[296] Corbett and Van Roy 2010, p. 354.

[297] Wilf 1999, pp. 1–2.

[298] From the guidelines of the Working Committee of the AIPPI, Project Q210 ('The protection of major sports events and associated commercial activities through trademarks and other IPR'; in a call for reports compiled for purposes of a draft resolution to be submitted to the AIPPI Exco meeting in Buenos Aires, October 2009), at 3—available online at the time of writing at https://www.aippi.org/download/commitees/210/WG210English.pdf

A useful starting point is to consider the following observations from the dissenting judgment of Kozinski J in the Court of Appeals decision in the *San Francisco Arts & Athletics* (the 'Gay Olympics') case[299]:

> The word Olympic has a meaning unique within our language. It connotes open and intense competition among non-professional athletes, usually involving the best and most accomplished athletes… I have great difficulty with the idea that Congress can deny all of us that word, and the idea it embodies, in connection with all public endeavours… To say that the word Olympic is property begs the question. What appellants challenge is the power of Congress to privatize the word Olympic, rendering it unutterable by anyone else in connection with any product or public event, whether for profit or, as in this case, to promote a cause… If Congress has the power to grant a crown monopoly in the word Olympic, one wonders how many other words or concepts can be similarly enclosed, and the extent to which our public discourse can thereby be impoverished.

This view, however, held little sway with the Supreme Court, where Powell J concluded that on a construction of the language of the Ted Stevens Act[300] the US Olympic Committee holds an exclusive right to the use of the word 'Olympic' in respect of the Games:

> When a word acquires value as the result of organisation and the expenditure of labour, skill, and money by an entity, that entity constitutionally may obtain a limited property right in the word. Congress reasonably could conclude that the commercial and promotional value of the word "Olympic" was the product of the USOC's talents and energy, the end result of much time, effort, and expense. In view of the history of the origins and associations of the word "Olympic", Congress' decision to grant the USOC a limited property right in the word falls within the scope of trademark law protection, and thus within constitutional bounds.

This approach has, not surprisingly, been criticised on the basis of its free speech implications:

> The elegant circularity… of course, is that Powell is using the results of a Congressional action to support the initial constitutionality of that action. Since 1950, when the legislation creating [USOC] was enacted, everyone but USOC has been legislatively prevented from using the term "Olympic" to promote athletic events. It is highly likely (though no empirical evidence was presented at trial on the matter) that most Americans nowadays, upon seeing the word "Olympic", do indeed conjure up a mental image of the games conducted under the auspices of USOC. But that reality is clearly a result of the word having been, as [Kozinski J] claimed, plucked from the dictionary and granted to one private entity. The question before the court, which Powell does not satisfactorily answer, is whether that initial plucking was constitutional.[301]

In the previous section we saw the lengths to which football governing body FIFA has gone in the past decade in order to claim (with varying success) trademark rights in Europe to the description of their 'World Cup' event. This is

---

[299] San Francisco Arts & Athletics, Inc. v USOC 789 F.2d 1320–1323. For more on this case, see the discussion in Sect. 4.4.10 of Chap. 4.

[300] See discussion in Sect. 4.4.10 in Chap. 4.

[301] Siegel 1994, p. 37.

not the first time that courts have encountered claims to the exclusive use of these words. The Delhi High Court, in the case of *ICC Development (International) Ltd. v Arvee Enterprises Ltd. & Philips*[302] was faced with an anti-ambush marketing claim by the plaintiff, which included a claim to protection for its use of the term 'World Cup' in the context of the ICC's World Cup cricket tournament in 2003. The court made short shrift of this claim, on the basis of the generic nature of the words in combination:

> Law in this regard is well settled. "Generic" words have dictionary meaning, and are neither specific nor special. These words belong to one genus. Such words are neither brand names nor have any protection by the registered trademark. 'World Cup' is a dictionary word. It means a tournament or event, where several nations participate. Thus, these words are generic and not capable of conferring any exclusive right. These are available to everyone. The genericness of these words can be judged from the fact that these words have been used to refer to several other international sporting events, namely, Football-FIFA World Cup, Hockey-FIH World Cup, Para gliding, Skiing, Horse Racing, Skateboarding, Rugby, Boxing. These words are not protected like the Olympics or its logo. Further, it is not contested that the Event was referred to in the years 1975, 1979 and 1983 as Prudential Cup; in 1987 it was referred to as Reliance Cup; and in 1991 it was referred to as the Benson & Hedges Cup. Even thereafter the names of major sponsors were associated with the plaintiff. In view of all this, prima facie, the words "World Cup Cricket" and "World Cup" have to be non-exclusive and generic.[303]

In light of the discussion earlier in this chapter of FIFA's attempts in the past decade to obtain special IP protection for its event marks relating to its 'World Cup', it is ironic to consider that FIFA earlier successfully challenged the registration of a 'World Cup' trademark before a South African court. In *FIFA v Bartlett*[304] the football governing body challenged the registration of the Respondent's mark, consisting of the words 'World Cup' and a representation of a globe (which had been registered in 1969), in terms of the provisions of section 18 of the then-applicable Trademarks Act.[305] This provision provided that if a mark 'contains matter common to the trade or otherwise of a non-distinctive nature', the registrar or court may require a disclaimer to be entered in respect of such matter. FIFA claimed that the words 'world cup' were common to the trade. The court agreed, and held that the words were descriptive of a number of sporting events and the mark was thus also non-distinctive in respects of the goods for which it was registered (the words 'world cup' were 'simply of a non-distinctive character in South Africa'[306]). Kelbrick pertinently asks, in light of the court's finding in *Bartlett* and in respect of FIFA's large number of registered trademarks in South Africa (she mentions that prior to 2008 FIFA was the proprietor of, or applicant for, over 500 trademarks in South Africa): How then has FIFA obtained a number

302 (2003) VII AD (Del) 405—see the discussion in Sect. 4.4.2 of Chap. 4.

303 At par. 18 of the court's order (by Agarwal J, dated 1 January 2003).

304 1994 (4) SA 722 (T)—as discussed elsewhere in Sect. 3.3.5 of Chap. 3.

305 Act 62 of 1963.

306 At 742E of the judgment.

of word marks consisting of the term 'World Cup' *simpliciter* or containing the words 'world cup', and what is the extent of their protection?[307] She explains that all the word trademarks registered by FIFA comprising or containing the words 'world cup' were registered subject to the following endorsement:

> Registration of this trademark shall give no right to the exclusive use of the words WORLD CUP except in relation to goods/services clearly connected with… the FIFA Football World Championship being the football competition held every 4 years under FIFA's authority.

However, Kelbrick explains that this disclaimer is rather strange, especially in light of FIFA's own argument in *Bartlett*:

> What is the effect of this disclaimer? In general, if a disclaimer is registered, it is not for the totality of the mark. For example, a disclaimer would cover the separate words in a word mark consisting of two or more words, or the words in ordinary, but not fancy, typescript… Here, the full mark appears to be effectively disclaimed: 'World Cup' is registered and the phrase 'world cup' is disclaimed. But one interpretation of this disclaimer is that the full mark is disclaimed except for use in respect of FIFA's event. In other words, it is no disclaimer whatsoever. So although FIFA, during litigation, stated that the phrase 'world cup' is non-distinctive and common to the trade, when someone else is using it, FIFA effectively maintains a monopoly on these words in respect of its own world cup.[308]

Sui generis event legislation aimed at protecting the commercial rights of event organisers and their sponsors, as we've encountered in Chap. 4, increasingly ring-fences words and terms, which are viewed as descriptive of the relevant event,

---

[307] Kelbrick 2008, p. 329.

[308] Kelbrick 2008, p. 329. It is interesting to note Swiss-based FIFA's view on its 'rights' to the term 'World Cup' in light of the following view expressed by the country reporters for Switzerland in the AIPP working committee (Q210—see discussion elsewhere in this chapter) process, when asked whether major sports events require less stringent trademark registration requirements in respect of the distinctiveness of marks:

'It is a fundamental function of a trademark to distinguish the goods and services of one enterprise from the goods and services of other enterprises (cf. art. 1 par. 1 Swiss Trademark Act). A non-distinctive trademark cannot distinguish the goods of one enterprise from those of another enterprise. Further, European and World Championships take place in numerous sports every year. It is not obvious at all why e.g. only the governing bodies of football should be allowed to use terms like "European Championship" and/or the corresponding abbreviations. Further, in some sports there is not even just one governing body, but many competing organisations (e.g. boxing). Thus, it is not justified to narrow the requirement of distinctiveness for marks which relate to Major Sports Events. In any event, it would disturb the proper balance of and contravene the rationale of trademark law to allow the monopolsation of descriptive terms as such. Such terms belong in the public domain. Inadequacies (if any) in particular situations may be remedied by the laws against unfair competition, if the third party behaviour should contravene the principle of good faith. Finally, separate trademark rules for certain right holders may not easily be justified and will result in other interest groups asking for similar benefits.' [The Swiss country report at 8–9—available online at the time of writing at https://www.aippi.org/download/commitees/210/GR210switzerland.pdf].

which are generic in nature. This may have significant free (commercial) speech implications[309]:

> There are many ways in which such terms, in particular when used on their own, could be used fairly without creating a likelihood of consumer confusion with the event marks or creating a false implication of endorsement or sponsorship. Thus, ambush marketing legislation often prohibits what would otherwise be allowable commercial expression, significantly interfering with the freedom of non-sponsors to communicate with their customers.[310]

Mouritz[311] examined the (then in Bill form) legislative protection against ambush marketing that was instituted for the 2010 Vancouver Winter Olympic Games, namely the Olympic and Paralympic Marks Act[312] (which I'll refer to as the 'Vancouver Act'—discussed in Sect. 4.4.7 of Chap. 4). Another commentator has chosen to call this Bill the 'Olympic Corporate Sponsor Protection Act' 'since its primary purpose is to protect the multi-million dollar investments of corporate sponsors'.[313] This legislation is described as *sui generis* legislation aimed, primarily, at addressing the practical problems in combating ambush marketing surrounding the event (especially the time factor; Mouritz points out that an objective of the legislation was to provide timely and sufficient relief against ambush marketing by means of preventive injunctions). However, Mouritz is of the view that the Canadian legislator, 'undoubtedly with all the best intentions in mind, seems to have gone overboard in some of its protective endeavours'.[314] The gist of the author's criticism of the Vancouver Act relates to the Act's apparent failure to provide exemptions for liability for the use of the protected trademarks (and generic terms); notably, it appears that the exemption of liability for non-commercial use is especially narrow and, in the author's view, problematic and nonsensical. Potential free speech implications[315] was a concern shared by Geist

---

309 Which will be further examined in Chap. 7.

310 From the International Trademark Association (INTA) resolution on ambush marketing legislation (November 2010), which is included as **Annexure A** at the end of this book.

311 Mouritz 2008.

312 Bill C-47; the Bill received Royal Assent on 22 June 2007, and entered into force on 17 December 2007.

313 Michael Geist, Canada Research Chair in Internet and E-commerce Law at the University of Ottawa, Faculty of Law, writing on his free speech blog ('Special interest law undermines the Olympic spirit', 19 March 2007—available online at the time of writing at http://www.michaelgeist.ca/index.php?option=com_topics&task=view&id=10041&Itemid=75&startmonth=&startyear=&endmonth=&endyear=&intersect=0&topic%5B%5D=10041&limit=10&limitstart=50).

314 Mouritz 2008, p. 10.

315 Similar concerns were expressed about the London 2012 Olympic Bill at the time of its passing, when Peers from all three major parties in the House of Lords attacked aspects of the Bill designed to stamp out ambush marketing, calling it a 'draconian constraint' and an 'interference with editorial freedom of expression'—from the report entitled 'London 2012 Olympic Bill called "draconian"', 16 January 2006, available at the time of writing on the web site of www.GamesBids.com at http://www.gamesbids.com/eng/other_news/1137514053.html.

(who observed that 'experience in other countries suggests that the legislation will create a chill for artists, bloggers, and social commentators who fear that their legitimate expression may lead to a date in court'), who also observed the following regarding a substantive shortcoming of the Bill:

> [T]he bill gives VANOC the power to obtain an injunction to stop the distribution of goods that might violate the law. This provision remarkably eliminates the traditional requirement to demonstrate irreparable harm in order to obtain an injunction. Canadian courts have set a high threshold for irreparable harm, typically requiring evidence that monetary damages alone will not fully compensate the injured party. In the case of ambush marketing, it is likely that VANOC would rarely meet that standard since the opposite is true—the damage likely could be quantified and appropriately compensated.[316]

For present purposes, however, I would like to focus on one specific aspect of the Vancouver Act, namely its apparent inclusion of non-IP protected matter (or things that IP law would normally not deem worthy or capable of protection). The Vancouver Act contains provisions regarding the protection of specific Olympic and Paralympic trademarks (as well as marks specific to the 2010 Vancouver event)[317] and, more problematically, certain 'generic Olympic terms'.[318] Mouritz points out that these last, especially, are rather problematic:

> [T]he generic terms listed in Schedule 3 [of the Bill] (the "Generic Olympic Terms") lack any … distinctive character and are therefore not regarded as intellectual property rights. For this reason these generic terms do not have statutory legal protection and remedies similar to intellectual property rights. None the less the Bill has prohibited the use of such generic terms as "Gold", "Winter", "Vancouver", "21st" and "Sponsor". These terms do not just lack any distinctive character, but are in fact common every day expressions. In ordinary life and under normal circumstances, one cannot forbid individuals and companies the use of such common expressions. The fear of ambush marketing at Olympic Games has sparked a certain creativity to try and limit the use of these generic terms where it is used in—mostly commercial—conjunction with the Olympics.

This Act provides a clear example of event-specific legislation that was passed in order to provide more protection than would normally be available to event organisers or sponsors in terms of, in this case, intellectual property laws. Where the net is cast wider than normal in such manner, it becomes especially important

---

[316] Geist (note 313 above).

[317] These are covered by section 3 of the Act, which provides as follows:

'No person shall adopt or use, in connection with a business, as a trademark or otherwise, an Olympic Trademark, or a translation thereof, or a mark that so nearly resembles an Olympic Trademark as to be likely to be mistaken for it.'

[318] This last in schedule 3 of the Act. Use of these terms is covered in section 4 of the Act, which provides as follows:

'No person shall, in association with an Olympic Trademark or other mark, promote or otherwise direct public attention to their business, wares or services in a manner that misleads or is likely to mislead the public into believing that (a) the person's business, wares or services are approved, authorised or endorsed by VANOC [the local organising committee] or any other Olympic body or, (b) there is a business association between the person's business and the Olympic Games, the Paralympic Games, VANOC or any other Olympic body.'

to consider the exceptions to liability for contravention of such unusual prohibitions and restrictions (which, as mentioned, Mouritz has argued are largely deficient in respect of this Canadian legislation).

Johnson[319] describes the 'London Olympics association right', created by the London Olympic Games and Paralympic Games Act 2006 (which I discussed in Sect. 4.4.3 in Chap. 4 and will refer to as the 'London Act'), as follows:

> The London Olympics association right is a *sui generis* right which was created to prevent people using innovative ways of making an association with the [London 2012] Games without the consent of the Organising Committee. It applies to any activity which takes place between 30 March 2006 and 31 December 2012. The London Olympics association right is an exclusive right which is actionable by the London Organising Committee. The right is to use any representation (of any kind) in a manner likely to suggest to the public that there is an association between the London Olympics [and Paralympics] and goods or services, or a person who provides goods or services... The representation can be of any kind and so it would include verbal representations ... The association created by that representation need not be intentional ... There is no requirement that the association is misleading and so it does not matter that consumers are not confused. Accordingly, the representation must objectively create the association.[320]

In light of the broad scope of what appears to be outlawed by this association right, Johnson considers whether the use of a disclaimer might prevent infringement:

> It was clearly the intention of the legislator to give a broad protection against association and it would seem somewhat perverse if this could be circumvented by the inclusion of a disclaimer. This is particularly the case as there is no requirement as to confusion and so any reader will be making the association and then, at best, subsequently discounting it. This being the case, it is suggested that no disclaimer would be effective.

The London Act makes use of certain specified combinations of words (as contained in schedule 4 to the Act) as indicators that a court may take into account in determining whether the association right has been infringed. It was proposed, when the London Act was in Bill form, that use of these terms should trigger a presumption of infringement of the association right, but this was watered down to the point where courts may take use of the terms into account for purposes of a finding of infringement. Interestingly, when considered in light of the Vancouver Act as discussed above, these are also mostly generic terms that do not enjoy intellectual property protection, outside of the Act: They include the words 'games', 'gold', 'silver', 'bronze', 'London', 'medals', 'sponsor' and 'Summer'. As Johnson points out, the following two phrases would likely constitute specified combinations in terms of the Act which could (strictly read) lead to a finding of infringement:

---

[319] Johnson 2007, pp. 129–130.

[320] Mouritz 2008 observes that the Vancouver Act, in its section 4 appears to have created a similar association right to the London Olympics association right.

'Come to London to see the Games'
'Sponsor of the 2012 FA Cup'[321]

Another example is that of the events company Brand Events, which runs a very successful international 'foodie' show called Taste Festivals that has seen 'Taste of…' festivals popping up in most of the world's big cities. The *Taste of London 2012* festival might run into some problems with the London Games organising committee; in terms of the London Act its name is surely a no-no and might be viewed to infringe the London Games association right. While there is clearly no connection or implication of a connection between the Games and the food festival, the London Olympics legislation would appear to outlaw the use of an unrelated and innocent use of words and numerals that are not the private property of the LOCOG.

The London Act does make provision for exceptions to infringement of the association right. Use of a representation (which causes an association) must be in the course of trade[322] within the United Kingdom, and without the consent of the London Organising Committee,[323] and the specific exceptions to infringement include registered trademarks (it is not an infringement of the association right to use a trademark in relation to goods or services for which it is registered, and an application to register a mark that includes a representation that would infringe the association right is not a basis for the refusal of a registration on absolute grounds); descriptive use (the London Act exempts from liability for infringement the use of a mark for descriptive purposes, provided such use is in accordance with honest practises in industrial or commercial matters[324]); and prior rights (the association right does not preclude the exercising of prior rights to e.g. symbols that a person may have had prior to the introduction of the association right[325]). Some of the other *sui generis* event statutes do not contain similar exceptions to liability for infringement of event organisers' rights (specifically, for example, the South African legislation).

New Zealand enacted its controversial Major Events Management Act (or 'MEMA') in 2007 in order to comply with the requirements of international sports federations (specifically the International Rugby Board) to, *inter alia*, establish a satisfactory legal framework for the combating of ambush marketing. Section 7 of MEMA provides for the declaration of an event as a major event, and s 8 for the

---

[321] Johnson 2007, pp. 131–132. Johnson does, however, point out that these two phrases would not likely be found to offend the association right and that a court is not obliged to take the specified combinations into account.

[322] Contrast the apparent lack of non-commercial use exceptions in the Vancouver Act as discussed by Mouritz 2008.

[323] Johnson 2007, p. 131.

[324] The London Act schedule 4 par. 7.

[325] Ibid. schedule 4 par. 10.

declaration of major event emblems or words that are protected.[326] Section 10 of MEMA prohibits the representation of association with protected major events:

> (1) No person may, during a major event's protection period, make any representation in a way likely to suggest to a reasonable person that there is an association between the major event and
>
> (a) goods or services; or
> (b) a brand of goods or services; or
> (c) a person who provides goods or services.
>
> (2) In subsection (1), a person who makes a representation includes a person who
>
> (a) pays for, commissions, or authorises the representation; or
> (b) receives consideration for the placement or the location of the representation.

Section 11 of MEMA provides for certain presumptions regarding the representation of an association and also provides that a disclaimer will not avoid liability for contravention of s 10.[327] A court may presume that a representation is

---

[326] Section 8 provides as follows:

'8 (1) The Governor-General may, by Order in Council made on the recommendation of the Economic Development Minister, declare any or all of the following:

(a) an emblem to be a major event emblem;
(b) a word, words if combined with other words, or a combination of words to be a major event word or major event words.

(2) The Economic Development Minister may only make a recommendation after consultation with

(a) the Commerce Minister; and
(b) the major event organiser; and
(c) persons the Minister considers are likely to be substantially affected by the recommendation.

(3) Before making a recommendation, the Economic Development Minister must take into account the extent to which, in relation to the major event, emblems and words require protection in order to

(a) obtain maximum benefits for New Zealanders;
(b) prevent unauthorised commercial exploitation at the expense of either a major event organiser or a major event sponsor.'

[327] Section 11 provides as follows:

'S 11 (1) The court may presume that a representation is in breach of section 10 if it includes any of the following:

(a) a major event emblem; or
(b) a major event word or major event words; or
(c) a representation that so closely resembles a major event emblem, a major event word, or major event words as to be likely to deceive or confuse a reasonable person.

(2) Subsection (1) applies even if the representation is qualified by words like "unauthorised" or "unofficial", or other words that are intended to defeat the purpose of section 10.'

in breach of section 10 if it includes 'a major event word or words'. Section 12(1)(d) of the Act provides for a non-commercial use exemption to liability.[328] It is an offence for a person to knowingly breach section 10 of the Act, and on conviction such person is liable to a fine not exceeding NZD 150 000.[329] The Major Event Emblems and Words (Rugby World Cup 2011) Order 2008,[330] which followed the declaration of the 2011 IRB Rugby World Cup as a 'protected event' under MEMA,[331] has declared a number of protected event emblems and words for the protection period of the rugby World Cup event stretching from 11 September 2008 to 21 November 2011. Part 1 of Schedule 2 of the Order lists a number of words and word combinations that are specific to the International Rugby Board and its World Cup event (and including the 'New Zealand 2011') designation, which are relatively unproblematic in light of its specific description of the relevant tournament (i.e. unauthorised commercial use of these words or word combinations would be indicative of rather blatant attempts to associate with the specific event). Part 2 of the second schedule of the Order, however, similar to the Vancouver Act and London Act referred to, contains two lists of words or word combinations (use of words in column A if used in combination with any words in column B is prohibited), which are more problematic. For example, column B includes '2011', 'host nation', 'host union', 'Two thousand and eleven' and Twenty eleven'.

The legislation has, predictably, been criticised for its effect on New Zealand society, with one website observing that the problem with MEMA-like protection of generic words 'is that the World Cup of whatever sport or activity is a celebration of the event and that [while] community support outside of the official sponsors is crucial for success this tends to amputate that type of support', and suggesting that readers should start referring to the 2011 event as the 'Global

[328] This section provides as follows:

'[Sections 10 and 11 do not apply if] in accordance with honest practises in industrial or commercial matters, the representation

(i) is necessary to indicate the intended purpose of goods or services; or

(ii) is made by an existing organisation continuing to carry out its ordinary activities; or

(iii) is for the purposes of reporting news, information, criticism, or a review (including promoting that news, information, criticism, or review) in a newspaper or magazine, or by means of television, radio, film, the Internet, or other means of reporting; or

(iv) in the case of a word or emblem (provided that the word or emblem is not being used in combination with other words or emblems with the intention of suggesting an association that breaches section 10), comprises the whole or part of

(A) the proper name of any town or road or other place in New Zealand; or

(B) the legal or trade name (not being used for the purpose of defeating the intention of this subpart) of the person making the representation; or

(C) an existing registered trademark.'

[329] MEMA s 13.

[330] SR 2008/250, an Order in Council issued 11 August 2008 (which came into force on 11 September 2008).

[331] By means of the Major Events Management (Rugby World Cup 2011) Order 2007.

Football Goblet' in order to avoid legal action by the event organisers.[332] Longdin, in turn, has observed that MEMA's protection of words which can be both generic and non-distinctive in trademark terms and which need not constitute an original copyright work has taken the sting out of the line of cases[333] which would deny copyright protection to individual words or a mere slogan or catch-phrase.[334]

Similar to some of the legislative provisions from other jurisdictions as mentioned above, we see that the protection afforded by means of section 15 of the Merchandise Marks Act (or 'MMA') in South Africa also appears to extend, very significantly, beyond what intellectual property law would normally protect. In fact, it appears that s 15A goes much further than the legislation from other jurisdictions referred to above.

We have seen that legislation such as the Vancouver Act and the London Act make use of generic terms that are not IP-protected. In the Vancouver Act, the use of such terms are prohibited in respect of the 'association right' contained in section 4 of that Act; in the London Act such generic terms may form specified combinations that a court may take into account in determining whether an infringement of the association right is present. The point, however, is that such generic terms are not terms that warrant intellectual property protection—they are e.g. not sufficiently 'original' for purposes of copyright, and not sufficiently distinctive for purposes of trademark registration. Section 15A (2) of the South African Merchandise Marks Act, which deals with the 'abuse' of a trademark relating to a protected event in terms of the Act, provides that during the period of protection of such event 'no person may use a mark in relation to such event in a manner which is calculated to achieve publicity for that trademark and thereby to derive special promotional benefit from the event, without the prior authority of the organiser of such event'. This provision prohibits the use by a trader of his or her own registered marks, even in circumstances that would not be objectionable or actionable in terms of the common law or IP statutes. For example, compared to the relevant trademark protection:

- Section 15A(2) does not limit its prohibition to the use of an identical mark to the mark(s) of an event organizer or official sponsor[335];
- The section does not limit its prohibition to trademark use that is 'likely to deceive or cause confusion' in respect of the marks of an event organizer or official sponsor[336]; and

---

[332] 'Be careful in New Zealand, free speech is no more, don't mention the World Cup', 14 August 2010, available online at the time of writing at http://rorybaust.wordpress.com/.

[333] Including *Exxon Corp. V Exxon Insurance Consultants International Ltd* [1982] Ch. 119, and *Francis Day & Hunter Ltd v Twentieth Century Fox Corp.* [1940] AC 112.

[334] Longdin 2009, p. 732 fn 45.

[335] In respect of the infringement provisions of the Trademarks Act, 194 of 1993, see section 34(1)(a).

[336] Ibid.; section 34(1)(a); section 34(1)(b).

- The section does not qualify liability in terms of the prohibition to use of a mark that is 'likely to take unfair advantage of, or be detrimental to the distinctive character or repute of' a well-known mark.[337]

The point is that s 15A(2) does not involve the concept of a trademark infringement, as it relates only to use of the 'ambusher's' own mark. Also, the section does not qualify unlawful use of such a mark in any way similar to traditional requirements for liability for a copyright infringement, i.e. reproduction in material form of a substantial part of an original work.[338] This provision is a strange creature indeed.

In light of what was said above regarding the protection of generic terms in other jurisdictions, it should also be noted that FIFA demanded similarly wide protection in respect of the 2010 World Cup. As was argued by the respondent in the *FIFA v Metcash*[339] matter:

> In addition to applying to the Minister to designate the FIFA World Cup 2010 as a protected event, [FIFA] sought a blanket prohibition in terms of section 15(1)(b) of the Merchandise Marks Act on "*the use of certain words and emblems in connection with any trade, business, profession, occupation or event or in connection with the trademark, mark or trade description applied to goods other than the use thereof by FIFA or its mandatories*" ... A consideration of FIFA's application in this regard shows that it sought an outright prohibition of any use of SOUTH AFRICA 2010 or indeed of the depiction of a football for any purpose and in any context other than use by the applicant or its mandatories but, interestingly, did not seek a prohibition on the use of the South African flag. It is precisely this type of blanket prohibition that the applicant is now seeking to enforce through these proceedings notwithstanding the fact that the Minister refused to grant such a prohibition and instead restricted the terms of the prohibition so as to exclude the SOUTH AFRICA 2010 emblem, the picture of a football and the word marks SOUTH AFRICA 2010 and SA 2010.[340] [Emphasis in the original]

This led the respondents in that matter to argue the following:

> [FIFA] is attempting to prevent any use without its permission of signs or symbols which might, however remotely or obscurely possibly have some reference to the FIFA 2010 soccer world cup. In these proceedings the applicant attempts to achieve a complete monopoly on the use of any reference to SOUTH AFRICA 2010, or variations of such reference, on any products in any context whatsoever, despite having sought and failed to secure such a blanket prohibition in terms of legislation.[341]

Section 15A (2) of the MMA also clearly provides more rigid protection than is found in e.g. the London Act. When one considers the exceptions to liability in respect of the London association right as mentioned in the text above, it is clear

337 Ibid.; section 34(1)(c).

338 See the Copyright Act 98 of 1978.

339 See the discussion in Sect. 4.4.5 of Chap. 4.

340 *Federation Internationale de Football Association (FIFA) v Metcash Trading Africa (Pty) Ltd* [2009] ZAGPPHC 123 Gauteng North High Court—Respondent's Heads of Argument par. 33–34.

341 Ibid. par. 7–8.

that these would not be available to a defendant in a claim of contravention of s 15A (2) (which, in fact, prohibits the use of a trader's own trademark). The restriction contained in s 15A (2) is much wider and more open-ended than anti-ambushing protection provided elsewhere. For example, it is doubtful that non-commercial use exemptions would apply in respect of this provision, as the wording of the section does not require commercial use. In respect of non-commercial use, one could also compare this provision to that found in the Australian Olympic Insignia Protection Act, 1987 (or 'OIP Act').

The OIP Act was enacted to regulate the use of certain symbols, devices and expressions related to the Olympic movement in order to facilitate the commercial application of these designs by the national Olympic committee to realise a substantial proportion of the funds needed to ensure Australia's representation at the Olympic Games. The Act makes provision for certain protected expressions, including listed words and phrases, and provides the exclusive right to use or licence such protected expressions to the Australian Olympic Committee (or AOC), by means of a prohibition on third parties to use such expressions for 'commercial purposes' (subject to certain exemptions such as media reporting and the activities of athletes and sports organisations).[342] A 2001 amendment to the OIP Act added a chapter 3, which aims to facilitate licensing by regulating the commercial use of certain Olympic-related expressions. Section 36(1) of this chapter provides that a person, other than the AOC or a 'licenced user' acting in accordance with their licence, may not use a 'protected Olympic expression[343] for commercial purposes'. Section 30 of the OIP Act provides that use of a protected expression for commercial purposes includes a situation where a person 'applies' a protected Olympic expression to their own goods or services; either for 'advertising or promotional purposes' or in circumstances 'likely to enhance the demand for goods or services'; and where such application would suggest to a reasonable person that the first person sponsors, sponsored, or is or was the provider of 'sponsorship-like support' for the AOC, the International Olympic Committee, organising committee, Olympic games, team or athlete. Case law considering the meaning of 'commercial purposes' [under the OIP Act and Australia's Sydney 2000 Games (Indicia and Images) Protection Act] suggests that 'a precise rather than general association must be proven for support to constitute "sponsorship" or [to be] "sponsorship-like"; the allegation of some 'vague, undefined connection' is insufficient.[344]

[342] From the report by Frontier Economics 2007, p. 24.

[343] These protected expressions are defined in s 24 of the Act as the words 'Olympic', 'Olympics', 'Olympic Games', 'Olympiad', 'Olympiads', and any other expression 'so closely resembling' any of those terms 'as to be likely to be mistaken, by a reasonable person, for such a protected Olympic expression'.

[344] From Frontier Economics 2007, p. 29, with reference to the cases of *Australian Olympic Committee v Baxter & Co Pty Ltd* (1996) 36 IPR 621 (decided under the Sydney 2000 Games (Indicia and Images) Protection Act) and *Australian Olympic Committee v ERI Bancaire Luxembourg SA* (2006) 69 IPR 135 (decided under the OIP Act).

While the provisions of the OIP Act are reminiscent of section 9 (as amended) of the South African Trade Practises Act as well as section 29 of South Africa's Consumer Protection Act, 2008, it should be clear to the reader that s 15A (2) of the Merchandise Marks Act goes far beyond the type of restriction contained in the above Australian legislation. The MMA does not appear to include any non-commercial use exemption, and the use of a trademark within the wording of this section (i.e. when calculated to achieve publicity for such mark and thereby deriving special promotional benefit from a protected event) also does not appear to specifically refer to commercial use only. It is submitted that a trademark can be used in this way in circumstances that may not necessarily be for a commercial purpose. Compare the hypothetical example of a protest march by a trade union or the World Wildlife Fund, in which trade unionists carry banners depicting the union's mark along with a slogan 'Stop FIFA 2010—Viva street traders!' or environmentalists carry banners with the WWF mark and a slogan 'Show FIFA 2010 the red card for its carbon emissions!'. I believe that both these instances might conceivably be considered to fall within the extremely wide ambit of the restriction contained in s 15A (2) of the Act. Don't assume that such examples would automatically be protected as free speech, though; just ask Durban academic Patrick Bond what happens to 'freedom of speech' when FIFA's commercial rights may appear threatened.[345]

When one considers, furthermore, that legislation such as that in Australia and the London Act are still aimed at prohibiting an 'association' with the relevant protected event(s) (compare also the wording of section 30 of the OIP Act above), section 15A (2) of the MMA clearly goes beyond this (and thus catches 'intrusion ambushes' in its net). Use of a trademark 'in relation to an event', even where such use only relates to alluding to an event, is restricted. This last, in this observer's opinion, illustrates not only the wide ambit of this provision but also the apparent irrationality of its prohibition. The fact that s 15A (2) does not require deception or confusion of the public or a representation of association with an event would make the use of a notice disclaiming such an association irrelevant for purposes of determining contravention of the provision. Accordingly, if a trader in using its trademark in an advertisement or even a public service notice (e.g. a brochure or newspaper insert providing information on expected traffic movement and volumes in a specified area during such protected event) merely refers to a protected event and also includes a clear notice to the public that it is in no way associated with such event, such conduct could still constitute the 'abuse of a trademark' and be a criminal offence subject to the substantial fines or imprisonment. This highlights the apparent irrationality of the similar approach of New Zealand's Major Events Management Act, 2007. As mentioned elsewhere, MEMA's section 11 provides that a court may presume that a representation is in breach of

[345] See Bond, P 'FIFA forbids free speech at World Cup Fan Fest', 11 July 2010, available online at the time of writing at http://www.counterpunch.org/bond07092010.html.

section 10 of the Act (i.e. is an unauthorised and prohibited representation of an association with the event) if it includes a major event emblem; or a major event word or major event words; or a representation that so closely resembles a major event emblem, a major event word, or major event words as to be likely to deceive or confuse a reasonable person.[346] Section 11(2) expressly provides that this presumption applies 'even if the representation is qualified by words like "unauthorised" or "unofficial", or other words that are intended to defeat the purpose of section 10'. I find this approach to disclaimers of an association rather mind-boggling. How can one rationally argue that a court may presume liability for an offence of 'associating' oneself with an event even where one has clearly and explicitly communicated that one is not associated with such event? This does not make sense, and all it implies is that a monopoly is provided in respect of use of the relevant event-related words or emblems referred to in the Act, irrespective of the actual context of use and the intention of the person using it.

Finally, it should also be noted that the protection afforded to the 2010 FIFA World Cup was for a much longer period than appears to be the norm elsewhere. The Minister's powers in respect of section 15A were extended specifically for purposes of the FIFA World Cup 2010, by means of the 2010 FIFA World Cup South Africa Second Special Measures Act 12 of 2006,[347] in terms of which the duration of protection for the event was extended from the one month period provided for in section 15A (1) (a) (ii) to a period of six months following the end of the event.[348] When compared to e.g. the Major Events Management Act in New Zealand, which provides that the declaration of an event as protected may not extend for more than 30 days after the completion or termination of major event activities,[349] it is clear that South Africa's anti-ambush marketing protection of the FIFA event was not only significantly more rigorous than is the case elsewhere, it also applied for a much longer period of time. South Africa's very extensive anti-ambushing protection as contained in the Merchandise Marks Act will be considered again where relevant in the rest of this book.

The general gist of the *sui generis* event legislation, in my opinion, constitutes an important example of the tendency of the world-wide monopolisation of language in a commercial sense and for commercial reasons, which is extremely worrying not only because of the event organisers' claims to such 'rights' of exclusive use but, more specifically, because of the law-makers' apparently largely uncritical acceptance of such claims and willingness to cement them into law. The

---

[346] MEMA section 11(1).

[347] In terms of section 2 of this Act, which provides as follows:

'If the Minister of Trade and Industry declares the 2010 FIFA World Cup South Africa a protected event in terms of section 15A (1) of the Merchandise Marks Act, 1941 ... he or she may, notwithstanding section 15A (1) (a) (ii) of that Act, stipulate by notice in the *Gazette* a date later than one month but not later than six months after the completion or termination of the final competition as the date on which the protection afforded by such a declaration ends.'

[348] The 2010 FIFA World Cup was scheduled to be played from 11 June to 11 July 2010.

[349] MEMA s 9.

previous sections of this chapter have attempted to illustrate the expansion of IP laws by such event legislation. The 'propertization' of language and of generic words and phrases, as discussed in this section, also shows how the protection of IP laws is increasingly becoming bloated and unmanageable. In fact, this is distinctly contrary to one of the claimed social benefits of trademarks, which Landes and Posner have identified, namely that they improve the quality of our language, by increasing our stock of nouns and by 'creating words or phrases that people value for their intrinsic pleasingness as well as their information value' (which, the authors claim, simultaneously economise on communication costs and make conversation more pleasurable).[350] In the *sui generis* event legislation we see that words and phrases which would otherwise not even be capable of carrying IP protection (particularly by means of trademark laws) have the exact opposite effect when it comes to considering their impact on the use of language, not to mention the freedom of speech of the public at large.

5.4 Evaluating the Legitimacy of 'IP+' Event Protection in Light of the Traditional Theories of IP Law

Intellectual property laws have always been the subject of a measure of criticism and, especially in recent years, there has been a groundswell of support for opposing views which reject the monopolies created (in what proponents of such views regard as privatisation of objects which belong to the intellectual commons) and the often significant free speech implications of restrictions of the use of intellectual property. There are good reasons for such criticism, which at least require the proponents of intellectual property laws to sufficiently explain and justify this form of legally-recognised 'property' and its 'ownership':

> The purpose of intellectual property law has always been to safeguard the integrity of intellectual objects, which are quite different from physical objects because they are not subject to scarcity. There are practical limitations to the number of physical objects one can own or reproduce, but the same can usually not be said about intangible forms of property. Laws that establish and protect intellectual property rights create artificial scarcity, and hence they require some justification from both an ethical and economic viewpoint.[351]

One result of this artificial scarcity in respect of ideas is 'the tendency, because the categories of [intellectual property] protection are open-ended, for "rights" to be ever expanded, at the behest of the most powerful lobby groups'.[352] It has also been observed that all justifications for IP protection, whether based in economics

[350] Landes and Posner 1987, p. 265.

[351] Spinello and Bottis 2009, pp. 4–5.

[352] Sumpter 2006, p. xi.

or morality, must contend with a fundamental difference between ideas and tangible property:

> Tangible property, whether land or chattels, is composed of atoms, physical things that can occupy only one place at any given time… [P]ossession of a physical thing is necessarily "exclusive"—if I have it, you don't… Ideas, though, do not have this characteristic of excludability. If I know a particular piece of information, and I tell it to you, you have not deprived me of it. Rather, we both possess it. The fact that possession and use of ideas is largely "non-rivalrous" is critical to intellectual property theory because it means that the traditional economic justification for tangible property does not fit intellectual property.[353]

Apart from the artificial creation of scarcity, which does appear to merit a different treatment of intellectual as opposed to physical property, intellectual property laws are essentially also about the creation of limited monopolies. The creator of a literary work and the inventor whose invention enjoys patent protection are afforded exclusive rights to commercial exploitation of such 'property'. Much has been made in legal literature of this difference between competition (or anti-trust) laws and intellectual property laws (such as patent law, trademark law and copyright law). Competition law is, by definition, aimed at promoting competition. Intellectual property rights created in terms of IP laws are aimed at creating a monopoly, albeit a limited one. As writer of this book I enjoy copyright in it, which provides a 'bundle of rights' all relating to my ability to control its use or, more accurately, commercial exploitation of any value it might have. The holder of a registered trademark or a patent, similarly, enjoys exclusive control over such mark or patent, which is by definition a right to exclude others. These limited monopolies are commonly justified by recourse to arguments relating to the traditional philosophies that underlie IP law (which will be examined more closely below), including the need to incentivise creativity or innovation, or to reward the intellectual efforts of creators and innovators.

It has, however, been noted that this traditional view raises internal difficulties, especially when one pursues the merits behind such justification of IP rights a bit further in the context of evaluating the need to provide 'special treatment' to IP rights compared to other forms of property. An example frequently used is that of a patent, which is commonly viewed as justified on the basis of the incentivisation argument,[354] but raises interesting questions especially from a competition perspective:

> The extent to which patent rewards are necessary to incentivise invention is unclear, and it is even less clear what incentive effect comes from any incremental increase in reward that would be produced by restraints associated with patents. One thus might doubt whether adjudicators have the capacity to balance any incremental incentives to innovate against the anti-competitive effects of the restraints at issue.[355]

---

[353] Merges et al. 2003, p. 2.

[354] See the discussion in the text below.

[355] Elhauge and Geradin 2007, p. 192.

Elhauge has suggested that one might dispute this entire way of framing the issue, and that it might be better to conclude, rather than referring to the monopolies created by IP rights, that patents (for example) are just another form of property right and should be treated no better or worse than any other property right:

> Patent rights in fact do not necessarily create economic monopolies or ban competition. They merely provide a right to exclude others from a particular innovation. Such patent rights often compete with other patents or methods of accomplishing the same goal, and thus may or may not enjoy any monopoly or market power. Whether a patent confers monopoly power depends entirely on how much value the patent has compared to other market options. This is likewise true for other intellectual property rights, like copyright… One could say exactly the same for physical property rights, like the right to exclude rivals from a firm's plant. Such rights to exclude may or may not preclude competition or confer monopoly power, depending on how valuable that plant is compared to other market options. Whichever sort of property right we are talking about, its ability to preclude competition or create monopoly power turns on its economic value compared to the property rights held by others, not on some metaphysical distinction between the natures of the property rights.[356]

This argument seems to turn on the availability of other, competing market options to the subject matter of the IP right concerned, and I will call it the 'market option approach' to the question of whether, or the extent to which, IP rights create or embody a monopoly. In essence, it means that if this book is the only one in existence on the subject, I will enjoy a monopoly right through my copyright in it. If other books on the subject exist (which are substitutable in the market for books on the subject), however, my copyright might provide no monopoly but simply a property right in the book (or, more specifically, the intellectual content of it in the form of the expression of such content, rather than the book in its physical form). This approach requires no discrete justification for such copyright as some special or fundamentally different type of property right, and the existence or not of the 'monopoly' depends on the market value of what is protected.

I may seem to have digressed, but there is a point to all this. In the discussion that follows I will examine the role of traditional justification arguments for IP rights in the context of commercial rights to sports mega-events. More specifically, I will examine the implications of such arguments for the nature and level of protection afforded by *sui generis* event legislation (and vice versa). But in doing so I would submit that one should bear the above reasoning in mind, and that this might affect the outcome of an evaluation of the legitimacy of such event protection. In Chap. 2 I discussed the modern model of commercial exploitation of mega-events, and in Chap. 6 I will argue that this model (due especially to its use of sponsorship exclusivity, but also for other reasons) raises some definite and real competition concerns. The event organisers are, generally, monopolists, and the product of the mega-event is supplied by a monopoly. In short, what I am getting at here is that if one subscribes to the reasoning of the above market option

---

[356] Ibid.

approach, which makes sense to me, it is important to consider the anti-competitive or monopolistic nature of the whole context within which IP rights to events exist and within which they are protected by means of *sui generis* event legislation. While one could thus argue that IP rights create a monopoly for event organisers but that such monopoly can be justified on traditional grounds relating to IP rights, more generally, I would submit that any such IP rights to mega-events automatically establish a monopoly for the rights holders, *in the whole context of the events*, simply because, by their nature, there are no competing and substitutable market options to the Olympic Games or the FIFA World Cup.

With that in mind I will briefly consider a few of the traditional theories used to justify IP rights and the law that protects them. Before I proceed, however, I should just include a brief disclaimer. Any meaningful examination of the philosophies behind IP laws is beyond the scope of this chapter (and this book). In modern times critics have increasingly questioned why we need intellectual property and laws which tend to provide monopolies to the few, often at the expense of the many. In fact, some observers question the very term 'intellectual property' as being inappropriate (as a collective term for the various rights which we know as 'IP rights', at least, and leaving aside the question of the status of such 'property' when compared to 'normal' property rights to tangible/corporeal things):

> There is no such unified thing as "intellectual property"—it is a mirage. The only reason people think it makes sense as a coherent category is that widespread use of the term has misled them. The term "intellectual property" is at best a catch-all to lump together disparate laws. Non-lawyers who hear one term applied to these various laws tend to assume they are based on a common principle and function similarly. Nothing could be further from the case. These laws originated separately, evolved differently, cover different activities, have different rules, and raise different public policy issues. Copyright law was designed to promote authorship and art, and covers the details of expression of a work. Patent law was intended to promote the publication of useful ideas, at the price of giving the one who publishes an idea a temporary monopoly over it—a price that may be worth paying in some fields and not in others. Trademark law, by contrast, was not intended to promote any particular way of acting, but simply to enable buyers to know what they are buying. Legislators under the influence of the term "intellectual property", however, have turned it into a scheme that provides incentives for advertising. Since these laws developed independently, they are different in every detail, as well as in their basic purposes and methods.[357]

My purpose with this section is simply to examine some of the principles which have, traditionally, been attributed as underpinning IP laws, and which have been formulated to explain the law's protection of the intangible and to justify the restrictions that such laws place on persons other than the creators of IP. My ultimate goal will be to briefly (and, quite possibly, rather superficially) examine whether or the extent to which the protections for event organisers and sponsors provided by *sui generis* event legislation are compatible with these underlying

---

[357] Richard M Stallman, software developer and software freedom activist who established the Free Software Foundation, writing on the web at http://www.gnu.org/philosophy/not-ipr.html.

theories of IP laws. We have seen that the legislation frequently (always?) significantly expands the scope and effect of IP rights. We now need to consider whether such expansion is justifiable in terms of first principles of law relating to the very nature of IP laws and the justifications for their existence.

Bearing in mind the broad nature of the topic, the proliferation of literature on the subject and the limited scope of this chapter, I will be extremely selective in my approach and choose as my point of reference for the following discussion the work of an eminent American scholar in the field of IP law. Harvard University's William W. Fisher III, writing in 2001,[358] summarised the four main 'theories' of IP laws as it has developed in the literature, judicial pronouncements and legislative writings:

(1) *The utilitarian theory*. This theory posits that 'lawmakers' beacon when shaping property rights should be the maximisation of net social welfare', and that the pursuit of that objective in the context of intellectual property requires lawmakers to strike an optimal balance between, on one hand, the power of exclusive rights to stimulate the creation of inventions and works of art and, on the other, the partially offsetting tendency of such rights to curtail widespread public enjoyment of those creations.[359] This theory shows a strong preference for the incentivisation of creation of intellectual property (i.e. that the protection afforded by the law to the creators of IP should serve as an incentive to encourage the creation of IP), although this is to be tempered in order to ensure a balancing act with the rights of others in society;

(2) *The labour theory*. This theory finds its genesis in propositions that a person who labours upon resources that are either un-owned or 'held in common' has a natural property right to the fruits of his or her efforts, and that the state has a duty to respect and enforce that natural right. These ideas, originate in the writings of John Locke and his theories of labour and property, and are widely thought to be especially applicable to the field of intellectual property, where the pertinent raw materials (facts and concepts) do seem in some sense to be 'held in common' and where labour seems to contribute so importantly to the value of finished products. An important point of contention, however, has been Locke's "famously ambiguous proviso", namely the proposition that a person may legitimately acquire property rights by mixing his labour with resources held "in common" only if, after the acquisition, "there is enough and as good left in common for others".[360] This last has generated much debate in respect of its implications for intellectual property laws (and, especially, the limitations that IP rights place on the rights and freedoms of persons other than the creator of IP[361];

---

358 Fisher 2001.

359 Ibid.

360 Ibid.

361 Ibid.; see also Gordon 1993; Waldron 1979; Becker 1993.

(3) The personality theory[362]; and
(4) The 'social planning' theory.[363]

Fisher observes that the judicial habit of conflating or blending these different theories in respect of their attribution as the driving force behind IP laws is well-illustrated by the US Supreme Court's judgment in *Harper & Row v Nation Enterprises*,[364] where the court said (in the context of copyright) that 'The rights conferred by copyright are designed to assure contributors to the store of knowledge a fair return for their labours.'[365] This implies that protection for copyright works is extended because of the creators' contribution to the store of knowledge (i.e. a rationale based on the IP creator's contribution to the betterment of society), but also incorporates not only a reward rationale but also an incentive rationale.

That being said, I will proceed to examine the *sui generis* event legislation with brief reference to justification for IP laws in terms of the first two theories that Fisher refers to, namely the utilitarian and labour theories. My reason for ignoring the other two (i.e. the personality theory and the social planning theory) is that I do not view these last theories as particularly (or potentially) apt in the mega-event rights protection context. In what may seem rather simplistic I will dismiss the relevance of the personality theory here simply on the basis that such theory is more appropriate in respect of the products of the creative efforts of natural persons, and less appropriate in the present context of mega-event organisers and the fruits of their labours in 'creating' a World Cup or Olympic Games event. The same goes for the large multi-national corporate sponsors. In this regard it may also bear mentioning that the very issue of the 'creation' of events in respect of e.g. the name of an event may lack the necessary characteristic of constituting

[362] Fisher 2001 describes this theory as follows:

'The premise of the third approach—derived loosely from the writings of Kant and Hegel—is that private property rights are crucial to the satisfaction of some fundamental human needs; policymakers should thus strive to create and allocate entitlements to resources in the fashion that best enables people to fulfil those needs. From this standpoint, intellectual property rights may be justified either on the ground that they shield from appropriation or modification artifacts through which authors and artists have expressed their "wills" (an activity thought central to "personhood") or on the ground that they create social and economic conditions conducive to creative intellectual activity, which in turn is important to human flourishing.' The personality theory has enjoyed specific support in European systems, which have tended to emphasise reputation and non-economic aspects of intellectual property (which has facilitated the wide-spread support for moral rights in copyright law).

[363] Fisher 2001 explains that this last theory is less well-established and 'does not even have a commonly accepted label', but 'is rooted in the proposition that property rights in general—and intellectual-property rights in particular—can and should be shaped so as to help foster the achievement of a just and attractive culture.

[364] *Harper & Row v. Nation Enterprises* 471 U.S. 539 (1985).

[365] Ibid. At 545–546.

'intellectual' property.[366] In respect of Fisher's 'social planning theory' I will simply suggest that I do not view the mega-event context as particularly appropriate in respect of this justification for IP rights. Although I am willing to admit that these events may have a significant social and cultural relevance and value, I would submit that such value lies outside the context of the primarily commercial aspects of such events. I can see little social or cultural benefit in protection of the narrow commercial interests of event organisers and their sponsors (beyond, possibly, the fact that the corporate investments in staging the mega-events and the protection of such investments for the benefit of the commercial actors involved may conceivably be necessary, fundamentally, in order to 'put on the show'—which issue I will examine in more detail in Chap. 9). It is easier to make the 'social planning'-type argument to defend the existence of copyright laws, for example, than it is to employ this theory in order to justify the exclusive rights provided to trademark proprietors.

So, let's consider the relevance and suitability of the utilitarian and labour theories of IP law when applied to the protection provided by the *sui generis* event legislation. The utilitarian theory encompasses the incentive argument, and the labour theory focuses on the reward argument.

The incentive argument has found special recognition in the United States, where the patent and copyright clause of the US Constitution is predicated on promoting the progress of science and useful arts,[367] and the Supreme Court has consistently accepted the incentive rationale for patent and copyright protection.[368] Prominent American IP law specialist Mark Lemley calls this theory an 'ex ante' justification for IP rights, because under this conception 'the goal of intellectual

366 Compare the finding of the German Federal Supreme Court (*Bundesgerichtshof* Case number I ZR 183/07 ('*WM-Marken*'), 12 November 2009) that the name of FIFA's World Cup event does not qualify for 'work title' protection in terms of German trademark law. 'Work titles' (*Werktitel*) are any distinctive designation of an intangible result of work, such as the title of a book, and are protected under the German Trademark Act, mainly under the same terms as trade names and other business identifiers. In contrast to trademarks, work titles are protected without registration as soon as they are used in trade, subject only to the condition that they are inherently distinctive (Clark, B 'World Cup trademark dispute: 1-0 says the German Federal Supreme Court' 8 January 2010, *Journal of Intellectual Property Law & Practice*—available online at the time of writing at http://jiplp.blogspot.com/2010/01/world-cup-trade-mark-dispute-1-0-says.html).The following was observed (an accurate prediction, it turned out) in this regard in the earlier Germany country report submitted to the AIPPI working group Q210:

'It is also questionable whether titles of events are protected as titles of work. The German Trademark Act acknowledges titles of work for printed publications, cinematographic works, acoustical works, stage plays or the "other comparable works". Only works which represent an "intellectual work result" deserve protection as other comparable titles of work. Although the Federal Court of Justice has confirmed that titles of work are protectable also in the area of software and games with "intellectual content", it has to be assumed that it would deny such "intellectual content" and thus the character of a work for titles of major sports events.'

367 United States Constitution, Article 1, clause 8.

368 See *Mazer v Stein* 347 U.S. 201 (1954).

property is to influence behaviour that occurs before the right comes into being', and he explains the incentive theory as follows:

> Ideas are public goods: they can be copied freely and used by anyone who is aware of them without depriving others of their use. But ideas also take time and money to create. Because ideas are so easy to spread and so hard to control, only with difficulty may creators recoup their investment in creating the idea. As a result, absent intellectual property protection, most would prefer to copy rather than create ideas, and inefficiently few new ideas would be created.[369]

He explains that different theories in justification of IP rights entail very different consequences for the scope, duration, and enforcement of such rights, and notes the following in respect of the incentive theory:

> Under the classical incentive story, intellectual property is a necessary evil. We grant creators exclusive rights in their works—permitting them to charge a supracompetitive price—to encourage them to make such works in the first place. This supracompetitive price in turn artificially depresses the consumption of the newly created work: some people who would be willing to pay more than the marginal cost of a copy of the idea will not be able to have access to it. Further, the exclusive control intellectual property rights grant to pioneers may stifle the invention of improvers. As a result, the incentive theory of intellectual property dictates that intellectual property rights should be granted only where necessary.[370]

The reward argument, which is aimed at providing a system through which the law's protection of the creator's idea or expression serves to reward the creator for the natural fruits of their labour, has a profoundly moral element: 'Flavouring many intellectual property cases, particularly those to do with filching trademarks and copyright plagiarism, are expressed or veiled references to the unauthorised reaper cashing in on the efforts of the original creator'.[371]

These two theories are, of course, not mutually exclusive, as it is conceivable that IP rights can be justified both on the basis of their wider incentive role as well as on the more 'personalised' basis of providing a reward to individual creators for work already performed and IP already created.

When one considers these theories in justification of IP in the context of the sports mega-event, and specifically the organisers' claims for protection of their commercial rights to events against ambush marketing, it is my contention that there are some conceptual difficulties with the aggressive rights protection framework provided by the *sui generis* event legislation. From the discussion elsewhere in this book the reader will note that event organisers have employed a combination of arguments that may resort under both the incentive and the reward theories, respectively, in their claims for special protection from law-makers and in their condemnation of ambushing of events. We have already encountered the

---

369 Lemley, M A 'Ex Ante Versus Ex Post Justifications for Intellectual Property' University of California—Berkeley Public Law and Legal Theory Research Paper Series Paper No. 144 (available online at the time of writing at http://levine.sscnet.ucla.edu/archive/refs4122247000000000492.pdf).

370 Ibid.

371 Sumpter 2006, p. xi.

argument that ambushing threatens the very existence of the mega-event (i.e. that ambushers' conduct threatens to alienate official sponsors by impinging on the exclusivity of their rights, and that in the absence of the sponsors' investment these costly spectacles could not be staged), which I will examine in more detail in Chap. 9. We have also, however, seen that the stigmatised view of 'ambushing' (which view tends to condemn conduct that may very well not be ambushing in the traditional sense of the term and may involve conduct that is not ethically or otherwise objectionable, in the absence of the special legislation which outlaws it) is often heavily motivated with claims of the 'free-riding' of ambushers and the fact that they have taken what they have not paid for—these claims will be further examined in Chap. 8. These claims clearly reflect incentivisation and reward arguments in support of the rights claimed by event organisers; namely 'we need protection in order to enable us to continue producing the events', and 'we need protection because the fruits of our labours are being filched'. I am, however, not convinced of the probity of such arguments. We have seen that the *sui generis* event legislation, generally, provides protection for event organisers that equates to protection which significantly expands on what IP rights would provide. Does the incentive or the reward theory provide justification for such protection?

As we have seen earlier in this chapter, the most important form of IP protection in respect of mega-events is the use of trademarks. We have also seen (and this will be examined in more detail later) that the 'association rights' to events as created in special event legislation, in essence, functions as a new statutory right akin to trademark rights. Lemley pointed (more than a decade ago) to the unconvincing nature of the incentive justification for intellectual property in the context of trademarks and, more specifically, in the context of what he refers to as the trend towards 'propertizing' intellectual property (as experienced primarily in the market for merchandising of logos and marks, which is especially relevant, and prevalent, in the professional sports industry):

> [T]here is an increasing tendency to treat trademarks as assets with their own intrinsic value, rather than as a means to an end. In part, this change reflects a broader trend towards "propertizing" intellectual property… Why should the law create property rights in trademarks, particularly the strong, unfettered property rights that seem to underlie the "trademarks as property" concept? We don't protect trademarks to encourage the creation of more trademarks, so the incentive rationale for intellectual property will not work here. Trademarks may be valuable as vehicles for efficient advertising; protecting their owners against the use of confusingly similar marks will encourage investment in brand quality and simultaneously protect consumers from confusion. But if we are to conclude that the trademark itself is valuable property, we need some rationale beyond these traditional justifications for trademark law.[372]

The author explains that this rationale is not an easy one to find:

> The new economic learning on brands and advertising ties trademarks to consumer search costs and experience characteristics. But none of these changes has undermined the basic differences amongst trademarks and other forms of intellectual property. Patents and

[372] Lemley 1999, pp. 1693–1694.

> copyrights are created for an instrumental purpose that is directly related to the subject matter of protection: We want more of the sort of works that patent and copyright law protect. One can construct from this an argument that we should vest the creators of those works with strong property rights, as rewards, incentives, or inducements to continued investment.'... The justifications for trademark law are different from those for other forms of intellectual property. We give protection to trademarks for one basic reason: to enable the public to identify easily a particular product from a particular source. Allowing this connection to be made in turn has secondary benefits: Consumer surplus is not diminished by fraud; producers can compete on the basis of experience characteristics of goods, and so on. There is no reason to believe that treating trademarks as property is particularly likely to further this goal. After all, we don't necessarily want more new trademarks as an end in itself. Indeed, we might all be better off in a world with fewer brands clamouring for our scarce attention, and less [artificial product differentiation]... Even if we did want more trademarks for some reason, it is far from clear that we would need government-provided incentives to create them.[373]

Others have also observed that the incentive argument is more suited to some forms of intellectual property than to others, as was noted in the context of the American right of publicity:

> The incentive-based rationale differs from the Lockean labour theory in that the latter focuses on reward for the actual labour performed rather than the motivation for such labour... The economic incentive rationale may be more applicable to copyright and patents, where a competitive monopoly is granted to creators whose artistic works and inventions enrich and benefit society. It is difficult to see how the right of publicity can lead to an increase in effort, creativity, and achievement in entertainment or sport that will benefit society, especially in an age where "celebrities" with dubious claims to fame are produced overnight by the media through a proliferation of reality television series such as *The Biggest Loser*, *Fear Factor*, and *Survivor*.[374]

Not only have event organisers attempted to claim 'special' trademark status for their event marks (compare the FIFA/Ferrero litigation discussed earlier in this chapter), we have also seen claims for extension of the international trademark classification in class 41 (for the organising of events to include merchandising of products and services in respect of such events). As pointed out above, the incentivisation argument provides poor grounds for such claims in respect of trademark protection. But another, more practical aspect, is the fact that event organisers have to date largely failed to prove their claims that ambush marketing of events, in fact, threaten the continued ability to host such events. Elsewhere I refer to the writing of Grady, McKelvey and Bernthal, who have observed the following in this regard:

> The Olympic movement's stated rationale for event-specific legislation is to protect the commercial value of its brand so that it continues to be financially valuable to official sponsors. Absent such legislation, it argues, ambush marketing will diminish the value of its sponsorship assets and ultimately result in companies not renewing their sponsorships or, at the very least, negotiating a lower price for their sponsorship. This presupposes that

373 Ibid. 1694.

374 Tan 2008, pp. 934–935.

ambush marketing actually has caused harm to the Olympic movement's sponsorship programme, or at least has the potential to do so.[375]

But the authors question the veracity of such claims:

This rationale has not, however, held up to scrutiny. Specifically, there is a notable lack of evidence that ambush marketing has ever been stated (at least publicly) as a reason for a company to opt not to participate in the Olympic movement's official sponsorship programme or to renew an existing Olympic sponsorship. Intuitively, one would expect that if a company cited ambush marketing as a reason for not becoming an official sponsor, or not renewing its official sponsorship, the Olympic movement would widely publicise this fact as 'proof' of the need for event-specific legislation.[376]

They refer to a recent academic study by Séguin et al.,[377] conducted within the context of the event-specific legislation for the 2010 Winter Games in Vancouver, which found little rationale to support the Olympic movement's need for such special event legislation. Through both a review of the ambush marketing literature and interviews with key figures associated with the Olympic movement, the researchers found little direct evidence of harm caused by ambush marketing, which could not be sufficiently resolved by the less aggressive and unobjectionable brand protection and education strategies'. They further argued that the IOC should not be able to use its negotiating power to impose legislation without unquestionable proof of damage'.[378] Grady et al. add that one must consider 'the rationale of enacting event-specific legislation designed to protect the revenue streams of a privately-run sport organisation that has demonstrated no tangible proof of harm or financial need that can be directly attributed to ambush marketing':

Olympic sponsorship revenue has grown consistently and substantially without such legislation, going from US$96 m for the 1988 Seoul Games to US$886 m for Beijing in 2008. This fact, coupled with the lack of substantiated harm associated with ambush marketing activity, raises legitimate questions as to the role or responsibility of government to protect the value and viability of the Olympics' sponsorship programmes through event-specific legislation. (This line of reasoning is also likely to apply for other highly profitable, privately-run sport organisations that demand event-specific legislation.) The closest analogy that one might suggest is the practise whereby state and local governments provide land and tax incentive packages to lure new companies and industry, with the intent of creating jobs, fuelling its economy, and even securing the psychic and economic benefits associated with the transaction. One can only imagine, however, the response of government officials and legislators if that company or industry demanded that the government also enact new business and trademark-related laws designed to give the incoming company or industry a decided advantage over companies or industries already doing business within the country.[379]

---

375 Grady et al. 2010, p. 151.

376 Ibid.

377 Séguin et al. 2008, pp. 99–101.

378 Ibid.

379 Grady et al. 2010, p. 152.

I would suggest that this failure by event organisers to provide unequivocal and convincing proof of the dire risks to the survival of their events posed by ambushing, and the resultant need for such far-reaching and extensive rights protection by means of special laws, serves to disqualify such strong rights protection from justification in terms of an incentive argument. In a related question, I believe that there is also insufficient proof of an incentive justification based on a wider socio-economic benefit in such strong commercial rights protection. Earlier in this chapter I have tried to show that the relevant event legislation generally does not require proof of consumer confusion in respect of infringement of association rights or prohibitions on the use of event-related words or symbols, and that this element of trademark protection and infringement proceedings is largely absent.

In respect of the reward theory, I would suggest that there are two main objections to its potential justification of the strong event commercial rights protection. The first, which is based on the practical experience of mega-events and of their commercialisation, is that event organisers already receive significant rewards for the staging of their events, primarily in the form of the prime source of revenue from such events, namely the sale of broadcasting rights. For example, FIFA reported in its 2010 annual financial report[380] that 93% of its revenues, over the 2007–2010 period, were event-related revenues. Of these revenues (totalling USD 3.89 billion), an amount of USD 2.448 billion was attributable to the sale of television rights over this period, of which the lion's share (USD 2.408 billion) were for the 2010 FIFA World Cup South Africa:

> The FIFA Congress passed a revenue budget of USD 3,200 million for the 2007–2010 period, which was exceeded by USD 605 million. This extra revenue is due to the very successful sale of TV and marketing rights of the 2010 FIFA World Cup South Africa™. This success underscores the huge appeal of FIFA's flagship tournament.[381]

The phenomenal commercial success of the Olympic Games in recent years is also well documented. I would submit that any claim to strong rights protection of event organisers' sponsorship programmes based on the reward for their labours in presenting the events is problematic, especially when considered against the substantial social and other costs of such strong legislative protection, as I discuss elsewhere in the chapters that follow.

My second objection to the justification for strong event rights protection based on the reward theory is the tenuous nature of event organisers' claims to rights based on the value associated with their events—this is an objection that is relevant to the issue of the subject matter of *sui generis* 'association right' protection, which I will consider in detail in Chap. 8. Rochelle Cooper Dreyfuss explains that there is no normative principle that equates value and private right (i.e. that once something has value it should immediately be assumed that someone should have a

---

[380] Available online at the time of writing at http://www.fifa.com/mm/document/affederation/administration/01/39/20/45/web_fifa_fr2010_eng[1].pdf.

[381] From the FIFA 2010 *Financial Report* (available online), *supra*.

right to it). She points out that, to the contrary, black letter law is that everyone is free to copy:

> Now, it is true that there are laws that depart from this baseline, but the justification for them is not "if value, then right." Usually, it is not even a principle of just deserts or a theory of natural rights. Rather, departures occur for instrumental reasons, when the creation of private rights is seen to further important social goals.[382]

She explains her view in terms of the copyright clause in the US Constitution, which (as mentioned earlier) gives Congress the power 'to promote the Progress of Science and useful Arts, by securing for limited Times to Authors and Inventors the exclusive Right to their respective Writings and Discoveries', and explains that this clause 'negates the reward theory with its first phrase and, by reason of the limited times provision, the natural rights idea as well'. The Clause articulates exactly what utilitarian goal exclusivity must further. Dreyfuss further articulates this understanding of the inappropriateness of mere value serving to justify the creation of special rights, in the (American) context of IP rights:

> Indeed, in the copyright context, the Supreme Court has often said that the ability to capture the economic value associated with works of creativity is secondary to the goal of building the domain of public knowledge. In patent law, where a great deal of economic literature has been devoted to the question of justifications, it has been posited that exclusivity is also useful for centralising research and promoting efficient development of new scientific fields. Of course, there is room to disagree that either profits or centralisation is necessary to produce the optimum level of creativity. However, those who disagree argue for more public access, not for a system of exclusivity based on the mere recognition of value. Similarly, functional goals lie at the core of trademark law… [C]ontrol over merchandising symbols gives buyers the ability to make effective choices amongst similar products and, ultimately, encourages investments in goodwill.[383]

I will show later that the recent experience of sports mega-events commercial rights discourse has been one where the event organisers have consistently claimed exactly such 'rights' to their events because of the value of such events in the marketing arena. Organisers appear to lay claim to the publicity value of their events, which I will argue has no basis in law, although law-makers have increasingly allowed them protection for such 'rights' and have even created some new 'rights' in this regard. I would suggest that this blind acceptance that value equates to right is unfounded and illegitimate; event organisers should not be entitled to claim, as a reward for the value of events which is due to their public nature and to other reasons (including the investment by governments, taxpayers and others), 'ownership' or rights to exclusive use of aspects which do not constitute private property in terms of normal legal principles. The significant expansion of IP rights by means of the special event legislation cannot be justified on the basis of a need to provide such ill-founded rewards to event organisers, and at such significant social costs.

---

382 Cooper Dreyfuss 1996, p. 142.

383 Cooper Dreyfuss 1996, p. 143.

5.5 Conclusion

This chapter has argued that the protection afforded to event organisers and their sponsors in *sui generis* event legislation, generally, significantly exceeds the protection found in traditional intellectual property laws. Event organisers are granted rights and remedies that they would not enjoy or be entitled to in terms of IP rights, which relates to both a broader scope of protection (e.g. protecting material which would not qualify for protection in terms of IP rights such as copyright or trademarks) and a relaxation of the requirements for the establishment of such rights when compared to IP rights. Such protection is also not in line with the fundamental principles or philosophies that underpin IP rights, and which are often raised in justification of IP laws and of the limits it places on the rights of others and on the greater common good.

The primary justification provided for this expansion of protection in respect of mega-events includes recourse to practical issues regarding IP enforcement, and relate to financial cost and the time factor in respect of pursuing legal action against 'ambush marketers'. While, as I have mentioned, one can understand the nature of such concerns over these practical issues which may in certain circumstances lead to a situation where rights holders are left without an effective remedy and the law's protection is in name only, I am concerned about an over-reach by legislatures who attempt to address such practical problems by means of significant re-writing of the substance of laws and which departs from accepted legal principles. I may be over-stating the point, but I believe that one can find parallels with other examples in the past where expediency has been raised to trump fundamental rights by means of draconian laws. Without wishing to express an opinion on matters beyond the scope of this book I believe one should bear in mind that, at heart, special mega-event laws are concerned with protecting the commercial rights of large corporations and powerful organisations in world sport, and that law-makers' flouting of fundamental principles of law in order to protect such narrow interests in ways which are suspect in respect of their impact on public interests and the rights of individuals is problematic, and requires much more active engagement by the legal fraternity than has hitherto been the case. The Canadian legislature, in enacting its Olympic and Paralympic Marks Act[384] for the 2010 Vancouver Winter Games, apparently subscribed to the belief that the existing general trademark legislation was insufficiently capable of legally regulating an event like the Olympic Winter Games, and Mouritz points out that the enactment of the legislation appeared to be on the basis of application of the principle of *lex specialis derogat legi generali.*[385] When one considers that the Vancouver Act made provision for outlawing non-commercial use of Olympic trademarks and generic terms, which is in conflict with Canada's Trademarks Act

[384] See the discussion in Sect. 4.4.7 of Chap. 4.

[385] Mouritz 2008, p. 14

(as well as the UK legislation and ECJ case law),[386] I would suggest that much more than recourse to the *lex specialis* doctrine is required in order to justify such significant extension of IP protection by means of special event legislation. It is one thing to employ this principle to explain anomalies between special and more general laws, but something completely different if it is used to seek to legitimise complete negation of generally-applicable laws and wholesale departure from established legal principles. The relevant special legislation still must conform to accepted principles of law; it is, after all, still 'law' (or, at least, purports to be so).

To return to an IP-related issue: The process that Lemley refers to as turning trademarks into 'property' holds the potential for dire risks which are especially important, and, I would submit, 100% germane, in the context of this book's consideration of the law's treatment of the private commercial interests of groupings and powerful entities which act as monopolists, constantly demanding greater and more expansive levels of protection at the cost of the public good:

> Even more troubling, propertizing trademarks comes at a rather significant cost to society. Sometimes that cost takes the form of lost opportunities: Important political and social commentary and works of art may be suppressed entirely. It may also take the form of higher prices: When we protect the design of products as trademarks, we prevent competition in the sale of those products, and the price goes up accordingly.
>
> Other social costs are more diffuse, but no less real: Our language and our culture are impoverished when we cannot use the most familiar words to discuss—or make fun of, or criticise—the products and companies that are the basis of our economy. At the very least, it becomes inconvenient to do so. And perhaps most important, trademark licensing is expensive. The more we propertize, the more transaction costs we impose on everyone. Companies and individuals will have to hire more lawyers, delay introducing their products, and spend money in merchandising fees to acquire the rights to use words, logos, or product configurations. Because trademarks so often overlap, propertization may also reduce certainty, making trademark searching and clearance more difficult and leading to more litigation.'[387]

Is anyone reminded of the issues which are increasingly frequently being raised in the media in respect of the commercialisation of the modern sports mega-event? I would suggest that the following rather strong words expressed by a South African IP lawyer in respect of what he characterises as 'the fascist and draconian' provisions of the South African Counterfeit Goods Act, 1997, are apt in describing much of the 'IP+' protection afforded to event rights holders:

> Some may rejoice in an act which is basically fascist as handing trademark owners a potent weapon in protecting their rights, but that view is short-sighted. When the checks and balances that underpin the very notion of justice, however vague a notion that is, are dispensed with, injustice follows. Where injustice reigns a reaction is inevitable and it typically is not kind to those who benefited from the injustice.[388]

---

386 See Mouritz 2008; Marcus 2010, p. 32.

387 See Lemley 1999.

388 Johannesburg attorney Ron Wheeldon, writing in a roundtable discussion on South African IP law ('Staying ahead in the rainbow nation' May/June 2007 *World Trademark Review* 38 at 42).

And[389]:

> Owners [of trademarks and IP] are inevitably partisan, but must be careful to be seen to be in favour of balance and equal rights, rather than greedy monopolists pushing endlessly for a tilted playing field[390]

When one considers the extent to which IP protection for sports mega-events has been expanded by means of the special event legislation, it is important to note that there also does not seem to be any clear prospect of such trend dissipating in the near future. This is surprising in light of the increasingly vocal criticism in the public discourse of event organisers' aggressive rights protection campaigns. In the mega-event rights protection debate one is faced with a skewed political environment when it comes to lobbying for ever-expanding IP and other event protection, where the following comments on the American IP regime are apposite:

> The advocates of increased intellectual property protection have consisted, for the most part, of creators, their surrogates (publishers, movie studios, etc.), businesses interested in protecting their trademarks, patent portfolios, or trade secrets, and celebrities eager to capitalise on their reputations. Most have had strong financial interests in statutory reform that would protect them against nonpermissive use of their "property." The interests of persons who would benefit from reduced intellectual property protection, by contrast, have tended to be more diluted. The largest and most important such group consists of consumers—each of whom typically has had only a small stake in the content of the pertinent laws. The result is that lobbying efforts have repeatedly been biased in favour of the expansion of intellectual property. Enthusiasts have made themselves heard, while sceptics have been largely silent.[391]

I believe the time has come for greater and more proactive engagement with the issues by critics of the activities of the 'mega-event tsars', and I hope that the discussion in the chapters that follow will lend further support for this view.

In conclusion I should just mention that some commentators have called for expansion of IP protection for events as a means of avoiding draconian *sui generis* anti-ambush legislation. I refer, in a number of places in this book, to the fact that most systems do not recognise a property right in an event. Copyright protection for events has also been denied on the basis of, primarily, the following considerations:

- The transitory or ephemeral nature of the spectacle;
- That it is unlikely that a spectacle can be property capable of being owned by anyone; and

---

389 Wheeldon, *supra*, commenting regarding the future of IP protection in South Africa, more generally.

390 Wheeldon *supra* 42.

391 William W Fischer III 'The growth of intellectual property: A history of the ownership of ideas in the United States' (at 18), Harvard University, paper available online at the time of writing at http://cyber.law.harvard.edu/people/tfisher/iphistory.pdf.

– Even if one were to recognise such a form of property in a spectacle, there is no authority to support a legally enforceable right to prevent anyone describing what they see of that property by viewing the spectacle.[392]

Corbett and van Roy, in their critical analysis of New Zealand's Major Events Management Act, are of the view that copyright protection for major events should be recognised, despite its ephemeral nature. They believe that '[t]he ability for sponsors to exploit their copyright by licensing or otherwise would provide sufficient return on their financial investments and would seem a more ready fit with traditional intellectual property principles than the kinds of protection afforded by MEMA.'[393] Aside from the fact that it is unclear why the authors appear to accept that such a copyright in an event would vest in the sponsors, as opposed to the event organiser, I do not agree that copyright protection for events is the answer. This suggestion is, of course, nothing new. As long ago as 1952, with the Gregory Committee's review of English copyright law, sports promoters argued that a sporting event should benefit from copyright protection comparable to that afforded to the creation of an artistic, musical, literary or dramatic work. In 1990, Portuguese law professor Jose de Oliveira Ascencao argued for an intellectual property right to an entertainment or event for its organiser, based on custom.[394] Elsewhere I refer to the fact that recent developments in Europe regarding calls for a 'sports event organiser's right' in the context of regulation of the sports betting industry are worrying. I believe that any means of attempting to provide a property (or intellectual property, such as copyright)-based entitlement for event organisers to control commercial exploitation of all down-stream aspects of 'their' events would be problematic. I would submit that the above-mentioned calls for such an organiser's right are, primarily, aimed simply at providing a more comprehensive basis for event organisers to exploit any and all possible commercial revenues which may derive from the event; this, I believe, is not sufficient justification for the expansion of copyright principles in this context, and would simply serve to exacerbate the anti-competitive effects of the modern mega-event sponsorship model and its protection by means of special anti-ambushing laws (which I'll consider in more detail in Chap. 6). Also, much of this book is concerned with the examples of apparent abuse of the monopoly that event organisers and their sponsors enjoy in respect of mega-events, specifically in terms of the *sui generis* legislation. In light of the experience to date in this regard I believe it would be dangerous to provide event organisers with any further legitimisation of such monopoly by means of rights of exclusivity relating to some form of special (intellectual) property. It remains to be seen where (and how far) law-makers will go with future regulation of the exploitation of commercial interests in respect of these events. While I agree with Corbett and van Roy regarding the many problematic aspects of MEMA, and of other special event legislation, I do not believe

[392] See Corbett and Van Roy 2010, p. 355.

[393] Corbett and van Roy 2010, p. 357.

[394] de Oliveira Ascencao 1990.

that development of a new or special form of 'copyright in a spectacle' would be in the public interest, or is the proper way forward. I hope that legislatures and courts will continue to deny such expansive protection to events, as the Court of Justice for the European Union confirmed in its recent landmark judgment on sports broadcasting rights in the cases *Football Association Premier League Ltd. & others v. QC Leisure & Others*; and *Karen Murphy v. Media Protection Services Ltd*[395] (even though the court appeared to leave the matter open to EU Member states to legislate for special protection if required, which I hope will not be the case in future in light of the above discussion[396]).

Mega-events are, in my view, at least unique in one sense. They are '*uncopyrightable*'—which is the longest isogram in the English language. And that's about as far as I believe their uniqueness should go.

References

All internet-based sources referred to, were last visited in or before December 2011.

Baird SR (1993) Moral Intervention in the Trademark Arena: Banning the Registration of Scandalous and Immoral Trademarks. Trademark Rep 83:661
Becker LC (1993) Deserving to own intellectual property. Chicago-Kent Law Rev 68:609
Beebe B (2005) Search and persuasion in trademark law. Mich Law Rev 103:2020

[395] Cases C-403/08 and C-429/08 (judgment delivered on 4 October 2011). The court observed as follows (at par. 96–99 of the judgment):

'[The Football Association Premier League] cannot claim copyright in the Premier League matches themselves, as they cannot be classified as works. To be so classified, the subject-matter concerned would have to be original in the sense that it is its author's own intellectual creation… However, sporting events cannot be regarded as intellectual creations classifiable as works within the meaning of the Copyright Directive. That applies in particular to football matches, which are subject to rules of the game, leaving no room for creative freedom for the purposes of copyright. Accordingly, those events cannot be protected under copyright. It is, moreover, undisputed that European Union law does not protect them on any other basis in the field of intellectual property.'

[396] The court observed as follows at par. 100–102 of the judgment:

'None the less, sporting events, as such, have a unique and, to that extent, original character which can transform them into subject-matter that is worthy of protection comparable to the protection of works, and that protection can be granted, where appropriate, by the various domestic legal orders. In this regard, it is to be noted that, under the second subparagraph of Article 165(1) TFEU, the European Union is to contribute to the promotion of European sporting issues, while taking account of the specific nature of sport, its structures based on voluntary activity and its social and educational function. Accordingly, it is permissible for a Member State to protect sporting events, where appropriate by virtue of protection of intellectual property, by putting in place specific national legislation, or by recognising, in compliance with European Union law, protection conferred upon those events by agreements concluded between the persons having the right to make the audiovisual content of the events available to the public and the persons who wish to broadcast that content to the public of their choice.'

Blackshaw I (2010) Protecting major sporting events with particular reference to the 2012 London Olympic Games. Entertain Sports Law J 7(2). http://www2.warwick.ac.uk/fac/soc/law/elj/eslj/issues/volume7/number2/blackshaw/blackshaw.pdf

Bollier D (2005) Brand name bullies: the quest to own and control culture. Wiley, New Jersey

Boyle J (2008) The public domain: enclosing the commons of the mind. Yale University Press, New Haven

Brookman AL (2003) Trademark law: protection, enforcement and licensing. Aspen Publishing, New York

Brown RS (1948) Advertising and the public interest: legal protection of trade symbols. Yale Law J 57:1165

Carrier MA (2004) Cabining intellectual property through a property paradigm. Duke Law J 54:1

Cooper Dreyfuss R (1996) We are symbols and inhabit symbols, so should we be paying rent? Deconstructing the Lanham Act and rights of publicity. Columbia VLA J Law Arts 20:123

Corbett S, Van Roy Y (2010) Events management in New Zealand: one law to rule them all? J Bus Law 4:338–362

Curthoys J, Kendall CN (2001) Ambush marketing and the Sydney 2000 games (indicia and images) protection act: a retrospective. Murdoch Univ Electron J Law 8(2)

Das PK (2000) Offensive protection: the potential application of intellectual property laws to scripted sports plays. Indiana Law J 75:1073

de Oliveira Ascencao J (1990) The right over an entertainment or event. Copyr Bull 24(2):3–13

Elhauge E, Geradin D (2007) Global competition and economics. Hart Publishing, Oxford

Ellis D, Scassa T, Seguin B (2011) Framing ambush marketing as a legal issue: an Olympic perspective. Sport Manag Rev 14(3):297–308

Ewelukwa UU (2006) Comparative trademark law: fair use defense in the United States and Europe—the changing face of trademark law. Widener Law Rev 13:97

Farley CH (2006) Why we are confused about the trademark dilution law. Fordham IP Media Ent LJ 16:1175

Fezer K-H (2003) Die Eventmarke. Festschrift für Winfried Tilmann 321. (as referred to in Lundgren FD 2010)

Fezer K-H (2007) Kennzeichenschutz des Sponsoring—Der Weg nach WM 2006, Zur Eintragungsfähigkeit von Veralstaltungsdienstleistungsmarken und Veranstaltungswarenmarken. Mitteilungen der deutschen Patentanwälte 5/2007, 193. (as referred to in Lundgren FD 2010)

Fisher WW (1988) Reconstructing the fair use doctrine. Harvard Law Rev 101:1659

Fisher WW (2001) Theories of intellectual property law. In: Munzer S (ed) New essays in the legal and political theory of property. Cambridge University Press, Cambridge

Franklyn DJ (2001) Owning words in cyberspace: the accidental trademark regime. Wis Law Rev 5:1251

Frontier Economics Pty Ltd, Melbourne (2007) Ambush marketing legislation review, a report prepared for IP Australia and the Australian government's department of communications. Information technology and the arts (October 2007)

Gardiner et al (2006) Sports Law, 3rd edn. Cavendish Publishing, London

Gordon WJ (1993) A property right in self-expression: equality and individualism in the natural law of intellectual property. Yale Law J 102:1533

Grady J, McKelvey S, Bernthal MJ (2012) From Beijing 2008 to London 2012: examining event-specific Olympic legislation vis à vis the rights and interests of stakeholders. J Spons 3(2):144–156

Haman M, Marriott D (2010) The 2010 World Cup—practical lessons in brand protection. World Trademark Rev 72–77

Heymann LA (2011) Naming, identity and trademark law. Indiana Law J 86:381

Johnson P (2007) Ambush marketing: a practical guide to protecting the brand of a sporting event. Sweet & Maxwell, London

Johnson P (2008) Look out! it's an ambush. Int Sports Law Rev 2/3:24–29

Kelbrick R (2008) The W***D C*P of 2*1*: FIFA's intellectual property rights in South Africa. J Intellect Prop Law Pract 3(5):327

Kobel P (2007) International report on question B: ambush marketing too smart to be good? Should certain ambush marketing practises be declared illegal and if yes, which ones and under what conditions? International report to the international league of competition law. Catania Congress 2007

Kunstadt RM, Kieff FS, Kramer RG (1996) Are sports moves next in IP law? Natl Law J c1

Kur A (2008) Strategic branding: Does trademark law provide for sufficient self help and self healing forces? In: Govaere I, Ulrich H (eds) Intellectual property, market power and the public interest P.I.E. Peter Lang, Brussels

Landes W, Posner R (1987) Trademark law: an economic perspective. J Law Econ 30:265

Lemley MA (1999) The modern Lanham Act and the death of common sense. Yale Law J 108:1687

Lemley MA, McKenna M (2010) Irrelevant confusion. Stanf Law Rev 62(2):444–446

Lessig L (2004) Free culture: the nature and future of creativity. Penguin Books, New York

Lewis A, Taylor J (2007) Sport: law and practice. Tottel Publishing, Haywards Heath

Longdin L (2009) Public law solutions to private law problems: major event regulation subverts IP's internal balance. J Intellect Prop Law Pract 4(10):726–742

Luepke MHH (2008) Taking unfair advantage or diluting a famous mark—A 20/20 perspective on the blurred differences between US and EU dilution law. Trademark Report 98(3):789

Lundgren FD (2010) Event marks: a necessary form of protection against ambush marketing? Thesis submitted to the Munich Intellectual Property Law Centre, 13 September 2010. http://oami.europa.eu/ows/rw/resource/documents/QPLUS/network/universities/felipe_danneman_lundgren_miplc.pdf

Marcus JT (2010) Ambush marketing: an analysis of its threat to sports rights holders and the efficacy of past, present and proposed anti-infringement programmes. Sport Law J 18(1):25

McKelvey SM (2006) Coca-Cola vs. PepsiCo: a "super" battleground for the Cola wars? Sports Mark Q 15(2):114–123

Merges RP, Menell PS, Lemley MA (2003) Intellectual property in the new technological age, 3rd edn. Aspen Publishers, New York

Mouritz A (2008) Challenging the legal enforceability of the Vancouver 2010 Olympic Games' anti-ambush marketing provisions. Sport Law J Issue 1(16):10–19

Ng CW (2008) The irrational lightness of trade marks. In: Bently L, Davis J, Ginsburg JC (eds) Trade marks and brands: an interdisciplinary critique. Cambridge University Press, Cambridge

Port KL (2008) Trademark extortion: the end of trademark law. Wash Lee Law Rev 65:585

Rayle R (2000) The trend towards enhancing trademark owners' rights—a comparative study of US and German trademark law. J Intellect Prop Law 7:227

Reichmann JH, Franklin JA (1999) Privately legislated intellectual property rights: reconciling freedom of contract with public good uses of information. Univ Pa Law Rev 147:875

Ross TP (2000) Intellectual property law: damages and remedies. Law Journal Press, New York

Scaria AG (2008) Ambush marketing: game within a game. Oxford University Press, Oxford

Schatte H (2009) Strategic branding—the difficulty of the term and trade mark 'Fussball WM 2006'. GRIN Verlag, Munich

Schwab F (2006) FIFA's trademark tactics. World Trademark Rev 3:6

Seguin B, O'Reilly NJ (2008) The Olympic brand, ambush marketing and clutter. Int J Sport Manag Mark 4(1):62

Séguin B, Ellis D, Scassa T, Parent M (2008) Who's ambushing whom? An examination of anti-ambush marketing legislation in Canada: the case of the 2010 Olympic and Paralympic Winter Games. In: Proceedings of the 16th European association for sport management conference, 10–13th September 2008, Heidelberg, Germany

Siegel P (1994) On the owning of words: reflections on San Francisco Arts and Athletics vs. United States Olympic Committee. In: Ringer RJ (ed) Queer words, queer images. New York University Press, New York

Spinello RA, Bottis M (2009) A defense of intellectual property rights. Edward Elgar Publishing Ltd, Cheltenham
Stim R (2010) Patent, copyright and trademark. Nolo Publishers, Berkeley
Stoll-DeBell K, Dempsey N, Dempsey B (2009) Injunctive relief: temporary restraining orders and preliminary injunctions. American Bar Association, Chicago
Storey S (2010) Pilfering, piracy and prevention: developments in combating ambush marketing. Sport Law J 18(1)40–54
Sumpter P (2006) Intellectual property law: principles in practice. CCH Ltd, New Zealand
Tan D (2008) Beyond trademark law: what the right of publicity can learn from cultural studies. Cardozo Arts Entertain Law J 25(3):913
Tawfik M (2008) When intellectual property rights converge: tracing the contours and mapping the fault lines 'case by case' and 'law by law'. In: Gendreau Y (ed) An emerging intellectual property paradigm: perspectives from Canada. Edward Elgar Publishing, London, p 267
Townley S, Harrington D, Couchman N (1998) The legal and practical prevention of ambush marketing in sports. Psychol Mark 15(4):333–348
Vaidhyanathan S (2003) Copyrights and copywrongs: the rise of intellectual property and how it threatens creativity. New York University Press, New York
Volokh E (2003) Freedom of speech and intellectual property: some thoughts after *Eldred*, *44 Liquormart*, and *Bartnicki*'. Houst Law Rev 40(3):697
Waldron J (1979) Enough and as good left for others. Philos Q 29:319
Wilf S (1999) Who authors trademarks? Cardozo Arts Entertain Law J 17:1
Williams TM (2009) *Winter v. NRDC*: A Stricter Standard for Irreparable Harm in Trademark Cases? 91J Pat Trademark Off Soc'y 571

Chapter 6
Mega-Event Rights Protection and Competition (Antitrust) Laws

> [W]here does protection against ambush marketing fit into general anti-trust legislation? Effectively, sponsors are paying to obtain a monopoly. There has been very little consideration of the relationship between the demands for extended protection and competition principles. Not surprisingly, the issue has been raised only by governments and public bodies, not by sports organizations.[1]

> The mere fact that protection against ambush marketing has been furnished on previous occasions is not a justification for its further protection. If there is a serious and responsible, competition-based reason for it, we should be told. And if the European Commission is content to allow such laws to hobble competition, perhaps it would be so kind as to explain why.[2]

6.1 Introduction

In Chap. 2 I briefly referred to potential competition law implications of the current system of commercial exploitation of sports mega-events, specifically of the system of category exclusivity of sponsorships to such events. I hoped to raise a number of issues regarding the competition implications of this system as background to considering ambush marketing of events, as the strategies (legal and otherwise) pursued by event organisers and their commercial partners to combat ambush marketing are essentially aimed at protecting such exclusivity of sponsors' rights, or what amounts to a commercial monopoly in the events. Scaria explains why competition law is so pertinent in this context:

> [S]ports have an intricate connection with contemporary economic and marketing strategies and nowadays it is almost considered as an economic activity by itself. The moment

---

[1] Kelbrick 2008, p. 48.
[2] Phillips 2006, p. 79.

A. M. Louw, *Ambush Marketing and the Mega-Event Monopoly*,
ASSER International Sports Law Series, DOI: 10.1007/978-90-6704-864-4_6,

event organisers engage in economic activities, the competition authorities will receive the *locus standi* to oversee them to ensure fair competition and to protect the interests of consumers. As many provisions of the event-specific legislation against ambush marketing contain elements of imposed exclusivity, they have to pass through the tests laid down by competition laws to assure fair competition in the market.[3]

Event organisers, just like their commercial partners (such as sponsors, suppliers and licencees), are 'undertakings' subject to competition law scrutiny, also in the context of the organisation of events[4] Commercial (and sponsors') rights to mega-events is, of course, not the only area in sport where competition law comes to the fore; examples of other such areas range from the collective selling of broadcasting rights (a major issue in the European Union during the last decade or so) to professional sports labour issues and franchise relocations in the United States. In fact, in a special issue in 2000 of the American Bar Association's *Antitrust* publication it was observed that three out of the four then sitting major professional sports league commissioners were prominent antitrust lawyers.[5] Coincidence? Maybe this is attributable to the fact that while antitrust issues pervade the industry of sport, most such issues are complex due to the very nature

---

[3] Scaria 2008, p. 117. Stephen Kinsella, in a speech to the *Rules of the Game* sports governance conference held in Brussels, 26–27 February 2001, observed the following in respect of the importance of competition law to sport:

'Competition law is very important for governing bodies' relationships with the competitors within its sport. When a governing body exercises its authority (because that authority is based on agreements between it and participants) it can potentially restrict competition and its actions can therefore be prohibited by Article 81 EC Treaty. In addition, sporting bodies have authority over how the sport in question will operate. This may place them in a "dominant position" within the meaning of Article 82 EC Treaty and therefore give them a special duty not to "abuse" their position.'

[4] Compare the case of FIFA, which the European Commission held to be 'an entity carrying on activities of an economic nature and [which] constitutes an undertaking within the meaning of Article 85 of the EEC Treaty' (92/521/EEC: Commission Decision of 27 October 1992 relating to a proceeding under Article 85 of the EEC Treaty (IV/33.384 and IV/33.378—Distribution of package tours during the 1990 World Cup)). The Commission considered the following as relevant factors in this regard relating to FIFA's organisation of the 1990 World Cup event (at par. 47–48):

FIFA is a federation of sports associations and accordingly carries out sports activities. However, FIFA also carries out activities of an economic nature, notably as regards:

- the conclusion of advertising contracts,
- the commercial exploitation of the World Cup emblems, and
- the conclusion of contracts relating to television broadcasting rights.

In the case of the 1990 World Cup, the sale of advertising and television broadcasting rights by FIFA accounted for some 65% of total World Cup revenue, estimated at Sfr 220 million.

[5] Commissioners Allan Bettman (NHL), 'Bud' Selig (MLB), David Stern (NBA) and Paul Tagliabue (NFL)—see Vol. 14 No. 2 *Antitrust* (Spring 2000) at 8 (available online at the time of writing at http://www.americanbar.org/content/dam/aba/publishing/antitrust_magazine/antitrust_14-2_full.authcheckdam.pdf).

of this industry. As one commentator observed regarding the recent (currently ongoing at the time of writing) American case of *American Needle Inc v NFL*, which will be examined in more detail below:

> *American Needle* offers the Supreme Court an opportunity to settle a longstanding source of confusion: how should antitrust law regulate the peculiar, perhaps incomparable, business entity known as a professional sports league?[6]

Having now also briefly considered ambush marketing (in Chap. 3), the special legal protection employed in various jurisdictions to combat ambush marketing (in Chap. 4) and the ways in which intellectual property (and 'IP+') commercial rights protection for events may serve to 'monopolise' language and elements of popular culture (in Chap. 5), we need to further consider aspects of competition law as they arise in this ongoing battle between rights holders and 'ambushers'. This chapter will continue to do so, with a specific emphasis on the potential competition law implications of special legal protection of commercial monopolies in mega-events.

The chapter will examine two main aspects of mega-event commercial rights protection against the backdrop of their potential competition law implications, namely the system of sponsorship exclusivity—a significant element of the commercial monopoly in mega-events—and the protection of events against 'ambushing' through the means of the *sui generis* event legislation discussed in the preceding chapters. I will conclude with some general observations regarding the potential competition law issues that may be relevant, and particularly problematic, in this context.

But first, just a brief disclaimer. I am not an expert on competition law (as the reader will surely soon realise), and my analysis will be a superficial one. I intend not to definitively answer the questions which I'll pose, but rather to just briefly explore the potential for mega-event commercial rights protection as discussed in this book to raise competition or antitrust issues. I hope that this exercise will inspire debate on the topic rather than promising any conclusions in this regard. The second caution relates to the scope of the review contained in this book, more generally. As shown in Chap. 4, the law relating to mega-event rights protection is varied and includes special legislation in a number of different jurisdictions. I cannot undertake any detailed discussion of competition laws in all such systems. As a result, I will proceed to discuss general principles in this area of law, mainly derived from the two major competition law regimes as found in the United States and in the European Union. The discussion that follows may appear to be some weird hotchpotch of laws from these two jurisdictions, but I hope that it will cover the main aspects of similarity and the differences in approach sufficiently, in the specific context within which I write here.

6 McCann 2009, p. 103.

6.2 Examining the Competition Law Implications of Mega-Event Commercial Rights Protection

From the preceding chapters it should be clear that the concept of competition is at the heart of the mega-event commercialisation model as well as the combating of ambush marketing. Sponsorship exclusivity is aimed, specifically and by definition, at limiting competition. Exclusive sponsors obtain (and pay for) rights which exclude their competitors and other marketers from involvement with the event. The value of such sponsorships is significantly dependent on exclusivity, and the sponsorship contracts with event organisers guarantee such exclusivity. From this flows the interest of sponsors in preventing ambushing from detracting from such exclusivity, and the event organisers' often aggressive anti-ambushing campaigns (FIFA is always a good example of this) derive from these contractual guarantees. When a sponsor has paid in the region of USD 100 million to be associated with a mega-event it is imperative for the event organiser to justify the large sponsorship fee which, as mentioned, is largely due to guarantees of exclusivity, and to protect the sponsors' investment by doing its utmost to ensure that no competitors of the sponsor will steal the show or other marketers clutter the marketing environment surrounding the event and thus detract from the exclusivity of the rights obtained by the sponsor or the value of its association with the event as a marketing platform for its brand.

This, however, does not mean that such inherently anti-competitive arrangements do not warrant scrutiny in terms of law, to determine whether they are in fact legal. Sports competition law literature and case law has focused mostly on other issues (primarily regarding sports broadcasting rights and, in the American context, issues of franchise relocations in professional sports and labour issues). I find the dearth of case law in this area rather surprising, especially as it will be noted from my discussion in the following section that I view the very concept of sponsorship exclusivity to be inherently problematic in the context of competition laws. A possible reason may be one advanced by some commentators, relating to the nature of the sports sponsorship market and the wealth of opportunities for sponsors to access sponsorship properties. One such commentator examined the issue of whether a recent sponsorship and naming rights deal in English football between Manchester City and Etihad Airways may have competition law (and other) implications. Andrew Nixon dismissed this on the following basis:

> [I]t is rare for a sports sponsorship deal to be caught by [competition] rules as, generally speaking, the same market exposure can be generated through alternative promotional arrangements. Any argument that the Etihad deal breached competition law would be based on the fact that it is for an unusually long period of time, and it is a 'blanket' arrangement, meaning that it encompasses both stadium naming rights and shirt sponsorship. This, nevertheless, would not be sufficient to foreclose the market to potential sponsors, and there are numerous football teams and indeed numerous other sports that a sponsor could use as a platform. An exclusive broadcasting deal of similar term would

inevitably catch the Commission's attention, but a complaint about a sponsorship deal, however long and wide ranging, is unlikely to get far.[7]

Elsewhere in this chapter I refer to others who have expressed similar sentiments, which appear to downplay or negate the potential anti-competitive effects of exclusive sponsorship arrangements. I believe, however, that this view is not applicable in the context of the sports mega-event, such as the Olympic Games or the FIFA World Cup, which I view to be quite different in respect of determining the relevant market as well as the anti-competitive effects of such arrangements, and will explore the issue further below. The mega-event sponsorship milieu has to the best of my knowledge not been the subject of significant analysis in this regard, and I will attempt to examine the issues, in broad strokes.

6.2.1 Is Sponsorship Exclusivity in Respect of Events Legal?

In Chap. 2 I briefly explained the working of the modern mega-event sponsorship model and, specifically, the phenomenon of exclusivity granted to sponsors in respect of product or service categories of sponsorship. I hinted there at the possibility that such system of exclusivity may not, in fact, be legal. The power to exclude others from commercial benefits relating to sports mega-events raise the possibility of anti-competitive implications of such arrangements falling foul of relevant competition or antitrust laws, and I will continue to consider this issue in more detail.

Category exclusivity clearly creates a highly artificial monopoly in respect of marketing of the relevant products or services in relation to an event. Fans who attend the games are subjected to restrictions and outright prohibitions on what they may wear or what they may eat or drink, or even the credit card they may use to pay for it all. But this not only applies for the 90 min period of a World Cup football match; local traders may be forced to effectively close up shop for a period of weeks if they're situated in an 'exclusion zone' in a host city or in the vicinity of a 'clean transport route', while many enterprises may be muzzled to a significant extent for months or even years in the run-up to a mega-event in conducting their marketing and advertising activities. During the 2003 ICC Cricket World Cup held in South Africa, schoolchildren attending a game were instructed to scratch the brand name off Coca-Cola cans because Pepsi was the official sponsor of the tournament, and a Johannesburg businessman was ejected from the Wanderers stadium for refusing to relinquish his six-pack of Coke when instructed to do so by security staff. At the time of writing of this book, the official web site for ticketing

[7] Nixon, A 'Sponsorship, FFP and Competition Rules' *The Sports Lawyer*, 11 August 2011—available online at the time of writing at http://www.mondaq.com/x/142396/Antitrust+Competition/The+Sport+Lawyer+Sponsorship+FFP+and+Competition+Rules.

for the 2012 London Olympics[8] proudly proclaims that '[i]n recognition of Visa's support of the Games, the London 2012 Olympic Games and Paralympic Games are proud to accept only Visa cards (debit, credit and prepaid), along with cash and cheques.' There are reportedly 91 million VISA cardholders in the UK compared to 40 million MasterCard and 4 million American Express cardholders, and it has been speculated that some potential buyers will struggle to obtain tickets. The deal also means they will not be able to withdraw cash from ATMs or make purchases at any Olympic sites unless they have cash, as the ATMs and payment terminals are also restricted to VISA cards. A London 2012 press officer was quoted as explaining the restriction by saying that the exclusive arrangement with VISA was not 'unusual in any way or form… As a sponsor, they gain exclusivity in their sector', and 'this has been the situation since [the Olympics in] Seoul in 1988.'[9] They conveniently neglected to mention that the European Commission previously examined the ticket sales for the 2004 Athens Olympic Games on competition grounds (in that case, tickets ordered via the Internet directly from the organising committee could only be paid for by VISA cards). Following modifications to the arrangements, which ensured that consumers were duly informed of the existence of alternative sales channels that did not require payment by VISA, the Commission closed the case without a decision. FIFA was also forced to amend its ticket payment provisions for the 2006 FIFA World Cup in Germany, after a complaint about similar rules which provided exclusivity for MasterCard in respect of payment for tickets, which decision was welcomed by the Commission.[10]

But the fans are not the only ones affected. Elsewhere I will include discussion of the potential impact of the legal measures imposed by host nation governments or host city authorities on members of the public in order to protect the commercial rights of event organisers and their official sponsors, which can be extremely

[8] http://www.tickets.london2012.com/.

[9] Insley, J 'London Olympics fans be warned—no Visa, no tickets', 24 June 2010—available online at the time of writing at http://www.guardian.co.uk/money/2010/jun/24/london-olympics-visa-card-tickets.

[10] The European Commission intervened following a complaint made in March 2005 by the UK consumer organisation, Which?, in respect of FIFA's ticket payment arrangements for the 2006 FIFA World Cup in Germany. Following discussions with the Commission, FIFA agreed to modify its arrangements for ticket payments for the latter stages of ticket allocation for the event, in terms of which more payment methods would be accepted in the second phase of ticket sales. Fans based in non-Eurozone countries in the European Economic Area (EEA) who did not have a MasterCard product or a German bank account could subsequently pay for tickets by making a domestic bank transfer in their local currency. Previously, some fans outside the Eurozone were faced with the high costs of making cross-border bank transfers into Euros. When assessing the ticket sales arrangements, the Commission looked at whether there was reasonable access to tickets to consumers throughout the EEA. See the Commission's Press Release IP/05/519 of 2 May 2005—available online at the time of writing at http://europa.eu/rapid/pressReleases Action.do?reference=IP/05/519&format=HTML&aged=1&language=EN&guiLanguage=en.

onerous and far-reaching but are often justified as being fleeting and insignificant in light of the 'big picture':

> Because we are limiting both the number and range of traders who are able to conduct their business in a particular area during particular periods, there will inevitably be an impact on competition. However, the regulations will apply to relatively small areas for short periods of time and, accordingly, the impact on competition will not be substantial, widespread or long-lasting[11]

One is tempted to say tell that to the kebab shop owner in central London or the informal street trader in Johannesburg, both of whom may be refused the right (and means) to earn a living for weeks at a time because the IOC or FIFA are in town. While dealing with the effects on competition of sponsorship exclusivity it should be remembered that the private commercial arrangements between event organisers and their commercial partners should not be viewed in isolation but within the wider milieu of event regulation by governments (which is discussed elsewhere), and that the potential effects on the broader public may be felt beyond the boardrooms of international sports organisations and a select group of wealthy multinational corporations.

Returning to the relationship of organiser and sponsor: By means of a contractual arrangement between exclusive sponsor and event organiser or rights grantor the field is effectively closed to potential competitors, whose only option would appear to be to face potential legal action for unlawfully 'associating with' an event of which it is not an official sponsor. Compare the ongoing Coca-Cola/Pepsi battles ('the Cola Wars') to obtain rights to events in order to exclude the competition from associating with it. An ironic example, which is also probably one of the first examples of such an exclusivity arrangement in practise, can be found in the context of the 1932 Olympic Games hosted in Los Angeles. An official bread supplier to the Olympic village (supplying bread to a number of the participating national teams), Helms Bakery of downtown Los Angeles (proprietor Paul H. Helms), had embarked on advertising and packaging its products with the inclusion of Olympic symbols and statements to the effect that it was the 'official' Olympic bread supplier. Even though there resulted a heated dispute between Helms and then US Olympic Association president (and later IOC president) Avery Brundage, spanning decades, Helms had merely capitalised on the Olympic authorities' procrastination in protecting its own intellectual property, by registering in all the U.S. states except Washington (and including the territories of Hawaii and the Philippines) the five rings insignia, the Olympic motto and the words 'Olympic' and its derivations. Helms encountered no resistance, as no previous attempts had been made to register this material, and proceeded to widely advertise its registration, to inform the Los Angeles

[11] From the UK Department of Culture, Media And Sport's consultation document on Regulations on Advertising Activity and Trading Around London 2012 March 2011 at 15—available online at the time of writing at http://www.culture.gov.uk/images/publications/ConDoc_Regulations_on_Advertising_and_Trading_London_2012-section1-7.pdf.

Organising Committee of the fact (no objection was made) and to place full-page ads in the LA papers advertising Helms's 'official Olympic products'. Helms also removed an injunction clause in the official supplier agreement with the organising committee, which clause prohibited suppliers from using the Olympic symbols in advertising; again, the organisers signed the contract with no objection. The real irony is to be found in subsequent events, when a competitor of Helms threatened to enter into a contract to supply competing nations not covered by the Helms contract. Helms had a blitzkrieg response: He had directed his lawyers to secure bond and warrants of attachment in advance, and he immediately informed the Los Angeles Organising Committee that if it interfered with his exclusive contract by granting supplier rights to his competitor or with his legally registered Olympic emblems, he would sue the Committee for USD 1 million damages on the basis of breach of (his duly signed) contract. The Committee caved and rejected the competitor's request for a supplier agreement.[12] Much has changed, and the IOC (and, subsequently, other event organisers) learned from the mistakes of these early years and tend to seek to avoid such problems by means of a veritable carpet bombing of pre-emptive trademark registrations and threats of legal action against would-be transgressors in the jurisdictions where events are to be hosted, often years in advance. However, the exclusionary (dare one say anti-competitive?) effects of the exclusivity of supplier or sponsor contracts are still of central importance to the parties involved in exploiting the commercial value of the events.

Marcus points out that restrictions on competition are not misplaced in the context of event sponsorship, because absent such restrictions, income-earning potential through sponsorship can be undermined with detrimental effect, and 'no sponsor will show alacrity in making future investments if there is no tangible benefit when current investments are made'.[13] However, such restrictions (e.g. restrictions on association with an event as provided for in the contract between sponsor and rights grantor) have wider implications than simply the contractual nexus between these commercial partners. This is inherent in the very term 'exclusivity', which by definition implies that others are excluded from the benefits transferred through such arrangement. Sponsorship exclusivity impacts on a number of stakeholders, specifically the consumer (in the sense of fans at matches,[14] and in the wider sense, the purchaser of event-related merchandise, etc.) and entrepreneurs (i.e. those businesses who may wish to be officially involved with the event but are excluded in terms of pre-existing arrangements with official sponsors). This last scenario, it is submitted, is especially relevant in respect of

[12] Barney et al. 2004, pp. 33–34.

[13] Marcus 2010, p. 30.

[14] See the discussion below regarding the views expressed by Fortunato and Richards in the American context.

small(er) businesses in the domestic context of the host nation or city, which may be excluded from even bidding for the right to participate in a 'domestic partner' programme due not only to the huge sponsorship fees, but also to the existing exclusivity of an incumbent global sponsor's rights. In fact, early experience in the Olympic movement's TOP programme appears to have facilitated a response that may have closed the door to many potential domestic sponsors:

> The organizing committees of the Games were as much a problem as the [National Olympic Committees in respect of the IOC achieving acceptance of the TOP programme]. They always believed they were being screwed by TOP and were convinced that they could have sold each sponsorship category for much more than they got from TOP... Whenever possible, they would try to sell sponsorships that encroached on the TOP categories. The most egregious example was what Sydney did to United Parcel Service (UPS) at the 2000 Games. The OCOG sold a category that was directly competitive with Olympic sponsor UPS to TNT, an Australian company, and simply refused to honor the TOP agreement, using pretexts, such as being unable to get the delivery envelopes ready in time, that were patently false as justifications for its behaviour. The result was that UPS withdrew from TOP and we lost an excellent international sponsor in a category that would be hard to replace, one that was not replaced for [the 2004 Athens Games].[15]

In the context of advertising, and specifically of the potential effect of exclusivity arrangements *vis a vis* smaller and un-established commercial enterprises, the following has been observed by a pair of American commentators:

> The trust, familiarity, and brand loyalty built by advertising, and their respective potential as important factors in the establishment and maintenance of a monopoly market position, serve as a backdrop for evaluating the role of sports sponsorship. Sponsorship through exclusivity agreements creates an opportunity for a dominant brand to promote and, in some cases, sell products to a contained audience, ensuring that subordinate brands remain impotent in their effort to achieve equivalent familiarity and trust.[16]

And:

> The issue of sports sponsorship exclusivity is an extension of the larger legal concern about how advertising, both as a form of communication and a factor in the economic marketplace of goods and services, fits within the protection of the First Amendment. Advertising is surely the exercise of free speech, but it also is a powerful economic tool, one capable of creating a regulatory tug-of-war between protecting free expression, while simultaneously controlling the excesses of capitalism. Indeed, at its worst advertising can be, and in this case appears to be, used in such a way that it clearly crosses the line and becomes a predatory business practice.[17]

Leaving aside for now the potential advertising and free (commercial) speech implications,[18] it is not clear how or why these commercial arrangements have

---

[15] Pound 2006, pp. 150–151.

[16] Fortunato and Richards 2007, p. 40.

[17] Ibid.

[18] For further discussion of implications for freedom of (commercial) speech and expression guarantees, see Chap. 7.

managed to avoid significant legal—specifically competition law—scrutiny to date. It is, I would submit, a surprising state of affairs. Sarantakes describes the unsuccessful attempt by then US President Jimmy Carter's legal advisor, at the time of the boycott of the 1980 Moscow Olympics, to institute a challenge to the IOC's control over the Olympic Games in terms of US antitrust laws.[19] While certain jurisdictions have seen high profile investigations and/or legal challenges to potential competition or antitrust implications of commercial agreements for the sale of sports broadcasting rights (which, as we've seen, constitutes the other major revenue stream for sports federations and event organisers), I am not aware of any such challenge specifically to the category exclusivity arrangements regarding sponsorship of mega-events.[20] I will not discuss competition challenges to sports broadcasting arrangements in this book, although this has been one area where the European competition authorities have been kept rather busy,[21] and where the issue of exclusivity of rights granted to broadcasters has been potentially problematic:

> The principle of exclusivity, the practice of selling sports rights on a territorial basis to one broadcaster, appears prima facie restrictive of competition as it segments the market on national lines and forecloses the market to those unable to access the content. Nevertheless, territorial exclusivity is a reflection of the national nature of the sports market and it is a protection much sought after by rights holders and purchasers. For the rights holder, exclusivity protects the value of rights thus allowing governing bodies to fulfil a wealth redistributive function. For the purchasers, exclusivity maximises profitability and allows broadcasters to invest with greater confidence in innovative programming. Exclusivity may therefore benefit the internal organisation of sport at all levels whilst allowing consumers to benefit.[22]

Elsewhere, there have been isolated and sporadic instances of legal challenge. The Australian Federal Court heard a competition challenge to restrictive conditions attached to tickets in respect of the sale of hospitality packages.[23] More

---

19 Sarantakes 2010, p. 128 *et seq.*

20 See, for example, Kobel 2007, p. 41:

'Writings on ambush marketing are usually more driven towards fighting ambush marketing for the benefit of sport. Writings and decisions on antitrust issues have usually focused on issues pertaining to the transfer of players, collective bargaining of TV rights and a few abuse of dominance cases in relation to the exploitation of rights related to an event. None really focused on sponsoring activities and the exclusivity granted to sponsors. As a result, not much was reported on these issues in the surveyed countries.'

21 See, for example, Parrish, R and Miettinen, S 'Sports Broadcasting in Community Law' (at 9–33) and Scheuer, A & Strothmann, P 'Sport as Reflected in European Media Law' (at 35–63) in Blackshaw et al. 2009.

22 Parrish & Miettenin in Blackshaw et al. 2009, p. 12.

23 *Australian Rugby Union Limited v Hospitality Group Pty Ltd* [2000] FCA 823.

directly relevant to sports sponsorship, however, and in the EU, the competition authorities had occasion to consider a challenge to the Danish Tennis Federation's exclusive ball sponsorship arrangements with Slazenger and Tretorn in the *Danish Tennis Federation* (or *DTF*) case, where the European Commission raised a number of objections and the DTF subsequently revised its arrangements (specifically in respect of setting up a competitive tendering process for the appointment of manufacturers or distributors as suppliers of equipment to its competitions, by limiting the scope of the designation rights obtained by such sponsors, and by limiting the duration of the sponsorships.[24] In the context of the FIFA World Cup in Italy in 1990 the European competition authorities considered a complaint by a Belgian tour operator who wished to provide package tours to the event (in the *Italia* case).[25] It was faced with an arrangement whereby FIFA had granted worldwide exclusive rights for the supply of stadium entrance tickets for

---

[24] A Commission press release (IP/98/355 of 15 April 1998) contained the following:

'The European Commission has just informed the Danish Tennis Federation (DTF) that its sponsorship agreements with its tennis ball suppliers no longer raise competition problems. This is the first time the Commission has come to a formal conclusion about the contents of such a sponsorship contract. The approval of the system follows acceptance of the Commission's conditions to guarantee full and fair competition on the market. The DTF will call for tender every two years to choose a sponsor. The selection will be transparent, non discriminatory and open to all suppliers. The selected sponsor will be granted the denomination "sponsor of the DTF" (but not "official") and will become the only tennis ball supplier for tournaments organised by the DTF during the two-year period. In exchange, it will supply a specified quantity of balls at a preferential price below the Danish market price.

The sponsorship agreements between the DTF and its tennis ball suppliers were challenged for the first time in the eighties. Following investigation by the Commission, these agreements have been considerably improved:

1. In the past, exclusivity contracts were allotted unilaterally by the DTF, without any objective selection criterion. From now on, there will be an open procedure for calls for tender with objective conditions.

2. Previously, players in official DTF tournaments could only use balls sold by the official network in Denmark could be used. Today, for team tournaments, which are the most interesting commercially, each team can obtain balls of the brand chosen by the DTF where it wishes, i.e. including abroad or via parallel imports.

3. Denominations such as "official ball" or "official supplier" have been abolished. Indeed, the use of such denominations can mislead consumers into believing that the products which benefit from them are technically superior to or of better quality than others, which is not always the case.

This type of agreement, which is increasingly widespread in the field of sport, can contribute considerably to the promotion of sport without threatening competition, provided that certain criteria for openness and transparency are met.'

[25] 92/521/EEC: Commission Decision of 27 October 1992 relating to a proceeding under Article 85 of the EEC Treaty (IV/33.384 and IV/33.378—Distribution of package tours during the 1990 World Cup.

the purpose of putting together package tours to the company '90 Tour Italia. The Commission found that this arrangement infringed the provisions of Article 81(1)[26] of the EC Treaty, in that the exclusivity precluded competition in the market of package tours to the 1990 World Cup (the market was narrowly defined as package tours to the event, including tickets to matches).[27] Elsewhere still, the Fair Trading Commission of Barbados states that it investigates complaints of the anti-competitive effects of exclusive sponsorship arrangements in respect of events in terms of the Fair Competition Act[28] (even though such Act does not expressly refer to sponsorship exclusivity arrangements),[29] but further information on any such cases that may have been encountered to date is not available to me at the time of writing. A recent American case, *American Needle, Inc v National Football League*[30]—which one commentator has described as 'arguably the most important sports law case in U.S. history and one that could dramatically reshape

[26] Article 81 (Article 101 of the Treaty on the Functioning of the European Union) prohibits agreements and concerted practises which prevent, restrict or distort competition, insofar as they may affect trade between Member States, unless justified by improvements in production or distribution in accordance with Article 81(3). The section provides as follows:

'(1) The following shall be prohibited as incompatible with the common market: all agreements between undertakings, decisions by associations of undertakings and concerted practices which may affect trade between Member States and which have as their object or effect the prevention, restriction or distortion of competition within the common market, and in particular those which:

(a) directly or indirectly fix purchase or selling prices or any other trading conditions;

(b) limit or control production, markets, technical development, or investment;

(c) share markets or sources of supply;

(d) apply dissimilar conditions to equivalent transactions with other trading parties, thereby placing them at a competitive disadvantage;

(e) make the conclusion of contracts subject to acceptance by the other parties of supplementary obligations which, by their nature or according to commercial usage, have no connection with the subject of such contracts.'

[27] Gardiner et al. 2006, pp. 367–368. The Commission held as follows (at par. 96 of its decision):

'All in all, by granting exclusive rights to 90 Tour Italia to supply entrance tickets to be included in package tours, alternative sources for the procurement of tickets not being available, the agreements concluded between, on the one hand, the local organizing committee in its capacity as a body belonging jointly to FIFA and the FIGC and, on the other, 90 Tour Italia, CIT and Italia Tour had the effect of restricting competition in the Community within the meaning of Article 85 (1) of the Treaty between our operators and between travel agencies on the market for the sale of package tours to the 1990 World Cup. The conditions of Article 85 (1) are thus met.'

[28] The Barbados Fair Competition Act Cap. 326C (text available online at the time of writing at http://www.commerce.gov.bb/Legislation/Documents/Fair%20Competition%20Act,%20Cap%20326C.pdf).

[29] From a report in the *Business Monday* newspaper, 26 July 2010—text available online at the time of writing at http://www.ftc.gov.bb/index2.php?option=com_content&do_pdf=1&id=197.

[30] *American Needle, Inc. v. National Football League*, 130 S. Ct. 2201 (decision delivered 24 May 2010).

how the NFL and other leagues conduct their business'[31]—may be the closest thing to an antitrust challenge of a category exclusivity sponsorship arrangement regarding a sports league. Note, however, that this relates to intellectual property licensing arrangements in the context of professional sports, and to the activities of a professional league rather than a mega-event such as the football World Cup or Olympic Games. The importance of this case (and why the May 2010 Supreme Court judgment was so breathlessly awaited) mainly concerns the NFL's attempt to obtain a blanket antitrust exemption for the league (and, potentially, other professional sports leagues) from the provisions of section 1 of the Sherman Act by means of its 'single entity' defence.[32] The Supreme Court, by way of Stevens J, rejected this defence. The case was remanded to the lower court (the Chicago district court) and currently, at the time of writing, is awaiting judgment in that court, although some commentators have already observed that the above-mentioned categorisation of the 'Armageddon' expectations of this case were overstated:

> [A]fter much sound and fury following the Seventh Circuit decision and leading up to the Supreme Court decision, *American Needle* has had little, if any, practical impact on the business of professional sports. The decision has preserved the status quo, leaving the NFL and other sports leagues in the same position—having to defend themselves under the rule of reason in antitrust suits...[33]

I will discuss the potential relevance and importance of the eventual outcome of *American Needle* in respect of the rule of reason analysis of whether the NFL's exclusive licensing arrangement at issue contravenes antitrust laws further below.

Also at the time of writing, a matter arising from an exclusive sponsorship agreement in Dutch badminton appears to be heading to court. The Dutch national badminton association, Nederlandse Badminton Bond, had in the interest of obtaining funding in order to raise the country profile in the sport and participating in a competitive fashion at the 2012 London Olympic Games, concluded a more than euro 3 million, 7-year exclusive sponsorship agreement with Yonex (to run from 1 January 2010 to 31 December 2016, with an option for renewal). In terms of this agreement, players sponsored by competitors (such as Dunlop) who refuse to play with Yonex equipment and to sport Yonex-branded apparel during tournaments are, *inter alia*, disqualified from selection in international competitions. In February 2011 this caused a furore amongst Dutch badminton fans, who protested

[31] McCann, M 'Why American Needle-NFL is most important case in sports history' 12 January 2010, *Sports Illustrated* online—available online at the time of writing at http://sportsillustrated.cnn.com/2010/writers/michael_mccann/01/12/americanneedlev.nfl/index.html.

[32] I.e. the NFL argued that its league constitutes a single entity, in terms of which the 32 NFL franchises function as one in respect of commercial decisions such as those relating to licensing deals involving NFL intellectual property. The argument went that, as a result, its conduct in respect of entering into an exclusive licensing arrangement does not constitute an agreement or collusion for purposes of the Sherman Act, and is therefore not subject to antitrust scrutiny in terms of the case brought by American Needle, Inc.

[33] Kishner and Albinsky 2011, pp. 8.

the planned exclusion of four Dutch national players[34] from the European Mixed Team Championships by means of an open letter to Yonex Japan. The matter had been taken to Utrecht district court[35] by Dunlop Slazenger International (a previous Dutch badminton sponsor) and a group of players who refused to sign the players' contract required by the Yonex sponsorship contract on the basis of their pre-existing agreements with other equipment sponsors (such as Dunlop and Forza Benelux),[36] in preliminary relief proceedings. The plaintiffs' case was that the Yonex sponsorship (and specifically clause 3 thereof, which contains the restrictions on players in respect of individual personal sponsorships and the use of equipment from competitors of Yonex) contravened section 6 of the Dutch Competition Act and Article 101 TFEU, as well as constituting abuse of dominance by the Dutch Badminton Association. The court,[37] on 20 March 2010, held that there was no evidence of a breach of competition law, apparently on the basis of a lack of evidence provided to this effect[38] (although it seems the court characterised the sponsorship contract as an exclusive purchasing agreement, which does not fall foul of the Treaty's competition provisions[39]). The court also held that Dunlop's arguments relying on the earlier-mentioned *Danish Tennis*

---

[34] Eric Pang, Yao Jie, Dicky Palyama and Judith Meulendijks.

[35] Court of Utrecht Preliminary Relief Proceedings, 20 March 2010, LJN BL6880.

[36] Including the highest ranked Dutch male badminton player (at the time ranked 20th in the world), who in 2008 had concluded an exclusive 5-year sponsorship agreement with Dunlop (in force until 31 December 2012).

[37] LJN BL6880, Rechtbank Utrecht, 281089/KG ZA 10-53; 282608 KG ZA 10-138 (judgment of 10 March 2010)—available online at http://jure.nl/bl6880.

[38] As explained by a commentator (Josine Potharst, Kennedy van der Laan newsletter, available online at http://www.kvdl.nl/PdfCreator.aspx?guid=%7BB0638478-CE9A-44C6-A498-FB9ECFC26FF3%7D):

'Dunlop and the players first argued that the sponsorship agreement concluded between [the Dutch Badminton Association] and Yonex is at odds with competition law. The Court in preliminary relief proceedings ruled that it is not likely that the cartel ban had been breached. One of the important factors in the ruling was that a factual investigation is required in the form of a market analysis, which is subject to high standards, in order to establish that an agreement has consequences distorting competition. As often in competition cases, it was not clear here what the relevant market is: the market for sports articles, for badminton articles or for badminton articles for top players? The players and Dunlop have not made sufficient assertions in this respect.'

[39] Case C 214-99, *NesteMarkkinointi Oy v Yötuuli Ky and Others*, where the ECJ held that the prohibition laid down by Article 85(1) of the EC Treaty (now Article 81(1) EC) does not apply to an exclusive purchasing agreement entered into by a motor-fuels supplier which the retailer may terminate upon one year's notice at any time where all that supplier's exclusive purchasing agreements, whether considered separately or as a whole, taken together with the network of similar agreements made by the totality of suppliers, have an appreciable effect on the closing-off of the market but where the agreements of the same kind as the agreement at issue in the main proceedings by reason of their duration represent only a very small part of the totality of one supplier's exclusive purchasing agreements, of which the majority are fixed term contracts entered into for more than one year.

Federation case were unfounded.[40] It further held that there was no abuse of dominance, apparently based on a view that players affiliated with the badminton federation are bound by its statutes, as well as the fact that the court found that the Yonex sponsorship had been concluded in the interests of the sport for both amateur and professional players.

This decision was reportedly received with shock by the sports community, and it was reported that the parties has initiated proceedings on the merits of the case which could promise a different finding in respect of the competition law implications of this sponsorship exclusivity arrangement..[41] I would suggest that the facts of this case provide a good illustration of the potential for abuse inherent in arrangements aimed at exclusivity of sponsors' rights, also in the context of athletes, and a further reason why the potential competition law implications of such deals require special consideration.

Apart from the handful above-mentioned cases, and to the best of my knowledge, no competition law challenge has been brought in respect of sponsorship category exclusivity agreements in respect of sports mega-events. As Kobel observes[42]:

> Writings on ambush marketing are usually more driven towards fighting ambush marketing for the benefit of sport. Writings and decisions on antitrust issues have usually focused on issues pertaining to the transfer of players, collective bargaining of TV rights and a few abuse of dominance cases in relation to the exploitation of rights related to an event. None really focused on sponsoring activities and the exclusivity granted to sponsors.

I would submit that this lack of critical antitrust scrutiny of such a central practise in respect of commercial exploitation of sport and events is surprising, especially if one considers, for example, that the European Commission's *White Paper on Sport*, in a section discussing antitrust, specifically mentions that rules protecting sports associations from competition represent 'a higher likelihood of problems concerning compliance with Articles 81 EC and/or 82 EC'.[43] I would submit that the very system of sponsorship exclusivity employed in respect of mega-events, as well as the demands for legislative protection of such exclusivity

---

[40] The court observed as follows (at par. 4.7.3 of the judgment):

'Ook op grond van de door Dunlop c.s. aangehaalde "Deense tennisballenzaak" kan niet worden geconcludeerd dat de afspraak dat spelers die deel uitmaken van één van de nationale selecties uitsluitend Yonex materiaal zullen gebruiken in strijd is met het mededingingsrecht. Uit het persbericht van de Europese Commissie van 15 April 1998 (IP/98/355) valt niet op te maken dat de Europese Commissie een exclusieve sponsorovereenkomst met een langere looptijd dan twee jaar ontoelaatbaar vindt. Bovendien geldt dat Dunlop c.s. onvoldoende heeft aangevoerd om te concluderen dat in deze zaak sprake is van een vergelijkbare situatie als in de "Deense tennisballenzaak".'

[41] See the report available online at the time of writing at http://217.114.90.55/nieuwsbrieven/nieuwsbrief_juni_2010/juni_11_en.aspx.

[42] Kobel 2007, p. 41.

[43] EC *White Paper on Sport*; Section 3 ('The Economic Dimension of Sport'); section 3.4 ('Anti-trust').

against 'ambushing', represent such protection of event organisers (and their sponsors) against competition, and as such are open to antitrust review. I will accordingly proceed to briefly consider the relevant issues.

6.2.1.1 The Monopolistic Position of Event Organisers

The Free Online Dictionary defines a monopoly as 'a company or group having exclusive control over a commercial activity', or 'exclusive control by one group of the means of producing or selling a commodity or service'. The US Supreme Court has defined 'monopoly power' as 'the power to control prices or exclude competition',[44] although the elements of this test have proven problematic and US courts in practise tend to determine the existence of monopoly or market power without requiring direct evidence of either of the two elements, and tend to use the alternative of inferring monopoly or market power from firm market shares (at least when coupled with evidence that entry barriers to the relevant market are relatively high).[45] A similar approach has been followed in the European Union in respect of its abuse of dominance provisions (Article 82[46] of the EC Treaty). A 'dominant position' has been defined as 'a position of economic strength enjoyed by an undertaking which enables it to prevent effective competition being maintained on the relevant market by giving it the power to behave to an appreciable extent independently of its competitors, customers and ultimately of consumers'[47] (although the ECJ warned that this last should not be used as a test on its own).[48] More recently, the EC cases have followed an approach similar to that of the US courts in inferring the requisite power from market shares:

> The existence of a dominant position may derive from several factors which taken separately are not necessarily determinative but among these factors a highly important one is the existence of very large market shares... Although the importance of the market shares may vary from one market to another, the view may legitimately be taken that very large market shares are in themselves, and save in exceptional circumstances, evidence of the existence of a dominant position.[49]

It has also been said that a monopoly in the strictest sense (a 'pure monopoly') occurs 'when a single firm or small group of firms who coordinate their activities controls the entire market supply of a good or service for which there are no close

---

[44] *Eastman Kodak Co. v Image Technical Services Inc.* 504 US 451 (1992).

[45] See Elhauge and Geradin 2007, pp. 244–245.

[46] Current Article 102 of the Treaty on the Functioning of the European Union.

[47] *United Brands v Commission of the European Communities* Court of Justice of the European Communities, Case 27/76 [1978] ECR 207, judgment of 14 February 1978, at par. 65.

[48] The ECJ, in *United Brands*, continued to warn that '[i]n general a dominant position derives from a combination of several factors which, taken separately, are not necessarily determinative' (at par. 66 of the judgment).

[49] Case 85/76, *Hoffman-La Roche & Co. AG v Commission* [1979] ECR 461; Elhauge and Geradin 2007, p. 246.

substitutes.'[50] Frank Fetter's classic work, *The Principles of Economics with Applications to Practical Problems*, contains the following description of a commercial monopoly[51]:

> Commercial monopoly, variously called contractual, organized, or capitalistic monopoly, arises where men unite their wealth to control a market, to overpower or intimidate opposition, and to keep out or limit competition by the mere magnitude of their wealth. These various kinds so merge into each other that they cannot always be distinguished in practice... A producing monopoly is one controlling the manufacture or the source of supply of an article; a trading monopoly is one controlling the avenues of commerce between the source and the consumers... Degrees of power to affect price result from varying extent of control; monopoly is a relative term. The term monopoly by its derivation has reference to a single seller; but there are other thoughts in the concept. Monopoly has reference also to the amount of the supply controlled... Ownership of an important fraction of an entire species of goods gives more power to affect value... [T]he test of monopoly is that a gain results from a higher price and fewer sales. It begins at the point where there is a motive to limit the supply in accordance with the paradox of value. The control of an entire species of goods gives price-fixing power, limited only by substitution of goods. Even though one person controlled all the coal and wood in any market, their prices still would be limited. If there were but one possible source of meat-supply, most people could live without meat.

It is interesting to consider the position in the market for the organisation of sports mega-events of sports governing bodies such as FIFA or the IOC, in respect of their mega-events. They produce a product (the event as an entertainment spectacle and as a competition to crown world champions, and the event as a spectacle which draws consumers the purposes of sponsors' marketing programmes as spectators, television viewers, internet fans, etc.), and control the only source for such product as well as the means of supply between the source and the consumer. In this way one could say that these organisations are both producing and trading monopolies. It should be noted that such a view is not based only on the scarcity of the relevant 'product':

> "Monopoly", whatever else it means, always conveys the idea of some exceptional kind of scarcity, scarcity due in part to some source or cause not ordinarily present... Monopoly is not merely superior economic power. Monopoly consists in unified control. The limitation connected with monopoly is not that of economic capacity but that of ownership and control.[52]

The mere fact that an organisation, such as FIFA, is the single monopoly regulator of the sport of football globally (and the IOC is the single custodian of the Olympic Movement and organiser of the Olympic Games) leads to exclusive control over the mega-event. The Fundamental Principles of Olympism may

---

[50] Harrison et al. 1992, p. 94; Miller 1999, p. 534.

[51] Fetter 1904, Section II: 'Kinds of Monopoly'.

[52] Fetter 1904, Chap. 33, Section I ('Nature of Monopoly').

declare that the practise of sport is a human right and that every individual must have the possibility of practicing sport, but it also clearly states that 'belonging to the Olympic Movement requires compliance with the Olympic Charter and recognition by the IOC'. We have already seen in the discussion in Chap. 2 that FIFA and the IOC also, in their charters and founding documents, claim ownership of 'property rights' to these events. Apart from claiming ownership of the property in the event, which for economic purposes relates to the subject of commercial exploitation (i.e. rights for commercial actors to associate themselves or their products and services with the event for purposes of marketing or otherwise), these organisations are also the sole purveyors of the supply of (access to) such property by means of licences and the granting of rights to sponsors, etc. FIFA exercises sole control over the product of its World Cup and its commercial exploitation while also claiming ownership of it as its property.

And in respect of the scarcity of the product and its supply, which provides the monopolist with price-fixing power and the power to exclude others from access to the product, one could argue that this position in the current context is not tempered by 'substitution of goods'. FIFA will not brook any upstart attempting to usurp its role of governing the global game of football, and no competing product (in the sense of a rival football world championship event) has any hope of getting off the ground. Similar attempts have (increasingly frequently) been made in a number of sports in recent years. Kerry Packer's attempts at establishing a 'World Series' to rival the international cricket authorities' test match competition in the 1970 s was met with rule changes and player bans. A similar attempt at a privately-organised Indian Cricket League (or ICL) was effectively smashed by those controlling international cricket (read: the Board for Control of Cricket in India), which orchestrated similar players bans imposed by domestic boards and responded by establishing its own, phenomenally successful and officially-sanctioned, Indian Premier League competition.[53] Other examples of such attempts abound, including the world motor sport governing body (the FIA)'s conduct in imposing conditions of participation on manufacturers, teams and circuits in order to protect its Formula 1 championship. This matter engaged the attention of the European Commission and was eventually settled, with the FIA agreeing, in light of its clear conflict of interest, to separate its regulatory functions from the commercial exploitation of the F1 world championship (which it proceeded to do by transferring its commercial rights to F1 to a company controlled by Bernie Ecclestone, a vice-president of the FIA, for a 100-year period). Not surprisingly,

[53] At the time of writing a case challenging the cricket authorities' response to the ICL tournament (*ICL (Essel Sports) v ICC and ECB*) is pending before the English High Court, although no further information is available to the author at this time.

this settlement has been characterised as 'legally... represent[ing] something of a mystery',[54] although European competition authorities viewed it as defensible.[55]

The role of international governing bodies as 'trustees' of their sport, in terms of a mandate provided by representative groupings from national member states on the basis of a monopoly, has proved to be 'the most successful model of organization and diffusion of a sports discipline'.[56] In the case of FIFA, as a leading exemplar of governance in the world's most popular sport, this system has developed into a model that has consolidated other organisational layers and is known today as the 'Pyramid of Football'. This structure is recognised as a prime example of the general European model of sport, whereby sport is organised in a hierarchical pyramid with international (European) sports federations at the top, having as their members national federations (one per country) which in turn have as members regional federations and, finally, clubs.[57] Outside the European context, this structure is also found in most sporting disciplines, where the relevant international governing body is found at the top of the pyramid.[58] Inherent in an international governing body's monopoly regulation of the sport is its control over the game in domestic jurisdictions, countries and territories of its member

[54] See Lewis and Taylor 2007, pp. 370–371 (par. B2.126–B2.130).

[55] Compare the following from the keynote speech ('Competition and Sport: The Rules of the Game') of European Competition Commissioner Mario Monti at the *Rules of the Game* conference on governance of sport, held in Brussels, 26–27 February 2001:

'Some may ask why the Commission should accept a sale of FIA's interest in Formula One to Mr Ecclestone's companies. Such a question betrays a misunderstanding both of the Commission's remit and, indeed, of its objections to the way motor sport were being regulated. It is not our role to determine who owns what part of the motor sport business, but rather to ensure that the regulatory and commercial arrangements comply with the competition rules. The combination of FIA divesting its commercial interests in Formula One, and FIA strengthening its rules to ensure that all potential motor sports organisers and participants are treated equally seems sufficient in principle to meet the competition objections raised.'

[56] Ducrey et al. 2004.

[57] *European Model of Sport*, Consultation Document of Directorate-General X of the European Commission (1998), at 2–3. Blanpain 2003, p. 2 also distinguishes between the East European and West European models of sport that existed between the end of World War II and the mid-1980s, where the former was ideologically-oriented and sport constituted a part of the propaganda machine.

[58] For example, Chapter 1 section 1 (read with section 3) of the International Sporting Code of the FIA describes its role and powers as follows:

'The [FIA] shall be the sole international sporting authority entitled to make and enforce regulations for the encouragement and control of automobile competitions and records, and to organise FIA International Championships and shall be the final international court of appeal for the settlement of disputes arising therefrom ... Each National Club or Federation belonging to the FIA, shall be presumed to acquiesce in and be bound by this Code. Subject to such acquiescence and restraint, one single Club or one single Federation per country ... shall be recognised by the FIA as sole international sporting power for the enforcement of the present Code and control of motor sport throughout the territories placed under the authority of its own country.'

FIA International Sporting Code (as amended—11 April 2005), available online at http://www.fia.com/resources/documents/1158037540__International_Sport_Code_a.pdf.

federations. This form of control has been characterised (in the context of a national sports governing body in American amateur sports governed by the Ted Stevens Act[59]) as 'monolithic control', which 'would normally violate the antitrust laws'.[60] Apart from the global governing body's power to make the rules of the game and of sanctioning 'official' competitions and to issue player bans for those who participate in unsanctioned competitions, the ultimate weapon in an organisation, such as FIFA's arsenal, is the absolute power to suspend or expel a domestic federation. These members of FIFA are bound by the rules of the organisation as embodied in its Statutes. Any attempt to break from FIFA's happy family and to participate in a rival competition (including a rival 'World Cup' international competition) can (and certainly would) be squashed in an instant, through the expulsion of the domestic federation (and, consequently, its national team). FIFA, for one, is not shy to threaten suspension or to actually suspend its member federations, although this happens most frequently due to claims of illegitimate 'political interference' in the game by member countries' governments.

Of course, this element of the monopoly control by FIFA is not in itself necessarily a bad thing, for a number of reasons. The sport of football requires a world champion, which presupposes a single, official, world championship (the sport of boxing is an example of the existence of an alphabet soup of 'official' world governing bodies, and the confusion regarding the official status of championship titles that this causes[61]). This uniformity and standardisation, in fact, would be one advantage of the monopoly of the international sports governing body. David Becker, at the time of writing the Head of Legal for the International Cricket Council, explains that the ICC's monopoly control of the game is constantly threatened by outsiders with often dubious credentials and motives to 'hijack' the game. He makes a good argument for the potential harm this would cause to the sport:

> Sports governing bodies take the argument that the monopolistic pyramid structure of sport is necessary and vital for the health of the sport, in that this structure protects the game and ensures that the revenues generated at the highest level of the sport flow down to grassroots sport. Those staging the unofficial events argue that players should be able to move between the 'official' and 'unofficial' leagues without sanction based on the principle of freedom of employment. We believe that the former argument should prevail, because if one considers the potential damage to the game by those who are 'free riding' on the efforts of others, and the lack of control private investment brings, it warrants protection and recognition of the monopoly… What most people don't' realize is the damage to the game. Firstly, the money

[59] See the discussion in Sect. 4.4.10 of Chap. 4.

[60] *Behagen v. Amateur Basketball Ass'n of the United States*, 884 F.2d 524 (10th Cir. 1989) at 529; *ChampionsWorld LLC, v. United States Soccer Federation, INC.*, et al.; N.D.Ill.; Case No. 06 C 5724, 2010 U.S. Dist. LEXIS 73253; 7/21/10.

[61] Currently there are four major sanctioning bodies, the World Boxing Council (WBC), the World Boxing Association (WBA), the International Boxing Federation (IBF) and the World Boxing Organisation (WBO), each of which sanctions matches and ranks fighters in 17 different weight divisions (i.e. it is possible to have four different 'world champions' in each such division)—see Andreff and Szymanski 2006, p. 365.

> generated by, say, ICL… does not go back into cricket. It goes back into the hands of private shareholders. Second, they have not invested in the players that will be attracted to play in the unofficial events. If these players, having been supported by the official cricket bodies, abandon them, they will begin to question why they are investing in them. Third, there is no way of ensuring that these events are properly regulated. As the international governing body, we require our Members to have in place Anti Doping policies, Anti Corruption codes, standards of conduct for players, pitches, venues etc. This 'control' is good for the game. We have no such control over the private entrepreneurs. An example is the poor stadia that were rife during the early days of ICL, the lack of doping procedures, corruption etc. Fourthly, ICL were one step away from arranging a Pakistan XI v Indian XI of "rebel" players. They were planning a triangular and then a World Series or World Cup. I am all for competition, but in sport this is very damaging to the legitimacy of the official structures. … There is a lack of cohesiveness and that results in lack of investment in the sport. I mention this point because it goes to the points raised about monopolies. Monopolies are, I agree, not always good for society. But in sport, they are generally regarded as being in the best interests of the regulation of the game.[62]

Not all monopolies are evil in every way—British poet and historian Thomas Babington Macaulay probably slightly overstated things a little more than 150 years ago when he said that one 'may safely take it for granted that the effect of monopoly generally is to make articles scarce, to make them dear, and to make them bad.'[63] One should give due credit to the benefits of a monopoly of control in the governance of sport,[64] and it is also argumentative to claim that the monopoly in respect of the organisation of mega-events necessarily serves to make the events themselves bad. Neither the extensive measure of control that governs their preparation and presentation, nor the gargantuan size and scope of the modern-day events that are paid for (at least in part) and made possible by the huge sums of money generated through the commercial programmes make the end product a bad one; in fact, the opposite is true. Although one must consider, in light of the vast costs of these events (and even though the costs of hosting are more often than not devolved upon host cities or nations) that monopolies may often show allocative and productive inefficiency—as it faces no challenge, it has no incentive to minimise costs and organise its resources effectively.[65] This would seem to be doubly

---

[62] From personal e-mail correspondence with the author, December 2011.

[63] Thomas Babington Macaulay, in a speech delivered in the House of Commons (5 February 1841), in *The Life and Works of Lord Macaulay: Complete in Ten Volumes*, Edinburgh ed. (Longmans, 1897), vol. VIII, 198.

[64] Compare the following, which was observed in the Opinion of Advocate General Kokott in the judgment of the European Court of Justice in *Motosykletistiki Omospondia Ellados NPID (MOTOE) v Elliniko Dimosio* Case C49/07 (judgment delivered 1 July 2008), at par. 92:

'[I]t is in the interests of the sportspersons concerned, but also of the spectators and the public in general, that, for each sport, rules that are as uniform as possible apply and are observed so as to ensure that competitions are conducted in a regulated and fair manner. This applies not only to the frequently discussed anti-doping rules, but also to the ordinary rules of sport. If rules varied greatly from one organiser to another, it would be more difficult for sportspersons to participate in competitions and to compare their respective performances; the public's interest in and recognition of the sport in question might also suffer.'

[65] Monti 2007, p. 56.

appropriate when the very commercial value of the events for their organisers lies in its potential promotional appeal, which clearly increases the bigger the event gets and the more money is put towards its organisation on such a grand scale. The event organisers may have a very real interest in the super-sizing of their product in order to maximise revenues from commercial sponsorship and broadcasting sources. I will revisit these issues in Chap. 9, when examining the arguments advanced by the event organisers in defence of their mega-event monopoly.

The point I wish to make, however, is that inherent or collateral benefits or the quality of the product does not detract from the determination of whether we are dealing with a monopoly with potentially significant anti-competitive effects, even bearing in mind that competition or antitrust laws generally require a 'rule of reason' approach which seeks to consider all aspects of a monopoly, both good and bad, in determining the lawfulness of the relevant restraint of trade or restriction on competition. And the point here, more specifically, is that there simply is no substitute for the product of the FIFA World Cup or the Olympic Games. The only potential danger that FIFA might face to its monopoly in the event is the possibility that the consumer of its product, the football fans, may elect to boycott the competition. This, however, is a frankly inconceivable notion when one considers the global popularity of football (and, similarly, the Olympic Games—in spite of widespread criticism and allegations of having sold out to commercialism, the Games still retains its stature as the world's premier international sporting event, with all its perceived social and cultural attributes).

The mega-event organising body offers a product that is unique. While monopoly power is normally measured with reference to, *inter alia*, a product market, which includes all products produced by different firms that have identical attributes, in the case of the mega-event there is no other 'firm' that produces an identical product against whom the monopoly power can be measured. The Commonwealth Games or Asian Games federations simply cannot produce Olympic Games; the International Cricket Council and the International Rugby Board may be similar 'firms' in respect of their global function in their relevant sporting codes, but the ICC cannot produce an international competition which crowns a world rugby champion, and vice versa in respect of the IRB's ability to produce such an event to crown the world's champion cricket team.

Apart from this rather exceptional nature of the mega-event organiser relating to the uniqueness of its product, the mega-event scenario presents another interesting characteristic which strengthens the view of a mega-event monopoly. It is a precondition for any amount of monopoly power to continue to exist in the long run that the market must be closed to entry in some way. One of the barriers to entry identified by economists is the ownership of resources without close substitute. Examples are rare (one being the case of a firm owning the entire supply of a raw material that is essential to the production of a particular commodity, as happened in the case of the pre-World War II Aluminum Company of America which controlled supply of the world's bauxite, an essential raw material for the production of aluminium).[66] As shown earlier, all the big boys (the IOC, FIFA and the other mega-event organisers) claim ownership in their events and all the self-proclaimed 'rights' that flow from such events. Having argued that the mega-event itself is a unique product, it should also be noted that the relevant organiser also appears to own the resources (the power to govern the game, to write its rules and to organise its competitions and crown world champions) to produce the product. As has been observed, FIFA actively suppresses any form of competition for its products:

> For the world's most important sport, football, the International Federation of Football Associations (FIFA) has a policy of sanctioning only one first division league in each country, of requiring that each team play only in its own national league (so leagues can not compete for teams), and of declaring all players and teams that engage in unsanctioned matches to be ineligible for international competition. Because of the financial and popular significance of the World Cup, the Champions' League, and other regional tournaments, no national governing body can afford to risk FIFA's sanctions by creating competitive First Division leagues or allowing a foreign team to join its top division.[67]

Never mind 'close substitutes', there is in fact *no* substitute for the resource 'owned' by the international governing body to produce its World Cup product. No other organisation or entity has the power to govern world football, and FIFA's Mr. Blatter need lose no sleep worrying about a competitor coming to the party with substitute resources to produce a product identical to FIFA's World Cup.

In the ways described above the sports governing bodies are clearly pure monopolists in respect of their mega-events, who exercise sole control over (and claim ownership of) the product of the mega-event as well as the supply of such product to the public and to businesses and entrepreneurs wishing to commercially exploit the appeal of such events for marketing purposes. FIFA enjoys a supremely dominant position, with a 100 per cent market share, in the market for an international, world championship football tournament. FIFA's World Cup or the IOC's Olympics are, quite simply, 'the only game in town.'[68]

---

[66] Miller 1999, pp. 534–535.

[67] Noll, R G 'Sports economics at fifty'—essay prepared for the Department of Economics and Stanford Institute for Economic Policy Research, Stanford University (2006) 20—available online at the time of writing at http://law.psu.edu/_file/Sports%20Law%20Policy%20and%20Research%20Institute/Noll%20Sports%20Economics%20at%20Fifty.pdf.

[68] Not only figuratively speaking, but also literally—FIFA, for example, does not allow any other relatively large-scale sporting competitions to take place in the host nation during or around the time of its event, in order not to detract from the splendour of its spectacle.

The US Supreme Court has defined the offence of 'monopolization' in terms of the Sherman Act[69] antitrust law as involving the following elements:

- The possession of monopoly power in the relevant market; and
- The wilful acquisition or maintenance of that power, as distinguished from growth or development as a consequence of a superior product, business acumen or historical accident.[70]

It could very well be argued that organisations, such as the IOC and FIFA, enjoy their monopoly power as a result of 'historical accident'.[71] In the context of antitrust adjudication in terms of section 2 of the Sherman Act this might serve to remove such monopolies from scrutiny. In *United States v Aluminum Co. Of America*[72] Hand J emphasised the distinction between the possession of a monopoly and unlawful monopolisation in terms of section 2, and that mere size does not determine guilt under the provision. A monopoly can result from causes that are not unlawful, such as 'by force of accident' (the firm may not have achieved monopoly, but may have had monopoly 'thrust upon it') or where a market is so limited it can profitably accommodate only one firm.[73] As mentioned above, not all monopolies are necessarily all bad. It has been observed that the language of the Sherman Act is broad and ambiguous, and that, viewed most broadly, one could interpret it to declare almost every type of agreement between two or more businesses as illegal. As a result the Supreme Court has held over the course of the last century that only those agreements that operate as an 'unreasonable' restraint of trade are in violation of the law, and has developed the 'rule of reason' approach.[74] The reason why a firm or undertaking enjoys a monopoly may be very relevant:

> If a firm makes a better mousetrap, and the world beats a path to its door, it may drive out all rivals and establish a monopoly; but that is a good result, not a bad one. Dominant market power normally reflects the fact that a firm is more efficient because of some cost or quality advantage over its rivals. If a firm has acquired that efficiency advantage through productive investments in innovation, physical capital, or organisation, then the additional profits it is able to earn might reasonably be thought to provide the right reward

---

[69] 15 U.S.C. § 1. The Sherman Act, in section 2, provides as follows:
'Every person who shall monopolize, or attempt to monopolize, or combine or conspire with any other person or persons, to monopolize any part of the trade or commerce among the several States, or with foreign nations, shall be deemed guilty of a felony, and, on conviction thereof, shall be punished by fine not exceeding USD 10,000,000 if a corporation, or, if any other person, USD 350,000, or by imprisonment not exceeding three years, or by both said punishments, in the discretion of the court.'

[70] *Broadcom Corp. v. Qualcomm Inc.*, 501 F.3d 297, 306-07 (3d Cir. 2007); see also *Grinnell* 384 US; *Kodak* 504 US 481; *Aspen* 472 US 596; Elhauge and Geradin 2007, p. 300.

[71] For more on the historical development and reasons for being of the international sports governing bodies (and of the power that they wield in modern times), see Louw 2007.

[72] 148 F.2d 416 (2d Cir. 1945)—as referred to in the text above.

[73] Ibid. At 429–430.

[74] Fortunato and Martin 2011.

for that investment, especially since any price premium it charges cannot exceed its efficiency advantage over other prevailing market options.[75]

Competition or antitrust laws focus rather on anti-competitive conduct that is used to obtain or maintain monopoly or dominant market power at levels that were not earned through productive efforts.[76] Where would one rate FIFA or the Olympic Movement in this regard? Have Mr. Blatter et al. earned their World Cup monopoly? What does FIFA bring to the modern world championship event that distinguishes it from potential rival football governance organisations that could, hypothetically, organise a similar event in its absence? Can it show any productive investment in innovation, physical capital or organisation that would distinguish it in this regard, or is its current market power simply the product of a serendipitous accident of history which placed it in the sole control of world football at the time when satellite television came to the fore and the resultant vehicle for massive global corporate sponsorship was born? And don't forget that, as mentioned, there are no 'other prevailing market options'; there is no alternative to FIFA's World Cup.

Be that as it may; I would contend, in any event, that these organisations are also constantly in the process of 'wilful acquisition and maintenance' of such monopoly or dominant power. Not only do the mega-event organisers create and protect their monopoly of control over the events in their own founding documents (which creates rules and contractual obligations that are binding on their member federations) and enforce such control through the terms of their contracts with commercial partners, the discussion elsewhere (see Chap. 4) has shown that they also demand protection for such monopoly by means of the law in host nations, specifically by demanding special legislation to protect their commercial rights as prerequisite for the privilege of hosting their spectacles. When evaluating the legality of a monopolist's dominant position it is not the dominance *per se* which rings the alarm bells, but rather the *abuse* of that dominance. It is debatable whether the rigid rights enforcement by event organisers, including such demands for special legislative protection, amounts to abuse of their dominance in the market. While the most objectionable provisions of some such legislation (which I'll discuss later) is, of course, mostly attributable to the over-zealousness of law-makers in those relevant jurisdictions, I have yet to encounter an instance where an event organiser has objected to such protection for its commercial interests or those of its sponsors as being too wide in reach or stringent in application. It should also be remembered that the above-mentioned element of wilfulness in the U.S. Supreme Court test does not require subjective intent; it is focused on the objective intent that can be inferred from the firm's conduct, and the U.S. courts

[75] Elhauge and Geradin 2007, p. 2.

[76] Ibid.

have on a number of occasions stressed that 'no monopolist monopolizes unconscious of what he is doing'.[77]

Apart from the role of the apparent basic premise of sole 'ownership' and control over the event, as described above, the very system of granting category exclusivity to sponsors and suppliers in the process of supplying the 'product' of the event also appears to be monopolistic in nature and serves to strengthen the perception of the governing bodies as monopolists:

> Monopoly is such a degree of control over the supply of goods in a given market that a net gain will result to the seller if a portion is withheld. Every producer has control over some agents and some portion of the supply of products; but ordinarily the portion controlled by any one is so small that withholding it entirely from sale would not cause the market price to rise in any appreciable degree… *As a reduction of supply results in a higher price, it is possible, as is seen in the paradox of value, for a situation to arise in the case of some goods, where a smaller number of units yield a larger sum in the market than a larger number of units. But the seller's interest lies not in the increase of total sales, but in that of net gains. Net gains, being the product of the number of units sold multiplied by the gain on each unit, increase at a much faster rate than do total sales.* The existence of monopoly power in any degree depends therefore on several factors: the effect of contraction of supply in raising prices, the effect on costs, the number of units remaining in the ownership of the one contracting supply, and the possibility of preventing others from increasing supply later to profit by the higher prices.[78] [My emphasis]

We have already seen that the very genesis of the modern Olympic sponsorship model resulted from a realisation by the organisers of the 1984 Games that the true value of sponsorship of the event lay in fewer sponsors with more valuable exclusive rights paying more for those rights (a trick missed by the organisers of the 1976 Montreal Games). The category exclusivity sponsorship model in terms of TOP and as employed for other mega-events is also clearly a manifestation of monopolistic supply of a scarce product by the governing bodies.

6.2.1.2 The Relationship of Event Organisers and Sponsors

Let us also consider the position of the sponsors and other commercial partners such as licencees of intellectual property in the context of event-related merchandising. The Free Online Dictionary defines a cartel as 'a combination of independent business organizations formed to regulate production, pricing, and marketing of goods by the members', or 'a collusive international association of independent enterprises formed to monopolize production and distribution of a product or service, control prices, etc.' The family of 'official sponsors' of the Olympics or the football World Cup, in my view, is just such a collusive association of independent enterprises formed to monopolise marketing and

[77] Elhauge and Geradin 2007, p. 301; see *United States v Griffith* 334 US 100 at 105; *Times-Picayune Publishing Co v United States* 345 US 594 at 626.

[78] Ibid.

distribution of products and services in the context of such mega-events.[79] They form an elite 'club' of rights holders with a high degree of exclusivity, and they often contractually undertake to support each other (e.g. through preferential rights relating to the sourcing of products or services from their fellow partners or, in the case of event broadcasting contracts, through the provision of rights of first refusal in respect of broadcast advertising). When considering the position of individual sponsors within the various product or service categories, it is also interesting to consider the actual categories that are allocated by event organisers. It would be one thing if categories were selected and allocated in some way relevant to the event and its target audience, but it often seems that categories are created purely based on the relevant sponsor who has indicated its willingness to pay the sponsorship fee. For example, Home Depot displaced Lowe's as the official 'home improvement warehouse' sponsor for NASCAR. While a home improvement or DIY supplier surely enjoys a measure of relevance in the (what I assume to be) primarily male demographical of NASCAR fans, one is often left with the impression that the sole purpose of the designation is to provide the sponsor (e.g. Home Depot) with a monopoly. The product category is only designated in order to protect the sponsor from competition. Weissman, tongue-in-cheek (I think), observes:

> The Olympics have auctioned off virtually every aspect of the Games to the highest bidder. In addition to multimillion-dollar sponsorship deals between the International Olympic Committee and international companies, smaller firms are paying for designations from "official home and industrial flooring supplier" to the "frozen dumplings exclusive supplier" of the Beijing 2008 Olympic Games.[80]

---

[79] It has been observed that the very organisation of e.g. the Olympic Games also involves a cartel structure in respect of the formal resource network—compare the following in respect of the 2008 Beijing Games:

'All mega-events have some central organizing authority… The central authority creates and enforces the rules for companies who seek to participate in the event. In the case of the Olympics, there are multiple authorities involved. The IOC is the international umbrella organization. The national Olympic Committee represents the country hosting the event, and it delegates its authority to the national organizing committee from the time of the winning bid announcement through the wrap-up of the event. For the Chinese Olympic Committee this entity was BOCOG (Beijing Organizing Committee for the Olympic Games). In addition, in the case of Beijing, the municipal and regional governments also participated as the financiers of major construction and infrastructure projects. These organizations and the networks they produce are organized as cartels. Cartels can be defined as combinations of independent organizations and businesses "whose object is to limit the scope of competitive forces within a market" … Cartel sourcing and contracting are not conducted (neither ex ante nor ex post) in a normal competitive market. While bidding and payments may be part of the process for admission to the cartel, the central authorities are not obligated to take the low bid, and there is no reason to think that these authorities are profit maximizers. There is convincing evidence of this for the Beijing Games.' See Dollinger, M J; Li, X; Mooney, C H 'Mega-events and entrepreneurial rents: Lessons from the Beijing Olympics' (draft document, April 2009—available online at the time of writing at http://www.indiana.edu/~rccpb/uschinacooperation/papers/P8%20Dollinger.pdf).

[80] Weissman, R 'The commercial Games: How commercialism is overrunning the Olympics', 17 August 2008—available online at http://www.corpwatch.org/article.php?id=15164.

There appears to be an almost unlimited potential for the expansion of sponsor categories to mega-events depending on what is on offer in terms of the interest from potential sponsors or others wishing to officially associate with the event. The London Organising Committee for the 2012 London Olympics even created the category of 'law firm sponsor' of the 2012 Games, which, together with other similar categories, extends the sponsorship concept quite significantly to professional organisations in return for their assistance in the provision of event-related services.[81]

This all raises the question of whether these monopolists and cartels are acting within the law, specifically competition or antitrust laws that have assumed such a prominent role in consumer protection in the modern age. Wise & Meyer[82] observed 15 years ago that sponsorship exclusivity is relatively unproblematic in the American antitrust context, but may be open to competition law scrutiny in the European Union:

> As a rule, the mere granting or receiving of exclusive license, sponsorship or distribution rights will not violate US antitrust law. That is not necessarily true under EC competition law. The EC Commission has consistently taken the position that the mere grant of exclusive rights to one company precludes the grant of similar rights to another enterprise, thus "may" violate Article 85(1) as a restraint of competition… The EC Commission has also attacked the acquisition of exclusivity where a company or group of companies secures overly extensive exclusive rights preventing other potential acquirers from having equal access to that market. Where a group or combination buys up extensive rights, how they share those rights and whether and on what terms they offer them to outsiders can raise antitrust issues… Official sponsors and/or official suppliers of goods and services to and for a European sports event may run afoul of EC competition rules… Once a sponsor secures the right to be identified as the sole sponsor or one of a limited number of sponsors of a major sporting event(s), it may, in the EC Commission's view, be in a dominant commercial position, and may be subject to more Commission scrutiny than its non-dominant competitors.

And the fact that the rights obtained by official sponsors relates mainly to rights to use event-related intellectual property (as discussed in the previous chapter above) may also open such arrangements to competition law scrutiny in respect of the conduct of sponsors in respect of such IP:

> Often, contractual exclusivity is buttressed by nationally granted intellectual property rights, such as trademarks and copyright. The EC Commission and European Court of Justice have clearly rules than an intellectual property holder's use thereof to divide up national market *(sic)* or prevent the development of new ones through the improper use of such rights or by refusing to grant a license can constitute an Article 86 abuse of dominant position. It might be mentioned that the EC Commission has recently adopted a close counterpart of the "essential facility" doctrine found in US antitrust law. Refusal to grant a license or demanding excessive royalties or unreasonable license terms, can violate Article 86. Any supplier holding a dominant market position refusing to supply an

81 With City of London law firm Freshfields as the official legal services provider for the Games—see the report dated 19 January 2012, available online at the time of writing at http://www.thegatewayonline.com/article/1087.

82 Wise and Meyer 1997, pp. 1996–1997.

established customer or to meet adequately market demand for the particular product or item, can infringe Article 86.[83]

Fortunato and Richards[84] have examined, in the American context, the relationship between sponsorship exclusivity and antitrust law in relation to the sports consumer (specifically related to venue exclusivity at stadia as opposed to the wider context of events, although the authors' comments are germane to both). They explain their concerns in the context of the impact of sponsorship exclusivity on fans of the major American professional sports leagues:

> How does this system of sponsorship exclusivity—that eliminates competition within a product category—impact the consumer? A sports stadium effectively can be defined and framed as a distinct marketplace. Some venues are extremely large marketplaces, capable of attracting over four million consumers each season. Additionally, these venues hold multiple exclusive sponsorship agreements for a variety of product categories at that location. Consumers are limited as to the brands to which they are exposed and in many cases also are limited in their brand purchase choices. In effect, sports stadiums operate as city-sized markets; markets that are, with respect to particular brands, devoid of competition.[85]

The authors observe that American antitrust laws 'exist to protect and promote the economic competitiveness of a marketplace', but that '[t]hrough the mechanism of brand exclusivity, corporate sponsorships… appear to create precisely the opposite effect.'[86] They use an example from America's no. 1 spectator sport, NASCAR motor racing:

> [T]he Indianapolis 500 Mile Race has an estimated attendance of 300,000 in a single day. The Allstate 400 NASCAR race, attracting nearly that many spectators on race day, is held at that same track. That race had been called the Brickyard 400 until 2005, when Allstate became the official sponsor. Pepsi holds the exclusive pouring rights at the track, having replaced a long-time sponsorship by Coca-Cola in 1998. On those single days, Pepsi has an absolute, unabated monopoly in a market equivalent in sheer size to a medium-sized city.[87]

Such exclusivity arrangements in sports mega-event sponsorship display a number of anti-competitive elements that beg the question of their legitimacy in terms of competition law. These are the following:

- The arrangements, by definition, are aimed at restricting competition by rival brands in respect of the relevant product or service category. Such exclusivity can extend across different activities (including, as in the example mentioned above, pouring rights at the venue for a soft drink or beer sponsor, or restrictions on the use of credit card brands by fans, and restrictions on advertising by rival

---

83 Ibid. at 1997.

84 Fortunato and Richards 2007, p. 33.

85 Fortunato and Richards 2007, p. 34.

86 Ibid. 35–36.

87 Ibid. 44.

businesses both at the venue and venue precincts as well as in broadcasts of the event);

- These rights are usually, as a result of their exclusivity, prohibitively expensive (compare again the sheer size of TOP sponsors' investment for the Olympic Games), in effect being available only to the big (multinational) corporations rather than smaller businesses. As mentioned elsewhere, the literature suggests that this feature of modern mega-event sponsorship may have been a prime reason for the emergence and flourishing of ambush marketing in respect of events; and
- Bidding for these rights does not take place very often, with long-term contracts being the norm. Compare VISA's contract for the Olympic Games—which has been extended to 2020[88]—and Coca-Cola's 28-year naming and pouring rights deal for one of its brands, Minute Maid, for the Houston Astros baseball stadium—signed in 2002, for an estimated price of USD 170 million.[89] [It might be surprising that the Astros would enter into another such long-term deal, seeing that it followed their catastrophic previous naming rights deal in respect of 'Enron Field' with Enron Corporation (a USD 100 million 30-year-deal signed in 1999) which brought the team much pain and reputational suffering following the Enron scandal; it is assumed that the Minute Maid deal contains lengthy and involved 'reverse-morals clauses'...[90]] Coca-Cola also holds non-alcoholic pouring rights to the FIFA World Cup through to 2022—a testament to the value of such rights.[91] In the *DTF* case referred to above the European Competition Commission specifically took issue with the fact that the official ball sponsorship arrangements were not subject to a bidding process and the application of objective selection criteria, and were not up for regular review. In the EU sports broadcasting context, it has been observed that territorial exclusivity of rights is not objectionable in itself, provided that it is not created but exists as the result of pre-existing market conditions. The use of such an arrangement has been sanctioned provided that artificial or unjustifiable barriers to trade were not erected[92]; one such unjustifiable barrier would be the granting of a long period of exclusivity for one broadcaster.[93]

In another example of the long-term nature of these sponsorships (and an illustration of how even public pressure regarding the sponsor's 'fit' with the sponsored property may be ignored in the interests of protecting existing exclusive

[88] See http://corporate.visa.com/media-center/media-kits/olympic.shtml.

[89] Fortunato and Richards 2007, p. 45.

[90] See Taylor et al. 2010.

[91] Schwab 2006.

[92] *Coditel SA v Cine-Vog Films SA* [1982] ECR 3381 (Case 262/81).

[93] Parrish & Miettinen in Blackshaw et al. 2009, p. 12.

relationships) it was reported in October 2011 that McDonald's and the IOC were close to finalising an extension of the restaurant chain's TOP sponsorship of the Olympic Games. The deal is reported to be valued at between USD 180 million to USD 200 million, and extends McDonald's membership of the programme and gives the company worldwide marketing rights to the Sochi 2014 Winter Olympics, the Rio 2016 Summer Games, and both the 2018 and 2020 Olympics, whose host cities have yet to be selected at the time of writing. It was reported that although McDonald's has been a TOP sponsor since 1996, an extension wasn't guaranteed. The company complained about a Subway advertisement on NBC during the Vancouver Games in 2010, which it considered to be ambush marketing, and complained to the IOC and US Olympic Committee about it, 'injecting tension into the partnership' between the company and the Olympic organisers. The IOC also reportedly faced pressure to discontinue its relationship with McDonald's, as 'its connection with a restaurant chain that built its empire on Big Macs and french fries drew increased scrutiny from the press and criticism from athletes'. Sources were quoted as remarking on the IOC's extreme loyalty to its existing sponsorship base, and, not surprisingly, 'both parties put those issues aside and reached a long-term extension in part because the IOC and USOC pledged to monitor ambush marketing aggressively, and the IOC's loyalty to long-term sponsors trumped any concerns about McDonald's food offerings'.[94]

When one considers the above characteristics of such exclusive sponsorship arrangements, it should be noted that the conduct of the parties involved may also be relevant in respect of assessing the potential anti-competitive impact of systems and processes which may otherwise appear to be 'competition-neutral'. First, let us consider the bidding for opportunities to enter into such sponsorship arrangements (the 'auction' of rights to mega-events). It should be noted that the bid processes in respect of commercial rights to major events are not always transparent and have, allegedly, at least once in the past been manipulated in an apparently anti-competitive manner by FIFA executives in respect of the football World Cup.[95] It has also been reported that Match Event Services, which was FIFA's exclusive official accommodation provider for the 2010 World Cup in South Africa and no stranger

[94] See Mickle, T 'McDonald's close to TOP extension', 17 October 2011—available online at http://www.sportsbusinessdaily.com/Journal/Issues/2011/10/17/Olympics/McD-TOP.aspx.

[95] See discussion of the bid process for the sale of television broadcasting rights to the 2002 and 2006 FIFA World Cups in Jennings 2006, Chap. 7.

to controversy, was allegedly appointed without any tender process at all.[96] It is interesting to note that the government of Brazil has implemented a system apparently aimed at addressing such problems. In May 2010 the Comptroller of the Union launched a website each for the 2014 FIFA World Cup[97] and for the 2016 Olympic Games,[98] through which all bids, contracts and projects will be available for public scrutiny and any citizen who identifies any irregularity in the proceedings may make a complaint. No similar mechanism exists, however, in respect of the bidding for rights to become event sponsors.

And then there's the issue of the term (duration) of sponsorship contracts, which is not only often for a long period (upwards of ten years is not unheard of) but also may often be further extended upon its expiry through a right of first refusal. MasterCard ran into some trouble with FIFA in 2006 over such a provision. MasterCard claimed that under a 'first right to acquire' provision of its 2002 contract with FIFA (MasterCard had sponsored the football World Cup since 1990), it held a right of first refusal to sponsorship rights, and FIFA could not offer those rights to another company within the same product category without first providing it with the opportunity to purchase rights on comparable terms. The clause in the 2002 agreement was worded as the 'first right to acquire, with respect to PRODUCTS (i.e., category), the package of advertising and sponsorship rights offered by FIFA.' Along with this phrase in Section 9.2 of the agreement was a specified 90-day notice of forthcoming offer required of FIFA, and in turn, a 90-day exercise period open to MasterCard to accept such rights as offered. Following the 90-day exercise period, FIFA was deemed 'free to grant to any entity such rights on comparable terms.'[99] In March 2006, FIFA sent MasterCard a 96-page agreement, which gave the company sponsorship rights for all FIFA competitions between 2007 and 2014, including the 2010 and 2014 World Cups. MasterCard signed the agreement, but FIFA, meanwhile, had also negotiated with VISA and decided to finalise a contract in which VISA was granted exclusive sponsorship rights to FIFA's competitions. Joe Cobbs explains that this strange state of affairs

---

96 Rob Rose writes (in Schulz-Herzenberg 2010, pp. 99–100):

'While [Match Event Services] officially warns accommodation providers to keep room rates low because tourists are 'sensitive to pricing', an investigation by the author has confirmed that tourists will have to pay Match 1000 per cent more than they would normally pay for accommodation in certain cases, such as for units at South Africa's Kruger National Park. Match Event Services is owned entirely by a family-owned UK-registered company called Byrom PLC. The circumstances of its appointment remain cloudy: there was never any public tender for the multi-million rand contract, for example. Riding on those coat-tails is the closely linked Match Hospitality, which has FIFA's official stamp of approval to provide exclusive hospitality packages to large companies seeking to impress clients at the South African event. Not only does Match Hospitality refuse to disclose its exact shareholding structure, but it has emerged that one of the four shareholders in the company is Infront Sports & Media, a company headed by Philippe Blatter—nephew and godson of the FIFA supremo.'

97 See http://www.portaltransparencia.gov.br/copa2014/.

98 http://www.portaltransparencia.gov.br/rio2016/_include/legislacao/.

99 Cobbs 2011 (my thanks to the author for providing me with an advance copy of the article).

stemmed from the demise of ISL[100] in 2001, the company to whom FIFA had previously outsourced the negotiation and sale of its marketing rights:

> ISL declared bankruptcy in 2001 and FIFA retained the sales function in-house. With adequate time to prepare for the next cycle of World Cup sponsorship negotiations, FIFA resolved to consolidate several of its sponsorship product categories (from 15 to 6) and package the rights into an eight-year cycle. In doing so, FIFA anticipated realizing greater returns from a more exclusive partner list over a longer timeframe. While this type of sponsorship rights restructuring is not uncommon in the sports industry, the manner in which FIFA proceeded to offer these rights within the ''payment services'' category was extraordinary, given their established relationship with MasterCard.[101]

It appears that the allegedly shady negotiations with MasterCard and VISA occurred on the watch of FIFA's then new marketing director, Jerome Valcke, who would later, probably surprisingly, become a blue-eyed boy within the organisation despite these events. Wikipedia reports that 'FIFA president Blatter had released Valcke in December 2006 from his job as marketing director after a New York court had found him guilty in the summer of 2004 in his role as marketing director for negotiating sponsor agreements with the rival VISA, despite the existing agreement of FIFA conducted with the longtime partner MasterCard and thus violated the right of first negotiation of MasterCard'. Valcke, at the time of writing, is FIFA's first non-Swiss born General Secretary, appointed to this position by the Executive Committee in June 2007, after being proposed by Blatter. Cobbs provides an informative and interesting narrative of the negotiations and deceptions in the FIFA/MasterCard/VISA debacle:

> MasterCard was still unaware of FIFA's dealings with rival VISA, and had an offer on the table from FIFA that was considerably different in contract length, breadth of product category exclusivity, and requested monetary commitment compared to past agreements. Cognizant of the 90-day exercise period laid out in the previous agreement, MasterCard retreated to undertake their internal analysis. Approaching the deadline of the exercise period, MasterCard requested, and was granted, a three-day extension by FIFA of the ''exclusive negotiating period.'' However, such a description was questionable on FIFA's part, given their ongoing negotiations with VISA. At one point during MasterCard's 90-day period, FIFA stated in a letter to VISA that ''(FIFA) could expect, and strongly recommend, that VISA and FIFA enter into an agreement.'' At the end of this first exercise period, MasterCard rejected FIFA's original offer and suggested returning to the original narrower product category definition that better described MasterCard's business interests. VISA reached a similar conclusion and FIFA was forced to scale down the package.
>
> With a reformulated ''financial services light'' package priced at US$180 million, FIFA remained true to form by presenting the sponsorship rights to VISA ahead of MasterCard (by two days) despite later admitting that a new offer consisting of terms not comparable to the original offer retriggered MasterCard's first right to acquire. This time, however, neither FIFA nor MasterCard referenced the 90-day stipulations of Section 9.2 of their current contract. FIFA completed a long-form draft agreement several months after the ''light'' package presentations and delivered a copy to VISA on August 22, 2005, and to

[100] See also the discussion in Sect. 9.4 of Chap. 9.

[101] Cobbs 2011.

> MasterCard on August 26, 2005. At this point in the concurrent negotiations, FIFA decided to openly discuss the progress of the MasterCard negotiations with VISA, while remaining silent with MasterCard regarding any contact with VISA. In later court testimony, one FIFA executive attempted to justify this strategy by comparing it to cheating on your wife and realising the benefits of waiting until ''the end'' to tell her, as opposed to the ''disruption'' incurred by telling her now. Despite FIFA's secret conduct opposing MasterCard, negotiations between the two parties reached a US $180 million cash agreement for the ''financial services light'' sponsorship package at the end of October 2005. Meanwhile, VISA's best offer to date consisted of US $154 million in cash and $16million in ''promotional value,'' which FIFA later admitted was of little interest to their enterprise. On October 26, 2005, the FIFA Board compared the two agreements and approved MasterCard as the financial service sponsor. The Board even stated in the meeting minutes that ''It is agreed to proceed with the final agreement for MasterCard.'' Similarly, on December 5, 2005, the FIFA Finance Committee also approved the agreement with MasterCard for the 2007–2014 term. Finally, on December 7, 2005, the FIFA Executive Committee granted the final FIFA approval for a MasterCard agreement. Had the chronology of events ended at this point, FIFA's conduct, while perhaps suspect, would most likely have been dismissed as overly aggressive negotiations. However, under the spell of undermined motivations, FIFA's sponsorship executives continued to push VISA to match or better MasterCard's FIFA-approved agreement. Three hours prior to FIFA's next Board meeting on March 14, 2006, and under pressure from FIFA's sponsorship executives, VISA verbally agreed to pay US$ 180 million in cash in addition to $15 million in marketing in-kind value for the ''financial services light'' sponsorship package. This turn of events enabled the FIFA Marketing Director, citing a (settled) trademark issue as the rationale for spurning MasterCard, to persuade the Board to approve the agreement with VISA. Further approvals were given by FIFA's committees in the following days and even still, MasterCard was not notified of the decision until VISA's Board approved the agreement on March 29, 2006. Upon finally being notified of the VISA agreement by FIFA, MasterCard promptly issued notice of a legal claim to both FIFA and VISA on April 4, 2006. Despite the forthcoming litigation, the FIFA agreement with VISA was executed on April 6, 2006, and contained some rights not comparable to those in the MasterCard agreement, such as certain World Cup on-site ATM rights, superior ambush marketing protections, and the ability of VISA to credit US$ 2.5 million of their cash commitment towards the purchase of sponsorship rights to World Cup qualifying competitions.[102]

Not surprisingly, the matter went to court, with MasterCard claiming an injunction (i.e. in effect an order for specific performance of its extended contract with FIFA). The US District Court issued an order blocking FIFA from 'implementing or otherwise proceeding with its purported 2007-14 FIFA World Cup sponsorship agreement with VISA', and ordered that FIFA 'be required to proceed with the 2007–2014 MasterCard Agreement that the parties agreed to'.[103] Judge Loretta Preska held that FIFA negotiators had failed to act in good faith (in fact, 'anything but fair play'), and had apparently lied repeatedly to MasterCard and

---

[102] Ibid.

[103] *MasterCard International Inc. v. Federation Internationale de Football Association (FIFA)*, 1:06-cv-3036, U.S. District Court, Southern District of New York (Manhattan) (7 December 2006). See the report by Glovin, D 'MasterCard beats Visa in court, can sponsor World Cup', 7 December 2006—available online at the time of writing at http://www.bloomberg.com/apps/news?pid=newsarchive&sid=aFu_VqYGZmLE&refer=home.

VISA when talks with both were under way. One FIFA executive, in court testimony, tried to justify FIFA's failure to inform MasterCard during the negotiation process of its contact with VISA by comparing it to 'cheating on your wife'—'realizing the benefits of waiting until "the end" to tell her, as opposed to the "disruption" incurred by telling her now'.[104] The court held that the sports body had breached its obligation to give the right to renew the contract to MasterCard, which spent almost USD 100 million over 16 years as official sponsor.

The ruling was reversed on appeal by the U.S. 2nd Circuit Court of Appeals[105] in May 2007, and MasterCard and FIFA subsequently settled the matter a month later, with FIFA agreeing to pay USD 90 million to MasterCard for ending its sponsorship arrangement for the World Cup (including settlement of a separate marketing dispute between the parties). MasterCard's counsel was subsequently quoted as stating that the settlement took into account the lower court judge's findings, which 'tell a story of a level of dishonesty and deceit' in FIFA's negotiations with both MasterCard and VISA.[106] Valcke, in a subsequent interview, appeared contrite but not convinced of the ethical or other concerns about the strategy in the MasterCard deal: 'I made the biggest mistake of my life by saying that in business we don't always say the truth and you could describe that as a commercial lie. And then I was dead. The day I [used the phrase] "commercial lie", I was out—completely destroyed by [MasterCard's] lawyer.'[107]

And so the way was opened for VISA to manage to obtain exclusive, long-term sponsorship rights to the world's two largest sports event properties, the FIFA World Cup and the Olympic Games, although it may be an uneasy partnership in the case of FIFA:

> [W]hen considering the deception FIFA also exhibited toward VISA, even going so far as to suggest at one point in the trial that VISA forged a signature on their FIFA agreement, it is somewhat surprising that VISA was still willing to not only engage in a partnership with FIFA, but also attempt to enter the legal battle with MasterCard as a necessary third party (which was denied). VISA's willingness to overlook such unethical practices by a promotional partner provides additional anecdotal evidence of the inherent value placed on corporate affiliation with the World Cup through category exclusive sponsorship.[108]

It is submitted that, even though I would argue (as I do) that the very nature and characteristics of the sponsorship exclusivity arrangements to mega-events are suspect in terms of their anti-competitive effect, a further factor that should be

---

[104] See Cobbs 2011.

[105] *MasterCard International Inc. v. Federation Internationale de Football Association* (FIFA), 06-CV-4433, U.S. Court of Appeals for the Second Circuit (New York) (25 May 2007).

[106] See Edwards, E 'MasterCard gets $ 90 million to end World Cup dispute', 27 June 2007—available online at the time of writing at http://www.bloomberg.com/apps/news?pid=newsarchive&sid=a5SAWGkesp8s.

[107] From a piece in *The Independent* by David Owen, 28 October 2007—available online at the time of writing at http://www.independent.co.uk/news/people/profiles/jr244me-valcke-he-scored-the-worstever-own-goal-now-hes-running-football-398086.html.

[108] Cobbs 2011.

considered is the conduct of sponsors, but more especially, of the event organisers in negotiating, implementing and enforcing such arrangements. This is particularly relevant in the context of these organisations' enforcement strategies. Compare, for example, the hard-nosed demands for special rights protection legislation in host countries (discussed in Chap. 4) as well as litigation against 'ambush marketers' (which will be discussed elsewhere), and it should also be noted that it has been observed that 'event organizers act concerned about ambush marketing at the time of contract negotiations but seem to have little power to stop it when it actually occurs'.[109] This may not only raise concerns for potential sponsors in light of the practicalities of rights protection but may also pose questions as to the bona fides of event organisers' negotiations with sponsors in the climate of ever-escalating rights fees based so substantially on promises of exclusivity.

Leaving aside such issues of the more practical experience of event rights negotiation and the resultant commercial contracts for partners such as sponsors, Fortunato and Richards are convinced that exclusive sports sponsorship arrangements have an anti-competitive affect:

> [T]hese deals… restrict consumer exposure to, and ultimately choice of, brands while at the event (for example, if a spectator wishes to purchase a beer, he can choose a Budweiser or a Bud Light). And the price in most instances reflects that lack of competition. There is little doubt that these exclusivity provisions are anticompetitive, as they are intentionally designed to limit consumers' choices to the sponsors' brands.[110]

It could be argued that these arrangements constitute 'abusive exclusionary conduct', although it appears that it is no mean task to properly determine what exactly constitutes exclusionary abuse in terms of the provisions of competition laws such as that contained in section 2 of the Sherman Act and Article 82 of the EC Treaty (Art. 102 TFEU):

> [T]the elaboration of appropriate tests for the assessment of exclusionary conduct of dominant undertakings poses an unprecedented challenge for academics and enforcement agencies. It seems that the different perceptions of consumer welfare and different views on the role of antitrust are more difficult to reconcile in the context of unilateral exclusionary conduct than in other areas of antitrust. This is probably because, in the case of exclusionary unilateral conduct, it is more difficult to determine to what extent a restriction of competition is due to superior performance or to mere exploitation of one's monopoly power. The American debate also demonstrates that designing rules for assessment of

[109] McKelvey and Grady 2008, p. 560.

[110] Fortunato and Richards 2007. The authors summarise (at 45–46) the anti-competitive effects of these exclusive sponsorship deals: 'These include, but are hardly limited to, completely foreclosing competitors from the market for extended periods of time and creating enormous barriers to entry when the sponsorship contract does eventually come up for renewal, both in terms of competition for promotional space of a brand to consumers within that marketplace and for actual sales to those consumers. That foreclosure lasts, in many or most cases, for several years, is yet another detrimental impact on competition. Most troubling is the fact that these exclusions further enhance the market power of those competitors already possessing the greatest share of power.'

exclusionary conduct which ensure both precision and administrability is an extremely arduous task, the accomplishment of which at this stage does not seem likely.[111]

The European Commission, in December 2008, issued a Guidance Paper[112] on abusive exclusionary conduct under the abuse of dominance provisions of Article 82[113] of the EC Treaty, which paper identified a general approach to be applied to all such conduct. The test proposed in the guidance paper envisages challenging a given conduct when the undertaking holds a dominant position in the relevant market and the conduct at hand, 'on the basis of cogent and convincing evidence', is likely to lead to anti-competitive foreclosure of rivals. Identifying an exclusionary abuse requires a finding that the relevant conduct led to (or is likely to lead to):

- Foreclosure of 'as efficient competitors' (or, under specific circumstances, 'not yet as efficient competitors'); and
- An adverse impact on consumer welfare, 'whether in the form of higher price levels than would have otherwise prevailed or in some other form such as limiting quality or reducing consumer choice'.[114]

Scaria expresses the following view regarding abuse of dominance in the context of ambush marketing, which I believe is important to note here:

> The question of "abuse of dominant position" by the event organisers in the context of anti-ambush marketing efforts needs to be analysed from the angle of elimination of competition, rather than elimination of competitors, even though competition law considers both with equal significance. The significance of the difference in approach lies in the fact that in most cases an event organiser is not engaged in abusive practices that eliminates its competitors, but in eliminating competition in a market place. For an event organiser, a competitor is another event organiser.[115]

I would agree that the abuse of dominance in issue here relates primarily to the elimination of competition (an express goal of sponsorship exclusivity arrangements). As I have observed above, I do not believe that event organisers, such as FIFA, have any competitors when it comes to organising the relevant event, sourcing sponsorship and combating ambushing. This should not, however, in any way detract from the aptness of competition law review of such conduct just because the effects are felt in more general elimination of competition in the mega-event market rather than of a specified or identifiable competitor; the effects of such elimination of competition are felt, potentially or in fact, by not only consumers but also by non-sponsor businesses. The above approach in terms of the European Commission's Guidance Paper emphasises that the main goal of the

---

111 Rousseva 2010, pp. 327–328.

112 European Commission *Guidance on the Commission's enforcement priorities in applying Article 82 (EC) to abusive exclusionary conduct by dominant undertakings*, 3 December 2008.

113 Current Article 102 of the Treaty on the Functioning of the European Union.

114 At par. 19 of the Guidance Paper.

115 Scaria 2008, p. 124.

application of Article 82[116] to exclusionary abuses is the protection of consumers, rather than competitors.[117] And as Scaria also says:

> Examples of [abusive practice by event organisers in the name of anti-ambush marketing efforts] are plenty… and an event organiser's conduct in imposing rigorous anti-ambush marketing efforts like preventing the entry of non-sponsors' products within and near the venue is one of the best examples of eliminating or lessening competition in a relevant market. The public outcry against such severe restrictions in most of the recent events adds more importance to this focus of discussion.[118]

While the sponsorship exclusivity arrangements do not, from the perspective of the event organiser governing body, foreclose the market for competitor governing bodies (as I have argued, there are no such competitor bodies in respect of the mega-events), we have seen that the limited access available for sponsors (and the exclusivity of the sponsorship deals) would seem to foreclose the market for potential competing sponsors. This seems to be borne out by the finding of the U.S. District Court in the above *MasterCard v FIFA* case, in respect of the requirement of proving irreparable harm to MasterCard through FIFA's conduct in granting the exclusive sponsorship rights to VISA, for purposes of an injunction. The court held that MasterCard would suffer the following irreparable harm if FIFA was allowed to continue with VISA as its exclusive financial service sponsorship partner:

> In the absence of an injunction, MasterCard would lose, for at least the next eight years, an undisputedly unique and irreplaceable sponsorship property;
>
> - In the absence of an injunction, MasterCard would lose indeterminate existing and prospective goodwill; and
> - In the absence of an injunction, MasterCard would lose a significant competitive advantage.[119]

Cobbs explains that this finding of the court recognises the value of exclusive sports sponsorship for the sponsors involved (and, I would suggest, obliquely, the potential anti-competitive effects of the very granting of category exclusivity):

> In this description of irreparable harm, a U.S. District Court is essentially recognizing that a specific sports sponsorship can be (1) irreplaceable, or inimitable in the language of the resource-based view of the firm, (2) a source of goodwill, and (3) the basis of a competitive advantage—all of which are supported, but not taken for granted in sponsorship theory. For instance, in proposing how sponsorship works, Meenaghan… suggests that sponsorship's ability to generate consumer goodwill differentiates sponsorship as a promotional tool from advertising. Yet, Amis et al.… point out that not all sponsorships entail

---

[116] Article 102 TFEU.

[117] American courts have on a number of occasions held that antitrust laws are aimed at protecting competition, not competitors—see *Brown Shoe Co v United States* 370 US 294 (1962) 320; *Brooke Group Ltd v Brown & Williamson Tobacco Corp* 509 US 209 (1993) 224; *Copperweld Corp v Independence Tube Corp* 467 US 752 (1984) 768.

[118] Scaria 2008, p. 125.

[119] See Cobbs 2011.

> the resource conditions necessary to generate a competitive advantage. Specifically, the sponsorship must be unique, difficult to imitate, inefficient to transfer, and supported by supplemental promotional assets that create barriers to competition. Elements of this theoretical foundation espoused by sponsorship researchers are clearly evident in the court's rationale summarized above for granting an injunction in the case. Without such a ruling, MasterCard would not only lose the goodwill generated by the World Cup sponsorship, but also be unable to leverage the affiliation toward a competitive advantage with supplemental promotional assets.[120]

And here one should bear in mind that FIFA's efforts at continually increasing the size of the World Cup commercial revenues cake has included a reduction in the number of its official sponsors in order to increase the exclusive sponsorship fees it can charge. Schwab observed the following at the time of the 2006 FIFA World Cup in Germany:

> Exclusive sponsorship deals with its 15 official partners and six official suppliers totalled nearly $900 million for the 2006 World Cup, and these figures are expected to rise for 2010 as FIFA increases the value of its sponsorship rights by lowering the number of official sponsors from 15 to six. Already, FIFA has earned over $1.5 billion for these rights, which lock in the exclusive partners until 2014, with the exception of Coca-Cola, which has a deal lasting until 2022. VISA alone has reportedly paid around $200 million for the right to take the place of its rival MasterCard for the 2010 South Africa World Cup.[121]

When considering the issue of foreclosure of the market to competing sponsors I do not think one should ignore the position of smaller business enterprises in the host jurisdiction of a mega-event. Elsewhere (in Chap. 8) I remark on the fact that, when it comes to determining the harm posed by 'ambushing' for purposes of evaluating the justification for far-reaching *sui generis* event legislation and measures, such as statutory 'association rights' to events, it should be considered that small (local) businesses who are often significantly affected by such legislation do not in fact pose a threat of significant harm to the event organisers and official sponsors. One reason for this is the fact that when one considers allegations of either 'free riding' by ambushers or of whether their conduct amounts to misappropriation of goodwill of the event, it should be remembered that these businesses generally do not qualify as potential sponsors of the event. The mom and pop store situated within a 'clean zone' in the vicinity of an Olympic venue, for example, simply cannot compete with the big multinational corporations in bidding for sponsorship rights running into millions of dollars. Accordingly, and apart from the what I believe to be negligible effect of event-related marketing by such a business on the event's goodwill, event organisers' argument that such 'ambushers' are receiving for free what other sponsors have to pay for ignores this practical fact. Bob's Pizzeria doesn't take something for free which it would otherwise have had to pay for, because it is precluded from even bidding for the right to buy access to such sponsors' rights. I would suggest that sponsorship

---

120 Ibid.

121 Schwab 2006, p. 7.

exclusivity arrangements (coupled with more practical considerations such as the generally long duration of such contracts as well as the prevalence of rights of first refusal and other ways to ensure perpetuation of such contracts) serve to foreclose the market to potential official sponsors in the form of large multinational corporations; in the context of smaller businesses the anti-ambushing laws serve to have the same effect on businesses that are excluded from bidding for 'official' rights and also prohibited from deriving any 'unofficial' commercial benefits from the events. I am convinced that these arrangements have a case to answer in respect of being unlawfully anti-competitive.

Apart from the potential anti-competitive impact on other (potential) corporate sponsors, it is, however, primarily the consequence on consumers of reducing (or completely removing) consumer choice as referred to above, it is submitted, which places such arrangements in jeopardy of constituting abuse of the dominant position of both the event organiser and the official sponsors. Gardiner et al., in the context of examining competition law implications in the European Union, observe that exclusivity is recognised as a commercial necessity for promoting sport, although the parameters must be carefully delineated:

- The duration or term of exclusive contracts must not be too long;
- The range of rights granted must not too wide (they observe that this is especially the case in respect of sports broadcasting arrangements);
- There must be no foreclosure of competition in the relevant market; and
- Longer periods of exclusivity may be allowed if justified by entry into a new market or developing new technology.[122]

Marcus, with reference to the above-mentioned *Danish Tennis Federation* case, expresses the opinion that 'exclusivity in and of itself is not illicit if there is a lawful tendering process'.[123] I would suggest, however, that more than just the matter of 'access to the club' of exclusive sponsors is at stake in determining the potential anti-competitive effects of sponsorship exclusivity. It is an important factor, indeed, but not the only one to be taken into account or subjected to scrutiny in determining the legality of such arrangements.

One must also ask whether the exclusive sponsorship arrangements for a mega-event may fall foul of the provisions of Article 81 (Article 101 TFEU). Article 101(1) TFEU prohibits all agreements between undertakings, decisions by associations of undertakings and concerted practises which may affect trade between European Union countries and which have as their object or effect the prevention, restriction or distortion of competition. Agreements between undertakings are caught by the prohibition rule of Article 81(1) when they are likely to have an appreciable adverse impact on the parameters of competition on the market, such as price, output, product quality, product variety and innovation. Agreements can have this effect by appreciably reducing rivalry between the parties to the

[122] Gardiner et al. 2006, p. 368.

[123] Marcus 2010, p. 30.

agreement or between them and third parties.[124] As an exception to this rule, Article 101(3) TFEU (ex-Article 81(3)) provides that the prohibition contained in Article 101(1) TFEU may be declared inapplicable in case of agreements which contribute to improving the production or distribution of goods or to promoting technical or economic progress, while allowing consumers a fair share of the resulting benefits, and which do not impose restrictions which are not indispensable to the attainment of these objectives and do not afford such undertakings the possibility of eliminating competition in respect of a substantial part of the products concerned. The assessment under Article 101 TFEU thus consists of two parts. The first step is to assess whether an agreement between undertakings that is capable of affecting trade between EU countries has an anti-competitive object or actual or potential anti-competitive effects. Article 101(3) TFEU becomes relevant only when an agreement between undertakings restricts competition within the meaning of Article 101(1) TFEU. In the case of non-restrictive agreements there is no need to examine any benefits resulting from the agreement. The second step, which becomes relevant only when an agreement is found to be restrictive of competition, is to determine the pro-competitive benefits produced by that agreement and to assess whether these pro-competitive effects outweigh the anti-competitive effects. The balancing of anti-competitive and pro-competitive effects is conducted exclusively within the framework laid down by Article 101(3) TFEU. The present guidelines[125] issued by the Commission examine the four conditions of Article 101(3) TFEU:

- efficiency gains;
- fair share for consumers;
- indispensability of the restrictions; and
- no elimination of competition.

Fortunato and Richards argue that the counter-balancing pro-competitive effects of sponsorship exclusivity arrangements, which a court would have to consider in an antitrust challenge, are hard to find. The exclusion itself may lower transaction costs for the venue, which might be argued enhances market efficiencies, but the authors point out that unless those savings are transferred to the consumer, the exclusion is not pro-competitive. While some sponsorship contracts have provisions that limit price increases or guarantee product supply to the venue, creating a more stable and predictable market, such effect varies, and the value to the consumer is uncertain. They argue that multiple suppliers would likely do more to guarantee a continuous supply of product to meet consumer demand than a contractual obligation placed on a single supplier.[126] They conclude:

---

[124] Par. 16 of the European Commission's Guidelines on the application of Article 81(3) of the Treaty (2004/C 101/08), 27 April 2004.

[125] Guidelines on the application of Article 81(3) of the Treaty (2004/C 101/08), 27 April 2004.

[126] Fortunato and Richards 2007, p. 46.

> The only foreseeable benefit to competition would be that the tremendous profits—to both the arena and the sponsor—resulting from these exclusivity agreements would virtually guarantee that neither would go bankrupt. And if that were sufficient benefit to justify anticompetitive actions, every antitrust case would be an exercise in futility.[127]

The interests of the consumer simply cannot be undervalued in the evaluation of the anti-competitive effects of sponsorship exclusivity, and this is just as true when one considers the potential anti-competitive effects of anti-ambushing laws which serve to protect such exclusivity. Corbett and van Roy argue that the protection provided against ambushing in New Zealand in terms of the Major Events Management Act, 2007 is anti-competitive: 'MEMA confers a benefit on authorised sponsors well beyond that which it would be possible to obtain under contract. The lack of competition is likely to increase prices to the consumer for the duration of the major event.'[128] This is rather ironic if one considers that many of the *sui generis* anti-ambushing laws passed in recent years do not appear to have as their focus or objective the protection of consumers against confusion or deception by 'ambushers' (which I will examine in more detail in Chap. 8). This just strengthens my conviction that special anti-ambushing laws, for the most part, are concerned mainly to protect event organisers' and sponsors' market control and profits. I will return to the issue of the potential role of countervailing pro-competitive effects of sponsorship exclusivity in Chap. 9, when I will examine the arguments so often raised by event organisers in justification of aggressive commercial rights protection for the events.

Moving away, for the moment, from the effects of these sponsorship arrangements on fans, it was predicted in 2007 (also in the American context) that sponsorship exclusivity in sports may provide a breeding ground for future antitrust litigation regarding access to sponsorship of teams in professional leagues:

> The next frontier of antitrust litigation in sport may be just on the horizon. Exclusive sponsorships, those that protect a sponsor from competitor advertisements, are getting bigger, covering more ground. Recent trends have sponsors buying the rights to entire leagues, not just specific events or single teams. It is not hard to anticipate that a potential sponsor, blocked by contract from attaching its name to any aspect of a sport will eventually view this as a conspiracy barring entry to a market. Whether the market is well defined is almost irrelevant, as that fact question may never be reached before an organization finds it prudent to settle… As more and more elements of sport become commoditized… exclusivity is sought over a broader and broader range. Sponsors are, with each contract iteration, seeking more value from their dollars. This value is generally created by guaranteed exclusivity. The wider the swath of competitors contractually barred from using their name with a team or a league, the higher the dollar value of the rights being granted. It is the scope of these ever-growing agreements that may lead to future antitrust trouble.[129]

---

[127] Ibid.

[128] Corbett and Van Roy 2010, p. 347.

[129] Barnett et al. 2007.

These remarks were made in the context of litigation at the time between telecommunications company AT&T and its competitor Sprint Nextel and NASCAR, in the case of *AT&T Mobility, LLC v. National Association for Stock Car Auto Racing, Inc.*[130] AT&T had bought wireless provider Cingular and was in the process of rebranding the company under the AT&T name. AT&T wanted to place the AT&T logo on a NASCAR car (Jeff Burton's No. 31 Richard Childress Racing Chevrolet) which, at the time, was branded with the Cingular logo in terms of a prior sponsorship agreement. NASCAR declined to permit AT&T to display its logo on the car because NASCAR asserted that this action would violate its contract with Sprint Nextel. In June 2003, Sprint Nextel Corporation reportedly paid USD 700 million for its exclusive sponsorship rights for the NASCAR Cup Series races over a 10-year period. The Nextel Sponsorship Agreement contained language defining competitors and specifically naming AT&T and several other telecommunications companies. Within the exclusivity clause in the SprintNextel/NASCAR contract was a list of competitors to be barred from advertising and sponsorships in connection with the now renamed NASCAR Sprint Cup Series. That competitor list included Alltel, AT&T, AT&T Corp., AT&T Wireless, SBC Communications, Bell South, and Cingular. However, both Alltel and Cingular had pre-existing agreements with individual racing teams. As a result, for the two teams adversely affected by the Nextel exclusivity deal, NASCAR modified its 'Driver and Car Owner Agreements', which contained the exclusivity clause. Following the SprintNextel exclusivity agreement, these contracts contained a clause that prevented teams from displaying any product or service identification from the category of wire-line and wireless communication services on the race car.

Competitors of SprintNextel were prohibited from advertising and sponsorships in connection with NASCAR Nextel Cup Series Events. However, at the time this agreement was executed, Nextel became aware that the Jeff Burton-driven car had been sponsored by Cingular Wireless since 2001. Accordingly, the Nextel Sponsorship Agreement carved out narrow exceptions to SprintNextel's exclusivity as an accommodation to those pre-existing telecommunications sponsors. The agreement permitted the Burton car to continue under its pre-existing sponsorship agreement with Cingular, under certain terms and conditions. NASCAR also agreed to take all legally permissible steps to protect Sprint Nextel's exclusivity. In 2007, NASCAR, the team owner and Burton were parties to the above-mentioned Driver and Car Owner Agreement, an addendum of which, designed to effectuate the narrow exceptions for Nextel's exclusivity, contained a grandfather clause permitting the team owner to 'renew its non-complying sponsorship so long as the sponsor's brand position is not increased on the… car.' This clause also provided that 'in the event the sponsorship relationship with Sprint Nextel Competitor is not renewed, [the team owner] will not be permitted to enter into a subsequent sponsorship agreement with a different Sprint Nextel Competitor.' In January

130 487 F.Supp.2d 1370 (2007).

2007, the team owner submitted approval for a paint scheme of the car that maintained the Cingular logo on the hood of the car, but also introduced the AT&T logo on the rear panel. NASCAR rejected this paint scheme as it violated the Sprint Nextel Sponsorship Agreement, prohibiting the display of the AT&T logo.[131]

AT&T's case was not based in anti-trust, but rather in contract, even though Cobbs observes that there were definite competition law implications that arose from the conduct of the event organiser and the title sponsor:

> [P]ursuant to rumors of mergers in the telecommunication industry, Sprint Nextel (ironically, given their own merger) and NASCAR negotiated an amendment to their own title sponsorship that explicitly prohibited a grandfathered product category competitor (i.e., Alltel and Cingular) from leveraging their existing team sponsorship under the brand of another excluded competitor. This created an interesting scenario where one firm, Sprint, was colluding with the controller of a promotional marketplace, NASCAR, to not only exclude category competitors by name, but also restrict the competitors' promotional outlets with the controller's affiliates, the racing teams. However, the legal case was not born out of an antitrust condition, but rather a contract law stipulation.[132]

The district court in Georgia[133] held that AT&T had demonstrated a substantial likelihood of success on the merits of its breach of contract claim as an intended third party beneficiary of the agreement (and its addendum) between the team owner and NASCAR, and granted AT&T a preliminary injunction to proceed to re-brand the car. In respect of the requirement of showing irreparable harm in order to obtain a preliminary injunction, AT&T argued that, without an injunction, it would suffer the loss of goodwill, consumers would be confused, and AT&T would lose the exclusive negotiation period outlined for the renewal of its agreement with RCR. The court agreed with all three arguments and went on to state that although a dollar value was placed on corporate affiliation with the #31 car, the court could not return to AT&T the goodwill lost if it was unable to feature its marks on the car. Further, it was deemed likely that NASCAR fans would be confused by the continued presence of the Cingular brand when in all other marketing mediums the brand was being phased out. Finally, without an indication from the court as to the possibility of transitioning the #31 car's branding to AT&T, any negotiations between AT&T and RCR in regards to a renewed agreement would likely remain in limbo, thereby disposing of the exclusive negotiating period. As a result, irreparable harm was found for AT&T and weighed against any harm done to NASCAR by a potential injunction.[134]

---

[131] From a summary of the facts of the case available online at the time of writing at http://blawg.scottandscottllp.com/businessandtechnologylaw/2007/08/nascar_says_not_so_fast_to_tel.html. See also the detailed discussion of the litigation in this matter in Cobbs 2011.

[132] Cobbs 2011.

[133] *AT&T Mobility LLC f/k/a Cingular Wireless LLC v National Association for Stock Car Auto Racing, Inc.* 487 F.Supp.2d 1370 (2007)(18 May 2007).

[134] See Cobbs 2011.

When the case was taken on appeal to the US Court of Appeals (11th circuit)[135] it was overturned (on the basis of a finding that AT&T in fact lacked the required third party standing under Georgia law) and remanded to the district court. Between the issuing of the district court's preliminary injunction and the reversal on appeal, NASCAR filed a countersuit against AT&T for USD 100 million when AT&T ran the re-branded #31 car in NASCAR Sprint Cup competitions. The NASCAR countersuit alleged breach of contract, fraud and misrepresentation, and conspiracy to aid and abet wrongful interference with NASCAR's category exclusive sponsorship with Sprint Nextel. While this action was still pending after the Appeals Court decision, AT&T and NASCAR settled their legal wrangling in September 2007 by agreeing to permit AT&T branding on the #31 car through the 2008 season, but no further (after Burton had raced the car in two races *sans* branding, similar to what had been done with Formula 1 cars with tobacco sponsorship in races where such sponsorships were banned). NASCAR agreed to let AT&T brand the car through the 2008 season, after which AT&T would leave NASCAR racing.

While, as mentioned, this case was not argued on the basis of an antitrust challenge to the relevant sponsorship arrangements between NASCAR and Sprint Nextel, it has been predicted that such future challenges may occur and, specifically, that this might necessitate careful drafting of sponsorship agreements:

> [In the context of the effect of exclusive sponsorship agreements limiting access to sponsorship of teams] allegations of anti-competitive action aren't far behind. How well-founded they may be could be irrelevant, if careless drafting creates fodder for a well pled complaint, organizations may find themselves funding their teams from sponsor dollars paid out in expensive settlements.[136]

Fortunato and Richards add a number of caveats to their view on the anti-competitive effects of sponsorship exclusivity, however, regarding the question of whether a court would find such anti-competitive effects (which, as mentioned, they identify specifically in respect of its impact on fans at matches) to violate antitrust law. The first relates to the important question of defining the relevant market for purposes of determination of the impact of the practise on competition. If a court views such market, for example, to include a wider area outside the sporting venue (remember that Fortunato and Richards focus mainly on the impact of sponsorship exclusivity on fans at matches) there may be no appreciable effect on competition. If the area is narrowly defined as the venue, however, the complete lack of consumer choice would be an important factor in determining the legality of such arrangements. Gardiner et al. observe the following in respect of market definition in sports sponsorship cases:

> Sponsorship is a form of advertising and as such competes with an almost limitless number of methods for promoting the brand, product or service at issue. Companies

[135] *AT&T Mobility, LLC v. National Association for Stock Car Auto Racing, Inc.* 2007 WL 2297832 (11th Cir. 2007), 13 August 2007.

[136] Barnett et al. 2007.

> seeking to promote particular products or services, or their "brand" generally, have a wide range of platforms from which to choose… Even if a sponsor insists on a sports-related platform, the range of "substitutable" possibilities is still enormous [these include endorsement deals with individual athletes, advertising at sports venues and sponsorship of a vast range of different events]… If a marketing department insists on [for example] a football-related platform rather than any other sport, there would still be a very wide range of promotional opportunities, each of which is broadly substitutable for the other… [I]t is possible to sponsor a broad range of different teams… and events… or event to create events of one's own… As a result of this broad range of market opportunities, an "exclusive" agreement of a breadth and length that would set alarm bells ringing in the broadcasting market is likely to raise little concern in the sponsorship market.[137]

It is submitted, however, that the position is quite different in respect of sports mega-event sponsorship. As argued above, there is a distinct lack of such 'substitutable marketing opportunities' in respect of these events, simply because of the unique nature of the product and the scarcity of the resources relating to the event (e.g. the ability to obtain sponsorship rights from only one entity, and the fact that sponsorship of the world championship football tournament that is FIFA's World Cup is only possible through the arrangements on offer by FIFA, and on the terms it sets in respect of its exclusive sponsorship arrangements). This should be considered in light of the special value that such event sponsorships, and their exclusivity, brings to the sponsors. As Cobbs observes in respect of the courts' findings of irreparable harm in both the *MasterCard/FIFA* and *AT&T/NASCAR* cases discussed above:

> In finding irreparable harm in both cases, the court essentially recognized that both NASCAR and the World Cup are unique promotional environments that cannot be sufficiently imitated by other marketing channels. Sponsors able to secure and defend a category exclusive relationship within these sports have the opportunity to leverage the official association with the sport as a brand differentiating factor. Recall sponsorship theorists' assertion that inimitability, together with heterogeneous distribution, imperfect mobility, and preemptive limits to competition, qualified sponsorship as a strategic tool for achieving a competitive advantage. The latter three qualities are inherent in multi-year product/service category exclusive sponsorship agreements; yet, the sponsorships characterized in the two legal cases dissolved acrimoniously.[138]

I would suggest that market definition for the mega-events is a different exercise from considering the marketing opportunities in respect of sports sponsorship more generally, which holds clear implications for the determination of dominance and abuse of such dominance as well as for the foreclosure of entry into this market by potential sponsors. As has been observed in the EU context, if a market is defined narrowly enough it is possible that a sponsorship arrangement may be deemed capable of having an appreciable effect on competition, in which case the Commission would try to ensure that arrangements do not foreclose competition in the market (typically, by considering the length and scope of the exclusivity granted, and by looking for evidence that the process of granting the sponsorship

---

[137] Lewis and Taylor 2007, pp. 419–420 (par. B2.307–B2.310).

[138] Cobbs 2011.

rights was fair and open to all competitors).[139] I would submit that, in this evaluation, one need also consider the interests of the consumer, and I would suggest that the implications of often draconian legislative enforcement of such exclusive sponsorship arrangements against members of the public (as will be discussed in the later chapters) should be an important factor in the determination of the potential anti-competitive effects.

The second caveat posed by Fortunato and Richards is that one should remember that fans attend matches voluntarily; even if the marketplace is defined narrowly (as the venue), the consumers subject themselves to decisions made by the sports league or team and their payment for the ticket can be construed as tacit approval for their range of experiences at the stadium. They are also only at that location for a limited amount of time and can voluntarily leave at any moment.[140] I am less convinced in this regard. The consent to such restrictions on the freedom of choice of sports fans wishing to watch a live match, where they have no choice but to buy a ticket and attend subject to the commercial arrangements in place with sponsors would appear to me to be a rather tenuous form of voluntary consent. At best I do not think this consideration should play an overly important role in assessing the potential anti-competitive effects of such sponsorship arrangements.

The authors conclude their review by expressing the opinion that sponsorship exclusivity arrangements are potentially anti-competitive and open to legal challenge. However, they pose the following conclusion, which highlights the complexity of the issue and deserves to be quoted in full:

> But if a court were to find exclusive contracts by sponsors to be illegal, there would be a monumental effect on sports and sports sponsorship throughout this country. Undoubtedly, a court would be reluctant to reach such a conclusion, regardless of how the law might direct such action, because of these potentially devastating consequences. After all, many companies would stop sponsoring sports if they could no longer secure exclusivity, which would probably undermine the financial security of some teams and facilities. Likewise, such a conclusion would almost certainly change the financial models used in the sports industries... [Should the courts] in fact amend the practice, especially in a capitalist economic system, where the exclusionary nature of the conduct is due largely to the cost of these sponsorships? The problem of sponsorship exclusivity is one that does not allow for a remedy that does not conflict with some other practical aspect of consumer rights, corporate rights, or the sports industry economics. Allowing the sponsorship situation to persist in its current state is a violation of consumer sovereignty. Yet forcing a sports team or league to advertise or sell products they do not want to can be a violation of democracy. The improbability that these agreements would be declared illegal should not let the government off the hook. Whether or not they are *found* illegal, they quite clearly eliminate consumer choice, and it is the central policy of both § 1 of the Sherman Act and § 3 of the Clayton Act against contracts which take away freedom of purchasers to buy in an open market. This practice, then, certainly violates at least the spirit of the antitrust laws, and some remedial action should be taken. At a time when sponsorship agreements are creeping into all public venues, even schools and public parks, failure to confront these issues may ensure that consumers eventually lose their sovereign rights in all public

[139] Lewis and Taylor 2007, p. 422 (par. B2.315).

[140] Fortunato and Richards 2007, p. 48.

> spaces. The courts typically interpret the antitrust laws as binary, all-or-nothing propositions. Either an action violates or does not violate the law. In this situation, though, neither decision is satisfactory, because of the damage caused at either extreme. A better approach would be to seek a middle ground, where damage could be limited but not eliminated. Some possibilities include limiting the extent to which stadiums and arenas can ban consumers from bringing in refreshments, limiting the terms of exclusivity agreements, and so forth. It is the spectator who makes it possible for the sponsors, the stadiums, the team owners, and the athletes to earn their livings. But in the current system, it is the spectator who is affected by these monopolies. It is time to stop taking advantage of them. The spectator's right of free choice deserves at least a modicum of respect and protection.[141]

It is clear that the issue is anything but a simple one. The current sponsorship exclusivity arrangements are not only fundamental to the commercialisation of mega-events, but also well established in the global mega-events culture and instrumental in respect of the funding of sport at the highest level (which, if the sports governing bodies' claims of the extent of 'trickle-down' of sponsorship revenues are to be believed, affects sport across all levels). Opportunities for commercial association with events through a system that is so extremely (and by definition) exclusive, and where rights are granted for long periods and in terms of bidding processes that are dubious in respect of their free access and equality of opportunities raise serious questions about their competition law implications. This, I would submit, is even more problematic when one considers the implications for the public (in the meaning of the fans as well as the citizenry of host nations or cities) of exclusive mega-event sponsorships. Event organisers love to claim that ambush marketing potentially threatens the very ability to stage these events, because of its potential to alienate the corporate sponsors (the 'survival of the Games' argument, which I'll examine more closely in Chap. 9). A recently-published discussion document of the UK'S Chartered Institute of Marketing notes that 'official sponsors to the 2012 Olympics are paying a total of £ 930 million, none of which is returned to the public purse which is funding the entire £ 9.298 billion cost of hosting the Olympics'.[142] It makes little economic (and moral) sense to allow such anti-competitive arrangements to be built upon the edifice of public investment and then, through the use of special laws, to protect such monopoly at the cost of the public interest (in what is 'by definition a cultural event, not a protected brand'[143]) as well as, increasingly, individual civil liberties. The implications for the public are truly significant in respect of the effects of the special laws that are increasingly being used to protect such commercial arrangements and to maintain the monopolies that exist. And one could also question the potential long-term impact on the public interest of the clear culture of egotism amongst event organisers in respect of their claims to the monopoly in

141 Ibid.

142 Chartered Institute of Marketing *Ambush Marketing and the Law* (April 2011) at 11—available via the CIM's website at http://www.cim.co.uk/resources/emergingthemes/home.aspx.

143 Ibid. 24.

their events. Elsewhere I will revisit issues regarding the public domain character of mega-events and the public interest dimensions *vis a vis* the maintenance and promotion of private commercial interests regarding such events. For present purposes one might just consider that the often ridiculed mentality of an organisation like FIFA, which through its aggressive and unapologetic pursuit of commercial exploitation of its events may appear to be hell-bent on lusting after world domination, may not be a healthy one even in a business sense:

> In business, egoist translates into monopolist: whatever I have created or bought is mine to own and control to the exclusion of everyone else. The vocabulary of creation and ownership is manipulated to downgrade prior arts and inputs, and to emphasise the overwhelming importance of my additions. If all firms behaved in this pathologically self-absorbed way, everyday moderately honest commerce would grind to a halt.[144]

On the other hand, however, one is confronted with claims by the stakeholders involved in this system that sponsorship exclusivity arrangements are a necessary evil in order to stage these events, and that without such exclusivity the very events would be in jeopardy in the face of the potential for sponsors to withdraw from the scene. These different arguments need to be considered in more detail, and I will revisit the justifications for the existing system in Chap. 9. For now I'll simply pose, for consideration, some remarks by Stevens J in US Supreme Court, writing in the context of the May 2010 *American Needle v NFL* judgment referred to in the section that follows below. While the court was charged with considering the 'single entity defence' raised by the league in that case (and which involved an exclusive licensing arrangement), I would submit that the following may be relevant in the context of consideration of the legitimacy of protection of sponsorship exclusivity in the mega-event context, in terms of its necessity for purposes of 'putting on the show':

> The mere fact that the teams operate jointly in some sense does not mean that they are immune [from anti-trust scrutiny]. [And in note 7 of the judgment:] In any event, *it simply is not apparent that the alleged conduct was necessary at all. Although two teams are needed to play a football game, not all aspects of elaborate interleague cooperation are necessary to produce a game. Moreover, even if league-wide agreements are necessary to produce football, it does not follow that concerted activity in marketing intellectual property is necessary to produce football.* [Emphasis added]

Kobel[145] refers to the important recent European Court of Justice sporting case of *Meca-Medina v EC Commission*[146] (which related to a challenge to a doping violation suspension) and states the following in respect of the competition law implication of sponsorship exclusivity arrangements by sports bodies:

---

[144] Vaver, D '"Brand culture: trade marks, marketing and consumption"—responding legally to Professor Schroeder's paper' in Bently et al. 2008, p. 187.

[145] Kobel 2007, p. 47.

[146] *David Meca-Medina and Igor Majcen v Commission of the European Communities* (Case C-519/04 P; judgment delivered 18 July 2006).

Contrary to anti-doping rules which are pursuing legitimate objectives consisting in securing the proper conduct of a competitive sport and to ensure healthy rivalry between athletes, exclusive attribution of exclusive sponsoring rights is not inherent to the organisation of the sport competition and necessary to ensure that sporting events take place and function properly. As a result, there is a strong probability that the restraint be subject to antitrust rules.

6.2.1.3 Of Football Caps and Video Games: A View from the United States on Exclusive Sports Licensing and Antitrust

At the time of writing the American courts are faced with an antitrust challenge to an exclusive licensing agreement in respect of merchandising of the National Football League (NFL) teams' intellectual property, in terms of sections 1 and 2 of the Sherman Act. The case was brought by American Needle, Inc, a headwear manufacturer based in Buffalo Grove, Illinois (a family-owned business since 1918 which started out manufacturing green celluloid visors for bank tellers and telegraph operators, until the owner's son approached the Chicago Cubs in 1940 with the idea of selling hats to fans at Wrigley Field and got the company into the licenced sports apparel business), against NFL Properties and Reebok International Ltd.

In the 1960s the NFL teams formed NFL Properties as a separate corporate entity charged with developing, licensing, and marketing the intellectual property the teams owned (such as their logos, trademarks, and other indicia), and with 'conduct[ing] and engag[ing] in advertising campaigns and promotional ventures on behalf of the NFL and [its] member [teams]'. The NFL teams authorised NFL Properties to grant licences to vendors so the vendors could use the teams' intellectual property for merchandising purposes (to manufacture and sell various kinds of consumer products that bear the teams' logos and trademarks—products such as team jerseys, shirts, flags, and, as pertinent in this case, headwear, like baseball caps and stocking hats). NFL Properties granted headwear licences to a number of different vendors simultaneously; one of those vendors was American Needle, which held an NFL headwear licence for over 20 years. In 2000, the NFL teams authorised NFL Properties to solicit bids from the vendors for an exclusive headwear licence. Reebok won the bidding war, and in 2001 the NFL teams allowed NFL Properties to grant an exclusive licence to Reebok for ten years. NFL Properties did not renew American Needle's headwear licence or the licences of the other headwear vendors.[147]

American Needle responded by filing an antitrust suit against the NFL, NFL Properties, the individual NFL teams and Reebok. American Needle claimed that the exclusive headwear licensing agreement between NFL Properties and Reebok violated § 1 of the Sherman Antitrust Act, which outlaws any 'contract,

[147] From the facts of the case as set out in the judgment of the 7th Circuit Court of Appeals (538 F.3d 736 (2008) at 737–738).

combination… or conspiracy, in restraint of trade', and/or § 2, which outlaws conduct by any person 'who shall monopolize, or attempt to monopolize, or combine or conspire with any other person or persons, to monopolize any part of the trade or commerce among the several States'.

The NFL's main defence was to claim summary judgment on the basis of a 'single-entity defence'; i.e. it claimed that the relevant provisions of the Sherman Act are not applicable because the NFL as league is a single commercial entity made up of the 32 constituent teams and, accordingly, it is not possible for it to enter into a contract or to conspire by virtue of its status as a single entity. This defence was worth a shot; as Fortunato and Martin observe, 'the [American] courts have been inconsistent in their rulings as to the question of whether professional sports leagues are a collective, singular economic entity or if teams are individual businesses'.[148] The Chicago district court granted summary judgment in favour of the NFL. American Needle took the matter on appeal to the 7th Circuit Court of Appeals, which affirmed the lower court's finding on the single-entity defence. The matter was further appealed to the U.S. Supreme Court,[149] where Stevens J, writing for the court in a unanimous judgment, observed that the court had only a narrow issue to decide (namely, 'whether the NFL respondents are capable of engaging in a "contract, combination…, or conspiracy" as defined by § 1 of the Sherman Act, 15 U.S.C. § 1, or, as we have sometimes phrased it, whether the alleged activity by the NFL respondents "must be viewed as that of a single enterprise for purposes of § 1"'[150]). The Supreme Court reversed, rejecting the single-entity defence and referring the case back to the district court for determination of American Needle's antitrust claims.

The case is currently awaiting judgment in the lower court on the merits of American Needle's antitrust claims, and I will not speculate as to the eventual outcome. I must admit, however, that I find the following finding by the Court of Appeals rather strange:

> [T]he failure of American Needle's § 1 claim [on the basis of the NFL's single-entity defence] necessarily dooms its § 2 monopolization claim. As a single entity for the purpose of licensing, the NFL teams are free under § 2 to license their intellectual property on an exclusive basis,… even if the teams opt to reduce the number of companies to whom they grant licenses,… ("To say that participants in an organization may cooperate is to say that they may control what they make and how they sell it: the producers of Star Trek may decide to release two episodes a week and grant exclusive licenses to show them, even though this reduces the number of times episodes appear on TV in a given market…."); ("An antitrust claim based solely on a single firm's denial of a license to a trademark

[148] Fortunato and Martin 2011, p. 78.

[149] *American Needle, Inc v NFL* 130 S.Ct. 2201 (2010)(judgment handed down on 24 May 2010).

[150] With reference to *Copperweld Corp. v. Independence Tube Corp.,* 467 U.S. 752, 771, 104 S.Ct. 2731, 81 L.Ed.2d 628 (1984).

would readily be dismissed…."). As such, American Needle has no colorable claim that the NFL teams and NFL Properties created a monopoly by awarding Reebok the exclusive headwear licensing contract.[151]

I, frankly, fail to follow this reasoning. How would a finding that the NFL constitutes a single commercial entity incapable of conspiring for purposes of § 1—even if correct—automatically exclude the possibility of its granting of an exclusive licence constituting monopolisation which may contravene § 2? It would appear that, in any event and apart from the Supreme Court's subsequent reversal on this issue, the Court of Appeals placed too much weight on its finding regarding the NFL's single-entity defence. The Supreme Court, in the course of its discussion and rejection of this defence, observed the following, which I would submit implies a rejection of the Court of Appeals' above reasoning:

> Directly relevant to this case, the teams compete in the market for intellectual property. To a firm making hats, the Saints and the Colts are two potentially competing suppliers of valuable trademarks. When each NFL team licenses its intellectual property, it is not pursuing the "common interests of the whole" league but is instead pursuing interests of each "corporation itself"; teams are acting as "separate economic actors pursuing separate economic interests," and each team therefore is a potential "independent cente[r] of decisionmaking,"… Decisions by NFL teams to license their separately owned trademarks collectively and to only one vendor are decisions that "depriv[e] the marketplace of independent centers of decisionmaking,"…, and therefore of actual or potential competition.

While private companies are typically allowed to engage in exclusive licensing agreements without violating the Sherman Act, American Needle argues that the Reebok/NFL Properties agreement limits competition by preventing apparel manufacturers from negotiating with individual NFL teams for the right to produce branded apparel and, as a result of exclusivity in apparel markets, allows Reebok to charge higher prices than it could with adequate competition[152] (the conspiracy claim in terms of § 1 of the Sherman Act). Aside from merely harming consumers through increased prices, the Sherman Act is also designed to prevent competitors from conspiring to limit consumer choice, which American Needle argues is a major concern when there is only one apparel supplier. I would suggest that similar potential anti-competitive effects may be experienced in respect of an alleged violation of the monopolisation provisions of § 2 of the Act.

It has been held, in a case relating to Major League Baseball which was very similar to the facts of *American Needle*, that centralised exclusive licensing of intellectual property by a league is not a 'naked restraint' and therefore not *per se*

---

[151] At 744 of the Court of Appeals judgment.

[152] As one source observed, one of the documents in the Supreme Court case quoted a Reebok executive as saying that 'caps that had sold for $19.99 a few years earlier were selling for $30' following the move to the exclusivity arrangement post 2000'—see http://www.scotusblog.com/2010/01/pro-sports-and-antitrust-argument-preview/.

illegal (and thus may only be subject to 'rule of reason' antitrust scrutiny).[153] Even though American courts apparently do not view the mere granting of an exclusive licence as potentially anti-competitive conduct,[154] I would suggest that the eventual outcome of *American Needle* may very well turn on the nature of the bidding for the exclusive rights which were granted to Reebok (and, possibility, the duration of such deal). I believe it is dismissive of the issues involved to reject the potential finding of an antitrust violation out of hand at such an early stage, when the courts have essentially only considered the NFL's narrow defence. I am, personally (and for selfish reasons related to my current attempt to evaluate the potential competition law implications of mega-event sponsorship exclusivity) less concerned about the 'status-of-the-league-as-licensing-entity' side of the equation, and more concerned about the effects on the relevant market of an exclusive licence such as the one provided to Reebok. I believe one should distinguish between a group licence (which may have pro-competitive benefits such as the reduction of transactional costs as opposed to separate negotiation of a numerous team licences in a league scenario) and an exclusive licence, and the potential anti-competitive effects that this last may hold. I would suggest that the strange reasoning of the Court of Appeals in *American Needle* as referred to earlier in respect of the above-quoted passage from the judgment derives from such an over-emphasis on the single entity defence in respect of the party granting the licence and an apparent failure to properly appreciate the potential nature and effects of the exclusivity granted to the licencee (Reebok in this case).

---

[153] See the decision of the district court in *Major League Baseball Properties v Salvino, Inc* 420 F.Supp.2d at 219. The district court noted in addition that courts have refused to apply the *per se* rule of liability to sports leagues because cooperation amongst teams, in addition to any anticompetitive effects, can have legitimate purposes, such as enabling and coordinating the contests. The 2nd Circuit Court of Appeals affirmed the applicability of rule of reason in this case—see *Major League Baseball Properties v Salvino, Inc* 542 F.3d 290 (2008), where the court concluded as follows:

'[W]e see no error in the district court's analysis of Salvino's claim under the rule of reason. The court noted that Salvino had proffered no evidence that the centralization of licensing in [Major League Baseball Properties] caused any actual injury to competition or any evidence that MLBP possessed power in the relevant market. The court stated that, "[i]ndeed, Salvino did not respond to MLBP's arguments regarding the rule of reason analysis and instead urged the Court to analyze its claims under the *per se* rule or quick look doctrine, neither of which would require Salvino to make a showing of adverse effect on the market"... On this appeal, Salvino has again argued solely that the court should have applied the *per se* or quick-look rule and has presented no basis for a ruling that, if rule-of-reason analysis was applicable, the district court erred in the conduct of that analysis. Our own examination persuades us that, on this record, the district court's analysis was correct.' (542 F.3d 290 (2008) at 334).

The court did, however, note the following:

'We express no view as to what the outcome would be of a case in which a plaintiff challenging the Clubs' centralization of licensing functions in MLBP as their exclusive licensing agent adduced admissible evidence as to the reasonableness of that practice.' (542 F.3d 290 (2008) at 334).

[154] See *Cook Inc. v. Boston Scientific Corp.*, 333 F.3d 737, 740 (7th Cir.2003), as relied upon by the 7th Circuit Court of Appeals in *American Needle* at 744.

As one observer (subsequently quoted on the internet) who attended the oral hearing of arguments in the Supreme Court, observed, 'Justice after Justice insisted strenuously that [the nature of the NFL as single entity or not, and its possible resultant immunity from antitrust scrutiny] is not really the issue, and that the case probably needs to go back to the lower courts for a potentially penetrating inquiry into what kinds of commerce are closely enough related to pro football that they escape antitrust liability'.[155] This same commentator expressed the following opinion:

> [Such apparent skepticism on the part of the Supreme Court Justices] doesn't mean, however, American Needle would win the case outright—indeed, they probably have a loser. But the sweeping legal ruling that the NFL won at the lower courts preempted further inquiry into the specific facts. A remand to the lower courts would allow the NFL to win the case on narrower grounds that would not have much application in other, future cases beyond this one. Moreover, such a ruling would absolve the Justices of the danger of deciding a case about the NFL that applies to a wide swath of joint business ventures throughout the country. (The NFL's argument was founded largely on its exceptionalism: We are the NFL and get this treatment, though no other business joint ventures should. That kind of argument is more persuasive on [ESPN's] *Around the Horn* than it is in the Supreme Court building.)

It should also be borne in mind that the U.S. Supreme Court, in the 1957 case of *Radovich v NFL*,[156] refused to uphold an argument calling for extension of baseball's antitrust exemption[157] to football, and held unequivocally that 'the volume of interstate business involved in organized professional football places it within the provisions of the [Sherman] Act'.[158]

By way of illustration of the potential effects of *American Needle* beyond just the NFL-licenced apparel industry, it has, for example, been speculated that the outcome of the case is being watched closely by the video gaming industry, with some parties being anxious to see whether a finding in favour of American Needle might augur an end to the monopoly of Electronic Arts Inc, the software company that markets sports video games under the brand label EA Sports, on NFL-licenced content in the form of its long-running *Madden NFL Football* game franchise (one of the highest revenue-producing video game titles of all time):

> While the effects of the Court's decision will be far-reaching, the primary concern for gamers will be over existing licensing arrangements for sports games. If the NFL loses the case, EA could lose its current position as the exclusive publisher of NFL-licenced games. Furthermore, the ways in which future game licensing agreements are negotiated would be forever changed. Rather than appealing to a single business or organization, such as [NFL Properties], publishers would be able to negotiate with individual teams. While this could

---

[155] Lyle Denniston, on the Supreme Court of the United States blog (or www.scotusblog.com), as quoted at http://smartfootball.com/grab-bag/recap-supreme-court-hears-argument-in-american-needle-v-nfl#more-785.

[156] *Radovich v National Football League* 352 U.S. 445 (1957).

[157] *Federal Baseball Club* v. *National League,* 259 U. S. 200 (1922); *Toolson v. New York Yankees, Inc.*, 346 U. S. 356 (1953).

[158] *Radovich* supra 452.

> lead to more competition in the sports gaming markets, it could also lead to really wonky arrangements—imagine EA releasing an NFL game with 20 NFL teams and a dozen or so fantasy teams to round out the roster while 2 K releases a game with the 12 NFL teams missing from EA's game and a handful of its own fantasy teams. However, it's also very likely that publishers would have no trouble securing the rights to each individual team for their games. In another interesting scenario, publishers could consider the cost to license individual marks and opt only to enter into agreements with the teams that seemed economically "worth it." After all, it is possible that a publisher does not derive as much value from including the Lions in their game as they do from including the Packers. While the *Madden* franchise will certainly continue to include the full "NFL experience," it's likely that another publisher may want to take advantage of individual licensing agreements to create a scaled-back football experience that only includes top teams. With the *American Needle* decision potentially affecting the NFL, NBA, and NHL (among others), gamers may soon be seeing some big changes in a significant portion of the industry.[159]

Not surprisingly, EA Interactive (whose USD 400 million, 5-year exclusive licensing deal with the NFL was struck in 2004 and was subsequently extended to run, at least, to 2012[160]) has supported the NFL in the litigation. In its *amicus* brief in support of the NFL's defence, EA Interactive declared that 'Licensees such as EA have always viewed NFL Properties as an efficient, one-stop-shop for NFL League intellectual property licenses'.[161] It argued that 'single-entity treatment of NFL Properties provides essential efficiency and certainty' (as for efficiency: 'by negotiating with NFL Properties a licensee such as EA may negotiate and contract with one entity rather than many, thereby lowering transaction costs and allowing

---

[159] Prestia, A 'What *American Needle v NFL* could mean for gamers', 13 January 2010, available online at the time of writing at http://www.lawsofplay.com/articles/what-american-needle-v-nfl-could-mean-for-gamers/.

[160] Good, O 'What the NFL antitrust ruling might mean for *Madden*', 24 May 2010, available online at the time of writing at http://kotaku.com/5546408/what-the-nfl-antitrust-ruling-might-mean-for-madden.

[161] A similar argument was advanced by Major League Baseball Properties (MLBP)'s expert economist in testimony in *Major League Baseball v Salvino, Inc* 542 F. 3d 290 2nd Circuit Court of Appeals (2008) at 303–304, which claimed pro-competitive benefits deriving from the MLBP's collective licensing of clubs' and teams' intellectual property:

'In the absence of one-stop shopping, licensees would incur substantial additional transaction costs; for some, these additional costs would be sufficiently large so as to prevent the licensees from producing some or all of the MLB-related products that they currently produce. Clubs would also incur greater expenses in the form of additional personnel costs to handle the added licensing functions for which they currently rely on MLBP and its centralized administration. Thus, *the absence* of one-stop shopping may well reduce output in the markets in which those licensees compete… one-stop shopping helps broaden the product offerings of MLB Intellectual Property, both to include products that require the use of intellectual property of all 30 MLB Clubs as well as to include product lines that Clubs would normally not spend the money to develop or license. Because it has centralized control over all consumer product licenses, MLBP can ensure that MLB Intellectual Property is licensed for use on a broad array of consumer products. Over the years, this has meant that MLBP has licensed MLB Intellectual Property for use in products such as video games, women's apparel, and household goods. Given the difficulties associated with product licensing and administration, absent MLBP, it is unlikely that the Clubs would ensure such a broad product offering.'

the licensee to pass those savings along to consumers'; and as for certainty: 'treating licensors as single entities allows licensees to negotiate just as they would with any corporate entity, without fear that a unilateral license would lead to an antitrust challenge').[162] The involvement of Electronic Arts in this litigation is even less surprising if one considers that the company is at the time of writing defending a class action law suit filed by purchasers of the *Madden NFL* game, wherein the plaintiffs are claiming that EA's exclusive licence agreement with the NFL violates § 2 of the Sherman Act, on the basis of, *inter alia*, the following claims:

> By signing the exclusive agreement with the NFL, Electronic Arts immediately killed off Take Two's NFL 2K5 software [a previously competing NFL-themed game], the only competing interactive football product of comparable quality to its Madden NFL franchise. Through its agreements with the NCAA and AFL, Electronic Arts prevented Take Two and others from re-entering the market with non-NFL branded interactive football software. Once again without a competitor, Electronic Arts raised its prices dramatically. Specifically, Electronic Arts raised the price of the Madden 2006 videogame (released in August of 2005) nearly seventy percent to $49.95. Electronic Arts currently sells interactive football software for up to $59.95.[163]

The district court in California denied EA's motion to dismiss the claim of violation of § 2, and the case is ongoing at the time of writing. Just to show the thickening of the plot, the plaintiff's lead counsel in this last case, David Paynter, was quoted as expressing the following opinion following the Supreme Court's reversal on the single entity defence in *American Needle*:

> "EA could have an antitrust claim against the NFL," Paynter said. "EA kind of publicly stated that the NFL was the one that insisted on an exclusive license to make one video game. And if so, EA could have a potential damages claim against the NFL, based on the difference between the huge licensing deal it signed, and the (less expensive) one it would have had if the NFL's teams hadn't gotten together and decided to agree to an exclusive group license."

One of the potentially most important areas where the outcome of *American Needle* might turn out to be extremely relevant is, of course, collective bargaining in American professional sports leagues:

> The potentially wider reach of the *American Needle* case, to other pro sports leagues, to league activities beyond trademark licensing, and to other industries is the theme of most of the amici briefs in the case. The players' unions in pro football, baseball, basketball and hockey argued, for example, that the NFL is using this case as "a Trojan horse designed to free sports team owners from Section 1 scrutiny so they can restrain competition with impunity in the market for player services." They predicted the loss of gains made by players over the years, and forecast "labor disputes and work stoppages" if the pro leagues and their team owners gain "broad single-entity" protection. The National Football

---

[162] At p 14 of the brief, a copy of which is available online at the time of writing at http://www.ualberta.ca/~bhumphre/an_docs/ea.pdf.

[163] *Pecover v Electronic Arts, Inc* 633 F.Supp.2d 976 (2009) at 980.

League Coaches Association also argued "that an NFL victory would effectively end competition in the "currently robust" labor market for professional coaches.[164]

The *American Needle* scenario, which quite clearly involves potential anti-competitive effects that may directly affect consumers (e.g. higher sports apparel prices due to the exclusive licensing arrangement with one vendor), probably has more potential to raise the ire of antitrust authorities than the exclusive sponsorship arrangements in respect of sports mega-events as discussed throughout this book. The reader may very well ask, 'why should we worry whether Coca-Cola is the exclusive soft drink sponsor for the Olympic Games and that Pepsi or any number of other producers may be excluded from involvement with the event?'. The short answer is that while the direct effects on consumers (e.g. in respect of the price of goods) may be less drastic in this last case, the potential effects on competition on the relevant market may very well be significant and may similarly demand competition law scrutiny. At the very least I would suggest that the American cases and current developments at the time of writing serve to enforce the view that exclusive sponsorship arrangements in respect of mega-events, just like exclusive licensing arrangements regarding sports-related intellectual property, are potentially problematic in terms of their competition law implications, and that future litigation is likely to follow.

6.3 *Sui Generis* Mega-Event Legislation and Their Potential Competition Law Implications

While the preceding discussion has focused on the potential competition law implications of exclusive sponsorship and other arrangements between event organisers and their commercial partners, it is submitted that one should also in this analysis consider the potential competition law implications of anti-ambush marketing legislation passed in order to protect such commercial interests. In a recent review of ambush marketing legislation commissioned by the Australian government, the following was observed in respect of the considerations that should be borne in mind by legislatures in considering the passing of such special event legislation:

> [T]here are difficulties when certain behaviour referred to as 'ambushing' appears to be little more than firms responding to changes in demand or reacting to their competitors. The difficulty is more pronounced when the said 'ambush' conduct is of type considered to be on the more benign end of the spectrum [i.e. intrusion ambushes]. There is a need to balance the interests of the organisers (assumed to require some intervention) against the interests of promoting competition in other markets (also assumed to require some

[164] Denniston, L 'Pro sports and antitrust: Argument preview', 12 January 2010, www.scotusblog.com (available online at the time of writing at http://www.scotusblog.com/2010/01/pro-sports-and-antitrust-argument-preview/).

> intervention). This reflects an inherent conflict and inescapable trade-off between the objectives of intellectual property law and competition policy. Nevertheless, given this trade-off and the stated objects of [anti-ambush marketing legislation], one would expect that the justification for restricting competition and economic activity would be weaker where the alleged 'ambush' conduct has little impact on the value of the rights being protected or the ability of the organisers to raise revenue.[165]

Lewis and Taylor characterised the special protection for the 2012 London Olympic Games as contained in the London Olympic and Paralympic Games Act, 2006 as 'the legislature not trusting the rights it would accord to businesses but effectively attempting to carve out a state monopoly of the subject matter of intellectual property rights in a way that avoids the pitfalls of the general law'.[166]

One needs to consider to what extent, if any, the anti-ambush marketing protections contained in *sui generis* event legislation as found in various jurisdictions (such as that discussed in Chap. 4) may have special competition or antitrust law implications.

6.3.1 Sui Generis Event Legislation as State Grants of Exclusive Rights: Some Guidance from the EU?

Reference has already been made in this chapter to the main competition law provisions found in the European Union, particularly Article 81 EC (Art 101 TFEU) and Article 82 EC (Art 102 TFEU), dealing with the prohibition on agreements and concerted practises which prevent, restrict or distort competition, and with abuse of dominance, respectively. These provisions are aimed at preventing and sanctioning harmful anti-competitive conduct between and/or involving firms or undertakings. The Treaty also contains a provision which is aimed at preventing anti-competitive behaviour by Member States of the EU themselves, which provision I submit may be relevant in the context of legal scrutiny of the protection afforded to event organisers and their commercial partners by means of the *sui generis* event legislation discussed elsewhere in this book.

Article 86 of the Treaty (Art 106 TFEU) applies to public undertakings and exclusive rights granted by Member States to private undertakings. This article does not have an independent application, and its applicability can only come into question in conjunction with another article of the Treaty, in particular in connection with the provisions of Articles 81 and 82. This provision has come to the fore in cases before the EU competition authorities dealing with claimed

---

165 Frontier Economics 2007, p. 41.

166 From Lewis and Taylor 2007, as quoted by Singer, J & Leadercramer, A 'What is "ambush marketing" in sport and does it represent perfectly legal and normal competitive behaviour?', in *Sports Sponsorship and the Law*—copy available online at the time of writing at http://www.imrpublications.com/Free-Samples.aspx?sid=25&rid=1.

anti-competitive conduct by public undertakings and firms involved in disparate fields ranging from telecommunications[167] to postal services,[168] broadcasting[169] and port freight services[170] to personnel recruitment,[171] and even exclusive rights to artificially inseminate cattle.[172] In light of this last I would suggest that it wouldn't be fanciful to contend that Article 86 may also, potentially, be relevant in the present context in respect of the law's protection of commercial rights to sports mega-events. Article 86 provides as follows:

> Art. 86 (1) In the case of public undertakings and undertakings to which Member States grant special or exclusive rights, Member States shall neither enact nor maintain in force any measures contrary to the rules contained in this Treaty, in particular to those rules provided for in Article [12] and Articles [81 to 90].
> (2) Undertakings entrusted with the operation of services of general economic interest or having the character of a revenue-producing monopoly shall be subject to the rules contained in this Treaty, in particular to the rules on competition, in so far as the application of such rules does not obstruct the performance, in law or in fact, of the particular tasks assigned to them. The development of trade must not be affected to such an extent as would be contrary to the interests of the Community.
> (3) The Commission shall ensure the application of the provisions of this Article and shall, where necessary, address appropriate directives or decisions to Member States.

Article 86(1) requires that a Member State shall neither enact nor maintain in force any measure that is contrary to the Treaty, and States have both a duty not to enact any measure which is contrary to the Treaty, but also a positive obligation to remove any such existing measure. I would suggest that the Article's application to 'public undertakings' is less relevant here than its application to 'undertakings to which Member States grant special or exclusive rights'. The following has been observed regarding this second category of undertakings:

> The second category of undertaking mentioned in Article 86 (1) is narrower and the phrase refers to undertakings not actually public but which have still been granted such special privileges in order to perform functions which are regarded as important by Member State governments. These kinds of undertakings are under the close influence of the State, by the granting of the special or exclusive rights, however the public authorities neither participate in them nor control their management. The special or exclusive rights are defined by legislation for purposes of [for example] the telecommunications sector as: 'the rights

[167] Case C-18/88, *RTT v GB-Inno-BM* [1991] ECR I-5941.

[168] Case C-320/91P, *Procureur du Roi v. Paul Corbeau* [1993] ECR I-2533.

[169] Case C-260/89, *Elliniki Radiophonia Tileorassi AE (ERT) v. Dimotiki Etairia Pliroforissis (DEP) and Sotirios Kouvelas* [1991] ECR I-2925.

[170] Case C-179/90, *Merci Convenzionali Porto di Genova SpA v. Siderurgica Gabrielli SpA* [1991] ECR I-5889.

[171] Case C-41/90, *Höfner and Elser v. Macrotron GmbH* [1991] ECR I-1979.

[172] Case C-323/93, *Société Civile Agricole du Centre d'Insemination de la Crespelle v. Coopérative d'Elevage et d'Insemination Artificielle du Département de la Mayenne* [1994] ECR I-5077.

granted by a Member State or a public authority to one or more public or private bodies through any legal, regulatory or administrative instrument reserving them the right to provide a service or undertake an activity'. The grant of an exclusive right is straightforward and exists where a monopoly has been granted by the State to one entity to engage in a particular economic activity on an exclusive basis.[173]

Enforcement of Article 86(1) may include, in terms of Article 86(3), a directive issued by the Commission addressed to a Member State that is responsible for an infringement to repeal offending legislation.

It has been observed that Article 86 poses a thorny issue within the scheme of the competition provisions of the Treaty, which are aimed at firms and undertakings rather than governments:

> Any interpretation of Article 86(1) in combination with Article 82 is obliged to confront a difficult legal problem: to make sense of combining a rule directed at Member States with a rule directed at undertakings. As far as Article 82 is concerned, the rule in Article 86(1) cannot simply be a reminder of pre-existing prohibitions directed at Member States, but instead that, in combination with Article 82, it has additional content. This additional content consists in some form of extension of the original scope of Article 82 to cover not only the behaviour of undertakings but also State measures. Different theories were developed in order to explain the application of Article 86(1) in combination with Article 82 of the Treaty. Nowadays, it is accepted without discussion that Article 82 imposes direct obligations on public and privileged undertakings, to which Article 86(1) adds complementary State responsibility.[174]

Accordingly, Article 86 would seem to provide an additional basis for EU competition authorities to prevent anti-competitive behaviour by dominant undertakings. Apart from the potential of legal challenge in terms of Article 82, the authorities are also empowered to take action against the governments of Member States where such governments, through their conduct (including legislation), facilitate or cause potential contravention of the abuse of dominance provisions of Article 82 (or the provisions of Article 81). It is here where I contend Article 86 is relevant to *sui generis* event legislation.

I have, in the preceding sections of this chapter, discussed the potential for abuse of dominance by event organisers and their commercial partners in respect of mega-event commercial rights exploitation. This can manifest in a variety of ways which may impact on consumers and/or other commercial enterprises (e.g. non-sponsor firms). These may relate to pricing (e.g. the charging of higher prices for tickets or event-related licensed merchandise) or to other forms of abuse (such as refusals to deal, 'tying', or limiting the market to the detriment of consumers).[175] And here Article 86 may become relevant:

---

173 Seferidis 2006, pp. 10–11.

174 Seferidis 2006, p. 22.

175 See, for example, Fortunato and Richards 2007, p. 33.

> Article 82 seeks to ensure, so far as possible, that the behaviour of the dominant undertaking does not result in the consumer being deprived of the benefits which could be expected to result from the normal play of market forces. Where the law of a Member State establishes such a monopoly and the body entrusted with its operation manifestly fails to satisfy the demand for the services in question, that failure constitutes an abuse of a dominant position within the meaning of Article 86...[176]

It is my contention that where such potential abuse of a dominant position in respect of the mega-event is facilitated, encouraged and promoted by means of special purpose (and special interest) legislation passed by a domestic legislature (in a Member State of the EU, of course), such legislation may conceivably fall foul of the provisions of Article 86. However, I would suggest that the principle of providing a basis for investigating and sanctioning the role of government facilitation of abuse of dominance should also apply outside the context of the EU. When one examines the legitimacy of special event legislation, as I do elsewhere in this book, I believe that the role of government patronage of the private mega-event monopoly through the means of *sui generis* legislation should be considered, critically. Seferidis observes:

> Exclusive rights confer dominant positions, and therefore the fact that they make possible abuses of a dominant position is obvious. However, in the absence of other factors... the mere existence of exclusive rights does not necessarily lead to abuses being committed by the undertakings benefiting from such rights.[177]

I have argued elsewhere in this book that the mega-event monopoly does, in fact, appear to go hand-in-hand with abuses of dominance by the event organisers and their commercial partners, and that this reality is only now starting to draw the attention of the legal fraternity and others in the form of critical consideration of the potential and real effects. The anti-ambush marketing provisions (and other provisions) contained in the *sui generis* event legislation in the various jurisdictions (as discussed in Chap. 4) are, by definition, aimed at protecting organisers' and sponsors' exclusive rights to events. As I have argued, the force of law is provided to private (contractual) arrangements; legislation is employed to protect and foster exclusivity in the commercial exploitation of rights ranging from sponsorship rights and broadcasting rights to the licensing of intellectual property for purposes of event-related merchandising, and to serious curtailment of individuals' freedom to trade in 'clean zones'. Anti-ambushing provisions—specifically the so-called 'association rights' to events—have the very purpose of prohibiting and sometimes criminalising competition in respect of marketing related to a protected event, and one might ask whether the following comment regarding the European Court of Justice's judgment in the *Corbeau* case[178] (an

---

[176] Seferidis 2006, p. 28, with reference to Case C-41/90, *Höfner and Elser v. Macrotron GmbH* [1991] ECR I-1979.

[177] Seferidis 2006, p. 32.

[178] Case C-320/91P, *Procureur du Roi v. Paul Corbeau* [1993] ECR I-2533.

Article 86 challenge regarding a Belgian postal service) is not entirely germane in this context:

> If the purpose with Article 82 is to prevent distortion, restriction or elimination of competition caused by the abusive behaviour of undertakings, a State measure which totally eliminates competition will have the same effects as such behaviour. Since the behaviour of undertakings would have been contrary to Article 82, such State measures are contrary to Article 86(1) in conjunction with Article 82.[179]

I will leave this issue here, as I am speculating as to the potential relevance of this section of the Treaty in the mega-event ambushing scenario. I do, however, suggest that this potential relevance be considered; as we have seen in the earlier chapters, the commercial rights arrangements (including sponsorship exclusivity) around mega-events are dubious in respect of their legal implications, including (as discussed earlier in this chapter) their considerable anti-competitive effects. The legislative bolstering of such commercial monopoly by governments and lawmakers, however, serves to expose such anti-competitive measures to an additional basis for competition law scrutiny. I would suggest that, within the meaning of Article 86(2) (Art. 106(2) TFEU), mega-event organisers are undertakings 'entrusted with the operation of services of general economic interest' (this would be bolstered by these organisers' frequent claims of economic benefits to host nations of the hosting of their events, and the fact that such events are significantly publicly funded) or 'having the character of a revenue-producing monopoly' (more will be said in this regard in Chap. 9). Active and far-reaching state support of such monopolies by means of the often controversial *sui generis* event legislation supports a finding that these organisers are undertakings to which states grant special or exclusive rights, and I view such scenario as subject to the these relevant Treaty provisions and that this may also provide some guidance to competition authorities in jurisdictions outside the European Union.

6.3.2 *The Potential Anti-Competitive Effects of Sui Generis Event Legislation: A Very Brief Overview*

I suggested in the previous section that the *sui generis* event legislation as passed by event host lawmakers to bolster the mega-event monopoly enjoyed by event organisers and their sponsors may be open to competition law scrutiny. It bears consideration, briefly, of how such special event laws and their provisions may be anti-competitive. The following discussion will be brief because all three the aspects to be discussed are covered in more depth in other chapters. In line with the general trend in this chapter I will just pose some general questions or point to potential issues of relevance in respect of competition law implications.

179 Seferidis 2006, p. 38.

The first measure as contained in special anti-ambushing laws relates to provisions regarding event organisers' rights to exclusive use of event symbols and words. I have discussed this in more detail in other chapters, and will here simply remind the reader of the apparent trend in recent years to establish a 'monopoly on language' in respect of mega-events (as discussed in Chap. 5). This holds significant free speech implications, but also, I would suggest, raises issues regarding restrictions on competition in the marketing industry. These exclusive rights limit access to the use of sometimes generic words which would, in the absence of such provisions, be in the public domain. I believe that their effects may require consideration from a competition law perspective.

The second measure, namely the creation by means of such legislation of 'association rights' to events, may also, in my view, have competition law implications. I will discuss these association rights in more detail in Chap. 8, but for now it simply bears mentioning that their purpose is to restrict marketing or other commercially-motivated conduct, and as such they may significantly affect both free competition within the marketing and advertising industries as well as businesses' freedom of trade, more generally. And when one considers the 'rule of reason' approach in determining justification of such restrictions and/or potentially anti-competitive effects of these rights, I would suggest that the apparent lack of a consumer protection rationale and of requirements for the enforcers of these rights to show harm by potential infringers (as I will discuss in more detail in Chap. 8) may be important factors to take into consideration and which may militate against a finding of pro-competitive effects outweighing the anti-competitive effects of such measures.

Finally, as mentioned in earlier chapters, one of the main mechanisms employed in recent years in mega-event host jurisdictions in order to combat ambushing of events is the declaration (and often aggressive policing) of demarcated geographical areas within host cities and in event precincts that are, for the duration of 'clean periods', to be kept free of advertising and trading which might potentially infringe anti-ambushing laws. These areas include so-called 'clean zones' and 'clean transport routes', in which advertising may be prohibited for certain periods (e.g. through the control of public billboard space) or trading (e.g. by street traders and other members of the informal sector) may be regulated or prohibited outright. These clean zones are controversial, mainly because they directly (and sometimes significantly) affect the rights of existing traders who may have no official or even indirect connection with events apart from their location. During the 2010 FIFA World Cup, for example, there was public outcry from traders, including 'mom and pop shops' in cities such as Durban. In October 2008 the British Columbia Civil Liberties Association (or BCCLA) filed a complaint with competition authorities against the buying up of billboard and other advertising space by the organisers of the 2010 Vancouver Winter Games, VANOC. The BCCLA claimed that VANOC's purchasing of outdoor advertising space for a ten week-period around the staging of the Games breached the Competition Act's prohibition on anti-competitive activities, including 'pre-emption of scarce facilities or resources required by a competitor for the operation of a business, with the object of withholding the facilities or resources from a market'. BCCLA claimed that this constituted 'an unconscionable effort to suppress other viewpoints', thus '[a]llowing government-sponsored organizations, like VANOC, to eliminate the right of others to put their message out before the public [which] is just as offensive as would be allowing monopolies in the press and media to do so generally'.[180]

These clean zones also, generally, appear to constitute a bit of an anomaly in the context of the event organisers' and host nations' own efforts at marketing the events. The unhappiness on the part of affected traders may be understandable not only due to the imposition, by law, of substantial curbs on freedom of trade, but also because of the mixed message that they often send. Compare the following, contained in a district council press release regarding the clean zones declared for the 2011 IRB Rugby World Cup matches to be played in the city of Roturua in New Zealand in September 2011:

> Retailers and other businesses are being encouraged to dress up their premises as part of the celebrations but need to be aware about government restrictions in place to guard against 'ambush marketing'—making commercial gains from unauthorised association with the tournament.[181]

Mention is made elsewhere (in Chap. 9, specifically) to a 'new' justification that has been advanced in respect of anti-ambushing measures by event organisers for recent events, namely the aesthetics argument which relates to protection of the 'celebratory look and feel' of the event. This has, specifically, been a basis for purported justification expressly relied upon by the UK government's Department of Media, Culture and Sport in respect of its advertising and street trading regulations published for the 2012 London Games (see Chap. 7). I believe that these arguments are tenuous, especially considering both the potential and real impact of these clean zones on fundamental rights of traders and others, but also because they seem to imply a certain weighting in favour of the 'official' message which event organisers and their sponsors which to send. There appears to be significant reliance on protecting an idealised notion of 'the Games' and to prevent crass commercialism; this in an environment where sponsor surveys (as referred to elsewhere in this book) appear to show that event organisers and their sponsors may, to a significant extent, be some of the worst sinners in this regard by causing large-scale advertising clutter through their own marketing activities. For the official sponsors this relates to efforts at saturation sponsorship; for event organisers this relates to the maximisation of revenues through possible over-extending opportunities for the granting of rights. I believe these are factors which would

---

[180] From the BCCLA press release dated 8 October 2008, available online at the time of writing at http://www.cba.org/cba/cle/PDF/INTL10_Holmes_paper1.pdf.

[181] "Clean zones" in Rotorua for Rugby World Cup 2011', available online at the time of writing at http://www.worldcup2011newzealand.com/2011/05/clean-zones-in-rotorua-for-rugby-world-cup-2011/.

bear consideration in consideration of justification for potential anti-competitive effects of such clean zones.

Clean zones have become par for the course as one of the main forms of anti-ambushing protections contained in *sui generis* event legislation. Examples are found in New Zealand's Major Events Management Act, 2007 (in section 16); the London Olympic and Paralympic Games Act, 2006 (in sections 19 and 25); and in the Host City By-Laws passed for FIFA's 2010 World Cup in South Africa. Their potential anti-competitive effects, however, may necessitate critical evaluation of their legitimacy as an anti-ambushing tool; remember that these measures are aimed primarily at combating 'intrusion ambushing', which by definition do not raise the much more convincing grounds for justification associated with the 'association ambush'. This should, undoubtedly, influence the determination of justification for any anti-competitive effects.

The UK government's Department of Culture, Media and Sport (or DCMS) recently (in September 2011) published an Impact Assessment document[182] which contained a number of arguments in purported justification of the draft London Olympic Games and Paralympic Games (Advertising and Trading) Regulations 2011, which had been published in early 2011 and had undergone a process of soliciting public comments. In an annexure to this document the DCMS dealt with a 'competition assessment' of such regulations. It did so with reference to revised guidelines for government departments in respect of competition assessments as published in 2007 by the Office of Fair Trading, which guidelines focus on the consideration of four questions:

(1) Do the proposed regulations 'directly limit number or range of suppliers'?
(2) Do the proposed regulations 'indirectly limit the number or range of suppliers'?
(3) Do the proposed regulations 'limit the ability of suppliers to compete'?
(4) Do the proposed regulations 'reduce suppliers' incentive to compete vigorously'?

The DCMS expressed the opinion that both the first two questions were to be answered in the negative:

> There is no exclusivity over supplying products to traders or advertisers. Wherever possible we are looking to authorise traders to continue to trade in the vicinity of Olympic venues and advertising space will be utilised. We are restricting any potential for new trade, illegal advertising and trading but for those legitimate traders we will make every effort to ensure they can continue to trade. For those we do restrict this will be for a short time and in a limited geographical space. We are not making a permanent change of business in the relevant areas.[183]

I would suggest that this justification for the restrictions misses the point, although it obliquely refers to it. The question is not whether 'legitimate' traders will be allowed to continue trading (or that 'every effort will be made' to ensure this), but rather the fact

[182] A copy of which is available online at the time of writing at http://www.legislation.gov.uk/ukdsi/2011/9780111515969/pdfs/ukdsifia_9780111515969_en.pdf.

[183] From Annex 2 of the DCMS Impact Assessment document (at 17).

that the inherently restrictive force of the regulations relates to determination of who such legitimate traders are and who does not qualify for this status. It is acknowledged that 'new traders' and 'illegal' traders and advertisers are restricted, and this is the crux of the anti-competitive effects of such regulations. The question is really what the anti-competitive effects are of the labelling of a trader as 'illegal' (i.e. an ambusher or otherwise unwanted trader) and the concomitant restriction of their trade. The only justification for the restriction on trade of such persons is that the restrictions are for a short time and in a limited geographical space. The fact that the regulations do not make a 'permanent change of business' in the relevant areas downplays the possibly extremely severe nature and effect of such restrictions on otherwise legitimate traders. In Chap. 7 I refer to the similar argument advanced by the DCMS in justification of the potential limitation of freedom of speech as occasioned by its proposed regulations, i.e. the limited time and geographical area for their application. I make the point there that this approach appears to ignore the nature and content of the rights so restricted. In the case of advertising restrictions on free commercial speech, the protected right includes the right holder's choice to use the event as a marketing platform, and the duration (or, for that matter, the geographical scope) of the restriction does not serve to make the restriction proportionate and justifiable. The gist of the anti-competitive effects of these regulations lies in its determination of who is or isn't a 'legitimate trader' (which is aimed primarily at protecting the commercial rights and exclusivity of official sponsors), and the justification for the then significant restriction in the form of a complete prohibition (i.e. an absolute negation) of the right to trade is not, in my view, sufficiently justified by means of recourse to the duration or geographical scope of such negation of the right in question. Bear in mind also that the pro-competitive effects of such restrictions are questionable. If competition law is aimed, primarily, not at protecting competitors but at protecting consumers against anti-competitive conduct, then the consideration of the pro-competitive effects of such regulations must include consideration of the benefits for consumers. In this regard I would suggest that something as flaky as the 'celebratory look and feel of the Games' is insufficient to tip the scales in favour of such regulations, and it is hard to imagine how the outright prohibition on certain traders and advertisers operating within clean zones, which, by definition, means a reduction in sources of supply of goods or services for consumers in such zones, is likely to benefit the consumer. When one considers venue ticket terms and conditions (as discussed elsewhere) relating, for example, to restrictions on what soft drinks or hamburgers a spectator is allowed to bring into the venue, it is clear that the consumer is faced, on the one hand, with a limited source of supply (e.g. only 'official' McDonald's burgers are sold in the clean zone) and the consumer may, on the other hand, not take any other burger into the stadium. As Fortunato and Richards have observed in the context of the implications of sponsorship exclusivity for free speech (as discussed elsewhere): '[I]t is the spectator who is affected by these monopolies. It is time to stop taking advantage of them. The spectator's right of free choice deserves at least a modicum of respect and protection.'[184]

---

[184] Fortunato and Richards 2007, p. 48.

In the Impact Assessment document the DCMS answered in the affirmative to questions 3 and 4 as quoted above. In respect of question 3 it expressed its opinion that 'Both advertising and trading will be limited in terms of what product they can promote however this limitation will only be in place within a restricted area and for a limited time. I would advance the same arguments as above in suggesting that this justification is simply insufficient to deal with the anti-competitive effects of the restrictions imposed. In respect of question 4 the following is expressed by the DCMS:

> We are restricting who may advertise or trade in specific areas so there will inevitably be an impact on competition. In addition we are limiting both the number/range of suppliers and their ability to compete. However, the restrictions are not substantial or long lasting enough to have a significant impact as they will only be applied to a tightly defined area for a limited period. The Games will generate a significant influx of new trade to the wider area and arguably there is scope for exploiting the market outside these areas. We therefore consider that this policy is unlikely to raise substantive competition concerns.[185]

I disagree. Apart from the reasons provided above (and specifically the apparent negation or, at least, complete ignoring of the interests of consumers in the determination of anti-competitive effects of the regulations) it is also, indeed, arguable whether 'there is scope for exploiting the market outside these areas' affected by the regulations. Remember that strict anti-ambushing legislation applies to the 2012 London Games, including the far-reaching 'association rights' to the event, and the above statement is a rather optimistic take on the ability of domestic businesses to derive any form of commercial benefit from the celebration that is the Games. This view ignores the wider context of the generally anti-competitive framework established by such legislation. If one considers other views expressed in purported justification of the regulations by the UK government (for example, in a short section dealing with the impact of the proposed regulations on small firms, the DCMS reiterates its above, rather narrow, argument though some hyperbole, by stating that 'whilst we prevent some traders from trading, this will only be for a limited period in less that 0,01% of the land mass of Great Britain, 1,2% of London') it is clear, to me at least, that these purported grounds of justification simply downplay the actual and substantial anti-competitive effects of these regulations in an extremely dismissive fashion.

Finally, and more generally, in considering the position of traders affected by clean zone regulations in host cities I am sometimes reminded of the defence found in the law of nuisance which is known as 'coming to the nuisance' (i.e. where the claimant has moved to a site where the nuisance has existed for a long time and subsequently complains). I have also elsewhere referred to an aspect of aggressive event rights protection which seems to rest on rather shaky ground, namely the practise of clean venues employed by event organisers (e.g. FIFA, which requires event venues to be exclusive use zones for the duration of their World Cup event and which necessitates existing stadium naming rights holders to

[185] The DCMA Impact Assessment document, Annex 2 at 18.

relinquish such rights). There appears to be no consideration given to the fact that existing rights should, in fairness, enjoy some measure of precedence over the event organiser's 'Johnnie-come-lately' status. I believe that it adds insult to injury for event organisers to insist on the enforcement of such severe restrictions on the rights of existing traders (e.g. the mom and pop stores or family businesses which may have been trading for generations) in event venue precincts, and for legislatures to then attempt to justify such draconian restrictions in such a dismissive manner and without recourse to full and properly argued justification which takes into account the interests of all the relevant stakeholders and not only those of the event organiser and its multinational corporate sponsors.

6.4 Conclusion

Andrew Carnegie was famously quoted as expressing the following view on competition:

> The price which society pays for the law of competition, like the price it pays for cheap comforts and luxuries, is great; but the advantages of this law are also greater still than its cost—for it is to this law that we owe our wonderful material development, which brings improved conditions in its train. But, whether the law be benign or not, we must say of it: It is here; we cannot evade it; no substitutes for it have been found; and while the law may be sometimes hard for the individual, it is best for the race, because it ensures the survival of the fittest in every department.

Ambush marketing is, essentially, all about competition, between the ambusher and the official sponsor (and event organiser). We have seen that the modern commercial rights programme in respect of event sponsorship is built around the concept of exclusivity. This very concept, then, is potentially and by definition anti-competitive. Event organisers earn millions of dollars by selling rights to associate with the event which fundamentally are aimed at excluding others from competing with the rights holders (motivated, to a significant extent, by the organisers' interest in maintaining and even increasing the level of rights fees). Those who attempt to compete with these sponsors without paying for the right to do so are accused of unlawfully competing, while the official sponsors pay for the privilege to sponsor the event in order to obtain a competitive advantage (which advantage is, of course, significantly enhanced by the exclusivity of the rights granted). Lingling Wei, in a recent paper presented at a European intellectual property policy conference, expressed doubts over the legitimacy of the promotion of competition as basis for combating ambushing:

> For those who engage in sponsorship activities, such companies focus on whether or not their competitors will benefit from the events at their expense. Thus their commercial rivals' ambush marketing (either by intrusion or by association), will irritate the former, and hamper them achieving the competitive advantage they expect. Competition, however,

is the designed function of the sponsorship and accordingly does not provide a legitimate reason for regulating ambush marketing.[186]

If one considers that not all forms of 'ambushing' are necessarily unethical or should be prohibited by law (as I have argued is the case in the earlier chapters), then the current blanket bans imposed by event organisers and the lawmakers who bow to the demands for stringent and far-reaching protection are inherently anti-competitive. It makes sense that not only the concept of sponsorship exclusivity but also any laws passed specifically to enforce or protect it may have an anti-competitive effect. Event organisers in the sports mega-event context are inherent monopolists who, due largely to an accident of history, enjoy a dominant position in the market for the brand that is the mega-event. The question is whether their granting of exclusive rights and, importantly, the ways in which such rights are granted, amounts to abuse of such dominant position. And the focus, in terms of a rule of reason approach, must be on the justification for any anti-competitive effects of this model of sponsorship and of the legal provisions employed to protect it.

As mentioned earlier in this chapter there is currently a dearth of case law, in all jurisdictions, specifically dealing with competition law issues in sports sponsorship, and especially in the context of mega-event sponsorship. My discussion has therefore been largely speculative. I will step off the subject by simply observing that I believe such challenges may present in future and that I do not view the mega-event sponsorship model as immune to such competition laws, by any means. When one considers that efforts to combat 'ambushing' are essentially aimed at restricting competition in marketing surrounding the events, I believe that this is one area of law which should play a more prominent role in future discourse on ambush marketing, especially in respect of combating 'intrusion ambushing'.

References

All internet-based sources referred to, were last visited in or before December 2011.

Andreff W, Szymanski S (2006) Handbook on the economics of sport. Edward Elgar Publishing Ltd, London

Barnett M, Smith S, Horvitz S (2007) Expanding exclusivity: AT&T v Sprint, NASCAR. Competition Law 360. Portfolio Media Inc, New York

Barney RK, Wenn SR, Martyn SG (2004) Selling the five rings. University of Utah Press, Salt Lake City

Bently L, Davis J, Ginsburg JC (eds) (2008) Trade marks and brands: an interdisciplinary critique. Cambridge University Press, Cambridge

[186] Lingling Wei 'Ambush marketing: Where is the base?'—paper presented at the European Policy for Intellectual Property association's 6th Annual Conference, September 2011, Brussels, Belgium (copy available online at the time of writing at http://www.epip.eu/conferences/epip06/papers/Parallel%20Session%20Papers/WEI%20Lingling.pdf).

Blackshaw I, Cornelius S, Siekmann R (eds) (2009) TV rights and sport: legal aspects. T.M.C. Asser Press, The Hague

Blanpain R (2003) The legal status of sportsmen and sportswomen under international, European and Belgian national and regional law. Kluwer Law International, The Hague

Cobbs J (2011) Legal battles for sponsorship exclusivity: the cases of the World Cup and NASCAR. Sport Management Review 14(3):258–268

Corbett S, Van Roy Y (2010) Events management in New Zealand: one law to rule them all? J Bus Law 4:338–362

Ducrey P, Ferreira C, Huerta G, Marston K (2004) UEFA and Football Governance: a new model. Int Sports Law J 1–2:85

Elhauge E, Geradin D (2007) Global competition law and economics. Hart Publishing, Portland

Fetter FA (1904) The Principles of Economics with Applications to Practical Problems. The Century Co, New York

Fortunato JA, Martin SE (2011) *American Needle v NFL*: Legal and Sponsorship Implications. Univ Denver Sports Entertain Law J 9:73

Fortunato JA, Richards J (2007) Reconciling sports sponsorship exclusivity with antitrust law. Texas Rev Entertain Sports Law 8:33

Frontier Economics Pty Ltd, Melbourne (2007) Ambush marketing legislation review, a report prepared for IP Australia and the Australian government's department of communications, information technology and the arts (October 2007)

Gardiner et al (2006) Sports law, 3rd edn. Cavendish Publishing Ltd, Oxford

Harrison B, Smith C, Davies B (1992) Introductory economics. McMillan Press Ltd, London

Jennings A (2006) Foul! the secret world of FIFA: bribes, vote rigging and ticket scandals. Harper Sport, London

Kelbrick R (2008) Ambush marketing and the protection of the trade marks of international sports organizations—a comparative view. CILSA 41(1):24–48

Kishner IA, Albinsky J (2011) Very much ado about… nothing: an analysis of the impact of *American Needle v NFL* on collective bargaining and merchandising in professional sports. Entertain Sports Lawyer 29(1):3

Kobel P (2007) International report on question B: ambush marketing too smart to be good? Should certain ambush marketing practices be declared illegal and if yes, which ones and under what conditions? International report to the international league of competition law, Catania Congress

Lewis A, Taylor J (2007) Sport: law and practice. Tottel Publishing, Haywards Heath

Louw AM (2007) An anomaly tolerated by the law: examining the nature and legal significance of the international sports governing body. S Afr Public Law 1:211–255

Marcus JT (2010) Ambush marketing: an analysis of its threat to sports rights holders and the efficacy of past, present and proposed anti-infringement programmes. Sport Law J 18(1):25

McCann MA (2009) *American Needle v NFL*: an opportunity to reshape sports law. Yale Law J 119:101

McKelvey S, Grady J (2008) Sponsorship program protection strategies for special sport events: are event organizers outmaneuvering ambush marketers? J Sport Manag 22:550–586

Miller RL (1999) Economics Today. Addison Wesley Longman Inc, Boston

Monti G (2007) EC competition law. Cambridge University Press, Cambridge

Phillips J (2006) 'Play the game, kill the competition', an editorial regarding anti-ambush marketing protection as contained in the London Olympic and Paralympic Games Act, 2006. J Intellect Prop Law Pract 1(2):79

Pound RW (2006) Inside the Olympics. Wiley, Canada

Rousseva E (2010) Rethinking exclusionary abuses in EU competition law. Hart Publishing, Oxford

Sarantakes NE (2010) Dropping the torch: Jimmy Carter, the Olympic boycott and the cold war. Cambridge University Press, Cambridge

Scaria AG (2008) Ambush marketing: game within a game. Oxford University Press, Oxford

Schulz-Herzenberg C (ed) (2010) Player and referee: conflicting interests and the 2010 FIFA World Cup™ monograph 169, South African institute for security studies, April 2010

Schwab F (2006) FIFA's trademark tactics. World Trademark Rev 3:6

Seferidis E (2006) Exclusive rights under article 86(1) EC. Masters thesis in European community law, faculty of law, university of Lund (Spring 2006). http://lup.lub.lu.se/luur

Taylor PL, Pinguelo FM, Cedrone TD (2010) The reverse-morals clause: the unique way to save talent's reputation and money in a new era of corporate crimes and scandals. Cardozo Arts Entertain Law J 28:65

Wise AN, Meyer BS (1997) International Sports Law and Business, vol 3. Kluwer Law International, Cambridge

Chapter 7
Mega-Event Commercial Rights Protection and Human Rights

> Brands… are often put to work by powerful corporations to crowd out equally legitimate expression. They tend to stifle the open and free flow of ideas. Brand building… sets out to occupy cultural space, social space and even one's own "headspace". Since, in time, marketing brands graduate to cultural icons, they should not be beyond the reach of public disclaim or indeed applause. The purpose of copyright and trade mark laws in an open and democratic society is not to shut out critical expression or to throttle artistic and other expressive acts in a manner that gives way to inordinate brand sway.[1]
>
> The legal/constitutional framework of each country in which anti-ambush marketing legislation is enacted will inevitably have an impact on the scope and boundaries of the rights created. Thus there may be significant differences in anti-ambush marketing protection from one jurisdiction to another… [T]he presence of meaningful constitutional rights and freedoms in a jurisdiction may further circumscribe the scope of anti-ambush marketing legislation or may raise issues down the road as to the legitimacy of the protection or the legality of its enforcement.[2]
>
> One person's ambush is another's free speech[3]

7.1 Introduction

The previous chapters have examined various legal implications of the commercial monopoly in sports mega-events as enjoyed by event organisers and sponsors, and of the laws used to protect a wealthy club of 'rights owners' against ambush marketing. The focus of much of my criticism of the existing position in this regard has been on the commercial interests of alleged 'ambushers' (i.e. in respect of intellectual property rights and competition law issues). The focus must now shift,

---

[1] The 'pith' of the applicant (on appeal)'s freedom of expression (and parody) defence to a trademark dilution claim, as expressed by Moseneke J in the South African Constitutional Court judgment in *Laugh It Off Promotions CC v South African Breweries International (Finance) BV t/a Sabmark International and Another* (CCT42/04) [2005] ZACC 7; 2006 (1) SA 144 (CC); 2005 (8) BCLR 743 (CC) (27 May 2005), at par. 13 of the judgment.

[2] Ellis et al. 2011, p. 304.

[3] Title of an article by Retsky, M L in *Marketing News* (30)14 (1996) 14.

A. M. Louw, *Ambush Marketing and the Mega-Event Monopoly*,
ASSER International Sports Law Series, DOI: 10.1007/978-90-6704-864-4_7,

more generally, to the effects of such monopoly and of the laws used to buttress it on Joe Soap, or the populace of host nations or cities in respect of these events. I will do so briefly (this is a short chapter) by examining some of the human rights implications of the commercially driven mega-event monopoly and of anti-ambushing laws. I believe that this is an area that has been largely neglected in scholarly literature, and my aim here is simply to provide a brief overview of potential grounds for human rights-based challenges to anti-ambushing laws with the hope that others will take up the task of further examining these issues.

Various aspects of the organisation and staging of mega-events implicate human rights. By way of example, consider the practice of 'spring cleaning' of event venue precincts, i.e. the forced removal of the homeless in terms of urban beautification projects (with cities such as Beijing, for the 2008 Olympics, and New Delhi, for the 2011 Commonwealth Games, being prime examples of the problems that may be encountered in this regard). Amnesty International, in June 2010, expressed concern over increased human rights violations in South Africa regarding the 2010 FIFA World Cup, including an increase in police harassment of informal traders, homeless South Africans and refugees and migrants living in shelters or high density inner city accommodation. Raquel Rolnik, special rapporteur on adequate housing for the United Nations Human Rights Council (and author of a March 2010 report on housing rights and mega-events[4]), was quoted in the media in April 2011 as accusing Brazilian officials of potentially violating human rights in cities such as Sao Paulo and Rio de Janeiro where families are being evicted ahead of the 2014 FIFA World Cup and 2016 Olympic Games.[5] In an online interview in August 2011 Rolnik expressed her thoughts on the seriousness of the threat posed by mega-events to the respect of human rights by host governments:

> FIFA is increasingly taking over the entire process of producing the event and signing protocols, and these protocols have already been signed off by the country and the cities to have the World Cup. Making demands not only to areas around the stadiums, but for the encompassing communities, requiring, for example, the exclusive sale of a certain brand of liquor in an area miles around a stadium. There are many violations that end up constituting a real state of emergency. That is, having the World Cup, a mega event, you basically justify not having to enforce human rights, environmental legislation? It's like they are suspended rights much like a state of emergency due to a war or a catastrophe. Increasingly, mega-events have been like this.[6]

---

[4] See the report of March 2010, which calls on FIFA and the IOC (and host governments) to ensure that mega-events such as the football World Cup and the Olympic Games do not lead to the displacement of the poor, through forced evictions, criminalisation of homeless persons and informal activities, and the dismantling of informal settlements—see the report entitled 'Olympics and World Cup soccer must take up cause of right to housing—UN expert', 9 March 2010, available on the web site of the UN News Centre at www.un.org [accessed 20 March 2010].

[5] See the report dated 28 April 2011 available online at the time of writing at http://www.gringos.com/brazil/un-special-rapporteur-calls-for-halt-to-olympic-and-world-cup-slum-clearances-in-brazil.html.

[6] See the interview, posted on 1 August 2011, available online at the time of writing at http://1mundoreal.org/residents-being-removed-for-world-cup.

Others have also engaged with the human rights implications of mega-events. Helen Jefferson Lenskyj, for example, states that '[t]he Olympic industry poses serious threats to free speech, in the form of a free press, and to freedom of assembly, in the form of peaceful protest'.[7] At the most extreme end of the spectrum, mega-events have in recent years also raised special concerns regarding human trafficking. And one should remember that sports mega-events (ironically, from the perspective of the event organisers and sponsors, if one considers the vast publicity machine and media coverage that is used to promote such events) offers an ideal vehicle for public protest also on non-event-related issues. As was observed in respect of the 2010 Winter Olympics:

> Vancouver's 2010 Olympic Winter Games can be seen as a compressed *time* and *space* in which broader relations of capital (along with imperialism, and repression) played out in a historically specific dynamic. This local, two-week mega-event represents the culmination—on a global stage—of many years and billions of dollars of corporate and publicly financed development, advertising, and merchandising; it thus presented activists with a poignant opportunity for critique and resistance.[8]

These human rights issues are increasingly making headlines nowadays, although it is also true that 'the profile of the events is such that… normal planning procedures are often suspended and the focus is on making the Games run well rather than their wider community and social impact'.[9] Such issues are often apparently swept under the carpet in the interests of the perceived greater good of putting on a good show, not unlike (I would suggest) the trampling of individuals' rights and even the rule of law in the context of protecting the party planning committee and its commercial benefactors by means of anti-ambushing laws. This chapter will not deal with these, more general, issues of human rights implications and civil rights violations in mega-event host jurisdictions. In keeping with the central theme of this book I will focus on the potential (and real) human rights implications specifically with reference to the commercial rights protection programmes and anti-ambushing measures regarding such events.

I will do so by using as my point of departure the example of fundamental rights as guaranteed in the Bill of Rights of one specific jurisdiction, South Africa. The reasons for this are, first, and from a practical perspective, my preference for engaging with the legal system with which I am most familiar. Second, the South African Constitution of 1996 (and its Bill of Rights) is generally viewed as being among the most progressive to be found anywhere in the world, and the South African Constitutional Court's judgments are studied with interest at universities in other countries. I believe that it makes sense to identify relevant human rights guarantees as contained in this instrument, and incorporating discussion of their

---

7 Jefferson Lenskyj 2008, p. 19. See also Jefferson Lenskyj 2000, Shaw 2008, Chap. 13.

8 Murray, K 'resisting the 2010 Olympics: Learning within the praxis of activism' 8th World Congress on Participatory Action Research and Action learning, 6–9 September 2010—available online at http://wc2010.alara.net.au/Formatted%20Papers/2.2.5.ICD.1.Paper.pdf.

9 Ritchie and Hall 2000.

treatment in other jurisdictions for the sake of providing a comprehensive overview which is relevant also beyond the context of this single jurisdiction. In light of the focus on South African law, the discussion in this chapter will also mostly focus on the recent 2010 FIFA World Cup South Africa, although the issues discussed now appear to be relevant at all mega-events.

I will proceed with an extremely brief overview of the South African Bill of Rights, and will then focus the discussion on three rights or fundamental guarantees which I view as most important for purposes of this chapter. These are the freedom of expression; freedom of trade, occupation and profession and the entrenchment of the fundamental right to property. In respect of the anti-ambush marketing measures which will be referred to here, I will focus mostly on two specific types:

(1) The prohibition on advertising which may be viewed as infringing anti-ambushing laws as contained in *sui generis* event legislation (this may include television advertising as well as advertising in print and other media); and
(2) 'Clean zones' surrounding event venues (such measures, and their potential impact on the human rights of individuals or entrepreneurs, include both prohibitions on advertising (e.g. in outdoor media) and prohibitions on trading).

First, though, some background on the South African Bill of Rights and how it works. section 2 of the South African Constitution[10] provides that any law or conduct inconsistent with its provisions is invalid. As mentioned, the South African Bill of Rights is particularly progressive and comprehensive, and it guarantees the fundamental rights of all South Africans and affirms the democratic values of human dignity, equality and freedom.[11] The Bill of Rights[12] applies to all law, and is binding on the legislature, the executive, the judiciary and all organs of state. It is also binding on natural and juristic persons if, and to the extent that, it is applicable, taking into account the nature of the right and any duty imposed by the right.[13] The fundamental rights as contained in the Bill of Rights may only be limited in terms of the provisions of the limitations clause contained in section 36

---

[10] Constitution of the Republic of South Africa, 1996.

[11] Constitution of the Republic of South Africa sec. 7(1).

[12] As contained in Chap. 2 of the Constitution. For detailed discussion of the rights contained in the Bill of Rights and case law regarding its interpretation and application, the reader is referred to more specialised texts on the subject—see Currie and de Waal 2005, Cheadle et al. 2005, Devenish 2005.

[13] Constitution of the Republic of South Africa sections 8(1) and (2). Section 8 of the Bill of Rights provides as follows:

> 8(1) The Bill of Rights applies to all law, and binds the legislature, the executive, the judiciary and all organs of state.
> 8(2) A provision of the Bill of Rights binds a natural or a juristic person if, and to the extent that, it is applicable, taking into account the nature of the right and the nature of any duty imposed by the right.
> 8(3) When applying a provision of the Bill of Rights to a natural or juristic person in terms of subsection (2), a court

of the Bill of Rights, and any 'limitation' of a right which does not comply with the provisions of this section will constitute an unconstitutional and invalid infringement of the applicable right.[14] 'Every court, tribunal or forum is enjoined to promote the spirit, purport and objects of the Bill of Rights when interpreting any legislation, or when developing the common law or customary law.[15] Courts are also obliged to consider international law, and may consider foreign law when interpreting the Bill of Rights.[16]

In the discussion, in the rest of this chapter I will frequently refer to the relevant fundamental rights in the South African context, with specific reference to the far-reaching South African anti-ambush marketing legislation.

7.2 Freedom of Expression

Discussion in the earlier chapters has referred to the limitations that are placed on corporations that are not official sponsors, and on marketers and advertisers in respect of the promotion of products and services with reference to major sporting events. It is clear that marketing involves (commercial) speech; the use of advertising and other forms of promotional activities by 'ambushers', by

---

(Footnote 13 continued)

(a) in order to give effect to a right in the Bill, must apply, or if necessary develop, the common law to the extent that legislation does not give effect to that right; and

(b) may develop rules of the common law to limit the right, provided that the limitation is in accordance with Section 36(1) [the limitation clause contained in the Bill of Rights] … .

[14] Section 36, the limitations clause, provides as follows:

S 36(1) The rights in the Bill of Rights may be limited only in terms of law of general application to the extent that the limitation is reasonable and justifiable in an open and democratic society based on human dignity, equality and freedom, taking into account all relevant factors, including:

(a) the nature of the right;
(b) the importance of the purpose of the limitation;
(c) the nature and extent of the limitation;
(d) the relation between the limitation and its purpose; and
(e) less restrictive means to achieve the purpose.

(2) Except as provided in subsection (1) or in any other provision of the Constitution, no law may limit any right entrenched in the Bill of Rights.

[15] Section 39(2) of the Bill of Rights provides a vehicle for the 'indirect' application of the Bill of Rights to disputes between private individuals or natural and juristic persons (e.g. contractual disputes), and states as follows:

When interpreting any legislation, *and when developing the common law* or customary law, every court, tribunal or forum must promote the spirit, purport and objects of the Bill of Rights …'[Emphasis provided].

[16] Constitution of the Republic of South Africa sec. 39(1).

definition, involves a form of expression which necessitates a consideration of whether restrictions on such expression in the form of anti-ambushing measures violate constitutional free speech guarantees. In respect of determining what, exactly, constitutes 'commercial speech', it is helpful to consider the position in the United States. The US Supreme Court has defined it narrowly as 'speech which does "no more than propose a commercial transaction"'[17] and as 'expression related solely to the economic interests of the speaker and its audience'.[18] In *Bolger*[19] the court confirmed that any consideration of whether speech is commercial should rest on 'the "commonsense" distinction between speech proposing a commercial transaction, which occurs in an area traditionally subject to government regulation, and other varieties of speech', and it proposed a test for the determination of whether speech is commercial which encompasses consideration of three factors:

(1) whether the speech in question is concededly an advertisement;
(2) whether it makes reference to a specific product; and
(3) whether it is motivated by economic interest.

The court stressed that a finding of just one of these factors does not make speech commercial; what is required is a combination of all three. The core question for determining whether speech is commercial is whether the speech proposes a commercial transaction.[20] In the ambush marketing context, advertising and other promotional activities by firms who are not official sponsors will invariably constitute commercial speech. It is such speech which is generally restricted or prohibited by *sui generis* event legislation (of which the exempted conduct, such as use of protected emblems or 'event words', generally is restricted to honest, non-commercial use). The commercial character of such speech is important primarily because the various jurisdictions generally provide some lesser form of constitutional free speech protection for such speech (although this is not universally the case). However, such speech does enjoy protection, and as I will show later, legislative limitations on commercial speech generally require the pursuit of a legitimate governmental interest and that any restriction should be proportional thereto. More on this later.

We have seen that freedom of commercial speech has on at least one occasion in the past been found to justify a case of alleged ambushing, when an Indian court held that opportunistic commercial exploitation of an event amounted to constitutionally protectable commercial speech and it was for the legislature to decide how far to curtail legitimate fair competition and freedom of speech.[21] Vassallo et al. have observed, in the American context, that '[t]he First Amendment also

[17] *Virginia State Bd.*, 425 U.S. at 762, 96 S.Ct. 1817 (quoting *Pittsburgh Press Co. v. Pittsburgh Commn. on Human Relations* 413 US 376, 385).

[18] *Central Hudson Gas & Electric Corp. v. Public Service Commission of New York*, 447 U.S. (1980) at 561.

[19] *Bolger v. Youngs Drug Products Corp.* 463 US 60, 66–67.

[20] See *US Olympic Committee v American Media, Inc* 156 F.Supp.2d 1200 (2001) 1207.

[21] *ICC Development (International) Ltd v Arvee Enterprises & Philips* 2003 (26) PTC 245 (Del).

plays a role in ambush marketing; indeed it may be a large part of the reason why the current legal remedies in the U.S. are lacking' and, with reference to earlier case law, the authors opine that 'the balance between free speech and trademark rights should generally tip in favor of free speech.'[22] Other commentators have also acknowledged the significant potential free speech implications of unchecked expansion of trademark law in respect of protecting sponsorship or affiliation (which I discuss elsewhere as being very relevant, and at least analogous, to the *sui generis* protection of 'association rights' to events).[23]

Event organisers have realised the potential free speech implications of their attempts to stifle event-related marketing by anyone not officially sponsoring their events. By way of example of the realisation of the potential role of free speech rights in anti-ambushing policies, compare the following from the 34th America's Cup 'Ambush Marketing Action Plan' for the 2012 and 2013 regattas, as published by the city of San Francisco for public comment in March 2011:

> This Plan is intended to address the intellectual property, sponsorship and rights owned or licensed by the Authority. Nothing in this Plan is intended to limit the individual free speech rights protected by the United States Constitution.[24]

Event organisers' recognition of the potential free speech implications of their anti-ambushing and other event protection strategies, however, may not be enough to prevent the stifling of free speech. Beijing Olympics organisers created dedicated spaces for public protest; the 2001 Tampa Bay Super Bowl saw extensive 'clean zone' restrictions but also the setting aside of a 'First Amendment Area' for people to assemble and speak out[25]; and the UK government has also proposed exceptions to the advertising and street trading regulations in respect of the London 2012 Games for 'demonstrations and related activities'.[26] The British Columbia Civil Liberties Association was less than enamoured, however, with VANOC's initiative in this regard at the 2010 Vancouver Winter Games, where the area designated for free speech was 'the tiny patch of green behind the Vancouver Art Gallery', which featured 'a pro-Olympic poster display, a provincial government log cabin, and a bobsled'.[27] Is it just me, or is the very concept of a 'free speech zone' (as VANOC called its new creation) something of an oxymoron?

Apart from event-related protest action or the facilitation of free speech at mega-events, anti-ambushing measures aimed at protecting purely commercial rights may significantly curb free speech. In Chap. 5 I referred to the creation of a

---

[22] Vassallo et al. 2005, p. 1341.

[23] See Lemley and McKenna 2010, p. 443–445.

[24] Copy available online at the time of writing at http://www.oewd.org/media/docs/03-31-11_Ambush%20Marketing%20Plan.pdf.

[25] McKelvey and Grady 2008, p. 568.

[26] See the consultation document dealing with sections 9 and 10 of the regulations, available online at the time of writing at http://www.culture.gov.uk/images/publications/ConDoc_Regulations_on_Advertising_and_Trading_London_2012-section9-10.pdf.

[27] See http://www.bccla.org/pressreleases/10Free_speech_zone.html.

'monopoly on language' for event organisers and sponsors. This, of course, holds significant potential free speech implications:

> The granting of exclusivity in the use of certain words [in anti-ambush marketing legislation] can negatively impact on the freedom of expression and political communication... While exceptions, such as that for press reportage, are one way of dealing with this issue, there may be broader questions when legislation limiting the use of words in common usage starts to impact on free speech.[28]

A case in point is that of New Zealand online wine and beer sales company, winesale.co.nz, who were threatened with legal action by the organisers of the 2011 IRB Rugby World Cup for using the following phrase in a promotion: 'The Rugby World Cup is getting closer!'.[29] I also referred, in Chap. 5, to the response to Robert Ronsson's *Olympic Mind Games* book. Coombe[30] would appear to agree about the pernicious effects of such a language monopoly regarding the use of e.g. Olympic indicia, arguing (with reference to the US Olympic Committee's refusal to allow use of its 'property' for purposes of the 'Gay Games'[31]) that the use of the law in this way enables a public authority to exercise its power in a discriminatory manner, by denying 'ownership' of common symbols to subordinated groups. Elsewhere I refer to the November 2010 resolution on ambush marketing legislation passed by the board of the International Trademark Association (or INTA). This includes the following:

> [A]mbush marketing legislation often extends sponsors' and organizers' rights well beyond the protection of traditional trademark and unfair competition laws, thus impeding existing trademark owners' rights by failing to appropriately balance the interests of official sponsors and event organizers with free commercial speech, fair use and the legitimate commercial activities of others.

The free speech issues are, however, not confined to ('ambush') marketers. There are clear and significant implications for consumers to be found in the restrictions on advertising and speech, which may include restrictions on how consumers interact with brands. Teresa Scassa explains:

> Limiting how individuals interact with brands may unduly limit their freedom of expression. The brand is a reputation that transcends the family of trademarks associated with the brand—it represents the intangible goodwill that is built by the brand owner. Increasingly, and in many contexts, brands are built by encouragement of public participation in their creation, manifestation, and articulation. Individuals are encouraged to wear clothing items bearing corporate logos and trademarks; they are encouraged to display brands on a wide range of other consumer goods. In many cases, the individual is encouraged to make the corporate brand an aspect of their individual image and identity. The brand is thus a highly

---

28 From Frontier Economics 2007, p. 95.

29 See the news clip, published 25 March 2011, available online at the time of writing at http://tvnz.co.nz/national-news/rwc-bosses-issue-yellow-card-warning-4087581/video#.

30 Coombe 1993.

31 See Symons, C & Warren, I '"David v. Goliath": The Gay Games, the Olympics and the Ownership of Language' *Entertainment and Sports Law Journal* (April 2006), text available online at the time of writing at http://www.bl.uk/sportandsociety/exploresocsci/sportsoc/mega/articles/clicklogo.pdf.

interactive space. Anti-ambush marketing legislation suppresses non-sponsor brands, and in doing so it may impact the freedom of expression of individuals.[32]

The South African Merchandise Marks Act's prohibitions as contained in section 15 and, specifically, section 15A(2) (restricting even the use by an existing trademark holder of their own marks), as discussed elsewhere in this book, are indicative of the type of restrictions that are increasingly being found in anti-ambush marketing legislation in the various jurisdictions (although it should be noted that more than one commentator has characterised South Africa as having amongst the most stringent protection against ambush marketing in the world[33]). Of course this raises the question of whether such (commercial) speech as constituted by advertising and other promotional efforts relating to major sporting events by 'ambushers' is protected in terms of the freedom of expression guarantees contained in section 16 of the South African Bill of Rights.[34] In other jurisdictions this question would, of course relate to the relevant free speech guarantees (for example Article 10[35] of the European Convention on Human Rights, or the First Amendment to the United States Constitution[36]).

---

[32] Scassa, T 2011, p. 366.

[33] Johnson 2007, p. 140; see also Kobel 2007, p. 14.

[34] Which provides as follows:

'Section 16. Freedom of expression:

1 Everyone has the right to freedom of expression, which includes
  a. freedom of the press and other media;
  b. freedom to receive or impart information or ideas;
  c. freedom of artistic creativity; and
  d. academic freedom and freedom of scientific research.

2 The right in subsection (1) does not extend to
  a. propaganda for war;
  b. incitement of imminent violence; or
  advocacy of hatred that is based on race, ethnicity, gender or religion, and that constitutes incitement to cause harm.'

[35] Which provides as follows:

Article 10—Freedom of expression:

1. Everyone has the right to freedom of expression. This right shall include freedom to hold opinions and to receive and impart information and ideas without interference by public authority and regardless of frontiers. This article shall not prevent States from requiring the licensing of broadcasting, television or cinema enterprises.

2. The exercise of these freedoms, since it carries with it duties and responsibilities, may be subject to such formalities, conditions, restrictions or penalties as are prescribed by law and are necessary in a democratic society, in the interests of national security, territorial integrity or public safety, for the prevention of disorder or crime, for the protection of health or morals, for the protection of the reputation or rights of others, for preventing the disclosure of information received in confidence, or for maintaining the authority and impartiality of the judiciary.

[36] 'Congress shall make no law respecting an establishment of religion, or prohibiting the free exercise thereof; or abridging the freedom of speech, or of the press; or the right of the people peaceably to assemble, and to petition the Government for a redress of grievances.'

7.2.1 'Ambush Advertising' and Freedom of Commercial Expression

The distinction between commercial expression (e.g. in its most prominent form, advertising) and other forms of protected expression appears to be of varying importance in different jurisdictions. A couple of South African commentators have observed that commercial speech is deserving of protection, for the following reasons[37]:

- It may be difficult to distinguish between commercial speech and other forms of expression, which means that restrictions on commercial speech may have a chilling effect on protected forms of expression;
- Due to the role of sponsorship by commercial speakers, protected speech may be made possible and restrictions on such commercial speech may have a knock-on effect and eventually undermine the role of the press and the media in a democracy;
- A market-orientated economy cannot function properly without commercial speech; and
- Commercial speech has been afforded constitutional protection in a number of open and democratic societies, such as Canada[38] and the United States.

After the US Supreme Court's initial denial of First Amendment protection for advertising in the 1942 case of *Valentine v Christensen*, later judgments brought about a sea change in the constitutional protection of commercial speech. The recognition of free speech protection in the later cases[39] has come with a view that '[t]he Constitution… affords a lesser protection to commercial speech than to other constitutionally guaranteed expression'.[40] The US Supreme Court has formulated a test for the constitutionality of governmental restrictions on commercial speech. In the often-cited *Central Hudson* case[41] the court formulated a four-prong test: This test asks, first, whether the commercial speech at issue is protected by the First Amendment (i.e. whether it concerns a lawful activity and is not misleading). Second, it asks whether the asserted governmental interest in restricting it is substantial. If the answer to both these questions is in the affirmative, then in order to be constitutional the restriction must, third, 'directly advance… the governmental interest asserted', and it must, fourth, be 'not more extensive than is necessary to serve that interest'. It was observed in 2009 that the US Supreme Court has applied the *Central Hudson* test in all the commercial speech cases it has decided since *Central Hudson*, and in nine of those cases the Court struck down

[37] Currie and de Waal 2005, pp. 379–380.

[38] See *Irwin Toy Ltd v Quebec (A-G)* (1989) 58 DLR (4th) 577.

[39] See *Virginia State Board of Pharmacy v Virginia Citizens Consumer Council, Inc* 96 S. Ct. 1817 (1976); *Bates v State Bar of Arizona* 433 US 350 (1978); *Bigelow v Virginia* 421 US 809 (1975); *Central Hudson Gas v Public Services Commission* 447 US 557 (1979); Weinberg 1982

[40] *United States v. Edge Broadcasting Co.*, 509 U.S. 418 (1993).

[41] *Central Hudson Gas & Electric Corp. v. Public Service Commission of New York*, 447 U.S. (1980) 566.

the challenged speech restriction (it has not upheld a commercial speech restriction since 1993).[42] A detailed examination of the protection of commercial speech in the USA is beyond the scope of this chapter. It appears, however, that there are prospects that the 'commercial speech doctrine' is slowly disappearing in favour of more robust protection for such speech notwithstanding its origin or commercial purpose.[43] In countries such as Canada[44] and India[45] it appears that a distinction between commercial and 'normal' speech for purposes of constitutional protection has become less important (while it has been argued that European courts such as the ECJ (or Court of Justice for the European Union) and the European Court of Human Rights have in principle recognised protection for commercial speech but 'in practice both Courts deny the protection by refusing to overrule limitations on commercial speech'[46]). In light of the wide interpretation of expression favoured by the South African Constitutional Court, it has been observed that all forms of commercial speech in South Africa are likely to be considered protected expression, and that any differentiation in treatment between commercial and other expression would occur at the stage of the limitations (i.e. justification) analysis in terms of section 36 of the South African Bill of Rights.[47] In line with the position

---

[42] Cohen, H *Freedom of Speech and Press: Exceptions to the First Amendment* Congressional Research Service Report for Congress, 16 October 2009, at 8—available online at the time of writing at http://www.fas.org/sgp/crs/misc/95-815.pdf.

[43] See *Sorrell v IMS Health, Inc* No. 10-779 (2011), where Justice Kennedy in the US Supreme Court held that there is no exception to the rule that government may not restrict speech based on content in the realm of commercial speech, and while the speech at issue in this case "results from an economic motive, so too does a great deal of vital expression." Deborah La Fetra has argued for the abolishment of the commercial speech doctrine:

> '[C]orporations and other business interests play a vital role in the American political economy, thus imbuing corporate speech with inherent value in our democratic society. Rather than treating such speech as a hostile intruder in public debate, it should be embraced as presenting a point of view that may well otherwise remain unexpressed.... [T]he line between commercial and noncommercial speech...is so blurred as to be indistinguishable. With greater frequency and subtlety, new technologies and innovative marketing strategies introduce corporate profit-motive into what otherwise would be fully-protected speech. The current commercial speech doctrine cannot predictably resolve disputes resulting from these new modes of expression. La Fetra 2004.

[44] *Irwin Toy Ltd v Quebec (A-G)* (1989) 58 DLR (4th) 577.

[45] *Tata Press Ltd v Mahangar Telephone Nigam Ltd* AIR 1995 SC 2438; *Hindustan Times v State of UP* AIR 2003 SC 250; *Sakal Papers (P) Ltd v Union of India* AIR 1962 SC 305.

[46] See Gassy-Wright, O V 'Commercial Speech in the United States and Europe' (2005). *LLM Theses and Essays.* Paper 13. http://digitalcommons.law.uga.edu/stu_llm/13. The US Supreme Court, in the 'Gay Olympics' case referred to elsewhere in this chapter, observed that 'Commercial speech receives a limited form of First Amendment protection', relying on *Posadas de Puerto Rico Assoc. v. Tourism Company of Puerto Rico,* 478 U.S. 328 (1986) and *Central Hudson Gas & Electric Corp. v. Public Service Comm'n of New York,* 447 U.S. 557 (1980).

[47] See Currie and de Waal 2005, p. 379. In *Laugh It Off Promotions CC v South African Breweries International (Finance) B.V. t/a Sabmark International & Another* 2006 (1) SA 144 (CC) Moseneke J declared the following (in par 62 of the judgment) regarding the distinction between 'normal' speech and commercial speech in the context of a constitutional freedom of

elsewhere, certain limitations on the freedom of commercial expression will likely pass muster as being justifiable.

Before one considers the relevant factors to be considered in testing the constitutionality of restrictions on commercial expression as per *sui generis* event legislation, it is pertinent to determine the form and extent of such potential restrictions. As discussed in earlier chapters, there are various ways in which such legislation restricts speech in the form of advertising by business enterprises (as well as, possibly, even normal discourse by individuals). Examples are found in restrictions on the use of major event emblems (compare the Olympic insignia), although this of course overlaps with intellectual property rights protection of logos, insignias and the like of event organisers. More worrying, possibly, is the trend towards restricting the use of language, for example by means of restrictions or prohibitions on the use of 'major event words'. In Chap. 2 I referred to the relevant provisions of the schedules to the London Olympic and Paralympic Games Act, 2006. I have also referred to criticism of the 2010 Vancouver Winter Olympics legislation and its restrictions on the use of generic terms and words which do not qualify for special legal protection in terms of intellectual property laws but was 'appropriated' by the event organisers with apparently little regard for free speech concerns. The Major Event Emblems and Words (Rugby World Cup 2011) Order, 2008 (which was issued in terms of section 8 of MEMA), for example, also contains a list of prohibited words in respect of the event (a total of 51 words or combinations of words in Part 1, and a total of 36 words in column A and 28 words in column B of Part 2 of the Order, which prohibits the combination of words from the two columns). Shortly before the start of the 2011 IRB Rugby World Cup the outgoing Governor-General of New Zealand extended these lists, by adding terms such as 'Live site', 'Fanzone', 'Fan Fest' and 'Fan Site'. These restrictions meant that, aside from sanctioned tournament partners, the terms could not be used for gatherings organised by individuals or businesses from 9 September 2011 until 21 November 2011, almost a month after the World Cup final. A breach of the Order carried a fine of up to NZD 150,000.[48]

(Footnote 47 continued)
expression defence to parodic messages on t-shirts which incorporated adaptations of well-known trade marks (*in casu*, a well-known beer brand), with reference to an argument advanced by an *amicus curiae* in the case:

'The amicus however draws our attention to the clear duality of the roles of the T-shirts—to sell and to make a social statement. It is the expressive role, the amicus argues, which engages the constitutional protection and is worthy of its shield. To limit valuable communication to non-commercial enterprises would further marginalise alternative and competing voices in society. In this way voices of the best resourced would tend to prevail. But also it is important to keep in mind the purpose for which the marks have been appropriated. What is being sold is not another beer or other product under the guise or on the back of the registered marks. What is being sold is rather an abstract brand criticism. T-shirts are not much more than the medium of choice.'

[48] See the report available online at the time of writing at http://www.stuff.co.nz/auckland/local-news/rwc-in-auckland/5561402/Squads-to-check-on-ambush-adverts.

Apart from such express prohibitions or restrictions on the use of specific language, the anti-ambushing legislation of course also restricts the use of language which might imply an association with a protected event. In Chap. 8 I further examine the wide reach of such provisions in, for example, the London Act. For present purposes just note that such an association may include any kind of contractual relationship, commercial relationship, corporate or structural connection or the provision of financial or other support for or in connection with the Games, and the Act prohibits the unauthorised making of 'any representation (of any kind) in a manner likely to suggest to the public that there is an association' with the event. MEMA's section 10 similarly provides that no person may, during a major event's protection period, make any representation in a way likely to suggest to a reasonable person that there is an association between the major event and goods or services (or a brand of goods or services or a person who provides goods or services). I have also frequently referred in the earlier chapters to the extremely wide reach of section 15A of South Africa's Merchandise Marks Act, which prohibits the use of a mark in widely phrased circumstances 'with reference to' a protected event. It should be clear that these provisions on their own (and the combination of their ambit) contain substantial limitations on freedom of speech, and of commercial speech. They are not only aimed at protecting intellectual property rights. As explained in Chap. 5, many (most?) of the words, for example, which habitually find their way into these lists of 'protected words', as well as a myriad of forms of normal language usage which may contravene 'association rights' provisions and constitute 'a representation of any kind', are not material that is capable of IP protection (e.g. as being generic for copyright purposes or descriptive for trademark purposes).[49] Accordingly, we are faced with clear restrictions on free speech, and the legitimacy of such restrictions needs to be determined in terms of accepted principles of law. And the fact that event organisers may vehemently defend any such restrictions on free speech by claiming that they protect, for example, trademarks in respect of their events, does not serve to remove them from constitutional scrutiny. Widmaier & Schechter, for example, refer to a recent case[50] in the American context which dealt with rights of publicity to conclude that the First Amendment can act as a bar to the assertion of even legitimate interests in protecting marks and designations relating to major sports events against commercial exploitation by unauthorised third parties.[51]

---

[49] See again Mouritz 2008.

[50] *C.B.C. Distribution and Marketing, Inc., v. Major League Baseball Advanced Media, L.P.*, 505 F.3d 818 (8th Cir. 2007).

[51] The authors of the country report on the United States prepared for the Working Committee of the International Association for the Protection of Intellectual property (AIPPI), Project Q210 ('The protection of major sports events and associated commercial activities through trademarks and other IPR'; reports compiled for purposes of a draft resolution to be submitted to the AIPPI Exco meeting in Buenos Aires, October 2009)—available online at the time of writing at https://www.aippi.org/download/commitees/210/GR210usa.pdf.

It is generally accepted (compare the *Central Hudson* test employed by the US courts, as referred to above and which will be discussed again below) that a threshold requirement for commercial speech in the form of an advertisement, for example, to be constitutionally protected would be that it must not be false, deceptive or misleading to the public.[52] Accordingly, and as Scaria argues,[53] ambush marketers will not be able to claim constitutional protection for false and misleading advertisements. This is in line also with the American position regarding free expression and trademark law, where it is accepted doctrine that the Lanham Act may restrict noncommercial speech 'where the public interest in avoiding consumer confusion outweighs the public interest in free expression'.[54] While Scaria's view is undoubtedly accurate in respect of association with ambush marketing, it is, however, submitted that the correctness of his conclusion is doubtful. He concludes that the inevitable result of bringing ambush marketing advertisements outside the purview of protection of commercial free speech is that anti-ambush marketing legislation such as the Sydney 2000 Games (Indicia and Images) Protection Act 1996 and the London Olympic Games and Paralympic Games Act 2006 will not be considered as unconstitutional on the grounds of violating commercial speech protection.[55] The point has repeatedly been made in this book that what is known as 'intrusion ambushing'—i.e. for example advertising by a nonsponsor of an event which refers to the event but without implying or causing any deception regarding association with such event[56]—must be considered in a different light. Where such deception regarding association is absent, it is

---

[52] Such advertisements are not constitutionally protected in the USA and India, for example—see the discussion by Scaria 2008, pp. 114–115. In the US context the following has been observed:

> [I]f the purpose of the Supreme Court's recognition of First Amendment protection for advertising is to further the dissemination of information, then it would not make sense to protect, false, misleading, or deceptive advertisements. But if the expression/advertisement is about a lawful activity and is not misleading, it is thought to deserve First Amendment protection… When the content of advertising crosses the line and becomes deceptive, it is the responsibility of the regulating body to minimize the resultant unfair competitive effects.—Wright 1999, 491.

[53] Scaria 2008, p. 115.

[54] *Rogers v. Grimaldi,* 875 F.2d 994, 999 (2d Cir.1989).

[55] Ibid.

[56] As pointed out previously, 'intrusion ambushes' may include a wide variety of activities which may otherwise not constitute legally or ethically objectionable conduct. An example is the marketing practice of running a promotional campaign in which tickets to an event are given away as prizes, a practice which has in recent years fell foul of anti-ambush marketing laws in a number of jurisdictions. This practice has increasingly been addressed by means of e.g. contract law (i.e. through the means of prohibitions contained on the tickets) or by means of specific legislation. In respect of the 2010 FIFA World Cup South Africa, the Minister of Trade & Industry published regulations prohibiting the resale and unauthorised promotion of tickets to the event (Government Notice 383 in Government Gazette 32123 of 14 April 2009—such regulations to serve as additional regulations in terms of section 2A of the 2010 FIFA World Cup South Africa Special Measures Act), which provide as follows:

submitted that an 'ambush marketer' should be able to claim constitutional free speech protection. Scaria concedes this (by referring to the example of a marketer who is able to show on proper evidence that it is merely conveying information through its advertisements), although opining that 'in the context of ambush marketing it is highly unlikely on the part of courts to accept such arguments.'[57] I would like to think that South African courts, at least, might be more open to such a finding, although the experience to date in this regard has been inconclusive (and, in my opinion, disappointing).[58] An interesting point to consider in this context of deceptive commercial speech relates to one of the grounds for the exemption of liability as found in some of the *sui generis* event legislation, namely the exemption for 'honest, non-commercial use'[59] (or, specifically in the context of the London Act's association right to the 2012 Games, the exemption of a statement 'which accords with honest practices in industrial or commercial matters, and does not make promotional or other commercial use of a representation relating to the London Olympics'). The emphasis on 'non-commercial' use clearly shows the primary purpose of such legislation, namely to prohibit competition in marketing around the event by 'ambushers'. The references to 'honest' use are interesting, however, in light of the fact that most of the *sui generis* event legislation does not require consumer deception or confusion for purposes of liability (a point I will explore further in Chap. 8). It would appear, I would submit, that the inclusion of such exemptions for honest, noncommercial use therefore, by definition, appears to ignore the fact that such use or conduct by potential 'ambushers' generally enjoys constitutional protection as honest commercial speech. In Chap. 8 I explain that a statutory creature such as an 'association right' to an event serves to remove wide swaths of matter which resorts within the public domain, and that the exemptions in

---

(Footnote 56 continued)

(1) No person shall, without the written authority of FIFA:

(a) Sell or otherwise dispose of a 2010 FIFA World Cup South Africa ticket, or any right pertaining to such a ticket, to another person, for commercial purposes;
(b) Use a 2010 FIFA World Cup South Africa ticket for advertising, sales or promotional purposes, or as part of a hospitality or travel package, or make it available or advertise it for any such purpose;
(c) Use a ticket transferred or acquired in violation of paragraphs (a) or (b) above.(2) Any person convicted of an offence in terms of section (1), shall be liable to a fine not exceeding R 15 000.00 for each article to which the offence relates, or to imprisonment for a period not exceeding five years, or to both such fine and imprisonment.

[57] Ibid.

[58] See the discussion of FIFA's legal challenges to ambush marketing in respect of the 2010 World Cup in Sect. 4.4.5 of Chap. 4. Compare also the following sentiment expressed in respect of the Canadian ambush marketing legislation in respect of the 2010 Vancouver Winter Games (by Geist, M 'Bill C-47 not in the spirit of the Olympics', *Toronto Star* 19 March 2007):

> [S]pecial interest legislation, particularly legislation blatantly designed to protect a select group of corporate interests at the expense of free speech, should have no place in a government focused on trust and accountability.

[59] See, for example, section 12 of the Major Events Management Act, 2007.

the relevant legislation mostly just serve to reclaim some such matter, in a limited way. Such 'honest, non-commercial use' exemptions thus do not, in my view, add anything to the general nature of exemptions, more generally, as a 'clawing back' of elements of the event that would otherwise resort within the public domain.

While I am on the subject of deception (or rather a lack thereof) in respect of constitutionally protected commercial speech, it also bears mentioning that the extent of free speech limitations imposed by event organisers is clearly illustrated in respect of a specific aspect of the relevant contractual arrangements in place for the 2012 London Olympics. The LOCOG is enforcing a December 2007 policy document entitled the *No Marketing Rights Protocol* for suppliers, consultants and contractors.[60] This is an interesting (I will say Orwellian) document which is aimed at curtailing the ability of *official* suppliers to the event organisers (note—these are the 'good guys') to benefit from any association with the event for which they did not pay. The main purpose of the protocol is explained as follows:

> Businesses supplying goods and services to the London 2012 Organising Committee, the [Olympic Delivery Authority] and other organisations involved in the delivery of the Games ("Suppliers"), will benefit from the experience and kudos gained from undertaking work in relation to, and/or providing goods and services for, the Games. However Suppliers do not pay to receive the benefits of being an official marketing partner of the Games; indeed, they are paid full value for the supply of their goods and services.[61]

The Protocol provides that many suppliers will be required to provide goods and services free of commercial branding (i.e. this is the case with all materials supplied to Olympic venues which will be 'visible to the public'). Goods or services being used at public events and documents created by suppliers which will be made public, should also be clean of any branding.[62] In order to prevent these official suppliers to the Games from sticking their hands in the cookie jar in respect of gaining unauthorised (and free) publicity, the Olympic authorities also employ a so-called 'London 2012 No Marketing Rights Clause' in their agreements with suppliers, which 'prevent Suppliers from marketing their involvement in the Games and also prohibit ambush marketing'. This creature is fascinating (and I would suggest hilarious) to behold, from a freedom of speech perspective. If you are ready for this (I hope you're sitting down), let us consider what official suppliers are faced with:

- Suppliers should not issue press releases, run advertising or undertake any marketing or PR campaigns around their involvement in the Games. They also must not promote themselves as a 'Supplier to the London 2012 Games/ODA' (or anything similar). They may also not say they are an official partner of the ODA or LOCOG;

---

60 This document is at the time of writing available as a download on the London 2012 website at http://www.london2012.com/documents/oda-publications/no-marketing-rights-suppliers-protocol-dec-2007.pdf.

61 The Protocol document at 3.

62 Ibid.

- Suppliers can undertake 'necessary internal communications' and make 'factual statements to staff' about the supplier's involvement in the Games. However, the protocol provides that such internal communications should be undertaken 'in an understated, proportionate and regular fashion which doesn't conflict with the spirit of the No Marketing Rights Clauses or the Protocol'. If the internal communication is likely to be made available publicly or is intended for wider circulation than just the supplier's staff, it should not refer to the supplier's involvement in the Games, unless this is permitted in accordance with the Protocol;
- The inclusion of the London 2012 Organising Committee/ODA/other Games Bodies within a supplier's list of clients is permitted, provided there are at least nine other clients mentioned in the list (*really?*); no special emphasis is placed on the Games (for example by highlighting, or emboldening the name); the official name of the client is used (i.e. 'Olympic Delivery Authority' or 'The London Organising Committee of the Olympic Games and Paralympic Games Limited' (not, for example, 'Olympics' or 'London 2012'); the client list consists of only a list of names of clients and, if required, a simple statement (no more than 20 words) on the nature of the work undertaken; the client list is only included in publications where it would be standard practice to include a client list (e.g. corporate literature or on a relevant page of the Supplier's UK website), and not within an advert, on the supplier's home page, within other 'more aggressive marketing materials' or on exhibition panels;
- An accurate factual statement may be included in annual reports and statutory reports as necessary to meet relevant obligations but these should not be embellished and should be 'in keeping with the spirit of the Protocol';
- Suppliers are allowed 'verbal responses': Suppliers may talk about the work they are undertaking on the Games in a social or informal business context, subject to any confidentiality restrictions. This does not apply 'where such "talking" is more akin to a marketing activity though'. This means that suppliers should not talk about the work they are undertaking on the Games if, for example, speaking to the media, or to a significant number of clients or potential clients;
- A statement (more detailed than that permitted within the inclusion of a client list) about the supplier's work undertaken in relation to the Games may be permitted with written consent, provided that the statement is succinct ('in most cases a limit of approximately 150 words will be applied'); it appears with at least five other examples of work undertaken for other clients; the statement is given equal weighting to those other five examples (no special emphasis is be placed on the Games); and the statement is only included in publications where it would be standard practice to include such case studies (e.g. corporate literature or on a relevant page on the supplier's website), and not within an advert, on the supplier's homepage, within a press release, on exhibition panels or within 'other more aggressive marketing materials' etc.; and
- Suppliers may, with written consent, be permitted to write an article in a trade journal etc. about the Games provided this does not amount to a marketing piece

for the supplier. Suppliers should 'not proactively seek the opportunity to submit such articles as a means of promotion' and the content of permitted articles will also be 'subject to review'.

It does not end there. The poor suppliers are allowed, of course, to engage in recruitment advertisements (after all, someone has to actually do the work they've been contracted for), but such job ads must not be 'Olympified' in any way through use of imagery or logos etc., or unduly emphasise the Games. The Protocol provides that, for example, an advert titled 'Olympic builders wanted' would not be approved but an advert titled 'Drain layers wanted' which then explained that they were needed to work on the Olympic Park may be approved. And finally, there are some further, interesting restrictions imposed:

- Suppliers may, with written consent, be permitted to speak at a conference or public event about the Games, provided the event is not attended by the Supplier for the primary purpose of publicising their involvement in the Games or for financial gain. These will be approved on a case by case basis and are 'audience dependent and event specific'. The content of permitted presentations relating to the Games will also be subject to approval;
- Suppliers may, with written consent, be permitted to use visual materials to accompany information provided in accordance with the Protocol. Prior approval must, however, be obtained in relation to use of *all* images, films, etc., *whether these are official London 2012 images or generic sporting images*;
- If a supplier performs work on a construction site, she is allowed to use a branded bull-dozer, for example, but manufacturer's branding, as would normally appear on equipment when purchased, is permitted 'provided the branding is reasonable and proportionate'; and
- Rather surprisingly in light of the above, suppliers are allowed to speak to the press. However: 'Except to confirm that they are a Supplier, Suppliers should not respond to media enquiries about the work they are undertaking on the Games, or provide any quotes or comments without first speaking to the London 2012 Organising Committee about this'.

When considering these frankly remarkable restrictions on free speech as imposed by the Olympic organisers, bear in mind that these relate *to official suppliers and to the communication of truthful and factual statements* (i.e. the fact that a supplier is an official Olympics supplier). There is no question here of deceptive 'ambushing' conduct, whatsoever, and the bottom line is that these suppliers have not paid for the privilege to associate themselves with the Games. Grady et al. observe that business groups have voiced frustration over these rules that prevent them not only from truthfully advertising and promoting their legitimate involvement as suppliers to the Games, but also have the effect of chilling commercial speech directed at their own employees. They note that this Protocol is 'even more draconian than that implemented for the 2010 [Vancouver Winter] Games, whereby VANOC has taken the unprecedented step of limiting its official suppliers to spending no more than CAN$ 5 m to promote their ties to the 2010

Games in order to prevent creating an appearance that such firms have made a bigger commitment to the Games than higher-level sponsors'.[63] If I were an Olympic supplier and subjected to these rules I would probably make sure to do some pretty shoddy work, to constantly leave my tools lying around and to generally make a real nuisance of myself (lunch breaks would be truly epic affairs).

To get back to consideration of advertising restrictions, more generally: Once the threshold requirement (a lack of deception) has been crossed, it remains to consider the legitimacy of anti-ambushing restrictions on advertising or other commercial speech as contained in *sui generis* event legislation. It appears (from a comparison of the gist of commercial free speech protection in the various democratic jurisdictions) that this exercise would generally require an evaluation of the state interest advanced in justification of such restrictions. As mentioned, the American courts require a substantial governmental interest and a restriction that is proportional (i.e. which does not go further than is necessary to achieve the objective of furthering such interest). In South Africa, the justification exercise requires that any limitation of the free speech guarantee must be reasonable and justifiable in an open and democratic society based on human dignity, equality and freedom (taking account of factors such as the nature of the right; the nature, purpose and extent of the limitation; the relation between the limitation and its purpose; and less restrictive means to achieve such purpose). In New Zealand, section 5 of its Bill of Rights requires that limits can be placed on its rights and freedoms only if they are 'reasonable' and 'demonstrably justified' in a free and democratic society.

When we seek a legitimate governmental purpose behind the often far-reaching legislative restrictions on advertising as contained in legislation such as MEMA, the London Act or South Africa's Merchandise Marks Act, we inevitably are confronted with the classic argument so often advanced by event organisers: 'Ambush marketing threatens the very existence of the mega-event, which cannot be staged without the substantial investment from official sponsors'. Coupled with this argument (which, as highlighted previously, for the most part of course relates to the protection of commercial rights created within a purely contractual relationship between an international sports governing body and a relatively small group of large multinational corporations), one finds the governmental response that the provision of such legislative protection is an absolute prerequisite in order to obtain the rights to host such an event.

I am not convinced. I believe that a legitimate governmental interest to restrict free speech (even if such speech is of a commercial nature) should be something more than either the protection of very narrow commercial interests of a small group of wealthy economic actors, or the apparently extortionate bid requirements which are often imposed on developing nations eager to take that first public relations step onto the global stage. I would suggest that the tenuous nature of these purported grounds of justification for limitation of free speech is illustrated

[63] Grady et al. 2010, p. 150.

when one considers them in terms of the above test as contained in the limitations clause of the South African Bill of Rights. And here it also bears considering the importance of the following characterisation of freedom of expression, more generally within a rights-based democratic society, as expressed by Moseneke J in the *Laugh it Off* Constitutional Court judgment[64]:

> [F]reedom of expression is a vital incidence of dignity, equal worth and freedom. It carries its own inherent worth and serves a collection of other intertwined constitutional ends in an open and democratic society.

I would suggest that, even if commercial expression may be subject to a lesser form of constitutional protection, it bears noting that the free expression guarantee is a key fundamental guarantee within the greater scope of a constitutional democracy (even though the same court said that it is 'neither paramount over other guaranteed rights nor limitless'[65]). This might necessitate a more stringent consideration of justification for limitation of such expression.

Ellis et al. refer to the potential role of the freedom of commercial expression guarantee in the Canadian context, with reference to anti-ambushing protection of the 2010 Vancouver Winter Olympics:

> The constitutional guarantee of freedom of expression in s. 2(b) of the Canadian Charter of Rights and Freedoms has been found to extend to commercial speech… While commercial speech may be regulated, any limitations imposed by government must constitute reasonable limits demonstrably justified in a free and democratic society. Thus, in Canada, legislation that prohibits expression because it merely suggests an association with an event might be difficult to justify as a reasonable limit. Although s. 4 of the 'Olympic and Paralympic Marks Act] is expressed in more constrained language than the right of association in the London Act, it does still place limits on commercial expression. In order to justify these limitations, the government must be able to demonstrate that the measure addresses ''an objective related to concerns which are pressing and substantial in a free and democratic society''… [T]he public policy justification for s. 4… is not entirely clear, and it may be vulnerable to constitutional challenge.[66]

The authors continue to examine whether, if a Canadian court were to accept that the legislation addressed a pressing and substantial objective, it would then find that the measures chosen were proportional. They quote the proportionality test as set by the Supreme Court of Canada in the well-known case of *R v Oakes*[67]:

> First, the measures adopted must be carefully designed to achieve the objective in question. They must not be arbitrary, unfair or based on irrational considerations. In short, they must be rationally connected to the objective. Second, the means, even if rationally connected to the objective in this first sense, should impair ''as little as possible'' the right or freedom in question. Third, there must be a proportionality between the effects of the

---

64 At par. 15 of the judgment.

65 Moseneke J in *Laugh it Off* supra at par. 17.

66 Ellis et al. 2011, pp. 303–304.

67 [1986] 1 S.C.R. 103 (at par. 70).

measures which are responsible for limiting the Charter right or freedom, and the objective which has been identified as of ''sufficient importance''.

They observe that legislation for which there is a poorly articulated purpose, or which is drafted in a vague or open-ended manner, will not fare well under scrutiny, as it will be difficult to argue that it impairs the freedom of expression as little as possible. When the law sets a standard that is unduly vague, it cannot be minimally impairing because it becomes difficult or impossible to know what conduct will be permissible and what will infringe the law.[68] Ellis et al. further identify the concern that over-breadth of a law (i.e. where a law is drafted in such a manner as to capture more conduct than is necessary to address the problem faced by the legislature) that infringes on protected Charter rights cannot be minimally impairing, and they speculate that section 4 of the Olympic and Paralympic Marks Act 'shares some of the deficiencies that may be found in legislation that does not flow from a strong grounding in public policy and that is drafted as broadly as possible so as to catch all manner of conduct that may be considered as encroaching on the newly created monopoly over the goodwill in an event'.[69] The same considerations apply, I would submit, to provisions of other *sui generis* event legislation such as New Zealand's Major Events Management Act and South Africa's Merchandise Marks Act.

As explained elsewhere in this book, the prohibition contained in section 15A of South Africa's Merchandise Marks Act is not aimed only at association ambushes, but also, more controversially, at 'intrusion ambushes'. An advertisement which contains use of a trade mark 'in relation to an event' that is 'calculated to achieve publicity for such mark' and which thereby 'derives special promotional benefit from the event', without the prior authority of the event organizer, is unlawful. As has been mentioned, this prohibition does not require the implication of an association with such event,[70] and accordingly also covers advertising that might not necessarily be false, deceptive or misleading in any way. It is submitted that the constitutionality of the restriction on commercial speech as occasioned by section 15A would have to be assessed purely on the basis of the reasonableness and justifiability test as contained in section 36 of the Bill of Rights—an exercise that is beyond the scope of this chapter—which in my opinion might very likely lead to a finding that the provision constitutes an unjustifiable limitation of commercial free speech in cases of 'intrusion ambush' advertising (especially where such advertising contains clear and unambiguous disclaimers denying any association with an event). It is disappointing to note that the court in *FIFA*

---

[68] Ellis et al. 2011, p. 304, with reference to *R v Nova Scotia Pharmaceutical Society* [1992] 2 S.C.R. 606.

[69] Ellis et al. 2011, p. 304.

[70] As opposed to the position under e.g. the Major Events Management Act, 2007 in New Zealand, which prohibits a 'representation of association' regarding a protected event—see the discussion in Sect. 4.4.4 in Chap. 4.

v Metcash Trading[71] dealt only cursorily with this constitutional challenge,[72] and it is submitted that the question is far from settled. I would suggest that similar considerations would apply to anti-'intrusion ambushing' advertising restrictions as contained in *sui generis* event legislation in other jurisdictions (including the association rights created in the legislation for the 2012 London Olympics as well as New Zealand's Major Events Management Act, for example).

In the run-up to the 2011 IRB Rugby World Cup New Zealand beer maker Lion Breweries, which owns the Steinlager brand, ran a nostalgic ad campaign entitled *We Believe*, which evoked the brand's 25 year association with the national All Blacks team as sponsor. The marketing campaign included bringing back an iconic white can for the product last seen in 1992 as well as a TV ad with a fictional celebrating fan from 1987 (the last, and only, time that the All Blacks had managed to win the rugby World Cup) proclaiming that he would save his can of Steinlager till the All Blacks win again. It was speculated that this marketing campaign by a competitor of Heineken, the official 2011 IRB Rugby World Cup sponsor, was the closest any major company had come to crossing the line of what is acceptable in terms of the Major Events Management Act. The ads did not show any rugby, but the connotation was clear to most. When questioned about its campaign (in light of the fact that the Steinlager brand had no links to the 2011 tournament), Lion's corporate affairs director was quoted as saying that 'the company believed the All Blacks brand was stronger than the Rugby World Cup brand and so "we believe that because we own the strongest property in the market this year, we will spend our time channelling our association with the All Blacks."'[73] (It appears these efforts were not very successful,

---

71 See the discussion in Sect. 4.4.5 of Chap. 4.

72 See par. 10 of Msimeki J's judgment:

'It has been submitted on behalf of [Metcash] that section 15A [of the Merchandise Marks Act] has to tazke cognisance of [Metcash's] rights to freedom of expression and "to use its products and trade marks in the manner and get up that it chooses". This argument, as is correctly submitted by [FIFA], loses sight of the fact that the interests of the general public must still be contended with. This … simply means that section 36 of the Constitution would allow and justify the limitation of [Metcash's] rights to freedom of expression or to intellectual property if their use would deceive or confuse the public and end up jeopardising an event such as the soccer world cup and at the same time prejudicing the sponsors and the licensees of the events. There is again, in my view, merit in this submission.'

It is submitted, with respect, that this is a rather shockingly superficial application of the limitations exercise in section 36 of the Bill of Rights, and that Metcash's freedom of expression challenge (see par. 12 of the order, where the learned judge states that it had been submitted on behalf of Metcash that section 15A has constitutional implications, and that '[t]he submission, in my view, is correct') appears to have been rejected on the basis of assumptions regarding facts and evidence which was apparently not before the court. It is submitted that deception of the public, potential 'jeopardising' of the World Cup as well as prejudice to sponsors and licensees were not proven.

73 Harvey, S 'Rugby World Cup advertising ambush expected' *Sunday Star Times*, 18 July 2011—available online at http://www.cmo.com/advertising/rugby-world-cup-advertising-ambush-expected.

however, as the Nielsen data for June and October 2011 indicating customer perceptions as to sponsorship of the IRB event showed Steinlager to be ranked in a lowly 15th place.) Such a campaign again raises the question of the limits to protection against either clever 'intrusion' advertising, which might refer to or connote in its audience's minds an event without direct reference thereto, or such advertising which directly refers to an event, but without any implication of association (or, even more troubling when it comes to anti-ambushing prohibitions, by expressly disclaiming non-association). I would venture to suggest, in light of its past form, that had FIFA been faced with this advertising campaign in respect of its World Cup event, cease-and-desist letters and/or litigation would very likely have followed.

One must ask whether even the possibility of such an 'intrusion' campaign being prohibited or subjected to litigation as being unlawful in terms of *sui generis* event legislation such as MEMA can be defended in light of freedom of speech considerations. The Steinlager campaign involved a clever leveraging of a long-time, existing association with the relevant sport (in respect of the national team in the world's leading rugby nation), timed to coincide with increased national (and international) attention for the World Cup event in New Zealand. It in no way involved the misleading of consumers regarding the brand's lack of affiliation with the event. I am reminded of the kulula.com (South African airline) marketing campaign in the run-up to the 2010 FIFA World Cup, which I will discuss later in this chapter, although the Steinlager brand could show such long-time association with the sport as an additional element favouring the legitimacy of its campaign and its timing. Any attempts to prohibit such campaigns by event organisers or official sponsors would, in my view, constitute illegitimate stifling of free commercial speech. And organisers and sponsors should not be allowed to defend such conduct on the basis of the 'ambusher's' commercial motive with such a campaign; the 'intrusion ambush' is often extremely successful simply because of the extensive publicity surrounding the mega-event, much of which is generated by the organisers and sponsors for their own commercial purposes. Again we are confronted with a scenario where complaints about such 'intrusion' into the realm of the event derive from the fact that the 'ambusher' did not play for the privilege (the free-riding argument). I will examine the fallacy of this argument in Chap. 8, when examining the boundaries of the thematic space of the mega-event and what sponsors actually buy for their large rights fees (and what organisers are entitled to sell).

Finally, in respect of the potential unconstitutionality of anti-ambushing provisions which may significantly limit freedom of commercial expression, it also bears considering another pertinent point raised by Ellis et al. I referred above to their discussion of the possible over-breadth of the Vancouver Act's anti-ambushing provisions. They continue to observe the following:

> In creating such broad measures governments must rely upon the good faith of those into whose hands they had placed enormous discretionary powers. However, under the [Olympic and Paralympic Marks Act] and the London Act, these hands are those of the event organizers, who were themselves under substantial direction and control from the IOC—bodies not accountable to any national government. In Canada, VANOC stated its role in these terms: "VANOC is legally obligated to the IOC and to its marketing

> partners to protect against unauthorized use of the Olympic Brand and ambush marketing in Canada". Perhaps aware of the exceptional rights and discretion it had been granted, VANOC assured the public that it: "will enforce its rights in a fair and reasonable manner, which will include pro-actively educating and engaging the public and implementing a fair process for assessing infringement and enforcing its rights". The attempt to articulate guidelines is important given the potential scope of the right and its ambiguity; it does not substitute, however, for a clearly delineated and measured legislative response.[74]

While it would seem that VANOC managed to achieve a rather admirable balance between the aggressive enforcement of its rights under the legislation (the traditional 'FIFA end of the spectrum') and the interests of the Canadian public, which I will revisit in Chap. 10, I believe the point is a relevant one. This devolution or delegation of discretion and reliance on the good faith of event organisers with a clear financial interest, is troubling, and I would suggest that it may be an important factor in any future judicial consideration of the justification for free speech limitations occasioned by such legislation.

Possibly even more troubling than the inherent restrictions on advertising and other forms of commercial speech by non-sponsors as found in legislative anti-ambush marketing prohibitions, it appears that major sports events organisers have in recent times also proceeded to increasingly impose sometimes harsh and wide-ranging restrictions on the dissemination of news and information regarding such events, through the use of e.g. ticket terms and conditions, athlete participation agreements and media accreditation regulations. It is one thing for team coaches to ban their players from using social networking tools such as Facebook and Twitter during events, as was the case with the All Black rugby team for the 2011 IRB Rugby World Cup (their coach apparently only found out about Twitter in 2009 when a player tweeted about being dropped from the team before it was reported in the media—coach Graham Henry was quoted as saying at the time 'I had to find out what bloody Twitter was. I thought it was a new guy playing five-eighth for England').[75] It is something else, however, when communication restrictions are imposed by event organisers. During the 2000 Sydney Olympic Games athletes were prohibited from talking to their hometown newspapers or from chatting online with journalists. Video streaming of events was banned and the IOC reportedly sued 1 800 'cyber-squatters' whose web sites supposedly used words 'owned' by the IOC.[76] The IOC's rather original (although, sadly, no longer unique) approach has been characterised as the assertion of a new 'centralised control over the outflow of information from the Olympic Games', and it has been observed that 'the IOC wanted to be paid for staging the competitions while controlling how they would be communicated to the world: a rather novel definition of "news"'.[77] Reference has been made elsewhere in this

---

[74] Ellis et al. 2011, p. 304.

[75] See the report entitled 'All Blacks impose social media blackout for the World Cup, 17 June 2011, available online at the time of writing at http://news.bbc.co.uk/sport2/hi/rugby_union/13808100.stm.

[76] See Bollier 2005, p. 171.

[77] Ibid. 171–172.

book to the International Rugby Board's 'draconian' media accreditation regulations for the 2007 Rugby World Cup, as well as the more recent *contretemps* between FIFA and the South African media (in the form of the SA National Editors Forum) regarding the accreditation provisions for the 2010 event. In August 2011 it was reported that two major publishers in Australia were in a dispute with the IRB regarding its journalist and press photographer accreditation provisions for the 2011 World Cup event. Fairfax Media and News Ltd refused to sign terms preventing them showing more than 90 s of footage on their websites or running advertisements before clips, despite Australian law allowing both under fair dealing exceptions to copyright protections for news reporting. The publishers claimed that the IRB is not entitled to seek to dictate what material may legitimately be used to report news, while Rugby World Cup Ltd said the dispute was about Australian newspapers intending to commercialise copyright material.[78] One report at the time explained:

> Publishers worry about setting a precedent in the digital age, with organisers seeking more revenue to cover costs through increasingly restrictive rights deals. The tournament has become a flashpoint for international media, drawing a line in the sand over increasingly prohibitive terms and conditions for access to matches and teams.[79]

The *Lei Geral da Copa* (the official FIFA 2014 World Cup and 2013 Confederations Cup legislation), which went to the Brazilian Congress in Bill form in September 2011, also contains controversial provisions regarding media reportage use of snippets of broadcasts of these events, which appears to have been a major point of contention between FIFA and the Brazilian government. Although (under section III of the Bill) FIFA is granted exclusive rights over the images and sounds of the events, it will be obliged to allow other broadcasters (in addition to the official broadcaster) to exhibit small passages of the matches and of the opening ceremony, as long as such broadcast is for informative purposes and restricted to 30 s. I would suggest that the following response (as found on the official FIFA World Cup 2014 website of the Brazilian government[80]) to the question of whether such provisions of the *Lei Geral da Copa* are detrimental to Brazil's national sovereignty is extremely dismissive and simplistic in respect of the potential free speech implications:

> No. Brazil signed the sovereign guarantees and no change [or] proposed rules offends the federal Constitution or the laws of our country. Other countries that have made the

[78] See the *Canberra Times* report available online at the time of writing at http://www.canberratimes.com.au/news/national/national/sport/publishers-tackle-rugby-world-cup-over-copyright/2269922.aspx.

[79] Dick, T 'World Cup tackled over restrictions on coverage' *Canberra Times*, 25 August 2011—available online at the time of writing at http://www.canberratimes.com.au/news/national/national/general/world-cup-tackled-over-restrictions-on-coverage/2269887.aspx.

[80] At http://www.copa2014.gov.br/noticia/conheca-o-projeto-de-lei-geral-da-copa-enviado-hoje-ao-congresso.

World Cup also signed guarantees similar to ours and passed laws specific to the World Cup.[81]

From a more practical perspective, I have referred, in an earlier chapter, to the often apparently masochistic attitude of event organisers to aggressive rights protection programmes, in the context of ambushing. Organisers often seem to create their own headaches through the extremely restrictive deals that they enter into with sponsors, thereby contributing to the 'ambushing' of events by those excluded from commercially benefiting from events. These problems are then compounded by aggressive promotion or enforcement of sponsors' rights by event organisers, often in a way that does more harm than good to the organisers from a public relations perspective. I would suggest that the above-mentioned media accreditation restrictions similarly relate to excessive attempts at ring-fencing potential sources of revenues and an apparent lack of appreciation of the role of the media in respect of conveying the message in marketing these organisers' events.

It appears, at least from this observer's perspective, that the clear concerns amongst major sports federations regarding the flow of information from events goes beyond merely the need to combat commercial (ab)use of information (e.g. for purposes of commercial ambush marketing campaigns); the impression is that these organisations frequently attempt to control the information purely for the sake of controlling the information. The reader is again asked to consider the fact that, in the South African jurisdiction as elsewhere, the event organisers do not enjoy a proprietary right to 'the spectacle' of such event. Also, it should be noted that other branches of the law—e.g. copyright law—does not protect information in the form of facts, *per se*.[82] It is submitted that these last-mentioned developments in respect of mega-events may constitute a relevant factor to be considered by a court if confronted with a challenge to the constitutionality of a free speech limitation in the context of an 'intrusion ambush' advertisement, in respect of determining the reasonableness of such a limitation in the meaning of section 36(1) of the South African Bill of Rights. In Chap. 10[83] I will briefly examine the potential future role of the internet and, specifically, social media in

---

81 Google translation from the original Portuguese text: Não. O Brasil firmou soberanamente as garantias prestadas e nenhuma modificação normativa proposta ofende a Constituição Federal ou a ordem jurídica de nosso país.

82 Although it should be noted that developments in some jurisdictions in respect of e.g. database rights have apparently opened the door to claims for protection of facts in terms of copyright laws—see the critical discussion by Bollier 2005, p. 160 *et seq*. Ironically, in the context of this book, a major battleground in this respect has been sports scores and statistics (see also the recent cases in the USA regarding fantasy leagues and access to player names and statistics—compare the litigation engaged in by Major League Baseball and the NFL Players' Association).

Hewitt 2005 discusses the failed lobby in England by the Association for the Protection of Copyright in Sports for the recognition of copyright in sports events similar to other types of 'works' under the applicable copyright legislation (e.g. literary, artistic and musical works), which was rejected in the 1952 Gregory Report (a report of the Committee on Copyright Protection which led to the Copyright Act of 1965).

83 In Sect. 10.4.2.

respect of ambushing of events. I refer there to the fact that event organisers, in keeping with their covetous attempts at market control and the arrogation of the whole thematic space of the mega-event (which is examined in more detail in Chap. 8) for the purpose of maximising commercial benefits; appear to claim 'the right to sell the conversation around their event'. This is something that is probably doomed to failure in the light of how social media function and what they are all about, but I would suggest that the potential free speech implications are clear and that this may become a major future issue in the mega-event human rights debate.

A final issue to consider is the role of *sui generis* event protection, coupled with (often widely reported) instances of aggressive rights enforcement by event organisers, in having a potentially very significant chilling effect on free (commercial) speech. The following was observed by a South African Constitutional Court judge in a case involving a parody defence to a trademark dilution claim,[84] which I view to be germane to the current discussion:

> Of… significance from a constitutional point of view is the manner in which even the threat of litigation can stifle legitimate debate. Large businesses have special access to wealth, the media and government. Like politicians and public figures, their trademarks represent highly visible and immediately recognisable symbols of societal norms and values. The companies that own famous trademarks exert substantial influence over public and political issues, making them and their marks ripe and appropriate targets for parody and criticism. Yet when applied against non-competitor parody artists, the tarnishment theory of trademark dilution may in protecting the reputation of a mark's owner, effectively act as a defamation statute. As such it, could serve as an over-deterrent. It could chill public discourse because trademark law could be used to encourage prospective speakers to engage in undue self-censorship to avoid the negative consequence of speaking; namely, being involved in a ruinous lawsuit. The cost could be inordinately high for an individual faced with a lawsuit aimed at silencing a critic, not only in terms of general litigation expenses, but also through the disruption of families and emotional upheaval. Such protracted vexation can have the effect of discouraging even the hardiest of souls from exercising their free speech rights.

I would suggest that these sentiments hold true also for FIFA and other mega-event organisers and for the special legislation passed by host governments to protect their commercial interests. And it is not only the legislation which may have this effect; consider the bulky advertising and marketing guidelines as published by FIFA and the Olympic organisers in the run-up to their events. Elsewhere in this book I refer to the wide scope of application of the new 'association rights' to events as contained in legislation such as the London Act for the 2012 Games and New Zealand's Major Events Management Act. One aspect of such rights which is especially problematic is the fact that determination of whether such rights have been infringed (or of whether the exemptions to such claims of infringement apply in any given case) is left to the extrajudicial discretion of event organisers, with the power to institute legal action or even criminal proceedings against alleged infringers and to potentially expose innocent persons to thousands of dollars of legal expenses to defend themselves against such claims. This same

[84] Sachs J in the *Laugh it Off* case *supra*, at par. 105–106.

danger, I would submit, also applies to these marketing guidelines, which are published ostensibly for educational purposes (and to avoid transgressions of rights or legal prohibitions), but may in fact have such a chilling effect based, again, on the interpretation of rights by a private entity with definite and partisan interests to protect. An example of this occurred in the run-up to the 2010 FIFA World Cup when a South African satellite TV channel, M-Net, postponed the broadcast of a new drama series after a FIFA football appeared in some scenes. The channel explained in a press statement at the time that '[u]pon reviewing FIFA's regulations around licensing for the World Cup during this time, M-Net and [the producers of the programme] realized that showing the scenes with the official FIFA ball would be against regulations'. It explained that experts were brought in to make the football scenes in the series 'as accurate and professional-looking as possible', but one of the experts brought an official FIFA ball and it was used in some of the takes. The producers subsequently reshot approximately nine minutes of the drama with the official ball replaced by a generic black and white one, and the broadcast was postponed for a couple of weeks.

The internet is awash with media reports from the past decade or so, in which dire warnings were posed to businesses and individuals in the run-up to sports mega-events protected by such legislation, regarding the need to curb their enthusiasm about the event in order to avoid falling foul of the law. While I continuously argue in this book that the 'intrusion ambush', as we have come to know it, is more often than not a perfectly legitimate, legal and ethical marketing device, we will probably never know how many such planned campaigns or witty and clever advertisements never saw the light of day as a result of the fears of sanctions or even gaol time in the face of the deterrent effects of such laws. The situation may be a patently unfair one for the small local business enterprise wishing to ride the wave of excitement surrounding a mega-event, as Ellis et al. observe:

> [W]hen ambush marketing is converted into a legal issue, the way in which the law is framed redefines the concept. Conduct which is captured by the terms of the law is illicit; but that conduct which falls outside the statutory language is legitimate. If a simple disclaimer of association is sufficient to make an advertisement unlikely to mislead the public into believing that a commercial relationship exists with event organizers, then ambush marketing that plays on the excitement or energy around the event while disclaiming formal association will be legitimate within the terms of the law. The type of legal advice necessary to permit companies to exploit legal loopholes is, however, only genuinely affordable by large corporations. This has the ironic effect of permitting them to continue to engage in ambush marketing while leaving small and even mid-sized local businesses to err on the side of caution and avoid all references, oblique or otherwise, to the event.[85]

Teresa Scassa also observes, with reference to the provisions of section 4 of the Vancouver Act,[86] that the nature of the remedies provided to event organisers may

[85] Ellis et al. 2011, p. 305.

[86] See the discussion in Sect. 4.4.7 of Chap. 4.

similarly have a chilling effect in respect of the decision of an alleged 'ambusher' to defend legal action taking by the event organiser:

> The combination of a lowered threshold for injunctions and the uncertainty over what conduct might infringe the right in s. 4 gives rise to some distinct issues of fairness. The new law creates an environment where very few cases may ever be heard on the merits, as the issues will become moot once an interlocutory injunction has been granted for the period of the event. An alleged ambusher would have to really wish to stand on principle to proceed with the costs of litigation to justify an advertising campaign whose time has long since come and gone.[87]

Legislatures who consider passing such laws should take due notice of the dangers and the constitutional implications of their actions. The event organisers and sponsors are highly unlikely to pause to consider these. As Louise Longdin explains in her example involving a matter in Australia[88] in the context of the 2000 Sydney Games:

> For example, an Australian animal rights activist was prohibited from distributing T-shirts and badges depicting an image of a hen in a cage with five eggs beneath it. The Sydney Organising Committee for the Olympic Games successfully obtained an injunction and an order for delivery up against her, convincing the court that the five eggs bore a close resemblance to the five-ring Sydney 2000 Olympic Games logo in which it had copyright. The fact that the respondent had accepted donations to her animal liberation organization's funds in return for the T-shirts and badges led the court to place no weight on any claim she might have made that she was using well-known symbols to attract attention to a political issue rather than attempting to pass off her goods as genuine logo bearing merchandize. The judge found the donations were a mere sham to disguise the reality of sale.[89]

In respect of the power of this example in highlighting the chilling of speech inherent in the powers granted to organising committees through widely drafted *sui generis* event legislation, Longdin observes:

> The point is here not whether SOCOG would have turned out to be right in its understanding that the law forbade such a satirical lampoon (had the substantive issue ever gone to trial), but that it had the capacity to shut down shallow pocketed protestors through intimidation aided by statutory ambiguity.[90]

And, as was observed in the UK Chartered Institute of Marketing (CIM)'s *The Event that Dare not Speak its Name: Marketing and the Olympics*[91] discussion document regarding marketing opportunities around the 2012 London Games:

> [W]hen the [LOCOG] itself decides what is and isn't an infringement of the [London Act] it is arguable that the only guaranteed safe way to respond for marketers will be to steer clear of anything associative at all. This would put SMEs in a largely no-win situation: they won't be able to afford to become a sponsor; being a supplier does not confer any

---

87 Scassa 2011, p. 361.

88 *Sydney Organising Committee for the Olympic Games v Pam Clarke* [1998] FCA 792.

89 Longdin 2009, p. 736.

90 Ibid.

91 Chartered Institute of Marketing *Shape the Agenda* Issue 14 (2008) 7.

exemptions to the rules; and by the nature of being an SME, few will be able to afford the risk, however small, of litigation.

7.2.2 'Clean Zones' and Freedom of Speech

An important battleground for constitutional free speech guarantees in the context of mega-events and anti-ambushing legislation is the increasingly common use of 'clean zones' around event venues. I have touched on this anti-ambushing measure elsewhere in the earlier chapters (including their potential anti-competitive effects in terms of competition laws in Chap. 7), and will simply mention a few examples of their use here, with a view to examining their potential for violating free speech guarantees. While activists were successful in forcing amendments to by-laws enacted for the 2010 Vancouver Winter Olympics after the filing of a suit against the Vancouver city council,[92] other recent mega-event host jurisdictions have, surprisingly, not seen much in the way of litigation against clean zone ordinances and other such measures which may impact significantly on the civil liberties of host nation citizens.

Ari Sliffman[93] has examined the NFL's clean zone requirements for the American Super Bowl with respect to their constitutionality. He explains that the enforced prohibitions by host cities on advertising in clean zones stand to be tested in terms of the US Supreme Court's commercial speech doctrine as developed in *Central Hudson Gas & Electric Corp. v. Public Service Commission of New York*[94] (where the state government enacted an ordinance prohibiting all advertising promoting the use of electricity in New York State). The Supreme Court held that, although the Constitution does not protect commercial speech to the extent of other forms of expression, the protection available for commercial speech depends on whether the speech itself is legal (more specifically, is not deceptive or misleading), as well as the governmental interests furthered by the regulation. In respect of this last component of the test, the question is whether the government asserts a legitimate interest for suppressing commercial speech, and also requires that the restriction on commercial speech 'must *directly* advance the state interest involved… [and] if the governmental interest could be served as well by a more limited restriction on commercial speech, the excessive restrictions cannot survive'. Finally, in terms of the First Amendment, any restriction on speech must directly further the asserted legitimate governmental interest and be narrowly tailored to achieve the asserted interests.[95]

---

92 See the short press release of the British Columbia Civil Liberties Association available online at the time of writing at http://www.bccla.org/pressreleases/10Activist_lawsuit.html.

93 Sliffman 2012—I wish to sincerely thank the author for kindly providing me with access to this document prior to its publication.

94 447 U.S. 557 (1980).

95 Sliffman 2012.

Sliffman explains the most likely legitimate governmental interests that might pass muster in respect of host city clean zone restrictions (with reference to the case law on state or city prohibitions on advertising[96]):

> The most common legitimate interests likely to be applied to a Super Bowl host city's clean-zone ordinance are community aesthetics and safety. Aesthetics lend to the quality of the city's appearance due to the absence of clutter or excessive off-site commercial signage, which has consistently been found a legitimate governmental interest. A municipality's desire to have a clean-looking presence is within its police power, so long as such restriction does not actually have an ulterior motive in restricting commercial speech. Community safety, whether related to traffic or otherwise, is a commonsense legitimate governmental interest.[97]

The author explains that Fort Worth, Texas, which successfully bid for the 2011 edition of the Super Bowl, enacted a clean zone ordinance on 23 January 2011 which followed the NFL's bid requirements exactly. Sliffman explains that the wording of the ordinance shrewdly dealt with the justification for its potential free speech implications, in light of the case law referred to above:

> The ordinance … states that Fort Worth found it necessary to enact the ordinance because the NFL informed city officials that difficulties have ensued in Super Bowl host cities where there was no regulation of "temporary outdoor advertising displays visible from public streets and sidewalks in the vicinity of Super Bowl related events resulted in pedestrian and vehicular traffic" safety issues. The safety concern is increased because of the large gatherings of people who enter the clean-zone area. Finally, the last purpose for enacting the ordinance was to "promote and protect good order and aesthetic quality and to protect the safety and convenience of drivers and pedestrians in and around downtown during the Super Bowl XLV and its related Super Bowl activities." This language set out aesthetics and public safety as likely legitimate governmental interests that would be furthered by suppressing otherwise legal commercial speech.

However, Sliffman argues that an additional factor relating to this ordinance makes it unconstitutional, in light of the courts' stance that providing an official with an unbridled discretion to permit or outlaw outdoor advertising is impermissible (e.g. if exercised for 'subjective or ambiguous reasons')[98]:

> Although Fort Worth's clean-zone ordinance specifically stated that its governmental interests were public safety and aesthetics, the fact that the phrase "unless approved by the NFL" appears throughout the ordinance suggests otherwise. Specifically that the NFL used its influence so that during the two weeks prior to the Super Bowl, to ensure that other interests—such as preventing otherwise legal ambush marketing—were met in addition to the legitimate aesthetic and public safety interests… Fort Worth's clean-zone ordinance, on its face, is unconstitutional. Applying the *Central Hudson* and *Metromedia* standards, a court may hold that aesthetics should not be a legitimate governmental interest because Fort Worth clearly had an ulterior motive; bowing to the demands of the

---

[96] With reference to *Metromedia, Inc. v. City of San Diego*, 453 U.S. 490 (1981); *City and County of S.F. v. Eller Outdoor Adver.*, 192 Cal. App. 3d 643 (1987).

[97] Sliffman 2012.

[98] With reference to *Atlanta Journal and Constitution v. City of Atlanta Department of Aviation* 322 F.3d 1298 (11th Cir. 2003); *Desert Outdoor Advertising, Inc. v. City of Moreno Valley* 103 F.3d 814 (9th Cir. 1996).

> NFL to secure the Super Bowl for the North Texas area. Furthermore, the clean-zone ordinance provides the NFL with unbridled discretion to determine what businesses may use outdoor advertising. This is in direct conflict with *Atlanta Journal & Constitution*. To avoid or defeat a constitutional challenge, future Super Bowl host cities should not include the language "unless approved by the NFL" with an enacted clean-zone ordinance.[99]

The author argues that aesthetics may not be a legitimate governmental interest in justification of a clean-zone ordinance where it can be shown that there was an ulterior motive. He states, in respect of the example under discussion, that it could be successfully argued that Fort Worth had an ulterior motive in enacting its clean-zone ordinance: 'Fort Worth effectively gave the NFL monopoly power over the clean-zone area to benefit the NFL's value for its official sponsors and to protect those sponsors from ambush marketing'.[100] Interestingly, Sliffman also argues that such ordinance might not be justifiable on the basis of the 'economic vitality' argument (i.e. that the legislature would be entitled to rely on the governmental interest of pursuing the economic benefits that an event such as the Super Bowl might bring):

> [I]t can be argued that, on its face, the ordinance restricts economic vitality rather than advances it. By prohibiting a restaurant located within the designated clean zone to place on-site and outdoor advertising of its products facing the public street may hinder the restaurant's business. It would effectively be prohibited to have outdoor advertising promoting any of the NFL non-official sponsor's beer specials it may have during Super Bowl week, or that it even sells the product. Fort Worth might argue that the ordinance's purpose, as related to economic vitality, is to grow the future prosperity of the city as a whole and businesses should not merely look at the short-term; however, hosting the Super Bowl generally has no actual economic effect on the host city. Additionally, any economic vitality interest would not be furthered by enacting the clean-zone ordinance, but only by hosting the Super Bowl. Therefore, economic vitality is likely not a legitimate governmental interest advanced by the clean-zone ordinance.[101]

Ultimately, Sliffman argues that the NFL would be advised to remove its '"unless approved by the NFL" language' in its bid package requirements (i.e. removing its unbridled discretion to authorise outdoor advertising by its official sponsors within clean zones) in order to pre-empt a constitutional free speech challenge. Additionally, he also observes that, in light of the dangers of ambush marketing, the NFL should not be blamed for flexing its muscle and 'recommending' that host bid cities promise to enact a clean-zone ordinance during the Super Bowl. Of course, it is debatable whether such 'recommendation' is merely that; as I have explained in Chap. 4, event organisers generally wield the sword of Damocles over those bidding for the rights to host events. Sliffman himself observes that '[i]f the North Texas Bid Committee failed to promise the NFL that Arlington and Fort Worth would enact clean-zone ordinances, one could likely assume that the NFL would look to other cities for hosting the Super Bowl because

[99] Sliffman 2012.

[100] Ibid.

[101] Ibid.

the NFL's interests in having an aesthetically-pleasing, safe, and ambush-free event would not be met'.

In respect of the issue of justification for restrictions on free speech occasioned by street trading and advertising regulations in 'clean zones', it is interesting to note the UK government's justification of its regulations for the 2012 London Olympic Games. In a 2011 consultation document published for public comment,[102] the UK government acknowledged the impact of its advertising and street trading regulations for the event on 'freedom of expression and protection of possessions'.[103] It listed three specific human rights implications in terms of the European Convention on Human Rights (or ECHR):

- Article 10 of the ECHR affirms the right to freedom of expression: 'During the London 2012 Games, the Regulations will restrict a person's ability to engage in advertising activity as well as some forms of trading that include an element of "expression" in small areas around London 2012 events. By doing so, the Regulations will interfere with the Article 10 rights of people who wish to engage in those activities.'
- Article 1 to the First Protocol to the ECHR ('A1P1') protects a person's 'possessions' from unjustified appropriation or interference by the State: 'The benefit of a licence, permit, certificate or consent (a "licence") to carry on a profitable activity can amount to a "possession" for A1P1 purposes. The Regulations will apply despite any licence granted before or after the Regulations come into force and will restrict a person's ability to engage in advertising activity and trading in accordance with an existing licence (in the small areas where the Regulations apply, during the Games period). Accordingly, the Regulations will arguably interfere with the A1P1 rights of current licensees.'
- '[T]he Regulations will limit the uses to which land and other property (again, within the small areas where the Regulations apply) may be put during the Games period. They will prevent, for example, a land owner from using his or her land (or allowing his or her land to be used) for advertising or trading activities. This may also amount to an interference with land or other property owners' A1P1 rights.'[104]

The UK government's views on justification of such impact on freedom of expression are explained as follows:

> An interference with freedom of expression will be justified under Article 10(2) of the ECHR where it is prescribed by law, where it furthers a "legitimate aim" referred to in Article 10(2), and where it is necessary in a democratic society. States are accorded a broad margin of appreciation under Article 10 for restrictions on commercial expression… The Regulations are intended to meet commitments given by the UK Government to the International Olympic Committee in London's bid to host the 2012 Games. The main aims are [t]o ensure all Olympic and Paralympic events have a consistent celebratory look and feel to them; [t]o prevent ambush marketing within the vicinity of venues; [and to] ensure people can easily access the venues. These aims are consistent with legitimate aims that

---

[102] At http://www.culture.gov.uk/images/publications/ConDoc_Regulations_on_Advertising_and_Trading_London_2012-section9-10.pdf.

[103] The consultation document *supra* at 91 *et seq.*

[104] Ibid.

> justify an interference with Article 10 and A1P1 rights. The Games are a once-in-a-lifetime occasion and it is reasonable for the Government to enact measures to facilitate the staging of the Games, even where those measures necessitate a limited and temporary interference with individuals' rights.[105]

The consultation document continues to explain that the regulations will 'further the interests of public safety at Games time by ensuring that competitors, officials, spectators and other people attending events are able smoothly to enter and exit venues'; of course, it also mentions that they will 'protect the rights of those that have made a commercial contribution to the staging of the Games (without which the Games could not take place) by preventing advertising and trading activities that amount to ambush marketing'. The document furthermore expounds that such restrictions on freedom of expression are reasonable and proportionate in light of their short duration and the limited geographical areas of their application.[106]

The above bases of justification, however, appear to be mostly cosmetic in nature. It is hard to imagine how the very extensive nature of such regulations in respect of their restrictions on advertising will contribute to the safety of event spectators (except in extreme cases of invasive placing of advertising materials on e.g. public transport routes or at venue entrances or exits). And I fail to fully understand how promotion of 'a consistent celebratory look and feel' for the Games can justify restrictions on freedom of expression. One assumes that the thinking behind this is that it is bad for the Games to be overtaken by crass commercialism in the form of commercial advertising—unless such advertising is by official sponsors? I believe this raises an issue regarding the role of the source of the advertising message, which bears consideration.

When one considers the issue of potential freedom of speech implications of commercial rights protection to mega-events it is important to also consider the potential content and nature of 'the message', the opinion or the expression that may be implicated or impacted upon. As we view the activities of 'official' sponsors and commercial partners compared to those of the 'ambushers', it is interesting to note that these two opposing camps appear to represent two poles of the public sphere inhabited by mega-events (the 'thematic space' of the event[107]) and of the opportunities they provide for public discourse surrounding the event. The following has been observed regarding such events in this context:

> Mega-events are… ambiguous. On the one hand they provide powerful media and occasions for elites both to network amongst themselves and with international elites, and to project and disseminate old and new hegemonic and "official" ideologies to "the masses". On the other hand, they also create opportunities—through information overloads, mixed messages, selective readings, message failures, creative responses by sections of the crowds which gather for the event, and also through some of the divisive and

[105] Ibid. at 92.

[106] Ibid. at 93.

[107] Which will be further examined in Chap. 8.

> exclusionary dynamics—for the development of "popular cultural" and occasionally "resistant" responses by members of the public.[108]

I would suggest that this characterisation neatly sums up one aspect of the conflict between the role, place and commercial message of the official sponsor, as opposed to that of the 'ambusher'. The official sponsor's role is that of supporter, partner or enabler—the event's very existence and success is attributable to its investment—while the 'ambusher' is a cheat, a free-rider and a destroyer—as a result of its contemptible conduct, the very existence of the event is threatened. We have examined the modern system of sponsorship exclusivity and how it functions. These corporations represent or reflect a homogenous group of disparate brands, bound through mega-event spin-doctoring to comprise a 'family' or 'movement' reflective of the ideology of the event (even though such links are sometimes extremely tenuous—much has been written about the involvement of fast food and soft drink peddlers like McDonalds and Coca-Cola with the athletic and clean-living culture of the Olympic Games, for example[109]). On the other hand, the 'ambushers' represent outsiders who bring 'popular cultural' and 'resistant' responses to the event, although such responses are consistently condemned by the elite and its official ideology. 'Ambushing', in this light, represents a diversity of opinions, a multiplicity of messages, which must surely contribute to rather than limit consumer choice. The elite's outright and reflexive condemnation of such alternative voice presumes a denial of the rights of the masses to an alternative experience of the event and what it represents. This is nothing new; the organiser of the first 'Gay Olympics'; in the United States (which I've referred to elsewhere), Dr Tom Waddell, was quoted in a 1982 issue of *Sports Illustrated* magazine—in criticising the IOC's alleged hypocrisy regarding the message of the Games—as stating that 'The bottom line is that if I'm a rat, a crab, a copying machine or an Armenian I can have my own Olympics. If I'm gay, I can't'.[110] When considered against the backdrop of the public domain element of mega-events, as discussed elsewhere in this book, the condemnatory and severely restrictive attitude of event organisers regarding alternative messages (including commercial ones) again highlights the contradiction inherent in the event organisers' and rights grantors' conception of ownership of what they view to be their private property. And inherent in this conception is an implication that the event organisers and official sponsors inhabit some moral high ground when it comes to disseminating any messages, commercial or otherwise, related to the event. This is

---

108 Roche 2000, p. 9.

109 Although the IOC does not appear to be overly bothered by such criticisms—compare the expected extension of the McDonald's TOP sponsorship of the Olympic Games through 2020, as reported in Mickle, T 'McDonald's close to TOP extension', 17 October 2011—available online at http://www.sportsbusinessdaily.com/Journal/Issues/2011/10/17/Olympics/McD-TOP.aspx.

110 As referred to by Symons, C and Warren, I "David v. Goliath": The Gay Games, the Olympics and the Ownership of Language' *Entertainment and Sports Law Journal* (April 2006), text available online at the time of writing at http://www.bl.uk/sportandsociety/exploresocsci/sportsoc/mega/articles/clicklogo.pdf.

ironic. In the run-up to the 2010 Vancouver Games CBC News Canada reported that, according to the IOC's Brand Protection Manual, VANOC would deploy 'brand protection teams of two or more members [to] conduct surveillance on foot, within and around each venue or cluster of venues, at neighbouring areas and in the city to ensure that venues are clean internally, to carry out surveillance for incidents of ambush marketing and to handle and report such activity in the appropriate manner with the goal of ceasing such activity'. It reportedly also included a 'how-to guide for keeping the Olympic venues free of political, ethnic or religious protest', including powers for such teams to confiscate material 'that violates the Olympic brand, and remove unauthorized banners or signs'.[111] The irony, I would suggest, is to be found in the response by VANOC's director of commercial rights management, who was quoted as defending the use of these 'black ops' teams as follows:

> We want this to be a celebration of sport…. We're not there singularly to prevent other messaging. We're there collectively to let the core message rise above… We're trying to preserve the environment for a core message, which is the athletic performance and the nation versus nation, individual versus individual. That's the story everyone's tuned in for. Other stories, forcing them on spectators and athletes, is unfair because that's not what they signed up for.[112]

Of course *that is* the message of the modern Olympics! It is also rather presumptuous (if not unexpected) to encounter this apparent assumption that spectators and athletes have in fact signed up to the (commercial) 'message' of the official sponsors and the event organiser. One commentator has observed that the modern spectre of taxpayer-funded infrastructure (e.g. stadia) which serves as platforms for advertising by corporate sponsors whose very investment is partially funded by the consumer, has occasioned a situation where the consumer is increasingly paying for the opportunity to be exposed to the sponsor's advertising.[113] The above attitude of event organisers sounds apropos; not only are we as fans/consumers obliged to submit to the marketing message leviathan that is the mega-event—often paying for the 'privilege'—we are also expected (in fact forced) to buy into the event organiser's perception of the ethical, moral and legal nature of 'ambush marketing'. Grady et al., in expressing reservations as to both the legitimacy and the efficacy of event-specific anti-ambushing legislation (in the Olympics context), observe the following:

> The requirement to enact event-specific legislation is foisted upon the host country's legislature, and the host country essentially must buy into the perspective of ambush marketing as defined by the Olympic movement. This view is increasingly at odds with the current conceptualisation of ambush marketing in the practitioner and academic literatures as an effective alternative to purchasing sponsorship rights. Whereas in the past ambush

---

[111] 'Roving teams shield Olympic brand', 15 September 2009—available online at http://www.cbc.ca/news/canada/british-columbia/story/2009/09/15/bc-olympic-advertising-protest-teams.html.

[112] Ibid.

[113] Schlossberg 1996, p. 176.

> marketing was largely viewed as an unethical business practice to be condemned, there has been a considerable shift in industry perspective, reflected in the academic literature, to an increasingly less negative and pejorative view of the practice.[114]
>
> One of the few notable exceptions remains the Olympic movement, which can maintain its un-wavering stance on ambush marketing because of the absolute leverage it holds over potential host cities throughout the bid process. As a result, by conceding to the requirement to enact event-specific legislation, governments not only embrace the Olympic movement's stigmatised definition of ambush marketing as unethical and immoral, but also threaten to make illegal competitive business behaviour that would otherwise be deemed normal, fair, acceptable and legal; again, part of the "normal cut and thrust" of business activity.[115]

I would suggest that this apparent, commercially-driven, control over the thinking of consumers and the host nation populace is an example of privatisation of elements of popular culture which is not in line with democratic principles:

> Private control over [merchandising images]—"commodification of the intertext"—can, therefore, do more than merely diminish expressive choices. Privatization can disturb the dynamics that are crucial to democracy.[116]

I would suggest that a very real purpose of the UK government's advertising restrictions for the 2012 Olympic Games, apart from combating 'ambushing', is to counter any potential message which is not in line with the 'celebratory look and feel' of the Games. Is the real purpose of guarantees of free speech not to allow those who feel they have less reason to celebrate the right to voice their views? I think the gist of the matter is really that event organisers (propped up by their host nation lawmakers) view the mega-event as their party, and while they cannot necessarily control who shows up when that party is held in the middle of a large cosmopolitan city, they can (and will) do their utmost to ensure that no party crasher upstages the host or 'brings down the vibe'. How else does one explain the arrest of social activists (on the basis of anti-ambushing laws) for handing out anti-xenophobia (i.e. decidedly *non-commercial*) pamphlets at a FIFA Fan Fest in Durban during the 2010 FIFA World Cup?[117]

---

[114] Grady et al. 2010, p. 154.

[115] Ibid. 151.

[116] Cooper Dreyfuss 1996, p. 140.

[117] See the report by Patrick Bond 'FIFA forbids free speech at World Cup fan fest', 9–11 July 2010—available online at http://www.counterpunch.org/bond07092010.html.

7.2.3 *Airlines, Dogs and Yoga Clothing: Of Parody and Common Sense*

A final aspect that merits some brief consideration is the issue of the law's treatment of parody[118] in advertising, and its potential relevance in respect of ambush marketing advertising. I will again focus, primarily, on the South African law and the experience of the 2010 FIFA World Cup. By way of illustration of the aggressive nature of FIFA's enforcement strategy in respect of the 2010 World Cup event, coupled with the apparently very wide scope of the conduct which the organisation views to be prohibited in terms of the South African legislation, is a promotional campaign launched by local airline kulula.com in early 2010. The airline launched a multi-media advertising campaign linked to low air fares during the World Cup event, which featured advertisements with the headline 'The Unofficial National Carrier of the "You-Know-What"', showing stylized drawings depicting what appeared to be the new Green Point stadium in Cape Town, soccer balls, vuvuzelas, a football player and the national flag. Following a letter from FIFA's lawyers, kulula withdrew the campaign. The airline's marketing manager was quoted as stating that the advertisement had been planned to be quirky and fun, in line with the airline's reputation for tongue-in-cheek and irreverent promotional campaigns, but that it had been decided to withdraw the ad as it appeared to have crossed FIFA's 'very strict line' in respect of ambush marketing. It was claimed that FIFA had objected to most of what was contained in the advertisement: 'They said we cannot depict the Cape Town stadium … soccer balls … the word South Africa, the national flag, can't make any reference to the World Cup and cannot use the vuvuzela.'[119]

In a similar vein, car manufacturer Suzuki had also been running a promotional campaign offering 'Off the Bandwagon' deals. This campaign, while not referring in any way to the 2010 World Cup event (which is probably the only reason why it has not invoked FIFA's ire), pointedly implied that the car maker was not joining all the other marketers who had gotten on the bandwagon in respect of promoting their wares with reference to football and the World Cup: no new car buyer would receive a free soccer ball or soccer boots.

It is submitted that advertising campaigns of this nature might be justifiable as parody, although not functioning in the traditional meaning of parody as a 'fair use' defence in respect of e.g. copyright infringement. In the United States, the social value of parody has been recognised, and the courts take parody as fair use

---

118 For an (as always) eloquent discussion of the meaning of parody, and its interaction with the law, see the judgment of Sachs J in the *Laugh It Off* case supra (especially from par 76 *et seq*).

119 Kulula.com marketing manager Nadine Damen, as quoted in the article by Dardagan, C 'Kulula flies into FIFA flak', 19 March 2010—available obline at www.iol.co.za [accessed 19 March 2010].

claims seriously when considering copyright infringement claims.[120] Parody can also constitute a defence to a trade mark infringement claim, i.e. that there is no likelihood of confusion because the parody will not be taken seriously.[121]

It is interesting to speculate whether section 15A of the MMA leaves room for a parody defence in respect of advertising such as the kulula.com and Suzuki campaigns. While, as mentioned, the point might be moot in respect of the Suzuki campaign (in which the only conceivable 'reference' to the football world cup might be the reference to soccer balls and boots), it is suggested that kulula.com may have been overhasty in pulling their campaign following FIFA's threatening stance. This brings to mind one American observer's remarks in the context of copyright: 'Because of widespread misunderstanding of copyright law, cease-and-desist letters carry inordinate cultural power and can chill if not directly censor expression.'[122] FIFA has been sending such letters to South Africans for years,[123] in the absence of the type of remedies provided in respect of 'groundless threats' as found in some other *sui generis* anti-ambushing events legislation.[124] One online report on FIFA's response to the kulula.com campaign contained the following:

> FIFA's office told *KickOff.com* that their lawyers contacted Kulula drawing attention to the fact that the advert breaches SA law against ambush marketing (s.15A Merchandise Marks Act) by seeking to gain a promotional benefit for the Kulula brand by creating an unauthorised association with the 2010 FIFA World Cup.

This is, of course, drivel. As has been shown, section 15A is not concerned with (and does not require) the creation of or an attempt to create an 'unauthorised association' with an event. The use of a mark in relation to an event which derives 'special promotional benefit' for such mark does not require or refer to an association with the event. While section 15A(3) provides that the use of a trade mark in terms of s 15A(2) *includes* use of the mark 'which in any way, directly or indirectly, is intended to be brought into association with or to allude to an event',

120 See *Campbell v Acuff-Rose Music, Inc* 510 US 569 (1994), and the discussion of this case in Vaidhyanathan 2003, pp. 146–148.

121 See the *Laugh It Off* case supra (and, in respect of a parody defence to trade mark infringement in the context of the constitutional freedom of expression guarantee, specifically the judgment in the Constitutional Court by Sachs J).

122 Vaidhyanathan 2003, p. 187.

123 For example, in 2006 the organisation admonished a local businessman who had registered five 2010 World Cup-related.co.za domains for an online travel and accommodation reservation, booking and information service (see the article by Glazier, D 'FIFA threatens World Cup domain owner', 5 October 2006 [available on the web site of http://www.itweb.co.za—accessed 8 April 2009)]. It appeared at the time that there was a lack of clarity regarding the legal position, as it appeared that FIFA's name and brand were not used, although FIFA's legal representatives were of the opinion that the domains were in contravention of the ambush marketing provisions of Section 15A of the Merchandise Marks Act, in light of the 'protected event' status of the 2010 World Cup. The eventual outcome of this dispute is unknown to the author at the time of writing.

124 Such as that found in Section 16 of the Olympic Symbol etc. (Protection) Act 1995 (and extended in Para 10(1)(h) of Schedule 4 of the London Olympic and Paralympic Games Act, 2006) in the UK—see discussion in Chap. 4.

the wording of the provision makes it clear that the prohibition also goes beyond such instances and is aimed at preventing non-association ambushes. It is submitted that kulula.com's advertisement did not, by any stretch of the imagination, imply *an association* with the World Cup. This was a clear case of the so-called 'intrusion ambush' which, in fact, incorporated a disclaimer in its reference to the 'unofficial' nature of its tongue-in-cheek status of national carrier for the 'you-know-what'.[125] It is suggested that FIFA's reported justification for its attempts to muzzle the airline (it was subsequently reported that FIFA had explained that its objection was not to use of the individual elements of the ad, but their combination) was overstated.

It appears that kulula got the last laugh, however. Following its recall of the advertisement, kulula unveiled a new advertisement including similar elements under the following thinly-veiled reference to '2010' in a prominent heading: 'Not next year, not last year, but somewhere in between'. This was followed shortly thereafter with a newspaper ad that appeared during the first week of the 2010 World Cup event, in which the airline offered affordable flights to everyone—except Sepp Blatter—during 'that thing that is happening right now'.[126] In a surprising about-turn, which appeared to show a measure of remorse towards FIFA, kulula subsequently offered to fly FIFA's president around the country for free for the duration of the event. As could be expected, a shrewd bloke soon saw a gap, and the rest is history (described as follows at the time on kulula's Facebook page):

> Sepp, a young Boston Terrier from Cape Town, is receiving free flights from low fare airline kulula during the next month following an offer to fly the president of FIFA around South Africa. Responding to an advert placed by the low fare airline in the *Sunday Times*, the dog's owners pointed out that the offer didn't specify which Sepp the ad, referred to, so their pet was eligible to take advantage of the free flights. Sepp (the dog) changed his name specifically to take up the offer. kulula has agreed to honour the promise of free flights during June and July and will be giving Sepp Blatter (the dog) a seat up front on any flight he wishes to travel on. The original advert was made as a conciliatory gesture towards the human Sepp following well publicised criticism from FIFA of previous kulula marketing during the World Cup period.
>
> "We really wanted to make a gesture to Sepp Blatter for putting on such a great show and to make up for our somewhat cheeky advertising telling people how reasonable our fares are. We were somewhat surprised that instead of flying the president of FIFA around we'll now be giving a seat to a Boston Terrier but he's really quite cute and very well behaved so why not," said Nadine Damen, Marketing Manager of kulula.

---

[125] Although it should be noted, of course, that the fact that s 15A(2) does not require deception or confusion of the public or a representation of association with an event would make the use of a notice disclaiming such an association irrelevant for purposes of determining contravention of the provision.

[126] According to the ad, kulula offered Mr. Blatter a free flight 'if he needs to be anywhere in the country in the most convenient way possible', provided he e-mails kulula at ImSeppBlatter@kulula.com.

As has been observed, kulula appears to have won first prize in respect of any promotional campaign, namely the achievement of publicity. FIFA's efforts at protecting its rights in terms of the letter of the law have probably just served to bring more attention to the ad campaign than would otherwise have been the case.[127]

This is reminiscent of similar events during the 2010 Vancouver Winter Olympics, involving a yoga-wear manufacturer, Lululemon, which was not an official sponsor of the event. Lululemon released a clothing line under the tag line 'Cool Sporting Event that takes place in British Columbia between 2009 and 2011', which was not well received by the Vancouver Organising Committee (VANOC). Both VANOC and Lululemon publicly admitted that no laws had been broken (the marketing campaign did not violate any provisions of the applicable Olympic and Paralympic Marks Act), and VANOC threatened a 'name and shame' campaign. As Jon Heshka observes, VANOC appears to have missed the plot and to have played into the hands of the 'ambusher', as holding press conferences to bring attention to Lululemon's campaign served little purpose other than further diverting attention from the official sponsors.[128] The VANOC response, just like that by FIFA in respect of kulula.com, shows little true appreciation for the realities of creative marketing campaigns. By using the proverbial sledgehammer to smash a pesky little nut, the organisations involved have done little more than display short-sightedness and a rather petulant schoolyard bully mentality in dealing with much smaller adversaries who appear to have the upper hand in the common sense department. Little wonder then that campaigns such as these (compare also the Bavaria beer campaign utilised at the 2010 FIFA World Cup, as discussed elsewhere in this book) often serve to draw a wry chuckle and some measure of admiration as well as sympathy from the public. This has been succinctly explained in the context of the Bavaria 'orange mini dresses' stunt and Nike's exceptionally successful 'Write the Future' and 'Write the Headline' campaigns as employed during the 2010 FIFA World Cup, and event organisers and official sponsors should take heed:

> Both the Nike and Bavaria examples demonstrate that the future of ambush marketing is very much archetypal guerrilla warfare, a small and highly mobile campaign supported by the public, acting against a larger unwieldy force. Ironically, the more that events rights holders rely on draconian and heavy handed statutory protections, the more they become fixed targets and therefore vulnerable to these sophisticated ambushes, particularly from social media. The adage of winning the hearts and minds of the population has just as much relevance here as it does in the military; by pursuing a criminal case against two women over what amounted to essentially a commercial dispute simply for wearing a plain orange dress, FIFA was always going to elicit sympathy for the underdog brewer.[129]

---

[127] See the article by Moerdyk, C 'Kulula is outwitting FIFA at every turn' (available at http://www.bizcommunity.com/Article/196/147/45942.html—accessed on 9 April 2010).

[128] Jon Heshka, writing in 'Rules and Rogues', *Marketing Magazine*, 1 February 2010, 37.

[129] Lines and Heshka 2010.

What is quite troubling (in the context of FIFA's apparently implied claim to 'rights' in respect of a depiction of a World Cup stadium during the kulula.com campaign), although I am speculating here, is the fact that it appears as if there may be some substance to concerns that have been expressed from some quarters that FIFA appears to have had the South African legislature in its back pocket for some time during the run-up to and staging of the 2010 event. It is interesting to note that in May 2010, shortly following media reports over the kulula.com ad campaign and its use, *inter alia*, of a depiction of the new Green Point World Cup stadium in Cape Town, the Minister of Trade and Industry published for public comment a notice in terms of s 13 of the Merchandise Marks Act, 1941 which proposed the prohibition of 'the use of words, devices, logos, pictures and drawings of the following stadiums, Nelson Mandela Bay Stadium, Peter Mokaba Stadium, Mbombela Stadium, Soccer City Stadium and Green Point Stadium or similar drawings which might cause confusion with any trade, business, profession or occupation or event or in connection with a trade mark, mark or trade description applied to goods, save where the use thereof is by or (*sic*) the authority of the relevant Metro/Municipality in which the above stadiums are situated.'[130] Apart from the possible implications of such a ministerial notice in light of FIFA's wrangle with kulula at the time, this notice is another example of a rather puzzling legislative product to emanate from the South African government during the 2010 event. One wonders how its proposed prohibition would be policed. Was there serious contemplation of a requirement that, for example, use of an aerial photograph of Cape Town (one of the world's favourite tourism destinations), incorporating the prominent World Cup stadium which FIFA reportedly insisted should be built on the Green Point site precisely because of the picturesque Table Mountain and city backdrop, would be prohibited on tourist brochures unless special consent is obtained from the relevant city authorities? While building designs may be copyrighted,[131] this would have taken attempts at monopolisation of the physical environment to rather ludicrous new lengths.

In determining the potential constitutional free speech implications of the anti-intrusion ambush restrictions inherent in s 15A of South Africa's Merchandise Marks Act, it is suggested that the following remarks by Moseneke J in the *Laugh It Off* case,[132] regarding the dilution provisions of s 34 of the Trade Marks Act in the context of the freedom of expression guarantees in the Bill of Rights, are germane:

> The reach of the statutory prohibition [contained in s 34(1)(c) of the Trade Marks Act] must be curtailed to the least intrusive [to the constitutional guarantee] means necessary to

---

130 'Prohibition of the Use of the Moses Mabhida Stadium and other Stadiums Intellectual Property Rights', Interim Notice 396 of 2010, *Government Gazette* No. 33197 (17 May 2010).

131 Compare the definition of an 'artistic work' in the South African Copyright Act 98 of 1978, which includes 'works of architecture, being either buildings or models of buildings'.

132 *Laugh It Off Promotions CC v South African Breweries International (Finance) B.V. t/a Sabmark International & Another* 2006 (1) SA 144 (CC).

> achieve the purpose of the section. *Courts must be astute not to convert the anti-dilution safeguard of renowned trade marks usually controlled by powerful financial interests into a monopoly adverse to other claims of expressive conduct of at least equal cogency and worth in our broader society.*[133] [Emphasis added]

It is submitted here, as elsewhere in this book, that FIFA's conduct against alleged 'ambush marketers' such as kulula.com, in light of legislative provisions such as s 15A of the MMA, serves to promote or maintain such a monopoly controlled by powerful financial interests which is adverse to other claims of expressive conduct, including commercial speech. It is suggested that kulula's exit stage left following FIFA's objections to this marketing campaign was premature (albeit prudent in light of the costs of potential litigation—remember, they also had to fork out the fare for flying a cute little dog around).

In conclusion on this issue, it is suggested that the very wide ambit of s 15A serves to subject it to especially rigorous freedom of expression scrutiny as opposed to similar provisions in legislation elsewhere. The following was observed in this context in respect of the Olympic Insignia Protection Act (or 'OIP Act') in Australia:

> [The OIP Act] include[s] a requirement that application [of a protected expression to goods or services] suggest to the reasonable person that there is sponsorship, sponsorship-like or other support. In addition, there are exemptions in [ambush marketing legislation], for instance for media reporting. In theory, these might reduce any impact on freedom of expression.[134]

As has been indicated, the provisions contained in s 15A of the MMA do not contain similar exemptions and in effect restricts a much broader spectrum of conduct and (commercial) speech.

7.2.4 Conclusions

As indicated in the text of the preceding sections, I believe that anti-ambushing laws have the tendency to infringe on constitutional free speech guarantees in the different jurisdictions. There are two forms of limitations on free speech which are relevant here, namely

- General restrictions on advertising with reference to an event by non-sponsors; and
- The so-called 'clean zone' restrictions on advertising, which have a more limited scope, geographically (within the precinct of event venues) and in terms of duration.

---

[133] At par 48 of the judgment.

[134] See Frontier Economics 2007, p. 96.

We know that advertising is viewed as commercial speech, and as such is generally protected in terms of free speech guarantees (although courts in different jurisdictions provide greater protection for, e.g. political and artistic speech as opposed to marketing with a commercial objective). As I have also pointed out elsewhere in the earlier chapters, cases of advertising which are claimed to constitute so-called 'intrusion ambushing' is generally not misleading or deceptive (i.e. falsely implying or representing an association or affiliation with an event as an official sponsor). Accordingly, these types of advertising clear the threshold hurdle for the protection of commercial speech.

The main issue to determine, therefore, is whether the resultant limitation of such free speech rights by means of either general advertising restrictions or clean-zone restrictions in terms of *sui generis* event protection legislation is justifiable. In this regard, the general requirements for justification in the various jurisdictions relate to three particular aspects of the restrictive measure. These are the following:

- Whether such measure serves a legitimate governmental purpose;
- Whether such measure is reasonable; and
- Whether such measure is proportionate in respect of the purpose it serves (i.e. the 'mischief' it is aimed at preventing), the means of pursuing the achievement of such purpose, and the effects of such measure on the rights of those hardest hit by it.

As I have argued, it is clear that the main and direct purpose of anti-ambushing advertising restrictions is to protect the commercial interests of event organisers and their official sponsors or commercial partners. In order to determine whether restrictions on fundamental rights which are aimed at protecting such narrow commercial interests are justifiable, I believe it must be shown that there is in fact a greater or weightier public interest at stake in this exercise. This also relates to the question of whether, or the extent to which, the passing of anti-ambushing laws to protect commercial interests of organisers and sponsors is a legitimate governmental function and responsibility (which I will examine more closely in Chap. 8). This brings one, inevitably, to the central justification for anti-ambushing measures most often raised by event organisers (and which I will examine in more detail in Chap. 9), namely the 'survival of the event' argument, i.e. that the very existence of mega-events are threatened by ambushing and that in the absence of aggressive rights protection the sponsors would withdraw and it would be impossible to obtain the financial support needed to stage these expensive events.

And here I suggest that one should cut through the often self-serving rhetoric and focus on the facts, namely to ask what empirical evidence exists to lend credence to the potential for such result to follow from unchecked ambushing. Remember, I am focusing on the role of intrusion ambushing. And in this regard one must ask: What are the real dangers posed by such alleged 'ambushes' in the form of advertising which refers to an event (remember: without attempting to deceive or mislead consumers)? I have already discussed the absence of a requirement to show harm in the case of many of the anti-ambushing provisions found in the *sui generis* legislation (especially also in those cases where 'association rights' have been created, such as in New Zealand and the UK). The absence of such requirement, in fact, is probably all that saves such legislative restrictions from clear legal challenge when it comes to restrictions on 'intrusion'-type advertising. As I've argued in Chap. 5 this absence of a requirement of harm, as well as the absence of a requirement to prove consumer deception, are not in line with accepted principles of trademark laws. If one adds to this the fact that the businesses or individuals often targeted or hardest hit by anti-'intrusion' restrictions are, in any event, not entities that would have contributed to the financing of events (or contributed to the profits made by event organisers)—I described the elite nature of the club of official sponsors in Chap. 2, and how difficult and expensive it may be to gain entry—one is left with the conclusion that there appears to be very little if any actual evidence to substantiate claims of a real potential threat to the survival of mega-events in the absence of such often draconian restrictions on advertising. My own view is that this last argument appears to rest solely on either the event organisers' perception of such potential threat, or on threats by sponsors in this regard, or both. Is this sufficient to justify advertising restrictions as reasonable and proportionate limitations on free commercial speech? I would say not, and I'm not the only person to hold that view.[135]

Finally, in respect of the arguments that advertising restrictions contained in 'clean zone' ordinances are proportionate because they are of limited geographical application and are only enforced for a relatively short period of time during the duration of an event (compare the UK government's justification of its advertising and street trading regulations for the 2012 London Olympic Games, as discussed earlier), I believe there is also little merit in such claims. In Chap. 8 I provide more detail regarding the nature and scope of the thematic space of the mega-event as a marketing platform. I believe these claims regarding the limited scope of restrictions lose sight of the fact that the express purpose of such restrictions on advertising is to prohibit certain businesses and persons from themselves using the event as a marketing platform (i.e. as the event organisers and official sponsors do). One should consider that (as I argue in the following chapter) the official sponsors who pay millions for the privilege (rights) of official association in their marketing with the event *only obtain certain, limited, rights in this regard*—the sponsorship contract is not an open sesame which provides 'ownership' of any and all aspects of the event. These parties (and the event organisers) do not own all publicity value of the event, thereby entitling them to ring-fence any and all references thereto, even if for commercial purposes. I am referring again, of course, to the intrusion 'ambush' scenario. Accordingly, what the advertising restrictions on reference to an event in fact does is simply to monopolise the event as a marketing platform for certain parties, and thereby removing vast swaths of references or allusion to the event from the public domain, for a commercial purpose. This, therefore, adds to the anti-competitive effects of the sponsorship

---

[135] See also Scassa 2011, p. 367.

model employed (see discussion of such effects of sponsorship exclusivity in Chap. 6). I would argue that for event organisers or lawmakers to argue that the fact that such restrictions are justifiable because they may be short-lived is tantamount to saying that the restrictions on freedom from torture occasioned by interrogations in a Guantanamo Bay-type facility are justifiable if such torture only lasts a short period of time. It ignores the nature and content of the human right so restricted. In the case of advertising restrictions on free commercial speech, the protected right includes the right holder's choice to use the event as a marketing platform, and the duration (or, for that matter, the geographical scope) of the restriction does not serve to make the restriction proportionate and justifiable.

7.3 Freedom of Trade

As is clear from discussion of the applicable anti-ambush marketing legislation in the different jurisdictions, restrictions on commercial activity related to protected events potentially limit the freedom of trade of private actors such as entrepreneurs. For example, section 15A of South Africa's Merchandise Marks Act prohibits the use of a trader's own marks in relation to an event. As indicated elsewhere in this book, such proscribed use may be nothing more than the normal use, in the course of trade, of a proprietor's own trade mark, in line with the normal function and purpose of a trade mark, but in relation to a protected sporting event. Section 22 of the South African Constitution entrenches the freedom of trade and provides as follows:

> Every citizen has the right to choose their trade, occupation or profession freely. The practice of a trade, occupation or profession may be regulated by law.[136]

The right contained in section 22 mirrors the concept of freedom to trade which is found in the South African common law, although this right is of a more limited ambit than its earlier counterpart in the interim Constitution of 1993.[137] This concept of freedom of trade has usually been expressed as a public policy consideration which must be taken into account when deliberating on claims to enforce restraints of trade or to prevent unlawful competition.[138] One dimension of this concept is that a free and competitive market requires that 'personal skills and

---

[136] The Section 22 right is only available to South African citizens (compare the wording of the section, and the Constitutional Court's finding in *Certification of the Amended Text of the Constitution of the Republic of South Africa, 1996 (2nd Certification decision)* 1997 (2) SA 97 (CC) that the right of occupational choice could not be considered a universally accepted human right—see Currie and de Waal 2005, p. 489).

[137] Section 26(1) of the Interim Constitution (Act 200 of 1993) provided that '[e]very person shall have the right freely to engage in economic activity and to pursue a livelihood anywhere in the national territory'. See Currie and de Waal 2005, p. 484 *et seq.*

[138] See Lagrange in Cheadle et al. 2005, Ch 17-1 note 2; *Magna Alloys & Research (SA) (Pty) Ltd v Ellis* 1984 4 SA 874 (A); *Sunshine Records (Pty) Ltd v Frohling* 1990 (4) SA 782 (A).

expertise can be freely bartered'[139]; a complementary dimension is that persons are entitled to trade without wrongful interference from others.[140,141]

The proviso in section 22 allows limitation of the freedom to practice a trade by 'law'. It is in this proviso that constitutional testing of alleged infringements of the right to freely choose a trade will usually find its substance—namely an evaluation of the legitimacy of any restriction of the right in question. The Constitutional Court[142] has held that an emphasis on freedom of participation in the economy did not implicitly include the right of unqualified persons to practice in professions requiring such qualifications nor did it entitle 'persons to ignore legislation aimed at regulating the manner in which particular activities are to be conducted, provided always that such regulations are not arbitrary.'[143,144] Regarding restriction of the right contained in section 22, Traverso J declared as follows in the case of *Coetzee v Comitis*[145] (a case involving domestic football transfer rules, reminiscent of the landmark *Bosman* judgment in the European Union):

> I accept that any profession must be regulated to a certain extent—these regulations can be internal or imposed by statute. Whatever the case may be, *a profession can only be regulated in a manner which is reasonable and in a manner which does not violate the constitutional rights of individuals.* [Emphasis provided]

It is clear that any alleged infringement of a person's choice to engage in economic activity in terms of section 22, which would constitute a limitation of such right, would have to satisfy the proportionality test under section 36 of the Bill of Rights. Any restriction falling short of such a limitation (in terms of the proviso to the right, namely a restriction regulating the manner of participation in such economic activity) must satisfy the 'rationality test', which, at least, demands that such restriction must not be arbitrary and that there must be a rational basis for the restriction. Where the restriction on the manner of participation also affects the choice to participate, the limitation test must be satisfied.[146] Such an analysis raises the importance of the policy issues underlying a regulatory measure, and specifically also the purpose of such measure.[147] In the context of a section 22-review it is also important to note that the presence of economic freedom does not mean that there can be no legitimate constraints on the exercise of economic activity—the section 22 right permits persons to be active in the economic domain

---

139 *Atlas Organic Fertilizers v Pikkewyn Ghwano & Others* 1981 (2) SA 173 (T) at 192F-193E, as quoted in Cheadle et al. 2005, Ch 17-1 note 2.

140 E.g. see *Patz v Green & Co.* 1907 TS 427 at 436-7; *Matthews v Young* 1922 AD 492.

141 Cheadle et al. 2005, Ch 17-1 note 2.

142 In *S v Lawrence; S v Negal; S v Solberg* 1997 (10) BCLR 1348 (CC).

143 Ibid, at par. 33 of the judgment.

144 Cheadle et al. 2005, Ch 17-4.

145 *Coetzee v Comitis and Others* 2001 (1) SA 1254 (C), at par. 27 of the judgment.

146 See Cheadle et al. 2005, Ch 17-4.

147 Cheadle et al. 2005, Ch 17-5.

with all its inherent constraints.[148] Such constraints and the bases for their existence must satisfy the thresholds for constitutional review. As has been observed:

> There are a host of constraints imposed by the kind of society that the constitution has brought into being, premised as it is on social democratic principles.[149]

When evaluating the justification for restrictive measures or laws which may impact on the freedom of trade, it is submitted that a fruitful analogy may be drawn with the approach to legislative regulation of vocational activity under the German Constitution of 1949 (which in article 12(1) contains a provision that is strikingly similar to section 22[150]). The approach regarding the regulation of vocational activity under the German Constitution has been summarised as follows:

> The general principles governing the regulation of vocational activity may be summarised as follows: The practice of an occupation may be restricted by reasonable regulations predicated on considerations of the common good. The freedom to choose an occupation, however, may be restricted only for the sake of compelling public interest; that is, if after careful consideration the legislature determines that a common interest must be protected, then it may impose restrictions to protect that interest—but only to the extent that the protection cannot be accomplished by a lesser restriction on freedom of choice. In the event that an encroachment of freedom of occupational choice is unavoidable, lawmakers must always employ the regulative means least restrictive to the basic right.[151]

And an added element to consider is the power wielded by the perpetrator (in the horizontal application of the right) of an alleged infringement of the right:

> In principle, the ability to argue the applicability of the right would seem to depend more on the market power wielded by the actor whose conduct is impugned rather than the status of that actor: *the more the power wielded enables that actor to control access to an entire market, the more vulnerable that power will be to constitutional attack.* This approach might well guide the courts when deciding the appropriateness of applying the right horizontally.[152] [Emphasis provided]

It is submitted that, on similar logic, an evaluation of the legitimacy of the limitation of the practice of someone's freedom to trade by a law that is aimed at protecting the rights or interests of specific entities such as sports event organisers and their commercial partners (as is the case with anti-ambush marketing legislation such as section 15A of the Merchandise Marks Act), should take into account the market power (and the exercise of such power) by these relevant entities. It is also submitted that the 'public interest' referred to should be applied, *mutatis mutandis*, in the context of anti-ambush marketing legislation and measures to refer to the 'public interest' in free participation in activities—including economic activities—related to major sporting events that are partly

148 See Devenish 2005, p. 139.

149 Ibid.

150 See Cheadle et al. 2005, Ch 17-1 note 2.

151 Kommers *The Constitutional Jurisprudence of the Federal Republic of Germany* 1997 at 287-8, as quoted in Cheadle et al. 2005, Ch 17-10 (note 38).

152 Ibid.

publicly funded from taxpayer money, and that also hold (frequently touted if not always evident) socio-economic upliftment implications. Here it should not be forgotten that section 15A(1)(b) expressly emphasises such socio-economic imperatives in requiring that 'the Minister [of Trade and Industry] may not designate an event as a protected event unless the staging of the event is in the public interest and the Minister is satisfied that the organisers have created sufficient opportunities for small businesses and in particular for those of the previously disadvantaged communities.' A related element to such public interest in this regard is not only the interest of the public (as supporters of teams and athletes within the relevant sporting code) in having access to the performances of such players at the highest level of competition, but to have the freedom to associate with the hype of the events and to express themselves (also through commercial speech) in this regard.

The above approach from German law aims to limit the regulatory infringement of the individual's freedom of choice through scrutiny of both the *purpose* of the limitation as well as the *proportionality* of the means chosen to effect such limitation. In this sense it is in line with the section 36 test under the South African Bill of Rights.

It should be obvious that anti-ambush marketing legislation does not, *per se*, constitute objectionable limitation of persons' freedom of trade; clearly such limitations on commercial freedom may be justifiable even though they have at their heart the purpose to protect, primarily, narrow commercial interests. Legislation aimed at prohibiting association ambushes clearly fortify already existing (and uncontroversial) common law protections against unlawful competition and passing off and protection against deceptive trade practices. The public interest in being protected against consumer confusion, at least, would be a worthy objective to pursue by means of such restrictions.

Once again, however, it is submitted that the same considerations do not apply in respect of 'intrusion ambushes', and the ways on which *sui generis* event legislation has attempted to combat such activities in the different jurisdictions. It has been repeatedly emphasised in this book that this latter type of marketing activity does not necessarily constitute legally or ethically objectionable behaviour; in fact, the only legal objections may stem from the relevant anti-ambush marketing legislation, in the manner of a self-fulfilling prophesy. Sports governing bodies lobby (and actively pressure) domestic legislators to legally sanction otherwise unobjectionable conduct, which in turn then provides grounds for arguing that such conduct is, even in the absence of such legislative prohibitions, illegitimate. An example of this, it is submitted, is to be found in the legal strategy pursued by FIFA's local legal representatives in their anti-ambush marketing litigation in the run-up to the 2010 football World Cup. Mention was made elsewhere in this book of the main pillars of the template for civil action in terms of this strategy,[153] which includes what has been described as 'groundbreaking

[153] See Sect. 4.4.5 of Chap. 4.

causes of action and arguments'.[154] What is of specific interest here is the following 'groundbreaking' argument:

> In particular, a method had to be devised to enable FIFA to pursue a civil claim against an ambush marketer based on the anti-ambush marketing provisions of s15A of the Merchandise Marks Act, that create a criminal offence. *An unlawful competition argument was formulated utilising the principle that, in breaching the criminal provisions and thus entering into direct competition with FIFA's sponsors for the 2010 World Cup, ambush marketers were perpetrating conduct which was objectively unlawful, being a criminal offence, and were causing damage to FIFA by prejudicing its relations with its sponsors.*[155] [Emphasis provided]

The Explanatory Memorandum to the amendment Bill which inserted s 9(d) of the Trade Practices Act[156] expressly stated that passing off would not be available under the common law in the event of a breach of trade practices law. It is unclear why or to what extent a similar consideration should not apply in respect of the Merchandise Marks Act.[157] Also, the alleged element of 'entering into direct competition with FIFA's sponsors' appears to be a bit of a stretch; s 15A(2) does not require a competitive relationship and (as has been pointed out above) also does not require prejudice to a sponsor—this appears to be implicit in the assumed 'filching' of publicity value around the event. Be that as it may, it should be noted that in respect of the conduct prohibited by s 15A of the Merchandise Marks Act—which clearly includes 'intrusion ambushes' which may otherwise constitute perfectly legitimate and non-deceptive conduct—it appears that FIFA has sought to obtain legislative criminalization of conduct which is not prohibited by the common law, and has then succeeded[158] in fabricating a contravention of the common law based on the contravention of such legislative provisions. The circular nature of the legitimization of this limitation of the freedom of trade of 'intrusion ambushers' is, in this observer's view, nothing short of ominous. While it has been observed that s 15A(2) does not require the representation of an association with a protected event, the common law passing off action does require this. Essentially, it is submitted, this argument creates an irrebuttable presumption of representation of an association, which is illegitimate.

Leaving aside such legal creativity, however, it remains to consider whether the South African anti-ambush marketing legislation (specifically, s 15A of the MMA in so far as it covers 'intrusion ambushing') might be open to constitutional challenge based on limitation of the s 22 right. I would submit that the restriction

---

[154] By Dr. Owen Dean, partner of Spoor & Fisher (one of the large intellectual property law firms representing FIFA in South Africa), writing in Dean, O 'FIFA scores opening goal' *Without Prejudice* May 2009 pp. 4–5.

[155] Ibid.

[156] The legislation that prohibits association ambushes—see discussion in Sect. 4.4.5 of Chap. 4.

[157] See Johnson 2007, p. 141 note 97.

[158] It appears from the rather sparse order in the *FIFA v Metcash* matter (see discussion in Sect. 4.4.5 of Chap. 4) that Msimeki J in the North Gauteng High Court found in favour of this argument by FIFA's legal team.

contained in the section clearly contains a limitation of a trader's freedom of trade in respect of the use of its own trade mark and the promotion of its goods or services. The question is whether this restriction is reasonable and justifiable in an open and democratic society, in light of the provisions of the limitations clause. As mentioned above, and in terms of the proviso contained in section 22, the restriction on the manner of practising freedom of trade must not be arbitrary and must have a rational basis. In this regard, I believe it is important to consider what, in fact, is the protected interest at which the prohibition against 'intrusion ambushing' in s 15A (and, specifically, s15A(2)) is aimed. As has been observed, this provision is not aimed at legislative bolstering of the common law protection against passing off, as it does not require deception or confusion of the public regarding an association with a protected event. Section 15A(2) specifically prohibits 'intrusion ambushing', and one must consider what it actually purports to protect. I will do so in more detail in Chap. 8, in consideration of the protected thematic space of sports mega-events.

In examining the freedom of trade impact of anti-ambush marketing measures regarding mega-events, one should also consider the impact of protection against ambush marketing of protected events outside of the specific legislation, in assessing the extent to which anti-ambush marketing measures limit the freedoms of individuals (including their freedom of trade). For example, let's consider the provisions of the host city by-laws that were passed by South African cities in respect of the 2010 FIFA World Cup. A respected South African constitutional law expert, in his *Constitutionally Speaking* internet blog, observed that events surrounding the enforcement of these city by-laws during the 2010 FIFA World Cup essentially meant that 'for the duration of the World Cup, the Municipality of each host city has in effect become the enforcement arm of a private company—FIFA—to protect that private company's image and profits'.[159] In considering the extent to which anti-ambushing measures limit the freedom of trade (as well as other personal liberties) of individuals, it is submitted that one need look no further than these—what I will call 'draconian'—provisions, which have been enacted in what I will characterise as an atmosphere of insufficiently motivated protectionism and extensive legislative overreach in respect of the World Cup event. As an example I will include some brief words on the 2010 FIFA World Cup South Africa™ By-laws adopted by host city Durban's eThekwini Municipality.[160] I will mention

[159] Pierre de Vos, writing at http://constitutionallyspeaking.co.za/on-the-fifa-world-cup-by-laws/ (posted 17 June 2010).

[160] Published in March 2009, in terms of the Municipal Systems Act 32 of 2000. Host cities are in terms of the Bid guarantees and following selection as host city required to pass such By-laws (which, to this author's knowledge, are based on a standard template drafted or commissioned by FIFA). This is explained in the preamble to the Durban By-laws:

> [T]he eThekwini Municipality … has assumed certain obligations with regard to the Competition and in particular, has agreed to ensure that appropriate by-laws are passed to enable the efficient running of the Competition. In this instance, the eThekwini Municipality is required to ensure that appropriate by-laws in the areas listed below are

only a few examples of the extremely invasive nature of the prohibitions and restrictions contained in these by-laws, which include the following:

(1) The By-laws provide that 'no person may, in any place owned, leased, administered by or under the control of the Municipality' engage in any Advertising or erect and/or position any Advertising Structure without the prior Approval of the Municipality.' This may seem relatively unproblematic in the context of the provision of 'clean zones' around event venues, until one considers the very loose (and wide) definition of 'advertising' in the By-laws. 'Advertisement' is defined in par. 1.1.3 of the By-laws as meaning 'a visual representation including but not limited to a sign, illustration, object, mark, symbol or device of any kind which is visible to the public from, including but not limited to, any street or any public place or any other vantage point or which is under or over-hanging from any bridge, building or other structure, including sky writing, used for advertising activity; or any combination of such elements with the object of transferring information' ('advertising' is, in turn, defined in par. 1.1.4 to mean 'the act or process of notifying, warning, informing, displaying, making known or *any other act of transferring information in a visual or oral manner*' [my emphasis]). It would appear that if I place my empty soda can on the sidewalk, I am 'advertising' to the public that my soda is finished, for which I need the Municipality's prior approval[161];

(2) The provisions on Controlled Access Sites[162] contain a number of rather severe prohibitions that, at the very least, may be difficult to police. For example, 'no person shall except with the written approval of the Municipality':
   - smoke, eat, drink or sleep in any Controlled Access Site where these activities are forbidden;
   - use abusive or otherwise objectionable language or behave in an abusive, objectionable or disorderly manner in a Controlled Access Site;
   - hamper, disturb, obstruct or harass any other Person using and/or entering any Controlled Access Site;
   - spill or drop any substance that may cause danger or harm to any user of a Controlled Access Site;
   - lie, sit, stand, congregate or walk, in a manner that otherwise causes an obstruction of any nature whatsoever, within any Controlled Access Site;
   - deposit or leave or cause to be left any object which may endanger or cause harm to or be a Nuisance to any user of a Controlled Access Site; or

(Footnote 160 continued)
promulgated and implemented, and become effective for the Term to enable an orderly and efficient staging and hosting of the Competition: Advertising; Controlled Access; Public Open Spaces and City Beautification; Public Roads and Traffic Guidance; as well as Street Trading.

161 Par. 2.1.1.2 of the By-laws.

162 As defined in par. 1.1.21 of the By-laws. Controlled Access Sites include stadia, official event locations, official training sites, team hotels, official hotels for the FIFA delegation, FIFA Fan Parks, and any other area so designated or demarcated by the Municipality, and including private property.

- throw any object, of any nature whatsoever, within or onto a Controlled Access Site.[163]

(3) In respect of the 'Public Open Spaces and City Beautification' provisions,[164] there are also quite stringent limitations on what one may or may not do. First, consider the provision requiring that 'all persons engaged in major construction during the term which is visible to the public view and close to major or concentrated transport centres or entertainment areas which will or may be used for the competition ... shall take all necessary measures at their own cost to cover and/or conceal such construction sites from public view to the satisfaction of the Municipality.[165] And beware if you are planning to 'plant any vegetation' in a Public Open Space[166] without the Municipality's prior express authorization, or 'capture or attempt to capture, chase, shoot at, injure, throw objects at, tease, molest or in any other way disturb any animal, fish, or bird or its nest or egg.'[167] That's not the end of it. 'No person shall at a Special Event or in a Public Open Space, in particular, or in any other area within the Municipality, in general, without the Approval of the Municipality' (*inter alia*)

- beg or solicit money in a Public Open Space;
- cause a Nuisance including play loud or offensive music;
- camp or reside;
- perform any action prohibited in terms of any sign erected by the Municipality in a Public Open Space; or
- consume any beverage from a glass container.[168]

(4) The provisions regarding street trading (note the definitions in this regard which appear to be rather circular and nonsensical[169]) are similarly extensive,[170] so much so that it is beyond the scope of this chapter to discuss.

These By-laws are characterised by what I view to be apparent blatant legislative overreach, even though this may be in part ascribable to rather sloppy drafting in places.[171] A cynical observer may be excused for reading between the

---

163 Par. 3.5 of the By-laws.

164 Chapter 4.

165 Par. 4.1.1.

166 This is defined in par. 1.1.62 of the By-laws.

167 Par. 4.6.

168 Par. 4.2.

169 'Street trader' is defined (in par. 1.1.74) as 'a person selling goods', and 'street trading' (in par. 1.1.75) as 'the selling of any goods by a street trader'.

170 See Chap. 6 of the By-laws.

171 For example, par. 1.1.18 of the definitions defines 'Competition' as including the 2010 FIFA World Cup as well as the 2009 Confederations Cup, which was not held in Durban. Another example is the word 'Culture', which is exhaustively defined in par. 1.1.22, even though the word does not appear anywhere in the By-laws. Also, as for over-inclusive drafting, see the definition of 'sign' as per par. 1.1.70.

lines to find a clear and rather sinister message from FIFA to the great 'unwashed masses': 'We're coming to your city. If you can't afford to buy a ticket to one of our games (where you'll have to wear what we allow you to wear and eat and drink only what we allow you to)—GET OUT NOW!'

Apart from the host city by-laws, other measures were also put in place to control aspects of trading around the FIFA event. In early 2010 the draft Liquor Control Policy for the 2010 FIFA World Cup was gazetted by the Department of Trade & Industry,[172] to be greeted by public outcry especially from the hospitality industry. Initial reactions to what was perceived as a requirement for existing liquor licence holders to obtain a costly special license during the event were highly critical (in reaction to the draft policy's wording, which requires venues hosting 'any public viewing event' where matches are broadcast 'to the general public or otherwise' to obtain a special license). The DTI attempted to set the record straight by explaining that the liquor control policy would only require a special license in respect of venues such as pubs, clubs, bars and restaurants that intended to charge an admission fee or similar surcharge for the screening of 2010 World Cup games (which establishments would require the permission of FIFA for this purpose). According to reports at the time, such license would have to be obtained at a cost of ZAR 50,000 each and 2% of traders' revenues. There were reports of proposed legal challenges to the policy, *inter alia* on the basis that it was alleged to be *ultra vires* of national government to regulate liquor licensing, which is a provincial competency in terms of the Constitution and relevant liquor legislation.

And then, finally, one must consider the impact of a combination of anti-ambushing legislation, other measures aimed at curbing commercial activities related to the World Cup and also the existing 'web' of contractual arrangements that FIFA had in place in respect of the 2010 event. For example, let's consider accommodation. FIFA's exclusive official accommodation provider for the 2010 World Cup, the controversial Match Events Services, had reportedly signed up 80% of the available rooms in South Africa's top hotel chains. It had by October 2009 finalised contracts for 40,000 rooms. Match was thus enabled to dictate prices to tourists, which has been defended as a measure to counter exorbitant pricing by local accommodation providers—a seemingly noble endeavour. Match's '2010 FIFA World Cup SMME (small, medium and micro enterprises) accommodation agreement' stipulated that guest houses were allowed to charge the rate they 'customarily' levied in June 2007, plus a 16 per cent mark-up. The guest house sells the room to Match, which then on-sells it to tourists as the only company allowed to market itself as FIFA's 'official' accommodation provider. Not surprisingly, this arrangement caused great unhappiness amongst a number of accommodation providers, who were faced with marketing their rooms 'unofficially' in a climate of stringent anti-ambush marketing laws as discussed in this book.[173] I do not know whether any of FIFA's famous cease-and-desist letters

[172] *Government Gazette* No. 32878 Vol. 535 (18 January 2010).

[173] See the discussion by Rob Rose in Schulz-Herzenberg 2010, pp. 101–108.

found their way to such accommodation providers. However, it bears mentioning that it subsequently emerged that Match (self/FIFA-appointed protector of the hard-earned dollars of foreign tourists) reportedly charged a 30% mark-up on rooms to guests over and above the price at which guest houses sold such rooms to Match. Also, in some cases (e.g. in respect of accommodation in the Kruger National Park) it appears that Match charged as much as 1,000% more than the normal rate for rooms during the World Cup event.[174]

In considering whether the relevant anti-ambush marketing legislation and other measures such as described above may constitute illegitimate infringement of the freedom of trade as encapsulated in section 22 of the South African Bill of Rights, one should consider whether such extremely invasive limitations are reasonable and justifiable in an open and democratic society, in terms of the limitations clause of the Bill of Rights. While this is an exercise that is beyond the scope of this chapter, I would submit that such legislation and measures would likely not pass the test of constitutionality, and are liable to be struck down. It is hard to imagine that a court would view, for example, the above-mentioned restrictions on what one may do in a World Cup 'Controlled Access Site' (e.g. to 'lie, sit, stand, congregate or walk, in a manner that otherwise causes an obstruction of any nature whatsoever') as justifiable in such a free and open democratic society based on the fundamental values of freedom, dignity and equality. Consider that these laws have as their objects the protection of the narrow commercial interests of an event organiser and its official sponsors, and it provides protection that is seriously disproportionate to the governmental protection provided to other traders in other contexts. Its restrictions may well apply only for a limited period of time and in a limited geographical space, but that does not detract from the extremely restrictive nature of such laws and their invasive impact on personal liberties. Consider also that the very persons affected by such laws also, through the working of the law, actually part-fund the event by means of their tax dollars. It is hard to think of any comparable aberrations of civil liberties in other contexts, and I would suggest that these types of mega-event regulations deserve proper legal challenge in any society based on the rule of law where they are sought to be enforced against host nation citizens.

In the context of the South African developmental state, it is of course especially poignant to consider the relevant anti-ambushing law's requirement that an event such as the 2010 FIFA World Cup may only be declared as a 'protected event' if the relevant government Minister is satisfied that the event is in the public interest and that sufficient (commercial) opportunities have been created 'for small businesses and in particular those of the previously disadvantaged communities'.[175] While restricting the activities of informal street traders selling counterfeit goods such as knock-off supporter clothing may be justifiable, it is a different proposition where such traders are prohibited from selling food or self-manufactured trinkets or

[174] Ibid.

[175] Merchandise Marks Act Section 15A(1)(b).

cultural arts and crafts. The protection of commercial interests of large multinational corporations such as Coca-Cola or Kia seems a dubious basis for restricting the freedom of trade of such individuals in so extensive and substantial a manner. I would suggest that the special importance of this public interest element also applies in other developing nations, and it may be interesting to consider future developments in a country such as Brazil in respect of its hosting of the 2014 FIFA World Cup and the 2016 Rio Olympic Games.

And, finally, one should not forget that street trading and 'clean zone' restriction provisions, generally, have what Longdin refers to (in the context of her criticism of New Zealand's Major Events Management Act) as 'enormous potential for overkill through over vigorous enforcement', and that the 'ultimate irony in such cases is that… an offender need not even be on the way to a major event activity, or even be the slightest bit interested in it'.[176] I have referred in Chap. 6 above to the UK government's apparently rather flimsy and dismissive rejection of claims that its draft street trading and advertising regulations published for the 2012 London Games offend competition laws. I would suggest that much more convincing evidence and argument must be brought by event organisers and the legislatures that pass laws which may significantly limit constitutionally guaranteed freedom of trade.

7.4 Rights to Property

In Chap. 5 I attempted to sketch the ways in which *sui generis* event legislation tends to very significantly expand the traditional scope of protection of intellectual property rights of event organisers and sponsors (what Phillip Johnson calls the provision of 'IP+' protection in respect of events). One should, however, not lose sight of the fact that these developments often go hand in hand with the concomitant (severe) restriction of the IP rights of others, namely those who have not paid the huge sponsorship fees to be officially associated with events. Anti-ambushing laws place significant limitations on the commercial marketing conduct of such non-sponsors, and sometimes this includes drastic restrictions on the use by such parties of their existing (intellectual) property such as trademarks. The relevance of constitutional protection of property rights must be considered in the context of such often extensive restrictions on the use of intellectual property as contained in anti-ambushing legislation. Also, and as recognised in respect of the UK's advertising regulations for the 2012 London Olympic Games, such laws may also impact on property rights and guarantees in two more ways, namely by depriving existing trading license or permit holders of the benefits of such

[176] Longdin 2009, pp. 737–738.

'property',[177] and by placing extensive restrictions on land owners (in 'clean zones') in respect of advertising activity on their land.[178]

The importance of constitutional property rights or fundamental guarantees relating to the use and enjoyment of property should not be underestimated in the context of considering the legitimacy of anti-ambushing laws, particularly because such rights and guarantees frequently fulfil a more important role in respect of (freedom of) trade than simply in protecting property. It has been explained, for example, that Article 17 of the EU Charter on Fundamental Rights, which entrenches protection of property rights, is an important guarantee for a number of reasons:

> [T]he right to property is recognised as a fundamental right, both to the extent that it is an aspect of personal identity (e.g. protection for the products of one's labour) and individual privacy (e.g. enabling persons to exercise a greater degree of privacy through the control of property) as well as to the extent that it is a necessary economic freedom (for the right to own property is an essential prerequisite to the acquisition, exchange and sale of property, and so on).[179]

Article 17(2) expressly acknowledges that intellectual property rights should be protected, and this acknowledgement is explained as follows:

> Protection of intellectual property, one aspect of the right of property, is explicitly mentioned in paragraph 2 because of its growing importance and Community secondary legislation. Intellectual property covers not only literary and artistic property but also patent and trademark rights associated rights. The guarantees laid down in paragraph 1 shall apply as appropriate to intellectual property.[180]

Article 1 of Protocol 1 of the European Convention on Human Rights similarly provides protection for the use and enjoyment of property, although it expressly provides that such protection 'shall not, however, in any way impair the right of a State to enforce such laws as it deems necessary to control the use of property in accordance with the general interest or to secure the payment of taxes or other

---

177 'Article 1 to the First Protocol to the ECHR ("A1P1") protects a person's "possessions" from unjustified appropriation or interference by the State. The benefit of a licence, permit, certificate or consent (a "licence") to carry on a profitable activity can amount to a "possession" for A1P1 purposes. The Regulations will apply despite any licence granted before or after the Regulations come into force and will restrict a person's ability to engage in advertising activity and trading in accordance with an existing licence (in the small areas where the Regulations apply, during the Games period). Accordingly, the Regulations will arguably interfere with the A1P1 rights of current licensees.'—see http://www.culture.gov.uk/images/publications/ConDoc_Regulations_on_Advertising_and_Trading_London_2012-section9-10.pdf.

178 'Further, the Regulations will limit the uses to which land and other property (again, within the small areas where the Regulations apply) may be put during the Games period. They will prevent, for example, a land owner from using his or her land (or allowing his or her land to be used) for advertising or trading activities. This may also amount to an interference with land or other property owners' A1P1 rights.'—see http://www.culture.gov.uk/images/publications/ConDoc_Regulations_on_Advertising_and_Trading_London_2012-section9-10.pdf.

179 See http://www.eucharter.org/home.php?page_id=92.

180 See http://www.eucharter.org/home.php?page_id=24.

contributions or penalties'. Inherent in the protection, therefore, is the possibility of governmental restriction and control of property rights and their use and enjoyment. This 'third rule' of the ECHR property right (as identified in the *Sporrong and Lonnroth v. Sweden* case[181]) is the most relevant here in the context of this discussion, in the sense that anti-ambushing laws constitute a form of state control over the use and enjoyment of (intellectual) property.[182] The Convention requires that any interference with the protected rights to property must be lawful (in accordance with the rule of law, which—importantly in the present context—might include a requirement for sufficient procedural safeguards in any law which interferes with an intellectual property holder's rights so as to ensure protection against arbitrary action) as well as being aimed at pursuing a wider interest (in respect of deprivation of property, the article refers to 'public interest', and in respect of control of use of property it refers to 'general interest'). Any interference with property rights must satisfy the requirement of serving a legitimate public (or general) interest (and must be proportional in doing so).[183]

One of the clearest instances of restriction of intellectual property rights by means of anti-ambushing legislation is to be found in the extensive and far-reaching provisions of the applicable South African legislation, particularly s 15A(2) of the Merchandise Marks Act, which has been referred to frequently in the preceding chapters. Section 25(1) of the South African Bill of Rights guarantees the right to property, and provides that 'no one may be deprived of property except in terms of law of general application', and 'no law may permit arbitrary deprivation of property'. According to section 25(4)(b), 'property' is not limited to land, and would include intellectual property (such as e.g. copyright or a trade mark).[184] South African courts have held that a deprivation of property includes any substantial interference with or limitation of the use, enjoyment or exploitation of private property which 'goes beyond the normal restrictions on property use or

[181] Application no. 7151/75; 7152/75, judgment 23 September 1982.

[182] As opposed to instances of the deprivation (or 'taking') of IP rights by the state—see, for example, discussion in the American context of this last in Price 2003, p. 150 *et seq*.

[183] As recognised as follows in the UK government's justification of the London Olympics advertising and street trading regulations (available at the time of writing at http://www.culture.gov.uk/images/publications/ConDoc_Regulations_on_Advertising_and_Trading_London_2012-section9-10.pdf):

> [A]n interference with possessions will be justified under [Article 1 Protocol 1 of the ECHR] where it is "lawful" (that is, imposed by sufficiently accessible, precise and foreseeable law), where it pursues a legitimate aim which is in the general interest, and where it is proportionate to that aim (that is, it strikes a "fair balance" between the general interests of the community and the individual's fundamental rights).

[184] "Property" for purposes of s 25 should therefore be seen as those resources that are generally taken to constitute a person's wealth, and that are recognized and protected by law. Such resources are legally protected by private law rights—real rights in the case of physical resources, contractual rights in the case of performances, and intellectual property rights in the case of intellectual property ... Should an individual's possession or exercise of any of these rights be interfered with arbitrarily or taken over without compensation, s 25 will be available to protect that individual.' Currie and de Waal 2005, pp. 539–540.

enjoyment found in an open and democratic society'.[185] The role of the term 'normal' has been criticised for being unclear, and it has been suggested that emphasis should rather be placed on the word 'substantial' rather than 'normal':

> Whether normal or abnormal, an interference with property must be of sufficient gravity, have sufficient impact on the rights of the property holder, to merit being considered a deprivation.[186]

Section 25(2) deals with the expropriation of property (which may only occur for public purposes or in the public interest, and against payment of compensation). An expropriation must be made with an expropriatory purpose; laws or conduct that have another purpose but that have the effect of taking of property do not qualify as expropriation. Accordingly, it would appear that a law such as s 15A of the MMA—even if ostensibly aimed at the public interest or for a public purpose (such as purporting to protect the commercial rights of event organisers and their commercial partners in order to facilitate the hosting of an event such as the 2010 FIFA World Cup), would not constitute an expropriation of the use and enjoyment of a trade mark that might be justified in terms of the Bill of Rights.

The 'arbitrariness' provision in s 25(1) requires that the deprivation of property by a law of general application must be both procedurally fair and not arbitrary in its substance; '[i]t requires state interference with private property, whether it amounts to expropriation or not, to be authorised by law and to meet a basic standard of justification'.[187] Furthermore, the courts have held that the requirement that a deprivation of property in terms of s 25 must not be arbitrary in substance is a demanding test; as a first step one must determine the reason for a deprivation, and then one must assess the sufficiency, as a matter of justice and logic, of the relationship between the deprivation and its purpose. Arbitrariness is assessed by means of a test that is specific to the property clause, and that falls somewhere between a mere rationality enquiry and the proportionality enquiry used to assess the limitation of rights in terms of s 36 (the general limitations clause of the South African Bill of Rights, as referred to earlier).[188]

It is beyond the scope of this chapter to attempt a detailed analysis of the question whether the prohibition on 'intrusion ambushes' as contained in s 15A(2) of the MMA constitutes a deprivation of property (in the meaning of the use and enjoyment by a trade mark holder of their mark in the course of trade) and, if so, whether such deprivation is procedurally or substantively arbitrary. I believe that this question at least bears consideration, in light of the extremely far-reaching nature of this provision as discussed elsewhere in this book. Section 15A(2) is not

---

185 *Mkontwana v Nelson Mandela Metropolitan Municipality* 2005 (2) BCLR 150 (CC) at par. 32 (per Yacoob J); see also *First National Bank of SA Ltd t/a Wesbank v Commissioner, South African Revenue Services* 2002 (4) SA 768 (CC).

186 Currie and de Waal 2005, p. 541 note 35.

187 Currie and de Waal 2005, p. 534–535

188 Ibid. at 545; *First National Bank of SA Ltd t/a Wesbank v Commissioner, South African Revenue Services* 2002 (4) SA 768 (CC) at par. 65.

based in the common law protections that exist in respect of deceptive and misleading marketing practices which would constitute passing off. The section requires no association or deception or implication of association between the 'ambush marketer's' mark and event organisers' marks; it requires no infringement of a trade mark, copyright or other intellectual property; and it requires no likelihood of confusion amongst the public regarding a connection between the mark and the protected event. In essence, the section places a restriction on a rights holder to use and enjoy their intellectual property 'in relation to an event', when such use is calculated to achieve publicity for such mark and thereby derives special promotional benefit from the event.

It is suggested that this section in fact facilitates the deprivation of property in the sense of constituting substantial interference with or limitation of the use, enjoyment or exploitation of intellectual property which 'goes beyond the normal restrictions on property use or enjoyment found in an open and democratic society', as referred to above. While it has been observed that the effect of a finding of a contravention of s 15A(2) of the MMA is that a trade mark holder is free to continue using its mark and must simply ensure that it is used in other ways without alluding to a protected event,[189] it is submitted that this is a rather simplistic argument. There is clearly a limitation of the use of such mark which may be substantial. It is submitted that regard must be had to the circumstances of the mega-event publicity and marketing machine: If one considers the virtual 'carpet-bombing' of publicity surrounding an event such as the football World Cup and the (what I have argued to be) illegitimately wide restriction as contained in s 15A(2) in respect of otherwise legally and ethically unobjectionable conduct by a trader in tapping into public interest and sentiment through its marketing efforts (as well as the long period of protection afforded by the legislation), the above argument may be tantamount to saying 'don't complain, you can still use your mark, just go do it on some island somewhere far away from the hype of this event and the existing market for your product or service.' This is reminiscent of the kulula airline's 2010 ad campaign which so upset FIFA and its legal team and which was referred to earlier. One might have sympathy for the creative director of this campaign, who responded by saying that he felt 'bullied and confused' seeing that '[i]t is hard to navigate the waters when we have to pretend that the World Cup doesn't exist… 2010? The year exists for everyone.'[190]

Without engaging with this issue in detail, it is suggested that a potential s 25 challenge may lie against the working of s 15A(2) of the MMA in respect of its effect on the rights of trade mark holders regarding the use and enjoyment of their intellectual property (and that similar challenges may lie in other jurisdictions in respect of the applicable constitutional property guarantees). In this regard it might

[189] See the blog posting by Owen Dean on 13 October 2009 on the afro-ip blogspot (available at http://afro-ip.blogspot.com—accessed on 9 April 2010).

[190] See Mnguni, H 'An industry "bullied" by FIFA' *News24*, 26 March 2010—available online at the time of writing at http://www.news24.com/SouthAfrica/News/Ad-industry-bullied-by-FIFA-20100319.

be relevant to remember that the South African Constitutional Court has held that the right to hold intellectual property is not universally accepted as a fundamental human right, and that it thus does not require recognition as such in the Bill of Rights.[191] However, this view has been criticised, and the same court, in a trade mark infringement by dilution action, in effect gave equal status to a statutory trade mark right and the fundamental right to freedom of expression as protected in the Bill of Rights.[192]

In conclusion, I wish to simply remark that I believe matters relating to deprivation of property in the form of IP rights to, for example, existing trademarks and related vested rights, may feature in the application and enforcement of *sui generis* event legislation aimed at protecting organisers' and sponsors' commercial rights. This adds an additional element to the problematic nature of such often far-reaching legislative restrictions on the liberties and rights of event host nation citizens, and may lead to legal challenge in future.

As regards the other possible types of limitations to property rights and fundamental guarantees relating to property as referred to above (e.g. interference with traders' licenses and permits, and restrictions on the use of land for advertising purposes in 'clean zones'), the UK government has tendered the following in justification of such restrictions as contained in its draft advertising and street trading regulations for the 2012 London Olympic Games:

> The Regulations are intended to meet commitments given by the UK Government to the International Olympic Committee in London's bid to host the 2012 Games. The main aims are:
>
> - To ensure all Olympic and Paralympic events have a consistent celebratory look and feel to them;
> - To prevent ambush marketing within the vicinity of venues; and
> - To ensure people can easily access the venues.
>
> These aims are consistent with legitimate aims that justify an interference with Article 10 and [Article 1 Protocol 1 of the ECHR] rights. The Games are a once-in-a-lifetime occasion and it is reasonable for the Government to enact measures to facilitate the staging of the Games, even where those measures necessitate a limited and temporary interference with individuals' rights.[193]

In addition, these regulations are claimed to 'further the interests of public safety at Games time by ensuring that competitors, officials, spectators and other people attending events are able smoothly to enter and exit venues'. Importantly, it

---

[191] *In re Certification of the Constitution of the Republic of South Africa 1996* 1996 (4) SA 744 (CC) at 799.

[192] *Laugh It Off Promotions CC v South African Breweries International (Finance) B.V. t/a Sabmark International & Another* 2006 (1) SA 144 (CC). See Dean 2006, p. 1-2A note 3 (and the authority cited there).

[193] From the UK government's 'Regulations on Advertising Activity and Trading around London 2012' document relating to exceptions, at p 92, as available online at the time of writing at http://www.culture.gov.uk/images/publications/ConDoc_Regulations_on_Advertising_and_Trading_London_2012-section9-10.pdf.

has also been claimed that they will 'protect the rights of those that have made a commercial contribution to the staging of the Games (without which the Games could not take place) by preventing advertising and trading activities that amount to ambush marketing', with the following rather ambitious claim:

> It is legitimate in a democratic society to take steps to protect commercial investments which have a public interest element to them. In this case, the social benefits of the Games could not be achieved without such commercial investments.[194]

It would be interesting to know what these 'social benefits of the Games' are, exactly, especially when one considers that the true extent of such benefits seems often to be in doubt when reviews of the economic and other benefits of mega-events are undertaken. Also, this statement is interesting in the light of sustained and widely reported criticism by marketing and other associations in the UK since the passing of the London Act, regarding the claimed unreasonable restrictions on the freedom of trade and commercial activities of small businesses and entrepreneurs. Which also forces one to critically examine the following unqualified (and dare I say biassed) view:

> The Regulations will be reasonable and proportionate. They will strike a fair balance between the community's general interests (as reflected in the objectives underlying the Regulations) and individuals' rights to freedom of expression and protection of possessions. They will interfere with those rights to the minimum extent necessary to meet the underlying objectives described above.[195]

I would suggest that more work needs to be done to determine the value of the actual social and other benefits which arise from an event such as the Olympic Games, and that such rather bald statements regarding the reasonableness and proportionality of measures which may severely restrict civil liberties but are self-confessed attempts to protect narrow commercial interests, should be further interrogated, especially by the legal fraternity (and, preferably, human rights lawyers).

7.5 Conclusion

I have attempted in this chapter to highlight a few fundamental human rights which may frequently be in the firing line in respect of the measures implemented (and laws passed) to protect the commercial rights of mega-event sponsors and event organisers. That is, of course, not to say that there are no other such fundamental rights that may be implicated. For example, the South African Bill of Rights, which has featured prominently in this chapter for the reasons expressed earlier, also contains a fundamental guarantee of freedom of association.[196] One might ask whether such a guarantee might be invoked by those accused of 'ambushing' an

194 Ibid. 93.

195 Ibid.

196 Section 18.

event in defence of their attempt to associate with the event. The next chapter will more specifically examine the thematic space of the sports mega-event, and particularly the emergence of 'association rights' to events (which I have referred to in the earlier chapters), which serve to clothe event organisers with an exclusive right to 'license' the right to associate with an event (for commercial or, apparently in some cases, *any* other reasons). Would such association rights be in contravention of a fundamental guarantee of freedom of association?[197] Clearly this would not be the case where the 'association' at issue involves consumer deception by an ambush marketer in respect of official affiliation of the event (i.e. the classic cases of 'association ambushes' which are aimed at deceiving consumers into believing that the ambusher is an official sponsor and has paid for the privilege). A constitutional guarantee of freedom of association may allow me to challenge a restriction on membership of a club, but it would not allow me to get around paying such club's membership dues. If I have to pay for the privilege of membership, the constitutional guarantee which provides me with the freedom to associate with such club and its members would not allow me to do so for free.

However, as I have stressed throughout this book, anti-ambush marketing measures and laws have long since progressed beyond prohibiting only the 'association ambush' in the above meaning. The more problematic 'intrusion ambush' is also hit by association rights as included in *sui generis* event legislation in the various jurisdictions. I would submit that these cases—where there is no element of deception as to official affiliation involved, and the 'ambush' relates solely to reference to the event without attempting to obtain the benefits of official sponsorship status without paying for it—might very well be protected in terms of such a constitutional guarantee of freedom of association. This question, however, is beyond the scope of this book. I mention it only to illustrate that other human rights or constitutional guarantees may similarly be implicated in respect of event commercial rights protection. In this regard, it also bears mentioning that constitutional equality rights may similarly be implicated. In the concluding section of the previous chapter I referred to the fact that ambush marketing (and efforts to combat ambushing) are essentially about competition in respect of the marketing of brands. With this in mind it bears consideration whether the often draconian and always 'special' *sui generis* event legislation aimed at combating ambushing possibly also have implications in respect of constitutional guarantees to equality before the law

---

[197] See, for example, Ellis et al. 2011, p. 304:

> [A] consequence of translating ambush marketing into a legal issue is that the legislative provisions inevitably set the boundaries of legitimate and illegitimate conducts. In other words, while in a context where there is no right of association, there may be debates about the ethics of certain forms of activity labelled as ambush marketing, in a system where there is a law that creates a right of association, marketing campaigns can be evaluated in terms of whether they fall foul of the law or not. In such a context, the approach of ambushers becomes one of the *(sic)* seeking legal advice on how to conduct an advertising campaign that will exploit any limitations or loopholes in the law.

and equal treatment by the law.[198] Such anti-ambushing laws significantly favour one group of competitors in the mega-event marketing milieu, namely the event organisers and official sponsors. These laws do so while significantly affecting the rights and freedoms of 'ambushers' and others. It is not inconceivable that such equality guarantees may be significantly infringed in the process.

More generally, and beyond only the vagaries of aggressive and heavy-handed legal responses to the 'intrusion ambush', event organisers have in recent years managed to create such a rigidly regulated environment surrounding their mega-events that the most basic of liberties of individuals—i.e. non-marketers—may also come under fire to a significant extent in the process of the purported protection of commercial rights. In the previous chapter I referred to the monopolistic control exercised over the freedom of choice of fans as consumers through, for example, pouring rights (and the concerns expressed by American commentators Fortunato and Richards in this regard). But that is the tip of the iceberg. As examined in Chap. 3 event organisers use their ability to control access to venues to impose obligations on ticket holders and others (such as journalists). These obligations may relate to normal conduct that goes hand in hand with the mere enjoyment of the celebration that is the sports mega-event; this does not gel well with the protection of the 'celebratory feel of the Games'-justification for aggressive rights enforcement as expressed by, for example, the 2012 London Olympics authorities. Ticket provisions may have some basis in protecting against ambushing but may also simply appear to be ludicrous attempts at control of all kinds of normally unobjectionable (and non-threatening) conduct. Consider the venue regulations in force for the 2011 IRB Rugby World Cup, which made use of a list of prohibited items which ticket holders were absolutely prohibited from bringing into a venue and which could be 'removed, confiscated and/or destroyed at the discretion of any authorised person'. A spectator could be 'requested to submit to a body check and/or a search of your possessions at any time to locate and remove any prohibited item'. Spectators were also expressly prohibited from 'using in and around the venue any unauthorised... commercial items or materials (of whatever nature)', whatever those may be. The list of prohibited items contains some whoppers (apologies to Burger King, although their products were expressly included in the prohibition on 'commercially produced takeaway food'). For example, one was prohibited from bringing into a venue any 'food other than a small amount of non-commercial food for personal consumption'. Woe betide anyone who attempted to bring to a match 'prams, strollers or pushchairs' or umbrellas, or 'car parts' (*really?*). Finally, of course, one could not bring any item which the organisers (in their 'absolute discretion') determined 'may cause... inconvenience to any other person'.[199] It really sounds much safer and less bother to just stay home.

---

[198] As, for example, entrenched in section 9 of the South African Bill of Rights.

[199] *IRB Rugby World Cup 2011 Venue Regulations and Prohibited Items List*, available online at the time of writing at http://tickets.rugbyworldcup.com/pdf/RWC2011VenueRegulations.pdf.

Of course, lawyers know that you can get away with just about anything if you can back it up with a contract, and that such ticket provisions are in fact deemed to be contractually enforceable against the poor saps who shelled out the big bucks to watch their favourite teams in action. But this is also indicative of how far the pendulum of power has swung from the sports loving fans to the commercially astute and ever-vigilant-when-there's-a-buck-to-be-made event organisers. How else have we come to the point where an event organiser can enjoy such a dominant bargaining position that it can, in these same 2011 IRB World Cup venue regulations, impose a ticket term that says that the organisers will determine (within their absolute discretion) whether a camera, photographic or other recording device is for personal and non-commercial use—failing which it may, of course, be removed, confiscated and/or destroyed—while simultaneously providing that 'your voice, image and likeness may be captured and recorded in and around the venue and publicly disseminated by any means and in any format and media, and you waive all rights on an irrevocable, worldwide and perpetual basis to object to such recording and dissemination'.[200] *Caveat emptor*, indeed. There is very little sign here of any parity in bargaining or respect for the autonomy of the individual, all in the name of the purported protection of commercial rights.

Any meaningful examination of the legitimacy of such invasive rules and draconian curtailment of liberty is beyond the scope of this book. Finally, however, it does bear mentioning that one should not forget that anti-ambushing laws also frequently contain provisions which may impact on civil liberties that are most familiar to criminal lawyers. These relate to the very act of criminalisation of 'ambush marketing' (as is the case with the South African legislation, The New Zealand legislation and also, it appears, in terms of the proposed 2014 FIFA World Cup Bill that is currently at the time of writing before the Brazilian Congress[201]). Louise Longdin is concerned about this:

> [T]here is every reason for trepidation when jurisdictions relinquish control over everyday, generic and non-distinctive words and emblems to private entities restricting or excluding time honoured judicial and legislative safeguards and move towards criminalizing activities that were hitherto actionable civilly (if at all), backing up that handover with heavy handed enforcement powers and criminal sanctions.

I am also extremely concerned. When one considers the often wide and unprecedented powers of search and seizure, forcible entry[202] or arrest and

---

[200] Ibid.

[201] The *Lei Geral de Copa* provides, in Article 19, for the criminalisation of 'intrusion ambushing' (defined as the act of exposing 'trademarks, businesses, establishments, products, services or to practice any promotional activities not authorised by FIFA or by a person indicated by FIFA, attracting, by any means, public attention in the Official Places of the Events, with the objective of obtaining economic or advertising advantage'), which would carry a penalty of 3 months to a year imprisonment, or a fine. My thanks to Felipe Dannemann Lundgren for kindly providing a translation of this provision from the Portuguese text of the Bill.

[202] Compare section 19 of the London Olympic and Paralympic Games Act, 2006, and section 24 of the Glasgow Commonwealth Games Act, 2008.

detention provided for anti-ambushing laws, it may appear that it would be much safer to decamp, post haste, from host cities when FIFA et al. arrive to put on their expensive and exclusive shows. As Corbett and van Roy observe, for example, New Zealand's Major Events Management Act provides for the establishment of a 'temporary and largely untrained enforcement army… given powers that exceed those given to any group other than the police', in order to achieve 'the objective of speedy resolution of ambush marketing problems'.[203] I am hoping that such laws and the trends of an ever-increasing chipping away at civil liberties, purportedly to protect the commercial interests of multinational corporations, will be subjected to judicial scrutiny to determine their constitutionality in a relevant host nation, sooner rather than later.

In stepping off the subject of human rights implications, I would suggest that we need to urgently avoid the danger that Ellis et al. refer to in their discussion of the potential role of the legal structure within host nations to curb ambush marketing through legislation:

> [W]hile [the Olympic and Paralympic Marks Act passed by the Canadian federal government for purposes of the 2010 Vancouver Winter Olympic Games] was deemed sufficient for the current needs of the Olympic movement, in the future will the inability of the Canadian government to extend the same broad legal protection as the [United Kingdom in the form of its legislation for the 2012 London games] hinder the country's chance to play host to the Olympic Games? By the same token, *it is possible that countries that have more restricted civil liberties and that demonstrate a willingness to implement more draconian measures against ambush marketing, including criminal penalties, may become more attractive sites for events. If indeed the legal requirements of the IOC became too stringent, the potential exists that fewer countries would be able to meet their prerequisites and a negative backlash may follow.*[204] [My emphasis]

I would suggest that this warning is even more poignant if one considers that a developed, democratic society such as the United Kingdom has seen its way open to include criminal penalties for ambush marketing around the 2012 London Games and, even more problematically, to incorporate a reversal of the onus in claims of contravention of the street trading and advertising regulations and a significant interference with the presumption of innocence. The UK government's draft Regulations on Advertising Activity and Street Trading around London 2012, referred to earlier, read with section 21(2) of the London Act of 2006, provide that a person who has an interest in or is responsible for a business, good or service, will be liable for a contravention of the Regulations by the business or if the contravention relates to the good or service. A person who owns or occupies land will be responsible for any contravention of the Regulations that takes place on the land. In both cases a person can escape liability *if they prove* that the contravention took place without their knowledge or despite their having taken all reasonable steps to prevent a contravention from occurring, continuing or recurring. In justification for this rather blatant contravention of the presumption of innocence as

[203] Corbett and Van Roy 2010, p. 361.

[204] Ellis et al. 2011, p. 306.

contained in Article 6(2) of the European Convention of Human Rights, the UK government explains[205] that the reverse onus provisions of the Regulations are justifiable because they further a legitimate aim and are proportionate to that aim. The legitimate aim is explained, of course, as the three objectives of the Regulations as mentioned earlier, namely to ensure the Olympic and Paralympic events have a 'consistent celebratory look and feel to them'; to prevent ambush marketing in the vicinity of event venues; and to ensure people can easily access the venues. I have dealt with these rather flimsy grounds for justification of such invasive regulations earlier. In the context of the reversal of the onus provisions, however, the UK government proceeds to add insult to injury. It declares that these provisions are reasonably proportionate to the achievement of those objectives, because 'the prosecution will be required to make out the main elements of an offence before the onus shifts to the defendant'. And then:

> In addition, once the onus is reversed, the matters that a person is required to prove in order to benefit from the defence are peculiarly within the knowledge of the person—that they did not know about the trading or advertising or that they took reasonable steps to prevent the trading or advertising from occurring. *The burden on the accused person would, accordingly, not be difficult for a person to discharge if they have no knowledge of the advertising or trading at issue* or took steps to prevent it.[206] [My emphasis]

It may well be easy to prove one's innocence, if an accused person is able to bring evidence of steps taken to prevent such unlawful trading or advertising. But the italicised part of the above quoted passage is, frankly, unmitigated drivel. What about the person charged with the offence who in fact has no knowledge of the trading or advertising (i.e. a truly *innocent* defendant—yes, UK government, you can't assume these guys don't exist)? Would it really 'not be difficult' for this poor sap to prove that he had no such knowledge? The mind boggles at the idiocy of declaring, in justification of this substantial negation of the presumption of innocence, that proof of a lack of knowledge-a notoriously difficult negative to prove-would apparently be easy.

This and other examples of anti-ambushing laws eating away at the heart of fundamental rights are extremely troubling. We (and the law-makers) should never lose sight of the following truths expressed by Scassa:

> Laws restricting civil liberties must… avoid vagueness: a law that is unduly vague will create an uncertain standard that makes it impossible for individuals to know what conduct will or will not fall afoul of the law. Not only do vague laws force citizens to err on the side of caution, thus suppressing more expression than necessary, they set uncertain standards that may lead to arbitrary application by authorities… Vagueness will undoubtedly be a problem with anti-ambush marketing legislation. The laws are drafted in a deliberately open-ended manner and their enforcement is left largely to the discretion of heavily invested organizing committees. Laws that infringe on rights are expected to do so

[205] See the document relating to exceptions (referred to earlier), at p 92, as available online at the time of writing at http://www.culture.gov.uk/images/publications/ConDoc_Regulations_on_Advertising_and_Trading_London_2012-section9-10.pdf.

[206] Ibid. At 95.

as little as possible to achieve the valid legislative objective. In other words, they must be tailored so as to achieve the purpose of the law without capturing conduct that lies outside their purpose... In short, anti-ambush marketing legislation and the emergent right of association are difficult to reconcile with a robust freedom of expression.[207]

In light of the reality of Johnson's vertical and horizontal 'creep' in respect of anti-ambushing legislation, one must consider the prospects of such serious and potentially invasive provisions regarding presumptions of guilt finding their way into future legislation in developing countries, and especially less democratic countries with quite possibly already questionable human rights records. Woe betide the 'ambusher'... and maybe even the innocent bystander.

References

All internet-based sources referred to, were last visited in or before December 2011.

Bollier D (2005) Brand name bullies: the quest to own and control culture. Wiley, New York

Cheadle MH, Davis DM, Haysom NRL (2005) South African constitutional law: the bill of rights, 2nd edn. LexisNexis, Butterworths

Coombe RJ (1993) Tactics of appropriation and the politics of recognition in late modern democracies. Political Theory 21:411–433

Cooper Dreyfuss R (1996) We are symbols and inhabit symbols, so should we be paying rent? Deconstructing the Lanham Act and rights of publicity. Columbia-VLA J Law Arts 20:123

Corbett S, Van Roy Y (2010) Events management in New Zealand: one law to rule them all? Journal of Business Law 4:338–362

Currie I, de Waal J (2005) The bill of rights handbook, 5th edn. Juta & Co Ltd, Claremont

Dean OH (2006) Handbook of South African copyright law (looseleaf—service issue 13). Juta & Co Ltd, Claremont

Devenish G (2005) The South African constitution. LexisNexis, Butterworths

Ellis D, Scassa T, Seguin B (2011) Framing ambush marketing as a legal issue: an Olympic perspective. Sport Manag Rev 14(3):297–308

Frontier Economics Pty Ltd, Melbourne (2007) Ambush Marketing Legislation Review, a report prepared for IP Australia and the Australian government's department of communications, information technology and the arts (October 2007)

Grady J, McKelvey S, Bernthal MJ (2010) From Beijing 2008 to London 2012: examining event-specific Olympic legislation vis à vis the rights and interests of stakeholders. J Spons 3(2):144–156

Hewitt I (2005) Commercialisation of major sports events: does the law help or hinder the event organiser? Sport Law J 13(1):32–33

Jefferson Lenskyj H (2000) Inside the Olympic industry: power. Politics and Activism State University of New York Press, Albany

Jefferson Lenskyj H (2008) Olympic industry resistance: challenging olympic power and propaganda. State University of New York Press, Albany

Johnson P (2007) Ambush marketing: a practical guide to protecting the brand of a sporting event. Sweet & Maxwell, London

[207] Scassa 2011, p. 367.

Kobel P (2007) International report on question B: ambush marketing too smart to be good? Should certain ambush marketing practices be declared illegal and if yes, which ones and under what conditions? International Report to the International League of Competition Law. Catania Congress

La Fetra DJ (2004) Kick it up a notch: first amendment protection for commercial speech, in symposium: *Nike v. Kasky* and the modern commercial speech doctrine. Case West Law Rev 54:1205

Lemley MA, McKenna M (2010) Irrelevant confusion. Stanf Law Rev 62(2):413

Lines K, Heshka J (2010) Blatter's drift: the battle for our hearts and minds in South Africa. World Sports Law Rep 8(8). http://www.e-comlaw.com/wslr/archive/volume_8_issue_8.htm

Longdin L (2009) Public law solutions to private law problems: major event regulation subverts IP's internal balance. J Intellect Prop Law Pract 4(10):726–742

McKelvey S, Grady J (2008) Sponsorship program protection strategies for special sport events: are event organizers outmaneuvering ambush marketers? J Sport Manag 22:550–586

Mouritz A (2008) Challenging the legal enforceability of the vancouver 2010 Olympic games' anti-ambush marketing provisions. Sport Law J Issue 1(16):10–19

Price PJ (2003) Property Rights: Rights and Liberties under the Law. ABC-CLIO, Santa Barbara

Ritchie B, Hall M (2000) Mega events and human rights. Brent Ritchie, University of Canberra, Michael Hall, University of Otago, NZ and Sheffield Hallam University, UK. In: How you play the game papers from the first international conference on sports and human rights, 1–3 September 1999. ISBN 1 86365 566 2

Roche M (2000) Mega-events & modernity: Olympics and expos in the growth of global culture. Routledge, London

Scaria AG (2008) Ambush marketing: game within a game. Oxford University Press, Oxford

Scassa T (2011) Ambush marketing and the right of association: clamping down on references to that big event with the all the athletes in a couple of years. J Sport Manag 25:354–370

Schlossberg H (1996) Sports marketing. Blackwell, Oxford

Schulz-Herzenberg C (ed) (2010) Player and referee: conflicting interests and the 2010 FIFA World Cup^{TM}, monograph 169. South African Institute for Security Studies, Pretoria

Shaw CA (2008) Five ring circus: myths and realities of the Olympic games. New Society Publishers, Gabriola Island

Sliffman AJ (2012) Unconstitutional hosting of the super bowl: anti-ambush marketing clean zone's violation of the first amendment. Marq Sports L Rev 22(1):257–285

Vaidhyanathan S (2003) Copyrights and copywrongs: the rise of intellectual property and how it threatens creativity. New York University Press, New York

Vassallo E, Blemaster K, Werner P (2005) An international look at ambush marketing. Trademark Report 95:1338

Weinberg J (1982) Constitutional protection of commercial speech. Columbia Law Rev 82:720

Wright JAYB (1999) The supreme court of the United States and first amendment protection of advertising. In: Jones JP (ed) The Advertising Business. SAGE Publishing

Chapter 8
'Jumping on the Brand Wagon': 'Association Rights' and the Thematic Space of the Sports Mega-Event

> Sponsors need to forget all about the posturing politicians and all of the event dignitaries and their proclamations of "lines in the sand" and look after themselves. Sponsors need to leverage every event fully and creatively and with absolute focus on adding value to the total fan experience, not just "owning" the event. Strategy will save the day, and if the IOC, FIFA, the IRB, the ICC, and the rest of the quadrennial anagrams really want to protect their sponsors, they will spend less time drawing up legal briefs and more time educating their sponsors.[1]

> As soon as the land of any country has all become private property, the landlords, like all other men, love to reap where they never sowed, and demand a rent even for its natural produce.[2]

> [A] celebrity like Madonna cannot say of her public image what the carpenter can say of his chair: "*I* made it." And because she cannot say this of her public image, she cannot lay a convincing moral claim to the *exclusive* ownership or control of the economic values that attach to it.[3]

8.1 Introduction

The *sui generis* protection of commercial rights to mega-events by means of special events legislation has in recent years morphed into the creation, by legislatures in host nations, of a new and rather strange legal creature, which is commonly referred to as 'association rights' to events. As we saw in the discussion of some of the mechanics of sports sponsorship in Chap. 2, the core of the commercial value

---

1 Marketing guru Kim Skildum-Reid, writing on her marketing blog in 'Why ambush marketing legislation will never work (and what will)', posted 5 August 2009—available online at the time of writing at http://blog.powersponsorship.com/index.php/2009/08/why-ambush-marketing-legislation-will-never-work/.

2 Scottish economist Adam Smith (1723–1790).

3 Madow 1993.

A. M. Louw, *Ambush Marketing and the Mega-Event Monopoly*,
ASSER International Sports Law Series, DOI: 10.1007/978-90-6704-864-4_8,

obtained by the corporate sponsor in terms of a sponsorship contract revolves around the rights it obtains to associate itself, its brand, product or service with the sports property. The mega-event serves as a marketing platform upon which the sponsor anchors its marketing campaign in order to leverage the rights for which it has invested the substantial rights fees. Anti-ambushing laws have started to specifically target this facet of mega-events against the involvement of outsiders. Whilst the London Olympic and Paralympic Games Act, 2006 (as discussed in Chap. 4) is the first of such legislation to expressly create a specific statutory association right (which vests in the London Organising Committee for the 2012 Games), other countries have similarly enacted provisions that limit the rights and freedoms of individuals and businesses to associate themselves or their products or services with the events. Such protection differs in scope and form, but the common thread is the increasing trend of legislatively regulating who may, or may not, 'associate' themselves with events primarily for commercial purposes.

In the earlier chapters I have subjected such *sui generis* protection for commercial rights to mega-events to legal scrutiny on the bases of traditional and accepted principles of intellectual property law and competition law, and with brief examination of some human rights implications. In this chapter I will consider, more fundamentally, the effect of such legislation on the basis of first principles of law. Specifically, I will ask (and try to answer) a number of questions:

(1) Is there any overriding public good served by such legislation (which, essentially, we must consider, is aimed at protecting private commercial interests by imposing often serious curtailment of the rights and liberties of members of the public and other commercial actors)?
(2) What, in fact, is such legislation trying to protect?
(3) What, exactly, does such legislation prohibit?
(4) What are the costs of such legislation in the greater scheme of the hosting of mega-events?

I believe that these association rights are an illegitimate extension of traditional principles of law in this context. They are, at first glance, an uncontroversial evolution of the traditional protection offered against 'association ambushes'; if one considers the traditional classical trinity of the passing off action (an important traditional mechanism to counter the association ambush), such association rights would appear to be a distillation of such action in statutory garb in that they are aimed at prohibiting misrepresentation regarding an association in order to protect the goodwill of the event or event organiser. If one considers these association rights more closely, however, we see that they tend to cast the net much wider than just that, and, much more controversially, they also outlaw the more problematic 'intrusion ambush', as discussed in the earlier chapters. This development of mega-event association rights has come to the point where mere reference to an event may be actionable (or even subject the 'ambusher' to criminal sanctions); a prime example of such extension of the scope for liability is the draconian provision found in section 15A(2) of South Africa's Merchandise Marks Act which deals with the 'abuse' of a trademark in connection with a protected event.

When potential liability for ambushing revolves around association with an event or even references to an event it becomes important to consider what, exactly, is the scope of the event that is so protected. Others have in marketing-speak referred to the thematic space of the event, and I will also use this terminology in examining this space in order to determine the limits of what may be protected or for which the event organisers and their official sponsors may rightly claim protection by the law.

First, though, I will say a few words regarding another controversial aspect of these statutory association rights, namely the fact they have made their way into special legislation with the force of law in order to protect private commercial interests and private contractual rights in respect of mega-events.

8.2 Is the Public Good Served By *Sui Generis* Protection of Commercial Rights By Means of Special Events Legislation?

Legislation is a mechanism by which the state creates laws of general application to its citizens, usually in order to address some mischief (real or perceived) in the interests of the state and, importantly, the public. The very basis for the wielding of legislative powers by the state in a democracy is the public good; i.e. laws should be used to protect the public and not serve narrow or selfish interests of the lawmaker or of special interest groups where such interests are served through laws which, on balance, do more harm than good to the broader public.

The commercial rights to mega-events, as discussed earlier in this book, are created in the course of private dealings between event organisers and their commercial partners (such as sponsors, licensees and broadcasters), and relate to private commercial interests. As pointed out earlier, such rights, for the most part, are creatures of contract. They are created by means of contracts between the relevant parties and are, in terms of general principles of contract law—and strictly speaking—applicable and enforceable only between such parties. Where legislation is passed to protect such rights, the public are involved (such laws are, in fact, passed in their name in the case of democratically elected legislatures) and directly affected; the state provides a mechanism by means of which such private rights are made enforceable against others, persons outside the private contractual nexus, and such personal rights are granted the force of law in the public dimension. As Louise Longdin puts it, the relevant legislation seeks to provide public law solutions to private law problems; as Scassa observes, '[a]nti-ambush marketing legislation reaches into areas once untouched by state law, and left largely to private ordering and market forces'.[4] And, strangely in the context of the

[4] Scassa 2011, p. 363.

legislative process, these developments appear to be anything but balanced, as has been observed in the context of the Olympic Games:

> By requiring countries to introduce legal measures to protect sponsors from ambush marketing, the IOC is able to protect their rights over those of all others despite the broader public policy obligations inherent in the creation of legislation.[5]

We must ask whether this extension of application of such private commercial 'rights' is justifiable. More specifically, what do members of the public gain from this? In essence, one must interrogate whether the following rather assumptive declaration is an accurate and justifiable expression of the role of the law in accommodating the interests of *all* the stakeholders in the mega-event milieu:

> [Proposed advertising and street trading regulations for the 2012 London Olympic Games] will … protect the rights of those that have made a commercial contribution to the staging of the Games (without which the Games could not take place) by preventing advertising and trading activities that amount to ambush marketing. It is legitimate in a democratic society to take steps to protect commercial investments which have a public interest element to them. In this case, the social benefits of the Games could not be achieved without such commercial investments.[6]

In examining these questions one must consider the role of governments and lawmakers, both more generally and also in the context of the hosting of mega-events, specifically in respect of the 'public interest element' referred to in the above quoted passage:

> At the most basic level, one can argue that one of the primary roles or functions of government (at least within capitalism based economies such as the UK and USA) should be to protect the commercial freedoms of its national and local business communities in order to ensure a fair and competitive marketplace. Towards this end, governments enact laws relating to trademark protection, honest business practices and fair competition. On a broader level, and particularly within the context of sport, one can argue that the government's role is to do what is prudent to secure the psychic and economic benefits of hosting an international mega sport event such as the Olympic Games… These two roles of government require it to engage in a delicate balancing act.[7]

In light of these two governmental roles, Grady et al. continue to question the legitimacy of such special events legislation:

> [O]ne must ask whether it is properly within the role of government to enact laws that substantially expand its existing business and trademark laws solely for the short-term benefit and protection of a privately-run sports organisation and its elite cadre of official sponsors (many of whom often have little or no commercial presence within the country/state).

---

[5] Ellis et al. 2011, p. 302.

[6] From the UK Department of Culture, Media And Sport's consultation document on *Regulations on Advertising Activity and Trading Around London 2012*, March 2011 (in Section 10: Human Rights Assessment, at 93)—available online at the time of writing at http://www.culture.gov.uk/images/publications/ConDoc_Regulations_on_Advertising_and_Trading_London_2012-section9-10.pdf.

[7] Grady et al. 2010, p. 149.

> This expansion ostensibly comes at the expense of the long-term interests of its own business community and citizenry.[8]

Miguel Portela, FIFA's head intellectual property lawyer, was quoted as explaining the problems it faced in bringing its showcase event and valuable commercial rights to deepest, darkest Africa in 2010:

> For South Africa, we did lots of training and education because it's a young country without a lot of IP legislation or experience for an event like this within the authorities or in the business community... So we took it upon ourselves to invest in that area and leave a legacy behind.[9]

While FIFA at the time may have failed to deal sufficiently (or at all) with some pretty important football-related issues, such as dicey refereeing and the use of goal-line technology in its World Cup games, it did indeed leave a legacy behind. A prominent South African intellectual property law expert, Wim Alberts, was critical of the extent of the South African legislature's protection of FIFA's commercial interests in respect of the 2010 World Cup event (with specific reference to the 'ambushing' campaign by local domestic airline kulula in early 2010, which is discussed elsewhere in this book):

> [The] objective [of the anti-ambush marketing legislation, namely that businesses should be protected in view of the significant amounts paid for the right to describe themselves as official sponsors and that monies earned would then be used for the development of football] is... not one traditionally classified as a governmental duty. Law enforcement, by contrast, is. Whereas the lack of law enforcement in general has been criticised, one now has the ironic situation where the simple act of painting a soccer ball can mean the difference between the words goal and gaol... [In the process of enforcing the law, state machinery is not directly involved]... One is confronted with a private adjudication system being allowed to operate parallel to the courts. FIFA is effectively the prosecutor, if not persecutor, judge and jury.[10]

Of course, it should be borne in mind that the decision whether or not (and to what extent) lawmakers should enter the fray in legislating for special event protection is largely a political one:

> To determine whether legislating is necessary or not, is a political question... [A]mbush marketing practices do not affect consumers. Any legislation is therefore purely for the benefits of [business-to-business] relationships and must be assessed within these parameters. [W]here the scope of a legislative intervention is limited to sports, one must be aware that macro-economic returns of mega sport events, have been questioned in the economic literature. They are often over stated (usually a gross calculation and not a net calculation taking into consideration the corresponding decrease in other spending) and sometimes set off by large public spending. The creation of jobs resulting from the organisation and construction of an infrastructure may be detrimental to other sectors of

---

[8] Ibid. pp. 149, 150.

[9] Portela, as quoted in Gannon 2010, p. 70.

[10] See the short article entitled 'Ambush marketing legislation: Contravention or constitutional?', 21 April 2010, available online at the time of writing at http://www.biz-community.com/Article/196/147/46893.html.

> the local industry, unless the economy is depressed. Last but not least, there are usually high follow-up costs to adapt, use and maintain the new infrastructures. The interest is most often political instead of economic.[11]

In fact, this political element to the process of legislating for events has been recognised in the context of one of the most stringent anti-ambushing statutes currently to be found, namely New Zealand's Major Events Management Act, 2007 (as discussed in Chap. 4). As MEMA allows for the imposition of restrictions on marketing practices harmful only to brand owners and sponsors rather than consumers, the framers of the Act 'have made some effort to impose internal political and bureaucratic controls on the decision to declare that an event is a major event', although some such internal controls are of dubious value in this regard.[12] Even so, legislation such as MEMA may be open to criticism of the use of legislative powers to protect private interests, as Longdin does when she calls MEMA a 'misguided attempt to provide a public law solution to a private law problem' and an example of '[t]emporary renting out of the coercive powers of the state' which reminds one of years gone by when 'a chronically cash-strapped Crown disbursed one-off privileges to those prepared to pay for them'.[13] Corbett and van Roy, also writing in the context of an analysis of MEMA, point to three important aspects in the consideration of the legitimacy of *sui generis* event legislation, namely—

- The fact that it usually deals with state regulation of matters which are not deemed as 'illegal' or as requiring intervention in terms of traditional laws;
- That it raises questions regarding the appropriateness of the state providing a special legal regime for certain businesses; and
- The fact that such legislation may affect the traditional balance between individual freedoms, the public interest and state coercion, as maintained by consumer and intellectual property laws (in the marketing context).[14]

These authors observe, correctly in my view, that if one considers the public interest justification for (special) legislation, there are surely 'other commercial organisations [rather than sports event organisers] that arguably are more concerned with genuine public interest products (for example power, fuel and telephone companies) and could therefore more appropriately claim to be entitled [to] special treatment from their own specific legislation'.[15] Another point that is worth raising here is the fact that the development in recent years of generic *sui generis* event legislation (i.e. which is not aimed at a specific event—compare the South African legislation and New Zealand's MEMA) is especially problematic. Teresa

---

[11] Kobel 2007, p. 57 (with reference to Baade R 'The economic impact of mega-sporting events' in Andreff and Szymanski 2006, p. 177 *et seq.*).

[12] Longdin 2009, p. 730.

[13] Ibid. p. 742.

[14] Corbett and Van Roy 2010, p. 339.

[15] Corbett and Van Roy 2010, p. 358.

Scassa observes that such generic legislating exercise 'removes the enactment of such legislation on an event-by-event basis from public debate by the legislature. The pressure to designate events touted as promoting some public interest will likely be high, and the opportunities for public input are diminished'.[16]

And one should not forget that the political element of the decision to host (or to bid for the rights to host) a sports mega-event may also involve private commercial interests, but have a disproportionate impact on private citizens:

> [U]nder the new urban politics imperatives, a decision to bid for mega-events, such as the Olympics, is not solely made by local or regional governments but often involves business corporations. In that sense, mega-sporting events are often credited with mobilising corporate elites and local politicians in profitable alliances that not only can boost local construction and retail and tourist industries but can also generate substantial infrastructure funding from higher levels of government. The practices of such alliances... usually involve campaigns to persuade the citizens of the host city that the event will transform their hometown into a 'worldclass' city, thus justifying the use of tax money. However, [an analysis of Toronto's bid for the 2008 Olympics] has claimed that taxpayers disproportionately bear the burden when they give consent for the use of tax money for the staging of mega-sporting events.[17]

In some countries—such as South Africa in respect of the 2010 FIFA World Cup—the involvement of local business interests and the interface with government may also lead to allegations of widespread corruption regarding aspects of the staging of events.[18] Indications at the time of writing of this book are that Brazil may be struggling with similar problems in respect of its preparation for the 2014 FIFA World Cup and 2016 Rio Olympic Games.

Apart from the (proper) role of governments and lawmakers in this context, let us examine the potential benefit for the public deriving from *sui generis* commercial rights protection by means of special events legislation more closely. Here we must pose the question whether such legislation, which is prohibitive in nature and serves to create both civil and sometimes criminal liability for contravention, actually serves to protect the public in some way. In order to attempt to answer this question I believe one should focus on the more traditional mechanisms of law that are most relevant in protecting sponsors and event organisers in the ambush marketing context. These are common law passing off (or unlawful competition) actions and the use of relevant intellectual property rights. I believe it is important to consider the public interest served by such mechanisms (why do we protect businesses against passing off, and why do we grant and require others to respect intellectual property rights?) in evaluating the significant expansion of protection occasioned by the *sui generis* event legislation. This legislation, and especially the new-fangled 'association rights' created by this means, have simply lost touch with the key consumer protection element (and justification) of these more traditional laws.[19]

---

[16] Scassa 2011, p. 359.

[17] Malfas et al. 2004, p. 216 (the study on the Toronto bid, as referred to, by Eitzen 1996).

[18] See the report by Schulz-Herzenberg 2010

[19] See, for example, Scassa 2011, p. 358.

The common law passing off action is aimed at protecting the goodwill of a plaintiff business (and therefore also the investment of the proprietor in such business), but it also encompasses an element of protection of the public against deceptive and misleading conduct by the defendant. While most jurisdictions protect the public against deceptive trade practices by means of legislation (compare South Africa's Trade Practices Act[20]), the passing off action reflects a common law cause of action which also provides a deterrent to deceptive trade practices such as e.g. misleading advertising. Trademark law, similarly has as one of its prime aims the protection of the public against confusion. A trademark is intellectual property, and the holder of such mark is granted certain exclusive rights relating to such mark and its use in the course of trade. But the philosophical basis for granting such a limited monopoly to the mark holder is premised on the public good function of a trademark—the benefit derived from a trademark which denotes the origin of goods or services lies in its ability to denote not only the source of the product or service to which the mark is applied (the consumer knows where it is coming from) but, consequently, the quality of such goods or services (the consumer knows what they're buying). The three rationales commonly cited to justify the legal mechanism of trademark protection are the following:

(1) Consumer protection—trademarks lower consumer search costs by distinguishing the desired goods or services of a desired trader from the goods and services of other traders (while also discouraging counterfeiting);
(2) Fair competition—trademarks and the laws that protect them facilitate the attraction of clientele for those traders who offer desired goods (and this promotes competition based on own built-up reputation); and
(3) Economic efficiency—'trademarks identify the goods in demand and help direct resources towards the production of those goods with the economic votes consumers cast by their patronage'.[21]

A trademark (and proper protection of such mark against infringement by competitors of the mark holder) serves to avoid consumer deception and confusion and, ultimately, also serves to protect the consumer. This represents the 'core of trade mark law' based on a model which can be called the 'information transmission model'—trademarks are devices for communicating product quality information to the market; the basic function of a trademark is to provide information to identify the source of a product or service in order to protect the consumer public (the object of protection) from deception and confusion.[22] While there is a difference of opinion on the true object of trademark law (i.e. marks are also seen as property of people who create them and invest in promoting a business—where the focus is on sellers, against misappropriation of their marks, and 'misappropriation of another's goodwill by using another's trademark or a close

[20] See Sect. 4.4.5 of Chap. 4.
[21] See Ng, C W 'The irrational lightness of trade marks', in Bently et al. 2008, p. 224.
[22] Spinello and Bottis 2009, p. 100.

imitation of the mark approached the idea of misappropriation of another's property and brought closer the related but different torts of trademark infringement and unfair competition'[23]), there is practical justification for the role of the 'information theory' (and its emphasis on consumer deception) as grounding for the law relating to such marks: 'Trademark law makes sense because it promotes the flow of truthful product information and leads to more efficient and competitive markets... Economically, trademark law reduces consumer search costs and facilitates investment in goodwill by protecting the accuracy of trademark-related investments in advertising and product quality.'[24] This conception of the true object of trademark law is more convincing than a 'property-based' approach which emphasises the trademark holder's interests as creator of a mark, especially if one considers trademarks in the context of other intellectual property such as copyright and patents: '[T]rademark law does not tie its prerequisites for protection to a need for additional incentives... we have no evidence to prove that society, or even an efficient market, needs more trademarks.'[25] The information transmission model does not gel well with the development of a goodwill-based conception of trademarks:

> The idea of protecting goodwill fits this model rather poorly. Goodwill protection has nothing directly to do with facilitating consumer choice or safeguarding the quality of product information. It has to do instead with protecting sellers from misappropriation. Goodwill on this view denotes the special value that attaches to a brand when the seller's advertising and investments in quality generate brand loyalty—a capacity to attract consumers over time. Trademarks are repositories or symbols of this goodwill, and trademark law prevents others from appropriating it by using a similar mark.[26]

In an earlier chapter I have referred to the fact that one of the main reasons for the special event legislation with which we are currently concerned (which, essentially and for the most part, is aimed at extending the protection traditionally provided by intellectual property laws), has been a realisation that such more traditional forms of legal protection often simply do not provide sufficient safeguards in such cases. I referred to what has been described as the 'third dimension' that events bring to the equation in the context of ambush marketing.[27] Traditionally, IP rights infringements involve, e.g. an infringement by X of Y's copyright in a work (for example, by means of unlawful copying or publication of the relevant work) or through X using, for example, a trademark that is confusingly similar to Y's registered trademark. In the case of ambush marketing of an event, however, the 'ambusher' would usually not be infringing the intellectual property

---

23 Ibid. p. 101.

24 Dogan and Lemley 2005, pp. 463, 466.

25 Spinello and Bottis 2009, p. 103.

26 Bone 2006, p. 4.

27 Shwetashree Majumder and Harsimran Kalra 'The ambush marketing debate', on the web site *Managing Intellectual Property*, 1 September 2010 (available online at the time of writing at http://www.managingip.com/Article/2665113/The-ambush-marketing-debate.html?ArticleId=2665113&p=2).

of its competitor (e.g. an official sponsor). The deception or confusion relates to association with *the event* and not with the official sponsor. The 'ambusher' is alleged to have created confusion over their (official) involvement or association with an event, which it is then claimed prejudices both the event organisers (rights grantors) and the official sponsors or commercial partners (rights holders) due to the dilution of the value of their investment and a potential loss of revenues that would otherwise have been payable in terms of an official rights grant contract (as well as negatively affecting the efficacy of the official sponsor's advertising through the creation of a cluttered marketing environment surrounding the event). When we enter the realm of ambush marketing of sports mega-events we are concerned, primarily, with issues which resonate with a specific branch of trademark protection that has developed in recent years, namely the law relating to use of a trademark to denote sponsorship or affiliation.

Lemley and McKenna[28] point to an important development in the US courts' jurisprudence regarding actionable source confusion in trademark cases (allied with the development of the law away from the earlier availability of trademark remedies only in cases of direct competitors), which later found legislative approval:

> Courts did something very similar to legitimate licensing practices. In order to distinguish uses by affiliated companies from infringing uses by third parties, courts began to hold that, even when it did not actually produce the products bearing its mark, a mark owner could be considered the legal "source" of those products if it exercised sufficient control over their quality… Congress later codified this understanding of source in section 5 of the Lanham Act, which provides that use of a mark by "related companies" inures to the benefit of the mark owner… A "related company" in this context is one "whose use of a mark is controlled by the owner of the mark with respect to the nature and quality of the goods or services on or in connection with which the mark is used"… Thus, in modern terms, the legal source of a product is not necessarily the actual producer of a product but instead the entity exercising control over the quality of products bearing a particular mark. That entity might be related to the actual producer only by contract.[29]

These developments formed the basis for recognition of trademarks as protecting sponsorship or affiliation, rather than merely the source of a product or service in the more limited, traditional, sense. And the authors are critical of such development:

> [T]he move to prevent confusion as to sponsorship and affiliation [in trade mark law] began with cases involving related goods that consumers might reasonably have assumed the trademark owner actually made. It expanded to include products that were not made by the trademark owner directly but that consumers might reasonably have believed the trademark owner stood behind or guaranteed, and ultimately it extended to include cases in which there was at most a business relationship between the trademark owner and the product maker but no belief whatsoever of a relationship between the trademark owner and the defendant's goods. We think the concept of sponsorship or affiliation, introduced

28 Lemley and McKenna 2010, p. 413.

29 Ibid. p. 426 n 52.

> to accommodate these broader claims, is to blame for much of what ails modern trademark law.[30]

They continue to suggest the following:

> [T]rademark rights ought to extend far enough to cover uses that confuse consumers about who is ultimately responsible for the quality of the defendant's goods or services. Some of those cases will be situations where consumers may not believe the plaintiff actually produced the goods or services at issue but nevertheless believe the plaintiff has played a role in guaranteeing quality. But "sponsorship" or "affiliation" could refer to virtually any relationship between the parties, and we believe it is precisely the vagueness of these terms that has led to … problems.[31]

Lemley and McKenna believe that a loose application by courts of confusion as to sponsorship and affiliation threatens to make the very scope of the application of trademark law overly wide:

> Confusion about some relationships simply shouldn't matter because it doesn't affect consumers decisions to purchase the defendant's goods or services. Yet the "sponsorship or affiliation" formulation allows for no such distinctions, threatening ultimately to swallow up all uses of another's mark.[32]

In fact, if one reads these criticisms they are reminiscent of the long and winding road followed in the development of a doctrine of trademark dilution (following Frank Schechter's seminal 1927 article on the subject), a doctrine which takes trademark law out of the realm of consumer confusion and can, at least by its critics, be viewed as an unjustified extension of the trademark holder's monopoly.[33]

Trademark law, of course, provides an important source of protection for event organisers and their commercial partners, in the context of the theme of this book; it is one of the traditional grounds for protection against ambush marketing of an event (specifically in the more blatant cases of ambushing where event marks are misappropriated, although these cases by sizeable and significant ambushers are extremely rare nowadays). That is not to say, however, that the event organisers are necessarily satisfied with the extent of such protection, far from it. Compare FIFA's unsuccessful attempts to obtain legal recognition of special trademark protection for its 'event marks' in Germany (in the protracted litigation against chocolate-maker Ferrero in respect of the 2006 FIFA World Cup Germany),[34] and its similarly unsuccessful attempt concerning Nike in the USA.[35] However, the

---

30 Ibid. pp. 427,428.

31 Ibid.

32 Ibid. p. 428.

33 Schechter 1927. For a useful exposition of the development of the dilution doctrine, see Bone 2008.

34 See the discussion in Sect. 5.2.2 in Chap. 5.

35 Compare the litigation in the US District Court for the District of Columbia in *Federation Internationale de Football Association v. Nike, Inc.* 285 F. Supp. 2d 64 (2003 U.S. Dist.), relating to FIFA's Women's World Cup USA in 2003.

point I am trying to make is that the *sui generis* protection of mega-events through special legislation is—at least ostensibly—similarly aimed at protecting against consumer confusion over sponsorship and affiliation.

The special event legislation we have looked at earlier generally protect against unauthorised 'association' (in commercial dealings) with a protected event. The London Act, for example, grants the Games organising committee, LOCOG, the capacity to regulate a right 'to use any representation (of any kind) in a manner likely to suggest to the public that there is an association between the London Olympic or Paralympic Games and goods and services, or a person who provides goods or services'.[36] The prohibited 'association' includes any kind of contractual relationship, commercial relationship, corporate or structural connection or the provision of financial or other support for or in connection with the Games.'[37] New Zealand's Major Events Management Act,[38] in section 10, similarly provides that no person may, during a major event's protection period, make any representation in a way likely to suggest to a reasonable person that there is an association between the major event and goods or services (or a brand of goods or services or a person who provides goods or services). Similarly, China's Protection of Olympic Symbols Regulations, 2002 (which were passed to meet its obligation to protect the Olympic intellectual property under the Host City Contract for the 2008 Olympic Games in Beijing) prohibits the use of Olympic names and logos for 'implied commercial purposes',[39] and prohibits 'activities that might be deemed by others as an existing sponsorship or other supportive relationship'.[40] It is clearly the relationship of sponsorship or affiliation (e.g. by means of licensing in the context of event-related merchandising) that is involved here. Such legislation prohibits deception of the public as to association in the form of sponsorship or affiliation, even though we see that deception (and actual confusion of the public) is often not required for purposes of infringement—compare the London Act, which does not require that the association caused by a representation should be misleading (i.e. it does not matter whether consumers are confused or not), the representation must objectively create the association. Two notable exceptions are, firstly, the legislation passed to protect the 2010 Vancouver winter Olympics. Section 4(1) of the Olympic and Paralympic Marks Act (or 'Bill C-47') states that no person shall, during the time period of the legislation, in association with the protected trade-marks or other mark, promote or otherwise direct public attention to their business, wares or services in a manner that *misleads or is likely to mislead the public into believing* that (a) the person's business, wares or services are approved, authorized or endorsed by any of the Olympic organizing committees, or (b) a business association exists between the person's business and the Games

---

36 Schedule 4, par. 1(1) of the Act.

37 Schedule 4, par. 1(2).

38 Public Act 35 of 2007, discussed in Sect. 4.4.5 of Chap. 4.

39 In Article 2.

40 In Article 9.

or any of the organizing committees. It should be noted, however, that protecting against consumer confusion was apparently not high on the agenda in the passing of the Olympic and Paralympic Marks Act:

> Section 4 of [the Act], which specifically addresses ambush marketing by association is embedded within a statute that also serves the more traditional role of protecting Olympic trademarks. The protection of trademarks is familiar territory, and is justified for… public policy objectives… In the Parliamentary debates surrounding [the Act], the objectives put forth for the enactment of the anti-ambush marketing provisions related specifically to the protection of the interests of the organizers and sponsors, with a public interest being identified in the commercial success of the games… No attention was given to the issue of consumer protection. This is not surprising, as ambush marketing does not give rise to the same issues of consumer harm as does trademark infringement. For example, a consumer is not likely to be misled in his or her consumption choices by the launch of a ROOTS line of Canada themed clothing shortly before the start of the Olympic Games in Vancouver. The clothing is made by ROOTS and the ROOTS brand is clearly marked. If there is any deception, it might be as to the relationship between the company and the Olympics—yet it is not evident that this results in a harm of any consequence to the consumer.[41]

The second example of an anti-ambushing provision which appears to emphasise the issue of deception of the public is contained in section 6(3) of the Russian Federation's 'Olympic and Paralympic Law'[42] passed for the 2014 Sochi winter Games, which provides as follows:

> Any advertising which contains false information concerning the association of an advertiser with the Olympic Games and the Paralympic Games, including in the capacity of a sponsor, or concerning the approval of consumer properties of advertised goods (works, services) by the International Olympic Committee, the International Paralympic Committee, the Olympic Committee of Russia, the Paralympic Committee of Russia, the Organising Committee "Sochi 2014", shall be deemed to be misleading.

This issue of consumer confusion[43] (or rather the lack of a *de facto* requirement of such confusion in most examples of special event legislation aimed at

[41] Ellis et al. 2011, p. 301.

[42] Federal Law No. 310-FZ (approved by the Federation Council on 23 November 2007)—see Sect. 4.4.8 in Chap. 4.

[43] In fairness, it should be noted here that some are of the view that trademark law has moved away from its traditional consumer protection rationale. Catherine Ng argues, rather convincingly, that developments in both the use of trademarks and in trademark laws have served to sideline the traditional requirement of consumer confusion as to the source of goods or services. These developments include the role of company law (i.e. modern corporate structures are often opaque and corporate management unknown to the public, which serves to 'alienate' the source of trademarked goods or services), the law's acceptance of trademark licensing (which, by definition, permits co-existence of multiple sources for one trademark) and franchising. She observes the following in arguing for a reassessment of the rationales for trademark law and a re-rationalisation of the boundaries for protection:

'Without a secure consumer protection rationale which presumes that consumer demand is trained more on the desirability of the goods than the desirability of their marks, the rationale [of trademark law] for advancing efficient distribution of economic resources… needs to be reconsidered. Where a mark is desired by and its goods incidental to the consumer, the consumer's economic votes may favour promoting the marks more than producing the goods

combating ambush marketing) raises an interesting question against the backdrop of Lemley and McKenna's criticism of the expansion of American trademark law to include confusion over sponsorship or affiliation. They argue that this expansion ignores a crucial requirement in terms of traditional notions of trademark protection, namely the *effect* of such consumer confusion on the consumer's actions, and that 'sponsorship and affiliation confusion has taken on a life of its own, leading courts to declare as infringing a variety of practices that might be confusing in some sense, but that do not affect consumers' decision-making process.'[44] In traditional terms, registered trademarks are intended to protect against consumer confusion because the use of an infringing mark (by a competitor or otherwise, depending on the circumstances) poses *a threat of actual harm to consumers*. Their confusion might lead them to decide to purchase the infringing party's goods or services, which may be of inferior quality or otherwise objectionable when not originating from the stable of the mark holder.

The association rights created by *sui generis* legislative event protection, arguably, create statutory protection that is akin to registered trademark rights (this was submitted recently by the London organising committee in a cyber-squatting dispute before the WIPO arbitration and mediation centre[45]). I would submit that the same criticism can be expressed in regard to such legislative protection and, more specifically, the fact that its focus is not on protecting the public (consumers) against harm deriving from confusion as to the origin of goods or services but rather the connection between the sponsor or merchandising licensee and the event organiser. What the legislation aims to protect is nothing more than the right (or ability) of the event organiser to license association with the event to sponsors or licensees. And claims that this type of consumer confusion may warrant such protection for event organisers are tenuous, at best, as Lemley and McKenna try to illustrate in the context of alleged infringement of the trademark of a producer where the use of a mark suggests to consumers a relationship of sponsorship or affiliation with such producer:

> [S]tudies suggest that any harm to producers [or event organisers in this context] from confusion about sponsorship or affiliation is quite attenuated: producers suffer no lost sales, and they are unlikely to suffer any reputational consequences absent additional information suggesting control over the partner. If a mall cookie vendor advertises that its cookies contain M&Ms, for example, consumers might or might not assume that Mars had entered into a deal with the cookie company, but whether they do or not they are unlikely to blame Mars if they don't like the cookies. *The only sense, then, in which a mark owner*

(Footnote 43 continued)
which fulfil material needs.' See Ng, C W 'The irrational lightness of trade marks', in Bently et al. 2008, pp. 223–237.

44 Lemley and McKenna 2010, p. 414.

45 *The London Organising Committee of the Olympic Games and Paralympic Games Limited v. H&S Media Ltd* Case No. D2010-0415 (the Administrative Panel decision dated 29 April 2010)—report available online at the time of writing at http://www.wipo.int/amc/en/domains/decisions/text/2010/d2010-0415.html.

is harmed by third-party uses that suggest sponsorship or affiliation is that third-party uses might interfere with the mark owner's own ability to develop and derive value from such relationships. In other words, the only likely loss to trademark owners from affiliation confusion is the loss of revenue the trademark owner could have made by licensing the mark to the putative affiliate. This is a claim to market control, not a claim of harm resulting from confusion or even an injury to consumers at all. We think this circular claim to licensing revenue is insufficient to justify trademark protection, particularly in light of the significant costs such protection entails... Our point is not that consumers can never be harmed by confusion regarding non-quality-related relationships. Rather, the point is that the sort of attenuated confusion at issue in sponsorship and affiliation cases does not *necessarily* or even often harm consumers or the market for quality products. The benefits of expanding confusion law to this class of cases are correspondingly smaller. [Emphasis added][46]

Let us not forget that, even without the role of an 'association right' as created by the 2006 London Act, the Olympic symbol is a special kind of special in the world of trademarks:

Real trade marks denote a commercial association between the goods or services bearing the mark and the owner. The only association between the Olympic symbol and any goods or services bearing the mark is that permission has been given by the IOC.[47]

And:

The [Olympic] symbol has wider protection than any ordinary trade mark. It is a merchandising right, pure and simple. When one sees the mark it denotes a chink in the distant cash register of the IOC and no more.[48]

I would submit that, similar to what Lemley and McKenna refer to, what association rights to events seek to protect is little more than the event organiser's loss of potential revenues from non-sponsors, where the point of departure is an assumption that the event organiser owns the whole of the thematic space around an event and is therefore entitled to control all reference to the event.[49] Allied to this is the substantial interest of event organisers to keep the existing sponsors happy by presenting a no-nonsense, 'zero tolerance' front against 'ambushers'. We see this view reflected in the frequent pejorative statements by event organisers about ambush marketing, where the emphasis is invariably on the fact that non-sponsors accused of 'ambushing' an event have not paid for the privilege. This attitude is, arguably, perfectly fine (although its basis in fact may be debatable) when one is faced only with a rights grantor responding to someone whom they clearly view as free-riding or misappropriating property (even where no such 'property' exists, legally speaking). It is more problematic, however, where this approach is given governmental recognition and cemented into legislation which often severely

46 Lemley and McKenna 2010, pp. 438–439.

47 Sir Robin Jacob in 'Trade Marks and the Olympic Games through the Years' [2001] *European Intellectual Property Review* 1 at 2 (as quoted by Kelbrick 2008, p. 327).

48 Ibid. at 3.

49 See Kobel 2007, pp. 7–8.

restricts the rights and freedoms of not only potential 'ambushers' of events but also members of the public, civic organisations and interest groups, etc.—this brings into the equation what Lemley and McKenna above refer to as the 'significant costs' of protection. I would suggest that, in the above-quoted words of these authors, such association rights to events represent 'a claim to market control, not a claim of harm resulting from confusion or even an injury to consumers at all.'

A related aspect which I view to be relevant here is that of the aptness in legal theory of liability of outlawing 'ambushing' in the absence of proof of consumer confusion. In Chap. 2 I referred to the fact that the commercial rights of sponsors of sports mega-events have their genesis in the sponsorship contract and, more specifically, the license provided by event organisers to use event logos and intellectual property for purposes of marketing the sponsors' products or services. The practical manner in which sponsors leverage these rights is through marketing and advertising campaigns which utilise such IP, and which employ the often-encountered notice to consumers that Coca-Cola, for example, is an 'official sponsor' or 'partner' of the FIFA World Cup. A recurring theme in my analysis in this book is the dubious nature of laws which outlaw forms of 'ambushing' which do not involve direct association with an event through the illegal use of event IP or deception of consumers by means of implied associations (which I generally lump under the accepted term of an 'intrusion ambush'). Pelanda,[50] for examples, refers to an example involving an advertising campaign by Nabisco at the time of the 2000 Sydney Olympics which resulted in litigation by Powerbar, Inc (an official Olympic sponsor) which was eventually settled out of court.[51] The gist of Powerbar's complaint about Nabisco's ad for its 'Fig Newton' cookies was that it depicted an ancient Olympic athlete throwing a discus, with accompanying text which read 'The ancient Olympians worshipped the fig and used it for energy during training'. Does (should) this constitute an ambush? Are consumers deceived into believing that there is an official sponsorship affiliation between Nabisco and the Games in the absence of any use of Olympic symbols or logos or of any words or other material which implies such an affiliation? I would suggest that courts faced with such claims should consider the fact that the consumer public is for the most part aware of the nature of sports event sponsorship (compare the reasoning in the South African case mentioned elsewhere which recognised the practice of character merchandising based on the public's knowledge of the practice[52]). If one were to accept that the consumer public is aware of the fact that official sponsors make no secret of their official association and will advertise the fact prominently (as they've paid a lot of money for the privilege), would this not militate against a finding that an ad such as that used by Nabisco

[50] Pelanda, B L 'Ambush marketing: Dissecting the discourse', undated 2011 paper available online at the time of writing at http://works.bepress.com/brian_pelanda/.

[51] *USOC v. Nabisco, Inc.*, Case No. C 00 3086 (N.D. Cal., Aug. 25, 2000).

[52] *Federation Internationale de Football Association (FIFA) & Others v Bartlett & Others* 1994 (4) SA 722 (TPD)—see the discussion in Sect. 3.3.5 in Chap. 3.

would by implication constitute an attempt at deceiving consumers into believing that such an unmentioned affiliation in fact exists? The claims that such marketing constitutes 'ambushing' are even more problematic in case of the use of clear disclaimers; yet, as we have seen, the special event legislation often outlaws marketing using such disclaimers as illegal. I would suggest that the role of consumer confusion (or, more accurately, the apparent lack of a requirement of proving such confusion for purposes of founding liability) in respect of much of what is called 'ambushing' is extremely problematic.

I argue elsewhere that the element of proven harm in ambushing cases is also conspicuously absent in respect of some of the *sui generis* event anti-ambushing legislation. I would call on event organisers to prove that what they often view as 'intrusion ambushes' (e.g. an advertisement by a non-sponsor which obliquely refers to an event, and which might include a clear disclaimer that it is not an official sponsor) actually threatens harm to consumers. It is doubtful that any such harm based on confusion as to the source or quality of such marketer's goods or services can ever be shown. McKelvey and Grady have remarked on some practical problems which also exist regarding the issue of proof of consumer confusion in respect of 'association rights' to events:

> The difficulty in defining the concept of "association" and in determining what evidence is needed to establish the requisite "association" to trigger a violation is often rather ambiguous, or in some cases completely absent in cases of required evidence, in many of the legislative models that have been proposed and adopted. Determining "association" depends largely upon an assessment of the degree or extent to which consumers are confused about the nature of the relationship between the non-sponsor and the event. This requires that the plaintiff present evidence of consumer confusion. However... typically plaintiffs seek to establish the confusion element through consumer survey evidence that is often faulty in its research methodologies including coverage, measurement and sampling, and non-response errors. Furthermore, the suspect manner in which courts currently assess the validity of survey evidence, coupled with the absence of a "benchmark level of confusion, accepted as providing evidence of deception," leads to survey evidence that is highly vulnerable in court... This results in significant challenges for event organizers seeking to establish the "association" element were it to pursue a lawsuit.[53]

There are other problems with such consumer surveys, not least of which for present purposes is that it is debatable to what extent even evidence of actual confusion translates to evidence of potential behavioural change amongst consumers:

> Most research into ambush marketing has examined consumers' attitudes, knowledge or beliefs, despite the fact that these variables are often poor predictors of behaviour. Given this, researchers' reliance on measures of consumers' attitudes towards sponsors, or their knowledge of official sponsors, seems unlikely to offer robust behavioural insights into the consequences of any confusion that might arise from alleged ambush marketing.[54]

---

[53] McKelvey and Grady 2008, p. 576.

[54] See Wood, Z; Hoek, J and Mossaidis, C 'Ambush marketing: A re-definition and research agenda', undated paper available online at the time of writing at http://smib.vuw.ac.nz:8081/WWW/ANZMAC2004/CDsite/papers/Wood1.PDF.

And Kobel has observed the following:

> When competitors [official sponsors who are competitors of the 'ambusher'] are affected, the negative effect is some dilution effect on the paid for association between the official sponsor and the event. As far as commercial objectives are concerned the effect should be measurable but the causal link between the ambush marketing practices and the absence of increased sales remains questionable. The situation is more difficult in relation to the institutional objectives: Institutional returns from sponsoring are hardly measurable and therefore effective damage cannot be demonstrated… At first sight, consumers do not appear to be harmed by ambush marketing practices. The issue whether company X is or is not an official sponsor has little bearing to the quality, composition, nature, etc. of a product or a service. So far, no one has reported any consumer organisation asking for legislation to prevent or fight ambush marketing practices. One cannot exclude though that consumers may decide to purchase company X's products under the mistaken belief that it is an official sponsor. The issue would be to determine how many of such consumers there are, to determine whether the likelihood to mislead consumers is material or not. One cannot exclude that over time, the communication campaigns launched by the main sport organisations contribute, and in particular with the change of generations, to increasing consumers' awareness of official sponsors and thereby the importance of that criterion in consumers' purchasing decisions. With that in mind, ambush marketing remains primarily a [business-to-business] issue.[55]

One should bear in mind that recent research suggests that consumers, generally, don't seem to care much about ambush marketing and seem to display a lack of empathy towards official sponsors when it comes to ambushing.[56] As one prominent marketing expert puts it, colloquially:

> What [surveys on the effects of ambush marketing] don't say is how ambush marketing impacts on actual buying habits and brand perceptions, and there is simply no evidence that ambush negatively affects either one… [T]he fact that serial strategic ambushers keep right on doing it and still manage to be strong, growing brands is ample evidence that when it comes to brand preference, consumers don't care if you've ambushed or not. [L]ook in your closet. Did the fact that Nike is one of the most prolific ambushers around stop you from buying their shoes? How about your wallet? Credit card companies are renowned for ambushing, as are airlines, but I bet that hasn't made you less likely to fly with them. Still drink Coke or Pepsi? Both are huge ambushers all around the world. The same goes for virtually every beer brand. People can go on and on about how unethical it is… but when it comes to actual purchase behaviour, the outrage is clearly a tempest in a teacup.[57]

It has been observed that this is one of the reasons why the Lanham Act in the United States might not provide satisfactory grounds for claims against ambush marketers (in the Olympic context):

> One of the problems with challenging ambush marketers under the Lanham Act is that the consumer protection-oriented approach may fail to provide courts with an appropriate rationale to find for trademark holders. Specifically, the "likelihood of confusion" analysis often does not apply to the facts of ambush cases. Ambushers often do not use or display

[55] Kobel 2007, pp. 8, 9.

[56] See the research referred to in Seguin and O'Reilly 2008, p. 77.

[57] Skildum-Reid 2007, pp. 31, 32.

the Olympic marks but instead create a false association with the marks and the Olympics. Additionally, survey evidence of actual consumer confusion may not be probative of whether consumers care about the identity of the actual sponsors or the impact it may have on their respective consumer behavior.[58]

It is doubtful that any implied sponsorship or affiliation would in fact affect consumers' behaviour in respect of their choice to purchase (and even possible confusion as to guarantees of quality would be absent in all but the rarest of cases). I will speculate that no event organiser will actually take up the challenge to try and justify aggressive rights protection—including the demands of governments to pass event legislation—on the basis of the potential harm of ambushing marketing for consumers. What I do expect is the old chestnut so often advanced (and which, as mentioned elsewhere, has never really been backed up with convincing evidence), namely that ambushing threatens the very existence of mega-events because official sponsors would likely withdraw from sponsoring such events if their competitors can get away with not paying the huge sponsorship fees. And I am less than convinced of the veracity of this claim, as I will explain in the following chapter. One is left with the conclusion arrived at by Seguin et al., that 'while "the ostensible purpose of legislation is to protect a country's citizens from harm … it can be argued that in seeking to protect the sponsorship rights of certain companies (i.e. legislation in place of proper brand protection), the government is, in fact, causing more harm than good" by depriving citizens of their basic rights.'[59]

Finally, before stepping off the point about the role (or lack thereof) of consumer confusion in respect of ambushing of events and of the use of statutory 'association' rights to events, it should be noted that others have echoed these sentiments. Phillips, commenting in the context of the 2012 London Olympics (and, specifically, the London Olympic and Paralympic Games Act), has observed—in a view that resonates with previous observations regarding the role of competition—that the consumer appears to be conspicuously absent from the system of sponsorship exclusivity to mega-events and of legislating to protect such sponsors and event organisers:

If we believe, as the European Commission believes, that advertising is good for consumers because it educates their choice and makes them more discriminating, what happens to their interest when special anti-ambush marketing [protection] kicks in? Is there an overriding interest in a viewer of Olympic events being able to receive information from only one manufacturer just when, stimulated by the achievements of Olympic competitors, he may be highly likely to go out and purchase sportswear? If so, we should be told about this overriding interest so that we may advocate it elsewhere… The mere fact that protection against ambush marketing has been furnished on previous occasions is not a justification for its further protection. If there is a serious and responsible, competition-based reason for it, we should be told. And if the European Commission is content to allow such laws to hobble competition, perhaps it would be so kind as to explain why.[60]

---

58 Schmitz 2005, p. 207.

59 Séguin et al. 2008, pp. 99–101—as quoted in Grady et al. 2010.

60 Phillips 2006.

The effect of association rights, as discussed, raises another issue related to trademark law which I view to be relevant in the current context. American courts have in the past few years recognised and protected so-called 'merchandising rights' relating to the use of trademarks on products (such as, for example, the sale of t-shirts by someone other than the trademark holder, depicting a car brand or the name of a sports team); which raises similar issues as those encountered in respect of the practice of 'trade mark licensing' (which 'permits trade mark owners to extend sales beyond their reach, and to extend product lines beyond their core competence'[61]) as found also in other systems.[62] Levy has explained this development as follows with reference to a recent claim of ambush marketing (for a ticket giveaway promotion aimed at Mexican fans) by Major League Soccer in the USA against power tool manufacturer Black and Decker:

> The case is reminiscent of a revenue grab by sports teams in the 1980's. At one time, anybody could make up a shirt that said "Dallas Cowboys" or "Boston Red Sox", and then wear it or sell it. The fans wearing those shirts didn't care one whit about whether the Cowboys or Red Sox made the shirt or had taken a cut of the shirt-makers' revenue. But Major League Baseball and the National Football League, armed with surveys created by consumer survey expert Jacob Jacoby, started filing lawsuits claiming that some minority of fans would automatically assume that the Cowboys or Red Sox had endorsed or at least approved of the shirt sellers. By winning a couple of cases, they created a new rule of law—you can't sell shirts showing support for a team without paying the team off for the privilege of doing so.[63]

These 'rights' present something of an anomaly in trademark law:

> When fans buy t-shirts with the name of their school, team, or rock band, they are almost always buying a product bearing an established mark entitled to some form of trademark protection. But the mark in these cases is rarely serving the traditional function of a trademark. Rather than indicating something to the consumer about the source or sponsorship of a product, the mark *is* the product—or at least is a critical part of what makes the product attractive. While the mark may, on occasion, also signal something about the source or sponsorship of the shirt, its function transcends the role of a traditional trademark. Merchandising cases therefore represent a kind of hybrid between product configuration and word-based trademark infringement claims: They generally involve protected marks, but the marks are more product features than brands.[64]

I would suggest that one can, again, draw a useful parallel between such use of trademarks as 'products' and the commercial rights protection to mega-events. Leaving aside for now the issue of actual trademarks to such events (e.g. event logos and symbols, event organisers' organisational marks, etc.)—which enjoy legal protection when registered—recent years have seen increasingly frequent

---

[61] Ng, C W 'The irrational lightness of trade marks', in Bently et al. 2008, p. 232.

[62] E.g. in the UK's Trade Marks Act, 1994.

[63] Paul Alan Levy 'Is "ambush marketing" a form of trademark infringement?', 29 December 2009, on Public Citizen's Consumer Law & Policy Blog, available online at the time of writing at http://pubcit.typepad.com/clpblog/2009/12/is-ambush-marketing-a-form-of-trademark-infringement.html.

[64] Dogan and Lemley 2005, pp. 471, 472.

claims by event organisers to protection for their events that goes beyond what trademark law allows. Mention was made earlier[65] of claims for protection of words and phrases that are not copyrightable or would not qualify for trademark protection (as being purely descriptive, for instance). Examples are found in relation to the 2010 Vancouver winter Olympics and the 2010 FIFA World Cup South Africa. In respect of the 2012 London Olympics, as we've seen, the legislature has also included guidelines in respect of potential infringement of the association right which include generic words (such as 'summer' and 'gold'); again, this represents words that are not susceptible to trademark protection in the traditional sense. I would submit that such claims for protection by organisers equates to claims that the actual event, as opposed to event marks that are registered trademarks, are deserving of protection *as if the event itself was a registered trade mark*. I would suggest that, by analogy with the merchandising rights referred to above, the event organisers appear to be claiming trademark protection for what is not a trademark, but the actual product. If I sell a t-shirt with some reference to the FIFA World Cup, which reference does not infringe any registered trademarks in the event, FIFA would claim trademark protection for the event where the event itself is in fact the product.

Legislative protection of events by means of the creation of 'association rights' in often draconian legislation is also worrying when one considers the precedent that it sets in respect of tailoring the law to advance the interests of a few select commercial entities at the expense of the greater public interest. Hylton observes (in the context of expanding protection of consumers through rules requiring free-to-air broadcasting of sports mega-events such as the FIFA World Cup) that '[s]port is a common commodity in the modern world, and laws should be designed to encourage the maximum amount of public involvement as both participants and spectators and not merely to enrich those who control the production of the premier sporting events'.[66]

I will end this section by simply observing that the justification for the need for special commercial rights protection by means of special purpose event legislation is weak, when one considers the public good and traditional notions of the role of legislation in jurisdictions based on the rule of law. Ellis et al. opine that '[a]t bottom, the most basic public policy objective underlying the enactment of [*sui generis* event] legislation was that of necessity. Legislation against ambush marketing is now a condition imposed by the IOC for any successful Olympic bid.'[67] The UK government has, in fact admitted this. In a 2011 Impact Assessment document issued by the Department of Culture, Media and Sport regarding the London 2012 advertising and trading regulations, it is unequivocally stated that

---

[65] See the discussion in Chap. 5.

[66] Hylton, J G 'The over-protection of intellectual property rights in sport' (Marquette University Law School/National Sports Law Insititute)—undated paper available online at the time of writing at http://shiac.com/files/arablexsportiva-presentations/004003.pdf.

[67] Ellis et al. 2011, p. 302.

'Our primary policy objective is to comply with the commitments made to the IOC and during the passage of the London Olympic and Paralympic Games Act 2006'.[68] I would suggest that something much more than this is required in justification of often invasive and draconian legislation aimed at protecting private commercial interests, and this governmental bowing and scraping to the whims of an international sports governing body is simply illegitimate in a modern democratic society. Ellis et al. explain why the public policy element to such event legislation is important:

> The purpose for which legislation has been enacted is a key element in the interpretation of legislation by judges. Further, in a constitutional democracy, the objectives of a piece of legislation may be scrutinized in determining whether the law unduly infringes upon protected rights or freedoms. A weak or insufficiently articulated public policy basis for legislation may have an impact on both the interpretation of the legislation and its ability to withstand constitutional scrutiny.[69]

I agree with these sentiments, and have criticised the superficial consideration of justification for alleged infringements of constitutional rights by means of anti-ambushing legislation in the judgment in the 2010 South African case of *FIFA v Metcash Trading Africa*, as discussed elsewhere in the earlier chapters. I can only hope that courts in future ambush marketing litigation in other jurisdictions will be more circumspect in this regard. As for the lawmakers in these future host jurisdictions I would suggest that a lot more circumspection is needed as well as proper co-ordination between such lawmakers and the authorities that bid for mega-event hosting rights. The above-mentioned 2011 UK government Impact Assessment document contains a brief consideration of the benefits and costs of three options which the government was faced with in respect of combating ambushing by means of street trading and advertising regulations. The first of these options, namely to preserve the *status quo* (i.e. 'do nothing and rely on existing legislation') was rejected by the government. The first of the listed potential costs of following this option is described as follows: 'The IOC could take legal action against the Government and other parties for failing to deliver on commitments made in the bidding process and contained in the Host City Contract'.[70] It is simply illegitimate for lawmakers to attempt to justify draconian laws based on promises made to event organisers in the bidding process; promises which probably shouldn't be made in the first place. Remember that, as mentioned in Chap. 2, these host city contracts and governmental guarantees are often contained in agreements which the public is denied access to (and that civil society and media organisations in some host jurisdictions have in the past had to resort to legal action to acquire access to such information, after the fact). The relevant parties to such agreements may be democratically elected, but public accountability is not a given. I believe that those compiling the bids and providing

---

68 The DCMS *Impact Assessment* document at 5—available online at http://www.legislation.gov.uk/ukdsi/2011/9780111515969/pdfs/ukdsifia_9780111515969_en.pdf.

69 Ellis et al. 2011, p. 302.

70 DCMS *Impact Assessment* document *supra* at 7.

governmental guarantees should not be allowed to disown knowledge of the potential for the need to pass such future laws when these promises are made, and when such laws are later passed the lawmakers should likewise not be allowed to justify the over-reaching of their legislative authority on the basis of such earlier governmental conduct. Such scenario is fundamentally at odds with the checks and balances required between the branches of government in a modern democracy, and I believe it taints the very legitimacy of such legislation.

By way of summary of the above: I believe that the justification for governments and lawmakers in host nations to pass special and often draconian legislation in order to protect commercial rights to events is arguable. It is not enough for such lawmakers to simply claim that 'the IOC or FIFA told me to do it'. Also, I would submit that the fact that such legislation is aimed at protecting private commercial interests of a select group of sports governing bodies and multinational corporations, often at a cost of imposing severe curtailments of the liberties of members of the public, calls for a greater and more convincing justification for this legislation than would be the case with other forms of legislative instruments aimed at protecting the public good. Such potential grounds for justification, if viewed from the perspective of the (consumer) public in the mega-event milieu, however, appear to be absent. In clear contrast with the more traditional mechanisms for protection of commercial rights to events, namely the common law passing off action and intellectual property rights, these laws attempt to ring-fence very broad rights of association with the events while failing to base the resultant radical curtailment of civil liberties and the rights of others on protection of the consumer or, even, a clear case that such legislation actually protects the beneficiaries against identifiable, real harm.

Accordingly, even though I would suggest that these laws are of dubious legitimacy for the above reasons, they might be saved if their proponents can show that they actually protect something that is worth protecting, and worth the social costs of the means employed. So, if their purpose is not directly to protect the consumer, let's consider exactly what the object of such legislation (and, specifically, of the association rights to events) is.

8.3 What, Exactly, Does Such Special Event Legislation Aim to Protect?

I have argued above that event organisers, when demanding from host governments the passing of special legislative protection for commercial rights to events, are in fact simply trying to protect and maintain market control in respect of commercialisation of the event. In fact, it appears that US courts have recognised this for years in the context of the Ted Stevens Olympic and Amateur Sports Act (which places exclusive power to license use of Olympic symbols in the hands of the USOC): 'courts have concluded that the primary purpose of [the Act] was to "insure the market value of licenses."'[71] In respect of the 2011 IRB Rugby World Cup in New Zealand, the City of Auckland Council compliance and licensing manager was quoted as saying that aggressive steps would be taken to counter possible ambushes, as 'official sponsors don't spend all this money on a tournament for other people to pop in and steal their thunder'.[72] This quest for control relates to the motive for pursuing such protection, but does not yet tell us what is the actual object of the claimed protection—i.e. what does such event legislation actually seek to protect? What is the actual object of the sponsors' 'thunder', and how deserving is it of legal protection?

In the preceding discussion in this and the earlier chapters I have frequently mentioned the event organisers' and sponsors' stigmatised view of ambush marketing, and the fact that most (if not all) definitions of ambush marketing and most (if not all) press releases and sound-bites on the subject which tend to emanate from these sources refer to the issue of 'free-riding' ('riding on coat-tails' or 'piggy-backing'), filching and misappropriation. These sources remain adamant that what is so ethically and morally wrong with 'ambushing' an event is that the 'ambusher' is, simply speaking, stealing; taking what is not theirs and for which they did not pay (while others did pay, and paid a lot). It should be obvious that this view proceeds from a very definite and specific premise, namely that the 'ambusher' is actually taking *something* which does not belong to them (and which, by implication, belongs to the event organiser, to sell or license, and/or the sponsors and other licensed commercial partners, to buy). As such, this approach implies that what the 'ambusher' takes is something that is susceptible of ownership or possession (or, at least, of a competency or even a right to control or exclude access to by others). Which brings us back to the central question: What, exactly, is it that the event organisers and sponsors are claiming as their own and which apparently needs the urgent, active and often drastic intervention of lawmakers to be protected from interference or 'misappropriation' by the 'ambusher'?

I have mentioned the apparent lack of a requirement of consumer deception (in cases of alleged infringement or contravention of the relevant provisions), in most of the *sui generis* commercial rights protection event legislation discussed in the earlier chapters. The South African legislation is a case in point. As mentioned, section 15A of South Africa's Merchandise Marks Act (or MMA) does not require any deception or confusion regarding an association with a protected event. Accordingly, it appears to be aimed solely at protecting the goodwill of event organisers and their commercial partners in respect of such an event. I would

---

[71] *Stop the Olympic Prison v. United States Olympic Comm.*, 489 F. Supp. 1112, 1120 (S.D.N.Y. 1980); *United States Olympic Comm. v. Union Sport Apparel*, 220 U.S.P.Q. 526 (E.D.Va. 1983); *United States Olympic Comm. v. Int'l Fed'n of Body Builders*, 219 U.S.P.Q. 353 (D.D.C. 1982); and *United States Olympic Comm. v. David Shoe Co., Inc.*, 835 F.2d 880 (6th Cir. 1987)—see Schmitz 2005, p. 204 n 12.

[72] Savage, J 'Officials ready for Rugby World Cup ambush marketing' *New Zealand Herald*, 8 September 2011—available online at http://www.nzherald.co.nz/business/news/article.cfm?c_id=3&objectid=10750200.

suggest that the concept of 'goodwill' should be more closely examined in this context, especially if one subscribes to the following school of thought:

> [G]ood will is somewhat vaguely considered as the favourable regard of the purchasing public ... But good will so construed certainly is not property in any technical sense; for no man can have ... such a proprietary right to the favorable regard of the public that he may exclude others therefrom.[73]

Leaving issues of the meaning and nature of goodwill aside, essentially the prohibition contained in section 15A of the MMA appears to be more akin to the common law unlawful competition tort of direct adoption of a rival's performance. If one considers the wording of section 15A(2), it is clear that—at least in terms of the common law—there is nothing objectionable about the use of a mark in relation to an event, which use is calculated to achieve publicity for such mark (this last is, in fact, one of the functions of a trademark). It appears that what is viewed by the legislature as objectionable is when such use of a mark '*derives special promotional benefit from the event*'. Note also that section 15A(3)(c) refers to the use of a trademark, in terms of section 15A(2), as including its use 'in promotional activities, which in any way, directly or indirectly, is intended to be brought into association with *or to allude to an event.*' Teresa Scassa observes the following regarding this remarkable legislative provision:

> Since most uses of a trademark by a trademark owner are calculated to achieve publicity for the mark, the focus would likely be on whether the defendant sought to derive "special promotional benefit from the event." This would seem to be a relatively low threshold to meet. The cause of action is triggered by the manner in which the defendant uses its *own* trademark, and not the trademark of a competitor or of the event organizer... The language used seems to be deliberately open-ended, as if it aims to catch a wide range of activities that might create an association with a protected event. The Merchandise Marks Amendment Act (2002) uses the term "association," although it does not explicitly create a "right of association."[74]

In essence, what is sought to be protected would appear to be the publicity value of the event ('popularity' may be a better word, or maybe what US Supreme Court Justice Frankfurter referred to in the context of trademarks as substantial advertising power or 'commercial magnetism'[75]). In trying to gauge the

---

[73] Hincks J in *Premier-Pabst Corp. v. Elm City Brewing Co.* 9 F.Supp. 754 (1935) at 757.

[74] Scassa 2011, p. 359.

[75] *Mishawaka Rubber & Woollen Manufacturing Co. v S SKresge Co.* (1942) 13 US 203, at 205: 'The protection of trade-marks is the law's recognition of the psychological function of symbols. If it is true that we live by symbols, it is no less true that we purchase goods by them. A trademark is a merchandising short-cut which induces a purchaser to select what he wants, or what he has been led to believe he wants. The owner of a mark exploits this human propensity by making every effort to impregnate the atmosphere of the market with the drawing power of a congenial symbol. Whatever the means employed, the aim is the same—to convey through the mark, in the minds of potential customers, the desirability of the commodity upon which it appears. Once this is attained; the trademark owner has something of value. If another poaches upon the commercial magnetism of the symbol he has created, the owner can obtain legal redress.'

legislature's intention with the use of the words 'special promotional benefit' I would suggest that, if one considers the common denominator in all of the myriad definitions of ambush marketing that have been formulated by the various commentators—namely the fact that an 'ambusher' derives benefit from its conduct without having paid for the privilege—it is this element that is uppermost in the mind. Official sponsors pay for the right to partake in (and contribute to) the publicity of an event and thus derive publicity for their brands through event-related marketing. The prohibited 'special promotional benefit' covered in section 15A(2) is promotional benefit in relation to an event for which the mark user did not pay.

By analogy with, for example, the common law action for misappropriation of a competitor's performance (which is available in South Africa) or the claim of parasitism, which is applicable to whoever takes advantage of another's reputation without authorisation (in jurisdictions such as France and Belgium), it appears that the legislature has prohibited the *misappropriation* of the publicity surrounding protected events, if one considers the publicity value of an event such as the FIFA World Cup as a product of FIFA—i.e. FIFA's organisation of the event, with the financial and other assistance of its commercial partners, produces a product in the form of the event; the goodwill in such event includes its significant publicity value. Considered in this light, one can draw an analogy with the *locus classicus* on misappropriation in American law, *International News Service v Associated Press*,[76] the 'Supreme Court's foray into creating a common law of unfair competition'.[77] The argument would go (I assume) that FIFA has put time, effort and labour into creating the event and its publicity value; a trader acting in contravention of section 15A(2) who acts in a manner that 'derives special promotional benefit from the event' is viewed as having filched the product of such labours, i.e. the publicity value of the event. This, it appears, was one basis upon which the U.S. Supreme Court upheld the US Olympic Committee's 'property right' in the word 'Olympic' in the 'Gay Olympics' case, referring to the 'image' of the event:

> The image the [San Francisco Arts & Athletics association] sought to invoke [by staging its 'Gay Olympics' event] was exactly the image carefully cultivated by the USOC. The SFAA's expressive use of the word cannot be divorced from the value the USOC's efforts have given to it. The mere fact that the SFAA claims an expressive, as opposed to a purely commercial, purpose does not give it a First Amendment right to "appropriat[e] to itself the harvest of those who have sown" [with reference to the *International News Service v. Associated Press supra].* The USOC's right to prohibit use of the word "Olympic" in the promotion of athletic events is at the core of its legitimate property right.[78]

The filching argument appears to hark back hundreds of years to the work of Adam Smith and his contention that protection of personal property is necessary to induce individuals to labour, and that labour and its fruits are the essence of

[76] (1918) 248 US 215.

[77] Cooper Dreyfuss 1996, p. 143.

[78] *San Francisco Arts & Athletics, Inc. v. USOC*, 483 U. S. 522 (1987) p. 541.

property ('The property which every man has in his own labour, as it is the original foundation of all other property, so it is the most sacred and inviolable'[79]) or Locke's labour theory of ownership.[80] This is, of course, one of the primary rationales that have traditionally been advanced for the state providing monopoly protection to the creators of intellectual property. But, it is submitted, it depends very much on the nature of the product of such labour and the circumstances of its production. If I produce a collection of original poems I am by law allowed to control its use by others, but if I somehow produce vast quantities of oxygen with some fancy machine out in a field on my farm, can (and should) I be legally entitled to prevent my neighbour from breathing it? Let's not forget the following astute observation about 'filching' arguments: 'The vivid maxim—made all the more powerful because of its biblical antecedents—that as you sow, so you should reap, may work well in matters agricultural but less so in matters intellectual.'[81] And, from a competitive free market perspective, it has been observed that 'A culture could not exist if all free riding were prohibited within it'.[82] Kratzke[83] has argued that to call competitive behaviour 'free-riding'—an apparent go-to argument for event organisers—is a conclusionary epithet, not a workable economic principle:

> Free riding is good—indeed, it is the essence of competition—unless there is some reason to think it will lead to a market failure. Were it not for free riding, everything we did, bought, or used would either be purchased at a monopoly price (probably with perfect price discrimination).[84]

To which Dreyfuss would add a warning against a morality-based abhorrence of 'piracy' playing too great a role:

> [T]here is an element of circularity in relying on commercial morality as the basis for creating exclusivity. After all, where there is a right to copy, so-called piracy is not immoral. It is only *after* it is determined that the norm is exclusivity that copying will appear to be wrongful.[85]

Burrell and Gangjee agree (in the context of 'free-riding' arguments in justification of trademark anti-dilution laws) that the economic arguments may be rather flimsy:

---

[79] Smith 1776, p. 138.

[80] See Spinello and Bottis 2009, p. 150 *et seq.*; Tan 2008, p. 928 *et seq.*; Wilf 1999, p. 24 *et seq.*

[81] From an address presented by Professor David Vaver, Reuters professor of Intellectual Property and Information Technology Law, Oxford University, at the Victoria University of Wellington, 30 August 2000—available online at the time of writing at http://kirra.austlii.edu.au/nz/journals/VUWLawRw/2001/2.html.

[82] Gordon 1992, p. 167.

[83] Kratzke 1991, p. 223.

[84] See Lemley 1999, p. 1694 n 33.

[85] Cooper Dreyfuss 1996, p. 144.

> [I]n real markets there are a vast range of positive externalities for which we do not seek to compensate. The person who buys and uses a handkerchief when suffering from a cold receives no compensation from acquaintances and passers-by who avoid becoming ill as a result; the person who invests time and money in developing an attractive garden receives nothing from neighbouring property owners who benefit from owning a house on a "well kept street". It is not enough to demonstrate that free riding has occurred; it must also be demonstrated that legal intervention promotes efficiency taking account of transaction costs, imperfect information, etc. This is an empirical question and the information necessary to calculate the effect of antidilution protection on the market has not been collected (and may well be uncollectable).[86]

I would suggest that the same holds true in respect of the (lack of) availability of information necessary to calculate the effect of ambush marketing on the market, when one considers the 'survival of the Games' arguments so frequently advanced by event organisers and sponsors (which I'll refer to again in Chap. 9). Let me leave the issue here by observing that, at the very least, as a 'catch-all' justification, misappropriation or filching arguments need to be considered more closely, and with special attention to the purported object of such claims.

At the heart of all the myriad generally accepted definitions of 'ambush marketing' is the perception in the minds of the consumer/public as to the ambusher's association with an event. The conduct of an ambusher can take a variety of different forms, of course, but what raises the hackles of event organisers and official sponsors is the (assumed) element of deception inherent in causing a false perception of official affiliation or association with the event, when the ambusher has not paid its dues for the right to be so associated and to reap the marketing benefits for which other sponsors pay big bucks. One of the earliest commentators on ambush marketing whose work is widely cited in the literature, Meenaghan,[87] suggested a definition for ambush marketing which emphasises this aspect, namely 'the practice whereby another company, often a competitor, *intrudes upon public attention* surrounding the event, thereby *deflecting attention toward themselves and away from the sponsor*' (my emphasis).[88] What this definition alludes to is the fact that the process of marketing (and sponsorship as a form of marketing, of course) is focused on grabbing the consumer's attention. Sponsorship, in fact, is often credited with being a form of marketing that has the potential to cut through advertising clutter in order to more efficiently achieve this object, because it is 'below-the-line' and concerned with consumer perceptions, and something different from advertising in the traditional media. 'Public attention', therefore, is the target of ambushers (and likewise of the official sponsors), and the key to the success of an ambushing campaign lies in the publicity it receives. It is this 'publicity', which is viewed as part of the publicity surrounding the event, which the event organisers and official sponsors seem to view as having been misappropriated by the ambusher who achieves the public's attention without having

[86] Burrell and Gangjee 2010, p. 7.

[87] Meenaghan 1994.

[88] Ibid. p. 79.

paid for the privilege; what Corbett and van Roy refer to as 'taking advantage of the captive audience, without contributing to the cost of staging the event'.[89] This has, in fact, received express legislative recognition in New Zealand's Major Events Management Act, 2007 (discussed in Chap. 4). Section 22 contains exceptions to the provisions of the Act which deal with unauthorised event-related advertising,[90] and contains the following specific exception:

> [The unauthorised advertising provisions] do not apply to advertising... on articles of clothing (including shoes) or other personal items being worn, carried, or used by... a member of the public, unless that item is being worn, carried, or used in co-ordination with other persons *with the intention that the advertising intrude on a major event activity or the attention of the associated audience*. [Emphasis added][91]

FIFA's required government guarantee on commercial rights protection for its World Cup event also contains the following boilerplate provision for incorporation in bid guarantees by successful host governments:

> [A]mbush marketing by intrusion in relation to the Events and/or FIFA, namely to practice, organise, approve, or sponsor any promotional, advertising, or marketing activities *through which one targets the audience of the Events, including ticket holders, in order to gain exposure* for its businesses, products or services without authorization from FIFA, will be prohibited by law. [My emphasis][92]

And consider the following, which was apparently pleaded by the International Cricket Council in its copyright claim against an ambusher in an Indian court in respect of the ICC Cricket World Cup 2003:

> *The entire advertisement or publicity value [of the event] is the exclusive property of the [ICC, the plaintiff]*, who in turn has authorised its sponsors to enjoy these rights. The plaintiff and sponsors have the right to commercially exploit the "persona" of the event and to derive the maximum commercial benefit of being associated with it.[93] [Emphasis added]

Having touched on the value of the sports mega-event as a 'marketing platform' for sponsors and others in Chap. 2, I believe it is important to consider this concept

---

[89] Corbett and Van Roy 2010, p. 338.

[90] Those provisions are contained in sections 18–20 of the Act.

[91] Section 22(b)(i) of the Act.

[92] From an undated draft letter by the Dutch government addressed to the president of FIFA, confirming the terms of Government Guarantee No. 6 ('Protection and Exploitation of Commercial Rights') in respect of the Low Countries bid for the 2017 FIFA Confederations Cup/ 2018 FIFA World Cup and/or the 2021 FIFA Confederations Cup/2022 FIFA World Cup—available online at the time of writing on the web site http://www.transparencyinsport.org/The_documents_that_FIFA_does_not_want_fans_to_read/PDF-documents/(6)Protection-and-Exploitation-of-Commercial-Rights.pdf An extract from this document is reproduced at the end of this book as **Appendix A**.

[93] *ICC Development (International) Ltd. v Ever Green Service Station & Another* 2003 IIAD Delhi 707, 102 (2003) DLT 723 (from par. 2 of the judgment).

of an event as platform just a little more closely here. Price[94] has engaged with the Olympic Games as a platform and its vulnerability to hijacking or piggy-backing by various groups and for various (including political and commercial, i.e. ambush marketing) purposes. He explains the modes of protection of such an event as a multi-purpose platform:

> Because of the ever-present danger of appropriation, one defining characteristic of significant platforms is the effort to protect them from unwanted or unremunerated uses. In the Internet world, platform software is created to protect a site from hacking. But what about complex platforms like the Olympic Games? These are protected through physical modes of security (limiting who may actually enter the Olympic facilities or who receives press accreditation for coverage). They are protected through assertion of intellectual property and contractual rights, using highly developed legal mechanisms to enjoin or impose high costs on those who seek to be free riders. The International Olympic Committee (IOC) sets terms for the uses of the platform (and limitations on those uses) by the organizers, the sponsors, and the athletic federations. And platforms are protected, most subtly, through intense management of narrative and response to efforts to subvert or countermand what is chosen to be dominant.[95]

This 'intense management of narrative' regarding the event as platform, I submit, is at the heart of efforts to control the publicity value of the event. There may be no clearer example of this publicity value of an event being the purported protected 'asset' than the wording of section 15A(2) of the South African Merchandise Marks Act, which refers to use of a mark in relation to an event which is calculated to achieve publicity for that mark and thereby to derive special promotional benefit from an event. The promotional benefit is 'special', I would assume, because it is viewed as having 'taken something' from the event or its organisers. If not, how could one punish the owner of a mark merely for the use of such mark? Compare also a provision which is reminiscent of the above South African provision, namely the anti-intrusion ambushing provision found in Article 19 of Brazil's *Lei Geral da Copa* (in Bill form currently before the Brazilian Congress at the time of writing), which criminalises a range of conduct which includes 'to practice any promotional activities not authorized by FIFA or by a person indicated by FIFA, *attracting, by any means, public attention* in the Official Places of the Events, with the objective of obtaining economic or advertising advantage'.

Let us get back to basics for a minute, and consider the dictionary meaning of the word 'publicity': One source defines the noun as 'the activity of *making certain that someone or something attracts a lot of attention from many people*, or the attention received as a result of such activity' (my emphasis).[96] Another source gives the following possible meanings:

---

[94] Price, M E 'On Seizing the Olympic Platform', in Price and Dayan 2008, pp. 86–114.

[95] Ibid. p. 89.

[96] As defined by Cambridge Dictionaries Online, at http://dictionary.cambridge.org.

(1) *Extensive mention in the news media or by word of mouth or other means of communication*;
(2) *Public notice so gained*;
(3) The measures, process or business of securing public notice;
(4) …
(5) The state of being public, or open to general observation or knowledge. [Emphasis added][97]

Publicity is, by definition, aimed at the public, is something that is public, cannot exist without being public, and is open to access by the public. The publicity around an event such as the football World Cup is clearly something that is created, not only by the organisers of the event and their commercial partners, but by others (e.g. the host government and local organising committee) and by members of the public themselves, and which, if done properly, persists notwithstanding the active promotional efforts to publicise the event. In this light, it appears nonsensical to argue that it is something that can be 'owned' in the traditional sense of the word, by the event organisers.

I have in the past written about 'image rights' (in South African law, specifically in the context of professional athletes) and unauthorised merchandising of celebrity, and have referred to the 'right of publicity' enjoyed by celebrities in a number of states in the United States of America.[98] I have argued for recognition of protection in South Africa based on the 'right to the earning capacity', as a species of 'personal goodwill' that attaches to those who are famous enough to be able to earn income from references to or use of aspects of their personas. I still believe that the law should recognise such an 'ownership' of the publicity value of fame in that context (largely because of the prevalence of unauthorised use of aspects of celebrity for gain, and the resultant need for recognition and protection by the law). However, in the context of the present discussion in respect of the publicity value of sports mega-events, I believe that one should distinguish the 'goodwill' of the event from the publicity value of the event. Of course, the publicity value is clearly an element of the goodwill (and, in monetary terms, would constitute something that would add value to the goodwill of an event, if/when quantifiable). However, I believe that one should distinguish the ordinary meaning of goodwill of a business undertaking as we understand it (also of the commercial undertaking that is the football World Cup, for example) and the fact that such goodwill relates to a spectacle, and a newsworthy one at that.

Let us take the example of the goodwill of a 'normal' business undertaking, let us say Coca-Cola. In the traditional meaning of the term as accepted (for example, in South African law), Coca-Cola's goodwill can be defined as 'the attractive force that brings in custom'.[99] This includes many aspects that add value to the brand of Coke (I am not a marketing or branding expert, and will leave the reader to

[97] Definition of 'publicity' as per Dictionary.com.

[98] Louw 2007.

[99] E.g., in South African law, see *Commissioners of Inland Revenue v Muller & Co.'s Margarine (Ltd)* 1901 AC 217 at 224; Neethling 2008, p. 99 *et seq*.

consider what these are). However, it is my contention that when one deals with an event such as the football World Cup, one should distinguish between the brand of the FIFA World Cup™ and the fact that the event itself is, well, *an event*—a spectacle. If one considers the above definitions of 'publicity', it is submitted that the publicity value of the brand (part of the goodwill of the business undertaking of FIFA's World Cup) should be distinguished from the publicity value of the event, i.e. of the spectacle. This distinction, with reference to trademark law, was pointed out by a South African intellectual property law expert commenting on FIFA's 2010 event and the legal protection granted to it:

> [T]he enforcement of the law has been extended to persons making any form of association with the World Cup. "This is the main weapon in FIFA's arsenal. However, there is a difference between someone making an association merely with the event, and someone attempting to make an association with FIFA—that is, to give the impression that the entity is a sponsor. This nuance seems to go unnoticed. In fact, the main objection against FIFA's enforcement campaign is the indiscriminate and mechanical view adopted towards perceived infringement cases. No wonder that FIFA had to take the unprecedented step of officially clarifying that the media would be 'permitted' to refer to the World Cup in coverage of the event.[100]

Sponsorship researchers refer to sports sponsorship as an investment by the corporate sponsor in exchange for the exploitable commercial potential associated with the sports event or property.[101] Price refers to appropriation of the narrative of the event as (marketing) platform; in the commercial context of the Olympic Games he refers to the narrative chosen by the TOP sponsors, who 'may have messages that subtly or less subtly reinforce attitudes toward consumption'.[102]I will call this 'exploitable commercial potential' of the event its publicity value. It is my contention that the publicity value of the event (as opposed to the goodwill of the event organiser) is in the public domain. It is not solely the product of FIFA and its marketing minions. It is a product of the efforts of FIFA, yes, but *also* of its sponsors (in leveraging their substantial investment in access to event logos etc.), of the host government, of the people of the host country, the football fans, the media and other sources (including this book, insofar as it discusses the FIFA event and is being read by you, the reader). In fact, and President Blatter would hate me for saying so, those who engage in 'intrusion ambush marketing', through their references to an event, also add to the publicity surrounding such event[103] (I'll stop short of suggesting that these persons should send event organisers a bill for such promotional activities). Having referred above to 'image rights', I believe there is much to be said for the applicability of the views of Michael Madow, writing about the American right of

---

[100] Wim Alberts, as quoted in the short article entitled 'Ambush marketing legislation: Contravention or constitutional?', 21 April 2010, available online at the time of writing at http://www.biz-community.com/Article/196/147/46893.html.

[101] See Meenaghan 1991.

[102] Price, M E 'On Seizing the Olympic Platform', in Price and Dayan 2008, p. 90.

[103] Kobel agrees, observing that 'by multiplying references to an event, ambush marketing is actually contributing to its publicity, popularity and fame'—Kobel 2007, p. 8.

publicity, in this context of mega-event publicity. Madow, in criticising the frequent claims that celebrities deserve special protection of their fame because such fame is due to their own labours, observes that this overlooks an elementary sociological truth about fame: '[F]ame is a "relational" phenomenon, something that is conferred by others. A person can, within the limits of his natural talents, make himself strong or swift or learned. But he cannot, in this same sense, make himself famous, any more than he can make himself loved'.[104] I would suggest that exactly the same principle applies to the goodwill and publicity value that surrounds the modern mega-event, and I'll continue to quote the following words of Madow (although, to serve my point here, I'll take the liberty of substituting some of the words he uses—mostly references to the 'celebrity'):

> [The FIFA World Cup]s public image is *always* the product of a complex *social,* if not fully democratic, process in which the "labor" (time, money, effort) of [FIFA or the event organisers] (and of the [mega-event] industry, too) is but one ingredient, and not always the main one. The meanings a star image [read: the publicity value and goodwill of the event] comes to have, and hence the "publicity values" that attach to it, are determined by what different groups and individuals, with different needs and interests, make of it and from it, as they use it to make sense of and construct themselves and the world.[105]

On a slightly more pragmatic level there are difficulties in identifying who, exactly, 'creates' an event:

> Who created the reputation and value of the event is actually a question in relation to sports as opposed to enterprises in other markets. In relation to the Olympic Games, it is not clear whether the "creator" is the IOC, the National Olympic Committees or the Organising Committees, or whether the created values are the outcome of the work and collaboration between all participating sport federations, athletes, teams or clubs. In some countries, right holders to the Games are the National Olympic Committee and/or the Organising Committee in addition or instead of the IOC. In practice, the reputation of events, like the Olympic Games or the World Cup or whatever large international championship is the outcome of a collective effort.[106]

The bulk of the publicity value of the World Cup is due to it being 'an event', and a major and newsworthy one at that. I do not believe that FIFA or its commercial partners can properly be said to 'own' this publicity value; more emphatically, I do not believe that they should have the power to restrain members of the public—the true 'owners' (or at least objects) of publicity?—from using such publicity, even for commercial purposes where such use relates only to mere reference to the event. Here I would like to pose the same question that Rochelle Cooper Dreyfuss asked back in 1996: 'Who should reap the benefits of images, those who introduce them into the popular culture or those in the culture who imbue them with enduring meaning?'[107] It has been observed that mega-events

[104] Madow 1993.

[105] Ibid.

[106] See Kobel 2007, p. 7.

[107] Cooper Dreyfuss 1996, p. 124.

(such as the Olympic Games and football World Cup) 'undoubtedly qualify as examples of "media-events"', and that (for example) television organisations typically consider that this type of event requires a special type of production treatment beyond the ordinary genres and categories of news and entertainment, and that media-event analysis is concerned with the media's 'witness-to-history' role.[108] Dayan and Katz[109] have argued that the success of media-events requires a 'negotiated' informal social contract and a consensus between three 'partners', namely the event organisers, television organisations and the viewing public. Roche adds two further 'partners' to this mix, namely the state (including host politicians) and the market (the corporate sponsors and advertisers willing to pay to use the event as their marketing vehicle).[110] When one considers the reality of mega-events it appears that this symbiotic relationship in fact depends, very significantly, on the viewing public as a 'senior partner' to the 'social contract'. Clearly, the event organisers are dependent on the sport-loving public (the fans) for the success of their competition; the broadcasters are dependent on viewers; the advertisers are dependent on the viewer as its aggressively targeted potential consumer; and, of course, the politician is (at least theoretically) dependent on the viewer as voter (and tax-payer who part-funds such events). However, when one considers the above approach of organisations such as FIFA in apparently claiming ownership of the publicity value of events, and that the *sui generis* event legislation in fact aims to protect such publicity by outlawing mere reference to an event by members of the public, it appears that the viewing public is relegated to the distant margins of the event 'contract'. We are consumers who are taken for granted, and our part of the event experience is dismissed as that of an unwitting target for the activities of the other partners while enjoying little tangible benefit beyond what we pay for as spectators and the purchasers of event-related merchandise or of the products and services branded with the event logos. This negation (or, at best, severe under-valuing) of the role of the consumer public in determining issues of legal protection of publicity value has been highlighted in the context of the American right of publicity afforded to celebrities and of unjust enrichment as a legal basis for protection:

> The plaintiff's right to sue in unjust enrichment depends on the plaintiff's proving that the defendant has been enriched at the expense of—or that economic value has been subtracted from—the plaintiff. There is no need to show interference with a proprietary interest. Therefore, one may validly argue that to award to the plaintiff a property right, on the basis that the defendant had gained some kind of an advantage or benefit, may, in fact, unjustly enrich the plaintiff. The grant of a property right connotes *exclusivity* of control on the part of the property owner. While this may be a desirable and convenient outcome for the celebrity individual and the culture producers—especially for advertising agencies and transnational corporations that rely on celebrity sponsorships, endorsements, and associations,—it does not account for the role of the audience that has participated in the

---

[108] Roche 2000, p. 163.

[109] Dayan and Katz 1992, as referred to in Roche 2000, p. 164.

[110] Roche 2000, p. 164.

> celebrity-creation process. This is where, according the right of publicity, the status of a full property right akin to that of land and chattel lacks a compelling doctrinal justification.[111]

The ironic consequence is that we, the largely ignored consumers/tax-paying event 'sponsors', in fact end up paying for the opportunity and the space (nay, 'the privilege'[112]) to be exposed to the marketers' advertising; or, we shell out our consumer dollars to become, as one observer put it, 'extras in somebody else's corporate video'.[113] Let me get (back) to the point, again with reference to Madow and his criticisms of publicity rights in the American celebrity 'market'. I believe that the following applies just as much to FIFA and the IOC:

> [A] celebrity like Madonna cannot say of her public image what the carpenter can say of his chair: "*I* made it." And because she cannot say this of her public image, she cannot lay a convincing moral claim to the *exclusive* ownership or control of the economic values that attach to it.[114]

Teresa Scassa expresses the apparent paradox well in her critical analysis of 'association rights' to events:

> The right of association belongs to the event organizers. Yet major international sport events require the efforts and participation of many stakeholders—public and private, corporate and individual—for their operation and success. These events are heavily subsidized by the public purse, and their success depends on the support and participation of a wide range of entities and individuals going far beyond official sponsors. The events take place in real time, within real communities. They require a host country, a host city, a great deal of local organization and participation, the participation of a large number of nations, the involvement of national sport organizations from around the world, and the hard, and often unrewarded efforts of thousands of individual athletes. Nevertheless, with anti-ambush marketing legislation, event organizers alone may exercise an extraordinary monopoly over an extremely broad concept of association with the event, and may exercise this right against other stakeholders.[115]

And let us not ignore the apparent double standard in respect of protecting the exclusivity of claimed rights to publicity value of events. Phillip Johnson[116] explains that while common law systems do not provide a 'right to a spectacle' to protect events (as discussed elsewhere in the earlier chapters), the law of confidence has developed significantly in recent years. With reference to the well-known *Douglas v Hello! Ltd*[117] case, he speculates as to the potential role for the law of confidence in order to protect against association with an event, but dismisses it for the following reason:

---

111 Tan 2008, pp. 933, 934.

112 See Schlossberg 1996, p. 176.

113 'Ambush marketing: War minus the shooting', *The Economist*, 16 February 2006, available online at the time of writing at http://www.economist.com/node/5536128.

114 Madow 1993.

115 Scassa 2011, pp. 365, 366.

116 Johnson 2007, p. 2, 3.

117 [2007] UKHL 21.

> Using the law of confidence to prevent ambush marketing is unlikely to be successful and, in many cases, would be of little value to the organiser or sponsors of the event. A sponsor wants as much coverage of an event as possible: saturation coverage being the ideal. This means that using the law of confidence to limit access to an event is not in the sponsor's interest and, to some extent, not in the interests of the event organiser.[118]

In effect, it is clear that sponsors (and event organisers, who charge extremely large sponsorship fees against promises of guarantees of exclusivity) naturally pursue maximum public exposure of the event, while claiming that their contractual rights of exclusivity means that only they (and the organiser) should be able to reap the benefits of such publicity. Surely there is some paradoxical notion inherent in such covetous self-centeredness? As pointed out above, it is trite that ambushing thrives on publicity, and that the aim of an ambushing campaign is to grab the attention of spectators and consumers, the mega-event audience. This is recognised by Ellis et al., who explain why the IOC has never been satisfied with trademark protection alone: '[A]mbush marketing does not need to exploit the marks of another to succeed. Discussion of various strategies for ambush marketing show, it is possible to 'ambush' an event simply by placing one's own mark in the spotlight generated by the event.'[119] This encapsulates the classic intrusion ambush, i.e. placing one's brand in the spotlight at stage left, in full view of the audience. While I accept the correctness of attributing such a key role for publicity in the ambush context, I have a conceptual problem with the resultant leap taken by event organisers (and host nation lawmakers) in then claiming (and providing protection for) some right to property or exclusive use of such publicity surrounding an event. I would suggest that this is tantamount to a government facing a gun control problem passing legislation expropriating (i.e. claiming ownership of) all firearms merely because they are a tool used to commit crimes. And one is left with the question: If, for official sponsors, saturation sponsorship is the ideal, what if they fail (either through the reality of the wide scope of the thematic space of an event, or through a failure to properly leverage sponsorship rights) to effectively achieve saturation? If there are remaining pockets of publicity surrounding the event which may provide a platform for marketing by outsiders, why should the law prohibit this? Only a conception of the event's thematic space which equates with traditional concepts of private property would allow for such a prohibition (i.e. even if I don't use a section of my farm every day, I am allowed to use the force of the law to prevent squatters from settling on it). Most jurisdictions, however, do *not* recognise such a property right in an event.

The effect of the provisions of section 15A(2) of the MMA in the South African context and of FIFA's attempts to enforce its 'rights' in terms thereof are, in my view an illustration of the following view that was expressed in respect of the special event legislation that was passed for purposes of the 2010 Vancouver Winter Olympic Games:

---

118 Johnson 2007, p. 3.

119 Ellis et al. 2011, p. 300.

> The primary goal of such legislation is to render illegal a wide range of previously legal activities and words, broadly described as ambush marketing. This type of event-specific legislation, in effect, broadens the concept of ambush marketing because it allows Olympic officials and event organisers essentially to redefine what activities will constitute ambush marketing at this particular Olympics depending on the language used in the special legislation and related bylaws.[120]

The mega-event (whether it be the FIFA World Cup or Olympic Games or other such grand spectacle) occupies a thematic space (which, in marketing terms, one can define as 'the definitional [category] within which products and services are positioned, categorized, and described, and within which they are, therefore, considered for purchase by consumers'[121]), and the question is whether such space is one that is in the public domain or whether it could be 'property' capable of private ownership (as the governing bodies like to claim). The father of the term 'ambush marketing', Jerry Welsh, has definite views on the subject:

> [I]n buying a sponsorship, a company buys only that specific, packaged product, offered as it is, with its constituent parts and attendant rights (and its liabilities). In sponsoring, *the company does not thereby purchase the rights to all avenues leading to the public's awareness of that property; and, more importantly, the company does not buy the rights to the entire thematic space in which the purchased property is usually only one resident.* In other words, all else other than that which is specifically purchased is up for commercial grabs.[122] [My emphasis]

He continues:

> If my competitor has just spent, say, [USD 100 million] to secure the Olympics sponsorship, that gives me roughly the same amount (assuming I want parity with my competitor in marketing expenditures) to get a similar benefit for my product or service without sponsoring the Olympics. So long as I do nothing to claim that I'm indeed an Olympic sponsor, and so long as I refrain from any other action or claim directly misleading to the public, then I'm free to pursue other Olympic-related activities (e.g., television advertising on the Olympics broadcasts, perhaps onsite events, and customer entertainment in the Olympic city), or non-Olympic—but nevertheless sports-related—activities and similar sponsorships (national teams, former Olympic athletes, children's athletic causes and programs in Olympic-featured sports) to underscore my company's support of, and dedication to, the thematic space which Olympic sports occupy. The argument that, if I'm an inventive non-sponsor, mining the sponsored thematic space in a clever way, the public may come to think of me as an Olympic sponsor, is not an argument supporting non-ambushing activities, but is rather a possible testament to the marketing skills of a non-sponsoring competitor. What the public perceives in the world of sponsorship is interesting grist for the marketing pollsters, but is hardly the stuff of which business morality should be gauged. Marketers routinely portray their wares in the best possible light; and in times when sponsored properties are on attractive display, the

---

[120] Grady et al. 2010, p. 148.

[121] See http://welshmktg.com/WMA_thematic_spaces.pdf.

[122] From Welsh, J 'Ambush Marketing: What it Is; What it Isn't', available online at the time of writing on the web site of Welsh Marketing Associates at http://welshmktg.com/WMA_ambushmktg.pdf.

> positive association with that thematic space—if not with the specific sponsored property—is the natural, and altogether legitimate, inclination of marketing professionals.[123]

Welsh concludes with rather strong-worded condemnation of the aggressive 'anti-ambushing' stance of the event organisers and their official sponsors:

> The… notion, put forward largely by sloppy event organizers, that non-sponsors have a moral or ethical obligation to market themselves totally away from the thematic space of a sponsored property, is simply nonsense which smart marketers have long recognized as a commercial non-starter, as well as an intellectual affront. Sponsors have bought a specific property; they have not bought a thematic space. Accordingly, they have no right to police, protect, and otherwise administer what they have not bought, have not created, and, therefore, do not own.[124]

There is a serious conceptual difficulty in claiming ownership of publicity or of the potential to grab the public's attention and, by extension, their wallets (unless terms such as 'ownership' and 'property' in this sense are understood more metaphorically so as to symbolize the fact that the courts will enforce a claim that has a pecuniary worth rather than attributing normal attributes of property thereto[125]). If one accepts such difficulty, as I do, then one should reconsider the legitimacy of the notion of an exclusive 'association right' to an event as created by special mega-event legislation. The best-known example of this is found in the London Olympics association right created by the London Olympic and Paralympic Games Act, 2006, which is discussed in Chap. 4. This right is to use any representation (of any kind) in a manner likely to suggest to the public that there is an association between the London Olympic or Paralympic Games and goods and services, or a person who provides goods or services.[126] This extremely wide definition of the right would appear to be susceptible to an interpretation which would include any marketing of a product or service within the thematic space of the event—while the definition clearly requires a 'representation', it would seem that infringement of the right may follow *even where no representation in the normal sense of the word is made*. Johnson points out that the representation can be of any kind (including a verbal representation); that it need not be intentional; and that there is no requirement that the association is misleading (i.e. it does not matter whether consumers are confused or not)—the representation must objectively create the association.[127]

The Free Online Dictionary defines a 'representation' as 'the act of representing or the state of being represented', and 'something that represents' as 'an account or statement, as of facts, allegations, or arguments'. Inherent in this last definition is the communication to others of something that is not in accordance with the facts. *In casu* the fact would be (official) association with the Olympics, which would be

---

[123] Ibid.

[124] Ibid.

[125] As the court observed in the famous American 'publicity right' case of *Haelan Laboratories, Inc v Topps Chewing Gum, Inc* 202 F.2d 866 (2d Cir. 1953)—see Tan 2008, p. 930.

[126] Schedule 4, par. 1(1) of the Act—see the discussion in Sect. 4.4.3 in Chap. 4.

[127] Johnson 2007, pp. 129, 130.

absent on the part of the person making a 'representation' who is not entitled to do so and thus would be infringing the right. The London Act, however, takes an extremely wide approach to the required association; it requires simply that the (also extremely widely defined) representation must be 'in a manner likely to suggest to the public that there is an association'. When I read these words I come to the inescapable conclusion that the Act goes much further than requiring the element of deception accepted in terms of traditional notions of 'ambush marketing' (i.e. a blatant untrue statement of being an official sponsor, or the use of event logos or symbols which deceive the public into believing there is an element of affiliation or association with the event). Bear in mind that the British advertising industry recommended three key revisions to improve a previous version of the London Olympic Bill (namely adding 'intent to create a false or misleading association,' distinguishing 'unfair association' from 'mere reference', and changing the language of the Bill to 'avoid prohibiting legitimate reference to individual sponsorship or merchandising deals with teams and stars'), but such calls were unsuccessful.[128] Seeing that a 'representation' is not defined in the Act, the wide concept of a 'representation' would include conduct beyond such traditional forms of ambushing; in fact it would appear to include conduct beyond actual *marketing*. Upon such an understanding of the term one could conceivably infringe the association right by means of any conduct (as long as it is 'likely to suggest an association' with the Games in the public mind), and such conduct does not even have to constitute marketing of goods or services. I hope that someone will buy this book (in which case I'll earn a small royalty—oh happy day!), and I sincerely hope that I won't be receiving a boilerplate threatening letter from the London 2012 organisers anytime soon.

The Act does, however, provide some guidance as to what would constitute exceptions to infringement (aside from exceptions relating to reporting on the event[129]):

> 'The London Olympics association right is not infringed by
>
> (a) the use by a person of his own name or address,
> (b) the use of indications concerning the kind, quality, quantity, intended purpose, value, geographical origin, time of production of goods or of rendering of services, or other characteristics of goods or services,
> (c) the use of a representation which is necessary to indicate the intended purpose of a product or service;
>
> provided, in each case, that the use is in accordance with honest practices in industrial or commercial matters.'[130]

The Act provides that an 'association' includes any kind of contractual relationship, commercial relationship, corporate or structural connection or the provision of financial or other support for or in connection with the Games.[131]

---

[128] McKelvey and Grady 2008, p. 578.

[129] Found in Schedule 4, par. 8.

[130] Schedule 4, par. 7.

[131] Schedule 4, par. 1(2)(a); Johnson 2007, p. 130.

As Johnson points out, the list is 'exemplary rather than exhaustive and so an association can occur in other cases'.[132] An infringement of the association right occurs if a person, in the course of trade, uses in relation to goods or services any representation (of any kind) in a manner likely to suggest to the public that there is an association between the London Olympics and the goods or services, or a person who provides the goods or services.[133]

It is my contention that the wide ambit of the definition of the association right and of prohibited conduct which could conceivably infringe such right, in fact, means that the London Act expands significantly on the traditionally accepted notion of what constitutes 'ambush marketing', and it does so by legislatively proclaiming—even if not in so many words—the thematic space of the event as no man's land for any commercial conduct in the course of trade which might conceivably overlap with or intrude on such space and thereby, automatically, be likely to suggest an association with the event.

By way of example, let us take a fictional advertisement for stylish open-toed sandals which appears in a London newspaper during the Olympic Games, consisting of a photograph of a pair of sandals against a black background with the words 'We love our athletes—let's treat them to comfort after a long day's slog', along with the sandal brand name. There is no direct reference to the Games, nor any implication of an association with the event as official sponsor or commercial partner. The ad also does not make use of any of the protected words or symbols in terms of the London Act. However, it is submitted that the reference to athletes, within the thematic space of the Games (i.e. the ad appears during the event, in a local newspaper, and it references sport), might be argued to constitute a representation which is made 'in a manner likely to suggest to the public that there is an association' between the Games and the sandals or the person providing the sandals. Has the marketer intended such an association, i.e. to deceive the public? It does not matter, as we have seen, as intention and deception are not requirements for an infringement of the association right. So what has the marketer actually done wrong here? They have included a reference to athletes in the advertisement, and everything athletic or sporting is taboo in light of the wording and ambit of the Act. When and while the Games are in town it is all-pervasive and omnipresent. It is so aggressively marketed to the public that the public, for want of a better term, has 'Olympics on the brain'. When one refers to 'athletes' within this climate and environment, can it not be argued that such reference is likely to suggest to the public that there is an association with the Games? I think yes, most definitely. And if one considers the combined effect of the very wide definition of a 'representation' and of an 'association' in terms of the London Act, I would suggest that the legislation may be inimical to both legal certainty and the rule of law, especially in light of the possibility that courts faced with allegations of ambush marketing in contravention of the Act may follow the lead of courts in various jurisdictions

[132] Johnson 130.

[133] Schedule 4, par. 2(1).

which have in recent years extended trademark protection to the controversial reaches of dilution and 'initial interest confusion' cases. After all, as some stern critics of these last extensions of traditional trademark principles observe: 'Some members of the public are capable of making the most extraordinary associations'.[134] Outlaw and even criminalise the consequences of such associations for marketers and individuals by means of widely-drafted legislation with insufficient exemptions to potential liability, and it will soon be a free-for-all where the sins of the stupid are visited on honest traders with the only possible winner the corporate sponsor or event organiser with deep enough pockets to be a serial litigator (or merely a user of the ubiquitous cease-and-desist letter or 'strike suit'[135]).

At this point, having touched on the possible parallels with trademark dilution law, I need to briefly consider the comments of Lingling Wei, who, in a paper delivered recently at a European intellectual property policy conference,[136] raises some interesting points. She observes that protecting against consumer deception is a legitimate (and traditional) justification for intellectual property laws, such as trademark law, but that this purpose is absent in respect of association rights protection against intrusion ambushing (as I have also argued above). She then proceeds to consider the justification for protecting consumer association with reference to another area where such consumer association is central, namely trademark anti-dilution law. She explains that dilution deals with the association which is detrimental to the distinctiveness or repute of the trademark, and that association is an essential element in dilution. With reference to ECJ case law on the dilution provision in the EU trademark directive,[137] the requirement is that 'the relevant section of the public makes a connection between the sign and the mark, that is to say, establishes a link between them even though it does not confuse them'.[138] Wei points out, however, that trademark dilution law has struggled to find a suitable basis of justification:

> The dilution law protects the advertising function of the trade mark. Trade mark owners' investment in building up the brand value of the trade mark seems to be a ready justification at the first glance. However, IP law does not protect the investment alone and the public good that will be brought by this protection needs to be proved as well. Dilution law fails to provide a satisfactory answer regarding how it contributes to public good. So will be the regulation of ambush marketing by intrusion. Although the investment in building up the Olympic brand is easy to prove, the contribution to the public interest through this regulation is a difficult question for host countries to answer.[139]

---

[134] Burrell and Gangjee 2010, p. 19.

[135] See Chaps. 3 and 5.

[136] Lingling Wei 'Ambush marketing: Where is the base?'—paper presented at the European Policy for Intellectual Property association's 6th Annual Conference, September 2011, Brussels, Belgium (copy available online at the time of writing at http://www.epip.eu/conferences/epip06/papers/Parallel%20Session%20Papers/WEI%20Lingling.pdf).

[137] Article 5(2) of Directive 89/104.

[138] *Adidas-Salomon AG v Fitnessworld Trading Ltd* [2004] E.T.M.R. 10.

[139] Wei (note 136).

As I have argued in Sect. 8.2, I would agree that this public interest element is currently severely lacking in the discourse around strong *sui generis* event commercial rights legislation. Wei continues to also reject free-riding arguments as justification for seeking to outlaw ambushing by intrusion, by asking how we can calculate the benefits of regulating this type of ambush marketing, and also how we can make the case that in the absence of such regulation by means of special event laws there is likely to be an underinvestment in the event sponsorship scheme. Finally, she explains the differences between trademark dilution law and regulation of ambush marketing by intrusion:

> Dilution protection conferred to the trade mark owner to prevent consumer association has its constraints built into prevent the over expansion of the protection. In the EU trade mark law, these constraints are revealed as being detrimental to or taking unfair advantage of the repute or distinctiveness of the mark. These are the requirements that trade mark owners have to meet in order to qualify for the protection to stop the consumer association… For the regulation of ambush marketing by intrusion, what damage [can] that event owner … prove in order to prevent the audience association? Without a constraint what the regulation is trying to achieve is the protection from pure audience association. There is no such precedent in IP law. In this sense, the criticism that the regulation is … overreach of IP law is well founded.[140]

I would suggest that what Wei refers to is further confirmation of the conclusion that what has thus been achieved by means of the introduction of 'association rights', as described above, is an appropriation of the whole thematic space occupied by the event, by means of legislation which encloses the event within a proverbial bubble which serves to suffocate and stifle the liberties and conduct of those caught within (or stranded without, not having paid a vastly inflated entry fee of dubious legitimacy). Undisputed 'king of horror', Stephen King, recently published a novel about a mysterious dome that appeared out of the blue one morning to envelop a small Maine town, leading, in true King tradition, to thrilling adventures and some nail-biting suspense.[141] The modern sports mega-event seems to create a comparable phenomenon, with event organisers attempting (and often succeeding) to artificially isolate the event and its locale in a controlled environment where access from the outside is exclusively regulated and the egress of news and information is carefully controlled. With exclusive use zones and clean transport routes, and with ambushing hit squads patrolling, one is reminded of an artificially-constructed, dome-like bubble overseen, in Jim Carrey's *The Truman Show* fashion, by a god-like behind-the-scenes director selling hotdogs, energy drinks and ad space. Carvajal[142] feels that the growing trend toward the enactment of special trademark legislation is the result of 'global sports organizations demanding to erect towering walls around their brands and word associations when host cities come courting'. Teresa Scassa explains the 'event bubble'

---

[140] Ibid.

[141] Stephen King's *Under the Dome* Hodder and Stoughton (2009).

[142] Carvajal, D 'Can't tell the sponsors without a scorecard' *International Herald Tribune* 31 May 2006 (as quoted in McKelvey and Grady 2008, p. 574).

well in reference to the New Zealand legislation, and gets the point across that this may be a very dangerous place to be:

> In MEMA, legislators have created a broad virtual space delimited by temporal and physical boundaries in which no one, regardless of their other relationships to teams, athletes, or organizations, may create any form of association with the event. If an organization is associated with an athlete, who in turn is associated with the event, the organization effectively risks liability by association.[143]

Scassa also points out that the law's resistance in most jurisdictions to recognising a property right to events[144] appears to have been circumvented by event organisers in their demands for special event laws. She refers to the Australian *Victoria Park Racing* case, which I have mentioned elsewhere, where the court declared that a party who objects to others looking onto his or her property can 'erect a higher fence'. Scassa observes:

> The court's response to the plaintiff in *Victoria Park* was to "erect a higher fence," something that organizations such as the IOC has been metaphorically doing for some time. The manifestations of this 'fence' are now legion. The fence is both a set of physical barriers (controlled entrance to venues, events, and facilities), as well as other barriers of private law ordering. Tickets to events contain detailed limitations on what can be done with the ticket, and on what can be worn or brought to the stadium. Event organizers are required to acquire and strictly control all advertising space within a certain radius of venues, and host cities may be required to limit certain advertising uses of private property close to venues. Flyovers may be prohibited, and other restrictions may be imposed by by-law or regulation on property use, permits to sell merchandise near venues, and a wide range of other activities. The fence gets higher, but it is apparently not high enough. In addition to these rights to control the physical space around an event, the new right of association has dramatically shifted the paradigm and created a kind of property right in the event itself.[145]

I would agree with Pelanda that much of what is often characterised as 'ambushing' of an event appears to derive from an overblown sense of entitlement on the part of organisers and their commercial partners as to what benefits their involvement in the staging of 'their' event should bring:

> [E]vent organizers and sponsors often allege that non-sponsoring companies have engaged in ambush marketing merely because those companies did any advertising at all in relation to the event. Event organizers such as the IOC and its corporate sponsors have demonstrated that they operate under the brazen assumption that they are entitled to a niche of the market free of any commercial competition whatsoever, and that no activity done in relation to their events or even the mere use of terminology evocative of the existence of their events could ever be fair or permissible without their authorization.[146]

---

[143] Scassa 2011, p. 362.

[144] An issue I have referred to in the earlier chapters and will briefly revisit in Chap. 10, in respect of recent developments regarding the recognition of a 'sports event organiser's right'.

[145] Scassa 2011, p. 365.

[146] Pelanda, B L 'Ambush marketing: Dissecting the discourse', undated 2011 paper available online at the time of writing at http://works.bepress.com/brian_pelanda/.

Sponsors are granted the keys to the city to peddle their wares and flood the area with their billboards and advertising (to the extent that city fathers will nowadays start buying up all available ad spaces even in the initial stages of event bidding, as required by bid requirements), even though the rights they have bought are in fact much more limited in scope than they may appear. In the words of Welsh, as quoted earlier:

> Sponsors have bought a specific property; they have not bought a thematic space. Accordingly, they have no right to police, protect, and otherwise administer what they have not bought, have not created, and, therefore, do not own.[147]

So, when Scaria describes the prime purpose of sponsorship from a commercial angle as being 'for enabling the sponsor to benefit from the marketing opportunities associated with the event',[148] it should be remembered that those sponsors are buying only the right to benefit from some of the marketing opportunities around the event. Why is it automatically assumed that sponsors have the right to exploit *all* potential opportunities? Surely, if an 'ambusher' identifies an opportunity which doesn't involve infringing any existing sponsor's rights or the rights of event organisers (e.g. in respect of event IP), such marketing is simply something involving aspects of the event which resort outside the organiser/sponsor relationship. If this involves something that the sponsor failed to negotiate and obtain rights for, that is their problem. And even though event organisers would undoubtedly love to sell rights to exploit such aspects of the event, if they have failed to do so (or simply because they can't) then why should the 'ambusher' be prohibited from pursuing such opportunity?

In this regard it should be noted that the same inherent, natural limitations in dealing with the thematic space of the event hold true also for the event organiser. The sponsor should have no legal right to police and exclude others from something that it has not bought. Similarly, the event organiser should not be allowed to aggressively police or exclude others from something it does not own and cannot sell in the first place. As one blogger observed in respect of the ambit of the advertising restrictions contained in New Zealand's Major Events Management Act:

> If sponsors want a monopoly on advertising within x kilometres of a venue, they have a very simple solution available: pay for it. But I really don't see why the government should be getting involved to support them. Event managers can promise "clean venues" all they like, but this is creating a clean *city*—something which simply is not theirs to sell.[149]

To which one could add the following view of the UK's Chartered Institute for Marketing as expressed in respect of the 2012 London Olympics:

---

[147] From Welsh, J 'Ambush Marketing: What it Is; What it Isn't', available online at the time of writing on the web site of Welsh Marketing Associates at http://welshmktg.com/WMA_ambushmktg.pdf.

[148] Scaria 2008, p. 16.

[149] From a posting titled 'Protecting corporate greed', 19 June 2007, on the No Right Turn blogspot (available online at the time of writing at http://norightturn.blogspot.com/2007/06/protecting-corporate-greed.html).

> It's one thing to argue that the sponsors who will be investing up to £930 m for 16 days' exposure should be protected from ambush marketers seeking to gain free publicity, but another thing entirely to assert that such big companies need protecting from small companies wishing to trade relatively harmlessly on the back of what is, by definition, a cultural event, not a protected brand.[150]

South African law recognises a principle that is not unknown in other systems, which is contained in the maxim *nemo plus iuris in alium transferre potest quam ipse haberet* (roughly translated, using the few remaining vestiges of Latin from my 1st year of law school, 'you cannot transfer to others more than what you yourself possess'). Event organisers and their sponsors appear to forget that, whatever special and technical arrangements their expensive sponsorship advisors may manage to negotiate, the law does not allow a party to appropriate that which is not open to private ownership or possession (i.e. which is *res extra commercium*) to start with, and others are not bound by the contracts entered into between organiser and sponsor. While the law would (and should) normally not provide these parties with a property right to such aspects of an event, the event organisers have managed to demand of (and obtain from) the lawmakers an extension of the existing 'property' in order to cover the whole thematic space surrounding and occupied by the event. If one considers that such thematic space, in marketing terms, constitutes the definitional category within which products and services are positioned, categorized, and described, and within which they are considered for purchase by consumers, one could characterise the conduct of event organisers as analogous to a situation where a lawnmower manufacturer attempts to claim 'ownership' of the whole category in the market of gardening equipment. It is an absurd notion, and it deserves the contempt of the law and lawyers rather than special legislation to compound the absurdity. As one observer put it in the context of ambush marketing: 'An official sponsor can buy the marketing space but not the consumer's mind'.[151] What event organisers are demanding is exactly that, an Orwellian utopia of near complete control of public thinking and expression relating to an event, and which they are not shy to defend:

> There is a moral argument that the World Cup is like summer—it comes and it goes—and it must therefore belong to everybody. FIFA's philosophical policy is "no". Somebody has to invest a lot of money. And that is FIFA, supported by countries and cities, to build streets and stadiums and pay security costs.[152]

---

[150] As quoted in 'Ambush marketing and the law: Protecting sponsors or harming small business?' 7 June 2011, available online at the time of writing at http://internationalbusinessblog.conversisglobal.com/2011/06/07/ambush-marketing-and-the-law-protecting-sponsors-or-harming-small-business/.

[151] From a posting by Saif, S on the *Management Punditz* web site—available online at the time of writing at http://management-punditz.blogspot.com/2010/06/you-can-buy-marketing-space-but-not.html.

[152] FIFA's Gregor Lentze, as quoted in 'Ambush marketing: War minus the shooting', *The Economist*, 16 February 2006, available online at the time of writing at http://www.economist.com/node/5536128.

I have referred above to the fact that 'filching' or 'free-riding' arguments in support of anti-ambushing laws and aggressive rights protection measures are not unproblematic. I would suggest, having considered in previous chapters the importance of trademarks (and trademark law) in the ambush marketing context, that these efforts by event organisers to prevent 'free-riding' on the coattails of their events are a manifestation of a dangerous rights holder mentality that appears to have crept into trademark law in recent years. This last relates to developments in respect of the law relating to trademark dilution in the different jurisdictions. Burrell and Gangjee, referring to the well-known *L'Oréal SA v Bellure* judgment of the European Court of Justice,[153] allude to the fact that 'there have been moves to bring pure misappropriation or free riding within the ambit of antidilution protection, that is, situations where the defendant appears to be taking advantage of the trademark owner's investment, but where there is no threat to the distinctiveness of the mark or its reputation'.[154] They mention that these cases have 'generated considerable unease'. I believe that I have convincingly shown in this and the earlier chapters that anti-ambushing laws appear to have strayed far from the rationale of protecting against consumer deception and confusion in recent years,[155] towards an apparent objective of protecting against free-riding, *per se*. I do not believe that sufficient justification for this exists in generally-accepted principles of law in most, if not all, of the jurisdictions.

Not to mention the fact that event organisers have also frequently come in for criticism of their apparent tendency to seek to claim some form of dominion over the geographic space of host cities (which reminds one of the approach of film crews shooting on location, who are notorious for harbouring the attitude of 'This may be your neighbourhood, but it's my film set'). In fairness, this attitude, of course, actually makes financial sense to the event organisers:

> FIFA has to go to great lengths to secure its lucrative rights through both preventative and reactionary efforts [against ambushing]. Euphemistic phrases such as "controlled territory" and "Rights Protection Programme", used by FIFA before and during the 2006 [FIFA World Cup Germany] tournament, demonstrate its desire to ensure exclusivity for its patrons—the official sponsors and suppliers of the 2006 World Cup. Why wouldn't it? The tighter the security and the more stringent the enforcement, the more valuable the exclusive rights become.[156]

What should bother the legal fraternity is the fact that not only do event organisers and their commercial partners consistently attempt (and obtain) this ring-fencing of 'rights' which may in fact not exist in actual terms, they also manage to coerce lawmakers in the potential host nations to coat this exercise with a thin sheen of legality through the means of special new laws. Pelanda succinctly touches on the problematic nature of this state of affairs:

153 *L'Oréal SA v Bellure NV* (C-487/07) [2009] ETMR 55 (ECJ).

154 Burrell and Gangjee 2010, p. 4.

155 See also Scassa 2011.

156 Schwab 2006.

> Both inside and outside the legal world, words matter, and the term "ambush marketing" is used too loosely both by commentators and event organizers and sponsors… Despite the glaring contradiction between the accepted definition of ambush marketing and its frequent application, the parties that stand to benefit from the overly broad use of the term nevertheless control the discourse. These parties are event organizers such as national Olympic committees in need of securing sponsorship contracts, and companies willing to invest in expensive sponsorship agreements. Although these parties claim that they are concerned with the consumer confusion supposedly caused by the marketing practices they label as "ambushes," what they seem to actually be concerned with is attaining the power to quell all unauthorized speech relating to the high profile athletic events that they promote, regardless of the likelihood of any such confusion. The controversy over ambush marketing has simply been manifested by the unrealistic expectation of being able to restrict the speech of third parties that event organizers and corporate sponsors have for the sponsorship contracts that they have negotiated.[157]

A proper understanding on the part of event organisers (and sponsors) as to what the full extent is of the rights sold and bought would limit the number of complaints over conduct that these parties love to label as 'ambushing' but which does not come close. If I'll be permitted a rather lame metaphor: A delusional gentleman, driving a cute little SmartCar while under the impression that it's a shiny big Cadillac, would be prone to flights of fancy at every turn, sweating the fact that other cars are continually going to hit him. If he realised that his steed is a much smaller target he would surely enjoy the drive a lot more. I would suggest that the apparent delusion as to the size of their 'property' makes event organisers paranoid (and it doesn't help that they undertake contractual liability to protect sponsors' 'rights' in order to justify the levying of the huge sponsorship fees). They do not own the whole thematic space of an event. Although the actual target for the true ambushers—that which the organisers actually do 'own' or can control—is of much smaller scope than they like to imagine, it is however not of any less value than what the organisers currently enjoy. The parts of the thematic space to which they have no rights are not something that earns them revenues. Placing a restriction on members of the public, civic associations or small businesses (who do not qualify to bid for expensive and very exclusive commercial contracts to sponsor the event) from referring to the event does not protect any potential income, as *none of these parties would have paid fees to the organiser in the absence of such restrictions*. And in this regard I believe the following view, expressed in a 2007 ambush marketing legislation review conducted in Australia, is apropos:

> There is a need to balance the interests of the [event] organisers (assumed to require some intervention) against the interests of promoting competition in other markets (also assumed to require some intervention). This reflects an inherent conflict and inescapable trade-off between the objectives of intellectual property law and competition policy. Nevertheless, given this trade-off and the stated objects of the [legislation], *one would expect that the justification for restricting competition and economic activity would be*

[157] Pelanda, B L 'Ambush marketing: Dissecting the discourse', undated 2011 paper available online at the time of writing at http://works.bepress.com/brian_pelanda/.

weaker where the alleged 'ambush' conduct has little impact on the value of the rights being protected or the ability of the organisers to raise revenue. [My emphasis][158]

Proponents of the strong anti-ambush marketing protection of mega-events by means of legislation such as that found in South Africa's Merchandise Marks Act (and, probably, the London Act and other such instruments) do not agree with such objections to monopolisation of the thematic space of events. Their approach to the issues can be well summarised as follows:

> [W]hen buying a sponsorship package, the sponsor is not only buying the tangibles of the event in terms of banners, advertising, clothing, etc., the sponsor is also buying the right to the perception of the event. Because everything we see, everything we choose and everything we believe is based on perception. So, in turn, this makes sponsorship not merely a claim to media platforms, but a claim to perception. This subliminal communication is one of the reasons that make major events so attractive, and therefore needs to be protected as much as any tangible association. Contenders for ambush marketing may argue that, in buying a sponsorship a company buys only that specific event. In sponsoring, the company does not purchase the rights to all avenues leading to the public's awareness of a property, and neither does it buy the rights to the entire consumer "mind space". The "mind space" here refers to the various associations—ideas, images, and events—that occur in the consumers' minds when they think of the sponsored space. This thematic space is not created by anyone, hence no one owns it. This is all very well, but when a company exploits a specific thematic space concurrently with a particular event, they are doing so with the deliberate intention of misleading the public... Each sponsorship property or vehicle has certain associated images in the consumer's mind that transfer to the sponsor. For example, using the thematic space of cricket at any other time other than at the time of the Cricket World Cup doesn't have the same effect—and marketers know that![159]

I have three specific objections to the above characterisation of the issues in the debate at hand. The first relates to the statements that, when buying sponsorship rights, the sponsor 'is also buying the right to the perception of the event', and 'this makes sponsorship not merely a claim to media platforms, but a claim to perception'. It is all very well to make such statements, but then one must clearly explain what is meant by the 'perception of the event'. The Olympic movement went through some turbulent times in recent years, with notable examples the Salt Lake City bribery scandal and the Tibet-related protests surrounding the Beijing Games. The public perception of the Games was, to put it mildly, less than positive in certain quarters. An Olympic sponsor clearly does not wish to buy such perception (if it was up for sale, I doubt there would be any takers—even the serial and serious ambushers are not that silly[160]). So what 'perception' is meant here?

---

[158] Frontier Economics 2007, par. 4.3.3.

[159] Dean-Wales, C and Dean, O, in an undated piece entitled 'Ambush marketing: Virtue or vice?', posted on the web site of South African brand advisors Scarab Origination, available online at the time of writing at http://www.scarabsa.com/news_ambush_marketing.htm.

[160] It was observed that due to all the chaos leading up to the 2010 Delhi Commonwealth Games many companies were very dubious and wary about letting their brand be associated with the Games. After the Games had been successfully launched, many companies were 'jumping on the band-wagon and ... practicing ambush marketing, with the sneaky entry of non-sponsor brands

At best the sponsor can buy the perception of being officially associated with the event, and this surely attaches to the rights bought and does not extend beyond what the sponsor has paid for. In the light of the sponsorship exclusivity model employed in respect of mega-events (which were discussed in Chap. 2), it is even more tenuous to suggest that the sponsor can claim rights to anything (including a 'perception') beyond the narrow confines of the rights bought. I would tend to agree with Rochelle Cooper Dreyfuss's view, in the context of intellectual property rights (specifically trademarks) that 'courts are too quick to equate value with right; to leap from recognizing that consumers attach value to trademarks to concluding that trademark holders ought to have the right to capture that value for themselves'.[161]

The second objection relates to the bald assumption that 'when a company exploits a specific thematic space concurrently with a particular event, they are doing so with the deliberate intention of misleading the public'. Apart from the blatant generalisation inherent in such an assumption of fault in the form of an apparently blameworthy intent, we have also seen that the special anti-ambushing legislation passed in certain jurisdictions simply does not require such an intention to mislead the public in order to found liability—both civil and also criminal in some instances—for the ambushers or 'infringers' of association rights to events. The event organisers are, in fact, provided much wider protection even in cases where such an intention may be completely absent.

The third objection is to the implication in the last line of the quoted passage that marketers' knowledge of the fact that use of a thematic space during an event as referred to (again, this knowledge is simply assumed) is somehow wrong, either ethically or legally. *Lawyers* need to be much more circumspect in labelling conduct, or knowledge, as wrongful based on a specific perception (the authors can't escape the important role that they themselves ascribe to perception in determining what we believe).

I would suggest that these commentators should reconsider their view, which is based on insufficiently motivated assumptions and flies in the face of first principles of law in civilised nations with developed legal systems (e.g. relating to notions of property and concepts of ownership, and to the prohibition of criminalisation of conduct by lawmakers even where *mens rea* is absent).

McKelvey and Grady (with reference to an article by Mallard[162]) point to the fact that, even though special legislation enacted for events often contains safeguards to protect ordinary citizens and local businesses, striking the proper balance

(Footnote 160 continued)
into the Games Village … being evident and pervasive'—see the short report available online at the time of writing at http://kozla.com/commonwealth-games-being-taken-over-by-ambush-marketing/224964.

161 Cooper Dreyfuss 1996, p. 124.

162 Mallard, T 'Close watch kept on ambush marketing' *The New Zealand Herald*, 30 April 2007.

is often difficult. They state, however, that if one considers the basic 'sponsorship protection rationale' of such legislation, the concepts 'seem straightforward':

> "[Official] sponsors do not want others to free-ride on their investments and trade off the goodwill and publicity surrounding an event, thereby undermining the value of their official sponsorship and the viability of obtaining sponsorship for future events". Thus, the legislation necessarily must address situations "when companies or advertisers make representations through advertising or other publicity that draw a connection in the public's mind with themselves and major events—without the authorization of the event organizers". The ongoing challenge in drafting such legislation is to properly and fairly achieve this objective without unduly impinging upon the rights of those parties not officially associated with the event.[163]

I would suggest that this challenging balancing exercise should not only involve legislative exemptions to liability and other exceptions to blanket bans on such a wide range of potential conduct by members of the public. I would suggest that, more fundamentally, a proper balancing of the rights and interests of the various parties concerned should include a re-evaluation of the very objective of the legislation. When one talks of 'free-riding' on 'publicity' surrounding an event—which event is publicised largely also by event organisers and the sponsors in order to leverage the sponsorship investment to the point of saturation—there should be due consideration of the fact that there are simply aspects of such publicity that should not be viewed as akin to private property carved out from the public domain within which the event and its publication takes place. I would submit that a proper balance will be absent until such time as event organisers and sponsors realise (or are told, authoritatively, by the law and lawmakers) that they are actually entitled to much less far-reaching protection than what they so love to claim. I will sum up the gist of the argument with the words of Kim Skildum-Reid, who cuts to the chase in her inimitably direct fashion:

> Event organisers control the event itself, the promotion of the event, event assets, and the IP belonging to the event. They control some of the content, although if we're talking about a number of teams and athletes, they have control over their own assets and IP and media also control some of the content. The upshot is, the event doesn't really control very much. On the other hand, we have the event experience, which is controlled by the people who make up an event's target market. Their experience includes everything from the first moment of anticipation to the last faded memory and everything in between. It is the atmosphere, pride, patriotism, the dramas and triumphs, the opportunities and inconveniences. It's newspapers and television and blogs and Facebook and Twitter. It's the stories, the rumours, and the scandals. It's the outrageous once-in-a-lifetime adventures with friends and the little moments that touch our hearts. It's the feeling of I-was-there and the memories of exactly where you were when something amazing happened. "Do you believe in miracles?!" is a moment I will cherish to my grave. Events don't own any of that. We do—the people, the fans. The residents of host cities and the tourists do. You don't have to attend an event to have an event experience. Event experiences happen in pubs and parks and living rooms and subway stations. They happen on computers and mobile phones and traffic jams. The event experience isn't owned by anyone, it is created by individuals. Making that experience better—amplifying the good stuff and lessening the bad stuff—is where

[163] McKelvey and Grady 2008, p. 578.

> strategic ambush lives and it doesn't require any access to IP or the event at all for it to work.[164]

Event organisers may need to be circumspect in their own marketing campaigns. While the final form of the expected Brazilian anti-ambush legislation is at the time of writing speculative, it might be problematic if it ends up containing provisions creating an association right in the mould of the London legislation, seeing that the 2016 Games organisers launched a new Facebook application in January 2011 designed to help supporters around the world get involved in its preparations for the Olympics and Paralympics. It would be a sad day if organisers were to blow hot and cold regarding the public's 'involvement' in the spirit of the Games (when those threatening letters start arriving in the post or the ambush hit squads come calling). This is no new phenomenon, however, as event organisers and host governments love to call on individuals and even small businesses to dress up their premises, their cars or themselves in order to promote the 'celebratory look and feel' of the event, while the ambushing hit squads wait in the wings to come down on those who go a bit too far.

Having argued above that proponents of the new 'association rights' to events are unable to definitively justify such rights with reference to the object of their protection, I would suggest that much more research should be done to try to obtain a more meaningful understanding of the size, scope and nature of the thematic space of the mega-event and its susceptibility to protection by law. A final problematic aspect of such *sui generis* laws as currently exist relates to the legitimacy of lawmakers passing such legislation in the absence of such a conception of what they are seeking to protect. I will end this section by saying that I believe the development of exclusive 'association rights' to sports events has been ill-founded and insufficiently justified. I believe there may be something in the following observation by Ellis et al.:

> A key concern with addressing ambush marketing in legislation lies in the difficulty of identifying with precision the objectionable conduct. [T]he term ambush marketing is often used to embrace a wide range of conduct and could be considered to be somewhat of a 'grey zone' causing much confusion among all marketing stakeholders in the sport community. While there remains no universally accepted definition of ambush marketing in the literature, one common thread seems to be the idea of an attempted, direct or indirect, legitimate or illegitimate 'association' being made by non-sponsors with events such as the Olympic Games. Organizations such as the IOC/OCOG have been successful at 'forcing' host countries to pass legislations with the aim of protecting the property from ambush marketing through any type of 'association(s)'. However, since association(s) can take numerous forms, statutes enacted to address ambush marketing may capture a varying range of conducts depending on the wording used.[165]

---

164 Kim Skildum-Reid, writing on her marketing blog in 'Why ambush marketing legislation will never work (and what will)', posted 5 August 2009—available online at the time of writing at http://blog.powersponsorship.com/index.php/2009/08/why-ambush-marketing-legislation-will-never-work/.

165 Ellis et al. 2011, pp. 301, 302.

I have serious concerns about basing such potentially invasive and draconian legislative protection for commercial interests on a measure of uncertainty in defining the perceived mischief which such legislation is supposed to address. And the problems are compounded when, as Ellis et al. observe, vagaries in the wording of statutes have the potential to capture 'a varying range of conduct'—some of which may be perfectly ethical and legal in the absence of such *sui generis* laws. It is truly troubling to consider these authors' observation that, with the passing of the London Olympic and Paralympic Games Act in the UK to protect the 2012 London Olympics, 'the Minister for Sport expressly admitted that the "right of association" created to counter ambush marketing was drafted in the broadest possible terms because there was no consensus as to what type of conduct it was meant to catch and because the future demands of the IOC for a legislative response to the public might change'.[166] *Nulla poena sine culpa*, anyone? Law-making of this ilk is destructive of the rule of law; it is illicit and simply abhorrent in a modern democracy.

8.4 What, Exactly, Does Such Legislation Prohibit?

In the previous two sections of this chapter I have examined, first, whether *sui generis* event rights legislation serves the greater public good beyond the commercial relationship existing between event organisers and sponsors, and secondly, what the actual object of such legislative protection is. I now turn to another aspect of a critical evaluation of such special legal protection, namely to examine what, exactly, is prohibited by statutory association rights. Of course, we have seen that it is the association or creation of consumer confusion as to association (in the form of sponsorship or affiliation of the event) which is nominally prohibited. We have also seen, however, that the relevant legislation does not always expressly require consumer confusion (unlike the protection afforded by other branches of e.g. intellectual property protection such as trademarks). What I wish to focus on now are two further aspects in this regard, which I've touched on earlier, namely the intention to deceive or create an association on the part of the alleged ambusher, and the element of harm arising from the relevant association. I will discuss these aspects with reference primarily to what I have previously characterised as the single most stringent and far-reaching 'association right'-type of statutory instrument currently found anywhere, namely South Africa's Merchandise Marks Act (or 'MMA'), specifically its section 15A. The comments that follow are, however, also relevant to other such legislation as discussed elsewhere in this book.

As mentioned, the first aspect of the legislative restriction contained in s 15 A (2) of the MMA that must be considered relates to the criminalisation of conduct and the imposition of criminal sanctions in light of the *mens rea* of an offender.

---

[166] Ibid. p. 302.

Strict liability where a sanction such as a fine or imprisonment is imposed would not be in accordance with a trader's constitutional rights (and the accepted principle of *nulla poena sine culpa*). Sanctions can only be imposed on the basis of culpability, taking into account the extent of fault in accordance with generally accepted principles of law, and an automatic criminal sanction would not be proportional and, thus, could be unconstitutional. According to the wording of section 15A (2), the element of *mens rea* which is required for a conviction appears to relate only to the intention to achieve publicity for a mark (i.e. where there is use of a mark in relation to an event 'which is calculated to achieve publicity for such mark'). As is pointed out elsewhere in this book in discussion of the MMA, this is in fact one of the normal purposes of trademark use. The intention required on the part of the trader does not appear to include the intention to derive special promotional benefit from an event (such promotional benefit is as a consequence of the use of the mark). I believe that the section seeks to criminalise insufficiently blameworthy conduct, and such criminalisation of private conduct is at odds with accepted principles of law. In this light it might be appropriate to refer to the following view as expressed by Morrison AJ in the South Gauteng High Court, with reference to the legislative force provided to the contractual obligations of the Local Organising Committee for the 2010 FIFA World Cup South Africa (a company) by means of the special event legislation and the event's designation as a 'protected event' by the Minister of Trade & Industry in terms of the MMA:

> [A] consequence of the law-makers of the country creating law to support the LOC's obligations is that the normal remedies provided for a breach of a term of a contract, usually only civil in nature, now have in certain instances the force of criminal sanction. Although this is not unique to the LOC, as the "protected event" notice legislation demonstrates, criminal sanctions for breaches of contractual rights are out of the norm. Where a private contract is breached the aggrieved contractual party can approach a civil court for enforcement of the contractual remedies against the other party or parties who may be in breach. In this case, however, as legislation has been passed encapsulating some of the LOC's contractual obligations to FIFA (such as those relating to ambush marketing and controlled access areas) it is the entire populace that is bound, and a contravention may be visited upon transgressors in the form of a criminal sanction, including imprisonment.[167]

The trend of criminalising insufficiently blameworthy conduct, however, is discernible much more generally in respect of ambush marketing protection for events in the various jurisdictions and the practice that has developed amongst the major event organisers (specifically FIFA and the IOC) to demand the demarcation of 'clean zones' or 'exclusion zones' and clean event venues, which has been referred to elsewhere. Compare again, in light of the above regarding the Merchandise Marks Act, the similarity with Article 19 of Brazil's *Lei Geral da Copa*,[168] which proposes to

---

[167] *M&G Media Ltd v 2010 FIFA World Cup South Africa Organising Committee Ltd* South Gauteng High Court Case No. 09/51422 (unreported at the time of writing) at par. 124.

[168] See Sect. 4.4.1 in Chap. 4.

make it a criminal offence 'to practice any promotional activities not authorized by FIFA or by a person indicated by FIFA, attracting, by any means, public attention in the Official Places of the Events, *with the objective of obtaining economic or advertising advantage*'. This, in my view, is simply insufficient to found criminal liability in the light of constitutional guarantees and the *nulla poena sine culpa* principle.

Mention was made earlier of the fact that the IOC has for many years demanded a completely clean venue for Olympic events, devoid of any extraneous advertising material such as e.g. billboards. FIFA has also, since its 2006 World Cup in Germany, demanded clean venues (not devoid of all advertising, but only of advertising by non-sponsors of its event) which have necessitated re-branding or the removal of advertising from existing stadia. Existing stadium naming rights holders, therefore, have seen their rights being severely restricted for the period of FIFA's 'exclusive use period' in respect of such stadia; by the obliteration of their names from stadia they suffer a severe diminution of the sponsorship value for which they have invariably paid large sums of money. One marketing group estimates that stadium naming-rights partners lost GBP 13.6 million in branding value *during each televised game* of the 2006 FIFA World Cup. The FIFA ban affected multiple venues in Germany and Austria and led to brands such as AOL and Allianz losing exposure (it was observed that for Allianz, which paid GBP 5.1 million a year for naming rights to the second-biggest stadium in Munich, the end of the 2006 FIFA World Cup could not come too soon).[169] Coca-Cola might have felt even more aggrieved at its loss of its GBP 30 million naming rights to Coca-Cola Park in Johannesburg, which it was forced to relinquish for the 2010 FIFA World Cup when the stadium reverted to its 80-year old name of Ellis Park, especially seeing that Coca-Cola is an official FIFA World Cup sponsor. It should be noted, though, that the naming rights deal had been concluded in 2008, well after the awarding of the 2010 FIFA World Cup to South Africa, so one must assume that Coke knew what it was doing and was willing to relinquish its rights.

A significant problem with such measures (which includes clean zones and stadium re-branding during exclusive use periods) is that it serves as a prime example of anti-ambushing legislation and practice completely ignoring legal requirements regarding the blameworthy intention of 'ambushers', which I've referred to above. By definition, existing rights holders (e.g. those who have paid substantial amounts of money for the rights to name stadia, or for billboard advertising in parts of host cities that form venue precincts) have no intention to ambush an event merely by exercising their existing contractual or intellectual property rights. If Nike is party to a 20-year contract which gives it the right to name a sports stadium, it would be hard to make a credible and rational argument that Nike's exercising of its rights ten years into such contract at the time that FIFA, for example, comes to town and uses such stadium for its World Cup

[169] See the short piece by Christian Sylt, writing on the website of Front Row Marketing Services (16 June 2010)—available online at the time of writing at http://www.frontrow-marketing.com/news-detail.aspx?id=142.

amounts to an intentional (and blameworthy) attempt to ambush the event. The same goes for the above-mentioned temporary loss of its stadium rights to its Munich stadium by Allianz (because Hamburg-Mannheimer Versicherung was an official supplier for FIFA's 2006 World Cup) and for AOL in respect of its stadium in Hamburg (because Yahoo! was an official FIFA sponsor).[170] Ditto, of course, for other non-sponsors wishing to exercise existing contractual rights in respect of billboard advertising near a venue (and, for that matter, existing participating team or athlete sponsors who are not official event sponsors, in the absence of a participation agreement through which such existing sponsors' rights may be curtailed). Marcus observes that, while the 'clean city' vision of event organisers is commendable and the search for 'commercial purity' in and around event venues is reasonably justifiable, the 'purging of an entire city is disproportionate'.[171] He opines that the concept of a 'clean athlete' (in respect of absence of branding) is most disturbing, when one considers the rights of existing sponsors:

> There is an inherent injustice when an entity has decided to invest in the growth and development of an athlete and through that support, the athlete achieves global acclaim. Now that the athlete has qualified for the Olympics, for instance, he has to divorce himself for two weeks from the very body that helped to harness his innate ability. Seemingly, this is justified because Brand Z, the athlete's sponsor, is not an Olympic sponsor. The solution herein is in the negotiation and conclusion of clearly defined contracts and carefully-drafted sporting rules that effectively consider the rights of athlete, sponsor and event organiser.[172]

The solution, surely, should not lie with stringent legislation that outlaws the sponsorship activities of such existing sponsor, in the form of a blunt instrument such as an event association right. There may be other conceptual, principled objections to the restrictions occasioned by such clean zones. One observer, writing about the clean zone regulations in place for the 2011 Super Bowl in Dallas, Texas, observed the following:

> It is interesting that Clean Zone/Ambush Marketing ordinances are designed to protect an investment in a trademark, whereas, trademark law, by its very nature, is designed to protect the consumer of goods and not the trademark owner.[173]

The current use of clean zones, etc. amounts to blatant overreaching by event organisers and legislators (and may also be indicative of a double standard and lack of consistency in respect of regulation by means of legislation[174]). This was,

---

170 See Schwab 2006, p. 8.

171 Marcus 2010, p. 31.

172 Ibid.

173 Bennett, T 'Ambush marketing and Super Bowl XLV', 31 January 2011—available online at the time of writing at http://ipandentertainmentlaw.wordpress.com/2011/01/31/ambush-marketing-and-super-bowl-xlv/.

174 See Wood, Z; Hoek, J and Mossaidis, C 'Ambush marketing: A re-definition and research agenda', undated paper available online at the time of writing at http://smib.vuw.ac.nz:8081/WWW/ANZMAC2004/CDsite/papers/Wood1.PDF:

'[P]urchase of media time and space that is legitimately offered for sale does not breach any

in fact, highlighted recently in the suggestion of the Emerging Issues Committee of the International Trademark Association (INTA) for a resolution regarding guidelines in respect of ambush marketing legislation[175]:

> [P]roperty owners and others are often forced to breach existing agreements and incur associated expenses for which there is no compensation. Such signs and advertisements that predate the special event are clearly not attempts by the owner or advertiser to interfere with the rights of the sponsors to a particular event and should not be considered "ambush marketing." Ambush marketing legislation should make reasonable accommodation for these pre-existing rights[176]

While a blameworthy intention (i.e. to deceive or to cause confusion) is generally not required in cases of alleged intellectual property infringement, it must be remembered that special anti-ambush marketing legislation is something more than IP protection (and not only in the sense of often providing 'IP+' protection for e.g. generic or non-distinctive terms, as referred to elsewhere). 'Association rights' are something different, even though they may sometimes be characterised as providing statutory rights that are 'akin to trade mark rights'. When one considers the penalties for contravention of such ambush legislation and their destructive effects on the pre-existing rights of affected parties or their chilling effect on the broader interests of the public (including free speech and freedom of trade),[177] it is clearly inappropriate to err on the side of requiring only flimsy grounds for alleged infringement. It is only right that the enforcers of such legislation in both civil and (especially) criminal proceedings should be called upon to show elements such as an intention to ambush (i.e. to create consumer confusion as to sponsorship or affiliation with the event, or to intentionally sabotage the official sponsors) and actual resultant harm to event organisers and sponsors from such conduct. We do not find this in clean zone regulations. We do not find it in an association right such as that created in the London Act, where no intention is required in the process of

(Footnote 174 continued)
statute, and competitive promotions characterise most trading environments, thus it is difficult to see why this should be acceptable in one arena and yet deemed unethical in another. It is even more difficult to see how the mere presence of competitive promotions could support an application for a "cease and desist" injunction.'

175 See the Resolution adopted by the committee calling on the Board of Directors of INTA to issue guidelines regarding ambush marketing legislation, dated 10 November 2010, available on the INTA web site at the time of writing at http://www.inta.org/Advocacy/Pages/AmbushMarketingLegislation.aspx.

176 Ibid.

177 It is worth noting that this chilling effect, in fact, to an extent deliberately forms part of event organisers' legal strategy to protect their commercial rights to events:

> 'Organisers of sport events usually make all-round [trade mark] registrations in all possible classes. That practice not only covers the main trademarks of the event organiser but a large number of expressions referring one way or another to the event, including words that are part of the public domain. The purpose is to prevent association with the event in general. The threat of litigation, justified or not, is considered to have a dissuasive effect on a large number of corporations which otherwise would take advantage of the event to make promotions and probably do not have the means to enter into long and costly legal battles.' See Kobel 2007, 54.

making a representation that is likely to suggest an association. And we do not find it in South Africa's Merchandise Marks Act whereby pre-existing trademark holders are prohibited from using their own marks in relation to an event in a way that is calculated to achieve publicity for that mark and derives special promotional benefit from such event. This last intention to use a mark in the way that it is supposed to be used, as I have argued, is insufficient to criminalise conduct that the law, normally, does and should not condemn. I have remarked in a number of places in the earlier chapters on the trend that an increasingly common feature of literature on ambush marketing generated by event organisers is the apparent acceptance of (and bald statements to this effect) the 'fact' that ambush marketing occurs with a blameworthy intention to deceive the public. Compare the following, to be found on the website of UEFA in respect of its commercial rights protection programme for its Euro 2012 football tournament:

> Ambush marketing usually consists of an unauthorised marketing, promotional, advertising and/or public relations activity relating directly or indirectly to the event in question. These activities are unauthorised *because they give (or are intended to give) the wrong impression that the event organiser has endorsed the relevant goods or services* and they take advantage of the significant value and goodwill established by the event organiser in connection with the event. [My emphasis][178]

As I argue elsewhere in this book, such definitions of ambushing and their implicit acceptance of an intention to deceive do not accord with the practical reality of so-called intrusion ambushes where the 'ambusher' does not necessarily have any intention to imply an association with an event beyond merely referring to it or to some aspects which might remind one of the event. The difference is not semantic; in light of the stringent event protection legislation we have encountered in the earlier chapters it could subject the 'ambusher' to significant and stringent legal sanctions. I believe this is extremely problematic, and needs to be reviewed as a matter of urgency in respect of the existing legislation or specifically considered by potential future host nation lawmakers.

The second aspect that deserves some attention here, which I will again discuss with specific reference to the South African legislation, is the element of the harm caused by a trader who may be convicted of an offence in contravening the relevant section of the MMA. This, again, is relevant beyond the South African legislation and relates to a common feature of ambush marketing legislation also in other jurisdictions. In referring to the 'filching' or misappropriation of publicity to an event (as referred to above), one must ask whether there is any harm in such conduct or, rather, whether the legislature intends for the substantial penalties to accrue even where no such harm can be shown. The ambush marketer is, after all, not accused of having stolen a loaf of bread, a car, or a plane. It is submitted that, if one wants to claim that publicity value is one's product, one should also be able to claim that any 'misappropriation' of such 'product' has in fact made one poorer in some form or

---

[178] Available online at the time of writing at http://www.uefa.com/uefaeuro2012/news/newsid=1612831.html.

other. And this, it is submitted, is completely absent from the restriction contained in section 15A(2). Consider the definition of ambush marketing as contained in the eThekwini (Durban) Municipality's By-laws for the 2010 FIFA World Cup, which also make reference to 'promotional benefit' regarding the event:

> "Ambush Marketing" means marketing, promotional, advertising or public relations activity in words, sound or any other form, directly or indirectly relating to the Competition, and which claims or implies an association with the Competition and/or capitalises or is intended to capitalise on an association with, *or gains or is intended to gain a promotional benefit from it to the prejudice of any sponsor of, the Competition,* but which is undertaken by a person which has not been granted the right to promote an association with the Competition by FIFA and whose aforesaid activity has not been authorised by FIFA Competition.[179] [Emphasis added]

Here we see an interesting variation on the words 'promotional benefit' as found in the Merchandise Marks Act. Section 15A(2) refers to 'special promotional benefit', without more, while the above definition of ambush marketing refers to 'promotional benefit ... to the prejudice of any sponsor'. Seeing that the same drafter did not draft these two provisions (and realising that one cannot use a method like comparing two simple mathematical equations), it is assumed that one cannot say that 'special' promotional benefit *a la* the Act refers to promotional benefit which prejudices a sponsor. It is submitted that this highlights the apparent irrationality of the restriction contained in section 15A (2). There is no requirement of harm to event organisers or sponsors (as would be the case in terms of the common law unlawful competition and passing off actions), and the restriction appears to relate simply to the use of publicity (or 'piggy-backing' on an event's popularity). Does the law (apart from this provision) really proscribe this? If so, *should* it?

It was recently mooted that special protection for major sports events might be required which deviates from the normal requirements of use of a trademark in trademark law. In guidelines published by a working committee of the International Association for the Protection of Intellectual Property (AIPPI), which investigated the desirability of special trademark protection for major sports events, the following was mentioned:

> It can be argued that the use of certain words by third party traders cannot be considered trademark use and that the requirement of use as a mark is therefore not fulfilled if it is accepted that non-official sponsors' use of certain words relating to Major Sports Events is considered infringing. Accordingly, it is relevant to consider whether it is reasonable to deviate from the general requirement of use as a mark in relation to trademarks which relate to Major Sports Events. For example, this may be done by having a provision as mentioned in Article 5(5) of the European Trademark Directive that deals with protection against the use of marks or signs for purposes other than distinguishing goods or services; such use may be opposed by a trademark owner *provided unfair advantage is taken from or detriment is caused to the repute or distinctiveness of his trademark.*[180] [Emphasis added]

---

[179] Par. 1.1.6 of the definitions section of the By-laws. For further discussion of the FIFA 2010 host city by-laws, see Chap. 7.

[180] From guidelines published by the Working Committee, Project Q210 ('The protection of major sports events and associated commercial activities through trademarks and other IPR'; in a

While the Directive referred to requires either detriment to the repute or distinctiveness of a mark or 'unfair advantage', it is suggested that no, or, at least, insufficient effort has been made by event organisers or lawmakers who pass special event legislation such as the MMA to explain such unfair advantage as a rationale for protection in (especially intrusion) ambush marketing cases. In the absence of such justification, protection for 'event marks' smacks of protection simply for the sake of protection, with no proper grounding in respect of the rationale for protecting commercial interests at the potential cost of curbing the freedom of expression, freedom of trade or even property rights of others (such as is the case with South Africa's MMA). It should be remembered that a view such as that expressed by the AIPPI above relates to the relaxing of requirements for infringement of a trademark (in respect of use of a mark), and as such provides an extension of trademark protection with a concomitant heavier burden on persons

---

(Footnote 180 continued)
call for country reports compiled for purposes of a draft resolution to be submitted to the AIPPI Exco meeting in Buenos Aires, October 2009), at 3 – available online at the time of writing at https://www.aippi.org/download/commitees/210/WG210English.pdf.

Reference is made to Article 5 of the First European Trademark Directive (89/104/EEC of the Council, of 21 December 1988), which provides as follows:

'The registered trade mark shall confer on the proprietor exclusive rights therein. The proprietor shall be entitled to prevent all third parties not having his consent from using in the course of trade:

a. any sign which is identical with the trademark in relation to goods or services which are identical with those for which the trademark is registered;
b. any sign where, because of its identity with, or similarity to, the trademark and the identity or similarity of the goods or services covered by the trademark and the sign, there exists a likelihood of confusion on the part of the public, which includes the likelihood of association between the sign and the trademark.

2. Any Member State may also provide that the proprietor shall be entitled to prevent all third parties not having his consent from using in the course of trade any sign which is identical with, or similar to, the trade mark in relation to goods or services which are not similar to those for which the trade mark is registered, where the latter has a reputation in the Member State and where use of that sign without due cause takes unfair advantage of, or is detrimental to, the distinctive character or the repute of the trade mark.
3. The following, inter alia, may be prohibited under paragraphs 1 and 2:

   a. affixing the sign to the goods or to the packaging thereof;
   b. offering the goods, or putting them on the market or stocking them for these purposes under that sign, or offering or supplying services thereunder;
   c. importing or exporting the goods under the sign;
   d. using the sign on business papers and in advertising.

4. Where, under the law of the Member State, the use of a sign under the conditions referred to in 1 (b) or 2 could not be prohibited before the date on which the provisions necessary to comply with this Directive entered into force in the Member State concerned, the rights conferred by the trade mark may not be relied on to prevent the continued use of the sign.
5. Paragraphs 1 to 4 shall not affect provisions in any Member State relating to the protection against the use of a sign other than for the purposes of distinguishing goods or services, where use of that sign without due cause takes unfair advantage of, or is detrimental to, the distinctive character or the repute of the trade mark'.

other than the mark owner. Such a development would need to be sufficiently justified, and the apparent standard approach of accepting a 'knee-jerk' aversion to 'ambushing' should not suffice. As Marcus points out in respect of the court's rejection of a claim against an alleged ambusher in the *New Zealand Telecom*[181] case:

> The ruling highlights the need for an event organiser or rights holder to prove the risk of actual damage, whether financial loss, damage to reputation or confusion in the public mind that leads to decreased revenue. A concern or "paranoia" about possible adverse ramifications is not sufficient.[182]

These two aspects of the anti-ambushing protection provided by the South African legislation (in respect of the lack of blameworthy intent and the lack of a requirement of harm) are also relevant in respect of the *sui generis* event protection in other jurisdictions. The legislation passed for the 2012 London Olympics is a case in point. Hussey and Snaith have highlighted the problematic role of the London Organising Committee (LOCOG)'s stance in respect of the association rights created in the 1995 and 2006 Acts (as discussed in Sect. 4.4.3 of Chap. 4):

> In relation to large scale ambush techniques… there are provisions in the legislation ensuring "clean venues" and preventing counterfeit Olympic related merchandise. There are sound economic reasons for addressing these two issues. However, [in respect of the Olympic Association Right (or 'OAR'), the Paralympic Association Right (or 'PAR') and the London Olympics Association Rights (or 'LOAR') as created by the statutes] the legislation and guidance from LOCOG goes further in addressing unauthorised associations generally. The economic and/or political justification for preventing such activity is less clear. It is clear that LOCOG views the association rights as separate and distinct from rights in trade marks (certain of the controlled representations and listed expressions are registered in the UK) and passing off. There is almost strict liability in relation to use of a controlled representation and infringement of the OAR/PAR. As regards infringement of the LOAR, LOCOG distils the test into one question, namely, has an association with the Olympic Games been created? This is clearly a lower threshold than what would be the equivalent test for misrepresentation under the law of passing off, i.e. has the marketer represented that they are an official sponsor of, or are otherwise affiliated with, the Olympics? Further, unlike the law of passing off, there is no requirement to show any damage as a result of the association. If the legislation is in fact directed at the mischief of marketers impinging on the rights of official sponsors, and is there to protect the funding of large scale events, then… the test should be more aligned to the passing off test above. If this were the case, then certain marketing activities that simply give a "nudge" or a "wink" towards the Olympics, and where the consumer does not perceive that the marketer is an official sponsor, would be permitted. Even in these circumstances, there could be still be remedies under trade mark law. Under this proposition, the OAR, PAR and LOAR are really more of a form of statutory passing off.[183]

---

[181] *New Zealand Olympic and Commonwealth Games Association, Inc v Telecom New Zealand* (1996) F.S.R. 757.

[182] Marcus 2010, p. 36.

[183] Hussey, G and Snaith, T 'Marketing With the London 2012 Olympic Games (or Not Associating With a Sporting Event to be Held in the UK Next Year)', January 2011, available online at the time of writing at http://www.bnai.com/MarketingLondon2012Olympics/default.aspx.

8.5 Those Magnificent Young Ladies with Their Little Orange Dresses: How Anti-Ambushing Laws Lose the Plot

Mention was made (in Chap. 2) of the claim of rights to events in the founding documents of international sports federations like FIFA (compare Article 74 of the FIFA Statutes currently in force at the time of writing). The organisation has been described as 'both the world governing body of association football and the lawful owner of the world-wide Marketing Rights, Media Rights and all other commercial rights in respect of the [World Cup] Competition.'[184] In determining the protected status of the publicity value of an event like the football World Cup it is submitted that this last statement must be interrogated more closely. The reader should remember that in terms of the current state of the law in most jurisdictions FIFA holds no property right to the event. The marketing rights referred to are simply a restatement of the fact that FIFA has the 'right' (i.e. is free) to create contractual rights in respect of sponsors and commercial partners. One observer pointed out, in the context of FIFA's 2010 World Cup, that South African law does not recognize a legally protectable 'marketing right' as such.[185] The underlying 'property' that forms the basis of such contracts and the rights they purport to create are intellectual property (i.e. the licensing of the use of copyright-protected material and registered trademarks) as well as common law remedies such as unlawful competition and passing off (i.e. FIFA's 'marketing rights' are 'rights' because the organization may (and does) prosecute civil claims in cases of unauthorized representations of association with the events). 'Media rights' are similarly based in contract—FIFA is not the 'author' of broadcasts relating to its events, but the copyright which would in terms of our law vest in the official broadcaster (who creates the copyrighted work) is, by means of an assignment in the broadcasting contract between FIFA and the broadcaster, automatically transferred to FIFA.[186]

Accordingly, it should be clear that such a claim of rights in the founding documents of an organization like FIFA does not create for itself a property right to the event or its publicity value. Apart from the intellectual property (e.g.

---

[184] In the preamble to the 2010 FIFA World Cup South Africa By-laws as published by the eThekwini Municipality for the host city of Durban.

[185] See Burrell, T 'FIFA's money grab a blatant foul', *Daily News*, 12 April 2010.

[186] Provided that the arrangement with any non-employee production crew/commentators contains appropriate copyright assignments (in terms of s 21(1)(e) of the South African Copyright Act 98 of 1978, for example), the broadcaster will normally be the first owner of the copyright in the broadcast (and accordingly the rights holder in respect of broadcasting of the live event footage and of highlights or clips). The event owner could obtain an assignment of the copyright arising from the broadcaster's production of match footage (which would be contained in the broadcasting rights contract), in return for the granting of a limited license to broadcast the event footage (See Lewis and Taylor 2007, p. 683). Such an assignment of copyright is the norm in broadcast rights license agreements, and copyright normally subsists in the relevant sports federation.

trademarks or copyright-protected broadcasts) and protection of goodwill by means of e.g. passing off claims, the 'marketing rights' that FIFA claims are in terms of the privity of contract not enforceable against third parties. These organizations, however, manage to obtain legislative legitimization of such 'rights', as mentioned throughout this book, by means of anti-ambush marketing legislation in the different jurisdictions. The reader should be under no illusions that this is due to sugar-coated 'lobbying': such legislation is obtained through straightforward pressure ('strong-arming') on governments in the bidding process for major events—the protection is demanded as a prerequisite for awarding of hosting rights (as discussed in Chap. 4). And, apparently, it does not end once the bid has been successful. FIFA was throughout the 5 years preceding the 2010 event credited with an apparent 'Plan B' in respect of the 2010 World Cup (Brazil and Australia were at different times rumoured to be potential alternate venues). South Africa's preparation for the event at all times proceeded under the proverbial dangling sword of Damocles, and Brazil currently seems to be in a similar position.

Viewed in the context of prohibitions on 'intrusion ambushing', sports governing bodies' justification for anti-ambush marketing efforts—namely the argument that the protection of sponsorship exclusivity is crucial for the attraction of sponsors and the consequent ability to stage such events—appears to be an assumption that big sponsorship money is required to create the publicity value of events. In my view this is fallacious: While the amount of hype (and, accordingly, the publicity value) surrounding an event is clearly influenced in part by the size and scope of the event, the real core of the publicity value of major sporting events lies in the actual nature and purpose of the event—i.e. the fact that an event like the football World Cup represents the pinnacle of international competition in the sport and produces, every 4 years, a world champion. It appears that the financial justification argument loses sight of the *raison d'etre* of such events, which has a very significant public domain character. Publicity value of the event is, of course, essential to the sponsors, as their investment requires publicity in order to market the product or service. It is, however, questionable whether (or to what extent) the objective of throwing lots of money at an event in order to increase its marketing value can or should serve to legitimize such a far-reaching prohibition on personal freedoms as contained in legislative provisions such as section 15A of South Africa's Merchandise Marks Act. One must again consider the fact that there is no requirement as to a representation of an association contained in section 15A(2), and that other jurisdictions are less willing to criminalise conduct by a trader which does not go this far. Compare the finding of the Delhi High Court in India in the matter of *ICC Development (International) Ltd v Arvee Enterprises & Philips*,[187] where Philips had offered ICC Cricket World Cup 2003 tickets in a promotional campaign. The court held that there was no likelihood of confusion that Philips was a sponsor of the event (which they weren't), and dismissed passing off and unfair trading claims. In respect of the practice of intrusion ambush

[187] 2003 (26) P.T.C. 245 (Del.).

marketing, the court held that this practice was distinguishable from passing off, as there is no element of deceit in intrusion ambush marketing but merely opportunistic commercial exploitation of an event. The court held that this is not contrary to the public interest, and that as long as an official sponsor's trademarks are not used, ambush marketing is not illegal and it is in line with commercial advertising as free speech in terms of the Indian Constitution.[188]

In its efforts to challenge ambush marketing before the South African courts, FIFA consistently claimed that it is the publicity value and goodwill of the World Cup event which is in fact being infringed. For example, in the *Metcash* matter[189] FIFA claimed that its World Cup tournaments have received significant publicity and public interest in South Africa and that, as a result of an enormous repute and goodwill in the 2010 event, there are 'strong common law rights in that event', which vest in FIFA.[190] One must, however, also ask, as I have done above, whether the publicity value of such an event is properly to be considered the exclusive property of the event organiser, and whether there is a legal basis for the legislative prohibition on deriving 'special promotional benefit' (e.g. also through mere allusion to the event[191]) from such an event. It is my view that there are some major impediments in the way of a claim to exclusive ownership of or entitlement to the publicity value of an event by the event organiser and/or its commercial partners. These include the following:

- Legal systems, generally, do not recognise a property right to the spectacle of a sporting event;
- In respect of the publicity value (and goodwill) of a major event, one must consider to what extent such publicity value is due solely to the efforts of the organisers; in this regard, the considerable role of public funding, infrastructure development etc. by host governments must be taken into account in determining the extent to which major events and their publicity value may be (at least partly) in the public domain;
- One must also consider the nature of the events, and the extent to which e.g. football's pinnacle of international competition resides in the public domain. This is in fact recognised by regulators in other contexts—compare the listing of major events as events of public interest in terms of sports broadcasting rights regulations, in order to prevent exclusive broadcasting rights to such events being sold to pay TV operators and to ensure access for the masses; and
- Finally, in light of the above analogy to the common law tort of misappropriation of a rival's product, one should consider whether or the extent to which 'intrusion ambushing' conduct (i.e. a marketing campaign in which reference is made to a protected event without claiming or causing confusion regarding the existence of an association with such event) constitutes filching of publicity or

188 Vassallo et al. 2005, p. 1347.

189 See discussion in Sect. 4.4.5 of Chap. 4.

190 At par. 11.1 of FIFA's heads of argument in the *Metcash* matter.

191 See Merchandise Marks Act section 15A(3).

mere reference to information which is (or should properly be) in the public domain—it is submitted that the catch-22 scenario that confronts an organisation such as FIFA is that its substantial efforts to market the World Cup as the world's biggest sporting event in fact causes such event to be extremely newsworthy. The sporting event becomes a major international event, and it attracts publicity as a result.

It should be noted that sporting mega-events hold the potential for increasing economic activity and for expanding economic investment in multiple areas (not only limited to infrastructure development and the construction of world-class stadia). Indeed, this is often touted in justification for the public funding required to host such events—compare the South African experience in respect of FIFA's World Cup. In this regard, it is interesting to note the following sentiments as expressed by the European Sponsorship Association (or ESA)[192]:

> [We believe] that protection should not be provided for the financial interests of a small number of major brands and events at the expense of wider economic benefits and indeed sponsors of other entities. Major events traditionally give rise to a large upswing in marketing spend across the board, with advertising campaigns themed around the event and a range of opportunities to exploit sponsorships of other properties that are not officially related to the event itself. Specific anti-ambush legislation should not be allowed to stifle the financial "dividend" generated in the wider economy generally, especially where the host nation has had to invest specifically in order to stage the event.

Mega-events, arguably, serve to stimulate such a financial dividend in the wider economy and, as such, stimulate trade. It is submitted that the legitimacy of limitations on the freedom of trade of individuals who attempt to reap the benefits of such dividend through otherwise legal and unobjectionable conduct (compare the 'intrusion ambushers') should be examined against this backdrop, and the rationale of protection of the public interest and common good which must underlie a justifiable limitation of the freedom of trade should be paramount.

While there may, therefore, be some grounds for justifying draconian anti-ambushing laws and their aggressive enforcement, these laws generally lose the plot when it comes to the more problematic forms of 'ambush marketing'. Strong legislative prohibitions may not seem overly problematic when viewed against the backdrop of what has been experienced in some jurisdictions in recent times in respect of blatant *association* ambush marketing, but it should be remembered that association ambushes would usually in any event constitute unlawful conduct that is prohibited in terms of either the common law or specific (e.g. IP) legislation, and which can (*should?*) be pursued in terms of such remedies. Scaria, in discussing potential competition law issues in respect of anti-ambush marketing protection, observes as follows:

> [E]ven the pro-competition bloc would appreciate the [anti-ambush marketing] restrictions which seem reasonable in light of the economic investments made by the sponsors and in

[192] From the European Sponsorship Association's *Position Statement on Ambush Marketing*, 14 October 2005.

> the necessity of defending the sponsorship value of an event. It is also essential not to overlook the very fact that most of the sponsorship contracts are awarded through a process of open bidding. Moreover, competition law by itself permits restrictions on false and misleading advertisements … If ambush marketing advertisements are considered as misleading advertisements, the regulations on such advertisements shall not fall within the purview of competition law.[193]

I have no objections to special anti-ambushing legislation to enforce existing common law protections, with the objective of addressing the practical hurdles posed by such traditional protection (e.g. the need for speedy procedures when faced with a mega-event with a limited window of exploitation in respect of association ambushing). The situation assumes a very different aspect, however, when one considers the fact that what may be termed 'intrusion ambushes' of events do not, necessarily, raise any concerns regarding the ethics or legality of the alleged 'ambusher's' conduct. A marketer can surely run a very successful marketing campaign through reference to a major event without actually deceiving (or even attempting to deceive) the public regarding an association with such event. An advertisement by Italian olive oil producer, Bertolli, during the 2006 FIFA World Cup—'If Italy wins over Ghana on June 12, Bertolli reimburses your groceries bought on that day'—did not offend the domestic laws.[194] Would it fly in other jurisdictions in the face of stringent 'association rights' and *sui generis* anti-ambushing legislation? What of the Indian restaurant owner who prior to the 2011 ICC cricket World Cup converted his restaurant 'into a cricket stadium', with a menu especially designed in a cricket theme for the World Cup?[195] Are we mad when we imagine such conduct as 'ambush marketing', something that the law should prohibit and for which civil remedies or even criminal sanctions are to be provided? The event organisers love to claim rights to sell approval of any 'association' with their events. Another word that has cropped up is 'affiliation'—compare the definition of ambush marketing as found in the agreement between the South African Football Association and FIFA for the organisation of the 2010 FIFA World Cup as meaning 'marketing, promotional, advertising and public relations activities in words, sound or any other form relating to the Championship, which are intended to capitalize on any form of association with the Championship, but which are undertaken by a person or an entity which has not been granted the right to *promote an affiliation* with the Championship by FIFA'.[196] A dictionary meaning of 'affiliation' is 'to associate oneself' or 'to become closely connected or associated' with something.[197] Do cricket-themed restaurant decor or a

[193] Scaria 2008, p. 118.

[194] Kobel 2007, p. 50.

[195] See the short report available online at the time of writing at http://www.andhranews.net/India/2011/Lucknow-restaurateur-promotes-World-Cup-themed-1749.htm.

[196] As quoted in *M&G Media Ltd v 2010 FIFA World Cup South Africa Organising Committee Ltd* South Gauteng High Court Case No. 09/51422 (unreported at the time of writing) at par. 108 note 42.

[197] According to the Free Online Dictionary at http://www.thefreedictionary.com/affiliation.

grocery give-away if a national team wins a World Cup match constitute attempts to 'promote an affiliation' with the relevant event? I would suggest such an implication is absurd; its outlawing by means of even criminal sanctions in special event legislation is obscene.

Reference was made (in Chap. 3) to a recent attempt by Chadwick and Burton[198] to classify ambush marketing into three main categories of conduct, each containing specific types of ambushing activities. It appears, however, that, generally-speaking, the type of activity which I am referring to here where reference is made to an event but not with the intention to deceive and simply in order to capitalise on the public's interest and the publicity value created by the event, does not seem to fit comfortably within any of the different types of ambushes described by these authors. The closest would seem to be some form of hybrid between what they call 'saturation ambushing' (where the marketer increases its advertising and marketing at the time of an event, but makes no reference to the event itself and avoids any associative imagery or suggestion) and 'associative ambushing' (the use of imagery or terminology to create an allusion that an organization has links to a sporting event or property). Clearly, however, these two types of ambushing appear to be mutually exclusive; the one involves no attempt to refer to an event, and the other very clearly does. This appears to highlight a gap in the suggested classification—it is submitted that a marketer may very likely wish to increase its marketing activities at the time of an event (in order to capitalize on the public's excitement and potentially increased susceptibility to advertising), and may also want to do so by referring to the event but without in any way attempting (or intending to attempt) to show a link to such event. These are the especially problematic cases, I would submit, i.e. the ones where the marketer is simply trying to tap into publicity surrounding the event and the climate for marketing created by it. I would argue that event organisers and rights holders cannot or should not be able to legitimately challenge such activity as constituting 'ambushing' of the event; at worst such marketing may lead to clutter in the marketing environment (which appears to be something that event organisers and official sponsors are often guilty of achieving without any help from 'ambushers'), but in the absence of an intention to deceive consumers or misappropriation of property such marketing should not be open to challenge. More emphatically, it should not form the subject of legislative criminalisation or potential civil liability in terms of anti-ambushing legislation.

By no means am I advocating the practice of 'intrusion ambushing'—I personally often find these TV ads and other such marketing efforts rather irritating. However, I am in favour of 'intrusion ambushers'' freedom to trade by producing such ads. The above consideration coupled with the severe—and yes, I will pointedly use the word 'draconian'—limitations on the rights and freedoms of

[198] Simon Chadwick & Nicholas Burton 'Ambushed' in *The Wall Street Journal*, 25 January 2010—available online at the time of writing at http://online.wsj.com/article/SB1000142405 2970204731804574391102699362862.html#articleTabs%3Dcomments.

individuals, business entities and entrepreneurs, forces one to ask whether such legislation does not in fact constitute an abomination of the very values and ideals underlying our developmental state and constitutional democracy.

I refer elsewhere[199] to the fact that American marketing expert Kim Skildum-Reid has suggested that event organisers simply cannot protect their rights holders against all forms of 'ambushing'. This is especially true of the type of marketing that I've described above. Her suggestion is that sports organisations and official sponsors should bite the bullet and rather focus their energies on better leveraging of the rights sold and acquired, in what she refers to as capitalising on the total 'event experience'. This view sounds eminently sensible and worthy of further investigation, and I hope that others will take up the call to do so.

Events during the early days of the 2010 football World Cup (in the week of 14 June 2010) made headlines worldwide and promised a potential diplomatic row between the Netherlands and South Africa, when FIFA filed criminal charges against two Dutch nationals in the country over an alleged ambush marketing campaign by Dutch beer maker Bavaria NV.[200] According to reports, Bavaria allegedly sent two Dutch nationals to South Africa to recruit (through a local promotions company) 36 young ladies, who attended the first-round match between the Netherlands and Denmark in Soccer City in Johannesburg as a group wearing orange 'Dutchy' dresses (which had been handed out in Bavaria gift packs in Holland ahead of the World Cup) bearing Bavaria's logo on a small purple tag on the side near the hemline. The Bavaria beer-maker was, of course, not an official sponsor (Budweiser was an event sponsor and Heineken a sponsor of the Dutch team). The women were reportedly escorted from the stadium by security staff during the second half of the match and, allegedly, interrogated by FIFA officials for three hours at nearby FIFA offices. The two Dutch women were subsequently arrested on charges of contravening the Merchandise Marks Act and provisions of the 2010 FIFA World Cup South Africa Special Measures Act,[201] and released on bail (pending trial in the Johannesburg Magistrates Court's 'special FIFA World Cup court'). It was reported at the time that the women had instructed a local firm of attorneys and were contemplating legal action against FIFA and the police, alleging that they were warned not to run as they might get shot, and that their hotel room was allegedly searched without a warrant and that personal items were taken.[202]

---

[199] See the section that follows in the text.

[200] During the previous FIFA World Cup in Germany in 2006, a similar episode occurred when approximately a thousand male fans who were clothed in orange lederhosen—also, reportedly, supplied by Bavaria—were asked to strip out of the outfits or leave the stadium during a Netherlands/Ghana match. A number of the fans reportedly stayed to watch the match in their underwear.

[201] The women were apparently charged with engaging in 'unauthorised commercial activities inside an exclusion zone' and 'enter[ing] into a designated area while in unauthorized possession of a commercial object'.

[202] From a report in Afrikaans newspaper *Beeld*, 18 June 2010.

The Netherlands government slammed the conduct of FIFA and of the SA Police Services for singling out the Dutch nationals and also for proceeding against the individuals involved rather than against Bavaria, with Dutch Foreign Minister Maxime Verhagen characterizing the arrests as 'disproportionate and not correct'. FIFA responded by reiterating its aggressive anti-ambush marketing stance and by stating that it had warned businesses prior to the event that it would clamp down on any attempts to ambush the event. While, at least according to reports, it appears that these events stemmed from a concerted and well-planned marketing campaign by Bavaria, it is submitted that they highlight the potential for rather absurd results through the confluence of anti-ambushing legislation such as that found in South Africa and the attitude of an organization like FIFA to its aggressive enforcement. In years gone by an episode of this nature would have prompted little more than a chuckle from right-minded persons and a small measure of admiration for a creative and colourful marketing campaign that added some spice to a major sporting event and its hype (especially at a time when the quality of football on the pitch during the opening round of the tournament had been rather disappointing). This might have been a case which could be described as 'the sort of situation where one pauses for a moment to laugh, and acknowledge the lateral thinking involved'.[203] In this day and age, however, it appears that the colour of one's dress could augur a lengthy jail term; one might be forced to exchange an orange mini-skirt for an orange prison jumpsuit because Budweiser happens to have a multimillion dollar contract with FIFA.

After vocal outrage from a number of sources following media reports of the criminal case against the two Dutch nationals, it was announced on 23 June 2010 that the National Prosecuting Authority had decided to abandon the prosecution, as FIFA had reportedly reached a settlement in the matter and 'had no further interest' in the prosecution of those involved. The settlement in this matter might reflect the fact that FIFA realised it was, with a criminal prosecution, less likely to triumph as it had managed to do through its top class and expensive local legal team in the civil suits that were pursued in South Africa against 'small fry' ambushers:

> Criminal sanctions were perhaps less popular as they can be imposed only if the court is satisfied beyond reasonable doubt that the marketer both intended to breach, and in fact breached, the ambush marketing provisions. The cynical view is that the criminal complaint procedure was less popular as it afforded FIFA less control over the handling and outcome of the case.[204]

It appears that the controversial events were belatedly recognized as a rather embarrassing publicity *faux pas* for the football governing body and South African prosecuting authorities, and was probably dropped for that reason. Not unexpectedly, Internet bloggers had a field day in blasting FIFA ('You don't talk back to Grandma, you don't argue with a bum, and you don't ever, ever, under any

---

[203] As per McGechan J in *New Zealand Olympics and Commonwealth Games Association v Telecom New Zealand Ltd* (1996) T.C.L.R. 167 at pp. 172, 173.

[204] Haman and Marriott 2010, p. 76.

circumstances, kick three dozen beautiful women out of a party…') and praising Bavaria ('Bavaria agreed to make no further comments on the matter, but if they could harness the power of smirks, they'd never need to pay another electric bill').[205] In fact, the FIFA/Bavaria *contretemps* was such a visible and highly-publicised one, that it gave rise to a rather half-baked (and ultimately thwarted) copy-cat 'ambush' in the run-up to the 2011 IRB Rugby World Cup at a Super 15 rugby match at the Eden Park stadium in Auckland, involving a number of young women dressed all in black (All Black?) who allegedly planned to take off their tracksuits to reveal 'skimpy clothing' branded with the logo of a rival to an official sponsor.[206] It appears that the Bavaria babes also inspired the owner of the *Mermaid* strip club in Wellington. Scantily clad women in stilettos and New Zealand All Blacks uniforms emblazoned with silver ferns handed out two-for-one flyers to male rugby fans after the city's first tournament match in the 2011 IRB Rugby World Cup (between South Africa and Wales on 11 September 2011). The flyers were distributed on the Wellington Regional Stadium concourse and at Wellington railway station, both designated 'clean zone' areas for the event. The club received a warning letter a few days later from the police, Wellington City Council and the Economic Development Ministry, accusing it of breaching the Major Events Management Act and a bylaw relating to sex industry advertising. The *Sydney Morning Herald* reported that the letter, which was at the time confirmed to be the only official warning issued in New Zealand regarding ambushing during the tournament, threatened that 'prosecution action will be considered should you engage in any further advertising or promotional activity within, or visible from, the Wellington Regional Stadium clean zone during the declared clean periods around future Rugby World Cup matches'.[207]

American marketing and sponsorship guru, Kim Skildum-Reid, has been rather direct and scathing in her assessment of FIFA's response to the Bavaria babes (and has included her opinion on the most effective way for event organisers to deal with ambushes of this nature):

> Good on you, FIFA! You've turned an inconsequential, cosmetic ambush into the biggest sponsorship story of the World Cup. Actually, FIFA's reaction was so predictable (as are all the various World Cup organisers and the IOC) that Bavaria was probably banking on FIFA to do all the heavy lifting for them! All the while, Nike is running rampant with viral video that actually is creating marketing value for them and reducing the effectiveness of Adidas' sponsorship. Wake up, organisers! It's time to stop dwelling on the inconsequential and start tackling the big issues in ambush marketing. When the ICC (Cricket's

---

205 See the blog by Victor Ozols on *Black Book*, 22 June 2010, available online at the time of writing at http://www.blackbookmag.com/article/drink-bavaria-the-new-official-beer-of-the-2010-fifa-world-cup/19949.

206 Savage, J 'Officials ready for Rugby World Cup ambush marketing' *New Zealand Herald*, 8 September 2011—available online at http://www.nzherald.co.nz/business/news/article.cfm?c_id=3&objectid=10750200.

207 See Miller, Mark J 'Rugby World Cup goes after strip bar for ambush marketing, posted 5 October 2011 at http://www.brandchannel.com/home/post/2011/10/05/Rugby-World-Cup-Strip-Bar-Ambush-Marketing.aspx.

global ruling body) started going through fans' coolers and dumping out their Coca-Colas, it made Cricket World Cup sponsor, Pepsi, look like a spoil sport. When organisers of major events make fans turn their T-shirts inside out, it makes both the organisers and the sponsors look petty and mean. Why do organisers do this? Because at least it looks like they're doing something. What they're not doing, however, is stopping the kind of ambush that hurts their sponsors. To do that would require them to admit that they can't control it, tell their sponsors that great leverage is their best defence, and to work and be flexible with those sponsors to find leverage ideas that will work across the entire event experience. Do I think this will ever happen? No, because being pedantic sabre-rattlers is easier.[208]

Skildum-Reid believes that event organisers like FIFA can do little to stop ambushes of this nature which are technically not in contravention of laws[209] (except, of course, where such conduct may contravene the draconian and far-reaching type of legislation as that passed in South Africa). Her suggestion is that the most rational response should be for the rights grantors to assist rights holders to more successfully leverage such rights in respect of what she refers to as the 'whole event experience':

Major events can't protect you. No matter what they say, the IOC, FIFA, or any other major event cannot protect a sponsor from ambush marketing. They can and should protect their rights and the immediate event, but they don't control the event experience. That experience is controlled and owned by the people, the fans, and the winner will be the brand that is most meaningful, most creative, and adds the most value to those fans. You don't need a high-priced TV schedule for that. All you really need is a lot of creativity and some strong communication channels—they could be product packaging, in-store activities, social media, and many many more.[210]

Sports marketing expert, Benoit Seguin, also observes that proper leveraging of the 'official' nature of an event sponsor's rights can be a powerful tool against potential ambushers, as he explains with reference to an example from Canada:

[S]ponsorship is the only way to have "authentic" association and sponsors must be strategic in providing promotional programs that take advantage of this 'authenticity'. This strategy was used by General Mills during the 2000 and 2002 Olympic Games. A Canadian Olympic Committee sponsor, General Mills leveraged its sponsorship by sponsoring "Team Cheerios" which consisted of a group of selected Olympians featured on cereal boxes (Cheerios). This included pictures, bios, and personal stories of the athletes. This was an excellent way for consumers to discover the athletes and 'connect' with them on a personal level. While competitor Kellogg's cereal brand "Victor" secured television

[208] From a posting ('How the World Cup ambushed itself', 18 June 2010) on Kim Skildum-Reid's blog at http://blog.powersponsorship.com.

[209] Shwetashree Majumder and Harsimran Kalra (writing in 'The ambush marketing debate', on the web site *Managing Intellectual Property*, 1 September 2010—available online at the time of writing at http://www.managingip.com/Article/2665113/The-ambush-marketing-debate.html?ArticleId = 2665113&p = 2) refer to the Bavaria stunt as an example of cases of ambushing by means of the use of trade dress, colours and other forms of association (i.e. less blatant forms of ambushing, which are harder to combat in terms of traditional IP laws)).

[210] From a comment posted by Skildum-Reid to an article by Chadwick, S and Burton, N 'Ambushed' in *The Wall Street Journal*, 25 January 2010—available online at the time of writing at http://online.wsj.com/article/SB10001424052970204731804574391102699362862.html#articleTabs%3Dcomments.

> advertising rights for both Olympics, General Mills' strategy was focused at the retail.[General Mills marketing agency's founder, Keith McIntyre, is quoted as explaining:] "We worked closely at developing relationships with key accounts at the retail, making sure they understood that we held the authentic association with the Olympic rings, the Games and the athletes, we owned the space!"[211]

The merits of this above-described approach appear to be borne out by the responses to a 2010 marketing survey conducted amongst leading sports marketers and executives from sports organisations and corporate sponsors.[212] 'Strategic activation' of sponsorships utilises the secret weapon at the disposal of those with 'official' status and rights:

> Official sponsors have a variety of defences at their disposal, the appropriate combination being unique to the type of property and violations they face. According to many of the marketing executives interviewed, going on the offensive with strategic activation of the sponsorship is the best protection against ambushing and copyright infringement—because official sponsors still have access to exclusive property content and intellectual property, they have the opportunity to create a level of authenticity that ambushers just cannot replicate.[213]

In light of the clear dangers inherent in the unchecked development of laws which facilitate such controversial incidents as FIFA's response to the Bavaria babes, it is submitted that there exists a very real (and, in my opinion, already thoroughly realized) danger that legislatures' bowing under what amounts to legalised extortion in respect of the enactment of legislative protections for what sports governing bodies claim as their own, simply serves to increase the demands of these same bodies to wider and wider protection. Johnson is of the view that this is indeed already the case (in respect of his criticism of 'vertical and horizontal creep' in the development of specific anti-ambushing legislation in different jurisdictions and in respect of different sporting events)[214] and I would suggest that a fruitful analogy can be drawn to criticism that has been expressed elsewhere regarding the protection of celebrity by means of the right of publicity in the USA:

> Granting property rights in fame is a dangerous proposition in no small part because celebrities tend to be control freaks … As their egos expand, so do their publicity rights. They conceive of their rights as granting them permission to ban any cultural expressions that tread on their alleged identity.[215]

---

211 Seguin, B '"Sponsorship in the trenches": Case study evidence of its legitimate place in the marketing mix' *The Sport Journal*—available online at http://www.thesportjournal.org/article/sponsorship-trenches-case-study-evidence-its-legitimate-place-promotional-mix.

212 A survey conducted by the Chief Marketing Officer (CMO) Council (a six-month qualitative and quantitative research campaign, 'Doing Away With Foul Play in Sports Marketing', aimed at sensitising sports sponsors and franchises to trademark trespassing, property rights violations and online scams, frauds and infringements) with the assistance of MarkMonitor. The CMO Council surveyed more than 180 senior-level sports marketers across relevant industries for an assessment of how brands are safeguarding themselves and whether those measures are effective. The study also drew from interviews with executives at top leagues and corporate sponsors.

213 Gannon 2010, p. 69.

214 See, generally, Johnson 2008, and the discussion in Chap. 4 .

215 Bollier 2005, at p. 135.

And I am reminded also, especially if one considers the 'Streisand effect' that appears to occur so often in respect of the highly-publicised anti-ambushing activities of an organisation such as FIFA, of the strongly worded comments made by Michele Boldrin and David Levine in the context of the 'evil of intellectual monopoly' in respect of abuse of IP laws:

> "Being a monopolist" is, apparently, akin to going on drugs or joining some strange religious sect. It seems to lead to complete loss of any sense of what profitable opportunities are and of how free markets function. Monopolists, apparently, can conceive of only one way of making money, and that is by bullying consumers and competitors to put up and shut up. Furthermore, it also appears to mean that past mistakes have to be repeated at a larger, and ever more ridiculous, scale.[216]

It is submitted that the time has come to say to the large international sports governing bodies that they will no longer be allowed to derive a mandate from the sport-supporting public to host events that are dependent on the support of such public, but in the same breath attempt to monopolise any and all commercial opportunities arising from such events and restrict members of the public from deriving any benefit apart from access to the spectacle, for which they of course have to pay (sometimes exorbitant ticket prices). And, more emphatically, the law should not be allowed to be abused as a means of protecting and maintaining such monopolies whilst the base generation of profits for a powerful few appears to be its main objective. We might find some guidance in the approach suggested by the European Sponsorship Association[217]:

> [We recognise] that major sporting and other events are a key element of modern culture and it is wrong to give an event organiser a complete monopoly over any references or allusions to the event. Major events have to operate along the lines of commercial businesses in order to fund themselves, but they are also part of a shared set of human experiences in the public domain. Companies, brand owners and their representatives should be allowed to refer to such events, provided that (a) intellectual property rights are respected; (b) official status is not implied when none exists; and (c) the reference is not unlawful in some other way (e.g. libellous, in breach of contract etc.).

However, while this suggestion does, I believe, constitute an approach to which we should aspire, it appears that very few members of the legal community have to date bothered to engage with some of the more sticky issues regarding the legitimacy of anti-ambush marketing measures and practices. This appears to be true, especially, in respect of governments and legislatures in the different jurisdictions. It is beyond the scope of this book to investigate the extent (if any) to which the South African government conducted an in-depth investigation into the pros and cons of adopting the relevant anti-ambush marketing legislation prior to the 2003 ICC Cricket World Cup or in the process (in terms of section 15A(1) of the MMA)

---

[216] Boldrin and Levine 2008, p. 89.

[217] In its *Position Statement on Ambush Marketing*, 14 October 2005.

of declaring the 2010 FIFA World Cup South Africa as a protected event.[218]. While the Minister of Trade and Industry may for all that I know be in possession of a lengthy report stating that the 2010 FIFA World Cup is 'in the public interest and … [that] the organisers have created sufficient opportunities for small businesses and in particular those of the previously disadvantaged communities' to benefit from the event,[219] I would suggest that the curious reader might want to poll the opinions of the various taxi associations (who had been involved in ongoing protest action against the South African government's unilateral imposition of a new Bus Rapid Transit system in the run-up to FIFA's event), informal street traders and the homeless (who were largely *persona non grata* in eight of South Africa's major cities in June and July 2010) and the owners of pubs, restaurants and other establishments that faced stiff liquor license fees for a special dispensation to screen World Cup matches while their patrons knock back a few. An undated government publicity document on preparations for the 2010 FIFA World Cup (circa 2008)[220] contains the following:

> Government aims for the [small and medium-sized enterprises] sector to benefit from the 2010 World Cup. The Department of Trade and Industry is supporting the SME sector to access economic benefits and opportunities brought by the 2010 FIFA World Cup™. Government negotiated that 30% of the budget of the Organising Committee should be allocated to Black Economic Empowerment and SMEs in terms of procurement policy.

The South African government has for more than a decade now enforced a so-called 'Broad-based Black Economic Empowerment programme' in terms of special legislation, which is aimed at addressing previous economic disadvantage caused by Apartheid. Even though there has been sustained criticism of the often mythical 'broad-based' credentials of this programme from various quarters, in respect of government procurement processes (and the nearly daily media reports on the activities of politically-connected 'tenderpreneurs' and the establishment of an ever-growing new black elite in the face of seriously defective service delivery by those awarded these government tenders), it is submitted that it is doubtful

---

[218] With specific reference to the proviso contained in s 15A(1)(b). Compare the following requirement for the declaration of a 'major event' in terms of s 7(4) of New Zealand's Major Events Management Act 2007:

'(4) Before making a recommendation [to the Governor-General to declare an event as a major event], the Economic Development Minister must take into account whether the event will—
(a) attract a large number of international participants or spectators and therefore generate significant tourism opportunities for New Zealand;
(b) significantly raise New Zealand's international profile;
(c) require a high level of professional management and coordination;
(d) attract significant sponsorship and international media coverage;
(e) attract large numbers of New Zealanders as participants or spectators;
(f) offer substantial sporting, cultural, social, economic, or other benefits for New Zealand or New Zealanders

[219] Merchandise Marks Act section 15A(1)(b).

[220] *Key Facts: Government Preparations for the 2010 FIFA World Cup South Africa*™.

whether the above initiative, in itself, satisfies the requirements for the designation of an event as 'protected' in terms of section 15A(1)(b) of the Merchandise Marks Act. I also recall controversy following media reports in February 2010 that the contract to produce toy figurines of the official 2010 FIFA World Cup mascot, Zakumi, had been outsourced to a reported sweat shop in China. The local South African contractor who had been awarded the contract is an African National Congress (ruling party) member of Parliament (ironically, a member of Parliament's economic development committee—tasked with the creation of new workplaces in South Africa—whose parliamentary profile reads 'We need more opportunities in order to bring more opportunities into the country').[221] It is suggested that the real experience of job creation and commercial opportunities for small and medium-sized enterprises in respect of the 2010 event has been largely illusive and, in this observer's opinion, does not play much of a role in tipping the scales in the determination of justification for the substantial limitations imposed on traders in terms of the anti-ambushing legislation. The interested reader is strongly advised to read a recently released monograph published by the Institute for Security Studies in South Africa regarding conflicts of interest and reported corruption regarding the 2010 FIFA World Cup, which makes for fascinating reading.[222]

In a 2007 ambush marketing legislation review conducted for the Australian government[223] the following was observed regarding the issues to be considered in respect of the passing of specific anti-ambush marketing legislation:

> Calls for legislative intervention in relation to sports and major event marketing generate two key questions:
>
> **What types of ambush marketing should be regulated?**
>
> This question involves the allocation of rights and the enforcement of rights. In allocating rights, there are clear trade-offs. As the set of rights allocated to the organisers of an event is widened, the set of rights allocated to other persons is narrowed. The government has to make a decision as to what might be a reasonable allocation of rights between different groups. The re-allocation and enforcement of rights may be a way of dealing with *perceived* problems of ambush marketing. However, governments need to consider whether the perceived problems justify the intervention, and whether legislation is the best option for addressing the problem. Other factors might also have a bearing on these questions, such as a host agreement in which an event's governing body requires certain protection of intellectual property and marketing activity for a country to stage an event.
>
> **How should legislative intervention be crafted?**
>
> Having identified that there is a need for legislation, the next stage is to determine the best way to respond to that need. The government has to decide, for instance: whether event-specific or general legislation would be more effective; the scope of the exclusive

---

[221] From a report entitled 'Zakumi, Proudly South African?' on *The Budapest Report*, 3 February 2010.

[222] Schulz-Herzenberg 2010.

[223] Frontier Economics 2007, pp. 20, 21.

> rights provided to the event organiser, including the range of subject matter protected; the limits of those exclusive rights, and the framing of any exemptions. The principal concern is in ensuring that provisions achieve their stated goals, but not in a way that unduly or unfairly affects the rights of third parties… [D]espite its pejorative connotations, the term 'ambush marketing' is used to cover a broad range of activities that include practices that are perhaps rightly not the concern of the law or may not justify government regulation.

Ditto. I have touched on issues such as the constitutionality of anti-ambushing measures (in respect of e.g. guarantees of freedom of expression) and their potential anti-competitive impact, but little critical work has been done in this regard. For example, the following is found in a relatively recent multi-national survey on the combating of ambush marketing, which covered a number of European and other jurisdictions:

> [The above-mentioned issues] are still relatively unexplored. Writings on ambush marketing are usually more driven towards fighting ambush marketing for the benefit of sport. Writings and decisions on antitrust issues have usually focused on issues pertaining to the transfer of players, collective bargaining of TV rights and a few abuse of dominance cases in relation to the exploitation of rights related to an event. None really focused on sponsoring activities and the exclusivity granted to sponsors. As a result, not much was reported on these issues in the surveyed countries.[224]

It is sincerely hoped that much more attention will be paid to such matters, if only in order to introduce serious consideration of these issues into the mainstream of thinking in the major events hosting bid processes. This might go some way towards guaranteeing more legal challenges in future to the (what I submit to be) largely unquestioned abuse of power by major sports federations and their pin-stripe-suited money men. At the very least, I believe that powerful reasons exist for demanding wider public consultation in future before any decisions are taken to bid for sports mega-events. The lack of clear evidence of tangible benefits from the hosting of such events does little to justify draconian anti-ambushing laws or their aggressive enforcement in situations where it appears as if everyone, including event organisers, host governments and even security forces, may have lost the plot.

8.6 Counting the Costs of Such Legislation in the Greater Scheme of the Hosting of Mega-Events

When considering the legitimacy of anti-ambushing protection we are squarely confronted with the effects of such measures on the interests of the broader public, as I have touched on above. Just two such potential effects are evident in the discussion of the anti-competitive effects of anti-ambushing legislation (and the current mega-event sponsorship monopoly) in Chap. 6, and in the human rights implications discussed in Chap. 7. Inherent in event organisers' frequent claims

---

224 Kobel 2007, p. 41.

that ambushing threatens the very ability to stage mega-events is a public good argument, which appears to imply that such events are in the public interest. This argument seeks to balance the narrow commercial interests of event organisers and sponsors against the public good and the premise is that some limitation of the rights and liberties of members of the public is justified in terms of such greater good. Host governments tend to attempt to downplay the potential impact on their citizens—compare the UK government's justification of its proposed advertising and street trading regulations for the 2012 London Olympics ('We are looking to extend our regulations no further than a few hundred metres around each venue's perimeter. This amounts to around 0.01 per cent of the overall land space across England, Scotland and Wales'[225]), while at the same time enacting laws that attempt to cover a broad range of conduct (for example, regulations to prohibit street trading near event venues that are so widely drafted that it necessitates a specific exemption to cover operating an established car wash business or providing a public sanitary convenience such as a public toilet[226]). But in order to succeed with such arguments, the actual impact on the rights of members of the public must be rationally and morally justifiable, and proportional.

In essence, and as I have referred to in the earlier chapters, anti-ambushing protection of mega-events by means of an increasingly narrow ring-fencing of 'rights' to events and event-related aspects is a form of 'propertizing' intangibles. A clear example is to be found in the new statutory association rights to events. I would submit that these developments are in line with the similar way in which trademark laws have expanded upon the more traditional common law protection provided by unfair competition law. Unfair competition law enhances the function of marks by protecting a mark from imitation only to the extent that its use in the market actually identifies the goods or services of a particular firm. Trademark laws, however, have tended to expand such protection in a number of ways. For example, federal trademark laws in the United States have allowed a firm that obtains registration of a mark to suddenly become the mark's proprietor in markets that the firm has never entered and might indeed have no interest in entering. Common law ownership of a mark in one part of the country can, through registration, become effective ownership of the mark in every part of the country, with the effect of giving the mark's owner the benefit of more than has been invested, by treating the mark as carrying significance in markets where it has none.[227] I also referred, earlier in this chapter, to developments in trademark law which have significantly moved away from the traditional source of origin functions of a trademark.

If we consider, on the one hand, this carving out of matter from the public domain by such arrogation of new-fangled and dubious 'property rights', and, on

---

[225] From the UK Department of Culture, Media And Sport's consultation document on Regulations on Advertising Activity and Trading Around London 2012 March 2011 at 6—available online at the time of writing at http://www.culture.gov.uk/images/publications/ConDoc_Regulations_on_Advertising_and_Trading_London_2012-section1-7.pdf.

[226] Ibid. p. 15.

[227] Carter 1990, p. 760.

the other hand, the effects of such laws on host nation citizens, we are obliged to ask whether such laws come at too great a cost. When the South African anti-ambushing legislation calls for the Minister of Trade and Industry to determine, before declaring an event to be 'protected', whether 'the staging of the event is in the public interest and the Minister is satisfied that the organisers have created sufficient opportunities for small businesses and in particular for those of the previously disadvantaged communities',[228] it is implied that in the absence of tangible proof of such benefits the legislative protection of an event would not be justified. When we place the various elements of *sui generis* commercial protection of events in the proverbial scales of justice, there appears to be a significant imbalance. On the one side we find draconian prohibitions and substantial civil and criminal penalties for insufficiently blameworthy conduct and a lack of requirement of actual harm for those in whose interest such legislation is enacted and enforced. On the other side we find often severe curtailment of civil liberties. How can this *status quo* be in the public interest? The event organisers would have to be able to show that the restrictions imposed actually benefit not only themselves and their commercial partners, but also hold wider benefits for society at large. The benefits should not only equate to closing off the market to potential competitors by means of naked restraints or to the maximisation of commercial revenues. What we are confronted with, in practice, is the argument that such stringent anti-ambushing laws are a *sine qua non* for the very ability to host the mega-events (and, impliedly, that the staging of such events is in itself in the public interest). The second, implied, argument is one that is beyond the scope of this book (although I have touched on it in places). The first argument I will deal with in more detail in Chap. 9.

Suffice it to say that the actual social and economic benefits of stringent anti-ambushing laws are controversial and not nearly as clear-cut as the event organisers would have us believe. As troubling, however, in considering the rationality of lawmakers passing such laws is the fact that these very laws may in fact not even be in the ultimate interests of the event organisers and the sponsors. One must ask whether such stringent and far-reaching anti-ambushing laws may, on a more fundamental level in respect of determining the value of event organiser's and sponsors' rights, serve to negatively affect such rights and the commercial value of the event for these parties. Eichhorn and Sahm[229] point to the value of the image of mega-events in the public perception for the value of sponsors' rights, in the context of the under-pricing of event tickets:

> [P]ublic support for the event usually exerts some positive externality on the demand in related markets, e.g. the one for sponsorship contracts. This externality can be explained as follows. People's empathy for the event has a decisive impact on its image. The image of the event, in turn, is transferred to the sponsors' products... Put differently, public support enhances the value of the event as a platform for advertisement and hence increases the

[228] Section 15A(1)(b) of the Merchandise Marks Act, 1941, as referred to elsewhere.

[229] Eichhorn and Sahm 2010, p. 38.

> demand and revenues in the market for sponsorship contracts. If the externality is strong enough, these additional profits may well offset the decline in gate revenues. Therefore, ticket underpricing may well be optimal in order to maximize overall profits of the organizer.

They also observe:

> The entertainment industry is well aware of the fact that the degree of acceptance for an event is an important (production) factor. Considerations of public support play a role for various decisions throughout the organization of an event, from the choice of the venues over the choice of PR measures (e.g. logos and mascots) to the pricing strategies.[230]

If the public image of events has this effect on sponsors' leveraging of their rights, one must ask whether or to what extent the increasingly frequent public criticism of the draconian nature of *sui generis* event legislation and how it impacts on the liberties of ordinary people may affect the public image of the event and, consequently, in fact detract from the sponsorship value of the event. I have referred elsewhere to the fact that such strong event rights protection by means of legislation may, by providing a safety net to organisers and sponsors, contribute to the failure of these parties to properly leverage their investment in the event (as is argued, for example, by Kim Skildum-Reid, to be a prime contributor to the success of 'ambushing' of events). Demands for strong event rights protection may, paradoxically, serve to prejudicially affect the value of the event as marketing platform for sponsors, and be counter-productive. Or, it is very possible that such draconian laws are simply part of the greater profit-making strategy of event organisers. Eichhorn and Sahm argue that vastly over-subscribed mega-event tickets are often under-priced precisely because this promotes positive public sentiment regarding the event, with the ultimate objective of making rights available in the market for selling sponsorships more attractive. I also referred in the earlier chapters to the often perceived lack of common sense on the part of event organisers who aggressively enforce anti-ambushing laws, and how this may in fact be nothing more than posturing aimed at keeping the sponsors happy (both in respect of justifying the ever-escalating rights fees charged and also to comply with the guarantees provided to sponsors in respect of the exclusivity of their rights). I believe that the costs to the public play a very subordinate role to event organisers' profit motive and revenue-generating strategies. Ultimately, these laws come at too great a price.

8.7 Conclusion

This chapter has considered the legitimacy of the 'association rights' created in *sui generis* legislation to protect mega-events in recent years, and I have argued that there appears to be little legal justification for this new and rather strange creature. To sum up, and in essence, recent developments in anti-ambush marketing protection worldwide equates to the following:

---

[230] Ibid. p. 40.

Legislation has been passed in a number of jurisdictions in order to prohibit association ambushes—this is in line with the common law protections already in place against unlawful competition, passing off and deceptive trade practices. Such legislation has in a number of instances, however, extended the protection of intellectual property beyond what IP law traditionally protects—the elements of deceptive use in terms of trademark law and the immunity of generic descriptions in terms of both trademark and copyright laws have apparently been abandoned by lawmakers in favour of all-encompassing protection against any form of association with events and event organizers, which have little foundation in accepted notions of law. The apparent trend towards the creation of association rights to events has gone beyond covering only 'association ambushes' in light of the wide application of the relevant legislative prohibitions—these 'rights' have apparently developed with no theoretical or jurisprudential underpinning. As referred to in this book, event organizers and their commercial partners hold no 'property right to a spectacle' in respect of such events in most if not all jurisdictions. By legally prohibiting an extremely wide and insufficiently explained 'association' with an event which extends to mere reference to the event (even when coupled with clear disclaimers of non-association) legislators have created unprecedented and illegitimate grounds for (criminal) liability of persons who are *de facto* not acting in contravention of established principles of law. Ironically, whilst there is a developing movement opposed to the abuse of traditional intellectual property laws, worldwide, the commercial monopolization of major sporting events and the legislative legitimization thereof in jurisdictions such as South Africa (with its truly bizarrely wide provisions as encompassed in the Merchandise Marks Act) has added a worrying new dimension to the mix. In the professed name of the common good and the public interest, huge commercial interests and undemocratic monopolies engaged in the governance of international sport have been granted legal license to 'strip-mine' the public domain and the public interest in what is one of the last remaining bastions of national and cultural pride in our globalised world—top-level international sporting competition. This state of affairs enjoys not only the positive protection of the law but is also frequently propped up by apparent immunity from both political scrutiny and legal prosecution. In this regard I will leave the reader with the words of one of FIFA's most avid critics (who has gone so far as to liken the organization to the Mafia with reference to the generally-accepted characteristics of organized crime):

> Legislators and public prosecutors have been cowed by FIFA's insistence that its affairs may not be meddled in by elected governments. Together with the IOC, FIFA claims 'autonomy' for sport with the thin argument that governments must not be permitted to interfere in the 'independence' of sports federations. The risible suggestion that these federations, so often tarnished by ballot rigging, corruption and ticket scandals, should be above the law, is accepted by most governments, most of the time.[231]

I believe that the legal fraternity, internationally and in the various domestic jurisdictions where the mega-events periodically encamp, have a special moral

[231] Andrew Jennings, writing in Schulz-Herzenberg 2010, p. 91.

obligation to engage critically with these issues in considering the future scope of protection for commercial rights for event organisers. It is probably sad (and a sign of a cynical nature) that I should have come to view an event such as the FIFA World Cup as the proverbial Trojan horse: the relevant sports governing body, commercial actors and (sometimes) corrupt officials in the host nation wheel and deal to turn a quick and very lucrative buck, while the populace is seduced by the promise of an exciting sporting spectacle—"while the sinners sin, the children play … how they play and play for that happy day".[232] Greed and opportunism are natural and sadly unsurprising human instincts, but what really worries me is when custom-made law is used to protect and promote such conduct and to legitimize these practices that probably hold little benefit for the common good. At the very least it should be recognised that the event organisers have to date not yet provided sufficient and convincing justification for the protection they claim in respect of its broader benefits beyond the commercial relationships they have with sponsors and other parties. Worryingly, these organisations have not really been called upon to produce such justification.

Organizations like FIFA and the IOC appear to soldier on unfazed, vigorously demanding the protection of the law for their commercial monopolies in the jurisdictions where they encamp for a few weeks every four years. It is rather ironic to consider the apparent arrogance of these Swiss-based organizations, seeing that Switzerland itself does not have specific anti-ambush marketing legislation (such measures are apparently limited to the domain of unlawful competition)[233] and, according to at least one report, there is a sentiment in that jurisdiction that small businesses should have extensive freedom to capitalize from marketing around major events.[234] In my opinion FIFA's arrogance and apathy towards the host nation and its people should be clear for all to see in respect of the hosting of the most recent instalment of its marquee event at the time of writing. Apart from its widely-reported and deep-seated Afro-pessimism regarding South Africa's ability to manage to build stadia and ensure that trains run on time to get

---

[232] From "Tea for the Tillerman" (Cat Stevens *Tea for the Tillerman* © 1970, A&M/Island Records).

[233] See the country report for Switzerland submitted to the AIPPI Working Committee, Project Q210 ('The protection of major sports events and associated commercial activities through trademarks and other IPR'; in response to a call for reports compiled for purposes of a draft resolution to be submitted to the AIPPI Exco meeting in Buenos Aires, October 2009)—available online at the time of writing at https://www.aippi.org/download/commitees/210/GR210 switzerland.pdf.

[234] Kobel observed the following regarding the relevant country reporters' views in respect of the sufficiency of anti-ambush marketing protection in Switzerland (Kobel 2007, p. 54):

> 'The Swiss Reporters believe that unfair competition protection is sufficient to deal with ambush marketing practices. They also think that small and medium size enterprises cannot play the same game as big enterprises and therefore are de facto excluded from bidding. They should therefore be able to make reference to the event for economic advantage.'

fans to matches, the organization appears to also have had some concerns that mascot figurines manufactured in South Africa might decide to explode and hurt a toddler (no such danger if the toy is produced in a Chinese sweat shop—as it subsequently turned out was the case—of course) or that Mr Blatter might have to take a pay cut if they allow a small-time vendor to sell local delicacies near a match venue. When FIFA commissioned a Hollywood-based events coordinator to organize the first-ever "Kick Off Celebration" music concert scheduled for the evening before the opening match of the 2010 event, it appeared to feel that very few local musicians are good (or popular) enough for its showcase. After vocal protest by the local Creative Workers Union (and suggestions voiced at a Cape Town musicians' conference for a free admission 'rebel' concert by local artists—which one industry member reportedly suggested should be called the 'Fuck FIFA' concert[235]), FIFA magnanimously allowed more South African artists on the programme for its musical extravaganza. It is evident that FIFA's overriding concern was that its 2010 World Cup should produce a 'cleansed' entertainment package for its European TV audiences; despite footing most of the bill, the 'host nation' plays little role in what is ultimately a FIFA event. Ironic, then, to consider that South Africa's President in April 2010 honoured Sepp Blatter with the award of the Order of the Companions of OR Tambo (a medal named after the ANC struggle stalwart, which is given to foreigners for friendship shown to South Africa) for Blatter's 'exceptional contribution to football' and support for the hosting of the World Cup in Africa. He was subsequently in March 2011 awarded the top spot by *The Times* in its 'Sport Power 100' list of the one hundred most influential people in sport (although his controversial comments on the alleged lack of racism in world football in November 2011 caused some to ask how much longer the game can afford the leadership of such a 'dinosaur').

The commercial monopolisation of sporting events and the resultant aggressive pursuit of anti-ambush marketing protection constitutes an important although insufficiently considered example of the whittling away of the public domain by large commercial actors such as multinational corporations. This ever-present tension between private (commercial) and public interests in events is critical to the evaluation of the legality of not only 'ambushing' but also of the legislative measures enacted to combat it:

> A relatively fundamental question raised by ambush marketing is to determine whether the values associated with the event stemming from the emotions, the pride, the charisma of the athletes, their contribution to the suspense of a competition should not remain public goods. Such a claim opposes any legal recognition of exclusive rights such as those

---

[235] During the playing of the 2010 football World Cup event there appeared to be a growing feeling of disillusionment and even anger at FIFA amongst South Africans. A Cape Town artist was reported as doing a brisk trade in 'Fick Fufa' t-shirts as a non-profit venture. Local satirical news site Hayibo.com was also selling a range of t-shirts that lampooned FIFA's copyright and other IP rights to phrases and other things, with the logo 'FEEFA 2.010 WHIRLED CUP SOWTH AFRIKA'—from a report by Raborife, M 'Fick Fufa!", *Mail & Guardian*, 18–24 June 2010.

claimed by official sponsors. Therefore any legal study of ambush marketing practices should first recognize that:

- Overall, ambush marketing practices are better qualified as a free rider issue instead of parasitism;
- competitors are not necessarily affected;
- mainly organisers are affected by ambush marketing practices;
- the values stemming from the event are the outcome of a collective effort;
- the damage, if any, is very difficult to quantify and the causal link between the said damage and ambush marketing practices is very difficult to identify;
- ambush marketing practices mainly concern business relations between undertakings, consumers are rarely affected;
- positive externalities such as the values conveyed by the event, perhaps belong to the public domain.'[236]

The role of the new 'association rights' to events should be considered much more critically by lawyers and lawmakers alike. I think this is urgently required, especially if one considers the following, which was observed regarding both the proof of 'association' and the need/proper role for legal intervention—in the context of a controversial area of trademark law, namely anti-dilution protection:

> Attempts have been made to use cognitive science to demonstrate that dilution does create higher costs for consumers. Cognition models rely on the hypothesis that the brain forms networks of association among ideas and images. Consumers then retrieve particular associations by accessing links in the network. Where a single term has multiple, non-confusing associations, dilution can increase the recall time for a pre-existing brand association because of the disambiguation required. One problem with such studies, however, is that they rest on laboratory tests that deprive consumers of real world contextual clues that may serve to eliminate increases in information costs. At a more fundamental level, however, very real questions remain about whether the law should take cognisance of the harm these studies purport to identify. For example, even if we were to accept that dilutive uses can increase the time it takes consumers to recognise the senior mark by 125 ms is this sufficient to warrant legal intervention and, if so, on what basis?... [A]t what point does a delay (of statistical significance) cause a change in purchasing behaviour (of legal significance)? To what extent is legal intervention necessary to ensure that consumers do not have their time wasted in such minute fractions?[237]

I hope that, in reading this last quotation, the reader will consider some of the points I've referred to in the preceding discussion: *Sui generis* legislation aimed at mega-event commercial rights protection generally does not require either proof of consumer confusion or actual harm to the event organiser/sponsor. The most problematic manifestation of this in respect of the 'intrusion ambush', in my view, is to be found in the fact that the legislation which creates these 'association rights' generally appears to expressly refuse any exemption from liability for 'ambushers' who make it clear that they are not 'associated with' the relevant event (by means of the use of disclaimers in advertising). I would suggest that this approach '[deprives] consumers of real world contextual clues [ugh, *clear disclaimers*] that may serve to

[236] Kobel 2007, p. 9.

[237] Burrell and Gangjee 2010, p. 9.

eliminate increases in information costs'. Also, and especially in this light, real questions abound as to 'whether the law should take cognisance of the harm [such legislation, and their event organiser/sponsor promoters'] purport to identify'.

There appears to be a chink of light at the end of the tunnel from within the marketing fraternity and elsewhere, though. I have referred (in Chap. 3) to an apparent paradigm shift in thinking in respect of the ethics of 'ambush marketing', a discernible move towards a pragmatic approach recognised by researchers in the last few years. There are also traces to be found of a dawning realisation of some of the conceptual, moral and jurisprudential problems, which I've tried to highlight in this chapter, in respect of *sui generis* event protection legislation. For example, the Emerging Issues Committee of the International Trademark Association[238] recently adopted a resolution to call on the organisation's Board of Directors to issue guidelines regarding ambush marketing legislation. The resolution was a result of a 4-year effort by the Emerging Issues Committee, during which period the committee reportedly received a favourable response to a more balanced approach through a survey of trademark owners on both sides of the issue and through submissions it developed for INTA to governments that were considering ambush marketing legislation. I reproduce this (rather lengthy) resolution as **Appendix B** at the end of the book.

Similarly, the International Association for the Protection of Intellectual Property (AIPPI) issued a resolution in October 2009 following a working committee's review of trademark and unfair competition protection for major sports events, in the following terms[239]:

> (1) Trade Mark and Unfair Competition law should not be amended just for Major Sports Events.
> (2) *Sui generis* rights for Major Sports Events extending beyond the generally applicable rules of Trade Mark and Unfair Competition law should be avoided.
> (3) However, where *sui generis* rights are created, they should provide a balance between the interests of all relevant parties, including sports governing bodies, organising entities, official event sponsors, other businesses and the public. In particular, such *sui generis* rights should:
> (a) be limited in time and start a reasonable time before and expire a reasonable time after the Major Sports Event has taken place;
> (b) only be infringed where an unfair advantage results from an association with the Major Sports Event;

---

[238] The organisation's web site (at http://www.inta.org) describes it as follows:

'The International Trademark Association (INTA) is a not-for-profit membership association dedicated to the support and advancement of trademarks and related intellectual property as elements of fair and effective commerce. The Association was founded in 1878 by 17 merchants and manufacturers who saw a need for an organization "to protect and promote the rights of trademark owners, to secure useful legislation and to give aid and encouragement to all efforts for the advancement and observance of trademark rights." Today, 5,700 trademark owners, professionals and academics from more than 190 countries make INTA a powerful network of powerful brands. Members of INTA find true value in the Association's global trademark research, policy development, and education and training.'

[239] AIPPI Resolution on Question Q210: 'The protection of major sports events and associated commercial activities through Trade Marks and other IPR', adopted at the AIPPI Executive Committee meeting in Buenos Aires, 14 October 2009—English version available online at the time of writing at https://www.aippi.org/download/commitees/210/RS210English.pdf.

(c) only be infringed by commercial activities;
(d) be subject to a balancing of interests with the right to freedom of expression; and
(e) recognise pre-existing intellectual property rights.'

I sincerely welcome the sentiments and aspirations expressed in such resolutions, but would like to call for broader engagement with the issues. The main problem is that these realisations have not yet permeated the thinking of event organisers and their legal advisors, of lawmakers and governments in host nations and of the international legal fraternity, more generally. I hope to see these stakeholders take on board some of these (very convincing) points and that we will shortly experience a major overhaul of the current monopolistic and anti-competitive system of both commercial rights exploitation of mega-events and of the law's protection and legitimisation of such commercial rights. Marcus, in discussing the protection of generic Olympic terms in the legislation passed for the 2012 London Olympic Games, observes that legislation can never capture every possible infringement, and that 'it becomes a matter of reasonable limitations and proportionate restrictions'.[240] My concern is that not only has the legal fraternity to date been less vocal than it could (should) be in the process of passing such legislation and in ensuring that proper limitations and restrictions are placed on event organisers' rights, there has been a remarkable lack of scrutiny of the more fundamental aspects of such legislation and of what they serve to protect. I would like to see a significant shift, not only in mindset but also in the (often pejorative) use of language, away from mere limitations on newly created statutory rights, towards more critical consideration of why these rights are created in the first place. Maybe I should conclude with the following words of Brian Pelanda, who does well to distil the gist of the objection against 'association rights' as a new creature of law:

> [M]arketing that capitalizes on the *occurrence* of an athletic event does not ipso facto create a wrongful *association* with that event or indicate an attempt to create a wrongful association with that event. If there is no likelihood that a particular marketing tactic has created a wrongful association with an event in the minds of consumers, then no problem exists and that tactic cannot fall into the category of ambush marketing… The real issue underlying most allegations of ambush marketing is the desire to prohibit *all* non-paid-for speech by competitors of official sponsors that in any way occurs during or references a sponsored athletic event, regardless of whether it creates any confusion as to association or sponsorship status.[241]

Lawmakers should, as a matter of course, not tolerate the continuing trend of allowing such illegitimate, ill-founded and self-centred covetousness—read: *Greed*—at such considerable potential costs to the public.

---

[240] Marcus 2010, p. 34.

[241] Pelanda, B L 'Ambush marketing: Dissecting the discourse', undated 2011 paper available online at the time of writing at http://works.bepress.com/brian_pelanda/.

References

All Internet-based sources referred to, were last visited in or before December 2011

Andreff W, Szymanski S (2006) Handbook on the economics of sport. Edward Elgar Publishers, Cheltenham

Bently L, Davis J, Ginsburg JC (eds) (2008) Trade marks and brands: an interdisciplinary critique. Cambridge University Press, Cambridge

Boldrin M, Levine DK (2008) Against intellectual monopoly. Cambridge University Press, Cambridge

Bollier D (2005) Brand name bullies: the quest to own and control culture. Wiley, Hoboken

Bone RG (2006) Hunting goodwill: a history of the concept of goodwill in trademark law. Law & Technology Scholarship Berkeley Centre for Law and Technology

Bone RG (2008) Schechter's ideas in historical context and dilution's rocky road. Santa Clara Comput High Tech Law J 24:469

Burrell R, Gangjee DS (2010) Trade marks and freedom of expression: a call for caution. University of Queensland TC Beirne School of Law Research Paper No. 10-05

Carter SL (1990) The trouble with trademark. Yale Law J 99:759

Cooper Dreyfuss R (1996) We are symbols and inhabit symbols, so should we be paying rent? Deconstructing the Lanham Act and rights of publicity. Columbia-VLA J Law Arts 20:123

Corbett S, Van Roy Y (2010) Events management in New Zealand: one law to rule them all? J Bus Law 4:338–362

Dayan D, Katz E (1992) Media events. Harvard University Press, London

Dogan SL, Lemley MA (2005) The merchandising right: fragile theory or fait accompli? Emory Law J 54:461

Eichhorn C, Sahm M (2010) Ticket underpricing and public support for mega-events' Ŕegion et D́eveloppement No. 31-2010 at 38. available online at the time of writing at http://region-developpement.univ-tln.fr/en/pdf/R31/6-Eichhorn_Sahm.pdf

Eitzen DS (1996) Classism in sport: the powerless bear the burden. J Sport Soc Issues 20(1):95–105

Ellis D, Scassa T, Seguin B (2011) Framing ambush marketing as a legal issue: an Olympic perspective. Sport Manage Rev 14(3):297–308

Gannon N (2010) Foul play in sports branding—the marketer's perspective. World Trademark Rev 27:67

Gordon WJ (1992) On owning information: intellectual property and the restitutionary impulse. Va Law Rev 78:149

Grady J, McKelvey S, Bernthal MJ (2010) From Beijing 2008 to London 2012: examining event-specific Olympic legislation vis à vis the rights and interests of stakeholders. J Spons 3(2):144–156

Haman M, Marriott D (2010) The 2010 World Cup—practical lessons in brand protection. World Trademark Rev 72–77

Johnson P (2007) Ambush marketing: a practical guide to protecting the brand of a sporting event. Sweet & Maxwell, London

Johnson P (2008) Look out! It's an ambush'. Int Sports Law Rev 2/3:24–29

Kelbrick R (2008) The W***D C*P of 2*1*: FIFA's intellectual property rights in South Africa. J Intellect Prop Law Pract 3(5):327

Kobel P (2007) International Report on Question B: Ambush Marketing Too Smart to Be Good? Should Certain Ambush Marketing Practices Be Declared Illegal and If Yes, Which Ones and Under What Conditions? Int Rep Int Leag Compet Law Catania Congr. http://www.ligue.org/publication.php?txtt=23&docc=4

Kratzke WP (1991) Normative economic analysis of trademark law. Memphis State Univ Law Rev 21:199

Lemley MA (1999) The modern Lanham Act and the death of common sense. Yale Law J 108:1687
Lemley MA, McKenna M (2010) Irrelevant confusion. Stanf Law Rev 62(2):413
Lewis A, Taylor J (2007) Sport: law and practice. Tottel Publishing, Haywards Heath
Longdin L (2009) Public law solutions to private law problems: major event regulation subverts IP's internal balance. J Intellect Prop Law Pract 4(10):726–742
Louw AM (2007) Suggestions for the protection of star athletes and other famous persons against unauthorised celebrity merchandising in South Africa. S Afr Mercantile Law J 19:272–301
Madow M (1993) Private ownership of public image: popular culture and publicity rights. Calif Law Rev 81(125):178–238
Malfas M, Theodoraki E, Houlihan B (2004) Impacts of the Olympic games as mega-events. Municipal Eng Issue ME3:209–220
Marcus JT (2010) Ambush marketing: an analysis of its threat to sports rights holders and the efficacy of past, present and proposed anti-infringement programmes. Sport Law J 18(1):25
McKelvey S, Grady J (2008) Sponsorship program protection strategies for special sport events: are event organizers outmaneuvering Ambush marketers? J Sport Manage 22:550–586
Meenaghan T (1991) The role of sponsorship in the marketing communications mix. Int J Advert 10:35
Meenaghan T (1994) Point of view: Ambush marketing—Immoral or imaginative practice? J Advert Res 34(3):77–88
Neethling J (2008) van Heerden-Neethling Unlawful competition (2nd edn). LexisNexis, Durban
Phillips J (2006) Play the game, kill the competition. J Intellect Prop Law Pract 1(2):79
Price ME, Dayan D (eds) (2008) Owning the Olympics: narratives of the New China. Digitalculturebooks, Michigan
Roche M (2000) Mega-events & Modernity: Olympics and expos in the growth of global culture. Routledge, London
Scassa T (2011) Ambush marketing and the right of association: clamping down on references to that big event with the all the athletes in a couple of years. J Sport Manage 25:354–370
Schechter FI (1927) The rational basis of trademark protection. Harv Law Rev 40:813
Schlossberg H (1996) Sports marketing. Blackwell, Oxford
Schmitz JJ (2005) 'Ambush marketing: the off-field competition at the Olympic games. Northwest J of Technol Intellect Prop 3(Spring):203
Schulz-Herzenberg C (ed) (2010) Player and referee: conflicting interests and the 2010 FIFA World Cup™ Monograph 169, South African Institute for Security Studies
Schwab F (2006) 'FIFA's trademark tactics. World Trademark Rev 6. http://www.worldtrademarkreview.com/Issues/Articles.aspx?g=faf17b21-f89a-473e-949c-bc1b25b93bad
Seguin B, O'Reilly NJ (2008) The Olympic brand, ambush marketing and clutter. Int J Sport Manage Mark 4(1):62
Séguin B, Ellis D, Scassa T, Parent M (2008) Who's ambushing whom? An examination of anti-ambush marketing legislation in Canada: the case of the 2010 Olympic and Paralympic winter games. In: Proceedings of the 16th European association for sport management conference, Heidelberg, Germany, 10–13 Sept 2008
Skildum-Reid K (2007) The Ambush marketing toolkit. McGraw-Hill, London
Smith A (1776) An inquiry into the nature and causes of the Wealth of Nations (Campbell, R H & Skinner, A S (eds.) Liberty Classics (1981))
Spinello RA, Bottis M (2009) A defense of intellectual property rights. Edward Elgar Publishing Ltd, Cheltenham
Tan D (2008) Beyond trademark law: what the right of publicity can learn from cultural studies. Cardozo Arts Entertain Law J 25(3):913
Vassallo E, Blemaster K, Werner P (2005) An international look at Ambush marketing. Trademark Report 95:1338
Wilf S (1999) Who authors trademarks? Cardozo Arts Entertain Law J 17(1):24

Chapter 9
In Defence of the Monopoly?

A Brief Look at the Arguments in Favour of Sponsorship Exclusivity and Aggressive Rights Protection for Sports Mega-Events

> Nowadays the rage for possession has got to such a pitch that there is nothing in the realm of nature, whether sacred or profane, out of which profit cannot be squeezed, and that not only by princes, but even by priests. In old days, even under the tyrants (when they were as yet untutored and did not know what tyranny really was) certain things were common to all—the seas, the rivers, the highways, the wild game. Now the great lords arrogate everything to themselves, as if they alone were men, or rather gods.[1]

> It will [at the 2012 London Olympic Games] cost up to £725 to see Usain Bolt hit his ultimate stride for appreciably less than 10 s and if you want an intimate view of the opening ceremony pageantry you have to part with more than £2,000... If there is ever a conflict of motivation in modern sport the one of profit will always sail through. The Olympics, like the World Cup which in South Africa last summer priced out so many of the local population, are supremely about money. It just means that when you get to stage one you have to pay twice. Once in your tax—and then when you want to see something more riveting than beach volleyball.[2]

9.1 Introduction

From the discussion in Chap. 2, we have seen that the modern sports mega-event is very significantly 'all about the money.' It costs a lot to put on the show, of course, and I do not intend to downplay that fact. These events may be expensive geese, but they do lay jumbo-sized golden eggs. Event organisers commercially exploit the publicity and 'feel-good' value of these entertainment spectacles by selling rights to corporate sponsors to associate their brands with the events for marketing

---

[1] Dutch humanist scholar and theologian Desiderius Erasmus (1466–1536), as quoted in Mann Phillips 1967, p. 45.

[2] Lawton, J 'Profit over people for Olympics and Champions League,' 19 February 2011, *The Belfast Telegraph*—available online at http://www.belfasttelegraph.co.uk/sport/columnists/james-lawton/james-lawton-profit-over-people-for-olympics-and-champions-league-15089828.html.

A. M. Louw, *Ambush Marketing and the Mega-Event Monopoly*,
ASSER International Sports Law Series, DOI: 10.1007/978-90-6704-864-4_9,

purposes. The sponsors pay hundreds of millions of dollars for these rights, and in return demand high levels of exclusivity in order to close the mega-event promotional market to their competitors. Because of these substantial investments in the events, ambush marketing by unlicensed outsiders frequently gets the hackles up for both sponsors and event organisers. The sponsors get upset because they feel a bit foolish (and envious?) having paid huge amounts of money when an 'ambusher' might be able to obtain the same or even greater marketing benefits for much less financial outlay. The more the sponsors pay; the more exclusivity they demand (understandably so). The event organisers, on the other hand, get upset because they are contractually obligated to make a big noise about ambushing and to appear actively (and proactively) to be on their toes in combating ambushes—after all, if you charge such huge amounts for promised exclusivity, you must at least appear able to deliver exclusivity. In order to achieve this goal the event organisers' single biggest weapon is the ability to demand special laws to protect their sponsors' rights. And they succeed in this because, possibly rather inexplicably, cities and host nations nowadays queue up to host the sports mega-events (even though their tax-paying citizens will have to foot much of the bill and the event organisers themselves will, generally, not be paying any taxes to such governments). This while Montreal smokers are probably still paying taxes on their cigarettes to finance the city's massive debt from the 1976 Olympic Games, and while Greece's current economic crisis has (at least by one observer) been placed at the door of the Olympic Games. Victor Matheson, on the *Sports Economist* group blog, has explained how Greece was forced to adopt austerity measures to reduce deficits in order to join the euro in 2000, but the 2004 Athens Olympic Games broke the bank. Government deficits rose every year after 1999, peaking at 7.5% of GDP in 2004, the year of the Games, thanks in large part to the 9 billion euro price tag for the Games. For a relatively small country like Greece, the cost of hosting the Games equalled roughly 5% of the annual GDP of the country.[3] As a South African tax-payer I will admit to being worried about how much longer I will have to pay for the costs of hosting FIFA's football extravaganza in 2010, and that it angers me when I read reports of how FIFA and its commercial partners managed to depart these shores not having paid taxes on the billions it raised from the event, this while trumpeting the developmental benefits of FIFA's first foray onto African soil (that is, an African first for its World Cup event; Mr. Blatter has personally visited the continent frequently in the past to garner votes for his presidential campaigns).

Against this background (and shameful declaration of my possible bias on the subject) we need to consider the veracity of the arguments advanced by event organisers in justification for their sometimes freakishly aggressive enforcement of commercial rights and its effects on others, especially when it comes to the *sui generis* event legislation discussed in the earlier chapters.

---

[3] Matheson, as quoted by Megan McArdle on *Business Insider*—available online at the time of writing at http://articles.businessinsider.com/2010-02-15/wall_street/30056382_1_greece-gdp-fun-olympic.

Let us get down to brass tacks and briefly examine the financial interests involved and how convincing the economic arguments against ambush marketing really are. This is a short chapter, and not only because I started running out of steam in writing this book. I also find very little of substance in the event organisers' justification for their often rabid rights protection efforts, and will mention that such arguments regarding the risks posed by ambushing appear to be based on very little in the form of empirical evidence. To be fair, though, I must point out to the reader that one industry insider does not agree with much of what I argue in this chapter. David Becker, at the time of writing the Head of Legal for the International Cricket Council, kindly read an advanced draft of this chapter prior to its publication. He has made some convincing arguments in respect of the economic justifications for anti-ambushing enforcement measures. I will include his views where relevant throughout this chapter, as well as in the concluding section at the end.

9.2 'Show Me the Money!'[4]: How Self-Proclaimed 'Non-Profit' Event Organisers Rake in the Mega-Event Profits

British newspaper *The Independent* reported in June 2010—2 days before the start of the 2010 FIFA World Cup in starry-eyed South Africa—that the Swiss-based organisation was set to make a killing from the event while leaving the host nation with a sizeable tab for the festivities:

> [FIFA's annual income from its marquee event] has leapt by 50 per cent since the last World Cup was staged four years ago in Germany. The non-governmental organisation is sitting on more than $1.1bn (£0.76bn) in equity, according to a provisional copy of its own financial report. The announcement of the huge pay day comes as the latest estimate of the cost of staging the finals comes to $8.6bn in a country where more than 40 per cent of the population live on less than $2 a day. Forecasts predict profits in excess of $2.5bn (£1.7bn) for the Swiss-registered charity, which means it will make more money from the World Cup than the host country will. The most optimistic predictions see the monthlong tournament giving the South African economy a 0.5 per cent bump in GDP–Fifa's profits would be equivalent to 0.7 per cent of South African GDP. Despite the immense geopolitical power that Fifa wields, the NGO is accountable only to the courts in Switzerland where it enjoys tax-free status. It refuses to answer questions such as the annual earnings of the organisation's Swiss president Sepp Blatter.
>
> "It's completely wrong and deeply improper that Fifa is making money out of this," said Stefan Szymanski, an economist at City University's Cass Business School who was called to advise the South African government after it won the bid in 2004. In the euphoria that followed the announcement six years ago that South Africa had won its bid, few questions were asked about the terms of the deal. In private, government officials are now accusing Fifa of acting like the "mafia" in sealing a one-sided licence to print money. "We told them it would be an economic disaster and that they should renegotiate the

[4] Apologies to Cuba Gooding's character 'Rod Tidwell' in Cameron Crowe's *Jerry Maguire*, TriStar Pictures (1996).

> contract as Fifa would never dare take the World Cup away after it was awarded," said Mr Szymanski. Under the terms of a confidential agreement signed between Fifa and Pretoria, the South African government takes no share of television, marketing deals or ticketing—the mega-event's main money spinners—and shoulders the cost of new sports stadia and related infrastructure. In addition, Fifa earnings are protected by a specially created "tax bubble" which means even the associated merchandising and match day events are untaxed and VAT on some items will have a "negligible impact" on tax receipts, according to the South African Revenue Service.[5]

In 2008[6] FIFA showed a surplus of USD 184 million.[7] Of its revenue of USD 957 million for the year, USD 903 million represented event-related revenue (i.e. 94% of total revenue, and up from USD 786 million in 2007). Of this amount, the organisation earned more than USD 550 million from the sale of television broadcasting rights in respect of the 2010 FIFA World Cup South Africa™[8] and USD 253 million from marketing rights (USD 246 million of this specific to the 2010 event).[9] It should be noted that it has been claimed that the organisation has,

---

[5] Howden, D 'Hosts see red as World Cup bill soars—but Fifa is £1.7bn in black,' 9 June 2010, *The Independent*—available online at the time of writing at http://www.independent.co.uk/news/world/africa/hosts-see-red-as-world-cup-bill-soars-ndash-but-fifa-is-16317bn-in-black-1994958.html.

[6] FIFA's *Financial Report 2008*.

[7] It was reported in March 2010 that FIFA declared a profit of USD 196 million and that it had increased its reserve fund to more than USD 1 billion in its *Financial Report 2009*. The organisation declared equity of USD 1.061 billion. It was reported that FIFA has focused on building its reserves in recent years to sustain it in the event that a World Cup is cancelled and commercial partners have to be repaid. It originally had a target of USD 800 million to be set aside by the end of 2010, but has already exceeded that—see the short report of 19 March 2010 available on the Business Report web site at http://www.busrep.co.za/index.php?fSectionId=552&fArticleId=5397601 (accessed 31 March 2010).

[8] The recognised revenue in 2008 from television broadcasting rights for the 2010 FIFA World Cup™ amounts to USD 550,085 million. The accumulated amount recognised (excluding hedge accounting effects, value-in-kind transactions and sales commissions) for the period 1 January 2007–31 December 2008 amounted to USD 1,105,360 million. Until 31 December 2008, the accumulated amount of USD 971,829 million had been collected—from Note 1: Revenue from Television Broadcasting Rights at 74 of the FIFA *Financial Report 2008*.

[9] Note F ('Revenue Recognition') of the Notes on the Consolidated Financial Statements contained in the FIFA *Financial Report 2008* explains the revenue relating to events as follows:

> Event-related revenue primarily relates to the sale of the following rights:
> – Television broadcasting rights;
> – Marketing rights;
> – Hospitality rights; and
> – Licensing rights.
>
> Under these revenue-generating contracts, FIFA receives either fixed royalty payments or royalties in the form of guaranteed minimum payments plus additional sales-based payments (profit share). Revenue directly related to the FIFA World Cup™ event is recognised in the income statement using the percentage-of-completion method, if it can be estimated reliably. The stage of completion of the FIFA World Cup™ event is assessed as incurred evenly over the project preparation period, which is 4 years. While this generally applies to fixed royalty and guaranteed minimum payments, additional

overall, earned significantly more income from sale of rights sources to the 2010 event than is reflected in the above figures for 2008.[10] In February 2011 FIFA president Sepp Blatter announced that the 2010 World Cup had been a bigger commercial success than the 2006 instalment in Germany, and had boosted the organisation's cash reserves to USD 1.2 billion.[11]

For the above period, event-related expenses constituted the organisation's largest item of expense, namely USD 441 million, of which USD 345 million represented expenses relating to the 2010 World Cup.[12] Thus, with event-related expenses making up 57% of total expenses and football development expenses of 17% of the total, FIFA proudly proclaimed that 74% of its overall expenditure for 2008 represented a direct reinvestment in football.[13] It is unclear whether the USD 462 million income in respect of events-related activities (i.e. the events-related revenue minus events-related expenses) was 'reinvested directly in football'; even if all the development project expenses for that year (USD 133 million) were financed directly from such event-related surplus, it appears that FIFA showed a surplus of USD 329 million from sources related to the organisation of events.[14]

(Footnote 9 continued)
sales-based revenue (profit share) is included in the percentage-of-completion method only when the amount is probable and can be measured reliably. Revenue relating to other FIFA events is deferred during the preparation period and is recognised in the income statement when the event takes place. Ticket sales in connection with the 2010 FIFA World Cup South Africa™ and the FIFA Confederations Cup South Africa 2009 are not recognised, since the 2010 FIFA World Cup Organising Committee South Africa is the beneficiary of the net revenue.

[10] Rob Rose (writing in Schulz-Herzenberg 2010, p. 118) observes as follows:

'For the 2010 World Cup, revenue generated through 'sale of rights' between 2007 and 2010 amounted to $3,2 billion, according to documents provided to the author. This was made up of $2 billion for TV rights (63% of the total), with $1 billion for the marketing rights, $120 million for the hospitality rights, and $80 million for licensing. World Cup sponsors, like beer brand Budweiser and cellular firm MTN, also pay FIFA a fee but this is included in the marketing rights.'

[11] See the *Guardian* report of 23 February 2011, available online at the time of writing at http://www.guardian.co.uk/football/2011/feb/23/fifa-world-cup-cash.

[12] Event-related expenses as recorded in FIFA's financial report are the gross outflow of economic benefits that arise in the ordinary activity of organising an event. Since FIFA organises the FIFA World Cup™ event over a period of 4 years, expenses relating to the event are recognised based on the stage of completion of the event, as determined for event-related revenue recognition purposes. The end of 2008 reflected a point roughly halfway in the 4 year period between the 2006 and 2010 world cup events.

[13] From FIFA's *Financial Report 2008*, as tabled at the 59th FIFA Congress, Nassau, 2–3 June 2009 (the most recent financial report for the organisation available on its web site at www.fifa.com).

[14] FIFA's published financial report for the year 2008 as discussed here does not clarify or itemise expenses related to either events or to development projects. It should be mentioned here, just as a matter of interest, that allegations have been made regarding an apparent decision by FIFA's executive committee, in or about sometime in 2000, that expense claims of members do not need to be supported by documentary proof. Andrew Jennings recounts one instance of an unnamed member who, allegedly, claimed a total of approximately USD 85,000 for travel and

Ultimately, the organisation's USD 184 million revenue surplus—i.e. *profit*-appears to have been largely attributable to income directly associated with the organisation of events, which is clearly FIFA's main stock-in-trade.[15] Its 2010 financial report (for the 2007–2010 financial period) claimed total event-related revenues of USD 3,890 million, with its second-biggest source of income being the sale of marketing rights worth USD 1,097 million, of which USD 1,072 million was generated by the FIFA World Cup. It reported a 'positive four-year result' of USD 631 million for the 2007–2010 financial period.

In this light, the motto of this 'Swiss charity'—*For the Game, For the World*—appears to presume that the world of football needs, primarily, big football events. In fact, one could be excused for assuming that FIFA's main role in world football is *not* to oversee the governance of the game (on which FIFA spent USD 46 million in 2008—interestingly, just marginally more than the USD 42 million spent on wages and salaries[16]), to write the rules of the game or to develop the game, but to organise big and expensive showcases for profit. On such a reading, FIFA's aggressive attempts to protect and exploit the commercial rights to its events appear to be understandable, even reasonable. I would suggest, however, that it bears closer scrutiny.

FIFA's current commercialisation model in respect of the World Cup event can be summarised as follows:

> In line with FIFA's marketing and TV strategy, FIFA sold the television broadcasting rights in the key markets for the final competitions of the 2010 and 2014 FIFA World Cups™ directly to broadcasters. For the 2006 FIFA World Cup™, the rights were sold in packages to intermediaries. In the area of marketing, FIFA has implemented a new strategy from 2007 onwards and now distinguishes between FIFA Partner, FIFA World Cup Sponsor and National Supporter. In this context, the number of FIFA Partners has been reduced from 15 in the 2003–2006 period to six for the 2007–2010 cycle. The revenue from television and marketing rights is received from large multinational companies and public broadcasters.[17]

(Footnote 14 continued)
accommodation expenses without providing any proof of the actual expenses incurred—see Jennings 2006, pp. 101, 102. Without expressing a view on such allegations, it is interesting to speculate to what extent income from events finds its way back into the game of football.

15 Compare Note E ('Income Statement') of the Notes on the Consolidated Financial Statements contained in the FIFA *Financial Report 2008*, which explains event-related revenue and expenses as follows:

'Event-related revenue and expenses are directly related to the organisation and realisation of the FIFA World Cup™ and other FIFA events. For accounting purposes, FIFA defines other FIFA events as all other football events, such as the FIFA Women's World Cup™, FIFA U-20 World Cup, FIFA U-17 World Cup, FIFA U-20 Women's World Cup, FIFA U-17 Women's World Cup, Olympic Football Tournaments, FIFA Futsal World Cup, FIFA Confederations Cup, FIFA Club World Cup, FIFA Beach Soccer World Cup, Blue Stars/FIFA Youth Cup, FIFA Interactive World Cup, etc.'

16 FIFA *Financial Report 2008* at 83.

17 See the FIFA *Financial Report 2008* at 96. FIFA 'Partners' are awarded the most comprehensive package of marketing rights; FIFA 'Sponsors' are granted the second most

In 2008, FIFA derived income from marketing rights specific to the 2010 FIFA World Cup South Africa™ in the amount of USD 246 million,[18] which was split as follows between the three main sponsorship categories:

- 'FIFA Partners,' USD 148 million;
- 'FIFA World Cup Sponsors,' USD 73 million; and
- 'National Supporters,' USD 8 million.

If one considers FIFA's profit from events and the rather paltry (in comparison) sum spent on football development as reflected for the 2008 financial year, one may be excused for finding the following statement, frankly laughable:

> FIFA was established in the legal form of an association pursuant to Articles 60ff. of the Swiss Civil Code. Pursuant to Article 2 of its Statutes, FIFA's objective is to improve the game of football constantly and promote it globally, particularly through youth and development programmes. FIFA is a non-profit organization and is obliged to spend its profits, reserves and funds for this purpose.[19]

In the recent ECJ judgment in the *MOTOE* case the court, in the context of an EU competition law matter, investigated the implications of an absence of a profit-making aim on the part of a sports governing body in respect of its classification as an 'undertaking,' and observed as follows:

> The fact that [a sports governing body] has the status of a non-profit-making association and operates without seeking to make a profit does not preclude the assumption that it pursues an economic activity and has the associated status of undertaking. Such organisations can also market their services in competition with other economic agents, irrespective of whether the other economic agents themselves operate without seeking to make a profit or on a commercial basis... It is true that an organisation cannot be classified

(Footnote 17 continued)
comprehensive package of rights, and FIFA 'National Supporters' are granted a package of specified marketing rights that are only exercisable within the borders of the host nation. In respect of the Olympic Games, the International Olympic Committee utilises six revenue-generating programmes:

- IOC-managed broadcast sponsorships;
- The TOP partners sponsorship programme (referred to elsewhere in this book, in Chap. 2);
- The IOC official supplier and licensing programme;
- Domestic sponsorship programmes run by the local Organising Committees for the Games (or 'OCOGS');
- Ticketing programmes in the host country; and
- Licensing programmes in the host country.

By way of example of the revenues generated through these streams between 2001 and 2004, broadcasting rights generated USD 2,232 million, the TOP programme USD 663 million, and domestic sponsorships USD 796 million—see Davis 2008, p. 157.

[18] According to the report (at 76), the accumulated revenue from marketing rights recognised (excluding value-in-kind transactions and sales commissions) in 2008 amounted to USD 437 million. The accumulated revenue from marketing rights collected in the period from 1 January 2007 to 31 December 2008 amounted to USD 474 million.

[19] Note K ('Income Taxes') of the Notes on the Consolidated Financial Statements contained in the FIFA *Financial Report 2008* at 67.

> as an undertaking where it confines itself to an exclusively *social or public-interest activity* which is not pursued on the market in competition with other economic agents. The rules on competition in the EC Treaty do not apply to an activity which, by its nature, its aim and the rules to which it is subject, does not belong to the sphere of economic activity. However, where the organisation concerned begins to *market* its services, it moves away from the sphere of exclusively social or public-interest activity; the mere fact that it continues at the same time to pursue an aim in the general interest [e.g. the promotion of sport] and does not seek to make a profit is no longer sufficient for it to be denied the status of undertaking within the meaning of competition law.[20]

I would suggest that a similar rationale applies to FIFA also in the context of evaluating its claims to special legal protection for its events, notwithstanding the claims of being a 'do-gooder' organisation (sometimes even referred to as a 'Swiss-based charity' in media reports) concerned primarily with bringing its big show to the masses. In light of what has been said regarding the apparent creation of a commercial monopoly in FIFA events and the aggressive steps taken to protect such monopoly, one might also find some food for thought in the statement that FIFA strives 'to prevent all methods or practices which might jeopardise the integrity of matches or competitions or give rise to abuse of Association Football.'[21] I am not the first to suggest that FIFA's non-profit credentials are rather suspect.[22] FIFA's above-mentioned substantial revenues have increased to these levels from a mere USD 8 million in 1989.[23] I would suggest that claims of being a 'non-profit' might have sat more comfortably back in those days, but are rather dubious today. Schwab declares, unequivocally, that '[i]n 2003, an important accounting year for 2006-related income, FIFA's profits were well over $100 million, even taking into consideration operating expenses for the 2006 World Cup and other FIFA events.'[24] *The Economist*, in May 2010, reported that FIFA's profits for the 2006 event were quite phenomenal and that even more was expected for the 2010 event:

> South Africans… are grumbling about the eye-wateringly large amounts of money that FIFA, the world football body that is the monopoly organiser [of the 2010 FIFA World Cup], is poised to make, even though South Africa is bearing most of the cost. FIFA is responsible only for the prize money paid to the teams along with the cost of their travel and preparation, which amounted to just $279 m in Germany, where the tournament last took place, in 2006. This week FIFA said it would contribute an extra $100 m to the South Africans to ensure that all the facilities are ready in time. Yet the event's main direct benefits, from television and marketing rights, all go to FIFA. According to Citi, the

---

20 *Motosyklesistiki Omospondia Ellados NPID (MOTOE) v Elliniko Dimosio*, Case C-49/07 at par. 41–43.

21 Article 2(e) of FIFA's Statutes (August 2009 version currently in force at the time of writing), entitled 'Objectives.'

22 Compare Andrew Jennings's entertaining read on alleged corruption within FIFA and world football, in Jennings 2006.

23 Schwab 2006.

24 Ibid. 7.

research arm of Citibank, FIFA's profit in Germany came to $1.8 billion, equivalent to 0.7% of South Africa's GDP.[25]

As mentioned above, FIFA subsequently declared that it had generated more than USD 4 billion (for the first time) over the 2007–2010 period, and had shown a USD 631 million 'surplus' in respect of the 2010 World Cup event (due in large part, one would assume, to its African 'tax bubble'). Internet reports, such as the one from *The Independent* quoted at the beginning of this section, displayed concerns about this, but the FIFA juggernaut managed to duck serious criticism (apart from the more tame concerns expressed over issues such as refereeing and the use of goal-line technology at the event). In this light it is interesting to note the following views as expressed by one of FIFA's most prominent local lawyers in South Africa, a year before the event—it is clear who is being identified as the ones who will allegedly be making the profits and have not paid their Swiss-based 'masters' for the privilege:

> The first match in the 2010 FIFA World Cup South Africa™ is scheduled to kick off on June 11 next year but football fans are already caught up in World Cup fever. As are those planning to make a profit from the event. That is fine with FIFA, as long as they agree to play by the rules and pay licensing and sponsorship rights. FIFA is well prepared for ambush marketers who think they can take advantage of the sporting event without paying their dues.[26]

Of course, in fairness, I need to mention that these observations regarding the non-profit credentials of FIFA may not be applicable or accurate in respect of all the mega-event organisers. The International Cricket Council, for example, may have a much stronger case that its quadrennial World Cup and other big events do in fact provide a significant share of funding for the game at grassroots level. I will revisit this later in the chapter.

In respect of other sports mega-events, it has been observed that the Olympic sponsorship (TOP) programmes established in the 1980s (as discussed in detail in Chap. 2) have flourished to such an extent that 'the Olympics became a thoroughly saturated commercial venture by the end of the twentieth century.'[27] The sheer cost of staging the Games now requires a dedicated commitment from sponsors and governments, and 'the withdrawal of one sponsor can seriously damage an organising committee's budget.'[28] The IOC has retained the right to license the exclusive use of Olympic symbols and insignia, while taking a percentage of sponsorship and broadcasting revenues raised by organising committees. In the midst of this arrangement the IOC remains removed from the everyday financing of the Games themselves, which is financed by the hosts (local, provincial and national

---

[25] 'South Africa's World Cup: Who profits most?,' 13 May 2010, *The Economist*—available online at the time of writing at http://www.economist.com/node/16117134.

[26] Owen Dean 'Defending its turf: FIFA combats ambush marketing' *WIPO Magazine*, July 2009—available online at http://www.wipo.int/wipo_magazine/en/2009/04/article_0003.html.

[27] Magdalinski and Nauright 'Commercialisation of the Modern Olympics' in Slack 2004, p. 194.

[28] Ibid.

governments) and the corporate sponsors.[29] This arrangement has been heaven-sent for the Olympic Movement, and the IOC has generated nearly USD 15 billion (yes, billion) through its marketing and licensing programmes from 1980 to 2000.[30] At the time of writing, the most recent instalment of the summer Games (Beijing 2008) generated some impressive numbers: The national government of China, the city of Beijing, and many associated public and private organisations spent more than USD 40 billion preparing for the games. The IOC received almost USD 900 million in financial support, in-kind goods, and services from the 12 TOP sponsors; broadcast rights totalled another USD 1.7 billion; and ticket sales amounted to around USD 150 million. More than USD 3 billion in revenue was reportedly taken in by the IOC directly.[31] Magdalinski and Nauright observe that the rise of corporate culture in the Olympics is illustrated by the IOC's response to the Games bidding corruption scandals of the 1990s (notably Salt Lake City), particularly after the threats by major sponsors to withdraw from TOP:

> The power of the sponsors to elicit reforms from a movement as opaque as the Olympics demonstrates the degree to which corporate interests have become germane to the central working of the Olympic movement.[32]

The Olympic Games 'are a commodity, the commercial outcome of an ongoing process that began when Coubertin first mooted the idea of organising an international sporting festival.'[33]

Of course, rapid (and rabid) commercialisation of major sports events is nothing new. The 'doyen of American sports law,' Jim Nafziger, prophesied as long ago as 1988 the important implications for the further development of international sports law by the International Olympic Committee's recognition of the 'inevitability and benefits of commercialisation.' The author did so following a comparison of dollar figures between the 1932 and 1984 Olympic Games, both of which were hosted in Los Angeles, and observed that ticket-sale revenue in 1932 was USD 1.5 million compared to USD 90 million in 1984.[34] Apart from the phenomenal role of the advent of television as a vehicle to bring sport to the masses of sports entertainment consumers, which has been mentioned elsewhere,[35] the role of sponsorship has been extremely significant in the modern commercialisation of sport. Grayson declared that modern day sport at the public entertainment level would be

---

[29] Ibid.

[30] Ibid.

[31] Dollinger, MJ; Li, X; Mooney, C H 'Mega-events and entrepreneurial rents: Lessons from the Beijing Olympics' (draft document, April 2009—available online at the time of writing at http://www.indiana.edu/~rccpb/uschinacooperation/papers/P8%20Dollinger.pdf).

[32] Magdalinski and Nauright in Slack 2004, p. 195.

[33] Ibid. 202.

[34] Nafziger 1988, pp. 155, 156.

[35] See Chap. 2.

'unimaginable' without certain companies attaching themselves to the sports and events such as the Olympic Games.[36]

It should not, however, be assumed that commercial activities such as sports sponsorship are such very modern phenomena; one of the earliest examples of corporate involvement in sport can be traced back to the Circus Maximus in ancient Rome where gladiators and chariot drivers dressed in the colours of their supporting merchants. Consider also the roles assumed by the names 'Wisden' in cricket[37] and 'Derby' in horse-racing.[38] In fact, sponsorship has been an instrumental part of sport for longer than many will care to admit.[39]

So, how should one judge the role and importance or, more tricky, the legitimacy, of commercialisation in modern sport? Does one take a 'purist' stance and, relying heavily on the purported values of Corinthian ideals and the supposed merits of amateurism, decide that big money in sport is all bad? Or does one recognise the many opportunities that are created by the revenues obtained from sponsors and broadcasters, to develop not only 'the game' but also, in countless instances, young and often disadvantaged talent, and to uplift whole communities? For example, while it was observed above that an organisation such as FIFA appears to be generating very substantial revenues from the organising of events and the licensing and commercial arrangements surrounding such events, one should not lose sight of the fact that, for example, FIFA contributes towards the travel and other expenses of qualifying teams for its world cup events[40] and also to tangible development efforts in member countries (e.g. through the development of pitches and facilities in rural and under-developed areas). It also makes an annual contribution towards the operating costs of its member federations.[41] Granted, the expenses related to such efforts appear to be a mere drop in the ocean in terms of the organisation's revenues, but some sponsor- and broadcaster-generated income clearly does find its way to the grass roots of the game and actually contribute to interests beyond those of the organisers and sponsors.

---

[36] Grayson 1999, p. 445.

[37] Grayson 1999, p. 446 describes how John Wisden, a Worcester sports outfitter, decided in 1863 to underwrite the publication of the *Wisden Cricketers' Almanack* (and how the name 'Wisden' has become more synonymous with cricket than with the sponsor's business).

[38] The word 'derby,' which has of course assumed much wider usage in modern times, originated from Lord Derby's financial patronage of horse-racing in England.

[39] For more on a brief history of sponsor involvement in sport, see Boyle and Haynes 2009, p. 44 et seq.

[40] From the FIFA *Financial Report 2008* (at 105):'FIFA organises the FIFA World Cup™ and other FIFA events. In connection with these competitions, FIFA offers financial support to local organising committees and compensates teams for travel and accommodation expenses. For the FIFA World Cup™, the qualifying teams also receive a subsidy to cover the cost of their preparations.'

[41] FIFA's Financial Assistance Programme is a financial aid programme, under which USD 1 million is granted to each member association and USD 10 million to each confederation during the 4-year cycle to improve their administrative and technical infrastructure—FIFA *Financial Report 2008* at 81.

The point, however, in evaluating the argument so often raised by organisations such as FIFA for aggressively combating ambush marketing—namely, that if sponsors' exclusivity cannot be protected, sponsors would withdraw and the events would be no more—is that it appears that only a relatively small portion of the current sponsor and broadcaster spend that goes towards the major events is actually required 'for the good of the game.' It is generally recognised that international sports governing bodies' traditional role as custodians of the game in the public interest has changed dramatically in the past few decades to incorporate a significant corporate profit-making character. The organisations, however, are less forthcoming in acknowledging this aspect. One struggles to find, for example, any use of the word 'profits' in FIFA's financial reports as referred to earlier. The terms used to describe the difference between revenues and expenditures include 'surplus,' and 'positive result.'[42] Much is made of the organisation's investment from such surplus in football development and payment to domestic football bodies and confederations. But does this change the character of such 'surplus' as representing profits from the events? If a large soft-drink manufacturer earns millions of dollars of profits and decides to donate part of such profits to charity, this surely does not change the nature of these surplus revenues as, well, profits.

The organisation of the 2012 London Olympic Games, in early 2011, saw an embarrassing public dispute between the local organising committee, LOCOG, and the British Olympic Authority (or BOA), over the sharing of profits from the event, in which one observer characterised the BOA's actions as having 'blown apart London's pre-Games spirit of unity.'[43] BOA demanded that it should share in the profits of the Games, while LOCOG insisted that such profits are only to be determined following off-setting of the significant expected loss from the costs of hosting the 2012 Paralympic Games against profits from the 2012 Summer Games. The IOC was called upon to provide clarity on the matter and, in the process, to define the term 'surplus' as found in the Joint Marketing Programme Agreement entered into by both parties in 2005. After the IOC ruled in favour of LOCOG, BOA angered the organisation by referring its dispute to the Court of Arbitration for Sport (which the IOC denied had any jurisdiction over the matter). Before the CAS could announce on whether it would hear the dispute it was reported that the parties had settled the matter, with BOA acquiescing in the IOC's position on the sharing of event-related profits in return for some other financial benefits (it was reported that, in terms of the settlement, LOCOG will help the BOA win corporate sponsorship deals after the Games, will help the organisation market merchandising items in the run-up to the Olympics and also waive its royalty fees on these items, and that the BOA will also be able to purchase additional Olympic

[42] See the *FIFA 2010 Financial Report* (at 14) available on the organisation's website at the time of writing at http://www.fifa.com/mm/document/affederation/administration/01/39/20/45/web_fifa_fr2010_eng[1].pdf.

[43] Blitz, R 'Olympic bodies resolve cash dispute,' 19 April 2011, *Financial Times*—available online at the time of writing at http://www.ft.com/cms/s/0/81bbb742-6a77-11e0-a464-00144feab49a.html#axzz1dOZuYJ6K.

tickets to give to British athletes who competed in previous games and help its fundraising appeal).[44]

This very public spat was embarrassing for the UK government and the Olympic authorities (IOC president Jacques Rogge was reportedly furious at the BOA for its decision to refer the matter to CAS) because it raised, again, the issue of the rampant commercialism of the Games. It also garnered public interest in the issue of the deriving of profits for the organisers from the staging of the event. I believe claims that FIFA, the Olympic authorities and other mega-event organisers do not make an often substantial financial profit from the commercial exploitation of their events—due in large part to the sale of marketing rights to sponsors—are disingenuous and are aimed at obfuscating the issues when it comes to considering the justifications advanced in favour of aggressive rights protection measures and demands for special laws to facilitate this. It should be noted that the Sochi 2014 Games organisers announced in October 2011 that more than USD 1 billion in domestic sponsorships had already been sourced and that there were hopes of securing a further USD 200 million in deals. Head of the organising committee, Dmitry Chernyshenko, declared that a 'surplus' of USD 300 million was expected from the event, and that no government money would be needed to finance the event. He was quoted as stating that 'we are really confident we will not apply for public money from the state. There is an obligation on the state to co-invest in the Games, but my goal is to have this money as profit of the Games.'[45] Well said, sir.

Not that the event organisers are necessarily the only ones who engage in the above-mentioned obfuscation tactic regarding the true objective with rights protection measures. James and Osborn, in writing about ticketing regulations passed by the UK government for the 2012 London Games, explain that a measure of window-dressing is to be found in such regulations regarding their real objectives:

> According to Richard Caborn MP, the government is 'concerned with catching people who want to make a fast buck out of 2012, not those who advertise legitimately, who exploit the Games in the right way, and from whom we receive benefit.' Put in these terms, it does not appear that consumer protection is high on the list of the government's priorities. Instead, it appears that they are concerned with profiteering, reduced profits and lost tax revenues. Although these are all issues with which any government should be concerned, in the case of the London 2012 Olympic Games, these provisions have been dressed up as being for the benefit of the consumer or justified on the basis that the IOC has forced the government's hand.[46]

It seems that there are frequent attempts to clothe measures and laws aimed at protecting or facilitating aspects of the commercial exploitation of mega-events with pseudo legitimacy, in terms of the protection of consumers, or with other laudable objectives which ostensibly are in the public interest but may be little more than merely commercially motivated (and redolent under a thin sheen of

---

[44] Ibid.

[45] From a report on the gamesbids.com website, 14 October 2011, available online at http://www.gamesbids.com/eng/other_news/1216135928.html.

[46] James and Osborn 2010.

greed). In this light I will proceed to briefly examine the above-mentioned stock argument advanced by event organisers in support of their stigmatised view of ambush marketing and the frequently alleged, urgent need to combat ambushing, which at its heart is a public interest argument but, in my view, lacks substance.

9.3 The 'Survival of the Games' Rhetoric in Support of Aggressive Anti-Ambushing Measures and Special Laws

The 'survival of the Games' argument referred to above has been frequently advanced by event organisers in the ambush marketing context (and are a regular feature of the 'name and shame' campaigns against alleged ambushers as referred to in Chap. 2), as well as in the legal and other literature relating to ambush marketing. One way to phrase this argument is to ask whether ambush marketing 'poses a serious threat to the longevity of sponsorship as a cost-effective marketing tool.'[47] Grady et al. succinctly describe this argument in the context of the Olympic Games:

> The Olympic movement's stated rationale for event-specific legislation is to protect the commercial value of its brand so that it continues to be financially valuable to official sponsors. Absent such legislation, it argues, ambush marketing will diminish the value of its sponsorship assets and ultimately result in companies not renewing their sponsorships or, at the very least, negotiating a lower price for their sponsorship. This presupposes that ambush marketing actually has caused harm to the Olympic movement's sponsorship programme, or at least has the potential to do so.[48]

The authors opine that this rationale has not held up to scrutiny, although it should be acknowledged that at first glance this argument does appear to make some sense. Sponsor investment is specifically linked with events, and if one recalls that sponsors pay for rights to associate their brands with the event for marketing purposes it is a fair assumption that the *quid pro quo* for the event organisers is the receipt of sponsorship fees for purposes of using such revenues to stage the events. In actual fact, however, I would suggest that this last assumption is not necessarily entirely accurate. We need to interrogate the extent to which sponsorship revenues in fact are employed to cover the costs of putting on the show or, alternatively, whether such revenues in fact largely go towards event-related profits for the organisers. If this last is the case, I would suggest that the 'survival of the Games' argument carries much less weight, especially if one considers the public interest element of the sports mega-event as referred to elsewhere in this book. It is one thing to say that we need often draconian special event laws in order to protect commercial interests which make the very staging of the events possible and that in the absence of such laws the organisers may be

---

[47] Tripodi and Sutherland 2000, pp. 412–422.

[48] Grady et al. 2010, p. 152.

unable to even stage the events (this at least implies that the public will ultimately benefit from the spin-offs from the event and that the limitations on civil liberties and other consequences of such special event legislation is a necessary price to pay in this regard). It is something very different, however, to argue that such laws are justified if they are used primarily to protect event organisers' ability to make substantial profits from the events. While detailed information about the financial aspects of event staging is not always publicly available, I will briefly consider these issues with reference to the limited writing available on the subject. In short, I will consider three (interrelated) questions, in an attempt to interrogate the veracity of the argument:

- To what extent is sponsorship money actually used to cover the costs of staging of the events?
- Is sponsorship money primarily a source of event-related profits for the event organisers?
- Do the ever-increasing size of and costs to stage the modern sports mega-event justify special anti-ambushing laws in terms of the 'survival of the Games' argument?

If one compares the position regarding the FIFA World Cup with the Olympic Games, it is interesting to note that the International Olympic Committee retains around 8% of revenues from the Games to cover its operating costs, and the remaining 92% is allocated to National Olympic Committees, international federations and the local organising committees for the Games events.[49] While the IOC may seem to be extremely generous in this regard—something worth considering in evaluating the profit-making activities of the organisation—it may not necessarily be an entirely accurate portrayal of its motives:

> One question that arises is why the [IOC] does not attempt to capture as much of the rent generated from the event as it can. The IOC clearly leaves money on the table. It does not appear to maximize its profit or revenues when it sets rates for sponsorships, fees for licensing, or rights for broadcasting. Of course, the central authority does not lose money either, and it generally increases its fund balances from year to year. Our supposition is that the IOC, rather than maximizing its own profits, maximizes the network's profits. By providing room for participant profitability and incentives for participant entrepreneurship, the IOC extends the Olympic network's reach and influence. The IOC is always cognizant of preparing for the next set of bids for the games and broadcast rights.[50]

It does at least appear that FIFA, for one, is much less generous in sharing revenues from its major events with the real stakeholders in the game of football. While FIFA has on occasion defended its efforts to draw maximum commercial benefit from the World Cup event on the basis that the revenues generated are needed to finance the organisation's activities in the 4-year period until the next

---

[49] Davis 2008, p. 157.

[50] Dollinger, MJ; Li, X; Mooney, C H 'Mega-events and entrepreneurial rents: Lessons from the Beijing Olympics' (draft document, April 2009—available online at the time of writing at http://www.indiana.edu/~rccpb/uschinacooperation/papers/P8%20Dollinger.pdf).

World Cup, it still appears as if a relatively small part of such revenues actually goes towards e.g. development and governance programmes. This does not stop FIFA from breathlessly making claims of imminent peril from ambushing of its commercial interests, and in strong language. Compare the following, found in Issue 1 (January 2011) of the *FIFA Public Guidelines for Use of FIFA's Official Marks* in respect of the 2014 FIFA World Cup Brazil[51] (note especially the wording of the passages I have emphasised):

> Any unauthorised use of the Official Marks not only undermines the integrity of the FIFA World Cup™ and its marketing programme, *but also puts the interests of the worldwide football community at stake*. The FIFA Rights Holders *will only invest* in the 2014 FIFA World Cup™ *if they are provided with this exclusivity* for the use of the Official Marks. If anyone could use the Official Marks for free and create an association with the 2014 FIFA World Cup™, there would be no reason to become a Rights Holder. *This would mean that FIFA and the LOC could not appoint any Rights Holders and could not secure the funding for the 2014 FIFA World Cup™ from such revenues*. Therefore, the protection of the exclusive rights *is crucial for the funding for the 2014 FIFA World Cup Brazil™* and FIFA asks that non affiliated entities respect FIFA's intellectual property and conduct their activities without commercially associating with the 2014 FIFA World Cup™. [Emphasis added]

I would suggest that some of these claims are overstated or, at least, not manifestly backed up by actual research data or empirical evidence to prove the effects claimed. And the reader should note that the organisation claims that allowing a free-for-all in terms of commercial association with the event would mean that FIFA 'could not secure the funding for the 2014 FIFA World Cup™ *from such revenues*.' It does not claim that such freedom of association would endanger the ability to host the event-clearly much of the money used for this purpose is derived from other sources—but only that it would not be able to use sponsor money for this purpose. Could one read this to mean that it is, actually, simply claiming that it will make fewer profits if it has to use other resources to fund the staging of the event? I think this interpretation does in fact show a verifiable consequence of potential loss of sponsors, although I doubt that it is sufficient justification for the aggressive rights protection laws considered in this book.

One finds a similar trend of hyperbole regarding the allegedly pernicious effects of ambushing amongst the commentators who defend commercialisation of the Olympic Games, especially the often less than objective ones:

> The challenge has always been to manage two issues. On the one hand, there is the organising committee's focus on generating enough revenue to avoid bankruptcy and balance the books. On the other, there is the IOC's need to ensure that the Games are successfully staged, and that the scramble for revenue does not undermine the overall Olympic ideal.[52]

The Games invariably (at least for its recent instalments since the late 1980s) generates significantly more revenues from commercial sources than what is

[51] Available on the web site of the organisation at www.fifa.com.

[52] Michael Payne, former IOC marketing director, writing in Payne 2006, p. 116.

needed to avoid bankruptcy and 'balance the books,' and one must assume that the continuing 'scramble for revenues' which exceeds this threshold limit and sees consistent and large profits from the event then, in fact, reflects part of the Olympic ideal. Yes, less sponsor money would undoubtedly mean smaller events, but it appears disingenuous to argue that the sport (e.g. FIFA's game of football, or the 'Olympic movement') would suffer significantly and irretrievably as a result. Would smaller events really be all that bad? At what cost the ever-escalating spectacles of opening and closing ceremonies and the other activities that surround the hosting of major sporting competitions? While, for example, the 2008 Beijing Olympics is generally recognised as an anomaly in respect of the vast scale of spending for the event, it has been speculated that a low estimate of the cost to stage the opening ceremony is in the region of USD 100 million (or about USD 476,000 per min and almost USD 8,000 per s, and more than twice the cost of the 2004 Athens Olympics opening ceremony!),[53] and the opening ceremony of the 2010 Vancouver winter Olympics was the most expensive for the winter instalment of the Games to date at USD 38 million.[54] These expensive productions are not uncontroversial. When FIFA commissioned a Hollywood-based events coordinator to organise the first-ever 'Kick Off Celebration' music concert in Johannesburg scheduled for the evening before the opening match of the 2010 World Cup event, it appeared to feel that very few local musicians were good (or popular) enough for its showcase. Only after vocal protest by the local Creative Workers Union (and suggestions voiced at a Cape Town musicians' conference for a free admission 'rebel' concert by local artists—which one industry member reportedly suggested should be called the 'Fuck FIFA' concert[55]), FIFA magnanimously allowed more South African artists on the programme for its musical extravaganza. And Price recounts how a UK academic's campaign to use the Beijing Games to highlight China's questionable role regarding Darfur spiralled into a Hollywood stand-off involving actress Mia Farrow and Steven Spielberg. Spielberg, who had been approached by the BOCOG to produce the opening and closing ceremonies of the Games, was confronted by Farrow, who asked in a 2007 editorial in the *Wall Street Journal*: 'Does Mr. Spielberg really want to go down in history as the Leni Riefenstahl of the Beijing Games?'[56] The political issues aside, the point is that event organisers see nothing wrong with and, in fact, actively

---

53 http://penguinsix.com/2008/08/09/how-much-did-the-olympic-opening-ceremony-cost/. Another online source puts the figure closer to USD 300 million—see http://www.sports-reference.com/olympics/blog/?p=9.

54 http://penguinsix.com/2010/02/13/vancouver-2010-opening-ceremony-cost-38-million/.

55 During the playing of the 2010 football World Cup event there appeared to be a growing feeling of disillusionment and even anger at FIFA amongst South Africans. A Cape Town artist was reported as doing a brisk trade in 'Fick Fufa' t-shirts as a non-profit venture. Local satirical news site Hayibo.com was also selling a range of t-shirts that lampooned FIFA's copyright and other IP rights to phrases and other things, with the logo 'FEEFA 2.010 WHIRLED CUP SOWTH AFRIKA'—from a report by Raborife, M 'Fick Fufa!', *Mail and Guardian*, 18–24 June 2010.

56 Price, ME 'On Seizing the Olympic Platform,' in Price and Dayan 2008, p. 106.

pursue their events being characterised by increasingly spectacular and expensive entertainment spectacles, to the point of involving Hollywood heavyweights, often ignoring the locale and socio-economic conditions in the host nation or city. Even the balloon show alone at the 2010 Commonwealth Games hosted in Delhi was reported to have cost around Rs 70 crore (or approximately USD 15 million)[57]—an ironic figure if one considers the controversy surrounding this event regarding the city's readiness to host it at the time and its reported negative impact on the poor and homeless—none of whom, I would venture to suggest, got to see the show or enjoy a Coke while watching the fireworks.

I submit (and this might sound simplistic), if one considers that the single biggest source of revenues in respect of the sport mega-event is the sale of broadcasting rights (and that actual event ticketing as revenue source has in recent years assumed a much less important role than was the case in the first half of the twentieth century), that the mega-event nowadays is primarily a mediated television product rather than a direct physical presence experience. In this light it makes sense to me that the spectacle of these events can be scaled down, in the interests of saving on the huge staging costs, without detracting overly much from the entertainment value. I would suggest that many of the spectacular visual effects put on and paid for by local organisers that have become *de rigueur* for opening and closing ceremonies, for example, can be accomplished by means of digital special effects in event broadcasts. Yes, this would make for a less spectacular show for the actual event spectators at the venue, but a *quid pro quo* could be significantly lower ticket prices (surely a big positive in the context of the modern mega-event where tickets have become prohibitively expensive for the local host populations—compare the ICC Cricket World Cup in the Caribbean, the 2010 FIFA World Cup in South Africa, the 2008 Beijing Games and what will in all probability also turn out to be the case with the 2014 FIFA World Cup and 2016 Rio Olympics to be held in Brazil). These ceremonies have become a source of bragging rights for host nations and cities as to what they can accomplish, but I would suggest that most right-minded local tax-payers would be happy to forgo them.

More to the point, does the maintenance of the huge (and ever-increasing in size) mega-events justify the apparent trampling of the rights of those outside the hallowed circle of event organisers and their commercial partners, as discussed elsewhere in this book? Schmitz does not appear to think so, in questioning the veracity of the very 'survival rationale' raised by event organisers in respect of combating ambush marketing:

> Critics of ambush marketing would suggest that the threat of ambush marketing could ultimately impair the ability of event organizers to host elaborate and successful Olympic Games if ambush marketing deters large multinational corporations from being official

[57] See the *Times of India* report of 7 September 2010, available online at the time of writing at http://timesofindia.indiatimes.com/india/CWG-balloon-show-at-opening-ceremony-to-cost-Rs-70cr/articleshow/6508276.cms.

> sponsors. However, the appeal to large corporations of the world-wide exposure that results from sponsorship of the Olympic Games will never be diminished by market imperfections such as ambushers to the point of threatening the budgets of event organizers. Additionally, as is evident from the ongoing efforts to stop ambushers, the practice of ambush marketing encourages organizers to work harder to thwart intellectual property violations, and raises the awareness of intellectual property rights globally—a long-term benefit to all intellectual property owners.[58]

Pelanda, who refers to this stock argument in favour of aggressive protection against ambushing as '"the sky is falling" hysterics,' recounts the argument of Steve McKelvey who questions the veracity of such alarmist claims in light of the Olympic experience—despite all the brouhaha around ambushing by the IOC, its sponsorship fees continue to escalate with each quadrennial, and Olympic sponsorship revenue 'has exploded in recent years, growing from nine TOP sponsors contributing $96 million in the 1985–1988 period to eleven sponsors contributing $866 million for the 2005–2008 period.'[59] The author concludes that 'It appears that the most serious threat posed by ambush marketing is the indiscriminate use of the term itself.'[60]

Which brings one to the need to evaluate the above argument regarding the economic necessity to eradicate ambush marketing in order to protect sponsorship investment and, ultimately, the continued existence of mega-events. FIFA's web site, for example, contains an item regarding the organisation's rights protection programme (which is aimed, primarily, at countering ambush marketing) and includes the following:

> In recent years, FIFA has been criticised for its rights protection programme in some sections of the media. However, it should always be remembered that protecting the various partners involved, whether that be the venues, the TV and marketing rights holders or the players on the pitch, ultimately ensures that *the staging of major events can be financed entirely from the private coffers of FIFA and the respective local organising committee*. [Emphasis added]

It appears that this statement is, at best, inaccurate, and at worst disingenuous. Huge amounts of public money (i.e. taxpayer-raised funding) in the host nation are utilised to stage the World Cup, with hundreds of millions or even billions of dollars usually required to build new or upgrade existing stadia as well as infrastructure, in order to meet FIFA's stringent hosting requirements as set out in the bid guarantees.[61] To claim that the billions of dollars of commercial revenue earned by FIFA is utilised to ensure that the event is 'financed entirely from the private coffers of FIFA' and of the local organising committee ignores this public

---

[58] Schmitz 2005, p. 208.

[59] Pelanda, BL 'Ambush marketing: Dissecting the discourse,' undated 2011 paper available online at the time of writing at http://works.bepress.com/brian_pelanda/, with reference to McKelvey et al. 2010, p. 23; Donatuti 2007, p. 207.

[60] Ibid.

[61] It has been reported that the organisers of the 2014 World Cup in Brazil estimate that infrastructure investment for the event will be in the region of USD 9.5 billion, or more than double the infrastructure investment for the 2010 FIFA World Cup South Africa.

investment in the event, and seems to seek to obscure the fact that FIFA earns a substantial profit from its commercialisation efforts. I subscribe to the following view expressed by Victor Matheson in a *Sports Economist* blog posting, which I believe exposes the fallacy of the above claim by FIFA, based on pure logic:

> FIFA and the IOC are able to generate such huge profits specifically because they don't bear the expense of building the sports infrastructure needed to host the event. If the governing bodies, rather than the host cities and countries, were on the hook for the sports facilities, we would see the Olympics rotate among a small number of locations, such as Los Angeles, with existing venues, and the 2022 World Cup would be headed to the United States, with its wealth of existing state-of-the art stadiums instead of Qatar, a country with almost none of the infrastructure currently in place to host the event.[62]

In similar vein to FIFA's claims, one commentator recently made the following rather bald statements in an article on the need for special anti-ambushing legislation in a particular jurisdiction:

> Another issue of concern to event organisers is that the practice of ambush marketing has jeopardized their ability to fund events due to their inability to retain top sponsors. Ambush marketing affects event organisers considerably and poses a substantial threat to their economic interests.[63]

In support of these statements the author refers to the fact that 'the worldwide sponsorship programme has increased the income of the IOC by 900% over a period of 20 years which makes the risk of losing sponsors colossal.'[64] I cannot agree with such brazen and uncritical acceptance (this is just one example from the literature) of the 'fact' that potential loss of sponsors in the face of ambush marketing—remember, there appears to be little or no empirical proof of the probability of this contingency actually occurring—would jeopardise the ability to fund events. I am not aware of any clear research data on the extent of investment by event organisers of sponsorship money in the staging of events as well as in development etc. of the relevant sport during the event quadrennium until the next cash cow event comes around. What is clear is that ambushing might, *if* it actually were to lead to loss of sponsors, pose a 'substantial threat' to event organisers' 'economic interests'—they will lose out on the currently huge profit margin in the face of the hundreds of millions of dollars that the IOC and FIFA rake in from sponsors. As has been observed:

> There is an argument, which host countries appear to be ignoring, that these often private and highly profitable businesses are changing the intellectual property laws of host nations to protect the event holders investment and profits. The IOC between 2005 and 2008 generated US$ 5,450,000,000 of which it claims to have kept 10%, still a staggering US$54,450,000.00.[65]

---

[62] Matheson, V 'Bad economics from FIFA,' 3 March 2011, *The Sports Economist*—available online at the time of writing at http://thesportseconomist.com/page/7/.

[63] Seth 2010, p. 456.

[64] Ibid. At 462 n 15.

[65] Palomba, M 'Is ambush marketing dead?' Reed Smith Advertising Compliance Team Client Update (May 2010)—available online at the time of writing at http://www.advertising

Another commentator's view also does not distinguish between the costs of hosting and the profits made, in the context of the Olympic Games:

> Although there has been a massive increase in sponsorship revenue over the past 20 years (TOP sponsors paid USD 95 million in 1988, rising to USD 866 million in 2008), this has to be considered in the context of the growing costs of hosting the event over the same period (with estimates that Seoul 1988 cost USD 4 billion, to Beijing 2008s USD 40 billion). Whilst modern Olympic Games can be profitable, this would not be feasible without the increasing sponsorship revenues. As such, the IOC is understandably anxious to protect what has become a valuable asset.[66]

This conflation of, on the one hand, costs of staging and, on the other hand, profit, is dismissive of the real issue and ignores the distinction, which is an important one when one seeks to determine the justification for legal protection of commercial rights to events. In light of the extremely restrictive and even draconian laws and measures that are frequently implemented in order to protect the commercial interests of event organisers and sponsors, as we have encountered in the earlier chapters, it is inconceivable that event organisers would be justified to claim such protection for purely a profit-making motive. I also find the following view, expressed in a country report on the United Kingdom for a 2009 review of trademark protection of major sports events by the International Association of Protection of Intellectual Property (or AIPPI), rather puzzling and lacking in substance:

> [I]n the UK, the Olympic Games (and Paralympic Games) and Commonwealth Games are the only major sports events to be granted separate and additional protection above that provided by UK trademark law. This is due in a large part to the unique nature and history of the Olympic Games *and the fact that funding is not profit making and spent on the event…* Although the Olympic and Paralympic Games receive funding through commercial sponsorship, *that money totally goes towards funding the costs of the events. The Olympic movement is not a profit-making venture and instead relies on such sponsorship as a means to put on the Olympics.* This is in stark contrast to the sponsorship of other major sports events where the monies received are often passed on to shareholders or interested parties. The Olympic Games are also generally part-funded by the national government of the host nation. The role of the Government and public funds, and the reliance on sponsorship necessitates the extension of intellectual property rights.[67] [My emphasis]

(Footnote 65 continued)
compliancelaw.com/uploads/file/10-097%20ReACTS%20-%20Is%20ambush%20marketing%20dead.PDF.

66 Ellen, L 'Protecting Sponsors at the London 2012 Olympics,' January 2010 (at 4), available online at the time of writing at http://www.mishcon.com/assets/managed/docs/downloads/doc_2413/Protecting_Sponsors_at_the_London_2012_Olympics_doc_(2).pdf.

67 From the country report on the United Kingdom prepared for the Working Committee of the International Association for the Protection of Intellectual property (AIPPI), Project Q210 ('The protection of major sports events and associated commercial activities through trademarks and other IPR'; reports compiled for purposes of a draft resolution to be submitted to the AIPPI Exco meeting in Buenos Aires, October 2009)—available online at the time of writing at https://www.aippi.org/download/commitees/210/GR210united_kingdom.pdf.

One commentator has observed that '[u]ltimately, the rationale that presides over repression of ambush marketing is not very much different from the rationale that explains the protection of pharmaceutical test data—such rationale is the protection of investment against its profiteering by opportunists, free riders.'[68] But this comparison seems to assume a similar societal importance for protection of the commercial investments in large sports events to that of R&D in the pharmaceutical industry. I beg to differ in this regard, and I don't believe that Pfizer and Coca-Cola should be viewed in the same light when one considers, on the one hand, the use of restrictive laws to protect investment in a health care-related field with, on the other hand, the use of such laws in the (bloated, commercialised) sports entertainment industry.

The arguments in favour of special legal protection invariably refer to the huge costs of staging the events and the trickle-down effect of profits being reinvested in the relevant sporting code or, for example, the Olympic movement. But how much of the sponsors' money actually goes towards hosting the events and developing the sport? What is the extent of the event organisers' financial outlay? The web site of the 2012 London Olympics, for example, proclaims that the Games are delivered by two key organisations, one private and one public. The organising committee, LOCOG, is the private sector company responsible for staging and hosting the 2012 Games. While it receives income from the IOC, it is stated that almost its entire GBP 2 billion budget is to be raised from the private sector. Its sources of revenue are declared to be income from sales of tickets, merchandise and, most importantly, a domestic sponsorship programme. The other key delivery organisation is the Olympic Delivery Authority (ODA), which is the public sector body responsible for the delivery of the new venues and infrastructure required for the London 2012 Games. The ODA budget is drawn entirely from the public sector. The ODA is funded by the Department for Culture, Media and Sport, the Greater London Authority, the London Development Agency and the Olympic Lottery Distributor (with GBP 2.2 billion of UK National Lottery funds helping to create the facilities to host the Games).[69] One observer commented as follows in 2008 on the subject of strong commercial rights protection as found in *sui generis* event legislation like the London Act:

> Supporters of this kind of legislation argue that it is necessary to protect official sponsors, without whose funding the taxpayer would be more heavily exposed; but this claim is difficult to sustain when the actual contribution of the official sponsors towards the overall cost of staging major events is taken into account. For example, of the total budget for hosting the London 2012 Games (9.3 billion [pounds sterling] at the time of writing), only about 10% is coming from corporate sponsors: the remaining 90% is coming from other sources, foremost among them the British taxpayer, especially Londoners, who are subject to a special levy. As the Institute of Practitioners in Advertising has pointed out, "local

[68] De Carvalho 2010, p. 52.

[69] Source: The London 2012 website, available online at the time of writing at http://www.london2012.com/making-it-happen/funding-the-games/index.php.

> businesses in particular will be paying for these events but will be deprived of benefiting from them because they will basically have to pretend that they are not happening."[70]

And host nation tax-base investment in order to physically stage the event apart, let us not forget that a large part of the publicity hype (and the thematic space of what a mega-event comes to represent—in the meaning of the discussion in Chap. 8) may in fact be attributable to the consumer audience itself rather than the organisers and sponsors:

> [O]nce symbols are introduced into a culture, they tend to be recoded by those who see and hear them. Audiences fit what they see and hear into their own cognitive frameworks, responding to signals and giving them meaning according to their own experiences, agendas and needs. In this way, signals become multidimensional. They come to convey not only the meaning ascribed to them by their initial purveyors, but also the new interpretations given them by listeners. Ultimately, there is no single reality.[71]

I would suggest that, while event organisers like the IOC and FIFA may continue to claim a dire need for lawmakers to protect its sponsors' and commercial partners' financial investment in the events (a claim which I examine elsewhere), it is fatuous for these organisations to claim that their own financial investments in staging the events are of such a nature that they deserve such special and often draconian new laws. The above-mentioned AIPPI, in a 2009 resolution, emphasised the role of special event legislation in protecting sponsors' investment, and its impact in respect of funding mega-events:

> [S]pecific *sui generis* rights are sometimes created by successful bidders for their major sports event *(sic)* such as Olympic and Paralympic Games. These *sui generis* rights supplement trade mark and unfair competition law with a view to creating a more valuable exclusive right for sponsors, and thereby a reduced demand on public expenditure.[72]

I believe that the apparent bald assumption that all revenues generated from sponsor investment (the object of the protection afforded by such legislation) are utilised for purposes of covering the costs of hosting these events needs to be further interrogated. In the context of often substantial profits earned by the event organisers it is problematic to assume, without proper empirical evidence—which, I would submit, the organisers have to date not produced and have not been called upon to produce by potential host governments—that significant chunks of such sponsorship revenue goes towards generating profits. And, if this is indeed the case, it makes for an interesting consideration to be added to the mix in the exercise of evaluating the legitimacy of often draconian event legislation and the balancing of the private versus public interests involved. Scaria, in examining the

---

[70] Leone, L 'Ambush marketing: Criminal offence or free enterprise?' Asser International Sports Law Centre (2008)—available online at the time of writing at http://www.thefreelibrary.com.

[71] Cooper Dreyfuss 1996, p. 139.

[72] AIPPI Resolution on Question Q210: 'The protection of major sports events and associated commercial activities through Trade Marks and other IPR,' adopted at the AIPPI Executive Committee meeting in Buenos Aires, 14 October 2009—English version available online at the time of writing at https://www.aippi.org/download/commitees/210/RS210English.pdf.

impact of ambush marketing and arguing that it leads to the loss of sponsorship value due to the loss of sponsors' exclusivity, observes the following:

> As it is an undeniable fact that corporate sponsorship is one of the biggest money-spinning sources of revenue for the event organisers, the loss in sponsorship value will definitely affect the financial strength of an event organiser. Hence, the most important argument against ambush marketing is that it dilutes the value of corporate sponsorships and thereby jeopardises the financial vitality of events.[73]

I agree. Of course a loss of sponsorship value (if that is the case) and the potential for this to lead to loss of potential sponsors would affect the financial strength of an event organiser. But he misses the point; the question should be what that financial strength refers to. If it refers to revenues required for the actual costs of staging the event there would be merit in this view. But if it relates primarily to the event organiser's profits from the event it is, I would submit, a very different story. The UK Chartered Institute of Marketing (CIM)'s April 2011 discussion document on ambush marketing and the 2012 London Olympics notes the following in response to the IOC's stigmatised view of ambush marketing and its assertion that it combats ambushing 'to preserve and promote the Olympic spirit':

> [O]fficial sponsors to the 2012 Olympics are paying a total of £930 million, none of which is returned to the public purse which is funding the entire £9.298 bn cost of hosting the Olympics. If there is an 'Olympic spirit,' surely it is tarnished at least as much by official commercialisation than ambush marketing. The literal reading of the IOC's view is that a company does not 'discredit' itself and does not 'threaten sport' as long as it pays sums of money that most companies would only dream of as their total marketing budget, to the organising body.[74]

I agree with this view, but the point I would like to highlight is the fact that it appears as if a substantial part of the corporate sponsorship income in respect of the Games is divorced from the costs of staging the event. The CIM document notes that Tier One sponsorship income (7 × £40 million) goes to the IOC, whilst Tier Two and Three income goes to the LOCOG, as part of the £2 billion budget to stage the Games. The £2 billion staging budget consists of £650 million anticipated final income from Tier 2 and 3 sponsors, £350 million from ticketing and merchandising, and £1 billion from the IOC. I think it is dismissive to simply assume that all sponsorship income is used to cover staging costs, and the significant component of such income which goes to the coffers of event organisers, as profits from the event, in my view puts a very different spin on the justification for often draconian special laws to protect such profit-making capacity of event organisers. In 2000, Tripodi and Sutherland observed that 'Without capital injection from sponsors, it is questionable whether the average tax-payer would be

---

73 Scaria 2008, p. 44.

74 Chartered Institute of Marketing *Ambush Marketing and the Law*, April 2011 at 10—see http://www.cim.co.uk/resources/emergingthemes/home.aspx.

willing to finance many of the current sporting events.'[75] I simply wish to point out that maybe that is already the case. I do not believe that current evidence shows unequivocally that sponsorship income is an indispensable requirement for the staging of the events.

And let us not forget that claims by event organisers that their 'surplus' (read: profits) from hosting the events are mostly ploughed back into development of the sport may not always be entirely accurate. FIFA, which consistently claims that around 75% of its revenues from its World Cup event finds its way to the grass-roots of world football, has been faced with claims that the money often seems to go into the pockets of officials and is used to buy votes rather than soccer balls for needy children:

> Senior former FIFA staffers describe an administration that is built around the specific purpose of delivering term extensions to Blatter. They talk euphemistically of the so-called "football development" funding as "questionable," since so little accountability is required of recipients. With FIFA distributing millions of dollars a year in central funding to its member associations, with so little visibility sought for what they do with it, it is hardly a surprise Blatter has proved so electable.[76]

Of course, as I pointed out earlier in this chapter, the position may be very different for other event organisers. David Becker of the International Cricket Council explains that the ICC does, in fact, have a strong justification for protection of its event-related revenues, which goes beyond a mere profit motive:

> The ICC, like many other international federations, is a non-profit organization. We collect the revenues from our events, deduct our costs, and distribute the revenues to our 105 Members around the world. Unfortunately the vast majority of our Member countries 'live on the breadline' so to speak. Very, very few actually make a profit (I have seen the figures). They rely heavily on these revenues for their survival, and more importantly, to fund grassroots cricket in their countries. I know it's hard to believe, but any material impact on these revenues has a big impact on the stability of our Member countries.[77]

Of course, one can still question the point of whether ambush marketing of events (and the ICC's Cricket World Cup has been no stranger to ambushing in recent years) has any 'material impact' on such revenues, in the light of possible other causes for financial harm, such as official sponsor advertising clutter. I will, however, concede David's point that the ICC can show a real and pressing need to safeguard revenues which may form the lifeblood of grassroots development of the game.

Ellis et al. refer to the 'anecdotal' nature of the 'survival of the Games' argument (i.e. which calls for protection of the expensive exclusivity of the rights

---

[75] Tripodi and Sutherland 2000.

[76] From Scott, M 'FIFA crisis: Storm clouds gather as big hitters fight to clear names,' 29 May 2011 in *The Guardian*—available online at the time of writing at http://www.guardian.co.uk/football/2011/may/29/fifa-crisis-storm-clouds-gather?INTCMP=ILCNETTXT3487.

[77] David Becker, at the time of writing the Head of Legal for the International Cricket Council, from personal e-mail correspondence with the author, December 2011.

of official sponsors in order to retain and attract such sponsors) so often advanced by event organisers in favour of aggressive rights protection for their events. I would suggest that the authors make some truly compelling points which deserve to be quoted in full here:

> The most consistent claims as to the necessity of anti-ambush marketing legislation relate to the need to protect the value of Olympic sponsorships. Yet if the dilution of the value of Olympic sponsorships is to be put forth as the public policy justification for the legislation, the link between ambush marketing and a decline in sponsorship values should be more than anecdotal. While ambush marketing is often asserted as a threat to sponsorship value, it is not clear that the value of Olympic sponsorships has indeed been waning. In fact, sponsorship investment has continued to increase significantly and is projected to break the $ 1 billion mark for the TOP program in the upcoming quadrennial. In addition the IOC has continued to sign international partners including Dow Chemical and Proctor & Gamble who have both committed to the TOP program until after the 2020 Games while VISA, along with Coca-Cola and Omega have already renewed their contracts until after 2020 Games. Further, any decline in sponsorship values may be attributable to other factors. As noted above, there have been a number of studies that have suggested that the IOC has struggled with brand management and has been criticized for causing harm to its own brand through excessive commercialization. High profile corruption and doping scandals linked to the Olympics, consumer cynicism over excessive commercialism, as well as concerns over human rights may also have an impact on the Olympic brand. Even if it were demonstrated that the value of sponsorships has declined in recent years, it would be difficult to demonstrate that any significant decline in value is due to ambush marketing as opposed to any one or a combination of the other factors mentioned. In light of this complex array of factors, the assumption that ambush marketing is a problem of significant enough dimensions to justify the creation of a very broad new intellectual property right can be questioned. However, one could also argue that this issue is not relevant in the eyes of the IOC whose primary concern is to protect their own brand as well as the exclusivity of their partners. Given the intense competition between cities/governments to host the Olympic Games, the IOC is in a favourable position to insist upon such legislation which has become an important element of their brand management strategy. By requiring countries to introduce legal measures to protect sponsors from ambush marketing, the IOC is able to protect their rights over those of all others despite the broader public policy obligations inherent in the creation of legislation. The IOC maximizes their benefits (i.e. revenue from sponsors) yet is able to keep the risks minimal with the financial burden of hosting the Games remaining with the host city/nation.[78]

Which, again, leads me to pose the question whether the rigid demands for special mega-event laws against ambushing are really aimed at protecting sponsors with a view to ensuring the 'survival of the Games,' or whether such demands simply represent a quest for market control by the event organisers. I have argued earlier (in Chap. 8) that the true object of event organisers' aggressive anti-ambushing rights protection programmes appears to be the monopolistic pursuit of market control, in the interests of maximising the potential commercial value of events with a clear profit motive. Price, in his analysis of the mega-event as platform and its 'hi-jacking' by those who attempt to appropriate the platform, distinguishes efforts to throw off the dominant narrative of the event ('competitive

[78] Ellis et al. 2011, p. 302.

use') from what he refers to as complementary use of the event; i.e. where such use is 'merely complementary (indeed reinforcing), in competition with or in contradiction to the accepted narrative (assuming that narrative can be specified)... in which the appropriator gains benefits, but those who built the platform bear no additional costs.'[79] He explains how ambush marketing is such a complementary use of an event such as the Olympic Games, and hints at the fact that attempts by the event organiser to combat ambushing are not necessarily linked to any real harm caused by such ambushing:

> [F]rom the point of view of the Olympics there is little difference between a complementary and a competitive user (where the dominant and alternate use are in more of a zero-sum game). Both are "free riders"—sometimes involved in what might be more gently called piggybacking, rather than hijacking, the platform. Free riders threaten the exclusivity of the platform and the underlying marketing theory that yields compensation for the IOC. Even where the free rider does not damage the Games or its family of participants, the IOC has an interest in capturing the economic benefit to the appropriator, thus internalizing the benefit of the Games and protecting those who pay for the privilege... These commercial appropriations are a way of thinking about the greater stories of the Olympic platform: because so much is spent, because the economy of the Olympics depends upon controlling them, and because there are lawsuits with extensive explanations, struggles in this sphere are better articulated than they are in connection to more substantial areas of competition. More is written about a sneaker manufacturer who is not an official sponsor trying to obtain market share, than about competition over the generalized narratives established by the IOC or the Organizing Committee.[80]

Other commentators have recognised that there exists very little evidence of the claims that ambushing actually threatens event funding through sponsorships, and I would suggest that what is actually under potential threat in many cases is mostly the huge profits made by FIFA et al.:

> Assuming that the IOC, FIFA and others of the same kind are the actual owners of the created reputation [of their events], they are the parties who may suffer [from] ambush marketing practices. The organiser aims at leveraging commercial value from the event and from the emotions and values generated in the public. The ambush marketer interferes in that process and reaps some of that commercial value. So far however, ambush marketing seems to have had little if no effect at all on the phenomenal growth in sports revenues. *The damage caused to the organisers, if any, may consist in loss of additional revenues only, i.e. those that would have existed if there had been no ambush marketing activity. This is a hypothetical loss because the sponsorship attribution process usually consists in a competitive bid system resulting in optimized prices and revenues. On the other hand, by multiplying references to an event, ambush marketing is actually contributing to its publicity, popularity and fame.*[81] [Emphasis added]

If the reader will permit me a brief flight of fancy, I will proceed to compare mega-event organisers such as FIFA and the IOC to well-dressed astronauts. No, that is not a typo, let me explain:

---

[79] Price, M E 'On Seizing the Olympic Platform,' in Price and Dayan 2008, p. 90.

[80] Ibid. 91–92.

[81] Kobel 2007, pp. 7, 8.

Naomi Klein,[82] journalist, author and outspoken critic of globalisation, has described the exertion of economic control in conditions that minimise corporate risk and accountability as 'a commercial race towards weightlessness.'[83] She explains this in the context of corporations' dumping of employees, outsourcing and the like, and the exponential growth in corporate expenditure on marketing and brand management. This phenomenon is taken to its limit in the case of companies that have been established on or are developed through the use of trademark licensing arrangements alone.[84] Klein uses the example of the Tommy Hilfiger fashion clothing brand, which is run entirely through licensing deals. It commissions all its products from other companies (Jockey International make Hilfiger underwear; Pepe Jeans London make Hilfiger jeans; Oxford Industries make Hilfiger shirts; and Stride Rite Corporation make Hilfiger footwear)—Tommy Hilfiger 'is less in the business of manufacturing clothes than he is in the business of signing his name.'[85] In this way, companies like Hilfiger, Calvin Klein and others are able to 'acquire virtual (or "weightless") production capacities through a network of licensing agreements':

> These agreements function on the basis of an exchange between the designer, who provides the product design and permission to use the brand name, and the licensee, who pays to make, distribute and sometimes advertise and sell the branded product on the designer's behalf. As their reward for the deal, the designers obtain a specific proportion of sales as well as guaranteed minimum payments each season. The licensee obtains the exclusive right to manufacture and distribute for a brand that has an established reputation and appeal among consumers.[86]

Such business model is facilitated by the law's recognition of trademark licensing[87] whereby marks become commodities in their own right, which has been characterised as an internal reversal in trademark law: 'While unfair competition law is based on the prohibition against palming off one's goods as the goods of another, licensing itself is essentially a "passing off".'[88]

If you will permit me to make the connection, I would suggest that the mega-event organisers such as FIFA and the IOC are similarly striving for 'weightlessness' in respect of exploitation of the commercial value of their events. We are confronted here with organisations that display the following characteristics in respect of the staging of their events:

- They mostly divest themselves of the costs of putting on the show and such costs are squarely devolved to others, namely host governments (and taxpayers) and corporate sponsors. The production costs for these event organisers are

[82] Klein 2000.

[83] See Lury, C 'Trade mark style as a way of fixing things,' in Bently et al. 2008, p. 206.

[84] Ibid.

[85] Klein 2000, p. 24.

[86] Ibid.

[87] In e.g. the UK's Trade Marks Act, 1994.

[88] Gaines 1991, p. 214, as referred to by Lury in Bently et al. 2008, p. 207.

limited to a significant extent to providing a framework for the sporting competition that forms the centre of the thematic space of the event (and includes, of course, the publicity and commercial value of the event as promotional vehicle for corporate marketing purposes);
- They deal, primarily, in a brand, and license the use of such brand to others (specifically the corporate sponsors and the merchandisers or licensees);
- Their reward for the use of their brand lies in huge sponsorship fees, and they make a (often substantial) profit from such use of the licensed brand. The sponsors and licensees, on the other hand, benefit from the commercial appeal of the mega-event for consumers and their exclusive rights to tap this appeal for marketing purposes.

I would suggest that FIFA, for example, must be very close to 'weightlessness,' although this might not be a very happy state of affairs for everyone else, and—crusty old cynic that I am—the *Hindenburg* comes to mind.

In light of the fact, as discussed above, that it appears as if revenues from corporate sponsorships most probably go more towards 'weightless' event organisers' profit margins than covering the actual costs of staging the events, I believe a further factor militating against these organisers' justification for condemning ambushing is to be found in the ever-increasing size of the huge sponsorship fees charged to sponsors. I have explained earlier how there is a vicious cycle at work here; sponsors expect and demand ever-increasing exclusivity, and event organisers demand ever-increasing fees to guarantee such exclusivity. This is, probably, the strongest claim that event organisers have to a protectionist stance by host governments and lawmakers, as the greatest risk posed by ambushers is probably that sponsors will eventually realise that they are being over-charged by means of the ever-escalating rights fees charged by organisers (if one considers that very few guarantees of exclusivity can actually be provided—a point I tried to make in Chap. 8 by arguing that event organisers simply do not and cannot control all elements of the thematic space of the event, as much as they may want to do so). Former *Financial Times* sports editor, David Owen, recently made the point in a tongue-in-cheek way:

> I recognise that getting excited—and, still worse, writing—about instances of ambush marketing constitutes deviant behaviour of the worst kind and may encourage activities that could ultimately undermine the whole Olympic edifice. After all, if official sponsors start to notice their main competitors parking marketing tanks all over their Olympic lawn free of charge, they might start to conclude that the steep ticket prices they have paid are no longer worth it.[89]

The more the sponsors pay, the more they demand. The question is whether this should not entitle ambushers to claim more leeway for accessing marketing

---

[89] Owen, D 'The great Olympic ambush—led by David Cameron,' 22 September 2011—available online at http://www.insidethegames.biz/blogs/14344-david-owen-the-great-olympic-ambush.

opportunities around the events. Arul Scaria does not subscribe to this view. He (rather dismissively) compares ambush marketers to copyleft activists:

> [Some who try to justify ambush marketing] argue that many a times the price of sponsorships is exorbitant and ambush marketing is a form of creative advertising for those companies who cannot pay exorbitant prices for exclusive rights packages. But when we analyse this argument in a comprehensive perspective, we see that it is an argument not only against the sports sponsorship packages, but also against the whole intellectual property rights system. It is an argument similar to that of the copyleft activists! Most of the music pirates and software pirates argue that they go for piracy because of the high price of original CDs and original software. But in today's world, where knowledge is the most powerful capital for any establishment, we see an obligation for its apposite protection. Hence, this argument based on the excessive prices for exclusive rights packages fails.[90]

I would suggest that there is at least one flaw of logic in Scaria's comparison of ambush marketing and IP piracy. Those who attempt to justify ambushing with reference to the prohibitive cost of 'official' sponsorship packages (not to mention the closed shop in respect of bidding for such packages, as I touched on in an earlier chapter) are not concerned with pirating IP in the sense of 'knowledge as capital,' as referred to. While I have discussed the role of IP in the context of ambush marketing elsewhere in this book it should be noted that, in this context, the term does not refer to knowledge (as reflected in the true sense in respect of traditionally protected 'intellectual' property) but rather to marks and brands as symbols employed for commercial exploitation. The modern, creative ambusher is more concerned with being afforded an opportunity to commercially exploit the marketing potential of the publicity that surrounds the mega-event, and in doing so will rarely actually misappropriate any property of the event organiser or official sponsor. As I have argued in the previous chapter, not all of the 'rights' to associate brands with mega-events, which are habitually sold to sponsors, are in fact susceptible to ring-fencing and commercial trade for consideration. I would suggest that this modern 'ambusher' should be allowed to justify its conduct on the basis that the mega-event monopoly and its exorbitant valuation of 'rights' leaves it with little if any room to compete in an open market without acting in a way that the event organisers despise. I think Scaria misses the point through a skewed perception of the ethics and legality of ambush marketing. Also, I think it is improper to allow event organisers to rely on the escalating costs of hosting events in order to justify aggressive protection against ambushing (as we have seen is invariably the case), and then simultaneously dismiss the possibility of such similarly escalating costs of sponsorship as providing any justification for the conduct of ambushers. And it should be noted that payment of these high sponsorship fees should not be seen as a license on the part of the official sponsors to object to every single example of what may be perceived as an 'ambush,' as the UK's Chartered Institute of Marketing recently argued in the above-mentioned discussion document:

---

90 Scaria 2008, pp. 46, 47.

> Preventing ['ambushers' who are not engaging in passing off and are simply attempting to gain legitimate exposure for their products or services] doing so is analogous to authorising a cartel or a monopoly to operate, with unfair competitive advantage enabled simply because the cartel or monopoly paid a fee.[91]

Earlier in this book I have referred to the fact that there appears to be a widespread recognition that ambush marketing has, at least in part, developed as a result of the prevalence of monopolisation of commercial opportunities around events and, more specifically, the phenomenon of sponsorship exclusivity. In Chap. 8 I argued that a covetous appropriation of elements of the thematic space of the mega-event by event organisers and official sponsors has led directly to the outlawing of conduct which would otherwise fall outside the regulation by laws, due to an overly broad perception on the part of 'rights holders' as to the true extent and content of such rights. Having also encountered the importance of the sports mega-event as a marketing platform (as touched on in Chap. 2) I would suggest that much of the prevailing attitude towards 'ambushing' on the part of the rights holders derives squarely from self-interested, exclusionary conduct which aims to arrogate such platform for exclusive use in the interests of obtaining market control. Price, in discussing the Olympic Games as a platform (not only for marketing purposes) explains that '[the] phenomenon of platforms exists in a world in which much clamouring for attention—to sell goods or alter political attitudes—encounters few effective channels to reach the desired audience. Furthermore, the existing channels are often tightly controlled and present significant barriers to entry.'[92] The exclusion of 'all others' from access to the platform has been a major cause of the growth in ambushing; escalating rights fees should not be used as justification for objecting to all sorts of conduct by outsiders as being 'ambushing' while simultaneously constituting a significant barrier to entry for opportunities to derive (commercial) benefits from events.

In conclusion in dealing with the 'survival of the Games' argument, Grady et al.[93] point out that there appears to be very little, if any, direct evidence of the veracity of such claims by sports governing bodies. In the Olympics context, a recent empirical survey amongst the TOP sponsors[94] by Seguin and O'Reilly[95] called into question whether ambush marketing is even the most important concern to the elite TOP sponsors; all those TOP sponsors interviewed 'referred to ambush marketing not in the traditional pejorative manner but merely as a "competitive marketing practice."'[96] The survey also found that these sponsors generally felt that sponsorship clutter 'that the Olympic movement itself has created' was their major

---

[91] Chartered Institute of Marketing *Ambush Marketing and the Law*, April 2011 at 7—see http://www.cim.co.uk/resources/emergingthemes/home.aspx.

[92] Price, M E 'On Seizing the Olympic Platform,' in Price and Dayan 2008, p. 88.

[93] Grady et al. 2010, p. 151.

[94] See Chap. 2 for discussion of the TOP sponsorship programme of the Olympic Games.

[95] Séguin and O'Reilly 2008.

[96] Grady et al. 2010, p. 151.

problem in respect of dilution of the value of sponsorships (through both an overemphasis on revenue generation and a structure that allows NOCs and national governing bodies to sign sponsors that are in direct competition with TOP sponsors), more so than ambush marketing. In fact, those surveyed appeared to believe that this situation 'results in scenarios whereby various governing bodies within the Olympic movement, in essence, are ambushing themselves.'[97] Tripodi and Sutherland made similar observations in a 2000 article.[98]

I am not aware of any definitive survey or other evidence that exists to provide real data to support the event organisers' claims in justification of aggressive anti-ambushing protection. I believe that the data showing the continuing trend of escalating sponsorship rights fees as well as the constant breaking of records in respect of the generation of marketing and sponsorship-related revenues for the successive instalments of events such as FIFA's World Cup and the Olympic Games, in fact, provide contrary evidence and give the lie to these claims.

Finally, I will just briefly refer to the fact that, apart from the 'survival of the Games' rhetoric, a second 'justification' for aggressive anti-ambushing protection has entered the language of mega-event organisers in recent years. The director of the Legal Affairs department of the Beijing Organising Committee for the 2008 Olympics (BOCOG), Lin Yanjung, was quoted as explaining that the BOCOG's main objective with anti-ambushing measures was the protection of sponsors' interests, but with a twist:

> On top of our agenda is *to guard the dignity of the Olympic Games and guarantee the solemnity, standardization and fairness of the Beijing Games*. We have to make sure that the companies supporting the Olympics are getting what they have paid for and receiving fair treatment. We won't let these Olympic supporters down.[99] [My emphasis]

In fact, this found its way into the very legislation passed to protect the 2008 Beijing Games, compare Article 1 of China's Regulations on the Protection of Olympic Symbols[100]:

> These Regulations are formulated for the purposes of strengthening the protection of Olympic symbols, safeguarding the lawful rights and interests of the right holders of Olympic symbols *and maintaining the dignity of the Olympic movement.* [My emphasis]

More recently, in the consultation document on Regulations on Advertising Activity and Trading around London 2012 (published for public comment in March 2011)[101] for the 2012 London Olympics, the UK Department of Culture,

---

[97] Ibid.

[98] Tripodi and Sutherland 2000.

[99] Yang, H 'Non-law enforcement methods to tackle Olympic ambush marketing,' *China Intellectual Property Magazine* (June 2008)—available online at the time of writing at http://www.chinaipmagazine.com/en/journal-show.asp?id=381.

[100] See the discussion in Sect. 4.4.9 of Chap. 4.

[101] Available online at the time of writing at http://www.culture.gov.uk/images/consultations/ConsDoc_Regulations_on_Advertising_and_Trading_London_2012.pdf.

Media and Sport emphasised that its proposed regulation of advertising and trading around the Games is based on three reasons, namely to ensure ease of public access to event venues; to prevent ambush marketing in the vicinities of venues; and *to ensure all Olympic and Paralympic events have a consistent celebratory look and feel to them.* Such claims as to a laudable intention to demand and invoke often draconian laws in order to protect and maintain the 'Olympic ethos' (which smacks of nostalgic longing for a time when the Games were less commercialised) are, frankly in my view, ludicrous—that horse bolted quite some time ago. The Olympics, just like FIFA's World Cup and most of the other mega-events, are in their modern guise a significantly commercial affair aimed as much at fans as consumers as at fans as sports lovers. It is not inappropriate that a banker, Brazil's former Central Bank President, was appointed in March 2011 to head the Olympic Public Authority organising the 2016 Rio Games... Sponsorship research referred to elsewhere in this book has shown that even the major multinational corporations that are the Olympic Movement's TOP sponsors believe one of the biggest problems they face to be the significant degree of marketing clutter surrounding the Olympics, which they themselves identify as not only being due to ambush marketing but also, to a significant extent, to the IOC's own proliferation of sponsorship categories in an attempt to maximize sponsorship revenues.[102] The Olympic organizers appear to be claiming protection for a problem they may have created themselves, and I would suggest that this latest justification for the often controversial efforts to combat ambushing rings as hollow as the 'survival of the Games' rationale. While I have argued in Chap. 7 that this 'look and feel of the Games' argument cannot serve to justify infringement of fundamental rights such as freedom of speech, I similarly do not view it, more generally, as a grounds for justification of aggressive anti-ambushing laws or measures.

9.4 'And in this Corner: The Squeaky-Clean Money-Men?'

When we examine the above questions regarding the arguments in justification of aggressive rights protection (and special laws), it is important to consider the origins of the massive commercialisation of mega-events as we encounter it today, which gathered heady momentum in the last decades of the previous century and currently shows little sign of tapering off or reaching a saturation point any time soon. As discussed in Chap. 2, a turning point in such developments was the 1984 Olympic Games hosted in Los Angeles, after which the then IOC president Juan Antonio Samaranch followed the lead of the head of the local organising committee, Peter Ueberroth, who had devised the new phenomenon of sponsorship exclusivity and categories of sponsorship as opposed to the open access model known theretofore (in terms of which anyone who wanted to sponsor an event

[102] See Séguin and O'Reilly 2008, p. 62.

could get involved). As mentioned, this notion of exclusivity[103] is generally recognised as a prime reason for the increased practices of 'ambushing' of events by non-sponsors who suddenly found themselves outside the candy store looking in. As has been observed, this evolution of sponsorship exclusivity in terms of what would develop into Samaranch's 'TOP' ('The Olympic Partners') model, which was initiated in 1985 and inaugurated at the 1988 Seoul Olympics, was devised at a time when the International Olympic Committee was experiencing serious financial problems and when hosting the expensive Games was not an attractive option for potential host cities (e.g. only Los Angeles bid for the 1984 Games, but it managed to report a USD 225 million surplus).[104] Since the inception of this new sponsorship model—which one observer has referred to as 'a corporatization and McDonaldization of the world sporting event'[105]—all subsequent instalments of the Olympic Games (except Athens in 2004) have either broken even or made a profit for its organisers.[106] In the 2005–2008 Olympic quadrennial, the 12 TOP sponsors paid a total of USD 866 million in sponsorship fees, of which revenues approximately 40% was allocated by the IOC to national Olympic committees and 50% to local organising committees.[107] At the time of the LOCOG/BOA dispute in early 2011 over profit-sharing in respect of the 2012 London Games as mentioned earlier, it was estimated by the BOA that the event would show a profit (or 'surplus') in the region of GBP 300 million.[108]

---

103 The following has been observed in respect of sponsorship exclusivity in the context of the United States sports sponsorship market:

> For sponsors of sport, categorical exclusivity is crucial for achieving [the objective of blocking competition] because it prevents the competition from entering into a sponsorship arrangement with a team, event, or governing body whose exposure is large and whose demographics fit the target market of the industry … [T]he pursuit of categorical exclusivity is driving service industry sponsorship within highly competitive business sectors such as banking, insurance and telecommunications. A survey of active sport sponsors found that almost half considered exclusivity to be an important aspect of their sponsorship agreements, with 40 percent indicating willingness to pay a 9 percent premium for the right to block the competition.

Irwin et al. 2008, pp. 169, 170.

104 See Johnson 2008, p. 24.

105 Gruneau, R 'The McDonaldization of the Olympics,' in Tomlinson and Whannel 1984, as referred to in Tomlinson, A 'The Making of the Global Sports Economy: ISL, Adidas and the Rise of the Corporate Player in World Sport,' in Silk et al. 2005, p. 36.

106 Ibid. 24–25. The Winter Games in Albertville in 1992 reportedly made a USD 57 million loss. By way of example, the Sydney 2000 Summer Games cost an estimated USD 3.24 billion to present (including a bid cost of USD 12.6 million) and broke even; The Salt Law Winter Games of 2002 cost an estimated USD 1.3 billion to present (including a USD 7 million bid cost) and showed an estimated USD 100 million profit—see Davis 2008, p. 68.

107 See Davis 2008, pp. 163, 164.

108 Nixon, A 'The Sport Lawyer—Olympic funding dispute heads to IOC mediation, 19 August 2011—available online at the time of writing at http://www.mondaq.com/x/140794/Arbitration+Dispute+Resolution/The+Sport+Lawyer+Olympic+Funding+Dispute+Heads+To+IOC+Mediation.

Also, one should consider that the process and rationale behind these developments appear to have had little to do with the 'good of the game.' If one critical observer is to be believed, developments around the commercial rights structure of the 1984 Games came in the wake of alleged secret dealings between űber-sports marketer Horst Dassler (son of sports shoe king Adi—'he of the three stripes') and Samaranch, through which Dassler had manoeuvred to instal Samaranch at the helm of the IOC and in return received the contracts to market the commercial rights in respect of more than a decade of Olympic Games through the mechanism of Dassler's rather shady International Sport and Leisure, or ISL (which, later, also managed to obtain the rights to market FIFA World Cup events).[109] After all, at the time of ISL's awarding (in 1985) of the exclusive contract to market the commercial rights to the 1988 Olympics it had only been in existence for 2 years. Which lends credence to reports that the contract was awarded to ISL on the basis of Dassler's 'political' activities in especially Africa and Asia, where sponsorship of national teams by the Dassler family's Adidas enabled him to wield considerable influence over key members of national federations and a number of IOC members.[110] In the view of the 'anti-establishment founding fathers' of Nike, who would become a major competitor and surpass the Dassler family product's success in sports marketing circles, Adidas was 'an elitist organisation that was deeply entwined with the corrupt and aristocratic international sports authorities of the day... the Adidas guys were "sports bureaucrats" who wined and dined league officials and international fat cats.'[111] A veteran IOC insider, who describes Horst Dassler as 'an inveterate sports politician,' has observed that '[r]umours abound as to the possible role of money to assist the winning candidates [both Samaranch in ascending to the presidency of the IOC and Joao Havelange in respect of FIFA] and the role of [Horst] Dassler in such activities.'[112] Patrick Nally,[113] former partner of Dassler at the West Nally media agency (who described Dassler as 'the puppet master of the sporting world') and one of the instrumental players in the development of the commercial programme for the FIFA World Cup, brokered (along with Dassler) the seminal global Coca Cola football sponsorship which was to be the first of its kind and a model for the development of global sports

[109] See Jennings 2006, Chap. 3.

[110] Slack, T and Amis, J 'Money for nothing and your cheques for free? A critical perspective on sports sponsorship,' in Slack 2004, p. 274.

[111] Katz 1994, p. 24.

[112] International Olympic Committee member Dick Pound, writing in Pound 2006, pp. 141, 142.

[113] The idea of selling exclusivity of marketing rights to a limited number of sponsors apparently predates Peter Ueberroth's efforts at the 1984 Olympics and originated in Britain in the 1970s with Nally and his associate Peter West's media agency, West Nally. Its executives went on to hold leading positions in a number of international sports federations, which earned the agency the title 'the global sports marketing university'—see Horne and Manzenreiter 2006, p. 7; Payne 2006, p. 21.

sponsorship as we know it today.[114] Nally has characterised this as his 'best deal' in a long sports marketing career; he first introduced FIFA and Coca-Cola in 1976 and it is the world's single largest sponsorship and still survives today.[115] It is truly interesting to note the views of this last 'insider' (who has been called a 'godfather of the sports marketing industry') about the effect of Coca Cola's involvement in football and its effect on the stature and status of major sports federations like FIFA:

> [The federations] … are in some ways, because of Coca Cola, beyond reproach. There's no government checking on them. There's *(sic)* no auditors checking them… They have the same aura [as Coca Cola] of credibility and extreme cleanness and Coca Cola helps that and yet they can get away with blue murder … but if the can of worms ever really got open and people started challenging why [the federations] have the ability to do what they do and why they are there and why do they get all these things …—then I think Coca Cola are going to get a lot of stick from it and Coca Cola's image is going to suffer immensely.[116]

This book will not investigate the frequent claims of wide-spread corruption in international sport and the organisations that govern them, but it is submitted that, in evaluating the justifications for commercial monopolies in events and the measures imposed to protect them, due regard should be given to the fact that 'for the good of the game' mantras must be considered in the light of what is, most probably, not a squeaky clean industry which has at its heart such lofty agendas as the promotion and development of sport for the benefit of the masses. I made mention (in Chap. 6[117]) of the saga around former Canal Plus executive and FIFA marketing director Jerome Valcke's 'commercial lie' in FIFA's deal with MasterCard in 2006; I would suggest that this episode may provide some insight into some of the less impressive aspects of the huge mega-event sponsorship arrangements. Valcke himself, in a subsequent interview, agreed that the payment of bribes or commissions was endemic in the sports rights business, although he believes things have changed in recent times:

> The old world was the system of commission. Twenty years ago… you were giving commissions to people in order to get market or to get product or whatever. Today the legal system has changed. I don't know if it's an improvement or not, I just say it has changed. You can't do it any more. I'm too young in a way to have been in this system, but I agree it was a system. The system was maybe changed in the 1990s… But in the '90 s you had younger people coming into the business. You had more and more people in charge who were from business schools—who were not just the son of the friends of [so and so]. When the money [began to come] in, it became a real business. When we

---

[114] Coca-Cola has, of course, long recognised the benefits of involvement in sport for building and maintaining its brand value; it is the longest running Olympic sponsor and has been directly involved in all the Games since 1928.

[115] From an interview with Patrick Nally available as 'Patrick Nally: Godfather to an Industry,' 7 January 2011 on the web site of Sports Pro Media at http://www.sportspromedia.com/quick_fire_questions/patrick_nallys_sports_business_answers/.

[116] Patrick Nally, as quoted by Tomlinson in Silk et al. 2005, p. 46.

[117] In Sect. 6.2.1.2 of Chap. 6.

launched Canal Plus in 1984, the [TV rights] agreements were just one page. Ten years later, the agreements are 150 pages and you are negotiating for months.[118]

Leaving aside issues of corrupt dealings, it is clear that commercialisation and the profit margin loom large in the minds of those who control and organise the major events. Tomlinson describes how FIFA took a leading role, through current president Sepp Blatter's predecessor Havelange, to establish new economic partnerships during the last few decades of the twentieth century which would become a template for the political economy of world sport[119]:

FIFA's capacity to generate such deals was premised upon its supra-national status. As an INGO (international non-governmental organisation)—a body with a global remit, but no accountability to any particular national government or governments ...—FIFA could offer the potential of worldwide markets to its commercial partners. And as an OFC (offshore financial centre)—"a centre that hosts financial activities that are separated from major regulating units (states) by geography and/or legislation"[120]—FIFA could assume a fiscal autonomy that could service a cosmopolitan and luxury lifestyle for its operatives and, crucially, broker distinctive deals for the marketing of the game. That the organisation was based in Switzerland, such a prominent international center for OFC dealing, expedited the pace and the scale of such transformative transactions.

[The FIFA of Havelange and Blatter] were not driven by any selfless goal of global equity within FIFA, more by the entrepreneurial motivation and machiavellian global networking of FIFA's bosses and their business allies ... In such contexts and circumstances, global markets for sports business and for major sponsors have expanded with little or no reference to the wider constituencies of sport, or to the ruling forum of individual sports organisations. Benefits may have accrued to under-resourced areas of the football world, but such expansion has been driven by the commercial interests of an incestuous network of sports leaders, administrators and commercial entrepreneurs.

The recent crisis within FIFA concerning its president Sepp Blatter and the ethics charges filed against him in May 2011 relating to allegations of bribes paid to CONCACAF officials saw UEFA and European football heavyweight Michel Platini quoted in the media as expressing the following view on FIFA politics:

I think that Fifa is like the International Olympic Committee was some years ago, I think we are at the end of a system based on politics. The future of this big international sports company is owned by people who are specialists—not political people like Juan Antonio Samaranch in the IOC, [Blatter's predecessor, João] Havelange, Blatter who comes from politics. I think it will finish in the next few years and we will have people from the sport. I think Fifa has to come back to football.[121]

---

118 From a piece in *The Independent* by David Owen, 28 October 2007—available online at the time of writing at http://www.independent.co.uk/news/people/profiles/jr244me-valcke-he-scored-the-worstever-own-goal-now-hes-running-football-398086.html.

119 Tomlinson, A 'The Making of the Global Sports Economy: ISL, Adidas and the Rise of the Corporate Player in World Sport,' in Silk et al. 2005, pp. 59, 60.

120 Quoting Hampton, M 'Where Currents Meet: The Offshore Interface between Corruption, Offshore Finance Centres and Economic Development,' in Harriss-White and White 1996.

121 Scott, M 'FIFA crisis: Storm clouds gather as big hitters fight to clear names,' 29 May 2011 in *The Guardian*—available online at the time of writing at http://www.guardian.co.uk/football/2011/may/29/fifa-crisis-storm-clouds-gather?INTCMP=ILCNETTXT3487.

Issues of sports politics aside, I believe that very little concrete evidence has emanated from the global sports industry in recent years to refute the view that the commercial profit-making motive is only very slightly tempered by the supposed 'greater good' benefits of major events. A number of studies have been done regarding the actual benefits to host countries and their peoples of mega-events such as, for example, the Olympic Games and FIFA World Cup.[122] Some have found that, historically, the actual net economic impact of hosting mega-events have been very small compared to initial estimates and predictions by those promoting the events[123] (it has been reported, for example, that members of London's legislative assembly have expressed the opinion that the originally estimated cost of USD 6 billion to host the London Olympics in 2012 is likely to escalate to approximately USD 29 billion[124]), while it has also been observed that the potential economic impact study which was prepared for the South African government prior to the 2010 FIFA World Cup bid was 'overly-optimistic.'[125] It was reported in April 2010 that the SA Revenue Service had confirmed that it was not expected that the World Cup event would add any revenue to the fiscus in the financial year.[126] Without wanting to appear unduly cynical, I would suggest that, at best, the jury is definitely still out on the extent to which, if at all, these major events provide real benefits apart from short-term promotional gains and commercial profits to the small inner circle of heavyweight corporate interests. It is unknown whether sufficient hard evidence exists of wider socio-economic and other benefits which would serve to justify commercial monopolies in events, especially in light of the competition law and constitutional implications of the effects of the severe restrictions on the freedoms of individuals and businesses

---

122 See, for example, Matheson and Baade 2004; see also the report entitled 'An African Football World Cup at Last! But what will be the effects? Maximising positive impact of the 2010 FIFA World Cup™' *Results of the International Symposium on the Impact of Mega Sports Events on Developmental Goals* 5–7 March 2008, Stellenbosch, South Africa; Mabugu and Mohamed 2008.

123 Compare Baade and Matheson 2004.

124 Davis 2008, p. 72.

125 See Bohlmann 2006, p. 13. Cottle ('Workers battle and CEOs cream it while World Cup costs soar' *Cape Times* 13 July 2009) observed the following:

'In 2004, the financial impact report for the South African World Cup bid committee (prepared by Grant Thornton) estimated the cost of infrastructure and stadiums to the taxpayer would be about R2.3 billion. By October 2006 this amount had increased to R8.35 billion. The current estimated costs to the taxpayer of the stadiums and related infrastructure is R17.4 billion.'

126 From a report on SABC News, 9 April 2010. This is rather surprising and disappointing, when one considers that the study commissioned by the South African bid committee for the (unsuccessful) bid to host the FIFA World Cup in 2006 reportedly claimed that the event would generate USD 483 million in tax revenues (see Alegi 2001, p. 11) and the bid committee in preparation of the successful 2010 bid reportedly predicted that the 2010 FIFA World Cup would generate USD 1 billion (see Bohlmann 2006, p. 13). The author is not in possession of figures in respect of the extent of the South African government's investment in the 2010 World Cup event (it was reported by the South African government in February 2008 that such investment in terms of contributions to the 24 World Cup projects amounted (at that time) to ZAR 28 billion).

that now characterise such events in all the jurisdictions where they are held. It is submitted that the following claim by FIFA in response to a freedom of expression challenge in its recent anti-ambush marketing litigation against Metcash in the Gauteng North High Court[127] is indicative of the organisation's apparent stance on the role of the public interest in respect of its commercial activities:

> [I]it is not only the interests of [FIFA] that have to be taken into account, but also ... the interests of the greater public ... A golden thread that runs through all trade mark intellectual property statutes, the common law relating to trade marks (notably passing off) and also, to a certain extent, section 15A of the MMA ... is also the right of the public not to be deceived ... If a respondent utilizes his freedom of expression rights or his own intellectual property in a manner that would deceive or confuse the general public *and, in addition jeopardize an event such as the Soccer World Cup and prejudice its sponsors and licensees* it would be a justifiable limitation on its rights to freedom of expression in terms of section 36 of the Constitution.[128] [Emphasis provided]

While I would agree with the first part of this claim regarding the public interest in prohibiting deception of consumers, it is submitted that FIFA's claim to the serving of a 'greater public good' in the protection of the commercial interests of its event and the monopoly that it enjoys along with its commercial partners is perched on much less solid ground.

At the very least it is hoped that organisations such as FIFA will in the near future be called upon to put forward a real case in this regard, if not before a forum such as the Court of Justice for the European Union or the international Court of Arbitration for Sport, then before domestic lawmakers in future host jurisdictions. It appears that domestic courts, also in South Africa, have been reluctant to rock the boat on those occasions where the huge commercial sports monopolies have been challenged by those small players who have attempted to obtain financial benefit from a partly taxpayer- and publicly-funded event such as the football World Cup. As I have argued above, I believe that there is little real and empirical proof of the veracity of the event organisers' 'survival of the Games' rhetoric in defending their substantial commercial interests, and I hope that the reader will consider the issue critically and with due regard for the nature of the modern global sports entertainment industry and its corporate power brokers.

In the meantime, as I put the finishing touches on the manuscript for this book prior to its submission to the publisher, both FIFA and the IOC are again in the news for their past dealings with ISL. *Sports Illustrated* reported in December 2011 that IAAF President Lamine Diack received a warning and African soccer head Issa Hayatou was given a reprimand after an investigation by the Olympic body's ethics commission. Although the commission's rulings cited conflicts of

---

[127] *Federation Internationale de Football Association (FIFA) v Metcash Trading Africa (Pty) Ltd* [2009] ZAGPPHC 123 (Gauteng North High Court)—see the discussion in Sect. 4.4.5 in Chap. 4.

[128] At par. 29.4—29.6 of the Applicant's Heads of Argument.

interest by both men, they currently remain full IOC members. Diack and Hayatou were investigated for receiving payments from ISL, which collapsed with debts of USD 300 million in 2001 (neither were IOC members at the time). The verdicts came just days after 95-year-old Joao Havelange resigned from the IOC executive to avoid suspension in the decade-old case dating to his days as FIFA president (Havelange was the IOC's longest-serving member with 48 years of service, and faced a possible 2-year suspension for allegedly taking USD 1 million from ISL in return for World Cup television contracts).[129] FIFA, meanwhile, was criticised from several quarters when it postponed publication of a Swiss court document naming soccer officials who took millions of dollars in kickbacks from World Cup broadcast deals. The 41-page document from the Zug court reportedly details a settlement announced in June 2010 whereby senior soccer officials admitted taking kickbacks from ISL and repaid USD 6.1 million. The officials repaid the money on condition that their identities remained anonymous. The BBC has reported that the document implicates former FIFA President Joao Havelange and Ricardo Teixeira, the 2014 FIFA World Cup Brazil organizing committee president, while FIFA president Blatter has claimed that he was cleared of any wrongdoing in all aspects of the ISL case. These events came in the wake of reports that the global anti-corruption watchdog Transparency International had walked away from its consultancy role with FIFA after citing a breakdown in their working relationship, saying that it could not accept that FIFA paid members of expert panels it appointed to advise on reforms. The anti-corruption body reportedly also insisted that reform task forces be allowed to re-examine past allegations, including claims of unethical behaviour during the 2018 and 2022 World Cup votes, but FIFA reportedly refused the request.[130]

9.5 Conclusion

The clumsy and blatantly illegal classic ambush tactic of deceiving the public into believing that an ambusher is an official sponsor justifies aggressive steps by event organisers to take legal action. I have nowhere in this book denied the rights of event organisers to protect their property such as trademarks against such conduct. However, as we have seen, these organisers claim extremely wide protection from lawmakers to extend the scope of what they call the 'intrusion ambush,' namely

[129] See the report entitled 'IOC members escape ethics scandal with hardly any punishment,' 8 December 2011—available online at http://sportsillustrated.cnn.com/2011/olympics/12/08/IOC-ethics-case.ap/.

[130] See the report entitled 'FIFA blames legal problems for delay to publish legal document in kickbacks scandal case' *The Washington Post*, 6 December 2011—available online at http://www.washingtonpost.com/sports/dcunited/fifa-blames-legal-problems-for-delay-to-publish-court-document-in-kickbacks-scandal-case/2011/12/06/gIQAvgPCZO_story.html.

marketing campaigns which simply grab the public's attention surrounding an event. Here the organisers are on much less solid ground. As shown, most legal systems provide no property right to the spectacle that is the sports mega-event. The organisers have no proprietary claim based on misappropriation (misappropriation of *what*, exactly?) and can, I would submit, not raise the public good justification of protection of the consumer public against deception if one considers that the *sui generis* event legislation generally does not require such deception or an intention to deceive in order to criminalise or otherwise outlaw the conduct of these 'ambushers.' We have also seen that such legislation does not require event organisers to prove harm in order for liability to follow for the 'ambusher.' This raises the question whether they in fact can prove such harm, even if not called upon to do so in terms of these special laws.

I have argued above that they cannot, or at least that they have not been able to do so to date. The claims that make up the 'survival of the Games' justification are largely anecdotal and devoid of any real, empirical evidence regarding the threats to the sourcing of future sponsorships. As pointed out above, some observers (such as Ellis, Scassa and Seguin) actually point to the opposite being true, and that sports mega-event sponsorship is only escalating, with some major multinational corporate sponsors being signed up until at least the 2020 Olympic Games and in very expensive rights deals. Yes, ambushing is by definition not good for sponsors (at least from the perspective of their having had to pay for certain privileges while others do not), but special laws require stronger justification than simply having been upstaged by clever marketers. While advertising clutter, sponsorship rights dilution and other fall-out from 'ambushing' might very well be prejudicial in some ways, the very significant, continuing growth of the mega-event sponsorship industry suggests that ambushing is not nearly the threat that the Olympic Movement or FIFA would have us believe. The current Head of Legal for the ICC is not convinced that my arguments which question the harm to event organisers (particularly the risk of losing sponsors) in this chapter apply to that organisation and its largest events:

> You have questioned whether lack of legislation and robust anti-infringement programmes causes lack of investment in the game, or a drop in the levels of investment. You are right to question that. But I can tell you that at negotiation time we come under huge pressure from our sponsors and broadcasters to disclose and address ambush marketing. But it goes further than that. After the first year of IPL (that's the official T20 league in India), which was backed by major sponsors, several of them pulled out because ambush marketing was rife and there was no action taken by the governing body (BCCI) to implement any effective controls. Those sponsors came across to ICC instead.[131]

I have no objections to the point made and the veracity of the example provided. I would, however, like to stress two things in response. The first is a point that I have made above, namely that such strong demands for protection of their rights by sponsors may be due to a significant extent to the promises and

[131] David Becker, from personal e-mail correspondence with the author, December 2011.

guarantees of exclusivity made by the event organisers to such sponsors. One wonders whether much of the problem might not be attributable to the organisers as a result of such promises which are made in order to justify well-documented, substantial escalation in rights fees in recent years. The second point is really the gist of my arguments in this chapter, namely that event organisers should be pertinently called upon by host nation lawmakers to *prove* (or at least make a case for) such potential harm from ambushing. I do not dispute that some event organisers may have valid claims for special protection; my concern is mainly that the experience of recent events does not seem to show that governments have required evidence of potential harm (e.g. potential loss of sponsors) before passing strong rights protection laws. And, as pointed out above, the relevant legislation does not require proof of such harm. If the ICC, for example, can make a case for this then I would be less concerned about the pernicious nature of such laws. I do, however, believe that FIFA, for one, may have a more difficult time proving its case in this regard.

Also remember that, as Ellis et al. point out, any decline in the value of sponsorships may be due to other factors. In the Olympic Games context, they observe that studies have shown that the IOC has struggled with brand management and has been criticised for causing harm to its own brand through excessive commercialization. They also cite other issues such as high profile corruption and doping scandals linked to the Olympics, consumer cynicism over excessive commercialism, and concerns over human rights, which may all very likely have impacted the Olympic brand. They suggest, and I agree, that even if it were demonstrated that the value of sponsorships has declined in recent years, it would be difficult to demonstrate that any significant decline in value is due to ambush marketing as opposed to any one or a combination of the other factors mentioned.[132] This view accords with that of Teresa Scassa, who also observes that actual harm due to ambushing is hard to prove (and may in fact not exist) and that this may raise a significant question for lawyers, namely that of causation in the context of such claims.[133]

I have argued elsewhere in this book that a major cause of the stigmatised view of ambushing emanating from the event organisers is the monopolistic quest for market control and the pursuit of profits. This attitude has been coddled by lawmakers in countries that fervently desire the right to host the events, and this vicious cycle of rigid demands and limp-wristed submission has contributed to the FIFA (and other event organisers) god complex when it comes to its commercial rights. Where are the practical and valid reasons for unusually severe and far-reaching special laws?

World sport (and the interaction of law and sport, more specifically) is no stranger to issues of pragmatism and necessity shaping the application of rules and laws which may have an extremely significant impact on individuals' rights,

[132] Ellis et al. 2011, p. 302.

[133] Scassa 2011, p. 364.

ranging from player transfer rules and national eligibility rules to gender testing. A prime example is the often controversial but apparently firmly entrenched strict liability rule in the international fight against doping (as manifested, for example, in Article 2.1.1 of the WADA Anti-Doping Code). Many commentators, over the years, have raised interesting questions regarding the legitimacy and legality of this no-fault approach in the light of generally accepted principles of law, such as *nulla poena sine culpa*. Yet the Court of Arbitration for Sport (CAS) has consistently upheld this relying on pragmatic reasons (the near impossibility to prove fault on the part of an anti-doping rule violator, or to rebut claims of no fault by such violators) and on the basis of the supreme importance of the maintenance of sporting integrity and fairness towards other athlete competitors, which may outweigh the interest of fairness to individual athletes.[134]

Earlier in this book I have referred to the fact that a prime justification for *sui generis* legislation to protect commercial rights to events is that the traditional legal bases for protection against ambush marketing are often viewed to be problematic and to have serious shortcomings which make them less than suitable to address cases of clever modern ambushes during events of a short duration (and for other reasons). This pragmatic justification for special laws holds some legitimacy on the basis of necessity, although, as I have argued, while I believe this might justify special procedural or infrastructural arrangements in order to address the issue of access to effective remedies for event organisers or sponsors in deserving cases, I do not view this pragmatic justification as providing convincing reasons to often significantly change the *substance* of laws. I refer here, *inter alia*, to special event 'association rights' which ignore the element of proof of consumer deception in an 'ambush' and completely ignore the element of harm to event organisers and sponsors while outlawing otherwise legally and ethically blameless conduct, often criminalising such conduct and even throwing the protection of civil liberties (by means of, for example, the presumption of innocence) out the window.

Still with reference to the anti-doping movement's justification for the strict liability rule, I also do not believe that commercial rights protection for mega-events can claim a similar supremacy of the integrity of sport or greater public good (i.e. encompassing also the interests of other stakeholders) in justification of the relevant laws. I have repeatedly emphasised in the earlier chapters that the *sui generis* event legislation appears, predominantly and fundamentally, to protect narrow commercial interests. We have seen that a number of commentators (including Longdin,[135] Grady et al.) have questioned the legitimacy of the enactment of legislation in free and democratic societies in order to protect these private commercial rights or interests. The jury appears to be out on this issue, although legislators continue to pass ever-increasingly far-reaching and draconian

---

[134] Compare the relevant and often-quoted sections from the *USA Shooting & Quigley v UIT* case (May 23, 1995 (CAS 94/129)).

[135] Longdin 2009.

laws upon the feeble basis that Johnson identifies, namely that other countries have done so or other events have been so protected. It sometimes appears to be a case of 'monkey see, monkey do.'

FIFA and the Olympic Movement, just like their counterparts in other codes and in respect of other events, have to date failed to make a convincing case for the need for such strong and legally questionable protection. The 'survival of the Games' rhetoric is getting old, but it has not gained any verity in its frequent retelling. Major international sponsors of sports mega-events also appear rather ambivalent, and may in any event be less than likely to abandon ship if proper leveraging of sponsorship rights can be achieved and the clutter caused by poor management of sponsorships by event organisers can be addressed. The development of ambushing has been laid at the door of these event organisers and attributed to the development of sponsorship exclusivity. Less exclusivity in future contracts—which is highly unlikely as it would directly affect event organisers' bottom line or, more accurately, profit margins—would not necessarily alienate these sponsors. Does anyone seriously suggest that Coca-Cola, Pepsi, MasterCard and the other big boys of international sports sponsorship will forgo this unique and extremely attractive marketing platform if they are afforded less scope to stifle the competition posed by their competitors? Surely not. What is highly probable, of course, is that these corporations would insist on paying much less for their rights. This would significantly affect the event organisers, and many a sleepless night may result in Switzerland and elsewhere, but I am not convinced that special laws of the kind examined in this book are the best or even the only answer. Thoughtful, realistic, transparent and professional management of sponsorships should be able to provide a satisfactory solution which would encompass and address the interests of *all* the mega-event stakeholders. If lower sponsorship fees due to less exclusivity are a result then event organisers should consider means of obtaining a broader sponsorship base (especially in the 'micro' market, domestically in host nations or cities) without causing unmanageable clutter. Or maybe ways should be considered in which increased leveraging of sponsors' rights could also provide a revenue stream for event organisers (with due recognition of the mutual benefits from a successful corporate marketing campaign which also feeds into the goodwill of the event organisers). What should be realised is that those aspects of events and of their thematic space which currently do not provide income for sponsors (due to inaccessible opportunities for small businesses in host nations to bid for rights) should remain open to entrepreneurs who conduct themselves within the law and without harming the rights and interests of other stakeholders. Coca-Cola's interests are not threatened in any significant measure by the mom and pop store situated a few blocks from the football stadium who sell their wares (including Coke's product) on a small scale to thirsty foot traffic on FIFA match days. Are there not more intelligent ways to ensure that such enterprises also benefit financially from the excitement and drawing power of the event, without viewing and treating them as an arch-enemy and alienating large swaths of the public (and football-lovers) in the process? I would suggest that there are, and that marketing and legal analysts should examine what these are and how best to implement them. Not to mention the lawmakers in future host jurisdictions, who should do so *before* they blindly pass ever more invasive future laws to protect and expand the illegitimate mega-event monopoly.

References

All Internet-based sources referred to, were last visited in or before December 2011

Alegi P (2001) Feel the pull in your soul: local agency and global trends in South Africa's 2006 World Cup Bid. Soccer Soc 2(3):1–21

Baade RA, Matheson VA (2004) The quest for the cup: assessing the economic impact of the World Cup. J Reg Stud 38(4):343–354

Bently L, Davis J, Ginsburg JC (eds) (2008) Trade marks and brands: an interdisciplinary critique. Cambridge University Press, Cambridge

Bohlmann HR (2006) Predicting the economic impact of the 2010 FIFA World Cup on South Africa. University of Pretoria, Department of Economics, working paper series, working paper: 2006–11

Boyle R, Haynes R (2009) Power play: sport, the media and popular culture. Edinburgh University Press, Edinburgh

Cooper Dreyfuss R (1996) We are symbols and inhabit symbols, so should we be paying rent? Deconstructing the Lanham Act and rights of publicity. Columbia-VLA J Law Arts 20:123

Davis JA (2008) The Olympic games effect: How sports marketing builds strong brands. Wiley, Singapore

De Carvalho NP (2010) The TRIPS regime of trademarks and designs. Kluwer Law International, New York

Donatuti J (2007) Can China protect the Olympics, or should the Olympics be protected from China? J Intellect Prop Law 15:203

Ellis D, Scassa T, Seguin B (2011) Framing ambush marketing as a legal issue: an Olympic perspective. Sport Manag Rev 14(3):297–308

Gaines J (1991) Contested culture: the image, the voice and the law. BFI Publishing, London

Grady J, McKelvey S, Bernthal MJ (2010) From Beijing 2008 to London 2012: examining event-specific Olympic legislation vis à vis the rights and interests of stakeholders. J Spons 3(2):144–156

Grayson E (1999) Sport and the law, 3rd ed. Butterworths, London

Harriss-White B, White G (eds) (1996) Liberalisation and the new corruption: IDS Bulletin, vol 27(2), pp 210–228. http://www.amazon.com/Liberalization-New-Corruption-Ids-Bulletin/dp/1858641942

Horne J, Manzenreiter W (eds) (2006) Sports mega-events: social scientific analyses of a global phenomenon. Blackwell Publishing Ltd/The Sociological Review, Oxford

Irwin RL, Sutton WA, McCarthy LM (2008) Sport promotion and sales management, 2nd ed. Human Kinetics, Champaign

James M, Osborn G (2010) 'Consuming the Olympics: the fan, the rights holder and the law' in the British library series. In: *Sport & society: the summer Olympics through the lens of social science*. http://www.bl.uk/sportandsociety/exploresocsci/parlaw/law/articles/consuming.pdf

Jennings A (2006) Foul! the secret world of FIFA: bribes, vote rigging and ticket scandals. Harper Sport, London

Johnson P (2008) Look out! it's an ambush. Int Sports Law Rev 2/3:24–29

Katz D (1994) Just do it: the Nike spirit in the corporate world. Adams Media Corp, Holbrook

Klein N (2000) No logo. Flamingo, London

Kobel P (2007) International report on question B: ambush marketing too smart to be good? Should certain ambush marketing practices be declared illegal and if yes, which ones and under what conditions? International report to the international league of competition law, Catania congress 2007
Longdin L (2009) Public law solutions to private law problems: major event regulation subverts IP's internal balance. J Intellect Prop Law Pract 4(10):726–742
Mabugu R, Mohamed A (2008) The economic impacts of government financing of the 2010 FIFA World Cup. Working paper of the Department of Economics and Bureau for Economic Research at the University of Stellenbosch, working paper 08/08
Mann Phillips M (1967) Erasmus on his times: a shortened version of the Adages of Erasmus. Cambridge University Press, Cambridge
Matheson VA, Baade RA (2004) Mega-sporting events in developing nations: playing the way to prosperity? S Afr J Econ 72(5):1069–1075
McKelvey S (2010) As games approach, time to reconsider ambush marketing. Sports Bus J 23
Nafziger JAR (1988) International sports law. Transnational Publishers, Inc, New York
Payne M (2006) Olympic turnaround. Praeger Publishing, Westport
Pound RW (2006) Inside the Olympics. Wiley, Toronto
Price ME, Dayan D (eds) (2008) Owning the Olympics: narratives of the New China. Digital culture books, Ann Arbor
Scaria AG (2008) Ambush marketing: game within a game. Oxford University Press, Oxford
Scassa T (2011) Ambush marketing and the right of association: clamping down on references to that big event with the all the athletes in a couple of years. J Sport Manag 25:354–370
Schmitz JJ (2005) Ambush marketing: the off-field competition at the Olympic games. Northwest J Technol Intellect Prop 3:203
Schulz-Herzenberg C (ed) (2010) Player and referee: conflicting interests and the 2010 FIFA World Cup™, Monograph, vol 169. South African Institute for Security Studies, Pretoria
Schwab F (2006) FIFA's trademark tactics. World Trademark Rev 6. http://www.worldtrademarkreview.com/Issues/Articles.aspx?g=faf17b21-f89a-473e-949c-bc1b25b93bad
Séguin B, O'Reilly NJ (2008) The Olympic brand, ambush marketing, and clutter. Int J Sport Manag Mark 4(1):62–84
Seth R (2010) Ambush marketing—need for legislation in India. J Intellect Prop Rights 15:455–463
Silk ML, Andrews DL, Cole CL (eds) (2005) Sport and corporate nationalisms. Berg Publishing, Oxford
Slack T (ed) (2004) The commercialisation of sport. Routledge, London
Tomlinson A, Whannel G (eds) (1984) Five-ring circus—money, power and politics at the Olympic games. Pluto Press, London
Tripodi JA, Sutherland M (2000) Ambush marketing—an Olympic event. J Brand Manag 7(6):412–422

Chapter 10
Conclusions

FIFA and its corporate sponsors and licensees certainly seem to have been the big winners of the 2006 World Cup in terms of money banked and increased brand awareness. However, the fact that FIFA's president Sepp Blatter was systematically targeted with a chorus of whistles when he was presented to the fans during the tournament should remind FIFA that the Italian team should be remembered as the true winners of the competition, and that an overemphasis on big business is likely to upset the fans and turn them even further against FIFA in the long run. FIFA must strike the right balance to ensure that the purity of the game, the enjoyment of the fans and the atmosphere of competition at the highest level are not overshadowed by excessive commercialism through monopolistic exclusivity and overzealous rights protection.[1]

[A] range of activities referred to by marketers as 'ambushing' do not necessarily breach fair-trading, trademark or passing off legislation. Instead of classifying all competing promotions as ambushing, it is more logical to think of a continuum, anchored by legitimate competition at one end and actionable behaviour at the other. The difficulty is not in identifying anchor points, but in determining whether activities falling between these are liable.[2]

10.1 Introduction

The reader of this or any other book on ambush marketing will know that it raises contentious and often very controversial questions, both from legal and ethical perspectives. If I have any say in the matter, this will always be the case. Ambush marketing is, at its heart, all about *competition*. Yes, the event organisers and official sponsors of events will always say that ambushing is 'fighting dirty', but the point is that it is, in fact, fighting—competition for the attention of consumers with the objective of 'selling the brand' more than one's competitor can manage to

[1] Schwab 2006, p. 9.
[2] Hoek and Gendall 2002, p. 87.

A. M. Louw, *Ambush Marketing and the Mega-Event Monopoly*,
ASSER International Sports Law Series, DOI: 10.1007/978-90-6704-864-4_10,

do. A criticism often expressed by official sponsors is that absent the large licensing fees spent by such sponsors to obtain their official rights, the ambusher is able to build a marketing campaign from the ground up with no such 'entry fee', and can thus obtain much more in terms of leveraging the marketing spend and translating it into consumer spend. It clearly makes commercial sense, and we have seen that some huge multinational corporations choose to habitually ambush events. But this apparent stamp of approval by the big players does not, however, make either the clumsy small-scale ambush or the orchestrated multimillion dollar ambushing campaigns 'right'. As Kim Skildum-Reid observes while explaining one of the drawbacks of ambushing (namely, the lack of a partnership with the event): It can be like choosing to be 'the other woman'—'It may be fun, but will it ever be as fulfilling as a real relationship?'[3]

Importantly, for the purposes of this book, the controversial nature of ambushing pertains also to the ways in which laws are used to combat ambushing. For example, and as should be clear from the previous chapters, I view my own native land's anti-ambushing laws (sometimes referred to as the most stringent to be found anywhere in the world, currently) as, frankly, despicable and illegitimate. I have throughout felt that it is apt that a South African should write this book. However, another observer, also a South African lawyer (although a much more respected IP specialist who was intimately involved with FIFA's efforts at protecting their 2010 World Cup event in terms of these same laws), views them as one respect in which 'South African law pertaining to brands and branding has been very pioneering and innovative and has set an international trend'.[4] I do not think that the two of us will ever see eye to eye on this matter, as I am rather worried about this trend and am not sure that it's something to be proud of. I do hope that this book will at least provide some food for thought in order to debate the legitimacy of these and similar laws as found in other mega-event host jurisdictions.

In this, the final chapter, I will briefly revisit the main issues and arguments contained in the previous chapters on the law's current treatment of ambush marketing in respect of sports mega-events and the commercial monopoly in these events. I will then briefly consider expectations for future developments in this regard, including, on the one hand, developments which would appear to indicate prospects of even more significant ring-fencing and monopolisation of commercial rights for event organisers, as well as, on the other hand, developments (primarily regarding the use of the Internet and social networks) which may augur an increased importance and prevalence for ambush marketing of events in future. Then I will attempt to suggest some ways in which the problems identified in this book regarding the legal treatment of ambush marketing and the mega-event commercial monopoly can be addressed. Finally, I will include some brief and

[3] Skildum-Reid 2007, p. 28.

[4] Owen Dean, legal advisor to FIFA in respect of the 2010 FIFA World Cup South Africa, quoted online in a piece entitled 'A perspective of intellectual property'—available online at the time of writing at http://www.brandsandbranding-online.co.za/a-perspective-of-intellectual-property-dr-owen-dean/comment-page-1/.

general thoughts on why I think the whole discourse on ambush marketing and the law has, to date, been fundamentally flawed. First, though, let us recap the discussion from the earlier chapters.

10.2 How Laws are Abused to Protect Commercial Rights to Mega-Events Against Ambush Marketing: A Summary

Ambush marketing has entered the annals of infamy in the past few decades precisely because of the traditional understanding of the term, namely that it constitutes something anathema to event organisers and their official sponsors, and, ultimately, to the interests of the (consumer) public. In the modern free market economy this conjures up something more than mere competition with such organisers and sponsors. Why did 'ambushing' not attract a different label, let us say something like 'alternative marketing' (in the meaning of an alternative to the process of paying for and obtaining official rights to be associated with an event)? The reason is simple and evident in the very use of the word 'ambush', which in its military sense denotes an attack (or, more correctly, a sneaky surprise attack). A true ambush marketing campaign is an ambush because it constitutes an attack on the commercial interests of the event organiser and/or its official sponsors, and it actually threatens their interests in an illegitimate manner.

The disconnect we have seen between this traditionally accepted notion of ambushing and the special laws that have been passed in recent years to combat ambushing is that these laws appear, for the most part, to ignore this fundamental nature of the ambush. As I have pointed out repeatedly in the preceding chapters, the modern day anti-ambushing laws more often than not do not require event organisers or their sponsors, when using such laws to defend against ambushers, to show any of these characteristics of an ambush to be present. They do not have to prove deception of consumers, or consumer confusion, or even harm as a result of the 'ambush'. What these laws appear to be, for the most part, are naked restraints on competition. But ambushing is not about mere competition; ambushing is supposed to be about something more; something sneaky and harmful and bad. These elements are, however, no longer required by event organisers who can now call on exclusive rights of association with an event while the public interest in protecting against the ambush (in the traditional sense) is absent, although the lawmakers and event organisers, paradoxically, love to claim such public interest in justification of these laws.

Ultimately, 'association rights' and statutory 'clean zones' are aimed primarily at creating and maintaining market power for event organisers and their commercial partners. These new legal creatures aim, for the most part, simply to restrict competition. While advertising restrictions on the use of billboard space in the event precinct, for example, clearly serve to protect official sponsors' rights by ensuring a clean palette for its own advertising, it is much less clear why or how restrictions on trading by small businesses and even informal traders serve this purpose in addressing any real and identifiable threat to the sponsors' commercial interests. We have seen that an organisation such as FIFA has called on governments and lawmakers to blur the line between the association and the intrusion ambush. I referred in an earlier chapter to the government guarantees (*inter alia* in respect of the protection of commercial rights) which FIFA demands of host governments. This includes a demand for legal prohibition of intrusion ambushing, which FIFA defines as 'to practice, organise, approve, or sponsor any promotional, advertising, or marketing activities through which one targets the audience of the Events, including ticket holders, in order to gain exposure for its businesses, products or services without authorisation from FIFA'. It is defining 'the audience' of the event which, of course, is the crux of the matter, with FIFA failing to explain how or why any marketing activities which are in no way connected with the event or aimed at implying an association with it should be subject to FIFA approval, just because it is aimed at the event audience. Remember, we are not limiting the restrictions here to the audience whose access to the event is controlled in the traditional manner (e.g. by means of a ticket or through the sale of rights to broadcast the event on television or through other media). If FIFA's record of enforcement is anything to go by it appears that its 'audience' includes any reference to the event entering the public's consciousness. Is the organisation implying that its goodwill in the event in some way includes a right to the attention of its audience in this broad sense? It is in terms of demands such as this that FIFA's lawyers can claim that an 'ambushing' campaign such as that run by South African airline kulula prior to the 2010 FIFA World Cup (which I discussed in Chap. 7), is unlawful. When an ad campaign contains clear disclaimers as to its 'unofficial' nature and, in fact, is in the form of a parody which takes clever pot shots at FIFA for its aggressive rights protection efforts, why should the organisation be entitled to demand that it be labelled unlawful simply because it is aimed at 'its' World Cup's audience? Laws which allow this type of response are patently absurd and illegitimate; Gandhi would have staged a sit-in.

The quest for monopolisation of opportunities to be 'associated with' the event has reached the point where an event organiser can actually demand that its own service providers must pay for the privilege to provide such services for the event. Compare the furore in 2009 when some of the UK's top advertising agencies withdrew after bidding for the 2012 London Olympics advertising contracts when 'they soon discovered that they would need to become a tier-three sponsor at a cost of nearly £10 million if they wanted the honour of developing the London Games' official advertising campaign', and 'would have to agree to doing millions of pounds of work in exchange for being named an official 2012 sponsor'.[5] These legal mechanisms as contained in the *sui generis* event legislation are no longer

[5] See the report by Amanda Andrews in *The Telegraph*, 28 March 2009—available online at http://www.telegraph.co.uk/finance/newsbysector/mediatechnologyandtelecoms/5067045/Advertising-agencies-withdraw-from-2012-Olympics-contract-over-sponsorship-fee.html.

justified as being in the public interest *because* they actually protect consumers. If they operated to simply bolster the contractual rights of sponsors and event organisers (i.e. by removing possible procedural hurdles to obtain quick and effective relief in cases of breach of contract) they would be justified, but they go so much further by expanding the protection from the confines of these private commercial arrangements to cover persons and business interests situated well outside the contractual relationship. In the process these laws constitute a radical departure from traditional principles of law, and in fact function to the clear detriment of members of the public (whose civil liberties are often radically curtailed) and consumers (who may be forced to pay inflated prices due to the anti-competitive effects of the mega-event monopoly and its central tenet of sponsorship exclusivity). In doing so they carve out vast swaths of the public domain and place them in the hands of wealthy sports organisations and a few multinational corporations, two of the least likely entities in our modern world to be labelled champions of human rights and civil liberties. Consider the perfect storm of such covetous commercialism that results when the manufacture of the mascot for football's pinnacle international competition is outsourced to a Chinese sweat shop, for example.

In the process of the commercialisation of sports mega-events in recent years it has become clear that the stigmatised attitude of event organisers and their commercial partners to 'ambush marketing' is rather ironic. It appears to me that, in respect of the frequently vehement (even vicious) criticism that is levelled at those who attempt to 'free-ride' on events and to derive marketing benefits for which they don't pay (read: For which they don't pay the event organisers)—which includes attempts to 'name and shame' the perceived culprits—the shoe seems to be very much on the other foot. To put it quaintly, this seems to be a case *par excellence* of the pot calling the kettle black.

I have tried to show that there appears to be growing recognition in marketing and (to a lesser extent, in legal) circles that what has traditionally been called 'ambush marketing'—with all the stigma attached to that label by the event organisers and their commercial partners—is a legitimate competitive marketing strategy, which holds few ethical objections. This is the case with the intelligent and often creative modern 'ambush', which does not deceive or attempt to deceive the public into an association with the event, and does not attempt to misappropriate the property (intellectual or otherwise) of the event organiser in an unlawful manner. Such campaigns are now often organised by large multinational brands such as Nike and Adidas, where millions are spent in clever (and legally savvy) ways of grabbing the public's attention in an environment where the official sponsors often seem to under-leverage their own investment and fail to capitalise on all the potential for exposure which they may have bought. Of course there will always be the tacky, fly-by-night operators who genuinely do attempt to reap where they have not sown, and in an underhanded manner. But the traditional laws are there to protect against these characters, as it always has been, and always should be.

On the other hand, however, it is suggested that the commercial monopolies and anti-competitive practices that are so ingrained in the mega-event commercialisation model (which, in fact, forms its very backbone in the form of the current system of sponsorship exclusivity) should rather be urgently subjected to legal scrutiny for what, I submit, is a system that is blatantly exploitative, overtly capitalist (with very little of the 'good stuff' associated with this), undemocratic, uncompetitive, contrary to accepted principles of the rule of law and, arguably, against public policy.

Sadly, everything in this world comes at a price. I would suggest that the price of the phenomenal commercial success of sports mega-events, and the billions of dollars of profits that the event organisers have consistently reaped in the past few decades, is the loss of the moral high ground in the debate about commercial rights exploitation of these events. No longer should we allow these organisations, such as the Olympic Movement or FIFA, to whine about the 'leeches' who try to make money off their 'pure' sports product. Things have changed—'The overwhelming cultural influence at the Olympics is now commercial culture; and the overwhelming informational message is: buy, buy, buy.'[6] We should not allow unquestioned recourse to age-old but less and less relevant 'Corinthean ideals', or nauseatingly persistent use of euphemistic rhetoric (e.g. 'The IOC, in accordance with the Olympic Charter, continues to ensure the priority of sport in a commercial environment'). If you have made your sport or competition into a brand or a product, little different from a drive-through hamburger, a fizzy soft drink or the latest model SUV, then you should bite the bullet and play with the big boys in the market that you chose to enter and are deriving significant benefit from. If that involves savvy marketers and advertising executives out-thinking and out-strategising you, do not run to the lawmakers crying for special treatment based on claims that you are 'special'. Learn to play the game, fairly, openly and intelligently. And, as the custodians of sporting codes, please learn a lesson that I would think these organisations, by definition, should have learnt many moons ago: Everyone should play to the same rules and you cannot change the rules to suit you when you realise that the other team is simply better at the game:

> There are also some who might argue that certain major events, such as the Olympic Games, are a special case, but I would suggest that if the Olympics are indeed a special case, which cannot cope with normal competitive pressures such as ambush marketing, then it is not the practice of ambush marketing which needs to be reconsidered but the business model for the Olympic Games.[7]

When the international sports governing bodies started to aggressively exploit the commercial potential of their mega-events, the playing field changed dramatically. While the traditional role of these organisations, the governance of the

---

[6] Weissman, R 'The commercial Games: How commercialism is overrunning the Olympics', 17 August 2008—available online at http://www.corpwatch.org/article.php?id=15164.

[7] Leone, L 'Ambush marketing: Criminal offence or free enterprise?' Asser International Sports Law Centre (2008)—available online at the time of writing at http://www.thefreelibrary.com.

sport, demands a monopoly, we have seen that the monopolistic attempts at market control by FIFA et al. are, in the commercial marketplace for the event, a prime cause of the potential anti-competitive effects which may expose these organisations to legal challenge. There are different rules at play in this marketplace where the event organisers peddle the event as a brand. These organisations, however, do not seem to have fully grasped these rules as yet. I would suggest that FIFA, for example, should consider the *22 Immutable Laws of Branding*,[8] as there are a few such laws that they seem to struggle with currently. First, there is the law of expansion, which says that the power of the brand is inversely proportional to its scope. Coupled with this is the law of contraction, which says that a brand becomes stronger when you narrow your focus. We have seen that event organisers, in an attempt to corner every inch of the market, register their trademarks in sometimes amusingly diverse and patently inappropriate classes of goods and services, considering the brand they are selling. We have seen that FIFA, specifically, has on occasion before the South African courts claimed goodwill in respect of goods in a market that it had never entered (and couldn't show any convincing intention to enter in the future). And we saw, in Chap. 8, how event organisers generally try to claim rights to their brand in all conceivable elements of the event's thematic space. I would suggest that less is more, and that such attempts at expanding rather than contracting the brand are a sure way to contribute to its demise; compare the growing backlash at aggressive rights protection to events, and the potential alienation of the consumer/fan public. Even more importantly, though, is the law of fellowship; in order to build the category, a brand should welcome other brands. Against the backdrop of the discussion of efforts to monopolise the mega-event thematic space in Chap. 8, the following rings a bell:

> Greed often gets in the way of common sense. The dominant brand in a category often tries to broaden its appeal in order to capture every last bit of market share. The law of contraction suggests the opposite. When you broaden your brand, you weaken it. Which brings us to the law of fellowship. Not only should the dominant brand tolerate competitors, it should welcome them. The best thing that happened to Coca-Cola was Pepsi-Cola… Choice stimulates demand. The competition between Coke and Pepsi make customers more cola conscious… Your brand should welcome healthy competition. It often brings more customers into the category.[9]

If these are truly the rules of the game that (should) apply in the mega-event brand marketplace, FIFA and the Olympic authorities seem like rank amateurs with little appreciation for how the game is to be played.

I could be charitable and downplay the apparent rapacious nature of mega-event organisers, by likening them to the experience of Mark Twain, who, from a reported attitude of disdain in his youth for the copyright of British authors,

---

[8] Ries and Ries 1998—summarised version available online at http://www.portugaliza.net/num06/The_22_Immutable_Laws_of_Branding.pdf.

[9] Ibid.

became a convert to the strongest forms of copyright after seeing his books flagrantly pirated. One could argue that the modern attitude of aggressive commercial rights protection and claims of 'ownership' of their events by the organisers may likewise be a result of the widespread 'ambushing' of these very events as encountered in the past few decades, a reaction to the conduct of others rather than indicating a deep-seated sense of greed or selfish and mercenary motives. The literature, however, shows that the prevalence of 'ambushing' (or, what the organisers like to designate as such) is more likely a result of the commercialisation practices involving exclusivity and overly ambitious contractual undertakings towards sponsors to justify the vast amounts paid for these rights. And *sui generis* anti-ambushing laws are, for the most part, in my view analogous to trademark dilution laws, at least to the extent where I would agree with two critics of the latter who express the view that the (sadly lacking, to date) 'debate attempts to cobble together an economic justification for a cause of action that was secured by brand owner lobbying' and which should 'move beyond knee-jerk reactions to "misappropriation"'.[10]

The sports mega-event may, justifiably, nowadays be viewed not only in terms of its historical, social and cultural role but also as a commercially valuable commodity. Much of this book has been about the mega-event as brand and the ways in which event organisers seek to market it. The International Rugby Board has recently amended its scheme in respect of bidding for its World Cup event, which, interestingly, I would suggest, shows the level of commodification of the modern sports mega-event. In late 2008 the IRB announced a new tournament fee structure for Rugby World Cup (or 'RWC') 2015 and 2019 bidders in order to give an added boost to the competitiveness of the process. The decision was reportedly made to reflect the current economic environment and feedback from the nine Member Unions who were tendering to host these tournaments at the time (England was subsequently awarded the 2015 event and Japan was awarded the 2019 event). A Deloitte report on the economic benefits of hosting Rugby World Cup highlighted the fact that it is one of, if not the most, cost effective major sports events in the world. RWC is estimated to have the potential to generate up to GBP 2.1 billion in economic benefits while capital expenditure costs are among the lowest for an event of this magnitude. IRB chairman Bernard Lapasset was quoted as explaining the new structure as follows:

> We have... had meetings with government officials from several of the potential host countries which have been very encouraging. However, in light of the current economic environment the IRB has decided to take a pragmatic approach on the tournament financial modelling to assist Unions in their future discussions with their respective governments and their delivery of competitive tenders. The IRB Council has agreed that the minimum tournament fee for 2015 be reduced to GBP 80 million from GBP 100 million and that the minimum tournament fee for 2019 be reduced to GBP 96 million from GBP 120 million. The IRB has also agreed to incentivise the Host Unions by building in a profit share formula for any tournament surplus it generates that exceeds the minimum guarantee. We

[10] Burrell and Gangjee 2010, pp. 12–13.

> are still looking to achieve a tournament fee of GBP 100 million from 2015 and GBP 120 million from 2019. The revised minimum requirements are just that, minimums. There is nothing to prevent one Union bidding the minimum guarantee of GBP 80 million for RWC 2015 and another bidding GBP 100 million.[11]

It appears that the Rugby World Cup bidding and hosting process equates to an invitation to bid to 'rent' the tournament, as a vehicle to make a profit. If you can provide a guarantee of how much money we will make, you can use our brand for a little while; break a leg! (but don't break our brand...). FIFA, for example, markets its '*other* World Cups' in a colourful brochure available on its website and aimed at its member associations.[12] In this document it encourages the associations to recognise the benefits of hosting FIFA events other than its prestigious World Cup, and it provides its 'products list' (no prices are mentioned—probably available on application—and it is not clear whether air conditioning and satellite navigation comes standard). These events include the FIFA U-17 World Cup, FIFA U-17 Women's World Cup, FIFA U-20 World Cup, FIFA U-20 Women's World Cup, FIFA Futsal World Cup, FIFA Beach Soccer World Cup and the FIFA Club World Cup. The brochure repeatedly pushes the potential financial benefits for member associations to host these events, which benefits include 'commercial and marketing initiatives', and comes to the cheery conclusion that 'In the end, it can only prove to be a worthwhile investment for any member association willing to take on this exciting challenge'. In a document that fleetingly, and only once expressly, mentions that these events are actually about sport (they deliver 'world-class sporting action'), FIFA proclaims the benefits of hosting them as including 'marketing/image management' (these events are 'an excellent opportunity for associations to invigorate partnerships with sponsors, media outlets and broadcasters') and 'monetary/economic advantages' ('A FIFA World Cup brings revenue opportunities, albeit depending on the efforts of the member association, through ticketing revenues, government and private funding, FIFA subsidy funding, food and beverage concessions and partnerships with national supporters'). The FIFA spin doctors finally come to the point:

> If your association is willing to accept the challenge, then FIFA cordially invites you to present a bid and join FIFA and the worldwide football family in its mission to: "*Develop the Game. Touch the World. Build a Better Future*".

Yeah, right. '*Touch the World*'? Did you also just grab your wallet just that little bit tighter?

The commercial benefits for mega-event organisers of strong contractual ties to major multinational corporate sponsors and aggressive commercial rights

---

[11] From a report entitled 'IRB boosts RWC bidding process', 26 November 2008, available at the time of writing on the IRB Rugby World Cup 2011 website at http://www.rugbyworldcup.com/mediazone/news/newsid=2027812.html.

[12] The elegantly titled 'The benefits of hosting FIFA's other World Cups', available online at the time of writing at http://www.fifa.com/mm/document/affederation/biddingforotherevents/01/30/02/09/bidcollateralbrochure_sebcs4.pdf.

protection (including the domestic anti-ambushing laws lobby) are clear to see. But what about the sponsors? What is in it for them?

As we have seen from discussion in the earlier chapters, large multinational corporations (such as the usual suspects, Coca-Cola, McDonalds, Adidas, Kia, and LG Electronics, to name a few) are willing to pay vast amounts of money for the rights to be officially associated with mega-events. When one considers what they receive from event organisers nowadays, this should come as no surprise. I have mentioned the exceptional nature and benefits of the sports mega-event as marketing platform. Add to this the following 'fringe benefits':

- The residual (although possibly fast disappearing) 'feel-good' factor of a sports (event) sponsorship—the 'Olympic ethos' or integrity of sporting competition, clean living athletes and good clean sportsmanship are all elements which, if nowadays sometimes more fiction than fact, are generally viewed by marketing researchers as beneficial to brands associated with these events;
- The expected (*demanded*) level of exclusivity provided to top-tier sponsors, as a matter of course in the case of the modern mega-event—this provides a marketing environment free from competition which must surely be hard to secure in any other context;
- The sometimes very long duration of such sponsorship contracts (often with very favourable rights of renewal); and
- The often draconian and very strictly-drawn anti-ambushing laws created in host nations as a prerequisite for hosting rights.

One is faced with what I would suggest is one of the most significant and jealously protected remaining examples of a legalised monopoly which is often criticised but remains largely immune from such criticism and from legal regulation. Not that one can really blame these sponsors for riding the wave of mega-event commercialism, which makes good business sense. When Coca-Cola forks out a 100 million dollars or more to sponsor the Olympic Games it truly receives a lot for its investment. Not only is it allowed, through its exclusivity arrangements with event organisers and the working of special anti-ambushing laws, to effectively exclude its main rivals from the market to a significant degree—remember that these sponsors generally engage in saturation marketing around many facets of the event—it is also allowed to do so for years at a time. And, lo and behold, it is often not even called upon to police its investment; event organisers promise the moon in respect of enforcement of its sponsors' exclusivity in order to justify the huge amounts paid for such rights. We have seen that on the few occasions when event sponsors had resorted to litigation against 'ambushing' (e.g. in India, New Zealand and Canada) things have gone less than well for them. Rather let the event organiser, contractually, bear the responsibility to enforce these 'rights'—'Heck, that's what we pay them for!'. And, come to think of it, who is better placed to do so than the organiser? After all, they are able to demand accommodating laws as a prerequisite for awarding hosting rights, which might go some way towards guaranteeing success if ever they need to take 'ambushers' to court. Or, better yet, they do not even have to go to court. If those laws, 'which we demand should be created if you want the right to host our party', are draconian enough—which appears to increasingly be the case—the inevitable barrage of cease-and-desist letters should be more than enough to put significant fear into the 'small fry' or anyone else with more brains than brawn who might baulk at unnecessarily expensive legal bills. It truly is hard to imagine a more satisfying win–win scenario for both event organisers and sponsors, and even host governments. It is just a pity about those pesky individuals or small businesses who may feel the burn of the activities of this elite club of power brokers and carpetbaggers who are propped up by unjust and ill-advised laws.

There is, however, a factor that one should consider in this scenario, which might militate against the aggressive rights protection for events (especially in the form of the ever-increasingly invasive special event anti-ambushing laws). In Chap. 2 I referred to the element of sponsor expectations that has come with the model of category exclusivity of sponsorships. This expectation has increased significantly in recent years in the light of event organisers' ability to demand special event laws as a hosting requirement. Ellis et al. observe (in the context of the Olympic Games) that this may have created a bit of a quandary for these event organisers:

> As anti-ambush marketing legislation has gradually become standard to the point where it must be guaranteed in the bid phase, its status as a value-added tool for sponsors is no longer relevant. Rather than something that can be used as a selling point, it is commonplace and expected. The question then becomes where does the IOC go from here? Legal protection is generally viewed as the ultimate deterrent and defence against objectionable behaviour. However, if as suggested above, the powers of such legislation can be critically limited by legal frameworks, loopholes, smart lawyers and creative marketing teams what is the next step to protect the brand and appease the needs of sponsors? The ability of the IOC to achieve authoritative management powers greater than those provided by legislation, either symbolically or literally, is implausible. Yet sponsors will continue to demand protection for their investment (e.g. exclusivity), and will expect the IOC to continue to expand and improve their program for combating ambush marketing as part of the sponsorship agreement. As the cost of the hosting the Games inevitably continues to rise and with it the need for greater sponsorship dollars, failure to meet the increasing expectation of sponsors could become progressively more dangerous to the funding of the movement as a whole.[13]

If I were to advise sponsors on a slightly more 'practical' note, divorced from the analysis of the legitimacy of laws to combat ambushing, I think there is much to be said for the following advice from a sponsorship lawyer:

> Ambushing is a creative science, so predicting what other sponsors might do and responding contractually is not always possible. The best advice is to do the best job you can with the sponsorship and your own leverage, so you own the event in proportion to your investment in the rights. If you are not prepared to do that, don't buy or don't complain.[14]

---

[13] Ellis et al. 2011, p. 305.

[14] Lionel Hogg, writing in Skildum-Reid 2007, p. 131.

My view on the position of the event organisers, however, is a little more hard-nosed, as I guess has probably been clear throughout this book. I tend to be less critical of the corporate sponsors who act (in seeking ever-increasing levels of exclusivity from their rights deals) in furtherance of undisguised motives of profit maximisation, which, let us face it, is justifiable at least in the sense that they owe a duty in this regard to their shareholders and, well, that is what we expect from large multinational corporations. The situation is, I would suggest, quite different for mega-event organisers. These organisations will always, at least notionally, be rooted in their traditional role and mandate of governing the relevant sporting code as 'custodians of the game' (and we all know that they generally love to resort to claims of acting in the interests of protecting this sacred duty). The vast opportunities for commercial exploitation of the events that are presented under their auspices have brought great benefits to sport, generally. But I have my doubts about the legitimacy of the profit maximisation motive when displayed so fragrantly by these entities. A multinational commercial giant like Coca-Cola makes billions of dollars from consumers. They are responsible to their shareholders, but beyond that, when they decide to do as they like (e.g. change their product... anyone remember New Coke?), the consumer soon shows its dissatisfaction and a drop in sales soon brings the corporation back into line. When the IOC or FIFA, however, does as it pleases, we are met with denials and circling of the wagons that often seems juvenile, and I often get the sense of an attitude of an implied untouchable status (*'Sports fans? We don't need no stinking sports fans!'*[15]). The irony, of course, is that Coca-Cola's product is a purely commercial one that is subject to the whims of the market and little else. The Olympic Games or FIFA's World Cup, however, is not merely a product produced by a corporation (although it may nowadays often seem that way). There is such a significant public interest and public domain element to what it represents and to the constituency that it proclaims to serve, that it is shameful that the powers that be in these organisations have been allowed to pay so little attention to public criticism. I believe it is ironic to consider that sports economists have observed that '[t]o justify on theoretical grounds public subsidies for mega-event infrastructure, such investments must exhibit substantial externalities or be construed as "public goods"'.[16] While, on the one hand, needing to proclaim and promote the hosting of the event as being in the public interest (in order to ensure that the host nation public will actually finance the staging of the event), on the other hand these event organisers are demanding laws which appear to largely ignore the interests of such public. And this is, primarily, in order to protect commercial interests of a small group of corporations in order to be able to charge enough to earn profits from the staging of the events.

---

[15] With apologies for borrowing, and misquoting, the widely misquoted line from John Huston's *The Treasure of the Sierra Madre* Warner Bros. Pictures (1948).

[16] Barros et al. 2002, p. 128.

At a recent international intellectual property law conference held at a South African university, the director of WIPO's Building Respect for IP division[17] (formerly the Enforcement and Special Projects division) spoke about the organisation's Recommendation 45 adopted under the WIPO Development Agenda at its 2007 General Assembly.[18] In doing so she emphasised the corporate social responsibility of IP rights holders, and stressed that 'you must be a corporate citizen where you want to enforce'. I would submit that an organisation such as FIFA falls far short of this recommendation, and its enforcement of its IP and other commercial rights in the territories where it stages its showcase events is sorely lacking and makes a mockery of the very concept of corporate social responsibility. Not to mention its 'sacred trust' as custodian of the game of football, which it owes to many millions of football lovers, all over the world? Arul Scaria, in consideration of the ethics of ambush marketing, opines that ambush marketers act in breach of corporate social responsibility obligations. He defines these obligations as 'arising from an implicit social contract between business firms and the society, which compels the firms to be responsive to society's needs and wants and business firms are required to tune its conduct in such a way as to maximise the positive and minimise the negative effects of its actions on the society'.[19] What about FIFA and the Olympic Movement and their counterparts in other sporting codes? Do these organisations not also have obligations to ensure that their activities in hosting and commercially exploiting their mega-events do not harm the public? Yet we see that the special legislation mandated by these organisations contain numerous examples of provisions of dubious legitimacy which often severely curtail the freedom and rights of individuals.

Finally, although by no means the least important, is consideration of the position and interests of the general public when it comes to the passing of often invasive and severely restrictive special legislation to protect commercial rights to mega-events. In the previous chapters I have often raised the issue of the impact of such special laws on members of the general public, and of the (lack of) wider public interest justification for many of the restrictions contained in such legislation. In this regard it is ironic to observe that the most stringent such anti-ambushing provisions currently to be found (as mentioned, those contained in South Africa's Merchandise Marks Act), are contained in a statute which also

---

[17] Louise van Greunen, speaking at the *New Horizons for Intellectual Property* conference (on the occasion of the establishment of the Anton Mostert Chair in Intellectual Property), University of Stellenbosch, 1–2 September 2011.

[18] Recommendation 45 commits the organisation 'To approach intellectual property enforcement in the context of broader societal interests and especially development-oriented concerns, with a view that "the protection and enforcement of intellectual property rights should contribute to the promotion of technological innovation and to the transfer and dissemination of technology, to the mutual advantage of producers and users of technological knowledge and in a manner conducive to social and economic welfare, and to a balance of rights and obligations", in accordance with Article 7 of the TRIPS Agreement.'

[19] Scaria 2008, p. 45.

provides that such provisions only apply to a 'protected event', and that the relevant Minister may only declare an event to be protected (and the anti-ambushing laws to be applicable to it) if the following is satisfied:

> The Minister may not designate an event as a protected event unless the staging of the event is in the public interest and the Minister is satisfied that the organisers gave created sufficient opportunities for small businesses and in particular those of the previously disadvantaged communities.[20]

Rather ironically (in my view), Corbett and van Roy disagree with the often-expressed view that the Merchandise Marks Act is the most draconian anti-ambushing law in the world, because it contains the above-quoted requirements for declaration of a protected event.[21] Sadly, we will probably never know whether any such review ever took place in respect of the 2010 FIFA World Cup, and to the best of my knowledge the South African government (or, for that matter, FIFA) has never been required to provide proof of this. I would suggest that, at least in practice, this last provision has largely gone unheeded to date. As Louise Longdin puts it in respect of the comparable provision in New Zealand's Major Events Management Act, because the Act 'allows for the imposition of restrictions on marketing practices harmful only to brand owners and sponsors rather than consumers, its framers have made some effort to impose internal political and bureaucratic controls on the decision to declare that an event is a major event'.[22] However, she observes that these relevant provisions of the Act make 'only the briefest of nods… towards the various limiting concepts contained in the law of copyright, trade marks, passing off, and trade practices, concepts carefully crafted over time to balance the gains to innovation, enterprise, and creativity against the rights of consumers and the needs of a competitive economy'.[23] I would suggest that the same applies to the above limiting provision of the South African legislation in respect of its true value in protecting the public interest.

While on the subject of the public interest element of mega-events, let us consider how this should play out in respect of combating ambushing. In the earlier chapters I have argued that a major problem with the existing special event laws is the fact that the interests of the public have been marginalised to a significant extent, especially in two respects. The first is that the traditional rationale for the law having a role in regulating ambushing, namely the interests in protecting consumers against deception and confusion through marketing that directly or indirectly implies an official connection or affiliation with the event, is largely absent from these special laws. The second is that the wide ambit and often draconian nature of the special event laws tend to disproportionally affect the interests of members of the public, which includes severe curtailment of civil liberties and fundamental rights. The effect of this is exacerbated by the fact that

[20] Merchandise Marks Act, 17 of 1941 (as amended), in section 15A(1)(b).

[21] Corbett and Van Roy 2010, p. 341.

[22] Longdin 2009, p. 730.

[23] Longdin 2009, p. 729.

lawmakers are at a loss to show a public interest sufficient to justify the passing of special laws which are aimed at protecting private commercial interests, but which have significant and troubling consequences for the wider public.

With this in mind, one is confronted with the question of the legitimacy of laws in this context, and I must ask that one considers the potential justification for such laws. In Chap. 6 I briefly examined the competition law implications of anti-ambushing laws, and I referred in passing to the American courts' treatment of monopolies, which, in terms of the rule of reason approach, to an extent requires that a monopoly should have been earned due to some technological or other investment which is, all things considered, sufficiently in the public interest to maintain in order to counteract the potentially anti-competitive effects of such monopoly. In the sports mega-event context, I think we should consider what FIFA and the other event organisers have in fact invested in staging their showcases, and whether this justifies legal protection of their monopolies. We have seen (in Chap. 9) that while this investment is mostly financial, it is debatable how much money the event organisers actually spend in putting on the show; I have argued that it appears that the costs of the events are mostly devolved to host governments and taxpayers. Against this, let us consider the 'investment' of the modern day, creative ambush marketer (in the meaning of an intrusion ambusher, as I have referred to in the earlier chapters). The question I would like to pose is whether lawmakers are justified in protecting such tenuously tangible and in any event mostly financial investments on the part of event organisers and sponsors, rather than using the mechanism of the law to ensure that the creative skills of marketers are protected as an arguably more valuable social commodity.

In conclusion here I doubt that I can phrase it any better than two other commentators have done. The first is the view of Phillip Johnson (from a 2008 law journal article), expressing reservations about the attitude of automatic entitlement for strong anti-ambushing protection for events on the part of event organisers and lawmakers:

> [E]ach escalation in brand protection equates to more money being demanded from sponsors and extra money leads to greater protection being demanded from governments. The spiral of protection will therefore continue onwards and upwards... The protection granted to events, and so to sponsors, to prohibit ambush marketing should be considered from a principled perspective by taking into account the interests of the public, other commercial enterprises, the media as well as the interests of sporting federations and the identified sponsors... Overly broad protection does not just hinder ambush marketers, but also legitimate traders, journalists and the public at large ...But this approach [of providing similarly restrictive protection to even small events, on the model of protection of the major events like the Olympic Games and the FIFA World Cup] does not take sufficient account of the public interest in allowing certain people, possibly even traders, to make associations with such a brand. Intellectual property law has always had at its heart the balance of interests between the rights holder and the public. Yet the justification for granting these pervasive rights is the expense and cultural importance of the major sporting events. It does not seem that sufficient consideration has been given to the appropriate threshold for protection. At some point it has to be possible to say: No, this event does not deserve protection.[24]

[24] Johnson 2008, p. 29.

The second view is that of Teresa Scassa, who observes that anti-ambush marketing legislation 'represents the point at which organizations recruit the coercive power of the state to reinforce their sponsorship agreements':

> The need for anti-ambush marketing legislation is not clearly established. Even if it were accepted that some additional protection is necessary, it is not clear that the very sweeping protections available in the new laws are warranted. Such protection amounts to a kind of corporate subsidy that may relieve organizers and sponsors of some of the responsibility they have traditionally borne for managing their brands and advertising campaigns, as well as for appropriate event management. At the same time, it removes from the community some of the benefits of hosting the event. Further, such legislation limits the range of expression available to corporate entities of all sizes who are not sponsors. It constrains the ability of individual athletes, teams, and national sport organizations to generate their own revenues to support their activities.[25]

10.3 Modern Challenges and Expectations for the Future

Discussion in the earlier chapters has referred to what Phillip Johnson calls 'horizontal and vertical creep' in respect of (legislative) rights protection for mega-events. We have seen that recent events have attracted increasingly far-reaching and stringent laws to protect such commercial interests of the event organisers and sponsors. At present the trend does not show any prospect of reversal anytime soon; legislation currently being considered in Brazil for the 2014 FIFA World Cup, for example, shows signs of perpetuating the trend of the organisation seeking the very stringent protection it enjoyed in South Africa for its 2010 instalment of the event.

Apart from the role of legislatures in respect of future mega-events (and I will try to include some suggestions for them when considering future special event laws, later in this chapter) one also needs to consider other, external factors which may play a significant role in both ambushing of future events as well as the capacity of event organisers to combat such ambushing. In this regard I believe there are currently three major issues which may play a significant role in future. The first relates to efforts by event organisers to strengthen their grip on the events they organise and to broaden the scope of their control over its commercial exploitation. I am speculating with this, but really do feel it bears watching. The second relates to the Internet as a potential vehicle for future ambushing of events, specifically the potential role of social media. The third relates to the fact that the focus and nature of ambushing of events might be changing, and this might require a different approach by the relevant stakeholders (and lawyers) in order to protect legitimate commercial interests. I will very briefly consider these issues in the following sections.

[25] Scassa 2011, p. 365.

10.3.1 *Expanding the Monopoly: The Evolution of a Potential 'Sports Event Organiser's Right'?*

As has been mentioned earlier in this book, most jurisdictions (notably, for purposes of this discussion, the UK, Australia,[26] Canada[27] and South Africa), do not recognise a proprietary right to a sports event. In the words of Latham CJ in the Australian High Court, a '"spectacle" cannot be "owned" in any ordinary sense of the word'.[28] While such a right to a sports event which is worthy and capable of protection against misappropriation appears to enjoy some recognition in the United States of America,[29] in the other countries mentioned the rights to broadcast a sporting event or to disseminate news regarding the results and action on the field of play must be protected by means of other mechanisms and/or through a combination of other, recognised, legal rights. While this position has not been significantly challenged in these systems to date, recent developments elsewhere bear scrutiny in light of the inter-related and significantly globalised nature of the international (professional) sports industry.

In terms of developments in Europe, and especially France, sports organisations have in recent times increasingly claimed what amounts to a 'right to offer bets' in the sports gambling arena. Apart from claims based on trademark infringement and database rights to prevent third parties from offering bets on events, or systems of direct taxation from betting activities for reinvestment in the sport, it appears that there have also been claims to an exclusive right to commercial utilisation of (what appears to be) virtually all downstream spin-offs of the events organised by such organisations.[30] While, as mentioned, these developments relate to gambling on sports events and are indicative of an example of sports organisations having apparently identified a largely untapped potential source of substantial revenues, this last claim raises interesting questions regarding the more general commercial monopolisation of events, also in the anti-ambush marketing context.

In France, Article L333-1 of the *Code du Sport*[31] provides for a 'droit d' exploitation' for sports federations in respect of the events they organise, and

---

[26] Compare *Victoria Park Racing and Recreation Grounds Co Ltd v Taylor* (1937) C.L.R. 479; *Australian Broadcasting Corp v Lenah* (2001) 208 C.L.R. 199. See also Wise 1996.

[27] See *National Hockey League v Pepsi-Cola Canada* (1995) 122 DLR (4th) 412.

[28] *Victoria Park Racing* supra at 497 (a case where the owner of a residential property adjacent to the plaintiff's racecourse allowed a radio broadcaster to erect a scaffolding tower on his front lawn, from where the broadcaster could view races and broadcast commentary).

[29] On the basis of the US Supreme Court judgment in *International News Service v Associated Press* 248 US 215, 63 L Ed 211, 39 S Ct 68 (1918); *Pittsburgh Athletic Co v KQV Broadcasting Co* 24 F Supp 490 (WD Pa 1937)—see also the judgment of the court of first instance in *National Basketball Association and NBA Properties Inc v Sports Team Analysis and Tracking Systems Inc* 939 F Supp. 107 (SDNY 3 September 1996) [overturned on appeal by the Second Circuit Court of Appeals in New York—105 F 3d 841 (2d Cir 1997)]; Lewis and Taylor 2003, pp. 405, 583 and 679; Johnson 2007, pp. 2–3.

[30] See Rohsler and Baudriller 2009.

[31] Law 84-610 (16 June 1984).

provides that '[s]ports federations and organisers of sporting events … own the right to exploit sporting events they organise'.[32] Article L333-1 provides such event organisers with the right to license audiovisual exploitation of events,[33] although recent case law has suggested that this monopoly to an event may have further reach than merely relating to sound and image rights.[34] In light of these provisions, the rules and regulations of events organised in France will often expressly reserve rights granted in terms of the Code in grant of rights provisions.[35]

In 2009 the courts in France and Belgium saw litigation relating to betting on the 'Roland Garros' tennis tournament, when the French Tennis Federation (or FFT[36]) sued betting operators Ladbrokes (in summary proceedings before the Liege courts in Belgium) and Unibet and Expeckt (in a suit on the merits before the Paris court of first instance). The Liege court dismissed the claim on the basis that unauthorised betting in respect of the event did not constitute a 'tortuous act', as the FFT had claimed. The federation was more successful in the Paris court, where it was held that, even though the defendants' conduct did not constitute a trade mark infringement in respect of the FFT's trademark in respect of the 'Roland Garros' event, the FFT's monopoly in terms of Article L333-1 of the Code extended to downstream markets such as the organisation of sports betting and that the unauthorised betting activity infringed on the federation's monopoly right, as well as constituting free-riding on the tournament's success which it was held constituted the tortuous act of parasitism.[37] The Paris Court of Appeal confirmed the judgment of the court of first instance in October 2009, when it upheld both the findings of infringement of FFT's monopoly rights as well as the finding of

---

[32] 'Les fédérations sportives, ainsi que les organisateurs de manifestations sportives … sont propriétaires du droit d'exploitation des manifestations ou compétitions sportives qu'ils organisent.'

[33] Which is further regulated in Articles L 333-2 to L 333-5 and Article R 333.

[34] See *ACO and ASAACO vs. Dragoon Editions, CCE* Tribunal de Commerce de Nanterre, 12 December 2002, implicitly confirmed in *FFT vs Hospitality Group* Tribunal de Grande Instance of Paris, 28 January 2004 (see Kobel 2007, p. 19); see also discussion of the FFT/Unibet matter in the text below.

[35] See, for example, the Supplementary Regulations of the Le Mans 24-Hour event held in April 2009, where the provision dealing with the royalty-free granting of image rights/rights to sound recordings by competitors to the organiser, Automobile Club de l'Ouest (or ACO), contained a specific proviso that '[t]he authorisation of use of the Images and Sounds granted by the Competitor hereby is fully and totally independent from the ACO's right to operate the events and sporting contests it organises, in accordance with Article L. 333-1 of the French Sport Code.'

[36] Fédération Française du Tennis.

[37] In the judgment of the President of the court in the Tribunal de Grande Instance de Paris, 30 May 2008. The tort of parasitism has been described as follows:

'The French jurisprudence created a parasitism doctrine on the basis of public liability principles. The theory of parasitism is applicable to whoever takes advantage of another's representation without authorisation. It is applicable even if the victim is not a competitor. The reputation of the sport event itself is apparently protected. That theory was successfully applied in several sports related cases.' Kobel 2007, p. 32.

parasitism, as well as overturning the finding of the court of first instance by holding that Unibet's activities had also constituted a trade mark infringement. The Court of Appeal awarded significant damages against Unibet of 3,00,000 euros in respect of the trademark infringement, 4,00,000 euros in respect of infringement of the FFT's exclusive right of exploitation and 5,00,000 euros in respect of the parasitism claim.[38] It was subsequently reported that the French government is pursuing a legislative amendment to broaden the scope of the exclusive exploitation right contained in Article L333-1 to the extent of providing sports federations with a right to charge betting operators for organising betting on matches, amidst reports at the time of Malta-based Unibet's intention to appeal the case to the Court of Justice for the European Union.

Within the European Union there appears to be a growing acceptance of recognition for such a 'sports betting right' for event organisers. The 'Schaldemose Report' of 2008[39] highlighted that sports bets are a form of commercial exploitation of sporting competitions and recommended that Member States protect sporting events from any unauthorized commercial use, by recognition of a specific right provided to sports organisers and by implementing agreements to ensure 'fair financial returns' for the benefit of all levels of professional and amateur sport. The European Commission, in March 2011, published a Green Paper on online gambling in the internal market for public consultation purposes.[40] The document alludes to 'a principle of return to event organisers' in respect of revenues from betting on their events, and declares that 'There is a broad consensus that sports events, on which gambling relies, should receive a fair return from the associated gambling activity'.[41] It also states that 'when gambling services are offered on an organised sport competition, the issue of whether the organisers... should be able to generate an additional revenue stream through the exploitation of their images or events by gambling service providers has been addressed by Member States. Given that without the use of their events the gambling services would not be viable, a fair return for the use of their events is sought.'[42]

It appears that, currently, the 'right to offer bets' as recognised in France in terms of Article L333-1 of the *Code du Sport* and bolstered by a government decree of 2010,[43] is unique in Europe. This new *sui generis* right implies that, before providing betting services on a specific event, betting operators must have reached an agreement with the organiser or the rights holder of the competition

---

[38] The judgment of the Cour d'appel de Paris, 14 October 2009.

[39] The *Report on the Integrity of Online Gambling* [2008/2215 (INI)] issued by the Committee on the Internal Market and Consumer Protection.

[40] European Commission *Green Paper on Online Gambling in the Internal Market* SEC (2011) 321 final, 24 March 2011—copy available online at http://ec.europa.eu/internal_market/consultations/docs/2011/online_gambling/com2011_128_en.pdf.

[41] The *Green Paper* at 32.

[42] Ibid.

[43] Decree No. 2010-614 (relating to trade agreements connected to betting operations in relation with sporting events).

which is the subject of betting activities. In consideration of the right to provide betting services on a specific competition, betting operators must provide a financial return to organisers of sporting competition proportionate to the amount of bids collected (calculated on a turnover basis).[44] Bretonniere observes that the French legislature had, surprisingly, not precisely defined the nature and scope of the Article L333-1 exploitation right over a sports event and that this task has been left to the courts. He observes that 'the organiser's exclusive right over the sporting event is said to include all patrimonial exploitations of such event, particularly audiovisual, marketing, publicity and merchandising rights and ticketing'.[45] Despite the uncertainty regarding the exact content of the new rights provided to event organisers, Bretonniere states that 'It is likely that this evolution in French law and the recognition of sports organisers' rights in France will be followed by other countries under pressure from major sports organisers, particularly the national football leagues'.[46]

I do not wish to express an opinion regarding such claims to a right for the appropriation of revenues in respect of sports betting activities, but I do find these developments (especially as they relate to claims to rights over all forms of commercial exploitation of events) troubling if they have the potential to impact, more generally, on the commercial monopolisation of events. We saw in earlier chapters that event organisers have in recent years increasingly demanded special treatment regarding issues of relevance to the commercial exploitation of their events (either through, for example, the Sports Rights Owners Coalition, or individually). Apart from the demands for special anti-ambushing laws for their events (as discussed at length throughout this book), such calls for special treatment range from calls for special 'event marks' with fewer procedural requirements for registration (and a lower threshold for protection), to a revamping of the international trademark classification system in respect of the services of organisation of sports competitions in Class 41 (i.e. calls to expand the classification of such organisation of events to include merchandising in relation to such events). It is submitted that, in light of the concerns that have been expressed in this book, it is a potentially dangerous contention to allow for such robust protection of commercial rights to a sports event. It should be clear that the process of awarding exclusive sponsorship and other commercial rights to events—often for a long term and through a bidding process that appears to lack transparency and to be very significantly skewed in favour of only the largest multinational commercial players—is not unproblematic, even when the commercial rationales of a need to generate substantial revenues in order to host large events and a need for

[44] See the report by Manasterski, A and Camilleri, M 'Corruption in Sports: The French Position', 24 January 2011—available online at http://www.gaminglaw.eu/news/corruption-in-sports-the-french-position/.

[45] Bretonniere, J F 'Building and Enforcing Intellectual Property Value 2011' (at 107)—available online at http://www.iam-magazine.com/issues/Article.ashx?g=110c2250-d9a7-411f-bbfb-fb82921bd71e.

[46] Ibid. 108.

exclusivity of rights in order to attract sponsors are often touted. As has been shown, such practices are specifically questionable in respect of their potential competition law implications, even though such legal challenges have largely been avoided to date. When viewed in light of the value and role of sport as a social activity, coupled with the traditional notion of the trusteeship of sport as the basis for the very authority and powers that sports governing bodies wield, it becomes apparent that further and critical consideration of the legitimacy of such practices is required. One must consider the potential implications, if such an 'event organiser's right' were to find its way into international sports governance practice and the event organiser's anti-ambush marketing arsenal (i.e. also in respect of the operations of governing bodies and the hosting of events in jurisdictions that do not recognise proprietary rights to events), especially bearing in mind that sports governing bodies already habitually flex their considerable economic and political muscle *vis a vis* governments in the bidding process to host major events.

10.3.2 Ambush by Social Media

An October 2011 *Financial Times* report speculated that the 2012 London Olympics, which has been billed as the first 'truly digital Games', is being threatened by the popular social media, which are 'outpacing the legal protection sponsors are promised'.[47] The report quoted sports business academic Simon Chadwick as stating that London 2012 'is going to be the first big Twitter Olympics', and that 'social media is a very, very difficult area [in which] to control the dissemination of information—it's fast-paced and hard for rights protection officers to track and monitor what is happening before it has already happened'. Another commentator was quoted as observing that the intricate and far-reaching special event legislation framework for the London Games (which we encountered in Chap. 4) may have met its match in the swiftly changing digital landscape: 'The framework is offline—it's old world'.[48] Not surprisingly, the IOC has issued social media, blogging and Internet guidelines for participants and accredited persons for the London 2012 Games.[49]

The capacity of social media to facilitate ambush marketing was succinctly explained by a VP for communications at Nielsen in connection with Nike's phenomenally successful *Write the Future* campaign surrounding the 2010 FIFA World Cup, which has been discussed elsewhere in the earlier chapters: 'Social media has made ambush marketing easier, simply because of the virality of it...

---

[47] Kortekaas, V 'Digital "ambush marketing" threatens Games', 9 October 2011, *Financial Times*—available online at the time of writing at http://www.ft.com/intl/cms/s/0/f1879b92-ee78-11e0-a2ed-00144feab49a.html#axzz1dg1w0GLD.

[48] Ibid.

[49] Available online at the time of writing at http://www.olympic.org/Documents/Games_London_2012/IOC_Social_Media_ Blogging_and_Internet_Guidelines-London.pdf.

Some people call it an echo chamber'.[50] Matt McDougall explains how easy it is to create an online ambush by means of social media:

> I guess using social media will become the new digital hunting ground for ambush marketing… find a fan page or online group and start to squat. Drip in new messages, photo and video content. Find the right groups/fan pages and you potentially have 10's of millions of pageviews and now new found exposure at little to no cost…[51]

Along with the 'traditional' social media other technological developments such as new Smartphone apps may also facilitate ambushing (for example by automatically sending marketing messages to Smartphone users when they enter a certain geographical area). Recently a South African mobile phone service provider, Cell C, ran a campaign on Facebook as the *Cell C Scoop* on the 2011 IRB Rugby World Cup, with postings of match day updates and interviews with players and ex-players in New Zealand for the duration of the tournament, and whereby fans could submit videos and other content to the Facebook page.[52] The campaign promised 'exclusive behind-the-scenes content' of the event, and also included a Cell C YouTube channel and updates from @cellc on Twitter. It is hard to pin claims of ambushing on such a campaign, where the marketer does not claim an official association and the focus is on the dissemination of news regarding an event. The purpose and character of such a campaign is, of course, commercial, so that such activities may very well fall foul of the far-reaching legislative prohibitions we have encountered in the earlier chapters. The question, however, is how susceptible such a campaign is to (legal) regulation.

Of course, savvy sponsors have also used social media, with various examples having hit cyberspace during recent mega-events. Just one such campaign was Budweiser's 'Bud House' in Cape Town during the 2010 FIFA World Cup, which saw a 'Big Brother'-type scenario of 32 football fans from 32 countries, both male and female, spending the duration of the event under one roof: 'They eat together. Sleep together. And watch every game together'. The fun and games were broadcast live on Budweiser's 'BudUnited' YouTube channel.[53] It remains to be seen how successfully official sponsors of events will be able to manage social media as an increasingly important means to properly leverage their sponsorship rights.

Undoubtedly, and inevitably, these official sponsors will claim exclusivity to areas of cyberspace, and I may have to revise my characterisation of a restrictive dome or bubble around the event, as contained in Chap. 8's discussion of the

---

[50] Alex Burmaster, as quoted in Klayman, B 'Ambush marketing gives Nike leg up for World Cup', 11 June 2010—available online at http://www.reuters.com/article/2010/06/11/us-soccer-world-nike-idUSTRE65A5AO20100611.

[51] A blog posting dated 4 March 2010, available online at http://www.sinotechblog.com.cn/index.php/component/content/article/48-direct-marketing/563-can-ambush-marketing-actually-work-online.

[52] At http://www.facebook.com/CellC.SouthAfrica?sk=app_163969547019187.

[53] At http://www.youtube.com/user/BudUnited.

mega-event thematic space, accordingly. But this would be especially inappropriate and illegitimate in the context of social media. In an earlier chapter I referred to the work of American commentators John Fortunato and Jef Richards on sponsorship exclusivity and anti-trust laws. They have expressed the following view, which resonates with the issue of the public's involvement in the sports mega-event and the impact on consumers of the exclusivity inherent in current event commercialisation practices:

> It is the spectator who makes it possible for the sponsors, the stadiums, the team owners, and the athletes to earn their livings. But in the current system, it is the spectator who is affected by these monopolies. It is time to stop taking advantage of them. The spectator's right of free choice deserves at least a modicum of respect and protection.[54]

This raises the issue of the role and place of the consumer (and sports fan) in the modern Internet society, when it comes to ambushing. I believe that there is increasing recognition (in the marketing literature, if not on the part of event organisers) of the role of the consumer/fan as a legitimate, and centrally important, stakeholder in the sports mega-event and its commercialisation. This raises questions regarding the power dynamic between event organiser, sponsor and fan, which assumes a new dimension in light of the prevalence of social media in the modern world. In Chap. 8 I attempted to demarcate the limits of the thematic space of the sports mega-event in the context of assessment of the reach and application of the new-fangled association rights to events as found in the *sui generis* event protection laws. I referred to the views of some marketing heavyweights regarding the limits on the ability (and legitimacy) of event organisers and official event sponsors to appropriate and seek to regulate the consumer's 'head-space'. In this context it is interesting to note that a recent Internet marketing blog posting highlights the role of social media and the fact that it might be 'the greatest ambush marketing technique ever'. The piece points out that social media make it much easier to create and maintain a long-term relationship with fans or other audiences—an affinity that could be stretched beyond the length of an official sponsorship—and provides a hypothetical example:

> Consider an automaker that has established itself as a sponsor in tennis through high-level partnerships with key tournaments and popular activation programs that have allowed it to build a targeted database of tennis-loving prospects from its key customer demographic. In the pre-digital age, if the company dropped its sponsorships it kept the contacts it had collected, but it was difficult to maintain a relevant dialogue without the assets and activation programs that came with its deals. But in the Internet era, we're no longer talking about names sitting in a database waiting for a direct mail piece. Today, the auto company can use its involvement with tennis to provide relevant content and build an online community of fans that it can continue to develop even if it doesn't renew its tournament deals. (It will be more difficult without the benefits of sponsorship, but nowhere near impossible.) This scenario crosses into ambush territory when another automaker comes along and takes over the event sponsorships. The original sponsor, with

[54] Fortunato and Richards 2007, p. 48.

its history of involvement and its ongoing conversation with fans is still hanging around the space, making it harder for the newcomer to gain its own foothold.[55]

I have argued in Chap. 8 that event organisers and their official sponsors generally display an attitude that every single element of the thematic space of the mega-event constitutes the property of those who stage the event and pay for putting on the show. I have argued that this is a fallacious conception of this space and that it urgently requires reassessment in the ambush marketing discourse, because this conception underpins, generally, the passing of special event legislation and, specifically, the controversial 'association rights' we now frequently see in such legislation. The question is whether social media may play a role in this regard, going forward. I believe such media have a definite role to play, because of its ability to grab and hang on to the consumer's headspace. As has been observed regarding the above example of perpetuation of a previously existing sponsorship, even after its demise:

From the property's perspective, there is really nothing a rights-holder can do to prevent a savvy company from maintaining an ongoing relationship with the people it met through its sponsorship. Providing access to a targeted audience is a key benefit of sponsorship, but unlike the rights to use a property's name or have a display space at a venue, it is not one that automatically ends when the contract does. This has always been the case, but social and digital media allow the sponsor to exploit it like never before.[56]

The marketer that manages to grab the public's attention through tapping into the *zeitgeist* and maintaining a narrative which 'keeps them coming back for more', would arguably be able to generate positive goodwill despite a lack of official sponsor status. I would suggest that when one talks about a Facebook, Twitter, YouTube or Flickr campaign which targets the thematic space of an event (but does not do so in a deceptive manner—remember, I am speaking of the modern day savvy and creative marketing which does not resemble the classic 'ambush'), one is confronted with issues of freedom of (consumer) choice, freedom of association and of expression. It is all about 'the conversation', as Rob Cotteringham explains in a recent blog posting, squarely implicating the potential free speech impact of anti-ambushing efforts as examined in Chap. 7:

One key implication of [the argument by event organisers such as FIFA that unauthorised association with an event is theft of goodwill] is that an organisation like FIFA or the IOC can sell—not just the right to put their logo on your brand's packaging, or to describe your company as an official sponsor—but something much bigger. They are, in a very real way, claiming the right to sell the conversation around their event. You want your business to participate in that conversation? Fork over a big chunk of cash or find yourself on the receiving end of a lawsuit (or at least a C and D letter). And implicit in that claim is the idea that the conversation is theirs to sell in the first place. But if the past decade or revolution in the social web and networked conversation has taught us anything, it's that you don't—can't—and, indeed, mustn't—own that conversation. Your users, members,

[55] Dan Schorr, as quoted on http://www.sponsorship.com/About-IEG/Sponsorship-Blogs/Jim-Andrews/October-2011/Is-Social-Media-The-Greatest-Ambush-Marketing-Tech.aspx.

[56] Ibid.

> customers, audience—whatever you want to call them—they own the conversation. If they want to have that conversation with the event convenors and sponsors, wonderful. But the more mind-share an event has managed to gain, the better the chances the audience will also want to have that conversation with others, and that includes competing brands and businesses.[57]

He continues to pose the question of how official sponsors should adapt to the challenge of this free-for-all conversation, and we again see that the advice to sponsors is to properly leverage what they have paid for, also in the wild and whacky frontiers of cyberspace:

> [Sponsors are advised to do] pretty much exactly the opposite of what event governing bodies have generally done in the past, which was to clamp down and try to assert more control. Organisations that gripe about others riding their conversational coattails need to become better—a lot better—at conversation themselves. Maybe that's by creating content that's worth talking about. And maybe it's by becoming more open, transparent and willing to engage. There's some good conversational advice in the adage "If you want to be interesting, be interested". A lot of the organisations complaining the loudest about "ambush" marketing haven't seemed terribly interested in what their audiences have had to say. And that has to change. In other words, bringing the most expensive cheese ball to the party doesn't mean everyone there has to talk to you and only you. But it can be a great conversation opener... if you're the social type.[58]

Social media may be just one more forum where official sponsors should ensure proper leveraging of their sponsorship investment. Apart from the above-mentioned sentiments regarding the open and eminently accessible nature of the conversation—which I, of course, completely agree with—event organisers are also faced with the very nature of the Internet, and the fact that it is in any event not the easiest thing to control. Eric Schmidt, chairman and chief executive of Google, was once quoted as observing that the Internet is 'the first thing that humanity has built that humanity doesn't understand, the largest experiment in anarchy that we have ever had'. One can only say good luck to FIFA and their mega-event organising brethren; the 'conversation' on social media around the event is one major element of its thematic space that will probably be a largely untouchable target for the ambushing hit squads. Yes, the IP lawyers can take action against cyber-squatters, but it is an entirely different question whether lawyers (or anyone else) can effectively control the discourse when the populace of 'digital natives' start chatting up a storm on the social media.

Finally, apart from the issue of commercially motivated ambushing campaigns through social media, one should also consider that this may serve as a new and very powerful soapbox or 'virtual town square' in which opposition to event commercialism (including aggressive anti-ambushing efforts by event organisers) may be voiced. The world was recently shocked by the toppling of oppressive regimes in the Middle East, with the process of the 'Arab Spring' significantly

[57] Cotteringham, R 'Is it ambush marketing, or conversation?', 23 June 2010—available online at http://www.socialsignal.com/blog/rob-cottingham/it-ambush-marketing-or-conversation.
[58] Ibid.

driven by social media ('Facebook, not fighter jets, can topple Iran's regime'[59]). FIFA et al. should take heed of the dangers of alienating the masses. After all, these people not only often pay for the infrastructure to stage their events and vote for the politicians who bid to host these events (and then write the laws that protect them). They are also, ultimately, the consumers of their mega-event brand, and money talks.

10.3.3 The Changing Face of the Modern Ambush

Having just referred to the fact that the Internet is one mechanism which may in future (and already as I write this) provide ambush marketers with increased exposure and simplified (and less expensive) means to ambush an event, it bears mentioning that the very nature of the ambush appears to be changing. This relates specifically to the targets of ambushing campaigns as well as the relevant commercial rights which are potentially affected.

David Becker, the author of a book on legal aspects of the organisation of sports events[60] and the current Head of Legal for the International Cricket Council, is convinced that this is the case. While ambush marketing has always been a dynamic practice and has evolved significantly in the past few decades, due in part to the creative nature of the successful ambush, he feels that the target of the modern ambush has also shifted. Becker, who has acted on both sides of the 'fence' (both as legal advisor to the ICC and to Nike in respect of the 2010 FIFA World Cup) believes that the biggest and most fundamental changes that have happened in the field of ambush marketing in the last 2 years are online piracy and commercialisation of broadcast footage of events. He explains, recounting the experience of the ICC in respect of its 2011 Cricket World Cup hosted on the Indian subcontinent:

> Online piracy is a growing headache for sports rights holders. I can get the figures for you, but we had something like 5,000 illegal streams during the Cricket World Cup 2011. We had to employ an agency to work 24/7 for 6 weeks. They were successful in taking down 80% of the streams, but not without a lot of effort. Online piracy is itself a form of ambush marketing. Because (a) it's passing off a commercial right (the right to broadcast) as their own and (b) because these illegal streams are being sponsored (that is now the primary source of income for the pirates). Our broadcaster, ESPN Star Sports, has failed to sell licenses in certain regions because of piracy. I am giving you a summary here, but online piracy is one of the top two ambush marketing issues facing sports today. And it is very hard to regulate and control. Legislation would be very useful in this area, but we are very far off it for a number of reasons.[61]

---

[59] Marcus, Y 'Facebook, not fighter jets, can topple Iran's regime ', 18 February 2011—available online at http://www.haaretz.com/print-edition/opinion/facebook-not-fighter-jets-can-topple-iran-s-regime-1.344135.

[60] Becker 2006.

[61] David Becker, from personal e-mail communications with the author, December 2011.

I referred, in Chap. 4, to the efforts of the Sports Rights Owners Coalition in respect of combating piracy, and the phenomenon appears to be a widespread one which promises to become even more prevalent (and harmful for rights holders) with the development of Internet and digital technologies and the social media (as referred to in the previous section).

Becker also points out that event broadcasts are now a major target for ambushing activities, which he believes has eclipsed the smaller scale ambush which is centred around an event venue or limited exposure in local media:

> The second issue, commercialisation of footage, is as fundamental and far reaching. This was the biggest issue facing us in the [2011 ICC Cricket World Cup], and it's beginning to face other sports too. What we are talking about here, is the placing of virtual advertising/sponsorship on our footage by news broadcasters, pirates, and national broadcasters alike. These people have quickly worked out how much money they can make from selling sponsorship in respect of our footage, when you have 40/50/100 million viewers watching. And now you will begin to realize why I am no longer so concerned about 30 people lining up outside the stadium in branded shirts or lederhosen. Because it is nothing compared to a news channel or broadcast licensee embedding a third party brand in the top right hand corner of the screen during the middle of an India/Pakistan World Cup semi-final watched by hundreds of millions of people.[62]

He again recounts the practical experience of the ICC in respect of its 2011 event, which appears to have necessitated currently pending (at the time of writing) legal action against offenders:

> During the [2011 ICC Cricket World Cup] we became aware of a number of channels that were [commercialising official broadcast footage without authorisation]. Apart from embedding branding on the footage itself, they were also producing 'magazine' type programmes with our footage and sponsoring those programmes with branding before during and after matches, providing sponsored score updates (more difficult to stop legally), and decorating their studios with branding even though they were official licensees of [the event's official broadcaster] ESPN Star Sports! Many of these companies also had accreditation at our Cricket World Cup matches. So I decided to pull their accreditation prior to the semi-final and final, which meant these representatives were not allowed into the grounds for the purposes of reporting on the game (they were still able to use our footage though). It caused a national uproar and the Minister of Broadcasting eventually got involved. We had a meeting in Delhi just before the semi-final and final but we could not resolve the matter. Essentially, the channels could not provide an undertaking not to provide the embedded branding and other sponsorship for the semi-final and final (a reasonable request we thought) because they had already sold those 'rights' for huge sums of money to third parties. The result was that we are now suing a few of those major channels and action will be instituted in the next week or two. In this case, there was no legislation, unsurprisingly, and we are going to have to rely on other legal remedies. Our broadcast partner, ESPN, is also joining the suit because they have the rights to sell sponsorship in respect of the broadcast. So their rights are in turn being infringed and diminished.[63]

---

[62] Ibid.

[63] Ibid.

In Chap. 9 I referred to the particular position of the ICC in respect of the funding of the sport and the role of event-related revenues in supporting grassroots development of the game in ICC Member nations. Becker explains the dire risks of such unauthorised commercialisation of broadcast footage and how the potential impact of the traditional 'ambush' (even a case such as the 'Bavaria babes' matter discussed elsewhere in this book) pales in comparison:

> Broadcasting rights generated and sold by the ICC make up about 85% of the world's cricketing revenues. We are talking about well over a billion dollars over an 8 year rights cycle. If we are unable to protect these rights adequately, we have a BIG problem. I can tell you for a fact that many of our Members will go bankrupt if these revenues are diluted. Grassroots cricket in countries like West Indies, Zimbabwe, Sri Lanka etc. will dissipate hugely, because there will simply be no money to fund it. Now I am not suggesting that legislation of the like implemented traditionally for major events is always the answer. However, the legislation and jurisprudence now needs to be in the area of online piracy and commercialisation of footage/news access regulations. Not about how many metres outside a stadium you can sell merchandise or brand a building! I don't give a damn about the latter. I now care about ambushing that is going to hundreds of millions of people, via Internet, TV and mobile. That is the future of ambush marketing.[64]

I believe that there is significant merit in these concerns and that the focus for event organisers, sponsors and lawmakers may need to shift in future in order to successfully combat ambushing of events. In fact, if special event laws in future focus more on these types of ambushes that Becker refers to, I would be less worried about such laws than I currently am in respect of the existing *sui generis* event legislation discussed in this book. The reason is that I believe that the relevant rights and interests threatened by online piracy or unauthorised commercialisation of official broadcast footage are much less controversial than some of the 'rights' claimed by event organisers and which are purportedly the subject of protection of such current *sui generis* legislation. I will explain this more clearly in Sect. 10.5.

10.4 How Do We Fix Things?

I have never claimed that this book would provide a definitive answer to the problems I have referred to in respect of ambush marketing and how the law is abused to combat it. In the great mega-event commercial rights arena there are valid arguments on both sides of the ambush marketing debate; on why ambushing is (un)ethical or (il)legal, and on why event organisers and the official sponsors should fight it tooth and nail. What I have tried to highlight here is that at the very least this is a contentious area and one in which more (and, I would suggest, more balanced) legal research is required. The marketing fraternity has in recent years produced a vast body of literature on ambushing. The lawyers have joined the fray

---

[64] Ibid.

more recently, and I do not believe that enough has been done in order to ensure that the law plays a positive role in this area rather than just to act as a blunt instrument which may increasingly be seen as working in a coercive and unfair manner, in classic capitalist tradition, to unduly protect narrow commercial interests at the cost of the greater public good. I, personally, would like to see more lawyers other than only the legal advisors of sports event organisers write on the subject.

Some commentators have come up with very helpful suggestions for fixing the current state of things. Sports marketing practitioner Andy Sutherden, for example, recently suggested that we should 'move the story on from a legal debate to a moral debate', and that official sponsors should be more creative in connecting with their audience and demonstrating the true value of 'official' sponsorship:

> Rather than continuing to spend time, money and positive energy in unscrambling the legal complexities of it all, ambushing the ambushers may simply come down to pricking consumer conscience and finding more compelling ways of selling the benefit of brands who actually pay to play.[65]

While I disagree as to downplaying the importance of the need for a legal debate (of an objective and unbiased nature, which I think has been largely lacking to date), I do think that there is something to the suggestion. We have seen that marketing experts like Kim Skildum-Reid and others have called for better leveraging of official sponsor rights rather than over-emphasis on the psychological safety net of draconian special event laws. Along with this we have seen that the Vancouver 2010 Winter Games organisers were praised for their educational campaign regarding sponsors' rights and ambushing, and for providing detailed guidance of where, exactly, the line was between legitimate and illegitimate marketing around the event.[66] I think Sutherden's suggestion fits well within this framework. It does not imply that ambushing is necessarily unethical (an issue which I examined in more detail in Chap. 3); it rather suggests that the actual benefits of official sponsorship investment can be used to make a moral argument to consumers. There are two aspects of this last which I think deserve special

---

[65] Sutherden 2011, p. 313.

[66] See, for example, Storch, J 'It's an ambush! Or is it?' *Marketing*, 17 May 2010—available online at http://www.macleoddixon.com/documents/Storch.pdf:

'When "The Olympic and Paralympic Marks Act" was tabled in 2007 there were breathless media reports about attempts to protect words such as "Winter" "Gold" and "Sponsor." Few of the media reports clarified that VANOC would only object to these words if used in a manner that would mislead, or be likely to mislead, the public that the user had a business association with the Games. VANOC's approach (after a rocky start in shaming Esso out of a hockey-based campaign around the time of the 2006 Torino Games) was educational and consultative and even included an ambush evaluation method with samples of what would be judged offending. This was a unique piece to Olympic ambush marketing that no other organising committee had ever contemplated, and resulted in keeping VANOC out of legal battles and their sponsors mostly happy. VANOC realized that amateur sport and its sponsors existed long before the Games came to Vancouver and VANOC would not be leaving much of a legacy if corporate Canada was not encouraged to invest in sport post-2010.'

mention. The first is the fact that it is a positive development to see such calls for the need to actually make an argument—it would be heartening to see event organisers embrace this concept of the need to make their case rather than continue with their current stance of demanding everyone to automatically and uncritically buy into their biased and stigmatised view of ambushing. The second point is that the strength of this moral argument would depend very much on event organisers being able to show that such sponsorship investment actually goes into developing the sport, towards grassroots development initiatives or other morally laudable causes. I am not convinced that these organisations have to date been able to do so, though (as I argued in Chap. 9), and that the public perception at least is that sponsorship money goes primarily towards large and tax-free event profits. This needs to change.

In the meantime, while we move towards this idyllic position of more thoughtful, critical and satisfactory treatment of the relevant issues, I believe there are a number of things that can, and should, be done in order to address the problems with the law's involvement in mega-event commercial rights protection. In the section that follows I will try and distil my own views, as expressed throughout the earlier chapters, in the form of a list of specific suggestions that I would make to lawmakers in future mega-event host nations, to consider before such draconian special laws are passed under coercion from the event organisers. Then I will conclude by providing a more controversial, and possibly unrealistic, suggestion for a more uniform solution to the legal regulation of commercial rights to mega-events and the fight against ambushing of events.

10.4.1 A Few Suggestions for the Host Nation Lawmakers

If this book makes it into the hands of those persons involved in bidding for or organising the staging of future instalments of sports mega-events, and in particular the host nation lawmakers, I would strongly urge due consideration of the following suggestions, which are listed in no particular order, in respect of the process of adopting and the content of any such future laws. Maybe this could be used as a rather simplistic checklist of elements of such potential laws which should, or should not, be employed, or to which very thoughtful consideration should be given when drafting new laws.

They've come to your house for a reason

Event organisers need to host their event in your country or city. Yes, there may be a few others bidding for the privilege to host the show, and such bidding wars may often turn quite ugly, but if FIFA were to stage every instalment of its World Cup in Germany because the stadia are already built and it will have a 'safe' and predictable legal climate for its show, things would get stale pretty quickly. It wants your local flavour and it needs the excitement which goes with the locale; it has also made lofty promises to its sponsors of the great benefits that will flow from their huge sponsorship investment, so it is also contractually obliged to make things interesting. If the tournament was only about 64 matches and what transpires on the field of play it could be hosted at any halfway decent local football facility and broadcast to the world. But the modern sports mega-event is about so much more than just the sport; it is a cultural event and a showcase of the global appeal of the game. So also take those threats of a 'Plan B' (they'll be taking everything away from you at the last minute if you even look like you'll screw up the arrangements) with a pinch of salt.

That being said, however, expect the event organiser to cherry-pick only the parts of your country and its culture (and, especially, its laws) which it likes and wants. It will likely demand that you provide it with a very special dispensation, relating to special commercial rights and IP laws; special immigration and entry rules; special measures to 'spring clean' the venue precincts (clearing it of undesirables such as the homeless and street children); special tax benefits and, generally, special treatment of its people akin to that usually reserved for visiting heads of state or royalty. Expect this, and be ready to say to them that they can't have their cake and eat it too. If you want to put on your party in my house, you'll have to put up with the noisy plumbing and the peeling wallpaper. You'd have to be satisfied with the colour I painted the walls and the drapes I picked for the dining room. More importantly, though, you also have to put up with my relatives and friends, and you can't invite only your VIP friends and expect 'my peeps' to go to their rooms. While we'll try our best to make your stay a happy one, it is very much a case of 'my house, my rules'. Live with it.

Avoid 'the creep'

I have referred to Phillip Johnson's colourful terminology in describing the horizontal and vertical 'creep' of special laws passed in recent years in various jurisdictions in order to protect events. Future host governments should actively avoid this process of automatically adopting and adapting laws passed in other countries for the same or similar events. This is especially imperative because of the differences between host nations; what may have worked in a highly developed democratic system may be less appropriate in a developing country with very different developmental needs and agendas, and vice versa. Specifically also avoid, at all costs, the coercion by event organisers who will demand that the level of protection that their event enjoyed the last time round in another country must be matched or even exceeded. Let the event organisers make their case and bring forward a convincing argument for the level of protection sought. The legislative process should demand a merit-based approach, where the passing of legislation which may have significant consequences for host nation citizens must be underpinned by a convincing show of the need for such a law. This should include a call to event organisers to show what harm they would likely suffer if commercial rights protection for their event were to be left solely to the existing laws of the country. Such proof of potential harm should not be mere claims of the potential loss of sponsors if nothing special is done to protect the value of their investments. If they want more protection they should show why this is required; if they can't then they shouldn't be allowed such potentially far-reaching appropriation of the legislative authority of the state for purely commercial purposes. Automatic adoption of the special laws as passed in other jurisdictions, under pressure from event organisers, equates to a marked lack of legislative sovereignty and may very well be *ultra vires* the powers of democratically elected lawmakers.

Demand to see some credentials before you open the door
Following on the previous suggestion, lawmakers should refuse demands for special laws unless the event organiser can first show how and why this is required. This should involve both the need to host the event, in the first place, but definitely also the need for special laws to protect commercial interests in such event. And this need should not relate purely to the commercial interests of the event organiser or its partners. The host nation government and, more importantly, its people, are also 'partners' in the event. In fact, the host nation's citizens and the many foreign tourists who may be drawn to the spectacle are ultimately the fans and consumers of the event brand. Accordingly, the need for special laws must include convincing proof that the public interest would be served by such laws. In line with provisions in some of the existing *sui generis* event laws [such as section 15A(1)(b) of South Africa's Merchandise Marks Act, and section 7(4) of New Zealand's Major Events Management Act], any special legislation should include real requirements to justify such laws with reference to the public interest. Such provisions must, however, be backed up by a real and transparent process of investigating how the public interest would be served by such legislation. This should not be a process reminiscent of the pseudo-science which often characterises economic impact assessments conducted for event bidding purposes. *Real and verifiable evidence should be required.* By borrowing Longdin's terminology in her evaluation of the New Zealand legislation, it should be ensured that such legislation is not merely a public law solution to a private law problem. And the exercise of demanding proof of justification for such laws should not merely pay 'lip service' to the public interest.[67] Lawmakers should be able to show that the mischief sought to be addressed by means of such legislation has a significant public interest element and that it not only would address private commercial interests. This may, importantly, require anti-ambushing provisions to have a strong consumer protection underpinning; anti-ambushing laws should have at their heart the outlawing of conduct by 'ambushers' which involves an element of consumer deception, rather than merely aiming to constitute a naked restraint on competition in the event marketing environment in order to protect vested interests of event organisers and multinational corporations.

Keep the balance
Still in keeping with the above suggestions for avoiding the automatic passing of special laws under coercion from event organisers and demanding a strong showing of justification for such laws as prerequisite, lawmakers should ensure that

[67] See Scassa 2011, p. 361.

whatever laws result maintain a good balance in respect of the rights and interests of the various stakeholders. For example, consider the nature, scope and extent of such laws in order to reflect the investment by the various stakeholders in the staging of the event. Where the event (especially infrastructure) is to a significant extent funded by taxpayers rather than by event organisers or sponsors, ensure that the legislation reflects the interests of such taxpayers in receiving a net benefit from their investment. The level of protection, which substantially involves or determines the extent of monopolisation of opportunities for commercial exploitation of the event, must be commensurate with the level of taxpayer investment in establishing the event's platform for such commercial opportunities. Any special event laws should mimic the suggested 'middle ground' approach advocated by Fortunato and Richards (in the context of American antitrust laws and event rights protection):

> The courts typically interpret the antitrust laws as binary, all-or-nothing propositions. Either an action violates or does not violate the law. In this situation [in evaluating the impact of sponsorship exclusivity on the sports consumer's freedom of choice], though, neither decision is satisfactory, because of the damage caused at either extreme. A better approach would be to seek a middle ground, where damage could be limited but not eliminated. Some possibilities include limiting the extent to which stadiums and arenas can ban consumers from bringing in refreshments, limiting the terms of exclusivity agreements, and so forth.[68]

The interests of the fan/consumer/taxpayer should never be relegated to the margins of the mega-event 'social contract'. When considering ways to ensure a balance between the interests of event organisers and sponsors, on the one hand, and fans/consumers/taxpayers, on the other hand, also consider the level of tax exemptions granted to event organisers. Instead of blindly allowing a 'tax bubble' through which event organisers can monopolise all revenues from the event and take it offshore, consider whether the provision of more far-reaching event laws could not be balanced by means of the imposition of some scheme by which taxes could be shared and, for example, channelled into small business development. While event organisers should be allowed to earn profits from their events, such profits should be insufficient to justify strong commercial rights protection unless it can be shown that some of the money (in the form of taxes, or otherwise) will be specifically reinvested in the development of those entities most directly affected by such laws. And I don't mean the building of a few token football fields in poor communities or an illusory Olympic legacy project that is good for little more than a few public relations ads. If the purpose of restraining trade and marketing by such small businesses is to enable the event organisers and sponsors to engage in their own marketing around the event, and these 'official' parties show a profit as a result, should some of these revenues not be trickled down to those persons whose legally-imposed sacrifice of their normal freedoms to compete in the marketplace actually enabled such profits?

'Old school' is best

Never forget what ambush marketing is all about. Avoid the illegitimate and ill-founded extensions of the concept as found in recent event laws, and ensure that

---

[68] Fortunato and Richards 2007, p. 48.

any legislation passed to protect an event against ambushing actually targets ambushing. At the heart of what should be treated as illegitimate marketing practices should be the element which makes it unlawful, namely the intentional deception of consumers or sabotage of official sponsors. Laws which lose sight of the need for event organisers or sponsors to prove the element of consumer deception are dangerous. When mere references to events are outlawed there are significant free speech issues at stake, and there can be very little by way of justification for any infringement of rights on the basis of rationality and proportionality where such a basis is absent. True ambush marketing is aimed at confusing consumers and causes actual harm to event organisers and sponsors. Anything less is not an ambush, and should not deserve special and invasive laws just because the event organisers would not be able to restrain such conduct if left to the normal principles of law (like everyone else is) because it wouldn't be able to prove its case. This would smack of a naked restraint on competition and ill-founded attempts to achieve market control.

If you can't define it you shouldn't outlaw it

When drafting laws to provide special protection of commercial rights to events, ensure that such laws are clear in their meaning in order to provide sufficient guidance to individuals and businesses as well as to those tasked with enforcing its provisions. If people are to be threatened as to what will happen if they cross the line, be sure that they know where that line is. If you are satisfied that traditional principles and rules of law do not provide satisfactory protection for rights holders or that there is some mischief which requires special treatment through the means of such legislation, ensure that use of vague and ambiguous language is avoided. If you cannot achieve certainty as to what is allowed and what isn't, you shouldn't be passing laws about it. In Chap. 8 I referred to a piece by Ellis et al. who recount how, in parliamentary debate over the special laws to protect the 2012 London Olympic Games, the Minister of sport declared that the 'right of association' created to counter ambush marketing was drafted in the broadest possible terms because there was no consensus as to what type of conduct it was meant to catch and because the future demands of the IOC for a legislative response to the public might change. This is a shameful use of legislative force in a modern democracy.

Know that when you engage in this law-making process you are likely to be asked to outlaw conduct which is not necessarily morally or ethically questionable (a prime reason why such conduct would have hitherto gone unregulated by law), and that any process of making laws which protect commercial rights to events involves the appropriation of elements of the event which may be in the public domain. You will through such legislation be allocating exclusivity of use and enjoyment of such elements to a select few. The carving out of such elements from the public domain should therefore be done sparingly and only once a clear case has been made out why only certain parties should be given the right to legally exploit them. It is unacceptable for a lawmaker to outlaw conduct which it labels as ambush marketing (and even to criminalise it) in a vague and nebulous way, especially if such an approach is due to the fact that ambushing is a dynamic phenomenon characterised by creativity on the part of the 'ambusher'. The grey zone of conduct within which many cases of 'intrusion ambushes' may fall might not be susceptible to be pinned down by black letter law. If you can't identify exactly what should be outlawed, it simply shouldn't be outlawed. Casting the net too wide in order to satisfy the demands of an event organiser, without proper justification, is destructive of the rule of law. And you would add insult to injury if you also include presumptions of liability or even reverse the burden of proof. If a wealthy and powerful event organiser or its corporate sponsors cannot prove what constitutes an ambush or the guilt of an alleged transgressor, it would be patently unfair to place a burden of disproving it on the little guy who gets caught in their crosshairs.

When prohibiting an 'association' with an event

… don't forget that the reason you've bid for and paid a lot of money to win the right to host the event is that you're hoping it will be a grand show. You've likely been promoting the expected benefits of bringing this show to your shores to your voters and taxpayers for years—after all, they'll likely be footing much of the bill—so don't suddenly ignore the fact that all of those promotional efforts mean that the event will pervade public attention and the public discourse for quite some time. So when you consider whether to include provisions in your legislation to prohibit persons from 'associating' with the event, also consider that you're actually acting a little like Dr Jekyll and Mr Hyde. This is much like giving a child a chocolate bar and then telling them not to eat it.

That being said, and if you really *have* to conjure up an association right, keep it simple and don't lose sight of the reason why an association with the event might be worthy of legal proscription. Do not make provision for the remotest likelihood of an association infringing such a right, and ensure that there is some objective standard to determine infringement (for example, what a reasonable person would believe). Ask the event organiser to explain why any such association which may be for a commercial purpose might harm its interests or those of its sponsors. Just because the person who makes such an association by, for example, referring to the event in the process of marketing its own product does not mean that it is an 'ambush' or should be treated as one.

Also, do not by implication treat your own consumer public like idiots; if an 'association' is anything less than an attempt at deceiving them about sponsorship or affiliation with the event, just don't prohibit it. And let's not get started on the use of disclaimers—if the 'ambusher' makes it clear to anyone but a 4 year-old that they are not an official sponsor, trust the consumer to decide from whom they want to buy the soda, the insurance policy or the mobile phone. They may decide to rather support the official sponsor, and maybe this will be because such sponsor has clearly communicated the message that its financial support of the event actually translates to tangible benefits for the sport and for its grassroots development or other such causes. But that would (and should) depend on market forces, and on the ability of the official sponsor to effectively leverage its sponsorship rights. Even though it would have paid a huge amount of money to the event organiser, it shouldn't be allowed an unfair advantage in the market caused by overly-zealous law-making.

What's good for the goose should be good for the gander

While you should not pass laws blindly, based on what other lawmakers have done in other jurisdictions in the past—and only if you really do have to pass such laws—at least do not ignore the history of the event as hosted in other countries or, as importantly, the conduct of the event organiser on those occasions. Event organisers will likely love to remind you of previous attempts to ambush their events. While you listen to the recounting of these sometimes amusing incidents, likewise consider how the event organisers have conducted themselves in the past. Be aware of the fact that the organisers often take a very aggressive stance on protection of the commercial rights which they sell at a premium to their sponsors, and that the reason you are being asked to pass laws specifically for the event is that the organisers plan to use them.

Also know that once those laws have been passed you will have little control over their use; many threats of legal action will probably be made and very few, if any, of these cases will ever reach a court of law where a judge will be able to pronounce on the fairness and legitimacy of such threats or legal action. You are being called upon to produce something which in the wrong hands may be very destructive and may have far-reaching and onerous consequences for the civil liberties and fundamental rights of your constituency of citizens, small businesses and entrepreneurs, taxpayers and voters. For any such law to be balanced and fair there should be reciprocity of remedies. Ensure, therefore, that if you do pass such laws they will also provide any persons who may be targeted through its enforcement with remedies against any groundless threats and legal action. And ensure that such remedies are effective and will have a deterrent effect. Let anyone think twice before signing their name to a cease-and-desist letter which can have a very significant chilling effect on free speech and on the exercise of the freedom to trade. Also, ensuring that your legislation takes a balanced approach and provides sufficient opportunity for those targeted in their enforcement might have some great PR value. There is no need for the host government to go down with the ship when the event organisers show such a tendency to be trigger-happy; after all, if you aren't going to share in the profits of the event (especially if you're planning on exempting the organiser from paying any tax on those earnings, which they will probably demand), why should you share the blame when rights enforcement programmes go overboard (as they often do)?

Don't ignore or undervalue existing rights

Although it probably will not feel that way while in the process of dealing with them and hosting their site inspection teams and advance guard of legal eagles, the sports event organiser will visit your shores only for a relatively short period of time. Once they've gone you may have to explain to your own citizens and small businesses why you suspended the rule of law and subjected them to a veritable police state for the duration. The fact that you will be stuck with your citizens long after the event organiser has decamped highlights the fact that those citizens were also here first. The event organiser is a Johnnie-come-lately who will descend on your jurisdiction and demand laws which ignore the existing rights of others. While it will make quite a song and dance about the importance and inviolable nature of its sponsors' rights (which is why it will demand that you pass special laws to protect these) it will show much less concern for the rights of others, including existing sponsors of local stadia or teams, for example. Where these are the same sponsors and they are happy to relinquish existing rights for the duration of the event, that's fine. But do not allow other parties to be steamrollered into giving up what is theirs, and be very careful in passing laws that force them to do so. Consider whether any alleged nuisance or threat of harm to the event organiser might be something that they have come to; let them make out a case why they require existing rights-holders' rights to be curtailed or taken away completely when, after all, they were here first. And do not accept as sufficiently persuasive any argument that the event organiser is contractually obliged to its sponsors to assist them in protecting their investment. Do not let the organiser get away with making promises that it probably shouldn't have made in the first place, or, at least, do not be complicit in transgressing the rights of others in order to help it keep those promises.

Thou shalt not monopolise language

If there is one thing about the sports mega-event that is clearly within the public domain it is the conversations generated by it. When you put on such a grand show people will talk about it, and they should be entitled to do so. While laws protect event symbols and other elements such as the Olympic Rings, attempts to prohibit the use of words which may describe the event or just conjure up associations with it tread on dangerous ground when it comes to considering the potential consequences for free speech guarantees. When use of words like 'games, 'summer' and 'gold' or other such generic terms is restricted by law the potential for severe limitations of persons' rights is evident, and public opposition can be expected. Lawmakers called upon to do so should be guided by principles of law, for example the traditional limits inherent in intellectual property laws regarding generic and descriptive terms. There are good reasons why these are generally not protected and monopoly rights to their exclusive use are not granted.

Furthermore, it should be noted that even restrictions on the use of words only in a commercial context are not necessarily unproblematic; consider that honest use may include honest commercial use. Most legal systems provide constitutional protection for commercial speech, and restrictions on such speech must be shown to adhere to thresholds of justification relating to the rationality, proportionality and necessity of such restrictions. The mere fact that words may be used in a commercial context or for a commercial purpose should not automatically justify the muzzling of marketers through laws which monopolise words for the benefit of event organisers and their sponsors.

Claims by event organisers to exclusive rights to the use of something as mundane as the year in which an event takes place may be indicative of the ego of such organisations and the covetous appropriation of as much of the thematic space of the event as it can gobble up. Require such event organiser to show how and why use of such material threatens to cause it harm, or to confuse consumers, before blindly allowing such patent arrogation of what is in the public domain.

Wherever possible, adapt procedures rather than change substantive laws

Proponents of strong anti-ambushing laws often complain of the feeling of helplessness when faced with traditional causes of action and legal remedies in order to address the dynamic nature and often short-lived lifespan of the ambushing campaign during the staging of an event. As I've observed in the earlier chapters I have a measure of empathy with these parties, and there is much to be said for this argument. This does not, however, mean that one necessarily has to change the very substance of laws in the face of practical necessity. Rather consider the viability of special procedural measures to facilitate effective remedies in combating an 'in-event' campaign; then use this to supplement less drastic changes to the substance of laws. The Ad Hoc division of the Court of Arbitration for Sport has for years operated a system of special-purpose arbitration tribunals at mega-events. The entry rules of the Olympic Games include an arbitration clause and CAS has created ad hoc divisions for every Olympics since 1996. Such ad hoc divisions have also been established for the European Football Championships, FIFA World Cup and Commonwealth Games, with arbitrations usually heard by a panel of three arbitrators who must render their decision within 24–48 h. A 'virtual' court was even established for the 2010 FIFA World Cup, for which arbitrators had to be accessible by video conference.

Would a similar forum tasked with adjudicating claims of ambush marketing during events, and with powers to impose possibly novel, time-sensitive remedies against ambushes, not be a possible solution to many of the above-mentioned practical problems which may arise from the working of 'normal' legal principles and procedures? Of course, the arbitrators or adjudicators should be independent, and should not represent the event organiser or its sponsors. They could consist of a diverse range of legal, marketing and even civil rights experts. And such tribunals would have to ensure that the interests of speedy resolution of disputes do not outweigh procedural fairness. Importantly, the *audi alteram partem* principle should be adhered to, and event organisers, official sponsors and the alleged ambusher should all be allowed an opportunity to present their respective cases.

Clean zones

Remember that a marketing 'clean zone' is, in fact, nothing of the sort. Event organisers are not calling for a zone free from any commercial messages, just a zone free from commercial messages not sanctioned by it and for which it has not been paid. The concept of such zones is not justifiable on the basis of avoiding the commercialisation of the event; it is a form of market control. When FIFA demands a host nation government to guarantee 'the creation and enforcement of a restricted advertising and street trading zone within, and in the airspace above, a 2 km zone around each stadium and other official sites used for the Events, in which the right to conduct commercial activities is subject to approval by FIFA or its appointees', make no bones about the fact that this is an extremely presumptuous demand. In the absence of such government creating such a zone FIFA would have no right at all to attempt to appropriate to itself control over 'the right to conduct commercial activities' where such activities are not in conflict with its rights in terms of traditional principles of law. Such a restriction goes much wider than prohibiting passing off or other harmful business practices which may conflict with FIFA's rights, and establishes a monopoly for the organisation at the significant cost of curtailing the existing rights and civil liberties of others. An event organiser should not be allowed any such blanket ban on other economic activity. If it wants the final word on whether anyone else may trade in a host city it should prove its case, in respect of every individual trader, as to why allowing it to trade would harm its legitimate commercial interests or those of its sponsors.

Guard the guardians

Insist on proper checks and balances within private organisations which exercise quasi-public powers. Local organising committees of sports mega-events are essentially private entities, but the powers they wield are considerable. Legislation which enables them to clamp down on speech, for example, or to threaten legal action against all and sundry, should include clear and comprehensive checks and balances to ensure that such power is not open to abuse. As mentioned above, this should include appropriate reciprocity of remedies. It could also include provision for mechanisms to pre-emptively control the exercise of such powers. Advertising standards authorities and other such industry watchdog organisations provide mechanisms to control potentially harmful marketing practices. These authorities generally function by means of procedures for the investigation of complaints by members of the public or consumers and by other marketers. It might be apt to consider building a similar system into the enabling framework of the organisation of an event by means of the relevant legislation. For example, provision could be made for a retired judge or an *independent* legal expert (such as an intellectual property lawyer) to vet claims of infringement of rights by local organisers, prior to the threatening of legal action. Such a person (or a panel of persons) could be called upon to consider claims of ambush marketing and to pronounce, on an urgent basis, on the potential lawfulness or otherwise of the relevant conduct, before the issuing of a cease-and-desist letter or summons (or other steps to institute legal action against an alleged transgressor). This could go some way towards dispelling the chilling effect on speech and trade of powers which enable event organisers to indiscriminately threaten legal action, without a requirement to show prospects for success or that such action is merited in any given case. Coupled with this should be clear and definitive guidance, which is easily accessible to the public, on what is allowed and what isn't. Similar to VANOC's reported detailed guidance of what types of marketing would likely infringe its rights in respect of the 2010 Vancouver Games, such educational campaign would contribute to certainty, would limit the potentially chilling effect of broad restrictions, and would lend legitimacy to threats of legal action and the relevant rights of organisers and sponsors.

Also, be careful to avoid the establishment of private armies to enforce commercial rights to events. Where powers of search and seizure and other traditional police powers are provided, ensure that those entrusted with such considerable ability to limit the rights of individuals are responsible and trained persons with the necessary experience of law enforcement. Ambush hit squads should not be made up of lay persons acting as enforcement officers who have not demonstrated the ability to exercise powers responsibly, or who are answerable only to a private entity tasked with protecting the commercial interests of an event organiser (and which, accordingly, has vested interests of its own). Also ensure that any and all warrants to search premises or persons and to seize goods or otherwise obtain evidence are subject to judicial controls no less strict than those required in the normal course of criminal investigations (where such powers are normally, and justifiably, to be found). And also try to incorporate some measure of common sense, although it's not always easy to know when the line has been crossed. A useful rule of thumb is that when hit squads start using masking tape to hide the maker's name on toilets in your shiny new stadium, you have a problem.

Do you really* need *criminal sanctions?
The fight against ambush marketing is situated squarely within the milieu of private commercial interests of event organisers, sponsors and alleged ambushers. An ambushing campaign normally does not raise any criminal law concerns, unless draconian anti-ambushing laws specifically criminalise the ambush. It is inappropriate to use a sledgehammer when surgical precision is called for, so do not employ the strongest measures that a lawmaker has at its disposal to target marketers and traders or even ordinary citizens. The mega-event is a huge (and yes, expensive) party; those who don't behave themselves should not avoid sanction, but they shouldn't end up behind bars. You can be sure that if you provide event organisers with the power to prosecute those whom they perceive to be ambushers, they will probably use such power. There will be a negative backlash and it will probably result in a public relations nightmare, and the host government will probably shoulder some of the blame. Let the protagonists in this commercial war slug it out in the civil courts. After all, they are probably not even paying you any tax for the privilege of using your criminal justice system as a blunt instrument.

Generally, I believe that the single most important principle for future event host nation lawmakers to adhere to is a conscious effort to avoid a blanket acceptance of event organisers'/sponsors' claims to rights, and the attitude that any form of marketing not authorised by such event organiser is in fact an ambush. Much is to be said for recognition of this as the first of the principles listed in the International Trademark Association's November 2010 resolution on ambush marketing legislation (reproduced as **Appendix B**), which provides that 'a reasonable balance should be struck between the interests of the organizers, sponsors, local businesses and property owners, the local community in which the event will be held, and trademark owners'. The ill-founded escalation in special laws to protect commercial rights to events is a result of a failure to adhere to this principle, and is due largely, in my view, to a failure on the part of such lawmakers to demand that event organisers or sponsors should convincingly prove the nature and extent of the threat allegedly posed to their interests by 'ambushers'. McKelvey and Grady believe that 'Ultimately, it is the responsibility of advocates of local businesses and its citizens to lobby against ambush marketing legislation that would seek to impinge the rights of these constituents while balancing the reasonable desires of event organizers to protect the investment of their official sponsors.'[69] I disagree. I do not think that a positive duty should be placed on these mentioned parties to actively oppose the passing of such special laws. Democratically elected lawmakers should not cave to demands for such laws in the first place, and it is the event organiser or sponsor who should have the ultimate responsibility to bring forth a convincing argument for such legislation, and with evidence to back up its claims.

10.4.2 A More Radical Suggestion for a Uniform Solution

Having included a few suggestions above for future host nation lawmakers to consider when called upon by event organisers to pass special laws to protect commercial rights to events, I will brave potential ridicule and go even further here. I would like to include a more radical suggestion, which may or may not be practically viable but which, I believe, does bear consideration. English barrister and author of an excellent book on ambush marketing, Phillip Johnson (whose work I have referred to frequently in this book), concluded a 2008 law journal article on ambushing with the following:

> The laws preventing ambush marketing by association have simply been developed too quickly and enacted too freely. This will soon undermine the legitimacy of such protection. *There is a need for multilateral agreement. If the standards set are more or less universal protection can creep no further*, but in the meantime it is clear that the present piecemeal approach and escalation of protection simply leaves ambushers watching their backs. The tables have been turned. The ambusher is now the ambushed.[70] [My emphasis]

I believe he might be on to something here, and he is not the only commentator to suggest this potential route.[71] In the earlier chapters I explained that the often

[69] McKelvey and Grady 2008, p. 573.

[70] Johnson 2008, p. 29.

[71] J. Tyrone Marcus suggests the following:

'[I]t is submitted that there should be a move towards the creation of a "World Anti-Ambush Code" of sorts. One of the latent benefits arising from the creation of the first World Anti-Doping Code in 2003 was the consistency and harmonisation brought to the fight against doping in sport. Extensive stakeholder consultation resulted in a working document that addressed a vast spectrum of needs expressed by athletes and regulators alike. A similar movement is recommended for the sports business industry, albeit on a scaled-down basis simply because the complexity of intellectual property law will make any major global Code on ambush marketing regulation difficult to harmonise. Perhaps, regional or continental Codes encapsulating IP, commercial and advertising law will be a useful starting point.' Marcus 2010, p. 37.

controversial and problematic special event legislation passed in various jurisdictions in recent years, and to which I have referred, has for the most part been passed under coercion by the relevant event organisers. It is now par for the course for such event organisers to demand special laws to be passed to protect them and their sponsors, as a prerequisite for the awarding of hosting rights to potential host governments. This is the case with the Olympic Games and with FIFA's World Cup event (we also saw that one of the key reasons for the failure of the Low Countries bid for the 2018 FIFA World Cup may have been the Netherlands government's refusal to pass such laws). We also saw the eventual success of the New Zealand rugby union's bid to host the IRB Rugby World Cup, which only materialised after the passing of the controversial Major Events Management Act. Such demands for special (and as Johnson observes, ever-escalating in scope and reach) event laws are now a fact of life.

In light of this reality the suggestions to potential host nation lawmakers which I included in the preceding section may seem like a waste of time; if the relevant government has no choice but to pass such laws, surely all these suggestions are of little value. The point I wish to highlight, however, is that I believe such demands and coercion by event organisers to be illegitimate, and a direct threat to the sovereignty of domestic legislatures and the rule of law. Others have written volumes about the tendency of sports governing bodies to claim an immunity from the application of laws, in various jurisdictions and with varying success (compare the so-called 'sporting exception' in European Union law, which was recently dealt a blow by the judgment of the then European Court of Justice in the *Meca-Medina* case). The sphere of ambush marketing and of commercial rights protection for events is rather ironic in this sense; here we see sports event organisers who often claim to be above the law actually succeeding in demanding that special laws be passed to protect them. Of course, where governments are so star-struck and adamant to host the event there is little one can do about it, apart from testing the legitimacy or even constitutionality of such laws in the domestic courts, an exercise which invariably must take place after the fact and once the event is done and dusted and the event organiser has moved on to other climes. This is hardly satisfactory, and I believe the time has come to put a stop to such cavalier lawmaking and unquestioned abuse of commercial power in the sphere of mega-events. So, how can we do this? I think Johnson's brief observation regarding the need for a multilateral agreement is something that warrants further scrutiny. Let's imagine such an agreement, possibly in the form of a multinational convention between governments, and what it would mean.

It is rather ironic to note that the sports mega-event which provided the locus for the development of the modern mega-event sponsorship model, the 1984 Los Angeles Olympic Games (as discussed in Chap. 2), may also provide an example of how current demands for special event laws could be avoided. It was widely reported that the commercial success of the 1984 Games and of Peter Ueberroth's new means of sourcing sponsorship investment and the resultant profit made by the organisers was due in no small part to the fact that no-one else wanted the Games at the time. Los Angeles was the only city to bid to host the Games, and this provided the organisers with unprecedented bargaining power in its negotiations with the IOC over the terms of the host city contract, especially regarding government guarantees to cover the costs of staging the event. This provides food for thought when considered against the backdrop of the modern-day demands for government guarantees by host nation governments. If one could remove the ability of event organisers to threaten to take their events elsewhere (if Brazil, for example, were FIFA's only choice to host its World Cup event in a given year) one would eliminate the coercive element in the bidding process, and one would eliminate the ability for the organiser to demand that special laws be passed to protect its event. This does not seem viable, however (how would one arrive at such a situation, would a 'lottery' of potential host nations ever work?). What one can do, however, is to remove not the ability of the event organiser to threaten to take its event elsewhere, but the temptation to do so. And the way to achieve this is by ensuring that wherever FIFA or the Olympic Movement might go it will be faced with substantially the same laws to protect its events. This would also put a halt to the ever-escalating 'creep' of such laws, as Johnson refers to.

An international convention between states on ambush marketing or on sports event commercial rights protection could contain a number of general principles (for example, a helpful starting point for drafters might be the International Trademark Association's November 2010 Resolution on ambush marketing legislation, referred to above in Chap. 8 and reproduced as **Appendix B**). It could, similar to some of the special event laws passed in recent years, cover specific aspects of commercial rights to events, including the protection of event-related intellectual property; advertising and trading restrictions in the vicinity of event venues; clear definitions (and a test) to determine what would constitute unlawful ambush marketing of an event; exemptions to liability for potential infringers; civil penalties for unlawful conduct (I do not believe criminal sanctions are appropriate and legitimate in this context); specific provisions regarding the balancing of event organisers' and sponsors' rights against civil liberties such as free speech guarantees; reciprocal remedy provisions such as those dealing with groundless threats of legal action; and other aspects worthy of protection. I will not suggest specifics here, but the point is that I believe such a multilateral instrument could provide what I will call a 'ceiling of protection' for event organisers. Their event will be protected, but no domestic lawmaker in a country party to such convention would be allowed to exceed the level of protection as provided for in the convention, either generally or in terms of specific elements. Association rights, as we have seen them in some of the domestic laws referred to earlier, should not form part of such legislation (or, at the very least, should be properly limited in their effect to cover cases of deceitful marketing aimed at causing consumer confusion over official affiliation to the event, and should be under- rather than over-inclusive in their reach).

In light of the prevalent role and importance of intellectual property rights in the context of event commercial rights protection and of ambushing, a prime organisation to drive the process to seek the establishment of such an instrument could be the World Intellectual Property Organisation, or WIPO. WIPO describes its mission as being dedicated to 'developing a balanced and accessible international intellectual property (IP) system, which rewards creativity, stimulates innovation and contributes to economic development while safeguarding the public interest'. I believe that lobbying of WIPO by stakeholder organisations (some of whom I've referred to in this book, for example the UK's Chartered Institute of Marketing, the European Sponsorship Association, the Association for the Protection of Intellectual Property and the International Trademark Association) could facilitate a process of review of ambush marketing laws and, at the very least, could result in proposals for a model law to protect sports mega-events. I will leave the issue here and will leave the details up to others who may have more energy for such a process.

If such a convention or other such instrument of international law were to be impracticable it is possible that other options may exist, specifically within the global sporting community. Simon Boyes has recently called for an investigation into the viability of what he refers to as a 'global sports charter', or a 'supra-national constitution for sport'.[72] He argues that, while the Court of Arbitration for Sport (or CAS) has acknowledged the need to adhere to generally accepted legal principle in its proceedings (which appear to be 'little more than the sort of rules ordinarily found in any system of administrative law: legality, legal certainty, legitimate expectation, fairness, non-discrimination, proportionality and respect for fundamental human rights'), it can lay little claim to having sufficiently acknowledged the peculiarities of sport:

> This is not to decry the development by CAS of broadly applicable administrative principles, which are certainly important and appropriate in the context of a system of regulation which requires consistency of application across a plethora of jurisdictions. However, what this amounts to is little more than a systemisation of rules by which disputes concerning sports regulations can be assessed. This in itself should not be lightly dismissed, but is representative of a relatively mundane function of the CAS… The reality is that what is 'special' about sport is not found so much in its governance and regulatory structures and practices, but in the nature of the enabling measures and facilitative arrangements that scaffold sporting activity. It is remarkable that, when identifying a *lex sportiva*, there has been so little comment about the special nature of sport *itself* as a basis for a particular and specialised jurisprudence of the CAS.

Boyes argues that the CAS might reasonably be considered to have taken on the role of a relatively one-dimensional tribunal for the resolution of contractual and quasi-contractual disputes, which has little opportunity to consider the validity of sporting rules rather than their application in disputes before it. He argues that 'athletes and other "private" litigants before the CAS are largely constrained from mounting any challenge to the overall validity of sporting federations' rules and regulations and, in most cases are limited to hoping for a favourable interpretation rather than a fundamental remodelling of the rules'. Boyes believes that this necessitates the creation of something along the lines of a global sports charter, as sports' claim to protection from legal intervention on the basis of its specific nature would be significantly strengthened were it to explicitly protect such values within

[72] In a short paper delivered at the *Law, Policy and the Olympic Movement* conference, Ithaca College, London, 13–14 May 2010. I wish to thank the author for providing me with a copy of this unpublished piece.

its own regulatory system. He believes that such an instrument should go beyond stating only the fundamental principles as contained in the Olympic Charter, which are 'of limited utility in the resolution of disputes where considerations such as solidarity, competitive balance, uncertainty of outcome, the development of young athletes, and the stability and sustainability of sports and competitions are principles with which sport would ward off legal attacks':

> A universal, binding charter in which these values were explicitly stated would provide a much more convincing basis from which to combat such challenges. Readily ascertainable, universally sporting principles which, above all, are effectively applied and accessible, would provide a clear and sustained rationale upon which sports regulations might be based. A tangible and overt set of principles stands a much greater chance of successfully limiting judicial temptation to activism in the sporting context. It would also offer the opportunity for sport itself to deal with the inevitable challenges arising to its regulatory schemes… "within the family of sport"; rather than being subject to the relative vagaries of the European Commission, Court of Justice or even domestic legal systems. As such it would be possible to avoid the sort of bifurcation between legal and regulatory systems that led to seismic events of the proportion of *Bosman*… In addition to facilitating the promotion of sporting values as being of a higher order and thus able to steer the substantive path of sports and federations, such a constitutional document might also incorporate the laudable, if mundane administrative law values already set out by the CAS. These, once established, would give a high degree of validity to the activities of sport and its federations; few courts could find reason to intervene in a system where sporting values were elevated alongside principles of good governance and the standards established in principle by the Olympic Charter.

I believe there is much to be said for this suggestion, not least being the fact that it would likely enjoy the support of the international sports governing bodies who so jealously seek to obtain either a measure of 'immunity' from domestic laws (with varying degrees of success to date) or recognition of the particularity of their activities. A prime example of this, of course, is the frequent calls for special treatment in the form of *sui generis* event legislation to protect commercial rights. These same organisations, however, would not be likely to agree to my suggestion that a uniform standard for event protection laws, as referred to above, should find its way into such a global sports charter. I believe that domestic federations would have to push for inclusion of such a model law, in a concerted manner, even though this may of course irk the international federations. The real drive for something along these lines would, however, have to come from the side of governments, as the bottom line is simply that both the international as well as the domestic sports federations must conduct themselves and the business of their events staging within the confines of domestic legal systems and the applicable laws and constitutional frameworks. It might not be bad idea for interested parties (possibly marketing industry associations or civil liberties groups) to petition their governments to initiate an impetus towards such a multilateral agreement. I believe that the objective should be to produce a model for lawmakers to follow, which should be drafted in the interests of producing a ceiling of rights protection, as referred to above. While the interests of all stakeholders should, of course, be accommodated within such a law—including the event organisers and sponsors—the aim should be to ensure that a cap is placed on the ever-escalating scope and nature of protections offered in special domestic events legislation. I will, again, leave the details to others with more energy, but would at the very least like to see further research conducted on the viability of such possible ways to curb the problems that characterise the current laws to be found in various jurisdictions.

10.5 Final Thoughts

At this point I am sure the reader has had enough of me, but I do want to just add one more angle to my analysis in this book. I will try to be brief. In researching this book I was struck by something which may sound quite elementary, although I think it has not received enough attention to date. I believe that the very basic premise of the approach to commercial rights protection for mega-events and of the discourse to date on ambush marketing (and the combating of ambushing by event organisers, sponsors and lawmakers), is fundamentally flawed.

A South African sports law academic, Steve Cornelius, recently wrote an interesting article on ambushing.[73] In his discussion he distinguishes between unlawful ambush marketing and parallel marketing, namely marketing which is 'innocent' and which simply coincides with the timing of the event and is in fact lawful. He argues for what he refers to as a simple 'context test' to distinguish the two. The question to ask is simply whether, if the marketing is taken out of the context of the major sports event and placed in any other day-to-day context, would it still make sense? If it does, the marketing amounts to lawful parallel marketing. If it does not, the marketing unlawfully appropriates the goodwill of the sports federation and amounts to ambush marketing.

I mention this here not to criticise Steve's work (it really is a good article), but only because it raises an issue which I believe is fundamental to the law's treatment of ambush marketing of an event and needs to be considered in more detail. I would argue that inherent in this distinction, and underlying the above-mentioned context test to determine the lawfulness of event-related marketing, is an ill-founded assumption. This assumption is that any reference to or mention of the event, or of something that conjures up the event in the mind—for example, the ubiquitous football-themed advertisement during the time of FIFA's World Cup—is wrong, or is enough to make the relevant marketing wrongful. This assumption, in fact, underlies the association rights created in some of the legislation mentioned earlier in this book, notably the London Act. Scassa does well to summarise what I would refer to as the 'traditional' approach to ambush marketing as found in the literature:

> The argument supporting anti-ambush marketing legislation is that the event organizers own any goodwill in the event, and that they alone should control the rights of other

[73] Which was published in Afrikaans in a local South African electronic journal (I am told that an English version of the work will soon be published).

> entities to associate themselves with it. Any unpaid association is an appropriation of this goodwill.[74]

The reasoning seems to be that any such reference to the event or even to things related to the general theme of the event thus may potentially harm the goodwill of the event organiser. In Chap. 7 I recounted an example from the 2010 FIFA World Cup, when prior to the event a local satellite TV channel postponed the broadcast of a new drama series after a FIFA football appeared in some scenes. The channel explained in a press statement at the time that upon reviewing FIFA's regulations around licensing for the World Cup during this time, the producers of the programme realized that showing the scenes with the official FIFA ball would be 'against regulations'. Clearly there is an assumption in such cases that such goodwill includes any and all references to the event, or, even more troubling, that it also includes things not referring to the event itself but to a wider theme that surrounds and/or encompasses the event (e.g., in my above example, the sport of football). But this is clearly wrong, and is not rationally or morally justifiable.

If we recall that most legal systems do not recognise any form of 'ownership' of a spectacle it is clear that the point of departure in our determination of the nature of the law's treatment of event-related commercial rights should, in fact, be that *anyone* is free to refer to the event or to use reference to it, even in their marketing. This would not only make sense in terms of legal principle, but it is also in line with the common sense suggestion that a sports mega-event is, at least in principle, something that is in the public domain. FIFA, for example, may for years now have monopolised the governance of the game of football (something I discussed in Chap. 6—and remember that I admitted that this is not necessarily a bad thing) and, in recent years, also the commercial exploitation of the game. This is definitely true of its World Cup event, at least. But the point is that despite all this, nothing FIFA has done or, I venture to say, can do, will change the fact that 'its' World Cup is the premier football competition in the world which crowns a world championship team once every 4 years. In fact, if it tried to change this, the event would lose its lustre and much of its relevance. How can this not make the tournament something that resorts squarely within the public domain for football lovers?

Furthermore, when considering the rationality of a 'propertization' of the thematic space of the mega-event, a default 'anything goes' approach also makes sense from the perspective that it militates against allowing event organisers to 'blow hot and cold' in respect of the publicity value of the event, as I referred to in Chap. 8. It does not make logical sense for the law to allow an event organiser to base the very attractiveness and popularity of the event on a strategy of saturation of publicity (i.e. to attempt to grab the public's attention on the vast scale that it does and which it also demands host governments to pursue), and then to say that any use of such publicity (for commercial, or sometimes other purposes) is restricted to only a small group of entities (the event organiser and its official

[74] Scassa 2011, p. 363.

sponsors). This is tantamount to staging a huge fireworks show in Sydney harbour to which you invite a select group of VIPs, and then asking—correction: *demanding*—all residents of the city to close their eyes for the duration of the show. This paradoxical anomaly would make a mockery of both the public interest in the hosting of an event (especially also where, as we have seen, much of the investment in the event in fact may derive from public taxpayer funding) and of the law's conception of the goodwill of a business undertaking. In determining the meaning and demarcating the content of FIFA's goodwill in its World Cup event, and when one considers the concept of the goodwill of business undertakings, generally, it is imperative to not forget that this is a *show*, not a coffee shop or a dental surgery. As referred to earlier, FIFA demands of a host government a guarantee that it will outlaw 'intrusion ambushing' in the form of 'to practice, organise, approve, or sponsor any promotional, advertising, or marketing activities through which one targets the audience of the Events'. In this way it is aiming to legally prohibit mere reference to its event (and to appropriate to itself a monopoly right to control such use of references to the event—remember, such conduct must be authorised by FIFA). Section 22 of the Major Events Management Act in New Zealand exempts certain 'intrusion ambushing' conduct from liability, unless there is shown an '*intention that the advertising intrude on... the attention of the associated audience*'; and the International Cricket Council argued in ambush marketing litigation in India that '[t]he *entire advertisement or publicity value [of the event] is the exclusive property of the [ICC as event organiser]*'.[75] These all display blatantly wrong conceptions of the goodwill of an undertaking, especially of a sports mega-event (both as a business undertaking and as a grand show). The law does not allow the proprietor of an undertaking to exercise any legal rights over the public's perception of its business or over mere reference to it, and these elements do not form any part of the goodwill to an event. I also doubt very much whether this above-described approach is morally justifiable.

I would suggest, therefore, that the basic assumption that all the significant parts of the sports mega-event can be reduced to a form of property and to which rights of exclusive use can be allocated or portioned off by an event organiser is fallacious. That is not to say that event organisers, let us again say FIFA, do not have the ability, in law, to take commercial control of *certain* elements of the event and to use such elements exclusively or to license their use exclusively to others. The first and most basic of such commercially viable elements is, of course, ticketing, i.e. charging spectators a fee for access to the event venue and the entertainment provided. This remains a significant source of income for the mega-event hosts, although it has, of course, been overtaken by technology and, as a revenue source, has been dwarfed by income from the sale of broadcasting rights to the event. In addition to these sources of income, event organisers have for many years granted contractual rights of exclusivity to their sponsors. The exclusivity, however,

[75] *ICC Development (International) Ltd. v Ever Green Service Station & Another* 2003 IIAD Delhi 707, 102 (2003) DLT 723 (from par. 2 of the judgment).

cannot logically amount to any rights to exclusive use of what is fundamentally in the public domain and which cannot form the subject matter of such a contract. The rights that the sponsor receives, therefore, must relate to something else (and something less than any and all of the publicity surrounding the event); this 'something else' is what the event organiser can give and can do for the sponsor in order to enable it to leverage its sponsorship investment. This is not the publicity value of the event—the organiser can allow the sponsor to derive publicity from the event and in the context of the event in order to market its products or services, but in terms of what I suggest is the logical basis of the mega-event commercialisation model, in terms of law, this does not mean that others cannot also do so. The event organiser can only legally undertake to give to or to do something for the sponsor that which it is legally within its power to give or do. *Nemo plus iuris in alium transferre potest quam ipse haberet.*

'Ambush marketing' has become the huge problem that it is because it has so often in the past been so phenomenally successful. These successful ambushing campaigns have been successful because—fundamentally—it is really so easy to ambush an event. If a sponsor's understanding of what it buys with its sponsorship fee is merely that it is a slice of the publicity surrounding the event (e.g. the right to refer to the event in its ad campaign) it should be clear to such sponsor that an 'ambusher' can with very little difficulty achieve exactly the same result without paying the sponsorship fee. If this is all that sponsorship was about, it would, in fact, make a mockery of the very concept of sponsoring an event. If an ambusher can achieve exactly the same result that an official sponsor can achieve even if its contract with the event organiser is fully performed and it receives 100% of what it has bought, then what has the sponsor in fact bought? If the event organiser has purported to sell something that anyone can pick up for free then what, if anything, has been the purpose of the sponsorship contract? This conception of what sponsorship of the event is all about is the genesis of modern anti-ambushing laws; the automatic answer for sponsors in the light of this is perceived to be to demand that reference to the event by anyone else be prohibited outright, so that all elements of the publicity surrounding the event are ring-fenced. That is how we have arrived at where we are today.

I want to suggest that we have all—event organisers, sponsors and even lawyers—simply approached the issue of ambush marketing from the wrong perspective. The automatic assumption—that deriving publicity for one's product from an event without paying for it is somehow wrong—is a fallacy. The event creates a limited set of opportunities for commercialisation for the organiser, namely ticket revenues, broadcasting rights sales, and the granting of sponsorship rights (and licensing or merchandising rights to produce event-related merchandise, which is less relevant here). In this light, we should rather, from the outset, ask *what the official sponsor has paid for and what the event organiser can sell to it in return for that sponsorship fee*. If we do this, we'll suddenly realise that not all 'ambushing' is in fact wrongful conduct. The 'intrusion' ambusher's timing or its reference to the spectacle should no longer make one cringe. Maybe these guys are, in fact and in all fairness, fully entitled to do so.

When we consider the sponsor's position we come to the crux of the matter. It has paid the event organiser for something while the ambusher has not. So what has it *not* received which it should be entitled to claim? The answer lies not in the outer reaches of the thematic space of the event or the publicity surrounding the event. It lies squarely within the four corners of the sponsorship contract. It is not the event organiser's goodwill in its event that might be affected or is at stake. It is the value that the sponsor has bought and which it has paid for, nothing more and nothing less.

So what is this value, exactly? What has the sponsor actually bought? The core rights granted in event sponsorship contracts relate directly to the sponsor's official commercial association with the event, in the form of access to the use of event marks (such as logos, emblems and mascots, for their use in advertising and other marketing) and designations (the right of the sponsor to describe itself as an official sponsor, partner, etc. in advertising and promotional literature and on product packaging and merchandising materials). There are of course myriad variations on how such rights may be granted, defined, packaged and exercised, as well as in respect of the guarantees provided by the event organiser to the sponsor, but these two main forms of rights are most common. The point I wish to make is that both these rights, generally, relate to matter that the event organiser is legally entitled to 'sell'. As I've explained previously the key nature of the sponsorship contract is that it constitutes an agreement by the event organiser not to sue the sponsor for conduct which would, in the absence of such agreement, constitute an unlawful infringement of the sponsor's rights. Access to event marks, therefore, relates to the licensing of the event organiser's intellectual property. Designation rights, similarly, relates to allowing conduct which would in the absence of such sponsorship agreement constitute an unlawful passing off. Interestingly, the astute reader will note that both these core sponsorship rights relate to matter which is protected by traditional legal principles or mechanisms, and they also represent what is *traditionally* understood in respect of the term 'ambush marketing' as the rights potentially infringed by such unauthorised conduct.

The problem that presents itself when we evaluate the legitimacy of the modern-day anti-ambushing laws (and especially as contained in the *sui generis* event legislation referred to throughout this book) concerns the extension of such anti-ambushing laws to cover issues beyond these core rights as provided for in the sponsorship contract. A point repeatedly made throughout this book is that the modern understanding of the legally savvy 'intrusion ambush' may include conduct which holds absolutely no implications for these core sponsorship rights. Where no IP is misappropriated and the 'ambusher' does not represent itself to be officially associated with the event as a sponsor or otherwise, the prohibited conduct has been taken out of the ambit of what the sponsorship agreement protects, what the sponsor has bought and the event organiser has purported to sell. More importantly, it goes beyond what the event organiser, in fact, *can* sell. Such an 'intrusion ambush' operates within the broader context of the thematic space of the event and thus functions within the space that is not susceptible to private ownership or the ring-fencing of rights to exclusive access and use. Two specific forms of 'intrusion ambushes' illustrate the point.

First, consider the advertisement which refers (maybe obliquely) to the event or, for example, includes a football- or other sports-themed reference which the event organiser claims to be unlawful. An example would be kulula's ad campaign prior to the 2010 FIFA World Cup in South Africa, as discussed previously. The event organiser cannot convincingly claim that an ad which proclaims that the airline is 'The Unofficial National Carrier of the "You-Know-What"' creates an association with the event, in the sense of conveying a deceitful misrepresentation as to official association with the event. This is an 'intrusion ambush', because what FIFA would claim is unlawful is that there is a *reference* to the event, and that such a reference without its authorisation is unlawful. Of course, in terms of the relevant South African legislation there may be merit in this view, but as I have argued this legislation is seriously flawed and should simply be struck down. Where such law creates a criminal offence for someone to use their own trademark 'in relation to an event' in a way that is calculated to achieve 'special promotional benefit' for such mark, there is a clear assumption that someone else (the event organiser) has the exclusive capacity and right to derive promotional benefit from the event. But this is not borne out by legal principle, as not all of the promotional benefit that derives from publicity of the event (or reference to it) actually accrues to the event organiser as goodwill. A similar example is the one so often referred to in the ambushing literature, namely the clever American Express ad campaign which ran during the VISA-sponsored 1994 Lillehammer Winter Olympics, with the strap line 'If you are travelling to Norway this winter, you will need a passport, but you don't need a visa'. Sarah Storey describes this 'ambush' as follows:

> This type of activity does not use any of the sports rights owner's intellectual property rights and therefore is not actionable under intellectual property rights legislation, nor is it misleading advertising because it does not make false statements or give the impression the sports rights owner endorsed the advertiser.[76]

I will (not surprisingly, I'm sure) respond by asking: What is wrong with this, then? But Storey concludes by stating that 'Nonetheless, it creates an association between the event and the advertiser'.[77] In the absence of ill-conceived statutory 'association rights' there is simply nothing rationally or morally justifiable in outlawing such an association as created through clever and creative advertising, and there is no basis in traditional legal principle to support this illicit extension of an event organiser's appropriation of the consumer's head-space through the arrogation of new-fangled 'rights' to such an association. Teresa Scassa explains the danger inherent in this by distinguishing the real target of anti-ambushing laws from the more traditional protection against consumer confusion (a point I argued in Chap. 8):

[76] Storey 2010, p. 48.

[77] Ibid.

> While it is clear that the harm sought to be addressed by [anti-ambushing] legislation is different from that addressed by other legal recourses, the law ultimately targets influences on the thoughts of consumers, and not necessarily on their actions. This is a difficult and dangerous target for legislation.[78]

If we scan the special anti-ambushing laws discussed in this book we find many references to the unlawful (commercial) 'association' purportedly targeted, and these provisions are often referred to as being aimed at combating the 'association ambush'. The problem, however, is that these same provisions and their enforcement in recent years has shown a clear tendency to also target the intrusion ambush. Prominent international advertising lawyer, Marina Palomba,[79] strongly opposed the London 2012 Olympics association right during the government consultations which led to the 2006 London Act (which Act, in Bill form, she characterised in a 2006 opinion piece as 'an attempt to ambush a fantastic event with draconian legislation'). She views this association right as 'a step too far', and echoes the sentiments I expressed in Chap. 8 and elsewhere in this book regarding the disconnect between such a strong event rights protection measure and the traditional role of consumer confusion in the context of ambush marketing:

> Go back to trademark law on confusion. If there is no confusion as to whether you're a sponsor, I would argue that people are not stupid—the general public knows [that there is no connection]. If you are blatant about not being a sponsor, but in some way are legitimately associating yourself with an event on your doorstep, where you have a legitimate right to get something from the goodwill of this major event, then I think you should be able to do so, provided there's no confusion.[80]

Webster's Online Dictionary provides a number of different definitions for the word 'association'. The above-mentioned one (of a commercial association such as sponsorship or other official affiliation) is one of these, but another is the use of the word as denoting a 'mental connection, or that which is mentally linked or associated with a thing'. American Express and kulula may very well have created such an 'association' with the relevant events with their above-mentioned ads, but this association is something that takes place and exists in the consumer's mind. Hands off, I say! This is not something that the law should entitle anyone to 'own' or attempt to control, and there is no convincing basis for it in law.

The second type of 'intrusion ambush' is one that is often targeted in 'clean zone' provisions in the *sui generis* legislation, namely trading in such a designated area in the vicinity of the event venue for a specified period of time. While it would be legitimate for lawmakers to protect official event sponsors by placing restrictions on advertising by others within such zones, it is a very different question whether normal (i.e. not intentionally aimed at ambushing) *trading* by non-sponsors in such areas should be the subject of such restrictions. Why does a

---

[78] Scassa 2011, p. 363.

[79] Marina Palomba, general legal counsel at McCann Erickson World Group, and former legal director of the UK's Institute of Practitioners in Advertising.

[80] As quoted in Smith 2011, p. 45.

fish-and-chips shop in central London threaten the interests of the Olympics organisers or their sponsors? How would its normal trading activities (that is, when it does not attempt to ambush the event, misappropriate IP or call itself a sponsor) actually threaten to harm the interests of the event organiser or official sponsors? The point is that it does not, but the event organiser will likely demand special laws to prohibit such commercial activity within a clean zone in order to signify to its sponsors an intention to protect their rights and fulfil exorbitant and ambitious rights protection guarantees in the sponsorship contract. The irony is, of course, that this does not relate to any rights bought or sold in such contract. The fish-and-chips shop's activities also take place outside the context of the elements of the event which were 'sold' in the sponsorship contract and, as such, again represent something that should not be within the power of event organisers and lawmakers to prohibit.

Not all of the different elements of the sports mega-event (the 'A to Z') are the property of the event organiser or of anyone else. Some such elements (let us call them A (ticketing), B (broadcast rights) and C (sponsorship rights)) are legally susceptible to ownership or the monopolisation of control over opportunities for commercial exploitation by the organiser or those licensed by it to do so. Anything outside the ambit of A, B and C should, as a matter of principle, be viewed as situated within the public domain of the event's thematic space, and any use of such element(s) which does not otherwise infringe on the legal rights of the event organiser or its commercial partners should not be actionable in terms of law. This understanding of what parts of the event, in fact, are susceptible to control and commercial exploitation by the event organiser and its partners also highlights the fact that much of what these parties claim to be ambushes in fact cause them no real harm. I remarked earlier that the *sui generis* anti-ambushing laws for the most part do not require any proof of harm, and the illicit nature of such laws is compounded by this fact, namely that there often is an absence of harm and thus, at least to my mind, no need for a remedy (and definitely not if this is in the form of a draconian criminal sanction, as is now often the case). This radical departure from the 'traditional' approach to ambushing and to what the event organiser owns or should be entitled to control has dire consequences, and these are not logically or morally justified:

> There is a cost to creating a "right of association" in public events that can be used to ban all unpaid associations. This cost is borne largely by the public, whose participation and involvement in the event is ironically necessary to its success. To appreciate the nature of this cost, it is important to step outside of the paradigm that sees every form of commercial association with an event as an infringement of a right of ownership. It is normal for people to reference events occurring in their community—particularly if the events are of an international scale and organizers have worked hard to draw their attention to the events. Local businesses are members of the community as well, and there is a fine line between policing unfair competition and prohibiting any references to public events. In addition, many businesses support individual athletes, as well as local and national sport activities and events. It is conceivable that some of the expression silenced by anti-ambush marketing legislation might actually have served to enhance the value of sponsorships.[81]

[81] Scassa 2011, p. 368.

The fish-and-chips shop in Hackney or the informal trader in Sao Paulo or Johannesburg does not merely through trading during an event, business as usual, cause FIFA or the Olympics organisers any harm, because their conduct does not fall within any of the elements of the event for which these organisers can legitimately claim exclusive rights of exploitation. The mere activity of trading is clearly none of FIFA's business, and it would be extremely far-fetched to argue that these small fry should have obtained sponsorship rights to the event (especially considering, as we have seen, that only large multinational or domestic corporations stand any chance of obtaining such very expensive rights). The event organiser is not harmed by such conduct because it relates to nothing that it owns or has a legal right to control.

I believe that if one considers this as an accurate description of the conception of what is legally protectable in respect of a sports mega-event, in terms of traditional and accepted principles of law (and of logic), then considering the modern anti-ambushing laws as contained in the *sui generis* event legislation in such light clearly shows up the many flaws of these laws and their core illegitimacy, as discussed throughout this book.

Others may not agree with my above characterisation of the fundamental flaws in the ambush marketing discourse. But there is one thing on which I am sure we will all agree, namely the unsatisfactory nature of the current state of the law when it comes to addressing ambush marketing of events. Event organisers will, of course, no doubt claim that more protection is needed. Others, such as associations of marketers, feel that the laws are too strict. I do not think that any right-minded person can deny that, at the very least, we have seen a significant escalation in the level and means of protection of commercial rights to events in recent years. That is a fact, not my opinion.

Earlier in this chapter I referred to the views of a legal expert and industry insider who believes that the nature of ambushing of events has changed, and that the two main and most dangerous forms of ambushing currently are and in future will be online piracy of event footage and unauthorised commercialisation of official broadcast footage of events. He has called for future event protection laws to focus on these issues rather than the more traditional forms of ambushing as targeted by the existing *sui generis* event legislation, due to the immense potential reach of such 'modern ambush'.[82] I expressed the view there that I would be less critical of such laws, simply because they would serve to protect conventionally recognised and much less controversial 'rights' to events, namely those rights relating to broadcasts. As pointed out above, these rights relate to an element of the commercial exploitation of the mega-event which I believe the event organiser should rightfully be entitled to control and claim protection for by law. However, my cynical view is that the experience of demands for aggressive rights protection by these event organisers to date shows that even if future laws will be passed to specifically protect this element of the event, the likelihood is that FIFA and other event organisers will not be satisfied, and that such laws will be demanded in addition to rather than in place of the

[82] See the discussion of the views of David Becker in Sect. 10.3.3.

existing type of anti-ambushing protection. I therefore feel that the criticism of these existing laws and of the many examples of their tenuous basis in legal principles as expressed in this book will remain relevant.

Schwab observed, back in 2006, that '[i]t remains to be seen whether the pendulum of corporate rights protection will swing further towards the draconian'.[83] The pendulum has continued to swing in that direction, and, unfortunately, still seems to have plenty of momentum to keep it swinging that way for years to come. One positive aspect of the increasingly aggressive protection of commercial interests by mega-event organisers is that, just like any other example of absolute power corrupting and feeding on itself to the point of saturation, these efforts and their consequences are starting to draw the attention of those who matter. In researching this book I found an impressive group of lawyers and academics in Canada who have in the last couple of years produced some quite critical work on ambush marketing laws. I wonder whether they have been inspired by the experience of the 2010 Vancouver Winter Olympics. I was, personally, inspired to write this book by the 2010 FIFA World Cup in South Africa. By that same token one might expect some important work by British lawyers and academics in the wake of the 2012 London Games.

I believe that the future is rosy for those who would like to see more critical engagement with the power dynamics at work in the world of sports mega-events commercial rights protection. If this book manages to strike a chord with just some of those readers who despise greed and the selfish and self-centred abuse of power, it might provide a basis in future for just the smallest of checks to address this slippery slope which leads towards the further monopolisation of elements of the public domain as it relates to sport. I think, in that case, that my job here would be done, and I would sleep a little more soundly at night. I might then actually even look forward, breathlessly, to the next time a sport mega-event is staged out in my neck of the woods. Personally, though, I would not support any bid by my government to host it—not least because I surely would not want to pay for it. That really is just my personal view.

References

All Internet-based sources referred to, were last visited in or before December 2011

Barros CP, Ibrahimo M, Szymansky S (2002) Transatlantic sport: the comparative economics of North American and European sports. Edward Elgar Publishing, Northampton

Becker D (2006) The essential legal guide to events. Dynamic Publishing Ltd, London

Burrell R, Gangjee D (2010) Trade marks and freedom of expression: a call for caution. The University of Queensland, TC Beirne School of Law, Legal studies research paper series No. 10-05

[83] Schwab 2006, p. 9.

Corbett S, Van Roy Y (2010) Events management in New Zealand: One law to rule them all? J Bus Law 4:338–362
Ellis D, Scassa T, Seguin B (2011) Framing ambush marketing as a legal issue: an Olympic perspective. Sport Manag Rev 14(3):297–308
Fortunato JA, Richards J (2007) Reconciling sports sponsorship exclusivity with antitrust law. Texas Rev Entertain Sports Law 8:33
Hoek J, Gendall P (2002) Ambush marketing: More than just a commercial irritant? Entertain Law 1(2):72–91
Johnson P (2007) Ambush marketing: a practical guide to protecting the brand of a sporting event. Sweet & Maxwell, London
Johnson P (2008) Look out! It's an ambush. Int Sports Law Rev 2/3:24–29
Kobel P (2007) International report on question B: ambush marketing too smart to be good? Should certain ambush marketing practices be declared illegal and if yes, which ones and under what conditions? International report to the international league of competition law, Catania Congress 2007
Lewis A, Taylor J (2003) Sport: law and practice. Cavendish Publishing, London
Longdin L (2009) Public law solutions to private law problems: major event regulation subverts IP's internal balance. J Intellect Prop Law Pract 4(10):726–742
Marcus JT (2010) Ambush marketing: an analysis of its threat to sports rights holders and the efficacy of past, present and proposed anti-infringement programmes. Sport Law J 18(1):25
McKelvey S, Grady J (2008) Sponsorship program protection strategies for special sport events: are event organizers outmaneuvring ambush marketers? J Sport Manag 22:550–586
Ries A, Ries L (1998) The 22 immutable laws of branding. HarperCollins Publishers, Inc, New York
Rohsler C, Baudriller M (2009) Creation of a "right to offer bets": analysis. World Sports Law Rep 7:10–11
Scaria AG (2008) Ambush marketing: game within a game. Oxford University Press, Oxford
Scassa T (2011) Ambush marketing and the right of association: clamping down on references to that big event with the all the athletes in a couple of years. J Sport Manag 25:354–370
Schwab F (2006) FIFA's trademark tactics. World Trademark Rev 6. http://www.worldtrademarkreview.com/Issues/Articles.aspx?g=faf17b21-f89a-473e-949c-bc1b25b93bad
Skildum-Reid K (2007) The ambush marketing toolkit. McGraw-Hill, Sydney
Smith A (2011) Ramping up trademark protection at the Olympics. World Trademark Rev 33:42–46
Storey S (2010) Pilfering, piracy and prevention: developments in combating ambush marketing. Sport Law J 18(1):40–52
Sutherden A (2011) Laying the law down on ambush marketing. J Spons 4(4):311–313
Wise A (1996) A'property right' in a sports event: views of different jurisdictions. Sport Law J 4(3):63

Appendix A

Extract from an undated draft letter by the Dutch government addressed to the president of FIFA, purporting to confirm the terms of Government Guarantee No. 6 ('Protection and Exploitation of Commercial Rights') in respect of the Low Countries bid for the 2017 FIFA Confederations Cup/2018 FIFA World Cup and/or the 2021 FIFA Confederations Cup/2022 FIFA World Cup:

General Measures and Protections

The Netherlands represents and guarantees to FIFA and ensures to FIFA that the following measures and protections will be implemented and operative on the federal, state, municipal, local and other relevant levels by no later than 1 June 2013, if necessary by the issuance of special legislation:

(i) the establishment of special "protected" status for the Competitions and in particular for FIFA's intellectual property rights relating to the Events, such "protected" status to bestow upon the intellectual property rights to [be] protected the equivalent rights as trademark registrations;

(ii) the unauthorised use, reproduction, imitation, counterfeiting, or modification of any official symbols of FIFA or the Events, or any other FIFA intellectual property in relation to the Events, as well as to import, export, sell, offer, expose for sale, or conceal official symbols or products resulting from unauthorized reproduction, counterfeiting, or modification of official symbols, will be prohibited by law;

(iii) the registration and use of domain names containing FIFA's trademarks will be prohibited by law;

A. M. Louw, *Ambush Marketing and the Mega-Event Monopoly*,
ASSER International Sports Law Series, DOI: 10.1007/978-90-6704-864-4,

(iv) ambush marketing by association in relation to the Events and/or FIFA, namely to promote, or otherwise direct public attention to businesses, products or services in a manner that may induce third parties into erroneously believing that those products or services are approved, authorised or endorsed by FIFA, or are connected to the Events, will be prohibited by law;
(v) ambush marketing by intrusion in relation to the Events and/or FIFA, namely to practice, organise, approve, or sponsor any promotional, advertising, or marketing activities through which one targets the audience of the Events, including ticket holders, in order to gain exposure for its businesses, products or services without authorization from FIFA, will be prohibited by law;
(vi) any and all acts of "unfair competition" or "passing off" in relation to the Events and/or FIFA, will be prohibited by law;
(vii) to hold, organise, approve or sponsor a commercial public viewing event related to the Events, unless expressly authorised in writing by FIFA, will be prohibited by law;
(viii) the resale or redistribution of match tickets or Event tickets, unless expressly authorised in writing by FIFA, will be prohibited by law;
(ix) the use of match tickets or Event tickets in advertising, sales, competitions, sweepstakes, give away, or other promotional activities, or as part of a hospitality or travel package, or the making available or advertising of match tickets or Event tickets for any such purposes, unless expressly authorised in writing by FIFA, will be prohibited by law; and
(x) the prohibitions listed above shall be sanctioned by a suitably severe penalty to deter any deliberate breach, subject to a written demand for penalty by FIFA.

Procedural Measures and Protections

The Netherlands represents and guarantees to FIFA and ensures to FIFA that the following procedural measures and protections will be implemented and operative on the federal, state, municipal, local and other relevant levels by no later than 1 June 2013, if necessary by the issuance of special legislation:

(i) the implementation of expedited examination and registration procedures for all FIFA's trademark, design and (if relevant) copyright applications related to the Events;
(ii) the implementation of expedited examination and opposition procedures for all third party trademarks, designs and (if relevant) copyright applications related to FIFA and/or the Events, filed without FIFA's written authorisation;

(iii) the grant of special powers to local law enforcement officers to enforce the prohibitions and restrictions outlined in this Guarantee, to seize or confiscate any materials that they reasonably suspect are being used in connection with the breach, and to dispose of/destroy goods used or created in connection with the breach (upon conviction for the breach);
(iv) the creation and enforcement of a restricted advertising and street trading zone within, and in the airspace above, a two kilometre (2 km) zone around each stadium and other official sites used for the Events, in which the right to conduct commercial activities is subject to approval by FIFA or its appointees;
(v) the implementation of expedited enforcement procedures, including judicial procedures, in relation to the enforcement by FIFA of its legal rights in connection with the Events;
(vi) the allocation of a suitable number of law enforcement officers to work with FIFA and physically participate in FIFA's rights protection programme, including the participation in patrol teams during the Events;
(vii) the allocation of sufficient numbers of customs officers to properly control the importation of counterfeit and pirate goods;
(viii) the establishment of a national rights protection programme committee to consist of members of the relevant national government departments and agencies (such as the department of trade & industry, the intellectual property office, customs service, public prosecutors office, law enforcement agencies, etc.); and
(ix) the establishment of regional rights protection programme committees for each host city, which are to consist of regional members of the relevant bodies as above.

Further Confirmations Regarding Commercial Rights

The Netherlands also represents and guarantees to FIFA that it unconditionally and irrevocably acknowledges FIFA's legal and beneficial, unrestricted and exclusive ownership of all media rights, marketing rights, ticketing rights and all other commercial rights related the Events, as well as of any marks and other intellectual property rights of FIFA related to the Events.

The Netherlands further represents and guarantees to FIFA, and will ensure, that the Netherlands will pass, to the extent necessary, special laws designed to ensure full protection of FIFA's ownership of all media rights, marketing rights, ticketing rights, other commercial rights, marks and other intellectual property and shall provide FIFA with the support of officers of relevant authorities, such as police and customs, to assist in the protection of the media rights, marketing rights, ticketing rights, other commercial rights, marks and other intellectual property of FIFA.

The Netherlands also represents and guarantees to FIFA, and will ensure, that there are and will be no legal restrictions or prohibitions on the sale, advertising or distribution of FIFA Commercial Affiliates' or FIFA Contractors' products, including food and beverages, in the stadiums or other sites for the duration of the Competitions and Events and that there are and will be no legal restrictions or prohibitions on the exploitation of the media rights, marketing rights, ticketing rights, other commercial rights, marks or other intellectual property of FIFA. The Netherlands agrees that any media, marketing, ticketing or other commercial laws or regulations which interfere with, or impinge upon FIFA's exploitation of the media rights, marketing rights, ticketing rights, and other commercial rights are suspended in respect of the Competition and that FIFA may exploit such rights unfettered in the Netherlands in a manner of its own choosing. FIFA shall, in particular without limitation, have the full and exclusive control over any news access or related rights, and fully control all access and accreditation rights to any official sites.

The Netherlands also represents and guarantees to FIFA that FIFA and each of the entities outlined below shall be permitted unconditionally to conduct business activities in relation to the Events in the Netherlands:

(i) FIFA / FIFA Subsidiaries;
(ii) FIFA Confederations and FIFA Member Associations;
(iii) Hosting Association and LOC;
(iv) FIFA Service Providers;
(v) FIFA Host Broadcaster, FIFA Commercial Affiliates and FIFA Contractors; and
(vi) other FIFA partners and their staff whose activities, services or deliveries are important for the organisation, staging, administering, marketing, rights implementation etc. in connection with the Events.

The entities outlined above shall be entitled, if required, free of charge and on an expedited basis, to register and establish themselves and legally recognised commercial entities in the Netherlands, to conduct trade and other commercial activities, to lease business premises, to own property (of all kinds), to employ staff, to enter into contracts of any nature and to conduct legal action in the Netherlands against third parties.

General Undertakings

The Government Declaration and the Government Guarantees No 1–8 shall be read together and interpreted as a whole. When the meaning, interpretation, scope and intent as set out in Chapter F of Government Guarantee No. 8 differs from or conflicts with a provision in this Guarantee, Chapter F of Government Guarantee No. 8 shall be given absolute priority and will prevail as the only applicable, valid and binding obligation, undertaking, guarantee or assurance by the Government of the Netherlands.

Nothing in this Government Guarantee may lead to or be interpreted as leading to a breach of Constitutional rules and principles or rules and principles of public policy applicable in the Netherlands, such as for example but not limited to the state structure, the separation of powers, the non-discrimination principle and the prevalence of international law.

The Government of the Netherlands represents and guarantees to FIFA and ensures that all special laws, regulations and ordinances necessary to properly fulfil the obligations under this Guarantee have been enacted or shall be enacted and enter into force in due time.

This Guarantee shall be valid and binding as of the date of its execution and shall remain valid and binding regardless of the fact that certain laws, regulations and ordinances will be enacted at a later stage. The necessary legal framework is in place to allow FIFA to impose enforcement of this Government Guarantee. The government of the Netherlands understands that all obligations under this Government Guarantee must be fulfilled and will take all necessary steps to ensure this.

If required, the government of the Netherlands, together with the LOC, will make all necessary arrangements to provide FIFA with an English translation of the relevant laws, regulations, ordinances (including circulars), other legal instruments and practice.

The government of the Netherlands confirm that all relevant correspondence and discussions shall be conducted in English language.

The signatories confirm to be competent to issue this Government Guarantee. Under the laws of the Netherlands, this Government Guarantee is and shall remain binding and valid against the Netherlands and its government and all other relevant authorities and bodies, up to, during and following the Competitions, irrespective of any change in the government of the Netherlands or in its representatives, or any change in the laws and regulations in the Netherlands.

The Netherlands

[Extract (Sect. A, the definitions section, omitted here) from a draft letter available online at the time of writing on the web site of the Dutch government at http://www.overheid.nl/]

Appendix B

Resolution on anti-ambush marketing legislation published by the Emerging Issues committee of the International Trademark Association (INTA), November 2010 (referred to in Sect. 8.7 in Chap. 8):

WHEREAS, organizers of major sporting and other entertainment events seek to generate greater revenues by preventing non-event sponsors from engaging in unauthorized marketing and advertising activities that create associations with the event (so-called "ambush marketing" activities);

WHEREAS, ambush marketing activities in many cases may be permissible under established trademark or unfair competition laws;

WHEREAS, the intense competition to become the host country for major events increasingly has led to the enactment of special legislation to prevent ambush marketing for such events as the Olympic and Paralympic games in the United Kingdom, Canada and Brazil; the Commonwealth games in Australia; and the World Cup in South Africa; and

WHEREAS, ambush marketing legislation often extends sponsors' and organizers' rights well beyond the protection of traditional trademark and unfair competition laws, thus impeding existing trademark owners' rights by failing to appropriately balance the interests of official sponsors and event organizers with free commercial speech, fair use and the legitimate commercial activities of others;

BE IT RESOLVED, that the International Trademark Association recommends that countries electing to adopt ambush marketing legislation relating to major events ensure that the legitimate rights of trademark owners and the public to use trademarks and descriptive terms fairly are balanced appropriately against the rights of event sponsors and organizers.

BE IT FURTHER RESOLVED, that the International Trademark Association recommends that ambush marketing legislation relating to major events should be based on the following principles and guidelines:

A. M. Louw, *Ambush Marketing and the Mega-Event Monopoly*,
ASSER International Sports Law Series, DOI: 10.1007/978-90-6704-864-4,

a. A reasonable balance should be struck between the interests of the organizers, sponsors, local businesses and property owners, the local community in which the event will be held, and trademark owners.
b. Prior to adopting ambush marketing legislation for the protection of a major event, event emblem or word, there should be consultation with potentially affected parties.
c. The special protections granted to organizers and sponsors of a protected event should be limited in time so that they are in effect only for a certain amount of time leading up to the event and for a reasonable amount of time following the event.
d. Restricted "ambush marketing" activities should be limited in scope and clearly defined so that only commercial activities that create or are likely to create a false implication of sponsorship or association for the non-sponsor or confusion among the public as to sponsorship are prohibited.
e. Remedies in ambush marketing legislation should minimize the risk of sponsors using overreaching rights of action to the detriment of bona fide trademark owners.
f. Special protection should not be granted to any single non-distinctive term or symbol and such terms and symbols should remain available for use by all traders, so long as use of such single term or symbol does not create a false impression of sponsorship of the event.
g. The validity of pre-existing rights, whether intellectual property rights, tangible property rights, contract rights, and others, should be recognized and reasonably accommodated, especially when establishing such restrictions as "clean zones" and "clean transport zones."
h. The effect of ambush marketing legislation on trademark applications, particularly for symbols, should be taken into account. For example, it may be appropriate to provide that a conflicting application remains in limbo pending expiry of a special protection period.
i. Ambush marketing legislation should make it clear that the organizers and/or sponsors of the event are the only entities responsible for bringing, or entitled to bring, civil actions to enforce the legislation.
j. Express exceptions to violation of ambush marketing legislation could include ongoing activities by existing organizations, registered trademarks and trade names. The categories of exceptions should be appropriately and carefully defined—for example the manner in which a registered trademark category is defined may also need to include device marks and "brand extensions." Pre-existing unregistered trademarks and trade names should be taken into account and descriptive and other permissible fair uses should also be excepted, so long as they do not create a false impression of sponsorship.
k. In the interests of appropriately balancing the respective parties' rights it would be preferable for ambush marketing legislation to avoid presumptions of violations and rather make the inclusion of protected emblems or words a factor to be considered in assessing whether a violation has occurred.

l. Ambush marketing legislation might provide for civil remedies as are available in other types of intellectual property matters, such as injunctions, damages, seizure of counterfeit goods, and corrective advertising, but should not provide for criminal penalties, such as criminal fines and imprisonment.'

[Reproduced with permission from www.inta.org/Advocacy/Pages/AmbushMarketingLegislation.aspx, Copyright 2010 International Trademark Association. Available online at the time of writing on the INTA's web site at http://www.inta.org/Advocacy/Pages/AmbushMarketingLegislation.aspx]

Glossary

Lanham Act United States federal trademark statute

Lei Geral da Copa Draft legislation before Brazilian Congress (at the time of writing) for the 2014 FIFA World Cup Brazil

London Act London Olympic and Paralympic Games Act, 2006, passed for the 2012 London Olympic Games

Pelé Act Brazil's general sports Act (Law 9615/98)

Sochi Act The Russian Federation's 'Olympic Law' (Federal Law No. 310-FZ) passed for the 2014 Sochi Winter Olympic Games

Ted Stevens Act Ted Stevens Olympic and Amateur Sports Act, 1998 (United States)

Vancouver Act Canada's Olympic and Paralympic Marks Act, 2007 (also referred to as 'Bill C-47'), passed for the 2010 Vancouver Winter Olympic Games

A. M. Louw, *Ambush Marketing and the Mega-Event Monopoly*,
ASSER International Sports Law Series, DOI: 10.1007/978-90-6704-864-4,

Index

A. M. Louw, *Ambush Marketing and the Mega-Event Monopoly*,
ASSER International Sports Law Series, DOI: 10.1007/978-90-6704-864-4,

MIX
Papier aus verantwortungsvollen Quellen
Paper from responsible sources
FSC® C105338

If you have any concerns about our products,
you can contact us on
ProductSafety@springernature.com

In case Publisher is established outside the EU,
the EU authorized representative is:
Springer Nature Customer Service Center GmbH
Europaplatz 3, 69115 Heidelberg, Germany

Printed by Libri Plureos GmbH
in Hamburg, Germany